"NO OTH

. . . THES

MW01672362

★ ★ ★ ★ ★ (5 star rating) "Crisply written and remarkably personable. Cleverly organized so you can pluck out the minutest fact in a moment. Satisfyingly thorough."

Réalités

"The information they offer is up-to-date, crisply presented but far from exhaustive, the judgments knowledgeable but not opinionated."

New York Times

"The individual volumes are compact, the prose succinct, and the coverage up-to-date and knowledgeable . . . The format is portable and the index admirably detailed."

John Barkham Syndicate

"They contain an amount of information that is truly staggering, besides being surprisingly current."

Detroit News

"These guides address themselves to the needs of the modern traveler demanding precise, qualitative information . . . Up-beat, slick, and well-put-together."

Dallas Morning News

". . . Attractive to look at, refreshingly easy to read, and generously packed with information."

Miami Herald

"These guides are as good as any published, and much better than most."

Louisville (Kentucky) *Times*

Other Books in the Get 'em and Go Series

Canada
Caribbean, Bermuda, and the Bahamas
Disneyland
Europe
Great Britain/Ireland
Hawaii
Mexico
South America
Walt Disney World

CONTRIBUTING EDITORS

Barbara Arau
Fred Baumeister
Tina Blackshare
Robert Bone
Al Borcover
James Bready
David Breakstone
Patricia Brooks
Anita Buck
Jeff Burger
William Burk
Robert Butler
Carol Campbell
Michael Carlton
Stacey Chanin
Marie Chesny
Shirley Christian
Thomas Coffey
Karen Cure
Sally Davy
John Doherty
Natilee Duning
Thomas Ellis
Luise Erdmann
Walter Evans
Brenda Fine
Sam Fletcher
Kathleen Fliegel
James Frank
Mark Gottlieb
Martin Grove
Paul Hagerman
Ben Harte
Willard Hazelbush
Patricia Hetrick
Rosemary P. Hinkle
Sam Jannerone
Lou Johnson
Michael Konon
Lori G. Kranz
Linda Lampman
Antoinette Martin
Alexandra Mayes
Timothy McEnroe
Donald McMillin
Anne Millman
Bill Millman
Teresa Morris
Laurie Nadel
Brooke Ramey Nelson
Marty Olmstead
Robert Pineda
Ann Pleshette
Mike Pulfer
Steve Roberts
Michael Robertson
Allan Rokach
William Ryan
William Schemmel
Ellen Sherberg
Art Siemering
Douglas Smith
Ronald Smith
Victoria Sprague
Michele Steege
Jean Stewart
Jack Swanson
Rick Sylvain
Charles Thurston
Diana Tittle
Robert Trumbull
Nikki Tureen
Jan Walker
Katherine Walker
Hesh Weiner
Robert Wells
Mimi Whitefield
Robert Wintner
Cathy Wood
Donald Woodward

ASSISTANT EDITOR

Denise DeGennaro

COVER

Paul Posnick

SYMBOLS

Gloria McKeown

A Get 'em and Go Travel Guide

UNITED STATES 1983

Stephen Birnbaum
EDITOR

Claire Hardiman
EXECUTIVE EDITOR

David Walker
ADVISORY EDITOR

HOUGHTON MIFFLIN COMPANY BOSTON 1982

For Alex

This book is published by special arrangement
with Eric Lasher and Maureen Lasher.

ISBN: 0-395-32875-6 (pbk)
ISSN: 0162-5497 (Get 'em and Go Travel Guides)
ISSN: 0162-2420 (United States)

Printed in the United States of America

W 10 9 8 7 6 5 4 3 2 1

Contents

GETTING READY TO GO

A mini-encyclopedia of all the practical travel data you need to plan your vacation down to the final detail.

When and How to Go

Preparing

On the Road

Sources and Resources

THE AMERICAN CITIES

Thorough, qualitative guides to each of the 40 cities most often visited by vacationers and businesspeople. Each section offers a comprehensive report of the city's most compelling attractions and amenities, designed to be used on the spot. Directions and recommendations are immediately accessible because each guide is presented in consistent form.

DIVERSIONS

A selective guide to more than 25 active and/or cerebral vacation themes, including the best places to pursue them. Our intent is to point out where your quality of experience is likely to be highest.

DIRECTIONS

This country's most spectacular routes and roads, most arresting natural wonders, most magnificent parks and forests, all organized into 66 specific driving tours.

Midwest

West

A Word from the Editor

The broadening sophistication of travelers has made it essential that guidebooks also evolve, if only to keep pace with their readers. So we've tried to create a guide to the United States that's specifically organized, written, and edited for the newly knowledgeable traveler, for whom qualitative information is infinitely more desirable than mere quantities of unappraised data. We think that this series is the first of a new generation of travel guides that are uniquely responsive to the needs and interests of today's travelers.

For years, dating back as far as Herr Baedeker, travel guides have tended to be encyclopedic, seemingly much more concerned with demonstrating expertise in geography and history than with any real analysis of the sorts of things that actually concern a typical tourist. But today, when it is hardly necessary to tell a traveler where Switzerland is, or that it was a noncombatant in both World Wars, it is hard to justify endless pages of historic perspective. In many cases, the traveler has been to Switzerland nearly as often as the guidebook editor, so the editor must provide new perceptions and suggest new directions to make the guide genuinely valuable.

That's exactly what we've tried to do in the new *Get 'em and Go* series. I think you'll notice a new tone to the text, as well as an organization and focus that are distinctive and different. And even a random examination of what follows will demonstrate a substantial departure from previous guidebook orientation, for we've not only attempted to provide information of a different sort, but we've also tried to present it in an environment that makes it particularly accessible.

Needless to say, it's difficult to decide what goes into a guidebook of this size — and, of course, what to omit. Early on, we realized that giving up the encyclopedic approach precluded the inclusion of every route and restaurant, and this fact helped define our overall editorial focus. Similarly, when we discussed the possibility of presenting certain information in other than strict geographic order, we found that the new format enabled us to arrange this data in a way that we think best answers the questions travelers typically ask.

Large numbers of specific questions have provided the real editorial skeleton for this book. The volume of mail I regularly receive continually seems to emphasize the fact that modern travelers want very precise information, and so we've tried to address ourselves to this need and have organized the text in the most responsive way possible. If you want to know the best restaurant in Chicago or the best tennis camp for improving a recalcitrant backhand, you will be able to extract that data easily.

Travel guides are, of course, reflections of personal taste, and putting one's name on a title page obviously puts one's preferences on the line. But I think I ought to amplify just exactly what "personal" means. I am not at all a believer in the sort of personal guidebook that's a palpable misrepresentation on its face. It is, for example, hardly possible for any single travel writer to physically visit a thousand restaurants (and nearly that number of hotels) in any given year and provide accurate appraisals of each. And even if it were physically possible for one human to get through such an itinerary in a single year, it would of necessity have to be done at a dead sprint, and the perceptions derived therefrom would probably be even less valid than those of any leisurely layman visiting the same establishments. It is, therefore, impossible (especially in an annually revised guidebook *series* such as we are developing) to have only one person provide all the data on the entire world.

I also happen to think that such individual orientation is of substantially less value to readers. Visiting a single hotel for one night, or eating one hasty meal in a restaurant, hardly equips anyone to provide meaningful appraisals that are of more than passing interest. No amount of doggedly alliterative or oppressively onomatopoeic text can camouflage a technique that is specious on its face. We have, therefore, chosen what I like to describe as the "thee and me" approach to restaurant and hotel appraisal, and in a somewhat more limited degree, to the sites and sights we have included in the other sections of the text. What this really reflects is personal sampling tempered by intelligent counsel from informed local sources, for these friends-of-the-editor are almost always residents of the city and/or area about which they are consulted.

We have also tried to be sure that our contributors have had a fair access to visitors so they may better solicit individual tourist reactions to the areas about which they contribute. It doesn't take long to discover whether a prospective contributor's tastes coincide with our own, and by the time we have assembled all the editors, researchers, writers, stringers, correspondents, and consultants that it takes to create an undertaking of this size, we have a fairly homogeneous group. We also find that these informed, insightful local correspondents are far more apt to hear about (or uncover) hard-to-locate gems that so often turn an ordinary visit into an exciting adventure. Furthermore, they are usually in the very best position to recognize and report on local consensus and consistency, and they represent a far better barometer of ongoing excellence than would any random encounter.

Despite this considerable number of contributors, very precise editing and tailoring keeps our text fiercely subjective. So what follows is designed to be the gospel according to Birnbaum, and represents as much of my own tastes and instincts as humanly possible. It is probable, therefore, that if you like your steak medium rare, routinely ask to have the MSG left out of Chinese food, and can't tolerate fresh fish that is overcooked, then we're likely to have a long and meaningful relationship. Readers with dissimilar tastes may be less enraptured.

I also think I ought to point out something about the person to whom this guidebook is directed. Above all, he or she is a "visitor." That means that such elements as restaurant choices have been specifically picked to provide that visitor with a representative, enlightening, hopefully exciting, and above all pleasant experience, rather than to provide an insider's guide for a constituency that already knows a city quite well. Since so many extraneous considerations can affect the reception and service accorded a regular restaurant patron, our choices can in no way be construed as a definitive guide to resident dining. We think we've got all the best in various price ranges, but they were chosen with a visitor's viewpoint in mind.

Just one example of how such choices were made is shown by the battle that waged over which French restaurant in New York City would be designated "best." Objective appraisals of the comparative cuisines of half a dozen perfectly marvelous Gallic establishments indicated that any one of them could reasonably qualify for the term, and there was hardly a perceptible difference in the quality of the quenelles or the hauteur of the hollandaise. But there *was* a perceptible difference in how unknown diners were received and treated by the staffs of these various restaurants, and our final choice of Lutèce was as much due to its unusual hospitality to strangers as it was a nod to an extraordinary group of cuisineurs. We think this is especially precious information for a traveler to have at hand.

Other evidence of how we've tried to modify our text to reflect changing travel habits is most apparent in the section we call DIVERSIONS. Where once it was common for travelers to routinely take a two-week summer vacation — one likely to be spent at some ocean or lakeside where the vacationer's most energetic activity was scratching his or her stomach — travel has changed enormously in recent years. Such is the amount of perspiration regularly engendered by today's "leisurely" vacationer that the by-product of a modern holiday is often the need to take another vacation immediately. So we've selected every meaningful activity we could reasonably evaluate and have organized this material in a way that is especially accessible to activists of either an athletic or cerebral bent. So whether your preference is breaking your body in a downhill hurtle over America's most difficult ski terrain or whether you have a particular penchant for music festivals around the countryside, we've organized lots of hard information about just that particular activity. It is no longer necessary, therefore, to wade through fifty states' worth of extraneous text to find the best golf resort within a reasonable radius of where you'll be vacationing.

If there is one single thing that best characterizes the revolution and evolution of current holiday habits, it is that Americans now consider travel a right rather than a privilege. No longer is a trip to the far corners of this country or to Europe or the Orient necessarily a once-in-a-lifetime thing; nor is the idea of visiting exotic, faraway places in the least worrisome. Travel today translates as the enthusiastic desire to sample all of the world's opportunities, to find that elusive quality of experience that is not only enriching but comfortable. For that reason, we've tried to make what follows not only helpful and enlightening but the sort of welcome companion of which every traveler dreams.

Finally, I should point out that every good travel guide is a living enterprise; that is, no part of this text is in any way cast in bronze. In our forthcoming annual revisions, we expect to refine, expand, and further hone all our material to serve your travel needs even better. To this end, no contribution is of greater value to us than your personal reaction to what we have written, as well as information reflecting your personal experiences while trying our suggestions. We earnestly and enthusiastically solicit your comments on this book *and* your opinions and perceptions about places you have recently visited. In this way, we are able to provide the best sorts of information — including the actual experiences of the travel public — to make that experience more readily available to others. Please write to us at 60 E 42nd St., New York, NY 10165.

We sincerely hope to hear from you.

STEPHEN BIRNBAUM

How to Use This Guide

A great deal of care has gone into the special organization of this guidebook, and we believe it represents a real breakthrough in the presentation of travel material. Our aim has been to create a new, more modern generation of travel books, and to make this guide the most useful and practical travel tool available today.

Our text is divided into four basic sections in order best to present information on every possible aspect of an American vacation. This organization itself should alert you to the vast and varied opportunities available in this country — as well as indicating all the specific data necessary to plan a trip in the United States. You won't find much of the conventional "blue skies and beautiful beaches" text here; we've chosen instead to use the available space for more useful and purposeful information. Prospective American itineraries tend to speak for themselves, and with so many diverse travel opportunities, we feel our main job is to explain them and to provide the basic information — how, when, where, how much, and what's best — to let you make the most intelligent possible choices.

What follows is a brief summary of our four basic sections and what you can expect to find in each. We believe that you will find both your travel planning and en-route enjoyment enhanced by having this book at your side.

GETTING READY TO GO

This mini-encyclopedia of practical travel facts is meant to be a sort of know-it-all companion that has all the precise information you need to understand how to go about creating a journey through America. There are entries on nearly three dozen separate topics, including how to travel, what preparations to make before you leave, how to deal with possible emergencies while away from home, what to expect in the different regions of the US, what your trip is likely to cost, and how to avoid prospective problems. The individual entries are specific, realistic, and, where appropriate, cost-oriented.

We expect that you will use this section most in planning your trip, for its ideas and suggestions are intended to facilitate this often confusing time. Entries are intentionally concise, in an effort to get to the meat of the matter with little extraneous prose. This information is augmented by extensive lists of specific sources from which to obtain even more specialized information and some suggestions for obtaining travel information on your own.

THE AMERICAN CITIES

Individual reports on the 40 US cities most visited by tourists and businesspeople, researched and written by professional journalists on their own turf. Useful at the planning stage, THE AMERICAN CITIES is really designed to be taken with you and used on the spot. Each report offers a short-stay guide to its city within a consistent format: an essay, introducing the city as a contemporary place to live; *At-a-Glance,* a site-by-site survey of the most important (and sometimes most eclectic) sights to see and things to do; *Sources and Resources,* a concise listing of pertinent tourist information, meant to answer a myriad of potentially pressing questions as they arise — from something simple like the address of the local tourist office to something more difficult like where to find the best night spot, to see a show, to play tennis, or to get a taxi; and *Best in Town,* our cost-and-quality choices of the best places to eat and sleep on a variety of budgets.

DIVERSIONS

This section is designed to help travelers find the very best locations in which to satisfy their fondest vacation desires without having to wade through endless unrelated text. This very selective guide lists the broadest possible range of vacation activities, including all the best places to pursue them.

We start with a list of possibilities that will require some perspiration — sports preferences and other rigorous pursuits — and go on to report on a number of more cerebral and spiritual vacation possibilities. In every case, our suggestion of a particular location — and often our recommendation of a specific resort — is intended to guide you to that special place where the quality of experience is likely to be highest. So whether you opt for golf or tennis, scuba or whitewater rafting, or tours of spectacular resorts or epic shopping areas — we've even got a guide to nude beaches (they call them "free" beaches nowadays) — each entry is the equivalent of a comprehensive checklist to the absolute best in America.

DIRECTIONS

Here are a series of 66 American itineraries, from Maine's coastal islands to Hawaii's hidden beaches, to take you along this country's most beautiful routes and roads, most spectacular natural wonders, through our most magnificent national parks and forests. DIRECTIONS is the only section of the book organized geographically, and its itineraries cover the highlights of the entire country in short, independent segments that each describe journeys of one to three days' duration. Itineraries can be "connected" for longer trips or used individually for short, intensive explorations. Whether you are planning a major family vacation to cover thousands of miles or simply want to escape to the country, the format is adaptable to your end.

Each entry includes a guide to sightseeing highlights; a cost-and-quality guide to accommodations and food along the road (small inns, out-of-the-way restaurants, country hotels, and off-the-main-road discoveries); and suggestions for activities.

Although each of the sections has a distinct format and a unique function, they have all been designed to be used together to provide a complete package of travel information. Sections have been carefully cross-referenced, and you will find that as you finish an entry in one section, you are directed to another section and another entry, with complementary information. To use this book to full advantage, take a few minutes to read the table of contents and random entries in each section. This will give you an idea of how it all fits together.

Pick and choose information that you need from different sections. For example, if you are interested in a camping trip of some sort but have never been camping and don't really know where to go or how to organize yourself, you might well begin by reading the short, informative section on camping in GETTING READY TO GO. This would provide you with plenty of ideas on how to find a campsite, how to organize the trip, where to go for more information, what to take along. But where to go? Turn to

DIVERSIONS for a listing of the best backpacking and camping sites in the country; a look through the selections will direct you to a route and a distance equal to your expertise. Perhaps you choose a walk along the Appalachian Trail in the Great Smoky Mountains. Turn next to DIRECTIONS for suggestions on what to see along the way, including the Cumberland Gap. Once there, you might well decide to take a break to visit some of the nearby cities, Nashville or Louisville, Atlanta or even Memphis; all are fully covered in THE AMERICAN CITIES.

In other words, the sections of this book are building blocks to help you put together the best possible trip. Use them selectively as a tool, a source of ideas, a reference work for accurate facts, and a guidebook to the best buys, the most exciting sights, the most pleasant accommodations and delicious food, *the best travel experiences* you can have.

GETTING READY TO GO

When and How to Go

When to Go

The decision of when to travel may be forced upon you by the requirements of your schedule; more likely, you will have some choice, and will make the decision on the basis of what you want to see and do, what activities or events you'd like to attend, and what suits your mood.

CLIMATE: Below is a general description of the climate in various American regions to help you plan (all temperatures are given in the Fahrenheit scale). For a brief, city-by-city review of weather, see the *Climate and Clothes* entry in each city report (THE AMERICAN CITIES, starting p. 65). Detailed rainfall and temperature charts, presented month by month for 350 locations in the US, Canada, Mexico, and the Caribbean, are offered in *The Climate Advisor* by Gilbert Schwartz (Climate Guide Publications, PO Box 323, Station C, Flushing, NY 11367, $7.90).

New England and Upstate New York:

Connecticut
Maine
Massachusetts
New Hampshire
Upstate New York
Rhode Island
Vermont

The seasons are sharply defined: cold, snowy winters with temperatures in the 20s or lower (much lower in the northern regions of Maine, Vermont, and New Hampshire); short, temperate springs; warm summers in the 70s and 80s, often clear but sometimes humid, especially along the coasts; clear, crisp autumns with brilliant red, yellow, and orange foliage. Tourist season lasts almost around the year: in winter, for skiing and winter sports; summer, for the lakes, coastal resorts, and historic areas; autumn (especially the last two weeks of September and first two weeks of October), for foliage. Least crowded is spring. Best foliage routes: Vermont's Rt. 9; northwest Connecticut around Litchfield; the White Mountains and lakes of New Hampshire; Mohawk Trail in Massachusetts.

Mid-Atlantic:

Delaware
District of Columbia
Maryland
New Jersey
New York City
Pennsylvania
Virginia
West Virginia

Temperatures ranging from below freezing in winter to upper 80s and into the 90s in summer, with cold, damp winters that can be brutal in windswept cities like New York. In the summer, humidity is high along the rivers, which is where many of the area's largest cities are located. Fall is pleasant with moderate temperatures. A long, temperate, flowering spring begins as early as March, continues into June, and is the region's finest season. Tourists visit the metropolitan areas in summer, when city dwellers spend their weekends in the country, and the cities are pleasantly uncrowded for visitors.

South:

Alabama	Louisiana
Arkansas	Mississippi
Florida	North Carolina
Georgia	South Carolina
Kentucky	Tennessee

Anytime is a good time to visit the South, but fall and spring are the most temperate seasons. Winters range from the 40s inland to the 60s along the coast. Summer temperatures are in the 70s, 80s, and into the 90s. Events in the South are usually scheduled from January to May and from mid-September to October.

Midwest:

Illinois	Missouri
Indiana	Ohio
Michigan	Wisconsin

Cold winters and hot summers mark the entire region. The northern states suffer the harshest winters, with heavy snowfalls and temperatures in the 0° to 20° range. In the more southerly parts of states — the Ohio River Valley section of Indiana, Illinois, Ohio, the southern tip of Illinois, and much of Missouri — winter temperatures average in the 30s. Summers across the region are hot, in the 80s and 90s, and can be blisteringly humid. Even so, summer is the most popular tourist season, when the colossal state fairs get into gear, and ethnic festivals are planned by towns large and small. Though the Midwest isn't as famous as New England for foliage, the leaves change just as dramatically, and are at their peak in mid-October in Manistee National Forest near Cadillac, Michigan, and in Mohican State Park in Ohio.

Plains:

Iowa	Nebraska
Kansas	North Dakota
Minnesota	South Dakota

The Plains states offer short, pleasant springs and autumns. In the northern areas, the summer days are warm, nights cool, with snowy winters. Farther south the winters become milder, and the risk of hot, dry, 100° days in July and August increases. Tourist season is generally spring through the end of summer.

Rockies:

Colorado	Utah
Idaho	Wyoming
Montana	

A region of great diversity, the Rocky Mountain states include mountains, deserts, and flatlands. Except in the deserts of Colorado and Utah, evenings even in summer are cool. Low humidity and dependable sunshine distinguish the entire area. November to mid-April is skiing season; sightseeing and touring begin in spring and continue until the snows announce winter. In summer, desert temperatures can reach 110° and more, and it is best to visit early in the summer season. The Rockies are most famous as a winter — skiing — destination, but a marvelous and uncrowded western vacation can be a summer tour of those famous ski resorts: Aspen/Snowmass, Steamboat Springs, and Vail in Colorado; Big Sky, Montana; Jackson Hole, Wyoming; Park City and Sun Valley, Utah.

Southwest:

Arizona	Oklahoma
New Mexico	Texas

This region boasts year-round sunshine and low humidity, as well as high temperatures. In Arizona and New Mexico, it can reach 110° and 115° in the summer, though temperatures in the northern sections are more likely to be in the 90s. The tourist season is December through April.

Far West:

Alaska	Nevada
California	Oregon
Hawaii	Washington

For our purposes, the Far West is a rather artificially contrived category which comprises everything from southern California and the Hawaiian Islands to the great expanses of Alaska in the Arctic Circle. Not only is the vast range of temperature, climate, and geography within this huge area impossible to characterize neatly, but even along the Pacific Coast, from California to Washington, weather and temperatures are unpredictable, because of the various sea currents which affect weather conditions. In general, California north of Sacramento, Oregon, Washington, and Alaska are best seen in late spring through summer, when outdoor temperatures are warm. The winters can be quite cold, and in some coastal regions, rainy. Plan to visit Nevada, which is mostly desert, from October through April. Southern California and Hawaii are pleasant throughout the year, offering springlike weather almost anytime.

SPORTS: In the South and Southwest from Palm Springs to South Carolina, any season is warm-weather-sports season. The rest of the country plays according to the weather.

Tennis and golf are underway by March in most of the country and last well into October. In the North, in New England and Minnesota, for example, it is often as late as May before the mud clears, and cold sometimes stiffens knuckles by late September.

Since the most famous mountain climbing, hiking, and wilderness trips are in the Rockies, the Pacific Northwest, and northern New England, participants in these sports usually wait until summer, when the snow is clear, the mountain air is warmer, and less gear is required. Canoeing and rafting enthusiasts follow much the same schedule.

Water sports, such as boating and sailing, get underway in the Northeast in late spring and continue through early fall,with most regattas and other events scheduled from July 4 through Labor Day. On the West Coast above Sacramento, the season lasts longer with regattas beginning in June and continuing into September.

The New England ski season starts in earnest around Christmas and lasts through March. A good year will bring skiers out much earlier, and if the snow lasts, the slopes will be busy into April. The season in the West is usually longer, beginning pretty dependably at Thanksgiving and lasting until early or mid-April. However, skiing conditions depend on the snow, and the determined skier should be prepared to make plans around the weather. Daily newspapers and radio shows in ski areas carry detailed daily, and sometimes hourly, ski reports. If you are planning to go a long distance for skiing and are uncertain of the conditions at your destination, call the management of the resort to get a complete report.

PARKS: Most national parks are open all year, closing only for Christmas and New Year's Day. However, many camping facilities in the parks close from October to April, and for a complete list of camping facilities and their opening and closing times, write the National Park Service, Department of Interior, Washington, DC 20240 (for a list of camping directories, guides, and other addresses for camping information, see the section on camping, p. 22). The most popular national parks, such as Grand Canyon, Zion, and Yosemite, keep some camping facilities open all year.

Parks will be crowded in the summer. Heaviest use is in July and August. To avoid crowds, consider a spring trip, when wild flowers are in bloom; or autumn, for changing leaves and clear weather. Two parks, the Everglades in Florida and Big Bend in Texas, are at their prime in winter.

CULTURAL EVENTS: The season for concerts, plays, art exhibits, dance, and other cultural events across the United States is October through April. New plays open on Broadway; regional theaters bring up their lights (see *Regional Theaters,* DIVERSIONS); major orchestras perform several nights a week; and art museums hold major exhibits, lectures, and film series (see *America's Great Museums,* DIVERSIONS). Schedules of events are available from the visitors and convention bureaus in most cities (addresses given in THE AMERICAN CITIES).

Summer programs are less formal, often outdoors, and usually less expensive (sometimes even free). Major cities offer full schedules of concerts and theater, as well as puppet shows and other entertainment for children. Many impromptu programs are set up in city parks. Exclusively summer events which cause national excitement are Saratoga Performing Arts Center, Saratoga Springs, NY; Tanglewood Music Festival in Lenox, MA; Wolf Trap Farm Park in Vienna, VA; Aspen Music Festival in Aspen, CO; and the Monterey Jazz Festival in California. (For a list of *America's Music Festivals,* see DIVERSIONS.)

FAIRS AND CELEBRATIONS: Tobacco-chewing contests, flower festivals, state fairs, rodeos, horse shows, Indian ceremonies, ethnic festivals, and an endless number of similar events bring people together in all parts of the country. To find out about the events that are taking place along your route or to get a list so that you can plan your trip around them, write the state tourist boards, most of which publish a calendar of events (addresses given on pp. 59–60 in this section). One source of events is *Mort's Guide to Festivals, Feasts, Fairs, and Fiestas* North American Edition (CMG Publications, Inc., Box 630, Princeton, NJ 08540, $3.75). This is a comprehensive guide, but dates and times should be double-checked and are not always up-to-date. For a selection of the craziest and most interesting celebrations, contests, and festivities in the US, see *Oddities and Insanities,* DIVERSIONS.

Touring by Car

DRIVING YOUR OWN CAR: Automobile travel is the most popular mode of transportation in the US, but not necessarily the cheapest. It costs 17¢ to 27¢ a mile to drive an automobile in the US (cost varies with size and condition of car, price of gasoline, city or highway driving, etc.); only 12¢ to 17¢ a mile to fly by commercial airline. Driving, however, becomes more economical with more passengers, and offers the great advantage of allowing you to explore inaccessible regions at your own pace and on your own schedule.

Automobile Clubs: To protect yourself in case of on-the-road breakdowns, you should consider joining a reputable national automobile club. Largest of these is American Automobile Association (AAA), with over 22 million members in local chapters around the country, but numerous other clubs offer similar services. Any club should offer three basic services:

1. On-the-road insurance covering accidents, personal injury, arrest and bail bond, and lawyer's fees for defense of contested traffic cases.
2. Around-the-clock (24-hour) emergency breakdown service (including reduced rates on towing to nearest garage). AAA provides a country-wide list of AAA-approved garages; other clubs allow members to call any local mechanic and reimburse for cost of towing at a later date.
3. Travel and vacation planning service, including advice and maps.

These are the basic forms of service; specific policies and programs vary widely from club to club. Before joining any one, get information and brochures from several national clubs, and compare services and costs to find services which match your travel needs. Most clubs cost between $25 and $50 a year and include spouse and family in membership. Listed below are several of the largest US auto and travel clubs:

1. *American Automobile Association* — Join through local chapters (listed under *Automobile Club of . . .* in the telephone book); information from national office, 8111 Gatehouse Rd., Falls Church, VA 22047 (703 222-6000).
2. *Amoco Motor Club* — Join through Amoco's office, 3700 Wake Forest Rd., Raleigh, NC 27609 (919 876-7500).
3. *Allstate Motor Club* — Run by Allstate Insurance; join through any Allstate agency; information from the Club, 3701 West Lake, Glenview, IL 60025 (312 291-5461).
4. *JTX Club, Inc.* — Run by the Insurance Company of North America, Box 13901, Philadelphia, PA 19101 (215 241-4000).
5. *Ford Auto Club* — Contact the Membership Services, PO Box 4219, South Bend, IN 46634 (800 348-5220 outside Indiana; 800 342-5744 in Indiana).
6. *Gulf Auto Club* — Join by writing PO Box 4189, South Bend, IN 46634 (800 348-5126 outside Indiana; 800 342-5666 in Indiana).
7. *Montgomery Ward Auto Club* — Join through credit manager at any Montgomery Ward store; national office, 2020 W Dempster, Evanston, IL 60202 (toll-free, 800 621-5151 outside Illinois; 800 572-5577 in Illinois; 312 973-7305 in Alaska).
8. *Motor Club of America* — Open to residents of 26 states (protection extends to members traveling in all states); national office, 484 Central Ave., Newark, NJ 07107 (201 733-1234).
9. *United States Auto Club Motoring Division* — National office, 1720 Ruskin St., South Bend, IN 46624 (800 348-2484 outside Indiana; 800 552-2320 in Indiana; or 219 236-3700).

Oil Company Credit Cards: All major oil companies offer credit cards which can be used nationwide to buy gas, repairs, and most car parts at their respective service stations. A credit card will reduce the amount of money that you must carry on your trip. Applications for cards are available at service stations (Mobil stations have applications for Mobil cards only, etc.), and you will be granted a card if you have proven credit-worthiness — another credit card of any kind or an established credit rating. They are issued free, and usually take about a month for processing after application.

Charges are handled in two ways, and it is important to be aware under which system your card is working. A few companies — Amoco, for example — allow cardholders to carry charges from month to month. The cardholder pays a minimum each month, and the balance is carried over. For this privilege the cardholder is charged an interest rate (usually about 1½% a month) on the carried-over balance. If you spent $300 on gasoline during a two-week trip, you could spread the payment of this $300 over several months — virtually a "travel now–pay later" system, but you will end up paying more than $300.

Other companies — an example is Gulf — insist that the cardholder pay the full balance due at the end of each pay period (usually a month). While there is no extended credit (except for large repair bills, for which special arrangements can be made), neither is there an interest charge. There are advantages to both systems; when you consider a credit card, know which way it works and decide which is best for you.

Preparing Your Car. Always have your car thoroughly inspected before you leave on a trip, paying special attention to brakes and tires (including the spare). Always have liability insurance. Other suggestions:

1. Consult road maps. Many automobile clubs offer their members free maps and precise routings. Other travelers can get road maps free by writing Exxon Touring Service, PO Box 10210, Houston, TX 77206; Texaco Travel Service, PO Box 1459, Houston, TX 77001; or state tourist boards (addresses on pp. 57–59). Maps are available at service stations, but due to budget cutbacks within the oil industry, most companies now charge for them. *Rand McNally's Road Atlas* (about $6) is excellent.
2. Make sure your car has the following equipment: spare tire, jack, wrench, and two wooden blocks; extra set of keys (well hidden); first aid kit; jumper cables/gloves; white towel for signaling and/or wiping windows.
3. Make the first days of your trip the shortest, and plan to drive 300–400 miles per day at the most (6–7 hours); this is a comfortable pace for most travelers.
4. For a state-by-state list of emergency telephone numbers, 24-hour gas stations, and other useful information, send $1 for the *Highway Assistance Directory* (National Highway Safety Foundation, Dept. P, 116 E State St., Ridgeland, MS 39157).

Breakdowns: If you break down on the road, immediate emergency procedure is to get the car off the highway, raise the hood as a signal that help is needed, and tie a white rag to the door handle or antenna, for the same reason. Don't leave the car unattended, and don't try any major repairs on the road.

In several states, some type of motorist-aid system exists: Connecticut, Iowa, Nebraska, New Mexico, North Dakota, and Tennesee. These "systems" usually involve a group of roving vehicles, looking out for motorists in distress. They are equipped with first aid supplies, and carry gasoline and oil.

Mechanics and Car Care: For any but the most simple malfunctions, you will probably need a mechanic. (Reliable mechanics are listed in THE AMERICAN CITIES section of this guide.) An excellent series of booklets on car care, mileage, mechanical problems and their sources is published by Shell Oil as its *Shell Answer Man* series, available from Shell dealers or directly from the company at PO Box 61609, Houston, TX 77208. Other suggestions for breakdowns and on-the-road car care:

1. Look for mechanics with certification. National Institute for Automotive Service Excellence (NIASE) has certified 100,000 mechanics, many of whom work for local stations. Automotive Service Council also certifies mechanics.
2. Have some idea what needs to be done. Oil needs to be changed approximately every 5,000 miles; a tune-up is needed every 12,000 miles (every 25,000 miles for transistorized ignition cars); spark plugs need to be changed every 25,000 miles; fan and air-conditioning belts, every 5,000 miles.
3. Get an estimate in writing on major repairs, and make sure there is a firm understanding that the mechanic will call you if any other problems arise. The average cost for service is between $15 and $35 per hour.
4. Be aware of dishonest practices. Some mechanics will cheat you. While checking oil they can "short-stick" the dipper so the full amount of oil in your engine doesn't register. Know your car's oil consumption, and watch while oil is being checked.
5. Recognize warning signals:
   - Fluid leaks — Spread paper and look for the following: brown or black fluid, *oil leak;* straw-colored fluid near wheel, *leaking brake fluid;* pink or reddish fluid, *automatic transmission leak;* colorless or greenish fluid near front, *radiator or hose leak.*
   - Car has trouble starting — May be a vapor lock caused by hot weather; a cold, wet rag on the fuel line and pump may help.
   - Rattle in rear — Loose muffler or tail pipe.
   - Rattling noise — Bent fan blade or loose pulley.
   - Loud squealing noise when wheel turns — Low power steering fluid.

6. If your car needs to be towed, agree in advance on the price and the station to which it will be towed. If you ask AAA clubs, they will often tell you which stations are not reliable.

SPEED-TRAPS: Watch your speedometer in small towns. Not only do speed-traps cost you a ticket, but they may also affect your future insurance rates.

SAVING ON GAS: Begin by planning your itinerary and making as many reservations as possible so that you don't waste gas figuring out where to go or stay. Drive early in the day when there is less traffic and heat. Leave your car at the hotel and take local transportation within cities. If it fits in with your plans, choose routes that are direct and avoid mountains or long hills.

Make sure that your tires are properly inflated and your engine is tuned correctly to cut your gas consumption. Avoid speeding — at 55 miles per hour, you can get 25% better mileage than at 70. You can also increase the number of miles you get per gallon by driving smoothly: Accelerate gently, anticipate stops, get into high gear quickly, and maintain a steady speed.

In times of a gas shortage, buy your gas during the day and on weekdays if possible, since more stations are likely to be open. For weekend travel, buy on Saturdays. Check with automobile clubs (like the AAA) for information on where gas is available. Also consult state police or highway patrols for gasoline availability information.

Make sure you have cash available for gas. Some stations are refusing credit cards — even those of their own company.

RENTING A CAR: No matter what the advertisements imply, renting a car is rarely as simple as signing on the dotted line and roaring off into the night. If you are renting for personal use, you will have to convince the renting agency that (1) you are personally credit-worthy; and (2) you will bring the car back at the stated time. This will be easy if you have a major credit card; all national agencies (see below) and most local rental companies accept credit cards in lieu of a cash deposit as well as for payment of your final bill. If you prefer to pay in cash, leave your credit card as a deposit and pay your bill in cash when you return the car.

If you don't have a national credit card, call the company several days in advance, give them your name, home address, information on your business or employer; the rental agency then runs its own credit check on you. In addition, you will have to leave a hefty deposit when you pick up the car — as much as $200 for each day you intend to keep the car. (Each company has a different deposit policy; look around for the best deal.)

Costs and Requirements: Renting is not cheap, but it is possible to economize by determining your own needs and then shopping around until you find the best deal. As you comparison-shop, keep in mind that rates vary considerably, not only from city to city, but also from location to location within the same city. It might be cheaper to rent a car at the airport rather than in the center of the city. Hertz might be cheaper in Tulsa, while Avis is more reasonable in New York. Ask about special rates or promotional deals such as weekend specials or 24-hour rates that include gas. Some companies have their version of the airlines' Super Saver fares — you can rent a car for as little as $100 a week with unlimited mileage if you reserve the car 7 days in advance. There are two typical car rental deals:

1. Per day, per-mile charge — You pay a flat fee for each day you keep the car (usually between $15 and $40) plus a charge for each mile you drive (15¢–40¢).
2. Per-day charge, unlimited mileage — You pay a flat fee for each day you keep the car, but are not charged for mileage (an alternative is to be given a certain number of miles free, and then charged on a per-mile basis over that number). If you plan to drive more than 100 miles, an unlimited mileage, flat fee is almost always the most economical arrangement.

Most rental firms require clients to be at least 21 years old and, of course, to have a valid driver's license.

Major national rental companies with toll-free telephone numbers:

1. *Ajax Rent-A-Car* — Continental USA except California, 800 421-0896; California, 800 262-1776.
2. *America International Rent-A-Car* — Continental USA except Texas, 800 527-0202; Texas, 800 442-5757.
3. *Avis Car Rental* — Continental USA except Oklahoma, 800 331-1212; Oklahoma, 800 482-4554.
4. *Budget Rent-A-Car* — Continental USA except Nebraska, 800 527-0700; Nebraska, 800 642-9910.
5. *Dollar Rent-A-Car* — Continental USA except California, 800 421-6868; California, 800 262-1520.
6. *Hertz* — Continental USA except Oklahoma, 800 654-3131; Oklahoma, 800 522-3711.
7. *National Rent-A-Car* — Continental USA except Minnesota, 800 328-4567; Minnesota, 800 862-6064.
8. *Sears Rent-A-Car* — Continental USA except Nebraska, 800 228-2800.

To economize on car rental, consider one of the firms that rent three- to five-year-old cars that are well worn but mechanically sound. One such company is Rent-a-Wreck (800 228-5958). While these cars often rent for half the cost of the cars from major companies, they probably consume more gas than would a new, economy-size rental car.

When budgeting for your car rental, remember to include the cost of gasoline, which these days can be considerable. You can save money by filling the tank yourself before you return the car since gasoline at the car rental pump is often quite expensive.

Traveling by Plane

It *sounds* expensive to travel across the country via air, but it could be the most economical way to go if you must get to your destination quickly. Plane travel is actually cheaper per mile than travel by car (12¢ to 17¢ per mile to fly on a commercial airline; 17¢ to 27¢ to drive your own car).

If you do decide to fly, there are some basic facts you should know about the kinds of flights available, the rules governing air travel, and bargain fares now offered.

SCHEDULED AIRLINES: A number of airlines offer regularly scheduled flights in the US. Within their ranks are all the well-known major companies and many smaller, regional companies that are not so familiar.

Fares: Today's air fares are changing so rapidly that even the experts have trouble keeping up with them. Budget-conscious consumers must shop around to come up with the best fare for what they need. The airlines must set their routes and rates within the guidelines of the Civil Aeronautics Board (CAB). Several years ago, the CAB simplified its regulations to foster competition among the airlines. Before this move, airlines could really only vie for passengers by offering better service than their competitors. Today, however, they can compete with price and schedule; this has opened the doors to a wide range of fares including the airlines' equivalent of clearance sales and introductory offers.

There are three categories of fares: first class, economy, and excursions, or discounts.

A first-class ticket is your admission to a special section of the aircraft with larger seats, more leg room, better food, free drinks, and, above all, lavish attention.

Like first-class passengers, people paying the economy fare are entitled to a reserved seat, and their tickets are sold on an open reservation system. This means that there are no advance booking requirements; you can buy a ticket for a flight up to the minute of takeoff if seats are available. If your ticket is round-trip, you can make your return reservation anytime you wish — months before you leave or the day before you return. You are not required to stay at your destination for any specified amount of time (tickets are generally good for a year, after which they can be renewed if not used). You can cancel your flight anytime without penalty.

Excursion, or discount, fares, which go by such names as Super Saver, are the airlines' answer to a sale. It costs airlines almost as much to run a full plane as it does a half-full plane. Thus, to make sure to fill their seats, the airlines offer lower prices to a limited number of people in hopes of attracting passengers who might not otherwise take the trip. These fares are between 20% and 50% lower than a regular economy-class ticket.

Generally, the more flexibility you have in your travel schedule and the farther in advance you can plan, the better the deal you can get. To begin with, there are only a limited number of seats on any plane set aside for these excursion fares, and at busy times like holidays they are sold quickly (make your holiday reservations months in advance). The airlines cut down on the number of reduced-fare seats when they expect more passengers and offer more of these seats when they expect business to be poor. The same is also true of the excursion rates themselves. You pay less for your ticket at the times of day and week and year when the airlines know a lot of empty seats will be available. Thus the traveler who can fly to a business destination late at night in the middle of the weekend is likely to be able to get a reservation at the excursion fare and also at the lowest possible fare.

The excursion, or discount, fares also have strings attached. Usually the more restrictive they are, the cheaper they are. Usually you must book the flight between 7 and 30 days in advance, depending on the conditions of your fare. Often you must pay for your ticket shortly thereafter. You may well have to stay at your destination for a specified period of time; for example, no less than 7 days and no more than 30 days. Finally, you do not have the option of changing your plans after a certain point without losing your money. Another kind of excursion fare is the "unlimited mileage" deals offered by Delta and Eastern airlines. For a flat fee ($576 and $640, respectively), a single traveler may fly anywhere in the US, logging in an unlimited number of miles. The restrictions are that: all stops must be scheduled 14 days in advance; the trip must take a minimum of 7 or a maximum of 21 days; the entire fare must be paid 14 days before departure; all legs of the trip must be flown on that particular carrier.

Airlines are apt to offer special promotional fares to make travelers aware of new services, to encourage travel in slow seasons or to increase their share of the market. Budget-conscious travelers should watch for deep discounts which, like other introductory offers, are limited to a given week or day or time of year. January and February are the favorite months for such promotional fares as "Kids Fly Free" or deep discounts for accompanying wives, husbands, or friends.

Many major airlines now offer a bonus system to frequent travelers. After the first 10,000 miles, for example, you might receive a first-class ticket for the economy fare; after another 10,000 miles you might receive a discount on your next ticket purchase. The value of the bonuses continues to increase as you log more miles.

To find out about the fares that are most useful to you, read the business and travel sections of your newspaper regularly or call the airlines directly. Ask about discount or promotional fares to the destination you desire; find out if there is a similar flight that would enable you to take advantage of a discount and ask about any conditions that might restrict booking, payment, cancellation, or change of plans before you make your reservations. Check the prices from cities nearby. Sometimes, for example, a promotional fare is offered in New York, but not in Philadelphia, and is enough of a bargain to warrant leaving from New York. Since not all discounts are advertised, you should check with several airlines. Call each airline desk several times; you may well receive varying quotes from different clerks. When you think you've obtained the lowest possible price, make your booking. Remember, the airline has no obligation to give you the lowest fare. That's up to you.

Several new airlines are operating flights at lower prices with fewer services. Such airlines as New York Air, People Express, Muse Air Corporation, and Southwest Airlines can offer these lower fares by such methods as charging for checking your bags, offering only beverages and light snacks during the flight, or putting more seats aboard the aircraft. Air Florida has experimented with nonrefundable tickets at a 20% discount off its regular price. While the tickets cannot be returned, they can be sold to someone else.

There are also many good package deals, including the fly/drive fare. Offered by virtually every airline, this is a land package, which you buy in addition to airfare. It can include car rental, hotel accommodations, dining or sightseeing features, and the combined cost of the package elements is always considerably cheaper than the cost of all of them purchased separately.

Some airlines also offer bonus elements with certain tour packages. For example, United Airline's discount card (called the Countdown Card) saves you 10% of the price of meals and many other purchases at over 1,100 restaurants, nightclubs, shops, and museums around the country.

To protect yourself against fare increases, purchase your ticket as soon as possible after you receive a confirmed reservation. Generally, domestic airlines will honor their ticket, even if the fare is lower than the going rate. If, however, fares are increased between the time you make your reservation and the time you purchase your ticket, you will have to pay the higher fare. If you have your ticket in hand when you arrive for your flight, it eliminates one more possibility of delay or problems.

It is important to remember on excursion or discount fares that when a reservation clerk or travel agent says that you must purchase your tickets by a specific date, this is a deadline. If you do not make the deadline, the airline may cancel your reservations without telling you.

Seats: Airline seats are assigned in advance or on a first come–first served basis at the time of check-in. Some airlines, such as United, permit you to request a seat when you make a reservation. You must decide if you want a smoking or nonsmoking section, a movie section, or one of the few nonreclining seats.

Some airlines furnish seating charts, which make choosing a spot much easier; but, in general, there are a few basics to consider. Airline representatives claim that most craft are more stable toward the front and midsection, while seats farthest away from the engines are quietest. Passengers with long legs should request a seat in the first row of a desired section or a seat directly behind emergency doors (as seats next to the exits are often removed). Bear in mind, however, that movie-watching from the first row is difficult and uncomfortable. A window seat protects you from aisle traffic and allows you a view, while an aisle seat enables you to get up and stretch your legs. Middle seats are the least desirable. If you want peace and quiet, it is probably a good idea to request a seat in the first section of coach (approximately rows 8–14). Some airlines have designated this area as the "quiet" or "business" zone. While other airlines do not have special quiet sections on domestic flights, once you are in flight, you are free to move to any available seat.

Meals: Just as seating can be arranged in advance, special meals can be ordered before flight time. Most of the major airlines offer kosher, salt-free, low cholesterol, vegetarian, and other special meals at no extra charge. You should order what you want at the time you make your reservation or at least 24 hours before your flight.

Getting Bumped: A special problem with scheduled flights is that the airlines often make more reservations than there are seats in order to compensate for people who don't show up for the flight. If the airline has oversold the flight and everyone with a reservation does show up, there are obviously not going to be enough seats. The Civil Aeronautics Board now requires that the airline first seek volunteers who will agree to be bumped from their seats if they are paid a sum set by the airline and given a seat on the next available flight. If, however, there are not enough volunteers, the airlines may bump passengers according to a priority seating plan approved by the CAB and available to passengers at all ticket counters. These passengers must be paid at least the full price of a one-way ticket to their destination, a minimum of $37.50 up to a maximum of $200. If the airline cannot get passengers who were bumped against their will to their destinations within two hours of their original arrival time, the airline must double this compensation. If you feel that being bumped cost you more than the airline is willing to pay at the airport, you can refuse its check and try to negotiate a higher settlement through its customer service department.

To protect yourself as best you can against getting bumped, arrive at the airport, allowing plenty of time to check in and get to the gate — an hour in advance if possible. If the flight is oversold, immediately ask for the written statement explaining the airline's policy on denied boarding compensation and its boarding priorities. If the airline refuses to give you this information or if you do not feel they have handled the situation properly, file a complaint with both the airline and the CAB (see address below).

Delays and Cancellations: Each airline has its own policy for assisting passengers whose flights are delayed or canceled or who must wait for another flight because their original flight was overbooked. Most airline personnel will make new travel arrangements if this becomes necessary. Generally, if the delay is longer than four hours, the airline will pay for a phone call or telegram, a meal, and in some cases a hotel room and transportation to the hotel. Make sure to ask about what the airline will do.

Caution: If you are bumped or miss a flight, insist that the bumping airline notify other airlines on which you have reservations or connecting flights. When your name is taken off the passenger list of your initial flight, the computer automatically cancels all of your reservations unless you take steps to preserve them.

Baggage: Each passenger is allowed only one carry-on bag, of which the total combined dimension of length, width, and breadth must be less than 45 inches. The bag must fit unobtrusively beneath the passenger's seat. First-class passengers are each allowed to put two bags in the cargo hold, neither one of which may exceed a total of 62 inches for its three dimensions. Economy passengers are also allowed only two bags each in the cargo hold, but the combined total of both bags may not exceed 107 inches, and no single bag may be more than 62 inches. Charges for additional or outsize bags are made at a flat rate, depending on the destination. If you plan to travel with a bike, skis, or other sports equipment, be sure to check with the airlines beforehand. Most have procedures for handling such baggage; however, you may have to pay a special charge for transport.

If your luggage is not in the baggage claim area after your flight has arrived or if it is damaged, report the problem to the airline personnel immediately (some airlines disclaim liability for missing or damaged luggage that is not reported in writing within four hours of the arrival of the flight). Next, make sure that the airline personnel fill out a report form on your lost or damaged luggage. Finally, hold on to your claim check until you receive your baggage. The airline is responsible for recovering lost luggage or must reimburse you for up to $750 for the loss or damage. Most airlines will give you some money at the airport for emergency purchases if your luggage cannot be readily located.

To reduce the chances of your luggage going astray, remove all tags from previous trips and doublecheck the tag that the airline puts on your bag to make sure that it is coded for your destination. Airlines also require that you label your bags inside and outside with your name and address, and suggest you include (inside) a person to contact at your destination if possible. Always lock your luggage.

CHARTER FLIGHTS: This type of program includes a seat on a specially arranged flight often coupled with a hotel room, meals, and other travel arrangements. Although charters were once clearly the best travel bargain available, today the scheduled airlines' discount and excursion fares (such as the Super Saver) generally offer tariffs that are just as low and often more flexible. Charter flights have been discontinued in many areas. To some popular vacation spots like Las Vegas and Hawaii, however, they can still be a good buy.

You pay in convenience for what you save in money on a charter. If you are forced to cancel your flight, you could lose most or possibly all of your money unless you have cancellation insurance, which is a *must* (see *Insurance* in this section, p. 37). Charters have little of the flexibility of scheduled flights; you must leave and return on the scheduled dates; if you miss the plane, you lose your flight and your money — no refund.

If you do take a charter, read the contract carefully and note specific stipulations for cancellations and penalties and the conditions under which the tour operator has the right to cancel the charter. Remember that if a tour is canceled, your money must be returned immediately.

Consumer Information: Consumers who do not feel that they have been dealt with fairly by airlines or charter companies should make their complaints known. Start with the Customer Service Representative at the airport where the problem occurs. If he or she cannot resolve your complaint to your satisfaction, write to the consumer office of the airline. In a businesslike, typed letter, explain what reservations you held, what happened, the names of the employees who were involved, and what you expect the airline to do to remedy the situation. Send them copies *(never the originals)* of tickets, receipts, and other documents that back up your claims. If this fails to produce results, write to the Civil Aeronautics Board, Bureau of Consumer Protection, Washington, DC 20428 (202 673-5990) and enlist its help. The CAB also offers consumers free information on the regulations governing the airlines. One of the many good publications you can write for is *Air Traveler's Fly-Rights.*

From a consumer standpoint, the need to select a reliable tour company has never been greater. While such selection requires time and investigation, care is absolutely imperative in the current atmosphere. Fortunately, you can check the number of complaints, if any, lodged against individual operators in the past, thereby uncovering the experience of other travelers. The two most obvious places to do this are the CAB and the Better Business Bureau in the home city of the company. When you consider a package tour, ask your travel agent who runs it and then check out the company. You're only protecting yourself.

Two excellent sources of general airline information are *Travel Smart,* a monthly newsletter (40 Beechdale Rd., Dobbs Ferry, NY 10522, $21 a year); and *How to Fly for Less* by Jens Jurgen (Travel Information Bureau, 44 County Line Rd., Farmingdale, NY 11735, $5).

Touring by Train

Almost all of the regularly scheduled passenger trains in the US are run by Amtrak, which serves most of the country's major cities and has made dramatic improvements in equipment and service. Routes, schedules, stations, sample fares, and a complete list of toll-free Amtrak numbers in every continental US state are given in the *National Timetable,* available at any Amtrak station or sales office (or through the national office at 400 N Capitol St., NW, Washington, DC 20001).

Accommodations and Fares: Amtrak fares are based on the quality of accommodation the passenger enjoys on the journey. Cheapest is basic transportation fare. Ordinarily this will buy a coach seat for the duration of the trip, but it guarantees only that the passenger has a right to transportation. Seats are allocated on a first come–first served basis. In addition to the seats, long-distance trains offer sleeping accommodations, for which the passenger pays significantly more. On most trains, there are three classes of these: slumbercoaches, private rooms with lounge seats that convert to beds and their own toilet and washstand; roomettes, larger rooms with chairs and fold-down beds; and full-sized bedrooms that can be combined into suites. The new Superliners have deluxe bedrooms; economy rooms, which are similar to a roomette with a toilet and washstand; and family bedrooms, which accommodate five people.

The cost of a coach seat — basic transportation fare — on a train will always be something more than the cost of a bus ticket to the same destination, and something less than coach fare on a plane. For example, the Amtrak coach fare between Chicago and Seattle is about $60 more than bus fare, $50 less than coach fare on a plane. However, the plane makes the trip in a few hours; the train takes two days, and it is likely anyone making the trip by train will want some kind of sleeping accommodations rather than just a coach seat. An economy room on that route costs about $85 more than the plane coach fare; and a deluxe bedroom about $200 more. So the cost of a train compared with that of a plane is very much relative to the level of comfort. From time to time, Amtrak also offers such promotional fares as a round-trip ticket for $10 more than the one-way fare.

Booking: Tickets may be obtained from Amtrak stations, travel agents, or on board the train (for an extra $3), and can be purchased with any major credit card or personal check. Reservations are mandatory for all club cars, sleeping cars, slumbercoaches, Metroliner coaches (high-speed electric trains that provide fast service between major cities), and on a number of other regular runs. Trains that require reservations are so marked in the *Timetable.* If you have difficulty reaching the reservation number, try early in the morning or late at night. Always allow extra time to make connections because trains are often late. If you have confirmed reservations and miss a connection because the train was late, Amtrak will provide overnight accommodations, if necessary. Passengers can stop anywhere along their route for as long as they like, so long as they reach their final destination before their ticket expires (most tickets are good for a year). Sleeping car attendants should be tipped $1 a night.

Baggage: In most stations baggage can be checked through to destination up to one hour before departure (and should be claimed within 30 minutes after arrival). On long-distance runs, you will be allowed to carry on only enough baggage for essentials during the journey; you are allowed to check three pieces of luggage weighing a total of 150 pounds. Attendants on the train, or Red Caps in most stations, will give you free help with your luggage (tip about 50¢). Amtrak urges you to deal only with Red Caps.

Tours: The USA Railpass is Amtrak's excursion rate. Not available to US citizens, it can be purchased only in Europe. The pass entitles the holder to unlimited coach travel on Amtrak trains and routes for periods of 7, 14, 21, and 30 days. For US citizens, Amtrak sometimes offers unlimited mileage and stopovers for a given time at a fixed fee. These are called Circle Fares. Amtrak also offers an incredible variety of package tours, from a trip along the Pacific Coast, Seattle to Los Angeles, to week trips through the New England foliage. Brochures and details on Amtrak tours are available from Amtrak stations, or travel agents. For Amtrak information; look in your phone book for their toll-free number or write Amtrak Tours, PO Box 311, Addison, IL 60101.

Touring by Bus

Crisscrossing America's highways to serve 15,000 cities and towns, bus companies easily comprise the country's most comprehensive public transport system. You can almost always get there by bus. Two major national bus companies, Continental Trailways and Greyhound, have depots in most cities across the country (listed in the Yellow Pages under "Bus"). Greyhound runs 4,600 buses over 100,000 miles of routes; Trailways' fleet is slightly smaller at 3,360 and covers 91,000 miles of highways. These two giants, with the many smaller independent firms in operation around the country, offer the most frequent, most economical transportation in America. Buses are undeniably slower than trains, planes, or private cars, and there is a trade-off of money saved for time spent en route.

Accommodations and Fares: The cost of a bus trip is 6¢ to 8¢ a mile, compared to 12¢ to 17¢ a mile by plane, and 17¢ to 27¢ a mile by private car. The real savings in bus travel are most evident on long-distance, return-trip journeys. The difference between the train and bus fares on a one-way, New York to Philadelphia trip is about a dollar (about $22 difference between bus and economy air fare). However, the difference between bus and train one-way rates from Denver to San Francisco is about $25. Lately the competition among bus companies is increasing, so that it is worth asking about promotional fares and checking fares with more than one company. Trailways, for example, has offered a family plan in which a spouse and children from 12 to 22 receive 25% off the child's fare. For those who can ride from 7 PM to 6 AM on certain routes, the company has offered 40% off the one-way fare, and on Tuesdays, riders receive 50% off the return portion of their round-trip ticket.

Bus passengers are allowed to make stopovers anywhere along their route, as long as their entire journey is completed before the ticket expires. Most regular bus tickets are good for 30 days. If you don't use the ticket within that time, it may be returned for a full refund, or replaced by another ticket.

Booking: Reservations are not necessary on most bus routes; companies usually send as many buses as are needed to handle all passengers. Sightseeing tours and special programs (see below) require reservations and are subject to slightly different stopover rules. Both Greyhound and Trailways have unlimited travel tickets that allow the ticket holder to travel anywhere in the US on company routes (and often on the routes of smaller, connecting bus lines) for specified periods of time (7, 15, and 30 days). Special prices for these unlimited travel deals represent considerable savings. Greyhound's program is called Ameripass; Trailways offers Eaglepass.

Services: Most buses are not equipped for food service. On long trips they make meal stops, and there is always food service of one kind or another in the terminals. It is not a bad idea to bring some food aboard. Almost all interstate, long-distance buses have air-conditioning, heating, toilets, adjustable seats, and reading lamps.

For Comfortable Travel: Dress casually with loose fitting clothes. Be sure you have a sweater or jacket (even in the summer air-conditioning can make buses quite cool). Passengers are allowed transistor radios for music or news, but must use earphones. Choose a seat in the front near the driver for the best view, or in the middle between the front and rear wheels for the smoothest ride. Avoid the back near the toilet unless you smoke. Smokers are generally restricted to the last rows of any bus.

Tours: Greyhound offers a wide variety of sightseeing bus tours. These include accommodations for overnight stays. For information on these tour programs, check with your local Greyhound office. Dozens of tour operators offer a wide variety of bus or motorcoach tours in the US. One directory is the *Official Domestic Tour Manual* published by Grace J. Talmage & Associates, PO Box 39, Abington, PA 19001, for $12.50.

Package Tours

A package tour is a travel arrangement that combines several travel services — transportation, accommodations, sightseeing, meals, etc. — into a one-price, one-booking package. The cost of the entire package is well below the combined price of the services if bought independently; and the passenger is freed from the bother of making any separate arrangements.

There are hundreds of package programs on the market today, offered by airlines, Amtrak, and the bus companies, as well as car rental companies, hotels, and travel companies. Many are built around sports activities like skiing. A typical package tour might include transportation to and from the destination, accommodations for the length of stay, a sightseeing tour of the area, and some meals. The price for this (especially if transportation were provided via charter flight) could be less than a round-trip economy airline ticket to the destination on a regularly scheduled flight.

One of the consumer's biggest problems is finding information about tour operators since you very seldom have direct contact. Usually, a retail travel agent intervenes between customer and tour operator, and much depends on the candor and cooperation of the agent.

You should ask your travel agent a number of questions about the tour he is recommending. For example: Have you previously used the packages provided by this tour operator? How long has the tour operator been in business? Is the operator bonded? Which and how many companies are involved in the package? Is there an escrow account in which deposits will be held, and, if so, what is the name of the bank?

This last question is very important. The law requires that tour operators deposit any charter passenger's deposit and subsequent payment in a proper escrow trust account. Money paid into such an account cannot legally be used except to pay for the costs of a particular package or as a refund if the trip is canceled. So to ensure safe handling of your money, make out your check to the escrow bank account. The law requires that it appear on any tour brochure, and it is usually found in that mass of minuscule type on the back. On the face of your check, write the details of the charter, including the destination and dates; on the back, print the words "for deposit only." Your travel agent may prefer that you make your check out to him, saying that he will then pay the tour operator the fee minus his commission. But it is perfectly legal to write your check this way, and the agent should have sufficient faith in the tour operator to trust him to send the proper commission. If you don't make your check out to the escrow account, you lose all protection should the trip be canceled or the tour operator or travel agent fail. If your agent objects too vociferously to this procedure, maybe you ought to take your travel business elsewhere.

Read package tour brochures carefully and with a grain of salt. Begin by assuming that the things that are not mentioned are not included in the price of the tour. Tour brochures often feature the lowest price at which a tour is offered, but this price may be available in off-season only, during midweek, at the cheapest hotel (which some travelers would not find satisfactory), or in such limited numbers that it is sold out at once. And remember: Prices quoted in brochures are based upon double occupancy (two people traveling together); if you travel alone, you may pay as much as 50% more (see *Hints for Single Travelers*). Tour brochures give prices of tours from the city of departure; if you don't live there, you must add transportation to and from that city.

Understand what is, and is not, included in a package. This may vary, but is generally spelled out in the fine print in the brochure. Read it and ask the following questions:

1. Does the tour include air fare (or other transportation), sightseeing, meals, transfers, taxes, baggage handling, tips, or any other services? Do you want all these services? If the brochure says "some meals" are included, exactly what does this mean — breakfast and dinner every day, or a farewell dinner the last night? Do you have a choice of food, or must you stick to a single menu?
2. What classes of hotels are offered?
3. Do you get a refund if you cancel? (If not — and stipulations vary widely between tour operators — get cancellation insurance.)
4. Can the operator cancel if not enough people join? (Usually the answer is yes.)
5. Is the price quoted in the literature guaranteed or can the tour operator increase it before departure?

Read the responsibility clause on the back page. Here the tour operator usually reserves the right to change services or schedules as long as you are offered equivalent service; this clause also absolves the operator of responsibility for circumstances beyond human control, like floods or famines, and of responsibility for injury to you.

Since tour programs vary so widely in quality and tour operators sometimes lack candor about their programs, travelers going to new areas really must rely on firsthand information from friends or a reliable travel agent to avoid disappointment.

Camping, Hiking, Biking, Recreational Vehicles

CAMPING: Fifty-eight million Americans go camping every year, and that can mean anything from backpacking with a pup tent to living in comfort in a plush recreational vehicle. There are almost 17,000 campgrounds serving these campers, some private, many in national or state parks and forests. Some excellent guides to campgrounds are, from Rand McNally: *Campgrounds & Trailer Parks* ($6.95), *Backpacking & Outdoor Guide* ($7.95), *Western Campgrounds & Trailer Parks* ($5.95), *Northeastern Campgrounds & Trailer Parks* ($4.95), and *Southeastern Campgrounds & Trailer Parks* ($4.95); from Woodall Publishing: *North American Campground Directory* ($8.95), *Eastern Campground Directory* ($5.95), and *Western Campground Directory* ($5.95). In addition, the AAA has free camping guides for AAA members which give practical camping hints as well as lists of campgrounds and facilities.

Where to Camp: Campsites range from private facilities to state and national parks. An organization called Camper 800 offers a toll-free reservation system for about 2,000 private campgrounds throughout the US for $1 a call, regardless of the number of reservations you make. The number: 800 828-9280 outside New York; 800 462-9220 within New York. Most national parks (even the famous ones like Yosemite, Grand Canyon, and Yellowstone) have adjacent extensive national forests with the same beautiful country. For a complete list of national forests, write for the free Forest Service brochure FS 13, "Field Offices of the Forest Service," US Forest Service, Office of Information, PO Box 2417, Washington, DC 20013.

The National Park Service also encourages campers to use lesser-known national parks in its brochure "Lesser Known Areas of the National Park System," usually available free from local offices of the Park Service, or for $4 from the Superintendent of Documents, US Government Printing Office, Washington, DC 20402.

Organized Trips: If you want to go far afield with an experienced guide and other campers, contact these organizations:

1. Yosemite Institute, PO Box 487, Yosemite, CA 95389 (209 372-4441).
2. American Wilderness Alliance, 4260 E Evans Ave., Suite 8, Denver, CO 80222 (303 758-5018).
3. American Forestry Association, 1319 18th St., NW, Washington, DC 20036 (202 467-5810).
4. Sierra Club, 530 Bush St., San Francisco, CA 94108 (415 981-8634).
5. Nature Expeditions International, 599 College Ave., Palo Alto, CA 94306 (415 494-6572).
6. Appalachian Mountain Club, 5 Joy St., Boston, MA 02108 (617 523-0636).

HIKING: If you would rather eliminate all the gear and planning and take to the outdoors unencumbered, park the car and go for a day's hike. There are fabulous trails in the United States (some of the very best are listed in *Wilderness Trips on Foot,* DIVERSIONS).

To make outings safe and pleasant, find out about the trails you plan to hike, and know your own limits. Choose an easy route if you are out of shape. Stick to the trails unless you are an experienced hiker or know the area well. If it is at all wild, let someone at the beginning of the trail know where you going, or leave a note on your car.

All you need to set out are a pair of sturdy shoes and socks, jeans or long pants to keep branches, poison ivy, and bugs off your legs, a canteen of water, a hat for the sun, and, if you like, a picnic lunch. It is a good idea to dress in layers, so that you can peel off a sweater or two to keep pace with the rising sun and replace them as the sun goes down. Make sure, too, to wear clothes with pockets or bring a pack to keep your hands free. Some useful and important pocket or pack stuffers include a jackknife, waterproof matches, a map, compass, and in snake areas, a snake bite kit.

BIKING: In choosing bike routes, long or short, look for ways to escape the omnipresent automobile and its fumes. Stick to back roads; use state highway maps (they cost a dollar or two at the most), which list secondary roads that the gasoline company maps ignore. Especially good riding is along old canal roads, abandoned railroad right-of-ways, and hard, packed beaches. Two sources of bike routes and roads are *The Bicycle Touring Book* by Glenda and Tim Wilhelm (Rodale Press, $12.95 cloth, $9.95 paperback) and *American Biking Atlas & Touring Guide* by Sue Browder (Workman Publishing, $5.95). For general biking information, try *All New Complete Book of Bicycling* by Eugene A. Sloane (Simon & Schuster, $19.95) and *Anybody's Bike Book* by Tom Cuthberton (Ten-Speed Press, $8.95 cloth, $4.95 paperback).

Road Safety: While the car may be the bane of cyclists, cyclists who do not follow the rules of the road strike terror in the hearts of automobile drivers. Follow the same rules and regulations as motor vehicle drivers. Stay to the right side of the road. Ride no more than two abreast, or single file where traffic is heavy. Keep three bike lengths behind the bike in front of you. Stay alert to sand, gravel, potholes, and wet surfaces; make sure to wear bright clothes and use lights at dusk or night.

Choosing a Bike: A bicycle is the correct size for you if you can straddle its center bar with feet flat on the ground and an inch or so between your crotch and the bar. (Nowadays, because women's old-fashioned barless bikes are not as strong as men's, most women buy men's bicycles.) Seat height is right if your leg is just short of completely extended when you push the pedal to the bottom of its arc. Experienced cyclists keep tires fully inflated (pressure requirements vary widely, but are always imprinted on the side of the tire; stay within five pounds of the recommended pressure), and pedal at an even pace. For roadside repairs, and especially on longer rides, carry a tool kit of a bike wrench, screwdriver, pliers, tire repair kit, cycle oil, work gloves.

Tours: For a variety of bicycle tours, contact: Country Cycling Tours, 95 W 95th St., New York, NY 10025 (212 222-6144), for greater New York and the Northeast; Vermont Bicycle Touring, RD 3, Bristol, VT 05443 (802 388-4011), for Vermont; Backroads Bicycle Touring Co., PO Box 5534, Berkeley, CA 94705 (415 652-0786), for California, Yellowstone, and the Grand Tetons; Colorado Bicycle Tours, PO Box 45, Pitkin, CO 81241 (303 641-4240), for the Colorado mountains; Suwannee River Bicycle Tours, PO Box 319, White Springs, FL 32096 (904 397-2757), for Florida. General biking information is available through biking clubs in almost every city in the country (listed in the Yellow Pages under "Clubs"); a national biking organization is League of American Wheelmen (PO Box 988, Baltimore, MD 21203, 301 727-2022).

RECREATIONAL VEHICLES: The term recreational vehicles (or RVs) is applied to all manner of camping vehicles, whether towed or self-propelled. The level of comfort in an RV is limited only by the amount of money you choose to spend: It can be nothing more than an enclosed space for sleeping bags, or it can be a home on wheels, requiring electrical hookups at night to run the TV and kitchen appliances.

Towed RVs: Tow vehicles are hitched to cars or trucks and pulled. At their simplest, they are fold-down campers, tents on wheels that unfold into sleeping spaces. Fold-down campers weigh about 1,100 pounds and cost between $2,100 and $4,700. More elaborate are travel trailers, 10 to 30 feet long (average is about 22 feet), weighing up to 10,000 pounds, and costing as much as $25,000 (they start around $4,000).

Self-Propelled RVs: There are several styles of self-propelled vehicles:

1. Truck campers are converted pickup trucks with covered living units built on the truck body, often with sections extending over truck cabs. Cost and weight depend upon the size of the truck; but the living units alone cost between $2,600 and $6,500.
2. Van campers are just like store delivery vans, modified inside for living, sleeping, and dining. They cost anywhere from $16,000 to $22,000.
3. Mini/Class A motor homes are homes on wheels, with varying degrees of size and luxury. A mini costs between $20,000 and $24,000; a Class A starts around $30,000 and can cost as much as $70,000.

Gas Consumption: An RV undoubtedly saves the traveler a great deal of money on accommodations, and, if cooking appliances are part of the unit, on food. However, any RV increases gas consumption. It is most expensive to tow a large trailer camper, which decreases auto mileage by 50%. More economical, because smaller, is the fold-down tow camper, which will reduce normal car mileage by about 10%–15%. Self-propelled RVs have no better mileage records. A truck camper gets about 20% less mileage than the same truck without camper, and an average Class A motor home gets only 7 to 12 miles per gallon of gas.

To reduce gas consumption, travel lightly (for every 100 pounds of weight, you use one percent more gas). Carry only the water you need on the road. Put everything inside your RV to reduce wind resistance and save on gas.

Renting: RVs are a poor choice for people who do not like to drive. They are not for people who want to leave housekeeping chores behind when they set off on vacation. They are sure to sour a person who cannot stand to do any maintenance or simple handyman chores, nor are they for people who need lots of privacy. The best way to introduce yourself to traveling by RV is to rent one. Some dealers will apply rental fees to the eventual price of purchase (check local Yellow Pages, and shop around for the best terms). For information on how to operate, maintain, choose, and use a recreational vehicle, see Jody R. Pallidin and Beverly Dubin's *Roll Your Own: The Complete Guide to Living in a Truck, Bus, Van or Camper* (Macmillan, $7.95). You might also consider subscribing to *Trailer Life,* 23945 Craftsman Rd., Calabasas, CA 91302 ($8.50 a year) or *RV Travel Magazine,* Woodall Publishing Company, 500 Hyacinth Pl., Highland Park, IL 60035 ($8.50 a year).

Preparing

Calculating Costs

A realistic appraisal of your travel expenses is the most crucial bit of planning you'll undertake before your trip. It is also, unfortunately, one for which it is most difficult to give precise practical advice. Travel styles are intensely personal, and style to a great extent determines cost. Will you stay in a hotel every night? Will you eat every meal in a restaurant? Are you camping or picnicking? The "average" per diem costs we offer below are based on certain assumptions — every night in a hotel, every meal in a restaurant — that are hardly graven in stone. Never let published figures on the cost of travel frighten you out of taking a trip. You can always make economies and travel more cheaply. On the other hand, never get lulled into the feeling that you don't need to budget before you go. No matter how lush your travel budget, you will discover that without careful planning beforehand, and strict accounting along the way, you will spend more than you anticipated.

If you spend every night in a hotel or motel, and *if* you eat every meal in a modestly priced restaurant, you can expect to spend about $45 per person a day traveling. This figure does not include transportation costs. It does include accommodations (based on two people sharing a room), three meals, some sightseeing and other modest entertainment costs. It is based on recent figures of the average amount that Americans spent each day on trips of 200 miles or more, adjusted for inflation. It is, therefore, a national figure, and if it seems a bit arbitrary, bear in mind that as a raw figure it should represent no more than the broadest kind of guideline for daily costs.

However, adjusted for regional price differences it produces some figures that are much more useful. For example, overall prices in the Mountain West indicate that a day's travel costs about 5% less than this national figure. Travel in New York and New Jersey costs about 30% more. Travel cost indices for different parts of the country are as follows:

AREA		TRAVEL COST INDEX
NEW ENGLAND		+15%
Connecticut	New Hampshire	
Maine	Rhode Island	
Massachusetts	Vermont	
NEW YORK/NEW JERSEY		+30%
MID-ATLANTIC		Same as national average
Delaware	Pennsylvania	
District of Columbia	Virginia	
Maryland	West Virginia	

SOUTH		Same as national average
Alabama	Louisiana	
Arkansas	Mississippi	
Florida	North Carolina	
Georgia	South Carolina	
Kentucky	Tennessee	
GREAT LAKES		+5%
Illinois	Minnesota	
Indiana	Ohio	
Iowa	Wisconsin	
Michigan		
MOUNTAIN WEST		−5%
Colorado	South Dakota	
Montana	Utah	
Nebraska	Wyoming	
North Dakota		
FRONTIER WEST		Same as national average
Arizona	New Mexico	
Kansas	Oklahoma	
Missouri	Texas	
FAR WEST		+25%
Alaska	Nevada	
California	Oregon	
Idaho	Washington	

You can use these travel cost indices to forecast a reasonably accurate picture of your daily travel costs, based on exactly the way in which you want to travel. Calculate how much it would cost, per day, to visit your home town, traveling just as you intend to travel (camping out occasionally, or splurging on the best hotel in town; eating out or renting a kitchenette and cooking your own meals; etc.). This is relatively simple to do because you have a day-by-day feeling for costs in your own area, and with a couple of local phone calls, you can check out accommodation rates

This home town travel cost figure becomes the "base rate" which you can use to calculate per-day costs at your destination, using the percentage point indices in the chart above. You must determine whether the area to which you are traveling is more or less expensive than your home town. To do this, locate your own state on the chart, and then your destination. If the area to which you are traveling has a higher travel cost index than your home state, find the difference. This represents the percentage by which your destination is more expensive than your home. To find the per-day cost of travel at your destination, you must multiply your home base rate by this percentage, then add the result to the base rate. The figure you get is the approximate per-day cost of travel at your destination.

If the area to which you are going has a lower index than your home state, find the difference. This figure represents the percentage by which your destination is less expensive than your home. Multiply the base rate by this figure, and then subtract the result from the base rate. The figure you get is the approximate per-day cost of travel at your destination.

Two hypothetical examples to clarify the method: Let us say your home town is Salt Lake City, Utah. After some brief research, you find it would cost you about $42.50 a day to visit Salt Lake City, staying at hotels and living the way you intend to live on your vacation. However, your real destination is New England. How does your base rate figure of $42.50 relate to costs in New England? Utah is a Mountain West state, with a travel cost index of −5%. New England is much higher, at +15%. New England is, therefore, a total of 20% more expensive than Utah (+15% − −5 = +20). Multiply your base rate by 20% ($42.50 × .20 = 8.50), and you discover you must add about $8.50 to your per-day costs. New England will cost about $51 a day.

Suppose you live in Evansville, Indiana. After some research, you decide that were you to visit your home town in the style in which you plan to travel, it would cost about $50 a day. Your real destination, however, is Wyoming and the Grand Tetons. Indiana is in the Great Lakes region, with a travel cost index of +5%. Wyoming is a Mountain West state, with an index of −5%. This means that Wyoming is actually 10% cheaper than Evansville (−5 − +5 = −10). Multiply the base rate by 10% (50 × .10 = 5.00); you discover that the Evansville base rate is about $5.00 more expensive than Wyoming, and so you must subtract that amount from the base rate. Thus, it should cost about $45.00 each day to visit the Grand Tetons.

For this calculation to work, remember always to subtract your home state index from the index of the state to which you are traveling. If you get a positive number, it means the state to which you are traveling is more expensive than your home state; a negative number means your destination is cheaper than your home area.

Calculating Transportation Costs: In earlier sections of GETTING READY TO GO we have discussed comparative costs of different modes of transportation, and the myriad special travel rates available through package tours, mid-week flights, train and bus budget deals. See each of the relevant sections for specific information. Transportation is likely to represent one of the largest items in your travel budget, but the encouraging aspect of this is that you can determine these costs before you leave. Fares will have to be paid in advance, especially if you take advantage of budget air travel or other special deals. Except for breakdown or repairs (for which you should budget something), car costs can be calculated by figuring mileage and average gas prices, based on your own experience.

A Note on Our Hotel/Restaurant Cost Categories: There are a great many moderate and inexpensive hotels and restaurants which we have not included in this book. Our *Best in Town* and *Best en Route* listings include only those places we think are best in their price range. We have rated our listings by general price categories: expensive, moderate, inexpensive. The introductory paragraph of each listing gives an indication of just what those categories mean within the context of local prices.

Planning a Trip

123 The merits of planning a trip carefully *before* you leave should be evident to even resolute nonplanners. But there are certain parameters within which each traveler must decide what to do, where to do it, how to get there, and how much to spend. You should consider these carefully even before you begin the time-consuming groundwork:

1. How much time do you have for the entire vacation, and how much of that do you want to spend in transit?
2. What interests and activities do you want to pursue (what makes the most pleasant break from your daily routine)?
3. What time of year are you going?
4. How much money is available for the entire vacation?

In addition, your general lifestyle will affect your decisions: What degree of comfort do you require; will you consider a tour, or do you want complete independence; how much responsibility for the trip do you want (will you consider a package trip)?

There is no lack of travel information in and on the United States. You can turn to travel agents, who specialize in planning and arranging trips (see p. 31), to travel clubs such as AAA and other motoring organizations which have tour centers, and to general travel sources like books, guidebooks, brochures, and maps. State tourist boards and city convention centers provide vast amounts of literature of this sort for the asking (for details on getting travel information, and a bibliography of travel books and sources, see this section, p. 57; for a list of state travel bureaus, p. 59; for city convention and tourist centers, see the *Sources and Resources* section of each city report in THE AMERICAN CITIES).

Make plans early. If you are flying and hope to take advantage of the considerable savings offered through discount fares or charter programs, you may need reservations as much as three months in advance. In high season, and in popular destinations, hotel and resort reservations are required months in advance (hotels inside Disney World, for example, often demand a year's notice). Hotels require deposits before they will guarantee reservations. Be sure you have a receipt for any deposit.

Household details before you leave:

1. Arrange for your mail to be forwarded, held by the post office, or picked up daily at your house. Someone should check your door occasionally to pick up any unexpected deliveries. Piles of leaflets, circulars, packages, or brochures are an announcement to thieves that no one is home.
2. Cancel all deliveries (newspapers, milk, etc.).
3. Arrange for the lawn to be mowed at the regular times.
4. Arrange for care of pets.
5. Etch your social security number in a prominent place on all appliances (televisions, radios, cameras, kitchen appliances). This considerably reduces their appeal to thieves, and facilitates identification.
6. Leave a house key, your itinerary, and your automobile license number (if driving) with a relative or friend, and notify police that you are leaving and who has the key and itinerary.
7. Empty refrigerator, lower thermostat.
8. Immediately before leaving, check that all doors, windows, and garage doors are securely locked.

To further discourage thieves, it is wise to set up several variable timers around the house so that lights and even the television go on and off several times in different rooms of the house each night.

Make a list of any valuable items you are carrying with you, including credit card numbers and the serial numbers of your traveler's checks. Put copies in your luggage, purse, or pocket, and leave one copy at home. Put a label with your name and home address on the inside of your luggage, to facilitate identification in case of loss. Put your name — but not your address — on a label on the exterior of your luggage.

Review your travel documents. If you are traveling by air, check to see that your ticket has been filled in correctly. The left side of the ticket should have a list of each stop you will make (even if you are only stopping to change planes) beginning with your departure point. Be sure that the list is correct, and count the number of carbons to see that you have one for each plane you will take. If you have confirmed reservations, be sure that the column marked "status" says "OK" beside each flight. Have in hand vouchers or proofs of payment for any reservations paid in advance. This includes hotels, transfers to and from the airport, sightseeing, car rentals, special events, etc.

If you are traveling by car, bring your driver's license, auto registration, proof of insurance, gasoline credit cards, and auto service card if you have them, maps, books, flashlight, batteries, emergency flasher, first aid kit, extra car keys, and sunglasses. (For more information on preparing your car, see p. 12).

Finally, if you are traveling by plane, call to reconfirm your flight. While this is not required on domestic flights as it is on international flights, it is always advisable.

How to Pack

Exactly what you pack on your trip will be a function of where you are going and when, and the kind of things you intend to do. As a first step, however, find out about the general weather conditions — temperature, rainfall, seasonal variations — at your destination. This information is included in the individual city reports of THE AMERICAN CITIES; other sources of information are airlines, travel agents, and *The Climate Advisor* by Gilbert Schwartz (Climate Guide Publications, $7.90) which includes very specific information on 350 locations (primarily cities) in the US, Mexico, and the Caribbean.

Throughout the United States life is quite casual, and only at the most elegant resorts will you be required to have dressy clothes. If you are planning to be on the move — either in a car, bus, train, or plane — consider loose fitting clothes that do not wrinkle. Lightweight wools, knits, and drip-dry fabrics travel best, and prints look fresher longer than solids. Bring styles and colors of clothes that can be matched to give you as much variety with as few articles of clothing as possible.

The idea is to get everything into the suitcase and out again with as few wrinkles as possible. Put heavy items on the bottom toward the hinges of the suitcase, so that they do not wrinkle other clothes. Candidates for the bottom layer include shoes (stuff them with small items to save space), toiletry kit, handbags (stuff them to help keep their shape), and alarm clock. Fill out this layer with things that will not wrinkle or will not matter if they do, such as socks, bathing suit, gloves, and underwear.

If you get this first, heavy layer as smooth as possible with the fill-ins, you will have a shelf for the next layer of the more easily wrinkled items like slacks, jackets, shirts, dresses, and skirts. These should be buttoned and zipped, laid along the whole width of the suitcase, with as little folding as possible. When you do need to make a fold, do it on a crease (as with pants), along a seam in the fabric, or in a place where it will not show, such as shirttails. Alternate each piece of clothing, using one side of the suitcase, then the other to make the layers as flat as possible.

On the top layer, put the things you will want at once: nightclothes, an umbrella or raincoat, or a sweater. With men's two-suiter suitcases, follow the same procedure. Then place jackets on hangers, straighten them out, and leave them unbuttoned. If they are too wide for the suitcase, fold lengthwise down the middle, straighten the shoulders, and fold the sleeves in along the seam.

Some Packing Hints: Cosmetics and any other liquids should be packed in plastic bottles, or at least wrapped in plastic bags and tied. Prepare for changes in the weather or for atypical temperatures; on abnormally hot or cold days, be able to dress in layers so that as the weather changes, you can add or remove clothes as required.

Some travelers like to have at hand a small bag with the basics for an overnight stay, particularly if they are traveling by plane. Always keep necessary medicine, valuable jewelry, travel documents, or business documents in your handbag, briefcase, or hand luggage. Never check these things with your luggage.

For more information on packing clothes, send a stamped, self-addressed envelope to Samsonite Corporation, Samsonite Traveler Advisory Service, Department US, PO Box 38300, Denver, CO 80238, for their free brochure "Getting a Handle on Luggage."

How to Use a Travel Agent

T.A. To make the most intelligent use of a travel agent's time and expertise, it is necessary to know something of the economics of the industry. As client, you pay nothing for most services performed by the agent; in most cases, any money the travel agent makes on the time spent arranging your itinerary — booking reservations, advising about the best beach — comes from the principals who provide travel services — the airlines, hotels, cruise companies, etc. These commissions currently run anywhere from 7% to 15% of the total cost of the services — not a king's ransom for the total amount of time a good agent can spend on your whole trip.

This tradition may be changing, so that in some cases a travel agent may ask you to pay a fee for services that do not include making reservations, but for the moment it is standard operating procedure for most agents across the country.

The commission system implies two things about your relationship with an agent:

1. You will get better service if you arrive at the agent's desk with your basic itinerary already planned. Know roughly where you want to go, what you want to do. Use the agent to make bookings for you (which pay commissions) and to advise on facilities, activities, alternatives within the parameters of the basic itinerary you have chosen. You get the best service when you are buying commissionable items. There are few commissions in a camping or driving-camping tour; an agent is unlikely to be very enthusiastic about helping to plan one. The more vague your plans, the less direction you can expect from most agents. If you walk into an agency and say "I have two weeks in June, what shall I do?" you will most likely walk out with nothing more than a handful of brochures. Do your homework.
2. There is always the danger that an incompetent or unethical agent will send you to a place offering the best commission rather than the best facilities. The only way to be sure you are getting the best service is to have faith in your travel agent.

You should choose a travel agent with the same care with which you would choose a lawyer. You will be spending a good deal of money on the basis of the agent's judgment, and you have a right to expect that judgment to be mature, informed, and interested. At the moment, unfortunately, there are no real standards within the industry itself. The quality of individual agents varies enormously. Several states are toying with the idea of licensing agents, which would at least ensure that anyone acting as a travel agent is honest, if not competent. There are no laws regulating travel agencies as yet, and so try to deal with a travel agency that is a member of the American Society of Travel Agents (ASTA), an industry organization that guarantees that any member agency has been in business at least three years. Any travel agent who has completed the two-year course at the Institute of Certified Travel Agents will carry the title CTA. This certification will at least guarantee a certain degree of expertise.

Perhaps the best way to find a travel agent is by word of mouth. If the agent (or agency) has done a good job for friends over a period of time, it indicates a level of commitment and concern in your favor.

Hints for the Handicapped Traveler

The travel industry has dramatically improved services to the handicapped in the past few years. Easy access facilities are far from universal, but the handicapped traveler can look to many new policies and a wide range of information sources to make traveling easier.

Planning: Your trip will be more comfortable psychologically as well as physically if you know that at the end of each day there are accommodations which suit your needs. For this you will need access guides to tourist facilities. Here are a few:

1. *A List of Guidebooks for Handicapped Travelers,* compiled and published by the Women's Committee, The President's Committee on Employment of the Handicapped (Washington, DC 20210, available free). This booklet lists 106 American cities and counties with accessibility guides to local facilities, with addresses to write for the guides. Because new guides are being published all the time, if you are visiting a city or area not mentioned in the *List,* write the local Easter Seal Society anyway; an accessibility guide may be available.
2. *International Directory of Access Guides,* a free listing of 275 domestic and international access guides (descriptions of the services in a particular locale that are barrier-free or have reduced barriers). RIUSA Travel Survey Department, Rehabilitation World, 20 W 40th St., New York, NY 10018 (212 869-9907).
3. *The Wheelchair Traveler* by Douglass R. Annand (Ball Hill Rd., Milford, NH 03055, $8.25 including postage and handling). A city-by-city, state-by-state accessibility guide to hotels and restaurants, including some in Mexico and Canada.
4. *Access to the World* by Louise Weiss (Chatham Square Press, $9.95). This is an excellent guide to handicapped travel, with airport access information.
5. *Rollin' On: A Wheelchair Guide to U.S. Cities* by Maxine Atwater (Dodd, Mead, $9.95). This guide offers general information on transportation and accessibility as well as specific information on major US cities.
6. *TravelAbility* by Lois Reamy (Macmillan, $11.95) gives vast amounts of information on finding tours — even adventure tours — for handicapped travel; coping with public transport; finding accommodations, special equipment, travel agents.
7. For train travel: *Access Amtrak: A Guide to Amtrak Services for Elderly and Handicapped Travelers* published by the National Railroad Passenger Corporation (400 N Capitol St., NW, Washington, DC 20001, available free).
8. For travel by car: *Highway Rest Areas for Handicapped Travelers* published by The President's Committee on Employment of the Handicapped (Washington, DC 20210, available free). Lists 400 accessible rest stops in 49 of the 50 US states.
9. On the national parks: *Access National Parks, A Guide to Handicapped Travelers* published by the National Park Service (Superintendent of Documents, US Government Printing Office, Washington, DC 20402; for $3.50; ask for stock number 024–005–00691–5).
10. For airline travel: *Access Travel: A Guide to the Accessibility of Airport Terminals* published by the Airport Operators Council International (1700 K St., NW, Washington, DC 20006, available free). Lists 118 airports, rating 70 features from location and size of parking spaces to width of corridors and accessibility of toilets.

For general information, write to the National Rehabilitation Information Center, Catholic University, 4407 8th St., NE, Washington, DC 20017 (202 635-5826).

An excellent aid to planning is offered by the Travel Information Center, Moss Rehabilitation Hospital (12th St. and Tabor Rd., Philadelphia, PA 19141, 215 329-5715). The center will provide detailed information on hotel accommodations, restaurants, touring sites, and other travel concerns. For a complete listing of travel information and tours available specifically for the handicapped, you may want to join SATH (Society for the Advancement of Travel for the Handicapped). Contact SATH, 26 Court St., Brooklyn, NY 11242 (212 858-5483).

Tours: Five travel organizations plan and sponsor group trips for handicapped travelers and also make arrangements for individual travelers. They are:

1. Flying Wheel Tours, PO Box 382, 143 W Bridge St., Owatonna, MN 55060 (507 451-5005 or toll-free, 800 533-0363).
2. Evergreen Wings on Wheels, Evergreen Travel Service, 19505L 44th Ave. W, Lynnwood, WA 98036 (206 776-1184)
3. Handy-Cap Horizons, 3250 E Loretta Dr., Indianapolis, IN 46227 (317 784-5777).
4. Helping Hand Tours, 175 Fifth Ave., New York, NY 10010 (212 674-3024).
5. Monte Tours, 349 Fifth Ave., New York, NY 10016 (212 679-9178).

By Car: Those traveling in their own cars will find that the problems are about the same as traveling locally. Hertz, Avis, and National have hand-control cars at some locations. There are only a limited number available; call well in advance.

By Plane: Airlines are now required to take all disabled people if they give advance notice and can be evacuated in an emergency. This represents no real change in airline policy: Most airlines have always been accommodating in dealing with handicapped passengers' problems. TWA, for example, publishes a booklet, *Air Travel for the Handicapped,* available from any TWA ticket office.

If you are handicapped, try to fly at less crowded times for greater comfort, and book nonstop or direct flights to keep boarding to a minimum. Tell the airline when you call for a reservation about your handicap, and give advance notice if you need a wheelchair. Arrive at the airport at least 45 minutes in advance.

Passengers in wheelchairs should get a luggage tag for their wheelchairs when they check in. They should stay in their own chairs until they are transferred to a narrower airline chair at the door of the aircraft. Their wheelchairs will then be sent down to the luggage compartment. (Some airlines have restrictions on battery-operated chairs; inquire beforehand.) Usually people in wheelchairs are asked to wait until other passengers have disembarked. If you are making a tight connection, tell the attendant.

By Train: Whether you are riding a reserved or unreserved train, call in advance to make special arrangements or to reserve Amtrak's special seats for handicapped travelers. The newer Amtrak cars, such as the Amfleet trains and Metroliners (on the New York to Washington route), are boarded on the level at most stations. In other parts of the country, you will need to get Amtrak personnel to help with steps. Wheelchairs are available at most stations. Amtrak's new cars have special seats, properly equipped bathrooms, and special sleeping compartments for the handicapped. Older equipment presents many barriers, and a traveling companion can make the trip much easier. If necessary, Amtrak will recommend a professional traveling companion. Handicapped passengers accompanied by travel attendants are given a 25% discount. Seeing-eye dogs may ride in the passenger cars at no extra charge.

By Bus: Both Greyhound and Trailways offer special handicapped tickets whereby the handicapped passenger and a companion travel for the price of only one fare. The handicapped passenger must have a doctor's letter certifying the handicap and stating that one companion is enough to help with getting on and off the bus. (If you can manage the bus steps on your own, you are not required to have a companion.) Both bus companies will carry nonmotorized folding wheelchairs for free.

Hints for Traveling with Children

Bring easily washed, stain-resistant clothes, and encourage each child to pack a small bag of toys and games. Have a toy or two close at hand for long waits and take simple snacks, like a small box of raisins or crackers, for those moments when hunger strikes and food is miles away.

Family Trips: An alternative to long car trips are holidays specifically planned for families, based on some adventure or activity exciting for all. A few examples:

1. A riverboat trip down the Mississippi on the *Mississippi Queen* offered by Four Winds Travel, 175 5th Ave., New York, NY 10010 (212 777-0260).
2. A train trip to Yosemite National Park organized by Amtour Corporation, Suite 390, 421 Powell St., San Francisco, CA 94102 (415 362-2177).
3. Rafting the Snake River in Idaho, with the Sierra Club, 530 Bush St., San Francisco, CA 94108 (415 981-8634).
4. Wagon train trip put together by L. D. Frome, Wagons West, Afton, WY 83110 (307 886-5240).

These are just a few of literally hundreds of vacations available throughout the country. One book of ideas, with the names and addresses of the companies that feature such adventures, is *Adventure Travel North America,* by Pat Dickerman (Adventure Guides, $7.95). Also see *Traveling with Children in the U.S.A.,* by Leila Hadley (Morrow, $4.95).

Consider trading houses or apartments with people in the area where you would like to vacation. Join an organization that fosters such arrangements, such as Vacation Exchange Club, 350 Broadway, New York, NY 10013 (212 966-2576); or Holiday Exchanges, PO Box 878, Belen, NM 87002 (505 864-8680).

Colleges and universities are opening campuses to travelers during traditional academic vacations and in the summer. Some offer accommodations only (usually very cheap, in dormitory rooms); others open their recreational facilities, gyms, and sports centers to visitors. Many are listed in *Mort's Guide to Low Cost Vacations and Lodgings on College Campuses* (CMG Publishing Co., PO Box 630, Princeton, NJ 08540, $6).

Try to find hotels that welcome children — that don't charge for children under a certain age, for example. In many of the larger chain hotels, the staffs are more used to noisy or slightly misbehaving children. These hotels are also likely to have swimming pools or game rooms — both popular with most young travelers. Write the hotel in advance to discuss how old your children are, how long you plan to stay, and to ask for suggestions on sleeping arrangements. Among the hotels known to welcome kids are *The Grand Hotel* on Mackinac Island in Michigan, the *Crown Center* in Kansas City, the *Houston Oaks Hotel* in Houston, the *Hyatt Regency* in Atlanta, the *Bonaventure* in Montreal, the *Polynesian Village* at Disney World in Orlando, Florida, and, of course, the *Plaza,* with its Eloise myth intact, in New York.

For another family pleaser, consider staying as a guest on a farm or dude ranch, lists of which can be obtained from state departments of agriculture (see *Vacations on Farms and Ranches,* DIVERSIONS). Write to state tourist bureaus for the names of parks with overnight accommodations and marinas where families can rent houseboats. Theme parks make good family vacations. They offer entertainment, rides, and games for the whole family and accommodate the hamburger-and-ice-cream tastes of children. (See *Amusement Parks and Theme Parks,* DIVERSIONS.)

Planning: If you are spending your vacation traveling, rather than visiting one spot or engaging in one activity, pace the days with children in mind; break the trip into half-day segments, with running around or "doing" time built in; keep travel time on the road to a minimum of four or five hours each day. Involve children in the initial planning stage at home; if they are as excited about the trip as you are, everyone will enjoy it more.

By Car: Traveling by car, you can be flexible — making any number of stops at souvenir shops or snake farms, and meeting moods and emergencies as they arise. You can also take more with you, including items like ice chests and charcoal grills for picnics. Frequent stops for children to run around make car travel much easier. So do games and simple toys, such as magnetic checkerboards or drawing pencils and pads.

By Train: Amtrak allows children under two (accompanied by an adult) to travel for free anytime. For older children it offers a series of programs that allow a family to travel by train at considerable savings by picking and choosing departure days. Children 2 through 11 travel for half price (that is, half the full adult fare) on Fridays and Sundays; on every other day, the cheapest rate for travel with children is by Family Plan — the head of household pays full fare, spouse and children 12 to 21 pay ½ fare, children ages 2 through 11 are charged ¼ fare. All long-distance trains with dining car service also offer special children's menus.

By Bus: On Greyhound and Trailways children 5 through 11 are charged half price (accompanied by an adult); one child under 5 may travel free on an adult's lap. Trailways offers a family plan in which a spouse and children 12 to 22 travel at 25% off the full price and children 5 to 11 travel at 25% off the child's fare. Be sure any bus on which you travel with children — even on short runs — has a bathroom.

By Plane: Generally, children under 2 travel free. For children 2 to 17, prices vary from 25 to 50% off the adult fare. Watch for promotions when children with an adult fly free or at a deep discount (usually during the months of January and February), or when family fares extend discounts to spouses as well. Avoid night flights. Since you probably won't sleep nearly as well as your kids, you risk an impossible first day at your destination groggily taking care of your rested, energetic children. Nap time is, however, a good time to travel, especially for babies. Avoid commuter flights, and try to travel during off-peak hours when there are apt to be extra seats. When the plane lands and takes off, make sure your baby is nursing or has a bottle, pacifier, or thumb in mouth. This sucking will make the child swallow and clear stopped ears. For a small child a piece of hard candy will do the same thing. Newborn babies, whose lungs may not be able to adjust to the altitude, should not be taken aboard an airplane.

You are entitled to ask for a hot dog or hamburger in lieu of the airline's regular dinner when you make your reservation. Some, but not all airlines, have baby food aboard. While you should make sure to bring your own toys, ask about children's diversions. Some airlines, like Pan Am, have terrific packages of games, coloring books, and puzzles.

Some airlines may refuse to allow a pregnant woman to board if she is in her eighth or ninth month, because they fear that something could go wrong with an in-flight birth. Check with the airline ahead of time and carry a letter from your doctor stating that you are fit to travel and indicating the estimated date of birth.

Things to Do: Special programs for children run the gamut from children's movies at museums and puppet shows in city parks to storytelling at a public library. Listings of these events, many of which are free, can usually be found in Sunday editions of city newspapers or at the city's visitors bureau or information center. Local or regional festivals, fairs, rodeos, parades, or other special events capture children's imaginations.

For a list of these events, write to the tourist bureaus in the states you plan to visit. And look in to discounts; children often get discounts on everything from movies to monuments. Many hotels offer large reductions to families who all stay in the same room.

Hints for Single Travelers

Most travel bargains — all-inclusive tours, resort packages, cruises — are based on *double occupancy* rates, which means the per-person price is offered on the basis of two people traveling together, to fill a double room (and concomitantly to spend a good deal more on meals and extras). For exactly the same package, the single traveler will have to pay a surcharge, called a "single supplement," which in extreme cases can add 50% to 75% to the basic per-person rate.

The only real alternative to paying this penalty is to find a traveling companion. Even special "singles' tours" which promise no supplements are based on individuals sharing double rooms. There are several travel agents and tour operators around the US who help get single travelers together to share costs; some charge fees, others are free. All serve a national clientele.

1. *Travel Mates* — For men and women of any age; arranges shares (on existing package tours) as well as organizing group tours for its own clients. Annual membership fee, $15. 56 W 45th St., New York, NY 10036 (212 221-6565).
2. *Gramercy Singleworld Travel* — More of a "swinging singles" agency than the above. No age limits, but about two-thirds of its clients are under 35 and more than half are women. Organizes singles' tours (on which shares can be arranged for a fee, from $16 to $45; if you don't share, you pay a single supplement). Also places sharers on existing package tours. Annual membership fee, $15. 444 Madison Ave., New York, NY 10022 (212 753-7595).

Certain cruise lines — Cunard and Commodore Cruise Lines, for example —have a sort of standby service for singles; you pay only the usual per-person charge for a double cabin if it has not been sold to a couple. One organization that caters exclusively to women is called Womantour. Run by feminist Estilita Grimaldo, it features group and individual travel programs for women. Annual membership fee, $15. 5314 N Figueroa St., Los Angeles, CA 90042 (213 255-1115).

A special guidebook for solo travelers has been prepared by Eleanor Adams Baxel. It offers information on how to avoid paying supplementary charges, how to pick the right travel agent, how to calculate costs, and more. Called *A Guide for Solo Travel Abroad,* it's available for $5.50 from The Berkshire Traveller Press, Stockbridge, MA 01262.

Hints for Older Travelers

No longer limited by three-week vacations or the business week, older travelers can take advantage of off-season, off-peak travel which is both cheaper and more pleasant than traveling in high season. Particularly attractive are cruises, wherein the crew takes care of all details, and special programs like the bus companies' Eaglepass and Ameripass, which offer unlimited travel for a fixed period of time (see this section, *Bus* travel).

Discounts: Senior citizens with identification are eligible for a huge variety of discounts in every city across the country. Although rules change from place to place and city to city, acceptable proof of eligibility (or age) is usually a driver's license, a membership card in a recognized senior citizens organization such as the American Association of Retired Persons (see below), or a Medicare card. Because senior citizen discounts are common but by no means standard, always ask about them before you pay — whether it's for a subway in Philadelphia or a campsite in Colorado. Discounts are available for local transportation in most American cities, for concerts, movies, museums, hotels, and dozens of other activities. Some states offer free hunting and fishing licenses to retired persons. Greyhound, Trailways, and Amtrak offer discounts. The airlines also have special fares. Depending upon local management, discounts are available in some Marriott, Holiday Inn, Sheraton, Howard Johnson, Days Inn, Rodeway, and Treadway Inn hotels.

The National Park Service has a free Golden Age Passport which entitles people over 62, and those in the car with them, to free entrance to all national parks and monuments as well as to discounts on campsites (available by showing Medicare card or driver's license as proof of age at any national park).

"Travel Tips for Senior Citizens," a free booklet with general advice, is available from Public Information Service, Room 4827-A, Department of State, Washington, DC 20520.

Package Programs: Many organizations and travel companies plan or organize tours designed for older travelers. Among the most active of these organizations are:

1. American Association of Retired Persons. Open to anyone 55 or older. Membership costs $5; from Membership Processing Department, 215 Long Beach Blvd., Long Beach, CA 90801 (213 432-5781).
2. National Council of Senior Citizens. Membership costs $6 for an individual, $7.50 for a couple, from the Council at 925 15th Street, NW, Washington, DC 20005 (202 347-8800).
3. National Association of Mature People. Membership costs $5 for one year, $12 for three years, from the association at PO Box 26792, Oklahoma City, OK 73126 (405 848-1832).

Numerous travel agencies and tour operators around the country specialize in organizing tours for older travelers. Three such are Gadabout Tours, 700 E Tahquitz, McCallum Way, Palm Springs, CA 92262 (714 325-5556); and on the East Coast, Groups Unlimited, 422 Madison Ave., New York, NY 10017 (212 765-8026) and Grand Circle Tours, 555 Madison Ave., New York, NY 10022 (212 688-5900).

For older adults on a tight budget, consider a camp for older people. These simple, inexpensive lodges with home-cooked meals are described in a free booklet by Vacations for the Aging, 225 Park Ave. S, New York, NY 10003 (212 777-5000).

Health: Medicare coverage is nationwide and will be honored by hospitals and doctors everywhere in the United States, Puerto Rico, and the Virgin Islands. If you have specific medical problems, bring prescriptions and a "medical file":

1. Summary of medical history, current diagnosis.
2. List of drugs to which you are allergic.
3. Most recent electrocardiogram, if you have heart problems.
4. Your doctor's name, address, and phone number.

For a complete discussion of health for older travelers, Rosalind Massow's excellent *Now It's Your Turn to Travel* (Macmillan, $4.95) has a chapter on medical problems.

Insurance

The amount and kind of insurance you carry when you go on the road depends in large part on your own feelings about traveling, the insurance policies you have already, and your method of transport. There are five basic types of insurance any traveler should consider, though by no means are all — or any — a necessity:

1. Baggage and Personal Effects Insurance
2. Personal Accident and Sickness Insurance
3. Automobile Insurance
4. Tour Cancellation Insurance
5. Flight Insurance

These are options to be considered after you have established that your current medical and homeowner's (or tenant-homeowner's) policies are up to date and paid.

Baggage and Personal Effect Insurance: Ask your agent if baggage and personal effects are covered by your homeowner's policy regardless of where you lose them. If not, find out about the cost and coverage of a floater to protect you while you are away. If they are not, you must decide if you need more protection than is automatically included in an airline, train, or bus ticket. (If you are driving, you must discuss protection from damage or theft of baggage with your insurance agent.) The airlines, Amtrak, and bus companies provide only limited protection against the loss or damage of baggage in their care. The limits of their liability are included as part of the fine print on every ticket, and are as follows: Airlines insure luggage and contents for a maximum of $750 on domestic flights, and $9.07 a pound on international flights; Amtrak takes responsibility for a maximum of $500 per passenger; and the buses assume responsibility for considerably less, about $250 maximum per passenger. These maximum payments are not automatic; payments will be based on the value of the baggage and its contents.

If you are carrying goods worth more than the maximum protection provided by these limits of liability, you should consider excess value insurance, available from the airlines for about 10¢ per $100 of protection provided (can be bought at the ticket counter at time of check-in) and from Amtrak for 50¢ for every $100 of protection. Travel agents have insurance packages which include excess value insurance (see below).

One note of warning: Be sure to read the fine print of any excess value or baggage insurance policy; there are often specific exclusions, such as money, tickets, furs, gold and silver objects, art and antiquities. And remember that ordinarily, insurance companies will pay the depreciated value of the goods rather than replacement value. To protect goods traveling in your luggage, have photos made of valuables, and keep a record of all serial numbers of such items as cameras, typewriters, radios, etc. This will establish that you do, indeed, own the objects. If your luggage disappears en route, or is damaged, deal with the situation immediately, at the airport, train station, or bus station. If an airline loses your luggage, you will be asked to fill out a Property Irregularity Report before you leave the airport. If your property disappears elsewhere, make a report to the police at once.

Personal Accident and Sickness Insurance: This insures you in case of illness on the road (hospital and doctor's expenses, etc.) or death in an accident. In most cases this is a standard part of life and health insurance policies, and anyone with average insurance coverage will be adequately protected while on vacation.

Automobile Insurance: Every driver is required by law to have automobile insurance. Minimum coverage is determined by state law, but it is almost always too low to protect you adequately. A professional insurance agent should determine the amount of automobile insurance you should carry, but there are several major kinds of coverage you should have:

1. Liability insurance — Protection if you are sued for injuring another person or that person's property.
2. Uninsured motorist insurance — Protection if you or passengers in your car are injured by another motorist without insurance.
3. Accident insurance — Protection against liability for medical bills, loss of pay, other expenses of people injured in an accident for which you are at fault.
4. Comprehensive and collision insurance — Protection against damage to your car.

There are several ways to save money on car insurance. Many policies offer discounts for cars used in car pools, cars with low annual mileage (or compacts), and drivers with good driving records. Some states (New York and New Jersey are two) publish free booklets on car insurance coverage, how much and what kind to buy. Write the Department of Insurance in your state capital for any available information.

Charter Flight Cancellation Insurance: Charter passengers are usually required to pay the full price of their tour (whether it is a flight only or a flight plus land accommodations — for full details on air charters, see *Traveling by Plane,* p. 14) well before departure. Although cancellation policies may vary, rarely will the passenger get more than 20% of this money back if forced to cancel within a few weeks of leaving. Therefore, if you are planning to take a charter tour, you should have cancellation insurance to insure full refund of your money should you, a traveling companion, or a member of your immediate family get sick and force you to cancel or return early from your trip. Cancellation insurance is available from travel agents and tour operators in two forms: as part of a short-term, all-purpose travel insurance package (sold by the travel agent); or as specific cancellation insurance designed by the tour operator for a specific charter tour. Generally, tour operators' policies are cheaper, but less inclusive.

Read either policy carefully before you decide which you want (both are bought from the travel agent at the time you book the charter). Be sure the policy you choose provides enough money to get you home from the farthest point on your itinerary should you have to book an economy scheduled flight, missing your charter home. And check the fine print definition of "family members" and "pre-existing medical condition." Some policies will not pay if you become ill from a condition for which you have received treatment in the past.

Flight Insurance: Before you hastily buy last-minute flight insurance from an airport vending machine (as many, many travelers do), consider the question in the light of your total insurance coverage. Do you really need more insurance coverage? (And remember, American domestic lines are demonstrably the safest in the world; you are safer in the sky in an airplane than in your bathtub at home. Don't be panicked into a needless purchase.) A review of your coverage may show that you have adequate coverage, and that your policy pays double or even triple for accidental death.

Airlines have carefully established limits of liability for the death or injury of passengers. On tickets for international flights these are printed on the ticket: a maximum of $75,000 in case of death or injury, for domestic flights, the limitation is established by state law, with some few states (California, New York, Illinois) setting unlimited liability. But remember, these limits of liability are not the same thing as insurance policies; they merely state the maximum an airline will pay in the case of death or injury, and every penny of that is usually the subject of a legal battle.

If you buy your ticket with an American Express, Carte Blanche, or Diners Club credit card, you are issued automatic life and accident insurance at no extra cost. American Express automatically provides $75,000 in free life insurance; Carte Blanche, $75,000; and Diners Club, $75,000. Each of these cards offers additional coverage at extremely reasonable prices. For $3, American Express cardholders can buy $250,000 of flight insurance; Diners Club members, $200,000; and Carte Blanche cardholders, $150,000.

Combination Policies: Many packages of short-term insurance are available to travelers. These policies, which protect you for the duration of the trip, include personal accident and sickness insurance, trip cancellation insurance, and baggage and personal effects insurance. They are available from retail insurance agencies.

Mail and Telephone

MAIL: Most main post offices are open 24 hours a day with at least a self-service section for weighing packages and buying stamps. In smaller cities and towns, hours are usually from 8 AM to 6 PM Monday through Friday and 8 AM to noon on Saturdays. Branch offices have shorter hours.

Stamps are also available at most hotel desks. There are vending machines for stamps in drugstores, transportation terminals, and other public places. Stamps cost more from these machines than they do at the post office, however.

Before you take a trip, fill in a change of address card (available at post office), which is the form you need to get the post office to hold your mail or send your first class mail to your vacation address. Generally, this free holding service lasts for a month, longer at the discretion of the post office. You can also have your third class mail sent on, but you will have to pay for this service.

If you want to receive mail in another city but do not know what your address will be, have it sent to you in care of General Delivery in the city or town you will visit. This is always the main post office in any large city. Have the sender put "Hold for 30 Days" on the envelope, and make sure that a return address is on the envelope so that the post office can return it if you are not able to pick it up. The post office will keep it only for 30 days. To claim this mail, go to the main post office in that city or town, ask for General Delivery, and present identification (driver's license, credit cards, birth certificate, passport). Mail must be collected in person.

If you belong to American Express or AAA, you can have mail sent to their offices in cities on your route. Envelopes should be marked "Hold for Arrival."

TELEPHONE: Public telephones are on hand just about everywhere if you are in a city or town. This includes transportation terminals, hotel lobbies, restaurants, drugstores, sidewalk booths, and along the highways. For a local call the cost is between 10¢ and 20¢.

Long-distance rates are charged according to when the call is placed: weekday daytime; weekday evenings; and nights, weekends, and holidays. Cheapest are calls you dial yourself from a private phone nights, weekends, holidays. It is always more expensive to call from a pay phone than it is to call from a private phone (you must pay for a minimum three-minute call). If the operator assists you, calls are more expensive. This includes credit-card, bill-to-a-third-number, collect, and time-and-charge calls, as well as person-to-person calls, which are the most expensive. Rates are fully explained in the front of the White Pages of every telephone directory.

If you are planning to be away for more than a month, you may be able to save money by asking the telephone company to temporarily suspend your home telephone service. You can also arrange to have your calls transferred to another number.

Hotel Surcharges: When you are calling from your hotel room, inquire about any surcharges the hotel may have. These can be excessive, and are avoided by calling collect or using a telephone credit card (free from the phone company).

Emergencies: 911 is the number to dial in an emergency in most cities. Operators at this number will get you the help you need from the police, fire department, or ambulance service. It is, however, a number that should be reserved for real emergencies only. If you are in one of the rare areas where 911 has not been adopted, dial "O" for the operator, who will connect you directly with the service you need.

On the Road

Credit Cards and Traveler's Checks

CREDIT CARDS: There are two essentially different kinds of credit cards available to consumers in the United States, and travelers must decide which kind best serves their interests. "Convenience" cards — American Express, Diners Club, Carte Blanche, are the most widely accepted — cost the cardholder a basic membership fee, but put no limit on the amount which the cardholder may charge on the card in any month. However, the entire balance must be paid — in full — at the end of each billing period (usually a month), so the cardholder is not actually extended any credit.

"Bank" cards, on the other hand, are generally issued free. Some banks now charge $12 to $15 for MasterCard, however. They are real credit cards in the sense that the cardholder has the privilege of paying a minimum amount (1/36th is not untypical) of the total balance in each billing period. For this privilege, the cardholder is charged an interest rate — about 1½% a month or 18% a year for the cards listed below — on the balance which is owed. In addition, there is a maximum set on the amount the cardholder can charge to the card, which represents the limit of credit the card company is willing to extend. It is determined at the time the card is issued. Major bank cards are Visa (formerly BankAmericard) and MasterCard (formerly Master Charge).

Getting any credit card will involve a fairly rigorous credit check; to pass, you will need a job (at which you have worked for at least a year), a minimum salary of $10,000 a year, and a good credit rating. In general, because no real credit is involved, it is easier to get a "convenience" card than a bank card, although an application for any credit card will be subjected to credit and reference checks.

1. *American Express* — Accepted at over 500,000 establishments; emergency personal check cashing at American Express or representative's office ($200 cash, $800 in traveler's checks); emergency personal check cashing service at participating hotels, car rental agencies, and airline counters; extended payment plan for tours and air tickets; travel service to plan trips and hold mail (domestic as well as international locations); low-cost travel and life insurance program; $35 membership, $20 for each additional card. PO Box 39, Church St. Station, New York, NY 10008 (212 323-2000).
2. *Diners Club* — Accepted at over 500,000 establishments; personal check cashing service ($250 maximum) for guests at member hotels; toll-free, guaranteed hotel reservation service; $40 membership for two cards, $10 fee for additional cards. 575 Lexington Ave., New York, NY 10043 (212 559-2900).
3. *Carte Blanche* — Accepted at 300,000 establishments; extended payment plan for airline tickets and tours at 18% per year interest; emergency personal check cashing up to $250 for guests at participating hotels; $75,000 travel accident insurance policy; $35 membership, $15 fee for each additional card for each family member. 3460 Wilshire Blvd., Los Angeles, CA 90010 (213 480-3210).

4. *Visa* (formerly BankAmericard) — Accepted at 3.3 million establishments; cash advances at 111,000 banks and subsidiaries worldwide based on credit limit; limits on charges and cash advances from $500 to $5,000; apply through participating financial institutions. Interest charge about 18% a year. PO Box 8999, San Francisco, CA 94128 (415 573-1012).
5. *MasterCard* (formerly Master Charge) — Accepted at 3 million establishments; cash advances at 80,000 affiliated banks worldwide; credit limits on charges and cash advances up to $5,000; apply through member banks. Interest charge about 18% a year. 888 Seventh Ave., New York, NY 10019 (212 974-5785).

TRAVELER'S CHECKS: With adequate proof of identification (credit cards, driver's license, passport), traveler's checks are as good as cash in most hotels, restaurants, stores, and banks. If you're traveling, they're even better because of their refundability; in the US, travelers can receive partial or full replacement funds the same day if their traveler's checks are lost or stolen and they have their receipt and proper identification. To avoid complications, keep your purchaser's receipt and an accurate listing by serial number of your checks in a separate place from the checks themselves. You can buy traveler's checks at any bank. Some companies offer more extensive services, making provisions for refunds on the weekends and after business hours. The following are charges and policies of the major traveler's check companies:

1. *American Express* —Purchase fee, 1%. Refunds usually available same day during business hours from American Express offices or banks that sell American Express traveler's checks. Night, weekend, and holiday emergency refunds of up to $100 available from Holiday Inns. To report lost or stolen checks, call toll-free in Continental US at 800 221-7282; in Alaska and Hawaii 800 221-4950; in New York State and Canada, call collect 212 248-4584.
2. *Thomas Cook*— No purchase fee at Cook's or AAA offices. Refunds available same day during business hours from Cook offices, AAA offices, or banks that sell Cook traveler's checks. To report lost or stolen checks, call toll-free 800 223-7373; in New York State call collect 212 754-2868.
3. *Citicorp* — Purchase fee, 1%. Refunds available same day during business hours from Citibanks and other banks offering Citicorp traveler's checks. To report lost or stolen checks, call toll-free 800 221-2566; in New York State call collect 212 559-6380.
4. *Visa* —Fees are determined by financial institutions selling the checks. They're free when purchased at Barclays Bank in New York City, for example. Refunds are available at authorized refund points with proper identification; emergency refunds during holidays or weekends are wired through Western Union. To report lost or stolen checks, call 800 227-6811; in California, 800 632-0520; in Alaska and Hawaii, 800 227-6830.
5. *Bank of America*—Purchase fee, 1%. Refunds available immediately during business hours at office where checks are sold; no weekend service. To report lost or stolen checks, call collect 415 622-3800 within Alaska or California; toll-free 800 227-3460 elsewhere.
6. *MasterCard*—For sales, refunds, theft, or loss, call collect to MasterCard for name and location of nearest agent: 212 974-5696.

Dining Out in America . . .

American cities are currently undergoing something of a restaurant revolution. In the last ten years, cities across the country, from Portland, Maine, to Portland, Oregon, have initiated renovation programs of the oldest sections of town. Often these are former port or warehouse districts, mercantile neighborhoods filled with fine 19th-century ironwork buildings which 100 years ago were in their prime and have since fallen into disrepair. Renovated, they become distinctive shopping areas, filled with gourmet food stores, art galleries, clothing or crafts boutiques, and . . . restaurants.

Built of simple wood and simpler bricks to accentuate the often stunning architecture of the original buildings, these restaurants — whether in Boston or St. Louis — have a slightly sinister similarity of look and design, but they represent a new era for the traveler. America's largest cities have always had a diverse collection of restaurants, but eating out in smaller American cities, especially in the South, Midwest, and Plains states, used to offer little variety. The new generation of restaurants is beginning to change that. Generally moderately priced, run by owner-managers who care about food, they offer an eclectic selection of cuisines (Oriental and traditional American, vegetarian and meat dishes, haute cuisine and simple) with great care and real pride. We have listed our favorites in the *Eating Out* section in THE AMERICAN CITIES reports.

Reservations: Restaurants vary widely on reservation policies. At some, it is requisite (especially at more expensive and popular places in larger cities); other equally fine restaurants refuse to take reservations at all; the patron simply goes, and waits at the bar until a table is free. If you are planning a big night out, it certainly is advisable to call the restaurant early in the day to make a reservation or find out its policy. After-theater restaurants in New York almost always require booking. Every restaurant listing in *Best in Town* gives reservation policy and a telephone number.

Hotel restaurants often have specific serving times; plusher hotels usually have coffee shops as well as restaurants, and the coffee shops will offer more flexible hours (and are often open 24 hours a day).

Hotels and Motels in America . . .

Americans who travel frequently to Europe complain that the United States has few of the centuries-old, privately owned and personally run, tradition-conscious "little hotels" which can so grace a European visit. To a great degree this is a fair observation: There are fine old hotels in the US — New England inns, Southwestern haciendas, frontier stagecoach rest stops (you will find our pick of them listed in *Best in Town* in THE AMERICAN CITIES and *Best en Route* in DIRECTIONS) — which have been in continuous operation for a century or more and which can match the amenities of any European find; but by far the majority of travelers in the US will be staying at hotels and motels only a few years old, which are often part of national (or international) chains, and which are, to some degree, standardized in price and quality.

There is one great benefit in this standardization: The basic level of acceptable accommodations in the US is much higher than anywhere else in the world. The tourist in America, arriving in an unfamiliar town (or driving through a new region), can be safe in assuming that nearby there will be safe, clean, comfortable accommodations in an acceptable price range.

You can choose for yourself just what price range is acceptable. Some chains — like the Hyatt and Hilton hotels — offer luxury accommodations with all possible amenities. The hotels themselves are beautiful, the service excellent, the facilities complete; and the prices, as you would expect, are high — as much as $115 or more a night for a double. On the other end of the scale is a relatively new phenomenon, the budget motel, designed to offer basic accommodations (a comfortable bed, clean bathroom, central heating and air-conditioning) without services, bar or restaurant, or elaborate lobby. A double for a night can cost as little as $15–$20. Watch for:

1. Days Inn (300 throughout the US) — 800 241-7200.
2. Econo-Travel Motor Hotels (about 130, East Coast and South) — 800 496-6900.
3. Motel 6 (more than 315 throughout the US).
4. Red Roof Inns (65 throughout the Midwest) — 800 848-7878.
5. Regal Inns (about 50 throughout the Midwest).
6. Superior Motels Best Value Inns (400 throughout the US) — 800 238-6059.
7. Budget Host Inns (over 125 throughout the US).

At hotels and motels in all price ranges, ask about minimum rates, weekend discounts, weekly rates, and discounts for business travelers.

Reservations: It is best to make reservations for accommodations in the major US cities, even if you are traveling off-season. Most cities have convention centers, and hotel space can be limited if a large convention is being hosted at the same time you visit. All the hotel entries in the *Best in Town* sections of THE AMERICAN CITIES reports include phone numbers for reservations. Resorts, country inns, dude ranches, theme park hotels, and other special places should always be booked in advance, regardless of the season. Most major hotel and motel chains have toll-free numbers for reservations, and any hotel within a chain can assure reservations for you at sister facilities. (For a useful listing of hundreds of toll-free numbers, including hotel chains, see *The Toll-Free Digest,* Warner Books, $4.95.) Many independent, nonchain hotels and motels are part of the American Reservation System (toll-free, 800 327-9157; except in Florida, where the toll-free number is 800 432-9109). Make sure to bring your reservation confirmation slip with you; it will increase your chances of getting a room if the hotel is overbooked. American Express, in conjunction with Hyatt and several other major hotel chains, offers an Assured Reservations Program. Any reservation made with an American Express credit card number will be held no matter how late you arrive. However, if you don't take the room, and fail to formally cancel, you will be charged.

Several organizations around the country have bed and breakfast networks that provide a more personable, and sometimes less expensive, alternative to hotels and motels. Accommodations range from private homes and lovely mansions to small inns and guesthouses with a continental breakfast included (usually no private baths are offered). The *Bed & Breakfast League,* 2855 29th St., NW, Washington, DC 20008 (202 232-8718); and *International Spareroom,* Box 518, Solana Beach, CA 92075 (714 755 3194) have nationwide listings. What follows are other, regional groups to contact for B&B information and reservations.

East: *Pineapple Hospitality,* 384 Rodney French Blvd., New Bedford, MA 02744 (617 990-1696); *New England Bed & Breakfast,* 1045 Centre St., Newton, MA 02159 (617 498-9819); *New Yorkers at Home,* 301 E 60th St., New York,

NY 10022 (212 838-7015); *Urban Ventures,* PO Box 426, New York, NY 10024 (212 662-1234).

South: *Bed & Breakfast Atlanta,* 1221 Fairview Rd., NE 30329 (404 378-6026); *Guesthouses Inc.,* 107 Bollingwood Ave., Charlottesville, VA 22903 (804 979-7264).

West: *American Family Inn,* 2185A Union St., San Francisco, CA 94123 (415 931-3083); *Bed & Breakfast International,* 151 Ardmore Rd., Kensington, CA 94707 (415 525-4569); *Bed & Breakfast in Arizona,* 8433 N Black Canyon Hwy., Suite 160, Phoenix, AZ 85021 (602 995-2831); *Bed & Breakfast Hawaii,* Box 449, Kapaa, HI 96746 (808 822-1582); *Digs West,* 8191 Crowley Circle, Buena Park, CA 90621 (714 739-1669); *Northwest Bed & Breakfast,* 7707 SW Locust St., Portland, OR 97223 (503 246-8366).

Religion on the Road

The surest source of information on religious services in an unfamiliar town is the desk clerk of the hotel or motel in which you are staying. In most cities, joint religious councils print circulars with the addresses and times of services of all the churches, synagogues, and temples in the city. These are often printed as part of general tourist guides provided by the local tourist and convention center, or as part of a "what's on" guide to the city. The local tourist council certainly can provide the information you need on services in the town. Many newspapers print a listing of religious services in their area in weekend editions. Often an entire page will be devoted to church and religious news.

You may want to use your vacation to broaden your religious experience by joining an unfamiliar faith in its service. This can be a moving experience, especially if the service is held in a church, synagogue, or temple that is historically significant or architecturally notable. You will almost always find yourself made welcome and comfortable.

Medical and Legal Help on the Road

MEDICAL HELP: You will discover, in the event of an emergency, that most tourist facilities — transportation companies, hotels, theme parks, and resorts — are equipped to handle the situation quickly and efficiently. Shout for help, and they will locate a doctor or ambulance. All hospitals are prepared for emergency cases, and even the tiniest of US towns has a medical clinic nearby. If you are on your own, you can get emergency help by dialing 911 or "0" (for Operator). You will be put into immediate contact with the service you require.

If you have a medical condition that may require attention on your trip, have your doctor at home recommend a physician in the areas you plan to visit. If you need a doctor unexpectedly, but it is not a severe emergency, you can call your own doctor for a recommendation in the area. If you are staying in a hotel or motel, ask for the house physician, who may visit you in your room or ask you to visit an office. (This service is apt to be expensive, especially if the doctor makes a "house" call to your room. Expect to pay $35 or more in larger cities for a house call, substantially less for an office visit.) In larger cities, many hospitals have walk-in clinics designed to serve people who do not really need emergency service, but who have no place to go for immediate medical attention. You can also go directly to the emergency room. A phone call to a local hospital requesting the name of a doctor will usually turn up a name; some hospitals actually have referral services for this purpose. The medical society in most towns (or counties) will refer you to a member physician in the specialty you need (listed in the telephone book under the city or county medical society; for example, Des Moines Medical Society).

If you wear glasses, make sure you have an extra pair with you as well as your prescription. Also carry prescriptions for any medicines you might need on the trip.

Medic Alert sells identification tags that specify that the wearer has a medical condition that may not be readily apparent to a casual observer. A heart condition, diabetes, epilepsy, or severe allergies are the sorts of things that these badges were developed to communicate — they are conditions that, if unrecognized at a time when emergency treatment is necessary (a time, incidentally, when you may be unable to speak for yourself), can result in tragic treatment errors. In addition to the identification emblems, a central file is maintained (with the telephone number clearly inscribed on the I.D. badge) where your complete medical history is available 24 hours a day via a telephone call. The cost of the I.D. bracelet or necklace depends on what sort of metal you select. For information contact: Medic Alert, PO Box 1009, Turlock, CA 95380 (209 668-3333).

Assist-Card International is sold only through travel agents and provides a number to call — 24 hours a day, 365 days a year — where complete emergency medical assistance can be arranged, including ambulance or air transportation to the proper treatment facilities, local lawyers for a case that is the byproduct of an accident, and up to $5,000 in bail bonds for a judicial proceeding that is similarly the result of an accident. They will also arrange for a flight home if the traveler is unable to complete his trip for medical reasons and will pay any fare differential that may be required. Fees for the Assist-Card vary according to the length of the trip abroad. The published schedule of fees calls for charges of $25 per card for a 5-day trip, $40 per card for a trip of 10 days, to a $150 fee for a 90-day itinerary. For information contact: Assist-Card Corporation of America, 745 Fifth Ave., New York, NY 10022 (212 752-2788 in New York, or toll-free elsewhere 800 221-4564).

Intermedic, a division of Executive Health Examiners, provides access to a directory of English-speaking physicians in 170 cities in over 90 countries. The fee is $6 per year for an individual and $10 a year for a family. Each physician listed has provided Intermedic with data on his medical education, his professional experience, and his hospital affiliation; and each has indicated a willingness to respond promptly to calls from traveling Intermedic members. They have also agreed in writing to a ceiling on fees for any initial visit. For information contact: Intermedic, Inc., 777 Third Ave., New York, NY 10017 (212 486-8974).

SOS provides a medical service program that covers medical emergencies while traveling. Again, members are provided with telephone access — 24 hours a day, 365 days a year — to a worldwide monitored multilingual network of medical centers. A phone call brings assistance ranging from telephone consultation to transportation home by ambulance or aircraft, and in some cases transportation of a family member to the place of hospitalization to assist in treatment or care. The service can be purchased for $12.50 a week, $36 a month, or $140 a year. Formerly available only on a corporate basis, the service is now being offered to individuals for the first time. For information contact: International SOS Assistance, Inc., 2 Neshaminy Interplex, Suite 208, Trevose, PA 19047 (toll-free 800 523-8930 or 215 244-1500).

LEGAL AID. The best way to begin looking for legal aid in an unfamiliar area is with a call to your own lawyer. If you don't have, or cannot reach, your own lawyer, most cities offer lawyer referral services (sometimes called attorney referral services) maintained by county bar associations. There are over 335 such referral services in the US, and they see that anyone in need of legal representation gets it at a reasonable fee. (They are listed in the Yellow Pages under Attorney or Lawyer. In smaller towns, you will usually find listed a toll-free number which connects you to the service in the nearest larger city.) The referral service is almost always free; expect the lawyer to whom you are referred to charge between $10 and $20 for the first half-hour of consultation. If your case goes to court, you are entitled to court-appointed representation if you can't get a lawyer or can't afford one.

Once you have found a lawyer, ask how many cases of this type the lawyer has worked on, and the arrangements to be made regarding fee and additional costs like medical or ballistics experts, transcripts, or court fees. For most violations, you will receive a citation at most. There are, however, the rare occasions when travelers find themselves in jail. Since obtaining a bond can be difficult away from home, the bail bonds offered by AAA and other automobile clubs are extremely useful. (See *Touring by Car,* p. 10.) If you do not have this protection, ask to see a copy of the local bail procedures, which differ from state to state. A lawyer will be able to advise you on the alternatives you have in the state in which you are incarcerated.

Time Zones, Business Hours, Holidays

TIME ZONES: East to west, the United States is divided into four time zones: Eastern, Central, Mountain, and Pacific. Each zone is an hour apart; when it is 8 PM in New York, it is 5 PM in Los Angeles. Alaska and Hawaii are both two hours behind Los Angeles time. To discover how these zones divide the country, check the map in the front of your telephone directory. Daylight Savings Time begins on the last Sunday in April and continues until the last Sunday in October. The only places that do not go on Daylight Savings Time are Arizona, Hawaii, Puerto Rico, the Virgin Islands, and parts of Indiana.

BUSINESS HOURS: Business hours throughout the country are fairly standard: 9 AM to 5 PM, Mondays through Fridays. While an hour lunch break is customary, employees often take it in shifts so that it rarely interrupts service, especially at banks and other public service operations. In Hawaii business hours run from 7:30 or 8 AM to 4 PM. Some California firms are also experimenting with these hours.

Banks are traditionally open from 9 AM to 3 PM Mondays through Fridays, although the trend is toward longer hours. In some areas they now open at 8 AM and stay open until 6 PM, especially at the end of the week. In addition they may remain open one evening a week until 8 or 9 PM, and some have hours on Saturdays.

Retail stores are usually open from 9:30 or 10 AM to 5:30 or 6 PM, Mondays through Saturdays. Most large stores, particularly department stores, are open *at least* one night a week until 9 PM. Blue laws, which close some stores, restaurants, and bars on Sundays, are controlled by cities in some areas, by states elsewhere. In major cities, grocery stores, delicatessens, and supermarkets are usually open Mondays through Saturdays from 9 AM to 9 PM, and some are open on Sundays as well. In fact 24-hour supermarkets are now operating in most regions. Drugstores are usually open from 8 AM to 9 PM, Mondays through Fridays. In major cities at least one is usually open until midnight, or all night, and on Sundays. Check the Yellow Pages.

HOLIDAYS: National holidays, when banks, post offices, libraries, most stores, and many museums are closed, include:

January 1, New Year's Day.
February, third Monday, George Washington's Birthday.
May, last Monday, Memorial Day (except in Alabama, Mississippi, and South Carolina, where it is not a legal holiday).

July 4, Independence Day.
September, first Monday, Labor Day.
October, second Monday, Columbus Day (except in Alaska, Iowa, Mississippi, Nevada, North Dakota, Oregon, South Carolina, and South Dakota, where it is not a legal holiday).
November, fourth Thursday, Thanksgiving.
December 25, Christmas.

Drinking Laws

Drinking is legal at 18 in Connecticut, Hawaii, Louisiana, Maryland, New York, Vermont, West Virginia, and Wisconsin. In Alaska, Arizona, Florida, Georgia, Idaho, Iowa, Minnesota, Montana, New Jersey, Tennessee, and Wyoming, legal age is 19. In Delaware, Maine, Massachusetts, Nebraska, New Hampshire, and Rhode Island, drinking is legal at 20. The legal age is 21 in all other states with the following exceptions: In Alabama, Mississippi, North Carolina, South Carolina, and South Dakota, it is legal to drink beer at 18; and beer and wine are legal for anyone 18 in Washington DC.

Laws on the availability of liquor run the gamut from Nevada's policy of "anytime, anywhere for anyone of age" to localities where drinking is strictly prohibited. Liquor laws are set by states, counties, and municipalities and towns, making generalizations terribly difficult. Regulations on the hours that bars and restaurants can serve liquor vary, though traditionally closing time in bars is between midnight and 3 AM.

Retail store sales are also restricted to certain hours in many states. Most states require liquor stores to close on holidays and Sundays. Some alcoholic beverages, however, may be purchased on Sundays (most often in restaurants) in almost all states. The following states, however, do not allow any Sunday sales: Alabama, Arkansas, Kansas, Louisiana, Mississippi, Oklahoma, and South Carolina.

Some states maintain their own system of state liquor stores, which are usually the only place where you can buy hard liquor, and sometimes wine and beer as well. These states include Alabama, Iowa, Maine, Montana, New Hampshire, North Carolina, Ohio, Oregon, Pennsylvania, Utah, Vermont, Virginia, Washington, and West Virginia.

It is possible to find dry counties or towns in all corners of the country. Usually, however, you will find a town just a few minutes away where the sale of liquor is legal. In Utah, beer is the only standard offering. Certain licensed restaurants are allowed to serve two-ounce bottles of mixed drinks, highballs, or wine, but only with meals.

Where the laws are tight, there are often private clubs. In states such as Kansas and Oklahoma, you can join private clubs through hotels and motels. Often you join the club with the price of your first drink. In localities that prohibit the serving of liquor, but not bottle sales, restaurants or clubs often furnish glasses, ice, and mix if the patron brings a bottle. This practice is also common in states where restaurants have difficulty getting liquor licenses.

Some states forbid the import of liquor: Arkansas, Georgia, Idaho, Michigan, and Pennsylvania. Some other states have quotas limiting imports to a quart or gallon. These are among the drinking laws least likely to be enforced. However, it is important to be aware of these laws, because if a state decides it is losing too much tax revenue to a neighboring state where liquor prices are lower, it will begin to crack down. It is wise, for example, not to buy a case of liquor in New Jersey in front of a policeman at the last liquor store before crossing into Pennsylvania.

Shopping and Tipping

SHOPPING: Large city or small town, wherever you travel there will be shopping centers, department stores, and small shops to provide the basic necessities (or that indispensable item you left at home). Many city department stores, like Filene's in Boston or Bloomingdale's in New York, are as much a part of the city scene as the very streets, and shouldn't be missed. Some suggestions: Jordan Marsh, Filene's in Boston; Lord & Taylor, Saks Fifth Avenue, Bloomingdale's in New York; Marshall Field in Chicago; Neiman-Marcus in Dallas; the May Company in Los Angeles.

Since supermarkets have become the most common source for food shopping, real farmers' markets have become tourist attractions. They are great places to take children, or to shop for picnics along the road. Several US cities have famous farmers' markets, including Haymarket in Boston, the Italian Market in Philadelphia, State Farmers' Market in Atlanta, and Soulard in St. Louis. (Some others are listed in individual city reports in THE AMERICAN CITIES.)

Other pleasant places to shop in the city are urban malls, such as Chicago's Water Tower Place, Salt Lake City's Trolley Square, or San Francisco's Pier 39.

Flea Markets: A growing phenomenon, especially on the East Coast, is that of flea markets, where all kinds of goods are offered in open stands. Located in country fields or empty parking lots, stadiums or skating rinks, some are occasional events advertised locally (watch the daily or weekly paper in the area in which you are traveling); others, usually in larger cities, are run on a permanent or semipermanent basis and advertised regularly. (See the entertainment section of the *New York Times*.) A few flea markets in the New York area:

1. Annex Fair and Antiques Flea Market, Ave. of the Americas at 25th St., New York, NY (212 243-5343, open Sundays April through October).
2. Barterama, Belmont Race Track, Elmont, NY (516 775-8774, open Saturdays, Sundays and Tuesdays).
3. Wallingford, Redwood Country Flea Market, exit 64 off the Wilbur Cross Hwy., Wallingford, CT (203 269-3500, open Saturdays and Sundays).
4. Lambertville Antique and Flea Market, rt. 29, Lambertville, NJ (609 397-0456, open Saturdays and Sundays).

Factory Outlets: Outlets are huge warehouse stores where companies unload their overruns and canceled orders at dramatically reduced prices — from 20% to 75% off the retail price. They also sell irregulars (slightly flawed pieces) and seconds (more severely flawed or damaged goods). These will be appropriately marked. Some companies, like Bass Shoes and Dansk housewares, have many stores, others just one or two. Factory outlets tend to be outside major urban areas, and several cities around the country have become known for having clusters of outlets nearby. Best known of these are Reading, Pennsylvania; Rochester, Minnesota; Sylvania, Ohio; and Louisville, Kentucky. Two urban areas known for outlets are Orchard Street in Lower Manhattan, New York City, and Fashion Row in Miami, Florida. The New England states are famous for blankets, leather, linen, and textiles; the Carolinas for furniture, linen, textiles, and towels; and Virginia and West Virginia for glassware and pottery.

At any factory outlet, be prepared for crowds, especially on Saturdays. Bear in mind that outlets are rarely centrally located and may take some time to find. (Usually you will need a car.) They can go out of business on short notice, so call in advance. Some of these factory outlets accept credit cards, but these are the ones that are likely to charge higher prices. To locate specific factory outlets, try these books:

1. *Factory Outlet Shopping Guide Series* by Jean Bird (available from PO Box 95-M, Oradell, NJ 07649, $4.95 each). Individual books cover Pennsylvania, New England, New Jersey, New York's Rockland County, New York City, Westchester County, and Long Island, North and South Carolina, Washington, DC, Maryland, Delaware, and Virginia.
2. *The SOS Directory* by Iris Ellis (PO Box 10482, Jacksonville, FL 32207, $9.95 including postage), listing 5,000 outlets throughout the United States.

Regional Specialties: In New England, New York, and Pennsylvania, look for good antiques. In addition to shops on Madison Avenue in New York or Pine Street in Philadelphia, you can find good buys in small antique stores along country roads if you are prepared to look through the junk and have a good sense of what items are worth. Vermont cheese and maple syrup, saltwater taffy along the New Jersey shore, and shoofly pie and pretzels in the Pennsylvania Dutch country are all specialties of their respective regions.

In the South there are interesting crafts, especially in the inland mountains. West Virginia is noted for handstitched quilts and quilted clothing and toys. Williamsburg, Virginia, reproductions of pewter, furniture, and other 18th-century items are justly famous. In Georgia you can buy local basketware, wood carving, handwoven wool, and ceramics. In the Blue Ridge Mountains, look for cornhusk dolls and a small wooden musical instrument called the Gee-Haw-Whimmy-Diddle. The Cherokees at Ocunaluftee Indian Village in North Carolina (see *A Short Tour of Indian America,* DIVERSIONS, p. 608) sell handmade tomahawks, bows and arrows, pottery, basketwork, rugs, and feather headdresses.

In the Great Lakes region, consider homemade jams and relishes (especially in Iowa's country stores); American antiques in Illinois; hand-painted ceramics in Clay County, Indiana; wheel cheese and lace in Wisconsin; and pipes, moccasins, and handwoven Indian tribal rugs in Minnesota.

In the Southwest, Mexican, Indian, and "Old West" items are especially good buys. Serapes, tree-of-life candlesticks, and wool rebozos from across the border make nice gifts. The Indian specialties are pottery, Kaibab squaw boots, Navajo rugs, and silver and turquoise jewelry, as well as drums, dolls, and headdresses. And, of course, cowboy boots and ranch clothes from Arizona, New Mexico, and Texas. In the Rockies the same "Old West" focus prevails in many of the shops. Consider buckskin jackets or pants and tooled leather belts, boots, or hats. The region is not without its Indian specialties, but most special is Rocky Mountain jade jewelry.

The Far West, Alaska, and the northern states are the places to buy Eskimo crafts, which include ceremonial masks, dolls, carved whalebone sculpture, and jade items. American Indian crafts are available in Oregon and Idaho as well as in northern Nevada. Merchandise from the Orient is available in San Francisco's Chinatown, and Hawaii.

A Special Hint: For some particularly interesting souvenirs and gifts, look in the shops of museums. Museum shops often carry beautifully made reproductions from their collections, anything from prints and posters to jewelry, silver goods, sculpture. And two shopping bonanzas: the United Nations Gift Center in New York City (in the United Nations building), with gifts from around the world.

Ask any store about mailing your purchases home; it may save on sales taxes and will mean less to carry with you.

TIPPING: While tipping is at the discretion of the person receiving the service, 25¢ is the rock-bottom tip for anything, and 50¢ is the customary minimum for small services. In restaurants tip between 10% and 20% of the bill. Waiters in good restaurants expect 20%; for average service in an average restaurant, 15% is reasonable. If you serve yourself in a cafeteria, for example, no tip is expected. Coat checks are worth about 50¢ a coat. For carrying luggage, tip bellboys $1 per person or couple, $2 if you have a lot of luggage. The doorman who unloads your car should receive $1. For any special service you receive in a hotel, a tip is expected — again 50¢ for a small service, ranging upward to $1 or more if someone really does something time consuming or out of the ordinary. Leave a hotel maid $1 a day.

Train personnel do not usually expect tips. The exceptions here are dining car waiters who expect 15% of the bill, sleeping car attendants who should get $1 a night, and porters, who expect 50¢ a bag, $1 if they do something extra. Taxi drivers should get at least 15% of the total fare, and expect 20% to 30% in larger cities.

Sources and Resources

Some General Notes on Sports

From Louisville, Kentucky, to Green Bay, Wisconsin, you can take in major seasonal sporting events during your travels. Here is some background on teams and events. See individual city reports in THE AMERICAN CITIES for specific ticket information.

Football: This most popular of American spectator sports is under the aegis of the National Football League (NFL). The season opens in September and culminates in the Super Bowl, which is held in mid-January in a warm-weather city like Los Angeles, Miami, Houston, or New Orleans, between the top teams of the two NFL conferences. The National Conference is made up of the New York Giants, Philadelphia, Washington, Atlanta, Detroit, Chicago, Green Bay, St. Louis, Minnesota, New Orleans, Dallas, Tampa, Los Angeles, and San Francisco. The American Conference consists of Cleveland, Baltimore, Pittsburgh, New York Jets, New England, Buffalo, Miami, Cincinnati, Houston, Kansas City, Denver, San Diego, Oakland, and Seattle. Information: the NFL, 410 Park Ave., New York, NY 10022 (212 758-1500).

College football competition also takes place throughout the country from September through December. The Rose Bowl, which is the championship game between the winner of contests among the Midwest Big Ten universities and the top team in the Pacific Conference schools, is held January 1. For tickets contact the Rose Bowl, Pasadena, CA 91103 (213 449-4100). Another famous college contest is the Yale-Harvard game, which takes place either in New Haven or Cambridge in November. It closes the Ivy League football season. For tickets, contact Department of Athletics, Yale University, New Haven, CT 06520 (203 436-1647), or Athletic Department, Harvard University, Cambridge, MA 02138 (617 495-2211).

Baseball: Another American spectacle is baseball; its season opens in April and continues through the World Series in October. The professional teams are divided into two leagues, the National League and the American League. The National League (at 1 Rockefeller Plaza, Suite 1602, New York, NY 10020, 212 582-4213) includes Atlanta, Chicago Cubs, Cincinnati, Houston, Los Angeles, Montreal, New York Mets, Philadelphia, Pittsburgh, St. Louis, San Diego, and San Francisco. In the American League (at 280 Park Ave., New York, NY 10017, 212 682-7000) are Baltimore, Boston, California, Chicago White Sox, Cleveland, Detroit, Kansas City, Milwaukee, Minnesota, New York Yankees, Oakland, Seattle, Texas, and Toronto.

Hockey: From October through May the ice is hotly contested by The National Hockey League, whose membership is composed of Boston, Buffalo, Calgary, Chicago, Colorado, Detroit, Edmonton, Hartford, Los Angeles, Minnesota, Montreal, New York Islanders, New York Rangers, Philadelphia, Pittsburgh, Quebec, St. Louis, Toronto, Vancouver, Washington, and Winnipeg. Its best teams compete for the Stanley Cup in May. For more information, contact: NHL, 1221 Ave. of Americas, 14th floor, New York, NY 10020 (212 398-1100); or NHL, 960 Sun Life Bldg., Montreal, Quebec, Canada H3B 2W2 (514 871-9220).

Basketball: Professional basketball gets under way each year in October and keeps its fans watching the hoops through the playoffs in late May or early June. The National Basketball Association (NBA) oversees the sport and is divided into two conferences. The Eastern Conference includes Atlanta, Boston, Chicago, Cleveland, Detroit, Indianapolis, Milwaukee, New York Knicks, New Jersey Nets, Philadelphia, and Washington. In the Western Conference are Dallas, Denver, Golden State, Kansas City, Los Angeles, Phoenix, Portland, San Antonio, San Diego, Seattle, and Utah Jazz. Information: the NBA, Olympic Tower, 645 Fifth Ave., New York, NY 10022 (212 826-7000).

Auto Racing: There are four major automobile races in the United States each year:

1. The Indianapolis 500 takes place on Memorial Day weekend each year at the Indianapolis Motor Speedway, 4790 W 16th St., Indianapolis, IN 46222 (317 241-2501).
2. The Daytona 500 is held yearly in February at the Daytona International Speedway, Daytona, FL 32015 (904 253-6711).
3. The United States Grand Prix is held in Watkins Glen every October, Watkins Glen, NY 14891 (607 535-7145).
4. The Long Beach Grand Prix is held each April in Long Beach, California; information from 100 E Ocean Blvd., Long Beach, CA 90802 (213 437-0341).

For information on other important races: the Automobile Competition Committee for the United States, FIA, Inc., 1701 K St., NW, Washington, DC 20005 (202 833-9133).

Horse Racing: Among the most prestigious national horse races are the Triple Crown races for three-year-olds. The Kentucky Derby is the first, held in early May at Churchill Downs (700 Central Ave., Louisville, KY 40208, 502 636-3541). Second is the Preakness Stakes run in May at Pimlico Race Course (Baltimore, MD 21215, 301 542-9400). The final leg of the Triple Crown is the Belmont Stakes held each year in June in Belmont Park (Elmont, NY 11003, 212 641-4700).

Golf: Professional-quality golf matches are held under the aegis of the Professional Golfers' Association of America (PGA). The three biggest matches on their tour include the Masters Golf Tournament held in April in Augusta, Georgia, the United States Open held in July at various courses around the country, and the Professional Golfers' Association (PGA) Championship also held at different courses in August. Write or call the PGA of America for details, PO Box 12458, 100 Avenue of Champions, Palm Beach Gardens, FL 33410 (305 626-3600).

Tennis: The major event in US tennis is the United States Open Tennis Championships at Flushing Meadow Park, which are held each year late in the summer. For specific information on this and other tournaments, contact the United States Tennis Association, 51 E 42nd St., New York, NY 10017 (212 949-9112).

Weights and Measures

The US may convert in the near future from the familiar "customary" units of measure (feet, yards, quarts, etc.) to the far easier and more logical metric system. Some highway signs, weight scales, and grocery labels already list both metric and US measurements. In anticipation of the changeover, we've included here a listing of metric conversions and equivalents.

APPROXIMATE EQUIVALENTS

Metric Unit	Abbreviation	US Equivalent
LENGTH		
millimeter	mm	.04 inch
meter	m	39.37 inches
kilometer	km	.62 mile
AREA		
square centimeter	sq cm	.155 square inch
square meter	sq m	10.7 square feet
hectare	ha	2.47 acres
square kilometer	sq km	.3861 square mile
CAPACITY		
liter	l	1.057 quarts
WEIGHT		
gram	g	.035 ounce
kilogram	kg	2.2 pounds
metric ton	MT	1.1 tons
ENERGY		
kilowatt	kw	1.34 horsepower

CONVERSION TABLES: METRIC TO US MEASUREMENTS

Multiply	by	to convert to
LENGTH		
millimeters	.04	inches
meters	3.3	feet
meters	1.1	yards
kilometers	.6	miles
CAPACITY		
liters	2.11	pints (liquid)
liters	1.06	quarts (liquid)
liters	.26	gallons (liquid)
WEIGHT		
gram	.04	ounces (avoir)
kilograms	2.2	pounds (avoir)

US TO METRIC MEASUREMENTS		
LENGTH		
inches	2.5	millimeters
feet	30.	meters
yards	.9	meters
miles	1.6	kilometers
CAPACITY		
pints	.47	liters
quarts	.95	liters
gallons	3.8	liters
WEIGHT		
ounces	28.	grams
pounds	.45	kilograms
TEMPERATURE		
°F = (°C × 9/5) + 32	°C = (°F − 32) × 5/9	

For More Information

Every city or region has at least one local guide — rarely available outside the area — which provides information on the nearby scene that is topical, detailed, and often amusing. While you are on the road, it will be well worth your time to browse the shelves of local bookstores. Before you leave on your journey, however, you can prepare by writing to city, regional, and state tourist authorities for information (see *State Tourist Offices,* p. 57, and *Sources and Resources* in THE AMERICAN CITIES section); and by perusing books relevant to your special travel interests. The variety and scope of travel information in the United States today is astounding; below, a partial list of publications we have found particularly useful. Refer to individual chapters of GETTING READY TO GO for further lists of sources on specific topics.

Newsletters: Provide up-to-date travel information in a simple format; most of the travel newsletters on the market today are monthly, eight-page reports that offer inside tips, detailed reports on destinations, and frank evaluations of travel bargains and opportunities in the US and abroad. Newsletters take no advertising, and can be good sources of disinterested — if subjective — judgments.

1. *Joyer Travel Report* (Phillips Publishing Inc., 7315 Wisconsin Ave., Bethesda, MD 20014; 12 issues per year, $25).
2. *Passport* (20 N Wacker Dr., Suite 3417, Chicago, IL 60606; 12 issues per year, $30).
3. *Travel Smart* (40 Beechdale Rd., Dobbs Ferry, NY 10522; 12 issues, $21).
4. *Travelore Report* (225 S 15th St., Philadelphia, PA 19102; 12 issues per year, $22).

Books: The list below is compiled of books which we have seen and think worthwhile; it is by no means complete. Check the card catalogue of your library for other titles. Prices may have increased slightly in most recent editions.

On Travel in the US:

1. *New America's Wonderlands: Our National Parks* (National Geographic Society, $12.95, cloth).
2. *Pictorial Travel Guide of Scenic America* by E.L. Jordan (Hammond Incorporated, $16.95, cloth).
3. *Rand McNally's Traveler's Almanac* by Bill Muster (Rand McNally, $7.95).
4. *Rand McNally's Vacation and Travel Guide* (Rand McNally, $6.95).
5. *Scenic Wonders of America* (W. W. Norton, Inc., $16.95, cloth).
6. *The U.S.A. Book* by Hans Hannau (Doubleday & Company, $8.95).
7. *Mobil City, Vacation and Business Guide* (Rand McNally, $4.95).
8. *Wilderness U.S.A.* (National Geographic Society, $9.95, cloth).
9. *Rand McNally's National Forest Guide* by Len Hilts (Rand McNally, $6.95).
10. *A Guide to the National Parks* by Laura and William Riley (Anchor, $9.95).

On Facts and Information:

1. *1001 Sources for Free Travel Information* by Jens Jurgen (available from Travel Information Bureau, 44 County Line Rd., Farmingdale, NY 11735, $5).
2. *How to Fly for Less* by Jens Jurgen (available from Travel Information Bureau, address above, $5).
3. *Rand McNally Road Atlas* (Rand McNally, $5.95).
4. *Oxbridge Omnibus of Holiday Observances Around the World* (Oxbridge Communications, $2.95).
5. *Simon's List Book* by Howard Simons (Simon & Schuster, $12.95, cloth; $5.95, paperback).
6. US Bureau of the Census, *Statistical Abstracts of the United States* (US Government Printing Office, Stock Number 003–024–02680–5, $11).

On Forests, Parks, and Camping:

1. *Rand McNally's National Park Guide* by Michael Frome (Rand McNally, $7.95).
2. *Rand McNally's Campgrounds & Trailer Parks* (Rand McNally, $6.95).
3. *Wheelers RV Resort and Campground Guide* (Print Media Services Ltd., 222 S Prospect Ave., Park Ridge, IL 60068, $6.95).
4. *North American Campground Directory* (Woodall Publishing Company, $8.95).
5. *Lakeside Recreation Areas* by Bill and Phyllis Thomas (Stackpole Books, $6.95).
6. *A Guide to the National Parks* by William H. Matthews III (Doubleday, $6.95).

On Walking and Backpacking:

1. *Off and Walking* by Ruth Rudner (Holt, Rinehart and Winston, $9.95 cloth; $4.95 paperback).
2. *Walking — A Guide to Beautiful Walks and Trails in America* by Jean Calder (William Morrow & Company, $3.95).
3. *The Compleat Backpacker* by Jerry Herz (Popular Library, $1.95).
4. *Guide to Backpacking in the United States* by Eric Meves (Macmillan Publishing Company, $5.95, paper).
5. *Rand McNally's Backpacking & Outdoor Guide* by Richard Dunlop (Rand McNally, $7.95).
6. *Outside* magazine (3401 W Division St., Chicago, IL 60651, $12 per year).
7. *Adventure Travel, North America* by Pat Dickerman (Crowell, $5.95).
8. *Worldwide Adventure Travel Guide* compiled by the American Adventures Association (Random House, $9.95).

On Bicycling:

1. *The American Biking Atlas and Touring Guide* by Sue Browder (Workman Publishing Company, $5.95).

2. *Bicycle Tours in and around New York* by Dan Carlinsky and David Heim (Hagstrom Company, $2.95).
3. *The New Complete Book of Bicycling* by Eugene A. Sloane (Simon & Schuster, $19.95).
4. *The Bicycle Touring Book* by Glenda and Tim Wilhelm (Rodale Press, $12.95, cloth; $9.95, paperback).
5. *Anybody's Bike Book* by Tom Cuthberton (Ten-Speed Press, $8.95, cloth; $4.95, paperback).

On Canoeing:

1. *Back to Nature in Canoes* by Rainer Esslen (Columbia Publishing Company, $6.95).
2. *A Guide to Paddle Adventure* by Rick Kemmer (Vanguard Press, $6.95).

On Theme Vacations:

1. *Adventure Travel North America* (A Dickerman Guide, $5.95).
2. *Farm, Ranch, and Country Vacations* (A Dickerman Guide, $7.95).
3. *Vacation* by Nancy Hayden Woodward (Penguin, $8).
4. *Learning Vacations* by Gerson G. Eisenberg (Acropolis, $7.95).
5. *America's Freedom Trail* by Victor M. Alper (Macmillan Publishing Company, $12.95).
6. *American Travelers' Treasury: A Guide to the Nation's Heirlooms* by Suzanne Lord (William Morrow & Company, $5.95).
7. *Fifty-one Capitols of America and Executive Mansions* by Jean H. Daniel and Price Daniel (Country Beautiful Corporation, $25, cloth).

On Food:

Where to Eat in America by William Rice and Burton Wolf (Random House, $7.95).

On Inexpensive Accommodations and Historic Inns:

1. *Hotel and Motel Red Book* (American Hotel Association, 888 7th Ave., New York, NY 10019, $35).
2. *National Directory of Budget Motels* (Pilot Books, 347 5th Ave., New York, NY 10016, $3.50).
3. *Country Inns of the Middle Atlantic States* by Anthony Hitchcock and Jean Lindgren (Burt Franklin, Pub., $4.95).
4. *Historic Country Inns of California* by Jim Crain (Chronicle Books, $6.95).
5. *The Inn Book* by Kathleen Neuer (Random House, Inc., $4.95).
6. *Country Inns and Back Roads: North America* (Berkshire Traveller Press, $7.95).

State Tourist Offices

Below is a list of state tourist offices in all the US states (city tourist and convention centers are listed in THE AMERICAN CITIES section of this guide). These state offices offer a wide variety of useful travel information, most of it free for the asking. For best results, request general information on state facilities (several states have "travel kits" which include lists of hotels, tourist attractions, maps, etc.) as well as specific information relevant to your interests: facilities for specific sports, tours and itineraries of special interest, accommodations in specific areas. Because most of the material you receive will be outsized brochures, there is little point in sending a self-addressed, stamped envelope with your request.

ALABAMA Bureau of Publicity and Information, 532, S Perry St., Montgomery, AL 36104 (205 832-5510 or toll-free 800 633-5761 outside Alabama or 800 392-8096 in Alabama).

ALASKA Division of Tourism, Pouch E, Juneau, AK 99811 (907 465-2010).

ARIZONA Office of Tourism, 3507 N Central Ave., Suite 506, Phoenix, AZ 85102 (602 255-3618).

ARKANSAS Department of Parks and Tourism, 1 Capitol Mall, Little Rock, AR 72201 (501 371-1511 or toll-free 800 643-8383 out of state or 800 482-8999 in Arkansas).

CALIFORNIA Office of Tourism, 1030 13th St., Suite 200, Sacramento, CA 95814 (916 322-1396).

COLORADO Office of Tourism, Division of Commerce and Development, Room 500, 1313 Sherman St., Denver, CO 80203 (303 866-2205).

CONNECTICUT Department of Econonic Development, Tourism Division, 210 Washington St., Hartford, CT 06106 (203 566-3977).

DELAWARE State Travel Service, Delaware Development Office, 630 State College Rd., Dover, DE 19901 (302 736-4254 or toll-free 800 441-8846).

DISTRICT OF COLUMBIA Washington Convention and Visitor's Association, 1575 Eye St., NW, Suite 250, Washington, DC 20005 (202 789-7000).

FLORIDA Division of Tourism, Department of Commerce, 126 Van Buren St., Tallahassee, FL 32301 (904 487-1462).

GEORGIA Tourist Division, Department of Industry and Trade, PO Box 1776, Atlanta, GA 30301 (404 656-3590).

HAWAII Visitors Bureau, 2270 Kalakaua Ave., Honolulu, HI 96815 (808 923-1811).

IDAHO Division of Economic and Community Affairs, Visitor Services, Room 108, State Capitol, Boise, ID 83720 (208 334-2470 or toll-free 800 635 7820).

ILLINOIS Office of Tourism, Department of Commerce and Community Affairs, 222 South College, Springfield, IL 62706 (217 782-7139).

INDIANA Tourism Division, Department of Commerce, 440 N Meridian St., Indianapolis, IN 46204 (317 232-8860).

IOWA Tourism and Travel Division, Iowa Development Commission, 250 Jewett Building, Des Moines, IA 50309 (515 281-3100).

KANSAS Travel and Tourist Division, Department of Economic Development, 503 Kansas Ave., 6th Floor, Topeka, KS 66603 (913 296-2009).

KENTUCKY Office of Tourism Development, Room 37, Capitol Annex, Frankfort, KY 40601 (502 564-4930).

LOUISIANA Office of Tourism, PO Box 44291, Baton Rouge, LA 70804 (504 925-3860 or toll-free 800 535-8388).

MAINE Publicity Bureau, 97 Winthrop St., Hallowell, ME 04347 (207 289-2423).

MARYLAND Office of Tourist Development, 1748 Forest Dr., Annapolis, MD 21401 (301 269-3517 or toll-free 800 638-5252 out of state or 800 492-7126 in Maryland).

MASSACHUSETTS Division of Tourism, Department of Commerce and Development, 100 Cambridge St., Boston, MA 02202 (617 727-3201).

MICHIGAN Travel Bureau, Department of Commerce, PO Box 30226, Lansing, MI 48909 (517 373-0670 or toll-free 800 248-5700 out of state or 800 292-2520 in Michigan).

MINNESOTA Bureau of Tourism, Department of Energy, Planning, and Development, 480 Cedar St., St. Paul, MN 55101 (612 296-5029 or toll-free 800 328-1461).

MISSISSIPPI Department of Economic Development, Division of Tourism, PO Box 849, Jackson, MS 39205 (601 354-6715).

MISSOURI Division of Tourism, 308 E High St., PO Box 1055, Jefferson City, MO 65102 (314 751-4133).

MONTANA Travel Promotion Bureau, Department of Commerce, Helena, MT 59620 (406 449-2654 or toll-free 800 548-3390).

NEBRASKA Division of Travel and Tourism, Department of Economic Development, PO Box 94666, Lincoln, NE 68509 (402 471-3111).

NEVADA Travel-Tourism Division, Department of Economic Development, Capitol Complex, Carson City, NV 89710 (702 885-4322).

NEW HAMPSHIRE Office of Vacation Travel, PO Box 856, Concord, NH 03301 (603 271-2343).

NEW JERSEY Division of Travel and Tourism, CN 384, Trenton, NJ 08625 (609 292-2470).

NEW MEXICO Commerce and Industry Department, Tourism and Travel Division, Bataan Memorial Building, Santa Fe, NM 87503 (505 827-5571 or toll-free 800 545-2040).

NEW YORK Division of Tourism, State Department of Commerce, 99 Washington Ave., Albany, NY 12245 (518 474-4116 or toll-free 800 342-3810 in state).

NORTH CAROLINA Travel and Tourism Division, 430 N Salisbuy St., Raleigh, NC 27611 (919 733-4171).

NORTH DAKOTA Tourism Promotion Division, 1050 East Interstate Ave., Bismarck, ND 58505 (701 224-2525 or toll-free 800 437-2077).

OHIO Office of Travel and Tourism, PO Box 1001, Columbus, OH 43216 (614 466-8844 or in Ohio, toll-free 800 B-U-C-K-E-Y-E).

OKLAHOMA Division of Marketing Services, Tourism and Recreation Department, 500 Will Rogers Building, Oklahoma City, OK 73105 (405 521-2406).

OREGON Travel Information, Department of Transportation, 101 Transportation Building, Salem, OR 97310 (503 378-6309 or toll-free 800 547-7842).

PENNSYLVANIA Department of Commerce, Bureau of Travel Development, 416 Forum Building, Harrisburg, PA 17120 (717 787-5453).

RHODE ISLAND Department of Economic Development, Tourist Promotion, 7 Jackson Walkway, Providence, RI 02903 (401 277-2601 or toll-free 800 556-2484, Maine-Virginia only).

SOUTH CAROLINA Department of Parks, Recreation and Tourism, Division of Tourism, Suite 113, 1205 Pendleton St., Columbia, SC 29201 (803 758-8735).

SOUTH DAKOTA Economic and Tourism Development, 221 S Central, Pierre, SD 57501 (605 773-3636 or toll-free 800 843-1930).

TENNESSEE Department of Tourist Development, PO Box 23170, Nashville, TN 37202 (615 741-2158).

TEXAS Travel and Information Division, Department of Highways and Public Transportation, PO Box 5064, Austin, TX 78763 (512 465-7401).

UTAH Travel Council, Council Hall, Capitol Hill, Salt Lake City, UT 84114 (801 533-5681).

VERMONT Travel Division, 61 Elm St., Montpelier, VT 05602 (802 828-3236).

VIRGINIA State Travel Service, 9th and Grace Sts., Richmond, VA 23219 (804 786-4484).

WASHINGTON Tourism Promotion and Development Division, State Department of Commerce and Economic Development, General Administration Building, Room G3, Olympia, WA 98504 (206 753-5607).

WEST VIRGINIA Office of Economic and Community Development, Travel Development, 1900 Washington St. E, Building 6, Room B564, Charleston, WV 25305 (304 348-2286).

WISCONSIN Division of Tourism, Box 7970, Madison, WI 53707 (608 266-2161).

WYOMING Travel Commission, I-25 at Etchepare Circle, Cheyenne, WY 82002 (307 777-7777).

Camera and Equipment

Vacations are everybody's favorite time for taking pictures. After all, most of us want to remember the places we visit — and show them off to others — through spectacular photographs. Here are a few suggestions to help you get the best results from your travel picture-taking.

BEFORE THE TRIP: If you're just taking your camera out after a long period in mothballs, or have just bought a new one, check it thoroughly before you leave to prevent unexpected breakdowns and disappointing pictures.

1. Shoot at least one test roll, using the kind of film you plan to take along with you. Use all the shutter speeds and f/stops on your camera, and vary the focus to make sure everything is in order. Do this well in advance of your departure so there will be time to have film developed and to make repairs, if they are necessary. If you're in a rush, most large cities have custom labs that can process film in as little as 3 hours.
2. Clean your camera thoroughly, inside and out. Dust and dirt can jam camera mechanisms, spoil pictures, and scratch film. Remove surface dust from lenses and camera body with a soft camel's hair brush. Next, use at least two layers of crumpled lens tissue and your breath to clean lenses and filters. Don't rub hard and don't use compressed air on lenses or filters because they are so easily damaged. Persistent stains can be removed by using a Q-tip moistened with liquid lens cleaner. Anything that doesn't come off easily needs professional attention. Once your lens is clean, protect it from dirt and damage with an inexpensive skylight or ultra-violet filter.
3. Check the batteries in the light meter, and take along extra ones just in case yours wear out during the trip.

EQUIPMENT TO TAKE ALONG: Keep your gear light and compact. Items that are too heavy or bulky to be carried with you will likely stay in your hotel room.

1. Most single lens reflex (SLR) cameras come with a conventional 50mm lens, a general purpose lens good for street scenes taken at a distance of 25 feet or more and full body portraits shot at normal distances. You can expand your photographic options with a wide-angle lens such as a 35mm, 28mm, or 24mm. These are especially handy for panoramas, cityscapes, and large buildings or statuary from which you can't step back. For close-ups, a macro lens is best, but screw-on magnifying lenses are an inexpensive alternative. Telephoto and zoom lenses are bulky and not really necessary unless you are shooting animals in the wild. If you want one such lens that gives a range of options, try a 35mm to 80mm zoom; it is relatively light, though expensive. Protect all lenses with a 1A or 1B skylight filter, which should be removed for cleaning only. And take along a polarizing filter to eliminate glare and reflection, and to saturate colors in very bright sunlight.
2. Travel photographs work best in color. The preferred and least expensive all-around slide films are Kodachrome 64, Fujichrome, and Agfachrome. For very bright conditions, try slower film like Kodachrome 25. In places that tend to be cloudy, or indoors with natural light (as in museums), use a fast film such as Ektachrome 400, which can be "pushed" to ASA 800 or 1600. Films tend to render color in slightly different ways. Kodachrome brings out reds and oranges.

Agfachrome mutes bright tones and produces fine browns, yellows, and whites. Fuji is noted for its yellows, greens, and whites. Anticipate what you are likely to see, and take along whichever types of film will enhance your results.

If you choose film that develops into prints rather than slides, try Kodacolor 100 or 400 for bright, sunny days. For environments where there isn't much contrast — in the shade or on dark, overcast days — use Kodak Vericolor. Remember that multiple prints made from slide transparencies are generally better than those made from print negatives.

How much film should you take? If you are serious about your photography, pack one roll of film (36 exposures) for each day of your trip. Film is especially expensive abroad, and any leftovers can be bartered away or brought home and safely stored in your refrigerator. Bring exposed film home for processing. It is cheaper and safer than developing it abroad. If you are concerned about airport security X rays damaging your film, store it in lead-lined bags sold in camera shops. In addition, always carry film on board with you to preclude the possibility of theft, loss, or damage. In case your camera will be inspected, keep it empty of film when passing through security.

3. A small battery-powered electronic flash unit is handy for very dim light or at night, but only if the subject is at a distance of 15 feet or less. Flash units cannot illuminate an entire scene, and many museums do not permit flash photography, so take such a unit only if you know you will need it. If your camera does not have a hot-shoe, you will need a PC cord to synchronize the flash with your shutter.
4. Invest in a broad camera strap if you now have a thin one. It will make carrying the camera much more comfortable.
5. A sturdy canvas or leather camera bag — not an airline bag — will keep equipment organized and easy to find.
6. For cleaning, bring along a camel's hair brush that retracts into a rubber squeeze bulb. Also, take plenty of lens tissue as well, and plastic bags to protect cameras against dust.
7. Pack some extra lens caps — they're the first things to get lost.

SOME TIPS: For better pictures, remember the following pointers:

1. *Get close* — Move in to get your subject to fill the frame.
2. *Vary your angle* — Get down, shoot from above, look for unusual perspectives.
3. *Pay attention to backgrounds* — Keep it simple or blur it out.
4. *Look for details* — Not just a whole building, but a decorative element; not just an entire street scene, but a single remarkable face.
5. *Don't be lazy* — Always carry your camera gear with you, loaded and ready for those unexpected moments.

THE AMERICAN CITIES

ATLANTA

When Jimmy Carter, at that time governor of Georgia, began getting national attention in the early 1970s, the media said he represented the best of the so-called New South, as if they'd just invented the term. Actually, Atlanta newspaper editor Henry Grady had first used the phrase as early as the late 19th century, when Atlanta was being resurrected from the ashes of General Sherman's Civil War siege. If you've seen the film "Gone With the Wind," you probably can conjure up a relatively vivid image of the blazing fire that reduced the city to cinders. In real life, too, the devastation was total, but rather than merely bearing the scars, the local populace returned to rebuild their city as the economic, political, and cultural capital of what would soon be the New South. Appropriately, Atlanta chose as its civic symbol the Phoenix — that mythological bird that dies by fire and then rises from its own ashes to claim freedom.

It's easy to enjoy this modern Phoenix, Atlanta's thoroughly modern metropolitan area — the fine restaurants, the shops that range from redneck chic to haute couture, the discos where no one will admit to being over 30 years old, the abundance of outdoor recreation, the skyline that's a seminar in modern architecture. If visitors find themselves slightly disconcerted by Atlanta's blend of old and new in a setting that shows so little of the city's 19th-century heritage, they should remember the fire — and the Phoenix — and look toward the future rather than the past.

First there was nothing, a section of frontier forest coaxed away from the Creek Indians by the state of Georgia in the early 19th century. A proposed rail route into the area from Tennessee was surveyed in 1837. A surveyor for the Western & Atlantic Railroad staked the southern terminus for the new right of way near where the Omni International complex now stands and called the railroad workers' camp that grew on the site simply the Terminus.

Pretty soon they started calling it Marthasville, after the daughter of the governor who boosted the rail project. Then someone with the Western & Atlantic feminized Atlantic into Atlanta and started using that name on railroad schedules. The city was chartered as Atlanta in 1847.

The state wanted the railroad to run through northern Georgia to help stimulate economic growth, and it did. As the US grew to the west, Atlanta's location became central in its region and even more rail lines were built.

Then came the Civil War, and with it, ultimately, General Sherman. Atlanta's rail facilities made it a prime center of Confederate supply and arms manufacture, so when the Northern (or Yankee, if you're a stickler for local idiom) armies started pushing east after their successes on the Mississippi, Atlanta became the primary target.

The battle for the city raged for months during 1864. In late summer, Sherman's army occupied the city. In November, the Northern commander pulled out, heading toward the coast on the infamous March to the Sea which would devastate much of Georgia. The man who proved that war is hell even before he made the quote famous issued a final order — destroy the city. Most of Atlanta's businesses, all of its rail facilities, and 90% of its 3,600 homes were burned. Five thousand of the city's 5,400 buildings were destroyed. They called it total war.

In 1866, Atlanta became federal headquarters for the Reconstruction. Many of the 20,000 residents who had fled during the burning flocked back, and, like the Phoenix, Atlanta undertook a new incarnation. City officials held several postwar national fairs to promote and stimulate the economy. General Sherman himself came to visit, and was so impressed he became an investor.

In Atlanta today, there are two impressive sculptures: one in front of the Broad Street entrance of the First National Bank, the other on Martin Luther King Drive next to Rich's Department Store. Both depict the Atlanta Phoenix. It is a symbol well chosen for the modern city. The energy to rebuild, to improve, and to create has never flagged. This is not a place to look for Confederate ghosts. Some 439 of the *Fortune* 500 largest corporations in the US maintain branches or headquarters in Atlanta. A sophisticated, cosmopolitan metro area of 1.8 million people, Atlanta is scattered with discos and sophisticated restaurants. Its "Little New York" shopping district offers branches of almost every major store from the Big Apple's Fifth Avenue.

Atlanta's architectural profile is modern in the best sense of the word. Clean-lined, functional skyscrapers are designed so that the inner space allows people to feel comfortable, rather than intimidated by overpowering monolithic anonymity. Peachtree Center's tree-filled atrium is more than just a beautiful place to relax — the greenery gives off oxygen. Atlantans are energy conscious, and their office parks are built with energy-efficient modifications (such as windows that are constantly in shadow to reduce air-conditioning costs). Office parks blend with the natural, living environment, with human needs and priorities integrated into the overall structure. Natural light is part of the new buildings, too: A downtown building like an ultramodern superprism of mirrored glass and sheer steel seems to be wrapped in blue light, sky, and clouds. Unlike any number of modern metropolitan centers, Atlanta is not a hostile city, imposing itself on its citizens and environment. It is a dramatic testament of ingenuity and enlightened planning by inhabitants for inhabitants. Atlantans, after all, have had some experience in rebuilding cities.

And the city still thrives as a distribution point for travelers. In the post–Civil War days, there was a familiar complaint about Atlanta: "Whether you're going to heaven or hell," people used to say, "you'll have to change trains in Atlanta." Today, it's a change of planes, but the city's role is the same. Because of Atlanta's geographic position in the complex web of interconnecting highways, interstates, railroads, and air routes linking different parts of this country, it is a stopover for people in transit from all over the world. Hartsfield International Airport is the second busiest airfield in the world (Chicago's O'Hare is first).

In another sense, too, Atlanta has taken a direct path since Reconstruction. Progressive political and civic leaders — especially in the 1890s, 1920s, and

1960s — have urged Atlanta to reach out to the rest of the country. The city has moved from regional to national to international importance. But as the reality of that progressive reputation has grown, it sometimes bumps into a Technicolor stereotype that's iron-magnolia strong: Southern belles in hoop skirts, white-columned and porticoed plantations in fields of cotton. And the plantations of this scene are all suspiciously alike, all named Tara.

You can't blame it entirely on Margaret Mitchell and *Gone With the Wind.* The ideal of a peaceful agrarian South, with a place for everyone and everyone in his place, had been kicking around since well before the Civil War. But Margaret Mitchell's three-handkerchief evocation of that sentimental South-that-maybe-never-was spread Atlanta's fame around the world on a scale that only peanut farmer President Carter has surpassed.

But if *GWTW* wasn't history at its most serious, it wasn't nonsense. Reverence for the land, respect for the past, a love of lost causes, a grave politeness in dealing with friend or stranger — some feel the modern South has sold these away in return for material prosperity. Atlantans feel they've kept the best of the past and purged the worst.

A key to that purging was the late Dr. Martin Luther King, Jr., an Atlantan who followed his father into the pulpit of Atlanta's Ebenezer Baptist Church, and who in the streets of Birmingham and Selma, Alabama, helped make the South think again. He was buried in Atlanta after his assassination in Memphis, and one of Jimmy Carter's most meaningful acts as governor of Georgia was placing Dr. King's portrait in the State Capitol (where it is still on display). Carter's respect for Dr. King, and his openness in demonstrating it, helped ease the stereotyped image of white Southerners during the decade of the '70s.

Visitors now quickly discover that Atlanta is more than a single city. It is certainly new and prosperous and sometimes a little gaudy, with a dazzling skyline and a cocky self-image as the next international city. High hopes for Atlanta have largely plateaued, however, and while it clearly is the capital of the Southeast — a by-product of a progressive business community led by "business mayors" Ivan Allen, Jr., William Hartsfield, and Maynard Jackson — the city has had its share of turmoil and disappointment in recent times. It remains to be seen what direction Atlanta will take under the stewardship of Andrew Young, the civil rights leader and former UN ambassador who assumed the office of mayor in 1982.

Despite its problems, however, there's still a grace to the city that survives behind and between its modern buildings, and there's a true Southern spirit that prevails amid modern urban concerns. So it's still possible to find something of that older Atlanta that stimulated the imagination of Margaret Mitchell. It just takes a bit more searching to find it.

ATLANTA AT-A-GLANCE

SEEING THE CITY: The view from the 70th floor of Peachtree Plaza Hotel's revolving *Sun Dial* restaurant is, in a word, spectacular. When the weather's clear, your eye sweeps from the planes arriving and taking off at Hartsfield International Airport (to the south) to the Blue Ridge Mountains (in the north). The *Sun Dial* can be reached only by an 80-second ride in one of the two glass elevators that skim up and down within the glass tubes affixed to the outside of the building. You will have to order something to eat or drink to spend any time admiring the view, and it's a good idea to make reservations before going up for a look. Open daily till 1:45 AM for cocktails. Peachtree at International Blvd. (659-1400).

SPECIAL PLACES: You can walk around downtown Atlanta without much difficulty, but be warned, the streets aren't laid out in a neat, orderly grid. They roughly follow the paths of early — and now extinct — rail lines, because the early streets ran parallel to the old tracks. The result is a tangled web with visitors often confused, as much by the erratic pattern as by the fact that at least half the streets seem to be named Peachtree, Circle, or Hills.

The good news is the public transportation system — MARTA — which is excellent, especially if you are downtown or near Peachtree Street. Not only are there regular buses cruising downtown, but a special circular loop route (with buses every ten minutes) connects the major hotels and convention sites; i.e., Peachtree Center, the Civic Center, the Omni complex, and the World Congress Center.

DOWNTOWN

Peachtree Center – Half a block from that spectacular 80-second glass elevator ride that transports you from the heights of the *Sun Dial* restaurant is Peachtree Center, the shopping "megastructure" that surrounds Peachtree Plaza. Mazes of escalators whisk you to different levels of unusual shops, such as Hans Frabel's handblown glass atelier. You'll find plants and vines hanging everywhere. There are lakes and fountains here, too. You can stop for a casual, relaxing meal in the Center's courtyard restaurant. Great for people-watching. Peachtree Center, 230-233 Peachtree St. NE (659-0800).

Central City Park – A few blocks south of Peachtree Center, Central City Park is a gift of Atlanta's best-known anonymous donor, Coca-Cola millionaire Robert W. Woodruff, whose six-figure civic generosity has done more to change the face of the city than cosmetic surgery has done for Hollywood. (Emory University's Medical School is another large beneficiary of his anonymous largesse.) At lunch, hundreds of officeworkers, street people, wandering preachers, and Hare Krishna folk swarm into the park — a gentle crowd. Grab a hot dog or plate of shrimp-fried rice at *Tokyo Shapiro's*, 62 Peachtree St., across from the park — and settle down on the grass. Peachtree, Edgewood, Pryor, and Auburn Sts.

Martin Luther King Memorial – In 1976, Atlanta's familiar Hunter Street was renamed Martin Luther King Jr. Drive. A more moving testimony is the Memorial at his burial place: "Free at last" reads the inscription on the tomb. The man who spent his life working for freedom lies here, next to the Ebenezer Baptist Church, where he preached, as his father had done before. King's mother was fatally shot here while attending Sunday services in 1974. 407 Auburn Ave. NE (688-7263).

Next door, the Institute for Nonviolent Social Change maintains an information center with papers, tapes, and other materials pertaining to the life of the late Nobel Peace Prize winner. 413 Auburn Ave. NE (524-4402).

Just down the road, Dr. King's birthplace is open daily except Mondays. Admission charge. 501 Auburn Ave. NE (523-0606).

Georgia Capitol – Walk southwest to Martin Luther King Jr. Drive, then west again to the State Capitol. You can't miss it — just walk toward the golden dome (regilded in 1981 with north Georgia gold leaf). If the legislature isn't in session, you can tour the Hall of Flags, the Hall of Fame in the rotunda, and the Museum of Science and Industry. Open Mondays–Fridays. Free. Capitol Square SW (656-2884).

Federal Reserve Bank – Remember the days when dollar bills were silver certificates, not Federal Reserve notes? The dollar was worth a dollar in silver then. Not these days. Not that we're complaining much — Federal Reserve notes seem to work just as well. If you want to see where they're made, walk over to Marietta Street, a few blocks west of Underground Atlanta, and take a look at the Corinthian-columned Federal Reserve Bank. Although the building is new, the Federal Reserve System's Sixth District headquarters has been located here since 1914. Tours of the Bank's operations and its Money Museum are available, but you must call in advance to schedule a visit. The tour takes an hour. Open Mondays–Fridays. Free. 104 Marietta NW (586-8747).

The Omni International Complex – Atlantans are fond of calling their office parks and shopping complexes megastructures, but if there really is such a thing, this extraordinary, futuristic design must be it. The total environment includes the *Omni International Hotel,* with a skating rink in the atrium lobby (see *Best in Town*), the 17,000-seat Omni Arena, six cinemas, scores of shops, discos, boutiques, and restaurants, and the World Congress Center, connected by a covered pedestrian bridge. Within the complex is the triple-tiered *International Bazaar,* with dozens of small specialty shops; and along the main concourse are some of the world's notables: *Givenchy, Hermès,* and *Rizzoli's*. The NBA *Hawks* play all their home games at the Omni Arena. The World Congress Center is the largest single-floor exhibition space in the US (eight acres or 350,000 sq. ft.). Because of its great size, the architects had to allow a ⅛-inch variance at each end of the structure to conform to the natural curvature of the earth. The 2,000-seat auditorium (and many of the meeting rooms) offer six-language simultaneous translation facilities. Also in the Center are well-done Georgia tourist and industrial exhibits, which include a free introductory film. 100 Techwood Dr. NW (681-2100).

SUBURBS

The Wren's Nest – The charming name was given to this Victorian cottage by its famous owner, Joel Chandler Harris, best known as the creator of Brer Fox, Brer Rabbit, and the other immortal Southern animal characters of the Uncle Remus stories. The house has original furnishings and lots of memorabilia from the life of the Atlanta newspaperman-turned storyteller. Open daily. Admission charge. 1050 Gordon SW (753-8535).

Chattahoochee Nature Center – The center is actually a 7-acre nature preserve on the peaceful banks of the Chattahoochee River, with animal exhibits and classes for both children and adults. Open daily. Voluntary admission charge. 9135 Willeo Rd., Roswell, 20 miles north of downtown (992-2055).

Grant Park Zoo – Although it's not one of the country's great zoos, Atlanta's does boast one of the world's largest reptile collections. Monkeys and big cats are well represented, too; and there are some natural-habitat exhibits, always a pleasant alternative to the traditional cage arrangements. In the "petting zoo," youngsters can actually touch the animals. Open daily. Admission charge. Grant Park, Cherokee, and Georgia Aves. SE (658-6374).

Fernbank Science Center – Often overlooked by nonparents, the Fernbank Science Center has the Southeast's third-largest planetarium, an observatory, and a nature trail leading through 70 acres of unspoiled forest. A see-and-touch museum, an electronic microscope laboratory, a meteorological laboratory, and an experimental garden also on the premises make this a fascinating place to spend an afternoon. Open daily. Admission charge. 156 Heaton Park Dr. NE (378-4311).

Piedmont Park – After watching the galaxies whirl, there's nothing like the feeling of firm, fresh earth under your feet. Fernbank Science Center is a short drive from Piedmont, the city's largest park. Playscapes, a children's sculpture and playground area, is a good place to let kids loose. In the spring, the Park is the site of the Piedmont Park Arts Festival. At Piedmont Ave., 10th St., and Southern Railway line NE.

Atlanta Memorial Arts Center – A few blocks from the northwest corner of Piedmont Park, the Atlanta Memorial Arts Center is dedicated to the more than one hundred Atlanta performers and artists who died in an air crash at Paris's Orly Airport in 1962, on their return from a European tour. The Rodin sculpture was donated by the French government to memorialize the crash victims. The Arts Center houses the High Museum of Art, which has a fine, eclectic representation of Renaissance, 19th- and 20th-century graphics, African, and Asian art. Open daily. Free. Here, too, you'll be able to hear the Atlanta Symphony, and see performances by the Atlanta Children's Theater and the Alliance Theater. 1280 Peachtree NE (892-3600).

Atlanta Historical Society – Proceed north along Peachtree Road to Andrews Drive, site of the Atlanta Historical Society's 18-acre complex. Showpiece of the Society is Swan House, built in 1928, and designed by well-known Atlanta architect Philip Shutze in the Anglo-Palladian style. It is a magnificent exercise in a popular Italian Renaissance mode and is handsomely furnished in 18th-century antiques, many of which belonged to the former owners, prominent Atlantans Mr. and Mrs. Edward Inman. Adults can enjoy a fine building; kids can look for the swan hidden in the decoration of every room. Also on the grounds is the Tullie Smith house, an authentic 1840s "plantation plain" Georgia farmhouse reconstructed on the property with all its attached buildings. Nearby is the Inmans' coach house, now a pleasant restaurant, gift shop, and art gallery. Also on the property is the McElreath Memorial Hall, which houses the Society's museum and its extensive Atlanta historical material, most of which is available to the public. A nature trail has been marked so you can learn about the region's ecology. If you want to do research, you'll find plenty of material on Atlanta history. Open daily. Admission charge for Swan and Tullie Smith houses. 3099 Andrews Dr. NE (261-1837).

Six Flags Over Georgia – Just outside the beltline (I-285), this 276-acre amusement park has over 100 rides and live shows, including the Great American Scream Machine (fastest, tallest, and longest roller coaster in the world — until 1976) and the Great Gasp parachute jump (666 feet tall), which lets you free-fall for 30 feet. During the summer, there's a free fireworks display at closing time (11 PM). Open daily, late May through Labor Day; weekends, late March through November. Admission charge. 10 miles west of Atlanta on I-20 (948-9290).

Stone Mountain Park – There's a bit of something for everybody here: a cable-car ride to the top, an old steam train, hiking trails, a lake where you can ride a riverboat or canoe, an 18-hole golf course, and an antebellum plantation. And that's not all. This is Mount Rushmore South. Confederate heroes Jefferson Davis, Robert E. Lee, and Stonewall Jackson have been drilled into the sheer face of a giant mass of exposed granite. The enormous bas-relief was begun — but not finished — by Gutzon Borglum, who carved Mount Rushmore. Resort facilities include campgrounds, restaurants, and motels. Open daily. Admission charge. 16 miles northeast of Atlanta on rt. 78 (469-9831).

Kennesaw Mountain National Battlefield Park – Kennesaw Mountain is the site of one of the most important battles of the siege of Atlanta. The 2,800-acre park holds a Civil War museum, 11 miles of earthwork defense lines, 18 miles of nature trails, picnic areas, and a tower with an excellent view of the battle site. On a good day, you can see downtown Atlanta. Open daily. Free. Old rt. 41, Marietta (427-4686).

Farmers' Market – Looking for that ole down-home feeling without trekking to Plains? Then drop down to the Georgia State Farmers' Market, the largest in the South. The colorful stalls and sheds spread across 146 acres, and for a buck-and-a-quarter you can still get a juicy, black-diamond watermelon or a mess of peaches. Just south of Perimeter Freeway on I-75. Take Thames Rd./Forest Park exit (366-6910).

Tara – We can't let you go on thinking we left it out, since just about everybody comes to Atlanta looking for the legendary white-columned mansion. But alas, Tara never existed, except in Margaret Mitchell's imagination and David O. Selznick's movie sets. If you're lucky, you'll be able to catch "Gone With the Wind" at a local movie theater. It's shown frequently around town, and there's no better place to see it. The "Gone With the Wind" Museum has a large collection of GWTW movie props and costumes as well as foreign editions of the book. Open daily. Admission charge. 152 Nassau St., downtown (522-1526).

■ **EXTRA SPECIAL:** Just 35 miles northeast of Atlanta, *Lanier Islands* are a group of islands that have recently been developed into a resort area with the help of state funds. The 1,200 acres of hills and woods contain golf courses, tennis courts, and facilities for horseback riding and camping. There are also sailboats and houseboats for rent. (Manmade Lake Lanier has 540 miles of shoreline.) There's a *Stouffer's Pine Isle Resort Hotel* on the grounds, too. Open daily. Admission charge. 35 miles north of the city on I-85 (Lanier Islands information, 945-6701).

SOURCES AND RESOURCES

For general information, brochures, and maps, contact Atlanta Chamber of Commerce, 34 Broad SW (521-0845); or Atlanta Convention and Visitors Bureau, 225 Peachtree NE, Suite 1414 (523-6517). Exhibits on Georgia tourism and industry are on display at the World Congress Center, Marietta and Magnolia NW (656-7000). A covered pedestrian bridge links the Center to the *Omni International Hotel.* Foreign visitors' information and language help are available from the Atlanta Council for International Visitors, 233 Peachtree NE, Suite 202 (577-2248).

Insider's Guide to Atlanta (Peachtree Publishers, $4) is the best local guide to the city. You can get one in advance by writing to *Guide*, 494 Armour Circle NE, Atlanta, GA 30324. Also available in local bookstores. *A History of Georgia* (University of Georgia, $12.50), with a foreword by Jimmy Carter, describes the state's development from a pre-colonial penal colony to present time. *Guest Quarters' Best of Atlanta* ($5.95) is a witty, informative insiders' guide to dining, shopping, and entertainment. *How, When and Where in Atlanta* ($8.95) is also a very good guidebook.

All telephone numbers are in the 404 area code unless otherwise indicated.

For Local Coverage – *Atlanta Constitution,* morning daily; *Atlanta Journal,* evening daily; *Atlanta* Magazine, monthly; *Brown's Guide to Georgia,* monthly.

For Food – *Atlanta* Magazine contains listings of most of the established restaurants and some newcomers. The Weekend section of the Saturday *Atlanta Journal-Constitution* offers complete dining, entertainment, and special events listings.

CLIMATE AND CLOTHES: Atlanta's temperatures vary from moderate winters to comfortable springs and falls to hot and humid summers. In the rainy winter months, December–March, it doesn't get much colder than 20°. May, September, October, and November tend to be the sunniest months. While Atlanta isn't exactly what you'd call dry, the average humidity hovers at 60%, which isn't intolerable either.

GETTING AROUND: Bus – MARTA (Metropolitan Area Rapid Transit) is the backbone of Atlanta's public transportation system. Bus routes interlace the city, with frequent stops at downtown locations. Exact fare required. A new rapid rail-line system now runs 12 miles east-west and 2 miles north-south, connecting at the Five Points station downtown. When it's completed, the system will have 50 miles of tunnel and grade-level track. Each station has been designed by a different architect and decorated with murals, photography, and collages. MARTA maintains information booths at the intersection of Peachtree and West Peachtree, near the *Hyatt Regency Hotel,* and at Broad and Walton NE (522-4711).

Taxi – Taxis generally cannot be hailed in the streets. There are cab stands at the major hotels, or you can call Yellow Cab (521-0200) or Diamond (521-0229).

Car Rental – All major national firms are represented.

MUSEUMS: The High Museum of Art in the Atlanta Memorial Arts Center, the Hall of Fame and Museum of Science and Industry in the State Capitol, and the Fernbank Science Center are described in *Special Places.*

Toy Museum of Atlanta, a delight for children. Thirteen rooms in this restored mansion are filled with antique dolls, trains, toy soldiers, and all sorts of games. Open daily. Admission charge. 2800 Peachtree Rd., 5 miles north of downtown (266-8697).

MAJOR COLLEGES AND UNIVERSITIES: There are nine important institutions of higher education in the metro area, each contributing to the cultural, as well as the academic, climate. They are: Atlanta University, 223 Chestnut SW (681-0251); Atlanta College of Art, 1280 Peachtree NE (898-1164); Atlanta College of Business, 1280 W Peachtree NW (873-1981); Agnes Scott College, E College Dr., Decatur (373-2571); Emory University (famous for its medical program), 1380 S Oxford Rd. NE (329-6123); Georgia Institute of Technology, 225 North Ave. NW (894-2000); Georgia State University, University Plaza NE (658-2000); Interdenominational Theological Center, 671 Beckwith SW (525-5926); Oglethorpe University, 4484 Peachtree Rd. NE (261-1441).

SPECIAL EVENTS: *Piedmont Park Arts Festival* takes place in the spring. In September, the *Atlanta Greek Festival* is a potpourri of Greek costumes, movies, gifts, art, dances, and food. Greek Orthodox Cathedral of the Annunciation, 2500 Clairmont Rd. NE (633-5870). Best of all is the *Dogwood Festival,* second week in April, when the city explodes in color (for information, call 892-0538). During the summer months, the *Atlanta Symphony Orchestra* plays outdoors in Piedmont Park on Sunday evenings.

SPORTS: A major-league city, Atlanta is home of the *Braves,* nest of the *Falcons* and *Hawks.*

Baseball – Atlanta *Braves* play at Atlanta–Fulton County Stadium, 521 Capitol Ave. SW. It's occasionally difficult to get tickets, but try at 522-7630.

Football – The Atlanta *Falcons* (588-1111) also play at the Atlanta–Fulton County Stadium.

Basketball – The Atlanta *Hawks'* home games are played at the Omni, 100 Techwood Dr. NW (577-9600).

Bicycling – Bikes (and roller skates) may be rented at *Skate Escape,* 1086 Piedmont Ave., NE, across from Piedmont Park (892-1291).

Ice Skating – *Omni International* (688-5993).

Fishing – There's good fishing at Lake Allatoona, Lake Lanier, and Lake Jackson.

Golf – The best public courses are at Stone Mountain and Lanier Islands.

Tennis – The best clay courts are at the *Bitsy Grant Tennis Center,* 2125 Northside Dr. NW (351-2774). Lanier Islands and Stone Mountain have good outdoor tennis courts, too. If you want to meet other players, drop into *Tennis Club Indoors* on weekends from 8 PM to midnight. They have ongoing round-robin mixed-doubles tennis parties. You can also rent a court anytime seven days a week. Tennis Club Indoors, 1000 E Side Dr. SE, Marietta (427-6606).

Whitewater Rafting – Burt Reynolds (with some help from poet James Dickey) made north Georgia whitewater famous in the movie "Deliverance." For an urbanized alternative, rent a raft at the Chattahoochee River Park at Hwy. 41 in NW Atlanta during the summer.

THEATER: For complete listings of performance schedules, check the local publications listed above. Atlanta has several professional theaters and any number of smaller groups performing in cabarets (see *Nightlife and Nightclubs*) and universities. Among the most prominent theaters are: *Memorial Arts Center* and *Atlanta Children's Theater,* Peachtree and 15th NE (892-3600); *Studio Theater* and *Alliance Theatre* at the Arts Center (892-2414); *Academy Theater,* 581 Peachtree St., NE (892-0880); *Fox Theater,* 660 Peachtree NE (892-5685); *Just Us Theater,* 1150 Peachtree St. (252-8960); and *Neighborhood Playhouse,* North Dekalb Mall (321-9844).

MUSIC: The halls are alive with the sound of everything from classical to country and western to pop. The *Atlanta Symphony Orchestra* plays at Memorial Arts Center, Peachtree and 15th NE (892-3600). Big-name, popular concert stars and touring companies play at the *Civic Center,* 395 Piedmont Ave. NE (523-1879), and at the Fox Theater, 660 Peachtree St., NE (892-5685). Classical concerts are frequently given at *Cathedral of St. Philip,* 2744 Peachtree Rd. NW (261-3810); Agnes Scott College, Decatur (373-2571); and occasionally at other colleges and universities. Check *Atlanta* Magazine for schedules. The *Atlanta Contemporary Dance Company* performs at Peachtree Playhouse, 1150 Peachtree NE (892-9511); and the nationally acclaimed *Atlanta Ballet* (873-5811) at the Fox Theater. New York's *Metropolitan Opera* performs for a week every May at the Civic Center.

NIGHTCLUBS AND NIGHTLIFE: Atlanta's nightlife covers the spectrum with most places open seven nights a week until 3 or 4 AM. There's excellent jazz at *Walter Mitty's Jazz Café,* 816 N Highland Ave., NE (876-7115). Disco thrives at *Another World* in the Atlanta Hilton (659-2000) and *Limelight,* 3330 Piedmont Rd., NE (231-3520). Live country and western bands are featured at *Scooter's Neon Cowboy,* 6521 Roswell Rd., NW (255-7295), and *Mama's Country Showcase,* 3952 Covington Hwy. (284-MAMA). Tea dancing to the big band sound of the 1940s packs the mall of *Colony Square,* Peachtree and 14th Sts., NE (892-6000), every Thursday evening. Young people perpetually crowd the *Agora Ballroom,* 665 Peachtree St., NE (872-4672), to enjoy local and internationally known rock groups. Cabaret-style shows are presented at *Upstairs at Gene and Gabe's,* 1578 Piedmont Rd. (874-6145). The *Wit's End Players*, a popular local satire troupe, appear at the *Off Peachtree Restaurant* in Peachtree Center (577-2300). One of the best places to meet people is *Harrison's,* 2110 Peachtree Rd., NE (351-7596).

SINS: Though *lust* in Atlanta has dissipated quite a bit, you just might be lucky enough to still catch a last glimpse of the action on the infamous stretch of Peachtree Street that runs north of downtown.

For *idleness,* it's hard to beat rafting on the Chattahoochee River. You can rent rafts at Atlanta-Rent-A-Raft, near the river (952-2824).

Atlanta's *pride* is its Dogwood Festival, held each year in April. During this citywide observance, tours are suggested through the dogwood-laden drives to see and smell the flowers and covet the elegant homes.

LOCAL SERVICES: Business Services – Team Concept, Inc., 1925 Century Center, NE (325-9754).

Mechanics – Don Davis Gulf Service, 359 W Ponce de Leon Ave., (378-6751); Joe Winkler's Gulf Station, 2794 Clairmont Rd. NE (636-2940).

BEST IN TOWN

CHECKING IN: Today, Atlanta visitors can pick and choose from the most fabulous assortment of hotels in the country. You can also stay in a Bed & Breakfast inn very inexpensively. These are private homes, all of which rent rooms with adjacent baths, and they're scattered throughout the city. For information and reservations: Bed & Breakfast Atlanta, 1221 Fairview Rd., NE, Atlanta 30306 (378-6026). Expect to pay $45 and up for a double in those we've classed as expensive; between $35 and $45 at places in the moderate category; under $30 in inexpensive places.

Peachtree Plaza – One hotel stands out on the Atlanta skyline. The 70-story Peachtree Plaza is the world's tallest hotel. The 1,100-room Plaza has a ½-acre lake in its 7-story lobby. Regrettably, its guest rooms are far less spacious and barely adequate. Atop the cylindrical structure is the *Sun Dial* restaurant and lounge, our choice for a bird's-eye view of the city and the surrounding countryside. There's also the *Inner Circle* nightclub and the *Savannah Fish Company* restaurant (see *Eating Out*). Peachtree at International Blvd. NW (659-1400). Expensive.

Omni International – Attached to the $70-million Omni complex, it resembles the set from a science fiction movie. Many of the 471 rooms have balconies overlooking all or part of the 14-story, 5½-acre Omni atrium, with its large ice-skating rink for a centerpiece. Several excellent restaurants vie for business. *Reggie's,* a melding of English pub and officers' club; *Burt's Place,* named after actor Burt Reynolds, with a decor of movie sets; *Bugatti's* (northern Italian cuisine); and the *French Restaurant.* One Omni International NW (659-0000 or toll-free 800 241-5500). Expensive.

Hyatt Regency – Each of the 800 guest rooms in the main building has an outside balcony as well as a window overlooking the inner atrium. The adjoining tower has 200 additional rooms. The 327-foot-high revolving rooftop restaurant, Polaris, is reached via glass elevator. 265 Peachtree NE (577-1234). Expensive.

Atlanta Hilton – The largest hotel in the city (and the Southeast), the tri-winged, 30-story, 1,250-room building has a group of small courtyards, each seven stories tall. At the top of the Hilton are Another World (see *Nightclubs and Nightlife*) and Nikolai's Roof (see *Eating Out*). The hotel provides 144 rooms for guests in wheelchairs or with other severe handicaps. Courtland and Harris NE (659-2000). Expensive.

Stadium Hotel – Formerly the Atlanta Internationale, redone in a contemporary style with sports as the major theme. Four of the meeting rooms are named for

Atlanta teams. There are 390 guest rooms, some of which are suites; almost all are being renovated. Swimming pool, restaurant, and nightclub lounge. 450 Capitol Ave. SE (688-1900). Moderate.

Atlanta Peachtree Travel Lodge – If you're looking for a smaller place, this 56-room facility could be what you want. It's not elegant, but it is comfortable. A swimming pool, too. 1641 Peachtree Rd. NE (873-5731). Moderate.

Radisson Inn Atlanta – Some 14 miles northeast of downtown, with two heated swimming pools, a café and lounge, lighted tennis courts for night play, racquetball courts, and a barber. Only one room is equipped for handicapped guests; the other 399 are standard. Pets are welcome. I-285, Chamblee-Dunwood Rd. exit (394-5000). Moderate.

Decatur Inn – Strictly a money-saver, this 34-room establishment in the suburbs won't cost more than $23 for a double. Don't expect luxury, but limited recreation facilities do include a pool. 921 Church, Decatur (378-3125). Inexpensive.

Georgia Motel – Another alternative to higher-priced accommodations, also with a pool. 41 units. 4300 Buford Hwy. NE (636-4344). Inexpensive.

EATING OUT: Ten years ago, hardly anyone ate out in Atlanta; people entertained at home. But the new lifestyles of the 1970s are affecting eating habits. Now, there's real diversification. The best place to get Southern cooking is still in a Southern home, but there are now some public places that run a pretty close second. Expect to pay $30 or more at restaurants in our expensive category; between $20 and $30 in the moderate range; under $20 at places noted as inexpensive. Prices are for a dinner for two, not including drinks, wine, tips.

Nikolai's Roof – With decor and atmosphere suggesting Czarist opulence, the Atlanta Hilton's rooftop restaurant was originally intended to heighten the establishment's prestige, and not to serve as a big money-making operation — which is why it seats only 67 diners. Reservations are necessary weeks in advance, but if you want personal service by waiters in Cossack attire (who have memorized the evening's five-course menu), you'll find it worth the necessary advance planning. The food is French, but then the old Russian courts were shamelessly Francophilic. Open daily. Reservations? Of course. Major credit cards. Atlanta Hilton, Courtland and Harris, NE (659-2000). Expensive.

Midnight Sun – Formerly known for Scandinavian specialties, its new management has created a sumptuous French menu. The restaurant's Danish modern decor—around a glass-enclosed fountain—is one of the city's most striking. Open daily. Reservations recommended. Major credit cards. Peachtree Center (577-5050). Expensive.

Savannah Fish Company – Fish and shellfish, flown in fresh from the Gulf of Mexico, the Pacific, and the North Atlantic, are the hallmark of this cozy restaurant in the Peachtree Plaza Hotel. Open daily. Major credit cards. Reservations recommended. Peachtree St. and International Blvd. (659-1400). Expensive.

Hedgerose Heights Inn – This is one of Atlanta's classiest new restaurants. Pheasant, veal, beef, seafood, and fowl are served with either a French, Swiss, or German flair, and complemented by a fine wine list and very good service. Closed Sundays. Major credit cards. Reservations recommended. 490 E Paces Ferry Rd. (233-7673). Expensive.

La Grotta Ristorante Italiano – Many knowledgeable Atlantans consider this elegant Northern Italian dining room to be the city's finest. Delicious veal, pasta, and seafood dishes are matched by some of Atlanta's most professional service. Dinner only; closed Sundays. Reservations recommended. Major credit cards. 2637 Peachtree Rd., NE (231-1368); and 647 Atlanta St. (US 19), Roswell (988-0645). Expensive.

The French Restaurant – The cuisine of the house is hardly a secret, but what won't be readily apparent from the name is the quality of the food, and the care with which it is prepared and served. Closed Sundays. Major credit cards. Omni International Hotel (659-0000). Expensive.

The Abbey – What a delicious confusion of the ecclesiastic and the secular: One of Atlanta's landmark churches has been converted into a "monastery" that serves French provincial dishes — escargots à la bourguignonne, tournedos à la béarnaise, coquilles St.-Jacques, etc. Dinner only. Reservations recommended. Major credit cards. 163 Ponce de Leon Ave. NE (876-8532). Expensive.

Coach and Six – You can get a good steak here and hearty black bean soup as well as seafood, veal, and very good drinks. American food "with no European pretensions." Open daily. Reservations suggested. Major credit cards. 1776 Peachtree Rd. NW (872-6666). Expensive.

Hugo's – Well-prepared Continental dishes are served without fuss, while harp music plays in the background. Open daily. Reservations recommended. Major credit cards. Hyatt Regency, 265 Peachtree NE (577-1234). Expensive.

Sidney's Just South – Unpretentious single-family cottage with additions tacked on over the years. First-rate Continental cuisine, good wine list, very friendly service. Open daily. Reservations necessary. Major credit cards. 4225 Roswell Rd. (256-2339). Expensive.

Nakato – This thoughtfully designed Japanese restaurant has separate dining rooms for teppan-yaki, sukiyaki, and tempura. Open daily. Reservations suggested. Major credit cards. 1893 Piedmont Rd. NE (873-6582). Expensive.

Pano's & Paul's – Classy restaurant hidden in suburban shopping center but catering to the more sophisticated diner. Continental and American cuisine served in turn-of-the-century eclectic decor. Kitchen promises it will prepare *anything* if requested far enough in advance. Dinner only. Reservations recommended. Major credit cards. West Paces Shopping Center (261-4739). Expensive.

Old Vinings Inn – This is a charming country cottage (about 20 minutes from downtown) full of delightful Gallic surprises. Hollandaises, béarnaises, and other delicious sauces complement the flavors of trout, dover sole, beef, veal, and fowl. Closed Sundays and Mondays. Major credit cards. Reservations recommended. 3020 Paces Ferry Rd., Vinings (434-5270). Moderate.

Anarkali – *Tandoori, biryanis,* curries, and other spicy Indian dishes are expertly prepared at two locations. Closed sundays. Reservations recommended. Major credit cards. 2115 North Decatur Rd. (321-0215); 3179 Peachtree Rd. NE (231-2276). Moderate.

The Corner Wine Bar – Chic little uptown café devoted to good wine sold by the glass or bottle and accompanied by quiches, salads, seafoods, and other light fare. Closed Sundays. Major credit cards. No reservations. 1040 N Highland Ave. NE (874-2082). Moderate.

Pittypat's Porch – Here's the Old South — its food, ambience, and even decor, right down to rocking chairs on interior balconies. The seven-course, family-style meal includes Pittypat's renowned "endless appetizer" salad buffet of fresh shrimp and oysters, as well as such traditional Southern favorites as roast Georgia quail and venison. Closed Sundays. Major credit cards. No reservations. 25 International Blvd. (525-8228). Moderate.

The Peasant Group – Some of Atlanta's favorite dining places are the locally owned Peasant restaurants, with innovative American/Continental meals served in a stylish and relaxed atmosphere. The group includes: *The Pleasant Peasant,* 555 Peachtree St. (874-3223); *The Country Place,* Colony Square, Peachtree and 14th sts. (881-0144); *Dailey's,* 17 International Blvd., downtown (681-3303); and *The Peasant Uptown,* Phipps Plaza, Peachtree and Lenox rds. (261-6341). Open daily. Major credit cards. No reservations. Moderate.

Dante's Down the Hatch – A late-night niche claiming a faithful coterie. Jazz lovers come to hear Paul Mitchell's Trio and assorted combos. The fondue/wine/cheese menu is an attraction on its own, and so is owner Dante Stephenson, who's usually there to recommend a vintage from his personally selected list. Decor resembles the inside of a sailing ship. Open till 1 AM Sunday through Thursday, and Friday and Saturday till 2 AM. Reservations required. Major credit cards. 3380 Peachtree Rd. (266-1600). Moderate.

Golden Buddha – A good place for a relaxing, filling meal. Definitely not elegant, but who goes to a Chinese restaurant to soak up atmosphere? (We go for the sweet and sour shrimp.) Closed Mondays. Reservations required for six or more. Major credit cards. 1905 Clairmont Rd. NE (633-5252). Inexpensive.

The Peking – If you're bored with Cantonese cooking, or find the spicier Szechwan more to your taste, hunt this one down. It's hidden around the left-hand corner of the Northeast Plaza Shopping Center in clean, nondescript quarters. The food is worth talking about and its reputation has spread by word of mouth. Closed Tuesdays. Reservations required for six or more. Major credit cards. 3361 Buford Hwy., Northeast Plaza NE (634-2373). Inexpensive.

Mary Mac's Tea Room – Most of the clientele are students, pensioners, and solid-community types. As soon as you're seated, you're handed a pencil and check so you can write your own order. You can eat amply for about $4.50. Try the President Pudding, a peanut custard. Closed Saturdays and Sundays. No reservations. No credit cards. 224 and 228 Ponce de León Ave. NE (875-4337) and (876-6604).

Le Gourmet – For that sweet tooth. This little deli is just a storefront on a shopping-center strip, so look carefully. Ask for the chocolate-filled "truffles." Closed Mondays. No reservations. 2341 Peachtree Rd. NE (266-8477). Inexpensive.

Excelsior Mill Dining Saloon – Founders of Atlanta's legendary Mellow Mushroom pizza chain bought this 19th-century building a couple of years ago. The place has since been renovated into a huge Continental beer-garden style dining room. Specializes in pizza, salads, sandwiches. Live music. Major credit cards. 695 North Ave. (577-6455). Inexpensive.

El Toro – The zippiest enchiladas, tacos, burritos, and other Tex-Mex dishes served hereabouts. Closed Sundays. No reservations or credit cards. 4300 Buford Hwy. NE (321-9502); 5288 Buford Hwy. NE. (455-9677); and 1775 Lawrenceville Hwy., Decatur (294-9906). Inexpensive.

Varsity – It's a scene right out of *American Graffiti* — a drive-in with singing car hops, an air of bedlam, and a menu of such All-American favorites as hot dogs, hamburgers, and sandwiches. Open daily. No reservations or credit cards. 61 North Ave. NW (881-1706). Inexpensive.

Gabriel's Midtown – This cheerful, primarily vegetarian restaurant broadens its range to include fish, chicken, quiche, lasagna, pizza, sandwiches, and some of the tastiest omelets in town. Beer and wine are also served. Open daily. Major credit cards. Reservations accepted. 112 10th St., at Peachtree St. (885-1502). Inexpensive.

BALTIMORE

You might expect to find residents a shade defensive about Baltimore. Slipped quietly between the great cities of the Atlantic seaboard, like a note between the pages of a novel, the world just didn't think much about it. Commerce among Washington, Philadelphia, and New York swings by on Baltimore's Beltway and Harbor Tunnel, and was so favorably impressed by the smooth efficiency of the freeway system that it used to by-pass the city every time.

But Baltimore has changed its image. Over the past decade, the city has undergone a miraculous transformation. The town has suddenly sparked to life with its dazzling new Inner Harbor, promenades, and marinas; a new modern downtown business district; a rash of new restaurants, pubs, and hotels; and a recently expanded airport.

The striking modern buildings and plazas of Charles Center, Baltimore's heart of business, Fort McHenry, the tiered iron stacks of the Peabody Library, the Sunpapers (among the nation's most distinguished newspapers), and the Johns Hopkins University and medical institutions provide the city with a contemporary cosmopolitan atmosphere, as well as a link to historic tradition. Perhaps best in Baltimore is the cuisine — the riches of the Bay, so to speak, in hard or soft-shelled crabs, oysters (raw and stewed), clams, rockfish, and shad roe — prepared in traditional Maryland style.

Baltimore's deep-water port on the Chesapeake Bay — the major Atlantic port for grain, coal, and spice — has always given residents a touch of smug satisfaction. Now its 45 miles of waterfront are further enhanced by a bright new centerpiece — Harborplace. This complex is the latest achievement in a long and concerted campaign to turn the city's decaying area of docks and piers into Baltimore's biggest asset. Once populated by derelict warehouses, debris, and pollution, the Inner Harbor is now the site of a pair of double-decker glass pavilions enclosing about 125 restaurants, cafés, and specialty shops.

South of the harbor, the city's neighborhoods are being rejuvenated and restored into elegant residential areas. Ten years ago, these blocks of rowhouses were the epitome of urban disaster. Through a city-sponsored program, countless rowhouses have been resold for $1 each to anyone who will restore the home and occupy it for 18 months. This successful homesteading program now extends across the city into Fells Point, Stirling Street, Otterbein, Patterson Park, and Ridgely's Delight.

Baltimore residents are busy these days toasting the new charms of their town and, as ever, celebrating the old. The city is proud of its architecturally impressive City Hall, completed in 1875 in French Empire style. It represents something of the city's style. For the building's centennial, Baltimore spent some $11 million renovating the interior, while preserving the best aspects of the old decor. Outside, the only change is that the small round dome now gleams with gold leaf. Like the building itself, the city's assets can be perceived and appreciated most readily from the inside — which explains why so many people who happen upon Baltimore for one reason or another like what they find and stay. But you don't have to be a resident to like Baltimore. You simply have to come here.

BALTIMORE AT-A-GLANCE

SEEING THE CITY: Baltimore offers its finest panoramic view from the top of the World Trade Center at the Inner Harbor. Downstream lies Fort McHenry, where the successful American repulsion of British forces in 1814 inspired Francis Scott Key to compose "The Star-Spangled Banner." To the northwest, the buildings and plazas of Charles Center stand out against the surrounding cityscape. At Pratt St. between South and Gay Sts.

SPECIAL PLACES: Most of the notable sights in Baltimore are concentrated in a few nicely designed areas. Consequently, the best way to see the city is by walking. Buses and taxis, which serve the entire city, are convenient means of transportation from one section to another; but parking in the lots downtown isn't too difficult or expensive.

CHARLES CENTER AND DOWNTOWN

Charles Center – Built during the past two decades to offset urban deterioration, Charles Center is a 33-acre plot of new office buildings, luxury apartment towers, overhead walkways, fountains, and plazas. Bounded by Lombard Street on the south, Saratoga Street on the north, Charles Street on the east, and Hopkins Place and Liberty Street on the west.

Within the complex are: One Charles Center, a 24-story tower of bronze-covered glass designed by Mies van der Rohe. Inside the Morris Mechanic Theater, such contemporary stars as Rudolph Nureyev and Lauren Bacall have performed; outside, this structure designed by John M. Johansen is intriguingly futuristic (Charles and Baltimore Sts.).

Hopkins Plaza is the scene for many events including everything from concerts by the Baltimore Symphony Orchestra to performances by lesser-known jazz ensembles and chamber groups (between Hopkins Pl., Charles, Baltimore, and Lombard Sts.). Center Plaza, an oval plaza modeled after Siena's Palio, features a 33-foot bronze sculpture in the shape of a flame, designed by Francesco Somaini, and presented to the city by the Gas and Electric Company (north of Fayette St. between Liberty and Charles Sts.). Pedestrian ramps link Charles Center to the Civic Center, a saw-tooth-roofed building which hosts circuses, ice hockey, and rock concerts (201 W Baltimore St.).

Edgar Allan Poe Home and Grave – The house where Poe lived in the 1830s; he visited Baltimore again in 1849 long enough to die and be buried. (Poe's grave is located nearby in the Westminster Presbyterian Church Cemetery at Fayette and Greene Sts.) Open Wednesdays through Saturdays noon to 4 PM. 203 Amity St. (396-4866).

City Hall – Still in use, the domed building is a monument to mid-Victorian design and craftsmanship. City Council meets in open session Monday evenings except in summer. 100 N Holliday St. For tour information, call 396-1151.

Lexington Market – Since 1782 this colorful indoor marketplace has provided stalls for independent merchants. Today it has 100 kiosks and shops in operation. You can lunch on Maryland seafood at its best — in the rough and at little expense — at *John W. Faidley Seafood,* one of the largest raw oyster bars in the world. Market is closed Sundays. 400 W Lexington St. at Eutaw.

MOUNT VERNON PLACE

This 19th-century bastion of Baltimore aristocracy now houses much of the 20th century's counterculture with its array of boutiques, plant stores, and natural food shops. Reminders of bygone days remain in the lovely 19th-century merchant prince housefronts, the stately squares, and outstanding cultural institutions.

Walters Art Gallery – This extensive collection owned by the Walters family (who also owned railroads), and bequeathed to Baltimore, offers an impressive span of art from Ancient Near Eastern, Byzantine, and Classical archaeological artifacts to Medieval European illuminated manuscripts and painted panels, Italian Renaissance paintings, and works of the Impressionists. Free. Charles and Centre Sts. (547-9000).

Museum and Library of Maryland History – Examples of 18th- and 19th-century clothing, furniture, and silver, and general exhibits. Closed Mondays. Library rich in genealogical material. Admission charge. 201 W Monument St. (685-3750).

Peabody Institute and Conservatory of Music – Worth a visit simply for a look at the magnificently designed library. Amidst pillars and balconies, this 19th-century interior holds 300,000 volumes on its tiered, iron stacks which spiral upward six stories. Free student concerts. Mount Vernon Pl. at Monument and N Charles Sts. (For concert information, call 659-8122.)

Washington Monument – The very first Washington Monument, designed by Robert Mills and completed in 1829. Washington's statue stands atop the monument's long shaft (a 228-step climb — there's no elevator) commanding an excellent view of the city, the harbor, and Mt. Vernon Pl. Small admission charge. Mt. Vernon Pl. (752-9103).

NORTH

Baltimore Museum of Art – Noted for two especially fine collections: the Cone Collection of the French post-Impressionist period, particularly rich in Matisse's work; and the Wurtzburger collections of primitive art and modern sculpture. Also has restored rooms from 17th- and 18th-century Maryland mansions, and a new wing featuring American decorative arts and an outdoor sculpture garden. Closed Mondays. Free. Art Museum Dr. near N Charles and 31st Sts. (396-7100).

INNER HARBOR

Harborplace – The dazzling kingpin in Baltimore's renaissance, Harborplace is carrying the heart of the city's business southward. In its two glass-enclosed pavilions you'll find a plethora of shops, restaurants, and market stalls — about 125 in all. On the first floor of the Light Street Pavilion is a marketplace where vendors hawk all manner of comestibles, while the upper level is chockablock with small eateries serving an overwhelmingly diverse range of foodstuffs — everything from hot dogs to Caribbean stews. And whether you're looking for a Peruvian mask or a collector's comic book, chances are it's in The Sam Smith Market, where merchants sell a raft of unusual wares from their pushcarts and kiosks (also on the second floor). The Pratt Street Pavilion has its share of restaurants, boutiques, and specialty stores. At Pratt and Light Sts.

The National Aquarium – Opened in summer 1981, this ambitious project was the brainchild of Mayor William Donald Schaefer. The aquarium has an impressive series of audio-visual displays on marine life with a total of 5,000 specimens on 7 different levels. "People movers" carry you past the exhibits, which include sharks and dolphins, puffins living in their natural habitat, the largest coral reef in the US, and a reconstruction of Maine's coast with a "hands-on" display of shellfish and other shoreline creatures; finally, on the top floor, you can wander through a tropical rain forest. Open daily. Admission charge. Pier 3, Inner Harbor.

Fort McHenry National Monument – Here in 1814, a young Maryland lawyer witnessed the successful resistance of American forces to heavy British mortar bombardment and was so inspired by the sight of the Stars and Stripes damaged but still fluttering against the morning sky that he wrote "The Star-Spangled Banner." Visitors can see the Fort, the old powder magazine, the officers' quarters, the enlisted men's barracks, and then walk along Francis Scott Key's famed ramparts overlooking the harbor. Open daily. During the summer, drills and military ceremonies modeled after those of 1814 are performed by uniformed guards. Free. South of Inner Harbor, at the end of Fort Ave. (962-4290).

United States Frigate *Constellation* – The US Navy's oldest warship (1797), the *Constellation* defeated the French frigate *L'Insurgente* in America's first important victory at sea and was in service through WW II. Now the ship, given its name by George Washington, has daily tours. Small admission charge. Pier 1 of the Inner Harbor (539-1797).

Maryland Science Center and Planetarium – Covers the vastness of outer space in the planetarium and the complexity of inner space in the walk-through model of a single human cell. Closed Mondays. Small admission charge. At the southwest corner of the Inner Harbor (685-2370).

■ **EXTRA SPECIAL:** 30 miles south of Baltimore on rt. 2 (Ritchie Hwy), lies *Annapolis.* The colonial charm of the first peacetime capital of the US is still preserved in Maryland's state capital. Around town are lovely 18th-century buildings, including the old State House which is still in use today, the Hammond-Harwood House, a Georgian home designed by William Buckland, and the campus of St. John's College, which appears much as it did to its most famous alumnus, Francis Scott Key. Also interesting is the United States Naval Academy. The remains of John Paul Jones lie in the crypt of the chapel. The full brigade of midshipmen passes in formal parade review most Wednesdays at 3:30 PM on Worden Field. In town, the harbor is flanked by fancy boutiques and restaurants.

SOURCES AND RESOURCES

The Baltimore Office of Promotion and Tourism offers useful tourist information, such as directions, maps, and brochures, and daily events listings. 110 W Baltimore St., in the Hilton Hotel (752-8632).

Baltimore, Annapolis and Chesapeake Country Guidebook by James F. Waesche (Bodine and Associates, Inc., $4.95) is the best local guide to Baltimore and the surrounding area.

All telephone numbers are in the 301 area code unless otherwise indicated.

For Local Coverage – *The Sun,* morning daily; *The News American; The Evening Sun,* evening daily; *The Sunday Sun* and *Sunday News American* list the coming week's events. *Baltimore* is a monthly city magazine with features on city life, listings of restaurants, and calendars of events. All available at newsstands.

CLIMATE AND CLOTHES: Baltimore weather is fickle, neither the rigorous clime of the North nor the mild South. Unpredictable rain and frequent changes in wind direction make umbrellas advisable, particularly in the summer and early fall. In the summer, the weather can be hot and muggy, though the Chesapeake Bay exerts a modifying influence and brings relief with nighttime breezes. The winter is cold with moderate snowfall. Spring is windy and pleasant.

GETTING AROUND: Bus – The Mass Transit Administration covers the entire metropolitan area. Route information and maps are available at MTA's main office, 109 E Redwood St. (539-5000).

Taxi – Cabs may be hailed on the street or called by phone. Major cab companies are Yellow Cab (685-1212), Diamond (947-3333), and Sun (235-0300).

Car Rental – Baltimore has offices of the major national firms. Reliable local service is provided by Baltimore Car and Truck Rental at 2303 N Howard St. (467-2900).

MUSEUMS: The fine collections of the Baltimore Museum of Art, the Walters Art Gallery, the Maryland Historical Society, and the Maryland Academy of Sciences are described in *Special Places*. Some other museums of note are:

B & O Railroad Museum, 901 W Pratt St. (237-2387). Closed Mondays and Tuesdays.

Babe Ruth Birthplace and Museum, 216 Emory St. (727-1539). Closed Mondays and Tuesdays.

Lacrosse Hall of Fame, on Hopkins' Homewood Campus in Newton H. White Athletic Center.

Peale Museum, 225 Holliday St. (396-3523). Closed Mondays.

Streetcar Museum, 1901 Falls Rd. (547-0264). Sunday, 1–5 PM.

MAJOR COLLEGES AND UNIVERSITIES: Johns Hopkins University, between 34th and Charles Sts. (338-8000), and Johns Hopkins Hospital and Medical School, 601 N Broadway (955-5000), are internationally renowned and have recently been pioneering in work on organ transplants and sex-change operations. Other notable schools are the Peabody Institute and Conservatory of Music, Mount Vernon Pl. (837-0600), Morgan State University, Hillen Rd. and Coldspring La. (444-3333), and Loyola, Charles St. and Cold Spring La. (323-1010). Goucher College is in suburban Towson on Dulaney Valley Rd. (825-3300).

SPECIAL EVENTS: The *Maryland House and Garden Pilgrimage* — Residents of Baltimore and its suburbs take pride in their own backyards, and it is lavishly demonstrated in this two-week, statewide event for garden lovers. Held during the last week of April and the first week of May, the Pilgrimage is a series of self-guided tours through a group of outstanding homes and gardens. For details, contact the Pilgrimage offices at 600 W Chesapeake Ave., Towson, MD 21204 (821-6933). Numerous ethnic fairs take place in warm weather and are usually held alongside Inner Harbor (see newspapers for listings). These festivities culminate in the *City Fair,* the third weekend of September, with everything from Old Country food to top-name entertainers. Merriment returns in May during the *Preakness Festival Week* of outdoor concerts, exhibits, and performances preceding the famous horse race. The *Harborlights Music Festival* is held every summer, usually July through September, at Baltimore's new 2,000-seat Pier 6 Pavilion. A variety of concerts —from symphony to pop—is given. For ticket information, call 727-5580. Pier 6 at Pratt St.

SPORTS: Football – The *Colts* play their home games at Memorial Stadium. The best bet is to purchase tickets as far in advance as possible at the Stadium or at the branch office at the Civic Center. Arrive half an hour to an hour early for parking or take the #3 bus from Charles and Baltimore Sts. downtown (allow one hour), 1000 E 33rd St. For ticket information, call 243-3611.

Baseball – The *Orioles* also play their home games at Memorial Stadium. Tickets for good seats may be hard to get (338-1161).

Lacrosse – The Johns Hopkins *Blue Jays* (Homewood Field, Charles St. and

University Pkwy.) are among the tops in the ranks of collegiate stickmen. Fans are old-family and rabid, but not particularly numerous, so seats are usually available.

Steeplechase – As for another specialty, point-to-point races (with timber barrier jumps) are run in the valleys north of the city (Western Run, Worthington, Long Green) on Saturday afternoons during April and May.

Horse Racing – The climax of the season is the *Preakness,* which ranks with the Kentucky Derby and the Belmont Stakes as one of the most important annual races. At the Pimlico Race Course, Belvedere and Park Heights Ave. (542-9400).

Bicycling – A brochure describing several tours through the countryside is available at the Physical Fitness Commission, 201 W Preston St. (383-4040).

Golf – Best public course is the 18-hole Pine Ridge, three miles north on Dulaney Valley Rd. (exit 27 on the Baltimore Beltway, 252-9837).

Tennis – There are many public courts in the city's parks. The best are at Clifton Park, Harford Rd. and 33rd St. (396-6101 for permit).

THEATER: For complete listings, see the publications cited above. Baltimore's theatrical offerings range from pre-Broadway tryouts or road shows at the *Morris Mechanic Theater,* Charles Center (727-4102) to resident productions at *Center Stage,* Calvert St. at Monument (332-0033), to dinner theaters such as *Bolton Hill* at 1111 Park Ave. (523-1000).

MUSIC: The *Baltimore Symphony Orchestra,* which is highly regarded nationally, performs at the Lyric Theater, where the music and exceptional acoustics can be appreciated in series concerts throughout the year, 124 Mount Royal Ave. (tickets, 837-5691). For those more attuned to a syncopated beat, there is the *Left Bank Jazz Society,* which performs Sunday afternoons at the Famous Ballroom, 1717 N Charles St. (727-8620). Other musical programs are presented by well-known visiting artists; check the newspapers.

NIGHTCLUBS AND NIGHTLIFE: *Girard's* is the popular place for late-nighters: the disco music is loud, lighting is dim, and the clientele is voguish. Food served in early evening. Five minutes from downtown at 1001 Cathedral St. (837-3733). *Shane's Restaurant-Cabaret* has a handsome turn-of-the-century decor and live entertainment. At 1924 York Rd. in Timonium (252-4100). The *Thirteenth Floor* in the *Belvedere Hotel* has a romantic piano bar and a great view of the city. 1 E Chase St. (539-7110). Entertainment at the many restaurants in Harborplace ranges from piano music to stand-up comics.

SINS: The town that *prides* itself on its row houses, Johns Hopkins University, and the Basilica of the Assumption of the Blessed Virgin Mary also has Blaze Starr — who was, in her time, the highest paid exotic dancer in the US. Her former home-away-from-home, the *2 O'Clock Club,* raunchy as ever, still thrives at 414 E Baltimore (752-5322), in the middle of Baltimore's version of Times Square — called the Block — just a hooker's stroll away from the city's police headquarters. The Block is where the boots-and-hot-pants set starts to swing, and to see how *lust* flourishes in an urban environment, visit the peepshow movies, pinball arcades, and pornographic-book stores along Baltimore Street that light up this murky strip of burlesque houses and strip joints.

Avarice claims its corner of Baltimore, too: in the Maryland lottery's daily draw, and at the betting windows at Pimlico Racetrack, Belvedere and Park Heights Aves. (542-9400), especially in May during the Preakness Stakes, the second race in the famous Triple Crown.

LOCAL SERVICES: Business Services – Able Temporaries, One Charles Center (685-8189).

Mechanic – Plotkin's of Franklin Street, 600 W Franklin St. (728-5533).

Babysitting – Elizabeth Cooney Personnel Agency (323-1700).

BEST IN TOWN

CHECKING IN: Downtown Baltimore has its share of moderately priced ($35 to $60 a night for a double room) accommodations in its chain hotels. Many motorists check in here and take advantage of the free downtown parking. There are more expensive luxury hotels ($60 and up) in outlying areas and several less costly hotels ($25 to $35) downtown. Our choices:

Cross Keys Inn – Five miles from downtown (12 minutes via I-83, Jones Falls Expressway). A stop on the airport limousine run, the Inn has a quiet atmosphere and is adjacent to the boutiques and specialty shops of Cross Keys Village Square. It has a good restaurant, coffee shop, lounge with entertainment, and a pool. 5100 Falls Rd. (532-6900). Expensive.

Hunt Valley Inn – Located in a suburban-industrial complex where office buildings and factories are attractively landscaped and discreetly set apart from one another, this is the place to stay if embarking on the Maryland House and Garden Tour or attending the spring's timber races in hunt country. In addition to the restaurant, bar, and breakfast-luncheon parlor, recreational facilities are available — a pool, tennis and golf courts. A Marriott Hotel. 200 rooms. Shawan Rd. at I-83, in the Hunt Valley Cockeysville Business Park (666-7000). Expensive.

Hyatt Regency Baltimore – Completing Baltimore's waterfront facelift is this glossy new Hyatt with 500 rooms, 27,000 square feet of meeting space, and a pathway connecting it to Harborplace and the Baltimore Convention Center. It's also only a short walk to The National Aquarium and the Maryland Science Center. Recreational facilities include tennis courts, jogging track, and swimming pool, and there's a coffee shop (with a waterfall) for snacks, a dining room in a park-like setting, and a formal restaurant on the rooftop level. 300 Light St., Inner Harbor (toll-free, 800 228-9000). Expensive.

Lord Baltimore Hotel – Like Charles Center where it is located, this 50-year-old hotel has undergone successful renovation. The scene of many conventions, the Lord Baltimore also caters to individual travelers. Facilities include a coffee shop, restaurant, bar and cocktail lounge, meeting rooms, and a ballroom. 450 rooms. 20 W Baltimore St. (539-8400). Moderate.

Sheraton Inn – This is the most convenient, respectable hotel for visitors to Johns Hopkins Hospital or School of Medicine, near Baltimore's colorful Fells Point. The Sheraton has a restaurant, a pub, a pool, and, as part of a package deal, car rental with unlimited mileage. 165 rooms. 400 N Broadway (675-6800). Moderate.

Abbey Hotel – This hotel is close to Mount Vernon Place and downtown. Air conditioned, TV, and free Continental breakfast. No restaurant or parking lot, and some rooms lack private bath; but the best prices in the area. St. Paul and Madison Sts. (332-0405). Inexpensive.

EATING OUT: If you like eating, you'll be happy in Baltimore. From its regional specialty, seafood in the rough, to the authentic dishes of its Little Italy, there are restaurants to suit most palates and pockets. Our selections range in price from $40 or more for a dinner for two in the expensive range,

$25 to $35 in the moderate range, and $25 or less in the inexpensive range. Prices do not include drinks, wine, or tips.

Café des Artistes – The fanciest of several eating places on the ground-floor level of Mechanic Theater. Classical French cuisine, handsome ornamentation. Veal, seafood, are warmly recommended. Closed Sundays. Major credit cards. Charles Center (837-6600). Expensive.

Prime Rib – A hangout for figures in the city's political and entertainment worlds. Its prime rib *is* great, but no more so than the crab imperial. Major credit cards. 1101 N Calvert St., in Horizon House (539-1804). Expensive to moderate.

Sabatino's – What looks like Napoli is really the heart of Baltimore's Little Italy. Veal and shrimp Marsala are the specialties, appreciated by the locals who refer to the place familiarly as Sabby's. Spiro T. Agnew and Marvin Mandel both ate here right after their respective court convictions. You'll do better. Open every day for lunch and dinner. No credit cards. 901 Fawn St. (727-9414). Moderate.

Obrycki's Crab House – Roll back your sleeves, put on your bib, grab a mallet, and you're ready for a bout at Obrycki's. Here you spend all evening battling steamed crabs. There's plenty of support along the way in the warm family atmosphere. Closed Sundays and Mondays. No credit cards. 1729 E Pratt St. (732-6399). Moderate.

Marconi's – The interior is drab to the eye, but the artistry is on the plate. The restaurant where, in a steady stream, Baltimoreans themselves go. The specialty of this Franco-Italian restaurant is filet of sole prepared in a variety of delicious ways. Open Tuesdays through Saturdays for lunch and dinner. No reservations. 106 W Saratoga St. (752-9286). Moderate.

Belvedere – The Falstaff Room has reopened, including the Owl Bar. Lunch, dinner, in the tradition of the decades when this was Baltimore's prestige hotel (it is now mostly given over to apartments). Major credit cards. N Charles St. at Chase (539-7110). Moderate.

Haussner's – Everything abounds in this German restaurant from the fat Tyrolean dumplings to the draft Bavarian beer, to the Barbizon paintings and busts of Roman emperors that cover the walls. The museum downstairs has a ball of string 25 miles long. Don't ask; we're just reporting the facts. Open Tuesdays through Saturdays for lunch and dinner. Major credit cards. Reservations accepted for lunch only. 3236 Eastern Ave. (327-8365). Moderate.

Tio Pepe Restaurant – Splendid Spanish cuisine, in the shadowy vaulted cellars of an old brick town house. The quality food, including paella à la Valenciana and the rock fish with lobster (not on the menu), and the excellent atmosphere and service make this a favorite haunt of residents. Dinner every day and lunch on weekdays. Credit cards. 10 E Franklin St. (539-4675). Moderate.

Ikaros – Greek as Greek can be with kalamari (squid), lamb in endless variations, wines, intricate salads, and sticky honey pastries. Closed Tuesdays. No credit cards. 4805 Eastern Ave. (633-9825). Moderate.

Pimlico Hotel – A center of Jewish community night life, complete with dancing. The food is neither kosher nor Jewish, but features beef, seafood, Cantonese Chinese. Open daily. Credit cards. 5301 Park Heights Ave. (664-8014). Moderate.

John W. Faidley Seafood – In the past hundred years, Faidley's has established itself as the place for oysters, crabs, and clams brought in fresh daily from the bay. The downtown lunch hour crowd regards a visit to Faidley's in Lexington Market — a vast assemblage of butchers and merchants — as the ultimate adventure. Closed Sundays. Open 9 AM to 6 PM. No credit cards. Paca at Lexington St. (727-4898). Inexpensive.

Harborplace – In addition to 33 food stalls, where you can find everything from

Buffalo wings to chocolate-covered strawberries, the following restaurants have good food, harbor views, and moderate prices. In the Light Street Pavilion are: *The American Café,* with a light American menu and frequent live entertainment (962-8400); *City Lights,* featuring French cuisine and homemade desserts (244-8811); *Jean-Claude's Café,* also with French food (332-0950); *Phillips Harborplace,* with Chesapeake Bay seafood and a piano bar (685-6600); and *The Soup Kitchen,* with homemade soups, good salads, and desserts (539-3810). In the Pratt Street Pavilion are: *The Big Cheese,* with international cheese specialties (332-0540); *The Black Pearl,* serving both hearty American fare and *nouvelle cuisine* (962-5050); *Tandoor,* featuring Northern Indian cuisine cooked in special tandoori ovens (547-0575); and *Taverna Athena,* with authentic Greek cuisine (547-8900).

BOSTON

On the map, the Boston peninsula curves up toward the northeast like a catcher's mitt, with Cambridge hovering above it, ready to plop down into its palm. Rich veins of history crisscross the blunt fingertips of this mitt. Here are the narrow cobblestone streets where Boston's colonists walked, the Common where their cattle grazed, the churches they prayed in, and the tiny burying grounds that shelter their bones to this day. Here, too, are the bold buildings of government, the fortresses of finance, the cool green of the wharfside parks, and the colorful chaos of the open market. Any Bostonian in an energetic frame of mind strolling briskly from the Common to the tip of the North End can traverse all this eventful terrain in less than an hour.

But he or she would be making a sad mistake. For Boston is a wonderful city to walk in, if you take your time. Here you will find very few of those brazen monstrosities that dwarf the human landscape; on the contrary, this is a city built on a personal scale. In Boston you must train your eye to look for the little things, the odd quirks of architecture, the bright spots of whimsy and caprice. Spend a couple of hours in the North End, wandering down twisting red brick streets barely wider than the ancient cowpaths they follow, or in the Back Bay, strolling along broad avenues lined with stately town houses, and you will see much that is lovely or curious or amusing. Keep a watchful eye out for the famous brass nameplates and gas lamps of Beacon Hill, the intricate wrought-iron balconies along Commonwealth Avenue, the bronze castings of orange peels, lettuce leaves, and other appropriate refuse set into the pavement near Haymarket.

What Boston offers her citizens, in addition to her physical beauty, her rich history, and her convenient pocket-handkerchief size, is a rare quality of civilized urbanity: a sense of ease combined with an abundance of delightful opportunities. Step out of your house or your hotel room, and Boston showers you with riches. Do you like museums? Boston's are among the finest in the world. Art? Her art schools are excellent, her galleries legion; a dedicated art fancier would be hard-put to keep up with all the openings in a single week. Music? The Boston Symphony is only the beginning. This is a town where baroque chamber music concerts are often sold out, where jazz fans can still sit through three sizzling sets in intimate underground cafés for a couple of bucks, where the biggest names in current folk and rock come back faithfully to sing in the local bars that gave them their starts. There are drum and bugle corps, barbershop quartets, Renaissance ensembles, Dixieland combos, and choral groups of all descriptions.

The Opera Company of Boston and the Boston Ballet need no introduction, but few people realize that Boston also supports dozens of contemporary dance companies that present frequent, innovative programs. Many pre-Broadway shows open here at less-than-Broadway prices, and local theater groups stage everything from Shakespeare to Japanese No plays. Besides the many commercial movie houses showing first- and second-run films, local colleges and cultural centers are always sponsoring film festivals where you can catch up with your favorite Chaplin or Dietrich or Bogart epic, or even the great old flicks from the pre-talky days.

These same colleges and cultural centers provide virtually unlimited opportunities for education and self-improvement, from sophisticated academic communities like Harvard, MIT, and Boston University to the dozens of excellent, lesser-known institutions. The list of stimulating lectures open to the public on any given day is overwhelming. You wonder who goes to them all. And then remember that Boston is an intellectual town, a city of serious thought. Whether you're interested in an advanced degree in nuclear engineering, or a six-week lunch-hour course in how to repair your car, somebody somewhere in Boston is eager to teach you, often for a nominal fee.

But for many, Boston is, above all, a sports town. Take baseball. A Red Sox fan can knock off early on a fine summer day, and thirty minutes later be eating hot dogs and guzzling beer at Fenway Park, right in the heart of Boston.

Fenway is the last of the great old urban ballparks, a cozy little stadium where the stands are so close to the action that between pitches you can almost hear the tobacco juice hitting the grass — and that's *real* grass, mind you. Basketball and hockey fans flock to the Boston Garden, just a few steps from Haymarket, where the Celtics and the Bruins generally put on dazzling virtuoso performances. Football followers have to drive down to Foxboro to watch the Patriots, but the distance doesn't seem to deter them. (Visitors should bear in mind that Boston loyalties are intense. If you must cheer for the opposition, cheer softly.)

For those who would rather play than watch, one of Boston's liveliest participatory sports is grocery shopping. The city delights in a wealth of ethnic communities, each with its own linguistic and culinary traditions, and shopping for dinner can become a fascinating cross-cultural odyssey. An enterprising Bostonian might buy provisions for a single cocktail party at a dozen little neighborhood shops all over town, picking up delicately flavored Chinese sausage, tangy Greek olives, braided Syrian cheese, sweet Portuguese bread, and crispy Italian cannoli. Certainly no visitor lucky enough to be in town on a Friday or Saturday should miss the vivid colors and high-pitched excitement of Haymarket, the traditional open market where generations of Bostonians have bargained zealously for their week's supply of fresh produce.

Boston is justly famous for its seafood, especially the ubiquitous scrod, which is actually young cod — or is it grown-up cod cut into fillets? Bostonians argue this — and everything else — fanatically, for they have the Irish tradition of impassioned and unswayable conviction, upheld by the equally Irish gift of agile tongues. Another time-honored and intense debate centers on the proper ingredients for chowder. There are those who hold with clams, and those who hold with fish (although the choice of haddock or pollock or both can take up an afternoon). Some feel strongly anti-potato, while others wouldn't dream of leaving out the spuds. Purists begin with fat salt pork, slowly rendered, while the lazy resort to butter or similar heresies. You hear tales, occasionally, of mean-minded cooks who skimp on pure fresh cream or who thicken with flour instead of crushed Cross crackers. A few, having read too many cookbooks, violate the chowder with pinches of this and that until it tastes like a foreign invention altogether. But one thing all true Bostonians are agreed on: There must be no trace of tomato in the broth. Heaven help the innocent tourist who refers, even in passing, to "Manhattan clam chowder," as if such a thing were not only a contradiction in terms, but a shame and a desecration.

It must be admitted that Boston's weather is less than ideal. Bostonians take perverse pleasure in claiming some of the worst weather in the world. True, spring and summer are balmy, autumn, gloriously crisp and red-golden; but there's no denying it, winter is foul. Sometime in November, the first, icy winds come swooping down from Canada, coating the naked trees with ice and penetrating even the stoutest coats. Sullen gray clouds close in over the rooftops, dumping soggy snow that piles up day after day into four-foot, six-foot, eight-foot drifts, immobilizing the city. Life becomes impossible for four months. Finally, in April, the winds relent, and suddenly every twig unfurls tender green buds, delicate shoots spring up through the last puddle of melted snow, and the air clamors with birdsong. Then all of Boston emerges from winter dens to take to the parks.

And no wonder. Thanks to the genius and foresight of Frederick Law Olmsted, Boston enjoys several miles of continuous parkland known as the Emerald Necklace. A visitor in Boston is never more than a few blocks from some kind of green oasis suitable for strolling or biking or jogging or picnicking or just for restful contemplation of living vegetation. Perhaps the prettiest of all is the Public Garden, with its ever-changing displays of luxuriant blooms arranged in intricate patterns and its graceful Swan Boats cruising the quiet pond. Much less artfully manicured, and less populous, are the broad peaceful stretches of the Fenway, perfect for picnics, and the endless acres of the Arnold Arboretum. One of the best places for both strolling and jogging — and Bostonians jog *everywhere* — is the long path along the Embankment of the Charles River, which provides plenty of aquatic as well as terrestrial scenery. In short, Boston is a dyed-in-the-wool Yankee town that nonetheless embraces an almost European breadth and depth of civilized pleasures.

BOSTON AT-A-GLANCE

SEEING THE CITY: There are two unparalleled posts from which to view Boston: the John Hancock Tower's 50th-floor Observatory, and the 50th-floor Prudential Skywalk. The Hancock Tower gives you a spectacular panoramic view that even includes the mountains of southern New Hampshire (weather permitting), telescopes, recorded commentaries, a topographical model of Boston in 1775 (which is a must — we promise you'll be surprised), and a seven-minute film of a helicopter flight over the city. (Take the subway, MBTA, to Copley Square or Arlington stop.) Open daily. Admission charge. 200 Clarendon St., Copley Sq. (247-1977). Like the Hancock, the Prudential Skywalk offers an excellent 360-degree view, but the Pru also has a restaurant on the 52nd floor, and a 50-minute multimedia show on eight giant screens on the ground floor. (MBTA, Auditorium stop.) Skywalk and restaurant are open daily. Admission charge. Prudential Center, between Huntington Ave. and Boylston St. (236-3318). For another kind of overview, the fascinating "Where's Boston?" exhibit and film (shown from 10 AM to 5 PM, on the hour) are open daily. Admission charge for film. 60 State St. (661-2425; 367-6090).

SPECIAL PLACES: Casting a friendly eye on its many visitors, the city of Boston has made it both easy and fun to track down the most fascinating sights in town. Just follow the red brick (or red paint) line set into the sidewalk. It's called the Freedom Trail, and it wanders in an erratic figure-eight path. It takes about two hours to walk its entire length without stops or side trips. Take the MBTA to Park Street and start from the Park Street Visitor Information Center, or take the MBTA to Government Center and begin from the City Hall Visitor Information Center. Both provide free maps.

Boston Common – A pastoral green, about which kind words are not now often spoken. The earliest Bostonians brought their cows and horses here to graze. Today, you'll find their descendants engaging in free-form pastimes that range from music-making to touch football, kite flying, and reading. We suggest starting your walking tour here, since this is the oldest park in the nation, founded in 1634. (It's advisable to walk in a group — and never at night — since the Common is often not adequately patrolled; you can park underneath the green in the Underground Parking Garage, open 24 hours daily.) MBTA, Park or Boylston stops. For information on activities on the Common, call 367-9275 or 338-1976.

State House – Fronting the Beacon Street entrance to the Common, the gold-domed State House dates back to 1795. The gold leaf was added in 1861. You can enter through the side door of the right wing (the main door is hardly ever used). Inside, you can pick up pamphlets in Doric Hall and visit the Archives Museum in the basement. The Archives contain American historical documents, among them the original Massachusetts constitution, the oldest written constitution in the world (727-2816). There is also a library (727-2590). Closed Saturdays and Sundays. Free. Beacon St. (727-2121).

Government Center – Passing the Boston Athenaeum, a private library founded in 1897, King's Chapel Burial Ground, and the back of Sears Crescent, a red brick 19th-century building where writers Emerson and Hawthorne used to meet, you'll come to the intriguing, angular shapes of the Government Center. Standing in the eight-acre City Hall Plaza, you'll see the twin towers of the John F. Kennedy Federal Office Building, designed by I. M. Pei. You can tour spacious City Hall on weekdays. The Visitor Information Center in Rm. 200 is open daily. Congress St. (725-4000 or 742-4528).

Paul Revere's House – In addition to having housed the legendary Revolutionary hero, this place has the distinction of being the oldest wooden house in Boston. Before Revere lived here, one of the previous occupants was a sea captain who spent time in a Puritan pillory for "lewd and vicious behavior." Revere moved here in 1770 with his wife, mother, and five children. He had seven more children by his second wife, which is why his house was the only one on the block that didn't have to quarter British soldiers. Open daily. Admission charge. 19 North Sq. (523-1676).

Old North Church – Affectionately known as "Old North," the official name of the church is Christ Church, built in 1723. On the night of April 18, 1775, sexton Robert Newman hung two lanterns outside to warn Bostonians that the British were coming by sea. His action and Paul Revere's famous ride were later immortalized by poet Henry Wadsworth Longfellow in a poem that you probably read in school. (The line you will want to remember is: "One if by land, two if by sea.") Services are still held on Sundays. Open daily. Free. 193 Salem St. (523-6676).

North End – Paul Revere's House and Old North Church are both snugly tucked away among the narrow red brick streets of the North End, a colorful, Italian-American community with a lively street life and some excellent little restaurants (see *Eating Out*). If you feel like sampling the specialties of the neighborhood, pick up a cannoli at one of the local pastry shops and take it to the *Caffe Paradiso*, 255 Hanover Street, where you can wash it down with a superb cappuccino. Leaving this ethnic enclave, go through a brightly decorated tunnel under the expressway, across Atlantic Avenue, by Haymarket, and then again follow the red-brick Freedom Trail to the rehabilitated marketplace area.

Faneuil Hall Marketplace – These three large buildings have been a market since 1826 and still house eleven of the original tenants. Redesigned and opened between 1976 and 1978, the market has become a much-copied prototype of urban renewal. One million people per month — natives and tourists — partake of its multiplicity of stalls, restaurants, and shops. Plan to spend time wandering around and sampling its food, drink, and chic wares. The market takes its official name from adjacent Faneuil Hall, a historic meeting house. Open daily (523-2980).

New England Aquarium – From *Faneuil Hall Marketplace*, walk down State Street, under the expressway, and you'll arrive at the Aquarium. Here, you can watch members of the world's largest shark collection cruising around in the world's largest glass-enclosed saltwater tank. (When the tank cracked in 1978, Aquarium officials had to move all the sharks.) There are also more than 2,000 other fish and marine animals, including performing porpoises. You can take the MBTA to Aquarium stop. Open daily. Admission charge; children under five free. Central Wharf, Waterfront (742-8870).

Waterfront – You can follow Richmond Street, in the North End, to the new waterfront park with its invigorating views of the harbor and shop in the boutiques along the wharves. On Long Wharf, the pier behind the Aquarium, you'll find the Customs House, built between 1845 and 1847, and boats for cruises to Provincetown, Cape Cod (see *Cape Cod,* DIRECTIONS), for harbor cruises and fishing excursions. For information, contact Baystate-Spray and Provincetown Steamship Company (723-7800) or Boston Harbor Cruises, Long Wharf (227-4320). Massachusetts Bay Line leaves from Rowe's Wharf (542-8000).

Beacon Hill – Another detour from the Freedom Trail. Leave the Trail at the State House and walk down Beacon Street one block to Joy Street, up Joy to Mt. Vernon Street, and left on Mt. Vernon. Here stand the stately old town houses that were (and are today) the pride of the first families of Boston. Look for the famous brass knockers, the charming carriage houses, and the intimate backyard gardens. A few blocks down Mt. Vernon Street is Louisburg Square, a rectangle of terribly proper houses facing a tiny park; this was once home to Louisa May Alcott and Jenny Lind, among others. From here you can retrace your steps to the Freedom Trail.

BACK BAY

Public Garden – A treasure among city parks, perfect for a serene afternoon. The Public Garden has fountains, formal gardens, and trees labeled for identification. It is a Boston tradition, dating from 1861. Ride the Swan Boats — they are exactly what their name says they are — boats shaped like swans, pedaled by park employees past the geese and ducks in the Frog Pond. (You might see some frogs, too.) The Public Garden is across the street from Boston Common. The Swan Boats are open daily April to September. Admission charge. Garden open daily. Free.

Arlington Street – Arlington is the first of an alphabetically ordered series of streets along which wealthy Bostonians built palatial homes, churches, and public institutions in the latter half of the 19th century. Looking at a map, Back Bay forms the fat palm of that catcher's mitt we mentioned in the essay, a part of Boston that got filled in during the mid-1800s. Since it was new, flat land, the broad streets and avenues were laid out in orderly, parallel lines, with narrower cross streets intersecting them at regular intervals. They are a joy to walk, and give a better feeling of Old Boston (Henry James' Boston) than any other part of the city.

Beacon Street – Here are some of those late-19th-century mansions, many of them now serving as college dormitories, or divided into professional offices.

Commonwealth Avenue – Make a left onto Berkeley Street, then a right onto stately Commonwealth Avenue. On the corner of Clarendon Street stands the First Baptist Church, a splendid Romanesque structure designed by H. H. Richardson and completed in 1882. Open daily. Free. 110 Commonwealth Ave. (267-3148).

Newbury Street – Turn left from Commonwealth onto Clarendon which intersects Newbury Street, where fashionable Bostonians shop for everything from edibles to etchings. Here, you'll find many art galleries and boutiques, as well as several outdoor cafés serving delectable, if pricey, repasts.

Copley Square – If you resist temptation and continue along Clarendon Street, you'll come to Copley Square, where in the olden days seagoing vessels used to drop their anchors. It was filled in about a hundred years ago, and it now harbors Richardson's magnificent Trinity Church. You can pick up a historical fact sheet inside. Open daily. Free. Copley Sq. (536-0944). The Boston Public Library is the oldest in the country. Be sure to step inside the Library's Copley Square entrance for a quiet moment in the lovely central courtyard. Closed Saturdays and Sundays. Copley Sq. (536-5400).

OTHER SPECIAL PLACES

John F. Kennedy Library – This presidential library opened on October 20, 1979. Designed by I. M. Pei, it sits on the edge of a point of land projecting into Dorchester Bay, with a magnificent view of the Boston skyline and out to sea. The museum includes a half-hour film and an exhibit of documents, photographs, and memorabilia of JFK and his administration. There's also a section on his brother Robert F. Kennedy. By car, take the Southeast Expressway south to the JFK Library/UMass exit. The route to the library is well marked. By MBTA, take the Ashmont train (Red Line) to Columbia; a shuttle bus takes you to the library. Open daily 9 AM to 5 PM (except holidays). Admission 75¢ for adults, children under 16 free (929-4523).

Museum of Fine Arts – This is one of the world's great art museums, with comprehensive exhibits from every major period and in every conceivable medium. Special shows come and go frequently, many of them mounted in the I. M. Pei–designed West Wing, which opened in 1981. The Monets are especially dazzling. Restaurant, snack bar, museum shop, and library. MBTA, Ruggles St. stop. Closed Mondays. Free Saturday mornings, other times admission charge. 465 Huntington Ave., along the Fenway (267-9377 — A-N-S-W-E-R-S).

Isabella Stewart Gardner Museum – Mrs. Gardner, the widow of a Boston Brahmin with lots of money, had the inspired idea of transporting this lovely Venetian *palazzo* to Boston, where she filled it with her extraordinary collections of tapestries, stained glass, fine furniture, and paintings by Masters like Rembrandt, Titian, and Corot. Chamber music concerts are held frequently in the courtyard. MBTA, Ruggles St. stop. Closed Mondays. Admission charge Sundays, other times free. 280 The Fenway (734-1359).

Institute of Contemporary Art – Exciting contemporary art in several media, including frequent series of interesting films. It's set in the halls of a 19th-century police station. Hours vary seasonally. Check before you go. MBTA, Auditorium stop. Admission charge. 955 Boylston (266-5151).

Museum of Science and the Charles Hayden Planetarium – A wide variety of superb exhibits illustrate the fields of medicine, technology, and space. Many exhibits involve viewer participation. You can watch a model of the ocean, and a simulated lunar module in action. There's a special medical wing with anatomical and medical history, and nutrition exhibits. Cafeteria and gift shop. MBTA, Science Park stop. Open daily. Admission charge. Science Park, Charles River Dam (742-6088).

The Boston Tea Party Ship and Museum – Here you can board the *Brig Beaver II,* a full-size working replica of one of the three original ships in the Boston Tea Party. If you feel like it, you can even throw a little tea into Boston Harbor. The adjacent museum houses historical documents relevant to the period, as well as films and related exhibits. MBTA, South Station stop. Open daily. Admission charge. Congress St. Bridge at Fort Point Channel (338-1773).

USS *Constitution* – View the famous "Old Ironsides," the oldest commissioned ship in the US Navy and the proud winner of 40 victories at sea (242-5670). The adjacent shoreside museum displays related memorabilia and a slide show. MBTA, City Square bus stop. Museum open daily till 3:30 PM. Admission charge. Boston Naval Shipyard, Charlestown (242-0543 or 426-1812).

Bunker Hill Pavilion – Witness a vivid multimedia reenactment of the Battle of Bunker Hill on 14 screens, with seven sound channels. We'll bet you thought the Americans won. Open daily. Admission charge. Adjacent to USS *Constitution* (241-7575).

The Arnold Arboretum – Contained in these 265 acres of beautifully landscaped woodland and park are over 6,000 varieties of trees and shrubs, most of them labeled by their assiduous Harvard caretakers. MBTA, Arborway or Forest Hills stop. Open daily. Free. The Arborway, Jamaica Plain (524-1717).

CAMBRIDGE

Harvard Square – Separated from Boston only by the whimsical meanderings of the Charles River, Cambridge nonetheless has a quality all its own. Buildings are lower here, houses smaller, streets a little wider and quieter; pedestrians amble along at a leisurely pace. You get a sense of a 19th-century village arbitrarily sprinkled with contemporary architecture. Harvard University, at its center, creates a permanent international cultural exchange. Cantabridgians, as Cambridge residents are called, routinely dress in saris, caftans, kilts, lederhosen, and blue jeans. Strolling on a hot summer evening, they are not surprised to find themselves serenaded by a Spanish guitarist on one corner, a bedraggled rock group on another, and a bunch of naked-scalped, orange-robed Hare Krishna troupers across the street. Take the MBTA to Harvard Square.

Harvard Yard – "I pahked my cah in Hahvahd Yahd." This sentence is invariably used to mimic the Cambridge-Boston accent (the speech pattern of the late President John F. Kennedy). However, you cannot pahk your cah, or park your car, in Harvard Yard since it's the main entrance to the oldest and most prestigious university in the country. Spend a few minutes walking through the quiet enclave of handsome 18th-century buildings which are both dignified and unpretentious. On Saturday afternoons in autumn, the classic collegiate euphoria is catching, as people prepare for the evening's parties. (If you're anywhere near college age, someone will probably invite you along.) For information on campus events, call 495-1573.

Fogg Museum – Said to be one of the richest university collections in the world, this comfortable little museum houses Harvard's paintings, drawings, prints, sculpture, and silver. The neo-Georgian building has constantly changing exhibits as well. Open daily. Closed weekends in summer. Free. 32 Quincy St. at Broadway (495-2397).

Peabody Museum – On one short block parallel to Oxford Street, the Peabody houses extensive anthropological and archeological collections, with an emphasis on South American Indians. There's also an exhibit on Africa and evolution. Open daily. Admission charge. 11 Divinity Ave. (495-2248).

Brattle Street – Returning to the center of Harvard Square, walk up Brattle Street.

On your left, about half a block past the distinctive modern shopping and office complex, you'll come to the *Blacksmith House*, where according to poet Longfellow, "Under the spreading chestnut tree the village smithy" stood. Today, it's a pleasant spot for a cup of tea and sinfully delicious Viennese pastries. There's a full selection at the takeout counter, too. Closed Sundays (56 Brattle, 354-3036). Up the street is the Longfellow House at 105 Brattle St. This is where George Washington and some of his troops billeted during those long nights at the beginning of the Revolutionary War. Longfellow became familiar with the house after that — as a student at Harvard he rented rooms there, and then bought it. Now it's a national historic site. Open daily. Admission charge (876-4491).

Radcliffe Yard – Until a few years ago, Radcliffe was a separate women's institution, the "sister school" of Harvard. Now it's fully integrated into the Harvard system. "Cliffies," as Radcliffe women are called, attend Harvard classes and receive Harvard degrees. Cliffies have a reputation for being terrifically intelligent and somewhat aloof, but like their brothers, they too will go out of their way to help visitors.

Old Burying Ground – Return to Garden Street and continue past Christ Church to the Old Burying Ground, also known as God's Acre. Graves here go back to 1635. Many Revolutionary War heroes and Harvard presidents are buried here. On the Garden Street fence, there's a mileage marker dating from 1754. Continue in the same direction for another block and you're back at the Harvard Square MBTA. The ride back to Park Street (Boston Common stop) takes only eight minutes, and as the train clatters over the Charles, it provides one of the finest views of Boston.

■ **EXTRA SPECIAL:** About 12 miles north of Boston on rt. 107 sits the town of *Salem.* The capital of the Massachusetts Bay Colony from 1626 to 1630, Salem earned a bitter name in American history as the scene of the witch trials, in which a group of women and children accused 19 villagers of witchcraft. The hysterical allegations resulted in the deaths of the accused. Several of the judges bitterly regretted their roles subsequently. Salem is also the site of Nathaniel Hawthorne's House of the Seven Gables (54 Turner St.). Hawthorne worked in the Salem Customs House and wrote the classic *The Scarlet Letter* at 14 Mall St. You can pick up a self-guiding cassette tour at the Chamber of Commerce, 18 Hawthorne Blvd. (744-0004). Like Boston, Salem has a history trail winding through its streets and port. The information booth provides maps and brochures. Open daily. Free. 18 Washington Sq. (744-0004).

While you're in the neighborhood, be sure to stop in at the Witch Museum, 19½ Washington Sq. N. Closed Thanksgiving, Christmas, New Year's. Admission charge (744-1692). The Witch House, site of some of the interrogations, radiates a claustrophobic, spooky feeling still, especially at night. (Some of the accused witches were confined here.) Open daily March to mid-December; other times by appointment. Admission charge. 310½ Essex St. (744-0180). (You can get in the mood for this tour by picking up a copy of Arthur Miller's play *The Crucible.*)

For a cruise in the harbor, walk down to Salem Willows Pier; Pier Transit Cruises (744-6311). The Peabody Museum has fascinating scrimshaw carvings and nautical regalia from the early days of shipping and far-off ports. Closed Thanksgiving, Christmas, New Year's. Admission charge. 161 Essex St. (745-1876).

A couple of miles east of Salem, the shipbuilding town of Marblehead has interesting colonial houses, places to sit and look at the harbor, and lots of boats. If you visit toward evening, you can watch Marblehead fishermen unloading the day's catch.

SOURCES AND RESOURCES

For tourist information, maps, and brochures, visit one of the Visitor Information Centers at City Hall, Boston Common, or the Hancock Tower, or call 338-1976. The Convention and Tourist Bureau and the Foreign Visitors' Center have helpful information, too. 15 State St. (367-9275).

All telephone numbers are in the 617 area code unless otherwise indicated.

For Local Coverage – *Boston Herald,* morning daily; *Christian Science Monitor,* Monday through Friday mornings; *Boston Globe,* four editions daily; *The Boston Phoenix,* weekly; *Boston* magazine, monthly.

For Food – *Robert Nadeau's Guide to Boston Restaurants* by Mark Zanger (World Food Press, $3.95) and *Boston* magazine's listings.

CLIMATE AND CLOTHES: Autumn is the best time to see Boston. Days are generally clear and brisk, with temperatures in the 50s and 60s. At night it can drop into the 40s, with chilly winds. Winter is formidable, with icy winds, snow, and sleet. If you intend to drive, make sure your car is properly equipped. Spring is glorious, in the 60s and 70s. In summer, the mercury climbs into the humid 80s, although nights are generally delightfully cool.

GETTING AROUND: Bus, Trolley, and Train – The Massachusetts Bay Transit Authority (MBTA) operates a network of underground trains, coordinated with a system of surface buses and trolleys. Exact change required. Service is fast and frequent during the day, less frequent at night, and nonexistent after about 12:30 AM. MBTA stations are marked with large, white circular signs bearing a giant capital T. For schedules, directions, timetables, and maps, call 722-3200.

Taxi – Boston has several taxi fleets, and you can hail them on the street, pick them up at taxi stands throughout downtown Boston, or call for them. Independent Taxi Operators Association (426-8700); Town Taxi (536-5000); Checker (536-7000); Yellow Cab, Cambridge (547-3000); Ambassador/Brattle Taxi, Cambridge (876-5600; 492-1100).

Car Rental – All major national firms are represented. Among the cheapest is American International Rent-A-Car, 209 Cambridge St. (Government Center MBTA stop, 523-5441) or 341 Newbury St. (MBTA, Auditorium stop, 267-6661).

MUSEUMS: For a complete description of the New England Aquarium, Museum of Science, Fogg Museum, Museum of Fine Arts, Institute of Contemporary Art, Gardner Museum, Peabody Museums (Cambridge and Salem), and Bunker Hill Pavilion, see *Special Places*. Other fine Boston museums are:

Museum of Transportation, Museum Wharf, 300 Congress St. (426-7999).

Children's Museum, Museum Wharf, 300 Congress St. (426-8855).

Boston Center for the Arts, 439 Tremont (426-5000).

Busch-Reisinger Museum, Harvard University (495-2317).

Ralph Waldo Emerson Memorial House, 28 Cambridge Turnpike, Concord (369-2236).

Gibson House (Victorian era), 137 Beacon (267-6338).

Museum of Afro-American History, Dudley Station, Roxbury (445-7400).

Society for the Preservation of New England Antiquities, 141 Cambridge (227-3956).

MAJOR COLLEGES AND UNIVERSITIES: Boston is the greatest college town in the country, with tens of thousands of students, professors, and visitors from all over the world pouring onto the campuses every academic year. There are literally dozens of educational institutions, including the aristocratic New England prep schools. Harvard University (see *Special Places*) is the most prestigious in the United States (Harvard Sq., Cambridge, 495-1000). MIT, just down the road, produces scientists in all fields, many of whom continue in government research and consulting positions. MIT is one of the few schools in the country where the computer center is open 24 hours a day, and it's *busy* on Saturday night! (77 Massachusetts Ave., 253-1000). In Boston, across the Charles River, Boston University emphasizes the humanities. Check out the bulletin boards and college newspapers for listings of campus events; Charles River Campus (353-2000). Other Boston area schools: Emerson College (130 Beacon St., 262-2010); University of Massachusetts/Boston (Park Sq. and Columbia Point, 287-1900); Brandeis University (415 South St., Waltham, 647-2000); Endicott College (376 Hale St., Beverly, 927-0585); Tufts University–Jackson College (Medford-Somerville, 628-5000); Lesley College (29 Everett St., Cambridge, 868-9600); Wellesley College (Wellesley, 235-0320); Suffolk University (41 Temple St., 723-4700); Wheaton College (Norton, 285-7722); Simmons College (300 The Fenway, 738-2000).

SPECIAL EVENTS: *Chinese New Year* is celebrated in Chinatown every February. *Patriots' Day* takes place the third Monday in April, which is also the day the famous 26-mile Boston Marathon is run. The *Battle of Bunker Hill* is commemorated on June 17. Male and female rowers compete in the Head of the Charles Races, the last Sunday in October. In even-numbered years, the *Harvard-Yale football game* is held in Cambridge.

SPORTS: No doubt about it, Boston is one of the all-time great professional sports towns. Whichever sport you follow, expect a fine team and a fiercely loyal crowd.

Baseball – Boston *Red Sox* play at Fenway Park, 24 Yawkey Way. MBTA, Kenmore stop (267-8661).

Football – The *New England Patriots,* Schaefer Stadium, rt. 1, Foxboro (262-1776).

Basketball – Boston *Celtics* play at Boston Garden, 150 Causeway St. MBTA, North Station stop (523-3030; 523-6050).

Hockey – Boston *Bruins* play at Boston Garden, too (227-3200).

Racing – Thoroughbreds race at Suffolk Downs, rt. C1, East Boston, January through December. Daily except Tuesdays and Thursdays (567-3900).

Fishing – Deep-sea fishing boats leave from Long Wharf. Contact Boston Harbor Cruises, Inc. (227-4320). You can rent boats, bait, and tackle from Hurley's Boat Rental, Houghs Neck, 136 Bay View, Quincy (479-1239); and Gamble's Landing, 15 Bayswater Rd., Quincy (471-8060).

Bicycling – Rent bikes from Herson Cycle, 1250 Cambridge St., Cambridge (876-4474).

Golf – There's a city course in Hyde Park, where the Parks and Recreation Department offers golf instruction. Contact George Wright Pro Shop, 420 West St., Hyde Park (364-9655). You can also take lessons at the Fresh Pond Golf Club, 691 Huron Ave., Cambridge (354-9130).

Skiing – There's cross-country skiing at Weston Ski Track on Leo J. Martin Golf

Course, Park Rd., Weston (894-4903) and at Lincoln Guide Service, Lincoln (259-9204). Lessons available.

Tennis – There are tennis courts at Tennis-Up, 100 Massachusetts Ave. (247-3051).

Sailing – You can rent boats from Marblehead Rental Boat Co., 83 Front St., Marblehead (631-2259); and in Boston at Boston Sailing Center, 54 Lewis Wharf (227-4198).

THEATER: For information on performance schedules, check the local publications listed above.

Catch a Broadway show before it gets to Broadway. Trial runs often take place at the *Shubert Theatre*, 265 Tremont St. (426-4520); the *Colonial Theatre*, 106 Boylston St. (426-9366); the *Wilbur Theatre*, 246 Tremont St. (423-4008); and the *Metropolitan Center*, 268 Tremont St. (482-9393). Or check out the *Charles Playhouse*, 74 Warrenton St. (426-6912). This is a much smaller and often livelier place, hosting consistently interesting contemporary plays. Curtain time for all four theaters is 8 PM. The *American Repertory Theatre*, 64 Brattle St., Cambridge (547-8300), is based at Harvard's *Loeb Drama Center* and features an ever-changing bill of plays during the school year. In addition, there are dozens of smaller theater groups, including several affiliated with local colleges. *Boston Ballet Company* gives performances at the newly renovated Metropolitan Center (see above; 542-3945 for ballet information). Tickets for theatrical and musical events can be purchased through Out of Town Ticket Agency, adjacent to the Harvard Square MBTA (492-1900); Ticketron, (542-5491); Bostix, Faneuil Hall Marketplace (723-5181).

MUSIC: Almost every evening, Bostonians can choose among several classical and contemporary musical performances, ranging from the most delicate chamber music to the most ferocious acid rock. The *Boston Symphony Orchestra* performs at Symphony Hall, September through April, 251 Huntington Ave. (266-1492). In summer they perform at *Tanglewood Music Festival* in western Massachusetts. Selected members of the Boston Symphony Orchestra make up the *Boston Pops*, performing light-hearted orchestrations of popular music under the direction of John Williams. The Boston Pops plays at Symphony Hall, April through July (266-1492), and gives free outdoor concerts in the Hatch Shell on the Charles River Esplanade in summer. The *Opera Company of Boston*, with Sarah Caldwell, finally has an elegant home at 539 Washington St. (426-5300). For jazz, try *P. B. Sharon's*, 14-20 Marshall St. (367-1540), and *Ryles*, Inman Sq., Cambridge (876-9330). Top-name blues and pop musicians play here, too.

NIGHTCLUBS AND NIGHTLIFE: A sophisticated and well-heeled crowd gathers nightly in the elegant *Plaza Bar* to listen to top-notch entertainers, Copley Plaza Hotel (267-5300). *Pooh's Pub* features outstanding jazz groups in the back room, relaxing atmosphere, 464 Commonwealth Ave. (262-6911). For vigorous popular music (mostly local) among an easy-going blue jean crowd, go to *Jack's*, 952 Massachusetts Ave., Cambridge (491-7800). TV celebrities, professional athletes, and those who want to meet them hang out at tiny, cozy *Daisy Buchanan's*, 240A Newbury St. at Fairfield St. (247-8516). *The Metro* features dancing to new wave music, has a video performance center, and is available for private parties; 15 Landsdowne St., Kenmore Sq. (262-2424).

SINS: An awe-inspiring display of *avarice* can be witnessed at Filene's Basement every Wednesday morning, about five minutes after the doors are opened. This is when bargain-mad shoppers storm the store, elbows out and aggression forward, searching for the special shipment of clothing that has just arrived from Neiman-Marcus or Brooks Brothers, marked way down.

Sloth is the word for lounging around the cafés of Harvard Square on a Sunday afternoon, slowly drifting through a copy of the *New York Times.* If you're up too late to find a *Times* left in any of the local stores, the *Boston Globe* will do. Especially slow-moving hangouts, ideal for this pastime, are the *Swiss Alps* and the *Blue Parrot,* named after Sydney Greenstreet's bistro in "Casablanca."

Boston drivers are notorious throughout the Eastern seaboard, and driving toward the Callahan Tunnel, the Tobin Bridge, or Cape Cod on any weekday afternoon after 3:30 PM will stimulate sufficient *anger* to make the reasons why all too clear.

LOCAL SERVICES: Business Services – Bette James & Associates, 1430 Massachusetts Ave., Cambridge (661-2622).

Mechanic – Ray and Tom Magliozzi, at the Good News Garage, will repair anything for a fair price, 46 Landsdowne St., Cambridge, between Central Square and MIT (354-8947).

Babysitting – International Sitting Service, 233 Harvard, Brookline (566-1972).

BEST IN TOWN

CHECKING IN: Boston has some fine, old, gracious hotels with the history and charm you'd expect to find in this dignified New England capital. There are also several modern places offering standard contemporary accoutrements. However, Boston accommodations are on the costly side. You can expect to pay $95 or more for a double room at those places we've noted as expensive; between $75 and $95 in the moderate category; and inexpensive, under $75.

The Ritz-Carlton – The great lady of Boston hotels, quietly elegant, impeccably correct, and conveniently situated on the Public Garden, within a few steps of the Newbury Street shops. The bar is the best place in town for a drink, and the upstairs dining room is superb. 265 rooms. 15 Arlington St. (536-5700). Expensive.

The Copley Plaza – This is a large, old hotel (450 rooms) on one of Boston's handsomest squares, convenient to the Prudential Center and to Newbury Street shopping. Single rooms are very small. Among its assorted restaurants, *Copley's* offers very good food in a series of rich Victorian rooms, while the *Plaza Bar* features the greatest names in jazz. Copley Square (800 225-7654 toll-free, or 267-5300). Expensive.

Hyatt Regency Cambridge – The 500-room Hyatt in Cambridge is an eye-catching piece of architectural engineering, featuring an enclosed central atrium with fountains, greenery, and glass-walled elevators. The revolving rooftop lounge offers a spectacular view of Boston, especially at sunset. Located on the Charles River, near MIT and Harvard (not easily accessible by public transportation). 575 Memorial Dr., Cambridge (492-1234). Expensive.

Sheraton Boston – A huge, 1,400-room modern hotel in the Prudential Center complex, surrounded by fine places to shop. Four restaurants, three cocktail lounges, and a year-round pool and health club provide plenty of diversion. Prudential Center (236-2000). Expensive.

The Colonnade – This is a distinguished 300-room hotel that tries very hard to emulate the European luxury tradition. There are large rooms, free parking, a (seasonal) rooftop pool, and *Zachary's* restaurant. Near the Prudential Center and Newbury Street. 120 Huntington Ave. (424-7000). Expensive.

The Meridien – Boston's newest hotel, which occupies and glorifies the old Federal Reserve Bank Building in the heart of the financial district, has 328 chic rooms capped with three glittering, glass-enclosed floors at the top. Its French café, *Fleuri,* is open for all meals, while its elegant dining room, *Julien,* serves more formal lunches and dinners. 200 Franklin St., Post Office Sq. (800 223-9918, toll free; or 451-1900). Expensive.

Dunfey's Parker House – This splendid, old 500-room hotel is located right on the historic Freedom Trail, within easy walking distance of the Boston Common, Faneuil Hall Marketplace, and the North End. Of the hotel's three restaurants, the *Last Hurrah,* a jolly Victorian room in the basement, is perhaps the best, with a lively, moderately priced menu, including, of course, the original Parker House rolls. Tremont and School Sts. (227-8600). Moderate.

57 Park Plaza Hotel Howard Johnson's – They're pretty much the same everywhere. This one offers free parking, a year-round pool, and a location convenient to downtown Boston. 351 rooms. 200 Stuart St. (800 654-2000 toll-free, or 482-1800). Moderate.

Sheraton Commander – This mellow old 178-room hotel is located directly on the Cambridge Common, within easy walking distance of Harvard University and Harvard Square. 16 Garden St., Cambridge (800 325-3535 toll-free or 547-4800). Inexpensive.

Howard Johnson's Motor Lodge – This is a modern, 205-room facility on the Charles River, a few minutes' drive from both Harvard and MIT (not easily accessible by public transportation). Sauna and paddle tennis court. 777 Memorial Dr. (492-7777). Inexpensive.

EATING OUT: Bostonians dine out less frequently than their New York neighbors; but when they do, they have their choice of several excellent restaurants, and far too many good ones to list here. Our selection is based on outstanding quality, reliable service, and value. Expect to pay $50 or more for two at one of the places we've noted as expensive; between $30 and $50, moderate; and $30 or under, inexpensive. Prices do not include drinks, wine, or tips.

The Voyagers – The imaginative Continental menu changes daily. Outstanding vegetables and herbs are grown in the young owners' gardens. Hanging greenery, trickling fountains, a superb wine list, comfortable chairs, and a pretty new roof garden dining area. Live classical music. Closed Mondays. Reservations necessary. Major credit cards. 45½ Mt. Auburn St., Cambridge (354-1718). Expensive.

Anthony's Pier 4 – This is a massive place, located right on the harbor and rigged out in a predictably nautical motif. There's a commodious waterfront deck where you can have drinks and enjoy the view while you wait for the loudspeaker system to announce your table. Good seafood, generous servings. Open daily. No dinner reservations accepted. Major credit cards. 140 Northern Ave., South Boston (423-6363). Expensive.

The Ritz-Carlton Dining Room – Large, lovely, and serenely elegant, the only place in town where you can enjoy a view of the Public Garden while dining with old-fashioned formality, served by an expert staff. The cuisine is Continental and familiar, but unfailingly excellent. Men must wear jackets and ties. Open daily. Reservations advisable. Major credit cards. 15 Arlington St. (536-5700). Expensive.

Locke-Ober Café – A splendid albeit somewhat stuffy tradition in probably the best-known of Boston's top restaurants. Until very recently it was a haven for businessmen who preferred to lunch without the presence of females. Today both sexes can eat at the stunningly handsome Men's Grill, with its glowing mahogany bar lined with massive silver tureens, its stained glass, snowy linens, and indefatigable gray-haired waiters. The food is identical in the less-distinguished upstairs room, heavy on German dishes and seafood. Closed Sundays. Reservations essential. Major credit cards. 3 Winter Pl. (542-1340). Expensive.

Nine Knox – Occupies two intimate little dining rooms in a fine old Boston town house. The rooms are beautifully appointed, the china and silver are lovely, and the menu, though very brief, is carefully prepared. On weeknights you may choose among half a dozen entrées. On Saturday nights, everyone eats beef Wellington. Closed Sundays. Reservations necessary. No credit cards. 9 Knox St. (482-3494). Expensive.

Harvest – This restaurant with a colorful dining room, lively bar, and (weather permitting) a secluded outdoor patio is tucked into a back corner of the former Design Research complex in Harvard Square. The ambience is distinctly Cantabridgian, with contemporary furniture. The menu features nicely executed international dishes in the *nouvelle cuisine* repertoire and fine salads and desserts. Open daily. Reservations advised. Major credit cards. 44 Brattle St. (492-1115). Expensive.

Café Budapest – Gorgeously decorated in the lavish Eastern European tradition, and renowned for fine Continental and Hungarian cuisine. Avoid it on Saturday nights, when no reservations are accepted and hordes of hungry diners sometimes wait hours for tables. On weeknights this is a wonderful place to linger over superb strudel and some of the best coffee anywhere. Open daily. Reservations necessary. Major credit cards. 90 Exeter St. (734-3388). Expensive.

Le Bocage – The creation of owner-chef Enzo Danesi, this restaurant has some of the most consistently good French food available in New England. Both regional and classic entrées grace the menu, which changes to suit the season. A bright, efficient staff and a fine wine cellar add to the pleasurable dining. Closed Sundays. Reservations advised. Major credit cards. 72 Bigelow Ave., Watertown (923-1210). Expensive.

Lenora – The area's newest elegant restaurant features a mélange of French and Continental food, prepared and served with skillful precision. Among its specialties are shrimp with lime, herbs, and champagne and the veal in mustard and green peppercorn sauce. Closed Sundays. Reservations. Major credit cards. 1812 Massachusetts Ave., Cambridge (661-0191). Expensive.

Ye Olde Union Oyster House – This is the real thing, Boston's oldest restaurant. Daniel Webster himself used to guzzle oysters at the wonderful mahogany oyster bar, where skilled oyster-shuckers still pry them open before your eyes. Full seafood lunches and dinners are served upstairs, amidst well-worn colonial ambience. Don't miss the seafood chowder. Open daily. Reservations necessary. Major credit cards. 41 Union St. (227-2750); and 142 Stuart St. (542-9091). Moderate.

Jimmy's Harborside – Slightly smaller than Anthony's Pier 4, but a whale of a spacious seafood vessel with a nautical bar overlooking the harbor. Jimmy's chowder is very special, as is his efficient, pleasant staff. Dinner reservations accepted weekdays only. Open daily. Major credit cards. 248 Northern Ave., South Boston (423-1000). Moderate.

Durgin-Park – Justly famed for generous servings of traditional Yankee roast beef, prime ribs, oyster stew, Boston baked beans, and Indian pudding. It's equally famous for its long, communal tables crowded with convivial diners and its brusque, no-nonsense waitresses. Open daily. No reservations. No credit cards. 340 Faneuil Hall Market Pl. (227-2038). Moderate.

The Warren Tavern – This is the closest any of us will come to dining in a real colonial tavern. Just a few minutes from downtown Boston, it offers a warm, pre-Revolutionary ambience, friendly service, and good New England food. Closed Sundays. Reservations advised. MasterCard and Visa. 2 Pleasant St., Charlestown (241-8500). Moderate.

Top of the Hub – This attractive restaurant on the 52nd floor of the Pru offers a spectacular view of the city, the harbor, and the planes landing and departing from Logan Airport. It serves an interesting assortment of international dishes as well as all-American favorites like prime ribs, broiled scrod, lobster. Arrive early for the fixed-price Sunday brunch, or be prepared to wait in a long line. Open daily. Reservations accepted for lunch and dinner. Major credit cards. Prudential Tower, Back Bay (536-1775). Moderate.

Chart House – This restaurant occupies the oldest building on the waterfront, and the interior is a strikingly handsome arrangement of lofty spaces, natural wood, exposed red brick, and comfortable captain's chairs. The menu lists abundant portions of steak and seafood, with all the salad you can eat included in the reasonable prices. Open daily. No reservations accepted, but the line moves pretty fast. Major credit cards. 60 Long Wharf (227-1576). Moderate.

The Seventh Inn – Macrobiotic food (vegetables, fish, fresh fruit) in a cheerful, informal red brick setting across the street from the Public Garden makes this an ideal place to refuel on nutritious meals. Everything comes with appropriately Japanese chopsticks except the magnificent ice cream desserts. Forks are supplied on request if you are uncomfortable fumbling at your salad with Oriental utensils. Closed Sundays. No reservations needed. MasterCard and Visa. 288 Boylston St. (437-1568). Moderate.

Houndstooth – The dining room of this Country French/Northern Italian restaurant overlooks the Common, and piano music fills the lounge. It's open for lunch Mondays through Fridays and for dinner daily. Reservations recommended. 150 Boylston St. (482-0722). Moderate.

Legal Seafoods – If you don't mind waiting in line and paying when you order, you'll find the seafood here plentiful, impeccably fresh, and well prepared. Open daily. No reservations. No credit cards. *Park Plaza Hotel,* corner of Columbus and Arlington (426-4444); in the Chestnut Hill shopping center, at 43 Boylston St. (547-1410); and 5 Cambridge Center, Cambridge (864-3400). Moderate.

Sanae – The emphasis here is on natural foods, prepared with a Japanese flair. Look for dishes like vegetables teriyaki and don't be afraid to try the noodles. The bread is home-baked. Open daily. Reservations are not necessary. No credit cards. 272A Newbury St. (247-2475). Inexpensive.

North End Restaurants – Modestly-priced Italian meals are available in literally dozens of little local restaurants in Boston's oldest section, the North End. *Felicia's* is the home of quite good northern Italian cuisine, and Felicia herself, friend of countless Hub celebrities, oversees the preparation of such specialties as *chicken verdicchio* and cannelloni. Open daily. Reservations. Major credit cards. 145a Richmond St. (523-9885). *Stella Restaurant,* right on the water by the Aquarium, serves dishes from all over Italy, and specialties include *veal cacciatore* and *lobster fra diavolo.* Open daily. Reservations. Major credit cards. 74 E India Row (227-3559). *La Principe* serves up large portions of good food. Open daily. No reservations. Major credit cards. 3 Prince St. (523-9475). Many locals swear the town's best pizza is tossed and baked at *Circle Pizza,* 361 Hanover St. (523-8787). Others claim the *European Restaurant* produces an even better pie. The *European* also has a large menu designed for the entire family. Open daily. Reservations. Major credit cards. 218 Hanover St. (523-5694). *Mother Anna's,* 211 Hanover St. (523-8496), and *Ida's,* 3 Mechanic St. (523-0015), are small-scale, home-style restaurants in the district noted for a fiercely loyal clientele and for authentic dishes cooked to order. Both are open daily, take reservations, and do not accept credit cards.

Elsie's – This incomparable place has been serving monstrous sandwiches to famished Harvard students for longer than anyone can remember. A great place to go when your feet are tired, or when you just want to fill up. Open daily. No reservations. No credit cards. 71 Mt. Auburn St., Cambridge (354-8781 or 354-8362). Inexpensive.

The F&T Delicatessen and Diner – The relaxed, friendly, 1930s-style atmosphere in this pair of eateries draws regular customers from all over town. Fresh, flavorful deli meals are complemented by some of the most elegant cuisine available in any diner in eastern Massachusetts. Early bird breakfasts are a special treat in both. Open daily. No credit cards. The deli and diner are both in the Cambridge Center section of Kendall Square in Cambridge at 304 and 310 Main St., respectively (547-3674, deli; 547-5820, diner). Inexpensive.

CHARLESTON, SC

Charleston residents used to joke that their city was "the best-preserved secret on the Eastern seaboard." Standing on a peninsula where the Ashley and Cooper Rivers flow into the Atlantic, Charleston's harbor is guarded by Fort Sumter, where the first shots of the Civil War were fired. (Charlestonians still refer to the War Between the States as "the Great War," and Robert E. Lee's birthday is observed as a holiday, as it is throughout much of the South.) With its architecturally gracious, historic buildings and magnificent gardens, Charleston had retained the flavor and charm of the Old South. But slow economic growth has been one of the consequences of this sleepy elegance. Charlestonians (like Bostonians or Virginians), however, tended to accept their city's lack of development as just another one of the continuing hardships of the post-Reconstruction era.

In their attempts to stimulate the local economy, city leaders tried to induce industry into the area, offering prime locations, tax incentives, and embroidered statistics about the available work force. But environmentalists opposed razing choice property for industrial parks. The conflict raged for years. The only common opinion was that tourism was not desirable. Charlestonians viewed tourists as long-necked, nosy people forever searching for bathrooms.

Then, early in 1975, Charleston was "discovered," like a rare, colorful, slightly chipped mollusk. Boosterism spread faster than the yellow fever in 1864. In the brief course of a year, "the best-preserved secret on the Eastern seaboard" metamorphosed into a national tourist attraction.

A new alliance of tourism-oriented entrepreneurs started a quarter-million-dollar promotion campaign. Old abandoned warehouses near Market Street were converted into boutiques, art galleries, studios, restaurants, and expensive town houses. Thirty new restaurants opened in 1976 (only half or a third are prospering), and the overall success of the Market Square renovation began to stimulate similar projects in other sections of the city.

In 1977, the Miss USA Beauty Pageant and the first Spoleto Festival USA were held in Charleston. More conservative Charlestonians regarded the pageant's toothy grins and skimpy swim suits as out of keeping with the city's traditional quaintness and suggested that events like the arts festival were preferable. As it worked out, the beauty pageant bombed — the city lost $70,000 — and any ideas about a repeat performance were abandoned. But the first American counterpart of Italian composer Gian Carlo Menotti's internationally acclaimed Spoleto Arts Festival was a great success, putting Charleston on the cultural map.

Even with its burgeoning renaissance, many of Charleston's 362,000 residents feel the city has a long way to go before it acquires enough cosmopolitan flavor to accompany the scenery and architecture. But, they say, Charleston is beginning to reclaim its cultural heritage.

CHARLESTON AT-A-GLANCE

SEEING THE CITY: Charleston is set in that sea-level peninsula of southeastern South Carolina known as the Lowcountry. There are no hills from which to get a good view of the city. Nicknamed the "Holy City" because of its many church spires, Charleston's best view is from the ground, looking up, especially at night, when floodlights illuminate the church spires.

For those determined to get a bird's-eye view, Holy City Air Tours will take a group of three or more over the city for a moderate fee (Aero Communication, 556-6015). You can also see the city from the harbor. Gray Line yachts depart daily from the King St. pier on the Battery. Admission charge (722-1112).

SPECIAL PLACES: The old city is approximately seven square miles, and even a five-day visit could be spent walking without covering the same street twice. An evening stroll is most popular with residents.

Fort Sumter – A national monument, the fort where the first shots of the Civil War were fired sits on a small manmade island at the entrance to Charleston's harbor. Under federal attack from 1863 to 1865, Fort Sumter withstood the longest siege in warfare. The Confederates gave up the fort in February 1865. To the Union, it represented secession and treachery; to the Confederates, it meant resistance and courage. The fort can be reached only by boat. Fort Sumter Tours leave Municipal Marina daily. Admission charge. Calhoun St. and Lockwood Dr. (722-1691).

Charles Towne Landing – Charleston was called Charles Towne in 1670 when the first permanent English settlers arrived. Now a state park, Charles Towne Landing has a number of restored houses, a full-scale replica of a 17th-century trading vessel, open-air pavilion with underground exhibits of artifacts found during archeological excavations, and an Animal Forest with indigenous animals. And plenty of picnic tables, bike trails, and tram tours, too. Closed Dec. 24 and 25. Admission charge. 1500 Old Towne Rd. (556-4450).

Middleton Place – The self-sustaining world of a Carolina Lowcountry plantation is recreated daily by people in 18th-century costume. Built in 1755, Middleton Place features the oldest landscaped gardens in the country, laid out by Henry Middleton in 1741. The 1,000-year-old Middleton Oak and the oldest camellias in the New World flourish on the lush grounds. Arthur Middleton, a signer of the Declaration of Independence, is buried here. A national historic landmark, Middleton House is the site of the Greek spring festival in May, the Spoleto Festival Finale in June, the Scottish Games in September, the Lancing Tournament in October, and Plantation Days (a dramatization of life on a plantation) in November. Open daily. Admission charge. 14 miles north on rt. 61 (556-6020).

Magnolia Plantation and Gardens – World-famous for its abundance of colors and scents, Magnolia Gardens' 30 acres abound with 900 different varieties of camellias, 250 varieties of azaleas, and dozens of different exquisite plants, shrubs, and flowers. Listed in the National Register of Historic Places, Magnolia Gardens has been the home of the Drayton family since the 1670s. In addition to the boat tours, a small zoo, and a ranch exhibiting a breed of miniature horse, Magnolia Gardens offers canoeing, bird-watching, and bike trails through its 400-acre wildlife refuge. On Monday, Wednesday, and Friday evenings, "*Magnolia by Moonlight*" dinners are held in the plantation house dining hall, followed by a torchlight tour of the gardens. Reservations essential. Open all year. Admission charge. 14 miles north on rt. 61 (571-1266).

Boone Hall – If you ever imagined yourself as one of those romantic characters in

Gone With the Wind, Boone Hall is the place where you can live your dream. The movie was actually filmed on the grounds of this 738-acre estate, formerly a cotton plantation. Settled by Major John Boone in 1681, Boone Hall has original slave houses intact. The ¾-mile Avenue of Oaks, planted in 1743, the famous restored mansion, and the 140-acre pecan groves attract visitors from all over the world. Open daily, except Thanksgiving and Christmas. Admission charge. Seven miles north on rt. 17 (no phone).

Charleston Museum – The Charleston Museum has moved from its original facility, built in 1773, to a new museum complex and courtyard. It is still the oldest municipal museum in the country, with impressive collections of arts, crafts, furniture, textiles, and implements from South Carolina's early days. Special film shows. Admission charge. 360 Meeting St. (722-2996).

Provost Dungeon – Another grim reminder of what history was really like. The Provost Dungeon dates back to 1780. Here, the British imprisoned American patriots during the Revolutionary War, and reconstructed exhibits show how they were treated during their detention. Attached to the Provost are excavations from the Half Moon Battery (circa 1690), the original city wall built by the British. Open Tuesdays through Sundays. Admission charge. East end of Broad St., under the Exchange Building (no phone).

Elfe Workshop – Thomas Elfe was an 18th-century cabinetmaker whose pieces now sell for as much as $80,000. Built between 1750 and 1760, the small scale of this mini-mansion's furnishings and rooms may make you wonder if Thomas Elfe really was one. You can ask. The guides are friendly and well informed. (See *Sources and Resources.*) Closed Sundays. Admission charge. 54 Queen St. (792-5020).

■ **EXTRA SPECIAL:** *Hilton Head Island,* a luxury resort area 110 miles south of Charleston off rt. 17, has 11 golf courses, pretty beaches, deep-sea fishing, tennis courts, private airstrip, and plenty of nightlife. Reservations advised if you plan to stay overnight. Sea Pines Plantation, a resort community of private villas and a 204-room, oceanfront inn, has beaches, 3 championship golf courses, tennis courts, bicycle paths with bike rental facilities, swimming pools, marinas, and a 625-acre forest preserve. For information write Sea Pines Plantation, Hilton Head Island, SC 29928 (800 845-6131, toll-free; 785-3333). The island's newest resort hotel, the 341-room Marriott, is on the ocean and adjacent to the racquet club and golf courses. 130 Shipyard Dr., Hilton Head Island, SC 29928 (800 228-9290, toll-free; 842-2400). For Information on Hilton Head activities, call the Chamber of Commerce (785-3673).

SOURCES AND RESOURCES

The Arch Building used to be a public house for wagon drivers entering the city, a tradition of hospitality which has carried over to the present. The Arch Building now houses the Visitor Center, where you can get advice or brochures on tours, hotels, and restaurants. The staff will assist you in making reservations. Open daily. Free. 85 Calhoun St. (722-8338) or write PO Box 975, Charleston, SC 29402.

For information on local events and performance schedules, call the Visitor Information Center (722 8338), the Charleston County Parks, Recreation and Tourism Commission (722-1681), or the Chamber of Commerce (577-2510).

The best local guide in Charleston isn't a book. It's Francis Brenner, a Southern gentleman who lives in the Thomas Elfe house, 54 Queen St. (722-2130). Mr. Brenner enjoys helping tourists, and he's probably an excellent source for accurate information.

All telephone numbers are in the 803 area code unless otherwise indicated.

For Local Coverage – *Charleston News & Courier,* morning daily; *Evening Post,* evening daily.

CLIMATE AND CLOTHES: Charleston's average temperature is 65°. Winters are mild, summers hot. March and April are the best months in the spring to visit, when the city is most accessible by foot and everything green and growing is a-bloom. In the fall, October and November are ideal.

GETTING AROUND: Bus – The South Carolina Electric and Gas Company operates the city bus system. 665 Meeting St. (722-2226).

Taxi – You can get anywhere within the city limits for $1, so taxis are a better bet than buses; they must be ordered by phone. Call Yellow Cab (577-6565).

Car Rental – Major national agencies are represented at the airport. The only agency in the city is National Car Rental, 200 Meeting St. (723-8266, 723-5729).

Horse-Drawn Carriages – You can pick one up at White Point Gardens (the Battery) or 96 Market St., daily, from 9 AM till dusk. Night rates available. Charleston Carriage Co., 96 Market St. (577-0042).

MUSEUMS: The Charleston Museum is the oldest city museum in the country. Some notable museums are:

Old Slave Mart Museum, 6 Chalmers St. (722-0079).

USS *Yorktown,* a WW II aircraft carrier, now a naval museum. East bank of Cooper River (884-2727).

Gibbes Art Gallery, 135 Meeting St. (722-2706).

Historical Houses:

Edmonston-Alston House (1828), 21 E Battery St. (722-7171).

Heyward-Washington House (1770), 87 Church St. (722-0354).

Joseph Manigault House (1803), 350 Meeting St. (723-2926).

Nathaniel Russel House (1808), 51 Meeting St. (723-1624).

Candlelight tours of historic houses are conducted by the Preservation Society in October (722-4630). The Historic Charleston Foundation will guide you through 85 historic houses by day or candlelight. Mid-March through April. Modest admission charge. 51 Meeting St. (723-1623).

MAJOR COLLEGES AND UNIVERSITIES: The Citadel Military College of South Carolina, founded in 1842, is one of the few state-run military schools in the country. A full-dress parade takes place Fridays at 3:45 PM. West end of Hampton Park (792-5000).

SPECIAL EVENTS: *Spoleto Festival USA* — the annual arts festival takes place in late May each year. For information, contact the Visitor Center, 85 Calhoun St., PO Box 975, Charleston, SC 29402 (722-8338).

SPORTS: Baseball – Charleston *Patriots* at College Park and Rutledge Ave.

Swimming – Close to the city, Sullivan's Island and the Isle of Palms have fairly nice beaches, crowded in summer. Folly Beach, at the end of Folly Road (rt. 171), usually gets a good crowd even though it's not well kept. North of Charleston, Capers Island and Dewees Island have more secluded beaches, probably because they're only accessible by boat. Both are state-owned wildlife refuges. Boats managed by Refuge Headquarters carry passengers to islands. For schedules call

928-3368. The prettiest beach in the area, Kiawah Island, is 25 miles south of Charleston.

Fishing – The Isle of Palms fishing pier is open spring through fall; it's generally crowded, but in fact, the fishing is unexceptional. For really good surf fishing, try Capers Island and Dewees Island. Charter boats for deep-sea fishing are available through the Municipal Marina, but the best fishing is in the estuarine creeks that swim with bass, sheepshead, flounder, and trout (in fall and winter). In summer and fall the creeks are full of crabs. Crab, oyster, and creek fishing are especially good on Capers, Dewees, Bulls, Kiawah, and Seabrook Islands. There are some public oyster beds closer to Charleston. For fishing and hunting regulations, write: South Carolina Wildlife Resources Dept., PO Box 167, Columbia, SC 29202.

Sailing – There's no place to charter sailboats in Charleston, but there are plenty of anchorages. Sailing regattas are held in the summer. If you're able to crew, go to the Municipal Marina. You'll usually be able to get on board for the day.

Biking – Many of Charleston's parks have bike trails. Bikes may be rented from Le Grand Tour, 173 Meeting St. (722-8168).

Tennis – Very good courts at the resorts on Kiawah and Seabrook Islands. Courts are open to the public, but can be expensive, and resort guests have priority.

Golf – Kiawah and Seabrook Islands have golf courses, but one of the most popular golfing areas in the country, Myrtle Beach, is only 98 miles north of Charleston on rt. 17. This year-round resort has 28 golf courses, innumerable miniature golf courses, and beaches. Golf lovers would do well to visit in January, when Myrtle Beach and other nearby resorts offer golf festivals, with special tournaments, exhibitions, and golf films. Hilton Head Island has 11 golf courses, including Harbour Town Golf Links, home of the annual Heritage Golf Classic (see *Extra Special*).

THEATER: Built in 1736, the *Dock Street Theater* is the oldest theater in the country. Frequent performances of original drama, Shakespeare, Broadway, and 18th-century classics. Closed Sundays. Closed Saturdays during July and August. On the corner of Church and Queen Sts. (723-5648). For up-to-date theater information and performance times, call the Chamber of Commerce (577-2510); the Visitor Information Center (722-8338); the Charleston County Parks, Recreation and Tourism Commission (722-1681). Schedules are erratic and subject to sudden change, so it's advisable to check in advance.

MUSIC: For *Community Concert Association, Symphony Orchestra*, and *Civic Ballet* schedules, call the telephone numbers listed above. The *Robert Ivey Ballet* performs regularly through the year (556-1343). For popular music schedules, call the WWWZ concert line (556-9132).

NIGHTCLUBS AND NIGHTLIFE: The best "happy hours" in town are at *No Name Cafe*, 4 Vendue Range (557-4508), and *Charleston Oyster Bar,* 70 State St. (723-1151). Both are within a two-block radius of Church and State streets. Also downtown is *Ashley's* in the new *Sheraton Charleston Hotel,* 170 Lockwood Dr. (723-3000), and, for an intimate atmosphere, try *The Best Friend Bar* in the *Mills House Hotel,* 115 Meeting St. (577-2400). The best nightspot north of town is the *Windjammer,* 1008 Ocean Blvd. (886-9336), a beer-and-billiards beach bar on the Isle of Palms. The *Atlantic House,* 303 W Atlantic Ave. (588-9563), on Folly Beach, south of town, is a restored beach house on pilings in the water. *Frances Willard's,* on Market St. (722-1960), often offers good jazz groups in the evening, as does *Myskyn's Tavern,* 83 Market St. (722-9288). *East Bay Trading Company* (corner East Bay and Queen sts.; 722-0722) is a converted warehouse filled with fun antiques and an unusual bar.

SINS: Look at the faces of the passengers in Charleston's romantic horse-drawn carriages, and you'll see the blissful glow of pie-eyed *sloth* that only the momentarily idle can experience.

Sometimes you can see *lust* on Folly Beach or the strands of Sullivan's Island, where the finest flowers of sweet-talking Southern womanhood spend weekends slathering each other with suntan oil. *Anger?* Watch the faces of the drivers of the cars forced down to the carriages' two-mile-an-hour clippity-clop. The city's *pride* is its collection of refurbished and immaculately maintained 18th-century homes.

LOCAL SERVICES: For information about local services, call the Chamber of Commerce (577-2510).

Business Services – Charleston Business Service, 227 King St. (577-7954). For 24-hour dictation service, Professional Word Processors, Inc., 315 Calhoun St. (577-0831).

Mechanic – Bowick Auto Service, 45 Pinckney St. (722-3923).

Babysitting – Baby Safe Sitters Club, 27 N Enston Ave. (723-7541).

BEST IN TOWN

CHECKING IN: Charleston has about a dozen hotels where you can get clean sheets and color TV, but you can also get old-fashioned Southern charm. Expect to pay $60 and up for a double room in one of the places we've noted as expensive; $30 to $60 in the moderate range; under $30, at places listed as inexpensive.

Battery Carriage House – A few doors away from the Provost Dungeon, facing the harbor, this elegant hotel provides guests with canopied beds, a fully stocked bar in each room, and Continental breakfast in bed. Free bicycles, and complimentary wine to be sipped in the wisteria-draped, walled garden. There are only ten rooms; make reservations well in advance. Price includes breakfast, all services. 20 S Battery (723-9881). Expensive.

Sword Gate Inn – In the heart of the old residential area, in a restored mansion. There are only four rooms, so reservations are required three to six months in advance for spring, one month in advance for the rest of the year. Breakfast and bicycles are included in the price of a room. 111 Trade St. (723-8518). Expensive.

Indigo Inn – Charleston's newest and most elegant hotel, the Indigo is furnished with 18th-century reproductions, and each of its 55 rooms has two 4-poster, queen-size beds. Centrally located at 1 Maiden La. (577-5900). Expensive.

Vendue Inn – Another new and beautiful hotel, it offers luxury and convenience. Each of its 18 rooms has 18th-century decor. Rates include Continental breakfast, as well as afternoon wine-and-cheese spread available in the garden lobby. 19 Vendue Range (577-7970). Expensive.

Sheraton Charleston Hotel – Near the historic district, this new *Sheraton* is set on the banks of the Ashley River, and some of its 350 rooms have balconies with river views. One of its dining rooms, the *Charleston Terrace,* emphasizes seafood and beef and offers a good selection of wines. Other facilities include pool, tennis courts, and jogging track. 170 Lockwood Dr. (toll-free, 800 325-3535). Expensive.

Heart of Charleston – Well run and conscientiously managed, the best thing about this 100-room contemporary motel is the people who own it. Within easy walking distance of the historic, shopping, and shipping districts, with a swimming pool, restaurant, and lounge. 200 Meeting St. (723-3451). Moderate to inexpensive.

Carr's Guest Home – A real "find" in Charleston, built in 1891 and similar to a European pension. Carr's has been a guest home for more than 50 years. Nine spacious rooms and a wide second-floor veranda overlook White Point Gardens and the harbor. It isn't ornate and will probably appeal to the more adventurous traveler. Reservations are requested two weeks in advance, one month for spring. 2 Meeting St. (723-7322). Inexpensive.

EATING OUT: Charleston used to be known as the kind of place where "you couldn't get a decent hot dog unless you knew somebody," but the times they are a-changing, and there are now more than enough interesting restaurants to whet your palate. Prices range from expensive ($35 or more for dinner for two without drinks, wine, or tips) to moderate ($20–$30) to inexpensive (under $20).

The Wine Cellar – The menu includes a choice of sautéed pompano almandine, roast duckling à l'orange, tournedos of beef, roast rack of lamb. Prix fixe for a six-course meal. Closed Sundays. Reservations required. Major credit cards. 35 Prioleau St. (723-3424). Expensive.

Robert's of Charleston – One of the city's top restaurants, the Châteaubriand prix fixe dinners are served by the owner-chef Robert Dickson. No extra charge for arias he sings as he serves. Closed Sundays and Mondays. Reservations required, preferably six weeks to two months ahead. Major credit cards. 42 N Market St. (577-7565). Expensive.

East Bay Trading Company – Whimsical antiques decorate this converted warehouse. The menu features beef dishes, seafood, soups, and homemade desserts (including ice cream). Closed Sundays from September through February. Reservations advised. Major credit cards. Corner of East Bay and Queen sts. (722-0722). Expensive to moderate.

Marianne's – The regular dinner menu is French and excellent: beef, veal, seafood, and lamb. A late supper is also available from 11 PM to 1:30 AM, and features appetizers, soups, steaks, and omelettes. A good wine list is available. Dinner reservations advised. Major credit cards. 219 Meeting St. (722-7196). Expensive to moderate.

Garibaldi – This small Italian café serves what may be best described as Italian home cooking. A regular fare of spaghetti dishes is offered daily, as are regular specials, including a seafood. Major credit cards. 49 Market St. (723-7153). Moderate.

Colony House Restaurant – Located in the same converted warehouse as the Wine Cellar, this is one moderately priced restaurant in Charleston that serves the best broiled or baked seafood in town. Open daily. Reservations advised. Major credit cards. 35 Prioleau St. (723-3424). Moderate.

The Last Catch – Some say that this place has the finest fresh seafood in town. Especially good is the *Coquilles St. Jacques.* Open daily for dinner only. Reservations advised. Major credit cards. Coleman Blvd. in Mt. Pleasant (884-2780). Moderate.

The Chart House – Set in the historic downtown section, this restaurant has an elegant atmosphere in which to enjoy steaks, seafood, and prime ribs. There's also a lounge with an outdoor courtyard for drinks. Open daily for dinner only Reservations not required. Major credit cards. 8587 Broad St. (722-6182). Moderate.

Sprouts and Krauts – A food emporium with a restaurant serving healthful sandwiches, salads, and cheesy casseroles. Open for lunch and dinner at its two locations: Marion Sq. (open daily; 722-6726) and Citadel Mall (closed Sundays; 571-0378). No reservations. Major credit cards. Inexpensive.

The Marina Variety Store – Overlooking the Municipal Marina, this is a local favorite, especially at lunchtime. A simple, no-frills restaurant (lunch and dinner) serving seafood, fried chicken, homemade soups, and good 85¢ burgers. Open daily. No reservations or credit cards. Municipal Marina (723-6325). Inexpensive.

CHICAGO

Ask a resident if Chicago has a soul, and you're likely to be greeted with a laugh. The second largest city in the country (the city proper has 2.9 million people; the metropolitan area, 7.6 million), ninth largest in the world, Chicago carries a long-standing reputation as a tough, cynical town. "Hog Butcher to the World," Carl Sandburg sang. Chicago lost that title to Omaha years ago, but it still remains one of the world's great cities. But despite its greatness, Chicago still suffers under a Second City inferiority complex, one that stems from the endless, inevitable comparisons to New York.

Yet there is a unique allure to the place. It has inspired musicians to create a Broadway musical comedy *(Chicago),* and has been the scene of any number of Hollywood films. One of the leading rock groups in the country has taken Chicago's name as its own. All of which can be viewed as especially ironic if you consider the fact that nobody really knows whether the Indian word *checagou* means "great and powerful," "wild onion," or "skunk." This long-standing linguistic controversy did not affect the songsters who created that legendary tribute to "Chicago, Chicago, that toddling town."

Chicago spreads along 29 miles of carefully groomed lakeshore. Respecting Lake Michigan, the people of Chicago have been careful not to destroy the property near the water with heavy manufacturing or industry. The lake is a source of water as well as a port of entry for steamships and freighters coming from Europe via the St. Lawrence Seaway. More than 82 million tons of freight are handled by Chicago's ports every year. The city is also the world's largest railroad center. The Chicago grain market is the nation's most important, and O'Hare Airport, its busiest. Nuclear research and the electronics industry came of age here. In 1942, the world's first self-sustaining nuclear chain reaction was achieved at the University of Chicago. Half the radar equipment used during WW II was made here, too. Today, Chicago does $90 billion in wholesale trade and $32 billion in retail. Its Association of Commerce and Industry proudly lists an amazing assortment of "number ones," in addition to those the city is most noted for: convention business, steel production, export trade, furniture marketing, mail order business, tool and die making, metal products, industrial machinery, household appliances, radio and TV manufacturing.

People from all over the world have come here to live. In 1890, 80% of all Chicago residents were immigrants or children of immigrants. There are more Poles in Chicago than in any Polish city except Warsaw, and healthy contingents from Germany, Italy, Sweden, and Ireland. People talk about "ethnic Chicago," which means you can find neighborhoods that will make you think you're in a foreign country. Chinatown stretches along Wentworth Avenue. Enclaves of Ukrainians and Sicilians live in West Chicago. The Greeks can be found on South Halsted and West Lawrence; Irish and

Lithuanians around Bridgeport and Marquette Park; Latinos in Pilsen; Italians in an area bounded by the University of Illinois Circle Campus, the Eisenhower Expressway, the West Side Medical Center, and the black community. Polonia, which looks like a set for a 1930s Polish version of *West Side Story*, is mostly along Milwaukee. Nearly every nationality has a museum, and at least some of its customs have become public domain as well. There's a splendid array of inexpensive ethnic restaurants where you can get a whole meal for the price of an appetizer in a ritzier joint. A lot of these places have no bar, no credit cards, and no atmosphere in the usual sense of the word, but they are great for when you want home cooking from "homes" like Poland, Greece, China, Eastern Europe, and South America.

This cosmopolitan center had unprepossessing beginnings. Marquette and Joliet, the French explorers who provided the first record of the area, knew it as the Chicago Portage, one landmark on their route to the Chicago River from the Mississippi. A trading post was established in 1679. In the 1812 Fort Dearborn Massacre, 53 people were killed by Indians. Eighteen years later, the first parcels of land were sold — $40 to $60 per 15,000-square-foot plot. The city, incorporated in 1837, began to look as if it might amount to something when the Union Pacific connected it to San Francisco in 1869 — two years later, on October 8, 1871, Chicago burned to the ground. Burning at the rate of 65 acres per hour ($125,000 damage per minute) and aided by a furious southwest wind, the Great Fire melted 15,000 water service pipes and 370 water meters, took 250 lives, left 90,000 homeless, and left 1,688 acres in rubble. The total damage was estimated at $196 million.

Like San Francisco after its earthquake, Chicago simply began to rebuild. And in the process, in the course of the following 50 years, a new urban architecture was born. Building quickly and furiously upon four square miles of charcoal, and abetted by simple clients whose aesthetics derived from their interests in the profits to be gained from efficient buildings rather than the glory to be garnered from neoclassical palaces, the Chicago architects *invented* the skyscraper; Frank Lloyd Wright pioneered the ground-hugging, prairie-style houses which became the prototypes for the suburban, single-family dwelling units we know today. In 1909, architect Daniel Burnham laid out a plan for the city's parks. Today, 576 of them stretch across 6,740 acres, not to mention 17 miles of clean public beaches and 35,350 acres of trail-crossed forest preserve on the outskirts.

The beaches are still clean and the forest acreage still pretty much unspoiled—a credit to the city planners who have, over the years, managed to keep Chicago alive and vibrant even as other downtown areas around the country have declined. While buildings elsewhere were being pulled down to make way for parking lots, Chicago was getting a handful of new skyscrapers surrounded by pedestrian plazas studded with magnificent pieces of sculpture by Alexander Calder, Marc Chagall, Pablo Picasso, Claes Oldenburg, and others. Lively programs of special events keep the plazas thronged with sightseers and Loop office workers alike throughout the summer; suddenly, brown-bagging lunch is as much fun, and as chic, as eating out.

In the same vein is the renovation of the venerable Marquette Building and the completion of the federally and city funded $17 million modernization of the State Street shopping area. So if you haven't seen Chicago for a while, you're likely to be astounded: Cars have been banned and buses only are permitted on the street — what's left of it. Sidewalks have been widened to nearly 50 feet and covered with hexagonal, battleship-gray paving blocks; open-air cafés have sprouted; and modern bus-stop shelters, subway entrances, light poles, and newsstands have been constructed of Cor-Ten steel. As part of the general facelifting, even Carson Pirie Scott, the turn-of-the-century department store designed by the celebrated Louis Sullivan, has restored its interior to match the rococo splendor of its well-cared-for façade. Chicago has also been experiencing an architectural renaissance with the construction of major new office buildings in the Loop, such as the Board of Trade Extension, the Xerox Building, and 3 First National Plaza.

If Chicago's modern-day face has improved with age, the same cannot be said of local politics. The successors to the late Mayor Richard Daley have not been able to maintain much of Chicago's old reputation as "the city that works," and municipal discord has become much more the order of the day.

Still, Chicago is quite a city, even if you consider just the ritzy Gold Coast and all those magnificent apartment buildings along the shore of Lake Michigan; the concert and lecture programs at its University of Chicago; the program of choral works at the neo-Gothic Rockefeller Chapel; the Rush Street bars; the Magnificent Mile — broad, shop-and-gallery-lined Michigan Avenue. There is the Chicago Symphony Orchestra, the Lyric Opera, and the Art Institute, which has a world-famous collection of Impressionist and post-Impressionist paintings. Chicago has a comfortable rhythm that is electric without being hectic, and a certain contagious, good-natured vitality. You can enjoy jazz and blues in late-night cafés till the wee hours of the morning. And if it's the kind of place that makes you want to sing — well, you won't be the first.

CHICAGO AT-A-GLANCE

SEEING THE CITY: What better place to see the city than from the world's tallest building? The 110-story Sears Tower maintains a Skydeck on the 103rd floor. Open daily. Admission charge. Wacker and Adams Sts. (875-9696). For a view from the north, visit the John Hancock Building (fifth largest in the world), fondly nicknamed "Big John." On the 95th floor, you'll find a bar and restaurant. Open daily. Admission charge. 875 Michigan Ave. (751-0900). If you can't stand heights, Wendella Sightseeing takes you by boat on the Chicago River and into Lake Michigan. Daily, mid-April through the first week in October. Admission charge. 400 N Michigan Ave. (337-1446).

SPECIAL PLACES: A sophisticated public transport system makes it easy to negotiate Chicago's streets. You can explore the Loop, the lakefront, and suburbs by El train, subway, and bus. Culture buses take you to the art, science, and ethnic museums on Sundays and holidays during the summer.

THE LOOP

"The Loop" generally refers to Chicago's business district, which is encircled by the elevated train known as the El.

The ArchiCenter – The Exhibition Gallery, opened in the spring of 1982, has changing shows that feature points of interest in Chicago. Guided walking tours of the Loop (and other neighborhoods) daily, May–Oct. 31, Tuesdays and Thursdays the rest of the year. Chicago Highlights bus tours, Saturdays. Admission charge for tours. 330 S Dearborn, 1st fl. (782-1776).

Art Institute of Chicago – Founded as an art school in 1879, the Art Institute houses an outstanding collection of Impressionist and post-Impressionist paintings, Japanese prints, Chinese sculpture and bronzes, and Old Masters. In the new Columbus Drive Addition, you can see some stained-glass windows by Chagall and the reconstructed trading room of the old Chicago Stock Exchange. Open daily. Admission charge; free Thursdays. Michigan Ave. at Adams St. (443-3500 for recorded information; or 443-3600).

Chicago Board of Trade – Largest grain exchange in the world. Stand in the visitors' gallery and watch traders gesticulating on the floor, runners in colored jackets delivering orders, and an electronic record of all the trades displayed overhead. A film and slide presentation explain the Board's operations. Open weekdays 9:15 AM to 1:15 PM. Free. Jackson at La Salle St. (435-3626).

Chicago Mercantile Exchange and International Monetary Market – The show is much the same, only here you can sit down. Trading here does not stop suddenly. Each commodity has its own opening and closing time. Open weekdays, 8:30 AM to 2 PM. Free. 444 West Jackson (648-1000).

Marshall Field's – Chicago's most famous department store. When it was built in 1892 — before electric lighting was common — it was designed in sections, with shopping areas on balconies overlooking a skylit central courtyard. Later, the skylights were covered over, one by a vivid blue and gold Louis Tiffany mosaic you can see by entering at the door on the corner of Washington and State Sts. The toy department, on Four, sells luxury items like $5,000 copper-roofed dollhouses. The Crystal Palace, on Three, serves unbelievable ice cream sundaes. Frango mint ice cream (a subtle mix of coffee, chocolate, malt, and mint) is a tradition. Closed Sundays. Wabash, State, Randolph, and Washington Sts. (781-1000).

NEAR SOUTH SIDE

Adler Planetarium – Exhibits on everything from surveying and navigation instruments to modern space exploration devices, plus a real moon rock and an antique instrument collection that is one of the three best in the world — the best in the Western Hemisphere. You can see it all before or after the sky shows, which are what most people come for. There are five in all. Open daily. Free; admission charge to the sky shows. 1300 S Lake Shore Dr. on Museum Point (322-0304).

Field Museum – Of the endless exhibits on anthropology, ecology, botany, zoology, and geology you'll find here, the most famous is the pair of fighting elephants in the Main Hall. Other standouts include the whole of Anniversary Hall, which explores the reasons for a natural history museum; the hands-on Place for Wonder, where youngsters can touch a dinosaur fish skeleton and try on ethnic masks; the full-scale model of a Pawnee earth lodge, where there are daily programs on Indian life; a display of prehistoric Egyptian tomb chapels; and an exhibit, Maritime Peoples of the Northwest Coast. The Hall of Chinese Jade and the display of Japanese lacquerware are also outstanding. Open daily. Admission charge; free on Fridays. S Lake Shore Dr. at Roosevelt Rd. (922-9410).

Shedd Aquarium – The largest aquarium in the world, this one has 198 fish tanks and a collection of over 5,000 specimens: sturgeon from Russia, Bahamian angelfish, Australian lungfish, and a coral reef where divers feed the fish several times a day. Closed Christmas and New Year's. Admission charge; free on Fridays. On Museum Point at 1200 Lake Shore Dr. (939-2426).

NEAR NORTH SIDE

Chicago Academy of Sciences – Exhibits on the natural history of the Great Lakes area. These are particularly lively and interesting, especially the reconstruction of a 350-million-year-old forest that stood on Chicago's present site, complete with humming insects and carnivorous dragonflies. There are also a "walk-through" cave and canyon. Open daily. Free. In Lincoln Park at 2001 N Clark St. (549-0606).

Chicago Historical Society – Pioneer crafts demonstrations, an outstanding collection of President Lincoln's belongings, and a Civil War slide show make this one of Chicago's most fascinating museums. Newest galleries focus on the city's beginnings and explore 19th-century American life through furniture and decorative objects. Open daily. Admission charge; free on Mondays. Clark St. and North Ave. (642-4600).

International College of Surgeons Hall of Fame – Full of medical curiosities: old examining tables, artificial limbs, an amputation set from the Revolution, a "bone crusher" used for correcting bow legs between 1918 and 1950 (!). Finally, a fascinating display of prayers and oaths taken by doctors in different countries. Closed Mondays. Free. 1524 N Lake Shore Dr. (642-3555).

Lincoln Park Conservatory – Changing floral exhibits and a magnificent permanent collection includes orchids, a 50-foot fiddle-leaf rubber tree from Africa with giant leaves, fig trees, and more ferns than you could ever imagine. Outdoors, Grandmother's Garden has more familiar flowers. Open daily. Free. In Lincoln Park, Stockton Dr. at Fullerton (294-4770).

Lincoln Park Zoo – The great thing about this zoo is that it has the largest group of great apes in captivity, now in a new Great Ape House. There are, of course, the standard houses of monkey, tiger, lion, bear, and bison, plus the zoo's popular farm. Open daily. Free. In Lincoln Park at 100 W Webster (294-4660).

Museum of Contemporary Art – This small museum has always offered lively changing exhibitions, both retrospectives of the work of contemporary artists and surveys of 20th-century art movements and avant-garde phenomena; but only since the recent completion of an expansion project has there been space enough to show off any appreciable portion of the fine permanent collection. The new area also houses shows by Chicago artists; and the symposia, poetry readings, and other special events that are so much a part of the museum's profile will continue. Closed Monday. Admission charge. 237 E Ontario (280-2660).

The Water Tower – This landmark, the sole survivor of the Great Fire of 1871, now serves as a visitor information center. Open daily except holidays. N Michigan and Chicago Aves.

Water Tower Place This incredible, vertical shopping mall with waterfalls and indoor plantings gets busier and better every year. Asymmetrical glass-enclosed elevators shoot up through an eight-story atrium, past shops selling dresses, books, gift items plus restaurants and a movie theater. Branches of Marshall Field, FAO Schwarz, and Lord & Taylor are here, along with the lovely *Ritz-Carlton Hotel,* stretching 22 stories above its 12th-floor lobby in the tower. The skylit *Greenhouse café* is great for tea or cocktails after a hard day of shopping. Michigan Ave. at Pearson St.

NORTH SIDE

Graceland Cemetery – Buried here are hotel barons, steel magnates, architects Louis Sullivan and Daniel Burnham — enshrined by tombs and miniature temples, and overlooking islands, lakes, hills, and views. A photographer killed while recording the controversial demolition of Louis Sullivan's celebrated Chicago Stock Exchange is buried in a direct line with the grave of Sullivan himself. Guidebooks can be obtained from the gatekeepers. Open daily. Free. 4001 N Clark St. (525-1105).

SOUTH SIDE

Museum of Science and Industry – Some 2,000 displays explain the principles of science in such a lively way that the museum is Chicago's number one attraction. Longtime favorites: Colleen Moore's fairy-tale castle of a dollhouse with real diamond "crystal" chandeliers, the cunning Sears circus exhibit, a working coal mine, a walk-through human heart, and a captured German submarine. Open daily, but a madhouse on Saturdays and Sundays. Free. S Lake Shore Dr. at 57th St. (684-1414).

Pullman Community – Founded by George Pullman in 1880 as the nation's first company town, this early example of comprehensive urban planning is now a city, state, and national landmark. Walking tours conducted on the first Sunday of the month from May through October give you the story in detail; at other times you can find the Greenstone Church and other important sites on maps available at the Florence Hotel, a Pullman-era structure that serves as a Visitor Center of sorts (and provides lunch on weekdays, breakfast and lunch on Saturdays, and brunch on Sundays). A number of the many privately owned row houses are shown on special house tours held annually on the second weekend in October. West of the Calumet Expy. between 104th and 115th (785-8181).

WEST

Garfield Park Conservatory – Four and a half acres under glass. The Palm House alone is 250 feet long, 85 feet wide, and 60 feet high. It looks like the tropics. There's a fernery luxuriant with greenery, mosses, and pools of water lilies. The cactus house has 85 genera, 400 species. At Christmas, poinsettias bloom; in spring, azaleas and camellias; at Easter, lilies and bulb plants; and in November, mums. Open daily. Free. 300 N Central Park Blvd. (533-1281).

OUTSKIRTS

Brookfield Zoo – Two hundred acres divided up by moats and natural-looking barriers make this one of the most modern zoos in the country. There are special woods for wolves, a bison prairie, a replica of the Sahara, and a dolphin show. Olga the Walrus languishes in a pool. Open daily. Admission charge; free Tuesdays. 1st Ave. at 31st St. in Brookfield, 15 miles west of the Loop (242-2630).

Marriott's Great America – An extravagant roller coaster and a double-tiered carousel are the highlights of a theme park full of rides, some wild, some tame. Musical shows are performed throughout the season, and there's a special giant participatory play area for kids. It is also home to the world's largest motion picture experience. Open daily Memorial Day through Labor Day, weekends in May and from September to mid-October. Admission charge. I-94 at rt. 132 in Gurnee (249-2020).

Lizzadro Museum of Lapidary Art – The collection of semiprecious stones and lapidary art is one of the most extensive in the US. About 150 exhibits show off cameos, jade carvings, minerals, and fossils. Closed Mondays. Free on Fridays, other times admission charge. 220 Cottage Hill, Elmhurst (833-1616).

Oak Park – Twenty-five buildings in this suburb, most of them remarkably contemporary looking, show how Frank Lloyd Wright's architectural style developed. The architect's residence/workshop and Unity Temple are open to the public, and there are daily tours (except on holidays). Admission charge. Edgar Rice Burroughs' and Ernest Hemingway's homes are here, too, along with numerous gingerbread and turreted Queen Anne–style palaces. The Oak Park Tour Center, headquartered in the Frank Lloyd Wright Home and Studio, operates most area walking tours as well as a visitors center at 158 Forest where you can see photo exhibits and take in an orientation program. At the Wright Plus Festival, third Saturday in May, ten private homes are open to the public. For more information, phone 848-1978.

■ **EXTRA SPECIAL:** You don't have to go very far from downtown to reach the *North Shore suburbs.* Follow US 41 or I-94 north. US 41 takes you through Lake Forest, an exquisite residential area, and Lake Bluff, site of the Great Lakes Naval Station. In Waukegan, *Mathon's Seafood Restaurant* has been delighting crustacean addicts since before WW II; two blocks east of Sheridan Rd. near the lake on Mathon Dr. (662-3610). Heading inland from Waukegan on rt. 120 will take you directly to lake country, past Gages Lake and Brae Loch golf course, Grays Lake, and Round Lake where rt. 120 becomes rt. 134, continuing on to Long Lake, Duck Lake, and the three large lakes — Fox, Pistakee, and Grass, near the Wisconsin border. All of these lakes offer water sports, fishing, golf, and tennis. On the northern border with Wisconsin, the 4,900-acre Chain O'Lakes State Park has campsites and boat rental facilities. Pick up Wilson Rd. north at Long Lake, then take rt. 132 past Fox Lake. This will take you to US 12, which runs to Spring Grove, site of Chain O'Lakes State Park (587-5512).

SOURCES AND RESOURCES

The Chicago Convention and Tourism Bureau, in the historic Water Tower at Michigan and Chicago Aves. (225-5000), publishes a downtown map that pinpoints major attractions and hotels. The Chicago Visitor Eventline gives taped information on theater, sports, and special events (225-2323). Also get copies of the Chicago Transit Authority brochures: "The Chicago Street Directory," which locates streets by their distance from State or Madison; the "CTA Route Map" of bus, subway, and El routes; and the "CTA Downtown Transit Map." These are available at El stations, subway stations, libraries. For details, contact the Illinois Adventure Center, 208 N Michigan Ave. (793-2094).

The best Chicago guidebook is *Sweet Home Chicago* by Tom Horwitz (Chicago Review Press, $4.95), an insider's look at the city for residents and visitors alike. For self-guided walking tours, see Ira J. Bach's architecturally oriented *Chicago on Foot* (Rand McNally, $7.95).

All telephone numbers are in the 312 area code unless otherwise indicated.

For Local Coverage – *Sun-Times,* morning daily; *Tribune,* morning daily; *Reader,* weekly; *Chicago* Magazine, monthly.

For Food – *The New Good (But Cheap) Chicago Restaurant Book* by Jill and Ron Rohde (Swallow, $2.95) and *Chicago* Magazine's section of restaurant reviews.

CLIMATE AND CLOTHES: They don't call it "the Windy City" for nothing. Fierce winter winds can knock you down, and wind-chill factors occasionally measure 47° below zero! Optimum visiting season is autumn, when temperatures are in the 60s and 50s; second best is spring (albeit pretty, spring does get damp). Summers are muggy, but the temperatures don't usually get higher than the 80s.

GETTING AROUND: Bus, Subway, and El – Chicago Transit Authority operates bus, subway, and El services. For information, call 836-7000. You can take a do it yourself tour on public transport. One good round trip by public transportation starts in the Loop, goes through Lincoln Park, past the Historical Society, and into New Town on the No. 151 bus. When you've ridden enough, get off and catch the same bus going in the opposite direction. On Sundays and holidays, there is also a Culture Bus which stops at the Art Institute, the Field Museum, the Shedd Aquarium, the Adler Planetarium, the Museum of Science and Industry, the Oriental Institute, and the DuSable Museum of African-American History. It operates every 30 minutes from 11 AM to 5 PM, June through August.

Taxi – Cabs can be hailed in the street or picked up from stands in front of the major hotels. You can also phone one of Chicago's taxi services: Yellow Cab (225-6000); Flash Cab (561-1444); Checker Cab (666-3700); American United (248-7600).

Car Rental – All major national firms are represented.

MUSEUMS: Chicago is paradise if you like going to museums. Those you see described in *Special Places* have plenty of company, including the following:

DuSable Museum of African-American History, in Washington Park, at 740 E 56th Pl. (947-0600).

Spertus Museum of Judaica, 618 S Michigan Ave. (922-9012).

The Telephony Museum, 225 W Randolph (727-2994).

Glessner House, 1800 S Prairie (326-1393).

Oriental Institute at University of Chicago, 1155 E 58th at University (753-2471).

Jane Addams' Hull House (National Historic Landmark), Halsted St. at Polk (996-2793).

The Balzekas Museum of Lithuanian Culture, 4012 S Archer (847-2441).

Polish Museum of America, 984 Milwaukee Ave. (384-3352).

Ukrainian Institute of Modern Art, 2320 W Chicago (227-5522).

Great sculpture and art can also be seen in the plazas of downtown skyscrapers. Bertoia's spellbinding *Sounding Sculpture,* at the Standard Oil Building, 200 E Randolph; *Flamingo,* a stabile by Alexander Calder, at Federal Center Plaza, Adams and Dearborn; Calder's gaily-colored mobile *Universe,* in the Sears Tower lobby, Wacker and Adams; sculptor Claes Oldenburg's 101-foot-high baseball bat, *Batcolumn,* at 600 W Madison; Chagall's *Four Seasons* mosaic, at First National Plaza, Monroe and Dearborn. (If you're there at noon, you might catch a free concert.) Chicago's Picasso (which is its formal title because no one could agree on a name), a giant sculpture, is at the Richard J. Daley Plaza, on Washington and Clark near the Chagall. (There are also free concerts at the plaza every weekday of the year.) Buckingham Fountain, a Chicago landmark in Grant Park at Congress Parkway, is illuminated from May to September.

MAJOR COLLEGES AND UNIVERSITIES: Although far too big to be called a college town, Chicago has many fine universities. The University of Chicago, known for its economics and social science departments, has its main entrance at 5801 S Ellis Ave. (753-1234); University of Illinois at Chicago Circle, at 601 S Morgan (996-3000); Illinois Institute of Technology, its Mies van der Rohe–designed campus located at 3300 S Federal (567-3000); Loyola University, at 820 N Michigan (670-3000) and 6525 Sheridan Rd. (274-3000); De Paul University, 25 E Jackson and in Lincoln Park at 2323 N Seminary (321-8000); Northwestern University at Chicago Ave. and Lake Shore Dr. (649-8649) and in Evanston (492-3741); Roosevelt University, 430 S Michigan Ave. (341-3500); Lake Forest College, Sheridan Rd., Lake Forest (234-3100). For information on concerts, sports events, films, and plays, call the individual campuses.

SPECIAL EVENTS: Summertime is festival time. In June, the *Old Town Art Fair* is held in Lincoln Park; in July, sailboats race on Lake Michigan; and in August, the *Western Open Golf Tournament* is played. The *Arlington Million,* the world's richest thoroughbred race, is held the last week of

August and is preceded by a 10-day festival. The *Chicagofest* — a major new 2-week-long musical event held along the lakefront in August — is bigger than ever thanks to Mayor Jane Byrne's energetic promotion. The *Ravinia Festival,* a series of outdoor concerts by the Chicago Symphony Orchestra and other headliners, runs throughout the summer in Highland Park (432-1236). The first week in September brings a jazz festival to the Grant Park Bandshell (free).

SPORTS: Plenty of major-league action in town.

Baseball – The *White Sox* play at Comisky Park, 35th and Shields, off the Dan Ryan Expy. (924-1000). The *Cubs* play at Wrigley Field, Addison and Clark (281-5050).

Football – The NFL *Bears* play at Soldier Field in Grant Park (663-5100).

Basketball – The NBA *Bulls,* 1800 W Madison (346-1122).

Hockey – The NHL *Black Hawks* play in Chicago Stadium September through April (733-5300).

Racing – Horses race at four tracks in the Chicago area:

Arlington Park, Euclid Ave. and Wilke Rd., Arlington Heights (255-4300).

Hawthorne, 3501 S Laramie, Cicero (652-9400).

Maywood Park, North and 5th Aves., Maywood (343-4800).

Sportsman's Park, 3301 S Laramie, Cicero (242-1121).

Polo – Summers at the Oak Brook Polo Club, 1000 Oak Brook Rd., Oak Brook (654-3060); during winter you can play indoors at the Chicago Armory, Chicago Ave. and Fairbanks.

Bicycling – Chicago has a glorious bike path along the shore of Lake Michigan, running from the Loop to Evanston — about 11 miles. You can rent bikes in summer from the concession at Lincoln Park.

Fishing – After work, people flock to the rocks along the shore, casting nets for smelt. The rocks around Northwestern University at Evanston are especially popular. There's also an artificial island, attainable by footbridge, around Northwestern.

Golf – Chicago has 10 golf courses, some along the lakeshore. The best municipal course is Waveland in Lincoln Park. The Chicago Park District offers golf instruction. For information, call 294-2274.

Hiking – Windy City Grotto, the Chicago Chapter of the National Speleological Society, organizes frequent field trips to cave country in southern Indiana and Missouri and meets at the Field Museum the second Wednesday of every month. For information, contact Windy City Speleonews, c/o Bill Mixon, 5035 N South Drexel, Chicago, IL 60615 (924-0441). Chicago Mountaineering Club organizes weekend expeditions and teaches safe climbing techniques. They meet at the Field Museum every second Monday. For information, write to PO Box 1025, Chicago, IL 60690. Sierra Club, 53 W Jackson (431-0158), also organizes outings.

Tennis – 620 outdoor municipal courts. The best are Waveland and Diversey in Lincoln Park. For tennis information, call 294-2314.

Swimming – Beaches line the shore of Lake Michigan. Those just to the north of the Loop off Lake Shore Drive are the most popular, and often the most crowded. Oak Street Beach along the "Gold Coast" is the most fashionable beach. If you go farther north, you'll find fewer people. The Chicago Park District offers swimming lessons at some of the 72 city pools. The best are at Wells Park and Gill Park. For information, call 294-2333.

Sailing – Lake Michigan offers superb sailing, but as experienced sailors can tell you, the lake is deceptive. Storms of up to 40 knots can blow in suddenly. Check with the Coast Guard before going out (219 949-7440). You can rent boats and take sailing lessons from City Sailors, Inc., 1461 W Cuyler (935-6145). There are a few marinas between the Loop and Evanston; others, along suburban shores. Highland Park is one of the most popular city marinas.

Skiing – There are more than 50 ski clubs in the Chicago area. For information, contact the Chicago Metro Ski Council, PO Box 7926, Chicago 60680.

Soccer – The *Chicago Sting* (NASL) plays at Soldier and Wrigley Fields, April through September (935-5608).

THEATERS: For information on performance schedules and tickets, consult the local publications listed above. Many Broadway-bound shows play Chicago before heading to the Big Apple. The main Chicago theaters are: *Shubert*, 22 W Monroe (977-1700); *Studebaker*, 418 S Michigan (435-0700); *Civic*, 20 N Wacker Dr. (346-0270); *Goodman Memorial*, 200 S Columbus Dr. (443-3800); *Blackstone Theater,* 60 E Balbo (977-1700); *Drury Lane Water Tower Place,* 175 E Chestnut (266-0500); and the *Apollo Theater Center,* 2540 N Lincoln (549-1342).

Among Chicago's thriving Off-Loop theaters are *Organic Theater*, 3319 N Clark (327-5588); the *Goodman Studio Theater*, 200 S Columbus (443-3800), where award-winning playwright David Mamet is associate artistic director; *St. Nicholas*, 2851 N Halsted (975-2300), founded by Mamet for new American dramatists; *Victory Gardens Theater*, 2257 N Lincoln (549-5788), which is dedicated to the promotion of Chicago playwrights; *Steppenwolf Theater,* 3212 N Broadway (472-4141); *Wisdom Bridge Theater,* 1559 W Howard (743-6442); and *The Body Politic Theater,* 2261 N Lincoln (871-3000).

There are several good dinner theaters, as well: *Drury Lane*, 2500 W 94th, Evergreen Park (779-4000); *Pheasant Run Theater*, Pheasant Run Lodge, rt. 64, St. Charles (584-1454); and the *Candlelight Playhouse,* 5620 S Harlem Ave. in Summit, the first dinner theater in the country (496-3000).

MUSIC: People who like music are discovering what a kernel of cognoscenti have known all along — that Chicago isn't the musical desert that the Midwest is generally thought to be. Good music (and lots of it) can be heard all over the place. The world-renowned *Chicago Symphony Orchestra* plays Orchestra Hall, 220 S Michigan, in winter (435-8111), and Ravinia Pavilion in Highland Park in summer (432-1236). Outdoor concerts are also played in the new Petrillo Musicshell, behind the Art Institute between Jackson and Monroe on Columbus Dr. (294-2420). The *Lyric Opera of Chicago* performs at Civic Opera House, 20 N Wacker (346-6111). The Auditorium Theatre, a landmark designed by Louis Sullivan and located at 70 E Congress (922-2110), is another major hall.

NIGHTCLUBS AND NIGHTLIFE: You can take in Chicago's blues, folk, and jazz scene in informal pubs, cafés, and taverns. Among them: *Barbarossa Lounge,* 1117 N Dearborn (649-1456); *Clearwater Saloon,* 3447 N Lincoln (935-6545), bluegrass; *Jazz Showcase,* 901 N Rush (337-1000); *Old Town School of Folk Music,* 909 W Armitage (525-7793); *Somebody Else's Troubles,* 2470 N Lincoln (929-0660); the *Earl of Old Town,* a Chicago institution; and *Agostino's* for an elegant, romantic atmosphere and dancing, 7 E Delaware Pl. (642-8540). *The Second City* revue ensemble, now in its twentieth year, performs original, improvisational, and satirical skits, 1616 N Wells (337-3992).

SINS: Great metropolis that it is, Chicago nurtures sin in all its forms. *Pride?* Listen to Chicagoans compare their Art Institute, their museums, their Magnificent Mile, and their sports teams to those of any other city in the country. *Anger?* Suggest to the same people that Chicago might just still be the Second City (second, that is, to New York).

And while Chicago has no sin center — red lights flicker here and there all over the vast metropolitan area — it is as important a site in the history of American *lust* as there is: It was here that Hugh Hefner took the stretch pants off the girl next door.

Playboy Enterprises still holds court just off Michigan Avenue, and the *Playboy Club* at 1960 Lincoln Park W (883-9090) is still mecca to timid Toms who like their curves and cleavage off-limits and covered up with satin and cottontails.

For a real pizza *glutton's* special — thickly crusted and slathered with toppings — check out *Gino's* or *Uno's*; for a marathon feed, go first to Gino's then to Uno's. Closet gluttons perch daintily on the wrought-iron ice cream chairs in Marshall Field's *Crystal Palace* on the third floor and order the giant special sundaes, which are so enormous that all but the very tallest ice cream freak has to bring the spoon down to his mouth instead of up.

LOCAL SERVICES:

Mechanics – ARCO station, 24-hour service, 665 N Dearborn (787-8164).

Babysitting – You can check at your hotel for reliable babysitting services.

BEST IN TOWN

CHECKING IN: There are quite a number of interesting hotels in Chicago, varying in style from the intimate clubbiness of the Tremont and Whitehall to the supermodernity of the Ritz-Carlton. Unless otherwise noted, all listed here have at least one restaurant; your choice of eating places increases with the price of your room and the size of the hotel. Big hotels have shops, meeting places, nightly entertainment. Rates in Chicago are higher than in most other midwestern cities: You'll pay $70 and up for doubles in expensive hotels (and $90 or more in the very deluxe establishments); $45 to $70 in those classified as moderate; and only as low as about $25 in those listed as inexpensive. If money is no object, ask for a room with a view. "Near north side" hotels put you close to New Town, Lincoln Park, and Water Tower Place; Loop locations (about ten minutes away, by taxi) are convenient to businesses and the fine, old downtown department stores.

Ritz-Carlton – Contemporary and chic, this beautifully appointed new 430-room luxury establishment, a member of the fine Four Seasons chain, rises 20 stories above its 12th-floor lobby. Located in the spectacular Water Tower Place shopping complex, the Ritz has all the accouterments of elegance, including a fine health club and skylit indoor swimming pool. A recent renovation has left it looking spiffier than ever. Near north side. 160 E Pearson (266-1000). Expensive.

Mayfair Regent – Quite a departure from the high-rise hotels opening these days, the recently renovated *Mayfair* (formerly the Lake Shore Drive Hotel) is small enough to offer the ultimate in comfort and style — the ratio of employees to guests is 1 to 1. Dinner here is quite an elegant affair: The rooftop *Ciel Bleu* offers classic French cuisine and romantic views of Lake Michigan; *The Palm,* on the ground floor, has steaks as prime as those served by its New York counterpart. 181 E Lake Shore Dr. (787-8500 or toll-free, 800 421-0530). Expensive.

The Westin Hotel, Chicago – Built in 1963, this growing deluxe near-north-side hotel has a swimming pool on the roof and a health club. Its rooftop restaurant, the *Consort,* is among the city's most elegant. Located near the Drake and the Hancock Center. N Michigan Ave. at Delaware (943-7200). Expensive.

Hyatt Regency Chicago – Over two thousand guest rooms in two ultra-modern towers. Conveniently located between the Loop and N Michigan Ave. Fine dining at *Truffles.* 151 E Wacker Dr. (565-1000). Expensive.

Hyatt Regency O'Hare – Ideal for a comfortable overnight stop between planes.

Health club. 1,150 rooms. South River Rd. exit off Kennedy Expy. (696-1234). Expensive.

Palmer House – A busy, 1,800-room giant, this is another Chicago tradition. The sumptuous, recently restored *Empire Room* is a visual delight; open for lunch only. You can also dine here at the *Palmer Steak House* and *Trader Vic's.* In the Loop on the new State Street mall. Monroe St. between State and Wabash (726-7500). Expensive.

The Tremont – The paneled lobby, with its elaborate moldings and chandeliers, is more like a private sitting room than a public foyer. Rooms are quite comfortable, with traditional elegance. Home to *Cricket's,* one of Chicago's best restaurants (see *Eating Out*). 100 E Chestnut (751-1900; or toll-free, 800 621-8133). Expensive.

Park Hyatt – Small, with 255 elegant guest rooms and suites, and as convivial as it is convenient to N Michigan Ave. and the historic Water Tower. Recently renovated. Formerly the Water Tower Hyatt. 800 N Michigan Ave. (280-2222). Expensive.

The Whitehall – Small, devoted to detail, and known for its elegance and its careful, courteous service. Its excellent restaurant is open only to members and registered guests. 226 rooms. 105 E Delaware Pl. (944-6300). Expensive.

Sheraton-Plaza – This 450-room gem, with 100 suites, recently was redecorated. Just off Michigan Avenue. 160 E Huron St. (787-2900). Expensive

Marriott – Health club, swimming pool, platform tennis. 1,179 rooms. Michigan and Ohio Aves. (836-0100). Expensive.

Drake Hotel – A 700-room institution, with a graciousness not often found in hotels these days. The *Cape Cod Room* is Chicago's finest seafood eatery (see *Eating Out*). Near north side. N Michigan Ave. at Lake Shore Dr. and Walton Pl. (787-2200). Expensive.

Holiday Inn — Mart Plaza – 526 rooms atop the Apparel Center, Chicago's answer to New York's garment district — and very spiffy. Free parking. 350 N Orleans (836-5000). Expensive to moderate.

Allerton – Close to museums and shopping on Michigan Avenue, 10 minutes from the Loop. The 450-room Allerton is an economical but quite pleasant choice — and a steal in this location. 701 N Michigan Ave. (440-1500). Expensive to moderate.

The Bismarck – The *Walnut Room Restaurant* is a long-standing noontime tradition for Chicago politicos. 537 recently renovated rooms and some nice suites. 171 W Randolph at La Salle (236-0123). Moderate.

Holiday Inn — City Centre – Architecturally more interesting than you might expect. Swimming pools and health club, indoor and outdoor tennis courts, racquetball, and free parking make this establishment's 500-odd rooms almost a bargain. 300 E Ohio (787-6100). Moderate.

Americana Congress – Not as large as the nearby Palmer House (1,000 rooms), this unit of the Best Western chain well deserves an excellent reputation for personal attention. It also boasts a kosher kitchen and fine views of Lake Michigan and Grant Park. 520 S Michigan Ave. (427-3800). Moderate.

Holiday Inn — Lake Shore – The best things about this 586-room Holiday Inn are its setting opposite the lake and Navy Pier and its relatively low rates, which are even more reasonable considering the outdoor pool. 644 N Lake Shore Dr. (943-9200). Moderate.

Holiday Inn — Downtown – The location is not Chicago's poshest — but then, you are not charged an arm and a leg, either. Convenient to Greektown, the Loop, and the expressways. The best surprise is no surprise. 412 rooms. Outdoor pool. Pets welcome. Free parking. 1 S Halsted (829-5000). Moderate.

Holiday Inn of Elk Grove – Convenient to O'Hare. With 159 rooms and an outdoor pool, it's an economical choice for an overnight stop. Pets welcome. Transportation to the airport. 1000 Busse Rd. (437-6010). Moderate.

Avenue Motel – This budget establishment has only 78 rooms, and few amenities, but it's good for a place to sleep close to town. Pets welcome. 1154 S Michigan Ave. (427-8200). Inexpensive.

Ohio House Motel – Another good choice if you're hoping to save money on accommodations. The 50-room Ohio House isn't centrally located, but the management provides a courtesy car to the Loop, daily from 8:30 AM to 4:30 PM. There's a coffee shop on the premises. Pets are welcome. 600 N La Salle St. at Ohio (943-6000). Inexpensive.

Grove Motel – An outdoor pool and low (for Chicago) prices make this 40-room motel a real find. Restaurant nearby. A half-hour drive from the Loop (longer in rush hour). 9110 Waukegan Rd., Morton Grove (966-0960). Inexpensive.

EATING OUT: Eating can be the best part of your Chicago stay. The city's restaurant business is booming, and some of the finest cooking in America can be found here. Expect to pay from $40 to $60 and up for two at those restaurants we've noted as expensive; between $30 and $40, for moderately priced meals; and under $30 at our inexpensive choices. Prices do not include drinks and wine, tips and taxes.

Le Perroquet – Subtle, sumptuous; undisputedly one of the best restaurants in the US. Expect a parade of wonders such as moules or a soufflé de crevettes Madras as hors d'oeuvres; salmon mousseline, venison filet, or quails as entrées; pastries to follow. Closed Sundays. Reservations necessary. American Express, Diners Club, and Carte Blanche. 70 E Walton (944-7990). Expensive.

Cricket's – In the Tremont Hotel. In the style of the "21" Club in New York, with red-checkered tablecloths, bare floors, low ceilings, and walls festooned with corporate memorabilia, and a menu that includes chicken hash Mornay and various daily specials. A very good choice for Sunday brunch. Ties and jackets required for men. Reservations essential. Major credit cards. 100 E Chestnut (280-2100). Expensive.

The Palm – Owned by the same people who run the well-known New York restaurants called *Palm* and *Palm, Too,* this eatery has a similar décor of sawdust-covered floors and walls hung with drawings of famous patrons. Also like its East Coast counterpart, the kitchen here specializes in producing great steaks and lobster. Open for lunch and dinner Mondays through Fridays; dinner only on Saturdays; closed Sundays. Reservations necessary. Major credit cards. 181 E Lake Shore (944-0135). Expensive.

Le Français – One of the country's foremost French restaurants — well worth the 45-minute drive from Chicago. The surroundings are elegant, the service exceptional, and the cuisine, prepared by the French chef-owner Jean Banchet, remarkable. Among the specialties are navarin de homard aux petites lègumes (lobster with sautéed fresh vegetables), aiguillette de canard à la rouennaise (roast duckling in red wine sauce with duck and goose liver), and millefeuille de saumon sauce crossonnière (fresh salmon in a pastry shell with spinach). Closed Mondays. Reservations essential. Major credit cards. 269 S Milwaukee, Wheeling, IL; take Kennedy Expy. to rt. 294 north, Willow exit (541-7470). Expensive.

Doro's – Quite elegant northern Italian cooking, much of it done at your table. Pasta made on the premises, superb veal, and four other categories of entrées, including grilled items, poultry, beef, and fish. Sautéed baby artichokes are excellent. Open daily for dinner. Reservations essential. Major credit cards. 871 N Rush St. (266-1414). Expensive.

La Cheminée – Rustic French, charming and small. Come here for great veal

Florentine, steak au poivre, duck à l'orange, which is the way it's supposed to be. The crabmeat-stuffed avocado and quiche Lorraine are perfect starters. Open daily for dinner. Reservations advised. All credit cards. 1161 N Dearborn (642-6654). Expensive.

Biggs – In a restored Victorian mansion. The prix fixe menu changes every day, but the selection often includes beef Wellington, duck à l'orange, roast rack of lamb persillade, tenderloin tips sautéed with fresh mushrooms and served on wild rice. An extensive wine list. Open daily for dinner only. Reservations necessary. Major credit cards. 1150 N Dearborn (787-0900). Expensive.

Jovan's – Prix fixe menus change daily depending on what's in the market; the cooking is taken very seriously. Pike mousse and quiche Lorraine are among the appetizers that appear frequently, along with interesting vegetables, dessert soufflés, and hand-dipped bonbons. Open weekdays for lunch; dinner daily except Sundays. Reservations required. American Express, Diners Club, and Carte Blanche. 16 E Huron (944-7766). Expensive.

95th – For food with a view, this is your best bet. Meals are elaborate, and everything is as elegant as the scene through the windows. Try the tournedos Rossini, and lobster specialties. Open daily; lunch and dinner Saturdays; brunch and dinner on Sundays. Reservations helpful. Major credit cards. 95th floor, John Hancock Center, 172 E Chestnut St. (787-9596). Expensive.

The Pump Room – Although now under the management of the "Lettuce Entertain You" restaurant chain, care has been taken to preserve *The Pump Room*'s winning formula of fine cuisine, diligent service, and lovely decor. Continental dishes are the mainstays, but there are some nouvelle cuisine specialties; both are complemented by the restaurant's good selection of wines. Open daily. Reservations necessary. Major credit cards. 1301 N State Pkwy. (266-0360). Expensive.

Gordon – This handsome restaurant attracts a chic young crowd and specializes in fresh, well-prepared fish. The menu changes every day—depending on what's available at the market—but a good bet would be the salmon with oyster sauce and the artichoke fritters. Reservations advised. Major credit cards. 512 North Clark (467-9780). Expensive.

The Bakery – Buoyant, bright, and busy. Nearly every night you can get pork roast stuffed with Hungarian sausage, beef Wellington, roast duck with cherry sauce. Seasonal entrées include stuffed lamb, bouillabaisse, roast pheasant or goose. There's no menu; the waiters recite the night's choices. Closed Sundays and Mondays. Reservations required. Major credit cards. 2218 N Lincoln (472-6942). Expensive.

L'Escargot – Unpretentious and pleasant, with an emphasis on provincial French cooking, including a cassoulet—white beans, sausage, pork, and goose. There's always fresh fish and homemade pastries on the menu. Reservations advised. Major credit cards. The Allerton Hotel, 701 N Michigan (337-1717), open daily except major holidays. Closed Sundays. Expensive to moderate.

Cape Cod Room – An institution. This seafood restaurant serves reliable fresh pompano, lobster, and other fish. Open daily. Reservations required. Major credit cards. 140 E Walton (787-2200). Expensive to moderate.

Chez Paul – Robert Hall McCormick's palatial mansion sets the scene for memorable meals of ris de veau Maréchal, salmon en croute beurre blanc, rognons de veau sautés Napoléon. Open weekdays for lunch; daily for dinner. Reservations essential. Major credit cards. 660 N Rush St. (944-6680). Moderate.

L'Epuisette – Small, with a good selection of seafood: turbot Véronique, crab in white wine and mushrooms, baked shrimp de Jonghe, red snapper Provençal. Open for dinner only; closed Mondays. Reservations advised. Major credit cards. 21 W Goethe St. (944-2288). Moderate.

Carson's – According to *Chicago* magazine (and us), the best spareribs in the city. Salads with a creamy, anchovy-flavored dressing and tangy au gratin potatoes are the other lures. Don't dress up, for bibs (supplied) are essential. No reservations, so expect to wait for a table. Major credit cards. 612 N Wells St. (280-9200). Moderate to inexpensive.

Blackhawk – This Chicago institution is famous for its thick cuts of prime ribs, aged sirloins, and fresh Boston scrod — all served with a salad mixed right at your table with appropriate flourish. Good cheesecake. Usually crowded. Closed Sundays. Reservations advised. Major credit cards. 139 N Wabash (726-0100). Moderate to inexpensive.

Lawry's The Prime Rib – The specialty here is prime ribs, served in three thicknesses with a big fresh salad with Lawry's special Famous French dressing. The salad is served with a chilled fork; the prime ribs, with Yorkshire pudding. And, of course, the seasoning salt that Lawry's made famous. Open daily; weekdays for lunch. Reservations suggested. Major credit cards. 100 E Ontario (787-5000). Moderate to inexpensive.

Berghoff – Another Chicago tradition. Although the service is rushed, the meals are bountiful and the selection wide-ranging: ragout, schnitzel, steak, and seafood. Closed Sundays. Reservations accepted for groups of five or more. No credit cards. 17 W Adams (427-3170). Inexpensive.

Greek Islands – A simple place where you can find thoughtfully prepared dishes such as gyros, squid, lamb, and fresh broiled red snapper. The decor isn't elegant, but the food is delicious. Open daily. Reservations are not necessary. Major credit cards. 766 W Jackson (782-9855). Inexpensive.

Febo's – A real "old neighborhood" restaurant where the northern Italian cooking tastes like it came out of a family kitchen. Try the antipasto, followed by linguine Alfredo, cannelloni, tortellini, or chicken Alfredo in mushrooms and lemon-herb wine sauce. Closed Sundays. Reservations suggested. Major credit cards. 2501 S Western (523-0839). Inexpensive.

The Great Gritzbe's, Lawrence of Oregano, R.J. Grunts, Jonathan's Seafood – These links in the "Lettuce Entertain You" restaurant chain are all sleekly contemporary in design and offer good food and fun at fair prices. Although they feature similar menus — salads, sandwiches, and entrées ranging from tacos to filet mignon — each has a distinctive and delectable "all you can eat" bar: desserts at *Gritzbe's;* salads at *R.J. Grunts;* and seafood at *Jonathan's. The Great Gritzbe's,* 21 E Chestnut (642-3460); *Lawrence of Oregano,* 662 W Diversey Pkwy. (871-1916); *R.J. Grunts,* 2056 N Lincoln Park W (929-5363); *Jonathan's Seafood,* 5419 N Sheriden Rd. (878-1846). Open daily. Major credit cards. Inexpensive.

CINCINNATI

Since most travelers know more about almost anything than they do about Ohio geography, here's a word of orientation for those contemplating a first trip to Cincinnati: Cincinnati is not Cleveland. Cleveland is in the north, on Lake Erie. Cincinnati sits snugly in a basin of the north bank of the Ohio River, in the southwest corner of the state, surrounded by tree-lined hills festooned with stately homes, on the border of Kentucky. Although resolutely businesslike and the headquarters of an unusually large number of well-known companies for a city its size (1.4 million people in the metropolitan area), Cincinnati does not feel itself to be as unredeemingly industrial as the cities of northern Ohio.

Originally called Losantiville, Cincinnati was founded in the 1780s and was renamed in honor of the Society of Cincinnati in 1790 by a member of that organization who happened to be passing through as the newly appointed governor of the Northwest Territory. "Losantiville!" he reportedly exclaimed. "What an awful name." The rest, as they say, is history.

Like river cities everywhere, Cincinnati had a lusty past. Soldiers were dispatched to protect its earliest settlers from the Indians, but the settlers soon came to fear the soldiers more than they feared the Indians. William Henry Harrison visited not long before he became President and pronounced it "the most debauched place I ever saw." As late as 1901, Carrie Nation arrived on a temperance crusade, but failed to smash a single saloon window. "I would have dropped from exhaustion before I had gone a block," she told curious reporters. But, in succeeding years, seemliness somehow got the upper hand and lust was banished. (Fear not, however. Lust is said to flourish across the river in northern Kentucky, which Cincinnati folks popularly suppose was created for just that purpose.)

Longfellow called it the "Queen City of the West," and Winston Churchill said it was "the most beautiful of America's inland cities." In 1976, the *Saturday Review* declared Cincinnati to be "one of the five most livable cities in the United States." Why the accolades? For one thing, Cincinnati's downtown is congenially vibrant, alive during the day and night. This is partly the result of substantial, continuing investment by the business community in an effort to stave off urban decay, the common enemy of cities. Leisure-conscious Cincinnati residents enjoy music, art, good food, and sports. Many are active volunteers on civic projects. The center of downtown is 19th-century Fountain Square, which surrounds the majestic Tyler-Davidson Fountain. Modern office buildings and ground-level shops line Fountain Square on the north and east. Across the street, Fountain Square South, one of the city's most ambitious private projects, is a brand new high-rise complex that has provided much-needed space for offices, hotels, and shops. The compact downtown area is easy to navigate. Because of its generally uncrowded streets and the skywalk, downtown Cincinnati can be easily explored on foot. Innumerable small restaurants, bars, and fast-food establishments exist to succor the foot-weary. Also within easy walking distance from downtown are Riverfront Stadium (home of the Cincinnati Reds baseball team and the National Football League Bengals) and the Coliseum (host to Cincinnati Tigers hockey, circuses, ice shows, rock concerts, and University of Cincinnati basketball).

Some 400,000 of the Cincinnati area's residents live in the city, many on the hillsides that ring the business district. Mt. Adams, to the northeast, and Clifton, directly north, are especially interesting. Mt. Adams is to Cincinnati what Greenwich Village once was to New York and Georgetown is to Washington: Bohemia at a price. Its slopes are covered by new and restored row houses, shops, and restaurants. Just north of Mt. Adams is Eden Park, in which the Cincinnati Art Museum, Museum of Natural History, and Playhouse in the Park are found. Clifton is the site of the 39,000-student University of Cincinnati, a campus set in a residential district of baronial homes and interesting shops. Between Mt. Adams and Clifton, Mt. Auburn is undergoing extensive restoration in an effort to recapture some of the area's previous grandeur. Cincinnati residents are justifiably proud, too, of the superb Cincinnati Symphony and Opera Company, both housed in Music Hall. The University's College Conservatory of Music also offers impressive musical programs. The Cincinnati Ballet performs at the downtown Taft Theater.

Cincinnati people are friendly, but reserved, sedately satisfied with their lives. Some residents will go so far as to admit the water tastes funny, but apart from that, they tend to be laconic. Although there are many excellent restaurants and expensive shops, "fashionably dressed" in Cincinnati is conservative by big-city standards. People tend to play it safe, rather than experiment, and this makes Cincinnati a city with class, but no glamour. Most Cincinnati residents speak standard Midwestern or Appalachian American English, with a couple of crucial exceptions. The expressions "three-way" and "four-way" do not refer to traffic signs; they refer to special toppings for native Cincinnati chili. "Please" is used to indicate that the listener did not understand a question and would like to have it repeated or clarified. "Square" is used interchangeably with "block" when describing directions or distances, as in "Shillito's is three squares north of Pogue's." A "Pony Keg" is a convenience store, mostly for the dispensing of beer for off-premises consumption. Either "Cincinnat*i*" or "Cincinnat*a*" is correct. No Berlitz courses are available as yet. But no matter what kind of English you speak, people in Cincinnati (or Cincinnata) will probably understand you. If you really get stuck, try a trusty international nonverbal: smile.

CINCINNATI AT-A-GLANCE

SEEING THE CITY: For the best view of Cincinnati, go to the top of the Carew Tower. You may see the original seven hills on which the town is said to have been built. Admission charge. Children under six free. Groups of 15 or more get in for half-price. 5th and Vine (381-3443).

SPECIAL PLACES: Cincinnati's relatively traffic-free streets make sightseeing on foot not only feasible but pleasant. There are many interesting shops and restaurants to stop at along the way.

Cincinnati Art Museum – This outstanding collection of paintings, sculpture, prints, and the decorative arts fills more than 118 galleries and exhibition rooms (with an exceptionally fine section on ancient Persia). Ancient musical instruments, costumes, and textiles are also on view. Closed Mondays and holidays. Admission charge. Eden Park (721-5204).

Natural History Museum – The cavern and waterfall exhibit here is the only one of its kind in the world. A wilderness trail features animals in their natural habitat. An Indian exhibit depicts early Ohio Indian life in life-size dioramas. Closed Mondays. Admission charge. 1720 Gilbert Ave. (621-3889).

Stowe House – Harriet Beecher Stowe, the author of *Uncle Tom's Cabin,* lived here while doing research on her famous novel. In addition to a collection of Stowe memorabilia, the house has a number of exhibits on black history. Open Tuesdays through Sundays. Admission charge. 2950 Gilbert Ave. (no phone).

Taft Museum – The boyhood home of the 26th president of the United States, William Howard Taft, is now a museum of paintings, Chinese porcelain, and Duncan Phyfe furniture. Portraits and landscapes by Rembrandt, Turner, Goya, Gainsborough, and Corot line the walls. Open daily. Free. 316 Pike (241-0343).

Riverfront Stadium – Cincinnati is the self-proclaimed baseball capital of the world, and sports fans will enjoy touring the dugouts and back rooms of this 80,000-seat, artificial turf stadium. Tours by appointment during baseball season. Admission charge. 2nd St. (352-3779).

Contemporary Arts Center – "What is art?" is a puzzler as old as the Cincinnati hills, and the Contemporary Arts Center keeps many people in this good city wondering. Not only are there constantly changing modern paintings and sculpture, the Center features multimedia exhibits aimed at dazzling the mind, the eye, and the mind's eye. Closed Mondays. Admission charge. 115 E 5th St. (721-0390).

Fire Department Museum – All kinds of old fire engines, paraphernalia, and some modern equipment, too. Closed Mondays. Children under 6 free. 329 E 9th St.

Cincinnati Zoo – The second oldest zoo in the nation, known for its expertise in the propagation of rare and endangered species. There are more than 6,000 animals here. The most popular exhibits are Big Cat Canyon with rare white tigers, the Bird of Prey Flight Cage, Outdoor Gorilla Exhibit, Children's Zoo, Insect House, and the Aquarium. Open daily. Admission charge. 3400 Vine St. (281-4700).

College Football Hall of Fame – A new collection of memorabilia of college football greats. The emphasis is on audiovisual displays and entertainment, including live shows, films, and computerized information banks. The College Football Hall of Fame is part of the Kings Island Theme Park complex, on I-71, 20 miles north of the city. Open every day but Christmas. (241-5410).

Sharon Woods Village – Life in 19th-century Ohio, with a representative group of buildings from the 1800s arranged in a village setting. Open Tuesdays through Sundays, summer only. Admission charge. Sharon Woods, off rt. 42 (721-4506).

Vent Haven Museum – For lovers of marionettes and talking puppets. This unique, entertaining museum across the state border in Kentucky has the largest known collection of ventriloquists' material in the world. In addition to about 500 puppets, there's a library of hundreds of books in eight languages, dating back to the 18th century. Summer tours by appointment. 33 W Maple Ave., Ft. Mitchell, KY (606 341-0461).

■ **EXTRA SPECIAL:** Just a couple of hours south of Cincinnati lies the best horse-breeding region in the United States — *Kentucky Bluegrass* country. The drive on

I-71/75 takes you through very green, rolling hills and beautiful breeding farms. Stop for lunch at the *Beaumont Inn*, a relaxing country inn, just west of Lexington, KY, in Harrodsburg. Open March through November. (606 734-3381).

SOURCES AND RESOURCES

For maps and brochures, write or visit the Convention and Visitors Bureau, 200 W 5th St. (621-2142), or the Chamber of Commerce, 120 W 5th St. (579-3100).

The best local guide to events and places of interest is *Cincinnati* Magazine, monthly, available at newsstands.

All telephone numbers are in the 513 area code unless otherwise indicated.

For Local Coverage – *Cincinnati Enquirer,* morning daily and Sundays; *Cincinnati Post,* afternoon daily.

For Food – *Cincinnati* Magazine's annual restaurant guide, available from the Chamber of Commerce, gives the best information on where to dine. The *Cincinnati Enquirer, Post,* and the magazine feature occasional restaurant columns and guides, too.

CLIMATE AND CLOTHES: It's damp in Cincinnati. Winters tend to be wet, in the 30s. Summers run into the sweaty 80s and 90s. Spring and fall, however, are more amenable, and a drive through the surrounding countryside in either season is a joy.

GETTING AROUND: Bus – Queen City Metro operates an excellent bus service. The bus stop signs carry numbers of the routes that stop there. Bus route maps are included in the "Visitors' Guide," obtainable at the Convention and Visitors' Bureau or the Chamber of Commerce, listed above. Queen City Metro, 6 E 4th St. (621-4455).

Taxi – Cabs are relatively scarce and expensive. The best way to get one is to call Yellow Cab, 1110 Kenner St. (241-2100).

Car Rental – Major car rental agencies are represented at the Greater Cincinnati International Airport.

MUSEUMS: Cincinnati's major museums — Cincinnati Art Museum, Natural History Museum, Taft Museum, Contemporary Art Museum, Fire Department Museum, and Vent Haven Museum — are described in detail under *Special Places*.

MAJOR COLLEGES AND UNIVERSITIES: Cincinnati's only major university is the University of Cincinnati, which has an astonishing 39,000 students from around the metropolitan area, the state, across the US, and around the world. Clifton (475-8000).

SPECIAL EVENTS: Ever since 1873, Cincinnati has been holding its annual *May Festival,* a series of choral and instrumental musical concerts at Music Hall, 1243 Elm (621-1919). In June, the *Ladies' PGA Championship* is held at Kings Island, Jack Nicklaus Sports Center, 3365 Kings Mills Rd. (398-9906). The last week in September, Cincinnati celebrates its German heritage with an *Oktoberfest,* along the lines of the famous Munich Festival, in and around Fountain Square.

SPORTS: Not only is Cincinnati one of the country's most enthusiastic baseball cities, it is also home to a National Football League team, the *Bengals.* Riverfront Stadium and Coliseum are easily accessible to downtown. For tickets and information call the following numbers:

Baseball: Cincinnati *Reds* (421-4510).

Football: Cincinnati *Bengals* (621-3550).

Basketball: University of Cincinnati (475-2287).

Horse Racing – Horse racing enthusiasts should check out the action at River Downs, 6301 Kellogg Ave. (232-8000); and Latonia racecourse, near the airport, 440 Price Pike, Florence, KY (606 371-0200).

Golf – For spectators and golfers, Kings Island is far and away the best — the Jack Nicklaus Sports Center, 3565 Kings Mills Rd. (241-5200).

Bicycling – Bikes can be rented, in the summer, from Airport Playfield, Lunken Airport, Wilmer Ave. (321-6500).

Fishing – There's moderately good fishing at Lake Isabella and Winton Woods, the largest of the county lakes. Serious Cincinnati fishermen and women drive four hours to Lake Cumberland and Kentucky Lake in southern Kentucky.

Swimming – There is a good public pool called Sunlite Pool at Old Coney Island just before River Downs on rt. 50 (231-7801). Call first to make sure it's open. You'll find lake beaches at nearby Hueston Woods in Butler County and Caesar's Creek in Warren County.

THEATER: Cincinnati has two theaters. The *Taft* features touring companies, and has a fall and winter season, 5th and Sycamore (721-0411). *Playhouse in the Park* is a professional regional theater specializing in modern American and European plays during the spring and summer, Mt. Adams Circle, Eden Park (421-3888). The *Beef'n'Boards* is a dinner theater offering a buffet followed by a comedy or musical comedy at Dry Fork exit #3 off I-74, then north ½ mile. Reservations required (367-4124).

MUSIC: The internationally famous *Cincinnati Symphony Orchestra,* founded in 1895, has a fall-winter season at Music Hall, 1243 Elm (621-1919). The *College Conservatory of Music* is one of the nation's oldest and most prominent professional music schools, located on the University of Cincinnati campus, Clifton and Calhoun (475-6638). The *Cincinnati Ballet* performs at the downtown Taft Theater in the spring, 5th and Sycamore (721-0411). The *Cincinnati Summer Opera* has been singing every year since 1921 at Music Hall.

NIGHTCLUBS AND NIGHTLIFE: Cincinnati is pretty much a couples' town. The most popular nightspots are *Tomorrows,* 5th and Race St., downtown (241-9555); *Sleep-Out Louie's,* 230 W 2nd St. on the riverfront (721-3636); *Lucy's in the Sky,* Holiday Inn Queensgate, 8th and Linn (241-8660); *Rookwood Pottery,* 1077 Celestial, Mt. Adams (241-4455); and *Conservatory,* 650 W 3rd St., Covington, KY (606 491-6400).

SINS: Cincinnati *gluttons* are smug in the knowledge that the city boasts some of the best restaurants in the tri-state area. Most notable is *La Maisonette,* 114 E 6th St. (721-2260), an excellent French restaurant that inspires you to ignore your pocketbook, don your toga, and grab your feather.

Lust in Cincinnati is something of a problem. For X-rated movies and other recreations, try Newport, Kentucky, just across the river.

The *pride* of the city is, of course, the Cincinnati *Reds,* also known as the Big Red Machine. This hearty team managed to take the World Series in both 1975 and 1976, making the fans about as cocky and prideful as any in the city's history. Home games are played at Riverfront Stadium, right in downtown Cincinnati, and you can be sure the locals turn out for them in droves.

LOCAL SERVICES: Business Services – Professional Secretarial Services, 322 E 4th (621-7724).

Mechanic – Irvine Tire Co., 405 Reading Rd. (241-4000).

Babysitting – Rock-a-Bye Sitters Registry, 7th and Vine (721-7440).

BEST IN TOWN

CHECKING IN: Although there are a few hotels that are comfortably elegant, Cincinnati does not offer any really outstanding accommodations. Stouffer's Cincinnati Towers is the most modern hotel in town. *President Motor Inn* across the state line in Ft. Mitchell, Kentucky, is the cheapest. You can expect to pay between $50 and $90 for a double at any of the hotels listed as expensive; $30 and $50 for those we consider moderate; under $30 at an inexpensive listing.

Stouffer's Cincinnati Towers – Corporate executives stay at this very modern, 462-room downtown hotel with a heated outdoor swimming pool, health club, sauna, lounge, restaurant, barber, beauty shop, and free parking because there is really no other choice. 5th and Elm (352-2100). Expensive.

Netherland Hilton – This beautiful, old, Art Deco building offers romantic atmosphere, in contrast to the ultra-modern, sophisticated Stouffer's. Its 685 rooms are quite spacious, parking is free, and you can bring your pets. 35 W 5th St. (621-3800). Expensive.

Westin – Opened in 1981, this is the newest of the downtown hotels. With 456 rather comfortable rooms, it is in the 17-story First National Bank Center. 500 Vine St. at Fountain Sq. (621-7700). Expensive.

Kings Island Inn – A favorite choice of golfers, since it's near the Jack Nicklaus course, this Alpine chalet-style inn offers good accommodations in an extremely attractive setting. In addition to its 194 rooms with queen-size beds, it has indoor and outdoor swimming pools, playground, tennis courts, game room, cocktail lounge with entertainment, dining room, and shuttle bus service to Kings Island Theme Park. 5691 Kings Island Dr., Mason (241-5800). Expensive.

Vernon Manor – A tasteful restoration of a faded beauty. Handsome modern decor in the bar, restaurant, and other public space; 115 elegant sleeping rooms, each with its own steam bath. Barber shop and beauty salon. No pets. 400 Oak St. (281-3300). Expensive.

Holiday Inn — Downtown – Long-time residents remember this Holiday Inn as the one across the street from the former stadium and the old railroad station. It's not in the greatest neighborhood, but if you're looking for a 247-room, functional place to rest your head, this could be it. It has a swimming pool, two dining rooms, bar, and a nightclub. 8th and Linn (241-8660). Moderate.

EATING OUT: Eating is one of Cincinnati people's favorite pastimes. They are nearly as proud of the city's fine restaurants as they are of its baseball team and music. Despite the city's varied origins, haute cuisine here is primarily French, Maisonette being its best restaurant. Cincinnati's most notable gastronomic eccentricity is its chili, which has little relation to the Southwestern product of the same name, perhaps because it was introduced to the city by a Bulgarian whose recipe was subsequently modified by the Greeks and Jordanians.

Cincinnati chili is served over spaghetti, to which may be added cheese ("three-way"), cheese and raw onions ("four-way"), or cheese, raw onions, and beans ("five-way"). At our one expensive listing, Maisonette, expect to pay at least $40 for two; between $15 and $20 at those places designated moderate; under $15 at places listed inexpensive. Prices do not include drinks, wine, or tips.

La Maisonette – It may seem in an unlikely spot, but it's one of the best French restaurants in the country. Its cuisine has consistently won every food award in the country. We recommend veal or lamb dishes. Unlike many fine places, the Maisonette is also an extremely friendly restaurant. New customers are treated like members of the family. Closed Sundays. Reservations required. All credit cards. 114 E 6th St. (721-2260). Expensive.

Mecklenburg Gardens – Known for its homemade soups, the Mecklenburg Gardens also offers an interesting selection of crepes and steaks. An attractive indoor dining room is complemented by a vine-covered garden, ideal for summer repasts. By the way, desserts here are excruciatingly lavish. Try the rum pie or Russian cheesecake. Closed Sundays. Reservations accepted. Major credit cards. 302 E University (281-5353). Expensive.

China Gourmet – Highly praised for its variety of Chinese food and superior Szechwan dishes, this small, friendly restaurant is tucked away in a little shopping mall in Hyde Park, about 10 minutes from downtown. One of the city's restaurant critics called it the best Chinese restaurant west of New York. Open daily. Reservations recommended. Major credit cards. 3340 Erie Ave. (871-6612).

Forest View Gardens – Waiters and waitresses sing your favorite operatic arias and serve tasty German food in a garden setting. Open Thursdays through Sundays. Reservations necessary. Major credit cards. 4508 North Bend Rd. (661-6434). Moderate.

Charley's Crab – Fresh fish is a rarity in landlocked Cincinnati, and this is one of the few places where it's available. The main selections are flown in fresh from the East Coast every day, and prepared simply and deliciously. Open daily. Reservations. Major credit cards. 9769 Montgomery Rd., 30 minutes from downtown on I-71 in Montgomery (891-7000). Moderate.

Samuri Japanese Steak House – Each table has its own Japanese chef, who cooks the meal before your eyes, with knives flashing and oil flaming. The performance is a large part of the fun, but the food is good, too. Open daily. Reservations accepted. Major credit cards. 126 E 6th St. (421-1688). Moderate.

Lenhardt's – Hearty food for the famished, leaning heavily on schnitzels and sauerbraten. Closed Mondays. Reservations accepted. No credit cards. 151 W McMillan St. (281-3600). Modcratc.

La Rosa's 580 – This is a convenient downtown spot for Italian food, from simple pizza and spaghetti to elaborate veal and chicken dishes. The easy, relaxed pace is especially good for vacationing kids who would otherwise be in danger of overdosing on Big Macs. Closed Sundays. Reservations accepted. Major credit cards. 6th St. between Walnut and Main (421-2025). Inexpensive.

Cricket Restaurant – Another German-American place, this huge restaurant serves very good, inexpensive steaks and well-prepared fish (frozen, not fresh). It's an ideal place for a low-cost, hefty, good meal. It's usually not crowded, but you can make a reservation. Open daily. Major credit cards. 6th and Vine (241-3949). Inexpensive.

Izzy Kadetz Delicatessen – The city's best deli, just a short walk from the middle of downtown. The food is standard fare. But the real attraction is Izzy, the spitting image of W.C. Fields. He stands at the register, and rather than quote prices from a menu, charges whatever he feels appropriate. His constant banter is a treat. Closed Sundays. No reservations. No credit cards. 819 Elm (721-4241). Inexpensive.

CLEVELAND

If you think there are no more chapters being written in the muscle-and-toil history of immigrant labor in America — that the story ended several decades ago with a final wave and the third generation — there is a book you should consult with some attention. It is called Cleveland, and you may find it a good deal more compelling than you'd expect.

Cleveland is a working city, and it always has been. Laid out in 1796 with strict attention to order and propriety by the surveyors of the Connecticut Company (led by Moses Cleaveland), its tidy New England pattern of straight streets around a public square was knocked into a cocked hat with the coming of industrialization. Cleveland's location at the confluence of Lake Erie and the Cuyahoga River provided a waterway which stimulated the growth of heavy industry — shipping, steel, iron, and construction. The city sprawled. Famous fortunes got their start. John D. Rockefeller parlayed an oil business into wealth beyond imagining; shipping magnates Sam Mather and Mark Hanna began their rise; the Van Sweringen brothers created a vast railroad and construction empire. But behind all this boom, and most of the money, was the muscle power of a largely immigrant work force that earned little more for its labor than the sweat of its own brow.

The workers have stayed, and so have the industries, and it is the continuing saga of their fortune together that makes Cleveland today something of a bellwether among middle-sized industrial US cities. For one thing, heavy industry is no longer the only game in town. Business competes with industry to place Cleveland high on the list of America's corporate centers. Of the largest 1,000 US corporations, around 35 have headquarters in or near Greater Cleveland. White collars are beginning to outnumber blue collars, and that is surely a token of things to come elsewhere as well. Not everyone is sorry to see the change. If the benefits of the city's industrial history have been great, so has the toll it's taken. Pollution and industrial waste have ruined the Cuyahoga and tainted the air, and the population of the inner city has diminished steadily over the last decade. Today, the city has a population of 600,000 within the city limits; Cuyahoga County, which includes the Greater Cleveland area, a ring of wealthy suburbs, has 1.5 million people. Among the 59 suburbs in the county is Shaker Heights, considered one of the most affluent towns in the country. There, on the site where the Shakers once threw off American industrial life to set up a rural commune, reside the most prosperous industry and business leaders; it is a haven of sorts still.

But don't think Cleveland is getting effete, or being abandoned by its industry. A drive along the Detroit-Superior Bridge over the flats shouldering the twists and turns of the Cuyahoga River — the steel mills belching flames into the sky, barges plunging up and down the river — shows Cleveland's muscles still flexing.

And that might be why, with all of its problems, there's something interesting about Cleveland. It's a city of the American Dream, bothered and bewildered, but with much to admire between the fret lines. Ethnocentricity is strong. Sons and daughters of immigrants who gladly took the toughest jobs at the poorest pay own their pieces of the suburbs, but the old neighborhoods live on. Buckeye Road, where the Hungarians once crowded in such numbers that Cleveland was second only to Budapest in the number of Magyars calling it home, is still a substantial Carpathian community. Little Italy is an East Side enclave; Chinatown is on the fringes of downtown; and Tremont is a mixed ethnic neighborhood where God accepts the worship of a bewildering number of denominations and faiths. When you get right down to it, there's something genuinely American about the crazy-quilt ambience of Cleveland's neighborhoods. (And if the underlying fabric appeals to you, you'll find a mix and match of business types and laborers at Chester Commons, a splash of green in downtown Cleveland that's a favorite lunch spot. Don't worry if you didn't bring lunch — just buy a steaming hot dog with the works from a vendor.)

You can buy anything you want in Cleveland, as a matter of fact, because somewhere, someone is selling it. The city has the attributes of a major cosmopolitan center. Besides the revitalized downtown shopping district, Coventry Road in Cleveland Heights is a smaller Greenwich Village, and Beachwood Place, a posh shopping mall in the suburb of that name, even boasts a Saks. The Cleveland Orchestra is world renowned, and the Cleveland Museum of Art has one of the richest collections in the country.

You might hear along the way that Cleveland isn't the town it used to be, but what place is? After more than 175 years, having survived industrialization, immigration, exploitation, and every other cultural shock wave to rattle urban America, Cleveland is a city not only still on its feet, but enthusiastic. It's a city where martinis for lunch are beginning to outnumber shot-and-beers at the bar; wing tips outnumber the steel-toed boot. Muscle still counts, but not as much as it once did. More people carry credit cards than lunch buckets to work.

What does it all add up to? Count on one thing for sure: Wherever Cleveland is going, much of the rest of urban America will be headed soon after. And that's what makes Cleveland worth your time.

CLEVELAND AT-A-GLANCE

SEEING THE CITY: Stouffer's *Top of the Town Restaurant* offers a panoramic view of Cleveland, the downtown, and Lake Erie with its heavy barge and shipping activity. To the east are the affluent suburbs of Shaker and Cleveland Heights; to the west, the Gold Coast, a row of ritzy apartment houses. 100 Erieview Plaza (771-1600).

SPECIAL PLACES: Many of Cleveland's most interesting sights are concentrated in the few areas served by public transportation. You'll want to stroll around, particularly in the University Circle area, which is the cultural heart of Cleveland, and in the lovely suburb of Shaker Heights.

DOWNTOWN

Public Square – In the heart of the business area, the Public Square is a good place to get one's bearings in Cleveland past and present. Statues pay tribute to the city's founder Moses Cleaveland, Tom Johnson, the populist reform mayor, and, with the flamboyant Soldiers and Sailors Monument, to Cleveland's Civil War dead. Dominating the Square is the 52-story Terminal Tower, built by the Van Sweringen brothers on the eve of the stock market crash that leveled their vast empire. Under construction is another tower that will be the world headquarters for the Standard Oil Company. Bounded by Euclid Ave., Superior Ave., and Ontario St.

The *Goodtime II* Boat Tour – The tour up the river is the best introduction to "the Flats" or industrial valley along the river basin where Rockefeller and shipping magnates Sam Mather and Mark Hanna made their fortunes. The 500-passenger boat goes up the Cuyahoga as far as the steel mills. Departures every day from May through October except Mondays. Admission charge. E 9th St. Pier (531-1505).

Old Arcade – This 19th-century marketplace is a multi-tiered structure topped by a stunning block-long skylight of steel and glass. Bookstores and galleries line the arcade (best of the galleries is *Feldman's*, 861-3580, where works of Andy Warhol, Rauschenberg, and others are displayed). 401 Euclid Ave. (621-8500).

The Mall – This spacious rectangular mall is the location of all the government and municipal buildings and a well-designed, fountained plaza. Buildings include City Hall, the Public Library (which has over three million volumes and many WPA murals), and the Cleveland Stadium, home of the Indians and Browns. Bounded by Lakeside Ave., St. Clair Ave., E 6th and E 4th Sts.

UNIVERSITY CIRCLE AREA

Cleveland Museum of Art – Among the best museums in the country, this Greek-style marble building contains extensive collections of many periods and cultures; particularly strong on the medieval period, Oriental art, and paintings of Masters including Rembrandt, Rubens, and Picasso. Overlooks the Fine Arts Gardens of Wade Park with its seasonal flower displays. Auditorium features free films, lectures, and concerts. Closed Mondays. Free. 11150 East Blvd. at University Circle (421-7340).

Western Reserve Historical Society Museum – Features the largest collection of Shaker memorabilia in the world, including inventions such as the clothespin, the ladderback chair, and various farming implements and furnishings. Also has exhibits on Indians and pioneers. Closed Mondays. Small admission charge. 10825 East Blvd. (751-5722). Associated with the Frederick C. Crawford Auto and Aviation Museum with 130 antique autos and 8 old airplanes. Displays trace the evolution of the automobile and describe Cleveland's prominence as an early car manufacturing center. Visitors can see how the old cars are given a new lease on life at the museum's restoration shop. Closed Mondays. Admission charge. 10825 East Blvd. at University Circle (721-5722).

Cleveland Museum of Natural History – Exhibits of armored fish and sharks found preserved in Ohio shales, a 70-foot mounted dinosaur, and skeletons of mastodon and mammoth are a must for those who thought that Cleveland had no natural history. Admission charge. Wade Oval Dr. at University Circle (231-4600).

Rockefeller Park – This 296-acre park features the Shakespeare and Cultural Gardens, a series of gardens, landscape architecture, and sculptures representing the 20 nationalities that settled the city. Between East Blvd. and Martin Luther King Jr. Dr. The Greenhouse displays include a Japanese Garden, tropical plants, and a Talking Garden with taped descriptions of plants for blind visitors. Open daily. Free. 750 E 88th St.

Hessler Road – This small brick-paved dead-end street of yellow and chartreuse frame houses is Cleveland's artists' colony. Picturesque any time but best during the annual weekend street festival in May when craft displays and live music highlight the events of Cleveland's counterculture. One block north is the New Gallery where the latest works of nationally known avant-garde artists are exhibited. 11427 Bellflower (421-8671).

EAST SIDE

Cleveland Health Museum and Education Center – A first of its kind, the Health Museum has exhibits on the workings of the human body and health maintenance. You can see everything here from the walk-through model of a human eye to Juno, the transparent woman, and the inspiring "Wonder of New Life" exhibit. Admission charge. 8911 Euclid Ave. (231-5010).

Lake View Cemetery – The plantings here are beautiful, the view fine, and the company illustrious. Among the natives buried here are President Garfield (you can't miss the monument), Mark Hanna (the US senator), John Hay (secretary of state under McKinley), and John D. Rockefeller (father of the fortune). Open daily. Free. 12316 Euclid Ave.

Coventry Road – For those who are wondering if there is life outside of New York City, this is Cleveland's answer to Greenwich Village. Colorful boutiques and shops feature the latest in fashions and crafts. For lunch, try a Mideastern sandwich and a milkshake at *Tommy's*, a local institution. 1820 Coventry Rd.

New Mayfield Repertory Cinema – This modernized old movie house in Cleveland's Little Italy features the classics of American cinema, a wine bar, and free parking. Open daily. Small admission charge. 12300 Mayfield Rd. (229-3875).

SHAKER HEIGHTS

One of the most affluent suburbs in America, Shaker Heights now houses Cleveland's elite in lovely big old homes on wide, winding, tree-lined streets. This is interesting because the area was originally Shaker Lakes, the rural commune established by the 19th-century religious sect who left American industrial life for a religious regime featuring strict celibacy. Their recruitment program eventually failed, and today all that remains of the Shakers is the Shaker Historical Museum with its collection of memorabilia (16740 South Park, 921-1201) and the Shaker Cemetery (Lee Rd. at Chagrin Blvd.). Shaker Heights is a fine place for a drive or a stroll down the shady streets.

■ **EXTRA SPECIAL:** 53 miles south of Cleveland along I-77 is *Canton*, home of the Pro Football Hall of Fame. You can't miss it — it's the only football-shaped building in town. Inside there are all kinds of memorabilia of the game and its players — costumes, helmets, team pictures, a recording of Jim Thorpe's voice, a film on football, and even a research library. Open daily. Admission charge. 2121 Harrison Ave. On the way, you may want to stop off in Akron, rubber manufacturing capital of the world, for a tour of the Stan Hywet Hall and Gardens. Built between 1911 and 1915 by Frank A. Seiberling, founder of the Goodyear and Seiberling Rubber Companies, the building is an excellent example of Tudor revival architecture, and the 65-room house contains original antique furnishings and artworks of the 14th through 18th centuries. The 70 acres of gardens are best in spring when thousands of tulips bloom. 714 N Portage Path, Akron.

SOURCES AND RESOURCES

The Cleveland Convention and Visitors Bureau is best for brochures, maps, and general tourist information. 1301 E 6th St. (267-1824).

The Cleveland Magazine Visitors' Guide to Cleveland (Cleveland Magazine

Co., $1.50) is the best and most comprehensive local guide to the Cleveland area.

All telephone numbers are in the 216 area code unless otherwise indicated.

For Local Coverage – *The Cleveland Plain Dealer,* morning daily; *The Cleveland Press,* afternoon daily; *Northern Ohio LIVE,* monthly; *Cleveland Magazine,* monthly. All are available at newsstands.

For Food – Check the monthly restaurant listings in *Northern Ohio LIVE* and *Cleveland Magazine*.

CLIMATE AND CLOTHES: Cleveland has cold and snowy winters which are followed by brief springs that give brief respite from damp winters and humid summers. Fall is generally the most pleasant season, with mild, sunny weather that often extends through November.

GETTING AROUND: Bus – Regional Transit Authority serves both downtown and the outlying areas. Complete route and tourist information is available from the downtown office, 615 W Superior Ave. (621-9500).

Taxi – Cabs can be hailed in the street in the downtown area around Public Square or ordered on the phone. Yellow-Zone Cab is the major company (623-1500).

Car Rental – Cleveland is served by the major national firms.

MUSEUMS: The Cleveland Museum of Art, the Western Reserve Historical Society Museum, the Cleveland Museum of Natural History, the Cleveland Health Museum and Education Center, and the Shaker Historical Museum are all described above in *Special Places*.

MAJOR COLLEGES AND UNIVERSITIES: Case Western Reserve University (University Circle), with two colleges and eight professional and graduate schools, is one of the city's principal educational institutions. Cleveland State University (Euclid Ave. and E 24th St.) is the area's largest school with an enrollment of 17,000 students.

SPECIAL EVENTS: During August, the *All Nation Festival* brings out Cleveland's ethnic groups in full force with exhibitions of crafts, music, amusement rides for the kids, and plenty of ethnic food and beer. Held on the Fountain Mall. On Labor Day Weekend the Mall is mobbed again because of the *Plain Dealer Barbecue Ribs Burnoff* — a contest to see who in Cleveland makes the best ribs. There's plenty of ribs to spare and share, as well as corn on the cob, sweet potatoes, and kegs of beer, and everyone joins in the revelry which culminates in the crowning of Rib King for a year.

SPORTS: Baseball – The American Baseball League's Cleveland *Indians* play their home games at the Municipal Stadium from April to September, W 3rd St. and Lakeside Ave. (861-1200).

Football – The Cleveland *Browns* play pro ball at the Stadium from August to January (696-5555).

Basketball – The Cleveland *Cavaliers* play at the Coliseum from mid-October to early April. At I-271 and rt. 303 (659-9100).

Bicycling – From U-Rent-Um of America, 6683 W 130th St (888-5100), or Easy Rider Bicycle Shop, 3974 E 131st St. (752-1748). The Cuyahoga Falls Reservation nearby has good biking trails.

Golf – Punderson State Park has the best public 18-hole golf course, at rts. 44 and 87 (564-5163).

Tennis – The best public courts are at Cain Park in Cleveland Heights, Superior Rd. at Lee Rd. (371-3000).

THEATER: For current offerings and performance times, check the daily and weekly publications listed above. Cleveland has a variety of theatrical offerings, some locally produced, others traveling shows. Best bets for shows: *Hanna Theater*, 2067 E 14th St. (621-5000); *Cleveland Play House*, 2040 E 86th St. (795-7000); *Karamu Theater*, 2355 E 89th St. (795-7070); *Great Lakes Shakespeare Festival,* Ohio Theatre (521-0090); *Eldred Theater,* Case Western Reserve University Campus (368-2858).

MUSIC: *The Cleveland Orchestra* performs with noted soloists and guest conductors from October to mid-May in Severance Hall, 11001 Euclid Ave. at East Blvd. (231-1111).

NIGHTCLUBS AND NIGHTLIFE: Current favorites: *Agora,* for rock or jazz, 1730 E 24th St. (696-8333); *Peabody's,* for folk or blues, 2140 S Taylor Rd. (321-4072); *The Front Row Theater,* for big-name entertainment, 6199 Wilson Mills Rd. in Highland Heights (449-5000); *Play House Square Association,* also for big-name entertainment, 1621 Euclid Ave. (771-4444).

SINS: In Cleveland, the vice squad keeps busy in that hotbed of *lust* along Prospect Avenue between 14th and 24th Streets (prostitutes, adult cinemas, massage parlors, and the New Era Burlesque, which has amateur nights). The *pride* of Cleveland's powerful, prideful Irish comes out in full force with a display of drunkenness on St. Patrick's Day; the wildest of the wild Irishmen are reeling by 10 AM, the Irish party at pubs through the night, and anyone sober enough to find the Cleveland Athletic Club crashes its annual bash.

Cleveland has two horse tracks — Thistledown Racing Club at Northfield and Emery Streets in North Randall, Ohio and Northfield Park Raceway on rt. 8 in Northfield. You can watch *avarice* in action at the betting windows on race days (Wednesdays through Sundays at Thistledown, daily at Northfield Park).

Where to play the *glutton*? *Boukair's*, 13968 Cedar Rd., University Heights (321-9191), over exotic ice cream sundaes big enough for two.

LOCAL SERVICES: Business Services – Kelly Girls, 33 Public Square (771-2800).

Mechanic – Park Auto Repair Co., 2163 Hamilton Ave. (241-7390).

Babysitting – Ba-B-Sit Service Enterprises, 592 Cahoon Rd. (871-9595).

BEST IN TOWN

CHECKING IN: Though Cleveland does not have much in the way of grand old hotels or interesting historic nooks, the city does have many accommodations which are attractive, comfortable, and reasonably priced. In addition to the usual chains, there is an assortment of modern, locally owned hotels. Our selections range in price from $40 or more for a double room in the expensive category, $30–$40 in the moderate range, and under $25 in the inexpensive list.

Bond Court Hotel – Cleveland's newest luxury hotel, a 22-story tower with a good view of Lake Erie, conveniently located near the convention center. The service is fine and other features include indoor parking, coffee shop, lounge with entertainment, color TV, and an elegant dining room. 526 rooms. 777 St. Clair Ave. (771-7600). Expensive.

Stouffer's Inn on the Square – This 60-year-old hotel recently underwent a $13 million facelift and is unlike most members of this pedestrian chain. Special new feature: a 10-story atrium complete with waterfall and swimming pool. 520 rooms and luxury suites. Four eating facilities. 24 Public Square (696-5600). Expensive.

Swingo's – Cleveland's home away from home for traveling entertainment and sports celebrities, a blend of contemporary chrome and Victorian bordello plush velvet, and excellent personal service. Near the revitalized theater district. Has king-sized beds, some huge suites with wet bars, coffee shop, entertainment lounge, and parking. Swingo's *Keg and Quarter Restaurant* has a flamboyant atmosphere. 146 rooms. 1800 Euclid Ave. (861-5501). Expensive.

Hollenden House – A favorite of business people because of its central location downtown. Features swimming pool and saunas, health club, free parking, color TV, coffee shop, lounge, and an excellent dining room specializing in aged beef and chops. 526 rooms. E 6th St. and Superior Ave. (621-0700). Moderate.

Marriott Inn – Near the airport, Cleveland's best motor inn. Its many recreational features include an indoor pool, therapy pool, sauna, miniature golf, putting green, volleyball, badminton. Also has free airport bus, lounge with entertainment, color TV, coffee shop, two dining rooms. 400 rooms. 4277 W 150th St. (252-5333). Moderate.

Park Plaza Hotel – This modern high-rise is conveniently located near University Circle, Cleveland's cultural center. Features include indoor swimming pool, health club, color TV, two coffee shops, lounge with entertainment, and an Old English dining room. 469 rooms. E 96th St. and Carnegie Ave. (791-1900). Moderate.

Beryl's – This motor hotel offers good clean accommodations at the best prices around, and throws in a free Continental breakfast too. Has TV, coin laundry, and proximity to cafés and restaurants. 40 rooms. 11837 Edgewater Dr., five miles west of city, one block north of US 6 (226-1616). Inexpensive.

EATING OUT: Cleveland was developed by over 20 different immigrant groups who brought with them distinctive old-country recipes and appetites. Restaurants reflect this diverse cultural background with fine ethnic cuisine and a wide range of styles; haute cuisine in shimmering elegance to solid hamburgers in a casual atmosphere. Our selections range in price from $40 or more for a dinner for two in the expensive range, $20 to $35 in the moderate, and $15 or less in the inexpensive range. Prices do not include drinks, wine, or tips.

Leonello's – This restaurant in Shaker Heights serves Continental cuisine in a surrounding of quiet elegance — Impressionist prints, low ceilings, and mirrored walls. The service by tuxedoed waiters is excellent, and the specialties are Châteaubriand and veal piccata. Closed Sundays. Reservations. Major credit cards. 16713 Chagrin Blvd. (752-6464). Expensive.

The Theatrical Restaurant – A favorite haunt of Cleveland's high rollers and flamboyant characters, from politicians to entertainers. The beef and Italian dishes are particularly good. Closed Sundays. Reservations. Major credit cards. 711 Short Vincent Ave. (241-6166). Expensive.

That Place on Bellflower – This place is the fleur-de-lis of Cleveland's French restaurants. Set in a charming century-old carriage house. Specialties are veal Oscar and fresh salmon renaissance. In the summer, dining is al fresco. Closed Sundays. Reservations. Major credit cards. 11401 Bellflower Rd., at University Circle (231-4469). Moderate.

The Samurai Japanese Steak House – A Japanese country inn, decorated with Far East silk screens and carvings. Each table is served by a Japanese chef who prepares shrimp, chicken, steak, or lobster tails with oriental vegetables. The food is excellent, done to the patron's own wishes. Open daily. Reservations. Major credit cards. 23611 Chagrin Blvd., Beachwood (464-7575). Moderate.

The Mad Greek – Moussaka, pastitsio, shish kabob, and Greek wine and liqueurs. Rustic inn atmosphere, with dining in the courtyard, weather permitting. Open daily. No reservations. Major credit cards. Cedar Rd. at Fairmont Blvd. (421-3333). Inexpensive.

The Balaton Restaurant – The atmosphere isn't much — bright lights and paper placemats — but the Hungarian food is the real thing. Specialties include home-made soups and strudel, dumplings, and Wiener schnitzel. No alcoholic beverages. Closed Sundays and Mondays. No reservations. No credit cards. 12521 Buckeye Rd. (921-9691). Inexpensive.

Corky & Lenny's – With a name like this, it could only be a deli, and it is. Cleveland residents claim that it's the best Jewish deli outside of New York City, and only New Yorkers may demur. Has the standard deli fare and plenty of the hustle-bustle as well. No reservations. No credit cards. 13937 Cedar Rd., University Heights (321-3310). Inexpensive.

La Fiesta Restaurant – The oldest Mexican restaurant in the city, this family-operated place features guacamole, tacos, tamales, enchiladas, chiles rellenos, chicharrones, and Mexican beer. Closed Mondays. Reservations only for parties of five or more. Major credit cards. 5110 Wilson Mills Rd., Richmond Heights (442-1445). Inexpensive.

Our Gang, Too – Amidst this plethora of ethnic restaurants, Our Gang, Too is America's representative with US culture served thick — shakes, burgers, huge onion rings, frozen yogurt — in a mildly anachronistic setting of stained glass, old pictures, plants, and a Victorian bar. Open daily till the wee hours. No reservations. Major credit cards. 20680 N Park Blvd. at Fairmount Circle, Shaker Heights (371-4700). Inexpensive.

DALLAS

Dallas is a paradox — both big city and small town. Gleaming glass monstrosities appear to rise daily in the downtown area, but Dallasites, at heart, are just down-home good ol' boys.

That is, if you can find a native Texan to talk to. Migration from the northern climes (with such major corporations as American Airlines relocating in the city) has doubled Dallas's population in 10 years. In less than 140 years, it has grown from a cabin on the banks of the Trinity River to a metropolitan area of almost 2 million (counting neighboring Fort Worth and surrounding suburbs). If Texas were a nation, Dallas would be its capital. More controversial is just how Texan it is; some residents claim it is quintessential Texas — the epitome of bigness and wealth. That claim has gained the city some enmity from other parts of Texas.

A few statistics: Dallas has more Cadillacs per capita than any major city outside the Arab world. Its gross annual sales exceed $2.5 billion, and its airport is larger than the island of Manhattan. These facts point to one thing: extraordinary wealth. Where does it come from? Oil, cotton, electronics, furniture, clothing, and insurance. It is this wealth, more than any other single factor, which determines what might be called the Dallas lifestyle. Historically, money was used to entice the railroads into the city. Today, it pays for glass skyscrapers that shine golden in the setting, rush-hour sun. It also stimulates leisure businesses, like discos and restaurants. At its best, the wealth has generated a number of progressive civic programs to improve the general quality of life. At its worst, it has led to a tasteless extravagance, and a preoccupation with power and influence.

In 1940 an unpublished book written as part of the Texas Writers' Project (for the WPA) described the typical Dallas resident as someone who "wants the latest fashions from Fifth Avenue, Bond Street, and Rue de la Paix; the newest models in cars; and the best in functionally constructed, electrified, air-conditioned homes, but prefers old-time religions with comfortable, modern trimmings and old-fashioned Jeffersonian democracy." If that picture is a touch too complacent to fairly represent contemporary residents, it nonetheless hits close to home. Dallas residents do have a fine sense of the good life, pursue it actively — and often achieve it. With an unemployment rate under 4% and a city manager and a school superintendent who both want to *lower* taxes, Dallas is a civic public relations director's dream.

There is a dark side to the dream, and though its impact diminishes year by year, it will not disappear. To millions of people throughout the world, Dallas is the city where President John F. Kennedy was killed on a November day in 1963. Memphis and Los Angeles bear no equivalent stigma for those similar tragedies — the assassinations of Martin Luther King and Robert Kennedy. But politically conservative, laissez-faire Dallas still suffers. Until recently, the mention of Dallas in any city outside Texas brought a free-association response of "Kennedy" or "assassination." Former Dallas Mayor Erik Johnson said, "In many places around the world, we became known as a city of hate — a city that killed a President." Years later, Dallas is still being silently blamed in the minds of millions, even though more than 25% of the city's residents weren't even alive in 1963. And tens of thousands have moved to Dallas since then, lured by the comfortable climate and jobs. But the place where President Kennedy was shot and the Texas Book Depository where Lee Harvey Oswald took aim have become sites to which visitors are obsessively drawn; the Texas Book Depository is the most-photographed site in Dallas — a bitter turn of events for a city that from the beginning has been an unabashed advertiser of its own virtues.

Dallas was founded in 1841 by a Tennessee lawyer named John Neely Bryan, who built a cabin at the junction of three forks of the La Santisisma Trinidad River (the Most Holy Trinity), and then set about building it into a city with circulars and much enthusiastic word-of-mouth advertising. Within nine years 430 people had joined him. In later years he was committed to an insane asylum — not, it should be said, for his part in the Dallas venture, though putting a city in such a flat, arid, landlocked place might have been used as evidence. But it worked. With the help of a lot of oil, cattle, manufacturing, and several fortuitous technological revolutions, Dallas has become the eighth largest metropolitan area in the country.

That is not to say that all is perfect with the world beneath the Dallas sun. Unemployment is low, but those without work are just as unemployed as those in high unemployment areas. The rate of crime is high enough to worry anybody but the criminally intent, and city politics are still, for some, a gentleman's diversion. The Dallas County commissioners, by contrast, are viewed as ruffians because they comport themselves with the bellicosity and street savvy of Chicago aldermen.

Significantly, Dallas has never had the kind of racial turmoil other cities have suffered, and when the school desegregation plan was implemented here in 1976 there were few problems. But the racial tensions and the racial separations that exist elsewhere exist here, too. They smolder and steam on street corners of this city's Southside, and they are a cold undercurrent that flows beneath the manicured lawns of affluent white Dallas.

Perhaps, in all, it is not so surprising to discover that at the heart of the bluff self-promotion that is so typically Texan and such standard Dallas-ese, there is a reflective reticence about the real nature of the city. Dallas is Texan, no doubt (the rest of the country can see that even if Texans can't agree); it is certainly American — in the problems it shares and the successes it enjoys and the future it mulls over. But the sum of these things does not quite equal the city itself. And it is this intangible "more" that fascinates residents — and keeps them thoughtfully silent.

DALLAS AT-A-GLANCE

SEEING THE CITY: For the best view of Dallas, go to the Hyatt Regency Tower with its revolving cocktail lounge, restaurant, and observation deck (admission charge). 400 S Houston St. (651-1234).

SPECIAL PLACES: Although attractions in Dallas are spread out, the museums are clustered together at Fair Park. There are several museums and gardens in Fort Worth, 35 miles away, and an amusement park complex in Arlington, halfway between Dallas and Fort Worth.

Fair Park – For 16 incredibly jammed days in October, Fair Park is the scene of the Texas State Fair, with all the superlatives you would associate with such an event: biggest, best, highest, widest, etc. For the rest of the year, Fair Park is the home of the Cotton Bowl, stadium for the New Year's Day college football game, and Fair Park Coliseum, home of the Dallas Black Hawks hockey team. Grand Avenue. For information on State Fair activities, call 565-9931.

Museum of Natural History – In order to attract the Texas Centennial Exposition to Dallas in 1936, the city fathers built a group of museums at Fair Park. The Museum of Natural History, a neoclassic, cream limestone building, contains a variety of fauna and flora from the Southwest. There are some interesting zoology and botany exhibits, too. Open daily. Free. Ranger Circle, Fair Park (421-2169).

Museum of Fine Arts – Exhibits of pre-Columbian art, African sculpture, 16th- and 17th-century Italian sketches, and changing exhibits on subjects like black American art. The museum has just acquired a new work, *Icebergs,* by American artist Frederic Edwin Church, which recently sold for $2.5 million, the highest price ever paid for an American painting. The art museum will be moving to a new home in a couple of years, thanks to the approval of a $24-million bond package by Dallas voters. Closed Mondays. Free. Ranger Circle, Fair Park (421-4187).

Aquarium – This one isn't the biggest or the best in the country, but it's the only one in Dallas. There are more than 325 species of native freshwater fish, cold and tropical-water creatures — finned, scaled, and amphibious. If you like watching the fish and sea animals being fed, be sure to get here early — around 8:30 AM. Open daily. Free. 1st St. and Forest Ave. (428-3587).

Garden Center and Health and Science Museum – Next to the Aquarium, the Garden Center has delightful tropical flowers and plants with Braille markers so that the blind can identify, as well as smell, them. Open daily. Free (428-7476). Just down the street, the Health and Science Museum features a fascinating series of anatomy, astronomy, and geology exhibits, including a talking transparent woman. A free planetarium show enraptures planet-watchers and stargazers. Open daily. Admission charge for Museum. Fair Park (421-2169).

The Midway and the Hall of State – As you walk along the Midway during the week, you will find it hard to imagine the frenetic carnival activity for which it is known. If you're here during the State Fair, or on weekends, you'll probably be swept into the frenzy, stopping only long enough to try winning a stuffed animal or doll at a shooting gallery or pitch 'n' toss. There is an assortment of spine-chilling, scream-inducing, turn you upside down and inside out rides for those who like thrills. There are also great food stands here — Greek, barbecue, and Mexican. At one end of the Midway, the Hall of State has paintings devoted to the heroes of Texas. It was built in 1936, for the Texas Centennial. If you like big art, you'll be happy with the giant murals. Open daily. Free. The Midway.

The Age of Steam Museum – Will bring a lump to the throat of anyone who ever loved an old train, with steam engines and other railroad nostalgia. Open Sundays and during the State Fair. Admission charge. The Midway (565-9931).

Neiman-Marcus – The shrine of commercial elegance, the Neiman-Marcus department store has been known to induce orgies of money-spending. If you have an insatiable craving for wave-making machines, a computer chess game, or a biorhythm calculator, this is the place to satisfy it. These games, however, are among the more conservative items in stock. The really exotic stuff is not on display; it's listed in the Christmas catalogue. Main and Ervay (741-6911).

Farmers' Market – This is raunchy, down-home, earthy Texas. From 6 AM, farmers drive into town in their trusty ole pickups to sell the fruit and vegetables of their labor. The market consists of a tin-roof shelter and dozens of stalls, with any number of colorful characters standing around. The vegetables are fresher and a bit cheaper than anywhere else in town. Open daily. In May there's a Flower Festival. 1010 S Pearl (748-2082).

Old City Park – This is one of the few places in Dallas where you can actually see what the place used to look like. Restored Victorian houses, railroad depots, and pioneer log cabins help give you some sense of the city's history. Slip away for a picnic. Closed major holidays. Admission charge. Gano and St. Paul (421-5141).

Texas Stadium – Cowboys fans go crazy here. (Not "giddyup" cowboys —the Dallas Cowboys.) This open 59,000-seat stadium packs 'em in during the Dallas Cowboys home games. It's constructed to give you the feel of being in a theater or auditorium, rather than a stadium, but critics point out that with the dome partially open, part of the field is always in shadow. On hwy. 183 at Loop 12 in Irving (438-7676).

L. B. Houston Park – One of the few wildlife areas in Dallas, with some woods so thick they appear to be woven, and beavers, opossums, gray foxes, rabbits, and raccoons scamper in the lush ferns. When you consider that this area was almost completely stripped of timber in 1900, the presence of so much natural splendor is especially overwhelming. Open daily. Free. Tom Braniff Dr., just off hwy. 114 near Texas Stadium.

Dallas Zoo – At one time an unkempt, run-down animal park, the Dallas Zoo has been rebuilt with newer facilities. It's now considerably more comfortable for the 2,000 mammals, reptiles, and birds that live within its 50 acres. Open daily. Admission charge; children free with adults. Marsalis Park, 621 E Clarendon Dr. (946-5154).

Texas School Book Depository – Known to millions of people around the world as the place where Lee Harvey Oswald hid, the Texas School Book Depository is the most photographed site in Texas. It's now the home of the Dallas County Commissioner's Court. 506 Elm.

John F. Kennedy Museum – A multimedia exhibit of "The Incredible Hours" showing events in the life of President John F. Kennedy, with particular emphasis on the day he was killed. Open daily. Admission charge. 501 Elm St. (742-8582).

John F. Kennedy Memorial – A 30-foot monument marks the spot where Kennedy fell. It has an indoor room for meditation, with the roof open to the sky. Main and Market Sts.

ARLINGTON

Six Flags Over Texas – A theme amusement park, Six Flags Over Texas motifs are based on different periods in Texas history: Spanish, Mexican, French, Republic of Texas, Confederacy, and the period since the Civil War. You can get a panoramic view of the Dallas and Fort Worth skylines from a 300-foot-high observation deck on top of an oil derrick. A narrow-gauge railway runs around the 145-acre grounds. Open daily May to September, weekends until Thanksgiving. Admission charge. I-30 (formerly the Dallas–Fort Worth Turnpike) at hwy. 360 (817 461-1200).

International Wildlife Park – A drive-through wildlife preserve, the only one of its kind in the Southwest. Thousands of animals roam freely around the 500-acre tract, and visitors can stop at many points along the six miles of safari trails. Open weekends. Admission charge. 601 Lion Country Pkwy., Grand Prairie (263-2201).

Southwestern Wax Museum – Definitely a cut above most of the genre. There are about 175 wax figures dispersed among 74 exhibits, including the car used by Bonnie and Clyde. This is a historical, not a horror, wax museum. Open daily. Admission charge, but children under six free. 601 E Safari Pkwy., Grand Prairie (263-2391).

FORT WORTH

Kimbell Museum – One of America's finest small art museums, the Kimbell has a permanent collection of works dating from pre-Columbian America to the early 20th century, with heavy concentration on European art. Will Rogers Rd. W, Fort Worth (817 332-8451).

Amon Carter Museum of Western Art – If you like pictures of the Old West, this is the place. Recent exhibits here have ranged from photographs of the Southwest by Ansel Adams to an exhibit on riverboats on the Mississippi. Open daily. Sundays free, other times admission charge. 3501 Camp Bowie Blvd. (817 738-1933).

Fort Worth Museum of Science and History – This differs from the Natural History Museum in Dallas because of its live animal exhibit and the Hall of Medical Science. There are exhibits on geology, natural history, and anthropology. Next door is the Planetarium, with shows that change every month. Both open daily. Museum free. 1601 Montgomery St. (817 732-1631).

Water Gardens – A water wonderland in the middle of downtown Fort Worth. Rivulets pour along concrete paths, forming gently moving streams and placid pools. Houston and 14th Sts.

Botanic Gardens – Another soothing environment, the Botanic Gardens blossom forth in a profusion of roses and garden flowers. Bonsai trees and wooden bridges form a tranquil Japanese garden; a hothouse creates the environment of the tropics; and a special section devoted to powerful scents is designed for the blind. Open daily. Free. 3220 Botanic Garden Dr. (817 870-7686).

Fort Worth Zoo – Although there aren't as many species here as in the Dallas Zoo, there are a number of imaginatively designed areas for viewing the animals. There's an aquarium, an underwater view of the seal pool, a rain forest with tropical birds, a children's zoo, and a super collection of snakes and reptiles. Open daily. Admission charge; children under 12 are free. 2727 Zoological Park Dr. (817 870-7050).

■ **EXTRA SPECIAL:** Fort Worth was once the home of the largest stockyards in the US, where thousands of cattle ran through town each day. That's why the city called Cowtown decided to honor its cattle legacy and restore the historical Stockyards area. The Stockyards features saloons, chili parlors, and a weekly rodeo at the Cowtown Coliseum. It's also home of *Billy Bob's Texas,* the world's largest honky-tonk (2520 Commerce; 817 625-6491). The Stockyards is at Main and Exchange Aves., on the city's north side.

SOURCES AND RESOURCES

For brochures, maps, and general information, contact the Dallas Chamber of Commerce. 1507 Pacific (651-1020).

The best local guide is *Guide Showcase,* the weekend magazine published every Friday in the *Dallas Morning News.*

All telephone numbers are in the 214 area code unless otherwise indicated.

For Local Coverage – *Dallas Times Herald,* evening daily; *Dallas Morning News,* morning daily; *D* Magazine, monthly.

For Food – *D* Magazine's restaurant section (monthly); and the Dallas restaurant guide in *Texas Monthly* magazine.

CLIMATE AND CLOTHES: Summers are blisteringly hot, with temperatures over 100. (Luckily, all indoor facilities in Dallas are air-conditioned.) Sudden thunderstorms punctuate the dry, blazing heat. From October to January, the weather is mild, although it can be in the 70s one day and in the 30s the next. From January to March, there are occasional sharp cold snaps, and between March and June you can expect rainstorms with westerly winds, and when it's not raining — dust storms.

GETTING AROUND: Bus – Dallas Transit Authority operates the bus service. For information, call 826-2222.

Taxi – There are taxi stands at most major hotels, but the best way to get one is to call Yellow Cab (426-6262).

Car Rental – All major national firms are represented.

MUSEUMS: For a full description of Dallas and Fort Worth museums, see *Special Places*. Another excellent museum is:

Fort Worth Art Museum – 1309 Montgomery St., Fort Worth (817 738-9215).

MAJOR COLLEGES AND UNIVERSITIES: Southern Methodist University (SMU) has a large campus with many activities (University Park, 692-2000). University of Dallas campus is located at 3113 University Ave. (579-5000).

SPECIAL EVENTS: Under planned special events, we list the *Texas State Fair,* in October in Fair Park. For more information call Bob Halford (565-9931). Another planned special event is the *Cotton Bowl* on New Year's Day. In May, *St. Seraphin's Annual Festival* features Ukrainian dancing and food at European Crossroads. 2829 Northwest Highway (358-5574). The *Flower Festival* at Farmers' Market is another May event, 1010 S Pearl (748-2082). Every January, Fort Worth hosts a rodeo at Will Rogers Coliseum, Lancaster and Montgomery (817 335-0734), with livestock exhibits and real cowboys roping calves and riding broncos. From November to April, there are weekly rodeos at Fort Worth's Cowtown Coliseum (817 332-7361).

SPORTS: Dallas has enough professional sports to satisfy just about everyone. A sampling:

Baseball – Texas *Rangers* play at Arlington Stadium, 1600 Copeland Rd., Arlington (265-3331).

Football – Dallas *Cowboys* play at Texas Stadium, Texas 183 at Loop 12 (438-7676). The Cotton Bowl is held every New Year's Day at Fair Park (565-9931).

Hockey – Dallas *Black Hawks* hit the puck around the ice at Fair Park Coliseum (565-0362). *Fort Worth Texans* play at Will Rogers Coliseum, Lancaster and Montgomery (817 332-1585). Fort Worth–Dallas hockey matches are worth seeing.

Horse Racing – Thoroughbred racing takes place at Louisiana Downs, Bossier City, Louisiana. Season runs from January to June. About three hours from Dallas on I-20 (800 551-8623, toll-free).

Basketball – Dallas's new NBA team, the *Dallas Mavericks*, plays at Reunion Arena, 777 Sports St. (748-1808).

Tennis – Tennis, however, is a year-round sport here, and it's terrifically popular. There are around 204 municipal courts. The best are at Sammuell Grand at 6200 Grand Ave. (821-3811) and at Fretz Park, Hillcrest and Beltline (821-1296).

Bicycling – Dallas has some pretty trails in the White Rock Lake–East Dallas areas. For outstanding biking, try Fort Worth's Trinity Trail, which begins downtown and then ambles along the river. You can rent bikes at River Ridge Pavilion (University Dr. at the river) and at both White Rock Lake and Bachman Lake (off Northwest Hwy. near Love Field).

Golf – There are several municipal courses in the Dallas–Fort Worth area. In Dallas, Tenison Memorial is best-known as the home of Lee Trevino. 3501 Samuell (823-5350). In Fort Worth, Meadowbrook is the best public course. 1815 Jenson Rd. (817 457-4616).

THEATER: For complete up-to-date listings on performance schedules, see the local publications listed above. The major Dallas theaters are: *Theater Three*, 2800 South in the Quadrangle (748-5191); *Dallas Theater Center*, 3636 Turtle Creek (526-8857). *El Centro College* presents touring companies of modern classics like *The Madwoman of Chaillot* at Main and Lamar (746-2262).

MUSIC: For information on concerts, check local publications or call the following numbers for information. *Dallas Symphony Orchestra* (692-0203); *Dallas Opera* (528-9850); *Dallas Ballet* (744-4430); *Fort Worth Symphony Orchestra*, Tarrant County Convention Center (817 921-2676).

NIGHTCLUBS AND NIGHTLIFE: Dallas crowds are so notoriously fickle that between the time of writing and the time of printing, everyone may have boogied down the road to another hangout. A currently popular place is *Café Dallas* at Old Town Shopping Center, Greenville (987-0066). A long-established private club, *elan* has a stiff one-night guest fee. Worth it, though. Visiting celebrities dance here. Expressway and Greenville Ave. (692-9855). The best jazz clubs are: *Strictly Tabu*, 4111 Lomo Alto (522-8101), and *Bagatelle*, 4925 Greenville (692-8224). On Thursdays and Sundays, Hal Baker and the Gloom Chasers play rousing Dixieland favorites at *Greenville Bar and Grill*, 2821 Greenville (823-6691). For country and western acts, there's the *Longhorn Ballroom*, 216 Corinth (428-3128), and the *Western Place*, 661 Skillman (341-7100). Number one rock club in Dallas is *Mother Blues*, 4015 Lemmon Ave. (528-1440).

SINS: Humility has never been Texas' greatest virtue, especially regarding things Texan. In fact, Texans' *pride* is *pride;* and all the "biggests" and "bests" have become something of a laughing matter, even among Texans — and no less in Dallas–Fort Worth than in other cities in the state. This metropolitan area's special claims to fame are the State Fair of Texas (16 days in October); the Dallas Cowboys Cheerleaders, who have been arousing *lust* in the hearts of men ever since they tried to cover themselves with those brief bits of satin that pass for shorts; and *Neiman-Marcus*, where you'll see the idle rich, among others, giving free rein to their acquisitive instincts, and hang the cost. Some dare call that *avarice* — but they're not the most popular people in Dallas, either.

LOCAL SERVICES: Business Services – ESP, Inc., 8585 Stemmons (661-8736).

Mechanics – For American cars, Exxon Car Care, 5748 Live Oak (823-1351). For foreign cars, World Auto Service, 11425 Denton Dr. (243-6441).

Babysitting – Babysitters of Dallas, Inc., 5622 Dyer (692-1354).

BEST IN TOWN

CHECKING IN: Dallas is the third most popular convention city in the country, and while it's not exactly overflowing with excellent hotels, it does have a considerable number of comfortable accommodations. Some hotels cater almost exclusively to conventions, so it may be difficult to book as an individual. It will save a lot of trouble if you inquire ahead of time. Expect to spend $85 and up a night for a double at those places we call expensive; between $40 and $60, moderate; under $30, inexpensive.

The Loew's Anatole – Loew's new addition to the luxurious hotel scene has two ultra-contemporary atriums with restaurants, bars, and tennis and racquetball courts. The red brick exterior looks more like a New York hospital than a Dallas hotel, but many residents find it a welcome change from monolithic rectangles of sparkling tinted glass. Located across the street from the Apparel Mart, it fills its 1,001 rooms during conventions. 2201 Stemmons Fwy. (748-1200). Expensive.

Fairmont – This is far and away the best hotel in Dallas. The morning paper is served with coffee, the restaurant is excellent, and you can generally indulge yourself at this luxurious 600-room hotel. The most expensive hotel room in Dallas is the $500-a-night Fairmont Suite. If you're willing to go that far, you might want to consider the Weekend Package, which includes a chauffeured limousine and dinner served in your suite — all for $1,000. Sunday brunch in the *Venetian Room* can give you a taste of elegance for considerably less money. 1717 N Akard St. (748-5454). Expensive.

Hyatt Regency – The Hyatt has become one of Dallas's most popular hotels and with the Fairmont and the Loew's Anatole, it gives the city a first-class triumvirate. It has an eye-catching silver-burnished exterior, a soaring atrium lobby, and a rooftop restaurant with a dynamite view. The second most expensive hotel room in Dallas is the $450-a-night Split Level Deluxe suite, with three connecting bedrooms, parlor, den, and wet bar. If you're just looking for someplace to shower, sleep, and perhaps watch television, it should be adequate. *Fausto's* restaurant has extravagant service, magnificent silver, with food that doesn't quite come up to the surroundings. 400 S Houston St. (651-1234). Expensive.

The Summit – The *Summit* is one of the most attractive hotels in the city. Its 379 rooms include many very expensive luxury suites. The six-story hotel contains *Gabriel's* restaurant and club, a sidewalk café, and a breakfast room. 2645 LBJ Fwy. (243-3363). Expensive.

Plaza of the Americas – Dallas's latest comer to the booming local-hotel scene is part of the British Trusthouse Forte chain. Management was given carte blanche to hire the best help available — and that they did, from the staff at the all-night restaurant to the chef in the posh *Café Royal,* which features nouvelle cuisine and a well-stocked wine cellar. The *Plaza* has brought class back to downtown Dallas after dark — something that has been sorely lacking. 650 N Pearl Blvd. at Bryan St. (747-7222). Expensive.

The Mansion on Turtle Creek – Dallas's newest luxury address exudes the kind of elegance and taste for which the *21 Club* management team is justifiably famous. Custom-made furnishings, opulent bathrooms, and attentive service make this the best of the city's deluxe hotels. 2821 Turtle Creek Blvd. (559-2100). Expensive.

Amfac Hotel – This hotel is another popular convention spot. In addition to meeting rooms, it has a swimming pool, bar, and 24-hour café. Kids under 13, accompanied by an adult, free. At the Dallas–Fort Worth Airport (453-8400). Expensive.

Adolphus – An elder giant among Dallas hotels, this 800-room colossus has a respectable dining room, supper club, café, and a sauna. 1321 Commerce St. (742-8200). Expensive.

Stoneleigh Terrace – A comfortable alternative to modern, mass-produced hotels, this 155-room older building has large rooms, a gracious exterior, and convenient downtown location. The two stone lions at the front entrance will make New Yorkers homesick for the Fifth Avenue library. 2927 Maple St. (742-7111). Moderate.

La Quinta Motor Inns – If you're looking for a clean, inconspicuous place to sleep, try any of these motels. 4400 N Central Expy. (821-4220); Dallas–Fort Worth Airport, 4105 N Airport Fwy., Irving (252-6546); I-30 at NW 19th St., Grand Prairie (641-3021); 13685 N Central Expy. (361-8200). Moderate.

Metro Park Inn – If you're coming to Dallas–Fort Worth to see the Texas Rangers or ride the roller coaster at Six Flags Over Texas, this also offers decent, simple accommodations. A good budget choice. 150 rooms. 1000 N Watson Rd., Arlington (817 649-8811). Inexpensive.

EATING OUT: The restaurant business is booming in Dallas. You can eat in a superlative place every night for a month and not repeat. Expect to spend $45 or more for two in those places we've listed as expensive; between $25 and $40, moderate; under $20, inexpensive. Prices do not include wine, drinks, or tips. (Parts of Dallas are "dry." Some restaurants serve drinks; at others, you must bring your own liquor. Call in advance to be sure.)

Pyramid Room – A lavish French restaurant in the Fairmont Hotel. The pheasant roasted in a clay crock, sealed with pastry, and the filet of sole with mushrooms, shrimp, and lobster baked in pastry are two of the exotic entrées regularly featured on the menu. The pompano flambéed in Pernod is superb, too, as are the famous soufflé desserts. The tab for two easily runs over $100. Open daily. Reservations a must. Major credit cards. 1717 N Akard St. (748-5454). Expensive.

The Mansion – As implied in the name, it's a refurbished private mansion, newly inaugurated by the management of New York's august *21 Club.* Quiet elegance, nouvelle cuisine, and polished service make dining here a memorable experience. 2821 Turtle Creek (phone: 559-2100). Expensive.

Mario's – This delightful restaurant offers a mixture of Italian and French dishes. The Scallopini alla Marsala — tender escallops of veal sautéed in butter and drenched in a rich wine-and-mushroom sauce — is the best in town. Major credit cards. 135 Turtle Creek Village (521-1135). Expensive.

Jean-Claude – This may be the best restaurant in Dallas. Main course dishes generally include stuffed lamb, roast duck with ginger sauce, medallions of veal in a cream-and-mushroom sauce, and pompano with a sauce mousseline. Reservations should be made at least 2 weeks in advance. Closed Sundays and Mondays. Most major credit cards. 2520 Cedar Springs (653-1823). Expensive.

Old Warsaw – One of the oldest restaurants in Dallas, with a special *Nouvelle cuisine* selection of low (or should we say lower) calorie dishes. Pâté of duck, côte de veau, and watercress purée are among the intriguing delicacies offered on the regular menu. Open daily. Reservations advised. Major credit cards. 2510 Maple (528-0032). Expensive.

Stagecoach Inn – For a taste of real Texas cooking, try this amiable eatery about one and a half hours' drive south of Dallas. Meals are served home-style, and after sampling the delicious fried chicken and homemade breads and pastries, you'll trundle away warm and satisfied. Reservations recommended. Off I-35 South, in Salado (817 947-5111). Moderate.

Houlihan's Old Place – A pleasant-enough branch of the Houlihan restaurant chain, with Tiffany glass and potted plant decor. Since it's open late, this is a good place for quiche, salad, dessert, or filling sandwiches. The frozen strawberry daiquiris should not be missed. Open daily. Reservations recommended at dinner. Major credit cards. 4 Northpark E (361-9426). Moderate.

Kirby's – A favorite choice of Dallas steak lovers, Kirby's is an old steak house with a warm and charming atmosphere. You might well fall in love with it and never want to eat anywhere else. It's a very relaxing, mellow place — and for many people it's the only place for steak and baked potatoes with all the trimmings. The creamy garlic salad dressing turns lettuce and other vegetables into a mouth-watering experience. (If you are not fond of garlic, you'd better skip it.) The "extra-cut" sirloin is tops. Closed Mondays. Reservations recommended. Major credit cards. 3715 Greenville Ave. (823-7296). Moderate.

Josef's – Some say that this is the best seafood restaurant in Dallas, with its Creole soup, smoked trout, and other fresh fish entrées. Open daily. Reservations advised. Major credit cards. 2719 McKinney (826-5560). Moderate.

Calluaud – This intimate restaurant in a lovely little frame house with wooden floors is run by Guy and Martine Calluaud, who are descended from a long line of master French cooks. The menu changes daily. The veal Normande with Calvados brandy is inebriating. Reservations advised. Major credit cards. 2619 McKinney Ave. (823-5380). Moderate.

Chiquita's – One of the best Mexican restaurants in town, this boisterous place isn't a Tex-Mex Americanized food joint — everything here is *really* Mexican. The carne asada Tampico-style is a filet sliced to triple its usual length and broiled over a hickory fire, then served with green peppers, onions, and soft tacos topped with ranchero sauce. Far and away one of the finest Mexican restaurants north of the border. Closed Sundays. Reservations are not accepted, but some major credit cards are. 3325 Oak Lawn (521-0721). Moderate.

TGI Friday's – The bastion of the Greenville Avenue nightlife scene, and one of the first restaurants to settle in that location. It specializes in the simple things: good food and drink at reasonable price, in a spirited atmosphere. Open daily. Major credit cards. 5500 Greenville Ave. (363-5353). Moderate.

Ranchman's Café – About an hour and a half's drive north of Dallas, you'll come to the town of Ponder (pop. 208) and one of the most splendid little home-town cafés in Texas. You'll swear you've stepped back into the era of Bonnie and Clyde. In fact, the bank building at the corner was used as a set in the film. The small restaurant's old wooden screen doors open into a room with longhorns and stirrups on the wall and an authentic country-and-western jukebox. Specialties are chicken-fried steak, T-bone steak, french fries, and possibly the best pecan pie in the country, along with other home-baked fruit pies. Open daily. No reservations. No credit cards. Main St. (479-8221). Inexpensive.

Angelo's – The best barbecue in Fort Worth has a huge stuffed bear wearing an *Angelo's* T-shirt holding his arms out to welcome you and a big moose head right inside the main door. The chopped beef barbecue is the best of all. Ribs served after 3:30 PM. Closed Sundays. No reservations. No credit cards. 2533 White Settlement Rd. (332-0357). Inexpensive.

Hunan – The best Chinese restaurant in the area, serving Szechwan hot dishes like sizzling rice soup, beef Hunan, Tung-an chicken, River Shang pork in black bean sauce, and spicy, crispy whole fish. Don't be alarmed by the flashy cuisine. The food is authentic. Open daily. Reservations suggested. Major credit cards. 5214 Greenville Ave. (369-4578). Inexpensive.

S&D Oyster House – The restaurant's decor will remind you of almost every cozy little seafood joint you ever found along the Gulf Coast. It's almost always crowded, and reservations are not accepted. Offerings include raw oysters, boiled and fried shrimp, and three kinds of broiled fresh fish. A house specialty is seafood gumbo. Only beer and wine. Major credit cards. 2701 McKinney Ave. (823-6350). Inexpensive.

El Taxco – Possibly the best Tex-Mex restaurant in Dallas and the proof is in the chili and hot sauce. The decor may not be much — plaster donkeys, paper flowers, and Day-Glo colors prevail — but it lends just the right amount of garish ambience. Owner Joe Navarro is available most nights to escort you to your table. No reservations. Some credit cards. 2126 N St. Paul St. (742-0747). Inexpensive.

La Cave – This is a French wine bar where you can get wine or champagne by the glass. For $1.50 cork fee, you can buy a bottle of anything in stock and drink it with your meal, to the music of Edith Piaf and other French artistes. Intimate, artistic, quiet, and *very* romantic. La Cave serves cheese, pâté, tureen du chef, and other cold entrées. Reservations recommended for parties of six or more. Major credit cards accepted. 2166 N Henderson (826-2190). Inexpensive.

DENVER

Denver sits a mile above sea level, sprawled across a sweeping plateau at the exact point where the high plains roll westward out of Kansas and Nebraska to splash against the Rocky Mountains. Those 5,280 feet give residents a healthy lift that must be more than just psychological, because first-time visitors invariably comment on how *healthy* everyone looks — with a smiling, rugged, outdoorsy appeal that speaks of long acquaintanceship with Mother Nature and the code of the Old West. It can't be true that all Denver residents (1.6 million in the metropolitan area) are old mountaineers, but a goodly number of them are up here, way above the plains, for just one reason — the city's envied, spectacular toehold on the foot of the Rockies.

To be in Denver is to be aware, first and foremost, of the perennially snow-capped mountains that form the Continental Divide. The mountains look deceptively close, and many an unwary visitor has got the notion to stroll over to the foothills. It's 30 minutes by six-lane, interstate highway, which is close enough by car or bus, but not a morning's promenade. The RTD (Regional Transportation District) sends buses past the foothills (see *Getting Around*) to serve the communities where thousands of people reside. It's called "living up in the hills."

These nearby hills are really responsible for Denver's reputation as a city with a phenomenal climate. People used to flock to Denver for its pure air. Nowadays, unfortunately, the city isn't much cleaner than any other large, urban area. The clean air is in the hills, and the climate that you'd like to take home with you comes from there, too. All those sufferers of emphysema and asthma who settled in the city 25 years ago are looking longingly toward Phoenix today, but their places are being taken by thousands of new immigrants looking longingly toward the mountains from the flatlands of the Midwest, the congested Eastern Seaboard, the rising New South, and even California. Even if it's true that downtown, as one disgruntled former resident complains, "on a clear day, you can see all of four blocks," there are plenty of folks who don't care.

Denver is a relatively young city, under constant construction. But even as buildings spring up around town in spurts of modern high-rises, efforts at renewing and recalling Denver's Wild West, lusty past grow apace. Larimer Square, on Cherry Creek (where the city's first tents and cabins appeared in 1858), has been remodeled into an artistic little corner of funky curio shops and cafés that irrationally manages to serve contemporary Denver while providing a sense of what the city used to be like. If you visit Larimer Square immediately after a drive through the outskirts of town, dressed as all town outskirts are with garish drive-ins and shopping centers, you will be especially struck with the vividness of this recreation.

And though Denver's a lot more like LA than the Old West, you'll still find plenty of people trucking through the streets in flannel shirts, blue jeans, cowboy hats, and boots. If this gives the impression that Denver is a cowtown, don't be fooled. It is not. The Union Stockyards are no longer here, and the only real cowboys and cowgirls on the streets come for a week in January to attend the National Western Stock Show and Rodeo. But people in Denver dress that way, perhaps because of the history of the place, and it makes them feel more at home to look the part. A lot of people drift into Denver to check out the action, and you'll no doubt see an interesting assortment of "Easy Rider" biker types, straight business people, long-haired ramblers on their way to look for jobs at the ski resorts, and the occasional chess hustler. (Chess hustlers, like pool hustlers, play the game for money, pretending at first that they don't know the moves. Denver is a hot town for chess hustlers, who are, as you might expect, a strange breed, often bearing PhDs in mathematics from places like MIT and Harvard. One of them recently brought home $300 after an afternoon at the board, and it was only his first day in town!)

Denver has come a long way since its beginnings as a group of log cabins and tents hugging the junction of the Platte River and Cherry Creek. The commercial center of the West, Denver houses more gold bullion than anywhere outside of Fort Knox (see *Special Places*). It has its own financial district, a new, modern art museum, Victorian mansions, and a zoo. But in spite of its green parks, small lakes, new 16th Street Mall, and tree-lined residential streets, there is no question that the best scenery is out of town. People come to Denver to get to the great outdoors, rather than to see the city environs. For instance, ten miles west of the city on I-70, you can see the futuristic house used as a location for Woody Allen's film "Sleeper." About eight miles further west, you can see the town of Idaho Springs, looking just like it did in "Downhill Racer." The old mining town is becoming a popular mountain retreat area, with houses sprouting from the hills, between the twisted scrub pine. The University of Denver ski team practices here in August, and it's a good place to watch, while you soak up some sun without having to go very far.

And that, in fact, is one of the best things about Denver: You don't have to go very far to find the legendary clear air, blue sky, and wide open spaces.

DENVER AT-A-GLANCE

SEEING THE CITY: The best view of Denver is from the top of the State Capitol rotunda, where you can see the Rockies to the west, the Great Plains stretching, like an ocean, to the east, and Denver itself sprawled below. On the 13th step of the State Capitol, you'll find an inscription informing you that you are exactly one mile above sea level. Between E 14th and E Colfax Aves. (866-2604).

SPECIAL PLACES: It's a pleasure to walk around Denver. The downtown section has a number of Victorian mansions, as well as the city's public institutions and commercial buildings.

United States Mint – Appropriately enough for a city which made its fortune in gold, Denver still has more of it than any place else in the country outside of Fort Knox. On the outside, the Mint is a relatively unimpressive white sandstone federal building with Doric arches over the windows. Inside, you can see money being stamped and printed, and catch a glimpse of gold bullion, although the stuff on display is only a fraction of the total stored here. Most impressive is the room full of money just waiting to be counted. Closed Saturdays and Sundays. Free. On Delaware St. between Colfax and 14th (837-3582).

Denver Art Museum – That imposing, rather odd building sparkling in the sun down the street from the Mint is the Denver Art Museum, a supermodern structure covered with one million glittering glass tiles. Designed by Gio Ponti, its interior is just as spectacular as its exterior. Be sure to visit the American Indian collection on the second floor — it has superlative costumes, basketry, rugs, and totem poles. You can stop for lunch or a light snack at the museum's outdoor terrace restaurant. Closed Mondays. Voluntary donations. W 14th Ave. and Bannock St. (575-2793).

Denver Public Library – This $3 million building houses books, photographs, and historical documents related to the history of the West. The lower level, known as the basement, contains a splendid children's collection. Exhibits on Western life are on display on the main floor, and rare book lovers willing to hunt for the special collections will be delighted. Closed Sundays in June, July, and August. Free. 1357 Broadway (573-5152).

Colorado History Museum – The new Heritage Center has exhibits on people who've contributed to Colorado history, period costumes from the early frontier days, and Indian relics. Many of the costumes were donated by members of old Denver families whose predecessors actually wore them. Life-size dioramas show how gold miners, pioneers, and Mesa Verde cliff dwellers used to live. Open daily. Free. 1400 Broadway (866-3682).

State Capitol – The rotunda looks like the dome of the Capitol in Washington, DC, coated with $50,900 worth of Colorado gold leaf (the Capitol's marble staircases are impressive enough to rate a look even if you don't want to climb to the top). Denver has such a wealth of federal agencies and workers that it's nicknamed "Little Washington." Open daily. Free. Between E 14th Ave. and Colfax, at Sherman Ave. (866-2604).

Molly Brown House – When gold miner Johnny Brown and his wife Molly moved into their Capitol Hill mansion, Denver society snubbed them as *nouveau riche.* But Molly earned her place in city history, and, ironically, it's her former house which is on the "most visited" list. She is remembered for her gutsy flair and keen intelligence, and for taking charge of a lifeboat when the *Titanic* sank, commanding the men to row while she held her chinchilla cape over a group of children to keep them warm. Which is how she came to be known as the "unsinkable Molly Brown." Open daily. Admission charge. 1340 Pennsylvania St. (832-1421).

Financial District – Seventeenth Street is the center of Denver's financial district, and there are quite a number of tall, modern bank buildings which will give you a proper sense of that economic stability and strength which characterizes such areas. During summer lunch hours, street musicians give outdoor concerts in the plazas outside the United Bank Center and the First National Bank of Denver. On top of the 30-story Security Life Building is the *Top of the Rockies* restaurant, another good place to get a bird's-eye view of the city. 1616 Glenarm Pl. (825-3321).

Larimer Street – Walk along the new 16th Street Mall to Larimer, Denver's most interesting shopping street. You'll pass the Daniels and Fisher Tower, a 1920s landmark said to be a copy of the campanile of Venice. It used to be the tallest building in town, but has been overshadowed by more modern edifices. Larimer Street is lined with fascinating art galleries, curio shops, silversmiths, and cafés. Most interesting is Larimer Square, where Mexican restaurants, crafts shops, and wine bars have been restored so that they retain the flavor of Denver's past (between 14th and 15th Sts.).

City Park – A 640-acre park with two lakes, spreading lawns, Denver's Museum of

Natural History known for its exhibits of animals in natural settings, and the Habitat Zoo. The museum was the first in the country to use curved backgrounds with reproductions of mountain flowers, shrubs, and smaller animals to give a real feeling of the natural environment. Exhibits of fossils, minerals, gold coins, and birds. Open daily. Free (575-3617). The Habitat Zoo has designed a number of natural mountain environments for its animals. Open daily. Admission charge. (575-2754).

■ **EXTRA SPECIAL:** There are so many gorgeous places to explore around Denver that it's almost unfair to single out any one in particular. *Rocky Mountain National Park* is, however, one of the most spectacular scenic areas of the United States, and it's a perfect choice for a day trip. Within its 264,000 acres are dozens of mountains over the 12,000-foot mark, among them Bighorn Mountain and Longs Peak. The interior of the park offers the opportunity to cross the Continental Divide. You can rent horses and camping equipment at Estes Park at the northeast corner of the national park. To get there, take I-25 north for 50 miles, then rt. 34 west. (See *Rocky Mountain National Park,* DIRECTIONS, for more information.)

SOURCES AND RESOURCES

For brochures, maps, and general information, contact the Colorado Hospitality Center, 225 W Colfax Ave. (892-1112). It will also provide up-to-the-minute reports on ski conditions, rodeos, and local festivals.

Guestguide Magazine is the best local guide to the Denver area, available at newsstands.

All telephone numbers are in the 303 area code unless otherwise indicated.

For Local Coverage – *Denver Post,* evening daily; *Rocky Mountain News,* morning daily; *Denver* Magazine, monthly; *Colorado* Magazine, monthly.

For Food – *Denver* Magazine; *Denver Post,* Friday edition.

CLIMATE AND CLOTHES: Because of the altitude, Denver is pretty dry. Even when the temperature hits the 90s and even the low 100s in summer, it won't be intolerable. Nights cool to the 70s. In fall and winter, the days are sunny and in the 60s, but nights can drop to the 20s. Denver is not usually hit by those mountain blizzards that the Weather Service reports as "sweeping the Rockies." And it only gets an average of 14 inches of precipitation throughout the year, so you'll hardly need an umbrella.

GETTING AROUND: Bus – RTD (Regional Transportation District) runs buses throughout the Denver area. For information, contact the Downtown Information Center, 1524 California St. (759-1000).

Taxi – Taxis cannot be hailed in the streets. Call Yellow Cab (892-1212) or Zone Cab (861-2323). There are cab stands at Brown Palace, Hilton, Fairmont, Marriott, and Cosmopolitan hotels, and at the airport.

Car Rental – All major national firms represented.

MUSEUMS: For a complete description of the Denver Art Museum, Colorado History Museum, Molly Brown House, Museum of Natural History, and Planetarium, see *Special Places*. Other notable museums are:

Buffalo Bill Museum, on Lookout Mountain is interesting, especially for children (526-0488). Buffalo Bill is buried on the grounds.

The Colorado Railroad Museum, 17555 W 44th Ave. (279-4591).

MAJOR COLLEGES AND UNIVERSITIES: The University of Denver makes its home within the city proper, at S University Blvd. and E Evans Ave. (753-1964). The University of Colorado is 20 miles northwest of the city on rt. 36, in Boulder (492-0111). The US Air Force Academy's bright, clean, spacious campus is 68 miles south of Denver on I-25, near Colorado Springs (472-1818).

SPECIAL EVENTS: The *National Western Stock Show and Rodeo* in January lasts a week, and attracts cowboys and cowgirls — cowfolk — from all over. The Denver Art Museum's annual exhibit of Western art runs from January through March. *Easter Sunrise Service* at Red Rocks Natural Amphitheater attracts thousands. In July and August, the University of Colorado at Boulder presents its annual *Shakespeare Festival.* And Larimer Square is the site of the *Oktoberfest* in guess what month?

SPORTS: Baseball – Denver *Bears* play at Mile High Stadium, 1700 Federal Blvd. (433-8645).

Football – Denver *Broncos* also play at Mile High Stadium, 1700 Federal Blvd. (433-7466).

Basketball – Denver *Nuggets* play at McNichols Sports Arena, 1635 Clay St. (893-6767).

Hockey – *Colorado Rockies* home rink is at McNichols Sports Arena, 1635 Clay St. (534-7825).

Racing – Greyhounds race at Mile High Kennel Club, 6200 Dahlia Rd. (288-1591). No one under 21 is admitted.

Bicycling – Bikes can be rented from Colorado Mo-Ped, 1515 E Colfax (832-6021), and LCA Bicycles, Inc., 4261 S Broadway (781-7772).

Fishing – There's good fishing at Dillon Reservoir west of Denver on I-70, and Cherry Creek Reservoir, a few miles south of the city on I-25.

Golf – Among the 50 golf courses in the Denver area, best are Kennedy, 10500 E Hampden Ave. (751-0311); Park Hill, 3500 Colorado Blvd. (333-5411); and Wellshire, 3333 S Colorado Blvd. (757-1352).

Skiing – Colorado ski country is famous all over the world. The slopes closest to the city are in Loveland Basin, 30 miles west on I-70; nearby Arapaho Basin; and Winter Park, west on I-70, then north on rt. 40. Former President Ford used to give news conferences on the slopes at Vail, a resort 60 miles west of Denver on I-70. Internationally acclaimed Aspen/Snowmass are about 135 miles southwest of Denver on I-70 and Hwy. 82. (See *Downhill Skiing,* DIVERSIONS, p. 486.)

Tennis – The best public courts are Tennis World, E Yale Ave. and S Monaco Pkwy. (758-7080), and Mountain Shadows Tennis Club, 2650 Alkire St. (279-2589).

THEATER: For complete up-to-the-minute listings on theatrical and musical events, see local publications listed above. The *Bonfils Theater* is home to the *Civic Theater Group*, which presents Broadway productions from October to June, E Colfax and Elizabeth Aves. (322-7725). *Elitch Gardens* is one of the oldest summer theaters in the country, 4620 W 38th Ave. (458-8801). The University of Colorado at Boulder hosts a *Shakespeare Festival* every summer (see *Special Events*). The *Helen G. Bonfils Theater,* which is part of the Denver Center for the Performing Arts, has a very good repertory company, 14th and Curtis Sts. (893-4111).

MUSIC: *Red Rocks Amphitheater* is the site of big-name rock concerts. Park of the Red Rocks, US 285 (575-2637). The *Denver Symphony* plays from October through May at Boetcher Hall, 14th and Arapahoe Sts. (292-1584). (Free concerts in City Park in June, July, and August.) *Heri-*

tage Square Opera House south of the town of Golden, west on rt. 6, stages opera (279-7881).

NIGHTCLUBS AND NIGHTLIFE: The best clubs in town are *Moulin Rouge,* Fairmont Hotel, 1750 Welton St. (571-5821), and *Turn of the Century,* 7300 E Hampden Ave. (758-4333).

SINS: To arrive in town only to discover that all the Texans got here first and that ground-hugging clouds of smog are a fact of life — that's an introduction to *anger* in Denver. Residents cool their outrage with *pride* thinking of Colorado's 52 mountain peaks at least 14,000 feet high. *Lust* flourishes even in the mountains: Sid King claims that the girls at his *Crazy Horse Bar*, 1211 E Colfax (831-9936), are the most beautiful in the world and nice enough to be your sister. No cover — top or bottom. Denver's red-light district is on East Colfax near the Crazy Horse.

LOCAL SERVICES: Business Services – Executive Services, 475 17 St. (534-3840); Record Executive Services, 11000 E Yale Ave. (750-8083).

Mechanic – May D & F Auto Center, 14th St. and Tremont Pl. (573-1502).

Babysitting – Columbine Sitters, 343 S Humboldt St. (722-8364); Holiday Governess, 9355 W Utah Pl. (988-9458).

BEST IN TOWN

CHECKING IN: Accommodations in Denver range from the ultra-deluxe, old-fashioned Brown Palace to the modern, comfortable Hilton, Radisson, and Marina. One of the best values for your dollar, we think, is the Holiday Châlet, an apartment hotel where two people can stay overnight for $30 or less. Expect to pay between $70 and $105 at those places listed as expensive; between $40 and $50 at those in the moderate category; about $35 at places noted as inexpensive.

Brown Palace – Built in the 1880s, it was one of the first hotels to have a nine-story-high atrium lobby with balconies rimming it on every floor. The 800 rooms have been remodeled several times. 17th St. and Tremont Pl. (825-3111). Expensive.

Hilton Hotel – With an outdoor swimming pool and an ice skating rink that becomes a terrace in the summer, the standard, self-contained Hilton environment naturally includes a dining room, coffee shop, and cocktail lounge with entertainment. 864 rooms. 16th and Court Sts. (893-3333). Expensive.

Fairmont Hotel – Recently opened in 1979, this $50-million, 26-floor beauty with 540 rooms has the latest of everything, including telephones in the bathrooms. Its *Moulin Rouge* dinner club and cocktail lounge has top entertainment, and the *Marquis Room* challenges *Palace Arms* as the swankiest and finest eating spot in Denver. 1750 Welton St. (571-1200). Expensive.

Downtown Marriott Hotel – Opened in February 1982, this is the newest in the worldwide chain and occupies the lower 20 floors of the 42-story Arco Tower in the heart of downtown Denver. Amenities include underground shopping and restaurants. 1701 California St. (825-1300). Expensive.

Denver Marina Hotel – If you like being around money, you'll love it here. The hotel is just opposite the US Mint. If your pets like being around money, they'll be happy here, too. The 260-room Marina has no restrictions on four-legged creatures. Facilities include a heated pool on the roof, a dining room, coffee shop, and lounge. 303 W Colfax (572-3623). Moderate.

Holiday Châlet – An inexpensive place to stay, with ten units, eight of which have two rooms with kitchenettes. You'll have to put your animals up at the Marina; the Holiday Châlet does not accept pets. 1820 E Colfax (321-9975). Inexpensive.

EATING OUT: Gone are the days when eating out in Denver meant broiling mule steak over an open fire and spicing your meat with gunpowder. (Salt and pepper were scarce in the Old West.) Nowadays, there's quite a cosmopolitan selection of cuisines, and two people can generally eat well for around $30. You can expect to pay more than that at the *Palace Arms* and *Marquis Room,* the only expensive places listed; between $30 and $35 at those places in the moderate category; inexpensive, under $20.

Palace Arms – Cuisine here might be called home-grown French. By which we mean Rocky Mountain trout meunière and Western steak with French sauces. The crowd here is very chic; dress up. Men are required to wear a coat and tie, even at lunch. Open daily. Reservations required. Credit cards. 17th and Tremont (825-3111).

Marquis Room – This restaurant in the Fairmont Hotel is the new and strong competition for the *Palace Arms.* It serves fine Continental and French cuisine in an elegant setting. Open daily for dinner; no lunch on Sunday. Reservations necessary. Major credit cards. 1750 Welton St. (571-5825). Expensive.

Downtown Broker – Tucked into an area that was once the basement vault and boardroom of a bank, you eat here in the cubicles people once used to peer into their safety boxes. This quaint touch of historical voyeurism heightens the palate, we think, and gives an added dimension to roast prime ribs and shrimp, both of which are house specialties. (A bowl of shrimp is included with dinner.) Reservations required. Closed Sundays. Major credit cards. 17th and Champa Sts. (893-5065). Moderate.

Buckhorn Exchange – Even though it's not located in a convenient downtown setting, you'll find the trip well worth the effort. Denver residents have been coming here for "umpteen million years," to feast on steaks in the shadows of big game trophy heads. A Denver tradition. Open daily. Reservations recommended. Major credit cards. 1000 Osage St. (534-9505). Moderate.

Fisherman's Cove – Although some people are cautious of inland seafood restaurants, the trout and lobster here swim in separate pools, and you can't get 'em any fresher than that, even in New England. Pick your own and enjoy it among Cape Cod knickknacks and fishnet lining the walls. Closed major holidays. Reservations required. Major credit cards. 1512 Curtis (893-1512). Moderate.

Gasho of Japan – Specializing in teriyaki, sashimi, and sukiyaki, the chefs here chop and prepare shrimp, vegetables, and other ingredients by your table. Open daily. Reservations advised. Major credit cards. 1627 Curtis St., at Prudential Plaza (892-5625). Moderate.

Emerson Street East – Sports pages decorate the walls, steak and prime ribs decorate the plates, and a lively crowd comes to savor the action. There's live music weekdays after 9 PM and generally a heavy crowd in the lounge. Open daily. Reservations recommended for dinner. Major credit cards. 900 E Colfax (832-1349). Moderate.

Apple Tree Shanty – A pristine cottage on Colfax. The house specialty is barbecue ribs, pork, and chicken, cooked tenderly over an apple wood fire, garnished with a mild sauce. Closed Tuesdays. No reservations. Major credit cards. 8710 E Colfax (333-3223). Moderate.

Mama Elena's – A small but authentic Mexican restaurant where most dishes are cooked to order. Closed Sundays in winter. No reservations. No credit cards. 4575 E Colfax Ave. (321-0146). Inexpensive.

Café Nepenthes – Exotic salads of spinach, carrot, fruit, artichoke, and greens fill a large portion of a mainly vegetarian menu, but if you insist on meat, there's turkey. The café offers live music at night, and is open till 4 AM Fridays and Saturdays. Open daily. Reservations are not necessary. No credit cards. 1416 Market St. (534-5423). Inexpensive.

DETROIT

Poor mercurial Detroit. When its auto industry is percolating, there is dancing in the streets. When it isn't, the bread line forms to the right. Gluttonous prosperity or hard times — Detroit has tasted both, and usually in larger doses than other big cities with a more diversified industrial underpinning. Cars have been both Detroit's lifeblood and its curse.

The inbound drive along Interstate 94 from Detroit's Metropolitan Airport provides more than subtle shadings of the Motor City, capital of the world's auto industry. Low-slung buildings of auto suppliers crowd the banks of the highway. At one bend is a giant tire the size of a ferris wheel. Farther along, the freeway skirts the leviathan Rouge manufacturing complex of Ford Motor Company, the largest industrial complex in the world, and the road's endless automobile billboards tick off auto production. But more than a digital readout, they are Detroit's electrocardiogram. During the last few years, a period of disastrously low sales and thorny labor disputes, Detroit's billboard odometers told the sad news. But Detroit always manages to hang in there, whether its vital signs are weak or strong.

Like most of the Great Lakes country, Detroit's roots are French. When the King of France started wearing a beaver hat late in the 17th century, everyone in French society had to have one, too. This made trapping and exporting beaver fur a very lucrative venture for French trappers around Montreal and Quebec. Like any successful business, the beaver trade fell prey to unscrupulous operators, and entire canoeloads of pelts were hijacked along the Great Lakes. In 1701, Antoine de la Mothe Cadillac — who was to have an automobile named after him 200 years later — arrived in Detroit to protect legitimate voyageurs and their cargoes. Cadillac picked the strait between Lake St. Clair and Lake Erie for Fort Pontchartrain d'Etroit ("on the Straits"). After the French and Indian War, the fort became British, and then was taken over by the Americans in 1796, 13 years after the Revolutionary War ended.

If its roots are French, subsequent Detroit history — its tree and branch — is indomitably American. Detroit's destiny was charted for it at the turn of this century when Henry Ford took the horseless carriage concept and applied mass production techniques. Detroit — and the world — hasn't been the same since. A historical plaque marks the site of the little two-story plant in uptown Highland Park where Model T's first sputtered to life.

Detroit's brontosaurus car-making plants went from wheels to weapons during World War II. Tides of war workers poured into the city and population zoomed. There was plenty of everything for everybody. That was, until Detroit fell into the same lockstep of other American cities. In the quietude of the 1950s, a middle-class exodus from the city began, and by the 1960s Detroit had become a case of classic American malaise: rings of wealthy suburbs around a neglected inner city — and its even more neglected residents. Degeneration of the core city has had severe consequences for Detroit. The mass exodus spurred city planners to allocate funds for endless concrete miles of freeways to connect the suburbs around the city, leaving the downtown area to shrivel.

At last something has been done, and Detroit is coming back. The city recently has seen an explosion of new restaurants. Downtown districts left for dead have been reborn. There is a profusion of new building, especially on the riverfront, and a recharged feeling among Detroiters, though not quite epidemic yet. Once again, downtown commands its share of nightlife.

Lording over the whole Detroit renaissance is the fittingly named Renaissance Center (known locally as RenCen), six circular towers of dark reflective glass surrounding an even taller tower, the 73-floor Westin Hotel, formerly the Detroit Plaza. The dramatic office-shopping-hotel complex soars regally on the lip of the Detroit River, which separates the city from Canada. Trollies bounce down Washington Boulevard past colorful sidewalk cafés to the riverfront and the doorstep of RenCen. Hart Plaza, on the riverfront, is for people-watching. Its centerpiece is the Dodge Fountain, and in summer, brown-bagging office workers flood the place on weekdays, while ethnic festivals take over on weekends. During the winter, a subterranean ice rink is popular.

Neighborhoods in the shadows of RenCen are enjoying new life. In Bricktown and the Warehouse District you'll find new restaurants hopping inside old buildings; Greektown is a long downtown block of some of Detroit's best restaurants, as Greek as Zorba and as energized as Disney World.

After cars, Detroit is a sports town. The Joe Louis Arena, named for one of Detroit's native sons, is home to Detroit's pro hockey team, the Red Wings, and, of course, to boxing. It's also on the revitalized riverfront, alongside sprawling Cobo Hall, the city's cavernous convention center. There's the Pontiac Silverdome, with the world's largest inflated roof, for football and basketball. Detroit's Cultural Center and its new Medical Center hug the city's main thoroughfare, Woodward Avenue, which separates Detroit's east and west sides.

Detroiters have a lot of good reasons to like themselves and where they live. After all, Detroit gave the world the Motown sound and the first ice cream soda and the first jazz club and cold duck and the most pistachios this side of the Middle East. Now, with the renaissance, there's even more to be proud of.

DETROIT AT-A-GLANCE

SEEING THE CITY: The best view of the city is from the top of the 73-story *Westin Hotel.* Part of the Renaissance Center, it is one of the city's most stylish and dramatic new creations. Views are from the hotel's top three floors, called the Summit, with a revolving restaurant and cocktail lounge and an observation deck. Philip A. Hart Plaza on Jefferson at St. Antoine (568-8000).

SPECIAL PLACES: Down on the ground, Civic Center is a good place to begin sightseeing. We've divided the city into Civic Center, Cultural Center, and other Special Places.

CIVIC CENTER

Renaissance Center – Detroit's very own Oz, this city-within-the-city dominates Detroit's skyline and dramatizes its rebirth. Dining, entertainment, designer boutiques, and more make RenCen tick. It's somehow tied together by a maze of walkways, atriums, gardens — even an indoor lake. Prediction: With seven circular buildings to walk around in, you'll get lost. Everybody does. Tours are available (568-7800). Jefferson Ave. between Randolf and Beaubien Sts.

Philip A. Hart Plaza – This once ragtag area of waterfront is now an upbeat people-place designed by international sculptor Isamu Noguchi. What it lacks in grass, this paved esplanade makes up in action. The $30 million Dodge Fountain spouts 30 computer-controlled water displays. It's also the home of Detroit's summer ethnic festivals of food and entertainment. The Detroit River is alongside, with Windsor, Ontario, in the background.

Cobo Hall — Washington Boulevard Trolley – A charming, antique trolley car wends its way south from Grand Circus Park along Washington Boulevard and east to the Renaissance Center. (The conductor wears 1890 regalia.) The trolley runs through a new downtown section of sidewalk cafés, specialty shops, and covered parkways, past St. Aloysius Church, the *Cadillac Hotel,* and various airline and travel agency offices.

CULTURAL CENTER

Detroit Institute of Arts – An unusual collection of Great Masters and modern artists lines the walls, halls, and gardens here. Walking through the Institute of Arts will give you the chance to examine Peter Breughel's Flemish masterpiece "Wedding Dance" and Mexican artist Diego Rivera's gripping, provocative frescoes on the industrial life of Detroit. In the garden is a bust of Lincoln by Gutzon Borglum, the artist who carved Mt. Rushmore. Closed Mondays. Donations accepted. 5200 Woodward Ave. (833-7900).

Detroit Public Library – This Italian Renaissance, white Vermont marble building houses books, paintings, stained glass windows, and mosaics. The Burton Historical Museum, an archive of material related to Detroit history, is one of the library's special collections. Closed Sundays, Mondays, and holidays. Free. Woodward and Kirby Aves. (833-1000).

Detroit Historical Museum – Collection of the early days of Detroit. There are models of early streets and railroads, period rooms, and exhibits on horseless carriages and automobiles. In the basement stands a permanent display of actual storefronts from bygone eras. Closed Sundays, Mondays, and holidays. Donations accepted. Woodward and Kirby Aves. (833-1805).

Wayne State University – Known for its innovative architecture rather than its football, a lot of new buildings have gone up on the campus in the past twenty years, among them a new medical center attached to the Wayne State medical school, reputed to be one of the best in the country. If you want a break from heavy culture, or if you enjoy a college atmosphere, take a stroll on campus. 650 W Kirby (577-2424).

Detroit Science Center – The "hands on" displays here allow visitors to demonstrate scientific principles for themselves. This $5 million complex also features a domed space theater. Closed Mondays. Admission charge. 5020 John R St. (833-1892).

Children's Museum – A planetarium and collections of puppets and small animals. Kids love the life-size sculpture of the horse near the entrance — it's made out of automobile bumpers. Closed Sundays. Free. 67 E Kirby Ave. (494-1210).

OTHER SPECIAL PLACES

Belle Isle – This beautiful island park in the middle of the Detroit River was originally allocated for pasture by Monsieur Cadillac himself. About two miles long, Belle Isle has a children's zoo; the Dossin Great Lakes Museum with displays of model ships (824-3157); an Aquarium with more than 300 different species of fish and crustaceans (267-7157); and the Remick Music Shell where the Detroit Concert Band plays for free in the summer. It's also a good place for picnics, biking, canoeing, and jogging. South of Jefferson, across the Gen. Douglas MacArthur Bridge (recreation office, 224-1180).

Boblo Boats – Every day between Memorial and Labor Days, two 1,200-passenger steamers leave downtown Detroit for Boblo Island. The 26-mile boat ride takes about an hour and a half each way — the most pleasant way to see industrial Detroit and Canada. At Boblo Island, you'll find a large amusement park, dolphins, sea lions, some historical exhibits, and local craftwork. Behind Cobo Hall, at 661 Civic Center Dr. (962-9622).

Greenfield Village and Henry Ford Museum – Local legend has it that when Henry Ford couldn't find a copy of McGuffey's *Reader,* he feared such examples of Americana would disappear entirely unless he founded a museum. The result is here — and as you might expect, it has hundreds of splendid, antique automobiles and thousands of early 20th-century machines. Next-door Greenfield Village is a unique collection of transplanted houses of historical interest. Henry Ford couldn't be stopped — he bought McGuffey's school and had it reconstructed, along with Thomas Edison's Menlo Park laboratory and the first boarding house to have electricity. An English shepherd's cottage and Noah Webster's house somehow found their way here, too. Separate admissions for Greenfield Village and Henry Ford Museum. South of Michigan Ave. between Oakwood Blvd. and Southfield Fwy., Dearborn (271-1620).

Fort Wayne – A friendly little fort, this one claims to have no battle scars. No one here ever fired a shot in anger through all the changes in ownership. French, British, American, and Canadian soldiers have all passed through this 15-acre fort in the line of duty. A museum focuses on Detroit's military history. Closed Sundays. Donations accepted. W Jefferson at Livernois, at the Detroit River (297-9360).

■ **EXTRA SPECIAL:** Detroit's biggest tourist attraction is just a mile away: *Canada.* In just a few minutes, you can enter a different country without having to go through the angst of getting a visa or changing money. You don't even need a passport if you're a US citizen — just a driver's license or birth certificate to prove citizenship. Don't expect any drastic change from Detroit, however. Windsor, Ontario, just across the river, is another automobile-producing city, with GM, Chrysler, and Ford Canadian plants. There's a great view of Detroit from Dieppe Gardens. If you're looking for bargains, Ontario is a great place to buy English woolens, glassware, and china. Windsor, Ontario, is literally on Detroit's doorstep, and you can get there by bus, tunnel, or the Ambassador Bridge. The bridge is like Rome — all freeways lead to it.

SOURCES AND RESOURCES

Metropolitan Detroit Convention and Visitors Bureau maintains a 24-hour "What's Line" directory of events (298-6262) and distributes free brochures and maps. 2 Jefferson Ave. (963-0879).

Visitor's Guide to Greater Detroit (Metropolitan Detroit Convention and Visitor's Bureau, free) is the best local guide to the area.

All telephone numbers are in the 313 area code unless otherwise indicated.

For Local Coverage – *Detroit Free Press,* morning daily; *Detroit News,* afternoon daily; *Royal Oak Tribune* and *Oakland Press* (Pontiac, both afternoon). There are also a number of suburban weeklies. *Key Magazine* is distributed free at hotels.

CLIMATE AND CLOTHES: Seasons usually procrastinate in Detroit. You might miss spring if you blink, and summer doesn't really peak until July. Autumn can be a day. The local joke is that if you don't like the weather, stick around because it'll change in five minutes. Temperatures range in the 70s and 80s in summer, and a light wrap might help for cool nights. Sub-freezing temperatures are often the rule in January and February, so bundle up.

GETTING AROUND: Bus – For information on bus routes and schedules, call the Department of Transportation (933-1300).

Taxi – Cabs can be hailed in the street, or picked up at the taxi stands in front of hotels. Some of the cabs are licensed to cross over to Canada. If you prefer to call for a cab, we suggest Checker (963-7000) or Radio Cab (833-1212).

Car Rental – Car rental agencies are plentiful, with all major firms represented.

MUSEUMS: Detroit's major museums — Detroit Historical Museum, Institute of the Arts, Children's Museum — cluster around the 5200 block of Woodward, and are described under *Special Places.*

MAJOR COLLEGES AND UNIVERSITIES: Wayne State University and medical complex, 650 W Kirby Ave. (577-3600); University of Detroit, 4001 W McNichols (927-1000); University of Michigan, 4901 Evergreen Rd. (271-2300); Oakland University, Walton Rd. at Squirrel Rd., Rochester (377-2100).

SPECIAL EVENTS: Some Detroit businesses offer tours. Though the list has shrunk in recent years, the Stroh Brewery, 909 E Elizabeth (961-5840), and the Hiram Walker Distillery, 2072 Riverside Dr. E, in Windsor, Ontario (519 965-6611), still offer a look around their plants. There are also good tours of Henry Ford's Fair Lane mansion, on the Dearborn campus of the University of Michigan (271-2300), and the Meadow Brook Hall mansion, Adams Rd., in Rochester (377-3140). *The Montreaux Jazz Festival* has become quite an event every year in the week surrounding Labor Day weekend. Concerts are held in Hart Plaza and at many other locations (259-8064, for details).

SPORTS: Detroit wouldn't be Detroit without its top major-league professional sports teams: the *Lions,* football; *Pistons,* basketball; *Red Wings,* hockey; and *Tigers,* baseball.

Football – *Lions* play in the 80,000-seat, covered Pontiac Silverdome. M-59 at Opdyke, Pontiac (335-4131).

Basketball – The *Pistons* play at the Silverdome, too (338-4667).

Hockey – *Red Wings* action is on the ice at Joe Louis Arena, Civic Center Drive (895-7000).

Baseball – Home base for the American League *Tigers* is Tiger Stadium, Michigan at Trumbull (963-9944).

Horse Racing – Thoroughbred and harness horses race at Detroit Race Course/

Wolverine Harness Raceway, Schoolcraft at Middlebelt, Livonia (421-7170); Hazel Park Harness Races, 1650 E Ten Mile, Hazel Park (566-1595); Windsor Raceway, fall and winter harness racing, Highway 18, Windsor, Ontario (519 961-9545).

Bicycling – Rent at Belle Isle Park (267-7115).

Fishing – Fishing is pretty good in the Detroit River, especially around Belle Isle. There are about 100 lakes in the area. We recommend Orchard Lake.

Golf – Two of the better public courses are Rackham, 10100 W Ten Mile, Huntington Woods (566-0739), and William Rogell, 18601 Berg Rd. (537-2150).

Tennis – The City of Detroit operates several public courts. The best are at Palmer Park and Belle Isle. Call Parks and Recreation (224-1180) for schedule information.

THEATERS: Detroit's active theatrical life provides audiences with entertaining choices. There may be a Broadway-bound hit breaking in at the *Fisher Theater* year-round. 2nd at Grand Blvd. (872-1000). The *Birmingham Theater,* 211 S Woodward, Birmingham (644-3533), features straight drama and comedy, as does the *Meadowbrook Theater* on the Oakland University campus. Their season runs from September to May at University Dr. east of I-75, Rochester (377-3300). Also very good are the *Hilberry Classic Theater,* 4743 Cass (577-2972), and the *Attic Theater,* 525 E Lafayette (963-7789).

MUSIC: You can find just about any kind of music in Detroit — symphonic, jazz, or soul. Detroit is the birthplace of *Motown,* the sound that made the Supremes famous. Rock and soul concerts are played at Cobo Arena, Jefferson at Washington Blvd. (224-1000); Pontiac Silverdome, M-59 at Opdyke, Pontiac (857-8000); Masonic Auditorium, 500 Temple (832-6648); and Ford Auditorium, Jefferson at Woodward (224-1070). The Ford Auditorium is home to the *Detroit Symphony Orchestra*, whose concert season runs from September to May. Orchestra Hall offers dance and classical and jazz concerts, 3711 Woodward (833-3700). "Brunch with Bach" is presented on most Sundays at the *Detroit Institute of Arts,* 5200 Woodward Ave. (833-7900). *Meadow Brook Music Festival* offers summer symphonies on Thursday, Saturday, and Sunday nights, and on Wednesdays and Fridays features pop and jazz artists, Oakland University campus (377-2010). Top-name entertainers perform at the outdoor *Pine Knob Music Theater,* Sashabaw, north of I-75, Clarkston (647-7790). *Music Hall Center for the Performing Arts* hosts traveling dance and music concerts, and is also the home of the *Michigan Opera Theater*, 350 Madison (963-7622).

NIGHTCLUBS AND NIGHTLIFE: *Gino's Surf Lounge* is a low-budget spot that has dancing and a floor show. The Italian/seafood menu is good, too. At 37400 E Jefferson, Mt. Clemens (468-2611). *Deejay's Lounge* at the *Westin Hotel* features rock 'n roll oldies; Renaissance Center (568-8000). *Baker's Keyboard Lounge* is the oldest jazz room in the country. Dizzy Gillespie, Les McCann, and Oscar Peterson play frequently; 20510 Livernois (864-2100). *Watt's Mosambique* features black jazz. 8406 Fenkell (864-0240). At the *Soup Kitchen Saloon,* the soup is homemade and the jazz, from Wednesdays through Sundays, is homegrown; 1585 Franklin (259-1374).

SINS: In the *London Chop House*, you can study *envy* as the diners on the east side of the salon (where you'll also find the men's room) watch the diners on the west side (where you'll find Henry Ford when he's in town). The restaurant is at 155 W Congress (962-0277). Its 300-item wine list isn't exactly the city's only *pride* now that photographs of the new Renaissance Center have been plastered all over every architectural magazine in creation; but when locals are trying to tell you how cosmopolitan Detroit really is, that wine list comes up every time.

Detroit is also a very wealthy city, full of business, businesspeople, and, as you'd expect, hookers of all shapes, sizes, and proclivities to provide room service in the hotels. Adult movie houses, adult bookstores, and adult streetwalkers pander to *lust* along Woodward Avenue in Highland Park and the 8 Mile-Schaeffer area. Patrons at Detroit's rowdy sports bar, the *Lindell A.C.,* often express *anger* over the city's teams.

LOCAL SERVICES: Business Services – For photocopying, try Likity-Split, 140 W Lafayette (963-1999). Macauley's, 157 Michigan (962-1347), has stationery and supplies.

Mechanic – Downtown Auto Service, 1200 Cass Ave. (963-2744).

BEST IN TOWN

CHECKING IN: If you're looking for spectacular accommodations, Detroit will suit you. Two hotels stand out: the Detroit Plaza, a 73-story hotel with indoor serial walkways, and the Hyatt Regency, near Ford Motor headquarters in Dearborn. It's a toss-up which is best; both are tops and both are expensive. So is the older Pontchartrain. By expensive, we mean between $60 and $80 for a double room. Our moderate selections are in the $40 to $50 range; sadly, we found no hotels that met our requirements for an inexpensive recommendation.

The Westin Hotel – "The best," "the newest," "the tallest" — accolades collect around this hotel like flotsam on a beach. Previously known as the *Detroit Plaza Hotel,* this 1,400-room, 73-story round building has style, no doubt about it. The lobby takes up the first eight stories, with fountains, trees, aerial walkways, specialty shops, and cocktail lounges which are served by a traveling trolley. Three levels of cocktail lounges and restaurants revolve. Unfortunately, the guest rooms are not nearly up to the standard of the public spaces. At the east end of Hart Plaza, on Jefferson at St. Antoine (568-8000). Expensive.

Hyatt Regency – With its spacious, airy rooms overlooking the landscaped park of the Ford world headquarters, the Hyatt Regency is a place you might want to stop by just to take a look. Round glass elevator pods lit up like rockets whisk guests to the upper floors, and a space-age peoplemover will take you to nearby Fairlane Shopping Center. You might like it because of its less hectic suburban environment. 800 rooms. Near Greenfield Village, Henry Ford Museum, and a University of Michigan campus, at Michigan and Southfield Freeway, Dearborn (593-1234). Expensive.

Pontchartrain Hotel – A landmark. Its 18th-century French antiques contribute to the aura of aristocracy and perhaps account for its popularity with visiting entertainers and minor royalty. Detroit residents call it the Pontch. The top of the 430-room Pontch offers a good view of the surroundings, although a few newer buildings have sprung up around it to partially block the panorama. There's also a popular dining and slow-dancing club; in summer months jazz concerts are held twice a week on an outdoor terrace. 2 Washington Blvd. (965-0200). Expensive.

Dearborn Inn and Motor Hotel – The prototype for a string of combined airports and inns designed by Henry Ford in the 1920s. At that time he was building the Ford Trimotor, a corrugated iron passenger plane affectionately known as the "Tin Goose." Ford envisioned an age of air travel, and knew people on the move would require different accommodations than the standard hotels of the 1920s. Thus the 180-room Dearborn Inn was born, and as such, occupies an important place in the history of the American hotel. 20301 Oakwood, Dearborn (271-2700). Moderate.

Book Cadillac Hotel – More than a half-century old and trying valiantly to cover its wrinkles, it has 796 rooms that are best described as done in old with a dash of modern. It fronts on the Washington Boulevard mall and the trolley stops at its doorstep. 1114 Washington Blvd. (256-8000). Moderate.

EATING OUT: Detroit has a number of moderately priced restaurants serving everything from steaks, crêpes, and pheasant to natural foods. And the nationalities represented include French, Middle Eastern, and Alsatian. Expect to pay $30 or more for two at expensive restaurants listed here; between $18 and $30, moderate; and under $18 in our inexpensive range. Prices are for two, and do not include drinks, wine, or tips.

London Chop House – Easily the best restaurant in town, due to the personal attention of owners Lester and Sam Gruber, who select the wines for their 300-wine list and change the menu daily. The restaurant is modeled after "21," with wood beams, leather banquettes, and celebrity caricatures. The Fords eat here, and the Chop was mentioned in a Paul Newman movie as "one of the world's greatest." If that's not testimony enough, the food will convince you. Specialties, obviously, are steaks and chops. By the way, status-conscious Detroit residents know who's important by checking out the west side of the bandstand. Anyone who gets seated there really rates. Closed Sundays. Reservations required. Major credit cards. 155 W Congress (962-0278). Expensive.

Tweeny's Café – New Zealander Yvonne Gill-Davis received her restaurant training in France, where she also spent a year working in the vineyards. The result of her studies is this posh establishment in the suburbs of Detroit. Excellent dinners are enhanced by pâtés, sauces, and sumptuous desserts served in elegant style. Closed Sundays and Mondays. Reservations necessary. Major credit cards. 280 N Woodward, Birmingham (644-0050). Expensive.

The Summit – Perched on the 72nd floor of the Westin Hotel and revolving to give diners a magnificent view of Detroit, the river, and Canada. The menu is limited to steaks, chops, and seafood. Open daily. Reservations recommended. Major credit cards. The Westin Hotel, Renaissance Center (568-8000). Expensive.

Charley's Crab – Part of a chain, but here, the wood-paneled dining room, once part of a now-razed Grosse Pointe mansion, lends distinction. We also like the ragtime piano player in the lounge, the iron anchor rescued from the New England coast, and the seafood. Open daily. Reservations accepted. Major credit cards. 5500 Crooks Rd. (at I-75), Troy (879-2060). Expensive to moderate.

Benno's – If you can get in, you'll find this a charmer. Benno Steinborn not only does the cooking, he comes out to bow from the waist when checking on your pheasant, beef Wellington, or whatever. The food here is Alsatian — French and German. Closed Sundays. Reservations. No credit cards. 8027 Agnes (499-0040). Expensive.

Joe Muer's Seafood – Some people say this place serves the best seafood west of the Atlantic. Others say it's even better. Extravagant praise, no matter how sincere, can never substitute for firsthand experience, especially where seafood is concerned. Be prepared to wait in line, though. Joe Muer's doesn't take reservations. (A waiter will bring you a drink while you're standing.) Major credit cards. Closed Sundays and holidays. 2000 Gratiot (567-1088). Expensive.

The Sheik – Hummus, pita bread, shish kebab, and other lamb delicacies, with a special reputation for salads. Closed Sundays. Reservations recommended. Major credit cards. 316 E Lafayette (964-8441). Moderate.

Pontchartrain Wine Cellars – Where cold duck was invented, with a unique French/New York style. Closed Sundays. Reservations recommended. Major credit cards. 234 W Larned (963-1785). Moderate.

Carl's Chop House – This place has been serving prime steaks about as long as there have been cows, and the walls are lined with blue ribbons to prove it. The large, open rooms have a distinctly masculine air, but the overall atmosphere is conducive to family dining. Open daily. Reservations advised. Major credit cards. 3020 Grand River (833-0700). Moderate.

La Cuisine – The flamboyant chef of this mite-sized French restaurant whistles up heavenly three-mustard kidneys, tasty fish soup, and more from his kitchen smack in the middle of the room. Closed Sundays and Mondays. Reservations necessary. Most major credit cards. 417 Pelissier, Windsor, Ontario (519 253-6432).

New Hellas – The hub of Detroit's 1-block Greek community is as Greek as Greek can be, with moussaka, kalamari (squid), and baklava. Most Greek of all are the late hours; whether you want a salad or dinner, you can get it until 3 AM. Open daily. No reservations. Major credit cards. 583 Monroe (961-5544). Inexpensive.

Spaghetti Company – Once a country roadhouse, it's been transformed into a quaint family restaurant but retains its original turn-of-the-century air. The Italian dishes are rarely priced above $5. Open daily. Reservations accepted. Major credit cards. 2593 N Woodward, Royal Oak (548-1600). Inexpensive.

HARTFORD

East Coast residents used to joke that Hartford was an oasis on the highway between New York and Boston. Hartford's unexpected beauty surprises many visitors. At first glance, the city's crystal skyscrapers, rising suddenly on the flat Connecticut River valley horizon, sparkle like Disney fantasy castles. However, the glitter is disarming. The majestic exterior of Connecticut's most dramatic cityscape masks one of the most pragmatic urban identities in the country. Hartford is the insurance capital of the United States. It is here, amidst the graceful towers, that nearly every major domestic insurance company makes its policy decisions regarding premiums and payments; decisions which, in some way or another, probably affect you. This bit of news is hardly likely to be first in your mind when you enter Hartford, however. Initial impressions are likely to be more aesthetic. But Hartford is more than just a pretty city, or the state's capital (and largest metropolitan area), or a thriving business center; it is beginning to generate a lot of excitement as a place in which to enjoy oneself.

Hartford was settled by the Dutch in 1623. For many years a lively port, here molasses, coffee, spices, and tobacco were stored in large warehouses, then shipped to other destinations on the Connecticut River. (An important tobacco-growing region, the Connecticut River valley was the site of the first cigar factory in the United States. Even today, the broad, green banks of the river stretch away, checkered by an intriguing patchwork of white cloth squares which shield the sensitive tobacco leaves from too much light.) Hartford is still the marketing center for Connecticut Valley tobacco. In the spring, when the river rises after the rains, farmers grow exceptionally fine asparagus in the waterlogged land.

In the middle of this productive agricultural area, Hartford retains the essence of a historic New England township, a source of joy for anyone curious about American architecture during our nation's formative years. Colonial, post-Revolutionary, and 19th-century houses sit in spacious gardens. The recently renovated Old State House, where statesmen gathered to debate issues of the day as far back as 1796, is open to visitors. Mark Twain, creator of Tom Sawyer and Huck Finn, spent many years in Hartford, and his home, as well as the nearby house of *Uncle Tom's Cabin* author Harriet Beecher Stowe, are favorite stopping points along Hartford's literary trail.

And juxtaposed in the same city is a dramatic, revitalized downtown area. Some 138,000 people live in Hartford. With Springfield, Massachusetts, 25 miles to the north, the urban area population climbs to more than one million.

Hartford's insurance business alone employs around 50,000 people. The Connecticut state government employs even more. Bradley International Airport, between Hartford and Springfield, gives northern New Englanders an alternative to the frenzy of Boston and New York airports. Visitors arriving from overseas can also be spared the more chaotic environment of the larger cities.

Hartford's Civic Center has sparked a proliferation of new restaurants and cafés, some in creatively restored buildings. Streets that used to fold up at nightfall are now alive with sports fans, bar-hoppers, diners, tourists, and residents of downtown apartments. With its new image, Hartford is fast becoming a sophisticated, enthusiastic visitors' center with a magnetism all its own.

HARTFORD AT-A-GLANCE

SEEING THE CITY: The top of the Travelers' Tower offers the best view of the city. It's 527 feet above the madding crowd in the Travelers' Insurance Company building. There are 72 steps to climb before reaching the very top. Open from May until the last Friday in October. Free. 700 Main St. (277-0111).

SPECIAL PLACES: Walking through Hartford can be highly enjoyable, especially since the city combines classical and contemporary architectural styles. Capitol Hill is a good place to begin.

Capitol Hill – The seat of the state government, the State Capitol atop the hill is distinguishable by its gold dome. Statues and bas-reliefs decorating the building commemorate events in Connecticut history. The governor and top state officials maintain offices here. Guided tours Mondays through Fridays. Near Capitol Ave. and Trinity (566-3662).

Bushnell Park – Bushnell is to Hartford what Central Park is to New York. In fact, Frederick Law Olmsted, designer of New York's Central Park, was also one of Bushnell's original designers. The Knox Foundation, a private charitable organization, has donated an antique carousel with Wurlitzer band organ to the Bushnell Park Carousel Society, a nonprofit corporation which charges adult carousel lovers $10 a year so that children can ride the merry-go-round for 25¢. Capitol Ave., High St., Asylum Ave., Jewell Ave.

Center Church – In 1636, Reverend Thomas Hooker of Cambridge, Massachusetts, led a group of 100 men, women, and children, and 160 head of cattle to Hartford, which at the time was a Dutch trading post. From the pulpit of the Center Church, he preached a revolutionary doctrine: "The foundation of authority is laid, first, in the free consent of the people." Hooker's ideas were incorporated into Connecticut's royal charter in 1662, and the Reverend became known as the founding father of the state. Outside the church is a cemetery, in use from 1640 to 1803. First Church of Christ on Main St. (728-3201).

Old State House – At one time an active meeting house for statesmen, this colonial building, designed by Charles Bulfinch, is now a museum. Colonial furniture and other exhibits date back to 1796, when Old State House was built. Now owned by a private group, the museum has recently been refurbished and has added a souvenir and craft shop. Open all year. Free. Main and State Sts. (522-6766).

Wadsworth Atheneum – The oldest art museum in the United States, with eclectic collections of prehistoric relics, paintings, sculptures, etc. Open all year. Admission charge (free on Thursdays). Main and Prospect Sts. (278-2670).

Avery Art Memorial – Attached to the Wadsworth Atheneum, Avery Art Memorial has an independent collection of Great Masters (Rembrandt, Wyeth, Daumier, Picasso,

Goya, Cézanne, Whistler, and Sargent). Open all year. 25 Atheneum Sq. N (278-2670).

Morgan Memorial – As the name suggests, this museum was started by the late J. P. Morgan, a Hartford citizen who left home to make his fortune. Fine collections of Middle Eastern and Oriental archeological relics, Meissen china, and firearms, especially those made by Colt, a local enterprise. Open all year. 590 Main St. (278-2670).

Nook Farm – A 19th-century writers' community, the former Nook Farm estate contains several authors' houses. Mark Twain lived in a riverboat-shaped brick, stone, and wood three-story house with brown and orange brick patternwork. Harriet Beecher Stowe, author of *Uncle Tom's Cabin,* lived only slightly less elaborately in a brick house next door. A 45-minute tour takes you through the premises. Closed holidays. Admission charge. Mark Twain Memorial, 351 Farmington Ave. (525-9317). Harriet Beecher Stowe House, 77 Forest Ave. (525-9317).

■ **EXTRA SPECIAL:** For a beautiful drive on winding, narrow roads through romantic pine forests and cozy New England towns, take a drive on *rt. 202*, going west. About 30 miles from the city is Litchfield, Connecticut, a dazzling village of huge, white mansions set around a classic American town green. Continue on rt. 202 for about 12 miles until you reach New Preston, on the shore of Lake Waramaug. *The Boulders' Inn*, a 30-room country inn, serves healthy, home-cooked meals. Closed Christmas (on rt. 45, New Preston, 868-7918). Continue south on rt. 47, one of the best antique centers in New England, for about 12 miles. In Woodbury, *Curtis House* claims to be Connecticut's oldest inn. Opened in 1754, it has 18 bedrooms, the majority of which have large, canopied beds. Large lunches and dinners include freshly baked hot muffins and lovely desserts (263-2101). Take rt. 6, going northeast, to return to Hartford.

SOURCES AND RESOURCES

The Hartford Convention and Visitors Bureau distributes brochures, maps, and general tourist information. 1 Civic Center Plaza (728-6789). A new information line that's helpful to visitors and residents alike is the Hartford Artline (247-4433), which has a rundown on things to do, sights to see, and entertainment possibilities.

All telephone numbers are in the 203 area code unless otherwise indicated.

For Local Coverage – *Hartford Courant* (the oldest daily newspaper in circulation), morning daily; *Connecticut Magazine,* monthly; *The Hartford Advocate,* a free alternative news and entertainment publication, weekly.

For Food – *The Complete Menu Guide to Hartford Restaurants,* by John A. Russo, Jr. ($3.95) lists menus for over 100 restaurants.

CLIMATE AND CLOTHES: Hartford's humidity is a problem in the summer when temperatures reach the 80s and 90s; winters are snowy, generally in the 20s and 30s; spring and fall are delightful.

GETTING AROUND: Bus – The state-owned Connecticut Company operates the municipal bus service. 53 Vernon St. (525-9181).

Taxi – It's very difficult to get a cab in the street. Call Yellow Cab, 8 Jewell Ave. (522-0234).

Car Rental – All major national firms are represented at the airport as well as downtown. Budget Rent-a-Car is the cheapest local service. 455 Farmington Ave. (249-5225).

MUSEUMS: Museum aficionados will love the abundance of art and historical collections in Hartford. Wadsworth Atheneum, the Avery Art Memorial, Morgan Memorial, Old State House are described above in *Special Places.* Other notable museums are:

Connecticut Historical Society, Elizabeth St. (236-5621).

Children's Museum, 950 Trout Brook Dr., West Hartford (236-2961).

MAJOR COLLEGES AND UNIVERSITIES: Trinity College, at Summit, Vernon, and Broad Sts. (527-3151); St. Joseph College, Asylum Ave. (232-4571); University of Hartford, 200 Bloomfield Ave. (243-4100).

SPECIAL EVENTS: The *Festival of Lights* is held every year on Constitution Plaza the day after Thanksgiving. Thousands of tiny white lights are turned on by a small child picked through a lottery. Santa Claus always makes a rather dramatic appearance. He arrives on top of the plaza's tallest building in a helicopter and descends in a window washer's gondola made up to look like a sleigh.

SPORTS: Hockey – The *New England Whalers* WHL team plays at the Hartford Civic Center (727-8080, for ticket information).

Tennis – The *Aetna World Cup Tennis Championship* also takes place at 1 Civic Center Plaza (566-6588). The best public courts are at Elizabeth Park, Prospect and Asylum Aves. Across the street from the State Armory on Capitol Hill, there are indoor courts at Intown Tennis (246-2448).

Swimming – The Connecticut River is polluted, and even though it may look tempting on a hot day, Hartford residents recommend swimming at the YWCA. Admission charge. 135 Broad St. (525-1163). YMCA, 160 Jewell Ave. (522-4183).

Fishing – For the best local fishing, try Wethersfield Cove.

Golf – There are 24 golf courses in the Hartford area. The best public course is in Goodwin Park.

Skiing – There's excellent cross-country skiing at the Metropolitan District Commission reservoir in West Hartford. Downhill enthusiasts like Mt. Southington, 20 minutes south on I-84; Powder Ridge Ski Area, 20 minutes south on I-91; and Mt. Tom, 35 minutes north on I-91.

THEATER: For complete listings of up-to-the-minute performance schedules, check local newpapers listed above. Hartford's main theaters are the *Civic Center*, 1 Civic Center Plaza (566-6000); *Hartford Stage Company*, 50 Church St. (527-5151); musical comedies performed at *Bushnell Memorial Hall*, 166 Capitol Ave. (246-6807); *Wadsworth Atheneum*, Main and Prospect Sts. (278-2670).

MUSIC: Concerts, operas, symphonies, and ballets are performed at Bushnell Memorial Hall, 166 Capitol Ave. (246-6807); Wadsworth Atheneum, Main and Prospect Sts. (278-2670); Goodspeed Opera House, in East Haddam, 30 minutes south of the city on Rt. 9 (873-8668).

NIGHTCLUBS AND NIGHTLIFE: Hartford's cafés are great places for listening to music. The selection varies from place to place, from night to night, so call ahead. *Mad Murphy's Café*, 22 Union Pl. (247-9738) is a favorite. A new night spot, *Shenanigan's,* 1 Gold St. (522-4117), has for a bar an authentic Art Deco diner that's been taken apart and rebuilt inside the restaurant. For disco dancing, try *Lorien,* 187 Allyn St. (525-1919). Most lively gay bar is the *Lost and Found Café,* 81 Pope Park Hwy., #4 (241-5000).

SINS: *Hartford's Civic Center* and surrounding *Constitution Plaza* are points of *pride* in the city; this complex of office buildings and shops bordering the Connecticut River is especially beautiful at Christmas, when it sparkles with thousands of tiny white lights. A good place to practice *sloth.*

Ditto for the magnificent carousel — a stained glass pavilion full of wooden horses assembled from merry-go-rounds of generations past — in Bushnell Park.

Teenage *lust* flourishes in the cars parked in the seclusion of Avon Mountain.

LOCAL SERVICES: Business Services – Miss Josephine's, 111 Pearl St. (247-7571).

Mechanic – Hartford Auto Repairs, 12 S Whitney St. (232-2236).

Babysitting – We Care, 687 Woolcott Hill Rd., Wethersfield (563-2346).

BEST IN TOWN

CHECKING IN: Hartford has an unexceptional collection of comfortable hotels. The Hartford Hilton does offer free local calls, free parking, and serves free coffee in guest rooms (some of which have water beds). Sonesta Hotel offers free in-room movies. In-room movies are also available at the Sheraton-Hartford. If you're looking for a place to sleep which has essential services, check into Governors' House/Best Western, where a double room is about as reasonable as can be decently had in town. Expect to pay between $50 and $60 at places noted as expensive, $40 and $50 at our moderate choices, under $40, inexpensive.

Sheraton-Hartford – Connected to the Civic Center, this 407-room hotel gives the indoor sports enthusiast a wider range of facilities than any other Hartford hotel. The indoor heated pool has a lifeguard on duty. There's also a whirlpool, sauna, exercise room, and recreation room. The café-bar features nightly entertainment and dancing. In-room movies are also available. There's a drugstore on the premises. Parking and cribs for infants are free. Trumbull St. at Civic Center (728-5151). Expensive.

Parkview Hilton – Formerly the *Hartford Hilton,* overlooking Bushnell Park and the State Capitol, it was completely refurbished in 1981 and offers 410 rooms, three restaurants, and an entertainment center. Ford and Pearl Sts. (249-5611). Expensive.

Sonesta – Located in the middle of Hartford's ultra-modern, exceptionally well-landscaped raised mall, Constitution Plaza. In addition to having a rooftop pool, café bar, drugstore, and dining room, the 302-room Sonesta offers free in-room movies. 5 Constitution Plaza (278-2000). Moderate.

Governors' House/Best Western – If you're looking for a centrally-located hotel with basic conveniences at a good price, you'll find the Governors' House/Best Western to be the best bet in Hartford. Its 96 rooms have recently been refurbished. It has a restaurant, café, and nightclub-disco. Banquet facilities are available and parking is free. 440 Asylum Ave. (246-6591). Inexpensive.

EATING OUT: The number and varieties of foreign cuisines available in the city are gradually increasing, but most of the best restaurants still feature traditional Hartford fare: American-Italian cooking, or the steaks-chops-seafood routine. With the exception of the Signature, where dinner for two can run as high as $50, two people can eat well for $30 or less (not counting drinks, wine, or tips). Expect to pay between $30 and $50 at restaurants designated as expensive; between $20 and $30 at those we've listed as moderate; $20 or less at inexpensive places.

Signature – Steaks, fish, shrimp, and lobster are standard, but there is also an unusually good selection of game: elk, venison, hare, and duckling. The house specialty is filet mignon stuffed with oysters and smothered in Béarnaise sauce. The 30-table restaurant can seat 200. Closed Sundays in July and August; open daily the rest of the year. Reservations are recommended. Major credit cards. Civic Center (249-1629). Expensive.

Honiss' Seafood Restaurant – The specialty is scrod. Thursdays, Fridays, and Saturdays the restaurant is especially crowded, so reservations are advised those evenings. Major credit cards. 44 State St. (522-4177). Moderate.

36 Lewis St. – This converted, centuries-old building serves lunch and dinner in three elegantly decorated rooms, one of which faces a garden and has a glass roof. Burgers, omelettes, salads, and zucchini are the specialties at lunch. At dinner, the menu includes prime ribs, top sirloin, stuffed shrimp, and fresh fish. The Captain's Room offers the Captain's Cut, a succulent 20-ounce prime rib. Open daily. Reservations are only accepted between 5 PM and 6 PM. Major credit cards. 36 Lewis St. (247-2300). Moderate.

Frank's Italian Restaurant – A favorite of state politicians; traditional Italian-American dishes. The manicotti is considered excellent, and the veal superb. Frank's is especially busy after hockey games, so call ahead for reservations. Closed Sundays in July and August; open daily the rest of the year. Major credit cards accepted. 159 Asylum Ave. (527-9291). Inexpensive.

The Marble Pillar – One of the friendliest restaurants in Hartford, serving German and American food. The waiters go out of their way to be helpful to visitors. The food is excellent, prices reasonable. Wiener schnitzel is the specialty of the house, and the seafood comes highly recommended. Free parking in the Travelers' Plaza garage. Closed Sundays. Reservations are not required. Major credit cards. 22 Central Row, behind the Old State House (247-4549). Inexpensive.

Brown Thomson & Co. – Located in the newly renovated Richardson building complex, which also includes a shopping mall, this antiques-encrusted restaurant offers the most extensive menu in town — 125 separate items. Sandwiches, Mexican food, and delicacies such as fried ice cream are included. This is where the young people of Hartford meet these days. 942 Main St. (525-1600). Inexpensive.

HONOLULU

Honolulu stretches along a 20-mile strip of land between the Pacific Ocean and the 3,000-foot mountains of Oahu, the major island of the state of Hawaii. In the past 20 years the city has outgrown this narrow strip and risen up the mountains along ridges and deeply cleft valleys; it reaches into the sea with a multitude of docks and marinas that run, off and on, from Pearl Harbor to the first grand sweep of magnificent Waikiki Beach — and magnificent it is, even poised against a backdrop of high-rise hotels that is several blocks deep. At night the homes up in the heights glitter above the city, and beyond them are the dank, tropical mountain rain forests as prolific and luxuriant as ever. Ten minutes from downtown Honolulu is rain forest.

Private sailors and yachtsmen know Honolulu as one of America's trimmest, cleanest port cities. To land-bound Americans it is something more — the country's most foreign metropolis, an American city which stubbornly refuses to quite feel like America. Small wonder, when you consider that less than 90 years ago — until 1893 to be exact — it was the capital city of a foreign country, and that foreign country was a monarchy ruled by a queen: a Pacific Ocean island nation with culture, arts, and world view rooted in the South Seas. In 1893 reigning Queen Liliuokalani was overthrown by Americans living in the islands, and five years later the islands were annexed as a United States territory. They became American, but they were — are — still the islands, and that ain't Baltimore. About 2,500 miles southwest of Los Angeles, Honolulu is just short of halfway between the continental US and Tokyo, a relationship that more than once has given rise to awe and some misgivings.

The sense of disorientation is not all one-sided. The "mainland" is what residents call the rest of the United States (and if you want to keep their respect you will never refer to it as "stateside" since Hawaii, too, is a state, and proud of it), and to many locals the other 49 states represent the strange and sometimes rather frightening culture of the *haoles.* Pronounced "howlies," this old Hawaiian word for outsiders has, in the 20th century, come to mean Caucasians — a segment of the population well outnumbered by Orientals and Polynesians in Hawaii. To native Hawaiians, haoles in the past have represented Yankees who don't understand pidgin, and who seem eager to bull their way into business and social success. The fact that they no longer automatically succeed in these objectives represents a change not uniformly felt, and sometimes overlooked, in the islands today.

Islanders in general, and Honolulu residents in particular, are unabashedly fond of dubbing their island home "paradise." But it is an uneasy Eden, with a history that has often been violent and tragic. Early-19th-century American missionaries experienced severe hardships here, but in the pitched battles between missionaries and western shippers and merchants for the hearts and minds of the native population, it was the Hawaiians who lost almost everything. They were converted to Christianity, and lost their culture; they were taught to read, write, and count, and were decimated by foreign diseases to which they had no immunity. Only today is the long-dormant pride of culture emerging among descendants of the original Polynesian Hawaiians.

Other groups came to live in the islands, of course, and as they did Honolulu grew cosmopolitan. When the economy required hard labor for the sugar plantations in the late 19th century, unskilled workers were recruited from all over, especially from Japan and China. When their contracts expired, many stayed on, marrying and spawning the lovely racial mix that characterizes contemporary Honolulu society. More than half the marriages in Hawaii today are interracial.

With the attack on Pearl Harbor — December 7, 1941 — Honolulu entered the consciousness of most mainland Americans. Martial law was declared throughout the islands, and for millions of American servicemen Hawaii became the jumping-off point for the Pacific theater. They called Oahu "the Rock," and they hated it.

They don't hate it anymore. Four million visitors a year pour into Honolulu airport, and drop $2 billion into the Hawaiian coffers as they come. Honolulu's green outback may be carpeted with sugar and pineapple plantations, but plantations no longer support the economy. Tourism is the vital juice of Hawaii, and most of it gets squeezed out in Honolulu. (And among the visitors are a goodly number of ex-GIs who hated the Rock. The most popular tourist destination is the beautiful memorial which floats over the sunken USS *Arizona.* One million people a year see it.)

Honolulu — 13th largest city in the country — is a modern metropolis struggling with modern problems. A few decades ago Waikiki was a sparsely settled jungle peninsula along a swamp, three miles southeast of town. There was an unobstructed view of Diamond Head, and the tallest structure in town was the ten-story Aloha Tower, from which ship traffic was controlled. No more, no more. Forests of high-rises dwarf the Tower and Waikiki has its share of dope dealers, pickpockets, and prostitutes. But in the center of town is still Chinatown, with noodle factories and small restaurants reminiscent of a port town 100 years ago. And within Honolulu is a taste of everything Hawaiian, and a flavor of far seas beyond.

HONOLULU AT-A-GLANCE

SEEING THE CITY: For an eye-popping view of the shoreline, walk across the long, private footbridge on the ocean side of the *Ilikai Hotel,* and take the outdoor glass elevator to the top. The view is a guaranteed knockout (1777 Ala Moana Blvd., 949-3811). For a wide-angle view of all Honolulu, drive along Tantalus/Round Top Drive to Puu Ualakaa State Wayside Park. Not many tourists know about it, so you'll have some privacy as well as scenic splendor.

SPECIAL PLACES: Although it is now considerably overbuilt, Waikiki is nonetheless an attractive center for wandering. We suggest getting to know your neighborhood first with a three-mile walking tour.

Diamond Head – Guarding the southeasternmost boundary of Waikiki, this 760-foot volcanic crater is a world-famous landmark. You can climb around the slopes of Diamond Head along the tricky trail that begins at a gate off Makalei Place or you can drive into the crater through a tunnel to a state park inside. For park information, call the State Parks Department at 548-7455.

Kapiolani Park – Most visitors making the pilgrimage to Diamond Head never get any further than this 100-acre park, named for the wife of Kalakaua, the last king of Hawaii. Within the park, you'll find enough special places to keep you busy for more than a few hours. The Waikiki Aquarium is one. At 25¢ per turn of the stile it's one of the best bargains in Honolulu (closed Mondays, 923-9741). A little further inland, just off Monsarrat Ave., the Kodak Hula Show is performed at 10 AM Tuesdays through Thursdays, and occasionally even Fridays. Get there early if you want a seat. Drift along toward the scent of the Kapiolani Rose Garden on the corner of Paki and Monsarrat. The subtle, exquisite odors are produced and maintained by the exotic fertilizers gathered from the Honolulu Zoo. Kalakaua Ave., named after the good king, begins here. Pronounced "ka-la-*cow*-wah," it is the principal thoroughfare of Waikiki.

Waikiki Beach – Just outside the park, alongside Kalakaua Ave., begins the famous, 2½-mile-long curve of Waikiki Beach. There are several places along the shore where you can rent surfboards for around $4 an hour, or take lessons for around $8. For thrills with fewer spills, try the surfing outrigger canoes. Well-tanned beach boys will take you on three waves over a ½ hour period for about $4. One-hour rides on the tamer, beachside catamarans cost about $6.

International Marketplace – For nearly two dozen years, shoppers have been poking around the outdoor stalls underneath the giant banyon tree festooned with lanterns. (A souk, Hawaiian style, is what we call it.) You can pick up all kinds of exotic junk and treasures you just can't live without. 2330 Kalakaua Ave.

Fort de Russy – Fort de Russy spreads across the grounds of what was once a coastal artillery headquarters. Stroll through the grounds, swim, surf, or ride an outrigger canoe. The Army Museum, in the battery, winds around inside the cells and magazines of the old artillery building. Open daily. Free (543-2639). On your way back, walk toward Diamond Head. If you start back at sunset, you'll be enchanted by the sky changing into myriad colors. The walk could be one of those moments in your life that you will never forget.

DOWNTOWN

Mission Houses Museum – Just across Kawaiahao Street, the Mission Houses Museum complex contains the earliest American buildings in Hawaii. The white, wooden frame house was shipped around Cape Horn in pieces, then reassembled in 1821 by the first missionaries. The buildings have been intelligently restored, and excellent guides are available (a good idea for a thumbnail sketch of basic Hawaiian history). Closed Mondays. Admission charge. 553 S King St. (531-0481).

Kawaiahao Church – Across the street from the Mission Houses, Kawaiahao Church is also known as the Westminster Abbey of Hawaii. It was designed by Hawaii's first minister and constructed out of 14,000 coral blocks cut from a local reef. King Lunalilo is buried in the front yard. Services are conducted on Sundays in English and Hawaiian. Open daily. Free. King and Punchbowl Sts. (538-6267).

Kamehameha I Statue – You might not be able to pronounce it, but you sure can't miss it. It's the giant black and gold rendering of the conquerer of the islands. On Kamehameha Day, June 11, it's adrape with leis of flowers. And would you believe this baby is a twin? The original statue was presumed lost when the ship carrying it from Italy sank. It was later recovered, and now stands on the island of Hawaii (Honolulu, we remind you, is on the island of Oahu) near Kamehameha I's birthplace.

Iolani Palace – With elaborate surroundings, Iolani Palace sits in state, receiving tribute from admirers. Highly revered by historians and sentimentalists alike, Iolani Palace was the final residence of monarch and songwriter Queen Liliuokalani. In fact she was imprisoned there following the 1893 revolution, and wrote some of her famous songs, including "Aloha Oe," while in detention. Iolani was built by King David Kalakaua in 1882. In 1883, he placed a crown on his own head in what is now Coronation Bandstand, where, every Friday at noon, the Royal Hawaiian Band gives free, informal concerts. Palace tours are given Wednesdays through Saturdays, and tickets should be reserved well in advance of your trip by writing to Iolani Palace, Box 2259, Honolulu, HI 96804. The palace is located on King and Richards Sts. (536-2474).

Hawaii State Capitol – Built in 1969, for $25 million, the capitol takes its inspiration from the natural history of the islands. All of its features — columns, reflecting pools, courtyard — reflect aspects of Hawaii's environment. Outside the capitol stands the controversial modern statue of Father Damien, the hero of the leprosy settlement at Kalaupapa on the island of Molokai. 400 S Beretania St. (548-2211).

OTHER SPECIAL PLACES

Ala Moana Center – This is one of the world's largest shopping bazaars. Built in 1959 when Hawaii achieved statehood, the Ala Moana Center has more than 200 stores selling quality clothing, antiques, carpets, furniture, fabrics, and art made at home and imported from other countries. Ala Moana Blvd. across from Ala Moana Park.

Arizona Memorial – More than a million people a year come to honor the Americans who perished on the USS *Arizona* when the Japanese bombed Pearl Harbor on December 7, 1941. You can take a free boat tour of the Memorial daily except Mondays. Tours leave from Halawa Landing. At Kewalo Basin near Waikiki you can buy a ticket for a half-day Pearl Harbor cruise. (471-3901).

Bishop Museum – Near the beginning of Likelike (pronounced vaguely "licky-licky") Highway, in the working-class neighborhood called Kalihi, the prestigious Bishop Museum houses the greatest collection of Hawaiiana in the world. Founded in 1899, the museum is the center for most of the anthropological research done throughout Polynesia and the Pacific. You can ride to and from the Bishop Museum on an old, red, London double-decker bus. Buy your ticket at the museum's shop in King's Alley in Waikiki. Open daily. Admission charge. 1355 Kahili St. (847-1443).

Foster Botanic Gardens – Often overlooked by tourists, this cool, tranquil retreat in the middle of the city is a living museum of growing things. The #4 bus from Waikiki will bring you close to the garden at Nuuanu and Vineyard. Open daily till 4 PM. Free. 180 N Vineyard Blvd. (531-1939).

Honolulu Academy of Arts – Across Thomas Square from Blaisdell Center, the Honolulu Academy of Arts has 5 open courtyards and 37 gallery rooms full of rare Oriental art and some European and American works. The eastern art is in the west part of the building, and the western art is in the east. Have lunch in the *Garden Café.* (For reservations call 531-8865.) Closed Mondays. 900 S Beretania St. (538-3693).

National Memorial Cemetery of the Pacific – Also known as Punchbowl crater, this cemetery is the Arlington of the Pacific. In prehistoric times it was the site of human sacrifices. Now, more than 20,000 servicemen lie buried among its 112 peaceful acres overlooking downtown Honolulu. Some commercial bus tours visit Punchbowl, but if you're on your own, you'll need a car or taxi. Take Puowaina Dr. to its end.

■ **EXTRA SPECIAL:** Honolulu is the great jumping-off point for *island-hopping* expeditions. Hawaiian Airlines (537-5100) and Aloha Airlines (836-1111) fly to the islands of Kauai, Maui, Hawaii, Lanai, and Molokai daily. Kauai, the oldest of the islands, is one of the least developed. Golfers come to play at its Princeville Resort course. Maui offers valleys, waterfalls, and beaches. You can take a half-hour helicopter tour over Maui's main sites, including a zooming, soaring look at the crater of the dormant Haleakala Volcano. Hawaii is the home of Mauna Loa, the world-famous volcano which last erupted in 1975. Scientists at Hawaii Volcanoes National Park say it's building up for another major eruption — any day now. (Don't say we didn't warn you.) On Lanai, only 17 miles long and once thought to be inhabited by ghosts, you'll see plenty of pineapples. The Dole Company owns most of the island, and most of the land is devoted to cultivating the spiny, delicious fruit. Molokai, 37 miles long, is a relatively untouched plantation island, and offers the opportunity to see Hawaii almost as it was.

SOURCES AND RESOURCES

For information, maps, and brochures, contact the Hawaii Visitors Bureau, 2285 Kalakaua Ave. (923-1811).

The best local guide to Honolulu is *The Maverick Guide to Hawaii* by Robert Bone (Pelican, $7.95).

All telephone numbers are in the 808 area code unless otherwise indicated.

For Local Coverage – *Honolulu Advertiser,* morning daily; *Honolulu Star-Bulletin,* evening daily; *Honolulu* Magazine, monthly.

For Food – *The Maverick Guide to Hawaii.*

CLIMATE AND CLOTHES: In ancient times, the Hawaiians had no word for weather. They did, however, have words for two seasons — winter and summer. Winter, which runs from about October through April, means daytime highs reaching the mid-70s and low 80s, dropping into the low 60s at night. There can be several short rains in a day. You can count on 11 hours of daylight — short by Hawaiian standards. Summer temperatures hover around the mid- to upper 80s; rains are less frequent, and you get about 13 hours of daylight, more vacation for your money.

GETTING AROUND: Bus – TheBus, as the municipal transit line is called, is the cheapest, most convenient way to get around Honolulu. You can get a map of bus routes in advance at your hotel, or from Honolulu Department of Transportation, Mass Transit Division, 725 Kapiolani Blvd. For information call 531-1611.

Taxi – There's some debate over whether taxis ought to be allowed to cruise the streets. At the moment, it's illegal, so if you want one, go to any major hotel or call one of the Honolulu cab companies: Charley's (531-1333); Sida of Hawaii (836-0011); Aloha State (847-3566).

Car Rental – The best local car rental firm is Tropical Rent-A-Car Systems, 2819 Ualena St. (836-1041). Major car firm rental agencies are represented at the airport and have stations in Waikiki.

Pedicab – These chromium versions of rickshaws, operated by healthy-looking college students, are available to the daring for short rides in the open air of Waikiki. Be sure to check rates with the driver before riding.

MUSEUMS: The Army Museum, Bishop Museum, and Honolulu Academy of Arts are described under *Special Places.* Another notable museum is *Polynesian Cultural Center*, 1½ hours from Waikiki in Laie (923-1861). Each of the seven model villages on the 42-acre grounds represents a Polynesian culture: Maori, Tahitian, Samoan, Fijian, Tongan, Marquesan, and Hawaiian. People live and work as they would on their native islands. At night, there's a dance and entertainment show. Closed Sundays. Admission charge. For information, call 923-1861.

MAJOR COLLEGES AND UNIVERSITIES: University of Hawaii, in Manoa Valley (948-8855); Brigham Young University, at Laie (293-9211); Chaminade University of Honolulu (735-4711).

SPECIAL EVENTS: Special events are year-round. Here are a few highlights:

January — The annual *Hula Bowl* College All-Star Football Classic is played in Aloha Stadium.

February — Early in the month, the nationally televised four-day *Hawaiian Open International Golf Tournament,* at the Waialae Country Club in the Kahala District.

March — The polo season opens early in the month at Mokuleia, at the east end of the North Shore of Oahu.

April — In late April, the *Flora Pacifica exhibition,* featuring flowers and plants, is held on the grounds of the H. Alexander Walker estate, 2616 Pali Hwy.

May — The last part of the month is reserved for events connected with *Fiesta Filipina,* a series of Philippine cultural events.

June — A 100-mile around-the-island canoe race starts from the Moana Hotel. On June 11, *Kamehameha Day* honors the conquerer of the islands with a long parade.

July — In odd-numbered years, the *Trans-Pacific Yacht Race* finishes off Diamond Head.

September — On Sept. 1, the *Waikiki Rough Water Swim* is held over a two-mile course, ending at Duke Kahanamoku Beach in front of the Hilton Hawaiian Village Hotel. The third or fourth week in the month is *Aloha Week,* Honolulu's biggest celebration. It features canoe races, luaus, balls, athletic events, parades and more.

October — On October 31, Waikiki comes spectacularly alive for Halloween, Honolulu's Mardi Gras.

SPORTS: Hawaii is one of the world's great centers for water sports. Surfing and swimming contests are held often. Aloha Stadium is the site of the Hula Bowl college football game each January, and other football and baseball games at other times. 99–500 Salt Lake Blvd. (487-3877). Basketball and boxing events are held at the Neal S. Blaisdell Center, 777 Ward Ave. (521-2911).

Bicycling – Bikes can be rented from Bicycle Rentals Hawaii, 2299 Kuhio Ave. (923-4768).

Fishing – Fishing enthusiasts from all over the world flock to Hawaiian waters. Fishing boats can be chartered from Sport Fishing Hawaii (536-6577), or Island Charters (536-1555). Most boats leave from Kewalo Basin, at the end of Ward Ave., just across Ala Moana Blvd.

Golf – There are 23 golf courses on Oahu. One of the best available to tourists is Hawaii Kai, on rt. 72 (395-2398).

Tennis – The best courts are at Ilikai Hotel, Waikiki Beach (949-3811). Anyone can play. There are 80 public courts on Oahu; the best are at Ala Moana Park and Koko Head.

Surfing – The quest for the perfect wave attracts surfers from all over the world. Most hotels along the Waikiki Beach have surfing instructors and concessions that rent surfboards, canoes, and catamarans. The most famous surfing beach is Sunset Beach on the other side of the island.

Skindiving – Skindiving Hawaii, 1667 Ala Moana (941-0548), rents diving gear and offers advice on Pacific diving conditions.

Swimming – When Waikiki Beach is overcrowded, head for Kahana Bay on the other side of the island. Though not as spectacular, it has as good a beach, and is off the tourist track. The *Maverick Guide* will pinpoint beaches dangerous for swimming.

THEATERS: You can get tickets at the door for most plays and musicals in Honolulu. The main theaters are *Blaisdell Memorial Center Concert Hall,* Ward and King Sts. (536-7334 or 521-2911); *Honolulu Community Theater,* Makapuu and Aloha Aves. (734-0274).

MUSIC: The *Honolulu Symphony* plays at the Blaisdell Center Concert Hall (536-7334). Rock musicians appear at the Blaisdell Center Arena (536-7332 or 521-2911) or sometimes at Aloha Stadium (487-3877).

NIGHTCLUBS AND NIGHTLIFE: Outside of Las Vegas, Honolulu is probably the biggest nightlife town in the country. With a large tourist industry to support it and a Hawaiian musical tradition to provide the raw material, it does indeed seem that Kalakaua Avenue — and plenty of side streets — swing from about 8 PM until dawn, most nights of the week. Hawaii's most famous singer and entertainer, Don Ho, plays the *Hilton Dome,* 2005 Kalia Rd., in the Hilton Hawaiian Village (942-3843). The *Prow Lounge* in the Sheraton-Waikiki Hotel (922-4422), and *Canoe House* in Ilikai Hotel, 1777 Ala Wai (949-3811) are popular nightclubs. Danny Kaleikini plays at the Kahala Hilton's *Hala Terrace,* 5000 Kahala Ave. (734-2211).

SINS: In the same way that black has become beautiful on the mainland, being a Polynesian-Hawaiian is a point of *pride* nowadays in Honolulu. You'll see a fine display of Hawaiian *anger* simply by saying, "I'm from the States." Islanders are too.

The city has go-go dancers, strippers, massage girls, and booksellers adept at pandering to every kink — everything, in short, you could ask of a self-respecting tropical paradise in the way of *lust.* It outdoes itself in that field at the *Club Hubba-Hubba*, 25 N Hotel St. (536-7698), in the center of the red-light district.

LOCAL SERVICES: Business Services – Una May Young, Suite 3206, Manor Wing, Sheraton-Waikiki Hotel, 2255 Kalakaua Ave. (922-4422).

Mechanic – Theo's 76 Station and Auto Repair Shop, 1489 Punchbowl St. (536-1545).

Babysitting – Merry-Go-Round Child Care Center, 4224 Keanu St. (737-5558).

BEST IN TOWN

Checking In: Some people say that Waikiki is almost wall-to-wall hotels today, but that's not quite true. Nevertheless, there are a confusing number to choose from. It works out to your advantage if your first choice happens to be fully booked. Pick your hotel well. It's not just a place you're merely overnighting, it will be your tropical headquarters during the Honolulu sojourn. Expect to pay around $50 or more for a double at those places we've listed as expensive; between $35 and $45 at those designated moderate; under $35 at hotels listed as inexpensive.

Kahala Hilton – A deluxe, prestigious 372-room modern resort located in the Kahala district, between Waialae Golf Course and Waialae Beach. The Kahala consists of two rectangular ten-story buildings with balconies (overflowing with bougainvillea). The 6½ acres of ground include an 800-foot beachfront and a tropical lagoon with dolphins and other aquatic playmates. The Kahala's reputation is based on excellent service. It seems to be addictive — people come back year after year. The Kahala is operated by the Hilton International Company. 5000 Kahala Ave. (734-2211). Expensive.

Hilton Hawaiian Village – Not to be confused with the Kahala, Hawaiian Village is owned by Hilton Hotels Corporation chain, and is a thing distinct. With 2,612 rooms, and more to come, Hilton Hawaiian Village is a gigantic resort campus with five main structures spread over 22 acres. The best rooms are, generally, in the Rainbow Tower. The widest, prettiest section of beach is right outside the door, where the Hilton's own rainbow catamarans dock alongside. The trees and plants on the grounds are labeled, so you can call them by name. The Rainbow Bazaar shopping area has tantalizing, unusual items on display. 2005 Kalia Rd. (949-4321). Expensive.

Royal Hawaiian – Fondly known as "The Pink Palace" or "Pink Lady," this 525-room hotel was *the* place to stay in the 1930s when luxury liners steamed into Honolulu with elegant passengers who stayed for months. The pink stucco Mediterranean-style building retains its glittering chandeliers and long corridors, although it has changed hands since its 1927 opening, and is now under the wing of the Sheraton-Waikiki. Its tradition of elegance is still highly respected on the island. The beach is wide and particularly nice, but the rooms vary. Avoid the new tower — it's awfully dull. The gracious, older rooms are really what give this place its charm. Make your reservations through the Sheraton-Waikiki, 2255 Kalakaua Ave. (922-4422). Expensive.

Ilikai Hotel – Frequently used as a location for the TV series "Hawaii Five-O," the 800-room Ilikai isn't exactly in the center of the action. It is pretty close to the Duke Kahanomoku section of Waikiki beach (you get there by crossing a long, private footbridge) and has a great view of the Ala Wai Yacht Harbor, a dynamite outdoor glass elevator, and a good restaurant, *Champeaux's.* There are also two swimming pools and seven tennis courts. 1777 Ala Moana Blvd. (949-3811). Expensive to moderate.

Moana Hotel – A Victorian grande dame perhaps a wee bit past her prime, the Moana hasn't changed much since opening in 1901. The Sheraton chain has taken over operations, but even so, the Moana clings to another age. In addition to its great location on the beach, the 390-room Moana is known for its Robert Louis Stevenson tree, more than 100 years old. Most rooms have no air-conditioning. 2365 Kalakaua Ave. (922-3111). Moderate.

Waikiki Surf – This is one of the "finds" of Honolulu. In a semi-residential part of Waikiki, it's friendly, clean, decorated in blue and green, quiet, and delightfully inexpensive. Some rooms have kitchenettes. Perhaps best of all, the 288-room Waikiki Surf has two companions — the 102-room Waikiki Surf East (422 Royal Hawaiian Ave.), and the 110-room Waikiki Surf West (412 Lewers St.) — owned and managed by the same people. The original Waikiki Surf is at 2000 Kuhio Ave. (switchboard for all three, 923-7671). Inexpensive.

EATING OUT: Strange though it seems, and disappointing though it is, there are only a few truly noteworthy Hawaiian restaurants in Honolulu. Every once in a while you can find a good Hawaiian dish in a non-Hawaiian restaurant. As long as Papeete, Singapore, Hong Kong, and Manila are around, Honolulu can never claim the title of Pacific headquarters of culinary excellence. But there are some interesting places with inviting menus and charming surroundings. Expect to pay $35 or more at those places we've described as expensive;

between $20 and $35 at those places listed as moderate; under $20, inexpensive. Prices don't include drinks, wine, or tips.

The Third Floor – One of the best restaurants in Honolulu, so named because it lives on the third floor of the Hawaiian Regent Hotel. The Third Floor has elegant parquet tables, high-backed rattan chairs, a small fountain, and a fish pond. The "Promising Start" buffet includes hearts of artichoke and shrimp vinaigrette. Entrées come with a generous relish tray, an excellent salad, an Indian naan bread, so you might want to skip the buffet. In addition to the scampi, shellfish special, rack of lamb, prime ribs, Châteaubriand, and saddle of venison, there are excellent curries and a number of daily specials. There's an inspiring selection of desserts, but all meals conclude with a serving of chilled bonbons dramatically presented on a "steaming" bowl of evaporating dry ice. Open daily. Reservations necessary. Major credit cards. 2552 Kalakaua Ave. (922-6611). Expensive.

Maile Restaurant – Manager Charleen "Charley" Goodness goes out of her way to see that all's well with her Continental menu. The roast duck with Grand Marnier sauce is superb. The view leaves something to be desired (the restaurant is under the lobby) and this is one of the few places in Honolulu where a jacket is required for men. Open daily. Reservations advised. Credit cards accepted. Kahala Hilton Hotel, 5000 Kahala Ave. (734-2211). Expensive.

Nick's Fish Market – Without a doubt, the best fish restaurant in Honolulu. Sitting under the lobby of the Waikiki Gateway Hotel, which makes it dark, it's the best place to try fresh island opakapaka, similar to a red snapper, and mahimahi, a traditional Hawaiian favorite. Open daily. Reservations advised. Major credit cards. Waikiki Gateway Hotel, 2070 Kalakaua Ave. (955-6333). Expensive.

John Dominis – This is the most extraordinary restaurant in Honolulu and is much favored by well-to-do Hawaiians. It stands at the end of a most unpromising street of warehouses and light industries on a promontory overlooking the Kewalo Basin and the Pacific. The smell of fresh fish is everywhere. At a central island lavishly laden with fruits of the sea, a chef shucks oysters, steams clams, and makes broth. In saltwater pools surrounded by substantial dining tables, spiny lobsters and carp clamber and swim around. Mainland specialties such as Maine lobster and Maryland crabs arrive at John Dominis fresh, but this is the ideal place to sample island seafood. *Ono* (wahoo), *hapuu* (grouper), and *opelu* (mackerel) are all available in season. The Cioppino stew of soft- and hard-shell seafood and fresh fish, cooked in tomatoes, herbs, and spices, is unbeatable. This is also one of the few restaurants in the city with a first-class bar serving decent drinks. Open daily for dinner; Sundays for brunch also. Major credit cards. Reservations necessary. 43 Ahui St. (523-0955). Expensive.

The Willows – It is quite simply the most famous restaurant in the state and the place to sample traditional Hawaiian dishes. *The Willows'* celebrated Poi Dinner offers many of these, including poi itself, steamed laulau, sweet potato, chicken luau, lomi salmon, limu kohu, green onion, fresh pineapple, and haupia. If these seem too exotic, the curry dishes, leavened with coconut milk, are superb. This is also the perfect place for wearing an aloha shirt or muumuu for the first time—the rural, tropical atmosphere of palm trees and thatched roofs seems to call for it. Open daily. Reservations necessary. Major credit cards. 901 Hausten St. (946-4808). Expensive.

Michel's – At most beachfront restaurants in Honolulu, the cooking takes a back seat to the view. *Michel's* is not one of them. For a start, the decor does not suggest a mere extension of sand and ocean. The dining room is elegant and subdued. Although there are occasionally deft local touches, such as prosciutto served with papaya, most of the dishes tend to be classic. Even the opakapaka is served véronique style with a champagne sauce added. The roast veal with cream sauce and the lobster bisque with cognac are memorable. Jacket required for dinner. Reservations necessary. Most major credit cards. In the Colony Surf Hotel at 2895 Kalakaua Ave., Diamond Head (923-6552). Expensive.

Canlis' – Sometimes called *Canlis' Broiler,* it is one of the most attractive restaurants in the city. An old timer on the Waikiki dining scene, it is famous for its salads and its desserts. The steak Pierre is a specialty. There are separate sections for men wearing jackets and men without, and a tie is not a bad idea, too. 2100 Kalakaua Ave. (923-2324). Expensive.

Bagwells – The fine Continental menu and gracious service at this elegant dining room on the third floor of the *Hyatt Regency Waikiki Hotel* makes a meal here worth the stiff price. Jackets are required for men. Open daily. Reservations advised. Major credit cards. 2424 Kalakaua Ave. (922-9292). Expensive.

Matteo's – An Italian restaurant popular with local and visiting celebrities in the Marine Surf Hotel. Generally considered the best Italian restaurant in town. Owner Matty Jordan also has Matteo's in Westwood, California. The chicken and veal dishes are terrific. You might want to try the pepper steak named after Frank Sinatra, with an antipasto to start. Open daily. Reservations advised. Major credit cards. Marine Surf Hotel, 364 Seaside Ave. (922-5551). Expensive to moderate.

Bon Appetit – This is one of the newest French restaurants on the Honolulu scene and fast becoming a favorite. It has the look of an elegant bistro in the French provinces, with its cane-back chairs and light pink linen. The menu is imaginative and includes an unusual snapper mousse, seafood soup with saffron, snails in puff pastry, and veal rib with coriander. Open daily for dinner. Reservations advised. Most major credit cards. In the Discovery Bay complex at 1778 Ala Moana Blvd. (942-3837). Moderate.

The Bistro – The escargots are consistently good, the house pâté is excellent, and the steak Diane flambé with Worcestershire, shallots, and brandy is in a class by itself. There can be a long wait at the bar even if you have reservations, and the $8.50 minimum per person for dinner doesn't include drinks, but the food is consistently good. Open daily. Reservations necessary. Major credit cards. 3058 Monsarrat Ave. (735-4444). Expensive.

Trattoria – A number of connoisseurs insist this is top entry in the Italian food category in Honolulu. At the very least, it's neck and neck with Matteo's. For one thing, Trattoria chefs don't overload the menu with tomato paste, and they cook many dishes al burro — delicately, in butter, instead of doused in olive oil. The lasagna in this charmingly decorated restaurant is well worth tasting. So are cotelctto di vitello alla Parmigiana and pollo alla Romana. The cannelloni Milanese is definitely a "don't miss." Open daily. Reservations advised on weekends. Major credit cards. Cinerama Edgewater Hotel, Kalia Rd. and Beach Walk (923-8415). Moderate.

Prince Kuhio's – The walls of this colorful Victorian-style restaurant are decorated with photographs of Hawaiian royalty, and the menu ranges from fine beef dishes to Hawaiian specialties. Conveniently located on the ground level of the Ala Moana Center facing the park, it's not to be confused with the Prince Kuhio Hotel in Waikiki. Closed Sundays. Reservations advised. Major credit cards. Ala Moana Blvd. (946-2102). Moderate.

Mon Cher Ton Ton – Don't be deceived by the French name. This is a Japanese restaurant, on the ground floor of the Ala Moana Hotel. At one end there is a "teppan island" where up to 32 can be served sautéed beef or similar dishes from the big teppan grill. At the tables you can sample delicious shabu-shabu, Japan's answer to Swiss fondue. You cook the beef yourself, holding each piece in boiling sauce for a few moments with chopsticks, then dipping it into special sauces. If you're really curious about how a Japanese dining spot got a French name, ask, but be prepared for a long story. Open daily. Reservations advisable. Major credit cards. Ala Moana Hotel (955-4811). Moderate.

House of Hong – Don't leave Honolulu without picking up chopsticks at least once, and this is as good a place to test drive the twin utensils as any. Work your way through standard Cantonese dishes like fried rice, lo mein, egg foo yung, and chop suey. Silent, attentive waitresses drift through the black and gold dining room, bringing you all the won lo bao (excellent) delicacies imaginable. Try the combination plate at lunch — you get a sampling of several dishes. Although prices are higher at dinner, two people can fill up for under $25. Open daily. Reservations recommended Fridays and Saturdays. Major credit cards accepted. 260A Lewers St. (923-0202). Inexpensive.

Mandarin – Honolulu also has several Mandarin or Szechwan-style Chinese restaurants. Here you are given huge portions of Shanghai steamed dumplings and Mongolian beef, sautéed with green onions and red peppers. The Mandarin makes its own noodles, great for gobbling. It's best to go with a group of four or more and order "family style" — passing around several different dishes. Open daily. Reservations advisable. Major credit cards accepted. 942 McCully St. (946-3242). Inexpensive.

King Tsin – This spicy favorite serves up very tasty hot and sour soup. The crackling chicken is chopstick-lickin' good, as is the Hunan pork sautéed with broccoli. Open daily. Reservations advisable. Major credit cards. 1486 S King St. (946-3273). Inexpensive.

Fisherman's Wharf – Tuna and charter boats tie up at the dock alongside this seafront restaurant where you'll be charmed by the nautical atmosphere and enchanted by the modest prices. (You'll find plenty of other people share your enthusiasm, so be prepared for crowds, and be kind to the waitresses — they're overworked.) The shrimp Louie salad in abalone shell is great. Open daily. Reservations not necessary. Major credit cards. Kewalo Basin (538-3808). Inexpensive.

Dickens – All the artifacts here, including the gorgeous bar, were once part of a city pub in Yorkshire, England. The food is every bit as successful as the decor: there's real steak and kidney pie, angels on horseback (grilled oysters and bacon), and genuine sausage rolls. Even the fish and chips, though not pub grub, strictly speaking, will make a Limey feel homesick. The bar sells beers from more than a dozen countries. Major credit cards. Open daily. 1221 Kapiolani Blvd. (531-2727). Inexpensive.

Wailana Coffee House – Anyone can find a restaurant in a Sheraton, but finding one that gives good value for the money usually is harder. Wailana Coffee House is one of those discoveries that will make it easier for you to enjoy your stay if you're on a budget. It's open 24 hours a day and serves sandwiches, snacks, full dinners. Most dishes are American, but this is one of those places where you can try Oriental food like steak teriyaki. Open daily. No reservations. Some credit cards. In the Wailana Apartment Bldg., 1860 Ala Moana Ave., across from the Hilton Dome (955 1764). Inexpensive.

HOUSTON

Houston is dazzling to the newcomer. Its downtown mushrooms unexpectedly from the flat Texas prairie in a striking display of modern architecture. The city stretches for miles in all directions, apparently without limits. Massive expressway systems, always busy, pump traffic in and out of the metropolis that's been called the "golden buckle of the Sunbelt." Construction activity is evident everywhere, "growth," an often-heard byword. Although a century and a half old, the past has been all but wiped out, overrun by a sense of newness and bravado of the prosperity in the here and now, and a promise of more to come. For Houston is the 20th century's incarnation of the 19th-century dream of industrial progress.

Houston is the fourth largest city in the country (metropolitan area population of 1.7 million) and the fastest growing. The economy is unaffected by national economic fluctuations; there are enough jobs to accommodate the 1,538 newcomers arriving each week. About 250 companies have relocated major operations in the city since 1970. Fueling much of this is oil, still the big word in the economy; but the key to the rapidly expanding commerce is diversity. Stoked by petro-dollars, finance, retailing, engineering, and construction have become major economic forces, and Houston ranks as the only Southern or Southwestern city included in the nation's top ten manufacturing centers.

Chaos has been one price of progress. Houston has grown faster than its civic services. There are no zoning laws, little evidence of city planning beyond the downtown, insufficient mass transit, congested traffic, and consequently, air pollution.

When a 19th-century traveler described Houston as a place "where one can no longer rationalize or explain what he sees," he spoke honestly not only of Houston past, but of Houston present, and undeniably, Houston future. It's the place where there are no state or city income taxes, but you still have to register cowbrands at the courthouse.

In Houston good luck comes in the form of oil, and that was as true in the founding of the city as it is today. In 1836, even before the first street existed, founders J. K. and A. C. Allen, two brothers from New York, were advertising their new town nationwide as the state's garden spot. In reality it was humid, marshy, and mosquito infested. People came anyway, enticed by the Allens' grandiose descriptions, cheap land, and the promises of great moneymaking opportunities.

Little did the newcomers realize how closely luck was following them. At the turn of the century, oil was discovered 90 miles away, and Houston found itself in the middle of the great Texas oil boom. In 1914, civic leaders built a ship channel 32 miles inland to the city, creating a fairweather port. By the 1960s the two — oil and port — combined to make Houston one of the world's major petrochemical centers creating the backbone of the city's economic strength.

Pure science as well as technology has reinforced this strength. The Lyndon B. Johnson Space Center has been the focal point of almost every manned space flight and has earned Houston the moniker "Space City." The Texas Medical Center, noted for cancer research, is one of the largest medical facilities in the country.

But the boom extends to more than science and business. Similar cultural growth has taken place, in large part due to those who've made fortunes in Houston. Their bullish attitude has provided the city with some of the best facilities for the performing arts in the Southwest. The Grand Opera, Houston Symphony, and Alley Theater, the established resident company, are highly acclaimed nationally. The arts are thriving, patronized by a citizenry that seems to be dedicated to making their home as renowned for cultural achievement as it is for business success.

It's been said that Houston has two seasons — eternal summer outside, and winter inside, borne on gusts from ubiquitous high powered air conditioners. The climate *is* hot, but being outdoors is a way of life, not a seasonal occupation. Municipal parks equipped with fine facilities for swimming, golf, tennis, and hiking are abundant. Open-air concerts, Shakespeare in the park, and sidewalk art festivals occur frequently year-round. Just 50 miles away, Galveston Bay and the Gulf of Mexico are a haven for water enthusiasts.

The city's emergence as an international business center has lent it a cosmopolitan image unique to the South. Over forty foreign consulates have offices here. In the streets, you'll still hear Texas drawls, but you'll also detect many foreign accents. Restaurants, especially those in the Montrose district, offer cuisine from all over the globe.

Things are happening at a furious, unpredictable pace. Houston is a city in the process of finding itself, an open frontier that draws new people like a magnet — where hard work is more the measure of success than family ties. Houstonians think of their city as America's next great city, and it's hard for a newcomer not to sense this after a day here. Given the positive economic forces at work, there's a fair chance that the newcomer will become a resident and help shape that future.

HOUSTON AT-A-GLANCE

SEEING THE CITY: The revolving *Spindletop* cocktail lounge atop the *Hyatt Regency* turns on the Houston panorama. One revolution takes in all of Space City. To the south stands downtown, to the north an industrial area and the ship channel, industrial sprawl to the east, and Houston's residential neighborhoods to the west. 1200 Louisiana (654-1234).

Stationary, but splendid for a view of the downtown skyline, is Sam Houston Park. Dominating the cityscape are the futuristic Pennzoil Towers designed by Philip Johnson, and the city's other big oil headquarters, Shell and Tenneco. 515 Allen Pkwy.

SPECIAL PLACES: A car is a necessity for mobility in the Houston sprawl. Mass transit is unreliable and not always accessible. Several of the attractions are concentrated in a few areas, so you can park and walk, but otherwise, you'll be driving from place to place.

Museum of Natural Science – Each of the 13 halls in the largest such institution of the Southwest pertains to a different natural science including two subjects near and dear to the wallets of Houstonians — oil and space. You can learn how oil is formed, see a model of an offshore oil rig, or manipulate a working model of a fault — by turning a wheel you can create an earthquake. The space exhibit includes reproductions of the lunar Rover (the real one is still up there) and a model of the space capsule used by John Glenn. Not as endearing, but also on display, are Ecuadorian shrunken heads and a Diplodocus dinosaur skeleton. The Museum of Medical Science displays the human body — yours. You can listen to the rhythm of your heartbeat or test your lung capacity, or, if you're too modest to put yourself on display, skip it and visit the Burke Baker Planetarium. Open daily. Free. 5800 Caroline St. in Hermann Park (526-4273).

Houston Zoological Gardens – One of the best zoos around, this abounds with some rarely seen animals in unusual settings. Vampire bats, flying squirrels, and bush babies inhabit a red light district where time is reversed and you can see the bats feeding on blood at 2:30 in the afternoon. The Tropical Bird House has over 200 exotic birds in a rain forest. But our favorite is the Gorilla House, where the royal couple of the jungle swing in primordial splendor complete with waterfalls, vines, moats, and skylighting. There's also a children's zoo where kids can make contact with creatures from four regions of the world. Open daily. Free. S Main at Bissonnet in Hermann Park (523-0149).

Museum of Fine Arts – With neoclassical beginnings and finishing touches by Mies van der Rohe, this structure could house most anything — and it does, including the Ima Hogg collection of Southwestern Indian art with pottery and Kachina dolls, an extensive collection of Frederic Remington's works, a pre-Columbian gallery, and a modern sculpture garden with Alexander Calder's "Crab." Closed Mondays. Free. 1001 Bissonnet (526-1361).

The International Strip – On the main drag of Montrose, one of the city's oldest residential neighborhoods, natives and visitors come to browse through antique shops, foreign bazaars, art galleries, boutiques, flea markets, and off-beat book shops. The art festivals held in October and April are the largest in the South. Sidewalk cafés and restaurants allow patrons to try dishes from around the world, linger in a wine-tasting shop, or just hang out in a tree house bar. A *Moveable Feast* is great for health food sandwiches (3827 Dunlavy, 528-8905) and for dessert, *Udder Delight* makes homemade ice cream (1521 Westheimer; 522-4436). The Strip is also the showplace for exotic nightlife, everything from bellydancing to body painting. More sedate, but also in the neighborhood is the Rothko Chapel, a meditation chapel with works by Russian-born painter Mark Rothko (3900 Yupon, 524-9839). The Strip extends from the 100 to 1800 block of Westheimer.

River Oaks – If you're wondering where all that oil money goes, you'll find that no one's trying to hide it. You can't miss the palatial mansions and huge estates, home of Houston's super-rich, who have it and flaunt it. River Oaks Blvd. between Westheimer and the Country Club.

Galleria Mall – This stunning, glass-domed, tri-level edifice shows how the wealth is spread, Houston style. Among the stores here are *Neiman-Marcus, Lord & Taylor, Sakowitz, Tiffany's,* and *Way Out West* (western wear), and across the street is *Saks Fifth Avenue.* There's also a skating rink on the ground floor. Open daily. 5015 Westheimer (621-0656).

Sam Houston Park – One of the few signs that there was an old Houston, this project of the Harris County Heritage Society encompasses a restored country church, homes, and shops, depicting the lifestyle of 19th-century Houstonians. The Kellum-Noble House is the oldest brick house in Houston, and contains pioneer equipment and furnishings, and the Cherry House is a Greek Revival home furnished with American Empire antiques. Tours begin at the office (515 Allen Pkwy., 223-8367). Open daily. Admission charge. Allen Pkwy. and Bagby St.

Astrodome – Besides serving as home for the Astros, Oilers, and the University of Houston Cougars, this $36 million domed stadium, big enough to accommodate an 18-story building (standing) or 66,000 spectators and the world's largest and most dazzling scoreboard (474 feet long and 4 stories high complete with pyrotechnical display when the home team scores), is Texas' most visited attraction. There are guided tours of the Dome at 11 AM, 1 PM, and 3 PM featuring a multimedia blowout on the scoreboard. Open daily. Admission charge. 4¾ miles southwest at I-610 and Kirby Dr. (799-9500).

Astroworld – Also part of Astrodomain, Houston's version of Disneyland offers 70 acres of entertainment including 11 theme amusement parks, water-skiing spectaculars, trained dolphin shows, and high-diving feats. The new Texas Cyclone Roller Coaster has been inducing its share of rave reviews, screams, and nausea. Open daily June through August and weekends during spring and fall. (Check locally for shortened or extended hours.) Admission charge. 9001 Kirby Dr., across from the Astrodome (748-1234).

San Jacinto Battleground – The 570-foot-tall San Jacinto Monument marks the spot where Sam Houston defeated Mexican General Santa Anna to win Texas' independence. The 460-acre state park also includes a Museum of Texas History tracing the region's development from the Indian civilization through Texas' annexation by the United States; the museum also houses the battleship *Texas,* veteran of both World Wars. Closed Mondays (open daily in the summer). Free. Farm Road 134, off Hwy. 225, 21 miles east of downtown Houston (479-2431).

Port of Houston – From an observation platform atop Wharf 9, visitors can see the turning basin area of this country's third largest port. To inspect some of the elaborate industrial-shipping developments, take an excursion along the ship channel aboard the MV *Sam Houston* (make reservations in advance). No trips on Mondays or in September. Free. Gate 8, off Clinton Dr. (225-0671).

Lyndon B. Johnson Space Center – Until you fly Trans-Universe to the moon, this is the closest you can get. This 1,620-acre campus-like facility is the training ground for the Gemini, Apollo, and Skylab astronauts, and the monitoring center for the NASA manned space flights. The Visitor Orientation Center displays craft that have flown in space, moon rocks, and a lunar module, and the Mission Control Center houses some of the most sophisticated communications computer data equipment in the world. You can visit the Control Center and the Skylab Training Room on guided tours, available by reservation. NASA films are shown throughout the day in the auditorium. Open daily. Free. 25 miles SE of downtown Houston via I-45 (483-0123).

■ **EXTRA SPECIAL:** Just 51 miles south of Houston along I-45 is *Galveston Island,* a leading Gulf Coast resort area. Stewart Beach is the principal public beach and there's good swimming, surfing, sailing, water skiing, and deep-sea fishing (reservations taken at boats on Piers 18 and 19 of the Galveston Yacht Basin). Seafood restaurants, art galleries, and restored turn-of-the-century homes are in the onetime vacation destination of the oil magnates clustered around Strand Blvd.

SOURCES AND RESOURCES

The Houston Convention and Visitors' Bureau is best for brochures, maps, and general information. 1522 Main St. (658-4200). Many banks also provide free visitor information kits as does the Chamber of Commerce. 1100 Milam (651-1313).

All telephone numbers are in the 713 area code unless otherwise indicated.

For Local Coverage – *The Post,* morning daily; the *Chronicle,* evening daily; the *Tribune,* weekly, published Thursdays. All are available at newsstands.

The revised edition of *Texas Monthly's Guide to Houston* by Felicia Coates and Harriet Howle (Mediatex Communications Corp., $3.95) is a comprehensive local guide. *The Intrepid Walker's Guide* to Houston by Eli Zal and Doug Milburn ($2.95) is the best guide to the network of underground tunnels connecting major downtown buildings, and other off-the-beaten-track walking tours.

For Food – Check *Best Restaurants Texas* by Ann Valentine, Derro Evans, and James Medlin (101 Productions, Inc., $2.95) and the *Texas Monthly Guide.*

CLIMATE AND CLOTHES: In the summer, Houston is hot and humid. Winds from the Gulf of Mexico create warm summer nights, and keep the winters and the rest of the year relatively warm. During the winter, light jackets are advisable. Dress is informal and lightweight clothes are most comfortable, but indoors air-conditioning is in full force during the hot months so you'd be wise to carry a sweater.

GETTING AROUND: Bus — Metropolitan Transit Authority of Harris County serves the downtown area and the suburbs, but the system can be confusing and unreliable. Mini-buses operate in the downtown shopping area. For route information contact the main office, 1212 Main (651-1212).

Taxi – Cabs can be ordered on the phone, picked up in front of hotels and terminals, or, with some difficulty, hailed in the street. Major companies are Sky-Jack's (523-6080); and Yellow Cab (236-1111). Be forewarned, however, that taxi rates are rather high, and a cab ride from the airport can run as much as $30.

Car Rental – Because Houston is a huge, sprawling city whose backbone is its extensive freeway system, a car is the most practical mode of travel. Try to avoid being caught in Houston's rush hour, during which traffic is impossibly snarled. All the major national firms serve Houston. Local service is provided by Greater Houston Leasing, Inc., 2888 S Richey (944-7130), and Thrifty Rent-A-Car at Hobby Airport (644-3351) and Intercontinental Airport (449-0126).

MUSEUMS: The Museum of Natural Sciences and the Museum of Fine Arts are described in some detail under *Special Places.*

Other notable Houston museums are:

Contemporary Arts Museum, 5216 Montrose at Bissonnet (526-3129).

Bayou Bend (early American furnishings), 1 Westcott St. (529-8773).

MAJOR COLLEGES AND UNIVERSITIES: Among Houston's educational institutions are Rice University (6100 S Main St., 527-8101), which has a good reputation for its engineering and science schools; University of Houston (4800 Calhoun Rd., 749-1011); and the Texas Medical Center (between Fannin St. and Holcombe Blvd., 792-2121).

SPECIAL EVENTS: Check publications listed above for exact dates. For two weeks in late February and early March, Houston cowboys come out of their closets in full force and descend on the Astrodome complex for the *Houston Rodeo and Livestock Show.* There's plenty of action — rodeo events and country and western concerts. During April and October, local and regional artists show their stuff in the Westheimer Art Show, an outdoor arts and crafts festival on Westheimer Rd. Hotels are filled within a 100-mile radius during the 4-day *Offshore Technology Conference,* the world's biggest oil industry show in late April and early May.

SPORTS: Tickets to professional games can be picked up at Ticket Connection, 2031 Southwest Fwy. (524-3687).

Baseball – The National League's Houston *Astros* play at the Astrodome from April to September, I-610 and Kirby Dr. (799-9555).

Football – The *Oilers* also play at the Dome from October to January (799-9555).

Basketball – The National Basketball Association's *Rockets* play from December to April at the Summit, 10 Greenway Plaza (627-0600).

Rodeo – On Saturday nights year-round, the *Simonton Rodeo* rounds 'em up with real live rodeo followed by country and western dancing, on Westheimer Rd., 45 minutes west of the city (499-1479).

Ballooning – The *Rainbow's End Balloon Port* sends 'em up weekend mornings at dawn when the winds are calm. You can watch the balloonists rise to the occasion, and if they don't, join them for breakfast. 18710 Montgomery Rd. (469-9615).

Bicycling – Rent from Recycled Cycles, 7921 Westheimer (977-1393). A good bike trail runs from the Sabine Street Bridge (just east of Allen's Landing) along Buffalo Bayou to Shepherd, and back along the Memorial side of the Bayou. The City of Houston Parks and Recreation Department offers a list of other bike routes. 2999 S Wayside (641-4111).

Fishing – Best for fishing is Galveston, where you can wet a line in the Gulf of Mexico off piers or from deep-sea charters that leave from Piers 18 and 19 of the Galveston Yacht Basin.

Golf – Best public course for the duffer is in Hermann Park, 6110 Golf Course Dr. (529-9788). The most challenging of the municipal courts is in Brock Park, 8201 John Ralston Rd., off Old Beaumont Hwy. (458-1350).

Tennis – The municipally run Memorial Tennis Center has 18 Laykold courts, showers, lockers, tennis shop, and practice court. 600 Memorial Loop Dr. (861-3765). There are free courts in most of the city parks.

Swimming – There are 42 municipal pools in Houston, open from June through Labor Day. The Hermann Park pool is convenient. 2020 Hermann Dr. (222-5525).

THEATER: For current offerings check the daily and weekly publications listed above. *The Alley Theater,* Houston's established and acclaimed resident company, performs everything from classical drama to experimental plays, October to May, at 615 Texas Ave. (box office, 228-8421). During the summer, the *Miller Outdoor Theater* offers a variety of entertainments, all free, ranging from pop concerts, *Frank Young's Theater Under the Stars* musical extravaganzas, to a Shakespeare Festival, at 100 Concert Dr. in Hermann Park (522-0701). *The Windmill Dinner Theater,* 390 Town and Country Blvd. (464-7655), offers light comedies year-round. Colleges and universities in the area produce plays and musicals.

MUSIC: Jones Hall for the Performing Arts provides a home for Houston's own companies as well as offering concerts and performances throughout the year by internationally renowned artists and companies. The nationally acclaimed *Houston Symphony Orchestra* performs there from September to May; the *Houston Ballet,* the only resident professional ballet company in the Southwest, from September to March; and the *Houston Grand Opera* from September to March at 615 Louisiana in Civic Center (222-3415). All give free performances at the Miller Theater in the summer. Big rock concerts are held at the Music Hall throughout the year. 810 Bagby in the Civic Center (222-3267).

NIGHTCLUBS AND NIGHTLIFE: Depending on what you want, you can unwind or recharge at one or more of Houston's nightspots. Current favorites for progressive country music, Texas style, and local color: *Steamboat Springs,* 4919 W Alabama (629-6650) or *Gilley's Club,* 4500 Spencer Hwy. in Pasadena on Houston's southeast perimeter (941-7990); for jazz, *Rockefeller's,* 3620 Washington (864-6242); *Diamond Lil's,* for ballroom dancing, 1700 W Loop S (960-0111); *Todd's,* for backgammon and folk music, 5050 Richmond (626-5990).

SINS: While conservative Dallas plods along congratulating itself on the Cowgirls, Houstonians are hustling bucks, and as you'd expect in a town with the sort of wide-open economy that is the city's *pride,* the seven deadly sins are prospering along with everything else. The Chamber of Commerce won't talk about it, but massage parlors, adult bookstores, and pornographic movie houses are flourishing all over town. One Houston banker likes to regale his out-of-town clients with lunchtime tours of the topless, bottomless, and middleless bars — and with a population full of such friends of *lust,* it's no wonder that so far attempts to pass the sort of city ordinances that keep the situation under control in other cities have met with defeat.

Avarice has drawn a lot of people here. Singles, for instance. Houston has more young people, and more single people, than most other American cities. There's no shortage of singles bars, and no shortage of action.

Everyone aspires to the good life in posh suburban River Oaks, portrayed in the recent best seller *Blood and Money* as rich folk getting their hair frosted, playing tennis, suntanning, and doing each other in. Some of the activities discussed in that book ring true; people might call it *sloth,* though it requires a lot of effort to do nothing elegantly.

Among those who haven't yet made it, the stupendous mansions constructed along River Oaks Boulevard provoke *envy.* A half-dozen all-you-can-eat buffet restaurants like the *San Jacinto Inn* give the Houston residents the chance to sublimate their frustrations with *gluttony.*

Anger? Check out the freeways at the rush hour, especially in the afternoon when it's bloody hot, and especially on the Southwest Freeway, on which you face the sun and the traffic crawls, for miles like a turtle speeding toward a soup tureen.

LOCAL SERVICES: Business Services – Business Services of Houston, 2537 S Gessner (780-7335).

Mechanics – Altenberg's Garage for American cars, 2306 Brazos (523-2837). For foreign cars, Barney Garver Motors, 7025 Old Katy Rd. (869-4853), or Poutous Auto Repair, 4601 Kelvin (524-4444).

Babysitting – Grandmothers Inc., 9821 Katy Fwy. (932-9553).

BEST IN TOWN

CHECKING IN: Whether you want to be treated like royalty (try the liveried service at the Warwick) or go rugged (YMCA), Houston hotels can suit you. But try to make reservations in advance because the influx of new residents and visitors fills most places to near capacity year-round. Expect to pay $100 or more for a double room in a hotel in the expensive range; $50 to $70 in the moderate; and $35 in the inexpensive category.

Warwick – The traditional favorite, and why not, with liveried service, marble statuary, and European styling. The atmosphere's pure plush, as are the fine shops in the lobby. Location is good, overlooking Hermann Park, and there are many frills — a dining room, café, dancing and entertainment, pool, golf, and tennis privileges, steam baths, and exercise room. 300 rooms. Pay garage. 5701 S Main St. (526-1991). Expensive.

Houston Oaks – Smack in the middle of the luxurious Galleria Mall, the ideal spot for someone on a shopping spree. And if you really want to splurge, for around $335 a night you can indulge yourself in the Crown Suite, a penthouse with a spectacular view of western Houston, two fireplaces, 2½ baths, a banquet table for 14, and a grand piano. There are plenty of extras even if you don't go all the way — a pool, café, entertainment and dancing, and access to ice-skating, a running track, and indoor tennis. 400 rooms. Pay garage. 5011 Westheimer Rd. (623-4300). Expensive.

Whitehall – This deluxe downtown hotel draws lots of corporate types and offers many amenities — shops, pool, café, dancing and entertainment, golf privileges, and a putting green. 325 rooms. Pay garage. 1700 Smith at Jefferson (659-5000). Expensive.

Inn on the Park – This hotel is an addition to the new Riverway complex and part of the Four Seasons chain. The hotel overlooks Houston's 1500-acre Memorial Park, and all 383 rooms have views of either the park and pool, or the lake. Other amenities include two restaurants, a cabaret, health club, outdoor jogging track, four tennis courts, and garage. In Riverway at Post Oak La. and Woodway Dr. (871-8181). Expensive.

Meridien Houston – Among the city's newest luxury hotels, this is part of the chain owned by Air France. And, as expected, the 363-room hotel has a certain Gallic style from its concierge to the nouvelle cuisine served in its restaurant, which some people are saying is the best in town. The *Meridien* is designed for the well-heeled tourist and upper-echelon executives. Downtown, in Allen Center (759-0202). Expensive.

La Colombe D'Or – A five-suite gem that was once the residence of Exxon founder Walter Fondreu. Each suite has its own bedroom, living room, and private dining room. Secretarial and limousine service are included in the room rate, plus a decanter of brandy. The hotel's restaurant is also first rate. 3410 Montrose Ave. (524-7999). Expensive.

Lamar – In the heart of downtown Houston, convenient accommodations. Shops, TV, café, free parking. 375 rooms. Main St. at Lamar (658-8511). Moderate.

The Plaza – Graceful and modest, with pleasant little touches — like the apple and a glass of sherry that are brought to your room every evening. The rooms are attractive with high ceilings and irregularly-shaped bathrooms. The location provides easy access to downtown. Café, bar, pay garage. 100 rooms. 5020 Montrose Blvd. (524-3161). Inexpensive.

Greenway Inn – More of the same, in the city's southwest sector. 2525 Southwest Fwy. (526-2533). Inexpensive.

EATING OUT: Besides offerings of fine regional foods — chili parlors and Mexican restaurants abound — Houston has a great variety of cuisines including seafood fresh from the Gulf of Mexico, Continental, Chinese, Greek, some down-home Southern meals, and even health food. Expect to spend about $50 for a dinner for two at restaurants in the expensive range, $20 to $35 in the moderate range, and $20 or less in the inexpensive range. Prices do not include drinks, wine, or tips.

Tony's – Owner Tony Vallone is on hand most of the time to see that his establishment remains a stronghold of elegance in this purposefully informal city. And it does, with punctilious service by waiters in black tie, understated wood-paneled decor, and fresh flowers providing the backdrop for excellent Continental food. The pâtés and salads are impeccable. Of the entrées, veal piccata with truffles and mushrooms, and red snapper noisette prepared with hazelnuts are the best. Have a Grand Marnier soufflé for dessert, but order it at the beginning of the meal. Closed Sundays. Reservations. Major credit cards. 1801 Post Oak S (622-6778). Expensive.

Maxim's – Consistently good haute cuisine and what is probably the most extensive wine cellar in the Southwest. The decor leaves something to be desired, but once you start eating, you'll forget all about the overtones of bordello red. The menu is weighted toward Gulf seafood, which is prepared well, but the beef is also prime. Chocolate mousse or brandy freeze for dessert are excellent. Closed Sundays. Reservations. Major credit cards. 802 Lamar (877-8899). Expensive.

Uncle Tai's Hunan Yuan – Uncle Tai made his name and reputation as an excellent Hunanese chef in New York. Recently, he gathered his family together and headed south to start his own place — and people in Houston couldn't be happier. This family-run restaurant has impeccable service, and from the Tricolored Lobster to Uncle Tai's Texas–Hunanese-style chicken, the food is wonderful. Open daily. Reservations advised. American Express and Diner's Club accepted. 1980 S Post Oak Rd. (960-8000). Expensive.

Ninfa's – A local must for Mexican fare that seems to be on everyone's list, so you may have to wait in line. But it's worth it, particularly for the tacos al carbon (tortillas wrapped around barbecued pork or beef) and chilpanzingas (ham and cheese wrapped in pastry, fried, and topped with sour cream). There are seven locations now, but the downtown site, near the Mexican community, is still the best. Open daily. No reservations on weekends. Major credit cards. 2704 Navigation (228-1175). Moderate.

San Jacinto Inn – This weathered old inn is adjacent to the San Jacinto Battleground. The freshly cooked seafood dinner comes in great waves of shrimp cocktail, stuffed crabs, tenderloin of trout or red fish, fried chicken, french fries, hot biscuits with fruit preserves, and, if you're still afloat, beverage and dessert. Closed Mondays. Reservations. Major credit cards. On Battleground Rd., off Hwy. 225 (479-2828). Moderate.

Zorba the Greek Café – Fried shrimp and seafood platters, and Greek dishes like tiropitakia (phylo filled with feta cheese), leg of lamb, and a great Greek salad. The place looks like a beer parlor, and is, but they also have retsina. Closed Sundays. No reservations. No credit cards. 202 Tuam (528-1382). Moderate.

Szechuan East – The rather ordinary decor belies some of the spiciest Chinese food around. The fowl dishes are especially good, and best of all is the spicy duck, which you can also order in milder versions. Open daily. No reservations. Major credit cards. 5300 N Braeswood (729-9443). Inexpensive.

Chili's – It's easy to guess the house specialty — the real hot stuff, served steaming, spicy, and thick, concocted from a secret Texas recipe. Otherwise, the jumbo hamburgers and homemade french fries make a solid meal at an easy price. Open daily. No reservations. Credit cards. 5930 Richmond (780-1654). Inexpensive.

The Health Seekers – To cool off from the combined heat of Texan, Mexican, and Chinese spicing, look here for refreshing salads, vegetable sandwiches and dishes, some meat platters, fresh juice drinks, and coolest of all, frozen yogurt. It's all good for you. Open daily. No reservations. Major credit cards. 2946 S Shepherd (526-9268). Inexpensive.

INDIANAPOLIS

Like quite a few other Midwestern cities, Indianapolis is not likely to excite you at first. There are those endless handsome neighborhoods — big trees, big yards, big houses — in an endless procession above 38th Street. Posh suburbs. Elegant shopping malls. The kind of city that might make you assume that it'd be a nice place to live — for a while.

But as in other cities, first impressions are deceptive. This is partly because of the lack of widespread information about the out-of-the-ordinary places that keep the citizens happy, partly because a lot of vociferous visitors left before they got to the heart of the place under the placid surface, partly because residents took their Indianapolis pleasures for granted. But in the last few years, all that taking for granted has come to a halt. At just about the same time the citizens of cities all over the Midwest were realizing that this part of the country was a pretty fine place to live after all, and talking up their cities, and patting themselves on the back for living there, and feeling smug and even holier-than-thou, Richard Lugar — a former Rhodes Scholar who had barely turned thirty — took over as Indianapolis' mayor.

He consolidated the city and county governments in an effort to smooth city finances. The downtown area — which had begun to decline only insofar as the movie houses had nearly all gone to the suburbs, and the better part of the more affluent shops and shoppers had followed them — began to blossom. The old city market — vaulted in cast iron and chockablock with fresh produce stands, fish stands, stands for meats, sausages, cheeses, spices, coffees, and tea — was among the first of the institutions to get fixed up instead of torn down. A Convention Center and elegant Hyatt Regency soon appeared, along with an arena nearby; the latter provides a home for the Indiana Pacers basketball team and such special events as concerts and ice shows. Monument Circle is being transformed into a clean park that's neatly surrounded by red bricks. City boosters call this effort the largest bricklaying undertaking in the world since the turn of the century.

Meanwhile, the excitement spread to the suburbs. Boutiques that had been quietly gaining fame and financial security during the preceding ten years have been joined by scores of others, particularly on the North Side. Broad Ripple — a village in its own right before the city grew around it and took it in — boomed as bath shops and kitchen shops took over quaint little frame houses along its side streets. The same thing is happening to Zionsville, another small village not quite part of Indianapolis' hustle and bustle. A new multilevel shopping center, Keystone at the Crossing, has added something like a bazaar to the city scene. Restaurants sprout, then flourish. The cornfield that some people had called Indianapolis is getting to look pretty lush.

INDIANAPOLIS AT-A-GLANCE

SEEING THE CITY: Indianapolis has some breathtaking vantage points. The highest point is in Crown Hill Cemetery, at the grave of author James Whitcomb Riley. (John Dillinger and Benjamin Harrison are also buried at Crown Hill, which is a National Historic Site.) Entrance at 3402 Boulevard Pl. (925-8231). Soldiers and Sailors Monument gives you the best overview of the layout of the city. Small admission. Monument Circle, downtown (631-6735). The view from *La Tour,* the 35th-floor restaurant at the top of the Indiana National Bank Tower, is also exceptional. 1 Indiana Square (635-3535).

SPECIAL PLACES: You'll find Indianapolis an easy place to get around. Numbered streets always run east and west, and the number of the streets represents the number of blocks north of Washington St. Most of the great places in Indianapolis are spread out north of Washington St.

Indiana State Museum – This really entertaining museum relates the natural and cultural history of the state. Free. 202 N Alabama, at Ohio (232-1637).

Scottish Rite Cathedral – A vast Tudor Gothic structure with a 54-bell carillon, two organs, and an interior that looks like 3-D lace turned into wood. Free tours on weekdays only. 650 N Meridian (635-2301).

James Whitcomb Riley Home – Indiana's underrated Poet Laureate lived in this comfortable house between 1892 and 1916; the whole area has been recently restored, as it might have been then. Admission charge. 528 Lockerbie (631-5885).

Benjamin Harrison Memorial Home – This 16-room Victorian mansion, built in 1875 for the 23rd US president, has been fitted out with the Harrisons' own furnishings. Admission charge. 1230 N Delaware (631-1898).

Indianapolis Motor Speedway – Minibuses will take visitors around the 2½-mile oval on which the 500-mile race is held every year on the last Sunday in May. You can also visit the IMS Museum, where race cars from the early days are on display. Admission charge. 4790 W 16th (241-2501).

Indianapolis Museum of Art – By any standards, a truly remarkable museum. Its Krannert Pavilion contains a wide-ranging collection of American, Oriental, primitive, 18th- and 19th-century European art. The Clowes Pavilion, adjacent, has rooms full of medieval and Renaissance art, plus some watercolors by Turner, ranged around a skylit, plant-filled courtyard. In the gardens are modern sculptures, including Robert Indiana's *LOVE,* and a wonderful, geometrical fountain. The museum grounds were originally the riverview estate of the Lilly family. Their mansion now shows off a collection of English, French, and Italian 18th-century decorative art. Admission charge for the third-floor and mansion exhibitions; the Pavilions are free. 1200 W 38th St. (923-1331).

The Children's Museum – This is the largest children's museum in the world. Kids can ride a turn-of-the-century carousel, spelunk in a simulated limestone cave, and see a real mummy and the largest collection of toy trains on public display. Also featured are antique fire engines, a furnished Hoosier log cabin, and two major galleries full of hands-on exhibits exploring the natural and physical sciences. Special programs are held regularly. Closed Mondays from Labor Day through Memorial Day. Free. 3000 N Meridian (924-5431).

Zionsville – A mid-19th-century restored village. The streets are now full of ritzy shops. Good for a long afternoon. 86th St. north to Zionsville Rd.

Conner Prairie Pioneer Settlement and Museum – A 25-building museum village portraying the life of central Indiana pioneers about 1836. Annual events include

Indiana Spring (late April), an old-fashioned Fourth of July bash, and quaint Christmastime festivities. Closed Mondays. Admission charge. 13400 Allisonville Rd., about 20 miles northeast of Monument Circle via rt. 37 and I-465 (773-3633).

SOURCES AND RESOURCES

The Indianapolis Convention and Visitors Bureau, 100 S Capitol (635-9567), and the Indiana Tourism Development Division, 440 N Meridian (232-8860), supply brochures and general tourist information.

All telephone numbers are in the 317 area code unless otherwise indicated.

For Local Coverage – *Indianapolis Star,* morning daily and Sundays; *Indianapolis News,* afternoon daily.

CLIMATE AND CLOTHES: Indianapolis has typical Midwest weather — beautiful springs, steamy summers, mild autumns, and moderately cold winters without much snow.

GETTING AROUND: You *can* do it by public transportation, but a car is more convenient since Indianapolis is a sprawling city.

Bus – Service has improved in recent years, and some lines operate 24 hours — but check before you go (635-3344).

Taxi – Phoning Yellow Cab (637-5421) is the surest way to get one.

Car Rental – You'll find all the big national companies.

MUSEUMS: The Indianapolis Museum of Art, the Indiana State Museum, the Children's Museum, and the Conner Prairie Farm are described in *Special Places.* Also interesting:

The Museum of Indian Heritage, 6040 DeLong Rd., in Eagle Creek Park (293-4488).

MAJOR COLLEGES AND UNIVERSITIES: The combined campus of Indiana and Purdue universities is modern and beautifully designed. 1100–1300 W Michigan (635-8661). The campus of Butler University is farther north at Sunset Ave. and W 46th St. (283-8000). The J. I. Holcomb Observatory and Planetarium sits at the campus's north end (283-9333).

SPECIAL EVENTS: *The Indianapolis 500 Race* — the world's biggest single-day sporting event — is held at the Speedway every Memorial Day weekend. One Saturday night in June, thousands crowd the Circle for the *Mid-Summer Fest,* a music fair. Almost as exciting is the *Indiana State Fair,* in August. In September, the *To Market to Market Ball* is held to benefit the City Market; you shop for your dinner at the food stalls and dance to the music of an orchestra outside. Indianapolis is also home to the U.S. *Open Clay Court Championships,* played in a new $7 million tennis stadium in August; and the *National Championship Drag Races,* held at Raceway Park every Labor Day weekend.

SPORTS: The N.B.A. Indiana *Pacers* play basketball in the Market Square Arena at 300 E Market (639-4444). The Indianapolis *Checkers* play hockey in the Coliseum, State Fairgrounds (923-3431); and the Indianapolis *Indians,* affiliated with the Cincinnati *Reds,* play baseball in Bush Stadium at 1501 W 16th (632-5371).

Fishing – Panfish at Eagle Creek Reservoir, 7840 W 56th (293-4827). Farther out of town: Geist Reservoir and Morse Reservoir, and, about two hours south and much larger, Monroe Reservoir, near Bloomington.

Golf – There are three good public courses near Riverside Park, 3501 Cold Spring Rd., and eight others around the city. For information on all of them, call the Parks and Recreation Department (924-9151).

Ice Skating – November to March at Ellenberger City Park, 5301 E St. Clair (353-1600) and Perry City Park, 541 E Stop 11 Rd. (888-0070). Also, October through the first of April, at the Coliseum, State Fairgrounds (923-3431), and year-round at the Carmel Skadium, 1040 Third SW (844-8888).

Tennis – Most area high schools' courts are open to the public. Municipal courts can be found throughout the city. For specific locations, call 924-9151.

THEATER: The professional *Indiana Repertory Theater* has grown by leaps and bounds in the last few years, 140 W Washington St. (635-5252). Indianapolis also has the *Civic Theater,* 1200 W 38th (923-4597), the oldest continuously active civic theater in the US. Community theater can be found at the *Christian Theological Seminary,* 1000 W 42nd (923-1516). For dinner theater, *Beef 'N Boards,* 9301 Michigan Rd., NW (872-9664), features stars of TV, Broadway, and Hollywood. Touring companies of Broadway shows appear at *Clowes Hall,* 4600 Sunset Ave. (924-1267). In July and August there are musicals under the stars at *Hilton U. Brown Theatron,* 304 W 49th (926-1581).

MUSIC: At Butler University in Clowes Hall. *Indianapolis Symphony Orchestra* plays most of its concerts there; Clowes is also the home of the recently formed *Indianapolis Opera Company.* (For info call 635-7464.) The *Butler Ballet* performs in winter and spring at Clowes Hall (283-9231).

NIGHTCLUBS AND NIGHTLIFE: For dancing: *Piccadilly's,* 2802 Lafayette Rd. (923-7625). Young singles patronize *Friday's,* 3502 E 86th (844-3355), and *Gritzbe's,* 8660 Bazaar Ln. (844-0088).

SINS: Ever since the Mayor's office found, in a survey a few years back, that the greatest obstacle to the growth of the Hoosier capital was its poor self-image, the city has been spitting and polishing, demolishing and building, and putting down those who don't talk it all up — with such enthusiasm that *pride* has routed humility. Justifiably, of course; ask anyone in town.

LOCAL SERVICES: Business Services – Manpower, Inc. of Indianapolis, 251 N Delaware (635-1001, main office).

Mechanic – Approved Auto Repair Service (924-5657), affiliated with AAA Motor Club, gives locations and phone numbers of reputable shops.

Babysitting – Most hotels can help you arrange for sitters. Failing that, contact *Kinder Care,* with several locations in the city (841-1944, headquarters).

BEST IN TOWN

CHECKING IN: You'll find all the usual chains — most of them immediately off I-465, which rings the city, or I-65, which cuts a diagonal through it. Inexpensive doubles run under $30, moderately priced rooms up to $40, and expensive rooms up to $60. Rates are usually higher during Indianapolis 500 weekend and the National Drags.

The Hyatt Regency Indianapolis – Elegantly designed in red brick around a 20-story central atrium lobby. 500 rooms, 5 restaurants, lounges, and shops. Washington, opposite the Convention Center (632-1234). Expensive.

The Hilton at the Circle – The elevator through the 425-room hotel is glassed in so that you can look out at Monument Circle as you ride; *Top of the Hilton* restaurant gives the same lovely view. 34 W Ohio (635-2000). Expensive to moderate.

The Atkinson – An older hotel downtown, with taste and style, and beautiful Empire antiques in the lobby. 233 rooms. Illinois and Georgia Sts. (639-5611). Moderate.

Sheraton Meridian – In a neighborhood of older but well-maintained apartment buildings, this 280-room hotel is close to the Children's Museum. Pleasant and modern, it has an indoor-outdoor swimming pool, a sundeck, and a health club. 2820 N Meridian (924-1241). Moderate.

Holiday Inn North – This hotel has a beautiful Holidome, a mini sports complex with a pool, Jacuzzi, saunas, and other facilities for overnight rest and relaxation. 3850 DePauw Blvd. (872-9790). Moderate.

Best Western–Classic – Directly opposite the Indianapolis Motor Speedway's new entrance. Outdoor pool. 4665 W 16th (248-9271). Inexpensive.

Days Inn South – That this establishment boasts a swimming pool makes the low rates especially noteworthy. On US-31 south and I-465 (788-0811). Inexpensive.

EATING OUT: Like most Midwestern cities, Indianapolis has always had more than its share of steak-and-baked-potato places; unlike many others, it also had a real dearth of ethnic eateries. But the number of interesting places to enjoy a meal is steadily rising. Excluding drinks, taxes, and tips, you'll pay $25 and up for a meal for two in restaurants listed below as expensive, $12 to $25 at those marked moderate, and less than $12 at inexpensive places.

Chanteclair sur le Toit – Entrées and desserts are flambéed at your table while strolling violinists entertain. Veal Oscar is among the Continental specialties. Open for dinner only, Mondays through Saturdays. Reservations recommended. Major credit cards. At the Holiday Inn–Airport, 2501 S High School Rd. (244-7378). Expensive.

La Tour – At the top of the Indiana National Bank Tower, this restaurant has a menu as ambitious as the view is gorgeous; and when the kitchen is good, it is very, very good. Closed Sundays. Reservations advised. Major credit cards. 1 Indiana Square (635-3535). Expensive.

The Glass Chimney – Some of the city's best Continental fare appears on the carefully set tables of this consistently fine establishment, newly situated in a charming old house about 25 minutes' drive from the Circle. Open for dinner only, Mondays through Saturdays. Reservations required. Major credit cards. 12901 N Meridian (844-0921). Expensive.

James Tavern – Warmly decorated in wood and gingham, here you can sit comfortably before one of many fireplaces and dine on steak, seafood, or deliciously prepared fowl. The pleasant waiters are also busy serving up house specialties like peanut soup and apple walnut pie. Open daily; brunch only on Sundays. Reservations recommended. Major credit cards. 8601 Keystone Crossing (844-7848). Expensive to moderate.

St. Elmo's – A local tradition for steaks and potatoes since 1902, and as wonderful as ever. Open for dinner daily except Sundays. Reservations recommended. Major credit cards. 127 S Illinois (635-0636). Expensive to moderate.

Adam's Rib – Prime rib is the specialty, but fresh fish is flown in daily, and the menu always lists one exotic viand like venison, rattlesnake meat, antelope, or the like.

The salad bar is one of the best in town. Open for lunch on weekdays, for dinner except Sundays. Reservations recommended. Major credit cards accepted. 40 S Main, in Zionsville (see *Special Places*). Phone 873-3301. Expensive to moderate.

New Orleans House – When you visit this relatively plain establishment, you need to do it on a very empty stomach: Unless you're ravenous, you simply can't do justice to the splendid all-you-can-eat seafood buffet. Allow 2½ to 3 hours to consume your fill of oysters and clams on the half shell, chowders and creole dishes, crab legs and lobster. Open daily for dinner only. Reservations required. Major credit cards. 8845 Township Line Rd. (872-9670). Expensive.

Captain Alexander's Wharf – Another good bet for seafood, prepared simply. Freshwater fish is flown in on Mondays, Wednesdays, Fridays, and Saturdays. The Sunday brunch — a huge spread featuring fresh fruits and juices, salads, fish and meat entrées both hot and cold, breads, cheeses, smoked salmon (lox), and desserts — is a standout. Open Mondays through Fridays for lunch, Sundays for brunch, and daily for dinner. Reservations required. Major credit cards. 6220 Castle Way W Dr. (842-4070). Moderate.

La Scala – The best place in town for Italian food. Closed Sundays. Reservations required. Major credit cards. 110 S Meridian (635-7415). Moderate.

The Iron Skillet – One of Indianapolis's several family-style restaurants, this is the kind of place to which, in pre-*McDonald* days, Pop would take Mom to give her a night away from the kitchen. Steaks, fried chicken, and vegetables in generous portions. Open Wednesdays through Sundays for dinner, for lunch on Sundays. Reservations suggested. Major credit cards accepted. 2489 W 30th (923-6353). Moderate.

Max and Erma's – Mostly for fun, this current hot-spot is known for the phones on the tables (for arranging after-dinner dates in the sunken bar), its make-your-own sundae stand (built into a refrigerated bathtub), and, on Sundays after 5 PM, a Bring-the-Kids night (free cake and ice cream for the under-12 set). Antiques dangle from ceiling and walls; pinball machines clang near the entrance; and hamburgers are the staple. Open daily for lunch and dinner. Major credit cards. 8930 Wesleyan Dr. (872-2300). Moderate to inexpensive.

Shapiro's – Indianapolis's best deli, with food served cafeteria style. Open daily for lunch and dinner. No reservations or credit cards. 808 S Meridian (631-4041). Moderate to inexpensive.

Rosa Corona – This Mexican restaurant serves very good fare from south of the border in an elegant and festive setting. There are also two bars, a greenhouse, and a lounge. Open daily. Reservations recommended. Major credit cards. 8650 Keystone Crossing (848-5202). Moderate.

Ayres' Tea Room – The waitresses in this genteel department store restaurant downtown wear black uniforms, white aprons, and matronly expressions; chicken velvet soup and ice cream desserts are scrumptious. Reservations recommended; no credit cards. Open for lunch 11 AM to 3 PM, except Sunday. 1 W Washington (262-2658). Inexpensive.

KANSAS CITY, MO

Kansas City owes a lot to its agricultural heritage. Surrounded by rich farmlands and grazing fields, agribusiness is the backbone of the economy. Kansas City is first in the nation as a farm distribution center and hard wheat market; second in grain elevator capacity; third as a feeder cattle market. However, don't expect to hear any of these sterling statistics from the average — and always helpful — Kansas City person-in-the-street. Residents are skittish as wild horses about anything that seems to reinforce Kansas City's ingrained "cowtown" image.

For most of its 130-year history, travelers have regarded Kansas City as "a one-night stand between the Rockies and Chicago." Residents, naturally, don't see it that way. With more than a million people tucked away in the urban area of rolling woodland, limestone bluffs, and the Kansas and Missouri Rivers, Kansas City is the heart of the "breadbasket of the world." It is called the City of Fountains, because of its hundreds of beautiful fountains, many of them European; some, centuries old. It is also a city of art. J. C. Nichols, developer of the Country Club Plaza and residential district, imported more than a million dollars' worth of statuary and other art in the 1920s, not for museums, but for the boulevards and parkways. In fact, Kansas City has more boulevards than Paris — 140 miles of wide, graceful, tree-lined streets and parkways.

But the resemblance to Paris does not extend to the cold, haughty condescension that Parisians show to outsiders. A visitor to Kansas City will inevitably be asked — and asked — what he or she thinks of the place. It may even get a little annoying, but Kansas City folk are self-conscious about their hick-town image and go out of their way to ask a lot of well-meaning questions to reassure you and make sure you're having a good time.

The Nelson Gallery of Art is one of the top museums in the United States. The Kansas City Philharmonic, repertory drama, and a wide range of concerts provide enough entertainment to keep anybody busy. Kansas City's breezy, contented lifestyle has a lot to do with its increasing popularity. Dynamic, without succumbing to a frantic pace, Kansas City has been experiencing a rapid but orderly growth cycle; one, however, that has not disturbed its fluid rhythm of life. It is a center of gracious living, magnificent mansions, and old wealth.

The city has certainly come a long way from the days of Rodgers and Hammerstein's musical *Oklahoma.* In those days, went the song, Kansas City "went and built a skyscraper seven stories high — about as high as a building ought to go." A number of private building ventures are still changing the skyline with complexes like the Crown Center, the overwhelming "city within a city," and Westport Square, which is filled with young shopkeepers and artisans who have recreated the charm of old Kansas City by restoring the old Victorian buildings. The nation's first shopping center, Country Club

Plaza, resembles a tile-roofed Moorish city, rather than an impersonal suburban behemoth of glass and brick. But some things Rodgers and Hammerstein wrote in *Oklahoma* still apply. Everything is "up-to-date in Kansas City," and visitors are more often than not delightfully surprised to find it beautiful as well.

KANSAS CITY AT-A-GLANCE

SEEING THE CITY: The best view of Kansas City is from the Observation Tower on the 30th floor of City Hall. Open Mondays through Fridays. Oak between 12th and 13th Sts. Free (274-2605, 274-2331).

SPECIAL PLACES: Kansas City's three major shopping complexes are self-contained units in which a visitor can be immersed for an entire day.

Crown Center – This $300 million development is the brainchild of Joyce Hall, founder of Hallmark Cards. We suggest starting out from the lobby of the super-elegant *Crown Center Hotel* (see *Checking In*), dominated by a tropical rain forest and waterfall that winds its way down the limestone hillside on which the hotel was built. Then move on to the Crown Center shops, where more than 50 stores offer everything from fine art to ski equipment. 2450 Grand (274-8444).

Westport Square – "Westward, ho!" was the cry that echoed across the field that is now Westport Square. It was here that pioneers outfitted themselves for the great journey west. Although times have changed, the tradition of seeking out supplies at Westport Square is solidly implanted in the consciousness of Kansas City residents. A lot of work has gone into restoring the old buildings, many of which date back more than 130 years. Broadway at Westport Square (924-6444).

Country Club Plaza – A few blocks south of Westport Square, Country Club Plaza is Disneyland for grown-ups with money to spend. More than $1 million worth of statues, fountains, and murals line the tree-lined walks of this spectacular Spanish- and Moorish-style residential shopping center with more than 150 shops, restaurants, and nightclubs. 4629 Wornall Road (753-0100).

Nelson Gallery of Art and Atkins Museum – The Nelson is renowned for its comprehensive collection of art, from the ancient Sumerian civilization (3000 BC) to works by contemporaries. Egyptian, Greek, Roman, and medieval sculpture and a reconstructed medieval cloister make this more than just a museum of Old Masters, although there are plenty of classics on the walls — Titian, Rembrandt, El Greco, Goya, the Impressionists, Van Gogh, and contemporary Andy Warhol. It also houses a fine Oriental collection. Closed Mondays, major holidays. Free Sundays. Other days, admission charge. 4525 Oak St. (561-4000).

Swope Park – This 1,772-acre park has two golf courses, a swimming pool, picnic areas, a zoo, and the Starlight Theater (471-5510), where popular musicals and concerts are performed in summer under the stars. 5600 E Gregory (444-4656).

Kansas City Stock Yards – At the nation's largest stocker and feeder market, you can see what a Kansas City steak looks like before it gets to your table. Depending on how you react to the cattlemen in action, you may or may not look forward to a hefty meal of the beef that helped make Kansas City famous. There are frequent cattle auctions at the stockyards. Visitors are welcome at the Sales Pavilion of the Livestock Building Tuesdays, Wednesdays, and Thursdays. 16th and Genesee (842-6800).

Benjamin Stables Trail Town – Benjamin Stables is a complex of barns, fields, and blacksmith's shop that recreates an early Western town. Horse-drawn carts, wagons, and carriages are visible everywhere. There are sleigh rides and hayrides, and horseback riding facilities for those who want to ride the old Santa Fe Trail. Call one day in advance for a tour. Open weekdays. 6401 E 87th at I-435 (761-5055).

Worlds of Fun – This 140-acre family theme park has more than 60 rides, divided by international themes (Scandinavia, Africa, the Orient, etc.). Worlds of Fun opens for weekends in mid-April to late May, then opens daily from May until early September. Open weekends September and October. Admission charge. On I-435, just north of the Missouri River, at Parvin Rd. (454-4545).

Missouri River Excursions – A relaxing way to spend a few hours. Cruises leave from Westport landing at the foot of Grand Ave. (842-0027).

■ **EXTRA SPECIAL:** Just eight miles east of downtown Kansas City in Independence, MO, is the *Harry S. Truman Library and Museum.* Remember his famous quote, "The buck stops here"? So should you, if you're a Harry Truman fan. Even if you're not, you might become one after a visit. Open daily except Thanksgiving and New Year's Day. Admission charge for adults; children and educational groups free. On US 24 at Delaware in Independence, MO (833-1225). While you're there, stop off for a meal at *Stephenson's Apple Farm* restaurant. Just up the road a piece from the Truman Library and Museum, you'll find *Fort Osage,* a reconstruction of the trading post established by explorer William Clark of the famous Lewis and Clark team. Open daily during daylight hours. Fort Osage is about 22 miles northeast of Independence on US 24, in Sibley, MO (249-5737).

SOURCES AND RESOURCES

The Kansas City Convention and Visitors' Bureau has a 24-hour hotline at 474-9600, for the latest information on Kansas City events. The Bureau also provides brochures, maps, and a restaurant and hotel guide. City Center Square Building, Suite 2550, 1100 Main St. (for further information, call 221-5242).

All telephone numbers are in the 816 area code unless otherwise indicated.

For Local Coverage – *Kansas City Times,* morning daily; *Kansas City Star,* afternoon daily.

For Food – *The Kansas City Restaurant Guide* (from the Convention and Visitors Bureau, free).

CLIMATE AND CLOTHES: Kansas City's Midwestern climate is notorious. It's fine in the spring and fall, but the winters are rough (frequently the thermometer never rises above freezing in January) and the summers are hot and humid. Rain is particularly likely in spring.

GETTING AROUND: Bus – The Kansas City Metro Bus covers the downtown area (241-0303).

Taxi – Call Yellow Cab (741-5000).

Car Rental – The best way to see Kansas City is by car. Major car firms are represented.

MUSEUMS: The Nelson Gallery of Art and Atkins Museum and the Harry S. Truman Library and Museum are described in *Special Places*. Other fine Kansas City museums are:

Kansas City Museum of History and Science, 3218 Gladstone (483-8300).

Wornall House, Civil War restoration, 61 Terrace and Wornall (444-1858).

1859 Jail and Museum, 217 N Main St., Independence, MO (252-1892).

Agriculture Hall of Fame, I-70 to Bonner Springs (721-1075).

Shawnee Methodist Mission and Indian Manual Labor School (Indian Mission), 53rd and Mission Rd., Fairway, KS (262-0867).

MAJOR COLLEGES AND UNIVERSITIES: University of Missouri – Kansas City, 51st and Rockhill Rd. (276-1000).

SPECIAL EVENTS: *American Royal Horse and Livestock Show,* November, at Kemper Arena, 1700 Wyoming (421-6460).

SPORTS: Kansas City has professional baseball, football, basketball, and indoor soccer teams.

Baseball – Kansas City *Royals,* Harry S. Truman Sports Complex, I-70 and Blue Ridge Cutoff (921-8000).

Football – NFL. Kansas City *Chiefs,* Harry S. Truman Sports Complex, I-70 and Blue Ridge Cutoff (924-9400).

Basketball – NBA. Kansas City *Kings,* Kemper Arena, 1700 Wyoming (421-6460).

Soccer – Kansas City *Comets,* Kemper Arena, 1700 Wyoming (421-7700).

Tennis – There are more than 200 public tennis courts in the Kansas City metro area. Most are free. Swope Park has good courts at the picnic area north of the Starlight Theater. For indoor tennis, try Airway Racquet Club, 10 Richards Rd. (471-7666). At 4747 Nichols Parkway, there are year-round courts. For reservations call 531-0761.

Golf – The best is at River Oaks, 140 and US 71, Grandview, MO (966-8111).

Bicycling – Bikes can be rented in summer at Shelter House One in Swope Park, at the main entrance, Swope Pkwy. and Meyer Blvd.

Horseback Riding – Benjamin Stables Trail Town on the old Santa Fe trail, 6401 E 87th at I-435 (761-5055).

THEATER: For the latest information on theater and musical events, call 474-9600. Most theater, music, and dance tickets are available through the computicket sales system by calling 421-3434. The city's Theater League (753-4675) presents touring companies of Broadway hits in the *Midland Center for the Performing Arts,* 1228 Main (421-7500). Dramatic and musical productions are also booked into the *Music Hall* in the Municipal Auditorium, 200 W 13th (421-8000); at the *Lyric Theater,* 10th and Central (471-7344); and the *Folly Theatre,* 12th and Central (842-5500). From July to September and January to March, the Missouri Repertory Company performs in the *Spencer Theater* on the University of Missouri campus (276-2704). The *Starlight Theater* in Swope Park, an under-the-stars amphitheater, features musical comedy and concerts with top-name stars from May to mid-September (471-5510). Kansas City has two dinner playhouses, *Tiffany's Attic,* 5028 Main (561-7921), and the *Waldo* (*not* Waldorf) *Astoria,* 7428 Washington (561-9876).

MUSIC: For up-to-date data on concert happenings, call 474-9600, or check the local newspapers. There are two *opera* seasons, in April and October at the Lyric Theater, 10th and Central (271-4933). The operas are in English. The *Kansas City Philharmonic* season runs from October to March (842-9300). Jazz still thrives in Kansas City. For information on who's playing at the clubs, check the "Now Showing" calendar in the arts section of the *Sunday Kansas City Star.*

NIGHTCLUBS AND NIGHTLIFE: In the last decade, Kansas City's after-dark scene has picked up so that now it's one of the most lively in the Midwest. The liquor laws are still a bit antiquated. Missouri bars close at 1 AM. Bars are closed on Sunday, although restaurants and hotels may serve drinks. Kansas taverns serve 3.2% beer and private clubs only may serve liquor by the drink. Singles action is liveliest at *Houlihan's Old Place,* 4743 Pennsylvania (561-3141), which also has good food. Best bet for out-of-towners is to park on the Plaza or near Westport Square and bar hop. There are dozens of clubs and bars — some with live entertainment — within easy walking distance of each other. Westport Square is very casual; the Plaza is a bit more formal, and some restaurant-bars require a coat and tie. The best gay bar is *Dover Fox,* 4334 Main (753-9777).

SINS: Kansas City may think of itself as the Paris of the Plains, and the citizens go apoplectic with *anger* when you suggest that their city is not quite as cosmopolitan as it pretends. But the fact of the matter is that in Paris, prostitutes are as easy to find as a good meal, and in Kansas City, they aren't. Which has less to do with food in Kansas City (*gluttony* flourishes there at places like *Arthur Bryant's*) than with an attitude toward prostitution that is as American as apple pie. But a few can usually be spotted along Main or on Troost between 31st and 39th streets.

As for overweaning *pride,* it depends on who you ask. Some folk will rave about the revolving restaurants and the fancy shopping malls; some people go bonkers over the boulevards and the fountains; some people get excited over the crispy burned ends of barbecue passed out for free at Arthur Bryant's Barbecue. Whatever you do, though, don't confuse Kansas City, Kansas, and Kansas City, Missouri.

LOCAL SERVICES: Business Services – Gal Friday, 1 E 45th St. (931-3933).

Mechanic – ABCO, 1515 McGee (421-0161).

Babysitting – Accepted Babysitting Services, 10041 Holmes (942-8900).

BEST IN TOWN

CHECKING IN: Expect to pay $40 and up for a double in hotels categorized as expensive; $30 to $40 in those places designated as moderate; and under $30 in the inexpensive range.

Crown Center Hotel – Built on a huge chunk of limestone known as Signboard Hill because of the commercial embellishments that used to decorate it, this 730-room ultra-modern hotel is part of the Crown Center complex. It integrates the limestone face of the hill into the lobby, where there is a winding stream, five-story waterfall, and tropical rain forest. It has seven restaurants, including *Trader Vic's,* and 86 shops and boutiques. 1 Pershing Rd. in Crown Center (toll-free, 800 228-3000; or locally 474-4400). Expensive.

Alameda Plaza – The *Alameda Plaza* is a sumptuous building with 359 elegantly appointed rooms in beautifully landscaped grounds on Country Club Plaza. Country Club Plaza (756-1500). Expensive.

The Hyatt Regency – Kansas City's fanciest hotel is also its most notorious since the collapse, in July 1981, of two of the three "skywalks" that spanned its huge, glass-topped lobby. The rubble of the disaster is gone, the three suspended skywalks have been replaced by a single elevated ramp resting solidly on pillars, and probably no other public building in America has undergone more inspections and safety tests. South of the downtown loop; McGee at Pershing Rd. (toll-free, 800 228-9000 or 421-1234). Expensive.

Hilton Airport Inn – Ideal if you're more interested in traveling than downtown sightseeing. In addition to 360 comfortable rooms, this Hilton has two heated swimming pools — one indoor, one outdoor; a sauna, whirlpool, health club, putting green, and tennis courts, as well as two dining rooms, a coffee shop, and bar with entertainment. I-29 and NW 112th St. (891-8900). Moderate.

Radisson-Muehlebach – The king of downtown hotels, acquired by the Radisson chain and given a facelift. Most of its 700 rooms have been redecorated, the lobby and restaurant have undergone a major overhaul, but the hotel's 1920s aura has been preserved. No pool or sauna here, but its style makes it popular with business people and conventioneers. 12th and Baltimore (471-1400). Moderate.

Sheraton Royal Hotel – Overlooking the Harry S. Truman Sports Complex in eastern Kansas City, the 300-room new Sheraton is popular with out-of-town sports fans who come to see the Chiefs or Royals. The sports motif extends to the decor — an easy chair shaped like a baseball mitt sits in the lobby. Only a few minutes away from the Truman Library and Museum in Independence. Facilities include swimming pool, sauna, and tennis. I-70 at Truman Sports Complex (737-0200). Moderate.

EATING OUT: Kansas City has great steaks and good French food. Its very best, however, is a barbecue restaurant, and that's a fact. You can select a high-priced haute cuisine restaurant, or one that will give you superb food at more moderate prices, although you'll find Kansas City prices to be reasonable everywhere. We recommend calling ahead for reservations at all the places listed below. Expect to pay $30 to $40 for dinner for two at those places we've listed as expensive; $20 to $30 at those places we've listed as moderate; under $20 at restaurants listed as inexpensive. Prices do not include drinks, wines, or tips.

American – Many Kansas City people say this is the best in town. Certainly, it's the fanciest. The *American* has French moderne decor and a menu featuring bluepoint oysters on the half shell, Nova Scotia salmon, Gulf shrimp creole with rice pilaf, fresh sea bass sautéed with mushrooms in white wine, rock salt hobo steak, Montana elk with lingonberries and mushroom caps, and braised South Dakota pheasant in juniper sauce. Open daily. All credit cards. In the Crown Center Hotel, Crown Center, 25th and Grand (474-4000). Expensive.

Alameda Rooftop Restaurant – The menu is oppressively pretentious, but this is a great place from which to see the glittering city spread below as you dine on excellent roast rack of lamb, seafood, and beef. The cold gazpacho is palate-tingling. Reservations are especially necessary if you want to sit near a window. Open daily. All credit cards. Ward and Wornall on the Plaza (756-1500). Expensive.

The Peppercorn Duck Club – This is a knockout restaurant in the new *Hyatt Regency* hotel. The decor is Olde English and the food is sumptuous, especially the roast duckling. The chocolate dessert bar is simply sinful and the service is attentive almost to a fault — you can hardly sniff without someone handing you a hankie. Reservations advised. Major credit cards. McGee at Pershing Rd. (421-1234). Expensive to moderate.

Bristol Bar and Grill – One of the best seafood restaurants in the Midwest can be found on the Country Club Plaza. A New York actress who eats here when she's in town says the fish is better than back home on Long Island. The decor is a pleasant blend of Victorian architecture and modern art; ask to be seated in the back room beneath the huge Tiffany leaded glass dome. The bar is a popular after-work watering hole for KC's upwardly mobile bunch. Reservations advised. Major credit cards. 4740 Jefferson (756-0606). Expensive to moderate.

Al Roubaie – Although in an unlikely part of town, this Mediterranean restaurant is a real treat, thanks to its specialty sauces and exotic-but-not-overpowering spices. The decor is so-so, but the food is great. Reservations advised. Major credit cards. 8241 Wornall (444-3460). Moderate.

Mr. Putsch's – If you like olde English taverns with ladies in décolleté costumes taking your orders, this is the place. Succulent roast prime rib of beef is the specialty here, and a good salad bar. Open daily. Major credit cards. 210 W 47th (561-2000). Moderate.

Golden Ox – In the heart of the stockyards, near Kemper Arena, where the wranglers who work the steers take their food breaks. Good, solid American cooking here, and arguably the best steaks in town, served with potato, garlic bread, and salad. Call to see if reservations are necessary. Open daily. All credit cards. 1600 Genesee (842-2866). Moderate.

Savoy Grill – A turn-of-the-century restaurant cherished by Kansas City residents that serves very fine seafood and steaks. The most outstanding feature of the *Savoy* is its 1903 Victorian mirrored bar and stained glass windows, giving you the feel of early Kansas City. Closed Sundays. Reservations accepted. Major credit cards. 9th and Central (842-3890). Moderate.

Stephenson's Apple Farm Restaurant – Down-home cooking has made this fine restaurant's reputation. Hickory-smoked pork ribs, chicken gizzards, beef brisket, steak, and homemade pie in a rustic American setting make this well worth a trip out to Independence, even if you have no interest in Harry S. Truman. Open daily. Here, too, reservations are recommended. Major credit cards. On US 40 at Lea's Summit Rd., South Independence (373-5400). Moderate.

Houlihan's Old Place – A casual dining spot serving soups, mushroom burgers, crab Newburg, eggs Benedict, quiches, omelets, roast duck, banana splits, and, of course, Kansas City steaks. Lavishly decorated in Gay 90s style, some people say it looks like a Wild West bordello. Decide for yourself. Open till the wee hours, daily. Reservations accepted. Major credit cards. 4743 Pennsylvania, Country Club Plaza (561-3141). Moderate to inexpensive.

Arthur Bryant's Barbecue – This eatery has acquired a reputation of legendary proportions, thanks in part to author Calvin Trillin's book *American Fried* (in which he says this is the best restaurant in America!). In fact, 95 pounds of Bryant's barbecued ribs and beef were flown to New York for Trillin's publishing party. To check it out, you'll have to wait in line — but the huge sandwiches, French fries, and free "brownies" (ends of brisket) make it all worthwhile. Closed Sundays and the month of January. No reservations. No credit cards. No atmosphere, but who cares? 1727 Brooklyn (231-1123). Inexpensive.

Winstead's Drive In – You can get a really good hamburger here with all the trimmings. There's nothing exotic about the place, but what do you expect from a good ol' American drive-in? If you're not crazy about hamburgers, try the chili and salad bar. Open daily. No reservations or credit cards. Winstead's, Country Club Plaza (753-2244). Inexpensive.

LAS VEGAS

The surface of Mars is at once hostile and beautiful. There may be no place on earth so forbidding and yet so alluring, but if there is, Las Vegas, that glittering oasis in the midst of mountainous Nevada desert, must be it. To some it's a 24-hour city of fantasy, to others an unending nightmare. How you feel about it may just depend on your tolerance for the phantasmagorical. But whether it's loved as a vacation paradise or damned as "Sin City," the maze of contradictions that are bred here make the place fascinating.

With the legalization of gambling in Atlantic City, and the probability of legalization elsewhere, a new age is dawning for Las Vegas. For three decades Las Vegas has reigned as the unchallenged gambling resort of the world, and it is not about to surrender its throne without a fight. A sense of competition has swept the city, and several of the older hotels have received emergency face-lifts, while the new structures that continue to spring up place special emphasis on "extras" and "freebies." But all this is simply adding more tinsel to what already is the ultimate in gaudiness; Atlantic City is going to be hard pressed to out-Vegas Vegas.

Visitors are shown one face of Las Vegas: the facade of "Entertainment Capital of the World." But this doesn't begin to describe it. The cavernous air-conditioned vastness of countless Strip casinos aims at total sensory bombardment with a maelstrom of sights and sounds: the ringing bells and flashing lights of the slot machines, the rolling wheels of fortune, the dice dancing on the green tables, the smoke-filled air mixed with a heavy undercurrent of free-flowing alcohol. Throngs of people crowd the casinos at every hour of the day and night. In Las Vegas, time doesn't matter. The casinos cater to circadian rhythms gone awry and offer breakfast and dinner 24 hours a day at such bargain prices that it might make sense to eat both at one sitting. Cocktail waitresses keep the thirst quenched by bringing drinks on the house for those gambling steadily. The casinos offer these extras so that Vegas visitors can spend their time indulging in the town's one overwhelming obsession — the desire to gamble. If gratification is not found instantly, there is a choice of a few hundred other places whose neon signs blare bigger and better attractions.

Just venture outside on the Strip (in Las Vegas, going outside is a big step) and you will see one after another huge hotel-casino: Caesars Palace, the Sahara, the Sands, Aladdin, MGM Grand. The names promise magic, but it's only an optical illusion. Underneath those imitation opulent exteriors and plush decors, there is only sand. Certainly, some of the biggest names in entertainment perform here and everyone flocks to see them, but the real business is gambling and anything else is done simply to draw people to the casinos. That's the real trick and that's what keeps Las Vegas going. Money is god here and it created poker chips in its own image. It also created some vast resort complexes — castles built on sand that promise paradise at the next throw of the dice.

And some of the extremes to which the casinos go to draw people in are truly amazing. Though ancient Rome wasn't built in a day, Caesars Palace was, and provides an authentic Roman atmosphere complete with air-conditioning, rock bands, and lots of waitresses running around in mini-togas. If you want Hollywood, there's the MGM Grand with its colossal movie atmosphere and a jai alai palace thrown in, too, to keep the ball rolling. And if you want to get away from it all, try the slot machine at the Union Plaza, where the big prize is an airplane.

But if you do manage to break the spell of the casinos and get outside — outside the Strip, outside town, back to where clocks are more than glittering, ticking anachronisms and have some relation to diurnal-nocturnal cycles — you will discover that the world outside is worth a good deal more than the few rounds of golf or tennis between poker games. Contrary to pre-conceived notions of the desert as a lifeless, joyless, uniformly bland stretch of rock and sand, you will value the treeless expanse for its incredible beauty — a magnificent variety of colors, and the utter freedom of its open spaces. Within miles of Las Vegas, but on the other side of the barrier of unreality, lie the dramatic red and white sandstone formations of Red Rock Recreation Area and the subtle desert colors of the Valley of Fire. These, with the nearby cool green mountains of Mount Charleston and the manmade Lake Mead, make the desert as attractive a proposition as the Strip.

LAS VEGAS AT-A-GLANCE

SEEING THE CITY: The *Top O' Mint Restaurant* offers a panoramic view of Las Vegas. As you ascend in the glass elevator, all of downtown Las Vegas glitters around you. As you reach the top, the expanse of surrounding desert appears, and your eye is drawn to the neon of the Strip, a long stream of hotels and casinos, and beyond to the south, the green heights of Mount Charleston in the distance. In the *Mint Hotel,* 100 E Fremont St. (385 7110). You can also try the *Top of the Landmark* for a spectacular 360-degree view. 364 Convention Center Dr. (733-1110).

SPECIAL PLACES: Gambling is the name of the game in Las Vegas. The cultural aspects of the city are undeniably limited, and its history has been all but obliterated by the rapid growth in the past three decades. But the surrounding area is rich in outdoor diversions that can fill visitors' days with a wide variety of noncasino pleasures, leaving the nights for the air-conditioned paradise of green felt, dazzling neon, and showgirl entertainment.

THE STRIP

If gambling is the game, the Strip is the place. Shining brightly in the desert sun, this five-mile boulevard just south of town glows more intensely at night, ablaze with the glittering opulence of a seemingly never-ending stream of hotels. The sky's the limit here, and one after another of the big hotels offer it — the *Sahara, Circus-Circus,* the

Riviera, the *Silver Slipper,* the *Sands, Caesars Palace,* and the *Dunes.* From slot machines, poker, and blackjack to the esoteric karo and baccarat of the casinos, to the production spectaculars with a cavalcade of stars in the main showrooms, to 24-hour breakfasts or dinners, it's all here and rolling around the clock. Las Vegas Blvd. just south of the city along US 91. Highlights are:

Caesars Palace – Las Vegas' stab at ancient Rome, Caesars Palace outdoes its namesake in gaming. The only other similarities are the Romanesque names of casino areas and showrooms, and the fact that cocktail waitresses and keno runners dress in distinctive mini-togas. Otherwise, it's the plushest of the plush, with more red velvet carpets than the total number of Caesar's battles. Superstars perform nightly, and if you're interested make reservations in advance. 3570 Las Vegas Blvd. (731-7110).

Circus-Circus – There's gambling on the ground and gamboling up above in this tent-shaped casino where trapeze and high-wire artists, clowns, acrobats, and dancers perform to the music of a brass band. The observation gallery at circus level is lined with food and carnival stands. Children are permitted in the gallery but not on the casino floor, so bring them along and everyone can have their own circus. Casino open daily 24 hours. Circus open 11 AM to midnight. Free. 2880 Las Vegas Blvd. (734-0410).

Convention Center – One of the world's major convention destinations, this is Las Vegas' center. This modern steel structure is a 785,000-square-foot complex which can seat 7,200 in the rotunda. On Paradise Rd. south of town, off the Strip (733-2323).

DOWNTOWN

Mint Hotel and Casino – A special tour here takes visitors behind the scene of the action, to where the real action is — coins and currency are automatically counted, slot machines are repaired, and security mirrors are used to view casino activities. Free instruction in the basics of various games. Tours given daily. Free. 100 E Fremont St. (385-7440).

Golden Nugget Gambling Hall and Rooming House – Newest among the leading casinos downtown, the Golden Nugget offers more of the same — plenty of shaking of the bones — with something slightly different: the decor of an Old West casino, complete with luxury wooden bar. 129 E Fremont St. (385-7111).

THE OUTDOORS

Hoover Dam and Lake Mead – Completed in 1936, Hoover Dam is an awesome monument to man's engineering capabilities, a 726-foot-high concrete wall that tamed the mighty Colorado River and supplies electricity to Las Vegas and California. Lake Mead, produced when the Colorado backed up behind the dam, is, at 115 miles long, one of the largest manmade lakes in the world. Fishing (bass, crappie, and catfish), swimming, and boating are available year-round. Tours of the dam are offered daily. Small admission charge. Visitors Center for Hoover Dam (293-8367) and headquarters of Lake Mead National Recreation Area (293-4041) are 30 minutes south of the city along Boulder Hwy. (US 93).

Mount Charleston – Just 35 minutes north of the city, Mount Charleston dramatically exhibits the effect of increased elevation with a wide variety of trees and wildlife. Plenty of cool fresh mountain air. During the winter months, snow covers the ground and temperatures often hover below freezing — even while vacationers swim in Las Vegas hotel pools just half an hour away. Tonapah Hwy. north to rt. 39.

Red Rock Recreation Area – A beautiful desert locale featuring red and white hues of sandstone formations, and spectacular views of steep canyons. Just a few miles farther west, the Spring Mountain State Park has Old West buildings, all located on a ranch that has belonged to such well-known capitalists as Howard Hughes and the German Krupp family (of armament notoriety). State rangers lead tours through the old buildings. Both located on W Charleston Blvd., 15 and 20 miles west of the city.

■ **EXTRA SPECIAL:** Just two hours northwest of Las Vegas lies *Death Valley.* The 120-mile-long Valley is the hottest, driest, and lowest area in the United States. It is also starkly beautiful. The high mountains surrounding the Valley have isolated it, and of the 600 species of plants that have been identified there, 21 grow nowhere else on earth. The variety of the colors and textures of nature in the raw is remarkable, from the jagged bluish rock salt formations of Devil's Golf Course, to the smoothly sculpted golden dunes of Mesquite Flat, to the rich reds and purples of Telescope Peak at sunrise. Scotty's Castle, an eccentric and intricate mansion built in the middle of this expanse by a Chicago millionaire, is the Valley's most incongruous wonder. Because of extremely high temperatures in the summer, the best time to visit the Valley is from November through April. Information on self-guided auto tours and planned walking tours and programs is available November through April at the Visitors Center at Furnace Creek (714 786-2331). Tonapah Hwy. north (I-95) to Beatty, then take the Death Valley Junction cutoff straight into the park. (See also *Death Valley,* DIRECTIONS.)

SOURCES AND RESOURCES

The Las Vegas Chamber of Commerce is best for brochures, maps, suggestions, and general tourist information. 2301 E Sahara Ave. (457-4664).

The Whole Las Vegas Catalog (BMA, $2.95) is the best local guide to Las Vegas and its environs. Includes a good dining-out section.

All telephone numbers are in the 702 area code unless otherwise indicated.

For Local Coverage – *Review Journal,* morning and evening daily; *Valley Times,* morning daily; *Las Vegas Sun,* morning daily. Several weekly entertainment guides are available at newsstands.

CLIMATE AND CLOTHES: In the middle of the desert, Las Vegas summers are hot and dry. Winters are pleasant and mild, and outdoor activity takes place year-round. Bring along a sweater for the indoors; high-powered air-conditioners are in use everywhere. Dress casually and comfortably during the day, but at night the stars come out, and showtime dress can be formal and elegant.

GETTING AROUND: Although Las Vegas is not really a large city, the heat, dust, and wind make walking difficult. If you are going any farther than a hundred yards or so, you'll probably do better on wheels.

Bus – The Las Vegas Transit System covers the downtown area and the Strip. The discount commuter ticket offers a real savings if you expect to use the buses frequently. Route information is available at 1550 Industrial Rd. (384-3540).

Taxi – Cabs can be hailed in the street, ordered on the phone, or picked up at taxi stands in front of hotels. Major companies are Western Cab (382-7100); Whittlesea Cab (384-6111); Yellow Cab (382-4444).

Car Rental – The large national firms serve Las Vegas, though the cheapest local service is provided by Dollar Rent-A-Car, at McCarran Airport (739-8408), and Abbey Rent-A-Car, 3745 Las Vegas Blvd. S (736-4988).

MUSEUMS: Las Vegas hotels have commercial art exhibits with works of well-known artists. One of the best commercial galleries outside the hotels is the *Adobe Galleries,* featuring a wide range of artwork from Indian crafts to abstract paintings. Open daily from 9 AM until midnight. 3110 Las Vegas Blvd. S (733-2941). *Herigstad's Gallery* has art shows as well as works for sale. Open Mondays through Saturdays from 10 AM to 6 PM. 2290 E Flamingo Rd. (733-7366).

The University of Nevada at Las Vegas has a Museum of Natural History with collections of Indian artifacts and live desert reptiles. Open daily. Free. 4505 S Maryland Pkwy. (739-3381).

The Mineral Collection, which is also on campus, displays 1,000 specimens from the area and around the world. Free. Closed weekends. Science Hall, room 103.

MAJOR COLLEGES AND UNIVERSITIES: The University of Nevada at Las Vegas is the largest school in the area, with an enrollment of 9,400. 4505 S Maryland Pkwy. (739-3011).

SPECIAL EVENTS: During the *Helldorado Festival* held for four days in May, the city celebrates its Western heritage with rodeos, parades, beauty contests, and, for those who want some slower-paced action, a beard-growing contest. The *Jaycees State Fair* takes place in August at the Convention Center and has carnival acts, magic shows, rides, livestock and craft exhibits.

SPORTS: Las Vegas offers a wide variety of sporting events and fine facilities.

Basketball – The University of Nevada at Las Vegas has fielded one of the finest collegiate basketball teams in the nation for several years. They play from November to February at Las Vegas Convention Center, on Paradise Rd. off the Strip (tickets, 739-3295). Tickets are scarce, but a pit boss or bell captain might be able to help you out if you tip generously or have been playing steadily.

Boxing – If punching is your bag, the major hotels promote many boxing matches. Major bouts between professional heavyweight contenders are held from time to time at Caesars Palace and the Hilton Hotel. Weekly bouts between talented unknowns take place every Wednesday at the Silver Slipper Hotel, 3100 Las Vegas Blvd. S (734-1212).

Jai Alai – Played daily except Mondays all year, at the MGM Grand fronton, 3645 Las Vegas Blvd. S (739-4682).

Betting – If you want to bet on almost any athletic event taking place outside of Nevada, numerous race and sports books dot the city. The facility in the Stardust Hotel is the most lavish on the Strip. 3000 Las Vegas Blvd. S (732-6111). Union Plaza's Book tops the downtown locales. 1 Main St. (386-2110).

Golf – Dozens of courses dot the desert landscape. Most of the Strip hotels have championship-quality courses, but the Sahara Country Club, 1911 Desert Inn Rd. (735-7070), and the Desert Inn Country Club, 3145 Las Vegas Blvd. S (733-4444), are the best. For lower prices, try the public courses. Best bet is the Municipal Golf Course which offers a reasonable challenge and good greens. Washington Ave. and Decatur Blvd. (878-4665).

Tennis – Almost all the Strip hotels have good tennis facilities open to the public. Best bet is Cambridge Tennis Club, 3890 Swenson Ave. (735-8153).

THEATER: For current performances, check the publications listed above. Outside of the entertainment at the Strip hotels, there is not that much in the way of theater. But a few new additions and old standbys keep the curtains raised. Best bets for shows are the *Repertory Theater at Judy Bayley Hall*, University of Nevada at Las Vegas campus (739-3641); the *Meadows Playhouse*, 4735 S Maryland Pkwy. (739-7525); *Aladdin Theater for the Performing Arts*, 3667 Las Vegas Blvd. S (736-0111). The Clark County Community College and other local companies are featured in *Theatre Under the Stars*, outdoors at the Spring Mountain Ranch in late June and early July. The creative sets make fine use of the environment, and the acting is first-rate. Tickets at the Ranch, on Spring Mountain Rd., 18 miles west on Charleston Blvd. (875-4141).

MUSIC: Symphony concerts, opera, jazz, and the Nevada Dance Theatre are featured throughout the year at *Artemus W. Ham Concert Hall* and the Judy Bayley Theatre on the UNLV campus. For ticket information call 739-3011.

NIGHTCLUBS AND NIGHTLIFE: When it comes to nightlife, Las Vegas is king. The city never sleeps, and can keep visitors who want to keep the same hours entertained all night. The Strip hotels offer a wide variety of entertainment. There are nightly production spectaculars, with dancing girls, lavish costumes and sets, and all kinds of specialty acts. Most extravagant are *Jubilee* at the MGM, 3645 Las Vegas Blvd. S (739-4111), and *Casino de Paris* at the Dunes, 3650 Las Vegas Blvd. S (737-4110). *Spice on Ice* at the Hacienda, 3950 Las Vegas Blvd. S (739-8911), and *Folies-Bergère* at the Tropicana, 3801 Las Vegas Blvd. S (739-2222).

In the main showrooms of all the other hotels on the Strip, a constant parade of stars perform twice nightly to audiences of 800–1,200 people in each hotel, either at the early show, when dinner is available, or later, when drinks are the rule. There's no cover charge but the minimum runs about $15 to $20 per person for dinner shows and $10 to $15 for late shows. You should keep a few things in mind when you are trying to get tickets to these big productions: Houseguests get first priority for many shows, so consider staying at the hotel which has the show you want to see. Always call early in the morning, or better still, go in person. Most hotels do not take show reservations more than two days in advance. The reservation booths open in the morning and stay open till show time, and the earlier you get there the better. If you've been gambling a good deal, ask the pit boss for assistance, and if you haven't you might try tipping the bell captain and hoping for the best.

Often overlooked are the casino lounges, where lesser-known performers (many of whom become better known) perform for just the cost of your drinks.

Favorite nonhotel clubs are: *Victoria's Disco,* 740 S Decatur Blvd. (878-8595); *Paul Anka's Jubilation,* 75 E Harmon St. (733-8822); *The Brewery* (also disco), 3824 Paradise Rd. (731-1050); *Top of the Landmark* has ballroom dancing, Landmark Hotel (733-1110); and the *Silver Dollar Saloon,* 2501 E Charleston Blvd. (382-6921), for live country-western music.

Las Vegas presents the best-known burlesque/striptease artists in the world. Tops (or topless, more likely) are: *The Royal Casino,* 99 Convention Center Dr. (732-2916); *Palomino Club,* 1848 Las Vegas Blvd. N (642-2984); the *Cabaret,* 4416 Paradise Rd. (733-8666); and *Bogie's* (for women only), 4375 Las Vegas Blvd. S (736-0668).

SINS: Sad to say, Las Vegas is not the sin capital it once was. Recently Lincoln County passed a law prohibiting prostitution, forcing several ranches of hard-working women into unemployment. This is not to say that *lust* has lost all its outlets. Fancy women who seem to linger too long on one spot, particularly barstools, are still likely candidates for a good time. And there are a number of bartenders and bellboys who continue to live by the motto, "Anything can be arranged." If all you really want to do is look, the floor shows in all the big hotels are still well stocked with long legs and full bosoms.

It is considered the height of *avarice* and gauche insensitivity to forget to tip the dealer working for you on your big win. Local protocol dictates that you toss a few big chips his way. Never openly hand him money. This could be considered even worse than ignoring him altogether, and he will not be able to accept the money.

LOCAL SERVICES: Business Services – Abacus and Quill, 3355 Spring Mountain Rd. (873-1552); Manpower Temporary Services, 314 Las Vegas Blvd. N (386-2626).

Mechanic – Caesar's Shell, 3496 Las Vegas Blvd. S (734-8740).

Babysitting – Sandy's Sitter Service, 24-hour service, 953 E Sahara Ave. (731-2086); Child Care Association of Clark County, PO Box 4855 (878-3271).

Wedding Bells Are Always Ringing in Las Vegas – If you are at least 18 (16 with parental consent), and you feel a sudden urge to get married, you can tie the knot on the spot (if you have someone to hold the other end of the string). Just apply at the Las Vegas Marriage License Bureau; there's not even a blood test or waiting period. Pay a modest fee, say "I do," and the deed is done. They don't call this place the "Wedding Capital of the World" for nothing. Open round the clock on Fridays and Saturdays; till midnight Sundays through Thursdays. Clark County Courthouse, 3rd and Carson Sts. (385-3156).

BEST IN TOWN

CHECKING IN: Although the city never sleeps, eventually bedtime catches the best of us. And when it does, there's a wide variety of places in which to rest up for the next round. In Vegas, the hotel's the thing. The Strip (Las Vegas Blvd. South) is a three-mile stream of hotel-casinos and motels, nearly matched in number, though usually not in quality, by the downtown "Glitter Gulch" area. Competition is fierce among the major hotels, and keeps room costs modest and on a par with one another. Expect to pay $60 and up for a double room per night in the expensive range; $25 to $50, moderate; around $18 to $25, inexpensive.

Caesars Palace – The unquestioned quality leader in Las Vegas since its construction in 1966, Caesars Palace is the ultimate Las Vegas hotel. Even the basic rooms are ornate, while the suites are sumptuous, with large classical statues to make you feel right at home in ancient Rome. The service is excellent, and the location — midway on the Strip — puts you in the middle of the action. But if you want action, you needn't leave the Palace. It has big-name entertainment, cafés, bars, restaurants, pool, tennis, golf privileges, meeting rooms, shops, and free parking. 1,236 rooms. Reservations are a must during the summer months, especially on holiday weekends. 3570 Las Vegas Blvd. S (731-7110). Expensive.

Las Vegas Hilton – With two completely new wings of rooms, it competes with the MGM Grand for the title of "Biggest in Vegas." The Hilton is a mini-city, with even a "children's hotel" to occupy younger guests while their parents attend to casino business. Located off the Strip near the Convention Center, the Hilton is not in the middle of the glitter, but neither is it in the center of traffic. Has star entertainment, café, bars, restaurants, large recreation center with pool, tennis, health club, putting greens and golf privileges, shops, free parking. 3000 Paradise Rd. (732-5111). Moderate.

Sahara Hotel – First stop on the Strip, and the flagship of the Del Webb fleet of hotels, the Sahara is unusual for its quietly elegant decor and its traditional sense of class. This friendly sophistication characterized Las Vegas a few decades ago but exists in fewer hotels each year. Here the service is personalized and excellent. Has star entertainment, café, bar, pools, health club, meeting rooms, shops. 1,000 rooms. 2535 Las Vegas Blvd. S (737-2111). Moderate.

Aladdin Hotel – The up-and-comer among Strip hotels, features a "Thousand and One Arabian Nights" atmosphere. Recently, Aladdin rubbed his lamp and out came upgraded facilities and a 7,500 seat theater. Also has cafés, bars, restaurants, pools, meeting rooms, shops, tennis, nine-hole golf course, free in-room movies. 1,000 rooms. 3667 Las Vegas Blvd. S (736-0111). Moderate.

Union Plaza – A large hotel, with the most complete facilities downtown, Union Plaza is situated at the entranceway to the downtown "Glitter Gulch" action. Some of the action starts right here with the hotel's dinner theater. Also has pool, café, bar, restaurant, shops, meeting rooms, and casino. 500 rooms. 1 Main St. (386-2110). Moderate.

Mint Hotel – Another Del Webb property, this modern high-rise combines a touch of class with good service amidst a dark and relaxing decor. The casino and dining areas have been expanded and are among the best downtown. Also has pool, amusement arcade for children, golf privileges, parking, and casino. 300 rooms. 100 E Fremont St. (385-7440). Moderate.

Golden Nugget – A new 600-room hotel has been added to this already bustling Old West–style casino. 129 E Fremont St. (385-7111). Moderate.

Circus-Circus Hotel – Of all the hotels on the Strip, the only one really dedicated to family entertainment (at family prices). With a full-scale circus operating above the gambling tables, complete with sideshows, there's something for everyone. Lots for the children — carousel, clown-shaped swimming pool; for the adults, cafés, bars, meeting rooms, health club, sauna. 800 rooms. 2880 Las Vegas Blvd. S (734-0410). Inexpensive.

Motel 6 – Offers good clean accommodations at the best prices in town. The bargain is worthwhile since hotel-motel rooms get little use in Las Vegas, and most of the time you're in them, you're asleep. Also, you get a pool for your money. 758 rooms. 196 E Tropicana (736-4904). Inexpensive.

Downtowner Motel – Offers standard accommodations with kitchenettes at low prices. 8th and Ogden Sts. (384-1441). Inexpensive.

Mini Price Motor Inn – Just as it says, mini prices, and located just off the Strip. 2550 S Rancho (876-2410). Inexpensive.

EATING OUT: Probably the only sure bet in Vegas is the food. Between hotels, restaurants, and casinos there's plenty to eat, and the food is much better than standard hotel or nightclub fare. From the Continental cuisine of the hotels' main restaurants to "all-you-can-eat" buffets, Las Vegas features quantity and quality. Though the offerings are basically American — steaks and seafood — there are a number of good ethnic restaurants. So eat up, and take advantage of the bargains in the casinos that are subsidized by gambling revenues; you're probably paying for them anyway. Our restaurant selections range in price from $45 or more for a dinner for two in the expensive range; $20 to $35 in the moderate range; and $15 or less, inexpensive. Prices do not include drinks, wine, or tips.

Palace Court – Considered the ultimate in dining grace in Las Vegas. Candelabra, vermeil flatware, and handblown crystal are the accouterments of an unforgettable experience. Sommeliers pour wine from the hotel's distinguished wine cellar. Wednesdays through Sundays, lunch, 11:30 AM to 2:30 PM, dinner nightly, 6:30 PM to midnight. Reservations. Major credit cards. 3570 Las Vegas Blvd. S (731-7110). Expensive.

Monte Carlo Room – Decorated in red velvet and crystal, this small hideaway in the Desert Inn Hotel has an almost homey atmosphere, though the home would have to belong to the Vanderbilts. Specialties include steak marchand de vin and veal dornandig, and the service is first-rate. Open nightly. Reservations. Major credit cards. 3145 Las Vegas Blvd. S (733-4444). Expensive.

Sabre Room – The Aladdin Hotel's main Continental restaurant offers an interesting twist. You can dine in your own private cave, a textured-cement-canopied alcove, on excellent Middle Eastern food — shish kebab, baked kibbe (veal), stuffed squash, and stuffed grape leaves (dolmades). Open nightly. Reservations. Major credit cards. 3667 Las Vegas Blvd. S (736-0111). Expensive.

House of Lords – The Sahara Hotel's try at a ritzy British pub serves fine steaks and seafoods. Best are sole, trout, and salmon, flown in from the Coast, and tournedos of beef if you really want to be swept away — thick chunks of filet mignon in a delicate hollandaise sauce. Open nightly. Reservations. Major credit cards. 2535 Las Vegas Blvd. S (735-2111). Expensive.

Don the Beachcomber – Another Sahara Hotel restaurant; Polynesian cuisine amidst tropical surroundings — real giant palms, flowing brook, and mellow background music. For a variety of flavors, try the High Chief Special — assorted appetizers including fried shrimp, egg roll and crab puff, main dishes of Cantonese pork, chicken with almonds, beef soya, with fried rice. Open nightly. Reservations. Major credit cards. 2535 Las Vegas Blvd. S (735-2111). Moderate.

Alpine Village – Best are the portions of good Swiss and German food — the wurst plates of all varieties, and the huge kettles of thick, dark German chicken soup which are meant for two but could actually feed the entire Swiss Family Robinson. Restaurant also features a Ratskeller with a piano player and lots of German beers. Open nightly. Reservations. Major credit cards. 3003 Paradise Rd. (734-6888). Moderate.

Battista's Hole in the Wall – Plentiful Italian pastas for dinner, helped along by all the wine you can drink, and an occasional Italian aria by Battista himself, to create the proper mood. Closed Sundays. Reservations. Major credit cards. 4041 Audrie, next to the MGM Grand (732-1424). Moderate.

Chateau Vegas – Continental cuisine amidst elegant surroundings, backed up by soft music and a harpist. Best are the Italian veal and any of the steaks. Open 24 hours a day. Reservations. Major credit cards. 565 Desert Inn Rd. (733-8282). Moderate.

Lobster Trap – The simple "come as you are" atmosphere belies some of the best seafood in town, from Maine lobster to a New England clambake. The ingredients of both are flown in from the East. Open nightly. Reservations. Major credit cards. 953 E Sahara St. (734-0023). Moderate.

Golden Steer – In a town that has to revise the phone books twice a year just to keep up with the comings and goings of things, 17 years in the same place attests to a strong tradition. The decor is luxurious: Western, and the offerings top-notch, from the steaks (try the Diamond Lil prime ribs) to the toasted ravioli, and the extensive wine list. If you give a day's notice, you can have a special delicacy: pheasant, goose, quail, chukar (partridge), or roast suckling pig. Open daily. Reservations. Major credit cards. 308 W Sahara Ave. (384-4470). Moderate.

Starboard Tack – For years, a local favorite. Now a sister restaurant, the Port Tack, also offers romance and good food in a larger setting with an attractive sunken fireplace. Open 24 hours. Reservations. Major credit cards. Starboard, 2601 Atlantic St. (457-8794). Port, 3190 W Sahara Ave. (873-3345). Moderate.

Viva Zapata – A cut above most Mexican places in price, but worth the difference. The atmosphere is modern and informal, decorated with baskets, fresh flowers, and posters. The food is excellent, and the flautas (tortillas stuffed with beef, vegetables, and cheese, and sautéed with avocado sauce) are really something special. Open daily. Reservations. Major credit cards. 4972 S Maryland Pkwy. (736-6630); and 3540 W Sahara (873-7228). Moderate.

Library Buttery and Pub – Located in an old mansion, the atmosphere is a combination of an expansive library and a traditional English pub. Extensive menu has a wide range of entrées, but best are chicken Angelo (done in tomato sauce with baby onions) and veal piccante. Open 24 hours. Reservations. Major credit cards. 200 W Sahara Ave. (384-5200). Moderate.

Carlos Murphy's Irish Mexican Café – Sounds strange, but with a touch of American nostalgia and multitudes of memorabilia, this warmly decorated café offers specialties such as quiche, crêpes, Irish stew, and Mexican dishes. Open daily. No reservations. Major credit cards. Moderate.

El Burrito Café – This small authentic Mexican restaurant seats only 30, but the quality of the food would keep it full if it were twice as big. Offers several fine combination plates. The chicharrones, burritos stuffed with fried pork bits, are extra special. Open daily. Reservations. No credit cards. 1919 E Fremont St. (385-9461). Inexpensive.

Golden Wok – This Chinese restaurant has been so successful that it now has a second location. Open daily. 4760 S Eastern (456-1868); 504 S Decatur (878-1596). Inexpensive.

Good Time Charlie's – With its prime location (about a mile from the convention center and strip), this local favorite serves up a splendid fare of super hamburgers, omelettes, and other incredible edibles as well as specialty drinks. Open 24 hours daily. No reservations. Major credit cards. 3107 S Maryland Pkwy. (737-0440). Inexpensive.

Vineyard – Located on the exterior of The Boulevard, one of Las Vegas's two enclosed shopping malls, this quaint Italian eatery offers a fine antipasto salad bar and specialties such as chicken cacciatore and veal cutlet Parmigiana. Open daily. Major credit cards. Reservations for six or more. 3630 S Maryland Pkwy. (731-1606). Inexpensive.

Buffets – If all-you-can-eat sounds good to you, you can spend all your time in Las Vegas doing just that. Virtually every Strip hotel and most of the downtown hotels have buffet lunches and dinners, where, for a couple of dollars, you can have as much as you can handle from an array of salads, fish, chicken, pasta, occasionally roast beef, and dessert. Best bets for buffets are the Holiday Casino, 3475 Las Vegas Blvd. S (732-2411); the Fremont, 2nd and Fremont Sts. (385-3232); the Mint, 100 Fremont St. (385-7440), downtown.

For something really special, try the weekend Champagne Brunch at Caesars Palace — a feast for the eyes as well as the tastebuds with its beautifully arranged selections of freshly baked pastries, fresh melons, eggs, bacon, ham, sausage, and all the champagne you can drink. 3570 Las Vegas Blvd. S (731-7110). Inexpensive.

LOS ANGELES

Los Angeles: the beginning of a dream or the end of the world? It depends on you and what you expect from the place. Perhaps more than any other American city — or any city in the world — Los Angeles capitalizes on illusion and desire. LA glitters, shines, and seems to embrace some ultimate, secret dream of golden success shared by millions. Los Angeles represents the possibility of achieving glamor, fame, and stardom, with the seductive promise of languishing on perennially sunlit beaches thrown in as an extra. Almost every kid in America spends some time longing to hang around with a sparkling, copper-and-bronze California beach crowd. Nearly every adult imagines speeding along palm-tree and mansion-lined boulevards in an elegant sports car, driving up the circular driveway of a Beverly Hills mansion, to be greeted by incredibly good-looking people with white teeth and smashing clothes, all drinking martinis around a swimming pool. This is the myth. To be more exact, this is *our* myth, the home-grown American legend that nurtures our collective imagination. Movie stars inhabit this new western Olympus just as Zeus, Hera, and the cast of hundreds of gods filled the mythological heavens of the ancient Greeks. As Olympus did to the Greeks, Los Angeles represents everything most Americans hope for and believe in. It is the land of make-believe come true, the home of the fantasy industry, where images are produced and sold around the world.

Like many self-images, LA's tend to conflict with reality. The beautiful weather is very often cloaked in yellowish smog that hangs sullenly over Hollywood like an extraterrestrial gas. The 172 miles of interlacing concrete ribbons of freeways linking the different communities of the 4,000 square miles called Greater Los Angeles can be snarled for hours. Critics say the phrase "urban sprawl" came into being just to describe Los Angeles. Once you get out of Hollywood and Beverly Hills, it begins to look like one endless shopping center and parking lot complex separated by apartment houses. To those who come yearning for that almost mystical fulfillment ascribed to the southern California environment, the letdown can be terrific. LA can be dehumanizing. Anonymous in a way unmatched by New York, San Francisco, or Chicago, city streets, residential streets with houses, sidewalks and roads all intermingle.

That perhaps is the major distinction between LA and most other big cities. There are no streets to speak of. Los Angelenos live in cars. They sleep in their houses (or in friends' houses), but they live in their cars. They're car freaks. There is no other reasonable way to conquer the distances between the Pacific shores, the rugged ridges of the Santa Monica Mountains, the vast San Fernando Valley, and downtown. It is nearly impossible to get from point A to point B without wheels. There is no viable public transportation. Buses are so infrequent that Los Angelenos joke about the skeletons on bus-stop benches — waiting patiently for their buses.

This is one reason Los Angelenos insist on driving. Another is the scarcity of taxis. You can get them, but because of the distances involved, they can be prohibitively expensive. Nor are there any plans to help residents relinquish their private cars. Past efforts to get people to switch to buses have invariably failed.

As you might imagine, rental car companies thrive in Los Angeles. Every independent car rental agency — big or small — wants a piece of the LA action. They even go so far as to pick up drivers at the service stations where they have just brought their cars in for repairs — drivers who are desperate for any wheels they can rent.

It takes longer to get to know LA than most other cities, and it can be frustrating for a first-time visitor. Most walks in LA start from, or lead to, parking lots. In LA, you have to know where you're going when you set out. If not, how will you know where to park? In San Francisco, for example, the main entrance of a building is its front door. Not so, LA. Here, the main entrance usually leads to and from the parking lot. For example, you really enter the Beverly Wilshire Hotel from its private drive-in entrance, not from its so-called front door on Wilshire Boulevard. Not only do most Los Angelenos never use the official front doors of the buildings they work in, many never even see those formal entrances. Many workers in LA drive directly into a parking garage beneath their office building, then take an elevator to the floor on which they work, completely by-passing the front door and main lobby. Some buildings in downtown Los Angeles were actually designed to provide access only by automobile. They don't take pedestrian traffic into account at all. This makes it particularly hard for a visitor who naturally expects the fronts of buildings to have doors. (Yes, that was silly of you, wasn't it?) But don't despair. It is possible to walk through compact, mansion-studded Beverly Hills. Another good place for walking is Westwood, although getting from Beverly Hills to Westwood can be very frustrating without a car.

Well-adjusted Los Angelenos take it all in stride. They regard this as just another aspect of life, and think nothing of driving an hour and a half for dinner in a certain restaurant. Creatures of whim, Los Angeles residents go with the flow of their own moods and enjoy the time they spend in their cars. For many, it is the only truly private time they ever have. Nobody can bother them while they drive. There are no phone calls to take, except for those status-seekers foolish enough to have telephones in their cars. There are no visitors dropping in, no mail or telegram deliveries. One's car is one's castle. Many a business executive dictates letters into a battery-powered tape recorder while inching along the freeway on the way to work. Others just use the time to sort out thoughts. Some put their private driving moments to different use. It is not unusual to see people screaming inside their cars. Because of the traffic noise, it's usually not possible to hear them scream, but the observant driver or passenger can easily figure out what they are doing. This type of therapy enables them to release tensions and hostilities that in other cities would remain bottled up inside. Consider the consequences of screaming in your apartment in, say, San Francisco — the neighbors would call the police in two minutes. Try screaming on a street corner in Boston for a few minutes. You'll be hauled off before you know what's happening. Or screaming out loud while riding the New York subways. (Dare we consider the consequences?) Only in Los Angeles is there a safe and comfortable place to scream in privacy.

Other behavioral characteristics distinguish Los Angeles residents from people in other parts of the country. They differ in at least one other important way: When they wake up in the morning they don't immediately look out the window. They don't have to. They don't go to bed worrying about what the weather will be when they awake. They *know* it will be pleasant and comfortably warm. *Always.* The local TV stations can make a big thing of giving detailed weather information, complete with satellite photos of cloud formations, but true Los Angelenos don't have to watch. They take the ideal climate for granted.

This is why LA residents hardly ever make contingency plans. For anything. Whereas a New Yorker will agree to reschedule a luncheon date in case of rain, a Los Angeleno never thinks about it. In his or her mind, there is never any possibility that the weather will be anything but ideal. The smog is always someplace else — never where the person you are speaking to actually lives, works, or plays golf. Smog is what other, less fortunate people suffer. Since everyone thinks this way, visitors are advised against making any honest observations about the climate. If you can't breathe, wheeze as quietly as you can, but don't dare suggest that the air quality is anything other than totally acceptable. It is very impolite to imply that sunny California isn't always all that sunny. Perhaps an even more sensitive topic than smog is that of rain. (What!?!) Rain. Although LA people profess a blithe unconcern for the torrents of water that suddenly stream down from the sky, they are quite aware of the dangers. As soon as the first drops hit the freeway, the oil-coated surface turns as slick as if it were black ice; the road becomes an ice-skating rink, and there can be incredible pileups, especially during rush hours. Los Angelenos, however, remain undeterred.

Such is life on the ultimate frontier. For most of the 10 million people in Greater Los Angeles, this is freedom, a state of mind as well as place. The majority of inhabitants came here from some other part of the country, precisely because LA is the Great Escape — the place where nobody watches and you can do what you want. It's the last stop. Many visitors, inebriated by the sudden sense of freedom, become swingers overnight. Others take one look and go home. The queen seductress of American cities, LA often deceives dreamers with her own brand of reality. She is, in one song, "the city of the fallen angels." In real life, there is no doubt she is a place of extremes, and your degree of delight or disenchantment will derive very much from your own judgments and yearnings. Dynamic, exciting, creative, flashy, vulgar, indulgent, or decadent — LA invites strong reactions. You'll probably either love it or hate it. One thing's for sure: Like many a well-publicized major motion picture, you won't soon forget it.

LOS ANGELES AT-A-GLANCE

SEEING THE CITY: There are at least three great places to go for a fantastic view of Los Angeles. The most famous is Mulholland Drive, a twisting road that winds through the Hollywood Hills. Another is the top of Mount Olympus, in Laurel Canyon, near Sunset Boulevard. The 34-story, 464-foot-high City Hall Tower has a sweeping view of downtown, the mountains, and the Pacific Ocean. Open daily. Free. City Hall East, near south end of Los Angeles Mall (485-2121 or 485-5620).

SPECIAL PLACES: A walk through Old Hollywood will delight the heart of anyone who loves the era of those great movies that made Hollywood known around the world. However, Hollywood is no longer the physical center of film production, and its glamor is, sadly, long gone. In recent years it has turned into a honky-tonk area. Keep in mind that most residents would never contemplate walking down Hollywood Boulevard after dark. During the daytime, however, most Hollywood streets are crowded, bustling, and safe. There is a lot to enjoy here, much of it for little or no cost.

OLD HOLLYWOOD: MEMORIES AND EMPTY BUILDINGS

Mann's Chinese Theater – Known to movie fans around the world as Grauman's Chinese Theater, this is probably the most visited site in Hollywood. If you wander down Hollywood Boulevard in the direction of Highland Avenue looking for the Grauman's sign, you'll never find it, though. Several years ago, Ted Mann took the theater over and added it to his movie chain. As the new proprietor, he felt within his rights to take down the sign that had made Syd Grauman famous, and replace it with his own. But it caused considerable local controversy. The Chinese Theater forecourt is world-famous for its celebrity footprints and handprints immortalized in cement. If you join the crowd of visitors outside the box office, you'll probably find your favorite star of the 1920s and 30s. If you buy a ticket to get in, you'll be treated to one of the world's most impressive and elaborate movie palaces. The ornate carvings, the very high, decorative ceiling, the traditionally plush seats, the heavy curtains that *whoosh* closed when the film ends, and the enormous screen itself are all part of a Hollywood that no longer exists. The Chinese Theater is one of those movie theaters that gives children some idea of what parents mean when they talk about how moviegoing has changed since their own childhood. 6925 Hollywood Blvd. (464-8111).

Hollywood Wax Museum – If the Chinese Theater makes you nostalgic for the faces belonging to the disembodied prints, stop in at the Hollywood Wax Museum. If you've been leery of wax museums ever since you watched Vincent Price coat his victims in wax in the famous movie "House of Wax," we hasten to reassure you that there is no such hanky-panky going on in the back rooms here. Marilyn Monroe, Clark Gable and Jean Harlow, Paul Newman, Gary Cooper, Barbra Streisand, Raquel Welch, and many more fill the star-studded display cases. There's also a horror chamber, a recreation of "The Last Supper," and a documentary about the history of the Academy Awards with film clips from winners like "Gone With the Wind" and "Mary Poppins." Open daily. Admission charge; children under six free. 6767 Hollywood Blvd. (462-8860).

Paramount Pictures – At one time, RKO studios adjoined the Paramount lot. After RKO folded in 1956, its studio became the home of television's Desilu Productions, which in turn sold its property to next-door Paramount. Close to the Bronson Avenue intersection with Melrose is the famous Paramount Gate, the highly decorative studio entrance that many people will remember from the film "Sunset Boulevard." The Gower Street side of today's Paramount was the old front entrance to RKO. At what used to be 780 Gower Street, you will now find nothing but an unimpressive back door to Paramount, painted in that dull, flat beige many studios use to protect their exterior walls. The door no longer bears its old marquee with distinctive Art Deco neon letters spelling out RKO, the numbers have been torn from the front steps, and the Art Deco front doors are gone. RKO is just a memory now. Paramount extends from Melrose Ave. on the south to Gower St. on the west, Van Ness Ave. on the east, and Willoughby Ave. on the north (468-5000).

Gower Street – This was once the center for so many small film studios that it became known in the film business as Gower Gulch. It was also nicknamed Poverty Row because so many of its independent producers were perpetually strapped for production money. Poverty Row's most famous studio was Columbia Pictures. It ultimately grew healthy enough to acquire most of the smaller parcels of studio real estate in the neighborhood. The old Columbia lot still stands in Hollywood, although Columbia moved out several years ago. Columbia found a new home in Burbank at the Warner Brothers Studio, which was then renamed The Burbank Studios (TBS). The two film companies operate TBS as a rental facility for film and TV production today. Columbia's old studios still stand at Gower Street and Sunset Boulevard. When Columbia vacated the property some of its sound stages were used for a time as indoor tennis courts. Today they have become film studios once more, available for rent to independent production companies.

Warner Brothers – In the late 1920s, when Warner's was introducing "talkies" to America, their pictures were filmed here. It was also the home of Warner's radio station at the time, KFWB. Today the old Warner Brothers studio is the headquarters for Gene Autry's KTLA–TV and KMPC radio. The stately southern-style mansion that served as the Warner's administration building still stands on Sunset Boulevard. Sunset Blvd. and Van Ness Ave.

Samuel Goldwyn Studios – Originally built by Mary Pickford and Douglas Fairbanks, the old Samuel Goldwyn studios became United Artists in 1919, when Pickford and Fairbanks were joined by Charlie Chaplin and D. W. Griffith. In 1980 Warner Brothers purchased the lot as a site for its television production activities. Santa Monica Blvd. and Formosa Ave., West Hollywood.

Selznick Studios – Nothing can compare with the old Selznick studios, where David O. Selznick produced "Gone With the Wind," "Rebecca," and "Intermezzo." It was originally built by silent film director Thomas Ince, a Southerner who wanted his administration building to look like a typical Georgia mansion. Millions of filmgoers have seen Ince's mansion as the opening logo of the Selznick film classics. The once beautiful Selznick studio is now a run-down rental facility, but it still retains some of its old majesty. If you imagine the gardens restored to their original condition and visualize the buildings freshly painted, it's possible to get a feel for how it used to be. It was here that Selznick filmed the burning of Atlanta in "Gone With the Wind." He had to film it before the other scenes so that the back lot could be cleared of sets and props to make room for other production activities. Jefferson and Ince Blvds., Culver City.

"HOLLYWOOD": ALIVE AND WELL

"Hollywood," as we refer to the film business, is no longer geographically located in the district bearing that name. If your nostalgic walking tour of Old Hollywood has made you curious about modern-day production methods, we suggest a tour of one of the following Los Angeles studios:

Universal Studios – The combination movie studio tour and theme park has been attracting more than three million people a year. In 1915, Universal Pictures established a mammoth studio on 420 acres of what was then a chicken farm. Land in the eastern part of the San Fernando Valley was pretty cheap, and Universal's founder, Carl Laemmle, was smart enough to buy a lot of it. As a result, the modern Universal, a division of MCA, Inc., found itself with more than enough room to make movies and television shows, as well as build a theme park. The Universal Studio tours, launched in 1964, are conducted on trams, complete with tour guides, and about 120 people per tour. Some of the tour highlights include a special stunt show, a working quicksand pit, a make-up show, a rock slide, a look at some of the 34 sound stages and other production facilities, a special-effects demonstration, a burning house, and a collapsing bridge. You'll also see the house used in Alfred Hitchcock's "Psycho," a street from "The Sting," the colonial street from "Airport 77," a flash flood, a runaway train, the parting of the Red Sea, an attack on the tour tram by the 24-foot "shark" from "Jaws," a waterfall, and the Doomed Glacier Expedition, where you get to plunge down an Alpine avalanche. If you're ready for all that, you can visit Universal Studios any day of the week. Admission charge; children under five free when accompanied by adult. Universal City (877-1311 or 877-2121).

The Burbank Studios – If you want something a little lower-key than the Universal extravaganza, try The Burbank Studios. Not only do you get to see some production, you also see a lot of behind-the-scenes action — scenery construction, sound recording, props, and wardrobe departments. You can also arrange to eat in the TBS commissary with the actors and actresses. Since TBS tours are limited to 12 people, with children under 12 not permitted, reservations are required. Open weekdays. Admission charge. 4000 Warner Blvd. (954-6000 or 954-1008).

NBC Television Studios – Another traditional behind-the-scenes tour, NBC offers you the chance to see television studios, set construction, special effects, make-up and wardrobe departments. Tours are escorted by NBC pages, who make no promises but very often guide you past a few stars. NBC takes you to the set of Johnny Carson's "Tonight Show," with the possibility of joining the show's audience for that night's taping. There are 25 people on each tour, which takes about an hour. Closed Sundays. Admission charge. 3000 W Alameda Ave., Burbank (840-4444).

20th Century–Fox – If you're interested in taking a peek at a working film studio other than on an official tour, you will be happy to know you can enter the 20th Century–Fox lot from Motor Avenue in Hollywood and drive the entire length of the cobblestone street from "Hello, Dolly!" before reaching the security-guard gate. (Carol Channing will not be there to sing for you, though.) The street was built for the 1969 musical, and is now being used for filming TV programs and commercials. The facades of the various buildings resemble New York in the 1890s, including the New York Public Library. It's one of the most interesting film studio sets in town, and it's free. Open daily. Pico Blvd. and Motor Ave., just west of Beverly Hills.

Beverly Hills – After a hard day on the lot, movie stars return to their Beverly Hills mansions for a good night's sleep. Even during the sunshiny daylight hours, Beverly Hills is remarkably tranquil, with nary a person walking on the residential streets. Without a doubt the most affluent and elegant suburb in southern California, Beverly Hills is a must-see. If you want to window-shop or purchase high fashion articles of clothing or leather, stroll along Rodeo Drive between Santa Monica and Wilshire Boulevards. If you want to make sure you don't succumb to an impulse to buy anything, go on Sunday, when the stores are closed. Gray Line offers bus and limousine tours. Call 481-2121 for information.

DOWNTOWN LOS ANGELES

To see a Los Angeles that most residents don't know about, take a walking tour through downtown LA. Your on-foot perspective will be radically different from that of auto-bound Los Angelenos.

The Plaza – If you ever wondered what the place looked like before shopping centers were created, step across the Plaza and marvel. The Plaza is a wide square. The Old

Plaza Church, built by a captured pirate in 1818, has a curious financial history. (It was partially paid for by the sale of seven barrels of brandy.) The city's first firehouse is here, too. The Plaza is the scene of monthly fiestas. For a complete repertory of colorful local anecdotes, take a narrated walking tour of the Plaza. For information, contact the Pueblo de los Angeles office on the Plaza (628-1274).

Olvera Street – Music from the Plaza fiesta spills into Olvera Street, a block-long pedestrian alley filled with colorful Mexican shops, restaurants, and spicy food stalls. The oldest house in Los Angeles is here — the 1818 Avila house, made of adobe. The first brick house is also here, but now it's a restaurant.

Los Angeles Mall – An unusually quiet, well-landscaped city mall, with tropical plants, gentle splashing fountains, and sculpture half hidden among the lush greenery. It's the first mall of shops and restaurants to be built on City Hall property. The Triforium tower of glass cylinders occasionally flashes brightly colored lights in time to music — a symphony of light and sound composed and conducted by a computer. For one of the best views of the city, make sure you get to the top of City Hall Tower at the south end of the mall. Open daily. Free (485-2121).

Third and Broadway – Several places in this area are worth noting. First is the skylit, five-story indoor court of the Bradbury Building. You can ride an old hydraulic elevator to the top balcony and walk down a magnificent staircase guaranteed to evoke visions of bygone splendors. Across the corner from the Bradbury Building is the Million Dollar Theater Syd Grauman's first. There's a sculpture gallery of the performing arts inside, but the exterior is pretty fascinating, too. Just south of the theater is the entrance to the Grand Central Public Market — a conglomerate of stalls selling food from all over the world. It's a great place to stop for a snack after your walk.

Central Library – To catch your breath, get out of the heat, or read for a while, walk to the Central Library, considered to be one of the first modern buildings in LA (built in 1926). Inside, in addition to the books, magazines, and periodicals, you'll find splendid murals of California history by Dean Cornwall. Closed Sundays and holidays. Free. 630 W 5th St. (626-7461).

Music Center – The best time to visit the Music Center is during a concert or performance, but it's worth seeing anytime. The Ahmanson Theater is host to touring companies from other parts of the country and England. The Dorothy Chandler Pavilion, a 2,500-seat auditorium trimmed in gold and red velvet, is home to the Los Angeles Philharmonic. The orchestra season runs from October to May. Other classical groups perform here the rest of the year. The Mark Taper Forum, a theater-in-the-round, houses the Center Theater Group, a well-respected professional repertory company specializing in modern and traditional classics. You can take a guided tour of the theaters. Hope and Temple Sts. (972-7211).

New Chinatown – New Chinatown has the usual assortment of restaurants, vegetable stores, and weird little shops selling ivory chess sets and acupuncture charts. N Hill and College Sts. (623-4479).

Farmers Market – "Eat your liver." No, we're not quoting your mother, we're quoting Yossarian, the hero of *Catch 22* (book by Joseph Heller, movie by Mike Nichols). Yossarian used to say "eat your liver" all the time, and at the Farmers Market you can do just that. You can also eat anything else within the realm of gastronomic imagination. You'll find 160 stalls of American, Mexican, Italian, Chinese, and vegetarian food, and any number of exquisite bakeries and fruit and candy shops. If you don't like to eat standing up, there are tables set among the aisles of this indoor, covered market. A great place to be hungry. Open daily. 6333 W 3rd St. and Fairfax (933-9211).

Griffith Park – If you thought Texas had the biggest of everything, you're mistaken. This is the largest municipal park in the country. (Eat your liver, Texas.) Griffith has five golf courses, a wilderness area and bird sanctuary, tennis courts, a miniature railroad, a carousel, and picnic areas within its 4,063 acres. Not only that — this is where you'll find the famous Los Angeles Zoo, home to 2,500 mammals, birds, and reptiles. We recommend a visit to the giraffes — they're always a calming influence. Open daily except Christmas. Admission charge; children under eleven free (666-4090 or 666-4650). If you like railroads, you'll love Travel Town, a unique outdoor museum of old railroad engines, cars, railroad equipment, and fire trucks. Open daily. Griffith Park Blvd. (662-5874).

Los Angeles County Museum of Art – There are special exhibits in the Armand Hammer wing, and a dazzling permanent collection which includes the Ahmanson Gallery's pre-Columbian and African art, tapestries, and paintings from the 18th century to today. The Leo S. Bing Theater offers special films. Closed Mondays. Admission charge. 5905 Wilshire Blvd. (857-6111).

Forest Lawn Memorial Park – A major tourist attraction, Forest Lawn is a huge cemetery calling itself a memorial park, which advertises on huge billboards overlooking the freeways. On the grounds you'll find a stained glass window depicting "The Last Supper" and spectacular artwork of the crucifixion and the resurrection. Forest Lawn is the home of the largest religious painting in the world, Jan Styka's 195- by 45-foot "The Crucifixion." Open daily. Free. 1712 S Glendale, Glendale (254-3131). Also, 6300 Forest Lawn Dr. (984-1711).

ORANGE COUNTY

Disneyland – For many people, the most remarkable thing about Disneyland is the number of people who go there. But if you've ever wished upon a star and longed to make your way toward the glittering spires of Fantasyland, a trip to this incredibly clean, colorful, and diversified amusement park is essential. You will undoubtedly encounter one of your favorite Disney characters promenading down Main Street, a re-creation of a typical 1890s American street. 40 minutes from downtown LA, Disneyland is open daily. Admission charge. 1313 Harbor Blvd., Anaheim (714 999-4565).

Movieland Wax Museum – About a ten-minute drive from Disneyland, with more than 230 movie stars in wax, molded into stances from their greatest cinematic moments. The original props and sets from many of the films are here, too. Closed Sundays. Admission charge; children under four free. 7711 Beach Blvd., Buena Park (714 522-1154).

Knott's Berry Farm – The theme is the Old West. An old-fashioned stagecoach and authentic steam coach will take you around the grounds, past the Corkscrew, Whirlwind, Log Ride, Sky Jump, Loop Trainer, and bumper cars. There are also paddle boats, burros, cable cars, and a mine train. Knott's Berry Farm has top country and western artists performing frequently, and a great ice show. Closed Mondays and Thursdays during winter months, open daily the rest of the year; closed Christmas. Admission charge. 10 minutes from Disneyland at 8309 Beach Blvd., Buena Park (714 952-9400 or 714 827-1776).

Lion Country Safari – If you've ever imagined a rhinoceros gently nudging your car's back bumper, and thought it might be an interesting experience, you'll spend many happy hours at Lion Country Safari. Rhinos, cheetahs, lions, tigers, hippos, and elephants stalk the grounds — more than 58 species of wild animals and 25 kinds of exotic birds. You remain in your car, driving at your own pace. A taped cassette tour is available, too. Open daily. Admission charge. San Diego Freeway (#405) south to Moulton Parkway exit, or Santa Ana Freeway (#5) to San Canyon exit. 8880 Moulton Pkwy., Laguna Hills, near Irvine (714 837-1200).

Marineland – Dolphins, killer whales, and acrobatic sea lions perform at this world-famous aquatic sea park. If you know how to snorkel, you can dive below the surface of Marineland's 540,000-gallon tank with a trained diver who'll show you a rare close-up of undersea life. A closed-circuit TV camera beams your special swim back to less-venturesome family and friends. The aquarium exhibits include walruses, otters, waterfowl, and an amazing assortment of fish. Open daily during summer months; closed Mondays and Tuesdays from September 12 to end of winter. Admission charge; children under four free. San Diego Freeway south to Hawthorne Blvd., Palos Verdes exit, or Harbor Freeway (#11) south till it ends. 6600 Palos Verdes Dr. S, Palos Verdes Peninsula (377-1571).

Queen Mary – Not far from Palos Verdes, the *Queen Mary* is docked in Long Beach. When launched in 1934, the *Queen Mary* was a luxury liner for the rich and famous. A transatlantic voyage on the *Queen* was the ultimate travel experience of the time. She was "relaunched" in 1971, after retiring from a long, exciting career on the high seas. You can tour the 81,000-ton ship from her berth in southern California, and can even spend the night — the original 400 staterooms are operated by Hyatt Hotels. Several fine restaurants serve lunch and dinner, a number of boutiques are now open, and on shore, undersea explorer Jacques Cousteau's Living Sea exhibit offers a fascinating look at underwater life. Open daily. Admission charge. Long Beach Freeway (#7) to *Queen Mary* exit (435-4747; for hotel reservations call 435-3511).

Catalina Island – It's two hours by boat from Long Beach to Catalina Island, where you can spend the day wandering around the flower-filled hills, looking at the ocean, swimming, sightseeing, playing golf, or riding horses. There are places to stay overnight. From December to April, special three-hour whale-watching cruises sail to scout for the annual migration of 10,000 gray whales. Boats to Catalina leave daily from Long Beach Terminal. Admission charge. Near *Queen Mary,* at 890 Queensway Dr., or from Los Angeles Terminal Building, foot of Harbor Freeway, San Pedro (775-6111; or call Catalina Cruises at 832-4521).

■ **EXTRA SPECIAL:** For one of the most spectacular drives in California, follow the Pacific Coast Highway (#1) north to *Santa Barbara,* about 95 miles from LA. Santa Barbara is a picturesque California mission town facing the Pacific, where bright bougainvillea flowers purple and magenta against classic white adobe houses, and small clapboard buildings recall the 19th-century settlers. A walking tour of the historic district might well begin at Ortega Street, named for an explorer who guided one of the first expeditions into California in 1769. From Ortega, it's six blocks along Spanish, vine-hung, hacienda-lined streets to State Street, where the architecture turns Victorian. Santa Barbara has a couple of interesting country inns. You can stay overnight at the *Upham Hotel,* an 1871 wooden structure furnished comfortably with antiques. The dining room can be found in another building, at the end of a vine-covered garden path. 1404 De La Vina (805 962-0058). The *Cold Spring Tavern,* about 10 miles northwest from Santa Barbara on rt. 154, goes back to the old stagecoach days. Chili is popular at lunch. At dinner, the menu tends more toward chicken and shrimp creole. Open daily for lunch and dinner. 5995 Stagecoach Rd. (805 967-0066).

SOURCES AND RESOURCES

For free information, brochures, and maps, contact the Southern California Visitors Council, 505 S Flower St. (628-3101).

The best local guides to Los Angeles are *Where Can We Go This Weekend?—1, 2, and 3-Day Travel Adventures in Southern California* (J. P. Tarcher, $3.95); *The Downtown L.A. West Guide* (ESE California, $2.45).

All telephone numbers are in the 213 area code unless otherwise indicated.

For Local Coverage – *Los Angeles Times,* morning daily; *Los Angeles Herald-*

Examiner, evening daily; *Los Angeles* Magazine, monthly; *California* Magazine, biweekly.

For Food – To keep absolutely up to date, check the restaurant listings in *Los Angeles* or *California* Magazine.

CLIMATE AND CLOTHES: Fog and smog continually act as deterrents to clear vision, although the dry, sunny days are so gloriously clear you will forget about the times when it's not. Temperatures are in the 90s in summer, dropping to the 60s at night; in the 70s during winter days, the 50s at night.

GETTING AROUND: Los Angeles is the best thing to happen to the automobile since Henry Ford. A car is essential for getting around with any degree of efficiency or comfort. But there *are* buses and taxis.

Bus – You can get from LA International Airport to West LA for 35¢ by taking the Line 3 bus of the Culver City Municipal Bus line. It takes 40 minutes to get to Westwood and Pico Blvds. For information call 837-5211. For other routes, Southern California Rapid Transit District (781-5890, 273-0910; information on the best routes, 626-4455).

Taxi – Beverly Hills Cab Co. (273-6611); Celebrity Cab Co. (278-2500); Yellow Cab (481-2345).

Car Rental – All major firms are represented throughout Greater Los Angeles.

MUSEUMS: The Los Angeles County Museum of Art is described in *Special Places.* Other fine museums in LA are:

George C. Page Museum, 5801 Wilshire Blvd. (933-7451).

Henry E. Huntington Library and Art Gallery, 1151 Oxford Rd., San Marino (792-6141).

Norton Simon Museum of Art, Colorado and Orange Grove Blvd., Pasadena (449-6840).

J. Paul Getty Museum, 17985 Pacific Coast Hwy. Malibu (454-6541).

SHOPPING: No single street on this planet so typifies consumer excess as Rodeo Drive in Beverly Hills. Few mortals will be able to afford the prices, but window-shopping along this street makes for as much fun as studying the boutiques along Paris's rue du Faubourg-St.-Honoré. In fact, many of the shop names are the same. By the way, *Giorgio* is supposed to have been Judith Krantz's model for the title store in her steamy bestseller, *Scruples.*

Here is a list of the top emporia along Rodeo and environs:

Abercrombie & Fitch – A trendy new version of the aristocratic old sporting goods store. 9424 Wilshire Blvd.

Bally of Switzerland – High-style shoes. 340 Rodeo Dr.

Brentano's – Books, adult games, posters, lithos. 9528 Wilshire Blvd.

Carroll & Co. – Ivy league clothing for men and women. 466 N Rodeo Dr.

Chess and Games Unlimited – Adult board games and electronic toys. 336 N Beverly Dr.

Alfred Dunhill of London – Tobacco and smoking accessories. 136 S Rodeo Dr.

Wally Findlay Galleries – Fine art. 339 N Rodeo Dr.

Cecil Gee – British clothing for men. 346 N Rodeo Dr.

Giorgio – Chic clothing for men and women; has stand-up bar and complimentary drinks for shoppers. 273 N Rodeo Dr.

Gucci – Italian leather goods, jewelry, clothing, accessories. 347 N Rodeo Dr.

Hermes – Fine leather goods from France. 343 N Rodeo Dr.

Fred Joaillier – Expensive jewelry. 401 N Rodeo Dr.

Jurgensen's – Gourmet foods. 409 N Beverly Dr.

Frances Klein – Antique jewelry. 310 N Rodeo Dr.
David Orgell – Silver and china. 320 N Rodeo Dr.
Superior Stamp & Coin – Gold coins and rare stamps. 9301 Wilshire Blvd.
Tiffany & Co. – Fine jewelry. 9502 Wilshire Blvd.

MAJOR COLLEGES AND UNIVERSITIES: There are three major university campuses spread through the LA area. in addition to dozens of colleges and junior colleges. The University of California (UCLA) is known to college football fans as the Bruins. UCLA's main campus is at 405 Hilgard, Westwood (825-4321). The University of Southern California (USC) has the Trojans. USC's downtown campus is at University Park, near Vermont Ave. (743-2311). California Institute of Technology's main campus is at 1201 E California, Pasadena (356-6811).

SPECIAL EVENTS: There are more special events than we could possibly list here. For complete listings, check the local publications listed above or call the Greater Los Angeles Visitors and Convention Bureau (628-3101). Among the major special events are: *Pasadena Rose Bowl,* the traditional New Year's Day gridiron spectacle; *Glen Campbell Open Golf Tournament,* Pacific Palisades, in February; *Camelia Festival,* Temple City, in February; *UCLA Mardi Gras,* in April; *Disneyland's Easter Parade; Sidewalk Arts Festival,* Westwood, in May; *All-City Outdoor Art Festival,* Barnsdall Park, in June; *4th of July* fireworks at Anaheim Stadium and Pasadena Rose Bowl; *All-Star Shrine Football Game,* Pasadena Rose Bowl, in July; *California International Sea Festival,* Long Beach, in August; *International Surf Festival,* Redondo Beach, in August; *Los Angeles County Fair,* Pomona, in August.

SPORTS: There is no question that southern California is a paradise for sports lovers. Professional sports teams play at the following locations:

Baseball – *Dodgers,* Dodger Stadium, 1000 Elysian Park Ave. (224-1400). California *Angels,* Anaheim Stadium, 2000 State College Blvd., Anaheim (714 634-2000).

Football – Two college teams face off in the Pasadena Rose Bowl every New Year's Day. UCLA and USC teams play at the Coliseum, 3911 S Figueroa (748-6131, 747-7111). The *Rams* play at Anaheim Stadium.

Basketball – The *Lakers* play at the Forum, Manchester Blvd. and Prairie Ave., Inglewood (673-1300, 674-6000).

Hockey – The *Kings* make their home at the Forum, too.

Horse Racing – If you like to spend your nights at the track, make tracks for Los Alamitos. The season runs from mid-May to late August. Take Freeway 605 south to Katella Ave. exit in Orange County (431-1361 or 714 995-1234). If you prefer daytime action, try Hollywood Park between mid-April and late July. Near Los Angeles International Airport between Manchester and Century Blvds. (677-7151).

Bicycling – Not on the freeways, but biking is great around the Westwood UCLA campus, Griffith Park, and the Santa Monica shore. You can rent from Bicycle Ville, 306 Pico Blvd., Santa Monica (392-6046); Westwood Cyclery, 1449 Westwood Blvd., West LA (478-8638); Europa Bicycle Center, 6203 Van Nuys Blvd., Van Nuys (785-6112).

Fishing – Fishing and sailing boats can be rented at 13560 Mindano Way, Marina del Rey (822-1868). Fishermen catch halibut, bonito, and bass off the LA shores. Sportfishing boats leave daily from San Pedro, 22 minutes from downtown Los Angeles, site of the LA port. You can also fish at Catalina Island (see *Special Places*).

Roller Skating – Skates can be rented from Cheapskates, 16856 Sherman Way, Van Nuys (786-9611).

THEATER: There is no shortage of stages in LA, despite the overshadowing presence of the film industry. Touring groups perform at the *Ahmanson Theater* at the Music Center. The *Center Theater Group*, a professional repertory company, makes its home at the Mark Taper Forum's theater-in-the-round. For information about either, call 972-7654. Other Los Angeles theaters include: *Huntington Hartford Theater*, 1615 Vine St., Hollywood (462-6666). The *Shubert Theater* is located in the ABC Entertainment Center, 2020 Ave. of the Stars, Century City (553-9000; for credit-card reservations, call 553-8101). The *Westwood Playhouse* is near the UCLA campus at 10886 Le Conte Ave., Westwood (208-5454). The *Pantages Theater* is at 6233 Hollywood Blvd. (462-3104). Tickets for all major theatrical events can be ordered from Mutual Theater Ticket Agency, 655 S Hill St. (627-1248), or Ticketron, 5151 W Imperial Hwy., Inglewood (642-5700, 670-2311).

MUSIC: All kinds of music can be heard in LA's concert halls and clubs. The *Los Angeles Philharmonic* plays at the Dorothy Chandler Pavilion, Music Center (972-7211). Rock superstars play at the Universal Amphitheater, Universal City (508-2515), the Greek Theater, 2700 N Vermont Ave. (660-8400), and the Roxy Theater, 9009 Sunset Blvd. (878-2222). For country and western music, check out the Palomino, 6907 Lankershim Blvd., North Hollywood (764-4010).

NIGHTCLUBS AND NIGHTLIFE: Anything goes in LA, especially after dark. Swinging nightspots open and close very quickly, since the restless search for what's "in" keeps people on the move for newer night scenes. *Doug Weston's Troubador Club* pioneered a number of top rock music acts, at 9081 Santa Monica Blvd., West Hollywood (276-6168). Another place which seems to be able to hold its own is *Whisky,* 8901 Sunset Blvd. (652-4202). For good disco action, stop in at *Dillon's,* 1081 Gayley, Westwood (208-5088). For good female impersonation acts, dining, and interesting gay clientele, *Queen Mary* is the place. It's at 12449 Ventura Blvd. in Studio City (506-5619).

SINS: Overindulging in the City of the Angels seems to be a native way of life. A good bout with *gluttony* is easy to arrange at any of LA's many Mexican restaurants around Olvera Street. You can either sit down to one enormous feast of tacos, chile rellenos, enchiladas, and tamales, or eat your way slowly from one end of the market to the other, stopping at each of the outdoor stands, and dripping hot sauce over the counters of embroidered blouses, huaraches, perfumed candles, and Mexican ceramics.

The beaches of LA offer plenty of space for a *sloth*ful falling out. You can find a few feet of sand, anywhere from Santa Monica to Leo Carillo Beach, and spread out your blanket or towel for a day in the sun. Cover your body with oil, turn on the radio or cassette recorder, lie back, close your eyes, and watch the yellow spots behind your lids. You needn't move until the sun has your head swimming or the passers-by have managed to slowly cover you in a gritty coating of sand. At that point it is straight into the water for a quick surrender to the force of the tides and waves, sometimes known as body surfing.

For *lust,* Los Angeles is prepared to accommodate any taste. Some of the more accessible scenes are at the empire of massage parlors (advertised in the *LA Free Press,* an underground newspaper) servicing everything from good health to the exotic to the ultimate kink; *Tony Roma's* or the *Rangoon Racquet Club* for a heavy dose of singles mixing; or simply the top of Mulholland Drive, looking out over the city below, where you have to arrange for companionship beforehand, but need only park and negotiate steering wheels and gearshifts for a good lusty time of your own.

LOCAL SERVICES: Business Services – Beverly Hills Secretarial Service, 433 N Camden Dr., Beverly Hills (275-1422); Century Secretarial Service, 2040 Ave. of the Stars, LA (277-3329); Just-a-Sec, 1888 Century Park E, LA (553-5693).

Mechanics – The best service is AAA, since mechanics will not come to tow you if you break down miles away. If you want to get your car checked, or need minor repairs, go to Richard Hoffman, Richard's Texaco Service, 18101 Ventura Blvd., Tarzana (705-9896).

Babysitting – Babysitters Guild, Inc., Agency, 6362 Hollywood Blvd., Hollywood (469-8246); Weston's Services Agency, 8318 W 3rd St., LA (274-9228); Community Service Agency, 14606 Victory Blvd., Van Nuys (781-2950).

BEST IN TOWN

CHECKING IN: Los Angeles is the city where you stand the best chance of checking in alongside a movie star, although, obviously, you'll be paying more for the possible privilege of rubbing shoulders with cinema royalty. If you're looking for someplace just to shower and sleep, you'll be happier at one of the smaller hotels or motor hotels sprinkled throughout the area. Generally speaking, accommodations are cheaper in the San Fernando Valley than in Hollywood or downtown. Expect to pay $80 and up for a double room at those places we've bracketed as expensive; between $50 and $80 at those places listed as moderate; under $50 at inexpensive places.

The Beverly Hills – A favorite home-away-from-home for movie stars. The *Polo Lounge* is a famous watering spot for movie moguls and producers — a place to be seen, if you're someone who people will know they've seen once they see you. The hotel has several fine jewelry shops and clothing boutiques, plus a good barber shop and beauty salon. We think the 255 rooms are a little on the musty side, but that's part of the charm. Show-biz action is pretty heavy at poolside. Stargazers can watch enraptured from a cabana, while eating lunch ordered from room service. A car is necessary for getting around. 9641 Sunset Blvd., Beverly Hills (276-2251). Expensive.

The Beverly Wilshire – You can walk out the door and into the middle of the elegant Beverly Hills shopping district. The mood here is more businesslike and subdued, less Hollywood flash, than at the Beverly Hills. In the new tower wing, all the rooms are done in different color schemes, furniture styles, and themes — but it's more expensive than the older wing. There are 500 rooms here, and an award-winning restaurant, *La Bella Fontana.* If you like to read, you'll be very happy with the Brentano's bookstore downstairs — it's open late. 9500 Wilshire Blvd., Beverly Hills (275-4282). Expensive.

The Beverly Hilton – Many Hilton fans say this is the best of the lot. It's not as convenient to downtown Beverly Hills as the Wilshire (you should have a car), but if you plan to spend a lot of time in the hotel you'll be happy here, as the Beverly Hilton is another one of those self-contained hotels which caters to your every need. *Trader Vic's* is a consistently good restaurant in the hotel. 9876 Wilshire Blvd., Beverly Hills (274-7777). Expensive.

Bel-Air – If you prefer intimacy to high-rise accommodations. The beautiful low building splashed with purple and magenta bougainvillea is surrounded by a splendid garden. This enchanting place is not for everybody — there are only 68 rooms, and as you would imagine, it's not as commercial as the other LA hotels. Located in a canyon; you'll need a car. 701 Stone Canyon Rd., West LA (472-1211). Expensive.

Le Parc – Ideally located between Beverly Hills and Hollywood, *Le Parc* has 152 guest suites in a quiet residential neighborhood. Each is tastefully appointed in contemporary designs and includes a fireplace, kitchenette, and full wet bar. The hotel's swimming pool and tennis court are on the roof. 733 West Knoll, West Hollywood (855-8888; toll-free in CA, 800 252-2152; toll-free elsewhere in the US, 800 421-4666). Expensive.

The Century Plaza – A 750-room hotel with a lot of convention business. There are several fine restaurants on the premises, the best being Japanese (*Yamato*), and plenty of shops to browse in. Because of its location in Century City, near the ABC Entertainment Center, a car is recommended, but there are usually cabs lined up outside. Ave. of the Stars, Century City (277-2000). Expensive.

Westwood Marquis – The current favorite among business folk who really know quality. Originally built to house UCLA students, it has now been converted to first-class digs. The 17 floors hold 250 suites, and the bustling college town of Westwood is all around. The *Garden Terrace Room* offers a terrific brunch, and the UCLA running track is not a half-mile away. 930 Hilgard Ave., Westwood (208-8765). Expensive.

Bel Air Sands – After a $3 million renovation, the Bel Air Sands has reopened completely refurnished with added amenities and a light, breezy atmosphere. All 163 rooms have balconies, and there are two swimming pools, tennis court, cocktail lounge, and dining room. Free parking and limo transportation to and from LA airport. 11461 Sunset Blvd. (476-6571; toll-free in CA: 800 352-6680; elsewhere in US: 800 421-6649 and 800 475-6640). Expensive.

The Bonaventure – This 1,500-room giant is the newest convention-oriented hotel. The hotel's mirrored towers are already a new LA landmark. Although the Bonaventure is convenient for downtown activities, you'll need a car to get anywhere else. 5th and Figueroa Sts. (624-1000). Expensive.

Hyatt Regency – Like the Hyatt Regencies in San Francisco and Atlanta, this one boasts a spectacular open-lobby design. This 500-room, super-modern luxury hotel is another convention favorite. *Hugo's V* is an expensive, Continental restaurant which is among downtown's best. 711 S Hope St. (683-1234). Expensive.

Sheraton Plaza–La Reina – This conference center is Sheraton's largest California hotel. It features 907 rooms and comprehensive convention facilities, and *Le Gourmet,* a fine restaurant. 6101 Century Blvd. (642-1111). Expensive.

L'Ermitage – No relation to the restaurant of the same name, this hotel has a European ambience, 116 suites, a rooftop jacuzzi and pool, a piano lounge, and its own fine *Café Russe.* It is very well run and blissfully low key. Parking available. 9291 Burton Way, Beverly Hills (278-3344). Expensive.

Beverly Rodeo – This small 100-room hotel is smack in the middle of Rodeo Drive, Beverly Hills' best shopping street. Gucci is right across the street, along with Courrèges, Hermès, and Céline. The hotel's restaurant, *Café Rodeo,* has a sidewalk café at lunch. If you plan to stay in Beverly Hills, you can get by without a car. 360 N Rodeo Dr. (273-0300). Expensive.

Safari Motor Hotel – If you're planning to visit The Burbank Studios, you'll find this more convenient than the Beverly Hills or downtown hotels. The management requires a minimum stay of three days. The spacious valley environment gives you more of a sense of being in the open. Only 57 rooms, so book in advance. 1911 W Olive Ave., Burbank (845-8586). Moderate to inexpensive.

Farmer's Daughter Motel – Across the street from the Farmers Market and CBS television studios, this 58-room Best Western hotel offers you the chance to be in the middle of an active part of town. There's also a heated pool, and some of the rooms have refrigerators. 115 S Fairfax (937-3930). Inexpensive.

Mikado Motor Hotel – The twisting canyon roads separating Hollywood from the San Fernando Valley are among the most scenic parts of LA. The Mikado is set between Coldwater and Laurel Canyons, where cottages and modern glass-and-wood homes hang dramatically from cliffs, propped up only by stilts. The 56-room Best Western Mikado has a pool, restaurant, and cocktail lounge. Pets are welcome, too. 12600 Riverside Dr. (763-9141). Inexpensive.

EATING OUT: In spite of the plethora of good restaurants in LA, finding one can be as hard as locating that proverbial needle in the haystack. A lot of places reward the unsuspecting first-timer with outstretched palms, unhonored reservations, and tables next to the kitchen door. Some of the places you've probably read about in the movie columns or heard about on television are among the worst offenders. With few exceptions, a restaurant's popularity with the show-biz crowd is inversely proportional to the excellence of its kitchen. If you have to spread cash around to crack the front door in hopes of sitting alongside someone famous, you can be pretty sure that neither the food nor the expected guests will be worthwhile. Our choices are below. Expect to pay $50 or more for two at those places we've listed as expensive; between $25 and $50, moderate; under $25, inexpensive. Prices do not include drinks, wine, or tips.

L'Ermitage – L'Ermitage is housed in a handsome old mansion, and a typical meal could start with the velvety-smooth mousse of duck livers laced with Armagnac, followed by very thin steak in Dijon mustard sauce, concluding with an individual chocolate soufflé. L'Ermitage is too special a place to waste on just an ordinary night, so celebrate something — anything — while you're there. (Maybe you could celebrate that you're willing to spend $100 for a dinner for two.) Closed Sundays and holidays. Reservations necessary. Major credit cards. 730 N La Cienega Blvd. (652-5840). Expensive.

Ma Maison – Known as the place where real power brokers break bread, and where film celebrities who like food go when they want to eat in peace. Like most of its patrons, you'll find the most imaginative French dishes in the list of daily specials, not on the menu. Reservations required. Major credit cards. 8368 Melrose Ave. (655-1991). Expensive.

Rangoon Racquet Club – This place gets two very different types of crowds. The swinging-singles set congregates in the Rangoon bar, but rarely stays to dine. An older and more elegant group turns up for lunch and dinner. Be sure to leave room for the huge stemmed strawberries and orange slices dipped in both dark and white chocolate. Closed Sundays. Reservations advised. Major credit cards. 9474 Santa Monica Blvd., Beverly Hills (274-8926). Expensive.

Perino's – Los Angeles doesn't get any dressier than this elegant, long-time favorite, with classic Italian dishes (fettucine Alfredo is simple and excellent). For dessert try the Grand Marnier or chocolate soufflé. Reservations required. Major credit cards. 4101 Wilshire Blvd. (383-1221). Expensive.

St. Germain – Another of our favorites. There is no written menu, and special selections vary from day to day. The filet of sole, veal kidney, and roast pork are delicious. Fresh fruit for dessert, as well as fancier sweets. Closed Sundays. Reservations required. Major credit cards. 5955 Melrose Ave. (467-1108). Expensive.

Le Restaurant – A quaint and unassuming decor provides the backdrop for yet another of LA's fine French establishments. All entrées, as well as appetizers, are carefully prepared. Service is just as meticulous. Closed Sundays. Reservations accepted. Major credit cards. 8475 Melrose Place (651-5553). Expensive.

The Bistro Garden – The very same Beverly Hills celebrities who have parked their Rolls-Royces up the street at *The Bistro* for years are now making its sister restaurant the "in" spot. Lunch is especially chic with popular fare like bratwurst with hot potato salad. Closed Sundays. Reservations required. Major credit cards. 176 N Canon Dr., Beverly Hills (550-3900). Expensive.

Palm – A local branch of New York's famous Palm steakhouse. The thick prime steaks and Maine lobsters are as succulent as their New York counterparts. Food is consistently good, and the service tends to be very friendly and attentive. Open daily. Reservations recommended. Major credit cards. 9001 Santa Monica Blvd., West Hollywood (550-8811). Expensive.

Tracton's – Fresh Florida stone crabs aren't easy to find in LA, but they're a specialty here, served — when in season — as an appetizer or as a super-giant-sized main course. And by all means try the green goddess dressing with the tomato and anchovy salad. Open daily. Reservations advised. Major credit cards. 16705 Ventura Blvd., Encino (783-1320), and 3560 S La Cienega Blvd. (931-1581). Expensive.

L'Orangerie – Under high ceilings and among the potted palms you'll find one of the city's most attractive dining rooms, and some of the most exciting dishes as well. The mostly French menu offers soft scrambled eggs, topped with caviar, a spicy fish soup, sea bass (with a touch of Pernod), and first-class desserts like the apple tart or a puff pastry, filled with raspberries and sweet cream. Open daily for dinner. Reservations required. Major credit cards. 903 N Cienega Blvd. (652-9770). Expensive.

Mr. Chow – The highly stylized Chinese cuisine here is even better than at Michael Chow's original London restaurant. Start with fried dumplings, Chinese noodles, or *gambei* (fried seaweed). Twice-fried beef is an excellent, if spicy, main course. Peking duck is best of all, and is often available even if not ordered in advance. There are numerous desserts, but the marjolaine cake is particularly good. Open daily. Reservations necessary. Major credit cards. 344 N Camden Dr., Beverly Hills (278-9911). Expensive.

Monty's – An all-around, mouth-watering favorite, Monty's serves great steamed clams, barbecued spareribs, the thickest, juiciest prime ribs in LA, tempting scampi, and shrimp Monty (bacon-wrapped and stuffed). The charcoal-broiled swordfish is habit-forming. Open daily. Reservations recommended. Major credit cards. 17016 Ventura Blvd., Encino (783-1660). Expensive.

Gladstone's – Select your own lobster for about $14 a pound. The steamed shrimp in their shells and a traditional New England clambake with Gulf shrimp are also terrific. Open daily. Reservations required. Major credit cards. 17300 Pacific Coast Hwy., Pacific Palisades (GL4-FISH). Expensive to moderate.

Scandia – One of the city's best, but we feel obliged to warn you that Scandia overbooks and sends everyone to the bar to wait for an eternity. The bar isn't large enough to handle crowds, so it's generally impossible to sit down or get close enough for a drink. Go at lunchtime, or after 10:30 PM, but by all means avoid the 7–10 PM crunch. A typical meal might begin with Scandia's Viking Platter (tiny blinis flavored with aquavit and topped with Danish caviar and sour cream), followed by virgin lobster (tiny fried Norwegian lobster tails), or tournedos Theodora (filet mignon split and garnished with goose liver). Closed Mondays. Reservations are necessary, but take our advice and avoid rush hour. Major credit cards. 9040 Sunset Blvd., West Hollywood (272-9521). Moderate.

Peppone – Possibly the best Italian restaurant in LA, tucked away in a tiny West Los Angeles shopping center. Splendid pastas and veal dishes are the cornerstones of the evening. Reservations absolutely required. Major credit cards. 11628 Barrington Ct. (476-7379). Moderate.

The Mandarin – Northern Chinese cooking in elegant surroundings instead of the usual plastic, pseudo-Oriental decor. Not on the menu, but well worth remembering as an appetizer is the minced squab wrabbed in lettuce leaves. Reservations recommended. Major credit cards. 430 N Camden Dr., Beverly Hills (272-0267). Moderate.

Madame Wu's Garden – Imaginative Oriental decor. Mostly Cantonese food, with some Szechwan selections. Tossed shredded chicken makes a good appetizer, and Wu's beef and cashew shrimp are fine entrées. One of our favorites is sizzling go ba, a bubbling combination of chicken, ham, shrimp, mushrooms, water chestnuts, shredded bamboo shoots, and other vegetables. Stay away from the sweet-and-sour pork. Open daily. Reservations recommended. Major credit cards. 2201 Wilshire Blvd., Santa Monica (828-5656). Moderate.

Musso & Frank Grill – It really is a grill, in Hollywood since 1919, and apparently not redecorated once (not that its regulars—film people, journalists, the moiling LA middle class—want it to change one iota). Orthodox American food and the kind of place the cachet of which is having no cachet; an LA classic. Reservations recommended. Major credit cards. 6667 Hollywood Blvd. (467-7788). Moderate.

Garden Terrace – This gazebo-like room with green and white decor suggests summertime dining all year. What really draws crowds are the elaborate Sunday buffet brunches, with omelettes prepared to order and freshly carved roast beef, ham, and turkey as well as platters laden with fresh fruit, pâtés, smoked salmon, and salads. Excellent dry champagne flows nonstop throughout the meal. Open daily. Brunch on Sundays only; reservations should be made days ahead. Major credit cards. Westwood Marquis Hotel, 930 Hilgard Ave., Westwood (208-8765). Moderate.

Stratton's – About as English as a restaurant this side of London can be. The menu includes English basics like roast beef with Yorkshire pudding, shepherd's pie, and sherry trifle with raspberries. Plum pudding with brandied hard sauce is served during the Christmas season. Closed Mondays. Reservations recommended. Major credit cards. Near UCLA at 10886 Le Conte Ave., Westwood (208-8880). Moderate.

The Tower – Atop the Occidental Center Building in downtown LA, with a bird's-eye view of the car-clogged freeways snaking throughout the city. Be thankful you're up here and not down there. Closed Sundays. Reservations required. Major credit cards. 1150 S Olive (746-1554). Moderate.

Cock 'n Bull – A legendary establishment, the Cock 'n Bull has held forth on Sunset Strip for more than 40 years. Lunch and dinner are served buffet-style. English brunch served Sundays. A great place for well-behaved kids who are always hungry. Open daily. Reservations required. Major credit cards. 9170 Sunset Blvd. (273-0081). Moderate.

The Gingerman – Hollywood celebrities have really taken to Patrick O'Neal and Carroll O'Connor's local branch of New York's Gingerman pub. At dinner the pepper steak is first-rate, and the country paté makes a fine starter. The Gingerman serves supper until 2 AM and usually musters a good crowd for those wee hours. Reservations recommended for dinner; not necessary for supper. Closed Sundays. Major credit cards. 369 N Bedford Drive, Beverly Hills (273-7585). Moderate.

Anna's – This is a good late-night place for Italian food. A highlight of the diverse menu is *linguine Sorrento al cartoccio* (linguine topped with shellfish, prepared in a bag, and served from it at your table). Open daily. Reservations advised. Most major credit cards. 10929 Pico Blvd., West LA (474-0102). Inexpensive.

Le Cellier – Another restaurant notorious for overbooking, but the prices are good and the quality makes it superior to many more-expensive restaurants. On Wednesdays only, there's a fresh salmon baked in brioche and topped with a light caviar sauce. Reserve a portion or two when you call to book your table. Be prepared to wait a half-hour or more, even with reservations. Closed Mondays. Major credit cards. 2628 Wilshire Blvd. (828-1585). Moderate.

Le Dome – One of the most interesting of LA's French restaurants. It opened as a brasserie with various grilled dishes (the thick veal chop is a wonderful introduction) but added more traditional haute cuisine in response to patron pressure.

The atmosphere is chic, understated, comfortable. Open daily, 11 AM to 2 AM. Reservations recommended. Major credit cards. 8720 Sunset Blvd. (659-6919). Moderate.

El Cholo – LA is glutted with places promising authentic south-of-the-border cooking, but this is the best, without question. Around for more than 50 years, and its burritos and combination plates are real knockouts. Open daily. There's usually a wait even with reservations; reservations are advised anyway. No credit cards, so bring cash. 1121 S Western Ave. (734-2773). Inexpensive.

Sida – Rather difficult to find in Canoga Park, and woefully short on charm, but it makes up for it with excellent Thai food, such as noodles made on the spot to complement chicken, cold meat, and vegetable dishes. A wonderful introduction to Thai food if you haven't met yet. Reservations not required. Visa and MasterCard only. 21109 Sherman Way, Canoga Park (703-9480). Inexpensive.

Lawry's California Center – From May to October, a unique steak fiesta with a Mexican scene is featured in an indoor garden surrounding the Lawry's (the sauce people) headquarters. Only two set dinners are served, beginning with a salad of crisp, crunchy vegetables accompanied by four superb Lawry's dressings. Then a Delmonico sirloin or salmon is barbecued to order, served with fresh corn-on-the-cob, a delicious sour cream tortilla casserole, a green vegetable, and tasty, hot, herb bread. Closed Mondays and Tuesdays. Reservations essential. Major credit cards. 568 San Fernando Rd. (225-2481). Inexpensive.

Nate 'n Al – Where unrepatriated Easterners go for a hot pastrami or a corned beef fix. Conveniently located a block or so from the *Beverly Wilshire Hotel.* No reservations. Diners Club only. 414 N Beverly Drive, Beverly Hills (274-0101). Inexpensive.

The Twin Dragon – Less formal than Madame Wu's, with a solid repertoire of top-notch northern Chinese food. A lot of families bring their children here, and it's pretty noisy. Open daily. Reservations are unnecessary. Major credit cards. 8597 W Pico Blvd. (657-7355). Inexpensive.

The Bicycle Shop – An informal café perfect for a leisurely lunch or a casual dinner. Paté, quiche, onion soup, and a wide variety of crêpes and sandwiches make up the menu. Older children may be intrigued by the many different types of bicycles hanging from the ceiling. Open daily. Reservations are not essential. Major credit cards. 12217 Wilshire Blvd., West Los Angeles (826-7831). Inexpensive.

Chicago Pizza Works – The pizzas are deep-dish style, and there is a wide range of toppings available. The lasagna, spaghetti, salads, and desserts are good, too. Open daily. Reservations not needed. Major credit cards. 11641 Pico Blvd. (477-7740). Inexpensive.

A Thousand Cranes – Besides having such a beautiful name, this Japanese restaurant is well versed in the traditional art of serving beautiful food. It has several tatami rooms and a western dining room. Reservations recommended. Major credit cards. In the *New Otani Hotel,* 120 S Los Angeles St. (629-1200). Moderate.

Hamayoshi – This restaurant, one of the reasons Japanese diplomats request an appointment in Los Angeles, is a sushi bar for connoisseurs, favoring flatfish of all kinds — a list not to be equaled at almost any other sushi house. The place is small and simple, and customers sometimes have to wait outside for a spot. Closed Sundays; no lunch on Saturdays. No reservations. Major credit cards. 3350 W 1st St. (384-2914). Inexpensive.

The Rib Joint – Known locally as "R.J.'s," this is the place for sumptuous spare ribs, seafood, and salads. Portions are very generous and best accompanied by the Anchor Steam beer on draft. The chocolate cake is colossal. 252 N Beverly Dr. (274-7427). Inexpensive.

And finally, for dessert, try the luscious ice cream at *Häagen-Dazs Ice Cream Shoppe,* 904 S Barrington Ave., West Los Angeles (820-1666) or 15615 Ventura Blvd., Encino (788-3118); or at *Swensen's Ice Cream Factory,* 231 North Beverly Drive, Beverly Hills (274-2660) or 16658 Ventura Blvd., Encino (784-8489).

LOUISVILLE

Everyone knows one thing about Louisville: Once a year the town is host to that amazing horse race and attendant carousal called the Kentucky Derby. There are two seasons in Louisville: Derby Week, the first week in May; and the rest of the year. But there is a good deal to that "other" season, and Kentucky's largest city is too often dismissed as a one-horse-race town.

Louisville (pronounced *loo-ee-ville* by visitors, and *looavul* — sounding a little like *interval* — by residents) combines aspects of the big city and the small town in its character. It is a blend of urbanity and provincialism, tradition and progressivism — the product of the city's traditional role as fence-sitter between North and South.

The fence the city sits on is the Ohio River, which also serves as the boundary between Kentucky and Indiana. The city has a population of 298, 000, but the metropolitan area extends into three Kentucky counties and two counties in southern Indiana, and so Louisville is the economic, social, and cultural center of 900,000 people.

Louisville's development as an industrial town is impressive. The city was actually settled in 1778 as an informal military base; it was the point from which George Rogers Clark drove the British and the Indians from the Midwest. The appearance of steamboats on the Ohio in the early 19th century turned a lazy river town into a booming port, and today, more tonnage passes through Louisville than through the Panama Canal. The city itself produces more than half the world's bourbon, as well as substantial amounts of such varied products as cigarettes, chemicals, and appliances.

It's a city of "has and has not." Actors Theatre of Louisville has been called the "Broadway of the Midwest" by national critics. The Louisville Orchestra is the only city orchestra in the world with its own recording label. And don't forget the lovely parks, the good old country cookin', or the leisurely cruises up the Ohio on the steamboat *Belle of Louisville.*

What it hasn't got is a variety of places to go after — or for that matter, before — the cruise. It's hard to find a good meal after midnight. In the city named for Louis XVI of France, good French restaurants are few.

Louisville keeps trying, though. Visitors will find its will to improve itself as inspiring as they find its reverence for tradition charming. In recent years, downtown has added a $2.3-million Riverfront Plaza, a natural history museum housed in a beautifully renovated 18th-century warehouse, and several classy restaurants. The most recent addition is a $135 million Galleria of stores and offices. A performing and visual arts center is under construction.

You get the feeling that Louisville wants to be a big city. In the Southern tradition, though, it's just taking its time.

LOUISVILLE AT-A-GLANCE

SEEING THE CITY: The *Top of the Tower Restaurant and Cocktail Lounge*, at the top of the 38-story First National Tower Building, offers the finest view of downtown Louisville, the Ohio River, and, when it's not too hazy, the fields of rural southern Indiana across the river. 5th and Main Sts. (585-2233).

SPECIAL PLACES: The best way to get around Louisville is by car. You can walk around downtown, but attractions like Churchill Downs, historic old homes, and the lovely surrounding countryside a few miles from the center of town require transportation.

Museum of Natural History and Science – Locally oriented exhibits trace the development of the Ohio River Valley from its geological origins to its modern status as the major waterway for four states. Open daily. Admission charge. 727 W Main St. (587-3137).

Belvedere-Riverfront Plaza – This open plaza overlooks an impressive expanse of the Ohio — two bridges spanning the river with barges and tugboats streaming down in between. North of Main St. between 4th Ave. and 6th St.

Louisville Zoological Gardens – The zoo offers a pleasant afternoon outing for the whole family, but be prepared to do some walking: Instead of cramped cages, the animal exhibits are spacious and attractive. There's also a children's zoo, a small train, and performances at an outdoor amphitheater. Open daily, except Mondays in winter. Admission charge. 1100 Trevilian Way (459-2184).

The Cloister – This large brick building with courtyard once housed a Catholic girls' school. It's now the home of small craft and curiosity shops, and of the *Chapel* restaurant (literally a former chapel). 800 E Chestnut St. (585-5929).

Belle of Louisville – You can board one of the last of the 19th-century-style steamboats for a cruise up the Ohio River as it winds its way east through rural fields of Kentucky and Indiana, into the river's navigatory past. Cruises leave once a day, Tuesdays through Sundays, and there is also a dance cruise Saturday nights. Memorial Day through Labor Day. Tickets at Steamer office at 4th Ave. and River Rd. or on the boarding line at the foot of 4th St. (582-2547).

Farmington – Constructed according to plans of Thomas Jefferson, the 19th-century home of Judge John Speed is an outstanding embodiment of the federal style of architecture. Striking Jeffersonian touches of this perfectly proportioned 14-room house are two central octagonal rooms and a secret stairway. Open daily. Admission charge. 3033 Bardstown Rd. (452-9920).

Old Louisville – The homes in Old Louisville (2nd to 6th Streets and Ormsby to Eastern Parkway) are fine examples of 19th-century Victorian architecture in various stages of restoration. The St. James Court Art Fair, the first weekend in October (between 4th and 6th Streets at Central Park), includes home tours. Enjoy Continental cuisine and tasty desserts year-round at *610 Magnolia,* 610 Magnolia (636-0783).

Locust Grove – Another fascination for architecture fans, this Georgian-style plantation was the last home of George Rogers Clark. Open daily. Admission charge. 561 Blankenbaker La. (897-9845).

Churchill Downs – By far Louisville's largest attraction, the Kentucky Derby draws some 100,000 people to Churchill Downs on the first Saturday in May. The twin-spired track is packed with fans sipping mint juleps, shedding a few tears at the singing of "My Old Kentucky Home," and if they're lucky, catching a glimpse of some of the world's most expensive horseflesh. If you can stand the unabashed sentimentality, the crowds, and the expense (accommodations Derby weekend can go higher than $100 a night), the Derby is worth the trip — at least once. Reserved seats for the race are hard to come by (they're held by box owners), but all you need to join the general admission party in the infield is $10 — and a lot of nerve. For information, write Churchill Downs, PO Box 8427, Louisville, KY 40208 (502 636-3541).

At other times, the grounds are open free to visitors except during races. The spring meet runs from late April to early July; the fall meet is in November, daily except for Sundays. The track's museum displays Derby memorabilia including photos and saddles of winners, and there, you too can be photographed in a garland of roses, a Derby champion. Open daily year-round. 700 Central Ave. (636-3541; museum, 634-3261).

■ **EXTRA SPECIAL:** About an hour and a half's drive from Louisville on US 64 is the restored *Shaker Community* at Pleasant Hill, Kentucky. The Shakers were a 19th-century communal religious group who believed in strict segregation of the sexes and celibacy. Although they are no longer in existence, they developed a distinct architecture, based on simple lines and sturdy functionalism. The state has taken over this village, located in scenic rolling fields and farmlands, and has restored 27 buildings including a meeting hall, homes, and shops. The *Shaker Town Restaurant* features good country meals, ham, chicken, garden-fresh vegetables, and Shaker Lemon Pie. No liquor or tipping. Since Shaker Town is a popular attraction, tourists are advised to make reservations for overnight visits and meals in advance (606 734-5411).

SOURCES AND RESOURCES

The Visitors Center provides lists of current events, maps, and other tourist information. Ask for the excellent Louisville Information Kit, Founder's Square at 5th St. and Muhammad Ali Blvd. (582-3732).

All telephone numbers are in the 502 area code unless otherwise indicated.

For Local Coverage – *Louisville Courier-Journal,* morning daily; *Louisville Times,* afternoon daily, publishes *Scene Magazine* on Saturdays with complete listings of the coming week's events. Available at newsstands.

CLIMATE AND CLOTHES: The general tendency is toward mild winters, brief but exquisite springs and falls, and overbearingly humid, long, and polluted summers. But save the bets for the thoroughbreds; a snow in April or a 65-degree day in December isn't too long a shot.

GETTING AROUND: Bus – TARC bus system serves the downtown area adequately during the day, but is limited in the suburbs and after dark downtown. Route information is available at the Transit Authority Office, 333 Guthrie St. (585-1234).

Taxi – Cabs must be ordered by phone, and are often slow to respond. The major company is Yellow Cab (636-5511).

Car Rental – Most national firms have offices at the airport, and Budget has a downtown office at 456 S 2nd St. (587-6974).

MUSEUMS: Museums not mentioned in *Special Places:*

American Saddle Horse Museum, 730 W Main St. (585-1342).

J.B. Speed Art Museum, 2035 S 3rd St., on the University of Louisville campus (636-2893).

Rauch Planetarium, also on campus, behind the museum (588-6664).
Zachary Taylor National Cemetery, 4701 Brownsboro Rd. (893-3852).

MAJOR COLLEGES AND UNIVERSITIES: University of Louisville, a four-year state school, is the area's oldest educational institution (between Eastern Pkwy. and Floyd St. south of 3rd St., 588-5555).

SPECIAL EVENTS: The week preceding the race, the *Kentucky Derby Festival* unwinds with a parade, music, hot-air balloons, and a race between the *Belle of Louisville* and *Delta Queen* steamboats. Many events free; write the festival, 621 W Main St., Louisville 40202 (502 584-6383). The free *Bluegrass Music Festival* is held the first weekend in June on the Riverfront Plaza.

SPORTS: Horse Racing – In addition to racing at Churchill Downs (April–July, November), the Louisville Downs has trotting races in the summer and after Churchill Downs' season is over. 4520 Poplar Level Rd. (964-6415).

Softball – This is the only other professional sport event, played by the Kentucky *Bourbons,* who belong to the American Slo-Pitch League. Listings of their games appear in the papers (or call 582-4361).

College Sports – University of Louisville's basketball and football teams play at the Kentucky Fair and Exhibition Center, off Watterson Expressway (I-264). (588-4192).

Bicycling – Rent from Highland Cycle Inc., 1737 Bardstown Rd. (458-7832). Cherokee Park has good bike trails in hilly terrain.

Fishing – For carp and gamefish, try the Falls of the Ohio River on the Indiana bank, off Riverside Dr. in Clarksville, Indiana.

Golf – Two good 18-hole courses are Iroquois Park (Newcut Rd. and Southern Pkwy., 363-9520) and Seneca Park (Taylorsville Rd. and Cannons La., 458-9298).

Tennis – The Louisville Tennis Center has the best outdoor courts in the area. Open during spring and summer, 3783 Illinois Ave. (456-4755). Indoor courts are available right across the river at the Kentuckiana Convention and Sport Center, 520 Marriott Dr., Clarksville, Indiana (283-0785).

THEATER: For current offerings, check the papers listed above. *Actor's Theatre*, a regional company, performs traditional productions and avant-garde plays from September through May, 316 W Main St. (584-1205). Touring repertory groups, including Broadway road shows, play at the *Macauley Theatre*, 315 W Broadway (589-2727).

MUSIC: The *Louisville Orchestra* (587-8681) and the *Kentucky Opera Association* (584-4500) perform at Macauley Theatre, 315 W Broadway. The *Louisville Ballet Company* (637-4725) performs at Memorial Auditorium, 970 S 4th St. Seasons run September through May.

NIGHTCLUBS AND NIGHTLIFE: Current favorites include *The Phoenix Hill Tavern*, which features popular music and a large rooftop beer garden, 644 Baxter Ave. (589-4957); *Peter Outlaw's,* for mixing and dancing to live music, 1930 Bishop La. (451-5377); *Kron's* for disco, 207 Wittington Pkwy. (425-1166); *Downtowner,* gay disco with female impersonators, straights welcome, 105 W Main St. (583-1166).

SINS: Clearly it is the Kentucky Derby and all the trappings that accompany it, like big hats, mint juleps, and shmaltzy renditions of "My Old Kentucky Home," that bring out the deepest *pride* in Louisville residents. Churchill Downs is the setting, the best horses in the racing game are the performers, and the citizens of the world are the spectators at this traditional and classic event.

Even *gluttony* has a racetrack flavor in Louisville. The concoction of chocolate, bourbon, and nuts called Derby Pie is a sure winner. The exact recipe is a secret and is protected by a patent. Only the original can be called Derby Pie on menus (so avoid "Famous Horserace Pie" or other imitators). Served at numerous restaurants.

LOCAL SERVICES: Business Services – Hospitality C Services, Legal Arts Building, 7th and Market Sts. (587-0933).

Mechanics – Sear's Auto, 820 W Broadway (587-2128); Smith Imported Car Service, 1250 E Broadway (583-4724).

Babysitting – We Sit Better, Inc., of Louisville, Starks Building, 445 River City Mall (583-7928).

BEST IN TOWN

CHECKING IN: Louisville's broad selection of accomodations ranges from standard large hotels to a resort-style motel with a lake and wave-making swimming pool. The more expensive hotels cost over $65 per night for a double room though they have some less expensive accommodations in the moderate category ($40 to $65). Inexpensive hotels are in the $30 to $40 range.

Hyatt Regency – Louisville's finest hotel features an 18-story atrium, spacious rooms, and several fine restaurants, including the revolving *Spire.* 320 W Jefferson (587-3434). Expensive.

Seelbach Hotel – The charm of a bygone era is combined with modern amenities in the *Seelbach.* A showplace in the early 1900s, the hotel has undergone extensive renovation aimed at recreating its turn-of-the-century appearance. Features include 324 guest rooms, a restaurant, 3 bars, a Georgian-style ballroom, 24-hour room service, and valet parking. The hotel adjoins the new Galleria shopping complex. 500 4th Ave. (585-3200). Expensive.

The Galt House – Though the decor is imitation extravagant — felt wallpaper, red plush carpets, and new "antiques" — the hotel is adjacent to Riverfront Plaza, has a fine view of the Ohio, and is convenient for downtown shopping. Facilities include two cocktail lounges, an outdoor swimming pool, and three restaurants, one with a revolving section (the view is better than the food). 140 N 4th St. (589-5200). Expensive to moderate.

Marriott Inn – This resort-style hotel features some unusual extras: a "Wave-Tek" ocean, which is really a huge swimming pool with mechanically created waves; a real 11-acre lake with boating and fishing; 10 lakefront villas; and a floating bridal suite on the lake. It also has a health club, babysitting service, and a restaurant and cocktail lounge. 505 Marriott Dr., Clarksville, Indiana (283-4411). Moderate.

Louisville Inn – This comfortable downtown hotel offers good service and excellent facilities for a modest price — indoor/outdoor swimming pools, a health club, two restaurants, and a cocktail lounge with entertainment. 120 W Broadway (582-2241). Moderate.

Howard Johnson's Motor Lodge – Good prices with all the standard features: pool, color TV, restaurant, and cocktail lounge. 100 E Jefferson St. (582-2481). Inexpensive.

EATING OUT: Our restaurant selections range in price from $40 to $60 for dinner for two in the expensive range, $25 to $40 in the moderate range, and $25 and below in the inexpensive range. Prices do not include drinks, wine, or tips.

Casa Grisanti – Louisville's finest restaurant offers carefully prepared Italian cuisine (try especially the veal), a good wine list, and attentive service. Reservations advised. Major credit cards. 1000 E Liberty St. (584-4377). Expensive.

New Orleans House – Eat all you want from an elaborate seafood smorgasbord of 15 different sea items, including crab legs, steamed shrimp, shrimp creole, smoked fish, and a wide variety of salads. The main course, if you can find a place to put it, is an excellently prepared filet mignon or lobster. Closed Sundays and Mondays. Reservations advised. Credit cards. 412 W Chestnut St. (583-7231). Expensive.

610 Magnolia – The Continental fare changes daily at this informal but sophisticated restaurant. A typical day's menu might include grilled swordfish, tenderloin in cognac and cream, chicken in Dijon sauce, and boned quail. Don't miss the desserts. Reservations advised. Major credit cards. 610 Magnolia Ave. (636-0738). Expensive to moderate.

Kienle's German Delicatessen and Restaurant – The food is wonderful and heavy — Wiener schnitzel, sauerbraten, and the homemade mushroom or cauliflower soups are highlights. Reservations required. No credit cards. Shelbyville Rd. Plaza (897-3920). Moderate.

Claudia Sanders Dinner House – It's a 25-mile drive, but worth it. The chicken, beef, country ham, and home-cooked vegetables served by the famous Colonel's wife will show you who *really* had the secret recipe. Major credit cards. US 60W, Shelbyville (589-0367). Moderate to inexpensive.

Hasenour's – Steaks are the specialty, but the seafood and daily specials are also reliable in this popular neighborhood restaurant. There's a wide variety in both food and price, and the drinks are among the most masterfully mixed in town. Credit cards. 1028 Barret Ave. (451-5210). Moderate to inexpensive.

The Nosh Box – Surrounded by thousands of country hams and Kentucky fried chickens, Louisville's biggest Jewish deli and restaurant stands out like a sour pickle. Features fresh bagels, great homemade kosher specialties — kreplach, borscht, blintzes, deli sandwiches, and short ribs. There's a wide variety of dinners and sandwiches, some imaginatively named with an eye to local history and attractions. Open late every night. Credit cards. Hurstborne Park Plaza at Shelbyville Rd. and Hurstborne La. (426-6824). Inexpensive.

MEMPHIS

Time magazine, not too many years back, blackened the collective Memphis eye by calling the city "a backwater river town." The outrage provoked by this cultural cut united Memphis residents as no other issue or event in recent years (with the possible exception of the death of Elvis). The wound was especially painful on two counts: It seemed, first of all, a willful misrepresentation of a quite genuine Memphis trait — that slow, unflustered approach to life entirely fitting in a town with the Southern credentials which Memphis carries; and, even more hurtful, there was an element of bitter truth in the epithet, an element which residents themselves had recognized and even begun to correct.

Everyone has heard the cliché that New York City is a great place to visit but you wouldn't want to live there. For a good while, Memphis was known as just the reverse: a great place to live, but you wouldn't necessarily want to visit. Moves had begun, however, to change that rap against this sleepy Southern city, which, almost despite itself, seems destined to move into the 20th century.

The 846,000 people in the Memphis area *do* live at a slower pace than people in other parts of the country. Sitting high on the bluffs overlooking the Mississippi at the mouth of the Wolf River, the city is bundled into the far southern corner of Tennessee, where the state shares the river with Mississippi and Arkansas. When Memphis was named in 1819 (for the Egyptian city of Memphis), it was one of the busiest ports in the United States and site of the largest slave market in the central South. Memphis lost its city charter for a year in 1878 when the yellow fever epidemic forced more than half its population to move to St. Louis (the half that could afford to move), but it survived as a shipping center. Today, more than one-third of the US cotton crop is still marketed through Memphis.

Memphis is basically a conservative town, both in politics and economics. One theory for this, advanced by residents, is that because the wealth in Memphis was accumulated over the decades through cotton, and because the process of accumulation was so slow, the community leaders are reluctant to spend. Memphis is *not* like Houston, with its fast-flowing oil money, or Atlanta, which leaped ahead of all Southern cities to become a tourist haven, in Memphis terms, almost overnight.

Memphis is a beautiful city with thousands of trees, magnificently landscaped lawns, and spacious parks, sitting atop the Mississippi bluff and surrounded by scores of fishing lakes. Outdoor activities (hunting, fishing, golf, water skiing, speedboat racing, auto racing, tennis, etc.) abound.

Two uniquely American phenomena are headquartered in Memphis, and both share peculiarities which are somehow typically Memphis-like. The late King of Rock, Elvis Presley, lived, and is buried, in his Memphis mansion, Graceland. It draws more visitors to the city than any other single attraction. And Holiday Inns — The World's Innkeeper — is based in Memphis, an organization built on a bedrock of shrewd business judgment and old-fashioned Southern faith. Not an unusual combination in this very Southern city.

MEMPHIS AT-A-GLANCE

SEEING THE CITY: The best way to see Memphis is by drifting along the legendary Mississippi. Captain Tom Meanley's *Memphis Queen* paddleboat takes you along the river and even gives you a chance to romp barefoot along a sandbar before returning to port. The cruise takes about an hour and a half. It leaves daily, from March through December, from Memphis Downtown Harbor, Monroe Ave. and Riverside Dr. (527-5694).

SPECIAL PLACES: A natural place to start a tour of Memphis is alongside the riverbanks. From there, you can wander through downtown, wending your way out to the suburbs.

Confederate Park – Once the site of Civil War battles, Confederate Park faces the river. Ramparts which were used to defend the Dixie forces against Union gunboats still stand. On the river at Front St.

Mud Island – Measuring one by five miles, legend has it that Mud Island was formed by mud deposits clinging to a gunboat sunk during the Civil War. Residents are sure it was a Union gunboat, because, they say, Confederate gunboats were unsinkable. Mud Island is the site of a $63 million tribute to the history and heritage of the Mississippi, with exhibits on its legends, music, and people; a 4,000-seat outdoor amphitheater; a five-block-long scale model of the river; and restaurants, shops, a marina, and a picnic area. Enter on Front St. between Poplar and Adams (528-3595).

Mid-America Mall – Breaking away from the riverfront, you can walk through this large multimillion-dollar mall, anchored on the south end by famous "Beale Street," where W.C. Handy gave birth to the blues, and on the north end by the Civic Center (formerly Main St.).

Civic Center – A series of modern government buildings surround a gigantic pool, in the center of which is a fountain that shoots water 60 feet in the air when it's turned on. Unfortunately it's not turned on as often as Memphis residents would like. At the north end of Mid-America Mall.

Victorian Village – Just off the Civic Center, this is an antiquity lover's paradise. Homes and churches in this concentrated area date back to the 1830s and feature a variety of architectural styles, among them late Victorian, neoclassic, Greek Revival, French, and Italianate. The Fontaine House and the Mallory-Neely House are open to the public seven days a week. 100 to 700 block of Adams St.

Memphis Museum – Although it's officially known as the Memphis Museum, nobody will know what you're talking about unless you ask for the Pink Palace. Really. The museum is built of pink Georgia marble, and features exhibits on the natural and cultural history of the mid-South. Closed Mondays. Admission charge. 3050 Central Ave. (454-5600).

Memphis Zoo and Aquarium – The complete range of lions, tigers, monkeys, and birds can be found in this well-designed city zoo. An aquarium adjoins the animal sections. Strollers and wheelchairs may be rented at the main gate. Closed Thanksgiving, Christmas Eve, Christmas, and icy days. Free hour, 9 AM to 10 AM Saturdays; other times, admission charge. Overton Park, off Poplar Ave. (726-4775, recording; for further information, 726-4787).

Graceland – Elvis Presley's home is the most popular site in Memphis. The white-columned Southern mansion is now open to the public, and Elvis fans can also stroll through the grounds of the 14-acre estate, well shaded by oak trees, and pay respects at the grave of Elvis, his mother, father, and grandmother. On the way out, don't forget to look closely at the Musical Gate at the foot of the winding circular driveway. It has a caricature of Elvis with guitar and a bevy of musical notes in ornamental iron. Open daily except Mondays. Admission charge. 3764 Elvis Presley Blvd. in Whitehaven, South Memphis (unlisted phone).

■ **EXTRA SPECIAL:** About 2½ hours away by car, *Shiloh National Military Park* lets visitors follow the sequence of a famous Civil War battle, the 1862 Battle of Shiloh. Points of interest are clearly marked, and visitors can walk or drive along a ten-mile route. Pre-Columbian Indian mounds are visible along the way. A 25-minute movie about the Battle of Shiloh is shown in the Visitor Center. Open all year. Off US-64 in Shiloh (689-5275).

SOURCES AND RESOURCES

The Convention and Visitors Bureau of the Memphis Area Chamber of Commerce is the best place for general information. 12 S Main St. (526-1919).

Key Magazine and the "Good Evening" column of the *Memphis Press-Scimitar* are the best guides to Memphis activities.

All telephone numbers are in the 901 area code unless otherwise indicated.

For Local Coverage – *Memphis Commercial Appeal,* morning daily; *Memphis Press-Scimitar,* evening daily; *Memphis* Magazine, monthly.

CLIMATE AND CLOTHES: Memphis humidity is formidable. Even though temperatures rarely drop below the 30s in winter, it's wet. The worst month is February, when it occasionally snows. July and August get dripping hot as the temperature climbs into the 90s and 100s; dress coolly.

GETTING AROUND: Bus – Memphis buses generally run between 5 AM and 9 PM during the week, with limited service on the weekend. Information, routes from Memphis Area Transit Authority, 701 N Main St. (523-2521).

Taxi – There are taxi stands near the bus station and at the airport. It's best to call Yellow Cab (526-2121).

Car Rental – The major national firms have agencies in Memphis. A reliable local firm is Thrifty Rent-A-Car, 2230 E Brooks (345-0170).

MUSEUMS: The Memphis Museum, known as the Pink Palace, is famous for natural history exhibits (see *Special Places*). Other local museums are the *Brooks Memorial Art Gallery* (American and European art), Overton Park (726-5266); and *Dixon Gallery and Gardens* (French and American Impressionist art) 4339 Park Ave. (761-5250).

MAJOR COLLEGES AND UNIVERSITIES: Memphis State University (454-2606); Southwestern at Memphis (274-1800); University of Tennessee Center for the Health Sciences (528-5500).

SPECIAL EVENTS: The *Memphis in May International Festival* stretches from late April into early June. Highlights of the Festival are the *Cotton Carnival,* the annual visit of New York's Metropolitan Opera, and *Music-Fest*, a 10-day extravaganza featuring top-name musicians and groups on four main stages at the Fairgrounds. Also in May, the *Danny Thomas Memphis Classic Golf Tournament;* in September, the *Mid-South Fair,* one of the ten largest fairs in the country. The Maid of Cotton is crowned in December and begins her worldwide trek promoting cotton. Also in December, two leading college football teams compete in the *Liberty Bowl.*

SPORTS: Baseball – Professional fans won't be disappointed in the Memphis *Chicks* (short for Chickasaw Indians, who once settled in the area) who play at Tim McCarver Stadium, renamed for the Memphis-born former catcher for the Philadelphia *Phillies.* The Chicks are a Southern League farm club for the Montreal Expos. Tim McCarver Stadium, Fairgrounds (272-1687).

Soccer – The *Memphis Americans,* of the Major Indoor Soccer League, play from November through April at Mid-South Coliseum, Fairgrounds (274-7400).

Golf – The $400,000 PGA Danny Thomas Memphis Classic is played on the Colonial Country Club, a private course 10 miles east of the city on I-40. The best public golf course is Galloway, 3815 Walnut Grove Rd. (685-7805).

Tennis – The best year-round public courts are at Audubon Tennis Center, 4145 Southern (685-7907) and John Rodgers Tennis Complex, Midtown (523-0094).

Swimming – Some of the lakes are polluted. The nearest good swimming pool is Maywood, which has a Florida white sand bottom. Maywood is just across the state line in Olive Branch, Mississippi. Admission charge. 422 S Maywood Dr. (601 895-2777).

Fishing – There are fish in the lakes, mostly crappies and catfish, the latter sometimes as big as 70 pounds (according to newspaper reports). Sardis Lake is a good bet; Meeman-Shelby Forest, a 14,000-acre park with two large lakes.

THEATER: For up-to-the-minute local listings, check daily and weekly publications listed above. *Playhouse on the Square,* Overton Square (726-4656); *Theater Memphis,* 630 Perkins Ext. (682-8323); *Orpheum Theater,* 197 Main St. (523-0122); *Circuit Playhouse,* 1705 Poplar Ave. (726-5521).

MUSIC: Big-name country-rock concerts are played at *Mid-South Coliseum,* Fairgrounds (274-7400), and *The Music Hall*, 469 Lamar (794-9111).

NIGHTCLUBS AND NIGHTLIFE: Memphis blues originated on Beale Street, with W. C. Handy, and is performed nightly at *Blues Alley,* 60 S Front St. (523-7144). For jazz, try the *Bombay Bicycle Club,* 2120 Madison Ave., Overton Sq. (726-6055); for the big-band sound, *Captain Bilbo's,* 263 Wagner (526-1966); and for '50s rock 'n' roll, *Dooley's,* 5100 Poplar (761-0771).

SINS: The aforementioned *Time* magazine article so riled residents that civic *pride* was rekindled, *sloth* ceased, *anger* diminished, and *greed* dismissed as residents met at a series of town meetings in 1981 to form a consensus on the best approach to community betterment. The redevelopment of downtown Memphis is a first step, with the Beale Street Development—several blocks of shops, restaurants, and nightclubs—opening in 1983.

Memphis also has its share of *gluttony.* Overeating is a contagious disease because the Bluff City is such a good town for food — both at the fine restaurants and at fast-food establishments. And *lust*? Well, Memphis women are endowed with Southern charm. But a word of caution: Don't be fooled by their gracious veneer; it masks a formidable and independent will.

LOCAL SERVICES: Business Services – Memphis Secretarial Service has been in operation since 1948, Sterick Bldg., 3rd and Madison (526-7848).

Mechanics – Lamb's Auto Service, 3343 Millbranch (345-5875); A.S. Martin & Sons, Inc., 411 Monroe (527-8606).

Babysitting – Crosstown Christian Daycare and Elementary School provides 24-hour, seven-day service for children 15 months and older. 1258 Harbert (725-4666).

BEST IN TOWN

CHECKING IN: Restoration of the 400-room *Hotel Peabody* is complete, and the construction of a new convention center hotel is in the offing. There's an abundance of Holiday Inns (eight, to be exact), the chain that makes its headquarters in Memphis. Other chains, such as Ramada, TraveLodge, and Sheraton, are also represented. Expect to pay between $60 and $90 for a double at the hotels mentioned here.

The Peabody – Mississippi author David Cohn wrote in 1935 that "the Delta begins in the lobby of the Peabody and ends on Catfish Row in Vicksburg." Built in 1925, the 13-story, 400-room hotel reopened in 1981 after a $20 million renovation. A focal point of the elegant Renaissance lobby is a travertine marble fountain in which the *Peabody* ducks—trained mallards—swim each day. Sixteen square marble columns support a mezzanine balcony; the ceiling is graced by ornate woodwork and stained-glass skylights. *Chez Philippe* is the hotel's fancy restaurant; *Dux,* its theme restaurant. (Incidentally, neither restaurant serves duck.) For music and dancing, there's the *Skyway,* a rooftop nightclub featuring top-name performers. The *Plantation Roof* affords splendid views of the river and city. The hotel's lower level has a pool, snack bar, health club, beauty shop, barber shop, and shoeshine parlor. 149 Union Ave. (529-4000). Expensive to moderate.

Hyatt Regency – This circular, 34-story all-glass structure is known affectionately as "the glass silo." The 400-room hotel, on the eastern outskirts of town, has a swimming pool, café, and bar with nightly entertainment and dancing, free parking, free cots, and cribs. Pets welcome. Children under 18 free. 939 Ridge Lake Blvd. (761-1234). Moderate.

Holiday Inn, Rivermont – The only high-rise Holiday Inn, sitting on the Chickasaw Bluff overlooking the Mississippi on the southwest flank of downtown Memphis. The 14-story, 550-room hotel manages to be rather imposing. Two swimming pools (one Olympic size), a 24-hour café, playground, beauty parlor, and laundromat. You can bring pets. There are two units for paraplegics. 200 W Georgia Ave., near Memphis-Arkansas Bridge (525-0121). Moderate.

EATING OUT: The city's natives are quick to say "There ain't no good eatin' places in Memphis," but this is a bum rap. While it's true there are hundreds of fast-food franchise outlets in every section of the city, the after-dark visitor can dine at one of the nation's top ten restaurants or enjoy home-cooked meals. Our restaurant selections range in price from $38 for two in the expensive range; around $20 for two, moderate; under $20, inexpensive. Prices do not include drinks, wine, or tips.

Justine's – Annually acclaimed as one of the nation's best restaurants, and deservedly so. The French cooking here is superlative. Baking is done on the premises. A rather formal ambience prevails in this antebellum mansion, however. Jacket and tie are required. So are reservations. Closed Sundays. Major credit cards. 919 Coward Pl. (527-3815). Expensive.

Folk's Folly – This is a steak house supreme, serving the largest steaks in Memphis. Vegetables are prepared Cajun-style — that's New Orleans French. Try the sautéed mushrooms or fried tomatoes. Humphrey Folk, a John Wayne type, owns the restaurant. According to local legend, he opened it to help his girlfriend, who always wanted to run a restaurant. After dinner, music lovers can hustle off to *Elan,* just around the corner. Open daily. Reservations advised. Major credit cards. 551 S Mendenhall (767-2877). Expensive.

Grisanti's – This northern Italian restaurant features spicy food and a chance to swap insults with owner Big John Grisanti, a legend on the city's nightlife circuit. The cannelloni, manicotti, and veal are highly recommended. The blind can order from a Braille menu. Closed Sundays. Reservations advised. Major credit cards. 1489 Airways Blvd. (458-2648). Moderate.

Rendezvous – Located in a basement in a back alley, this classic little place is chock full of thousands of dollars of Memphis memorabilia. It's as much of a museum as it is a restaurant, and it serves the best barbecue ribs, beef, and pork in town. Closed Sundays and Mondays. Reservations advised. Major credit cards. General Washburn Alley, off S 2nd and behind the Ramada Inn (523-2746). Inexpensive.

Captain Bilbo's – Have a drink at the bar and listen to nightly entertainment while viewing beautiful sunsets on the Mississippi River. And don't be surprised if an Illinois Central Gulf Railroad train rumbles past—the railroad track is only 22 feet from the restaurant's windows. Next, enjoy the excellent salad bar, seafood gumbo, steaks, and fish. Reservations not accepted. Major credit cards. 263 Wagner (525-1966). Moderate.

Pete and Sam's – Pound for pound, the best all-around restaurant in town; serves dynamite Italian-American food. Order anything, the steak is as good as the pizza. There are five Memphis locations, but try the original on Park Avenue. Open daily. Reservations are a good idea. Major credit cards. 3886 Park (458-0694). Inexpensive.

MIAMI

Difficult as it is to find adults actually born in Miami, practically all residents regard themselves — somehow — as natives. The year-round population of Miami is 1½ million. This figure swells to an incredible 13 million during the winter months when "snowbirds" arrive. ("Snowbird" is a tricky term as used in Miami; it refers primarily to tourists escaping the Northeastern freeze, but can just as easily describe South Americans in town for a mid-summer shopping spree.) Sprawling across 2,054 square miles of land (the metropolitan area also encompasses 354 square miles of water), Miami is a huge and cosmopolitan metropolis; yet it has managed to maintain a provincial quality in spite of commercialized efforts to identify it as a tropical New York City.

This is in part due to the way in which the metropolitan area is organized. Greater Miami (actually Metropolitan Dade County) is composed of 27 municipalities and a scattering of totally unincorporated areas. This breeds something of a small-town attitude in residents who have a chauvinistic interest in their own small enclaves. They identify with the whole city — it is, after all, all Miami — but they live where they live.

In even larger part, it is due to a deeply rooted tradition of hospitality and neighborliness that can only be described as somehow "Southern" — even while admitting that a large number of those residents who display it most openly are either recent arrivals or part-time snowbirds.

From an early small settlement consisting primarily of Indians, Miami only began to grow after one Julia Tuttle tickled the fancy of a railroad tycoon with some orange blossoms. According to the story told here, Tuttle was an early settler who was eager to see Miami become part of a railroad hookup with the rest of the state. She petitioned railroad magnate Henry Flagler to extend his Florida East Coast Railroad from Palm Beach to Miami. He seemed in no great hurry to do so until the Big Freeze of 1894 devastated most of Florida's fruit and vegetable crops. Most, but not all. When he received a box of frost-free orange blossoms from Tuttle, he suddenly got her point. Soon enough Miami had rail access to the rest of the world.

It wasn't long until the rest of the world was glad of access. Attracted by year-round warmth and sunshine, thousands of new residents began pouring into the area, only one step behind hundreds of shrewd and even occasionally honest entrepreneurs. In 50 years Miami was — has been — transformed from a coastal area of mangrove swamps and saw grass seas, to the metropolitan complex it is today. Not an entirely happy change — the draining of the area has severely threatened the beautiful and mysterious Everglades swamps to the west — but one that today is tempered with a real understanding of the ecological issues at risk.

Jolted a few years ago into the realization that their fun and sun city had begun to lose its good reputation, the municipal government began implementing a series of major programs dedicated to restoration and redevelopment. Renewing the beaches, sprucing up oceanfront hotels, cleaning up the Miami River, expanding the park system, and enforcing strict environmental laws to protect the delicate marine ecology reflected a determination to keep the good life good.

That Miami still has the good life is attested to by the waves of new residents who settle in one or another of Miami's municipalities each year (a fact that sits uneasily with long-time residents, torn as they are between the need for steady economic growth and the desire to maintain the quality of life). Today, the majority of these new residents are Spanish-speaking, many of them from the steady flow of refugees from Cuba, others fleeing violence in Central America, while still others are affluent Venezuelans and Colombians who occupy their Miami homes only part of the year. This has turned metropolitan Miami into a city where you can buy anything from fried bananas to Chilean wine and where more than 40% of the year-round inhabitants speak Spanish as their first language. However, there is also an only slightly smaller tide of new resident and regular visitors from the Caribbean islands, Britain, and Europe, bringing Miami such things as Jamaican-Chinese restaurants, Haitian grocery stores, and elegant French restaurants with Paris prices.

Coral Gables is Miami's prestigious planned community, conceived and built by a poet, George Merrick. Elegant gates to the city are still standing in various spots around the Gables, relics of Merrick's grand scheme to build "a place where castles in Spain are made real." Strict building codes prevail here, and woe to the newcomer who tries to put a flat roof on his home. (Everyone knows that Spanish castles have angled roofs.) In a county where almost all the streets are laid out in a simple north-south-east-west numbered grid, Coral Gables sticks to its Spanish and Italian street names and layout. (Get a map.)

South Miami, adjacent to the Gables, is reminiscent of an Anywhere, USA, crossroads town. Further south, in an unincorporated part of Dade County called Kendall, lie expensive estates with pools and tennis courts, where barely 20 years ago, there were only extensive mango and avocado groves.

Nearer to downtown Miami is the area known as Coconut Grove, a base for wealthy year-round and winter residents, and not so wealthy colonies of artists and writers. Here, crafts shops stand next to expensive boutiques, health food stores sit alongside posh restaurants, and old Florida houses of coral rock nestle close to modern high-rises. Luxurious yachts and sailboats lie in Biscayne Bay, and the Grove's younger generation lies all over Peacock Park. Further up the line, Miami proper begins, an area making a comeback from the decline the city experienced following a mass exodus to the suburbs. Little Havana is part of this center city but is really a small world unto itself with its Latin culture intact.

Also in a class by themselves are the communities of Miami Beach and Key Biscayne. Besides its glittering hotel row, the Beach (and the small manmade islands between it and the mainland) houses some of the most luxurious waterfront homes in Greater Miami. Cuban refugees who arrived during the boatlifts a few years ago have begun to share South Beach with retired and semi-retired Northeasterners. Key Biscayne has rows of luxury high-rises, simple bungalows, and excellent beaches.

With a mean annual temperature of 75.3°, with 40,000 registered boats, miles of improved beaches, 57 marinas, 11,829 acres of parks, 354 square miles of protected waters, and 3,200 more of sheltered waters, Miami's vital statistics support its reputation as a sunny water-oriented resort. Yet in recent years, the city has become a major urban area with an economic diversity associated with cities of comparable size. To a large extent, this is a result of the Latin American–Caribbean connection. Population has grown by 37% over the past 15 years, and employment has doubled in local business and industry. Although tourism is still the big business, the export trade is rapidly gaining on tourism and is expected to overtake it sometime in this decade.

Just over 80 years ago this city — if the tiny settlement here could qualify as a city — could only be reached by foot along the beach from the north, or by boat from Key West. It is hard to imagine a more isolated and undeveloped part of the American continent than the small village that was stuck on the side of a swamp, barely surviving from hurricane to hurricane. It is probably not true, as an old Florida legend claims, that a race of giants once lived here. But it surely is true that Miami today is the product of a gigantic will, an intention to grow.

MIAMI/MIAMI BEACH AT-A-GLANCE

SEEING THE CITY: Miami spreads out before your eyes from the top of several buildings. The *Omni Gallery Lounge* at the Omni International (1601 Biscayne Blvd.) looks out over downtown; the *700 Club* atop the David William Hotel (700 Biltmore Way) in Coral Gables offers a panoramic view of the area; *Horatio's,* on the roof of the Coconut Grove Hotel (2649 S Bayshore Dr.) commands a fine view of Biscayne Bay.

SPECIAL PLACES: The best way to see Greater Miami is by car. The points of interest are spread out, but an extensive system of highways and expressways makes them easy to reach, if you have an automobile.

Port of Miami – Every week thousands of people depart on Caribbean cruises from here — over a million travelers a year, making Miami the country's largest cruise port. Cruises aren't free, but watching the tourist-laden ocean liners turn around in the narrow channel that leads to the open sea is. Open daily. Ships leave Fridays, Saturdays, and Sundays from 4 to 6 PM.

Miamarina – Sightseeing and charter boats berth in this downtown marina. You can board the *Island Queen* for a two-hour circle cruise of Biscayne Bay, viewing waterfront estates and residential islands daily (379-5119). Admission charge. (For information on boat tours see "Tours" in *Sources and Resources*). Miamarina is open daily. Free. At 5th St. and Biscayne Bay.

Bayfront Park – This splash of green along Biscayne Bay lined with royal and coconut palms plays host to open-air concerts and special events year-round, but is also a nice place to sit and watch the world of Miami sail or stroll by. The John F. Kennedy Memorial Torch of Friendship symbolizes the relationship of the United States and Latin American countries. Open daily. Free. NE 5th to SE 2nd St.

Little Havana, Calle Ocho (Eighth Street) – The real Latin Flame, however, burns in this community, founded by Cubans who left Cuba after Castro's takeover. A recent rejuvenation program has transformed the area into a thriving social, economic, and cultural center. Shops feature handmade jewelry, dolls, and works of art. Fruit stands, bakeries, restaurants, and coffee stalls offer authentic Latin food. Try *La Tasca* for lunch or dinner — roast pork with rice and black bean sauce (2741 W Flagler St.) and then a cup of strong black coffee at a sidewalk coffee stall. You can watch cigars being hand-rolled by Cuban experts in exile at Padron Cigars (1564 W Flagler St., 643-2117). Around 9 PM, the nightlife begins, and the beat goes on until the small hours.

Metro Dade Zoo – This is Miami's new zoo and at this writing is open only on weekends and holidays and only partially stocked. Eventually, however, it is to be home for Bengal tigers, pygmy hippos, baby lions, and the rest of the more than 1,200 animals who once were available to the public at the Crandon Park Zoo on Key Biscayne. Admission charge. 12400 SW 152nd St. (251-0401).

Planet Ocean – The International Oceanographic Foundation maintains this multimillion-dollar permanent exhibition that tells the story of the world's oceans in films and exhibits (including a real submarine and a real iceberg). Open daily. Admission charge. 3979 Rickenbacker Causeway, Virginia Key (361-9455 or 361-5786)

Seaquarium – Once you've learned all about the oceans, you can see who lives there at the world's largest tropical marine aquarium. Among the 10,000 creatures swimming around the tidepools, jungle islands, and tanks under a geodesic dome are killer whales, sharks, sea lions, and performing seals and dolphins. The real stars, though, are Flipper, who performs with aquamaid assistants on the original TV set, and Lolita, a killer whale. Open daily. Admission charge. On Rickenbacker Causeway across from Planet Ocean (361-5703).

Miami Marine Stadium – This 6,500-seat roofed grandstand on Biscayne Bay hosts Miami's big shows as well as powerboat races, water shows, outdoor concerts, and fireworks displays. Check papers for special events. 3601 Rickenbacker Causeway (579-6956).

Vizcaya – This palatial estate is where International Harvester magnate James Deering reaped his personal harvest. Now the Dade County Art Museum, the 70-room Venetian palazzo is furnished with European antiques, precious china, and artworks spanning 18 centuries, and is surrounded by 30 acres of formal gardens with fountains, pools, and statuary. Open daily. Admission charge. 3251 S Miami Ave., just off US 1 (579-2708; 579-4626).

Museum of Science and Space Planetarium – Exhibits on a coral reef and the Everglades are enlightening, and there's a new participatory science arcade. The planetarium has several shows daily, and if you are really inspired you can search for the stars yourself with the Southern Cross Observatory telescope atop the building in the evenings. Open daily. Admission charge. 3280 S Miami Ave. (854-4242).

Historical Museum of South Florida – More on Indian civilizations, and exhibits on the Spanish exploration, and maritime history including relics of Caribbean underwater exploration and antique maps. Open daily. Free. 3280 S Miami Ave. (854-4681).

Fairchild Tropical Gardens – Founded by a tax attorney with a touch of the poet in him, this might just be one of the most lyrical tax shelters imaginable — 83 acres of paradise with tropical and subtropical plants and trees, lakes, and a rare plant house with an extensive collection of unusual tropical flora. Tram rides are available through the grounds complete with intelligent commentary. Open daily. Admission charge. 10901 Old Cutler Rd. (667-1651).

Parrot Jungle – More of the tropics, but this time, screaming, colorful, and talented. Not only do these parrots, macaws, and cockatoos fly, but they also ride bicycles, roller skate, and solve math problems. If you don't believe it, just wait till you see the flamingoes on parade — all amidst a jungle of huge cypress and live oaks. Open daily. Admission charge. 11 miles south off US 1 at 11000 SW 57th Ave. (Red Rd.) and Killian Dr. (666-7834).

Monkey Jungle – The monkeys wander, run free, and swing from trees as monkeys will. Naturally, some chimp stars perform, and there are also orangutans, gibbons, and an Amazonian rain forest with South American monkeys in natural habitats. Open daily. Admission charge. 22 miles south off US 1, at 14805 SW 216th St. (235-1611).

Serpentarium – An intriguing collection of reptiles, including a king cobra. Owner Bill Haast is considered an authority on snakes and snakebites. Frequent demonstrations of venom extractions. Open daily. Admission charge. 12655 S Dixie Hwy., south of Miami off US 1 (235-5722).

Orchid Jungle – Jungle trails wind through this huge orchid display, more species and colors than you thought existed. Open daily. Admission charge. South of Miami off US 1 in Homestead, 26715 SW 157th Ave. (247-4824).

Bird-Heinlein Fruit and Spice Park – These 20 tropical acres feature over 250 species of fruit, nut, and spice trees and plants. Guided tours by Parks Department naturalists include samplings of seasonal fruits. Open daily. Free. 35 miles southwest of Miami off US 1 at the intersection of Coconut Palm Dr. and Redland Rd. (247-5727).

Miami Beach – Some folks aspire to heaven, others to Miami Beach, an eight-mile-long island between the Atlantic Ocean and Biscayne Bay, lined with hotels that try to outdo each other in opulence. The architectural styles represented include Mediterranean, art deco, streamlined, Tuscan, and Venetian Gothic, with plaster castings, and pink and beige tints to reduce glare. But what the colors offset, the neon doesn't — ride down the main drag, Collins Avenue, at night and the glare is stronger than the Florida sun is during the day. The real draw is the beaches. There are big-name hotels with big-name entertainment and big-time resort facilities, but one of the best shows of all is free — watching the action in the lobby of the luxury beachfront hotels, where people from all walks of life step out for a few days, dressed either to kill or to be camouflaged from the glitter. If you feel at a disadvantage, you can actually rent a fur or vicuña (there are such places in Miami Beach) and join the parade. If you've seen enough glittering rococo, the Miami Beach Garden Center has a beautiful display of Florida's native flora. Open daily. Free. 2000 Garden Center Dr. The Bass Museum of Art has a permanent collection ranging from the Old Masters to the Impressionists. Closed Sundays and Mondays. Admission charge. 2100 Collins Ave. at 21st St. (673-7530).

■ **EXTRA SPECIAL:** After a few days in Miami, you'll probably want to get back to where things are real, and if you do, head south and you'll leave it all behind you. Along US 27 you'll drive through miles of Miami's little-known farmlands. You can stock up on fresh fruits and vegetables at numerous stands or go right out into the U-Pic fields and choose your own. Forty miles south of Miami (turnoff on US 1) is the *Everglades National Park,* a unique and extremely diverse subtropical wilderness with some of the best naturalist-oriented activities anywhere in the world. This 1½ million-acre preserve features alligators, raccoons, manatees, mangroves, and thousands of rare birds, all in their natural habitats. For complete details see DIRECTIONS. Farther south along US 1 stretch the *Florida Keys,* a chain of islands connected by an Overseas Highway. Here you'll find everything from the only living coral reef in the continental United States (which you can see in all its glory only by skin diving, snorkeling, or in a glass-bottom boat) at John Pennekamp State Park in Key Largo, to great fishing possibilities, and better food: turtle steak, conch chowder, and Key lime pie. For complete details see DIRECTIONS.

SOURCES AND RESOURCES

The Metro Department of Tourism is best for brochures, maps, and general tourist information; open weekdays. 234 W Flagler (579-4694). Just down the street, the Miami Office of Information and Visitors Department of Tourism Office can also provide information. 150 SE 2nd Ave. (579-6327). For information on fairs, art shows, and seasonal events in the area's parks, call the Dade County Leisure Line (547-PARK).

All telephone numbers are in the 305 area code unless otherwise indicated.

For Local Coverage – *Miami Herald,* morning daily, publishes the *Weekend* section on Fridays with a schedule of upcoming events; *Miami News,* afternoon daily. *Miami* Magazine, monthly, includes a "What's Going On" section with calendar of events for every day of the month. All are available at newsstands.

For Food – Check *Guide to Restaurants in Greater Miami* by Harvey Steinman (Brooke House, $4.95), a listing and evaluation of the area's restaurants.

CLIMATE AND CLOTHES: There is good reason why Miami is the major retirement and vacation destination in the country. It's warm all year with average daily temperatures of 75.3° and lots of sunshine. During the day, summer clothes and beach attire (if you're headed that way) are most comfortable, and at night medium-weight clothing and sweaters should be worn as the temperature drops outdoors, and air-conditioning prevails indoors. In the big hotels, men dress in jackets and ties, and women wear anything from cocktail dresses to evening gowns and fur wraps.

GETTING AROUND: Bus – The Metro Transit Agency serves downtown Miami, Collins Avenue on Miami Beach, and links the two, as well as Coral Gables. There are also connections between the Gables, Coconut Grove, and South Miami as far as Dadeland, but the routes tend to be slow and complicated. A special shuttle bus covers the central downtown area, linking shopping streets and waterfront parks in a continuous loop throughout the day. For information on routes, schedules, and fares, call 638-6700.

Taxi – You can sometimes hail a cab in the street, but it's better to order one on the phone, or pick one up in front of any of the big hotels. Major cab companies are Courtesy Cab, for South Dade County (545-6300), and Yellow Cab, for North Dade County (945-7777).

Car Rental – Miami is served by the large national firms. Good local service is provided by Shamrock Auto Rentals, 2701 NW LeJeune Rd. (871-6311).

TOURS: Boat – Miami is largely a waterfront city and one of the best ways to get to know it is by boat. Besides the *Island Queen*, which leaves from Miamarina (see *Special Places*), Nikko's Gold Coast cruises set sail out of Haulover Marina, 10800 Collins Ave. (945-5461), several times every day.

Bus – A tour of Miami highlights is given by American Sightseeing Tours, 4300 NW 14th St. (871-4992).

Air For a different view of the city, you can take a helicopter flight over Miami Beach from Watson Island or MacArthur Causeway. Open year-round (377-0934).

MUSEUMS: Vizcaya, the Museum of Science and Space Planetarium, and the Historical Museum of South Florida are described in some detail in *Special Places*. Other notable Miami museums are:

Metropolitan Museum and Art Center, 1212 Anastasia Ave., Coral Gables (442-1448).

Lowe Art Museum, 1301 Stanford Dr., on the University of Miami campus in Coral Gables (284-3535).

Grove House (this gallery is a nonprofit cooperative for artists and craftsmen, featuring the works of award-winning Florida artists in many mediums), 3496 Main Hwy., Coconut Grove (445-5633).

MAJOR COLLEGES AND UNIVERSITIES: The University of Miami in Coral Gables (1200 San Amaro Dr.) has an enrollment of 17,000. Florida International University is a four-year degree college with two separate campuses (SW 8th St. and 107th Ave., NE 151st St. and Biscayne Blvd.). Miami Dade Community College has three separate campuses and is the largest junior college in the country (11380 NW 27th Ave., 11011 SW 104th St., and 300 NE 2nd Ave.).

SPECIAL EVENTS: Check the publications listed above for exact dates. Miami is the site of the annual *Orange Bowl Parade,* nationally televised from Biscayne Blvd. each New Year's Eve as a prelude to the *Orange Bowl* football classic played on New Year's Day. Two of the country's largest boat shows are held each year, the *Dinner Key Boat Show* in Coconut Grove in October, and the *International Boat Show* at the Miami Beach Convention Center in February. Miami Beach hosts the *Festival of the Arts* each February, and the *Coconut Grove Art Festival* in the same month draws many away from the beach. In March, in Little Havana, natives and visitors alike head for Calle Ocho (8th St.) for *Carnaval Miami,* a 9-day festival.

SPORTS: Football – Miami is home to the NFL *Dolphins* and Dolphin-mania infects the entire city during the football season, so for good seats go to the Orange Bowl, 1501 NW 3rd St., Gate 14, in advance (643-4700). The University of Miami Hurricanes also play football at the Orange Bowl; for tickets and information, contact the University of Miami ticket office, 5821 San Amaro, Coral Gables (284-2655) or go to the Orange Bowl.

Baseball – Fans can watch preseason games of the Baltimore *Orioles,* whose spring training camp is in Miami; they often play the New York *Yankees,* who train in Fort Lauderdale. For information call 635-5395.

Jai Alai – From December through April there's jai alai (a Basque game resembling a combination of lacrosse, handball, and tennis) and betting action nightly at the Miami Jai-Alai Fronton, the country's largest. You can pick up tickets at the gate or reserve them in advance, 3500 NW 37th Ave. (633-6400).

Horse and Dog Racing – Betting is big in Miami. Hialeah racetrack, 4 E 25th St., Hialeah (887-4347), is worth a visit not just for the action, but to see the beautiful old grounds and clubhouse, and the famous flock of pink flamingoes (you can't bet on them). There is also thoroughbred horse racing at Gulfstream Park, US 1 at Hallandale (944-1242), and at Calder, 21001 NW 27th Ave. (625-1311). Greyhound racing is held at Flagler, 450 NW 37th Ave. (649-3000) and Biscayne, 320 NW 115th St. (754-3484). Check the racing dates before heading to the track.

Swimming – With an average daily temperature of 75°, and miles of ocean beach on the Atlantic, Miami Beach and Key Biscayne offer some great places for swimming, all water sports, and another prime activity, sun worshiping. Some of the best beaches are:

Crandon Park Beach – A two-mile stretch lined with shade trees, picnic tables, barbecue pits, ample parking. Drive to the far end for private cabanas rented by the day or week. Rickenbacker Causeway to Key Biscayne.

Bill Baggs State Park – This long, wide beach with sand dunes, picnic areas, fishing, boat basin, restored old lighthouse, and museum is a favorite of residents. At Cape Florida, the far south end of Key Biscayne.

Virginia Beach – Popular with skin divers and swimmers. Near the Seaquarium and Plant Ocean on Virginia Key, reached via Rickenbacker Causeway.

Miami Beach – Several long stretches of public beach at various places, including South Beach for surfers (5th St. and Collins Ave.), Lummus Park with lots of shaded beaches (north of South Beach on Collins Ave.), the newly restored North Beach with landscaped dunes and oceanfront walkway (71st St. and Collins Ave.). There are also small public beaches with parking facilities hidden in the midst of Hotel Row.

Haulover Beach – Long stretch of beautiful beach, good for surfing and popular with families. Marina, sightseeing boats, charter fishing fleets, restaurants, and fishing pier. A1A north of Bal Harbour.

Matheson Hammock – Large, peaceful park with wading and swimming beaches, tidal pools, picnic areas, wooded trails, bike paths, guided nature walks, refreshment stand, marina, sailing instruction. South of Miami Beach, next to Fairchild Gardens.

Bicycling – Rent from Dade Cycle Shop, 3043 Grand Ave. in Coconut Grove (443-6075). There are over 100 miles of bicycle paths in the Miami area, including beautiful tree-shaded lanes through Coconut Grove down beyond Matheson Hammock. A self-guided bicycle tour of Key Biscayne originates in Crandon Park. Dade County Parks Department will provide more information (call 579-2672).

Fishing – Surf and offshore saltwater fishing is available year-round, and there's always plenty of freshwater action in canals and backwaters, including the Everglades and Florida Bay. Charter boats offer a half day and full day of deep-sea fish, snapper, grouper, yellowtail, pompano, and mackerel trips from Miamarina, Bayfront Park at 5th St. (374-6260); Crandon Park Marina (361-5421); and Haulover Marina, 10800 Collins Ave. (947-3532).

Golf – More than 35 golf courses are open to the public. Some of the best are Crooked Creek, 9980 SW 104th St. (274-1044); the 27-hole Kendale Lakes, 6401 Kendale Lakes Dr. (382-3930); and Key Biscayne, 6700 Crandon Blvd. (361-9129).

Tennis – Many hotels have courts for the use of their guests and there are also public facilities throughout the county. Some of the best are Flamingo Park with 13 clay courts, 1245 Michigan Ave. (673-7761); Moore Park, 765 NW 36th St. (635-7459); and Tamiami, 11201 SW 24th St. (223-7076).

Boating – Greater Miami is laced with navigable canals, and has many private and public marinas with all kinds of boats for rent. Sailboats are available from Dinner Key Marina (on Bayshore Dr., in Coconut Grove).

Skating – Roller skating is big with Miami kids and they roll year-round at Kendall Lakes Skating Center, 8700 SW 137th Ave. (387-9100), and Tropical Roller Skating Center, 8750 SW 40th St. (226-2050). For outdoor roller skating, Coconut Grove is the place. You can rent skates at Sandy's Skates, 3001 Grand Ave., Coconut Grove (447-8888). For hard-hit snowbirds, there's year-round ice skating at the Polar Palace, 3685 NW 36th St. (634-3333)

Nature Walks – There are nature walks at Fairchild Tropical Gardens and Bird-Heinlein Fruit and Spice Park, but the Parks Department offers frequent guided tours through natural hammocks, tree forests, bird rookeries, and even through water (a monthly marine walk and nature lesson and dousing at Bear Cut-Off, Virginia Key). For information contact the Park Department office (949-3134).

THEATER: For current offerings, check the publications listed above. Miami's resident repertory company, *The Players,* performs everything from classical plays to experimental theater from October to April at the Coconut Grove Playhouse, 3500 Main Hwy. (442-4000). *The Miami Beach Center of the Performing Arts* offers touring plays and musicals, including some pre- and post-Broadway road shows, 1700 Washington Ave. (673-8300). The Gusman Cultural Center, 174 E Flagler St. (374-2444), and the Dade County Auditorium, 2901 W Flagler St. (642-9061), book theatrical and cultural events year-round.

MUSIC: The *Florida Philharmonic* performs with internationally acclaimed soloists and guest conductors from winter to spring at the Gusman Cultural Center and at the Miami Beach Center of the Performing Arts, where the *Miami Beach Symphony Orchestra* plays from winter to spring. The *Greater Miami Opera Association* stages several major productions annually, 1200 Coral Way (854-1643). The *Miami Ballet Company* performs with local dancers and guest stars in three yearly productions at the Dade County Auditorium, 2901 W Flagler St. (545-3395).

NIGHTCLUBS AND NIGHTLIFE: What they now call Las Vegas–style entertainment in Miami used to be called Miami–style entertainment in Las Vegas. During the winter season, some of the beach hotels feature big names and glittering star-studded revues. There are also discos, jazz spots, singles bars, and Latin entertainment.

Nightclubs in the *Diplomat*, 3515 S Ocean Ave., Hollywood (949-2442); and *Sheraton Bal Harbour* hotels, 9701 Collins Ave. (865-3119) offer the biggest of the Las Vegas/Miami style. Live bands play at the *Fontainebleau Poodle Lounge,* 4441 Collins Ave. (538-8811), and there's nightly entertainment at the *Doral,* 4833 Collins Ave. (532-3600). *Jazzery,* 777 Curtis Pky., Miami Springs (887-2621) for Latin music and jazz; *Village Inn,* 3131 Commodore Plaza, Coconut Grove (445-8721) for reggae; *Reflections on the Bay,* Miamarina (371-6433), for a great view and piano music; *Tuttle's,* 600 NE 36th St. (576-7676) and *Casanova's,* for disco, 740 E 9th St., Hialeah (883-8706); *Baturro,* for Latin music and dancing, 2322 NW 7th St. (642-9043); *Ginger Man,* for a jazz quartet, in the Mayfair mall, 3390 Mary St., Coconut Grove (448-9919); *Rollo's,* 9100 S Dixie Hwy. (665-0161) for rock 'n' roll; *Sebastian's,* for female gays, 2492 SW 17th Ave. (854-9216).

SINS: The city whose *pride* is the Orange Bowl also welcomes visitors with enough rudeness (at Miami International Airport) and traffic jams (on Collins Avenue) to fill the most mild-mannered visitor with *anger. Avarice* gets plenty of encouragement at Hialeah Race Track, 4 E 25th St. (887-4347), where the thoroughbreds race and the hopeful place their bets; and *gluttony* is alive and well, thanks to platterfuls of stone crabs at *Joe's Stone Crab*, 227 Biscayne St. (673-0365). Miami is also as long on pulchritude as the publicity photos would like you to believe, and to judge from the action in the *Poodle Lounge* at the Fountainebleau Hotel, not all Miami visitors are too old to *lust* after a pretty woman. Miami's red light district can be found in northeast Miami, along Biscayne Boulevard and NE 2nd Ave., between NE 50th St. and the 79th St. Causeway.

LOCAL SERVICES: Business Services – Stephan Secretarial Services, 2731 Ponce de Leon Blvd., Coral Gables (446-9500).

Mechanics – Martino, for foreign and American cars, 7145 SW 8th St. (261-6071). Lejeune-Trail Exxon, for American makes, 801 SW 42nd Ave. (446-2942).

Babysitting – Thelma's Angels, 16263 NW 2nd Ave. (940-0301).

BEST IN TOWN

CHECKING IN: Finding a place to stay in Miami can be difficult because of the area's growing popularity with Latin American and European tourists. Winter is the busy season, and reservations should be made at least 2 months in advance. In winter, a double room in the expensive range would run $90 and up per night; $60 to $85 in moderate; and $35 to $50 in inexpensive. In summer, some hotels cut their rates, so shop around.

Omni International – This 10.5-acre complex with a five-story atrium lobby includes 165 shops, six movie theaters, ten restaurants, an amusement park, tennis courts, a sundeck, and rooftop pool. There are 500 rooms and suites. 1601 Biscayne Blvd. (374-0000). Expensive.

Key Biscayne – The Key's first and still most delightful hotel with a quiet and peaceful atmosphere amidst soft tropical decor. Features a long private beach, tennis courts, pitch-and-putt golf course, and a good dining room. 103 rooms. 701 Ocean Dr., Key Biscayne (361-5431). Expensive.

Four Ambassadors – Right on Biscayne Bay, near downtown Miami, this hotel offers a saltwater and heated pool, two whirlpools, a marina, a restaurant, and other fine facilities. There are 181 rooms and suites, and in the winter, some of the condominiums here are rented as well. 801 S Bayshore Dr. (377-1966). Expensive.

Fontainebleau Hilton – A new owner, a new manager, a new face, and a mere $14 million have given this old classic a whole new style and a new constituency. It is still the glittering standard by which most "flabbergast" hotels are measured, but for the first time there is a sign outside telling passersby its name. The assumption that you never want to leave the hotel is no longer the operating credo, but there is still plenty to do here. 1,250 rooms. 4441 Collins Ave., Miami Beach (538-2000). Expensive.

Doral-on-the-Ocean – At the top of this high-rise is the *Starlight Roof Supper Club,* but the beach gets top billing here. Other highlights include shops, pool, and free bus to the Doral Country Club in West Miami, built around a championship 18-hole golf course with tennis, sauna, and health club. 420 rooms. 4833 Collins Ave., Miami Beach (532-3600). Expensive.

Sheraton River House – The newest hotel near Miami International Airport features resort facilities — tennis courts, golf course, pool, and boat dockage — and a lounge. 408 rooms. 3900 NW 21st St. (871-3800). Expensive to moderate.

Coconut Grove – A 20-story high-rise looking out on Biscayne Bay and Dinner Key marina. The rooftop restaurant has a beautiful view. 2649 S Bayshore Dr., Coconut Grove (858-2500). Expensive to moderate.

Marina Park – This is a pleasant new hotel just across from Biscayne Bay and the port of Miami near the downtown area. 340 Biscayne Blvd. (371-4400). Moderate.

University Inn – Across from the University of Miami, this motel is a good stopping-off place for visitors to the southwest area. The rooms are comfortable and there's a pleasant waterway restaurant, on the Coral Gables Waterway (boat dockage available). 1390 S Dixie Hwy. (667-2437). Moderate.

EATING OUT: There are thousands of restaurants in the Greater Miami Area ranging from haute cuisine at haute cost to inexpensive outdoor cafés in Little Havana. Much of Miami socializing centers around eating out, so beware the long waiting lines during the winter season (December through

April) when snowbirds swell the ranks of regular diners. Residents always make advance reservations. Although the restaurants are generally scattered, there are quite a few concentrated in Coconut Grove and Little Havana, so to make your own finds you can stroll around here, and particularly around 8th Street. Expect to pay $45 or more for a dinner for two in the expensive range; $30 to $40 in the moderate; and $25 or less in the inexpensive range. Prices do not include drinks, wine, or tips.

Café Chauveron – Transplanted from New York City to Bay Harbor without a rippling of its famous soufflés. A French restaurant in the grand manner. Everything is beautifully prepared, from coquille de fruits de mer au champagne to soufflé Grand Marnier. Docking space if you arrive by boat. Open daily but closed in summer season (June through early October). Reservations. Major credit cards. Two locations: 9561 E Bay Harbor Dr., Bay Harbor Island, Miami Beach (866-8779); and 3390 Mary St., Coconut Grove (446-0134). Expensive.

Le Parisien – During winter in Miami you can have a taste of springtime in Paris. Fresh flowers and impeccable service complement the classic French cuisine, memorable for its mousse de saumon, fraisen aspic, and duckling Montmorency. Closed Sundays and in late summer. Reservations. No credit cards. 474 Arthur Godfrey Rd., Miami Beach (534-2770). Expensive.

Raimondo's – In its new brick building in Coral Gables, *Raimondo's* doesn't offer much atmosphere, but the food is as good as ever. Many Miamians swear chef Raimondo is *sans pareil.* Daily specials are posted on the blackboard, but spaghetti carbonara, red snapper meunière, and fried zucchini are also excellent. Open daily. Reservations. No credit cards. 4612 S LeJeune Rd. (666-9919). Expensive.

Joe's Stone Crab – By now, this famous old (since 1913) South Beach restaurant is a Miami tradition, big, crowded, noisy, and friendly (get there by 6:30 or you'll have to wait). The stone crabs are brought in by Joe's own fishing fleet. Scenes of early Miami Beach and antique clocks are about the only decorations — people come here for serious eating. Open daily; closed May 15–October 15. No reservations. Major credit cards. 227 Biscayne St., Miami Beach (673-0365). Expensive.

Miamarina – There are two restaurants here, both on the bay. The *Dockside Terrace* is pleasant for an indoor or alfresco lunch. For dinner, go upstairs to *Reflections on the Bay* with its panoramic bay-and-skyline view. Florida seafood is the specialty. Closed Sundays. Reservations. Major credit cards. 301 NE 5th St. (358-6419 or 371-6433). Expensive to moderate.

Vinton's – Spread across the ground floor of the old La Palma Hotel, an elegant choice, with foot pillows and fresh flowers for the ladies, and sherbert served midway through dinner to refresh the palate. Superb bouillabaisse, lots of flambéeing at tableside. Closed Sundays. Reservations. Major credit cards. 116 Alhambra Circle, Coral Gables (445-2511). Expensive to moderate.

Gatti – In Miami Beach since 1924, this family-owned restaurant remains in its original stucco house. The northern Italian cuisine is excellent and the waiters are mostly from Italy's Piedmont province. Closed Mondays and June through October. Reservations. Major credit cards. 1427 West Ave., Miami Beach (673-1717). Moderate.

La Belle Epoque – The secret of success is chef/owner Denis Rapy who, before starting his own restaurant, worked at Maxim's in Paris and the Plaza Hotel in New York. Continental specialties include poulet Josephine en croûte (chicken breast in pie crust with mushrooms, ham, cheese, and cream sauce), veal en croûte, and La Belle Epoque soufflé, made with Grand Marnier and chestnuts. The wine list is extensive, including such items as a $1300 bottle of Château Margaux (1887). Open daily. Reservations. Credit cards. 1045 95th St., Bay Harbor, Miami Beach (865-6011). Moderate.

Kaleidoscope – Indoor-outdoor dining amidst palms and hanging plants on the second floor of a Coconut Grove building. Good shrimp and duckling for dinner; tasty salads for lunch. Reservations necessary for dinner. Major credit cards. 3112 Commodore Plaza (446-5010). Moderate.

Prince Hamlet – Danish smorgasbord loaded down with black and red caviar, smoked salmon, sturgeon, whitefish, raw oysters and clams, and herring, all included with the price of the entrée (duck Danoise and veal Oscar are excellent). Open daily. Reservations. Major credit cards. 8301 Biscayne Blvd., Miami (754-4400). Moderate.

Centro Vasco – Next to jai alai, this is Miami's favorite Basque import. Specializes in snapper in green sauce and chicken Basquaise. You can even order take-out paella here. A great sangria is made right at your table. Open daily. Reservations. Major credit cards. 2235 SW 8th St. (643-9606). Moderate.

Jamaica Inn/English Pub – These two restaurants share a building and ownership, but there the resemblance ends. The Jamaica Inn is set in a miniature rain forest with a giant skylight, and is known for Jamaica duckling, prime ribs, and fresh Everglades frogs legs. The Pub, dismantled in England and shipped here, is dark, atmospheric, and . . . pubbish. Both open daily. Reservations. Major credit cards. 320 Crandon Blvd., Key Biscayne (361-5481). Moderate to inexpensive.

Captain's Tavern – A neighborhood restaurant serving super-fresh seafood. Go early or expect to wait. Look for the fish of the day posted on the blackboard. Native fish is always good, but fresh clams, oysters, and Maine lobsters are also available, with generous servings of salad. Open daily. No reservations. Major credit cards. 9621 S Dixie Hwy. (666-5979). Moderate to inexpensive.

Marshall Major's – Some people call Miami the Bronx with palm trees. Whether or not that's true, Major's ranks with New York delis — pastrami, corned beef, home-style flanken, boiled chicken and vegetables, all served in huge portions. There's an Early Bird Special for dinner. Open daily. No reservations. Major credit cards. 6901 SW 57th Ave. (665-3661). Moderate to inexpensive.

Versailles – Authentic Cuban food and a lively ambiance characterize this Little Havana landmark. A favorite of Latins and knowledgeable gringos. Wonderful Cuban sandwiches, black beans, and rice. Open daily till the wee hours. Major credit cards. No reservations. 3555 SW 8th St. (445-7614). Inexpensive.

Shorty's Bar-B-Q – This family-owned restaurant can't be matched for barbecued ribs, chicken, and fresh corn on the cob. Open daily. No reservations. No credit cards. 9200 S Dixie Hwy. (665-5732). Inexpensive.

Café Cardozo – Across the street from the Atlantic Ocean, this pleasant little café is in a restored Art Deco hotel. Its period interior features lilac-colored walls and flowers on each table. Especially good are the artichoke pie, salads, and hearty sandwiches. Closed Mondays. No reservations. Major credit cards. 1300 Ocean Dr., Miami Beach (538-5750). Inexpensive.

The Spiral – The best bets at Miami's first vegetarian restaurant are tempura (shrimp, vegetable, or combination), salads, and vegetable sandwiches. Open daily. No reservations. Major credit cards. 1630 Ponce de Leon Blvd., Coral Gables (446-1591). Inexpensive.

La Crêpe – A small French café in the middle of the Dadeland Shopping Mall with fine crêpes, soups, and desserts at low prices. Open daily. No reservations. Major credit cards. N Kendall Dr. at Palmetto Expy. (661-6051). Inexpensive.

El Gaucho – A little bit of Argentina in Little Havana, where the specialties are traditional steaks and mixed grill. The house wine is served in penguin-shaped pitchers made in Argentina. Closed Tuesdays. Reservations necessary on weekends. Major credit cards. 3494 SW Eighth St. (444-6968). Inexpensive.

MILWAUKEE

Milwaukee is the kind of place that grows on you gradually, like contentment with a cold glass of beer. And beer is the word you immediately associate with Milwaukee. Only in 1889 was brewing the city's principal industry, but Milwaukee residents loyally claim they consume more beer than anyone else in America. Two of the nation's four largest breweries are making beer in the city that grew up around a French-Canadian trading post, and their presence is so pervasive that you smell malt in the air.

The city's role as a lake port was primarily responsible for its early growth. Here, Lake Michigan receives the waters of the Milwaukee, Menominee, and Kinnickinnic rivers. With so much water around, it's easy to see why Milwaukee used to be a swamp. But the resourceful pioneers who arrived in 1833 discovered plenty of gravel left by a departing glacier ten thousand years earlier. They were fast with a shovel, and before long, New Englanders were parceling off Milwaukee real estate and selling it to each other.

The sailing ships brought loads of immigrants in the 19th century — first the Irish, fleeing the potato famine; then the Germans, including those who left home after the abortive revolutions of 1848; and in years following, a variety of ethnic groups, among them the Poles, now Milwaukee's second largest ethnic group. (The Poles gave the city kielbasa sausage, a dietary staple on the South Side.)

During the latter half of the 19th century, Milwaukee called itself the German Athens. It's not really true that the shops on North 3rd Street had signs reading "English spoken here," but as late as the 1880s two out of every three Milwaukee residents literate enough to buy a daily paper chose to read the news in the language of Goethe. The city's Germanic era ended in a flurry of divided loyalties and ill will during World War I. The Deutscher Club changed its name to the Wisconsin Club and sauerkraut became liberty cabbage. A statue of Germania which graced the front of what is now called the Brumder Building was quietly taken down and hidden away, although the towers, which resemble Prussian spiked helmets, remain.

Although Milwaukee's European heritage has been considerably diluted over the years, stubborn local conviction insists that food ought to be piled high on the plate, that no one ought to thirst for long, and that a householder who doesn't keep his lawn cut is a menace to civilization. With a downtown district that seems too small for a metropolitan population of 1.3 million, and an Old World respect for homely virtues and tidy streets, Milwaukee impresses a lot of people as an overgrown small town. Where else but in Milwaukee would everyone quit work for a sausage break, as employees of Usinger's wiener works do each morning, to sample the product? Where but at County Stadium would a bratwurst be nearly as popular with hungry fans as a hot dog? A bratwurst on a poppy seed roll in one hand, a beer in the other, and the home team hitting homers while Bernie Brewer slides down a chute next to the scoreboard into an oversized imitation stein of lager — now that's Milwaukee living!

Of course, there is more to the place than sauerbraten and suds. Milwaukee's lakefront has been compared to the Bay of Naples — not, it must be admitted, by the Neopolitans, but by the people who live here. Much of the shore belongs to the local taxpayers, including those who fish there for everything from smelt to coho salmon. (Milwaukee residents claim that no one lives more than half an hour from where the fish are biting.) When the weather is warm, the beaches within five minutes of downtown are crowded even though Lake Michigan is generally too chilly for leisurely swimming.

Everyone celebrates the annual opening of Wisconsin's deer season, with thousands of hunters scurrying toward the woods and North Country taverns. Milwaukee County is proud of its park system, its zoo, its golf courses, and horticultural exhibits in glass domes that rise south of the Menominee Valley. The Milwaukee Symphony plays at the Performing Arts Center, and there are first-rate repertory and ballet companies. A downtown natural history museum and an art museum on the lakefront round out the city's cultural life. Urban problems are less severe in Milwaukee than in other cities of comparable size. The odds are pretty good you won't get mugged walking downtown after dark, and any political scandals you hear about are likely to be mild in comparison to those of other major cities. Milwaukee works hard to uphold its tradition of honest politicans and upright public servants.

Still, as nearly anyone you ask will admit, the city is no San Francisco, New Orleans, or New York. And ever since the early days, when a rival lakeport pulled ahead in the competition to attract settlers, it's been clear it's no Chicago. But the people who live in the community that made beer famous take comfort in that.

MILWAUKEE AT-A-GLANCE

SEEING THE CITY: The 41-story First Wisconsin Center, Milwaukee's tallest building, anchors the eastern end of Wisconsin Avenue at Lake Michigan. Arrange a free visit to the top-floor observatory deck by calling 765-5733. 777 E Wisconsin Ave.

SPECIAL PLACES: Milwaukee River divides the downtown area into east and west segments of unequal size (walking east you soon run into the beautiful Lake Michigan shoreline).

DOWNTOWN WEST

Wisconsin Avenue West – Walking west from the bridge along Wisconsin Avenue, Milwaukee's principal shopping street, you pass *Gimbel's,* on the same site that John Plankinton, a pioneer butcher, started his career with one cow and boundless ambition. He became a millionaire, and gave a start to packing tycoons Philip Armour and Patrick Cudahy. The blocks between Gimbels and the Boston Store have been converted into a downtown shopping mall. Just to the west is the *Marc Plaza Hotel,* home of a good jazz spot, the *Bombay Bicycle Club* (271-7250).

Joan of Arc Chapel – On the campus of Marquette University. This is the medieval chapel where Joan of Arc prayed before being put to torch — not here in Milwaukee, but in the French village of Chasse, from whence the chapel was transported stone by stone. One of those stones reputedly was kissed by Joan before she went to her death, and is said to be discernably colder than the others. Open daily, 10 AM to 4 PM. Free. 601 N 14th St. (224-7700).

The Alex Mitchell Home – Now quarters of the Wisconsin (formerly Deutscher) Club, this was originally the house of General Billy Mitchell's grandparents. A Scot, Alex Mitchell arrived in Milwaukee with a carpetbag full of money and established the first bank. Banks were illegal at the time, but that didn't stop him. He called it an insurance company. Later he became a railroad president. 900 W Wisconsin Ave.

Milwaukee Public Museum – Has the fourth largest collection of natural history exhibits in the country, including a "Streets of Old Milwaukee" section showing the city in the 19th century. Discreetly hidden away in an upstairs bedroom is the sink that once belonged to Kitty Williams, a famous Milwaukee madam. Open daily except major holidays. Admission charge. 800 W Wells St. (278-2700).

Milwaukee County Historical Museum – Built in a former brewer's bank (pre–WW I), this is the most interesting part of the Convention Hall/MECCA Complex, which includes an arena for sports activities and facilities for meetings. The museum has an archive and numerous exhibits on the city's history, several of which are especially entertaining for children. Open daily. Free. 910 N 3rd St. (273-8288).

Père Marquette Park – Between the museum and the river, this park is named after the explorer-priest who stopped briefly in Milwaukee during a canoe trip through the Great Lakes area. Local legend insists that he landed here, which at the time was part of an extensive tamarack swamp in the basin of the lake and surrounding rivers.

DOWNTOWN EAST

Wisconsin Avenue East – Wisconsin Avenue, east of the river, is a shopper's haven, with numerous fine stores. Shops on several nearby cross streets have been lovingly restored to their 19th-century origins. Across from the *Pfister Hotel* is the Milwaukee Club, whose members are Milwaukee's ruling elite.

Milwaukee War Memorial, Milwaukee Art Museum – Located on the lakefront, where Lincoln Memorial Drive crosses Wisconsin Avenue. The original building was designed by Eero Saarinen. The Art Museum has recently doubled its size; its permanent collection includes Old Masters, contemporary art, and primitive painting and sculpture. It also runs the Villa Terrace Decorative Arts Museum at 2220 N Terrace Ave. Outside, Lake Michigan provides a powerful backdrop for sculpture. The Art Museum is closed Mondays. Admission charge. 750 N Lincoln Memorial Dr. (271-9508).

Cathedral Square – Between Jackson and Jefferson Streets, this square dates back to Milwaukee's territorial days. Except for the tower, St. John's Cathedral in the square was nearly destroyed by fire in 1935. On the west side of the square, Skylight Theater offers musical plays and vest pocket operas. If you feel like a snack, turn left on Jefferson to number 761, where *George Watts & Son's* interesting silver shop has a restaurant tucked away on the second floor.

City Hall – Milwaukee's best-known landmark, this building with the tall tower (393 feet) was designed in 1895 so taxpayers could drive their buggies up in the rain to pay real estate taxes without getting wet. In the tower above the arched entry, Old Sol, a 20-ton bell, gathers dust. In 1922 citizens complained about the noise of Old Sol tolling, and city fathers ordered it stilled. N Water St. at Wells St.

OTHER SPECIAL PLACES

Annunciation Greek Orthodox Church – The last major building designed by Wisconsin-born architect Frank Lloyd Wright. You can tour the saucer-shaped structure daily except Sundays. Admission charge. 9400 W Congress St. (461-9400).

Whitnall Park – One of the larger municipal parks in the country, Whitnall includes the 689-acre Boerner Botanical Gardens, with sunken gardens, nature trails, and exhibits. Open daily. Free (425-1130). Also on the park grounds is the Todd Wehr Nature Center, a wildlife preserve for hikers and strollers. Open daily, closed Sundays in winter. Free (425-8550).

Milwaukee County Zoo – Among the most famous zoos in the country, this one allows the animals to roam free in natural habitats. Samson, the world's largest captive gorilla, is the zoo's captivating king. Kids adore the miniature railroad and children's zoo. Open daily. Admission charge. 10001 W Blue Mound Rd. (771-5500).

Schlitz Audubon Center – The 180 acres of undisturbed grazing area once provided pasture to brewery horses weary from pulling beer wagons. It's a good place to wander and wonder at days gone by. Admission free to members of Audubon Center. Admission charge for visitors. Closed Mondays. 1111 E Brown Deer Rd. (352-2880).

Harbor Cruises – Iroquois Boat Line offers two-hour trips along the Milwaukee River. Daily from Memorial Day through Labor Day. Admission charge. Clybourn Street Bridge dock (354-5050).

■ **EXTRA SPECIAL:** For an interesting day trip, take I-94 west for 78 miles to *Madison, Wisconsin*, capital of the state and home of the *University of Wisconsin*'s 1,000-acre, Big Ten campus. Drop in at the information center at Memorial Union on Park and Langdon streets to pick up a map and find out what's happening on campus. You'll find more than enough to keep you busy here, with an art center, geology museum, planetarium, observatory, and arboretum to see. The four lakes around Madison — Lakes Mendota, Monon, Waubesa, and Kegonsa — are great for fishing and swimming. If you continue driving west (toward the Iowa border), you'll find yourself in Wisconsin cheese country.

SOURCES AND RESOURCES

For information, maps, and brochures contact the Visitor Information Centers at 828 N Broadway and 161 W Wisconsin (273-3950, 276-6080). The public service bureau in the lobby of the Journal Building, 4th and State, is also helpful.

All telephone numbers are in the 414 area code unless otherwise indicated.

For Local Coverage – *Milwaukee Sentinel,* morning daily; Milwaukee *Journal,* afternoon daily.

CLIMATE AND CLOTHES: Summer and fall are generally pleasant, but expect sudden change when the wind shifts to the east. Even in July or August, pack a sweater. In winter, be prepared for bitter winds. The sub-zero cold is formidable.

GETTING AROUND: Bus – During the summer, a shuttlebus runs from the lakefront to the courthouse, mostly along Wisconsin Avenue. For information on bus schedules, contact Milwaukee County Transit System, 4212 W Highland Blvd. (344-6711).

Taxi – There are taxi stands at most major hotels, but we recommend phoning Yellow Cab Co-op (271-1800).

Car Rental – Most major car rental firms are represented. For a reliable local car rental agency, contact Selig Ford, 10200 W Arthur Ave., West Allis (327-2300), or Econo-Lease, 3504 W Wisconsin Ave. (933-1040).

MUSEUMS: The Milwaukee Public Museum, Milwaukee County Historical Society Museum, and Milwaukee War Memorial and Art Center are described in *Special Places*. Milwaukee has other museums a-plenty, among them:

Experimental Aircraft Association Museum, 11311 W Forest Home Ave. (425-4860).

Brooks Stevens Auto Museum, 10325 N Port Washington Rd. (241-4185).

Old World Wisconsin, 25 miles SW in Eagle, Wisconsin (425-4860).

MAJOR COLLEGES AND UNIVERSITIES: Marquette University (13,000 students) 11th and 18th Sts. on Wisconsin Ave. (224-7700); University of Wisconsin–Milwaukee (25,000 students) Kenwood Blvd. and Downer Ave. (963-1122).

SPECIAL EVENTS: *Summerfest* is held every June and July on the lakefront. Amusement park rides, rock and jazz concerts are part of the celebrations. *Lakefront Festival of the Arts* is held outdoors near the Milwaukee Art Center in the middle of June with music, food, arts and crafts exhibits. The *Wisconsin State Fair* takes place for two weeks in mid-August on the fairgrounds adjoining route I-94 west of downtown. The weekend before Thanksgiving, *Holiday Folk Fair* features ethnic food, music and entertainment. MECCA complex, Kilbourn Ave.

SPORTS: Baseball – Milwaukee *Brewers* play at County Stadium, 201 S 46th St. (933-9000).

Football – Green Bay *Packers* play at County Stadium, 201 S 46th St. (342-2717).

Basketball – Milwaukee *Bucks* and Marquette *Warriors* play at the Arena, 500 W Kilbourne Ave. (271-2750).

Hockey – Milwaukee *Admirals* also play at the Arena.

Polo – Sundays in summer Milwaukee's polo teams compete at Uihlein Field, Good Hope Rd. and N 70th St. (no phone).

Bicycling – Bikes can be rented from East Side Cycle and Hobby Shop, 2031 N Farwell Ave. (276-9848); Wilson Park Schwinn Cyclery, 2033 W Howard Ave. (281-4720).

Fishing – Salmon and trout as big as 30 pounds are caught in Lake Michigan, from shore and breakwater. You can use launching ramps at McKinley Marina and near South Shore Yacht Club for $3 to $5. Half-day boat charters cost about $125 for a party of six, including bait and tackle, and are offered by numerous firms (see Yellow Pages under "Fishing Parties — Charter").

Golf – The best public golf course is at Mee-Kwon Park, 6333 W Bonniwell Rd., Mequon (242-1310).

Skiing – Currie, Dretzka, and Whitnall parks have ski tows, and mostly beginners' trails. Cross-country skiers may use all county parks. The Whitnall Park trails are particularly good.

Tennis – Try North Shore Racquet Club, 5750 N Glen Park Rd. (351-2900), or Le Club, 2001 W Good Hope Rd. (352-4900). In warm weather, numerous county parks have courts available for nominal fee.

Swimming – Seven public beaches along the lakefront have lifeguards and dressing facilities. The water is usually chilly, even in August. For information on the 17 public pools, call 278-4343.

Ice skating – In winter, many parks open rinks. For year-round ice skating (indoors), try Wilson Park Center, 4001 S 20th St. (281-4610); Northridge Ice Palace, 9225 N 76th St. (354-1751).

THEATERS: For complete listings on theatrical and musical events, see local publications listed above. *Milwaukee Repertory Theater* is based at Performing Arts Center, 929 N Water St. (273-7121). *Pabst Theater* stages a variety of shows, 144 E Wells St. (271-3773). Other theaters include: *Skylight Theater,* 813 N Jefferson St. (271-8815); *Melody Top* theater featuring musicals in summer (271-8815). Tickets and information are available through Sears stores as well as theaters' box offices.

MUSIC: *Milwaukee Symphony, Milwaukee Ballet Company,* and *Florentine Opera Company* play at Performing Arts Center, 929 N Water St. (273-7121). "Music Under the Stars" concerts are held in Washington and Humboldt Parks on Friday and Saturday nights in July and August.

NIGHTCLUBS AND NIGHTLIFE: For jazz, visit *Bombay Bicycle Club,* Marc Plaza Hotel, 509 W Wisconsin Ave. (271-7250); *Jazz Gallery,* 932 E Center St. (263-5718).

SINS: When it comes to *lust* in Milwaukee, you may find yourself in something of a bind (no pun intended).

Gluttony takes rather a strange form in this Midwestern city, with Milwaukee boasting the largest per capita consumption of popcorn anywhere in the world. If this sounds sissy to you, you might consider it is also the largest consumer of brandy in the entire US, though residents make a habit of cutting their drinks with 7-Up or sugared club soda.

If you want a *sloth*ful afternoon, grab your binoculars and head off to the *Schlitz Audubon Center*, 1111 E Brown Deer Rd. There are plenty of nature walks to stroll along and an amazing variety of birds to spy on. And when the exertion gets to be too much for you, it is easy enough to find an old reliable tree to curl up under for a lazy afternoon nap.

LOCAL SERVICES: Business Services – National Business Offices, 2300 N Mayfair Rd. (259-9110); also at 2040 W Wisconsin Ave. (933-0636); Central Dictation Service, 610 N Water St. (271-6040).

Mechanics – Midtowne Mobil Servicenter, 2630 W Wisconsin Ave. (342-7726); Suburban Motors, Cedarburg (377-1000); for foreign cars, Tosa Imports, 6102 W North Ave. (771-2340).

Babysitting – A-Able Baby and Child Care Service (276-4083), or see newspaper classifieds.

■ **THE BEERS THAT MADE MILWAUKEE FAMOUS:** If you're wondering where the smell of malt is coming from, follow your nose to one of the big breweries, where you'll be escorted through the facilities and given samples of the frothy wares (unless you're a child, in which case you only get to look): Miller's, 3939 W Highland Blvd. (931-2000); Pabst, 917 Juneau Ave. (347-7300). All welcome visitors except on holidays when everyone stays home testing the product.

BEST IN TOWN

CHECKING IN: Milwaukee's hotels range from the elegant, older Pfister and the new Hyatt Regency to the functional Red Carpet Inn near the airport. You can expect to pay between $50 and $80 for a double at those places designated expensive; between $35 and $45 in the moderate category; between $20 and $30 at inexpensive places.

Pfister – Catering to visiting and local elite since the 1890s. For a while, it looked as if the 330-room establishment was sliding gently downhill, but the new owners have brought it back to the level of elegance which enchanted Enrico Caruso and several presidents. The bronze lions in the lobby are named Dick and Harry, by the way, and the best views of the lake are in rooms 8, 9, 10, or high up in the new tower. 424 E Wisconsin Ave. (273-8222). Expensive.

The Marc Plaza – The largest hotel in Milwaukee since 1927; its 540 rooms have gone through extensive renovation during their long career. Updated facilities include a heated indoor swimming pool and sauna. With advance notice, the Marc Plaza will accommodate pets, too. 509 W Wisconsin Ave. (271-7250). Expensive.

Hyatt Regency – This $28 million, 18-story luxury hotel is the first large new hotel to be built in Milwaukee in many years and has helped to end a chronic shortage of rooms for conventions. And, by no coincidence, it is located next to the downtown convention center. Topping the 485-room structure with its atrium lobby is a revolving restaurant. 4th and Kilbourn (toll-free, 800 228-9000). Expensive.

Marriott Inn – Stands out among the many motels on the outskirts of town. It has 254 rooms (one especially equipped for paraplegics) and an indoor heated pool. 375 S Moorland Rd., Brookfield (786-1100). Expensive to moderate.

Red Carpet Inn – Near the airport, adjoining a convention hall, with 400 rooms, two heated swimming pools, handball, tennis and racquetball courts. If you're intrigued by Milwaukee's favorite sport, you'll be delighted to find out the Red Carpet Inn is close to a bowling alley. 4747 S Howell Ave. (481-8000). Moderate.

Hilton Inn – Overlooking the Milwaukee River, this 164-room hostelry includes such amenities as king-sized beds and an indoor pool. The adjoining *Anchorage* restaurant is noted for its seafood. On the Milwaukee River, near the Hampton Ave. exit of Interstate 43. Expensive.

EATING OUT: Visiting Milwaukee without sampling the Wiener schnitzel would be like going to New Orleans' French Quarter and living on Big Macs. You could do it, but your sanity would be suspect. There used to be a saying that you could get any kind of food in Milwaukee as long as it was German, but these days you can feast at Polish, Chinese, Italian, Serbian, and American restaurants as well. Expect to pay between $25 and $35 for two at those places listed as expensive; between $20 and $25, in the moderate category; under $20 in the inexpensive bracket. Prices don't include drinks, wine, or tips.

Karl Ratzsch's – Ranked as one of Milwaukee's top dining spots for many years, specializing in Teutonic cuisine since the days when the city called itself the German Athens. Open daily. Reservations advisable Fridays and Saturdays. Major credit cards. 320 E Mason St. (276-2720). Expensive.

Mader's – Another family-run place going back to shortly after the century's turn, decorated in Bavarian style. For years, Gus Mader offered a reward to anyone who could finish his 3½-pound pork shank. The prize? Another 3½-pound pork shank, to be eaten in the same sitting. Open daily. Reservations recommended on Fridays and Saturdays. 1037 N 3rd St. (271-3377). Expensive.

John Ernst's Café – Even older and still a favorite of members of the brewing aristocracy, serving since 1878. Decorated with steins, German clocks, and posters. You can get steak, but to do as the local populace does it's better to order sauerbraten mit dumplings, ja? Closed Mondays. Reservations advisable Fridays and Saturdays. 600 E Ogden Ave. (273-5918). Expensive.

Pfister Hotel's English Room – We might as well warn you from the outset — this place is fairly exotic for Milwaukee. If you suddenly develop an overwhelming craving for crêpes flambées or pheasant with truffles, this is the place. Flaming dishes are prepared at your table with appropriate theatrical flourish. Open daily. Major credit cards. Reservations necessary on Fridays and Saturdays. 424 E Wisconsin Ave. (273-8222). Expensive.

La Rôtisserie and Polaris – These two new restaurants are located in the new *Hyatt Regency* hotel. The former overlooks the 18-story lobby/atrium and specializes in duck roasted on a spit. The latter, revolving slowly atop the *Hyatt's* roof, offers a more limited menu but a better view. Open daily. Reservations recommended. Major credit cards. 4th and Kilbourn (276-1234). Expensive.

Kosta's White Manor – Milwaukee's best Greek restaurant, Kosta's is known for its shish kebab, rice, souvlaki, and bellydancers. You eat the shish kebab, rice, and souvlaki, and you watch the bellydancers. Open daily. Reservations necessary on weekends. Major credit cards. 1234 E Juneau Ave. (272-4029); and at 146 W Michigan (224-0910). Moderate.

Public Natatorium – Back in the days when indoor plumbing was a luxury, this was a public bathhouse. Now dolphins cavort in the pool while tropical birds perch overhead and guests watch from two dining levels. Light meals — sandwiches, hamburgers, and quiche — are served on the lower level; and full course dinners — steak, seafood, and veal variations — on the upper. Open daily. Reservations recommended. Major credit cards. 1646 S 4th St., just off Interstate 94 (645-4449). Expensive to inexpensive.

Toy's Chinatown – The family that owns this elaborate downtown Chinese restaurant has been serving Milwaukee residents for three generations, so when you eat here, you're not just getting egg rolls, you're getting tradition. Unless you order hundred-year-old duck eggs, you can be sure of fresh Cantonese dishes, like sweet and sour shrimp, spare ribs, and chow mein. Open daily. Reservations recommended on weekends. Major credit cards. 830 N 3rd St. (271-5166). Moderate.

Old Town – This is a Serbian restaurant where you can dine to the tune of tinkling tamburitzas. Fine, you say, but what is Serbian food? Well you might ask. We did, and were delighted to find it means sizzling lamb dishes cooked somewhat spicier than similar Greek and Turkish dishes. Closed Mondays. Reservations advised on weekends. Major credit cards. 522 W Lincoln Ave. (672-0206). Moderate.

Jake's Delicatessen – If corned beef on rye appeals to you more than goose à la Tivoli or souvlaki, head for Jake's Delicatessen. All kinds of people eat here, from local millionaires to penniless kreplach lovers. You can sit at a booth, at a counter, or take your pastrami sandwich with you in a paper bag. Try the specials — they're giant knockwurstlike sausages. Open daily. Reservations advised. No credit cards. 1634 W North Ave. (562-1272). Inexpensive.

Bavarian Inn – This inn sits in a park owned by Germanic clubs, but its dining room is open to the public daily except Mondays. The food is good, the atmosphere informal, and Sunday buffet is one of the best bargains in town. You can help yourself to as much as you like, so make sure you bring a big appetite to do it justice. Closed Mondays. Reservations advised on weekends. Major credit cards. Take the Silver Spring exit from I-43 north, turn south on N Port Washington Rd., then west on Lexington to 700 W Lexington Ave. (964-0300). Inexpensive.

MINNEAPOLIS-ST. PAUL

Describing the Twin Cities is like describing your children: They can be very different and yet you love them for their unique qualities; and you can never forget that they are products of much the same history. Vibrant and culturally eclectic, Minneapolis and St. Paul complement one another, each lending something extra to the other's character.

Just how these characters differ may not be as apparent to the visitor as it is heartfelt by the resident. But even long-time Minneapolis residents get lost in St. Paul (or say they do), and they are quick to reassure the outsider that people from St. Paul get just as confused in Minneapolis.

Minneapolis is the larger of the two cities, and has been for almost a century, but St. Paul is the state's capital. St. Paul is the older, settled in the 1850s by Irish and German Catholics, the city with a tradition of "old wealth" that, by reputation at least, looks down its nose at nouveau riche Minneapolis; but as an old industrial and railroad center, St. Paul suffers more pollution than its twin, which has cleaner industries and more room to grow.

In the past decade, however, St. Paul has enjoyed an enthusiastic revival. A large-scale redevelopment brought $903 million in new buildings to the downtown area. Town Square Park is a four-level, glass-enclosed park, filled with flowing streams, waterfalls, and trees. Fine shops and enticing eateries are just a skywalk away from 100 retail stores, professional services, and government offices. Grand Avenue and the Ramsey Hill redevelopment combine 2 miles of epicurean delights and innovative shops with restorations of Victorian architecture in F. Scott Fitzgerald's old stomping ground.

As for the flamboyant twin, Minneapolis, Nicollet Mall is the hub and heart of downtown shopping and business. The city retains its natural beauty through an outstanding park system, while creating residential neighborhoods of distinct character and ethnic variety.

Located at the junction of the Mississippi and Minnesota Rivers, the Twin Cities region was discovered by French explorers in the late 17th century. It remained relatively undeveloped until the 1850s, when the Indian territory west of the Mississippi was opened for settlement. Situated at the first navigable point on the Mississippi, Minneapolis and St. Paul became major shipping points for timber, flour, furs, and other natural resources.

South of Franklin Street, St. Paul and Minneapolis are divided by the Mississippi, but Twin Cities residents don't perceive the river as the boundary. The University of Minnesota campus spans both sides of the river, but retains a Minneapolis address. About 50 miles in diameter, the metro area absorbs diversified industries and businesses that have spread out throughout the two cities; St. Paul has attracted more of the steel and chemical plants over the years, while Minneapolis is home of cleaner industries like electronics. Traditional rivals, in recent years the two cities have opted for a joint approach toward solving mutual urban problems. Water, pollution, sewage, and transportation are dealt with efficiently on a "metro area" basis.

Although St. Paul initially led in population, Minneapolis surpassed its twin around 1880 and has been Minnesota's largest city ever since. With a population of 2 million, the unified Twin Cities metro area is the third fastest growing urban region in the United States — and the fifteenth largest. Its 936 lakes and 513 parks contribute to Minneapolis–St. Paul's unusual pastoral beauty.

Part of the charm of the metro area can be directly attributed to an almost religious sense of tithing on the part of the more responsible corporations and their principals. They feel, perhaps, that the quality of life in the Twin Cities is unique and worth supporting. The first car pools in the United States were started by the 3M Corporation to help employees conserve energy. Corporate and individual response to the arts is exemplary; perhaps business leaders realize that the relative isolation of the Twin Cities (at least 400 miles from another major city) requires a full measure of cultural and sports activities to provide the nonbusiness pleasures demanded by talented employees.

The cultural scene in Minneapolis–St. Paul is outstanding. The world-famous Guthrie Theater makes its home here, as does the Minnesota Orchestra — a full-time symphony. The only full-time chamber orchestra in the United States, the St. Paul Chamber Orchestra, performs to packed houses. The Minneapolis Institute of Arts, the Walker Arts Center, the Twin Cities' two science centers, the Minnesota Opera, and the cities' many historical collections and art galleries are responsible for Minneapolis–St. Paul's reputation as the cultural center of the Midwest. And the Minneapolis radio program *Prairie Home Companion,* a delightful take-off on the Grand Ole Opry that is broadcast Saturdays on National Public Radio, is attracting a national audience.

Minneapolis–St. Paul residents don't even mind the severe winter weather. They enjoy it with a vigor by snowmobiling, ice fishing, and skiing. Twin Citians like where they live no matter what the season.

MINNEAPOLIS–ST. PAUL AT-A-GLANCE

SEEING THE CITY: From the top of the controversial 57-story IDS (Investors Diversified Services) building (Nicollet Mall and 8th St., Mpls.), you'll be able to see the entire metro area spread below. You can't miss the IDS center — it's 20 stories higher than anything else. St. Paul is built on seven hills, like Rome, and while there's no place as romantic as Hollywood's Mulholland Drive, there are a few drives with good views. One of the best is the Pennsylvania Avenue hill.

SPECIAL PLACES: The most extraordinary feature of downtown Minneapolis and St. Paul is their interior skyways, an interconnected belt of pedestrian malls and escalators lacing in and out of shops, banks, and restaurants at the second-story level. When it's below zero, you may still walk around comfortably without a coat. At street level, courtyards, gardens, fountains, and sculpture form attractive plazas. In Minneapolis, travelers may check in at one of three hotels connected to the skyway, the *Marquette,* the *Radisson,* and the *North Star Inn.* St. Paul's skyway connects to the Radisson Plaza (see *Checking In).*

MINNEAPOLIS

The Minneapolis Institute of Arts – Architecturally classical, the Institute houses Old Masters, Chinese and Egyptian art, Revere silver, and historical exhibits. In addition to the museum collections, the Institute's Society for Fine Arts presents classical films, recitals, and lectures. A model for other arts institutions around the country, the Institute is also the home of the Minneapolis College of Art and Design and the Children's Theater Company and School. Open every day. Admission charge. 2400 3rd Ave. S (870-3131).

The Guthrie Theater – Internationally acclaimed for its superb productions, the Guthrie Theater features a resident professional repertory company which presents ensemble productions of classical and modern drama. The contemporary theater building can seat more than 1,400 people in a 200-degree arc around an open stage. After a nationwide search for a hospitable metropolitan environment in which to locate a repertory theater, Sir Tyrone Guthrie selected Minneapolis. His choice has been borne out by the enthusiastic, loving support of audiences and patrons. The theatrical season generally runs from May to February. Concerts are performed throughout the year. 725 Vineland Pl. (377-2824).

Walker Arts Center – Named after T. B. Walker, a local patron of the arts, the Center, located in the Guthrie building, complements the classical Institute of Arts by focusing on post-Impressionist and contemporary art. The Walker also features alternating exhibits, innovative film programs, and concerts. Pretheater dinners are served in the Walker restaurant. Closed Mondays. Free except for special exhibits. 725 Vineland Pl. (375-7500).

Minnehaha Park – In his poem "Hiawatha," Longfellow immortalized the "laughing waters" of Minnehaha Falls along the Mississippi. In addition to the splendor of the Falls, you can picnic near a statue of Minnehaha herself and brave Hiawatha. Free. Minnehaha Pkwy. and Hiawatha Ave. S.

Minneapolis Grain Exchange – An ornate hall the size of a large school gym, the Exchange is a loud, hectic place where futures and samples of actual grains are bought and sold. You can take a guided tour through the world's largest grain exchange, but you must make reservations in advance. Visitors' balcony open daily. Tours, Mondays–Fridays. 400 4th St. S (336-6361).

Orchestra Hall – Music has had an appreciative audience in the Twin Cities since the turn of the century. The Hall houses the Minnesota Orchestra, formerly the Minneapolis Symphony, an orchestra which played its first concert in 1903 and has been playing classical and symphonic pop music to responsive audiences ever since. Though spartan in appearance, the new Orchestra Hall is renowned for its superior acoustics. 1111 Nicollet Ave. (371-5656).

Minnesota Zoo – Set in the rolling hills of Apple Valley, the new Minnesota Zoo opened in Spring '78. This 500-acre, state-funded zoological park provides a natural environment for Siberian tigers, musk oxen, moose, and other northern animals. A pair of beluga whales joins other aquatic species in the Aquarium, and a five-story indoor tropical environment houses jungle fauna and flora. Zoo lovers will find this one among the nation's best. Open daily. Admission charge. 12101 Johnny Cake Ridge Rd., Apple Valley, 25 minutes south of city on Hwy. 35 (432-9000).

ST. PAUL

Como Park – Vividly beautiful, Minneapolis–St. Paul has a multitude of parks. The largest is St. Paul's Como Park which dates from Victoria's reign. A 70-acre lake, a small zoo, a golf course, and children's rides contribute to Como Park's popularity. In addition, there are special floral gardens and a conservatory where summer concerts are held. Open daily. Free. Lexington Pkwy. and West Como Blvd. (zoo: 488-4041; floral: 489-1740).

State Capitol – St. Paul is Minnesota's political center, and its capitol is one of the most important buildings in the state. Set on a hill, the giant dome of the capitol — a replica of one designed by Michelangelo in Rome — is one of Minnesota's outstanding landmarks. More than 25 varieties of marble, limestone, sandstone, and granite were used to construct the building. The Minnesota Historical Society building sits on the edge of the capitol grounds. Founded in 1849, ten years before Minnesota became a state, the Society houses records of pioneer days. Open daily. Free. University Ave. between Wabasha and Cedar Sts. (296-2881).

St. Paul's Cathedral – The center of the Roman Catholic archdiocese, this Cathedral is a replica of St. Peter's Cathedral in Rome. Architecturally noted for its 175-foot-high dome and a central rose window, the Cathedral has a special "Shrine of the Nations" where visitors from all around the world can meditate and pray. Open daily. Free. 239 Selby Ave. (225-6563).

St. Paul Arts and Science Center – This three-and-a-half-million-dollar complex combines a 635-seat theater for the performing arts, a 300-seat auditorium, an art gallery, a rooftop lounge, and the pièce de résistance, the science museum. Featuring natural history, environmental, geological exhibits and films, the science center is immensely popular with residents. Open daily. Free. 30 E 10th St. (221-9488).

William L. McKnight Science Center – The Science Center — named after the founding father of the 3M Company — is among the most advanced science centers in the US. Part of the Science Museum of Minnesota, the high point of this new science complex is its "omnitheatre" — a floor-to-ceiling hemispheric screen surrounding the audience and tilted at 30° so that viewers will see the screen in front of them rather than above, as in conventional planetarium-type theaters. Closed Mondays. Admission charge. 505 Wabasha (221-9488).

Fort Snelling State Park – The oldest landmark in the Twin Cities, one of the first military posts west of the Mississippi. Not very far west, however: Fort Snelling sits high on a bluff overlooking the junction of the Mississippi and Minnesota Rivers. You can see what life was like here during the 1820s. People in costume demonstrate early crafts, and parade in military formation. Fife and drum bands perform in summer. Open daily June to September, weekends in May and October. Free. Highways 5 and 55, six miles southwest of the city (726-9430).

■ **EXTRA SPECIAL:** *St. Croix Valley,* 25 miles northeast of Minneapolis–St. Paul, offers several stops for a day's outing. Stillwater, Minnesota's first town site, is within easy striking distance of the Afton Alps, Trollhaugen, and Snowcrest mountains for skiers. In Stillwater, visit the *Grand Garage and Gallery* on Main Street, with shops and galleries. It has food, but a better eating-stop is *Brine's Meat Market and Lunchroom,* which has *The Employees Lunchroom* upstairs, open to *anybody* employed *anywhere,* with great bratwurst, pastrami, and chili. On the Wisconsin side of the tour is Somerset, which has one of the greatest summer activities in the entire world: tubing down the Apple River. You get carted upriver about four miles, plunked into an inner tube, and sent drifting back to Somerset. The river flows quickly at the outset but widens and slows down, and the ride is tranquil into town.

SOURCES AND RESOURCES

The Greater Minneapolis Chamber of Commerce and the Minneapolis Convention and Tourist Commission have an information booth in the IDS building, 15 S 5th St. (348-4330). For a free copy of the Minnesota Calendar of Events, contact the Minnesota Tourist Information Center, 480 Cedar St. (296-5029).

All telephone numbers are in the 612 area code unless otherwise indicated.

For Local Coverage – *Minneapolis Tribune,* morning daily; *St. Paul Pioneer Press,* morning daily; *St. Paul Dispatch,* afternoon daily. *The Reader* (distributed free in the Mall and downtown hotels) lists activities in the Twin Cities. *Mpls.–St. Paul* and *Twin Cities* magazines, available monthly at newsstands, give full details on who's who and what's what.

Twin Cities: Guide to "Where It's At" by Ann Ryan (Dorne, $5.95).

For Food – Check *Whitman's Restaurant Guide to Minnesota* (Nodin Press, $2.45).

CLIMATE AND CLOTHES: In winter, be prepared for the worst. The average winter temperature is 19°, but it can drop to 35° below zero, and snow has been known to fall as early as October. Summer temperatures are generally in the 70s and 80s.

GETTING AROUND: Bus – Minneapolis–St. Paul bus systems are a model of efficiency studied by other cities. They run from 6 AM to 1 AM. Express buses make the trip between Minneapolis and St. Paul in 15 minutes. Passengers' queries handled by an extensive switchboard. Metropolitan Transit Commission, 3118 Nicollet Ave., Mpls. (827-7733).

Taxi – As in many other cities, taxis are impossible to get when you really need them and plentiful when you don't. Most are radio-dispatched. There are some taxi stands. The largest cab company is Yellow Taxi, 127 1st Ave. NE (379-7171); in St. Paul, 1759 Selby Ave. (222-4433).

Car Rental – All major firms represented. A good local agency is Dollar Rent-A-Car, at the airport (861-2232).

MUSEUMS: The pride of Minneapolis–St. Paul is the Twin Cities' cultural wealth, and a visit to the many fine museums is well worth it. The Minneapolis Institute of Arts, the Walker Arts Center, the St. Paul Arts and Science Center, and the new McKnight Science Center are described in greater detail in *Special Places*. Some others are:

Science Museum and Planetarium, 300 Nicollet Mall, Mpls. (372-6543).

Bell Museum of Natural History, 17th and University SE, Mpls. (373-2423).

Minneapolis Transportation Museum, W 42nd St. and Queen Ave., S Mpls. (no phone).

Minnesota Museum of Art, 305 St. Peter St., St. Paul (227-7613).

Ramsey House, 265 S Exchange St., St. Paul (296-0100).

Musical Instruments Museum, 1124 Dionne, Roseville (a suburb of St. Paul) (488-4303).

Mayo Clinic Medical Museum, in Rochester, 90 miles southeast of Mpls.–St. Paul.

MAJOR COLLEGES AND UNIVERSITIES: About 55,000 students attend the University of Minnesota, one of the Big Ten universities; the campus sprawls across the east and west banks of the Mississippi. Escorted tours are available. University Ave. SE (373-1099).

SPECIAL EVENTS: The *Aquatennial Festival* in late July, features sailboat races, a torchlight parade, and "Queen of the Lakes" beauty contest. *Minnesota State Fair,* 11 days, ending Labor Day at Como and Snelling Aves., St. Paul. *St. Paul Winter Carnival,* late January or early February, is a citywide celebration.

SPORTS: Professional Sports – The new 60,000-seat Hubert H. Humphrey Stadium houses major-league baseball and football teams. The Stadium is at 500 11th Ave. S, and for information on games call: *Twins* (baseball, 854-4040), *Vikings* (football, 941-9060). The Metropolitan Sports Center, 7901 Cedar Ave. S, is home of the *North Stars* hockey team (853-9300).

Golf – There are nine courses in Minneapolis–St. Paul. Best is Meadowbrook Golf Course, 201 Meadowbrook Rd. at Goodrich Ave., Mpls. (927-2077).

Fishing – Twelve fishing lakes in the Twin Cities metro area; the best is Lake Minnetonka which has 177 miles of shoreline. 15 miles west on Hwy. 12. Within the city limits, Lake Calhoun has a fishing dock.

Skiing – Best are Afton Alps Ski Area, Inver Hills, and Buck Hill.

Biking – There are bike trails around Lake Harriet, Lake Calhoun, and Lake of the Isles in Minneapolis, Lakes Como and Phalen in St. Paul. Bicycles may be rented from Pedals and Spokes, 1611 W Lake St., Mpls. (822-2228) and at Lake Como, St. Paul (488-1477).

Swimming – There are public swimming beaches at 23 lakes in and around the Twin Cities area. Open June to August.

Ice Skating – The cities clear, test, and maintain outdoor rinks on many of the lakes. Indoor ice arenas offer some free time for public skating. Consult telephone directory for locations and numbers.

Tennis – There are many lighted, outdoor courts as well as indoor courts (ranging from $6.50 to $9 per hour) available throughout the cities.

THEATER: In addition to the *Guthrie,* Minneapolis–St. Paul has more than a dozen theaters. The universities and colleges also produce plays and musicals. Best bets for shows: *Guthrie* (377-2224); *Children's Theater Company* (874-0400); *Chimera Theater,* 30 E 10th St., St. Paul (222-4300).

MUSIC: For a complete schedule of musical happenings, check local newspapers, *St. Paul Dispatch* "Entertainment" on Thursday; *Minneapolis Star-Tribune* "Preview" on Friday. There are outdoor summer concerts at Lake Harriet in Minneapolis and at Lake Como in St. Paul.

NIGHTCLUBS AND NIGHTLIFE: *Gallivan's Downtown* in St. Paul, 354 Wabasha (227-6688), features professional entertainment and a piano bar. The *Registry Hotel,* 7901 24th Ave. S., Bloomington, provides dancing to the big band sound on Sundays. *Scotty's* is a café and disco named for F. Scott Fitzgerald, 36 S 7th St., Minneapolis (338-8311). *Duff's* caters to a sports crowd, 21 S 8th St., Minneapolis (332-3554); The *Carleton Celebrity Room,* 8350 24th Ave. S, Minneapolis (854-9300) has Las Vegas–style dinner theater with top-name performers. Bob Dylan began his singing career in the West Bank area near the University of Minnesota, where there are a number of small clubs and cafés.

Singles flock to *Maximilian's* disco club, 7717 Nicollet Ave. (866-3431), or *Ichabod's,* 7800 Computer Ave. S (831-4498).

SINS: The twin cities are blessed with one of America's finest regional theaters, the Tyrone Guthrie. *Pride* in this 1,487-seat repertory showplace reaches six to eight peaks a year, once for each production staged. It would be criminal for people who consider themselves cultured to visit Minneapolis and not see at least one of these highly professional masterpieces. Or to be in St. Paul without attending a performance of the world-famous St. Paul Chamber Orchestra.

The sin of *anger* grips Twin Citians on two main issues. The new Minnesota Zoological Garden, created by an act of the state legislature, was to be self-supporting, but instead has required continued appropriation of funds to keep it going.

The $55 million domed Hubert H. Humphrey Stadium, opened in April 1982, raises some voices as well. Twin Citians paid a liquor tax for several years for a stadium with 60,000 seats but no parking facilities or air conditioning.

LOCAL SERVICES: Business Services – Northstar Telephone and Secretarial Services, 10299 University, SE, Mpls. (784-3136); A–1 Secretarial Services, American National Bank Building, St. Paul (225-6597).

Mechanics – Fisher Shell and Towing Service provides excellent 24-hour road service at extremely reasonable prices. 1022 Hennepin Ave. (338-6953). Pat's Mobile Service, 1010 W 7th St., St. Paul (292-8482).

Babysitting – Dayton's department store, 700 Nicollet Mall, has a three-hour sitting service during store hours (375-2288). YWCA cares for children from three months to five years old. You have to make reservations 24 hours in advance. Minimum sitting assignment is four hours. 1130 Nicollet Ave. (332-0501). We Sit Better is part of a nationwide service organization, with 200 sitters on its Minneapolis staff. Minimum assignment is four hours (three at motels), and you're required to pay the sitter's transportation (375-0932). St. Paul Day Care (298-4260).

BEST IN TOWN

CHECKING IN: There are a number of places near the Minneapolis–St. Paul International Airport in Bloomington, a thriving new suburb which is quickly surpassing the downtown centers in popularity. Expect to pay around $50 or more for a double room in one of the hotels we've listed as expensive; $30 to $40 in the moderate range.

***L'hotel Sofitel* –** The first North American link in the French hotel chain offers a concierge, the latest issues of Parisian magazines, and real croissants for breakfast. Many of the 300 rooms have bidets. Continental elegance includes an indoor heated pool, sauna, babysitter service, bars, and dancing. Children under 12 admitted free, but for the rest of us it's pricey. I-494 and Hwy. 100, Bloomington (835-1900). Expensive.

***Marquette Inn* –** Connected to the interior skyway in the IDS center, the Inn offers gracious, spacious accommodations in the middle of downtown. Princess Margaret has stayed here. Steam baths in rooms. Bar, beauty shop, drugstores, café, babysitter service; 285 rooms. 710 Marquette Ave. (332-2351). Expensive.

***Sheraton-Ritz* –** An elegant modern 304-room hotel in Nicollet Mall with a top-floor cabaret and a fine view of the Mississippi. When the Metropolitan Opera plays Minneapolis–St. Paul, the cast stays here. Heated pool, barber, beauty shops, babysitter service, free parking. Children under 17 free. *The Stradivarious* restaurant offers ambitious Northern Italian food. 315 Nicollet Mall (332-2357). Expensive to moderate.

Normandy Inn – Located in the heart of downtown Minneapolis, the Normandy offers a cozy atmosphere in the midst of a metropolis. The 150-room complex occupies a full block, with adequate parking, pool, conference and banquet rooms, whirlpool and sauna. Two dining rooms; one serves full dinners, the other light lunches. 405 S 8th St. (370-1400). Expensive to moderate.

Radisson Hotels – Connected to the Minneapolis skyway, the Radisson has 533 rooms. Its cabaret features eight strolling guitarists. 45 E 7th St. (333-2181). The *Radisson South* is the tallest and largest hotel in Bloomington with 408 rooms, an indoor heated pool, a wading pool, therapeutic pool, sauna, café, bar, dancing, entertainment, free parking. I-494 and Hwy. 100, Bloomington (835-7800). *Radisson St. Paul* has 480 rooms, indoor heated pool, café, bar, entertainment, dancing, barber, beauty shops, sundeck, cabanas, in-room movies. (Three rooms for paraplegics.) 11 E Kellogg Blvd. (292-1900). The *Radisson Plaza* has 252 rooms in a 16-story solar atrium and indoor garden court and swimming pool. Town Square Park, St. Paul (291-8800). All expensive to moderate.

EATING OUT: You can find almost any kind of food in the Twin Cities area, from high-priced, exquisitely prepared Continental cuisine to Japanese food or kosher delicatessen. In fact, Minneapolis–St. Paul is considered a great eating-out town. We include a few of the better places, with prices ranging from $40 or more for a dinner for two in the expensive range, $20 to $30 in the moderate, and $20 or less, inexpensive. Prices do not include drinks, wine, or tips.

Blue Horse – Winner of innumerable awards over the years, St. Paul's most gracious, intimate restaurant is consistently cited as the Twin Cities' finest. The chef devotes full, loving attention to every dish. The pasta is specially prepared and comes highly recommended. Closed Sundays. Reservations are necessary. Major credit cards. 1355 University Ave. (645-8101). Expensive to moderate.

Lowell Inn – The closest thing to a New England inn that you'll find in the Midwest. Gracious, family-style Minnesota meals. The menu includes beef fondue and gigantic drinks are another special feature. Open daily. Reservations essential. Major credit cards. Located in Stillwater (northeast suburb of St. Paul) at 102 N 2nd St. (439-1100). Expensive.

Chouette – One of the metro area's newest French restaurants, started by a Frenchwoman who fondly remembers dining in Paris as a teenager. Her Paris-trained executive chef insists on quality preparation and presentation. The menu offers calves' brains, veal tongue, and rabbit, as well as more conservative cuisine. Closed Sundays for dinner; open for afternoon brunch. Reservations a must. Major credit cards. 739 E Lake St., Wayzata (473-4611). Expensive.

The Orion Room – High atop the IDS Center, the view from three seating levels 50 stories up is magnificent. Specialties, including rack of lamb, Châteaubriand, wild rice soup, pheasant, and Dover sole, and impressive tableside presentations enhance the spectacular setting. Open daily. Reservations suggested. Major credit cards. IDS Center, 80 S 8th St., Mpls. (372-3772). Expensive.

Charlie's Café Exceptionale – Long touted as one of the best in the Twin Cities, this restaurant has won numerous awards from *Holiday* magazine. Traditional favorites are prime ribs, sweetbreads, and poached sole. Closed Sundays. Reservations a must. Major credit cards. 701 4th Ave. S, Mpls. (333-1616). Moderate.

Fuji Ya – If you're in the mood to sample the gentle, tranquil mood and food of Japan, then this is the place. Reiko Weston, who came to the Twin Cities as a war bride, charmed discriminating diners first with conventional Japanese fare and then with showbizzy teppan yaki cuisine. The view of Lock #1 on the Mississippi complements the settling effects of the food and service. Closed Sundays. Reservations a good idea. Major credit cards. 420 1st St., Mpls. (339-2226). Moderate.

Lexington Restaurant – An unpretentious neighborhood restaurant in St. Paul, with steaks, prime ribs, lamb shanks, and seafood. Well-prepared cocktails. Reservations recommended. No credit cards. 1096 Grand Ave. (222-5878). Moderate.

Anthony's on Main – An entire development of eating establishments and specialty shops on rustic Main Street, on the Mississippi. *Anthony's Wharf:* East Coast cuisine comes to Minneapolis, offering fresh lobster, fresh scallops, rainbow trout, and swordfish. No reservations. Major credit cards. 201 SE Main St., Mpls. (378-7058). Moderate. *GuadalaHARRY's:* This popular restaurant captures the true south-of-the-border atmosphere and offers Mexican pizza and chimichangas. No reservations. Major credit cards. 201 SE Main St., Mpls. (378-2233). Inexpensive. For dessert, stop by *Häagen Dazs* for all-natural, out-of-this-world ice cream.

Peter's Grill – The definitive downtown Minneapolis café, Peter's is a hometown restaurant — B.F. (before franchise). No liquor, but plenty of pies, great homemade soups. Dinners include vegetable and salad. Prewar decor and prices. A family of five can dine for under $20. Weekdays only. No reservations necessary. No credit cards. 85 S 9th St. (333-1981). Inexpensive.

Black Forest Inn – Near the Institute of Arts, the Inn serves bratwurst and sauerkraut dinners, Wiener schnitzel, and other honest, substantial German fare. The restaurant evolved from a tavern which used to serve only beer. It still offers German beers, and you can enjoy drinking in the outdoor beer garden. The jukebox plays opera. Open daily. Reservations advised. Major credit cards. 1 E 26th St. (872-0812). Inexpensive.

Chi Chi's – Though there is often quite a wait, taking in the restaurant's famous Margaritas and its lively atmosphere, with rotating fans, sprawling plants, and stucco walls, may make the wait enjoyable. Specialties include chimichangas and Mexican fried ice cream, served in large portions and reasonably priced. Open for lunch and dinner. No reservations. Major credit cards. 7717 Nicollet Ave., Richfield (866-3433). Inexpensive.

Forepaughs – The charm and elegance of the Victorian age is preserved in this home-turned-restaurant. Both American and Continental cuisine are served in a gracious 19th-century atmosphere. Reservations advised. 276 Exchange St., St. Paul (224-5606). Inexpensive.

NASHVILLE

Hundreds of thousands of hero-worshipping country music fans from around the country come to Nashville every year, by the busload, for the afternoon or the weekend, to take a tour of the homes of the stars and cruise past the houses where Minnie Pearl, Pat Boone's parents, and dozens of others live. Afterward, when the final "ooh" is "ahed," they take in a performance of the Opry.

The Grand Ole Opry, a two-and-a-half-hour country music extravaganza which takes the title as the longest-running radio program in the US, is justifiably Nashville's biggest drawing card. Something which inspires so many people can't be all bad, and even if you hate country music, you can't fail to be moved by the spectacle. Up on stage in the very fancy Grand Ole Opry House — completed in March 1974 to the tune of some $13 million — there are guitarists in glittery, rhinestoned leisure suits; busty female vocalists with curly manes and slinky dresses (or little-girl outfits that seem strangely incongruous with the bodies underneath), or square dancers who stomp up a storm in a blizzard of ruffly white petticoats. Every time a new performer comes onstage, the fans whistle, clap, jump up and down in their seats, then scramble up the aisles to be the first to get an autograph or snap a picture. Sometimes so many flashbulbs pop off at once that it seems as if a giant strobe is flickering over the audience. Onstage, friends and families of the performers look on from church pews moved from the old Ryman Auditorium, where the Opry spent the better part of 30 years, or mill around in the wings, never bothering to make themselves inconspicuous. It's hard to tell the hangers-on from the stars, who, meanwhile, are twanging away onstage, signing autographs in the manner of true professionals.

Which they all are. If you've seen Robert Altman's film "Nashville," you've got a pretty fair idea that this city is far from being the simple hillbilly heaven portrayed in the songs that pour out of the one-square-mile area of South Nashville known as Music Row. The country music business, which is concentrated here, is a multi-million dollar industry, getting bigger all the time. There are over 70 recording studios, 250 music publishers, 100 talent agencies, and countless record pressing plants, marketing firms, and production houses. The Opry House is the largest broadcast studio in the world. TV shows by the score are taped in Nashville. The odds are even that when you come for a visit you can sit in on a taping, and when you do, you'll find out why audiences you hear at the beginning of some live TV shows are clapping so madly: Studio people close to the stage urge them on like cheerleaders.

But for all that, Nashville is also a Southern city, with all the traditions of gentility that characterize the breed, and you don't have to stay here for very long before you understand from whence came the nickname, "the Athens of the South." The town that annually goes berserk for the Country Music

Fan Fair is also home to many colleges and universities, countless plantation mansions, and the world's only replica of the Greek Parthenon. There are symphony orchestra concerts and lovely old suburban neighborhoods which, by no stretch of the imagination, could you call nouveau riche. A Nashville botanical garden boasts one of the finest growths of boxwood in the US.

Like other American cities of half a million, Nashville has its slums. And its eyesores: highways lined with what seems like an endless procession of fast-food joints, chain coffee shops with plastic signs, streams of neon lights, and garishly illuminated used-car lots. But beyond that, and beyond the occasional silliness of the country music mania, there is something about the place that can't fail to catch your imagination. There's unabashed, unpretentious good humor almost everywhere you go. There are dozens and dozens of nifty little Southern-cooking restaurants (not much to look at, but how they do cook) and hole-in-the-wall nightclubs with stages so small that fiddlers can barely keep from bowing the banjo players.

NASHVILLE AT-A-GLANCE

SEEING THE CITY: On a clear day, from the observation deck on the 31st floor of the Life & Casualty Building, you can see 26 miles in all directions. Even rainy days can be interesting: A peculiarity of the building's L-shaped design makes raindrops fall up instead of down. Admission charge. 4th and Church Sts. (244-9300).

SPECIAL PLACES: The outstanding attractions are clustered within a couple of miles of the downtown area, and ranged along the southern and eastern outskirts of the metropolitan area.

DOWNTOWN

Fort Nashborough – A partial reconstruction of the pioneer fort where present-day Nashville began back in 1779, when a small band of settlers under the leadership of James Robertson arrived on the west bank of the Cumberland River. In five cabins, costumed guides show how the settlers chopped wood, tended gardens, carded and spun wool, made candles and lye soap, cooked meals (in pots hanging from iron hooks in immense stone fireplaces), and entertained themselves with singing and square dancing. Closed Sundays and Mondays. Free. 170 1st Ave. N at Church St. (255-8192).

The Ryman Auditorium – Home of the Grand Ole Opry between 1943 and March 16, 1974. You can climb up onto its creaky wood stage, and see mementos of the stars of days gone by. The Ryman, Mecca to country music lovers, was built in 1891 by a riverboat captain, Tom Ryman, who had found religion and wanted to help others do the same. Admission charge. 116 5th Ave. N (749-1422).

The Country Music Hall of Fame and Museum – Memorabilia of country music stars (Elvis Presley's solid gold Cadillac, comedienne Minnie Pearl's straw hat complete with dangling price tag, Chet Atkins' first guitar, etc.) — interesting more for the reverence with which your fellow visitors view it all than the objects themselves (unless you're a country music fan). Admission charge. On Music Row at 4 Music Square E (244-2522).

Studio B – Elvis Presley, Chet Atkins, Charley Pride, Eddy Arnold, and a score of other greats recorded for RCA at this famous studio in the 50s and 60s. Guides will tell you its history, talk about the Nashville recording industry, and let you act as a recording engineer at a "mix-down" session, in which the 16 tracks recorded by the artists are put onto two tracks before delivery to the record presser. Admission available only to Hall of Fame visitors. Small charge. 806 17th Ave. S (242-9414). Note: Not many active recording studios admit guests. If any open sessions exist, you'll find them by telephoning individual studios, listed in the Yellow Pages.

The Parthenon – A full-scale replica of the ancient Greek building; the building material is not marble but a steel-reinforced conglomerate. Its four bronze doors are the largest in the world. Inside, displays include reproductions of the Elgin marbles, plus pre-Columbian art and various changing exhibits. Closed Mondays. Free. In Centennial Park at 25th Ave. N and West End Ave. (259-6358).

EAST

The Grand Ole Opry – Over 55 years old, this long country-music-star-studded spectacular is well worth the planning it takes to get tickets. More than a third of the 60-odd acts under contract to the Opry will perform in a given night, and you're bound to like some if not all of them. There are shows Fridays at 7:30 PM and Saturdays at 6:30 and 9:30 PM, and matinees and a second Friday show during the peak season months when Opryland USA is open. Reserved-seat tickets sell out months in advance for summer shows, weeks ahead the rest of the year. General admission tickets go on sale Tuesdays at 9 AM the week of the show, at the box office only. The nearer to summer, the closer to box office opening time you must arrive to get a ticket. Information Center, 2802 Opryland Dr. (zip 37214; 889-3060).

Opryland USA – Music from Broadway and the hit parade and just about any other kind of melody that has ever been called music, along with foot-tapping bluegrass, carry out the American-music-is-great motif at this new-style family theme park. Open daily in summer, and weekends in spring and fall. Admission charge. Information Center, 2802 Opryland Dr. (889-6611).

SOUTH

Belle Meade Mansion – Inside the century-old rock walls that edge the 24-acre estate, Belle Meade Mansion is just a shadow of its former self, but even its shadow is impressive enough: There are immense pillars, a beautifully balanced portico, ornate plaster cornices outside, and, inside, Adamesque moldings and a splendid double parlor. The estate was once the home of Iroquois, a horse who until 1954 was the only American-bred winner of the English Derby. Open daily. Admission charge. Harding Rd., US 70 S (352-7350).

Travellers' Rest – The remarkably finely detailed home of John Overton, one of Nashville's first settlers, restored, expanded, and filled up with furniture, letters, and memorabilia that tell the story of Tennessee's settlement and civilization. Open daily. Admission charge. 636 Farrell Pkwy. six miles south of downtown Nashville via Franklin Rd., which is US 31 (832-2962).

Tennessee Botanical Gardens and Fine Arts Center – Cheekwood, a Georgian-style mansion built in the 1930s, is now a museum with art shows and traveling exhibits. You may be more impressed, though, by the elegant Palladian window, or the chandelier (once the property of a countess), or the swooping spiral staircase (which used to be a fixture of Queen Charlotte's palace at Kew). Outdoors: formal gardens, a wisteria arbor, wildflower gardens, a Japanese sand garden, greenhouses, horticultural exhibits, and an outstanding boxwood garden. Closed Mondays. Admission charge. Cheek Rd., seven miles west of town on rt. 100 (356-3306).

■ **EXTRA SPECIAL:** You'll see the announcements for tours of the homes of the stars on big billboards on the way into town, and even if you ordinarily hate group excursions, you may like these. While you're getting a glimpse into what makes Nashville tick, you can also enjoy some delightful Southern-accented speech and the colorful language that seems to be the mark of Nashville citizenry. Each of the following offers several all-day, half-day, or evening tours: Gray Line, 501 Broadway (244-7330); Grand Ole Opry Tours, 2810 Opryland Dr. (889-9490); Sound City Tours, 25 Music Sq. W (269-3080); Country and Western Tours, 2416 Music Valley Dr. (883-5555); and Stardust Tours, 1504 Demonbruen St. (244-2335).

SOURCES AND RESOURCES

For brochures, maps, general tourist information, and all kinds of other help, your best bet is to write the Nashville Area Chamber of Commerce, 161 4th Ave. N, Nashville 37219; to phone 259-3900; or to stop in at the official Tourist Information Center at Exit 85 on I-65 N just east of downtown. The *Nashville Visitor's Guide,* published annually by the Chamber in conjunction with *Nashville!* Magazine, is as comprehensive a city guide as you'll see anywhere.

All telephone numbers are in the 615 area code unless otherwise indicated.

For Local Coverage – The *Tennessean,* morning daily; the *Nashville Banner,* afternoon daily. The former publishes a complete events listing on Fridays and Sundays; the latter on Thursdays. *Nashville!* Magazine publishes a monthly events calendar. All are available at newsstands.

For Food – Check the *Nashville Visitor's Guide* or *Nashville!* Magazine for ideas.

CLIMATE AND CLOTHES: Nashville's weather hovers around the 80s in summer, dropping into the 40s and 30s between December and February. It gets humid in the summer, and you can expect thunderstorms from March through late summer.

GETTING AROUND: Bus – You need a car to manage conveniently. However, buses are available (route information, 242-4433).

Taxi – Nashville's principal cab companies are Yellow (256-0101) and Checker (254-5031).

Car Rental – Major national car rental agencies can be found in Nashville.

MUSEUMS: In addition to those described above in *Special Places*, you'll want to investigate the following:

The Tennessee State Museum, in the Tennessee Performing Arts Center (741-2692), with a branch devoted to military history in the War Memorial Bldg., 7th and Union Sts. (741-5383).

The Cumberland Museum and Science Center, 800 Ridley Ave. (259-6099).

MAJOR COLLEGES AND UNIVERSITIES: Of the dozen-plus colleges and universities in Nashville, Vanderbilt, West End at 21st Ave. (322-7311), is perhaps the most famous as its nickname, "the Harvard of the South," would suggest. However, the city is also home to Fisk University, 17th Ave. N (329-8500), one of the most noted of the predominantly black colleges in the US.

SPECIAL EVENTS: The *Annual Opryland American Music Festival* brings bands, choruses, and lots of extra music to the theme park every year in May (see *Special Places*). Also in May is the *Tennessee Crafts Fair*, one of the largest shows in the South. For information, write PO Box 120713, Nashville, TN 37212 (833-9075). The second Saturday of May is the *Iroquois Steeplechase,* the daylong series of eight races that's the oldest amateur steeplechase meet in the US. Old Hickory Blvd. in Percy Warner Park, 11 miles south of Nashville. For information: PO Box 22711, Nashville 37202 (373-2130). The *International Country Music Fan Fair,* a June event, brings thousands for five days of spectacular shows, autograph sessions, concerts and a Grand Masters Fiddling Contest. For more information write: Fan Fair Information, Grand Ole Opry, 2808 Opryland Dr., Nashville 37214 (889-3060). In October, there's the *National Quartet Convention,* five days of top-name gospel singing at the Nashville Municipal Auditorium. For information: National Quartet Convention, PO Box 23190, Nashville, TN 37202 (242-4457). December's *Trees of Christmas* at Cheekwood is an exhibition of Christmas trees from around the world. Information: Horticultural Society of Davidson County, Botanic Hall, Cheek Rd., Nashville 37205 (356-3308 or 356-3306).

SPORTS: Stock Car Racing – NASCAR-sanctioned racing on a ⅝-mile track at the Tennessee State Fairgrounds every Saturday night from April through Labor Day, Wedgewood Ave. between 4th and 8th Aves. S (242-4343).

Baseball – The Nashville *Sounds,* a New York Yankees farm team, plays in a new stadium on Chestnut, between 4th and 8th Aves. S (242-4371).

Golf – There are six public courses in Nashville. Best 18-holers are at Harpeth Hills, Old Hickory Blvd., off rt. 431 S (373-8202); McCabe Park, 46th Ave. N at Murphy Rd. (297-9138); Shelby Golf Course, 20th Ave. and Fatherland St. (227-9973); and Two Rivers Course, Two Rivers Pkwy. near Opryland (889-9748).

Tennis – The major public facility is in Centennial Park, West End and 25th Aves. N, where there are 13 courts open from March through October. Admission charge. For further information, call 259-6399.

Fishing and Boating – Three Army Corps of Engineers lakes — Old Hickory, Cheatham Reservoir, and Percy Priest — are a 20-minute drive from downtown and six others are within an hour or so. Black bass, rock bass, striped bass, walleye, sauger, northern pike, crappie, bluegill, and sunfish are the standard catch. The Tennessee Wildlife Resources Agency, PO Box 40747, Ellington Agricultural Center, Nashville 37204 (741-1512), can provide details.

Swimming – Wave Country, on Two Rivers Pkwy., near Opryland, is the Southeast's largest surf-producing swimming pool. Open May–September. Admission charge. For more information, call 885-1052.

Ice Hockey – The Nashville *South Stars,* the farm team for the Minnesota North Stars, plays from October through April at the Municipal Auditorium, 417 4th Ave. N (248-1986).

THEATER: For touring Broadway shows and regional companies: the new *Performing Arts Center,* 505 Deaderick St. (741-7975). Lively children's theater and classics for adults: the *Nashville Academy Theatre* (the city's only professional resident company), 724 2nd Ave. S (254-9103). For dinner theater: the *Barn Dinner Theater,* 8204 Hwy. 100 (646-3111).

MUSIC: The Nashville Symphony Orchestra holds concerts from September through May in the new Tennessee Performing Arts Center. The symphony box office is at 1805 West End Ave. (329-3033). Friday and Sunday nights during June, July, and August, there are musical programs at Centennial

Park. For information, phone the Parks and Recreation Department's activities number (259-6399). *Chamber music* is offered at Cheekwood on weekends, at Fisk, and at Blair School of Music on the Vanderbilt campus. Often, it's free.

TV SHOW TAPINGS: "Pop Goes the Country" and "Hee Haw," among others, are taped irregularly in the TV studio behind the Opry House. National network specials and syndicated shows are also taped frequently in the Opry House itself. The schedules will be handed to you when you enter Opryland, or you can call ahead (889-6611). Tickets are always free.

NIGHTCLUBS AND NIGHTLIFE: For music, this is a hard town to beat. Even motels can sometimes turn up good entertainers. Check newspapers and the *Nashville Visitor's Guide* for a thorough rundown of places to hear country music.

For the best in a concentrated area, however, visit Printer's Alley down town, where, along with some strip-tease joints and seedy-looking bars, there are standouts like the *Captain's Table,* a silver-and-white-linen-tablecloth sort of place (251-9535), and *Boots Randolph's,* which features Boots and his incomparable saxophone (256-5500). More good music can also be heard at the *Four Guys Harmony House,* 407 Murfreesboro Rd. (256-0188); it is named after, and features, one of the more popular Grand Ole Opry acts. *Wind in the Willows,* nearby at 2205 State St., just off Elliston (320-9154), presents different music on different nights, but it's always informal, a beer-only kind of place. For bluegrass, try the *Blue Grass Inn,* located at the rear of 1914 Broadway at the edge of the Vanderbilt campus (320-0624), or the *Station Inn,* 402 12th Ave. S (255-3307). Saturday nights, the institution is the *Midnight Jamboree,* a sort of continuation of the Opry held at the Ernest Tubb Record Shop: You browse through the record shop while Ernest Tubb, in person, and his compatriots perform up front, 2414 Music Valley Dr. (889-2474). Three places to hear local talent play jazz, rock, country, and folk music are: *Cantrell's,* 1900 Broadway (327-2356); *Springwater,* 115 27th Ave., N (320-9512); and the *Bullpen Lounge* at the Stock-Yard Restaurant, 901 2nd Ave. N (255-6464).

SINS: The *pride* of Nashville is heard throughout the world on every jukebox, dance floor, and radio station. It is country music supreme, with headquarters at the *Grand Ole Opry*. But music abounds throughout the city in honky-tonks, bars, music clubs, and an enormous number of recording studios that produce the largest number of top-selling albums in the world.

Lower Broadway is the place for *lust* with massage parlors, peep shows, and topless joints.

LOCAL SERVICES: Business Services – Executive Park Office Services, 4741 Trousdale Dr. (331-2300); Nashville Secretarial Services, 1612 Church St. (329-2436).

Mechanics – People come from all the way across town to have their domestic cars fixed at Garrett Amoco Service, 2600 Lebanon Dr., Donelson, near Opryland (883-1386); for foreign cars, try Stubblefield Brothers, 317 6th Ave. S (255-5453). Also good is Robinson's Chevron, at Exit 96 off I-65, about 5 miles north of downtown (859-2816).

Babysitters – If you think you might need one, your best plan is to ask your hotel or motel to make the arrangements at the time you book your room.

BEST IN TOWN

CHECKING IN: There are dozens of new motels in Nashville, some parts of large chains, some parts of small chains, and a few independents. Prices generally range from $60 and up per night for a double room in an expensive hotel; $35 to $55 for accommodations in hostelries we've classified as moderate; and as low as $25 in an inexpensive place.

The Hermitage – Built in 1910, this showpiece structure of Beaux-Arts classic design is now a luxury hotel featuring 112 suites—with three phones and two color TVs in each. *The Hermitage* also has an oak-paneled bar, a fine dining room, and a Rolls-Royce as the hotel limousine. 231 6th Ave. N, downtown (244-3121). Expensive.

The Hyatt Regency – Like its fellows in the chain, this 480-room hotel has glassed-in elevators to whisk you up through a vast skylit lobby, the elegant *Café Troubadour* (great for desserts and specialty sandwiches), and a good restaurant, *Hugo's.* 623 Union St., downtown (259-1234 or toll-free 800 228-9000). Expensive.

The Opryland Hotel – This 615-room hotel is convenient to the Opry and Opryland (but 20 minutes from downtown). Good entertainment at its *Stagedoor, Saloon,* and *Staircase* lounges. 2800 Opryland Dr. (889-1000). Expensive.

Hermitage Landing Beach Cabins – On Percy Priest Lake, with lake activities — fishing, boating, swimming — at your doorstep. There are 20 units with kitchenettes. (Five have fireplaces.) Rt. 2 on Bell Rd. (889-7050). Expensive to moderate.

Holiday Inn–Vanderbilt – Standard Inn high-rise — but close to Vanderbilt University and a horde of good restaurants, and across the road from the Parthenon and Centennial Park. This 300-room Holiday Inn is near some good night spots, and home to a lively bar of its own. 2613 West End Ave. (327-4707). Moderate.

EATING OUT: Nashville is, as they say, a good eating town, with lots of small unpretentious restaurants where you'll find fried chicken and shrimp, steaks, home-style vegetables, and the like. An inexpensive meal will cost two of you $15 or less, a moderate one about $15 to $25, and an expensive one anywhere from $25 up. Prices do not include drinks, wine, or tips.

Julian's – Sophisticated French cuisine, featuring duckling in peach sauce, trout meunière, and veal aux champignons. The restaurant is located in an old house, complete with white columns and plants. Note that prices appear only on men's menus. Closed Sundays. Reservations recommended. Major credit cards accepted. 2412 West End Ave. (327-2417). Expensive.

Mario's – Owner Mario Ferrari serves up zuppa di pesce (shrimp, crab, lobster, clams), lasagna, and a variety of Italian veal specialties — alongside photos of himself taken with celebrities who stop in when they're in town. Open for dinner Mondays through Saturdays. Reservations recommended. Major credit cards. 1915 West End Ave. (327-3232). Expensive.

Arthur's – Seven-course Continental gourmet dining and plush decor characterize this chic eating place. The menu changes daily, but specialties include Dover sole, beef Wellington, and veal Normandy. Closed Sundays. Reservations recommended. Major credit cards. 9 Belle Meade Plaza (383-8841). Expensive.

Crown Court – The fine Continental fare (veal Oscar, steak Diane) and melodious piano music are enhanced by the remarkable view of downtown Nashville from this dining room atop the *Maxwell House Hotel.* Open daily for lunch and dinner. Reservations recommended. Major credit cards. 2025 MetroCenter Blvd. (259-4343). Expensive.

The Stock-Yard – This is the refurbished Union Stockyard in the downtown area. Corn-fed beef is the house specialty, and *The Stock-Yard*'s particular brand of beef stew accompanies each dinner. Open daily for dinner. Major credit cards. 901 2nd Ave. N (255-6464). Expensive to moderate.

Captain Ray's Sailmaker – This pleasant seafood place, where on Sunday nights you can buy all the shrimp you can eat for just about $7, also boasts one of the city's most extensive salad bars. Open for lunch Mondays through Fridays, for dinner daily. Major credit cards. 4243 Harding Rd. (298-2645). Expensive to moderate.

Houston's – Hamburgers with special toppings, quiches, fine spinach salads, and exotic desserts make the menu at this singles spot one of Nashville's more interesting. Open daily for lunch and dinner. No reservations accepted. Major credit cards. 3000 West End Ave. (269-3481). Moderate.

The Dynasty – Quiet conversation, soft lighting, and good Cantonese cooking. Open daily. Reservations recommended on Fridays and Saturdays. Major credit cards. 3415 West End Ave. (269-0188). Moderate.

The Belle Meade Motel Restaurant – The Formica-topped tables wouldn't win any design prizes, but the country ham, fried chicken, steaks, pork chops, and fresh vegetables are filling and delicious. Open daily. Reservations are not accepted here. No credit cards. 5133 Harding Rd. (352-9917). Inexpensive.

The Gaslight Beef Room – Located at Opryland USA, this steak and baked potato place is convenient if you're going to the Opry. Best are the homemade rolls. Open any time Opryland is open (see *Special Places*). Reservations are not necessary. Major credit cards. 2802 Opryland Dr. (889-6611). Inexpensive.

Loveless Motel Restaurant – Fried chicken, homemade biscuits, and peach and blackberry preserves, plus country ham (salty the way it's supposed to be) with gravy. Breakfast anytime; reservations recommended. Closed Mondays. No credit cards. Rt. 5, Hwy. 100 (646-9700). Inexpensive.

Satsuma Tea Room – At this long-time local favorite for lunch in downtown Nashville, you'll find fresh-cut flowers, Southern cooking, and homemade breads and desserts. Open Mondays through Fridays for lunch only. No reservations. No credit cards. 417 Union St. (256-5211). Inexpensive.

NEW HAVEN

To most visitors, New Haven is Yale, and Yale is New Haven. Certainly, the university dominates the city center, with 200 buildings spreading across much of New Haven's downtown section. And as the city's largest single employer, Yale could qualify as New Haven's major industry, if the production of literate graduates can be properly called an industry.

But there was a New Haven long before there was a Yale. The city was established in 1638; Yale moved to New Haven from Old Saybrook, Connecticut, in 1716, and wasn't even called Yale until a year later. And the city has always had the kind of diverse population that Yale discovered as a goal to work toward in the late 1960s.

An early trading center with a good harbor on Long Island Sound, New Haven really established its character in the 19th century, when the construction of the New Haven Railroad and the arrival of Irish, Italian, Polish, and Eastern European Jewish immigrants provided all the ingredients for heavy industry (the first repeating rifle was a New Haven product, which, like a number of young, ambitious Yale students, helped settle the frontier).

Today New Haven is a city of strong contrasts. There is the "Hill Section," a miserable slum of ugly old wooden buildings, once occupied by Irish railroad workers; but there is also Hillhouse Avenue, described by Dickens as the loveliest street in America. The avenue is flanked by beautiful Victorian mansions of red brick, set back from the street by spacious landscaped gardens. One of the homes, the Aaron Skinner house, is an outstanding example of Greek Revival architecture.

Many of New Haven's neighborhoods have retained their particular ethnic characteristics, although the city has undergone a population loss in recent decades, down about 25,000 from a high of 163,000 in the late 1930s. Neat wooden houses line the streets of Fair Haven, where many Irish live, and the Wooster Square area, with its large Italian population. Lace-curtain Irish and aristocratic Yankees live in the exclusive homes in Westville and on Wooster Square itself. The efforts of city officials were the principal factor in keeping these neighborhoods intact and desirable during the 1950s and 60s, when New Haven was confronted with deterioration and the threat of wholesale suburban exodus. New Haven was not allowed to degenerate into a massive slum surrounding an Ivy League enclave.

New and modern buildings standing side by side with the genteel 19th-century homes create a sharp contrast of architectural styles. But the presence of Yale creates an even more distinct mixture of cultures. The university and city have coexisted for two and a half centuries, sometimes on good terms, sometimes not. Currently the two administrations are battling over finances; as a nonprofit educational institution, Yale is exempt from taxes, but the city wants money in lieu of taxes, which the university is reluctant to give. Nevertheless, town and gown are on good terms, mostly due to the efforts of A.

Bartlett Giamatti, Yale's president since 1978, who is a home-grown product and originally went to Yale on a scholarship.

Yale gives the town a number of its valuable libraries and galleries —the Peabody Museum of Natural History, the Yale Collection of Musical Instruments, the University Art Gallery, and the Center for British Art. The town, in turn, supplies the university with workers, and complements its collections with three beautiful churches on the Green, the New Haven Historical Society, and a score of good restaurants. Like an old married couple that has suffered bitter disappointments in the past and still harbors ancient grievances, the bond between town and university is hardly perfect; but if this particular marriage wasn't made in heaven, it was most certainly contracted on the New Haven Green, around which town and gown are intertwined, presumably forever. Despite what others may think, both "Yalies" and "townies" know that New Haven wouldn't be New Haven without Yale and Yale really wouldn't be Yale outside New Haven.

NEW HAVEN AT-A-GLANCE

SEEING THE CITY: Once used by the Quinnipiac Indians for smoke signals, the 359-foot summit of New Haven's eastern cliff in East Rock Park still commands a panoramic view of the area — the city centered around the Green, the Yale campus, the harbor, and, on a clear day, 18 miles down Long Island Sound to Bridgeport.

SPECIAL PLACES: New Haven, the first architecturally planned city in the US, was designed for walking. Laid out in nine squares, the Green is still the main square. Almost everything of interest is located nearby in a 30-block area whose cultural and historic scope transcends its geographic limits.

The Green – The 16-acre square of grass, trees, and shrubbery in the city center remains today the focal point of New Haven activity as it was for early-17th-century settlers. Originally all public buildings were on the Green, as well as cows and pigs to keep the grass down. All the animals are now gone. The only buildings left are three churches, two of Georgian and federal style and one Episcopal church of Gothic Revival, all built between 1812 and 1815.

New Haven Historical Society Museum – A large model offers a look at New Haven of 1640, and other collections span the city's historical development over the past three centuries. Closed Mondays. Free. 114 Whitney Ave. (562-4183).

City Hall – Only the clock tower remains of the Victorian brownstone that served the city for more than a century. A new city hall is being built behind the tower at 161 Church St., facing the Green.

Yale Campus and Facilities – Named for East India trader and donor Elihu Yale, the university, founded in 1701, is one of the most distinguished educational institutions in the world. The campus is lovely with its ivy-covered Gothic-style buildings, charming green courtyards, and examples of contemporary architecture. The best way to see the campus is to take a free university tour led by student guides well versed in college lore and anecdotes. The tour begins at Old Campus with its Gothic and Romanesque structures, including the oldest of the ivy-covered buildings, Connecticut Hall, the Memorial Quadrangle to Harkness Tower, and the newer Yale structures such as the Payne Whitney Gymnasium, a huge physical education complex, and the Art and

Architecture building. Tours are given twice daily throughout the year starting at the University Information Office, Phelps Archway, 344 College St. (436-8330).

In addition to the campus itself, Yale has a wealth of museums and collections of great interest:

Peabody Museum of Natural History – Exhibits on evolutionary history: a huge skeleton of a brontosaurus, the Pulitzer Prize–winning "Age of Reptiles" mural by Ralph Zallinger, the Hall of Mammals. Open daily. Small admission charge. 170 Whitney Ave. (436-0850).

University Art Gallery – Fine collection includes John Trumbull's original paintings of the American Revolution (though the artist was a Harvard man). Samples of ancient Greek and Roman art and architecture. Closed Mondays. Free. 1111 Chapel St. (436-0574).

Yale Center for British Art and British Studies – The latest university addition, the center, designed by Louis I. Kahn, features works of Hogarth, Constable, Turner, Stubbs, and Blake. The paintings are hung in bright, open galleries which create the atmosphere of an English country house and provide optimal viewing. There are more British works here than anyplace outside of Britain. Closed Mondays. Free. 1080 Chapel St. (432-4594).

■ **EXTRA SPECIAL:** 60 miles east of New Haven on I-95 is the town of Mystic where the fastest clipper ships and the first ironclad vessels were built in the 19th century. The town has been restored as a 19th-century seaport. You can stroll along the waterfront of the Mystic River or down the cobblestoned streets lined with reproductions of quaint, 19th-century seaport homes. The Mystic Seaport Museum has an outstanding collection featuring the *Charles W. Morgan,* a large wooden whaling ship built in the 19th century and in service more than 80 years, and the *Joseph Conrad,* one of the last squareriggers ever built. For more information, see DIRECTIONS.

SOURCES AND RESOURCES

The New Haven Office of Public Information is best for maps, brochures, and general information; downtown at 157 Church St. (787-8228). Exit 47, off I-95 (436-2016). Yale has its own information center at Phelps Archway, 344 College St. (436-8330).

Enjoying New Haven, A Guide to the Area by Jane Byers and Ruth McClure (Round the Town Publications, $4.95), is a good guide to the city. *Best Restaurants in New England* by Patricia Brooks (101 Productions, $3.95) has many New Haven listings.

All telephone numbers are in the 203 area code unless otherwise indicated.

For Local Coverage – The *New Haven Journal-Courier,* morning daily; the *New Haven Register,* evening daily and Sundays, the Friday *Register* lists the coming week's attractions. Available at newsstands.

CLIMATE AND CLOTHES: Umbrellas are an important item in New Haven. Located on Long Island Sound, the city gets a lot of rain. The sea breeze, which gives some pleasant relief during the humid summers, the spring, and the fall, becomes raw and biting during the cold and snowy winters.

GETTING AROUND: Bus – Connecticut Transit serves the downtown area and the suburbs. Route information and guides are available at 470 James St. (624-0151).

Taxi – Cabs can be ordered on the phone or picked up at stands located all around the Green. They can be hailed in the street, but free taxis are rare. The largest company is Yellow Cab (562-4123).

Car Rental – New Haven has offices of all the national firms.

MUSEUMS: With Yale's fine collections, and New Haven's Historical Society, all cultural bases are loaded in the city. Two specialized collections reach interests further afield:

Yale Collection of Musical Instruments, 15 Hillhouse Ave. (436-4935).

Beinecke Rare Book and Manuscript Library, 121 Wall St. (436-8438).

MAJOR COLLEGES AND UNIVERSITIES: Yale University (see *Special Places*). Other educational institutions in the area are the University of New Haven, 300 Orange Ave. in West Haven (934-6321) and Southern Connecticut State College, 501 Crescent St. (397-4000).

SPECIAL EVENTS: At the end of June, the Green is filled with a lively ethnic fair, the *Mayor's Festival,* celebrating the city's cultural diversity. The ethnic groups come out in full force with Old Country food, dances, music, craft shows, and fireworks. Check the newspapers for exact dates. In late November of odd-numbered years, the Harvard-Yale football game takes place, with all the fanfare of a traditional rivalry, at the Yale Bowl. The 100th anniversary of "the game" is in 1983.

SPORTS: Hockey – The New Haven *Nighthawks* of the American Hockey League play from October to April, home games at New Haven Coliseum, 275 S Orange St. (772-4330).

Football – Yale has teams in all major sports, but the biggest are the *Bulldogs,* who play football at the Yale Bowl. Between Derby Ave. and Chapel St. Call the Athletic Association for tickets (436-0100).

Skiing – Best facilities are at Powder Ridge in Middlefield, 21 miles on I-91 (exit 16) to E Main St. in Meriden; from there follow the signs to Powder Ridge.

Tennis – There are many good outdoor courts for the public in the city. Municipal courts at Bowen Field (Munson St. between Crescent St. and Sherman Ave.) are free while the College Wood Courts (Orange and Cold Spring Sts.) have a small fee. Yalies get preference at university courts but the public is welcome. Yale Ave. and Chapel St.

THEATER: For up-to-date offerings and performance times, check the publications listed above. New Haven is the home of a well-known professional repertory company: the *Long Wharf Theatre Company,* with productions of classics and experimental theater, in a former warehouse in the meat and produce terminal. Closed in the summer. 222 Sargent Dr. (787-4282; see *Regional American Theater,* DIVERSIONS). *Yale Repertory Theatre,* 1120 Chapel St. (436-1600), also has experimental theater and classic plays.

MUSIC: The *New Haven Symphony Orchestra* gives concerts from September through March at Woolsey Hall on the Yale campus (information, 865-0831). For information about the Yale chorus, student groups, and visiting artists, call University Information at 436-8330.

NIGHTCLUBS AND NIGHTLIFE: Nightspots come and go in New Haven. The *Top of the Park,* at the Sheraton Park Plaza Hotel, has the best view of the city at night, and no cover charge, at 155 Temple St. (772-1700). *Toad's Place,* 300 York St. (777-7431), features top-name entertainment. *Partners,* mostly for gays, has drag entertainment, 365 Crown St. (624-5510).

SINS: In New Haven, Yale is the city's *pride* — the kind of pride that can easily precede a fall. University people think they're better than townspeople; townspeople strike out at the university by withholding permission for new dorms. It's not that such strained town-and-gown situations are unusual among college cities, but New Haven manages to be a little worse than most because the pride of Yalies is so fierce. Here, when the going is roughest, the only place you'll spot the twain meeting is in Wooster Square, in the heart of the city's huge Italian neighborhood, over pizza at diners like *Sally's, Pepe's*, and the *Spot*. (Each has its loyal following; *gluttony* flourishes at each.) The city has a perennial problem with the world's oldest profession in the Chapel-Howe area, bumping smack up against Yale, with enough streetwalkers to rival Place Pigalle in Paris. Yalies, however, are usually above such things and the business is mostly from locals and out-of-towners. At Yale, it is still boy-meets-girl, although occasionally a minor scandal errupts.

LOCAL SERVICES: Business Services – Audubon Copy Shoppe, 50 Whitney Ave. (865-3115).

Mechanic – Libby's Sales and Service, 60 Printer's La. (772-1112).

Babysitting – The bulletin board at the Yale Information Center posts cards of interested students, Phelps Archway at 344 College St. (436-8330).

BEST IN TOWN

CHECKING IN: Everything is easy to find in New Haven, but you will certainly get lost searching for the grand old hotel — it's simply not there. What is there is as easy to find in New Haven as anywhere else — branches of the chain hotels which offer moderately priced accommodations ($65 to $75 per night for a double room). There are also inexpensive rooms downtown ($30 to $40 per night) which can be a real find if you've seen one too many chains. Our pick of New Haven's best:

Sheraton Park Plaza Hotel – Located downtown, with a rooftop restaurant which features a view of New Haven at night, music, and dancing. 155 Temple St. (772-1700). Moderate.

Holiday Inn – Also downtown, with heated pool, a restaurant, and live entertainment on the weekends. 30 Whalley Ave. (777-6221). Moderate.

The Colony Inn – The old Midtown Motor Lodge, closed for several years, has been completely refurbished and opened as The Colony Inn. As close to Yale as you can get without being in a classroom. 1157 Chapel St. (776-1234). Moderate.

Hotel Duncan – A small, old hotel near Yale (so near, in fact, that students sometimes live here). But there are rooms available for visitors, travelers, and the student-at-heart. 1151 Chapel St. (787-1273). Inexpensive.

EATING OUT: If you consider eating more important than sleeping, New Haven is the place for you. What the city lacks in overnight accommodations, it makes up for in its abundance and variety of restaurants. A two-minute walk through the center of town will turn up several worthwhile restaurants tucked away in basements and unlikely corners. Because there are many potential diners-out in the city, restaurants are highly competitive, and prices are reasonable. Most of the restaurants are in the moderate ($20 to $30 for a dinner for two) to inexpensive range ($15 and under) though there are a few that are more expensive ($40 and up). Prices do not include tax, drinks, or tip.

Leon's – Though located in the impoverished "Hill Section," this is a family-run restaurant rich in Italian food. The specialty is chicken Eduardo, prepared in a light butter and garlic sauce, but mussel and clam dishes are also good. You should drive to Leon's (it has a parking lot). Closed Mondays. Reservations for large parties in private rooms only. Major credit cards. 321 Washington Ave. (789-9049). Expensive.

Sherman's Tavern on the Green – French classic food in an authentic colonial atmosphere, the home of Roger Sherman, first mayor of New Haven and a signer of the Declaration of Independence. Same management as the city's original French restaurant, *Poor Lad's,* which burned down. Always fresh fish and you should try oysters Anton. No lunch on Saturdays; closed Sundays. Reservations advised. Major credit cards. 1032 Chapel St., across from old Yale Campus (777-2524). Expensive.

Delmonaco's – The decor is strictly Valentino — Valentino posters on the wall and sometimes an old Valentino silent film to dine by. And the food is southern Italian. Inspired by the atmosphere, the chef has created two dishes designed to raise passions in the blood, fresh fish on linguine topped with a whole lobster, and a variety of meats mixed with peppers and onions, cooked in a secret sauce. Both terrific, both called the Chef's Specials. Open daily. Reservations. Major credit cards. 232 Wooster St. (865-1109). Expensive.

Basel's – Everyone and everything here is Greek, from the large portions of moussaka to the waitresses in flowery peasant dresses, who dance to the live Greek bouzouki music (Thursday through Saturday nights) and get everyone into the act, Greek or not. Closed Sundays. Reservations. Major credit cards. 993 State St. (624-9361). Moderate.

Old Heidelberg – One of the city's basement restaurants, this one has a real Yale flavor, complete with students, beers, steaks, and pictures of generations of varsity heroes lining the walls. Open daily. Reservations. Most major credit cards. 1151 Chapel St. (777-3639). Inexpensive.

New Haven Restaurant – Formerly the Shubert Theater, its past is depicted by scenes on the wall murals. Food ranges from hamburgers and sandwiches to full entrées, and the salads are unbeatable. Comedy night is on Thursdays, usually with talented performers. Open daily. No reservations. Major credit cards. 986 Chapel St. (777-1272). Inexpensive.

Fitzwilly's – This place is always jumping with students, residents, and visitors. Good quiche, homemade soups, and complete dinners are offered. Open daily. No reservations. Major credit cards. 338 Elm St. (624-9438). Inexpensive.

Claire's Corner Copia – Sitting unobtrusively on the corner of College and Chapel streets, *Claire's* looks beat-up and is always jam-packed. Here you'll find the best homemade food away from home. Soups are nothing short of wonderful, as are the breads and cakes (the carrot cake is widely acknowledged to be the finest in the city). Open daily. No credit cards. No reservations. 1000 Chapel St. (562-3888). Inexpensive.

Pepe's – Pepe claims to have invented the pizza. You might not believe him but you'll have to agree that in an area where pizza-making is fine art, Pepe's takes the pie. Closed Tuesdays. No reservations. No credit cards. 157 Wooster St. (865-5762). Inexpensive.

NEW ORLEANS

Jazz musicians call it the Big Easy, and down in New Orleans jazzmen are called professors. If anyone can transmit a feeling for New Orleans, it is probably the professors. Not because they are formally educated — they're not, and some can't even read music — but they can *improvise;* and in New Orleans, that's what it is all about.

The past has been a double-edged sword for New Orleans. Not even its port on the Mississippi — second in trade only to New York City harbor — has shaken it out of a certain Old South torpor. The city (metropolitan population of 1,094,000) lacks manufacturing and heavy industry, and throughout its long history as a center of trade and source of great wealth for some, it has maintained a European, 18th-century air. For the rich it has ever been a sophisticated, cultured haven; for the poor — many of whom are black — it has offered little hope of betterment over the years. The poverty just seems to roll along like the river; and little has appeared to change it. But at the same time, this torpor has managed to protect the city's charms, where in a different place they might have fallen long ago before the trumpet of civic progress.

Initially, New Orleans was something of a hot property, traded back and forth between governments. The French were first attracted in the early 1700s by the area's deep, swift harbor; named for the Regent of France, Philippe, Duc d'Orléans, it served as the capital of the French territories in America from 1723 to 1763, when a Bourbon family pact transferred it to Spanish rule, until it was ceded back to France in 1803. Two important things developed from all this swapping and ceding: the Creole culture, unique to the New World and descended from French and Spanish parents; and one of the greatest bargains of the century. Napoleon deeded New Orleans and the entire Louisiana Purchase to the United States for $15 million in 1803, doubling the size of the United States' territory. In 1815, to protect this wily investment, General Andrew Jackson and his Kentucky militiamen teamed with anyone and everyone — including pirate Jean Lafitte, the Choctaw Indians, numerous Creoles, and some black slaves — to defeat the British in the Battle of New Orleans. The War of 1812, unfortunately, had ended, some time earlier, somewhat dampening the victors' spirits. (News of the peace had not yet reached the combatants.) Jackson secured the Mississippi River for America, and New Orleans began to grow as a major port for the cotton, sugar cane, and indigo crops grown on surrounding plantations and as a kind of Old World cosmopolitan center in the midst of the deep South. The terrain is basically flat plains of the river delta — the Mississippi flows to the south, and the sea-sized Lake Pontchartrain borders the city on the north.

Today, the Vieux Carré or French Quarter, the main area of interest in New Orleans, reflects and preserves the New Orleans style. Protected by a powerful Vieux Carré Commission which regulates construction and modification of the area, the architecture is a blend of French and Spanish colonial (and their hybrid, Creole) standing side by side. A fine example of the mixture of cultures and styles is the Cabildo, the one-time headquarters of Spanish colonial rule. The impressive structure features wide Spanish arches and a French mansard roof. Nearby, flanking the European-style Jackson Square, are the imposing St. Louis Cathedral and the Pontalba apartments which contain a French-style arcade, and beautiful cast ironwork on the balconies, of a kind seen throughout the French Quarter. And there is a lot more — the renovated French Market, with a history dating back 200 years, still has a colorful atmosphere and some of the best café au lait on either side of the Atlantic. The way to see the French Quarter is also old-fashioned — by strolling down the cobblestoned streets and allowing your eyes to direct you. It's the kind of place where you relax and take it easy — the charms surround you.

In New Orleans, though, you don't just see and feel the city, but you must taste what it has to offer — Creole food, a highly developed regional style blending classical French cuisine with Spanish and American Southern, enhanced by spices and seasonings from American Indian, African, and West Indian recipes. The results are so good that they say down in New Orleans when a Creole goes to heaven, the first thing he asks Saint Peter is where he can find the jambalaya (a fragrant stew of shrimp, oysters, tomatoes, and rice) or gumbo filé (a spicy soup of shrimp, crabmeat, okra, oyster, herbs, and rice). Seafood is a Creole staple, as are fresh vegetables and veal, and the city is rich in fine restaurants which serve it up in style.

And then there is the Carnival Season — an extravagant blow-out that begins shortly after Christmas and builds up steam till Mardi Gras (Fat Tuesday) preceding Ash Wednesday. The tradition of Mardi Gras in New Orleans was begun over one hundred years ago by a social club, the Mystick Krewe of Comus. Other private clubs picked up the idea and thus began a series of elaborate balls and parades whose tradition continues today. The balls are still the principal event of New Orleans society. A well-known businessman is crowned King; the Queen is a debutante from a prominent family. But all the world loves a parade, and the Mardi Gras has gone public (though private balls still are held). In addition to the traditional parades with elaborate floats, marching jazz bands, doubloons and trinkets tossed to the crowds, the entire French Quarter, St. Charles Ave., and Canal Street are jammed. And celebrate they do in all manner of the word. Also parading on Mardi Gras is a black krewe, led by King Zulu, who shares some of the spotlight with the Big Shot of Africa. Zulu meanders throughout downtown New Orleans throwing painted coconuts, doubloons, and beads. The annual He Sheba costume competition for transvestites colorfully jams already jammed Bourbon Street. Each year, two parades of magnificently decorated trucks follow the Rex parade, with the occupants throwing trinkets just like the maskers on the floats. Costumed marching clubs dance and weave their way toward Canal St. behind small Dixieland jazz bands before Rex takes to the streets. In recent years, new krewes parade in the suburbs on Mardi Gras after the Rex parade.

Mardi Gras is both the best and the worst of times to visit New Orleans. The revelry and spectacle reach great heights, but so, too, do the hotel prices and the frenetic pace. There are other festivals which offer New Orleans in a different mood, without the crowds of the Mardi Gras (see *Special Events*).

The Jazz Heritage Festival is a special event, but there's no dearth of music anytime. The place that started off such great jazzmen as Louis Armstrong, Buddy Bolden, Joe "King" Oliver, Kid Ory, and Jelly Roll Morton still swings. The Old Mint, which is being renovated and is scheduled to open in 1982, will be the permanent home for excellent exhibitions on how it all began with a merging of Afro-American and European rhythms, and at Preservation Hall Dixieland jazz is played every night; and in countless honky-tonks on Bourbon Street the beat goes on. New Orleans still has brass band funerals where a marching band accompanies the procession from the church to the cemetery, playing solemn marches and hymns. As soon as the services are over, the rhythm picks up and the theme changes to something like "I'll Be Glad When You're Dead You Rascal You." The mourners begin prancing and cavorting behind the band, picking up others who join in the "Second Line" though they probably don't even know who died. But it doesn't really matter because when you leave the Big Easy, New Orleans folk act like you're on your way to the Bigger Easy, and send you off easily. Regardless of where you go afterward though, while you're there, it's hard not to join in. And why not? As they say in New Orleans, if you ain't gonna shake it, what did you bring it for?

NEW ORLEANS AT-A-GLANCE

SEEING THE CITY: The revolving bar in the *Top of the Mart* restaurant, at the International Trade Mart, offers the best view of the city, the Mississippi River as it cuts the crescent shape of New Orleans, and the barges, ocean liners, and ferries as they move up and down the river. 2 Canal St. at the river (522-9795).

SPECIAL PLACES: Nestled between the Mississippi River and Lake Pontchartrain, New Orleans' natural crescent shape can be confusing. North, south, east, and west mean very little here; New Orleans residents keep life simple and use "lakeside" or "riverside" as directions.

VIEUX CARRÉ

Jackson Square – This stately square was once the town square of the French colonial settlement, and the scene of most of New Orleans' history, from hangings to the transfer ceremony of the Louisiana Purchase. Rebuilt in the 1850s with the equestrian statue of Andrew Jackson, the hero of the Battle of New Orleans, the square is a pleasant place to sit and watch New Orleans go by, against a setting of charming brick facades of the surrounding buildings. Heads no longer roll here, but an occasional open-air jazz concert does, and the only hangings are on the iron fence bounding the area, where local artists display their work, and some draw portraits. Traffic is usually rerouted from the area, leaving a pedestrian mall. 700 Chartres St. bordered by Chartres, St. Ann, St. Peter, and Decatur Sts.

St. Louis Cathedral – Built in 1794, this beautiful Spanish building features towers, painted ceilings, an altar imported from Belgium, and markers for those buried in the sanctuary in French, Spanish, Latin, and English. Tours given daily. Donations requested. 700 Chartres St., across from Jackson Square (525-9585).

The Cabildo – Once the headquarters of Spanish rule and the site of the Louisiana Purchase and now part of the Louisiana State Museum. The architecture reflects the Spanish influence in its wide arches; the French influence with its mansard roof; and American with the emblems near the roof. Exhibits focus on New Orleans' interesting heritage with historical displays on French and Spanish colonial Louisiana (including portraits and documents, and even a death mask of Napoleon Bonaparte). Between the Cathedral and the Cabildo is Pirate's Alley, a narrow passageway that is the scene of frequent outdoor art shows. Small admission charge. Closed Mondays. At the corner of Chartres and St. Peter Sts. (568-6968).

The Presbytère – Used as a courthouse during the Spanish colonial period, it now houses the Louisiana State Museum Mardi Gras displays, and holds court with memorabilia of the festival's past kings and queens — costumes, ball invitations, and other odds and ends. Closed Mondays. Small admission charge. At the corner of Chartres and St. Ann Sts. (568-6968).

Pontalba Apartments – Built in the 1850s, this row of town houses features distinctive cast ironwork on the balconies, and a French-style arcade. Rich in New Orleans history, the Pontalba apartments and shops have seen the comings and goings of the French aristocracy, Jenny Lind, Sherwood Anderson, and William Faulkner. Today, ice cream parlors and small shops line the ground floors and some very fortunate New Orleans residents live above. Jackson Square at St. Ann and St. Peter Sts.

The Moon Walk – Named for former mayor Moon Landrieu, the title's a bit misleading. But this promenade alongside the Mississippi River shows "Ol' Man River" at its best as it winds its way along the crescent shape of the city (the only resemblance Moon Walk has with the moon). The Mississippi is deep and swift at New Orleans and the port, which can accommodate oceangoing vessels, is second in tonnage only to New York. Across the levee from Decatur St. at Jackson Square.

French Market – A farmers' market for two centuries, the French Market still has a colorful atmosphere with stands under large old arches offering everything in the way of fresh vegetables and fruits (try the Louisiana oranges, sugar cane, and the sweet midget bananas), meats, and fish including live crab, turtle, shrimp, catfish, and trout. The covered section has cafés, candy shops, and gift shops. The *Café du Monde* is a New Orleans institution featuring marvelous café au lait (half coffee and chickory, and half hot milk) and beignets, square-shaped French donuts. The café never closes, and the market is open daily. Extending down Decatur St. from St. Ann.

Beauregard-Keyes House – Although George Washington never slept here, almost everyone else lived in this federalist-style house including novelist Frances Parkinson Keyes, chess player Paul Morphy, and Confederate General P. G. T. Beauregard; quite a few of another sort died here in a Mafia battle in 1909. The house has period furniture, a collection of dolls, and Keyes memorabilia. Admission charge. Closed Sundays. 1113 Chartres St. (523-7257).

Madame John's Legacy – Built in 1727 and survivor of the great fire of 1794, this house is one of the oldest remaining in the Mississippi Valley. The house is an excellent example of the Creole "raised cottage," with its brick-paved first floor used for storage below the dwelling area and for protection against floods and dampness, a service wing with a double stairway, and a courtyard. The Louisiana State Museum has renovated the house and furnished it with early Louisiana pieces as an example of 18th-century New Orleans lifestyle. Closed Mondays. Small admission charge. 632 Dumaine St. (568-6968).

Royal Street – There really was a streetcar named Desire, and in the 19th century it used to run along Royal St. Though the streetcar is gone, desire for the old days remains and some of it can be fulfilled by a stroll down this street, famous for its antique shops and highly distinctive architecture.

Old Mint – Opened in 1982, the Mint contains a collection of jazz memorabilia. Jazz lovers will find souvenirs of the patron saints of jazz — Louis Armstrong's first horn, Bix Beiderbecke's cuff links, and instruments played by members of the Original Dixieland Jazz Band. Fine exhibits trace the development of jazz from its Afro-American rhythms and the European brass band tradition to current progressive strains. 400 Esplanade Ave.

Preservation Hall – What's recorded in the jazz collection at the Mint still happens every night at Preservation Hall. Features traditional New Orleans Dixieland played by a different band from a group of six. No booze, sparse surroundings, but the real jazz thing. Open nightly from 8:30 to 12:30. Small admission charge. 726 St. Peter St. (523-8939).

Bourbon Street – Though the street was named for the French royal family, it actually has a lot more in common with the drink, which, along with anything else potable, can be found here in abundance (and New Orleans establishments have added many drinks to the bartender's list, including the absinthe frappe, and the Hurricane, which has been rumored to devastate entire populations). Round the clock the honky-tonks offer live jazz, which gets wild in the wee hours, and live booze, which gets wicked the morning after. A hot strip since the post–WW II years, Bourbon Street also has lots of strip joints and peep shows, where, even if you stay outside, you'll get more of an eyeful than a peep as the hawkers swing the doors open to lure customers. Among the hottest spots is *Lafitte's Blacksmith Shop,* 941 Bourbon St., where pirate Jean Lafitte is purported to have had a blacksmith shop, now a bar where the forge is still flaming; others are the *Old Absinthe House,* 240 Bourbon St., a barroom since 1826, and *Crazy Shirley's,* for open-air Dixieland jazz, 640 Bourbon St.

St. Louis Cemetery Number One – Last stop in the Vieux Carré, this old New Orleans cemetery with its aboveground tombs designed by earlier architects is literally a diminutive necropolis. The marshy ground dictated above-the-ground burial, and the monuments are interesting for their structure, inscriptions, and number of remains inside (to solve the overcrowding problem, tombs are opened, and the remaining bones are moved further into the vault to accommodate new arrivals). If you're interested, the caretaker will give you a tour and can tell you as much about the procedure as you'll want to know. Among the prominent buried here are Étienne de Boré, the first mayor of New Orleans; Paul Morphy, the chessplayer; and Marie Laveau, a 19th-century Voodoo Queen. Open daily. Free admission, but small charge for tours. 400 Basin St.

DOWNTOWN AND THE GARDEN DISTRICT

Canal Street – Where the French Quarter ends, the business district begins, and the transition is sharp, from narrow cobblestoned streets to a wide, main boulevard. The International Trade Mart, a glass skyscraper, is the center of companies dealing in foreign trade and home of the Louisiana Maritime Museum (with good exhibits on the Mississippi's navigatory past, and a fine collection of models of battleships, steamers, sailboats, naval weapons and equipment). Open daily. Small admission charge. River Wing of 2 Canal St. at the river (581-1874).

River Tours – On the free ferry you can ride back and forth to Algiers. The *Mark Twain* steamboat gives a tour down through the bayou country to Bayou Barataria, home of the pirate Jean Lafitte. Open daily. Admission charged. The big side-wheeler steamboat, the *President,* tours up and down the river daily, and Saturday nights has a dance cruise, with a 1930s-style ballroom and lots of jitterbugging. Admission charge. Boats leave from the dock at the foot of Canal St. (586-8777 or 525-6311).

Garden District – Above Canal Street and the business district is the lovely Garden District, once the center of 19th-century American aristocracy, still preserving its old style. The houses, mainly Victorian and Greek Revival in design, are set back from the street with wide, shady gardens of oak, magnolia, camelia, and palm trees. The District is a great place to stroll anytime (or take the St. Charles Ave. streetcar), but during the two-week Spring Fiesta in April, there are tours of the private homes. For information contact Spring Fiesta Headquarters, 529 St. Ann St. (581-1367). Bounded by Magazine St., St. Charles Ave., Jackson Ave., and Louisiana Ave.

CITY PARK AND LAKE PONTCHARTRAIN

New Orleans Museum of Art – This attractive Greek Revival building has fine permanent collections including the Samuel H. Kress Collection (Italian renaissance and baroque masterpieces), 19th-century French salon paintings, works by Degas, pre-Columbian art, African art, and Spanish colonial paintings. Closed Mondays. Admission charge. In City Park (488-2631).

Lake Pontchartrain – New Orleans' other body of water, this large saltwater lake has swimming and fishing at the beach, on Lake Shore Drive. Best is the drive over the Lake Pontchartrain Causeway, the longest overwater highway bridge in the world — 24 miles across open water, and for eight miles in the center, you are completely out of sight of land; there's only Lake Pontchartrain for as far as the eye can see. I-10 leads to the Causeway. Toll.

■ **EXTRA SPECIAL:** Somewhere out there in Louisiana country was once the heart of the *Old South,* and it still beats faintly along the banks of the Mississippi. Little over 100 years ago sugar cane was king in Louisiana, and large plantations established commercial empires, as well as an entire social system, around it. A few of these plantations have been restored and are open to visitors who want to see what that period was like, at least for the people on top. And the life that the Southern gentry created for themselves really is something to see. The most interesting plantations are within an hour's drive of New Orleans. Houmas House (72 miles west on River Rd.), which was used for the filming of "Hush, Hush, Sweet Charlotte," looks just like a plantation should — a big, white mansion with stately columns, and lovely grounds with huge, old oak trees and formal gardens. There is an excellent tour through the house which has a circular staircase, rare antiques, a widow's walk for river gazing, and outside, garçonnière, little windmill-shaped structures where young men were sent to live independently when they came of age. San Francisco (42 miles west along River Rd.) is an attractive structure — flamboyant Steamboat Gothic with lots of Victorian trim, elaborate ceiling paintings, and, over the front door, a mirror that reflects the Mississippi River.

SOURCES AND RESOURCES

The New Orleans Tourist Information Center provides a wealth of information on the city's attractions, including maps, brochures, and personal help. 334 Royal St. (566-5011).

New Orleans by Carolyn Kolb (Doubleday and Co., $3.95) is the most comprehensive local guide to New Orleans and the surrounding area. Another good source is *The Pelican Guide to New Orleans* by Tommy Griffin (Pelican Publishing Co., $2.95).

All telephone numbers are in the 504 area code unless otherwise indicated.

For Local Coverage – *The New Orleans Times-Picayune/The States-Item,* daily.

For Food – Check *The Revised New Orleans Underground Gourmet* by Rima and

Richard Collin (Simon and Schuster, $3.95), and *New Orleans Restaurant Guide* by Rima and Richard Collin (Strether and Swann, $3.95).

CLIMATE AND CLOTHES: New Orleans weather is subtropical with high humidity, temperatures, and substantial rainfall. Moderated by the Gulf of Mexico winds, summer temperatures hover around 90°, while winter temperatures rarely drop to freezing. Summers can get unbearably sticky; fall and spring are more pleasant.

GETTING AROUND: Bus – New Orleans Public Service provides efficient bus and streetcar service throughout the city. The St. Charles Ave. streetcar offers a scenic ride through the Garden District (board at Canal and Baronne Sts.). Complete information and free transit maps are available at the New Orleans Public Service office, 317 Baronne St. (595-2192).

Taxi – Cabs can be ordered on the phone, hailed in the streets, or picked up at stands in front of hotels, restaurants, and transportation terminals. Major cab companies are Yellow Cab (525-3311); United Cab (522-9771); Checker Cab (943-2411).

Car Rental – All major car rental companies have offices in New Orleans.

MUSEUMS: The New Orleans Museum of Art, the Old Mint, the Louisiana State Museum exhibits, the Historic New Orleans Collection, and the Louisiana Maritime Museum are described above in some detail in *Special Places.* Other notable New Orleans museums are:

Confederate Museum, 929 Camp St. (523-4522).
Pharmacy Museum, 514 Chartres St. (524-9077).
Wildlife Museum, 400 Royal St. (568-5841).

MAJOR COLLEGES AND UNIVERSITIES: Tulane University, 6400 St. Charles Ave. (865-5000), is New Orleans' most prominent educational institution, known primarily for its medical and law schools. Loyola University, 6300 St. Charles Ave. (865-2011), which has an enrollment of over 4,000 students, is also in New Orleans. The University of New Orleans, the Lakefront (286-6000), is the area's largest school.

SPECIAL EVENTS: When it comes to special events, none tops New Orleans' *Mardi Gras,* an extravagant succession of parades, carnivals, and balls that begin January 6 and continue through Ash Wednesday. (For a fuller description, see p. 293).

As if the Mardi Gras is not enough, two weeks later, the *Spring Fiesta* begins with "A Night in Old New Orleans." After the coronation of the queen, there is a carriage parade through the French Quarter. For the next two weeks the town is literally laid open. For information, contact the Fiesta Association, 529 St. Ann St. (581-1367).

Since 1969 New Orleans has been driving home the point that there just ain't no better place for jazz than the *New Orleans Jazz and Heritage Festival,* held every May. The top names in jazz perform at a number of places throughout the city, while all kinds of bands — ragtime, traditional New Orleans Dixieland, Cajun — and folk and blues musicians entertain outside on the Fair Grounds. All come together as jazz stars join in late night jam sessions in the French Quarter. More than just music for the soul, the Heritage includes something for the stomach and plenty of it. All kinds of Creole and Cajun food, the New Orleans specialties, are available at booths on the Fair Grounds — jambalaya, crawfish pie, file gumbo, po'boy heros, muffalettas, frogs legs, and smoked sausage on a stick, just to get you going.

The *New Orleans Food Festival* is in June. An afternoon of eating: everything listed above and more, served up at numerous booths in the French Quarter for about a quarter a shot, so why not? And at night, there's an elaborate banquet. *La Fête* is New Orleans' newest summer festival, celebrating the city's heritage with music, food, and cultural programs during the first 2 weeks in July.

Check the papers or write the Tourist Information Center for specific dates.

SPORTS: The biggest thing in New Orleans sports is the Superdome, the world's largest domed stadium. You can take 15-minute tours daily of the 27-story-high arena with a capacity of 97,000. The Superdome hosts the *Sugar Bowl* football classic.

Football – The NFL's New Orleans *Saints* play at the Superdome from August to December. Tickets are available at the Superdome box office. 1500 Poydras St. at La Salle St. (587-3664).

Horse Racing – There are two seasons for racing and parimutuel betting: winter season at Fair Grounds Race Track, 1751 Gentilly Blvd. (944-5515) from Thanksgiving Day to April 5; summer season at Jefferson Downs, Kenner La. (466-8521) from April to November 1.

College Football – The Tulane University *Green Wave* team plays at the Superdome from late September through November (for tickets and game information, call 861-9283).

Bicycling – Both City Park and Audubon Park are good for riding.

Fishing – On Lake Pontchartrain, and within easy distance of the Gulf of Mexico, New Orleans is a fishing paradise (for fishermen, not fish). Best spot is Empire, 52 miles south on rt. 23 where you can rent boats or take a charter to go after king mackerel, white trout, and red snapper, at Battistella's Marina (523-6068). You can fish in Lake Pontchartrain for bass, speckled trout, and red fish off the seawall along Lake Shore Drive or rent a boat from Ed Lombard's bait center at Chef Menteur.

Golf – Golf is popular year-round in New Orleans, and the best courses for the public are the four 18-hole courses at City Park, Esplanade Ave. southwest of French Quarter (283-3458 or 482-8991), and the course at Audubon Park, 6300 St. Charles Ave. (861-9513).

Tennis – City Park has 38 good public courts of various composition, open year-round; they charge a small fee. For information, call 482-2230.

Swimming – You can swim during the summer at the public beach of Lake Pontchartrain along Lake Shore Drive or else at the Olympic-sized pool in Audubon Park, St. Charles Ave. (899-4373).

THEATER: For up-to-date offerings and performance times, check *The New Orleans Times-Picayune/The States-Item.* New Orleans has several theaters which offer performances, some locally produced, others traveling shows. Colleges and universities in the area also produce plays and musicals. Best bets for shows: *Theatre of the Performing Arts,* 801 N Rampart St. (586-4624); *Beverly Dinner Playhouse,* 217 Labarre Rd. (837-4022); *Saenger Performing Arts Center,* 143 N Rampart St. (524-0876).

MUSIC: *Classical concerts* and *opera* are heard at *Theatre of the Performing Arts,* 801 N Rampart St. (586-4168); *New Orleans Opera Guild* has eight productions from September to May (525-7672); the *New Orleans Philharmonic Symphony* performs from September to May at the *Theater of the Performing Arts,* 801 N Rampart St. (524-0404). Jazz is the big story in New Orleans music, and when it comes to jazz, it's time for:

NIGHTCLUBS AND NIGHTLIFE: New Orleans is a night town, and the jazz gets better and the drinks stronger (at least it seems that way) as the night wears on. At any one time there is an astonishing array of jazz being played in the city: top names and talented local musicians playing traditional New Orleans jazz, progressive, blues, rock, or folk music. Check the newspapers listed above for up-to-date information on who is where.

Current Favorites: *Al Hirt Night Club* features the big trumpeter when he's in town, 809 St. Louis St. (525-6167); *Crazy Shirley's,* for Dixieland, 640 Bourbon St. (581-5613); *Maple Leaf Bar,* for ragtime, 8316 Oak St. (866-9359); *Pete Fountain's Night Club,* Poydras St. at the Mississippi River (523-4374) for New Orleans jazz; *Ole Man River's*, 2125 Hwy. 90, Avondale (436-3001) for jazz and rock; *Preservation Hall,* for pure jazz (no drinks) by traditional New Orleans bands, 726 St. Peter St. (523-8939). Favorite bars: *Napoleon House and Bar,* 500 Chartres St. (524-9752); *Lafitte's Blacksmith Shop,* 941 Bourbon St. (523-0066); *Old Absinthe Bar,* 400 Bourbon St. (561-9231); *Pat O'Brien's* (home of the Hurricane), 718 St. Peter St. (525-4823).

SINS: The Big Easy, as the "professors" or jazzmen of New Orleans call their city, is one of the hottest and funkiest places in the US. And it is not difficult for its uniquely complicated citizenry to find a lot in which to have *pride.* From the French, Spanish, African, and native American roots that form New Orleans' culture, a variety of music has been born and nurtured that is richer, more imaginative, and more influential than that from any other single source in the Western Hemisphere, and possibly the world. *Preservation Hall* is the Dixieland capital of the world. The Jazz Heritage Festival and the Old Mint's jazz exhibit are formal acknowledgments of this city as the home of jazz. And Mardi Gras is a time when all the other musical forms, such as combined Indian-African chanting hymns, suddenly emerge in public places, letting outsiders in on a kind of music they can hear nowhere else in the world. And as if this isn't enough to engender a deep sense of pride, the New Orleans cooking, language, architecture, and pace of life are as unique and wonderful as the sounds it has come to invent.

The cooking will particularly interest visitors who are up for a chance to indulge in a little *gluttony.* There aren't many places as well equipped to satisfy. If you start the day with poached eggs and crab meat, turtle soup, and a slice of peanut butter ice cream pie, how far do you have to go to achieve the goal of overindulgence? There is still gumbo, jambalaya, stewed okra, oyster loaf, and shrimp rémoulade to get to at lunch and dinner. And it's easy to find, well prepared, comfortably priced, and delicious.

Lust is the main business of Bourbon Street in the French Quarter, though it may be the music that made its name. On both sides of the street and in every other doorway you will see a lady of the night ready to offer her services to any taker in town. There is nothing undercover or oblique about the action here, that is not New Orleans' way. Uninhibited, up front, and in the same spirit as the rest of the city's goings-ons, the philosophy is, "If you got it, use it. And if you want it, get it!"

LOCAL SERVICES: Business Services – Dictation Incorporated, open 24 hours, seven days a week, 1552 Washington Ave. (895-8637).

Mechanic – Advance Automotive Service, 3900 Canal St. (488-9907).

■ **GET YOURSELF SOME OF THAT OLD BLACK MAGIC:** If there's anything you desire, or you just have a bad case of the Basin Street blues, try some of the original New Orleans Voodoo. Visit the grave of Voodoo Queen Marie Laveau (St. Louis Cemetery No. 1, 400 Basin St.), snap your fingers, stamp your feet, mark an X on the tomb with brick dust, and make a wish. Then hope for the best.

BEST IN TOWN

CHECKING IN: Hotels in New Orleans are usually more than just places to stay after spending a day and half the night seeing the city. Many of the hotels reflect the influence of French, Spanish, and Louisiana colonial architecture, and often a measure of charm. The service in these hotels is generally excellent, and in some cases, the owner even lives in to ensure that it is. No matter where you stay or what you pay, make reservations in advance, particularly during Mardi Gras and the Carnival season, from Christmas to Ash Wednesday (this includes Sugar Bowl Week, which precedes the football classic on New Year's Day). Slightly higher rates prevail during these periods. Out of high season, expect to pay $75 to $85 for a double room for a night in the expensive range, $50 to $60 in the moderate scale, and $35 to $45 in the inexpensive category.

Pontchartrain Hotel – Provides excellent service and 100 individually decorated rooms and suites with many French provincial antique furnishings. Favorite of celebrities and traveling dignitaries. Has an excellent restaurant, the *Caribbean Room* (see *Eating Out*), serving Creole specialties, and a café with a jazz pianist nightly. The owner lives right here and oversees everything. 2031 St. Charles Ave. (524-0581). Expensive.

Royal Orleans Hotel – Located on the site of the famous St. Louis Hotel amidst the hustle and bustle of the Vieux Carré. The lobby is luxurious Italian marble, most rooms are elegantly furnished, and there is conscientious service. Features the *Esplanade Lounge,* popular with the late-night crowd, *Café Royale, Touche-Bar,* a tri-level nightspot, the fine *Rib Room* for dining, a rooftop pool, shops, garage. 386 rooms. 621 St. Louis St. (529-5333). Expensive.

Prince Conti – Converted from an old mansion, this inn retains all of its charm from the carriageway entrance through the lovely French château lobby to the rooms with authentic antique furnishings and some fine reproductions. In the morning, Continental breakfast is brought up to the room; in the afternoon, *Le Petit Bar* serves cocktails. 50 rooms. 830 Conti St. (529-4172). Expensive to moderate.

The St. Louis Hotel – This small, elegant hotel is one of the city's newest. In the tradition of hotels of Paris, it offers personalized service, rooms with French period furnishings, tastefully landscaped, fountained courtyards, and even a concierge. *Le Petit Restaurant* features French cuisine, and formal dining for breakfast, lunch, and dinner. 77 rooms. 730 Bienville St. (581-7300). Expensive.

New Orleans Hilton – This is the city's newest; a downtown resort located at the river. There's a fine view, and the International Rivercenter is an entertainment development which includes a cruise ship terminal, a tennis club, and a luxury shopping mall. Also has pool, health club, sauna, and garage. 1,200 rooms. Special features are the *Le Café Bromeliad's* Sunday champagne brunch; *Rainforest Club* with a computer diet buffet (a calorie count on each item); *Pete Fountain's* nightclub, featuring the famous jazz clarinetist; and *Winston's* (main dining room), offering five-course gourmet dinners of *nouvelle cuisine.* 2 Poydras St. at the Mississippi River (561-0500). Expensive.

Fairmont – They say New Orleanians wept when its predecessor, *The Roosevelt,* was sold to the Fairmont interests. But they weep no more. The Fairmont's owners have successfully wedded the charm of San Francisco and New Orleans and produced an efficient enterprise. At the fine *Sazerac Restaurant* you can sample the Sazerac cocktail or the famed Ramos gin fizz. The *Blue Room* has dinner dancing and top acts. *Bailey's* is a 24-hour restaurant-bar. Also a rooftop pool and two tennis courts, and 800 rooms. University Pl. (529-7111). Expensive.

French Quarter Maisonnettes – A converted Vieux Carré mansion with carriageway drive of flagstones and a spacious patio, the inn is a quaint and friendly place to stay. Each room is luxuriously private and situated on the patio. The owner presents each guest with a printed, personalized folder listing places to go, what to see and do in the city, and offering advice and suggestions for activities. 10 rooms. 1130 Chartres St. (524-9918). Moderate.

Monteleone Hotel – At the gateway of the Vieux Carré. This large old hotel maintains a friendly atmosphere while offering the amenities of a larger operation. Features rooftop pool, revolving lounge with Dukes of Dixieland Band, *Steaks Unlimited Dining Room, Le Café,* garage. 600 rooms. 214 Royal St. (523-3341). Moderate.

Cornstalk Hotel – This old Victorian home is surrounded by a New Orleans landmark — a cornstalk wrought-iron fence showing ripe ears of corn shucked on their stalks, ready for harvest, and pumpkin vines. The interior is something of a landmark, too — a grand entrance hall and lobby with antique mirrors and crystal chandeliers. The rooms feature fourposter beds, and you can take Continental breakfast there, in the front gallery, or on the patio. 14 rooms. 915 Royal St. (523-1515). Moderate.

Quality Inn Midtown – Convenient and modestly priced, with an excellent restaurant featuring Maine lobster, boiled Creole beef brisket, and shrimp cocktail. Pool, café, bar, meeting rooms. 100 rooms. 3900 Tulane Ave. (486-5541). Inexpensive.

EATING OUT: The city abounds with restaurants. Most are good. Many are excellent. And all reflect the distinctive cuisine of New Orleans, Creole cooking — shaped through the years by the cultures of France, Spain, America, the West Indies, South America, African blacks, and the American Indian. Seafood is king in Creole cooking and the nearby waters are a rich kingdom, providing crabs, shrimp, red snapper, flounder, Gulf pompano, and trout. Vegetables in season, fowl, veal, fresh herbs and seasonings are culinary staples that fill out the court and have made this strongly regional style royal art. There are many fine expensive and moderately priced restaurants. Inexpensive restaurants and even department stores serve up New Orleans specialties, gumbo, po' boy sandwiches, and red beans and rice on Mondays, a New Orleans tradition. Our restaurant selections range in price from expensive at $45 or more for a dinner for two, $25–$35 in the moderate range, and $15 or less in the inexpensive range. Prices do not include drinks, wine, or tips.

Le Ruth's – Far and away the best restaurant in New Orleans. Owner and chef Warren Le Ruth has spent his career in New Orleans preparing French and Creole food, never leaves the kitchen, and will serve only consistently fine dishes — oysters and artichoke soup, soft-shell crab with lump crabmeat and meunière sauce, veal Marie with crabmeat, frogs legs meunière, homemade desserts, mandarin ice, or the exquisite almond torte. He also bakes his own bread. The menu is something special. So is the elegant Victorian decor and the service. Closed Sundays. Reservations a must. Major credit cards. 636 Franklin St. in Gretna, LA, 4½ miles across the Mississippi River Bridge from Canal St. (362-4914). Expensive.

Antoine's – Established in 1840, and one of the oldest restaurants in the country, still offering a grand gastronomic experience. The waiters know the daily fare well and it pays to listen to their suggestions. Specialties include tournedos with Creole red wine sauce, pompano en papillote, oysters Rockefeller, filet de boeuf Robespierre, soufflé potatoes, and baked Alaska. Though the decor is somewhat sparse

— white tiled floors and mirrored walls — Antoine's has a great wine cellar and picturesque private dining rooms. Closed Sundays. Reservations. Major credit cards. 713 St. Louis St. (581-4422). Expensive.

Caribbean Room – The Pontchartrain Hotel's exceptional dining room serving French and Creole cuisine. The menu is imaginative, and specialties are beautifully served — trout Véronique (poached and topped with green grapes and hollandaise sauce), crabmeat Biarritz (lump crabmeat with whipped cream dressing and topped with caviar), pompano Pontchartrain (with soft-shell and buster crabs), and, if you can go the distance, mile-high ice cream pie. An elegant buffet is served Sunday nights and major holidays. Everything (including the pie) is prepared under the watchful eye of the owner and founder who lives in the hotel and dines in the Caribbean Room. Open daily for lunch and dinner. Reservations. Major credit cards. 2031 St. Charles Ave. (524-0581). Expensive.

Galatoire's – No matter who you are or who you think you are, you stand in line on the sidewalk like everyone else when the house is full. But both the wait and the possible humiliation (depending on who you think you are) are worth it. This favorite of New Orleans residents has great French and Creole dishes, a distinctive atmosphere with ceiling fans and mirrored walls, and knowledgeable waiters. Specialties include trout Marguery with shrimp, shrimp rémoulade, oysters en brochette, eggs Sardou (artichokes and spinach over poached eggs), and crêpes maison filled with apple or grape jelly. Closed Mondays. Open for lunch and dinner. No reservations or credit cards. 209 Bourbon St. (525-2021). Moderate.

Brennan's – Although some say that its quality and service have been slipping lately, others still claim that you haven't really had a full day in New Orleans unless you've started it with breakfast at Brennan's — poached egg specialties with hollandaise and marchand de vin sauce, creamed spinach, or New Orleans style with crabmeat, turtle soup, and maybe bananas Foster (bananas with ice cream and liqueur) for a flaming dessert, and certainly café Brulot (coffee with Curaçao and orange rind). Make reservations in advance. Open daily. Major credit cards. 417 Royal St. (525-9711). Moderate.

Versailles – This relative newcomer to the New Orleans scene improves each year. Its menu is a good mix of French, German, and Creole. One fine appetizer is the Versailles escargots en croute — classic snails bourguignon served in a hollowed-out bun made of New Orleans French bread. Main course specialties include duck à la Flamande, rack of lamb persillade, veal financière with sweetbreads, bouillabaise Marseillaise, and veal farci with crabmeat. On the ground floor of the Carol Apartments at the edge of the Garden District. Valet parking. Closed Sundays. Reservations advised. Major credit cards. 2100 St. Charles Ave. (524-2535). Moderate.

Commander's Palace – This long-time favorite has been operated for the past several years by a branch of the Brennan restaurant family. The unusual "jazz brunch" offered on Sundays features traditional and exotic poached egg dishes accompanied by New Orleans jazz. Dinner specialties include trout pecan, crabmeat imperial, turtle soup, lemon crêpes, and filet mignon. Located in an old mansion in the Garden District. Open daily. Reservations advised. Major credit cards. 1403 Washington Ave. (899-8221). Moderate.

Arnaud's – This once noble Vieux Carré restaurant, founded in 1918 by Count Arnaud Cazenave, has rejoined the ranks of New Orleans' best. Its traditional menu has been shortened and strengthened: Many dishes were eliminated; some that originated here and became famous were retained; a few were added. You can't miss with shrimp Arnaud (a spicy rémoulade), trout Meuniere, and caramel custard. The dining areas also have been refurbished, but not at the sacrifice of the old France–old New Orleans decor — crystal chandeliers and flickering gas lanterns. Open daily. Reservations advised. Major credit cards. 813 Bienville St. (523-5433). Moderate.

Masson's – This elegant French restaurant near the lakefront has a strong local following. Chef-owner Ernest Masson visits France frequently to bring back recipes for the latest in haute cuisine. He tries them out for a while and if they are assez haute, he adds them to the offerings on the already fine menu — oysters Albert, seafood crêpes, and marinated rack of lamb. Open daily. Reservations. Major credit cards. 7200 Pontchartrain Blvd. (283-2525). Moderate.

Alonso's – This is a typical New Orleans neighborhood restaurant and bar, specializing in seafood. The main attraction is the very large, very good, and very cheap seafood platter. It contains the traditional hot seafood, plus a few seasonal items like crayfish or soft-shell crab, and some boiled shrimp or crab tossed in for good measure. Don't expect your party to be served together — you get it while it's hot. Extremely crowded on Friday nights. Closed Sundays. No reservations. No credit cards. 587 Central Ave. (about 6 miles from Canal St.) (733-2796). Inexpensive.

K-Paul's Louisiana Kitchen – One of the city's most celebrated chefs, owner Paul Prudhomme, dishes up dozens of tempting Cajun specialties, including 17 varieties of gumbo. The *pièce de résistance* is a hot Cajun martini served in a Mason jar. Closed Saturdays and Sundays. No credit cards. No reservations. 416 Chartres St. (524-7394). Inexpensive.

Ye Olde College Inn – In the University section, daily dinner plates, shrimp rémoulade, red beans and rice, oyster loaf, French fried onion rings, and a good bar. The Creole vegetables, especially the eggplant, and stewed okra are at the top of their class. Open daily. No reservations. Major credit cards. 3016 S Carrollton Ave. (866-3683). Inexpensive.

Mandina's – In a city where the list of places that offer poor boy sandwiches is probably longer than the welfare rolls, this small family-style restaurant does it best with Italian sausage and roast beef. If you are yourself a poor boy (or girl), the large servings of meatballs and spaghetti, gumbo, and jambalaya will not take too big a bite out of your pocket. Open daily. No reservations. Major credit cards. 3800 Canal St. (482-9179). Inexpensive.

Gumbo Shop – This pleasant little shop in the Vieux Carré serves up some of the best gumbo around, and in Gumbo City, that's saying something. Open for lunch and dinner except Sundays. No reservations. Major credit cards. 630 St. Peter St. (525-1486). Inexpensive.

D. H. Holmes – You can get a good and filling lunch or snack at this department store for just a few dollars. The daily specials are usually good, and the turtle and vegetable soups are great. Closed Sundays. No reservations. No credit cards. 819 Canal St. (561-6321). Inexpensive.

NEW YORK CITY

A first-time visitor trying to capture New York City in a single phrase may find a situation similar to the legendary blind man who tried to describe an elephant. Your first impression of this enormously diverse city can easily be distorted by the specific neighborhood in which you happen to land. An uninitiated tourist in the Tottenville section of Staten Island would likely surprise neighbors back home with descriptions of rolling farmland, rural ambience, and settings seemingly more appropriate to Iowa than to this country's most cosmopolitan center. That same stranger standing amidst the ruins of the South Bronx would horrify home-town friends with tales of a "war zone" reminiscent of Dresden after the firebombings. And seeing the corner of 59th Street and 5th Avenue for the first time, our fledgling traveler couldn't help but be impressed with the incredible elegance of surroundings whose gaudy opulence has few equals in the world. The question, then, is which is the real New York?

The answer has to be that New York is all these things. In a way, a visitor has his choice of the New York City he wishes to visit, and it's a simple matter to be insulated from all potential unpleasantness. A tourist's terrain in New York is traditionally limited to Manhattan and, indeed, generally bordered by the Hudson and East Rivers and 34th and 96th Streets. Within this relatively narrow geographic area stand New York's most famous hotels, its conglomeration of elegant restaurants, and its most famous theaters, cinemas, museums, and fine shops.

It is, therefore, sometimes difficult for a New York City visitor to reconcile the entertaining New York of his own experience with the troubled and troublesome New York about which he so often reads. It is hard to understand matters of civic bankruptcy while craning one's neck up the canyons of Park Avenue, and hard to understand want and welfare while window-shopping through the chic, dramatic boutiques of Madison Avenue. But in fact the tourist's New York and the most crowded residential areas of the city seldom intersect, and it is unlikely that the reality of New York's municipal malaise will ever intrude on the tourist's consciousness — unless he or she specifically sets out to see the city's other face.

For those not heavily into social consciousness, New York offers an array of distractions unequaled anywhere on earth. Nowhere are there more museums of such a consistently high quality. Nowhere are there restaurants of such striking ethnic diversity. Nowhere is there more diverse shopping for more esoteric paraphernalia, and nowhere in the world does the pace of city life and the activities of the populace more dramatically accent a city's vitality and appeal.

Just as Americans hardly ever refer to themselves simply as Americans — tending to describe themselves as Southerners, Texans, Californians, and the like — New York's seven million residents are similarly chauvinistic about the specific enclaves within the city in which they reside. Though in theory New York is composed of five boroughs — Manhattan, Queens, Brooklyn, the Bronx, and Richmond (Staten Island) — everyone understands that Manhattan is "The City."

So a visitor to New York should not feel at all self-conscious about his insular orientation, since residents of Flushing (in Queens) talk of going to the city with the same undertone of long-distance travel adventure as do residents of Kansas City. Brooklynites have been known not to cross the East River for years at a time, and many think of themselves as living in some relatively rural hamlet quite separate and entirely distinct from the evils of the Big Town. And there are farmers on Staten Island who haven't ventured into Manhattan in a generation. Yet all are lifetime New Yorkers, and all are filled with especially fierce pride in the area of the city in which they live.

Indeed, New York is truly the capital of this country in almost every way, and the presence of the United Nations enclave in the middle of Manhattan makes it possible to describe the city as the capital of the world as well. It is likely that you will find more French people in Paris, more Japanese in Tokyo, and more Africans in Dakar, but it is *unlikely* that any other city in the world boasts so large a representation of these cosmopolitan cultures, races, and ethnic entities as New York. And one has only to pick any of a broad range of midtown restaurants to experience dining elbow-to-elbow with the very same figures who, just hours before, were deciding everything from the future of world commerce to the maintenance of world peace.

New York is also the communications capital of the planet; from the Avenue of the Americas come most of the decisions that determine television viewing — not only in this country, but around the world — and while TV production facilities are firmly headquartered in California, the decisions about what will be produced are usually made in executive offices in Manhattan. New York has the same dominance in radio broadcasting and magazine publishing, and though the city is now down to only three daily newspapers, at least two of them — the *New York Times* and the *Daily News* — have national impact. Books, records, and even motion pictures all depend on New York–originated decisions for everything from creativity to advertising and financing, and they reflect what has often been described as the bias of the Eastern establishment. The capital of that establishment is clearly New York.

There is, in addition, widespread perception that for any creative artist to succeed, she or he must gain recognition in New York. In the theater, every actor, writer, director, designer, singer, dancer, musician, and composer feels the magnetic pull of Broadway. Painters, sculptors, writers of every description, cartoonists, jingle rhymers, artists, and charlatans all focus their creative and financial yearnings toward New York. Whether one wants to make it on the stage, on the screen, on the airwaves, in bookstores, or on billboards, the path to success must eventually traverse New York.

Just as hard to characterize as the geography of this diffuse city is the attempt to stereotype a typical New Yorker. The city is notable, first of all, for its immense ethnic diversity, and there are large segments of the city where the English language is hardly ever heard. From the obvious examples of

Chinatown and Little Italy to the less apparent Slavic and Hasidic enclaves, centuries-old tradition is maintained through rigid authoritarianism and purposeful segregation. Though New York's ethnic ghettos are initially invisible and completely unofficial, they are often most stringently maintained by the residents who live within their boundaries.

Other New Yorkers use these enclaves to their own benefit and regularly visit ethnic neighborhoods to attend "foreign" festivals during the year. The Chinese New Year is nowhere more intensely celebrated than on Mott Street, and one would be hard pressed to develop a more authentic case of Italian indigestion than can be suffered during the San Gennaro Festival on Mulberry Street each fall. New Yorkers, whose culinary horizons probably reach farther afield than any other civic population on earth, regularly plumb the depths of such exotica as Greek specialties wrapped in grape leaves, Lebanese shish kebabs, Slavic pirozhkies, and German wursts. A visitor who does not follow the local lead (and try to immerse himself in as many ethnic cuisines as possible) is indeed wasting a once-in-a-lifetime opportunity.

New York's cultural and gastronomic leadership is only slightly less important to the nation and the world than its financial ascendancy. Just walking through the Wall Street area provides a dramatic impact and reaffirms that the city's own financial problems have in no way lessened its hold on world commerce. Visitors' galleries at the New York Stock Exchange and certain of the commodity exchanges provide the unique opportunity to watch capitalism in action in its wild state, and nowhere is the sense of the enormity of American industry and the scope of commercial trading more intensely felt.

Trading has a long history in New York City, for it was here that the original $24 worth of trinkets and baubles bought the island of Manhattan from the Indians who may (or may not) have been its owners. Depending on one's point of view, the Indians were either boldly deceived on the price or they made one of the best real estate deals in the city's history.

That original island of Manhattan, a near wilderness traversed by several streams and rivers, bears little resemblance to the island as it presently exists. Various landfill and reclamation projects have enlarged it over the years, and just a brief glance today at the west side of the Battery Park area (at the southernmost tip) indicates that expanding the island's real estate is still very much an active enterprise.

Through the years, New York has resisted any exclusive European identification, and its current cast indicates very little influence of the passage from Dutch hands to English and the subsequent ascendancy of first one group of immigrants and then another. In this sense, it is a singularly liberated city, feeling little allegiance to any single ancestor or antecedent. From this polyglot past springs the New York feeling that it is really a nation unto itself.

In all the world, New York has no equal. Its ability to prosper in spite of its monumental problems testifies to its strength and resilience more dramatically than can any analytic essay. That its residents choose to continue to live amid its many municipal shortcomings highlights the fact that its benefits far outweigh its discouragements, and the inclination of tourists from all over the world to visit its halls and byways continues to make it the single most popular tourist destination in this hemisphere. This ongoing appeal amply justifies New York's avowed preeminent attraction and ensures its continued attraction as the greatest magnet in America. It is, above all, a city that revels in its ability to excite the curious and strongly attract the interest of those who live elsewhere.

NEW YORK AT-A-GLANCE

SEEING THE CITY: New York is, to put it simply, the most complex city in the world. People who have lived here all their lives don't even know all of it — its size and diversity challenge even the most ambitious. The best bet for the visitor who wants to feel the magic of New York and to understand how the city is laid out is to take it all in from one of several vantage points:

Brooklyn Promenade – Standing on this walkway at dusk, with the lights of Manhattan shimmering across the East River, you'll get an idea of the magnitude and beauty of the city. On Lower Manhattan the towers of the World Trade Center rise before you, and the Brooklyn Bridge spans the river to your right. Farther north stand the Empire State Building and the United Nations Secretariat Building, landmarks of midtown. The easiest way to get here is via the IRT 7th Avenue subway line, Clark St. stop.

World Trade Center – The elevator to the observation deck of Two World Trade Center whisks you more than a quarter of a mile above the street. There is an enclosed deck on the 107th floor and a promenade on the roof above the 110th floor. Manhattan spreads out to the north, Brooklyn is on the east, on the west is New Jersey, and to the south lies New York harbor, leading to the Atlantic Ocean. Open daily from 9:30 AM to 9:30 PM. Tickets are sold on the mezzanine level of Tower Two. Liberty and West Sts. (466-7377).

Empire State Building – Although many tourists prefer the newer and higher World Trade Center observation deck, the old queen of New York attracts more than 1.5 million people a year — the Art Deco design is more romantic than anything in the World Trade Center (even if Deborah Kerr never kept her appointment with Gary Grant here in "An Affair to Remember"). You can feel the breeze from the 86th floor or ascend to the glass-enclosed 102nd floor. Don't be surprised if in the evening the top of the building is bathed in colored lights — it's the city's newest way to commemorate holidays and special occasions. Open daily from 9:30 AM to midnight. Admission charge. 34th St. and 5th Ave. (736-3100).

Statue of Liberty – The view from the small windows in the great lady's crown is not really worth the climb (the elevator only goes partway to the top) up 12 stories of narrow, cramped, winding staircases, but the views from the island itself are lovely. Take the Circle Line (269 5755) from Battery Park to Liberty Island (formerly called Bedloe's Island); the cost of the trip includes admission to the statue and to the Museum of Immigration (732-1236) at the base. You can see the statue from a distance and the southern tip of the city by riding the Staten Island Ferry. For 25¢ round trip, it's also the best way to beat the summer heat. The Ferry Terminal is located next to Battery Park (the South Ferry stop on the IRT 7th Avenue line).

Views from Above and Below – You get some of the most dramatic views of New York when entering the city by car. The three western access routes have special features: the Holland Tunnel access road from the N. J. Turnpike, leading into lower Manhattan, offers a panorama of the southern tip of the island; the Lincoln Tunnel access road offers a view of Manhattan's West Side; and the George Washington Bridge, linking New Jersey and the Upper West Side, has spectacular views of the Hudson, the city's long shore along the river, and the New Jersey Palisades, as well as being a work of art itself, best seen from a distance, from the river, or while driving north on the West Side Highway.

The Streets – On Saturdays, Sundays, and holidays, you can see New York on the Culture Bus. Loops I and II will take you to New York's major museums, tourist attractions, and historical sights. For a map and a schedule, pick up a pamphlet at the Information Booth at Grand Central Station, Penn Station, or at 370 Jay St., Brooklyn (9 AM to 5 PM, weekdays), or call the NY Transit Authority (330-1234). This information is also available on the buses.

Tours – Many of the tour companies in the city will help you get your bearings before setting out on your own. Gray Line, 900 8th Ave., between 53rd and 54th Sts. (397-2600), provides good bus tours. Circle Line Cruises offers an interesting three-hour guided boat trip around Manhattan from the middle of April until mid-November. Boats leave from Pier 83 at the foot of W 42nd St. and the Hudson River (563-3200). Most spectacular is Island Helicopter's ride around Manhattan. Though the price is considerable, you won't forget this trip soon. At E 34th St. and the East River (683-4575).

SPECIAL PLACES: Manhattan is a 12 ½-mile-long island stretching 2 ½ miles at its widest point. Avenues run north and south, streets run east and west. Fifth Avenue is the dividing line between addresses designated east and those designated west. For example, 20 E 57th Street is in the first block of 57th east of 5th Avenue; 20 W 57th Street is in the first block west of 5th Avenue. New York grew from south to north, street by street and neighborhood by neighborhood. The oldest parts of the city are around the docks in Lower Manhattan and in the financial district.

The best way to discover the city and enjoy its incredible variety and ethnic diversity is by direct contact — walking through the neighborhoods. You will want to take taxis or public transport between areas — distances can be great — but have no hesitation about walking once you've arrived. The much-touted reputation of New Yorkers for aloofness and unfriendliness simply isn't true. Just watch what happens when you ask directions on a bus or subway (except during rush hours, when things are, admittedly, a bit primitive). We suggest a copy of the *Flashmaps! Instant Guide to New York* (Flashmaps, Inc., $2.95), which has the most accessible and best-organized series of maps of New York neighborhoods that we've encountered.

LOWER MANHATTAN

Ellis Island – Before you begin exploring Manhattan, you may want to take the Circle Line to this island, which served as a processing center for immigrants from 1892 to 1924. The trip provides a fascinating introduction to what the city is all about. More than 24 million people passed through this island on their way to a new life in the land of opportunity; these aging shells of buildings were the sites of joy and heartbreak; many immigrant families were separated here when some members were refused entry to the US because of bad health or lack of money. Tours led by National Park rangers take one hour and give a lasting impression of the experience. Boats leave four times a day from Battery Park, from the end of April to the end of October (269-5755).

Governors Island – You can visit this island in New York harbor on special occasions. Now a Coast Guard base, the island's two pre-1800 structures are the Governor's House and Fort Jay. Free tours for groups of ten or more (no individual tours) can be arranged by writing to the Special Services Division, US Coast Guard Support Center, Governors Island, NY 10004 (668-7255).

Battery Park – Twenty-one acres of green, overlooking New York harbor, this is the spot for picnics on hot summer days. There's a statue of Giovanni da Verrazano, the pilot of the *Dauphine,* the ship that reached Manhattan in 1524 (Verrazano was later killed by cannibals in the Caribbean). Castle Clinton was build as a fort in 1807 and has functioned as an opera house, an immigrant landing depot, and as an aquarium at various times. Bordered by State St., Battery Pl., and the river.

Battery Park to Wall Street – This area is a lovely place to wander on weekends, when the empty streets emphasize the incongruity of the Chase Manhattan building and the World Trade Center surrounded by the 17th- and 18th-century buildings on Pearl Street, Bowling Green, and Hanover Square. Two buildings of particular note are the India House on the south side of Hanover Square (1837) and the old US Customs Houses (the new Customs House is in the World Trade Center), which was built in 1907 in neoclassic style. Another turn-of-the-century building at 56 Beaver St. until recently housed *Delmonico's Restaurant,* the meeting place of the elite of lower Manhattan.

Fraunces Tavern Museum – This building was the site of Washington's farewell to his officers in 1783, and contains memorabilia of the American Revolution (including Washington's hat). The *Fraunces Tavern* restaurant occupies the ground floor. Most of the area around it is slated for eventual renovation as a historic area. Open daily. Free. 54 Pearl St. (425-1778).

New York Stock Exchange – A tree stands in front of the stock exchange to commemorate the tree under which the first transaction took place in 1792. Today, close to 1,600 corporations are listed on the big board. You can observe the action from a glass-enclosed gallery reached via the visitors' entrance at 20 Broad St. Open weekdays. Free. (623-5168). The American Stock Exchange is located at 86 Trinity Pl. and also offers free explanations of the business on the floor. If you want to see real emotion, though, head for the New York Cocoa Exchange, 127 John St., or the New York Coffee and Sugar Exchange, 4 World Trade Center (938-2800), which makes the Stock Exchange seem like a London tea party.

Federal Hall – This national historic site served as the British headquarters during the Revolution and was later the seat of American government. George Washington was sworn in as president here in 1789. Open weekdays. Free. At the corner of Wall and Broad Sts. (264-8711).

Trinity Church – The church faces Wall Street, which is appropriate, because it has been a wealthy parish since it was first granted a charter by William III in 1697. One of the local citizens who aided in building the church was Captain Kidd, the notorious pirate who was hanged in London in 1701. The present building was completed in 1846, but the graveyard beside the church is even older. William Bradford, Jr., Robert Fulton, and Alexander Hamilton are buried here. For years, the Trinity Church steeple was the highest point on the New York skyline. During the summer, the church sponsors lunch-hour entertainment, called the Noonday Café, for downtown workers in the south courtyard. Classical concerts are held year-round on Tuesdays at 12:45 PM in the church. At Broadway and Wall Sts. (285-0800).

St. Paul's Chapel – The oldest church building in Manhattan, this fine example of colonial architecture was erected in 1766 on what was then a field outside the city. George Washington worshiped here. North of Trinity Church on the corner of Broadway and Fulton St.

World Trade Center – A world in itself. At 1,350 feet each, its two towers are not the tallest buildings in the world (the CNR Tower in Toronto is at 1,815 feet), but close to it. In order to build the center, 1.2 million yards of earth and rock were excavated (they're now in the Hudson River). The concourse has shops and some excellent restaurants (see *Best in Town*), including *Windows on the World, The Big Kitchen,* and the *Market Dining Room.* Not all World Trade Center businesses involve trade, but the Customs House is located here, as is the Commodity Exchange and the Cotton and Mercantile Exchanges. The *Vista International* hotel, a recent addition to the center, is the first hotel to open up in this area in over 100 years (see *Best in Town*). Open daily. Free. Bounded by West, Church, Liberty, and Vesey Sts. (466-4170).

City Hall – This is the third City Hall of New York; it was built in 1803 and contains the office of the Mayor and the City Council chamber. The original construction cost half a million dollars, and in 1956 the restoration cost some $2 million (times change). The building was a site of great importance to New York's and America's history: Lafayette visited in 1824; Lincoln's body lay in state in 1865; and, in the 1860s, City Hall and Tammany Hall (Park Row and Frankfort St.) were controlled by Boss Tweed, the powerful corrupt political figure who dominated New York politics until the 1870s.

Other city government buildings nearby include the Municipal Building on the northeast corner of City Hall Park, the United States Court House, across from Foley Square, the New York County Courthouse next door, the Federal Office Building on the other side of Lafayette St., and the Hall of Records. City Hall Park has a statue of Nathan Hale, the patriot of the Revolution, who was executed here in 1776. Today, protestors of every persuasion gather in the park to welcome the Mayor when he ventures downtown. Open weekdays. Free. In a triangular park between Park Row, 250 Broadway, and Chambers St.

Fulton Street – The eastern end of the street is alive and well. Most of the action is between Fulton and Beekman Streets. Fish is now shipped in by truck instead of taken off the boats, but the wholesale market is still a wild place. It comes alive from midnight until 8 or 9 in the morning. It is rough and ready, not exactly a tourist spot; but if you don't mind fishheads whizzing past you at high speeds or getting up early, you'll see a part of the real New York.

South St. Seaport – A lovely place to spend hot summer days. The area includes two piers and two blocks of buildings, all of which preserve a flavor of the seafaring days of early New York. The Visitors Center is a good place to start exploring. The seaport gallery has shows of maritime art, a recreation of a 19th-century print shop, a model room of a steamship, and shops. Of greatest interest are the ships, including the *Peking,* built in 1911, the *Lettie Howard,* a fishing schooner from 1893, and the *Ambrose Light Ship* of 1907. Open daily. Voluntary contribution to enter the museum and admission charge to board the ships. Fulton St. at the East River. (766-9020).

Brooklyn Bridge – You can stroll from Manhattan to Brooklyn by crossing the Brooklyn Bridge on a pedestrian walk. You'll get a good view of the city, and a close look at this engineering feat. The 6,775-foot bridge, which spans the fast river at a height of 133 feet, was completed in 1883 and cost $25 million to build. Many workers were seriously injured during its construction, and a number of people have since committed suicide by jumping from it. Always open. Free, unless someone succeeds in selling you title to the bridge. Take the IRT Lexington Ave. line to Worth St.–Brooklyn Bridge station.

Chinatown – The best way to get the feel of New York's Chinese neighborhood is to hit the streets, especially Mott, Bayard, and Pell. More than 10,000 people live in this area of crowded, narrow streets, and the Chinese population spills into neighboring Little Italy. Although the Chinese community here is not as large as the one in San Francisco, it is authentic. You'll know when you reach Chinatown by the pagoda-shaped telephone booths and stores that sell shark fins, duck eggs, fried fungi, and squid. Herbs are lined up next to aspirin in the pharmacies. This is where Chinese shop, and uptowners and out-of-towners are following their lead. Don't miss the good, cheap restaurants, the tea parlors, or the bakeries. Try the dim sum at lunchtime (steamed or fried dumplings filled with seafood, pork, or beef). Sundays are a good time to visit the area, but if you can, come during the Chinese New Year (held on the first full moon after January 21). The celebration is wild and woolly, with fireworks, dancing dragons, and throngs of people. While you'll get the best sense of Chinatown from the streets, if you want historical perspective, stop by the Chinese Museum, which houses exhibits from the first dynasty to the present. Open daily. Admission charge. 8 Mott St. (964-1542).

Little Italy – Italian music from tenement windows, old men playing bocce, old women dressed in black checking the vegetables in the markets, store windows with religious articles, pasta factories, and the ubiquitous odor of Italian cooking fill this neighborhood, which has the reputation of being one of the safest areas in the city. Mulberry Street is the center of Little Italy, but the area stretches for blocks around and blends into parts of SoHo and Greenwich Village. Even Bleecker Street, toward 7th Avenue, has a decidedly Italian flavor, with bakeries selling cannoli and cappuccino sandwiched between Middle Eastern restaurants and stores selling Chinese window shades. Little Italy is thronged during the festivals of San Gennaro and St. Anthony. In late September, San Gennaro covers Mulberry Street from Spring to Park. St. Anthony fills Sullivan Street, from Houston to Spring, in mid-June. The festivals attract people from in and out of the city with game booths, rides, and most of all, enough food and drink (both Italian and "foreign") for several armies. Bordered by Canal and Houston Sts., and the Bowery and Ave. of the Americas.

The Bowery – There is nothing romantic about New York's Skid Row. On this strip are people who have failed — alcoholics and dope addicts, both old and young. If you drive west on Houston Street, you'll get a look at some of the inhabitants — they'll wipe your windshields whether you like it or not and expect some change for their trouble. Recently, however, the Bowery has had some new settlers; a few theaters and music places have moved in. The area also has some good places to shop; specialties include lamps and restaurant supplies. The stores have moved into this area because of the proximity to one of the most interesting shopping markets in the world: the Lower East Side. Between 4th St. and Chatham Sq.

The Lower East Side – This area is probably the largest melting pot in the city. Its Sunday market is an experience that shouldn't be missed. Eastern European Jews, many of whom are Hasidim (an ultra-religious sect, easily recognizable by their earlocks, called pais, and their fur hats and long black coats), sell their wares for rock bottom prices; you'll have to bargain if you want the best prices, and these merchants are formidable opponents. The area is also home to Puerto Ricans, blacks, and various other groups; you will hear Yiddish, Spanish, and even some Yiddish-accented Spanish.

The Lower East Side was where the Jews from Eastern Europe, fleeing Czarist persecution and pogroms, first settled during their massive migration from 1880 to 1918. Many of the streets, including Rivington, Hester, Essex, and Grand, still look the way they did then. To really get a taste of the area, try the food at the *Grand Dairy Restaurant* (341 Grand St.), knishes at *Yonah Schimmel's* (137 E Houston St.), hot dogs at *Katz' Delicatessen* (205 E Houston St.), or a Rumanian "broilings" at *Sammy's* (157 Chrystie St.).

SoHo – The name means "South of Houston Street" (pronounced *How*-stun by natives). SoHo leads a double life. On weekends, uptown New Yorkers and out-of-towners fill the streets to explore its trendy stores, restaurants, and art galleries. During the week, SoHo is a very livable combination of 19th-century cast-iron buildings, spillovers from Little Italy, off-off-Broadway theater groups, and practicing artists. At night, the streets are empty and you can see into the residential lofts of the old buildings; some are simple, open spaces, others are jungles of plants and Corinthian columns. *Fanelli's,* on the corner of Mercer and Prince streets, is one of the oldest around and a hangout for residents. Many artists are now moving to Tribeca (the triangle below Canal, get it?), which is located south of SoHo farther west and has better loft pickings. SoHo is between Canal and Houston Sts., Broadway and Hudson St.

The East Village – Famous during the 60s as the center of the New York counterculture, this section is now the home of poor artists, poor — though often very accomplished — theater groups, and various ethnic groups (the largest of which is Ukrainian, but there are also Armenians, Czechs, Germans, Russians, Poles, Jews, blacks, and Hispanics, many of whom live in low-income housing projects). East 8th Street, once the city's psychedelic capital, is now pretty burnt out, although some streets are still lively, with cheap restaurants, shops, and movie theaters. (Don't wander here after dark unless you know where you're going.) Astor Place, on the border between the East and West Villages, is the site of Cooper Union (good for free concerts and lectures) and the Public Theater, 425 Lafayette St. (598-7150), Joe Papp's creation, where you'll find some of the best serious drama (both contemporary and classical) and experimental theater as well as progressive jazz. You might want to have a drink at *McSorley's,* 15 E 7th St. (473-8800), a fixture in the East Village for years, and until recently a bastion for male drinkers. A few blocks north is the spiritual home of the village, St. Mark's-in-the-Bouwerie, on the corner of 2nd Ave. and 10th St. St. Mark's still sponsors community activities, especially poetry readings by some of the best poets in New York. The East Village has been home to many writers, from James Fenimore Cooper (6 St. Mark's Pl.) to W. H. Auden (77 St. Mark's Pl.) to LeRoi Jones — now Imamu Baraka (27 Cooper Sq.). Bounded by Lafayette St. and the East River, Houston and 14th Sts.

GREENWICH VILLAGE

You can and definitely should wander around the West Village (as residents know it) at night. The area is filled with surprises. You've probably heard of Bleecker Street, the slightly tawdry gathering place of tourists and the high school crowd from the suburbs, or of Washington Square Park, with its musicians, mimes, and street people. But you might not have pictured Grove Court, the lovely and secluded row of 19th-century houses near the corner of Grove and Bedford Streets (where O. Henry lived), or the Morton Street pier on the Hudson River, from which you can see the Statue of Liberty on a clear day. But the Village is more than this. It is an activist neighborhood, struggling to keep control of this famous, much-loved neighborhood. There are meat-packing factories from the 1920s, old speakeasies turned into restaurants, a miniature Times Square on W 8th Street, and immaculate (and expensive) brownstones on quiet, tree-lined streets. Get a map (you'll need it — there's nowhere else in Manhattan where W 4th Street could bisect W 12th Street) and wander. Or you can ask directions— villagers love to help and it's a nice way to meet them. You can eat, go to the theater, sip cappuccino in an outdoor café, hear great jazz, and find your own special places. Bounded by 5th Ave. on the east, the Hudson River on the west, Houston St. on the south, and W 14th St. on the north.

Washington Square – A gathering place for students from New York University, Frisbee aficionados, volleyball players, modern-day Bohemians, and people who like to watch them all. The Arch is New York's answer to the Arc de Triomphe. Buildings surrounding the square include the New York University library, administration buildings, and law school. The north side of Washington Square has some lovely homes, including number 7, where Edith Wharton lived. Bounded by extensions of W 4th St., Macdougal St., Waverly Pl., and University Pl.

Bleecker Street – Strolling down Bleecker Street from La Guardia Place to 8th Avenue you'll pass outdoor cafés, head shops, falafel parlors, jazz clubs including the *Village Gate* (Bleecker and Thompson Sts.), Italian grocery stores, and a myriad of restaurants. You should also wander down some of the side streets, like Thompson, Macdougal (Bob Dylan's old stomping ground), and Sullivan. Have a cappuccino at *Caffè Reggio* (119 Macdougal). Beyond 7th Avenue, the side streets become more residential; try Charles Street, W 10th Street, and Bank Street for examples of how the upper middle class lives in the Village. You'll also pass Christopher Street, the center of gay life in Manhattan (although the toughest part of it comes alive on West Street, by the West Side Highway, on weekend nights).

Fifth Avenue – Where the wealthy Villagers live. The Salmagundi Club, built in 1853 at 47 5th Avenue (near 12th Street), is the last of the imposing private mansions that once lined the avenue. On the streets between 5th and the Avenue of the Americas (which the natives call 6th Avenue) you can see expensive brownstones. The New School for Social Research, 66 W 12th St., has courses on everything from fixing a leak to ethnomusicology. From Washington Sq. north to 14th St.

Avenue of the Americas – One of the most unusual buildings in the village is the Jefferson Market Library, on 6th Avenue and 10th Street, with a small garden alongside. Built in 1878 in Italian Gothic style, it served as a courthouse for many years. Nearby is *Balducci's,* 424 6th Ave., an Italian market with a wide variety of exotic foods, plus fresh fruit and vegetables. *Ray's Pizza* at 465 6th Ave. — the place on the corner with the long lines — is considered to make some of the best pizza in the city by queues who know their pies.

Farther west (between 6th Ave. and Hudson St. and W Houston and Christopher Sts.) is a series of small winding streets with some especially interesting places to visit. At 75½ Bedford Street is the house in which Edna St. Vincent Millay and John Barrymore once lived (not at the same time) — it's only nine feet wide. *Chumley's,* 86 Bedford St., used to be a speakeasy during Prohibition and still has no sign on the door — but it does have good food and poetry readings inside. Commerce Street is a small side street lined with lovely old buildings, including the Cherry Lane Theater, one of the city's oldest. Morton Street, one block south, is often mistaken for Hester Street, because it was the site of the filming of "Hester Street," the 1975 film about the Lower East Side Jewish immigrants. Another block south is Leroy Street with St. Luke's Place, a row of 19th-century houses. Number 6 Leroy was built in 1880 and was the home of New York Mayor Jimmy Walker. If you walk to the end of the block and north on Hudson Street, you'll come to the *White Horse Tavern,* 567 Hudson St., which was Dylan Thomas' hangout on his trips to New York City. Go in and have a drink.

14TH STREET TO 34TH STREET

Gramercy Park – A few blocks north of Greenwich Village, Gramercy Park is one of the few places where you can get a feel for what Manhattan used to be like. The park itself is open only to local residents, but on a sunny day you can see nannies with their privileged young charges sitting on the benches in the shadows of the 19th-century mansions that surround the park. A few blocks north of Gramercy Park on Lexington Avenue are dozens of little Eastern Indian shops selling splendid assortments of spices, saris, cotton blouses, jewelry, and food. E 21st St. and Lexington Ave.

Chelsea – An eclectic residential neighborhood in the West 20s, between 7th and 10th Avenues, where you can find elegant brownstones next door to run-down, four-story, walk-up tenements. The *Chelsea Hotel,* W 23rd St. and 9th Ave., has earned an important place in literary history. Thomas Wolfe, Brendan Behan, Dylan Thomas, and Arthur Miller slept and wrote in its rooms. Andy Warhol made a four-hour movie about its raunchier inhabitants. For a sojourn into tranquillity, step into the inner courtyard of General Theological Seminary, a gift to the city in 1817 by Clement C. Moore, author of "A Visit from Saint Nicholas." Open daily from 2 to 4 PM. Free. 175 9th Ave. (243-5150).

MIDTOWN (34TH STREET TO 59TH STREET)

West 34th Street – A major shopping street, this is the home of the traditional mercantile giants *Macy's* and *Gimbel's,* as well as *B. Altman's* (technically on E 34th St.), and scores of boutiques selling blue jeans, blouses, underwear, shoes, records, and electronic gear. The main shopping district runs along 34th Street from 8th Avenue east to Madison Avenue, with a number of smaller, expensive shops lining the street as far east as Third Avenue. The hub of 34th Street is Herald Square, where Broadway intersects the Avenue of the Americas (6th Avenue).

Madison Square Garden, the Forum, and Penn Station – A huge coliseum-arena, office building, and transportation complex. The Garden's 19,500 seats are fully packed when the New York Knicks (NBA basketball) and the New York Rangers (NHL hockey) play home games, when the Ringling Brothers and Barnum & Bailey Circus comes to town, or whenever there is a major exhibition, concert, or convention. The Felt Forum is a 5,000-seat hall attached to the Garden, used for boxing matches, concerts, and smaller exhibitions. Penn Station is Amtrak's major New York terminal (for Amtrak information, call 736-4545). There are no guided tours. 4 Pennsylvania Plaza, W 33rd St. between 7th and 8th Aves. (564-4400 for Garden and Forum information).

Garment District – The center of the clothing and fashion industries. On any weekday during office hours, you can see racks of the latest apparel being pushed through the terrifically hectic streets. Along 7th and 8th Aves. from 30th to 39th St.

The Empire State Building – The first skyscraper in New York to be attacked by King Kong. The 102-story building was erected in 1931 and became the symbol of the city for decades. There is an open-air observation deck on the 86th floor to which millions of tourists have been whisked over the years to gaze in awe at the surrounding New York skyline and another glass-enclosed viewing area on the 102nd floor. Open daily, 9:30 AM to midnight. W 34th St. and 5th Ave. (736-3100).

Times Square – Every New Year's Eve, Times Square is where thousands of New Yorkers and visitors welcome in the New Year. Although the height of mad celebration reaches its pinnacle at that time, Times Square is always crowded. The quality of the crowds, however, leaves much to be desired. In spite of its reputation as one of the major crossroads of the world, Times Square is mainly the hangout of drug pushers, pimps, hookers, junkies, and assorted street peddlers attempting to fence stolen jewelry. It is also the center of the city's sex industry. To the naked eye, it is nearly wall-to-wall porn shops and hard-core movies. Proposals for rehabilitation have been almost as numerous as the prostitutes on parade. The latest involves a new John L. Portman hotel, to be built on the site of the Helen Hayes and Morosco theaters, now demolished. W 42nd St., where Broadway crosses 7th Ave.

Broadway and the Theater District – Just north of Times Square, you'll find the glamorous marquees and billboards for which New York is famous. The lights are still pretty dazzling, twinkling on and off in a glittering electric collage. On most nights, the streets are jammed with people. The legitimate theaters are between W 42nd and W 50th Sts. to the east and west of Broadway.

New York Public Library – A couple of blocks east of Times Square, this dignified old building is a good place to sit and catch your breath. Sit on the front steps, between the famous lion statues, or in Bryant Park behind the library, where there are lunchtime concerts during the summer. The park is not, however, very safe after dark. New Yorkers generally prefer to sit on the steps near the stone lions. Inside the library is New York's largest reference collection of books, periodicals, and exhibits of graphic art, as well as a gift store, and a Gutenberg Bible worth $3 million. Closed Thursdays and Sundays. Free. E 42nd St. and 5th Ave. (790-6161).

The Chrysler Building – The princess of the skyline. Its distinctive, graceful spire, decorated with stainless steel, now sparkles with more than its usual brilliance since the recent installation of hand-blown fluorescent lights around its peak. Although it has long ceded the title of tallest on the skyline, this twinkling building of the 1930s remains, to many New Yorkers, the most beautiful of all. Since there are no tours or observatories, it is best seen from a distance. E 42nd St. and Lexington Ave.

The Ford Foundation Building – If you happen to be wandering through New York at sunrise and climb the stairs between 1st and 2nd Avenues on 42nd Street, you'll see the bronzed windows of the Ford Foundation building catch the first rays of the sun, reflecting copper-colored light into the sky. At other times, the building is just as dramatic. Built around a central courtyard containing tropical trees and plants, it is the only place in Manhattan where you can feel like you're in a jungle. Pick up an egg roll at the *Wunam Kitchen* on E 43rd Street and 2nd Avenue and munch away in the steamy garden. It's one of the great New York experiences — especially on snowy afternoons. Open weekdays. Free. 320 E 43rd St. (573-5000).

Tudor City – A nearly forgotten pocket of the city, this 1920s neo-Tudor apartment complex is one of the most romantic parts of the city. An esplanade overlooks the East River and the United Nations. Home to many diplomats and UN employees, Tudor City serves as an international campus. (According to local legend, Tudor City used to be where executives and industrialists housed their mistresses in the 1930s and 1940s.) The long, curved staircase leading to the sidewalk opposite the United Nations is known as the Isaiah Steps because of the Biblical quote carved into the wall. Between E 42nd and E 43rd Sts. at 1st Ave.

The United Nations – Although the UN is open all year, the best time to visit is between September and December when the General Assembly is in session. That's when delegates from nearly 150 nations gather to discuss the world's problems. Sessions are open to the public. The UN delegates' dining room is also open to the public for lunch weekdays throughout the year. Overlooking the East River, the dining room offers a lovely international menu and the chance to listen in on intriguing conversations. (Reservations for lunch are essential; call 754-7625). There are guided tours of the UN. Open daily. Admission charge for guided tour. 1 Dag Hammerskjold Plaza, E 42nd St. and 1st Ave. (754-1234).

Rockefeller Center – A group of skyscrapers originally built in the 1930s, Rockefeller Center is best known for the giant Christmas tree (always said to be the tallest in the world) on display in December, for its ice skating rink, and for Radio City Music Hall, a theatrical landmark and home of the Rockettes (757-3100). There are tours of the Center and the observation tower. Closed Sundays. Admission charge. 5th Ave. between 48th and 51st Sts. (489-2947).

St. Patrick's Cathedral – A refuge from the crowds of 5th Avenue. The most famous church in the city, dedicated to Ireland's patron saint, stands in Gothic splendor across the street from Rockefeller Center in the shadow of the skyscrapers. Resplendent with gargoyles on the outside, stained glass windows and gold sacraments on the inside, St. Patrick's is a good place for rest, contemplation, and prayer. Catholic services are held daily. 5th Ave. between E 50th and E 51st Sts. (753-2261).

Sixth Avenue – Officially known as Avenue of the Americas, but no New Yorker calls it that. Sixth Avenue between 42nd and 57th Streets is particularly breathtaking at dusk when the giant glass and steel buildings light up. In the basement of the McGraw-Hill Building, 6th Ave. and W 48th St. (869-0345), is "The New York Experience," a dazzling multimedia show about the Big Apple. You travel through a replica of an old-fashioned "El" train to get to the show. Open daily. Admission charge.

Museum of Modern Art – A must. The masterpieces of modern art hanging on the walls include Wyeth's "Christina's World," Monet's "Water Lilies," and Van Gogh's "Starry Night." Throughout the year, the museum presents films from all over the world. Closed Wednesdays. Admission charge. On Tuesdays admission is on a pay-as-you-wish basis. 11 W 53rd St. (956-6100).

Fifth Avenue – Although the street runs from Washington Square straight to Spanish Harlem, when New Yorkers refer to 5th Avenue they usually mean the stretch of the world's most sophisticated shops between Rockefeller Center at 50th Street and the *Plaza Hotel* at the southeastern corner of Central Park at Central Park South (E 59th Street). *Sak's, Gucci, Tiffany's, Cartier, Bergdorf Goodman,* and, for children, *FAO Schwarz* make walking along the street an incredible test in temptation. Stop in at *Steuben Glass* on the corner of 55th Street and marvel at its permanent collection of sculpted glass depicting mythological and contemporary themes. Fifth Avenue is the dividing line between east and west in New York street addresses. It is the only New York avenue that runs perfectly straight along a north-south axis.

Grand Army Plaza – No New Yorker knows its official name, but this baroque square, with its central fountain at the southeast corner of Central Park, faces the regal *Plaza Hotel,* the General Motors Building, and the hansom cabstand where horse-drawn carriages (guided by drivers in top hats and tails) wait to escort clients through Central Park. If you have a lover, be sure to arrange to meet here at least once. Be sure, too, to take at least one ride through the park in a hansom cab, preferably at dusk or very, very late. Central Park South and 5th Ave.

Central Park – More than 50 blocks long but only three blocks wide, this beloved stretch of greenery is used by New Yorkers for jogging, biking, walking, ice skating, riding in horse-drawn hansom cabs, listening to concerts and opera, watching Shakespearean plays, demonstrating, flying kites, boating, gazing at art, and playing all kinds of ball games. It's literally one of those places where anything goes. The Central Park Zoo, between E 61st and E 65th Sts. on 5th Ave., has elephants, lions, monkeys, sea lions, and street performers and is most outrageous on Sundays. The zoo may be closed for renovation during part of 1983. Open daily. Free. Central Park is bounded by Central Park South (W 59th St.) on the south, W 110th St. on the north, 5th Ave. on the east, and Central Park West on the west. (For information on events in Central Park, call 755-4100.)

UPPER EAST SIDE

The Metropolitan Museum of Art – Perhaps the finest museum this side of the Louvre, more than two million people make the pilgrimage to these halls every year. You could easily spend days walking through the impressive sections displaying the costumes, ceramics, metalwork, armor, mummies, paintings, drawings, sculpture, photographs, and mosaics of dozens of different periods and countries. The special exhibits are really special. There is a cafeteria and gift shop. Films and lectures are presented throughout the year, and a distinguished concert series (570-3949) is held from September through May. Closed Mondays. Admission charge. On 5th Ave. at 81st St. (535-7710).

The Guggenheim Museum – Designed by Frank Lloyd Wright, this white curved building has spiraling ramps along its inner walls so you can travel through the collections on display by following the curves of the building. While it is given over primarily to exhibitions of contemporary art, some patrons feel that its architecture is more impressive than the collection it houses. Closed Mondays. Admission charge. 5th Ave. between E 88th and E 89th Sts. (860-1313).

Yorkville and Gracie Mansion – An interesting ethnic neighborhood of mostly German and Eastern European families. There are plenty of restaurants, beer halls, and delicatessens selling Wiener schnitzel, sauerbraten, wurst, and kielbasa. Gracie Mansion, the official residence of the Mayor of New York, sits in a garden that is part of Carl Schurz Park alongside the East River. The park is popular with joggers and dog-walkers. The best time to visit is at dawn, when the eastern sky comes to life. Yorkville stretches from E 80th to E 89th Sts. between Lexington and York Aves. Gracie Mansion and Carl Schurz Park are located at E 88th St. and East End Ave.

Roosevelt Island – A self-contained housing development in the middle of the East River. Accessible only by tramway, Roosevelt Island offers a unique view of midtown Manhattan. A loop bus encircles the island, which has restricted automobile traffic. The aerial tramway leaves each side every 15 minutes daily except during rush hours, when it leaves every 7½ minutes. The tram costs 75¢ (subway tokens are also accepted). Manhattan terminal at E 60th St. and 2nd Ave. (753-6626).

UPPER WEST SIDE

Columbus Circle and New York Coliseum – The southwestern corner of Central Park is dominated by a statue of Christopher Columbus and a traffic circle. On the western side of the circle stands the New York Coliseum, the site of major exhibitions such as the annual auto, boat, and antiques shows. Admission charge for events. W 59th St. and Central Park West (757-5000).

Lincoln Center – If you have ever seen Mel Brooks' film "The Producers," you have probably retained an image of the glowing lights of a fountain shooting into the air with an exuberance to match the enthusiasm of actors Zero Mostel and Gene Wilder. That's the Lincoln Center fountain, and it's just as magnificent in real life. The pulsing water and light are dramatically framed by the Metropolitan Opera House, a contemporary hall with giant murals by Marc Chagall. The performing arts complex also contains Avery Fisher Hall (home of the New York Philharmonic), the New York State Theater, (home of the New York City Ballet), the Vivian Beaumont Theater, the Juilliard Building, and the Library and Museum of the Performing Arts (see *Theater* and *Music* sections, below). Guided tours through the major buildings are conducted daily and last about an hour. Admission charge for tour. Broadway and W 66th St. (877-1800).

The Museum of Natural History – A cornucopia of curiosities. The anthropological and natural history exhibits in the form of life-size dioramas showing people and animals in realistic settings have made this one of the most famous museums in the world. The dinosaurs on the fourth floor are the stars of the show. Free guided tours leave from the main-floor information desk. Open daily. Donations accepted. Central Park West and W 79th St. (873-1300).

Hayden Planetarium – An amazing collection of astronomical exhibits on meteorites, comets, space vehicles, and other galactic phenomena. The sky show, in which constellations are projected onto an observatory ceiling, is one of the great New York sights. Subjects of the sky shows include lunar expeditions, the formation of the solar system, and UFOs. On Wednesday, Friday, Saturday, and Sunday evenings, Hayden Planetarium presents "Laserium," a light and sound display using laser beams. Open daily. Admission charge. Central Park West and W 81st St. (724-8700).

The Cathedral of St. John the Divine – The largest Gothic cathedral in the world, with a seating capacity of 10,000. It is irreverently nicknamed St. John the Unfinished, for a chronic shortage of funds has allowed only two-thirds of the impressive church to be completed since work began in 1892. Stonemasons, who most recently put down their trowels in the late 30s, picked them up again in 1979, with plans to finish the interior of the Crossing and the two towers' spires by the year 2000. There is a stunning collection of Renaissance and Byzantine art inside, and an exquisite time to see it all at its best is on Christmas Eve at midnight mass. Free guided tours are conducted daily. Open daily. Free. Amsterdam Ave. and W 112th St. (678-6888).

Columbia University – The Big Apple's contribution to the Ivy League. Although more than 27,000 students attend classes here, the campus is spacious enough to avoid a sense of crowding. Around the campus are a number of interesting bookstores, restaurants, and bars. The *West End Café,* Broadway and W 113th St. (666-8750), is a long-standing student favorite, and it was from here that Jack Kerouac went forth to lead the Beat Generation of the 1950s. On weekdays at 3 PM, from September through May, free guided tours of campus leave from 201 Dodge Hall. Open daily. Free. Broadway and W 116th St. (280-2845).

Riverside Church – Perched on a cliff overlooking the Hudson River, Riverside is an interdominational Christian church with a functioning carillon tower and an amazing statue of the Angel Gabriel blowing the trumpet. The white building next to the church is known as "the God Box" because many religious organizations (among them, the National Council of Churches and the Interfaith Council on Corporate Responsibility) are headquartered here. The carillon tower is open daily; free guided tours of the Church Sundays at 12:30 PM. W 120th St. between Riverside Dr. and Claremont Ave. (222-5900).

Grant's Tomb – Who is buried in Grant's tomb? (If you don't know, we're not going to tell you.) Suffice it to say, You-Know-Who and his wife, Mrs. You-Know-Who, are entombed here in a gray building topped with a rotunda and set in Riverside Park. A word about the park: Don't wander in after dark. Grant's tomb is officially known as General Grant National Memorial. Closed Mondays and Tuesdays. Free. Riverside Dr. and W 122nd St. (666-1640).

The Cloisters and Fort Tryon Park – Without a doubt one of the most unusual museums in the country, if not in the world, the Cloisters is a monastery that actually consists of sections of cloisters that originally belonged to monasteries in southern France. It houses an inspiring collection of medieval art from different parts of Europe, of which the Unicorn Tapestries is the most famous. Recorded Medieval music echoes through the stone corridors and courtyards daily; Medieval and Renaissance concerts are held on Sundays in November, December, March, and April. Set in Fort Tryon Park along the Hudson River, the Cloisters offers a splendid view of the New Jersey Palisades, the George Washington Bridge, and the Hudson River. Closed Mondays. Admission charge. Washington Ave. and W 193rd St. (923-3700).

Harlem – Most visitors to New York — black or white — get uncomfortable at the thought of entering Harlem, and it is intimidating. But there is much to see there, and a visit has the undeniable effect of shattering the monolithic association with threat and violence that attends most people's image of the community. Harlem, starting in earnest at 110th Street and stretching to about 160th Street, is a community filled with neighborhoods of families as concerned about community problems as families in other neighborhoods throughout the city.

In the words of a New York police officer: "The best way to see Harlem is by driving or in a cab. Take a bus rather than a subway if you are using public transportation." The nicest part of Harlem is the landmark block called "Strivers Row" — 138th Street between Seventh and Eighth avenues — a string of turn-of-the-century brownstones designed by Stanford White. Penny Sightseeing Company conducts three-hour guided tours of Harlem on Mondays, Thursdays, and Saturdays, from March through December. For reservations, contact their office at 303 W 42nd St. at 8th Ave. (247-2860).

BROOKLYN

Mention Brooklyn to most Manhattanites and you'll probably hear, "Oh, I never go to Brooklyn" or some similar wise-aleck remark. People who do not know the borough think purely in terms of the book *A Tree Grows in Brooklyn* or 1930s gangster movies in which Brooklyn-born thugs make snide remarks out of the sides of their mouths while chewing on cigars. Actually, Brooklyn has a lot of trees (more than Manhattan) and some charming neighborhoods that are more European in character than American. Not only is it greener, it is also considerably more peaceful than Manhattan, even though it has 3 million people and bills itself as "the Fourth Largest City in America."

Brooklyn Heights – The most picturesque streets of classic brownstones and gardens can be found in this historic district. Not only does the Promenade facing the skyline offer the traditional picture-postcard view of Manhattan, but the area behind it retains an aura of dignity that characterized a more gracious past. Montague Street, a narrow thoroughfare lined with restaurants and shops selling ice cream, candles, old prints, flowers, and clothing, runs from the East River to the Civic Center, a complex of federal, state, and municipal government buildings. To get to Brooklyn Heights from Manhattan, take the IRT 7th Avenue line to Clark Street; or, better yet, walk across the Brooklyn Bridge and bear right. The district extends from the Brooklyn Bridge to Joralemon Street and from Court Street to the Promenade. For information on events in the Heights, contact the Brooklyn Heights Association, 157 Montague St. (858-9193).

Atlantic Avenue – Lebanese, Yemeni, Syrian, and Palestinian shops, bakeries, and restaurants line the street, purveyors of tahini, Syrian bread, baklava, halvah, assorted delicious foodstuffs, Arabic records, and books. There is even an office of the Palestinian Red Crescent, an official branch of the International Red Cross that has been helping victims of the wars in Lebanon. Occasionally, women in veils make their way to and from the shops, some incongruously carrying transistor radios. The most active street scene takes place between the waterfront and Court Street along Atlantic Ave.

Park Slope – An up-and-coming restoration district, the Slope resembles the Chelsea section of London, with many beautiful, shady trees and gardens. It feels more like a town than part of the city, especially at night, when the only sounds are the birds and the wind rushing through the trees. A large part of Park Slope has been designated a historic district and there are some truly impressive town houses here. Grand Army Plaza, a colossal arch commemorating those who died in the Civil War, stands at the end of the Slope that extends along the western edge of Prospect Park. Seventh Avenue, two blocks from the park, is an intriguing shopping street where you can get old furniture, stained glass, ceramics, houseware, flowers, health food, vegetables, and toys. Saturday afternoons get pretty lively. To get to Park Slope from Manhattan, take the IRT 7th Avenue line to Grand Army Plaza or the IND D train to the 7th Avenue exit.

Prospect Park and the Brooklyn Botanic Gardens – More than 500 acres of gracefully landscaped greenery with fields, fountains, lakes, a concert bandshell, an ice skating rink in winter, a bridal path, and a zoo. The Botanic Gardens contain serene rose gardens, hothouses with orchids and other tropical plants, cherry trees, a Zen meditation garden, and hundreds of flowers and shrubs. Closed Mondays. Free. (622-4433). To get to Prospect Park and the Brooklyn Botanic Gardens from Manhattan, take the IRT 7th Avenue line to Grand Army Plaza and walk up the hill along Flatbush Avenue or take the IND D train to Prospect Park.

The Brooklyn Museum – In addition to its outstanding permanent anthropological collections on American Indians of both the northern and southern hemispheres, this museum hosts terrific traveling exhibits. In the permanent collection are fine exhibits of Oriental arts, American painting and decorative arts, and European painting. The roster of artists whose work is permanently displayed includes Van Gogh, Rodin, Toulouse-Lautrec, Gauguin, Monet, and Chagall. Closed Mondays and Tuesdays. Suggested donation of about $1.50. To get to the museum from Manhattan, take the IRT 7th Avenue line to Eastern Parkway. Eastern Pkwy. and Washington Ave. (638-5000).

Bay Ridge – Although Brooklynites have been fond of this Scandinavian waterfront community for years, it took the film "Saturday Night Fever" to bring it to national attention. Bay Ridge is dominated by the world's longest suspension bridge, the Verrazano-Narrows Bridge, which connects Brooklyn with Staten Island. (Some people say this bridge goes from nowhere to nowhere else, but they fail to appreciate its finer aesthetics.) Although chances are you won't see John Travolta tripping down 4th Avenue, you will see a lot of people who look like the character he played in the film, and you'll also get to see the bridge rising over the tops of houses, shops, restaurants, and discos. A bike path runs along the edge of the Narrows from Owls Head Pier, the pier of the now-defunct Brooklyn–Staten Island ferry, all the way to the Verrazano Narrows Bridge. The pier has recently been renovated and is a great place for fishing, watching the ships come in, and looking at a wide-angle view of Lower Manhattan. To get to Bay Ridge from Manhattan, take the BMT RR train to 95th St.

Coney Island – If you've seen the classic film "The Beast from 20,000 Fathoms," you no doubt remember the climactic final scene in which the beast is shot down from the top of a roller coaster called the Cyclone. As the monster falls, he destroys half of Coney Island. But fear not, gentle reader, Hollywood's illusion is a far cry from reality, although some disenchanted local residents wish it were a lot closer to the truth. Now a long strip of garish amusement park rides, penny arcades, hot dog stands, and low-income housing complexes, Coney Island is jam-packed in summer, eerily deserted in winter. Weekends in the summer are the worst time to visit. Weekday evenings are considerably less frenetic. You can ride the Cyclone, one of the most terrifying roller coasters on the East Coast, and the Wonder Wheel, a giant Ferris wheel alongside the ocean, but the parachute jump, which is Coney Island's landmark and can be seen for miles, is no longer operational. There are honky-tonk bars along the boardwalk, where country and western singers compete with the sound of the sea. If you get a sudden craving for Italian food, head for *Gargiulo's,* 2911 W 15th St. (266-0906) for some good Neapolitan dishes. The ultimate offbeat New York treat is to have hot dogs at *Nathan's* at 3 or 4 in the morning. Surf and Stillwell Aves. Take IND F, D, or B trains to Coney Island from Manhattan.

Sheepshead Bay – More like a New England fishing village than part of New York, fishermen sell their catch on the dock in the early afternoon. Charter boats that take people out for the day leave very early in the morning. For the best view of the scene, cross the wooden footbridge at Ocean Avenue and walk along the mile-long esplanade. A few blocks south of the bay is Manhattan Beach, one of the smaller city beaches. Brighton Beach, a few blocks to the east, joins Manhattan Beach with Coney Island. To get to Sheepshead Bay from Manhattan, take the IND D train to Sheepshead Bay.

THE BRONX

If you intend to visit the Bronx, don't ask for directions from someone from Brooklyn. Because of a local prejudice, residents of these boroughs look down on each other. With 1.5 million inhabitants, the Bronx is smaller than Brooklyn, and the only borough in the City of New York that is joined to the mainland. Although all the points of interest listed here are safe for visitors, some sections of the Bronx are the most dangerous parts of New York City. The South Bronx, for example, has been nicknamed Fort Apache by the New York Police. One police officer advises staying clear of any place south of Fordham Road.

Bronx Zoo – One of the most famous zoos in the world. More than 3,000 animals live in the 250 acres set aside for them. Elephants, tigers, chimps, seals, rhinos, hippos, birds, and buffalos are the favorites. To get to the Bronx Zoo from Manhattan, take the IND D train to 177th St. Open daily. Admission charge Fridays through Mondays; Tuesdays, Wednesdays, and Thursdays free; parking, $2.50. At Fordham Rd. and Bronx River Pkwy. (367-1010). (220-5100).

The New York Botanical Gardens – Adjoining the zoo to the north, the 230-acre gardens have an unspoiled, natural forest area. This is what New York looked like BP (before people). The Enid A. Haupt Conservatory (closed Mondays) with its 11 pavilions — each with a totally different environment — is a special treat. Other highlights include a rose garden, azalea glen, daffodil hill, conservatory, botanical museum, and restaurant. Well worth the trip, especially in the spring. From Manhattan take the IND D train to Bedford Park Station. Open daily. Admission charge for the Conservatory, except Wednesdays; parking, $2.50. Kazimiroff Blvd. between Bedford Park Blvd. and Mosholu Pkwy. (220-8777).

The Van Cortlandt Museum – One of the few remaining 18th-century Dutch estates, this one is lovingly preserved with carefully restored furnishings. Women in colonial garb escort you through the premises. Take the IRT 1 train from Manhattan to W 242nd St. Closed Mondays. Admission charge for adults only. In Van Cortlandt Park north of W 242nd St. and Broadway (543-3344).

The Bronx Museum of Art – This relatively new (1970) museum in the Bronx County Courthouse features art organized around themes such as the history of the Chinese community in the United States, women, social class, and other documentary subjects. Contemporary paintings and photography generally make up the bulk of the changing exhibits. Classical music concerts, film programs, poetry readings, and dance concerts are held throughout the year. From Manhattan take the IRT 4 to W 151th St. Closed Fridays and Saturdays. Free. W 151th St. and Grand Concourse (681-6000).

The Edgar Allan Poe Cottage – A tiny cottage, adequately cramped to inspire claustrophobia in anyone larger than a gnome, sits incongruously in the middle of the Grand Concourse. It once housed the great American poet Edgar Allan Poe during his final unhappy years. You can see Poe's personal belongings and some manuscripts inside. Closed Mondays. Free. Grand Concourse and Kingsbridge Rd. (no phone).

Yankee Stadium – A landmark. Here, in this recently renovated 70,000-seat stadium, batted the late, great Babe Ruth, Joe DiMaggio, and dozens of other baseball stars. Take the IND D train from Manhattan to 161st St. Open during baseball season. Free. 161st and River Sts. (293-6000).

The Hall of Fame – Bronze-cast busts of great American presidents, poets, and people noted for achievement in the sciences, arts, and humanities. About 100 busts stand on podiums set atop columns. The Hall is on the Bronx Community College campus; from Manhattan take the IND D train to 183rd St. Open daily. Free. W 181st St. and University Ave. (220-6187).

STATEN ISLAND

Located much closer to New Jersey than New York, Staten Island is the Big Apple's most remote borough and, with 250,000 people, its least populous. Since the Verrazano-Narrows Bridge opened in 1964, Staten Island has been filling up with suburban housing developments and shopping centers. However, a few farms remain in southern Staten Island. To find them, take the bus marked Richmond Ave. at the ferry terminal. Getting around Staten Island by public transportation takes a long time. Driving is recommended if at all possible.

Staten Island Zoo – Although considerably smaller than the Bronx Zoo, here the specialty is reptiles. Snakes of all descriptions coil and uncoil in glass cases. The zoo is set near a lake in Barret Park. Open daily. Wednesdays free, other times admission charge. Broadway and Clove Rd. (442-3100).

Jacques Marchais Center for Tibetan Art – One of the esoteric treasures of the city, this is also one of the best-kept secrets in the metropolitan area. A reconstructed Tibetan prayer hall with adjoining library and gardens with Oriental sculpture, the Center sits on a hill overlooking a pastoral, un–New York setting of trees. The Tibetan *Book of the Dead,* other occult tomes, prayer wheels, statuary, and weavings are on display. Open April through November; weekends only. Admission charge. 338 Lighthouse Ave. (987-3478).

■ **EXTRA SPECIAL: SHOPPING IN NEW YORK** This city is like no other for acquiring material possessions. It is the commercial center and the fashion capital of this country, and styles that originate here set the trends for fashionable folk from Portland, Maine, to Portland, Oregon. The scope of the merchandise available approaches the infinite, and the price range can fit every budget. Whether you want to buy Ukrainian Easter eggs or a Moroccan caftan, somewhere, someone in New York is selling it.

Knowing how to shop here is something of a fine art — a function of taste, style, and budget. Being a smart shopper is knowing where to go for what and when; knowing that the dress that's in *Bloomingdale's* on Wednesday might just turn up on Orchard Street on Sunday, with 50% off the price (or more if you speak good Yiddish). If shopping is high art, window shopping is a form of popular entertainment, New Yorkers' favorite outdoor activity. But whether you want to buy, browse, or bargain, you'll find a myriad of places to suit your fancy. The following are some of the highlights.

***Bloomingdale's,* A World unto Itself** – This is the place for fashionable Upper East Siders and anyone else who aspires to those heights. Whether you want to pick up satin running shorts, a sheer evening gown, or someone clad in either, you'll probably find them here. Saturdays on the main floor is something of a social event — anyone who cares to be anyone is here shopping and being seen. Lexington Ave. at 59th St. (355-5900 or 223-7111).

Bookstores – The publishing capital of the world, New York has a wealth of literary worth. Leaders among its outlets include *Barnes and Noble,* 5th Ave. and 18th St. (807-0099) and 600 5th Ave. at 48th St. (765-0590), which carries a wide selection at bargain prices. On 5th Avenue, near the Barnes and Noble branch, you'll find a cluster of other stores, including *Scribner's,* 597 5th Ave. (486-4070), *Brentano's,* 586 5th Ave. (757-8600), *B. Dalton,* 666 5th Ave. (247-1740) and at three other Manhattan locations, and *Doubleday,* 673 5th Ave. (953-4805), all of which carry a broad variety of new titles and trade books. *The Strand,* 828 Broadway at 12th St. (473-1452), has a huge collection of old and used books and even some rare manuscripts. *Rizzoli,* 712 5th Ave. (397-3700), is best known for its collection of art books.

Boutiques – Madison Avenue in the 60s and 70s is lined with boutiques that carry haute couture at haute prix. If you buy, you might well be getting one-of-a-kind fashion, but looking is free. The names are an encyclopedia of style: *Halston, Valentino, Veneziano,* and the like, to say nothing of *Saint-Laurent. Ménage à Trois,* 760 Madison at 65th St. (249-0500), has fine shirts for men and women in linen and silk.

Department Stores – *Macy's,* Broadway at 34th St. (695-4400), is the quintessential New York department store. You can buy what you need and choose from a large assortment of high-quality, stylish goods, but most people come here for the total experience of shopping — browsing, watching, and buying. Macy's basement emporium, The Cellar, is designed as a street lined with shops, which carry everything from fruits and vegetables to housewares, and restaurants, including a replica of *P.J. Clarke's* bar, which has great hamburgers, lots of beer, and atmosphere. *Gimbel's,* at 33rd St. and Broadway (736-5100), just down the block, has a wide selection of goods, though less quantity than Macy's. *B. Altman,* at 5th Ave. and 34th St. (689-7000), has a good selection of women's and men's clothing and housewares. *Alexander's,* 731 Lexington Ave. at 58th St. (593-0880), carries medium-quality goods, though you can find some excellent buys there during its numerous sales and markdowns. *Abraham and Strauss,* 420 Fulton St. at Hoyt St. in downtown Brooklyn (875-7200), carries a complete stock of moderately priced goods.

Jewelry and Gems – The ultimate in absolute luxury! Diamonds are a girl's best friend, they say, and so as not to limit ourselves, we'll include emeralds, rubies, sapphires, gold, silver, and other precious metals. And so as not to discriminate, we'll include men, too. Without a doubt, the most famous of all luxury emporiums is *Tiffany & Company,* 5th Ave. and 57th St. (755-8000). If you must have something from Tiffany's but can't afford a necklace or ring, you can purchase a novelty like a silver bookmark or toothpaste roller. Across the street, *Harry Winston,* at 5th Ave. and 56th St. (245-2000), has display cases, but most of the jewels are kept in an inner sanctum. After conferring with a salesperson, the items you wish to see are brought for your inspection. *Cartier,* at 5th Ave. and 52nd St. (753-0111), is renowned for highly polished silver and some of the world's finest jewelry and accessories. For bold Brazilian jewelry, stop in at *H. Stern* on 5th Ave. between 51st and 52nd Sts. (688-0300). For splendid glass sculpture, bowls, trays, and goblets, go to *Steuben Glass,* 5th Ave. and 56th St. (752-1441). And for the ultimate in European style and craftsmanship, there's no jeweler who exceeds the talent of *Bulgari*, 5th Ave. and 61st St. (486-0086).

If your budget is limited, you may want to do your gem shopping along 47th Street between 5th and 6th Avenues. That's the heart of New York's wholesale jewelry district and the best place to find sparkling stuff at mortal prices. *Colon's* (27 W 47th St.) is an especially worthwhile stop for quality and fair prices; and if you're planning to get married (or even reaffirm your vows), *Bill Schifrin* (Booth No. 86 at the National Jewelers Exchange, 4 W 47th St.) has the largest collection of wedding rings and bands in the world.

Kitchen Equipment – The Bowery is New York's kitchenware and lamp district, where large wholesale houses such as the *Federal Restaurant and Supply Company,* 202 Bowery St. (226-0441), offer some commercial products at very reasonable prices. At *Professional Kitchens,* 18 Cooper Sq. (254-9000), which is a retail outlet for Bowery supply companies, you will find a good, complete selection of the kitchen equipment from the Bowery. *The Bridge Company,* 214 E 52nd St. (688-4220), has four floors of kitchenware. You can find every possible domestic and imported item here, from cherry pitters to egg slicers. Selecting a single pot or pan could occupy several hours or a full day, given the number and variety on display.

Knickknacks – Shopping in *Azuma,* 415 5th Ave. at 37th St. (889-4310), is like wandering through a gigantic bazaar. It has abundant displays of low-priced Japanese novelties, colorful imported gift items, decorative household goods, and unusual personal ware. Smaller branches of Azuma are at 666 Lexington Ave. at 55th St. (752-0599), 387 Ave. of the Americas between Waverly Pl. and 8th St. (989-8690), 251 E 86th St. at 2nd Ave. (369-4928), and 25 E 8th St. at 5th Ave. (673-2900).

Begun in Harlem, the unique *Ashanti Bazaar* is now at 872 Lexington Ave. at 65th St. (535-0740). In this beautifully appointed shop, traditional African motifs influence modern design, and the results in their clothing, objets d'art, jewelry, and rugs are sensational. *Jenny B. Goode,* 1194 Lexington Ave. at 81st St. (794-2492), sells amusing nostalgia and contemporary adaptations (soft-sculpture penny candy, mugs with gorgeous gam handles, transistors disguised as giant Oreo cookies) that are a serendipitous delight. Round the world in a unique way with a trip to *The United Nations Souvenier Shop,* UN Building, 1st Ave. at 47th St. (754-7702), featuring handicrafts, ethnic clothing, native jewelry, indigenous toys — lots of beautiful things from every UN nation.

The Job Lot Store, at 140 Church St. between Chambers and Warren Sts. (962-4142), is the ultimate for bargain hunters. This massive discount retail shop is filled with merchandise of every sort, in perfect condition, in an atmosphere resembling Times Square on New Year's Eve.

Luggage – You'll have no trouble finding a wide selection of high- and low-priced luggage and leather goods in New York. For elegant, luxury luggage from reputable manufacturers, *Crouch & Fitzgerald,* 400 Madison Ave. (755-5888), *Mark Cross,* 645 5th Ave. (421-3000), *T. Anthony,* 480 Park Ave. (750-9797), *Saks Fifth Avenue,* 49th St. and 5th Ave. (753-4000), and *Gucci,* 685, 689, and 699 5th Ave. (826-2600), are hard to top for quality and price. Along cheaper lines, you will run into several reasonable leather goods and luggage stores during your strolls around the East and West Sides and the Lower East Side.

Men's Clothes – *Brooks Brothers,* 346 Madison Ave. (682-8800), and 1 Liberty Plaza, downtown (682-8595), *J. Press Inc.,* 16 E 44th St. (687-7642), and *Chipp's Inc.,* 14 E 44th St. (687-0850), all offer high-quality traditional and basically conservative men's styles at high prices. At *Burton's,* 475 5th Ave. (685-3760), you can usually find Brooks Brothers–type clothes for somewhat less. (Both *Burton's* and *Brooks Brothers* also have women's clothing.) *Paul Stuart,* Madison Ave. at 45th St. (682-0320), offers a less conservative but highly stylish and elegant selection of top-quality men's fashions at top prices.

Poster and Print Shops – *The Old Print Shop,* 150 Lexington Ave. at 29th St. (683-3950), has a huge collection of early American prints, watercolors, and paintings ranging in price from $10 to $20,000. For contemporary theater posters and some collector's items, try the *Triton Gallery,* 323 W 45th St., between 8th and 9th Aves. (765-2472).

Records – There are a number of places where you can get good prices on records.

The most famous is *Sam Goody's,* at 235 W 49th St. (246-1708) and branches throughout the city. Goody's stocks new labels, classical, jazz, and foreign music as well as audio equipment. Two chain stores, *King Karol* and *Disco-Mat,* carry a lot of labels, including the latest in pop and disco at prices lower than standard retail stores. Disco-Mat's main store is at Lexington Ave. and E 58th St. (759-3777). King Karol's main store is at 126 W 42nd St. (354-7684). *J & R Jazz Mart* at 33 Park Row (349-8400) has the best selection of new and hard-to-find old jazz records at very good prices. *House of Oldies* at 35 Carmine St. (243-0500) specializes in discs from the past. *Colony Record and Radio Center* at 1619 Broadway (265-2050) carries out-of-wax records that are no longer being made.

Sheets and Pillowcases – For good buys on top-brand and designer sheets and pillowcases, New York is definitely the place. At *Ezra Cohen,* 307 Grand (925-7800), *H & G Cohen Bedding Company,* 306 Grand St. (226-0818), and *J. Shachter,* 115 Allen St. (533-1150), you can find all the major brands at a 25% to 30% discount. J. Shachter also specializes in custom comforters that can be made from any fabric you wish. (All are closed Saturdays and open Sundays; typical of the stores on the Lower East Side).

Shoes – For expensive, imported women's shoes, go to *I. Miller* at 5th Ave. and 57th St. (581-0062) or *Charles Jourdan,* 769 Madison Ave. (628-0133). For well-made men's boots and shoes, stock up at *McCreedy and Schreiber* at 37 W 46th St. (719-1552) or 213 E 59th St. (759-9241). *Chandler's Shoe Store* at 695 5th Ave. (688-2140) has a wide selection of good women's shoes at reasonable prices.

Special Shopping Districts – The ultimate shopping experience is on the *Lower East Side* of Manhattan, if you're up to it. Along Orchard Street, Delancey Street, and all the side streets, you'll find incredible bargains in all manner of clothing, housewares, foam padding; but finding them is only half the battle. Then you have to fight for them, and the haggling begins. The merchant says something along the lines of, "I couldn't give you this for a penny less than $12," to which you respond that it's not worth more than 50¢, and usually you come to terms, apparently unsatisfactory to both of you. A lot of the selling is done in a mixture of Yiddish, English, and Spanish — particularly the counting — and if you know any or all three, you'll do better than wholesale. See the *Special Places* section for more on the Lower East Side.

Specialty Shops – For high-quality fashion and designer clothes (domestic and foreign), visit New York's finest shops. Although there is a certain amount of overlap in the labels and styles carried, each store has a distinctive style. Prices at all tend to be expensive, but you are paying for the best. *Lord & Taylor,* 5th Ave. and 39th St. (391-3344), has a unique, modern elegance that makes browsing through the designer collections a particularly enjoyable experience. The salespeople are friendly, and the store is never so crowded that you feel as though you are in the subway. *Saks Fifth Avenue,* 5th Ave. and 49th St. (753-4000), can get rather hectic, but this is one place where you can be sure you'll get the latest in whatever style is chic this season. *Bergdorf Goodman,* 5th Ave. and 57th St. (753-7300), is the epitome of elegant shopping. In some haute couture salons, you sit in a room like a parlor, overlooking Central Park, while salespeople bring merchandise for you to examine and escort you to the fitting rooms. *Henri Bendel's,* 10 W 57th St. (247-1100), carries an impressive selection of trendy clothes for only the slimmest of people. If you have a model's figure and want to wear the latest dramatic fashions, this is your place. Cosmetics counselors and hair stylists have branches here, too. *Lane Bryant,* 5th Ave. at 40th St. (532-0200), has fashionable clothing for larger women.

Sporting Goods – *Herman's,* New York's best-known sporting goods chain, has everything, but *Paragon* says it has more. At either one, you can find just about every piece of sporting gear and wear under the sun. Herman's stores are located at 110 Nassau (233-0733), 135 W 42nd St. (730-7400), and 845 3rd Ave. (688-4603). Paragon is located at 867 Broadway at 18th St. (255-8036).

Thrift Stores – The most celebrated area for thrifting in New York is the Upper 80s along 1st, 2nd, and 3rd Aves. *Stuyvesant Square Thrift Shop,* 1704 2nd Ave. (831-1830), has a good selection of clothing for men and women of all ages, household items, and appliances in good condition. Unfortunately, many of the secondhand clothes stores in New York carry the price tags of fine antique stores. *Granny's Attik,* 2310 Broadway (595-3980), is a shop where you can usually find some good old rags at moderate prices.

Toys – Once immersed in the enchanting world of children's toys at *FAO Schwarz,* 745 5th Ave. at 58th St. (644-9400) adults have as difficult a time as children leaving empty-handed. They have every kind of toy — from precious antiques and mechanical space ships to simple construction sets and building blocks. The prices are very high. Many of the large department stores, particularly *Gimbel's* and *Macy's,* also have an enticing selection.

Teachers as well as parents favor *Childcraft's* two stores — 155 E. 23rd St. (674-4754) and 150 E. 58th St. (753-3196) — for educational toys, games, and crafts, many of which, including the anatomically correct dolls, are made in Europe and are unique in the US.

Trendy Gear – There are several large outlets in New York for the stylish military attire that has put practical army surplus clothes and gear on the fashion pages. The best stores for work shirts, pea jackets, navy pants, jeans, combat boots, and other surplus attire, which have the unique combination of being both "in" and inexpensive, are *I. Buss,* 738 Broadway (242-3338), *Unique Clothing Warehouse,* 718 Broadway (674-1767), and *Hudson's,* 3rd Ave. at 13th St. (475-9568).

Uniquely New York – Probably nowhere else on earth could you find everything from plugs with which to stuff your ears at night to fine silver under one roof. You might have to go some to figure out how to use some of these gadgets, but *Hammacher Schlemmer,* 147 E 57th St., between 3rd Ave. and Lexington (421-9000), has it all. And what they don't have, whether it's a chotchka or a real white elephant, they'll try to order.

Loehmann's, 19 Duryea Pl., off Flatbush Ave. in Brooklyn (469-9800) and 9 W Fordham Rd. (near Jerome Ave.) in the Bronx (295-4100), carries some of the best bargains in women's clothing found anywhere. You can get designer clothing, with the labels removed, at 25% to 50% off the retail prices, and what's more, doting personal service. You will know whether the garment looks good, because the salespeople will tell you.

SOURCES AND RESOURCES

The New York Convention and Visitors Bureau, 2 Columbus Circle (397-8222), is an excellent source for tourist information and assistance. Its office carries hotel and restaurant information, subway and bus maps, descriptive brochures, and current listings of the city's entertainment and activities, and it is staffed with multilingual aides. Tourist information is also available at the Information Desk, 30 Rockefeller Plaza, in Rockefeller Center (489-2950). (Note: If you are thinking of moving to New York, you may want more details on the city and its environs. A service called *Instant New Yorker* focuses on 350 communities within a 50-mile radius of Manhattan, and covers in detail a number of important topics, including transportation, taxes, school systems, shopping, religious denominations, median income, and so on. Although this portfolio is usually purchased by corporations who are transferring employees to the metropolitan area, individuals may also inquire. Contact: *Instant New Yorker,* 950 Third Ave., New York, NY 10022; 212 355-1045.

For Local Coverage – The *New York Times,* morning daily; the *Daily News,* morning daily; and the *New York Post* morning and afternoon daily; and the Sunday *New York Times,* with its enormous entertainment section. Also, the weekly magazines *New Yorker* and *New York.* An interesting book about the city is *New York: A Guide to the Metropolis* (subtitled *Walking Tours of Architecture and History*), by Gerald Wolfe (New York University Press, $10.95).

For Food – *Restaurants of New York,* by Seymour Britchky (Random House, $7.95); *The New York Times Guide to Dining Out in New York,* by John Canaday (Atheneum, $3.95); *The All New Underground Gourmet,* by Milton Glaser and Jerome Snyder (Simon and Schuster, $3.95); *Best Restaurants New York,* by Stendahl (101 Productions, $3.95).

All telephone numbers are in the 212 area code unless otherwise indicated.

CLIMATE AND CLOTHES: The best times to visit New York are in the spring — mid-April to mid-May — and in the fall — mid-September through October — when temperatures are comfortable, in the high 60s to low 70s. Winter and summer are extreme, averaging in the 80s and up in July and August, in the 20s or below during the months of hard winter. However, the weather should not determine your visit since most of what makes New York great takes place indoors, and air-conditioning and central heating are standard. Like people in the rest of the country, New Yorkers dress informally for almost all events. Anything in good taste goes. Remember, there is no rainy season as such — it can happen any day of the year. Be prepared. And during the warm months, a sweater or a wrap is usually welcome after an hour or so of sitting in an air-conditioned place. Wintertime is very cold; boots, hats, gloves, and a heavy coat are necessities.

GETTING AROUND: – The fare on New York City buses and subways (and the Roosevelt Island tramway) is 75¢, no matter how far you travel.

Bus – New York City buses run frequently. There are more than 200 routes and over 4,500 buses in operation. Although slower than subways, buses bring you closer to your destination, stopping about every two blocks. The main routes in Manhattan are north-south on the avenues, and east-west (crosstown) on the streets, as well as some crisscross and circular routes. Check both the sign on the front of the bus and at the bus stop to make sure the bus you want stops where you are waiting. Be sure to have exact change for the basic fare (subway tokens are acceptable), and ask for a transfer, should you need one, when you board the bus. Bus drivers do not make change nor do they accept bills. Bus rates are half-fare from 6 PM Saturdays to 1 AM Mondays. Transfers (called Add-a-Rides) should be obtained from the bus driver at the time of paying your fare, and cost half the regular fare. Buses run 24 hours a day throughout the city.

An innovative plan is the Culture Buses I and II, which run on weekends and holidays, each making over 20 different stops at sites and attractions of special interest. Free bus maps are available at Grand Central and Penn Station, or by sending a stamped, self-addressed envelope to the New York Transit Authority, 370 Jay St., Brooklyn, NY 11201, Attn.: Maps.

Subways – No doubt about it, the New York subway system is confusing. But that is no reason to avoid it. Its convenience and speed can't be duplicated by any other form of transportation, and the intelligence of its overall design is awesome. Basically, there are three different subway lines, with express and local routes serving all city boroughs except for Staten Island (reached via the Staten Island Ferry). The most extensive line is the IRT, which originates in Brooklyn and transverses Manhattan en route to the Bronx. The IRT has two main divisions: the 7th Avenue line, which serves the West Side of Manhattan, and the Lexington Avenue line, which covers the East Side. You can go from east to west (crosstown) on the shuttle (SS) between Grand Central Station and Times Square. The IND serves Brooklyn, Queens, Manhattan, and the Bronx. The BMT serves Brooklyn, Queens, and Manhattan. The subway is the most heavily used means of city transportation (over 4 million people ride it daily on 230 miles of track) and is mobbed during rush hours, weekdays from 7:30 to 9:00 AM and from 4:30 to 7:00 PM. You can pick up a free subway map at the Convention and Visitors Bureau, or check the complete map in the Yellow Pages of the Manhattan phone book, or the maps posted in every station and in each subway car.

From 6 PM Saturdays until 1 AM Mondays, subway riders receive free transfers. The subway system operates 24 hours a day. For further information, call the NY Transit Authority (330-1234).

Taxi – The handiest and most expensive way to get around the city is by cab. Cabs can be hailed almost anywhere, and are required to pick you up and deliver you to your specified destination. Cabs can be identified by their yellow color, and are available if their light is on. Cabbies expect a 20% tip. There is a 50¢ surcharge on fleet cab fares between 8 PM and 6 AM; red and white stickers are on both front doors of cabs that impose the extra charge.

Car Rental – New York is served by all the major car rental companies as well as a host of small local firms. Find them listed in the Yellow Pages and do a little comparative shopping.

MUSEUMS: The Guggenheim, Museum of Modern Art, Metropolitan Museum, Hayden Planetarium, Museum of Natural History, the Cloisters, the Brooklyn Museum, the Jacques Marchais Center for Tibetan Art, and the Fraunces Tavern Museum are described in *Special Places.* Other notable New York museums are:

Asia House, 725 Park Ave. (288-6400).
Cooper-Hewitt Museum (textiles and material arts), 2 E 91st St. (860-6868).
El Museo del Barrio (Hispanic art), 1230 5th Ave. (831-7272).
Fire Department Museum, 104 Duane St. (570-4230).
The Frick Collection, 5th Ave. at 70th St. (288-0700).
Japan House, 333 E 47th St. (832-1155).
The Jewish Museum, 1109 5th Ave. (860-1888).
Museum of American Folk Art, 49 W 53rd St. (581-2474).
Museum of the American Indian, Broadway at 155th St. (283-2420).
The Museum of the City of New York, 5th Ave. at 103rd St. (534-1672).
American Crafts Museum, 44 W 53rd St. (397-0630).
Museum of Holography, 11 Mercer St. (925-0526).
New-York Historical Society, 170 Central Park West (873-3400).
The Pierpont Morgan Library, 29 E 36th St. (685-0008).
The Studio Museum in Harlem, 144 W 125th St. (864-4500).
The Whitney Museum of American Art, Madison Ave. at E 75th St. (570-3600).

MAJOR COLLEGES AND UNIVERSITIES: New York City has a variety of leading institutions of higher education, some offering a broad-based liberal arts curriculum, others concentrating in areas of specialization, and all of them enriching New York as a center of culture and learning. Among them are: Barnard College, Broadway and W 116th St. (280-5262); the City College of City University, Convent Ave. and W 138th St. (690-6741); Columbia University, Broadway and W 116th St. (280-1754); Cooper Union, 3rd Ave. and 7th St. (254-6300); Fordham University, Columbus Ave. and 60th St. (841-5100), and at E Fordham Rd. and 3rd Ave., Bronx (933-2233); Hunter College, 695 Park Ave. (570-5118); Jewish Theological Seminary of America, Broadway and W 122nd St. (678-8000); Juilliard School of

Music, Lincoln Center Plaza (799-5000); Mannes College of Music, 157 E 74th St. (737-0700); New School for Social Research, 66 W 12th St. (741-5600); New York University, Washington Sq. (598-1212); Parsons School of Design, 5th Ave. and 12th St. (741-8900); Pratt Institute, 200 Willoughby Ave., Brooklyn (636-3600); Queens College, 65–30 Kissena Blvd., Queens (520-7000); Union Theological Seminary, Broadway and W 120th St. (662-7100); Yeshiva University, Amsterdam Ave. and W 186th St. (960-5400).

SPECIAL EVENTS: January–February, *Chinese New Year Celebration and Dragon Parade,* Chinatown; January, *National Boat Show,* Coliseum; March 17, *St. Patrick's Day Parade,* 5th Ave.; May and September, *Greenwich Village Outdoor Art Show,* Washington Square; First Sunday in June, *Puerto Rican Day Parade,* 5th Ave.; June–August, free *Shakespeare Festival,* Delacorte Theater, Central Park; free performances, *NY Philharmonic, Metropolitan Opera,* all boroughs; *Dr Pepper Central Park Music Festival,* Wollman Rink, Central Park; July, *Newport Jazz Festival,* throughout city; July 1–4, *Harbor Festival,* Parade of Ships, Old NY July 4 Celebration, Lower Manhattan; September, the ten-day *Festival of San Gennaro,* patron saint of the Neapolitans, Mulberry St.; October, *Columbus Day Parade,* 5th Ave.; mid-October, *Annual NYC Marathon;* early November, *Horse Show,* Madison Square Garden; *Macy's Thanksgiving Day Parade,* Broadway, Herald Square; December, *Christmas Tree Lighting,* Rockefeller Plaza; November–January, *The Great Christmas Show,* Radio City Music Hall.

SPORTS: New York is a sports-minded city, offering a great variety of spectator and participatory activities. It is the home of the *Yankees* and *Mets, Jets* and *Giants* (though technically they play in New Jersey), *Rangers* and racetracks, and countless tennis players, swimmers, bikers, runners, joggers, and walkers, to name but a few of the major activities.

Baseball – The season, April through early October, features the *Mets* (National League) at Shea Stadium, Flushing, Queens (672-3000), and the *Yankees* (American League) at Yankee Stadium, Bronx (293-4300). Tickets are usually available at the many Ticketron outlets throughout the city (central ticket information, 977-9020).

Basketball – Features the *Knicks*, playing at Madison Square Garden (564-4400), and the *Nets*, just moving into their new home in Brenden Byrne Arena at the Meadowlands Sports Complex in East Rutherford, NJ, during the regular season from late October to early April (201 935-8888, for ticket and schedule information).

Bicycling – There are over 50 miles of bike paths in the city, with Central Park in Manhattan and Prospect Park in Brooklyn the two most popular areas. Most roadways within the parks are closed to traffic from May through October, except in rush hour, during the week and on weekends year-round. Bikes can be rented in the parks or on nearby side streets.

Billiards and Bowling – Extremely popular with many New Yorkers. Pool halls and bowling alleys are plentiful throughout the city. Consult the Yellow Pages for the location most convenient to you.

Boxing – Although not as popular as it once was, major bouts are still fought at Madison Square Garden, and the *New York Daily News* continues to sponsor the Golden Gloves competition every winter.

Football – During the September–December season, the *Jets* play at Shea Stadium and the *Giants* at Giant's Stadium at the Meadowlands Sports Complex in East Rutherford, NJ (about 6 miles from midtown). Tickets to any of the NFL games are hard to get due to the great number of season subscribers. Columbia University leads the collegiate football scene, with its games played at Baker Field (280-2541).

Golf – For up-to-date information on current golf tournaments, call the Metropolitan

Golf Association (914 698-0390). The Department of Parks (472-1003) can provide a complete list of public courses and how to get on them.

Handball – Try Central Park's courts, north of the 97th St. transverse, or call the city's Parks Department (472-1003) for other locations.

Hockey – Tickets are expensive and scarce during the early October to early April season, featuring the *Islanders,* at the Nassau Coliseum (516 794-9100), and the *Rangers,* Madison Square Garden (564-4400).

Horseback Riding – Horses can be rented and boarded at the Claremont Riding Academy, 175 W 89th St. (724-5100). There are almost 50 miles of bridal paths in the city, most in Central Park.

Horse Racing – Harness racing is at Yonkers Raceway, in lower Westchester County, nightly except Sundays (562-9500), and at Roosevelt Raceway in Westbury, Long Island (895-1246). The Meadowlands, E Rutherford, NJ (201 935-8500), has both harness and flat racing nightly, except Sundays. Thoroughbreds also run during the day at Aqueduct Race Track in Queens (641-4700), or Belmont Park Race Track in Elmont, Long Island (641-4700). Aqueduct and Belmont are never open at the same time; closed Tuesdays.

Jogging – Undoubtedly the most popular sport in New York, with enthusiastic runners in all the city parks; paths at Riverside Park, near W 97th St., around the Central Park Reservoir, 85th St., and the promenade along the East River, between E 84th and 90th Sts.

Skating – Ice skating is a popular pleasure from October to April at the famous Rockefeller Center rink (757-6230), at the Wollman Memorial, 59th St. in Central Park (360-8260), open mid-November to April, and at Skyrink, 450 W 33rd (695-6555), for indoor skating.

Soccer – The New York *Cosmos* play at the Giants' Stadium, E Rutherford, NJ (in New York, 265-8600). There are also 26 playing fields scattered throughout the city parks.

Swimming – Several dozen indoor and outdoor pools are operated by the City Parks Department. Indoor pools are open most of the year, except Sundays and holidays, and usually until 10 PM weekdays. Call the Parks Department for particulars (472-1003). Check the Yellow Pages for pools at the YMCA and YMHA.

Ocean swimming is a subway or bus ride away. Jones Beach State Park, Wantagh, Long Island, 30 miles outside the city, is the most popular. It is a beautifully maintained, enormous stretch of sandy beach, and includes surf bathing, swimming and wading pools, lockers, fishing, outdoor skating rinks, paddleball, swimming instruction, restaurants, and day- and nighttime entertainment. Beaches maintained by the city are Orchard Beach in the Bronx; Coney Island Beach and Manhattan Beach, Brooklyn; and Riis Park and Rockaway Beaches in Queens.

Tennis – Courts maintained by the City Parks Department require a season permit. One of the larger privately owned clubs that will rent by the hour is the Midtown Tennis Club, 341 8th Ave. (989-8572). Check the Yellow Pages for other locations.

THEATER: There are devoted New York theatergoers who wouldn't dream of stepping inside a Broadway theater. They prefer instead the city's prolific off-Broadway and off-off-Broadway circuit, productions less high-powered but no less professional than the splashiest shows on Broadway. On the other hand, there are theater mavens who've never seen a performance more than three blocks from Times Square and who can remember every detail of the opening night of *My Fair Lady.* If their reminiscences don't have you running to the nearest box office for front-row seats to the season's biggest hit, you are made of stone.

Broadway signifies an area — New York's premier theater district, the blocks between Broadway and 9th Avenue running north of Times Square from 42nd Street —

and a kind of production — the "big show" that strives to be the smash hit of the season and run forever. The glitter of the area has turned a bit tacky since the halcyon days of the Great White Way, but a renovation of the area is in the planning stage and may eventually turn things around. In any case, the productions remain as stellar as ever.

Off-Broadway and off-off-Broadway signify types of theater (playhouses producing shows that qualify as off-Broadway are strewn from the Lower Village to the Upper West Side) that have developed in response to the phenomenon of Broadway. Off-Broadway productions are smaller in scale, with newer, lesser-known talent, and are likely to feature revivals of classics or more daring works than those on Broadway. Off-off-Broadway is more experimental still, featuring truly avant-garde productions with performances in coffee houses, lofts, or any appropriate makeshift arena. Off-Broadway often costs half of the price of a Broadway ticket, and the price of a seat in an off-off-Broadway performance may be only what you choose to contribute.

You should take advantage of all three during a visit. The excitement of a Broadway show is incomparable, but the thrill of finding a tiny theater in Soho or the West Village in which you are almost nose to nose with the actors is undeniable. Planning your theater schedule is as easy as consulting any of the daily papers (they all list theaters and current offerings daily, with comprehensive listings on Fridays or Saturdays) or looking in the "Goings On About Town" column in *The New Yorker* or "Cue" Theater Guide in *New York Magazine,* which lists current theater fare under headings of "Broadway," "Off-Broadway," and "Off-Off-Broadway."

Broadway tickets can be quite expensive (they average $15 to $40 depending on where you sit and when you go), but that needn't be a deterrent to seeing as many shows as you would like. The TKTS stands (47th St. and Broadway at Times Square and 100 Williams St. in Lower Manhattan) offer half-price tickets for a wide range of Broadway, off-Broadway, and off-off-Broadway productions; tickets are sold on the day of performance after 3 PM for evening shows, after 12 noon for matinees. You must line up for the tickets; there are no reservations.

Theater Companies – *Brooklyn Academy of Music,* 30 Lafayette Ave., Brooklyn (636-4100); *Chelsea Westside Theatre,* 407 W 43rd St. (541-8394); *Circle Rep,* 99 7th Ave. South (924-7100); *Manhattan Theatre Club,* 321 E 73rd St. (472-0600); *NY Shakespeare Festival,* Public Theatre, 425 Lafayette St. (598-7150); *Phoenix,* 221 E 71st St. (730-0794); *Ridiculous Theatrical Company,* 1 Sheridan Sq. (691-2271); and *Roundabout,* Stage Two, 333 W 23rd St. (924-7160). All can provide a schedule of offerings and performance dates.

MUSIC: New York is a world center for performing artists. It presents the best of classical and nonclassical traditions from all over the world, in a variety of halls and auditoriums, filled with appreciative, knowledgeable audiences.

Lincoln Center for the Performing Arts, completed in 1969, represents the city's devotion to concerts, opera, operettas, and ballet, and is located on Broadway and 65th St. (for general information, 877-1800). Its buildings are: *Avery Fisher Hall,* home of the *NY Philharmonic* (874-2424); *NY State Theater,* featuring the *NY City Ballet* and *NY City Opera* (870-5570); *Metropolitan Opera House* (580-9830); *Damrosch Bandshell,* an open-air theater used for free concerts; the *Juilliard School* for musicians, actors, and dancers (799-5000); and *Alice Tully Hall,* home of the Chamber Music Society (362-1911). In addition, all the auditoriums in Lincoln Center present other musical events and recitals. While in the area, visit the *NY Public Library at Lincoln Center,* a unique ultramodern library and museum of the performing arts (930-0800). Guided tours of Lincoln Center are available daily (877-1800).

Other major halls are: *Carnegie Hall,* 57th St. and 7th Ave. (247-7459); *City Center Theatre,* 131 W 55th St. (246-8989); *Eastside Playhouse,* 334 E 74th St. (861-2288);

Kaufmann Auditorium, 92nd St. and Lexington Ave. (427-6000); *Grace Rainey Rogers Auditorium,* 5th Ave. and 82nd St. (879-5512), in the Metropolitan Museum; and *Brooklyn Academy of Music,* 30 Lafayette Ave. (636-4100). Also check music and dance listings in the newspapers, and *New York* and *The New Yorker.*

NIGHTCLUBS AND NIGHTLIFE: The scope of nightlife in New York is as vast as the scope of daily life. Cultural trends strongly affect the kinds of clubs that are "in" at any given time and their popularity has a tendency to peak, then plunge rather quickly. Old jazz and neighborhood clubs, on the other hand, remain intact, catering to a regular local clientele. They offer various kinds of entertainment, and many stay open until the wee hours of the morning serving drinks and food. It is a good idea to call all the clubs in advance to find out when they are open and what shows or acts they are offering; or consult the "Cue" listings in *New York Magazine.* Many of the city's nightclubs with live entertainment and/or dancing have cover charges of about $10, more or less, but this usually includes one or two drinks.

The current focus of the younger crowd is on clubs that offer rock and New Wave music — most also manage to sneak in some disco and oldies — along with a few bars and lots of room for dancing. The liveliest of these are: *The Ritz,* 119 E 11th St. (228-8888), mostly featuring live rock music; the *Underground,* 860 Broadway at 17th St. (254-4005), with two floors of bars, lounges, and dancing to live and taped music; and the very avant-garde *Danceteria,* 30 W 21st St. (620-0515), with three levels of dance space, live bands, taped music, a restaurant, and video games.

The revival of the big band sound has sent people searching for clubs where they can lindy and jitterbug the night away. The place to go is the *Red Parrot,* 617 W 57th St. at 12th Ave., with its own "swing" orchestra and a stereo system playing the most unusual assembly of recorded music in town. The *Red Blazer Too,* 1576 3rd Ave. (876-0440), also features swing bands on most nights.

Among the nightclubs with food and drink that feature live pop music — including rock, soul, rhythm and blues, reggae, jazz and top 40–type music — are *Ones,* 111 Hudson St. (925-0011); and *Mikell's,* 760 Columbus Ave. (864-8832). You can eat, dance to, and hear country-style music and bluegrass at *O'Lunney's Steak House,* 915 2nd Ave. (751-5470). Programs at *The Other End,* 149 Bleecker St. (673-7030), and *The Bottom Line,* 15 W 4th St. (228-7880), often offer traditional blues and rock. Country music notables entertain, and are entertained, at the *Lone Star Cafe,* 61 5th Ave. (242-1664), when they come to New York. The *Eagle Tavern,* 355 W 14th St. (924-0275), is also good for country and bluegrass.

Even though discos are no longer the city's hottest spots, there are still a fair number of chic places where it's offered, such as *Regine's,* 502 Park Ave. (826-0990); *Leviticus,* 45 W 33rd St. (564-0408); *Xenon,* 124 W 43rd St. (221-2690); *Magique,* 1110 1st Ave. (935-6060); *Bond's,* 1526 Broadway (944-5880); and the less flashy *Library* at the Barbizon Plaza, Ave. of the Americas between 58th and 59th Sts. (247-7000). The famous Brooklyn hangout where the movie *Saturday Night Fever* was filmed, *2001 Odyssey,* 802 64th St. (238-8213), still draws a crowd. For dancing to a Latin beat, try *Cachaca,* 403 E 62nd St. (688-8501); the *Corso Latin Ballroom,* 205 E 86th St. (534-4964); and *Chateau Madrid,* Lexington Ave. at E 48th St. (752-8080), where there's a floor show. If you prefer disco on wheels, try the *Roxy Roller Disco,* 515 W 18th St., between 10th and 11th aves. (675-8300), or *Empire Rollerdome,* 200 Empire Blvd., Brooklyn (462-1570). As for good, clean traditional ballroom fun with American and Latin live dance music, the famous *Roseland Dance City,* 239 W 52nd St. (247-0200), definitely deserves a whirl — it holds up to 4,000 dancers. *Lorelei,* 233 E 86th St (722-9926), is another large, family-style dance hall where you can waltz, jitterbug, swing, bop, and even polka.

For a low-key, elegant evening, try the *Pyramid Club,* Avenue A between 6th and

7th Sts. *Jimmy Weston's,* 131 E 54th St. (838-8384), adds dancing to live music to a good show and dinner. The *Rainbow Room,* 30 Rockefeller Plaza (757-9090), also has good cheek-to-cheek dancing music and one of the most dazzling views of the city anywhere; its *Rainbow Grill* has an entertaining — if somewhat risqué — floor show and a dance floor.

For small, intimate, after-theater or late-night clubs with good food, a nice, informal atmosphere, and low-key, quality entertainment, we recommend the *Café Carlyle,* in the Carlyle Hotel, 35 E 76th St. (744-1600); and *La Chansonette,* 890 2nd Ave. (752-7320). Talent scouts often go to search for new talent and potential stars in the lively, casual "showcase" clubs, where singers, dancers, and performers of all kinds test their new material on reliably loud but not always appreciative audiences. Two such clubs, which often cook until the early morning hours, are *The Improvisation,* 358 W 44th St. (765-8268), and *Catch a Rising Star,* 1487 1st Ave. (794-1906). *The Magic Towne House,* 1026 3rd Ave. (752-1165), is a unique weekend spot where you can catch some good magic acts.

The largest concentration of singles bars in New York can be found on 1st and 2nd (some on 3rd) Avenues, between 61st and 80th Streets. If you walk along either one of these you will probably find a likely looking place. Be sure to check out the *Adams Apple,* 1117 1st Ave. (371-8650); *Maxwell's Plum,* 1185 1st Ave. (628-2102); *T.G.I. Friday's,* 1152 1st Ave. (832-8512); and *Septembers,* 1442 1st Ave. (861-4670). Maxwell's Plum is particularly noted for its food and decor. If you like sitting around a piano, listening to, requesting, and even singing your favorite tunes, *The Village Green,* 531 Hudson St. (255-1650), *Knickerbocker Saloon,* 33 University Pl. (228-8490), and *Oliver's Restaurant,* 141 E 57th St. (753-9180), can fill the bill as well as satisfy your appetite.

The Village Vanguard, 178 7th Ave. S (255-4037), *The Village Gate,* Bleecker and Thompson Sts. (475-5120), *Sweet Basil,* 88 7th Ave. S (242-1785), and *Seventh Ave. South,* 21 7th Ave. S (242-4694), feature top-name current jazz artists.

The more recent loft scene, offering contemporary, avant-garde jazz, is centered in SoHo. Some of the more casual, neighborhood-type jazz clubs with reasonable prices and a relaxed atmosphere are *The Cookery,* 21 University Pl. (674-4450); *Arthur's Tavern,* 57 Grove St. (242-9468); *The Angry Squire,* 216 7th Ave. (242-9066); *Bradley's,* 70 University Pl. (228-6440); *The West End Jazz Room,* 2911 Broadway (666-8750); *Lush Life,* Bleecker and Thompson Sts. (228-3788); *Blue Note,* 131 W 3rd St. (475-8592); and *Jazzmania,* 40 W 27th St. (532-7666). For nostalgia and the more traditional jazz sounds heard in the 20s, 30s, and 40s, try *Eddie Condon's,* 144 W 54th St. (265-8277); *Michael's Pub,* 211 E 55th St. (758-2272); *Jimmy Ryan's,* 154 W 54th St. (664-9700).

Gay bars are scattered throughout New York, but the Upper West Side, in the 70s, and Christopher Street in the West Village distinguish themselves as gay areas. *Harry's Back East,* 1422 3rd Ave. (249-6991), is a regular hangout for gay men, and *Ty's* on Christopher Street is a noted cruising bar.

SINS: New York is a city of vast extremes, with an opulence equal to any metropolis in the world and poverty harsh enough to force people to live in steam tunnels, bombed-out shells of old cars, doorways, and on park benches. One might expect *anger* to seethe throughout this urban madland, but while it's not uncommon to see people walking down the street talking fiercely to themselves, a much more violent response can be raised by visitors who blithely announce, "It's a great place to visit, but I wouldn't want to live here."

For all their normally frenetic pace, New Yorkers can be seen at their *slothful* best at lunchtime in Central Park or in such vest-pocket enclaves as Paley Park (between Madison and 5th Avenues on 53rd Street).

New York fairly boils over with *lust,* mostly of a very unattractive variety. The 42nd Street–Times Square area, extending up 8th Avenue as far as 50th Street, includes both homosexual and straight pornographic establishments, including peep shows, strip shows, massage parlors, and street women. Pornographic cinemas dot the city, with conglomerations around the Times Square area and Penn Station. Bars that serve weak beer (or apple cider when their liquor licenses have been revoked) proliferate on the West Side between 34th and 52nd Streets. Be forewarned: Street prostitutes in New York are among the most dangerous in the world, and muggings and robbery are a frequent by-product of an encounter with one of them.

There are numerous "baths" for gays (gay *men* only; only one such establishment has tried to cater to gay women, but it closed within a few months) like *Man's Country* on W 15th Street. Public sex centers for so-called swinging heterosexuals are just being opened, the most famous being *Plato's Retreat* on W 34th Street. (Males must be accompanied by a woman.) Perhaps the most bizarre sex scene in New York is along the old West Side Highway across from the piers in Greenwich Village. Numerous after-hours sex clubs for gays — featuring heavy sadomasochistic rituals — compete for the attention of adventurers with the dark, ruined piers themselves, through which the men roam amid the wreckage.

New York could well be called the *gluttony* capital of the world. Ice cream freaks craving banana splits, sundaes, floats, or frosted, should head for *Agora's* (corner of E 87th and 3rd Ave.), *Serendipity* (E 60th between 2nd and 3rd), or *Swensen's Ice Cream Factory* (E 59th St. between Lexington and 3rd). Pessimists can satisfy their gloomy perspectives as well as their appetites by dropping into *Mary Elizabeth's* (E 37th between 5th and Madison) and asking for the most delicious donut holes ever baked. And for cheesecake fanciers, New York's creamiest is in Brooklyn at *Junior's* (Flatbush Ave.).

You'll have all you can do to keep your *envy, avarice,* and consummate *greed* in check as you romp through such palaces of the privileged as *Gucci, Cartier,* and *Tiffany's*. It is scant comfort to know these are but three of the nonpareil shops that will stir your basest instincts.

And when it comes to *pride,* New York chauvinism is rivaled only by the amount of criticism the city takes. From Yankee Stadium to the World Trade Center, you will hear again and again that New York has the best of everything — restaurants, museums, shopping, art, theater, music and dance, career opportunities — and the most interesting cross section of American culture in the country.

LOCAL SERVICES: Business Services – World-Wide Business Centers, Inc. (486-1333), and Molly's Professional Typing Service (268-7900). Let Millie Do It! (532-8775) is a service run by Millie Emory, who will run just about any kind of errand ("as long as it's legal and moral") for which you don't have time.

Mechanics – 24-hour road service and minor repairs: City-wide Auto Repairs, 606 W 47th St. (265-5353).

Babysitting – Ask at the hotel desk for recommended babysitting services.

Limousine Service – If you'd care to cavort in a Rolls-Royce, call *Cooper* (929-0094). If you're content to settle for a mere Cadillac, we've gotten top service from *London Towncars* (988-9700).

BEST IN TOWN

CHECKING IN: New York City is still one of the hardest places in the world to find an empty hotel room, and a rash of new properties have opened up to alleviate the problem. *Halloran House,* a high-rise Howard Johnson franchise; Hyatt's renovation of the old *Commodore* (now called the *Grand Hyatt*); and the *Harley* have added some 1,500 rooms to the Grand Central area. The super-deluxe *Palace Hotel* incorporates a shiny glass tower with the landmark Villard houses at Madison and 50th Street. However, don't expect this increased supply to offset inflation's upward push on room rates in the foreseeable future. Do expect to pay $100 or more — often lots more — for an expensive room for two in Manhattan; $70 to $90 for a moderately priced room; and $70 or less for an inexpensive one. These prices include no meals. (Note: Many of these hotels offer special weekend packages for relatively low rates. The packages include a variety of amenities — from just a room to a room plus breakfast/dinner, champagne, theater tickets, and parking. Reservations are always required, so write or call for information well in advance.) An alternative to taking a standard hotel room is a new Bed & Breakfast plan run by *Urban Ventures, Inc.* Accommodations are in private homes, include a Continental breakfast, and cost from $28 to $60 per night. For a brochure, contact Urban Ventures, Inc., 322 Central Park West, New York, NY 10025 (662-1234).

The Pierre – The most luxurious stopping place in midtown, with the most august clientele. The elegance is low-key, but consistent, and the rooms with a park view command the highest of already heady prices. Located on the most attractive corner of the city, it is *the* place to stay. 5th Ave. and 61st St. (838-8000). Expensive.

The Regency – Where the movers and shakers of America now stay when they're in New York. More business is probably conducted in the dining room here at breakfast than in all of the rest of the country during a normal business day. A relatively new addition to the New York hotel scene, its modern architecture does not detract at all from its appeal. Park Ave. and 61st St. (759-4100). Expensive.

The Carlyle – The leader among luxurious uptown hotels, where the Kennedy family traditionally stays. Noted for its quiet and serenity, with prices to match the high level of service. 35 E 76th St. (744-1600). Expensive.

The Plaza – You won't find Eloise romping in the halls anymore, but it's hardly an effort to "skipperdee" up to one of the rooms facing Central Park. Recent refurbishing has restored most of the old elegance, and this is the first hotel NYC visitors think of when they imagine a luxurious urban hostelry. 5th Ave. and 59th St. (759-3000). Expensive.

The Sherry-Netherland – It's a little less renowned than the Plaza and the Pierre (its immediate neighbors), but the accommodations here are hardly less elegant. The location is superb, and this is a luxurious stopping place truly worthy of the description. 5th Ave. and 59th St. (355-2800). Expensive.

The St. Regis – Right in the heart of the best New York shopping, a favorite with international visitors. The *King Cole Bar* is a popular late-afternoon rendezvous, and there are still legacies from the days when John Jacob Astor built this hotel just after the turn of the century. 5th Ave. and 55th St. (753-4500). Expensive.

The Waldorf-Astoria – A legend on Park Avenue, divided between the basic hotel and the more opulent Towers. The degree of comfort delivered here is consistent with the hotel's reputation. *Peacock Alley* is a favorite cocktail rendezvous, and the clock in the middle of the lobby may be New York's favorite meeting place. Well equipped to deal with foreign visitors. 301 Park Ave. (355-3000). Expensive.

The Tuscany – Located in the middle of attractive Murray Hill, it is a name not often known outside the city's immediate environs. Guests who know it well treasure the service and atmosphere. 120 E 39th St. (686-1600). Expensive.

The United Nations Plaza – The design of this modern hotel is beautifully integrated, from the sleek, green-tinted glass exterior through the dark green marble reception area to the top 10 floors, where the subtly hued rooms are a foil for magnificent city views. Both a truly international staff and exceptional facilities — including a tennis court, heated pool, and exercise room — are provided to pamper you. 44th St. and 1st Ave. (355-3400). Expensive.

Mayfair Regent – For those New York visitors who stay at the *Gritti* in Venice and the *Hotel du' Cap* in the south of France. There are just 150 suites, plus the nonpareil *Le Cirque* restaurant. Uncompromising elegance and superb service. Park Ave. at E 65th St. (288-0800). Expensive.

The Helmsley Palace – The *Palace* combines the landmark Henry Villard houses with a 51-story high-rise and has old-fashioned but beautifully restored public rooms decorated elegantly in marble, crystal, and gold, as well as modern, clean-lined guest rooms. You must use the 50th Street side entrance for checking in, but thereafter be sure to make your way into the hotel through the wrought-iron gates on Madison Avenue. 455 Madison Ave. at 50th St. (888-7000 or toll-free, 800 221-4982). Expensive.

The Grand Hyatt – If you've come to New York for glitter, you won't find more dazzle east of Broadway than at the *Hyatt.* Formerly the *Commodore Hotel,* it has been reincarnated with sleek modern lines, mirrored glass, and shiny chrome. The centerpiece of the multilevel lobby is the tiered, marble fountain crowned by a 77-foot bronze sculpture. On the lobby's upper level is the *Sungarden,* a glass-enclosed bar and cocktail lounge that overhangs the hotel's entrance and the busy 42nd Street traffic. The 1,400 guest rooms are dressed in rich, earthy tones that are brightened up daily with fresh flowers. Park Ave. at Grand Central Station (883-1234 or toll-free, 800 228-9000). Expensive.

The Berkshire Place – Originally built in 1926, the old *Berkshire* hotel has been resuscitated with dash and considerable understated flair. Most impressive is the Atrium Lobby, a mirrored lounge accented with soft shades, creating a quite comfortable and intimate atmosphere. Gaining momentum on the culinary scene is the pretty *Rendez-vous Restaurant* serving both classic French and nouvelle cuisine. 21 E 52nd St. (753-5800 or toll-free, 800 228-2121). Expensive.

The Harley of New York – The nationwide chain of Harley Hotels now has its third Manhattan address with the addition of a shining glass skyscraper on 42nd Street. This is an executive-oriented facility with special services available for the business traveler — secretaries, telex, photocopying, meeting rooms, and other extras. For dining, there's *Mindy's,* and for drinks and piano music try *Harry's New York Bar.* 212 E 42nd St. (888-1624 or toll-free, 800 221-4982). Expensive.

Hotel Parker Meridien – Billing itself as New York's "first French hotel," this establishment provides guests with the elegance of a European hostelry. There are 600 luxurious rooms plus apartments, bars, and *Le Restaurant Maurice* serving nouvelle cuisine. The sports-minded will enjoy Club Raquette for racquetball, handball, and squash, and the rooftop running track that encircles the enclosed pool where the views of Central Park are lovely. The hotel also has banquet and meeting facilities. 118 W 57th St. (245-5000). Expensive.

Vista International – The first hotel to be built in Manhattan's Wall Street vicinity in over 100 years, it sits between the World Trade Center towers and, since it faces New York Harbor, many rooms overlook the Statue of Liberty. A full range of special services is available for business travelers, and the hotel's shuttle bus makes frequent runs uptown. Other highlights include the indoor Executive Fitness Center, with first-rate sports equipment; the *Greenhouse* and *American Harvest* restaurants, offering very good American regional specialties; and the *Tall Ships Bar,* a popular after-work meeting place. 3 World Trade Center (938-9100). Expensive.

The New York Hilton – An enormous modern structure located near Rockefeller Center and one of New York's largest hotels. A bit antiseptic in ambience, but about as efficiently run as any hotel with more than 2,000 rooms can be. A favorite meeting and convention site. Pets allowed. 1335 Ave. of the Americas between 53rd and 54th Sts. (586-7000). Expensive.

The Mayflower – A favorite with ballet and concert buffs, this older hotel used to be a residential operation only, but now caters solely to a transient trade. Guests enjoy large, comfortable rooms with pantries that once served the permanent residents. All rooms have traditional, tasteful furnishings. Quite close to Lincoln Center. 15 Central Park West, between 61st and 62nd Sts. (265-0060). Expensive.

The Barbizon Plaza – Free bikes are provided for forays across the street into Central Park, and a charming café serves snacks as well as complete meals from 7 AM to midnight. Excellent maintenance and a warm welcome make this commercial hotel a wise buy for the location. 58th St. and 6th Ave. (247-7000). Expensive.

The Roosevelt – The hotel has recently changed ownership and undergone redecoration and restoration. The accommodations are clean and comfortable and its *Crawdaddy* restaurant has one of the area's most popular after-work bars. A good choice for business travelers. Madison Ave. at 45th St. (661-9600). Expensive to moderate.

Sheraton City Squire Hotel – This 50-story modern monolith has recently been taken over by the Sheraton chain. From here it's a short walk to the theater and the rooms are quite comfortable. 811 7th Ave. between 51st and 52nd Sts. (581-1000). Expensive to moderate.

The Algonquin – Long known as a favorite among literary types, the hotel's reputation is most closely connected to the days of the "round table" in its fine restaurant. The personal attention accorded by the management is visible everywhere, and, if anything, the hotel has improved with age. 59 W 44th St. (840-6800). Moderate.

The Ramada Inn – A typical member of the Ramada chain, this hotel offers modern units with air-conditioning, phones, and TV. The rooftop pool is a real bonus in the summer, and free parking is a bonus year round. 790 8th Ave., between 48th and 49th Sts. (581-7000). Moderate.

The Salisbury Hotel – Run by the Calvary Baptist church, this hotel has a small, welcoming lobby and newly painted, nicely sized pastel rooms (all with refrigerators and pantries, but no stoves). The Salisbury is a favorite with buyers and musicians, who like the hotel's location near 5th Avenue and Carnegie Hall. 123 W 57th St. (246-1300). Moderate.

Milford Plaza – Out-of-towners usually come to Manhattan for Broadway's bright nightlife and the *Milford* is smack in the center of New York's exciting theater district. All kinds of money-saving tour packages are available, and while rooms aren't too big, they're pleasant. You won't find a nicer place for the price. 270 W 45th St. (869-3600). Moderate to inexpensive.

The Royalton Hotel – Midtown hotels can be budget-benders, but this one — conveniently located in the theater district, and spic-and-span with color TV and telephone — is quite reasonable. 44 W 44th St. (730-1344). Moderate to inexpensive.

Excelsior Hotel – Nicely situated near Central Park and the Museum of Natural History, the *Excelsior's* clean and cheery rooms are enhanced by their even cheerier low prices. Rooms are pleasantly decorated — some have pretty park views — and have color TV and telephone. The coffee shop is also quite good. 45 W 81st St. (362-9200). Inexpensive.

Hotel Empire – Across the street from Lincoln Center, accommodations here are sufficiently comfortable and clean, and the food service pretty good. 44 W 63rd St. (265-7400). Inexpensive.

The Prince George – Located near toy, gift, and textile wholesalers as well as near the garment district, the Prince George attracts hordes of buyers. Of course, with air-conditioned rooms, color TV, and two restaurants, the hotel is a good buy in itself. 28th St. and Madison Ave. (532-7800). Inexpensive.

The Olcott – By no means plush, but certainly comfortable and adequate, this is a typical New York residential hotel that offers some transient accommodations. Spacious facilities and a homey atmosphere are the advantages of staying in this type of establishment. Most rooms are suites, with a living room, bedroom, kitchen, and bathroom. All rooms have air-conditioning. Reservations should be made several weeks in advance. 27 W 72nd St., only one block from Central Park (877-4200). Inexpensive.

The Gorham – The variety of room-and-bed combinations possible, together with the fact that all units contain a kitchenette, dining table, and color TV, make the Gorham a great boon to families traveling with children. 136 W 55th off 6th Ave. (245-1800). Inexpensive.

The Piccadilly – The gradual disintegration of this theater district standby has abruptly halted; new furniture and colored sheets have replaced chipped chairs and spotted spreads. Although the renovation probably cost a mint, the price is still right. 227 W 45th St. (246-6600). Inexpensive.

The Century Paramont – The enormous lobby is always alive with flight crews and tour groups — about 70% from abroad. Most of the 700 air-conditioned rooms are smallish but cheerful. 235 W 46th near Broadway (246-5500). Inexpensive.

The Chelsea – A New York architectural and historic landmark where Dylan Thomas, Arthur Miller, Lennie Bruce, Diego Rivera, Martha Graham, and others have made their New York home. The atmosphere in this 19th-century structure is distinctly unmodern, unhomogenized, and unsterilized. There is a large permanent occupancy, with about 200 rooms available for transients. Rooms vary in structure, price, and facilities — some have kitchens, fireplaces, and bathrooms and others have none of the above. For the adventurous only; make reservations well in advance. 222 W 23rd St. (243-3700). Inexpensive.

EATING OUT: New York City is, plain and simply, the culinary capital of the world. It is possible that there are more good French restaurants in Paris or more fine Chinese eating places in Taiwan, but no city in the world can offer the gastronomic diversity that is available in New York. If there is one compelling reason to come to New York, it is to indulge exotic appetites that cannot be satisfied elsewhere, and it is not unusual for dedicated eaters to make several pilgrimages to New York each year simply to satisfy their sophisticated palates.

Regrettably, New York's tastiest cuisine does not come cheap, though there are places to dine around the city where you need not pay in 30-, 60-, and 90-day notes. But as in most places, you get what you pay for, and you should expect to pay $75 or more for two in the restaurants that we've noted as expensive. Moderate restaurants will run between $50 and $75 per couple, and in inexpensive establishments you can expect to spend about $25 for a meal for two. These price ranges do not include drinks, wine or tips. Unless otherwise noted, reservations are essential.

Lutèce – New York's (and perhaps this country's) finest French restaurant, with service and atmosphere to match the extraordinary cuisine. Of all the premier

French restaurants in New York, this is the one most hospitable to strangers willing to pay the price for deluxe French food. If you have the option, dine in the comfortable upstairs room, though the enclosed garden is a treat in New York City. André Soltner runs this incredible bastion of gastronomic delight with a firm hand, but you'd still best be prepared for a check that will total into three figures. This is, however, one of those instances where what you get is worth the price. Make reservations at least 2 weeks in advance. Closed Sundays. Accepts only American Express and Diners Club credit cards. 249 E 50th St. (752-2225). Expensive.

La Caravelle – A traditional bastion of French haute cuisine with all of the attendant hauteur to go with it, this is often the choice of New York's smartest set. Menus are unalteringly interesting, and the kitchen is not merely competent but quite innovative. Closed Sundays. Major credit cards. 33 W 55th St. (586-4252). Expensive.

Dodin Bouffant – Bobby and Karen Pritsker have crafted just about the best new French restaurant that New York has seen in many a moon. The new premises give the Pritskers an opportunity to demonstrate their expertise in the Big Apple after a great success in Boston. Specialties include vegetable sausage with hazelnut butter and magret du canard — boned, sautéed duck in a pastry shell. The desserts, which heavily reflect a predilection toward chocolate, are especially notable. Closed Mondays. Major credit cards. 405 E 58th St. (751-2790). Expensive.

Palm – The best sirloin steak in New York in an atmosphere so unattractive that it's the restaurant's prime appeal. Sawdust covers the floor, tables and chairs are refugees from a thrift shop, but the steaks are just great. The largest (and most expensive) lobsters in New York are served here. *Palm, Too,* across the street, is a branch serving identical food and takes care of the overflow. Closed Sundays. Major credit cards. 837 2nd Ave. (687-2953). Expensive.

Christ Cella's – Palm's only rival in the top sirloin steak sweepstakes. The decor is attractive, the service is efficient, and it's a popular favorite of advertising and publishing types. Closed Sundays. Major credit cards. 160 E 46th St. (697-2479). Expensive.

The Palace – The most expensive restaurant in America, clearly dripping chic and cachet. This is a high roller's heaven, where the opulent surroundings make the rapid thinning of your wallet as bearable as possible. The menu is impressive and superbly prepared, and it's a prix fixe dinner that is not only a singular experience but almost worth the prix. Major credit cards. 420 E 59th St. (355-5150). Closed Sundays. Expensive.

Windows on the World – Somewhat overpriced (though interesting) menu that is extremely ambitious, but the food is less a lure than the best view of Manhattan that exists. Try to sit along the north wall, where you'll have all of glittering Manhattan spread out at your feet. If you don't care to spend the price of dinner, stop for a drink in the bar and enjoy the superb hors d'oeuvres. Open daily. Major credit cards. 1 World Trade Center (938-1111). Expensive.

Coach House – The best "American" restaurant in New York. The black bean soup is only superb, and people cry (with delight) over the chocolate cake. The Greenwich Village location is also an attraction, as it sits across the street from some of the most appealing federal-style row houses in the country. Closed Mondays. Major credit cards. 110 Waverly Pl. (777-0303). Expensive.

The "21" Club – The legendary atmosphere and unquestionable cachet are what lure most visitors, but the preparation of fresh game here happens to be among the finest in this country. Ties are required, and this is not the place to wear your leisure suit or white socks. The upstairs dining room is more elegant and quiet, but those who wish to see and be seen usually adorn the wall on the left as you enter the downstairs bar and dining room. Closed every Sunday and weekends during the summer. Major credit cards. 21 W 52nd St. (582-7200). Expensive.

The Russian Tea Room – With enough blinis to float you down the Volga, this unique restaurant is an almost obligatory stop for any visitor who will be in the city for any length of time. This is a place to abide by the waiter's suggestions and to let your Slavic instincts have free rein. Open daily. Major credit cards. 150 W 57th St. (265-0947). Expensive.

The Four Seasons – The Pool Room is perhaps the most beautiful dining room in the city, with a proprietorship that is not only creative but extremely able. Although the menu is interesting from top to bottom, desserts deserve special mention, and there's one called Chocolate Velvet that is merely ecstasy. The Grill Room is currently a luncheon favorite of New York's power elite. Closed Sundays. Major credit cards. 99 E 52nd St. (754-9494). Expensive.

Gloucester House – The most inspiring seafood in the city. Fresh biscuits are a particular delight and help salve the impact of some frankly staggering prices. A fine seafood restaurant, but a real budget-bender. Closed only Thanksgiving and Christmas. Major credit cards. 37 E 50th St. (755-7394). Expensive.

Peter Luger – The best T-bone steak in town lurking in the shadows under the Brooklyn side of the Williamsburgh Bridge. The neighborhood is hardly fashionable, but the food is first class. No menu, but try the thick-sliced onions and tomatoes under the special barbecue sauce, and be sure to taste the best home-fried potatoes the city has to offer. Open daily. No credit cards. Cash only. 178 Broadway, Brooklyn (387-7400). Expensive.

Maxwell's Plum – Actually three establishments in one: New York's most popular singles bar, a streetside café, and an elegant dining room. Decor consists of cut glass of every color and variety, and there's not a more visually spectacular dining room in the city. This is the New York City scene about which you've read. Open daily. Major credit cards. 64th St. and 1st Ave. (628-2102). Expensive to moderate.

Tavern-on-the-Green – One of New York's most beautiful dining establishments. In winter, the snow-covered trees trimmed with tiny white lights outside the Crystal Room make a dazzling display. Only slightly less spectacular in summer. Open daily. Major credit cards. Central Park West and 67th St. (873-3200). Expensive.

Trattoria da Alfredo – One of those superb small restaurants found only in a city like New York, offering the finest Northern Italian fare. Special, inventive pasta dishes are featured in an alternating group of specialties not found on the menu, and these should be your focus when you dine here. Reservations are hard to come by, so plan your visit early. It's well worth the forethought, and bring your own wine. Make reservations a week in advance. Closed Tuesdays. No credit cards. 90 Bank St. (929-4400). Moderate.

Grotta Azzurra Inn – The traditional bastion of Sicilian specialties in the heart of Little Italy. Lobster fra diavolo exacts an awesome price, but it's worth the tariff. The garlic bread is like no other in this world, and it guarantees that you won't be bothered by vampires for years. Closed Mondays. No reservations. No credit cards. 387 Broome St. (226-9283). Moderate.

Shun Lee Palace – Chef T. T. Wang is one of New York City's two most talented Chinese cooks, and his menu here includes the most exciting Oriental temptations ever inscribed. If you can somehow round up a group of ten to dine together, you might be interested in ordering Wang's special Chinese feast. It's beyond belief. Open daily. Major credit cards. 155 E 55th St. (371-8844). Moderate.

Sichuan Pavilion – At the moment, perhaps New York's most interesting Chinese restaurant. Diplomats from the neighboring U.N. fill the tables at lunch and dinner, and other city citizens have discovered the allure of an innovative and always tempting menu. Try the dumplings and sichuan-style spare ribs for an appetizer, and the chicken with peanuts as a main dish. But beware of hot peppers and very spicy seasonings — you can order dishes "mild" if you'd like to spare your stomach lining the first time around. Open daily. Major credit cards. 322 E 44th St. (986-3775). Moderate.

Richard Mei's King Dragon – The best of New York's Chinese restaurants that offer the kind of Cantonese cooking that was once thought to be all that Chinese cooking was about. Nothing remarkably creative, but the old favorites are prepared well. Open daily. Major credit cards. 1273 3rd Ave. (988-3433). Moderate.

Tovarisch – So what if the chef's name is Boris Blech! This is the most authentic Russian food available in midtown, and host Marvin Safir keeps the ambience lighthearted and supremely pleasant. Closed Sundays. Reservations necessary. Major credit cards. 38 W 62nd St. (757-0168). Moderate.

Kitcho – The restaurant that Mimi Sheraton (of the *New York Times*) describes as "the most serious and authentic Japanese restaurant I have found." Soups are notably delicate, and teriyaki grills of meat or fish are tastefully seasoned with ginger and sweet sake (rice wine). Try such delicacies as *kushi-katsu* — crisp, deep-fried chunks of pork — or *to-banyaki* — marinated and grilled meat or fish with broiled vegetables. Closed Saturdays. American Express and Diners Club only. 22 W 46th St. (575-8880). Moderate.

The Market Bar and Dining Room – The less known (but superior) of the two world-class restaurants in the World Trade Center. An interesting menu with equally interesting atmosphere and superb service. Portions are extremely large; pay particular attention to the daily specials. Closed Sundays. Major credit cards. 1 World Trade Center (938-1155). Moderate.

Café des Artistes – One of New York's most romantic restaurants, in a West Side apartment house. Appetizers and main dishes are all first rate, but the real lure are the desserts. Save room, for they've an unusual special offering that includes a sample of every dessert on the menu. For those with a sweet tooth, it's visiting paradise. The most beautiful Sunday brunch in town. Open daily. Major credit cards. 1 W 67th St. (877-3500). Moderate.

Frankie and Johnnie's – A fine steak house in the middle of the theater district, where it's not always easy to find a good restaurant. Hash-brown potatoes and salads are specialties. Closed Sundays. Major credit cards. 269 W 45th St. (245-9717). Moderate.

Gaylord – The most accessible of a rapidly increasing number of restaurants featuring Indian food. Considered the most British of the Indian restaurants, and most comfortable for neophyte experimenters. Try the special Tandoori Mix, an amalgam of small helpings of almost everything on the menu. Drink beer here, not wine. Open daily. Major credit cards. 50 E 58th St. (759-1710). Moderate.

Shezan – Perhaps the most beautiful Indian restaurant in New York and the favorite of the gentleman who designed the cover for this book. He says it's the best Indian table in the city, and since he designs pretty good covers, maybe he knows. Closed Sundays. Major credit cards. 8 W 58th St. (371-1414). Moderate.

Cockeyed Clams – The best seafood-per-dollar value in New York. Tables are close and the dining room can get quite noisy, but you won't find a better lobster or piece of snapper in the city for these prices. Open daily. No credit cards. 1678 3rd Ave at 94th St. (831-4121). Equally good, with the same menus and management, are the *Butterfish Hole,* 1394 3rd Ave. at 79th St. (879-0991), and *Hobeaus,* 963 1st Ave. at 53rd St. (421-2888). Moderate.

Oh Ho So – Quong and Mary Lum, owners of this SoHo Chinese restaurant, have used a great deal of imagination in setting up and running this unusual establishment. The food is founded on Cantonese cooking, but with a variety of fruits, honey, innovative sauces, and lots of poetic license thrown in. Specialties include such dishes as Orange Steak and Honey Prawns. The decor is strictly contemporary SoHo Loft — 18-foot ceilings, large open spaces, exposed beams and pipes, and rather incongruous but lovely antique tables and chairs. There's only one catch — there's no readily visible sign outside. Check the address. Open daily. Reservations. American Express only. 395 West Broadway (966-6110). Moderate.

Village Green – Don't be dismayed by this restaurant's rather shabby-looking Hudson St. location. Inside, you'll find the two-story dining room elegant yet cozy: linen-draped tables shining with crystal and silver and a fire snapping away in the hearth. The menu is Continental, the food always well prepared, and the service friendly. Open daily. Major credit cards. 531 Hudson St. (255-1650). Moderate.

Sweets – New York's oldest seafood restaurant, with an atmosphere that truly harkens back a couple of centuries. The cooking is wonderful and the value is better than normal. Open weekdays. No credit cards. No reservations. 2 Fulton St. (825-9786). Moderate.

Vienna '79 – The cuisine at this small (15 tables) modern eatery is Viennese and the specialties served are *taselspitz* (boiled beef), duckling, and (of course) Wiener schnitzel. Open daily for dinner. Major credit cards. 320 E 79 St. (734-4700). Moderate.

Lüchow's – Often mistaken for a Chinese restaurant, but actually a popular center of traditional German fare. The beer and schnitzel flow freely while the violins play and the oompah band toots in the background. Especially exciting at Christmastime, when the dining room holds the city's largest indoor tree. Open daily. Major credit cards. 110 E 14th St. (477-4860). Moderate.

Sammy's Roumanian Steak House – The last remaining survivor of a long, Lower East Side tradition of ethnic meat restaurants. Traditional Eastern European favorites are featured, as is old country music of a sort you're not likely to hear in any other establishment. The makings for egg creams are set right on the table, and this is an experience you don't usually find this side of Anatefka. Open daily. American Express. 157 Chrystie St. (475-9131). Moderate.

Vasata – An authentic Czechoslovakian restaurant that is a wonderful experience at relatively low prices. Genuine Czechoslovakian Pilsner beer is only one of the substantial allures, and you should order your dessert of palacinky filled with either apricot jam or chocolate sauce. Closed Mondays. Major credit cards. 339 E 75th St. (650-1686). Moderate.

Gage & Tollner – Holding forth at this stand since 1889, so they must be doing something right. It's worth a visit, if only to watch the gaslight glowing in the evening. The hashmarks on the sleeves of the waiters indicate their years of service, and some look like they're about to run out of arms. Among the specialties are 15 separate styles of potatoes. Open daily. Major credit cards. 372 Fulton St., Brooklyn (875-5181). Moderate.

Poletti's – Fresh pasta's a current craze, and carefully arranged trays of green and yellow noodles are filling up shop windows and restaurants all over town. *Poletti's* one-ups most of them by making its fresh noodles in full view of the diners. Pasta dishes are augmented by a selection of other Italian specialties. Open daily. No reservations. Major credit cards. 2315 Broadway (580-1200). Moderate.

Pierre au Tunnel – Onion soup, mussels, frog's legs, and minute steak typify the French provincial dishes featured by this theater district bistro since 1950. Jacqueline and Jean-Claude Lincy, the daughter and son-in-law of the founders, now run *au Tunnel.* The original high standards have not changed a whit. Closed Sundays. American Express only. 306 W 48th St. (582-2166). Moderate to inexpensive.

Pastrami & Things – Though it's recently changed hands, it's still got the best corned beef or pastrami sandwich in New York. The 23rd Street branch is superior to the large Rockefeller Center incarnation, though we wouldn't turn our noses up at the pickles from either place. Open daily. No credit cards or reservations. 297 3rd Ave. (683-7185); 30 Rockefeller Plaza (247-4700). Inexpensive.

Sloppy Louie's – Right in the heart of the Fulton Fish Market, this is a place to try at lunchtime, when you'll sit at long tables with all the Wall Street brokers and bankers. The experience of eating here is the equal of the fresh fish, which has only to be delivered from across the street. Open weekdays. No credit cards or reservations. 92 South St. (952-9657). Inexpensive.

V & T Pizzeria – Merely the best pizza in town, located just across the street from the Cathedral of St. John the Divine. A favorite of generations of Columbia University students, and a genuine discovery for those who thought they knew what good pizza was. Other good Italian dishes, too. Closed Mondays. No credit cards or reservations. 1024 Amsterdam Ave. (663-1708). Inexpensive.

Green Tree – For a taste of the old country, head to this family-run Upper West Side establishment. Hungarian waiters load down your table with specialties of their homeland — chicken or cold cherry soup, stuffed cabbage, and Hungarian goulash. For dessert try the palacsintas, crêpes filled with cheese or apricot jam. Closed Sundays. No reservations. No credit cards. 1034 Amsterdam Ave. at 111th St. (864-9106). Inexpensive.

Ukrainian Restaurant – On the ground floor of the Ukrainian National Home, this restaurant is very much like home, if yours happens to be the Ukraine. Slavic diners of all ages come here for the food their mothers used to make — pirogen, noodle dumplings stuffed with cheese, cabbage, or meat and kasha (a buckwheat grain); borscht; boiled beef; and cherry blintzes. This is a good place to eat before or after attending a show at the Public Theater. Open daily. No reservations. No credit cards. 140 2nd Ave. between 8th and 9th Sts. (533-6765). Inexpensive.

Hunan House – Among Chinatown's best, this pleasant restaurant specializes in the subtly spiced food of the province of Hunan. Start off with fried dumplings or hot and sour soup, then have some Hunan lamb, prepared with scallions; Changsha Beef, done in a hot sauce with broccoli; or Confucius Prawns with cashews. Open daily. No reservations. American Express only. 45 Mott St. (962-0010). Inexpensive.

Madras Woodlands – This restaurant is a cheap and convenient lunch stop for tourists—just steps away from the United Nations and a quick cab ride to the Broadway theaters. The food served here is South Indian vegetarian; you can choose from a number of delicious curries, breads, and vegetable pastries. Open daily. Major credit cards. 310 E 44th St. (986-0620). Inexpensive.

Harvey's Chelsea Restaurant – Etched-glass windows, polished brass rails, and baroque wood paneling make this turn-of-the-century bar a delightful oasis in an otherwise dreary neighborhood. The best choice on the menu is the tasty fish and chips, accompanied by a frosty draft. Reservations advised. Major credit cards. 108 W 18th St. (243-5644). Inexpensive.

OKLAHOMA CITY

April 22, 1889. On that day the United States opened the theretofore protected federal lands of central Oklahoma to settlement by white men. Between dawn and dusk more than 10,000 people poured across these unrelieved prairie midlands staking claims and laying out homesteads as if pursued by the Furies. By nightfall a city of flickering campfires and roughly marked claims outlined the farthest extents of the city born so abruptly, and in such a fever, on the open prairie.

If it was a moment of dreams fulfilled for the settlers, it was the bitter end of a promise to the Indians who had been "given" Oklahoma years before. The area had become American in 1803 as part of that most fabulous of real estate deals, the Louisiana Purchase. Almost immediately, it was declared Indian Territory, and tribes throughout the US were compulsorily moved there (see *A Short Tour of Indian America,* DIVERSIONS). From the forests of New England and the bayous of the South, what remained of the Indian tribes were moved to the Territory. The land was owned and administrated by the federal government, but dedicated to use for, and by, the Indians. This commitment lasted all of about 60 years. By the end of the Civil War, the area was halved, the western half becoming Oklahoma Territory, the eastern half remaining Indian Territory. From then until 1907, when both territories became the state of Oklahoma, the Indians lost land as the open and to-be-settled areas were extended.

But for the settlers, the area that was to be Oklahoma City represented one precious commodity — space, cheap land on which to establish homes. Just how ambitious they were, and how many of them there were, are still evident: By area Oklahoma City is one of the largest American cities, with 621 square miles within its municipal borders. And more than ambitious, they were lucky: Beneath the surface of their jealously guarded homesteads percolated a sea of oil, and Oklahoma became the city with oil derricks downtown (and even in front of the State Capitol). Oil meant money, and with the money came sophistication that a prairie town could scarcely have expected.

Today Oklahoma City has a population of over 800,000 people. Oil is still a mainstay of the economy, but the giant Oklahoma City Air Materiel Area (Tinker Air Force Base) employs more than 19,000 civilians and 3,600 military personnel. The FAA Aeronautical Center, including the Civil Aeromedical Institute, is located at the city's bustling Will Rogers World Airport. More than two million passengers fly to and from Oklahoma City annually. The city is also a shipping point for wheat and cotton grown in surrounding areas. The OKC feeder market is the third largest cattle market in the country. The University of Oklahoma School of Medicine with its affiliate hospitals, Research Building, Medical Research Foundations, and Veterans Hospital is considered one of the best in the nation.

Sports and religion play a big part in the lives of residents. OKC (or Oke City, as residents refer to it) is practically the center of what is commonly known as the Bible Belt. More than 45 denominations are represented in the city's 500 churches, from Zen Buddhist to Baptist (admittedly more Baptist than Buddhist). The fervor of spirit is not all religious, however. Every autumn, "Big Red" fever sweeps the city as the University of Oklahoma starts the football season.

Because of its wide-open spaces, Oklahoma City is mainly residential, with plenty of yard to mow between the homes. Real estate is a comparative bargain. A house and land that would cost more than $100,000 in the eastern part of the country costs about half that here. The residential area is surrounded by lakes which are great for fishing, sailing (even ice sailing), and swimming.

OKLAHOMA CITY AT-A-GLANCE

SEEING THE CITY: *Eagles Nest* restaurant, on top of the 20-story United Founders Life Tower, offers a view of the city as well as fine seafood specialties. 5900 Mosteller Dr. (840-5655).

SPECIAL PLACES: Because Oklahoma City spreads across such a vast expanse of land, many of the major visitor attractions are not within walking distance. You'll need a car.

State Capitol – This is one of the few capitols in the nation that does not have a dome. It's probably the only one with an active oil well on the grounds. (The Capitol was built before prospectors struck oil. When it was, derricks went up everywhere.) The Capitol complex consists of four buildings. Most interesting is the main building, of granite and limestone, with pillars and a wide staircase in front, a statue of a cowboy in the lobby, and murals of Oklahoma history in the halls. Open Mondays through Fridays. Free. Lincoln Blvd., between 22nd and 23rd Sts. (521-2011).

Oklahoma Historical Society – An astounding collection of Indian artifacts, presenting aspects of Indian history from diggings that go back from AD 400 and 500 to the days of Custer and Buffalo Bill. The library has one of the most complete archives of historical documents on American Indians in the US. Open daily. Free. On the southeastern section of State Capitol grounds, 2100 Lincoln Blvd. (521-2491).

Omniplex – The only Egyptian mummy in Oklahoma makes its home here. Part of the Foundation complex, the Gerrer Museum and Art Gallery has a number of curios from ancient times, as well as some Renaissance paintings, carved ivory figurines, and contemporary Americana. The Kirkpatrick Planetarium presents sky shows and hosts traveling Air Force exhibits. Open daily. Admission charge. 2100 NE 52nd (424-5564).

Oklahoma City Zoo – Captivity seems to agree with the more than 2,000 animals, birds, and reptiles here, perhaps because they're left to wander freely in natural settings. The zoo has been so successful in raising animals in captivity that many are sent here from other parts of the country to breed. (You might catch a couple of baboons on a wild weekend.) A Safari train covers the exhibits. There's also an Iron Horse train. Open daily. Admission charge. East Ave. and NE 50th St. (424-3343).

National Cowboy Hall of Fame – Hi-yo, Silver! Cowboys, real and fictional, line the halls of this good-natured museum. In addition to art and scupture, there are dioramas, relief maps showing migration paths, and a model village of early days. Also, plenty of saddles and exhibits on movie cowboys. Western heroes visit at least once a year. Open daily. Admission charge. 1700 NE 63rd St. (478-2250).

SOURCES AND RESOURCES

Oklahoma City Tourism and Convention Center has brochures and maps. Main and Gaylord (232-2211). The best local guides to the city are the Tourism and Convention Center brochures.

All telephone numbers are in the 405 area code unless otherwise indicated.

For Local Coverage – *Daily Oklahoman*, morning daily; *Oklahoma City Times*, afternoon daily.

For Food – *Downtowner* Magazine, weekly.

CLIMATE AND CLOTHES: The weather is very changeable. Changeable means that in winter it can be 12° in the morning and 45° or 50° in the afternoon. In the summer it's often 100° or higher, but the wind keeps it from being totally unbearable. The winds often gust from 35 to 40 miles an hour. Oklahoma exemplifies the aphorism that you don't find oil where there's nice weather.

GETTING AROUND: Bus – Mastran operates frequent buses. Their main office is at 300 E California (235-7433).

Taxi – There are taxi stands in front of the big hotels and at major intersections, but they are difficult to find at need. For dependable service, call Yellow Cab (232-6161).

Car Rental – Every major national firm is represented.

MUSEUMS: National Cowboy Hall of Fame and Oklahoma Historical Society, are described in *Special Places*. Other Oklahoma City museums are:

National Softball Hall of Fame, 2801 NE 50th St. (424-5266).

Oklahoma State Firefighters Museum, 2716 NE 50th St. (424-3440).

Oklahoma Art Center, 3113 Pershing Blvd., Fair Park and Plaza Circle (946-4477).

MAJOR COLLEGES AND UNIVERSITIES: University of Oklahoma (Norman, 325-0311); Oklahoma State University (Stillwater, 624-5000); Oklahoma City University (2423 NW Blackwelder, 521-5000).

SPECIAL EVENTS: College football season, September-December; *National Rodeo Cowboys of America Championship,* November and December; *Spring Arts and Azalea Festival,* April.

SPORTS: Baseball – The *'89ers* play at All Sports Stadium, Fairgrounds Park, 10th and May (946-1453).

Football – College football games are held at Lewis Stadium, University of Oklahoma, Norman, and Oklahoma State University, Stillwater (624-5000).

Hockey – The Oklahoma City *Stars,* members of the CHL, play at Myriad Gardens (236-0420).

Fishing – The best fishing is at Lake Hefner and Lake Overholser, twin lakes 20 miles northwest of the center of town, between McArthur and Council Rds. There's also good fishing at Lincoln Park, Eastern Ave. and NE 50th St.

Golf – The best city course is at Lincoln Park, Eastern Ave. and NE 50th St.

Tennis – There are good public courts at Memorial Park, 32nd and Classen.

Sailing – There's good sailing (and ice sailing) on Lake Hefner and Lake Overholser.

THEATER: *Oklahoma Theater Center* is an ultra-modern complex with two stages, 309 W Sheridan (239-7333). *Gaslight Dinner Theater* has good food and touring acting companies at reasonable prices, 2804 NW 122nd St. (751-4343).

MUSIC: *Oklahoma Symphony Orchestra* and traveling entertainers play at the Music Hall, Civic Center, 201 Channing Sq. (231-2584). Oklahoma City University music school sends opera singers to the Met. Check out their performance schedules by calling 521-5000.

NIGHTCLUBS AND NIGHTLIFE: For country and western music, try *Cowboys,* 4300 W Reno (942-6300). *Michael's Plum,* at NW 63rd in Glenbrook Center (848-8659), has dancing to mostly disco music; and *Bianca's,* 2874 NW 63rd in French Market Mall (848-3217), has jazz.

SINS: In Oklahoma City, people used to brag about the fact that its 900 square miles made it the largest city in the world in terms of area; since Tokyo edged it out, that's no longer true, and the citizens' one point of *pride* these days is the fact that just about everybody owns a home.

LOCAL SERVICES: Business Services – Kelly Services, 50 Penn Pl. (848-8545).

Mechanic – Burke Chevrolet (all makes), 700 N Broadway (236-8501); Ray's Tire and Auto Service, 5201 N Pennsylvania (842-1427).

Babysitters – There are no registered sitter services. Oklahoma City University students are sometimes available. Call 521-5000.

BEST IN TOWN

CHECKING IN: Expect to pay $80 and up for a double room at hotels listed as expensive and about $60 in the moderate category.

Sheraton Century Plaza – This modern hotel has 625 rooms, brightly splashed in orange, rich brown, and beige tones. Indoor pool, disco, and two restaurants — both average and both expensive. 1 N Broadway (235-2780). Expensive.

Skirvin Plaza – A landmark. Built by the father of Perle Mesta, the legendary "hostess with the mostess," this was The Hotel for many years. Rooms have all been completely remodeled. *Perle Mesta Room* serves a buffet with fresh orange juice, choice of champagne or bloody Mary. Excellent steak and pastries, too. 460 rooms. 1 Park Ave. (232-4411). Expensive.

Holiday Inn Downtown – If you're looking for convenience, this is probably your best bet. Sitting right in central downtown, it's closest to the Civic Center Music Hall and theaters. Outdoor pool. Pleasant, reasonable restaurant. 300 rooms. 520 W Main (232-4444). Moderate.

EATING OUT: Oklahoma City is known for its choice steaks. Restaurants are spread out across the city, rather than concentrated into one area (in the case of the Haunted House, getting there is half the fun!). Expect to pay $40 at an expensive restaurant; between $15 and $20 at those we've classed as moderate; under $15 at the inexpensive one. Prices are for a meal for two, without drinks, wine, or tip.

The Haunted House – A local legend. Two murders were actually committed in this classic "house on the hill" about 25 years ago. The bullet holes are still visible. There have been reports of strange noises, but you'll have to decide for yourself. The house specializes in fresh veal prepared in a variety of ways (scallopini is one of the best), and lobster and steak. All meals come with special Caesar salad mixed at your table. When you make your reservations, manager Art Thebo will give you directions. It's hard to find. Open daily. Major credit cards. 1 mile east of Cowboy Hall of Fame, just off I-66 (478-1417). Expensive.

Junior's – This Victorian-style restaurant draped in red velvet serves steak, giant lobster, and fried chicken. *Junior's* also has a piano bar and a private club. Closed Sundays. Reservations recommended. Major credit cards. 2601 NW Expy. (848-5597). Expensive.

Alberta's Tea Room – A restaurant with a quiet atmosphere and fine food and service. Although it's called a tea room, the portions are substantial. Open for lunch only; closed Sundays. Reservations advised. Major credit cards. French Market Mall at 63rd and North May (842-3458). Moderate.

Molly Murphy's House of Fine Repute – Waiters and waitresses here are actually performers who dress up like comic- and story-book characters and sit and chat while they take your order. The menu features steak and chicken, and the Bacchus feast, a platter of chicken, vegetables, and other foods, easily feeds four. Open daily. No reservations. Major credit cards. 1100 S Meridian (942-8588). Moderate.

Pistachio's Café et Bistro – Decorated with handsomely framed 1920s advertising posters and Tiffany lamps, known locally for fresh spinach salad with house dressing, omelettes, burgers, and the ubiquitous steak and lobster. Open daily. No reservations needed. Major credit cards. 50 Penn Place (340-3247). Moderate.

El Zocalo – Very fine Mexican (not Tex-Mex) food, specializing in chiles rellenos and dishes prepared with sour cream. Open daily. Reservations not necessary. Major credit cards. 4600 W Reno (947-8665). Inexpensive.

OMAHA

Whenever a stand-up comic wants to take a shot at a cowtown, he invariably aims at Omaha. Omaha has got a lot of cows, and cows are a sure laugh. The blizzards and thundershowers are funny, too, but they obscure the target. What the comic fails to mention is that the Wizard of Oz also came from Omaha (as he admits when he's been debunked), and though it's no Emerald City, it has appeal.

Nebraska's largest city (metropolitan population of 377,000) strikes a nice compromise between the friendly ways of a small town and the cultural sophistication of a bigger city. Omaha is the industrial center of the Great Plains and maintains one of America's largest shopping centers, but also has relatively clean air, a low crime rate, and free-flowing traffic. A good art museum, an ambitious opera, a symphony, and a zoo, provide evidence that Omaha is no longer just an overgrown cowtown, though the cows continue to be pretty important citizens.

Omaha is located on the west bank of the Missouri River, and, with its suburbs, spreads out across 89 square miles of rolling Midwestern terrain. The river, which runs 2,723 miles from southwest Montana to join the Mississippi north of St. Louis, has played an important role in the city's historic and economic development. Founded in 1854 by a ferryman from Council Bluffs, the raw young river town bristled with gunfighters and gamblers. In 1868, saloon keepers outnumbered teachers, and undertakers outnumbered clergymen. But its location on the river, and the naming of the city by President Lincoln as the eastern terminus of the transcontinental railroad in 1862, assured Omaha's future prosperity. During the following decades, the prairie gave way to stockyards, plants, and warehouses. Today barges transport grain, farm products, and machinery on the Missouri, and the transcontinental railway lines converge in the home of Union Pacific. Omaha is a major center of grain and livestock markets, meatpacking, insurance, and is the headquarters of the Air Force's Strategic Air Command.

Despite its advantageous position, Omaha's collective ego is sensitive about being so far removed from America's cultural capitals. But this situation, too, has its assets. Residents are proud that many silly notions ballyhooed elsewhere never really catch on in Omaha. And some of them never even arrive. Swinging nightspots are not that common, but the sunsets are beautiful. The Gerald Ford Birthsite is now a pleasant park. And there are many places to rustle up an Omaha steak, which is a carnivore's justly celebrated slab of pleasure.

Though the downtown area has been in a slow state of decline for twenty years, and many of the businesses have moved out to West Omaha which sprawls with shopping centers, fast-food chains, and apartment complexes, recently, a "Return to the River" movement has generated renewed interest in the downtown area. New government and university buildings and a library have already been built. In place of deteriorated buildings near the river, a mile-long Central Park Mall is under construction, lined with stores, fountains, and even an artificial stream to stretch to the river.

OMAHA AT-A-GLANCE

SEEING THE CITY: *Caniglia's World Restaurant*, at the top of the area's tallest building, offers the best view of Omaha — the metropolitan area, the Missouri River, and further eastward to the small industrial town of Council Bluffs and the bluffs themselves, which are wind-blown deposits of soil which have formed steep hills, unusual for Midwestern terrain. 1700 Farnam (344-3200).

SPECIAL PLACES: Omaha's a spread-out city. You can walk around the downtown area or take the bus, but it's best to have a car to visit the places of interest on the outskirts of town, and in West Omaha, which is the thriving business center.

Central Park Mall – Reclaimed from a decayed commercial and warehouse district, this new urban park will stretch a mile east to the Missouri River when completed. Lined with an artificial stream, pond, and waterfall, the Mall is already the site of festivals and free concerts in nice weather. 14th and Douglas Sts.

Union Pacific Historical Museum – Located in Union Pacific National Headquarters, the museum recalls this line's colorful history as a transcontinental trailblazer, displaying everything from thumbcuffs, used by railroad detectives to disable miscreants, to President Lincoln memorabilia (including a replica of his funeral car). Closed Sundays. Free. 1415 Dodge St. (271-3530).

The Old Market – Once Omaha's wholesale produce center, the market is now an ever-changing collection of small shops, restaurants, pubs, art and craft galleries, pinball arcades, and plant stores. Among the most interesting of the galleries is *Artists' Cooperative*, which features contemporary and abstract prints, sculptures, and paintings by 30 of the area's best artists. At *Spaghetti Works*, you can have lunch or dinner — all the spaghetti you can eat and as much of the works (bread, salad, sauces) for an inexpensive price. 11th and Howard Sts.

Antiquarium – Near but not part of the Old Market, the Antiquarium has the real old stuff, from rare 19th-century manuscripts to over a half million used books at bargain prices. Closed Sundays. 1215 Harney St. (341-8077).

Joslyn Art Museum – This monolithic chunk of pink marble holds some of the finest Midwestern and Western collections around, as well as exhibits of international art through the ages. Features the Maximilian-Bodmer Collection of paintings done while on the Belgian Prince's Upper Missouri River Expedition of 1833–34. Also has 19th-century Western landscapes of Albert Bierstadt, and paintings by Remington, Russell, Catlin, and the Stewart Miller Collection focusing on the Great Plains of the 1830s. Closed Mondays. Admission charge. 2200 Dodge St. (342-3300).

Boys Town – Internationally famous institution for homeless boys, founded in 1917 by Father Flanagan, in the belief that there is no such thing as a bad boy, given a good Christian upbringing and education. Self-conducted tours of the campus, which has 65 buildings including grade and high schools, a trade school, gyms, a fine philatelic and numismatic center, and 350 good boys. Open daily. Free. 138th and W Dodge Rd. (498-1350).

■ **EXTRA SPECIAL:** 50 miles southwest of Omaha along I-80 is *Lincoln*, the state's capital and second largest city. The University of Nebraska State Museum (14th and U Sts. in Morrill Hall) has excellent displays of the geology and animal life of the Great Plains from prehistoric to modern times, as well as the world's largest *mammoth.* The 400-foot State Capitol is an impressive sight, visible for miles around, and features a glazed dome with the Indian Thunderbird design, topped by a 32-foot statue of "The Sower."

SOURCES AND RESOURCES

The Omaha Convention and Visitors Bureau (444-4660) publishes brochures and maps of attractions that are available in all the hotels.

All telephone numbers are in the 402 area code unless otherwise indicated.

For Local Coverage – *Omaha World Herald,* morning and evening daily, publishes Sunday *Entertainment* magazine which lists the coming week's events; *Sun Newspapers,* weekly paper; *Omaha* magazine, monthly. All are available at newsstands.

For Food – *Omaha* magazine offers current information (price range, hours, credit cards) on area restaurants.

CLIMATE AND CLOTHES: Seasons are distinct and there is daily variety, perhaps a bit too much for some when the mercury drops to 15° below or rises to 105° above. Omaha is mostly sunny, with evening showers and thunderstorms occurring frequently between April and September.

GETTING AROUND: Bus – Metropolitan Area Transit provides efficient service for the city and Council Bluffs. For route information contact Metro Area Transit, 2615 Cuming St. (341-0800).

Taxi – Cabs can be picked up at taxi stands in front of major hotels or at the airport, or can be ordered on the phone. Major companies are Happy Cab (339-0110 or 331-TAXI); Checker Cab (342-8000); Safeway Cab (342-7474); and Yellow Cab (341-9000).

Car Rental – Omaha has offices of the major national firms and inexpensive service is provided by Thrifty, 2323 Abbott Dr. (345-1040).

MUSEUMS: In addition to the Joslyn Art Museum and the Union Pacific Historical Museum (see *Special Places*), there are the Strategic Aerospace Museum (12 miles south on US 75, open daily, 292-2001); and the Western Heritage Museum (801 S 10th St., closed Mondays, 444-5071).

MAJOR COLLEGES AND UNIVERSITIES: The University of Nebraska at Omaha at 60th and Dodge Sts. (554-2800), with an enrollment of 15,000, and the Medical Center, 42nd St. and Dewey Ave. (559-4000) are both part of the University of Nebraska system. Creighton University (enrollment 5,000) is a private institution founded in 1878 by the Creightons, who were early settlers of the territory, 2500 California St. (280-2707).

SPECIAL EVENTS: The Ak-Sar-Ben *World's Championship Rodeo* in late September features bull riding, calf roping, wild broncos, livestock collections, and country-and-western entertainers.

SPORTS: Baseball – The American Baseball Association's Omaha *Royals* play their home games at Rosenblatt Stadium from May to September, tickets at Stadium Office, 13th St. and Murphy Ave. (734-2550). In June, the stadium is the site for the National Collegiate Athletic Association Baseball

World Series. Tickets available at City Auditorium, 1804 Capitol Ave. (346-1323).

Horse Racing – For racing and parimutuel betting, Ak-Sar-Ben is ranked among the country's finest tracks. The season is from April through July, 63rd and Center Sts. (554-8800).

Golf – There are two excellent public golf courses; Benson at 5333 N 72nd St. (571-5940) and Applewood at 6111 S 99th St. (339-2020).

Tennis – Dewey Park has fine outdoor public tennis courts, at 500 Turner Blvd. (342-5609), and Hanscom Park offers indoor public courts, 3200 Creighton Blvd. (345-2966).

THEATER: For current offerings, check the publications listed above. The *Omaha Community Playhouse*, where Henry Fonda got his start, puts on a large variety of productions year-round, using amateur performers and a professional staff, 6915 Cass St. (553-0800). The *Firehouse Dinner Theater,* 514 S 11th St. (346-8833), has professional local and outside actors who perform in comedies and dramas throughout the year.

MUSIC: The *Omaha Symphony* performs with featured guest artists from September to May, and *Opera/Omaha* presents three operas from November to April, both at the Orpheum Theater, a restored vaudeville palace at 409 S 16th St. The City Auditorium has entertainment all year from rock and pop concerts to Triumph of Agriculture shows. Tickets for all Orpheum and Auditorium events are available at the Auditorium Box Office, 1804 Capitol Ave. (346-1323), or at Brandeis Stores ticket centers.

NIGHTCLUBS AND NIGHTLIFE: *The Howard Street Tavern* is a two-fisted bar with the best in blues, jazz, rock, and bluegrass music, at 11th and Howard Sts. (342-9225). Other hotspots are: *Arthur's Le Grille,* 8025 W Dodge Rd. (393-6369); *Chicago,* 3529 Farnam St. (346-7300), for chatting up; and *Club 89,* 89th and H Sts. (339-5445), for cabaret.

SINS: *Lust* is alive, if not exactly kicking, in Omaha. Ladies of the night once again ply the streets of downtown after dark, thanks to a recent change in state law that reduced their crime to a misdemeanor. For a pornographic book or movie, though, you'll still have to cross the state line to Council Bluffs, Iowa. As for other vices, any old-timer can probably recommend a spot where people fish illegally. *Gluttony* has never had a problem in Omaha, however, and flourishes at the city's several bountiful buffets. *V. Mertz Restaurant,* 1022 Howard (345-8980), offers an elegant, inexpensive Sunday brunch.

LOCAL SERVICES: Business Services – Superior Office Services, 310 S 72nd St. (393-1992).

Mechanics – Anderson's Standard Service, 7140 Dodge St. (553-7750).

BEST IN TOWN

CHECKING IN: Several of the national chains have good setups in Omaha and the local highlight is the Granada Royale Hometel which features two hours of free cocktails each evening. Our selections range in price from around $55 and up for a double room per night in the expensive category, $35 to $50 in the moderate range, and $30 and under, inexpensive.

Granada Royale Hometel – A Spanish-style building with a gleaming tiled fountain courtyard and indoor garden. Suites have kitchens, living rooms, hide-a-bed couches, free full breakfasts. Facilities also include wet bars, indoor heated pool, whirlpools, and sauna to dry it all out. 188 suites. 7270 Cedar St., 1½ miles north of I-80 exit 72nd St. (397-5141). Expensive.

Red Lion Inn – Its location across the street from City Auditorium makes it Omaha's busiest convention hotel. The rooftop restaurant's revolving bar offers a panoramic view of the city. Free parking in adjacent garage. 456 rooms. 1616 Dodge St. (346-7600). Expensive.

New Tower – Centrally located, the New Tower has good standard accommodations with modern furnishings and design. Features a domed indoor pool, saunas, whirlpool baths, and a cocktail lounge. 340 rooms. 7764 Dodge St. (393-5500). Moderate.

Holiday Inn – Nebraska's largest hostelry, Holiday Inn features two restaurants, two lounges with live entertainment, "Holidome" (enclosed swimming pool), putting green, electronic games, shuffleboard, and bar. 503 rooms. 3321 S 72nd St., just north of I-80, exit 72nd St. (393-3950). Moderate.

Continental Towers – Downtown high-rise suites with kitchens and full living rooms. 87 suites. 2121 Douglas St. (346-4920). Moderate.

Thrifty Scot Motel – A brand-new addition to one of the city's busiest hotel areas, Thrifty Scot's brand of basic hospitality includes color television, free Continental breakfast, plus *Perkins' Cake and Steak* restaurant next door. 7101 Grover, just north of I-80, exit 72nd St. (391-5757). Inexpensive.

EATING OUT: There really are a lot of cows out here, and when you eat out you learn why. Omaha restaurant offerings run the gamut from prime ribs to hamburgers. Steaks are big here, and folks are proud of it — the beef is terrific. It is not fertile ground for vegetarians. Besides steakhouses, there is a variety of ethnic places as well as a handful of Continental restaurants. Our selections range in price from $40 up for a dinner for two in the expensive range, $25 to $35 in the moderate, and $20 and under in the inexpensive range, without drinks (wine only).

The French Café – Of Omaha's three restaurants that specialize strictly in French cuisine, this one carries an aura of glamour and buzzes with excited conversation. Specialties include veal, rack of lamb, a daily fresh-fish dish, French onion soup, rich desserts, and an extensive wine list, all served in an elegant yet comfortable atmosphere. It's decorated with antiques, brassworks, and fresh flowers. Closed Sundays. Reservations advised. Major credit cards. 1017 Howard St. (341-3547). Expensive.

To corral a prime Omaha steak, try either of Omaha's classic steakhouses, ***Johnny's*** or ***Ross***'. In both places all is the way it should be, big and heavy, from the cowtown decor, where huge tables and chairs leave plenty of room to rassle with the cow, to that pure slab of pleasure itself, which can weigh in at as much as 20 ounces (not including the potato, spaghetti, bread, and salads that come along with the fight). Johnny's (4702 S 27th St., 731-4774). Ross' (909 S 72nd St., 393-2030). Both closed Sundays. Both take reservations and credit cards. Expensive to moderate.

Salvatore's – A restaurant that serves a wide range of Italian dishes as well as other fine Continental cuisine. There's a notable wine list and the owner sometimes sings opera. Closed Sundays. Reservations. Major credit cards. 4688 Leavenworth St. (553-1976). Expensive to moderate.

Gallagher's – Long menu runs the gamut from light to hearty fare — burgers to quiche. Opulent decor is set off by a stained-glass skylight. Open daily. Reservations. Major credit cards accepted. 10730 Pacific St. (393-1421). Moderate.

Imperial Palace – An artfully decorated alternative to the usual Chinese storefront restaurant. Menu embraces the cuisines of Northern China and the sinus-clearing specialties of Szechuan. Although a newcomer, Imperial Palace has gained a reputation as Omaha's best Oriental restaurant. Open daily. Reservations. Major credit cards. 627 N 109th Plz. (496-1888). Moderate.

Firmature's Sidewalk Café – At this green oasis within the city's most elegant shopping center, the all-encompassing menu ranges from lighter fare — omelettes, crêpes, and such — to steaks and seafood. Specialty of the house is Omaha's most coveted prime rib. The New Orleans Brunch served on Sundays is worth missing a sermon for. Open daily. Reservations. Major credit cards. 153 Regency Fashion Court (397-9600). Moderate.

Mister C's – Although the decor here might be a little tacky — twinkling lights reminiscent of Italian street carnivals, an iridescent mural of Venice on one wall, a backlighted diorama of a Sicilian village on another — the food is quite good. Specialties are Omaha steaks and Italian pasta; homemade soup appears on every table nightly except Saturdays and strolling musicians play requests 7 nights a week. Mister C's may be the busiest steakhouse in Omaha and despite the place's formidable capacity, there's often a wait to get in. Mister C himself greets one and all. Open daily. Reservations advised. American Express and Diners Club only. 5319 N 30th St. (451-1998). Moderate to inexpensive.

Bohemian Café – Besides an impressive collection of Jim Beam bottles, which speaks for itself, the café features a full line of Eastern European specialties, like boiled beef in dill gravy, sweet and sour cabbage, roast duck, liver-dumpling soup, and kraut. Open daily. Reservations. Major credit cards. 1406 S 13th St. (342-9838). Inexpensive.

Michaels' II – When *mamacitas* do the cooking, they do it right. Consistently excellent Mexican food — spiced to sting, but not to start a fire — served in an unpretentious bar atmosphere. Open daily. No reservations. No credit cards. 1919 Missouri Ave. (733-9666); and 108th and West Center Rd. in Rockbrook Village (393-7373). Inexpensive.

PHILADELPHIA

An American visiting Philadelphia for the first time is bound to leave with a new appreciation of what the United States stood for when it was founded. It's not merely a question of the neatly preserved pockets of historic buildings. It has to do with Philadelphia residents themselves. They have a way of talking about "our history" that naturally seems to include a visitor, even if your first reaction is to think "Our history? I don't live here." A few hours spent walking through streets that look like illustrations in history books you read as a child will bring home the notion that this is, truly, the America you learned about in school.

But it's not a textbook experience. The tradition in which the city was born, the inextricable marriage of politics and conscience, is everywhere evident. Even on bitterly cold days, you are likely to see human rights vigils at Independence Mall, across the street from the buildings in which the Bill of Rights and the Constitution were drafted, and where the Declaration of Independence was signed. Residents don't pass even small demonstrations without at least slowing down to read the signs; and a protest too small to warrant media attention in New York is often reported in detail here. A 25-year-old resident, an opponent of the Vietnam War, says he often comes to gaze at the Tomb of the Unknown Revolutionary Soldier in Washington Square. "I just come to read the inscription ('Freedom is a light for which many men have died in darkness'). I ask myself what I would have done then. Of course, I can't say. But I do know that those people acted on their conscience. They had to fight. They weren't heroes, so much as real people making ethical decisions. Like we did during the Vietnam War."

When William Penn founded Philadelphia in 1682, on a flat, fertile site between the Delaware and Schuylkill Rivers, he advertised his colony as a place of religious freedom, christening it "The City of Brotherly Love." Thousands of persecuted Europeans left their homes and came to this New World city to create lives for themselves which would enable them to live in accord with their beliefs. By 1750, Philadelphia was the leading city in the colonies. In 1752, the Liberty Bell emerged from a foundry in England. It had been designed to mark the 50th anniversary of William Penn's Charter of Privileges. A precursor of later documents, such as the Universal Declaration of Human Rights, the Charter declared, "Proclaim liberty throughout all the land, unto all the inhabitants thereof." When the colonies broke away from Great Britain in 1776, the Bell cracked, upon being put to use. (It was recast by a Philadelphia foundry.) From 1790 to 1800, the first Congress of the United States met in Congress Hall. Philadelphia only abdicated as the nation's capital when the District of Columbia became permanent headquarters of the federal government.

Today the city has a population of 1.6 million (5.5 million in the metropolitan area). To this day the city follows Penn's original plans, laid out around four spacious parks (one in each quadrant of the city). Contemporary Philadelphians still live in the city's 18th-century town houses, trimmed with cream-colored wooden shutters, and they pray in the same churches as did George Washington, Benjamin Franklin, and John Adams. You begin to discover Philadelphia as you walk along the narrow red brick, dovetail-patterned sidewalks that lead through narrow alleys to reveal hidden gardens and courtyards. These parts of the city look remarkably like the 18th-century sections of London.

And it's not all solemn. Walking along Market Street between the river and City Hall, you will discover a quickening pace amid a typical hodgepodge of chain stores selling clothing, drugs, novelties, pastries, ice cream, nuts, records, stereos, and radios. Market Street can suddenly start to pulse with disco music, while the street vendors peddling incense, balloons, and pretzels dance in place to the beat; at the same time, an old blind man with a tin cup in front of a 5¢ and 10¢ store wails the blues in a voice strong enough to be heard over the electronic music, the rushing crowds, and the buses. Throughout the day, people wander through Wanamaker's, one of the city's oldest and most prominent department stores. A delightful place for shopping and browsing, it boasts the city's most famous meeting place — the bronze bald eagle statue on the main floor of the store's seven-story atrium. The holiday season brings a special tradition to Wanamaker's, when people congregate around the eagle to gaze at a brilliant show of lights and to listen to resounding triumphal strains that sound like a cross between a church and an ice skating rink. You can't see the organ, hidden somewhere behind the six layers of white balconies trimmed with gold and covered with magenta velvet drapes, but you can catch a glimpse of the gold pipes under a cupola topped by a statue of the archangel Gabriel blowing two horns.

Almost directly behind Wanamaker's is the city's most famous landmark, William Penn's statue on City Hall. Crowning a dome which, in turn, caps what can only be described as an architectural extravaganza of portholes, turrets, wedding cake statuettes, Ionic, Doric, and Corinthian columns and pillars, Billy Penn's statue (as residents call it) is, by law, the tallest fixture on the skyline. Nothing in the city can be built higher than 548 feet, the height of the statue of Philadelphia's founder. Diagonally behind Penn's left shoulder stands the giant clothespin — yes, a sculpted clothespin — which dominates the plaza in front of the Atlantic Richfield building. The old-fashioned wooden clip clothespin towers several stories above street level, in funny juxtaposition to the solid, ornate City Hall.

Philadelphia's sense of humor cuts loose every New Year's Day, when the Mummers Parade struts down Broad Street, playing tunes like "Oh Dem Golden Slippers." A tradition since 1901, it is Philadelphia's Mardi Gras, incorporating the ebullient New Year's customs of several ethnic communities. Mummers' suits (don't call them costumes) are extraordinary fantasies of brightly colored silk, sequins, gold braid, feathers, pointed hats, and veils. Prizes are awarded for the best, some of which are on display at the Mummers Museum, and on top of Penn Mutual tower, where you can also listen to a recording of parade music. How do you get to be a Mummer? According to a former resident, you have to be invited to participate by one of the Mummers Clubs — usually a storefront social club in the predominately Italian neighborhoods of South Philly (where the movie "Rocky" was filmed). Because of the competitiveness among rival clubs and neighborhoods, coming from West Philly makes you ineligible. Once you're in the club, you can spend the rest of the year practicing an instrument like the ukelele or banjo, learning the songs and steps to the Mummers Strut. Mothers in the neighborhood often spend the year designing and sewing the suits, although there are some commercial establishments like Pierre's on Walnut Street which supply outfits.

In recent years Philadelphia, like so many cities, has been in the course of restoration. Slums have been swept away, and crumbling chunks of the business district have fallen to the wrecking ball, giving way to better housing and commercial facilities. This, in turn, has stimulated residents to return to the city from the suburbs. The Society Hill riverfront restoration project is a case in point. Named for the Free Society of Traders, an early British company, Society Hill had deteriorated over the years. But with ingenuity, determination, and creative use of space, it was transformed into what has since been called "the textbook example of how to improve urban environment in America." Concern for keeping the city livable has resulted in rezoning some of the downtown streets into traffic-free pedestrian malls. Now, you can browse along Chestnut Street, Philadelphia's popular shopping street, without breathing in exhaust fumes, or dodging in and out of traffic to cross to the other side. And you can wander along the Delaware River, taking in the sights and sounds of the riverfront shops on Front Street, and the boats berthed in the docks.

Philadelphia has recently cleaned up its political scene as well. In early 1980 the very controversial and powerful Mayor Frank Rizzo was swept from office, and a new man, William Green, promising reform, was sworn in. He has, at the very least, managed to cool much of the polarized passions of Rizzo's regime.

Every July, Philadelphia celebrates the signing of the Declaration of Independence. The Bicentennial celebrations of 1976 focused national attention on the place where it all began. But when the firecrackers stopped, and the 200-year anniversary became just another page in the calendar, the Bicentennial exhibits were not torn down; they were, instead, integrated into the network of historic sites which people come from all over the world to see.

Philadelphia residents used to joke that the next-door state of New Jersey had been created only so that Philly residents would have somewhere to go on the weekend. But nowadays people joke, "I went to Philadelphia on Sunday — and it wasn't closed."

PHILADELPHIA AT-A-GLANCE

SEEING THE CITY: You don't have to run up the steps of the Philadelphia Museum of Art the way Sylvester Stallone did in his hit movie, "Rocky." You can walk up to get the same far-reaching view of the skyline. Inside, you'll find an impressive collection of paintings, drawings, sculpture, and graphic art from all periods and countries. Open daily except Mondays and holidays. Admission charge (for the museum, not the view). 26th and Parkway (763-8100).

The 22nd-floor observatory of Penn Mutual's Philadelphia office offers a 20-mile view on clear days. The elevator has a porthole that lets you see the dome and weathervane of Independence Hall, Benjamin Franklin Bridge, and what looks like half of New Jersey on your way to the top. Definitely not for acrophobics. The rooftop lounge has historical memorabilia, marked observation posts, multimedia exhibits, and intelligent guides to answer your questions. Open daily May through October; closed Sundays and Mondays the rest of the year. Admission charge. Independence Square, 6th and Walnut Sts. (629-0695). Or, you can hop on a riverboat for a two-hour narrated cruise. Closed in winter. Admission charge. Penns' Landing, at the foot of Delaware Ave. (925-7640).

SPECIAL PLACES: Philadelphia's main places of interest are clustered in Independence Hall National Historical Park, and around Fairmount Park in West Philadelphia.

INDEPENDENCE HALL HISTORICAL AREA

Independence National Historical Park – "The most historic square mile in America." This is what everyone comes to see. Within the park, you'll find the major colonial and Revolutionary era buildings, which we've listed separately, below. Open daily. Free. Bounded by Franklin Square, Vine, 6th, 2nd, Walnut, Chestnut, Dock Sts., and Washington Square. (597-7132).

Independence Hall – When you think of Philadelphia, this is probably the first image that comes to mind. The solid tower, massive clock, and graceful spire are unmistakable. Early colonists called it the State House. Here, the Declaration of Independence was signed, and 11 years later, the Constitution was written. Carriage tours of Old Philadelphia depart from here daily, weather permitting, from March through October; by appointment only in January and February. (Admission charge for tours; for more information call 922-6840.) Independence Hall is open daily. Free. 5th and Chestnut (597-7079).

Congress Hall – The first US Congress met here, between 1790 and 1800. George Washington delivered his final congressional address in these halls; here, too, the Bill of Rights was adopted. In 1800, the seat of federal government moved to the District of Columbia. Open daily. Free. 5th and Chestnut (597-7079).

Old City Hall – The first US Supreme Court issued judgments from the bench inside this building. The Court moved to new headquarters in Washington, DC, in 1800. Inside, an audiovisual show gives you an idea of what life was like in post-Revolutionary Philadelphia, with an emphasis on the formative years of the federal judiciary. Open daily. Free. 5th and Chestnut (597-7079).

Independence Mall – Across the street from the Halls, this leafy stretch of grass, fountains, and tree-lined walks contains the glass pavilion housing the Liberty Bell. It was moved from Independence Hall so more people could see it and touch it. Open daily. Free. Market and 5th Sts. (597-7624).

Carpenters' Hall – So named because it housed the Carpenters' Company Guild during the colonial era (before unions). The oldest building organization in the US still owns the Hall, and early carpentry tools are on display. In 1774, the First Continental Congress met here to list grievances against King George. Closed Mondays; also closed on Tuesdays in January and February. Free. 320 Chestnut (925-0167).

Todd House – Before Dolley Madison married James, the fourth president of the United States, her name was Dolley Payne Todd, and she was known as a great hostess. The home in which Philadelphia society partied was built in 1775. Guided tours are available by reservation only. To arrange tours, stop at the Visitors Center (see below).

Phone reservations are not accepted. Open daily. Free. 4th and Walnut (597-2800).

Visitors' Center – This is a good place to ask questions of the park guides, and to pick up brochures. Candlelight Strolls and other walking tours leave from here. Open daily. Free. 3rd St. between Walnut and Chestnut (597-8974).

Christ Church – Benjamin Franklin sat in pew 70. George Washington prayed here, too. The original church was built in 1695; this, a larger one was erected in 1745. It's still in use. Open daily. Donation suggested. 2nd St. above Market St. (922-1695).

Betsy Ross House – Where, tradition says, George Washington directed Elizabeth Ross, an upholsterer's widow, in the stitching of the first American flag. According to the Philadelphia Historical Commission, however, Betsy Ross never lived here and had nothing to do with the first US flag. Make up your own mind, after you've seen this tiny cottage filled with household items and memorabilia allegedly pertinent to Mrs. Ross. Open daily. Free. 239 Arch (627-5343).

Elfreth's Alley – Oldest continuously occupied residential street in America, dating back to 1690. Only one block long, six feet wide, it is lined with 200-year-old houses. Usually the first weekend in June, Elfreth's Alley holds its annual pageant. North of Arch St., between Front and 2nd Sts.

Headhouse Square – Only survivor of the many middle-of-the-street markets that once flourished in the city. Built in 1775, it is dotted with good restaurants and revitalized shops. In summer, there are crafts demonstrations and concerts. 2nd and Pine.

Mummer's Museum – Philadelphia pop history is lovingly preserved in this memorial in South Philadelphia, in the heart of where Mummery began. The outside is tile as dazzling as a Mummer's suit. Inside are memorabilia, history, sound recordings. Closed Mondays. Admission charge. 2nd St. at Washington Ave. (336-3050).

Franklin Court – Benjamin Franklin came to Philadelphia in 1723, a skinny, 17-year-old runaway. Considered the most brilliant among a community of remarkable men, in his later years Franklin resided in a brick house on this site. He died here in 1790. Although the house itself is no longer standing (it was destroyed in 1812), three of the surrounding Franklin-designed houses are here, along with an 18th-century garden with some mulberry trees planted by Franklin. An underground museum has Franklin stoves, papers, and a phone where you can "dial-an-opinion" of Benjamin Franklin. Open daily. Free. Orianna St. between Chestnut and Market (597-8974).

Christ Church Burial Ground – Throw a penny on the grave of Benjamin and his wife Deborah Franklin. It's a Philadelphia custom. Tours by appointment. Open daily April through September. By appointment only October through March. 5th and Arch Sts. (922-1695).

USS *Olympia* – Oldest steel-hulled American warship afloat, the *Olympia* was Commodore George Dewey's flagship at Manila Bay in the Spanish-American War. Open daily. Admission charge. Pier 11 North, Delaware Ave. and Race St. (922-1898).

Boathouse Row – A collection of Victorian boathouses used by collegiate and club oarsmen. The hub of many national competitions. On east bank of the Schuylkill River.

WEST PHILADELPHIA

Fairmount Park – Approximately 8,000 acres of meadows, gardens, creeks, trails, and 100 miles of bridle paths. Philadelphia residents love this park and refuse to allow new buildings to interfere with its present layout. Joggers, bicyclists, softball players, fishermen, and picnickers hang out here in good weather. The Fairmount Park Trolley Bus, a replica of a Victorian conveyance, takes you through the grounds, with stops at the zoo, museums, and historic mansions. Open daily. Admission charge. The park's ten historic mansions are: Cedar Grove, Sweetbriar, Lemon Hill, Mount Pleasant, Strawberry, Woodford, Letitia Street House, Solitude, Hatfield, and Laurel Hill. (Closed Mondays. Admission charge. For information on guided tours, call 763-8100, ext. 305). Park open daily. Free. The park begins at Philadelphia Museum of Art and extends northwest on both sides of the Wissahickon Creek and Schuylkill River (686-1776).

Philadelphia Zoo – Established in 1874, this is the nation's oldest. More than 1,600 animals, reptiles, and birds make their home within its 42 acres. There are several natural habitat exhibits, a children's zoo, and a safari monorail aerial tram. Open daily, except holidays. Admission charge (free on Mondays in January and February). 34th St. and Girard Ave. (387-6400).

Philadelphia Museum of Art – Outstanding collections of all periods and schools, housed in a sweeping Greco-Roman building. Closed Mondays and holidays. Admission charge (Sundays free until 1 PM). 26th and Parkway (763-8100).

Franklin Institute Science Museum – Ben Franklin would have traded his kite for one day of browsing through this remarkable science museum, with Fels planetarium and four huge floors jammed with exhibits on anatomy, aviation, and space exploration. Open daily. Admission charge. 20th St. and Parkway (564-3375; planetarium, 563-1363).

Rodin Museum – Sculpture, sketches, and drawings (including the famous sculptures *The Thinker, The Gates of Hell,* and *The Burghers of Calais*). This is the largest collection of Auguste Rodin's work outside France. You can easily spend an afternoon wandering through the halls and gardens. Foreign language tours available by appointment. Open daily. Free; donations accepted. 22nd and Parkway (763-8100).

OTHER SPECIAL PLACES

City Hall – The most distinctive landmark in Philadelphia. Critics have called it"an architectural nightmare." Others praise its elaborate decor: sculpture, marble pillars, alabaster chandeliers, ceilings with gold leaf, carved mahogany, and walnut paneling. The Tower, at William Penn's feet, looks out to the Delaware and Schuylkill Rivers (smog permitting). The business district fans out from City Hall. Guided tours of the tower and offices are offered Mondays through Fridays. Free (686-4546).

Rittenhouse Square – Named after David and Benjamin Rittenhouse, who designed the first astronomical instruments in the United States toward the end of the 18th century. Today, Rittenhouse Square is one of the loveliest, most elegant residential areas of the city. Handsome brownstones and high-rise apartment houses surround a green park, where people from all over town congregate. Art shows, flower shows, and concerts take place here in spring and summer. Bounded by 18th, 20th, Walnut, and Spruce Sts.

United States Mint – Watch coins being minted. This facility can produce 10,000 coins per minute. At each marked observation post, a pushbutton activates a taped commentary on the different stages of the minting process. Historic coins are exhibited in the Relic Room, and a special counter sells proof sets and medals. Guided tours for senior citizens and the handicapped. Open Mondays through Fridays. Closed federal holidays. Free. 5th and Arch Sts. (597-7350).

Edgar Allan Poe House – The poet composed his epic to the raven, and his chilling story "The Murders in the Rue Morgue" in these quarters. He lived here for three years, with his mother-in-law and young bride. A must for Poe addicts. Open daily except major holidays. Free. 530 N 7th (597-8780).

Pennsylvania Horticultural Society – The formal gardens of the 18th century are recreated here, with flowers, shrubs, and pruned trees typical of the era. This is the oldest horticultural association in the US, with a library devoted to botanical subjects. Open Mondays through Fridays. Free. 325 Walnut (625-8250).

Reading Terminal Market – Shoppers of all persuasions come to foray for fresh ground horseradish, study French brie, and snack at oyster bars. Check out the homemade soups and hot-from-the-oven shoofly pie. Ice cream at *Bassett's* is a must. 12th St. just north of Market (922-2317).

Italian Market – Also known as Rocky's market. This is part of Sylvester Stallone's famous jogging trail. It's located in South Philly. 9th St. and Washington Ave.

■ **EXTRA SPECIAL:** Even if you've never played the song "Washington at Valley Forge" on a kazoo, you've undoubtedly heard of the place. General George Washington and 11,000 Revolutionary troops retreated to *Valley Forge* during the winter of 1777–78. The site of their camp and training grounds is now a state park. Closed Mondays, Thanksgiving, Christmas, and New Year's Day. Free. Take Schuylkill Expressway to Valley Forge exit (about 20 miles). Take route 363 north to the park (783-7700).

SOURCES AND RESOURCES

Right in the heart of the city, only steps from City Hall, is the Visitors Information Center, with maps, brochures, and tourist information. Ask specifically for four free brochures: "Visitor's Guide Map of Philadelphia," the "Cultural Loop Bus," "The Liberty Walk Through Historic Old Philadelphia," and the "Philadelphia Shopping Guide." 1525 John F. Kennedy Blvd. (574-7800).

Foreign visitors can stop in at the Council for International Visitors, Civic Center Blvd. at 34th St. (387-1414); International House, University of Pennsylvania, 3701 Chestnut (387-5125); or the Nationalities Service Center, 1300 Spruce (893-8400) for information and social activities. International House cafeteria is open to the public Mondays through Fridays.

Enjoy Philadelphia (Philadelphia Magazine, $3.95) is the most comprehensive local guidebook, and includes nearby Valley Forge, Pennsylvania Dutch country, and the New Jersey shore.

All telephone numbers are in the 215 area code unless otherwise indicated.

For Local Coverage – *The Inquirer,* morning daily; *The Daily News,* afternoon daily; *Philadelphia* Magazine, monthly.

For Food – *Philadelphia* Magazine's restaurant listings or *Philadelphia — The Great American Experience* (Philadelphia Convention and Visitors Bureau, $1.95), available at the Visitors Information Center.

CLIMATE AND CLOTHES: Winter temperatures in Philadelphia generally hover in the 20s and 30s. Spring and autumn are the best times to visit — temperatures then are usually in the 60s and 70s. Summer tends to be hot and sticky, with temperatures in the 80s.

GETTING AROUND: The first thing to do is get out of your car and onto your feet. Philadelphia's tight city blocks and narrow streets make it great for walking but not driving. Streets are laid out in checkerboard fashion and easy to understand, but they are always choked with traffic. It's best to park your car at your hotel.

Bus – SEPTA (Southeastern Pennsylvania Transportation Authority) will take you everywhere, by bus, trolley, or subway. A good SEPTA map showing routes for all public transportation is available at newsstands (call 574-7800 for information). The Cultural Loop Bus takes you to ten well-known attractions, among them Independence Hall and the Rodin Museum of Sculpture, with off-and-on privileges.

Taxi – Costly, but for short hops to transport three or four people, it's worth it. Hail them in the street or do as Philadelphians do and pick them up in front of the 30th Street train station or the nearest hotel, which is where most of them wait for customers. Call Yellow Cab (922-8400) or United Cab Association (854-0750).

Car Rental – Philadelphia is served by all the national firms.

MUSEUMS: Independence National Historic Park, Philadelphia Museum of Art, Rodin Museum, and the Franklin Institute Science Museum, described in *Special Places,* are only a few of Philadelphia's museums. Some of the other notable museums are:

Afro-American Historical and Cultural Museum, 7th and Arch (574-3670).

Art Alliance, 251 S 18th St., Rittenhouse Sq. (545-4302).

Alverthorpe Manor (rare books), 515 Meeting House Rd., Jenkintown (884-5000).

Athenaeum (library and historic documents), 219 S 6th St., Society Hill (925-2688).

Attwater Kent Museum (local history), 7th, between Market and Chestnut sts. (922-3031).

Barnes Foundation, 300 N Latch's La., Merion Station (667-0290).

Civic Center Museum (art), 34th and Civic Center Blvd. (823-7400).

Fireman's Hall Museum, 2nd and Quarry sts. (923-1438).

Institute of Contemporary Art, University of Pennsylvania, 34th and Walnut (243-7108).

Library Company of Pennsylvania (rare books), 1314 Locust (546-2465).

Historical Society of Pennsylvania, 1300 Locust (732-6200).

Philadelphia Maritime Museum, 321 Chestnut (925-5439).

Perelman Antique Toy Museum, 268–70 S 2nd St. (922-1070).

Norman Rockwell Museum, 6th and Sansom (922-4345).

Please Touch Museum (terrific hands-on exhibits for children 7 years and under), 1910 Cherry St. (963-0667).

Print Club, 1614 Latimer (735-6090).

Rosenbach Museum (former private house containing porcelains, antiques, graphic art), 2010 Delancey Pl. (732-1600).

University of Pennsylvania Museum, 33rd and Spruce (243-4000).

Academy of Natural Sciences, 19th St. and the Parkway (567-3700).

Wagner Free Institute of Science, 17th St. and Montgomery Ave. (763-6529).

MAJOR COLLEGES AND UNIVERSITIES: Philadelphia's colleges and universities are among the best in the country. Foremost is the University of Pennsylvania, founded by Benjamin Franklin in 1740. Information center, 3541 Walnut (243-5000). Others include: Temple University, Broad St. and Montgomery Ave. (787-7000); Drexel University, 32nd and Chestnut (895-2000); La Salle College, 20th and Olney (951-1000); St. Joseph's College, 54th and City Line Ave. (879-7300); Haverford College, Haverford (896-1000); Swarthmore College, Swarthmore (447 7000); Bryn Mawr College, Bryn Mawr (645-5000); Villanova University, Villanova (645-4500)

SPECIAL EVENTS: *The Mummers Parade,* a Philadelphia tradition on Jan. 1, is eight hours of string bands strutting up Broad Street in elaborate costumes. *Super Sunday,* usually the second Sunday in October, is a day of free culture at institutions along the Benjamin Franklin Parkway with folk dancing, flea markets, music, pop foods, and mobs of people.

SPORTS: Whether you like to watch or do it yourself, there's enough sports activity to satisfy even the fanatics. First, the spectator sports:

Baseball – From May to September, the *Phillies* chase the pennant at Veterans Stadium, Broad St. and Pattison Ave. (463-1000).

Football – The *Eagles* play also at the Vet, and almost always before a sellout, but try 564-5500 for tickets, or be prepared to pay a scalper's price outside the gates on game day.

Basketball – Pro basketball's *76ers* pack them in at the Spectrum, Broad St. and Pattison Ave., from October to April (339-7676).

Bicycling – Rent from the Fairmount Bicycle Rental behind the Art Museum, Boathouse Row and E River Dr. (978-8505). Some 10.6 miles of Fairmount Park are devoted to bike paths.

Boating – Within the city you can rent rowboats and canoes for the Schuylkill River at the East Park Canoe House on E River Dr. (228-9336).

Boxing – The Spectrum hosts frequent big-name bouts.

Golf – Try to get invited to a country club. If you can't, your next best bet is to try the public city course at Karakung, 72nd and Lansdowne Ave. (877-2724).

Hockey – Hardest to get are tickets to the *Flyers*, who play ice hockey at the Spectrum, too, from October to May. Best bet is to try a center city ticket agency (or call 755-9700).

Horse Racing – There is one parimutuel thoroughbred track in the city, Liberty Bell Park, at Knights and Woodhaven Rds. (637-7100).

Skiing – Everybody goes to the Pocono Mountains, two hours away. Best bets: Camelback Mountain, Tannersville, PA (923-4010), Big Boulder, Lake Harmony, PA (717 722-0101), and Jack Frost, Whitehaven, PA (717 443-8425).

Tennis – The nation's number one indoor event, the US Pro Indoor, is held annually at the Spectrum in late January. The city owns more than 100 all-weather courts and Fairmount Park also has that many. Call the City Recreation Department at 686-3600.

THEATER: Check the daily newspapers for up-to-the-minute information on schedules and performance times. Broadway-bound, off-Broadway, or Broadway reruns are all performed at four major houses and a dozen other theaters. *Forrest Theater* at 1114 Walnut (923-1515) has year-round offerings, as do the *Shubert* at 250 S Broad (735-4768), and the *Walnut Street Theater,* 9th and Walnut (574-3550).

MUSIC: The *Philadelphia Orchestra* under new conductor Carlos Muti (living legend Eugene Ormandy has retired) performs at the Academy of Music, a classic 1847 building at Broad and Locust sts. (893-1930). In summer, they play at the Mann Music Center, Fairmount Park (567–0707).

NIGHTCLUBS AND NIGHTLIFE: There's a full range of live artists in lively spots — but Philadelphians prefer cabarets to Las Vegas–type shows. Best bets: *Bijou Café,* 1409 Lombard St. (735-4444), an intimate club showcasing big-name entertainers; *Café Borgia,* 406 S 2nd St. (574-0414), a subterranean café with left bank ambience and sophisticated jazz; *Rick's Cabaret,* 757 S Front (389-3855), features an assortment of live entertainment and dancing; and *Middle East,* 126 Chestnut (922-1003) has bellydancers. Comics perform upstairs from the *Middle East* at the *Comedy Works* (922-5997) and at *The Comedy Factory Outlet,* part of Cavanaugh's bar and restaurant at 32nd and Market sts. (386-4889). *Palumbo's,* 824 Catherine (627-7272), is a long-time citadel of family-style entertainment with big names like the Four Aces.

SINS: If you want to see *sloth* at its well-dressed best, take a stroll around City Hall, at Broad and Market Streets. Not only is the building replete with 19th-century statuary goddesses, but the offices exude the vapors of languishing bureaucrats, the product of an ancient and still thriving patronage system.

Across from City Hall, at 15th and Market Streets, is Claes Oldenburg's *Clothespin,* a piece of sculpture that produces real *anger* among the city fathers, who think it is fashionable to hate contemporary art. If you hate contemporary art, the 45-foot chrome and steel monument to laundry and the Eiffel Tower will probably make you mad, too.

Gluttony can be indulged in many forms in Philadelphia. You can start genteelly, sipping a strawberry daiquiri made from fresh fruit, at *Wildflowers*, 516 S 5th St., move on to an orgy of coffee ice cream at *Bassett's* in the Reading Terminal Market, 11th and Filbert Sts., and then get down to the gritty Philly reality of the Italian Market, 9th St. at Washington Ave. Here you will find staggering quantities of the good things in life, just waiting to be taken home. Mussels come by the bushel in large brine-filled barrels; rice and exotic golden grains pour from their sacks; skinned rabbits, hot Italian sausage, and provolone cheeses swing from the ceilings; and there is plenty to nibble on while you are picking and choosing.

You can also treat your *lust* to the temptation of your choice on Walnut and Locust Streets around 13th.

LOCAL SERVICES: Business Services – CPS Services, Philadelphia Center Hotel, 1725 John F. Kennedy Blvd. (563-1542).

Mechanic – Center City Service, 427 N Broad (922-7021), is a 24-hour garage.

■ **TAKE SOME PHILADELPHIA HOME WITH YOU:** "Tastykakes" are what exiled Philadelphia residents dream about. The little packages of cakes and pies are available at most grocery stores. (Great for munching on your way to the top of Penn Mutual.) But the biggest food thrill is Bassett's ice cream, available around the city. You can't take it with you, but you can eat a lot of it while you're there.

BEST IN TOWN

CHECKING IN: Hotels range from durable, famous places to sleek, new spots with loud, lively lobbies. But there are very few really good inexpensive hotels. Expect to pay between $75 and $100 for a double in any of those places we've listed as expensive; between $50 and $70, moderate; under $50, inexpensive.

The Latham – A favorite of business people who seek a central location and good service. Its café, *Bogart's* (see *Eating Out*), and bar are places to see and be seen. 145 rooms. 17th and Walnut (563-7474). Expensive.

Marriott Hotel – Comfortable modern decor with four restaurants, two outdoor swimming pools, one indoor pool, and ice skating (weather permitting). An array of stores, restaurants, and nightspots lines the highway near the hotel. 750 rooms. City Line Ave. and Monument Rd. (667-0200 or 800 228-9290, toll-free). Expensive.

The Barclay – A quiet, stylish stalwart, only steps from Rittenhouse Square and the Walnut Street shops. Its restaurant is a favorite with the monied Main Line crowd. Though the 200 rooms are not regal, they are comfortable and tastefully furnished. Rittenhouse Square East (545-0300). Expensive.

The Hilton – Slightly away from the mainstream with its Civic Center location, but close enough to most sites to be convenient. Rooftop restaurant, discotheque, coffee shop, and indoor pool. 400 rooms. Civic Center Blvd. at 34th St. (387-8333). Expensive.

Bellevue-Stratford – After a year as *The Fairmont,* the city's most famous hotel went back to its original name. Totally refurbished ($22 million went into its facelift), it is now more handsome than ever. The Victorian edifice is the same, but inside the lobby has been enlarged, primarily to accommodate a tea room for high teas; meeting rooms have been added as well as dining rooms and a supper club, and new bathrooms installed in all guest rooms. (By the way, don't let the well-publicized episode about Legionnaire's Disease keep you from staying here. The Center for Disease Control in Atlanta has reported that the strange illness was caused by a virus infection that simply spread from one conventioneer to another.) Broad St. at Walnut (893-1776). Expensive.

Franklin Plaza – Opened late in 1980, this large, lavish gem is not only the newest but perhaps the best, judging from early reviews. Only four blocks from city hall and a few steps from the parkway, its location is good. So are its amenities: 800 modern rooms, racquetball courts, health club, underground parking, meeting rooms, and four restaurants. 17th and Vine Sts. (448-2000). Expensive.

Holiday Inn–Midtown – Small, scrupulously maintained motor inn with a good location, a swimming pool, and surprisingly, kennels. Near theaters, and just a stroll away from all the best shops. Free indoor parking. 160 rooms. 1305 Walnut (735-9300). Moderate.

Holiday Inn–Center City – Good location, near the Penn Center complex. Indoor pool, standard amenities. Within walking distance of major museums, one mile from Independence Mall. Free indoor parking. 304 rooms. 20th and Market (561-7500). Moderate.

Holiday Inn-University City – Convenient to the University of Pennsylvania campus, the hotel has free parking and a restaurant called *Smart Alex,* which features live country and western entertainment. 370 rooms. 36th and Chestnut sts. (387-8000). Moderate.

Penn Center Inn – Pioneer high-rise motor inn that was built in 1962, and continues to keep house competently. Has the biggest indoor pool and sundeck in the city. Free indoor parking. 304 rooms. 20th and Market (569-3000). Moderate.

Philadelphia Center – With 24-hour room service, three restaurants, airline ticket booths, and rent-a-car counters. Free parking. 860 rooms. 1725 John F. Kennedy Blvd. (568-3300). Moderate.

Howard Johnson's – Situated near Valley Forge, with an outdoor pool, restaurant, cocktail lounge, entertainment, babysitting service, and free in-room movies. 168 rooms. Rt. 202, N and S Gulph Rd., King of Prussia (265-4500). Moderate.

George Washington Motor Lodge – We're certain George Washington would have preferred staying here during his cold Valley Forge encampment. Its facilities include a restaurant, cocktail lounge, entertainment, indoor pool, and babysitting service. 407 rooms. Routes 202 and 23, King of Prussia (265-6100). Moderate.

Best Western Roosevelt – About 30 minutes' drive from downtown in northeast Philly. Two restaurants, cocktail lounge, entertainment, and outdoor pool. 170 rooms. 7600 Roosevelt Blvd. (338-7600). Inexpensive.

EATING OUT: Once, not so long ago, the only meal you could look forward to was a seafood dinner at tradition-encrusted Old Original Bookbinders'. Now, however, the city has some outstanding restaurants. Although there were fears that when the Bicentennial crowds departed, the new restaurateurs would pack up their pots, pans, and potted plants, they have stayed, and if anything, improved. Expect to pay $50 or more for two in those places we've listed as expensive; $20 to $40 in the moderate category; $10 or less, inexpensive. Prices do not include drinks, wine, or tips.

Le Bec Fin – The best in town, and clearly one of the best restaurants in the country. Imaginative French food by Lyon-born Georges Perrier, a master chef. Quenelles de brochet is exceptionally good. Closed Sundays. Make reservations well in advance as the restaurant seats only 30. No credit cards. 1312 Spruce (732-3000). Very expensive.

Old Original Bookbinder's – Philadelphia's most famous restaurant, with mahogany and gleaming leather. Many love it, many hate it. The seafood is as much of a legend as many of the celebrities who dine here. Open daily. Reservations recommended. Major credit cards. 125 Walnut (925-7027). Expensive.

La Panetière – Another excellent French restaurant. The filet de boeuf, rack of lamb, and wine cellar are outstanding. Elegant, period French decor, and a devoted clientele which has made of the place a local cult. Closed Sundays. Reservations necessary. Some major credit cards. 1602 Locust (546-5452). Expensive.

Restaurant Maureen – Owner Maureen Horn greets and seats you at this tiny but top-notch French restaurant; husband Stephen in the kitchen skillfully prepares *nouvelle cuisine.* The duckling with fresh strawberry sauce rates a four-syllabled "*incroyable!*" Closed Sundays and Mondays. Dinner only, from 5:30 PM. Major credit cards. 11 South 21st St. (561-3542). Expensive.

La Terrasse – A glass-enclosed terrace where a tree grows amid the dining tables is the focal point of this small, lively French restaurant near the University of Pennsylvania campus. Favorite of artistic and scholastic types (scientists and professors, doctors and joggers). Good for Sunday brunch or late night snacks. Open daily. Reservations advised. Major credit cards. 3432 Sansom St. (387-3778). Expensive.

Top of Center Square – Expansive windows in each of the four dining rooms here provide a panoramic view of the city. Request the east dining room to see the beautifully lighted City Hall and Billy Penn statue towering above. There is a varied and delicious menu of meats and seafoods. Open daily. Major credit cards. Reservations advised. 1500 Market St. (563-9494). Expensive to moderate.

The Fishmarket – A gourmet seafood restaurant, it's always crowded at lunch, so get there early. Entrées vary according to the day's catch, but the high quality of preparation never varies. The crab quiche is fabulous. Reservations recommended. Open daily. Major credit cards. 124 S 18th St. (567-3559). Expensive to moderate.

Bookbinder's Seafood House – The better (and cheaper) of the two restaurants bearing this famous name. Happy, bustling, serves the same well-prepared, simple food, fresh from the ocean. Open daily. Reservations advised. Major credit cards. 215 S 15th (545-1137). Moderate.

Bogart's – Like the movie set of "Casablanca," with wooden ceiling fans and tinkling piano. You won't find Bogie belting one down at the bar, but you will find Continental dishes, and a well-dressed crowd. Open daily. Reservations necessary. Major credit cards. Latham Hotel, 17th and Walnut (563-9444). Moderate.

The Garden – Seafood and French country cooking in a stylish old town house. You can eat outdoors in the courtyard when the weather's good, or station yourself at the cozy Oyster Bar in the front room. Closed Sundays. Reservations advised. Major credit cards. 1617 Spruce (546-4455). Moderate.

The Frog – The blackboard menu changes constantly, but is generally adventurous. Expect dishes like duck à l'orange, cold poached striped bass, and an extraordinary chocolate mousse. A favorite hangout for newspaper, TV, and modeling crowds. Open daily. Reservations necessary. Major credit cards. 264 S 16th (735-8882). Moderate.

The Imperial Inn – An ambitious, well-prepared menu of Mandarin and Szechwan dishes. Located in Chinatown. Open daily. No reservations. No credit cards. 941 Race (925-2485). Moderate.

Miss Headly's Wine Bar – A classical guitar is played beneath a gypsy wedding tent while the customers slurp their peanut soup in this upstairs revelation in the old city section. Spend a quiet time among wines, cheeses, desserts, and special dishes. Open daily. Major credit cards. 56 S 2nd St. (922-0763). Moderate.

H. A. Winston & Co. – Dozens of ways to have your burger, in an atmosphere that's warm, cozy, and comfortable. Open daily. Reservations are not necessary. Major credit cards. Front and Chestnut sts. (928-0660) and 1500 Locust St. (546-7232). Inexpensive.

Ragozzino's – Connoisseurs agree this little shop is *the* place to get that fabled Philadelphia sandwich, the Hoagie: Italian bread sliced lengthwise and filled with ham, provolone, salami, onions, tomato, and condiments. Closed Sundays. No reservations. No credit cards. 737 S 10th at Fitzwater (923-2927). Inexpensive.

Famous Delicatessen – Famous among Philadelphia residents. Monstrous hot pastrami, roast beef, and corned beef sandwiches. No-frill eating, the food comes on paper plates. Open daily. No reservations. No credit cards. 700 S 4th St. (627-9198). Inexpensive.

PHOENIX

Phoenix: the Los Angeles of the future? If it sounds unthinkable, consider these facts: In 1960, Phoenix had a population of 439,000; now it's over 900,000. It's among the fastest growing metropolises east of California. Its major industries are electronics and aerospace, both businesses coming of age with the coming millennium — not just future-oriented, but damn near futuristic. People are flocking to the Southwest, and in many cases landing in Phoenix and its environs. If residents view this turn of events with some satisfaction, they are not oblivious to the dangers ahead. Most people come here for just one thing — the environment: smog-free, clear, boiling in summer but beautiful for the lungs. Nothing threatens the environment like numbers, and the numbers of Phoenicians keep growing. And not one is willing to sacrifice oxygen or scenery to the future.

The scenery is frankly spectacular. The city takes a back seat to the awesome beauty of the Valley of the Sun (as the area around Phoenix is called). From the top of nearby South Mountain one sees the Valley stretch away in all directions, with the checkerboard of Phoenix's main avenues crisscrossing far into the northern horizon. East and west, suburbs extend for 50 miles (Glendale, Avondale, Sun City, and Youngtown to the west; Scottsdale, Tempe, and Mesa eastward toward the fabled Superstition Mountains). In the northeast, there's no mistaking the Valley's most distinctive landmark, Camelback Mountain. If you were to draw an imaginary line down its rugged, red haunches, you'd have the boundary between Phoenix and Scottsdale, the city's fashionable, artistic suburb.

As the eye follows the palisades of the Superstitions along the eastern horizon, it picks out the far mountain chain which cradles the crashing Salt River, lifeblood of the city and the Valley. The Salt has been irrigating the Valley for more than 1,000 years, and some of its canals follow water paths created by ancient Hohokam Indians.

What ancient history Phoenix has is associated with its first residents, the Indians. The city itself is little more than 100 years old, and Arizona has only been a state since 1912. But it cherishes its Indian past. Ringed by reservations, Phoenix has a number of museums devoted to indigenous cultures, as well as art galleries featuring the work of local Indian artists.

If you think the desert is all sand dunes, you'll be delightfully surprised by the abundance of plant life. There are at least a dozen different species of cactus, one of which, the saguaro, with its thick, tall torso and upraised arms, is the state symbol. You'll also be surprised by residents' attitude toward distance. They consider it nothing to drive 200 miles for a picnic or a swim. (By the way, you'll need a car to get around here. Everything is spread out.)

Everything is also dependent on the weather, generally fantastic in winter and *incredibly* hot in summer. In winter, the Valley bustles with thousands of "snowbirds" escaping the northern and eastern cold. Except for the occasional cold snap or cloudburst, it's possible to play tennis and golf all winter. But make no mistake. It gets cold after dark. Sometimes, the temperature drops below freezing. Even during the daytime, coats or sweaters are almost always necessary. Oddly enough, though, Phoenix gets most of its rain in the summer — what little there is.

By June, Phoenix metamorphoses into an oven. The snowbirds forsake the mountain-rimmed bowl to return to their spring gardening, and residents scurry from air-conditioned house to air-conditioned car to air-conditioned office. Daytime temperatures climb over the century mark most days through September. On a really cool night the mercury might plunge to 70°! On weekends, Phoenix becomes a ghost town as people flee to the cooler mountain forests. You'll understand why Arizona is the only state in the nation that doesn't have daylight savings time. Arizonans can't wait for the sun to go down.

The heat also generates some tall local legends. One of the hottest-selling items in souvenir shops is an ordinary-looking twig called a "lizard stick." An accompanying tag informs the buyer that this stick is used by Arizona lizards during the summer. The crafty critters, it alleges, carry the stick in their mouths as they run from burrow to burrow. When their feet get too hot, they jam the stick into the sand, and climb it to give their feet a rest. It won't be taken amiss if you raise a skeptical eyebrow at these gadgets. They sell a lot of them here, but save your wonder for the fabulous Phoenix desert.

PHOENIX AT-A-GLANCE

SEEING THE CITY: As you look out on Phoenix from South Mountain ponder on the words of an Indian prayer to Corn Mother and Sun Father: "Oh, it is good, you provide. It is the ability to think. It is the wisdom that comes. It is the understanding."

SPECIAL PLACES: Street numbers start at zero in the center of downtown. Central Avenue, the business-financial district, runs north and south, bisecting the city into east and west. Numbered avenues lie to the west of Central; numbered streets to the east.

State Capitol – The building will give an idea of what granite from the Salt River Mountains looks like when it's being put to constructive use. The murals inside depict Arizona's discovery and exploration in the 16th century. The Department of Library and Archives on the third floor contains historical material. Closed Saturdays, Sundays, and holidays. Free. W Washington and 17th Ave. (271-4900).

Heard Museum – A fascinating anthropological collection of artifacts from ancient Indian civilizations in Arizona. The Kachina doll collection, donated by Senator Barry Goldwater, is consistently interesting for neophytes as well as experts. Changing exhibits feature contemporary Western paintings and drawings, and modern Indian art. Intriguing. Open daily. Admission charge. 22 E Monte Vista (252-8848).

Phoenix Art Museum – Specializes in contemporary art from the Southwest; other collections lean toward North American art in general (including Mexican), with a small permanent exhibit of Renaissance, 17th-, and 18th-century material. Some fine Chinese porcelain as well. Closed Mondays. Free. 1625 N Central (257-1222).

Pueblo Grande Museum and Indian Ruins – Pueblo Grande is on the site of a former Hohokam Indian settlement. By climbing to the top of a mound marked into seven stations, you can see the ruins which are believed to have been occupied from 200 BC to AD 1400, when the Hohokam Indians vanished without a trace. Phoenix municipal archeologists are continuing their excavations. Open daily except Sundays and holidays. Free. 4619 E Washington (275-3452).

Legend City – About three miles east of Pueblo Grande is Legend City, the largest amusement park in the Valley of the Sun. Hardly surprising, its rides have Wild West–rodeo themes, with antique cars, a replica of an Old West city, and a steam engine train. Open Saturdays, 2 to 10 PM. Admission charge. 56th and Washington (275-8551).

Desert Botanical Gardens – Just across the road from Legend City, Desert Botanical Gardens take up a sizable part of Papago Park. Half of all the different kinds of cactus in the world are planted on the grounds, and there are self-guiding tours and booklets to help you identify the prickly flora. Open daily, 9 AM to sunset. Admission charge. Papago Park (941-1217).

Phoenix Zoo – When you're done walking around the Botanical Gardens, take a leisurely drive through desert rock formations to Phoenix Zoo, in another section of Papago Park. (You can stop to picnic in the park.) The zoo covers more than 125 acres. Two of the most popular attractions are the oryx herd, and Hazel, the gorilla, and her offspring Fabayo. There are more than 1,000 animals altogether. Open daily. Admission charge. Papago Park (273-7771).

Scottsdale – This recreated Western community with hitching posts is a haven for artists and art lovers. Scottsdale's Fifth Avenue is lined with galleries featuring Indian art, handicrafts, and jewelry. Every Thursday evening from 7 to 9 PM, October through May, the community sponsors a promenade, with music and wine to regale you as you stroll. In Scottsdale, taking a walk is an aesthetic adventure. McDowell Rd. east to Scottsdale Rd. north.

Cosanti Foundation – If you want to see what architecture of the future will look like, architect Paolo Soleri maintains a workshop here, with a model of Arcosanti, his megalopolis of the era to come. His sculpture and windbells are on exhibit, too. Open daily. Reservations required. $1 donation. 6433 E Double Tree Ranch Rd., Scottsdale (948-6145).

Taliesin West – The future owes its shape to the innovative imagination and technical expertise of the late Frank Lloyd Wright, master architect. Wright's former office and school, Taliesin West (pronounced tally-essen), offers you the chance to see what goes into planning and designing those marvelous, ultra-modern structures. Closed on rainy days and holidays. Admission charge. Scottsdale Rd. north, to Shea Blvd. east, to 108th St. north, to Taliesin West (948-6670).

■ **EXTRA SPECIAL**: For a picturesque day trip through open desert, take the Black Canyon Highway north, to Cordes Junction, then travel west through the old territorial capital of Prescott, to *Sedona*, famous for its dramatic red cliffs. At Sedona, take a breathtaking drive up Oak Creek Canyon to *Flagstaff*, or complete the circle by driving back to Verde Valley, where you return to Black Canyon Highway. Be sure to stop in *Jerome*, the ghost town too ornery to die. A community of artists now lives in the old wooden buildings that cling precariously to the steep mountainside of this former copper mining town. Jerome has great curio and antiques shops specializing in mining paraphernalia and one of the best restaurants in Arizona, the *House of Joy*. The food is Continental, the prices are ridiculously inexpensive, and it's open only on weekends (so reservations are a must, call 634-5339).

SOURCES AND RESOURCES

For maps, brochures, and information, contact Phoenix and Valley of the Sun Convention and Visitors Bureau, 2701 E Camelback (957-0070), or Arizona Office of Tourism, 3507 N Central Ave. (255-3618).

The best local guide is *Amazing Arizona* (Arizona Office of Tourism, free).

All telephone numbers are in the 602 area code unless otherwise indicated.

For Local Coverage – *Arizona Republic,* morning daily; *Phoenix Gazette,* evening daily; *New Times,* weekly; *Phoenix* Magazine, monthly.

For Food – *100 Best Restaurants in the Valley of the Sun,* by John and Joan Bogert (ADM, $2.25).

CLIMATE AND CLOTHES: Try not to visit in summer, when it's more than 100°. Fall, winter, and spring are dry, warm, and sunny. Temperatures range from daytime highs of between 60° and 80°, to nighttime lows of about 35° to 50°.

GETTING AROUND: Getting around Phoenix is next to impossible without a car.

Bus – There are buses, but service is sketchy, with interminable waiting periods, erratic schedules, and no buses at all at night and on Sundays. However, you can call Phoenix Transit System (257-8426) for schedule information. Sun Valley Bus Line runs buses to Tempe and Mesa (248-4040).

Taxi – Call Yellow Cab (252-5071).

Car Rental – All major national firms are represented. Bargain Bug (244-0366) is among the cheapest.

MUSEUMS: Heard Museum, Phoenix Art Museum, and Pueblo Grande Museum, are described in *Special Places*. Other museums in Phoenix are:

Arizona Mineral Museum – 1826 W McDowell (255-3791).

Hall of Flame Museum – (no kidding), a collection of firefighting paraphernalia from 1725; 6101 E Van Buren. (275-3473).

MAJOR COLLEGES AND UNIVERSITIES: A lot of concerts and plays take place on local campuses. Check publications listed above for details. The largest and most active campus is Arizona State University, Apache Blvd., Tempe (965-9011). Phoenix College, 1202 W Thomas Rd. (264-2492), and American Graduate School of International Management, 59th Ave. and Greenway Rd., Glendale (978-7011), sponsor concerts and activities, too.

SPECIAL EVENTS: *Phoenix Open Golf Tournament* takes place in January; other golf tournaments are played throughout the year. In mid-March, the *World Championship Rodeo* is held at Veterans Memorial Coliseum, 1826 W McDowell. In October, the *Arizona State Fair* fills up the State Fairgrounds. In November, the annual *Thunderbird Balloon Race* takes place at the American Graduate School of International Management in Glendale.

SPORTS: The year-round sun makes Phoenix ideal for watching or participating in outdoor athletics. (In summer, get up early and play before it gets too hot.) In winter and spring, there's dog racing at Greyhound Park, 40th and E Washington Sts. (273-7181), and horse racing at Turf Paradise, 19th Ave. and Bell Rd. (942-1101).

Basketball – NBA Phoenix *Suns* play at Veterans Memorial Coliseum, 1826 W McDowell (258-7111). The Arizona State University *Sun Devils* have come to national attention during the past few seasons (965-9011).

Bicycling – You can rent bikes from Salem's Cyclery, 3839 N 7th St. (277-6764), and Wilbur and Orville, 4400 N Scottsdale Rd. (949-1978).

Fishing – Trout, bass, and crappie can be caught at Apache Lake and Salt River.

Swimming – The Salt River is good for swimming, too. There are 40 municipal pools in Phoenix. Every large park has one. Try the pool at Coronado Park, N 12th St. and Coronado Rd.

Tubing – Arizona's most popular summer sport. On any given weekend, as many as 20,000 residents strap beer-filled ice chests and their behinds to old inner tubes and float down five or ten miles of free-flowing Salt River below Saguaro Lake just north of Mesa. The trip is free and you can buy tubes — the bigger the better — at gas stations and stands along the route. This utterly relaxing pastime is called "tubing down the Salt."

Golf – There are 68 courses in Phoenix. The best public course is Encanto Municipal (253-3963).

Tennis – Phoenix Tennis Center has 22 lighted courts for night games, 6330 N 21st Ave. (249-3712).

Inland Surfing – If you've always wanted to surf, but can't quite brave the force of the ocean, Big Surf at 1500 N Hayden Rd. in Tempe is a good place to break in. There are artificial beaches and waves, and you can rent equipment. Closed Mondays, May-September; open weekends only March-April. Admission charge (947-2477).

Horseback Riding – Hourly rentals at Ponderosa Stable, 10215 S Central (268-1261), and South Mountain Stable, 10001 S Central (276-8131). All Western Stables, 10220 S Central (276-5862), also rents horses by the hour.

THEATER: There's quite a lot of drama in Phoenix and Scottsdale. World-renowned performers like Sir Michael Redgrave have come to play Shakespeare in the past. Check the local publications listed above for schedules. The major theaters include: *Phoenix Little Theater*, 25 E Coronado Rd. (254-2151); *Gammage Auditorium*, a Frank Lloyd Wright building on the campus of Arizona State University in Tempe (965-3434). Scottsdale has a *Shakespearean Festival* in September, with three plays presented by the Old Globe Theater Company of San Diego. Scottsdale Center for the Arts, Civic Center Plaza, Scottsdale (994-2787).

MUSIC: *Phoenix Symphony* and *Arizona Opera Company* play at Symphony Hall, 225 E Adams (262-7272); *Scottsdale Symphony* and *Arizona Ballet Theater* play at Scottsdale Center for the Arts, 7383 Scottsdale Mall (994-2787). Traveling dance troupes play Gammage Auditorium and Scottsdale Center for the Arts. Nationally known rock performers and classical musicians appear at Gammage Auditorium. Rock groups also give concerts at Veterans Memorial Coliseum, 1826 W McDowell (258-6711).

NIGHTCLUBS AND NIGHTLIFE: One of the most popular nightspots in town is *Bogart's*, 4821 N 20th St. (957-1684), where the atmosphere and opportunities to meet people are legendary. Other good meeting places are: *Oscar Taylor* at Biltmore Fashion Sq. (956-5705); *TGI Friday's*, 1851 E Camelback (277-6205) behind the Colonnade Shopping Center, with the biggest martinis anywhere and an exceptional menu.

SINS: The assassination of Phoenix newspaper reporter Don Bolles *angered* journalists around the country. Angry at what they saw as a pretty absolute move to deprive their colleague of First Amendment rights as guaranteed by the US Constitution, a group of journalists from all parts of the country converged on Phoenix to finish the work that Bolles had begun. The Arizona Project, one of the most intensive cooperative investigations in the history of American journalism, spawned a new national organization committed to informing the public: Investigative Reporters and Editors, Inc.

As a visitor, practice real Phoenix *gluttony.* Gorge yourself on fresh air and sunshine. All you have to do is go outside and take a deep breath. It's not fattening and it's free. And to enjoy *sloth,* take a chest full of ice-cold beer out to the Salt River north of Mesa and plunk it onto an old inner tube. Plunk yourself right down next to it and let the tube and the river do all the work. Tubing down the Salt allows you to remain utterly inert while you travel, guzzling beer all the way.

LOCAL SERVICES: Business Services – Alison's Secretarial Service, 3270 E Camelback Rd. (955-3542).

Mechanic – Johnson Shell Service, 1519 N 7th St. (254-0495).

Babysitting – Arizona Babysitters Service, 4214 N 48th Dr. (247-0260).

BEST IN TOWN

CHECKING IN: If you're coming to Phoenix on business, you'll probably want to stay downtown. If it's a pleasure visit, you can't beat the resorts, which offer full recreational activities and Valley tours. Meals are included in the price of a room at a resort. You can expect to pay between \$40 and \$110 for a double room at an expensive resort; between \$30 and \$45 at an expensive hotel; between \$20 and \$30 at a moderate hotel; and around \$20 at an inexpensive hotel.

***Arizona Biltmore* –** The first and most luxurious resort in the Valley, first class in every way. Golf and tennis facilities are outstanding, and so are the swimming pools. Horseback riding trails too. The dining room serves the finest Continental cuisine in the state. 314 rooms. 24th St. and Missouri (955-6600). Expensive.

***Camelback Inn* –** This is the largest resort in the state — 413 rooms, in two-story cottages. It's set among the beautiful Camelback Mountain foothills and has swimming pools, golf, and tennis facilities. The cowboy cookouts are great fun. 5402 E Lincoln Dr., Paradise Valley (948 1700). Expensive.

***The Phoenix Hilton* –** A Phoenix fixture, previously known as the Adams Hotel. The 538 large rooms all have magnificent views and there's an old-time feeling at the quaint bar, with swimming pool, good coffee shop, and a fair dining room. Central and Adams (257-1525). Expensive.

***Hyatt Regency* –** You can play night tennis, swim, or relax those aching muscles in the whirlpool. This elegant, 711-room newcomer has a fine restaurant and an overpriced coffee shop. 2nd and Adams (257-1110). Expensive.

***Doubletree Inn* –** This new, modern, centrally located 139-room hotel near the financial district has a swimming pool, whirlpool, and an excellent restaurant which features nationally known jazz groups on weekends. Pets are welcome. 2nd Ave. at Osborn (248-0222). Expensive to moderate.

***Fiesta Inn* –** Only five minutes from the airport by courtesy bus, this 149-room inn is perfect for an overnight stopover. Lavishly decorated interiors, tennis courts, and swimming pool. 2100 S Priest, Tempe (967-1441). Moderate.

***Friendship Inn 6* –** Smaller and quieter than the others, this 68-unit inn is also kinder to your budget. Two of the rooms are suites; there's a coffee shop so that you can eat without having to hit the highway in search of a diner. There's also a heated swimming pool. 201 N 7th Ave. (254-6521). Inexpensive.

EATING OUT: Best bets in Phoenix are Mexican food and steaks. Expect to pay $25 or more for a meal for two at an expensive restaurant; between $18 and $25 at a moderate restaurant; under $18 at a selection noted as inexpensive. Prices do not include drinks, wine, or tips.

Vito's Scampi – Everything on this all-around Italian menu is good, but the Guaymas shrimp are exceptional. The dining room decor is elegant. Closed major holidays. Reservations recommended. Major credit cards. 4515 N Scottsdale Rd., Scottsdale (946-1031). Expensive.

The Golden Eagle – Although this restaurant is quite expensive, the view over the valley and the quick and attentive service make you feel it's worth it. The Continental menu features some Southwestern specialties, including roast buffalo and pheasant; also try the stuffed trout. Since men are routinely handed the menu with the price listings, women should specify whether they wish one also. Open daily. Reservations recommended. Major credit cards. 201 N Central, atop the Valley Center (257-7700). Expensive.

Monti's La Casa Vieja – A Valley landmark. Serves the best steaks anywhere. It's always crowded but the service is good. Side dishes are plentiful. Closed Christmas and New Year's. Reservations accepted. Major credit cards. 3 W 1st, Tempe (967-7594). Moderate.

Asia House – A unique concept offering meals at one price, with different rooms devoted to Chinese, Japanese, and Mongolian cuisines. Select the type of meal you want when you call to make reservations. The Japanese room has low tables; the Mongolian, a circular table set under a yurt (a Mongolian tent). All the food is excellent, but the Mongolian meal is an experience. Closed Mondays. Reservations essential. Major credit cards. 2310 E McDowell (267-7461). Moderate.

Tuba City Truck Stop and Country Club – For a big slice of Arizona color in pictures, song, and flavor, try the one-of-a-kind hangout of Dolan Ellis, Arizona's official balladeer. Ellis, one of the original New Christy Minstrels, has been recording the look and feel of the West for 15 years. He sings original songs with lush background slides in the lounge. The restaurant features steaks and seafood. Barbecued ribs are a standout. Special children's show and menu Sundays at sundown. Closed Christmas Eve. Reservations accepted. Major credit cards. 7419 E Indian Plaza, Scottsdale (945-2672). Moderate.

Lunt Avenue Marble Club – If the name isn't enough to draw you in, it has great deep-dish pizza, too, and one of the best crêpe and sandwich selections in the state. Lunt's has four locations. Open daily. No reservations. Major credit cards. 1212 E Apache Blvd., Tempe (967-9192); 6202 N Scottsdale Rd., Scottsdale (998-3505); 2 E Camelback Rd., Phoenix (265-8997); 2770 W Peoria (863-9791). Moderate.

Pinnacle Peak Patio – No trip to Arizona would be complete without a visit to a real, by-God Western cowboy steak house. This one's the oldest and most famous, with two-pound Porterhouses broiled over mesquite coals and served with sourdough bread and pinto beans. Open daily. No reservations. Major credit cards. 10426 Pinnacle Peak Rd., Scottsdale (949-7311). Moderate.

The T-Bone – An out-of-the-way real find. Never crowded. It has basically the same menu as Pinnacle Peak but with a fantastic night view of the Valley. Food is brought by entertaining, gun-totin' waitresses, and you get to help yourself to a filling salad. Open daily. Reservations unnecessary. Major credit cards. End of 19th Ave. on South Mountain (276-0945). Moderate.

Tee Pee Mexican Food – You can spend twice the money for half the food at posher restaurants, but you won't find better quality. On the outside, it looks like a biker hangout, but it's a good family restaurant. Closed Sundays, Thanksgiving, Christmas, and New Year's. No reservations. Major credit cards. 4144 E Indian School Rd. (956-0178). Inexpensive.

The Original Hamburger Works – If all you want is a good burger, wander over to the vicinity of Phoenix College and partake of giant hamburgers with all the fixin's. The decor is rustic 1880s, with advertising posters from the turn of the century on the walls. Open daily. No reservations. No credit cards. 2801 N 15th Ave. (263-8693). Inexpensive.

Rosita's Place – Want a *really* authentic Mexican restaurant with great food and the lowest prices in town? This one's only four blocks from Sky Harbor Airport and a well-kept local secret. Service is slow but worth it — few dishes on the menu are over $3. The menus are in English but the waitresses only speak Spanish. Open daily. Reservations not required. No credit cards. 1914 E Buckeye Rd. (262-9372). Inexpensive.

PITTSBURGH

Pittsburgh is one of the most important industrial cities in the world. Without Pittsburgh, Detroit could not survive. One-fifth of all the steel produced in the United States is made here. Steel capital, USA, however, is not the city's only title. It's also the world's largest manufacturer of steel rolls, rolling mill machinery, air brakes, plate and window glass, aluminum and safety equipment. Within the one-half square mile which comprises the downtown area known as "The Golden Triangle," 16 of the world's 500 leading corporations maintain offices. The top six bring in more than $1 billion revenue annually. Pittsburgh is also an international leader in the fields of chemical, plastic, nuclear, and general scientific research.

If this sounds like Pittsburgh as you've always imagined it, pause for a moment over the classified columns in the back pages of any recent *Pittsburgh* magazine. There you will find ads for singles, clubs; piano, violin, and English horseback-riding lessons; workshops in printmaking, human sexuality, Arica self-development, Zen; and a variety of services including tree pruning, parliamentary procedure, and house cleaning. You can buy stained glass windows, antique music boxes, tropical fish, and custom-made harpsichords ($1,800 and up). All of which indicate a healthy range of interests. If that surprises you about Pittsburgh residents, it's time for a visit; if it doesn't, perhaps you've recently returned.

This city of 450,000 spreads out around the confluence of the Allegheny and Monongahela Rivers; they intersect the city's streets to form a watery wishbone. The Point, where the rivers join to make the Ohio River, has been strategically important as far back as the years predating the French and Indian War. This confluence was a point of contention, and later, the site of vicious conflict between France and Great Britain, at that time colonial rivals. It was not far from the Point, in 1754, that young George Washington, then an ardent British officer, ordered an attack on a French encampment, thereby inadvertently triggering the Pennsylvania phase of the French and Indian War. In 1758, British troops managed to secure control of the river forks, which enabled them to ensure their domination of North America. They built the formidable Fort Pitt at the Point, naming the battlement in honor of England's Prime Minister at the time, William Pitt.

Even as Fort Pitt's military usefulness declined, Pittsburgh developed as a commercial town and river port. The center for transporting westward-bound pioneers and supplies, the city did a thriving business, selling flatboats loaded with glass, home furnishings, hardware, drygoods, and farm products. In 1760, the largest coal seam ever struck in the United States was discovered on Mount Washington. With this coal, and iron ore that was shipped from nearby, Fort Pitt became industrial, as well as commercial. Iron foundries multiplied, and in the Civil War, Pittsburgh was the "arsenal of the North." It was also a magnet for magnates. The roster of tycoons who made their fortunes in Pittsburgh includes Thomas Mellon, Andrew Carnegie, and Henry Clay Frick.

But unrestricted industrial development left its scars. By the time WW II ended, Pittsburgh was an urban slag heap, known to millions of Americans as "Smoky City." The image of a grimy, factory-ridden town choked with smoke still prevails, although a rigorous clean-up campaign waged immediately after the war successfully cleared the air and introduced extensive civic improvement urban renewal programs.

The cleaner environment heightens the enjoyment of Pittsburgh's many-faceted cultural activities, many of which are the legacy of the giants of industry. Thomas Mellon and Andrew Carnegie endowed several arts institutions; Henry Clay Frick gave the city a museum, and the Henry Heinz family of the famous "57 varieties" contributed a performing arts center. In the final analysis, the intellectual character of this city is more interesting than its physical appearance, and if it takes steel and iron, air brakes and window glass, rolling mills and research centers, factories and the Golden Triangle to maintain that character, residents are content to be vigilant, and enjoy.

PITTSBURGH AT-A-GLANCE

SEEING THE CITY: Go to the top of Mount Washington for a sweeping view of the intersection of the Allegheny, Monongahela, and Ohio Rivers. Take Duquesne Incline or Monongahela Incline to the top. Duquesne is at W Carson Street (381-1665); Monongahela, in operation since 1870, is at E Carson St. (231-5707). Pittsburgh's first blast furnace can be seen on the south side of the Monongahela River, between the two inclines.

SPECIAL PLACES: There are three main sections of the city in which you'll find most of Pittsburgh's places of interest. The Golden Triangle encompasses the downtown area; North Side, old homes, the restored "Mexican War Streets," and parks; Oakland, museums and cultural institutions.

GOLDEN TRIANGLE

Point State Park – At the tip of the Golden Triangle. Covering 36 acres of broad walks and spacious gardens on the banks of the river junction, Point State Park contains Fort Pitt Blockhouse, a 1764 fortification, and Fort Pitt Museum, with exhibits on the French and Indian War and early Pennsylvania history. The park is free and open daily (281-9284); the museum is open Tuesdays through Sundays. Admission charge.

Bank Center – Once a financial hub, these four turn-of-the-century buildings are now an indoor bazaar. Under a stained-glass skylight and amid marble columns and gleaming brass, there are shops, cinemas, and restaurants. "Do" the boutiques, then have espresso, antipasto, or quiche at *Café Cappuccino* as you watch the parade pass by. 307 Fourth Ave.

Tamburitzans Cultural Center – Pittsburgh's 19 ethnic communities contribute to the surprising diversity of the cultural scene. Specializing in folk arts from Eastern Europe, Tamburitzans, near Duquesne Univeristy, displays peasant skirts, hats, balalaikas, and other unusual musical instruments. Guided tours by appointment. Free. Closed weekends. 1801 Blvd. of the Allies (281-9192).

Heinz Hall – A very classy movie theater in 1926, Heinz Hall has undergone renovation and is now an acoustically balanced, stately auditorium, home of the Pittsburgh

Symphony, Pittsburgh Opera, and Civic Light Opera, and host to performing arts troupes. Worth a look for its ornate decorations. Guided tours by appointment. Admission charge. 600 Penn Ave. (392-4800 for tour; 281-5000 for tickets).

NORTH SIDE

To get to the North Side from the Golden Triangle, cross Sixth Street Bridge, then proceed north to Allegheny Center Mall. Crosstown buses leave from *Horne's* at Penn Avenue and Stanwix Street.

Allegheny Observatory – Acclaimed as one of the best observatories in the world, Allegheny offers amateur astronomers the chance to scan the skies with a powerful telescope. Illustrated lectures help you to identify constellations. Open Tuesday through Friday evenings by appointment, April through October. Free. Riverview Park, off Perrysville Ave. (321-2400).

West Park Conservatory–Aviary – Another surprise. Tropical birds in jungle trees, twittering away like a Tarzan soundtrack. A good place to escape from 20th-century urban America with the advantage that you can slip back into it once you've had your fill. Open daily. Free Saturdays, other times admission charge. Ridge Ave. and Arch St., Allegheny Commons (322-7855).

Pittsburgh History and Landmarks Museum – North Side was Pittsburgh's prime residential district in the 19th century. Here you can see what it looked like then. Discriminating, sprightly collections of antiques, toys, musical instruments, clothing, and furnishings are on display. Pick up a self-tour pamphlet on historic architecture and explore. Admission charge. Closed Mondays. Allegheny Square (322-1204).

Buhl Planetarium – One of the first sky shows in the country. These entertaining exhibits on astronomy and other branches of science allow you to pedal a bicycle to generate electricity, push a button to activate the rotation of planets in our solar system, and monitor voice patterns on an oscilloscope. A weird-looking Zeiss projector is used for "Sky Dramas" in the Theater of the Stars. Open daily. Admission charge. Adjacent to the Landmarks Museum, Allegheny Square (321-4300).

OAKLAND

Cathedral of Learning – Part of the University of Pittsburgh, this imposing 42-story Gothic tower is the only skyscraper of classrooms in the country. A unique first-floor display composed of 19 Nationality Rooms is devoted to each of the major ethnic groups in Pittsburgh. Open daily. Free. Bigelow Blvd. and 5th Ave. (624-6000).

Carnegie Institute – Behind the Cathedral on Forbes Avenue, this vast, internationally distinguished arts and cultural center contains an art museum, a natural history museum, and an extensive library. Be sure to see Segal's *Tightrope Walker,* balancing 15 feet from the floor. You'll enjoy browsing in the Carnegie Library. Open daily. Free Saturday. Other times admission charge. 4400 Forbes Ave. (622-3289).

Phipps Conservatory – Rare tropical and domestic fragrant blossoms flourish in the hothouses and gardens of this 2½-acre conservatory. The 13 hothouses here are only a fraction of the greenery of surrounding Schenley Park, which covers 422 acres. Schenley has a lake, tennis courts, baseball fields, a golf course, an ice skating rink, picnic areas, and nature trails. Conservatory and park open daily. Admission charge (free Saturdays). Schenley Park (255-2375).

Historical Society of Western Pennsylvania – Curious bottles of antique glass, hand-carved furniture, and other memorabilia line the halls, walls, and shelves. You can peruse old documents on Pennsylvania history in the library. A journey into the past. Closed Sundays and Mondays. Free. 4338 Bigelow Blvd. (681-5533).

Pittsburgh Zoo – Not only does this zoo have more than 2,000 animals spread over 75 acres, but an indoor Aquazoo as well, with tanks full of domestic trout and pike, and esoteric species like penguins and piranhas. Nocturnal animals are on display in the Twilight Zoo. Open daily. Saturdays free, other times admission charge. Highland Park (441-6262).

Frick Art Museum – A magnificent Renaissance-style mansion houses Great Masters from the Renaissance through the 18th century. Marie Antoinette's furniture is on display in an ornate living room. The eclectic collection comprises Russian silver, Flemish tapestries, and Chinese porcelains. Closed Mondays and Tuesdays. Free. 7227 Reynolds St. and S Homewood Ave., Point Breeze (371-7766).

■ **EXTRA SPECIAL:** For a total change of environment and mood, drive across the state border to *West Virginia*, still a relatively isolated part of the country — ¾ of the state is forest. Take I-70 to exit 6 (Washington, Pennsylvania) and then follow rt. 18 to rt. 844. In West Virginia, the road becomes rt. 27, and it will take you to *Drovers Inn* in Wellsburg, West Virginia, where you can feast on hearty, home-cooked American food (304 737-0188). *Wellsburg* is near Meadowcroft Village, in Avella, Pennsylvania, a restored early-19th-century farming community spaciously rebuilt on a wide tract of land. Open daily June–October, and Saturdays and Sundays in November; closed December–June. Admission charge (2½ miles off rt. 231, 587-3412). In Wheeling, West Virginia, there are outdoor summer concerts in Oglebay Park (304 242-3000); and country music concerts at Brush Run Park near the airport (304 232-1170).

SOURCES AND RESOURCES

For information on places of interest and events contact the Visitor Information Center in Gateway Center, The Golden Triangle. The VIC is run by the Pittsburgh Convention and Visitors Bureau, 200 Roosevelt Building (281-7711). For recorded information on daily events, call 391-6840.

The Convention and Visitors Bureau offers a variety of free city guides.

All telephone numbers are in the 412 area code unless otherwise indicated.

For Local Coverage – *Post-Gazette,* morning daily; *Press,* evening daily; *Market Square of Pittsburgh,* weekly.

For Food – The restaurant sections of *Pittsburgh* Magazine and *Key — This Week in Pittsburgh* magazine.

CLIMATE AND CLOTHES: Pittsburgh has a moderate climate with frequent precipitation year-round. Summer temperatures climb into the 80s; winters drop into the 20s. About 200 days of the year are cloudy.

GETTING AROUND: Bus – Port Authority Transit provides efficient bus service (231-5707).

Taxis – To get a taxi, call Yellow Cab (665-8100).

Car Rental – All major national firms are represented.

MUSEUMS: The Fort Pitt Museum, Tamburitzans Cultural Center, History and Landmarks Museum, Buhl Planetarium, Carnegie Institute, Historical Society of Western Pennsylvania, and Frick Art Museum are described in *Special Places*.

Other museums worth noting are:

Art Institute of Pittsburgh, 536 Penn Ave. (263-6600).

Old Economy Museum and Village, 14th and Church Sts., Ambridge (266-4500).

Pittsburgh Center for the Arts, 5th and Shady Aves. (361-0873).

MAJOR COLLEGES AND UNIVERSITIES: University of Pittsburgh, Forbes Ave., Oakland (624-4141); Chatham College, 5th Ave. and Woodland Rd. (441-8200); Duquesne University, Blvd. of the Allies (434-6000); Carnegie-Mellon University, Schenley Park (578-2000).

SPECIAL EVENTS: From the last weekend in May through the first Sunday in June, the *Three Rivers Festival* takes place in Gateway Center and Equitable Plaza. Simultaneously, the *Folk Festival,* an international extravaganza, is held at Civic Arena and Exhibit Hall. *Shadyside Art Festival* takes place in Shadyside in early August. Around the same time, *Butler County Fair* in nearby Prospect has the usual assortment of fairground activities. Phipps Conservatory holds three flower festivals a year — in spring, fall, and at Christmas. Point State Park is the site of celebrations over July 4th and Labor Day weekends.

SPORTS: Pittsburgh's professional sports teams are among the best in the country.

Racing – Enthusiasts flock to Ligonier, 40 miles east of the city, in the Laurel Mountains, for the Rolling Rock Hunt Steeplechase in September.

Harness Racing – Fans have a choice of the Meadows, Washington, PA (563-1224), or Waterford Park, Chester, WV (304 387-2400).

Baseball – *Pirates* play at Three Rivers Stadium, Stadium Circle, North Side (323-1150).

Football – *Steelers*' home grid is also at Three Rivers Stadium (323-1200).

Hockey – *Penguins* play at Civic Arena, Washington Pl., Center and Bedford Ave. (765-3939).

Tennis – The best municipal courts are at Highland Park. There are excellent suburban courts at North and South Parks.

Bicycling – There are no bike rental shops in town, but the county parks (like North and South Parks) have rental facilities.

Fishing – The City Parks and Recreation Department runs a group fishing program at Panther Hollow in summer. You can rent rods and reels (255–2355).

Swimming – There are swimming pools throughout the city. Ream Playground has a good one, Merrimac and Virginia (431-9285).

Hiking – There are quite a few hiking programs. For information on Parks Department nature tours and programs for the handicapped, contact Schenley Nature Center, Schenley Park (681-2272). For information on hiking, backpacking, canoeing, and camping in the area contact the Sierra Club (561-0203).

Canoeing, Kayaking – You can canoe and kayak through exciting whitewater rapids in the Laurel Highlands. Canoe, Kayak and Sailing Craft offers lessons and guided tours, 701 Wood St., Wilkinsburg (371-4802).

Scuba Diving – In Pittsburgh? Check it out. Sub-Aquatics gives a 36-hour course in essentials with tips on local lakes and water-filled quarries, 1593 Banksville Rd. (531-5577).

Horseback Riding – Hit the trail in Boyce Park. You can rent a horse or sign on for a hayride at the stables (793-1578; 793-5525). If you bring your own horse to Pittsburgh, you can board it at Boyce Park stables.

THEATERS: For information on performance listings and schedules, check the local publications listed above.

Pittsburgh's theatrical scene is pretty lively, especially in summer when *Park Players* and *Pittsburgh Puppet Theater* take to the parks. For information, call 521-1474. *The Pittsburgh Public Theater*, Allegheny Square (323-1900), and *Heinz Hall*, 600 Penn Ave. (281-5000), are the city's most prestigious theaters. *Pitts-*

burgh Playhouse Theater Center produces adults' and children's plays, 222 Craft Ave. (621-4445).

Carnegie-Mellon Theater Co. performs at Kresge Theater, Carnegie-Mellon University, Schenley Park (578-2407). *Chatham College Theater* presents modern classics (441-8200). There are dinner theaters at *Apple Hill Playhouse*, Lamplighter Restaurant, Delmont (468-4545), and *Little Lake Dinner Theater*, rt. 19 south, Donaldson's Crossroads (745-6300, 745-9883).

MUSIC: André Previn conducts the world-famous *Pittsburgh Symphony Orchestra* from September through May at Heinz Hall, 600 Penn Ave. (281-5000). Summertime the air fills with music. The *American Wind Symphony* performs at Point State Park (281-8866). Jazz can be heard at the Aviary, string ensembles at the Conservatory, and folk music on Flagstaff Hill. The Parks Department coordinates schedules (255-2390). Touring opera, ballet companies, symphonies, and entertainers perform at Heinz Hall.

NIGHTCLUBS AND NIGHTLIFE: *The Georgetown Inn* offers a glittering nightscape, 1230 Grandview Ave., Mt. Washington (481-4424). *Holiday House Supper Club* hosts entertainment headliners, 3755 William Penn Hwy. (824-4000). For disco there's *Heaven,* 105 6th St. (243-2836).

SINS: It's a long way from Shady Side and Fox Chapel, the affluent areas to which the *avaricious* in Pittsburgh aspire, to Liberty Avenue; but from the look of that street's massage parlors, peep show palaces, and other strongholds of *lust* in the city, some of that money must be filtering down. Pittsburgh's point of *pride?* The *Bank Center*, an old bank building at 4th and Wood that has been renovated to house shops, restaurants, and cinemas, and discos.

LOCAL SERVICES: Business Services – Allegheny Personnel Services, Jenkins Arcade (391-2044).

Mechanic – Grandview Mobil, 1 Virginia Ave. (431-2952).

Babysitting – All hotels except *William Penn* have babysitting services. There are no independent child care services, however.

■ **WHILE YOU'RE IN THE NEIGHBORHOOD:** The Pittsburgh Astrology Association meets the third Tuesday of every month at 300 6th Ave., downtown Pittsburgh (681-3700).

BEST IN TOWN

CHECKING IN: For a city of this size, the hotel choices are surprisingly small, and the level of accommodation runs only from fair to mediocre. Expect to pay $60 or more for a double at those places we've listed as expensive; $50 to $60, moderate; inexpensive, under $50.

Hyatt Pittsburgh – Conveniently located near Civic Arena and Exhibit Hall, the 400 rooms here have all been redecorated. The improvement is very apparent, and the top two "Regency" floors offer the best accommodations in town. *Hugo's Rotisserie* serves a moderately priced lunch and buffet dinner, with roast duckling the specialty of the house. You can get an inexpensive meal at *QQ's Café.* Both open daily. Chatham Center (391-5000). Expensive.

Marriott Inn – The Marriott livens up its 500-room facility with three swimming pools (indoors and out), a putting green, tennis under roof or sky, a whirlpool, sauna, and exercise room. You can enjoy entertainment or disco nightly in the *Trolley Bar* or dinner at the *Inside Track.* 101 Marriott Dr., Crafton (922-8400). Expensive.

Pittsburgh Hilton – Standing at the edge of Point State Park with an incomparable view of the three rivers, this is currently the leader in a town where great hotels are notable by their absence. Some of its 800 rooms overlook the park, others face the Gateway Center mini-parks. Boutiques on the premises are the best in the city. Gateway Center (391-4600). Expensive.

The William Penn – Once the city's best, but no longer at the top of the list. This 800-room property has been undergoing a refurbishing for some time, and guests should be sure to ask for a room that's been redone. But even these are hardly deluxe. Public rooms are better than the bedrooms. Mellon Sq. (281-7100). Expensive.

Sheraton Inn — Station Square – This 300-room riverside hotel has a health club with a swimming pool, cocktail lounges, and restaurants. *The Wharf* serves a good seafood buffet on Thursdays and Fridays; *The River's Edge* has a sumptuous Sunday brunch. Near Station Square's shops and restaurants. Smithfield and Carson sts. (261-2000). Expensive.

EATING OUT: The city's restaurant choices are far better than its selection of hotels, and there is a broad spectrum of ethnic eateries all over the landscape. These are most recommended, for they offer a level of food preparation far higher than that found at the anonymous "Continental" restaurants. Expect to pay $30 or more for two at a restaurant we've noted as expensive; between $20 and $30, moderate; under $20 at a place listed as inexpensive. Prices don't include drinks, wine, or tips.

Hyeholde – Just a few minutes from the Pittsburgh airport, there is a medieval castle. Or at least what looks like one, with wooden beams, slate floors, European tapestries, and spacious grounds. Dinner menu changes daily but consists of classical recipes — filet mignon, trout, breast of fowl — prepared with the freshest ingredients. Bread and desserts are homemade, and don't pass up the Hyeholde trifle. The wine list is the most extensive in the area. Closed Sundays. Reservations. Major credit cards. 190 Hyeholde Dr., Coraopolis (264-3116). Expensive.

La Plume – The main restaurant in the *William Penn Hotel* offers fine Continental food, coupled with friendly and able service. The menu wisely sticks to basics, and the cooking is truly first-rate. The size of the shrimp cocktail is prodigious, and well worth its price. Roast beef is also a prime choice. Mellon Sq. (281-7100). Expensive.

Park Schenley – Dine on succulent filet mignon sautéed in butter and flambéed in brandy at your table nestled in a balconied tier. Poulet d'azur (chicken cooked in sauterne) is accompanied by grand helpings of vegetables. Business lunch is the best deal with sole Véronique and mixed grill leading the bill. Closed Mondays Reservations required. Major credit cards. 3955 Bigelow Blvd., Oakland (681-0800). Expensive.

Tambellini's – The outstanding selection here includes lemon sole, lobster tail, scallops, shrimp, oysters, crabmeat and frogs legs. The spinach salad is crunchy, and the homemade gnocchi irresistible. Closed Sundays. No reservations accepted. No credit cards. 860 Saw Mill Run Blvd. (481-1118). Expensive.

Top of the Triangle – Atop the 64-story, triangular-shaped US Steel Building, this restaurant gives you a gorgeous three-mile panoramic view. The oak walls add a certain warmth which modern decor often lacks. There's nightly entertainment in the glass-enclosed cocktail lounge. Stouffer's provides the food. Open daily. Major credit cards. Reservations advised. 600 Grant St. (471-4100). Expensive.

Arthur's – Though one of Pittsburgh's newest, this small restaurant, in the city's oldest office building, provides an attractive early American decor with four working fireplaces. The menu includes Continental and American dishes; the smoked meats and fish are excellent (all smoking is done on the premises). Some specialties are German Onion Beer Soup and veal stuffed with smoked scallops and mozzarella cheese, served with spinach noodles in a Marsala wine and mushroom sauce. Closed Sundays. Reservations. Major credit cards. 209 4th Ave. (566-1735). Expensive to moderate.

Grand Concourse – This elegant remake of the old Pittsburgh and Lake Erie Railroad Terminal is the best thing to happen to Pittsburgh's restaurant scene in years. Beautiful wood, stained glass, and gleaming brass surround diners who devour excellent seafood — oysters, shrimp, clams, crab — and especially a tangy seafood chowder that is served in a pewter tureen. One Station Sq. (261-1717). Expensive to moderate.

The Pilot House – A riverboat restaurant. Sitting at the foot of Wood Street at the Monongahela Wharf, it's decorated like an old Mississippi riverboat, and serves steaks, seafood, and Italian dishes. Open daily. Reservations suggested. Major credit cards. Wood St. and Monongahela Wharf (281-2203). Moderate.

Timberlink Steak-Out – Select your own prime steak and broil it yourself over a charcoal pit, concoct a fantasy from the salad bar, and complete the course with warm, crusty bread and a pot of baked beans. You can play golf on the Timberlink nine-hole course or tour Storybook Forest in adjacent Idlewild Park. Open daily. Reservations. Major credit cards. 40 miles east on route 30, Ligonier (238-9880). Moderate.

Tequila Junction – A short walk from the city, across the Smithfield Street Bridge, will take you to the Freight House Shops at Station Square, where you can lunch or dine south of the border. In a romantic brick and adobe inn, sip a strawberry Margarita followed by one of the many tasty Mexican entrées, such as crabmeat enchilada or chili Colorado. Open daily. No reservations. Major credit cards. Freight House Shops, Station Square (261-3265). Moderate.

Mad Anthony – Another suburban choice. A German tavern that serves hearty sauerbraten, Wiener schnitzel, and knockwurst with German beer. In summer, you can sing along with a German band in the outdoor biergarten. Waitresses are in costume. Near Old Economy Village, a preserved 19th-century estate. Open daily. Reservations aren't necessary. Major credit cards. 12 miles west of Pittsburgh on rt. 65, at 13th and Merchant Sts., Ambridge (266-9662). Inexpensive.

Bimbo's – Great for hungry families. Informal, spontaneous atmosphere combined with excellent pizza, Italian food, burgers, sandwiches, imported beers, wines, and soda fountain creations. Steel City Stompers entertain while guests participate in music and patter. Open daily. Reservations aren't necessary. No credit cards. 1539 Washington Rd. (343-8333). Inexpensive.

Cornucopia – The vegetarian specialties here include stuffed mushrooms, string bean stroganoff over brown rice with cheese sauce, stir-fry vegetables, non-alcoholic beverages, frappes, and a spectacular banana dessert with coconut-walnut glaze. It's in a fascinating, multi-ethnic neighborhood, and has a simple, pleasant atmosphere. Closed Mondays. Reservations aren't necessary. No credit cards. 328 Atwood St., Oakland (682-7953). Inexpensive.

Samreny's – Actually the full name is Samreny's Cedars of Lebanon Restaurant. And there's a full menu of Middle Eastern dishes, like shish kebab, stuffed cabbage and grape leaves, kibbi nayaa (rice with pignolia nuts), heaping green salads, baklava, and other rich, rare pastries. The decor includes a delightful collection of antique water pipes. Open daily. Reservations accepted. No credit cards. 4808 Baum Blvd. (682-1212). Inexpensive.

PORTLAND, OR

One of the most important things to bear in mind when you visit Portland is that it's likely that you will be made to feel welcome. Under no circumstances, however, must you let on that you'd actually like to live here. Of course you *will* want to live here, if you've got any sense, even after just one visit; but lie about it. Portland residents are that sensitive.

They're not unfriendly, mind you. It's simply that the city is beautiful — number one choice in a recent study of 243 cities for "quality of life" — and with an enlightened government and determined citizenry, it's getting better all the time. Even the eruptions of Mt. St. Helen's haven't left any scars.

Portland stretches along the Willamette River (one of the few rivers in the country that flows north) just below the point where it joins the Columbia. The confluence provides Portland with a deep, freshwater port that serves oceangoing vessels, and because the city straddles the Willamette, ships dock beneath downtown bridges. Some 110 miles from the ocean, Portland is a seaport. Around the whole metropolitan area, like the brackets of parentheses, are the Northwest's two most imposing mountain ranges — the Cascades in the east, the Coast Range to the west.

The city is divided neatly into its east and west side by the Willamette; each side has its own atmosphere (east side, homey; west side, posh. The elegant, downtown shopping district is very west side). The two segments of the city are connected by 11 bridges. The whole city is then divided into five large sections: North, Northeast, Northwest, Southeast, Southwest. Sounds confusing, but it actually makes finding places very easy with a local map, since every address includes an area designation (SW, NE, N, etc.).

For the most part, the city is flat, hugging its major waterways, lakes and ponds, with hundreds of parks spread across its metropolitan area. Now and then, a group of forested hills raises an imperious eyebrow — some residential, others intentionally undeveloped. In the east, the city holds up three fingers of small, residential mountains, as if pointing to the great mountains to the east, and 11,235-foot Mt. Hood in the Cascades, an hour away.

The Greater Portland Area stretches from the foothills of Mt. Hood to the western plains of the Coast Range; more than one million people live in this four-county area.

The city was incorporated in 1845 by New England settlers — it's named for Portland, Maine. When the great crash of 1893 closed banks across the country, one pioneer Portland merchant, Aaron Meier, took his bags of gold to banker Henry Corbett. The next morning, as the rest of the nation's banks failed, Corbett stood tall and firm in the middle of his bank's lobby — properly attired in frockcoat and top hat — with Meier's gold piled conspicuously around him. There was no closure in Portland that day.

When Scottish shipper Donald Macleay bequeathed 107 acres to the city at the turn of the century, it was with the stipulation that no wheeled vehicle *ever* be allowed to enter the premises. The city agreed, and has even expanded Macleay's trust. Today, Macleay Park stands mid-city, untouched by exhaust fumes or bicycle tread, a part of more than 30 miles of dense forest that are completely contained within the city — a green velvet buffer for hikers, bird-watchers, and nature lovers.

Macleay anticipated the attitude of modern Portlanders with admirable skill. In recent years, the city has torn up some 24 blocks right out of the heart of the west side business district to build a brick-covered, tree-lined pedestrian mall, spotted with fountains and sculpture. Along the Willamette River, which creates the city's natural seaport, the old factories have been razed, and greenways are spreading out with smug brilliance. By order of the people, the Willamette River has been cleaned up and riverboating, salmon fishing and waterskiing are now commonplace on weekdays.

Along with the rest of the state, Portland has banned the sale of aerosol sprays, abolished the sale of beer and soda in nonreturnable cans and bottles, and is seriously discussing mandatory use of seat belts in all automobiles. Portland is a potent force in civic activism.

After taking a long look at the first 40-story building to go up in its business area, Portland moved swiftly to assure that no other such building would be built higher. It has thus saved its panorama of mountains and wooded hillsides for succeeding generations.

The City of Roses, Portland has also proven a thorn in the side of some industry. All new buildings must pass inspection as early as the planning stages, and the powerful Historic Landmark Commission works constantly to protect Portland's historic buildings. On its list of protected properties are several iron-fronted buildings, plus one sycamore and one elm tree, each planted by founding parents and each continually bursting the seams of downtown sidewalks.

PORTLAND AT-A-GLANCE

SEEING THE CITY: Portland offers several exceptional vantage points from which to see the city, the valley in which it lies, and the mountains beyond. Two of the best are:

Pittock Acres Park – The grounds of the former Pittock Mansion (see below), 1,000 feet above the city. At your feet are the port, business section, the Willamette River, and the southeast residential areas. In the distance are the Cascade Mountains — Mt. Hood in Oregon, Mt. Rainier and St. Helens in Washington. 3229 NW Pittock.

Washington Park – The best view is from the International Rose Test Gardens, looking east toward mountains in the background. 228 SW Wright.

SPECIAL PLACES: Portland was made for walking. Her founders frequently built homes in the west hills and walked to work along the waterfront. Especially on the west side, major points of interest are within walking distance of one another.

WEST SIDE

Portland Art Museum – Features an outstanding permanent collection of Northwest Indian art, a representative group of Oregon's prolific contemporary artists, and a wide variety of traveling shows. The outdoor Sculpture Mall is especially appealing in summer. Closed Mondays. Donations accepted. SW Park and Madison (226-2811).

Oregon Historical Society – Exhibits on Oregon history, before and after the arrival of the white man. Also a fine series of dioramas on Indian life, plus a research library with open stacks for browsing; pioneer craft demonstrations for children. Closed Sundays. Free. 1230 SW Park (222-1741).

Ira Keller Fountain (and Civic Auditorium) – A series of pools and waterfalls a block wide, facing the Civic Auditorium. In hot weather, so many people splash around in its tons of swirling water that the city has obligingly hired lifeguards. Designed by Lawrence Halprin, it is widely known as "the people's fountain." On SW 3rd Ave.

Pioneer Courthouse – The first federal building in the Pacific Northwest, completed in 1873, and now restored to its original Victorian splendor. The interior includes a working post office, an elegant Victorian courtroom (where the U.S. Court of Appeals meets), and adjoining rooms for the judges. These private chambers can be seen by asking the judges' secretary for a convenient time. 555 SW Yamhill (no phone).

Old Town – When the Pioneer Courthouse was brand new, some folks thought it much too far from the downtown business section — a whole six blocks. Now "downtown" is called Old Town, and it's being restored into a shopping and browsing area filled with craft, art, and antique shops. The area runs from Second to Fifth Avenues, on both sides of Burnside. Artists from all over the state sell their work at the Sunday and Saturday markets, under Burnside Bridge, from 10 AM to 5 PM, May to December.

Worth noting on Ankeny, south of Burnside: *Dan and Louis Oyster Bar* (see below, *Eating Out*), and *Le Panier,* on SW 2nd, whose Parisian chefs serve fresh French bread and croissants every day. North of Burnside, Couch Street and beyond, are numerous specialty shops. Best buys are Indian artifacts, toys, spinning and weaving supplies, original jewelry.

Washington Park – One of the city's oldest parks, with 145 acres, all part of the 30-mile park system that thrives within city limits. There are four points of special interest on the grounds: the Rose Test Gardens, the Oregon Museum of Science and Industry, the Western Forestry Center, and Tera One, a totally solar home, as well as some magnificent views of the city and countryside. Plan to spend some extended periods of time here, but be forewarned: The only eating accommodations are hot dogs and hamburgers at the zoo, so think about bringing along a picnic for lunch (*Rian's Breadbasket* will prepare one for you; see *Eating Out*).

The Rose Test Gardens offer hundreds of varieties of roses, all generously identified. June and September are the best months for seeing Portland's roses at their peak. From the Gardens, you can take the zoo train to the zoo (admission is included in the price of the train ticket), which (among other exhibits) has a children's petting zoo (kids can play with the animals and talk to the birds), and a Ladybug Theater for children. There are also animal "teaching machines," which humans can use to communicate with the animals. You can also send friends a unique, if perhaps unappreciated, gift. "Zoodoo" — solid elephant dung from the zoo's herd, processed and odorless. Open daily.

The zoo is part of a complex that includes the Oregon Museum of Science and Industry (OMSI), the Planetarium, and Western Forestry Center. OMSI is open every day except Christmas; offers a giant walk-through reconstruction of a human heart, an authentic ship's bridge, simulated airplane ride, various traveling exhibits. Admission charge. Western Forestry Center has displays, exhibitions on Oregon's largest industry. Admission charge. The entire complex is on SW Canyon (OMSI, 248-5900; zoo, 226-1561; Forestry Center, 248-5900).

Pittock Mansion – The imposing French Renaissance home built by Henry Pittock, a poor boy who made good as editor of *The Oregonian* at the turn of the century. The grounds are open daily, and are free; the house is open Sundays through Wednesdays in the afternoons. Admission charge. 3229 NW Pittock Dr. (248-4469).

Tryon Creek State Park – The state's first metropolitan park, two miles south of central Portland, with 600 acres of wilderness for biking, hiking, and naturalists (horses are welcome, but there are none for rent). Adjoining Lake Oswego (636-4550).

EAST SIDE

The Grotto – An outdoor chapel, built in a grotto with a ten-story cliff, monastery, and gardens at the top. Fifty-eight acres of grounds are open for contemplation, quiet walks, solitude. Sunday noon mass (from Mother's Day to Labor Day) is held in the Grotto chapel. 8804 NE Skidmore (254-7371).

Crystal Springs Gardens – More than 2,000 rhododendron plants, maintained by the Portland chapter of the American Rhododendron Society. No Portlander would miss the gardens during April and May when first the azaleas, then the rhododendrons, reach their peak. Adjacent is the campus of Reed College. SE 28th Avenue near SE Woodstock.

Mt. Tabor Park – Believed to be the only extinct volcano within a US city's limits. Some of the best views of the city. Between Yamhill and Division, east of SE 60th Ave.

■ **EXTRA SPECIAL:** *Sauvie Island,* largest island in the Columbia River, just north of Portland on US 30. Devoted primarily to farmland, the island is ideal for biking, hiking, picnicking, fishing, or just lolling about for a day. Here, the Oregon Historical Society maintains the *Bybee Howell House,* a restored pre–Civil War farmhouse, open to the public from May to October (free, with donations appreciated). The last Saturday of September is the "Wintering-In" picnic and celebration at the House, when local farmers sell harvest goods.

Columbia River Highway runs east and west of Portland. Drive east for a view of the Columbia River Gorge, with its 2,000-foot cliff and 11 waterfalls.

SOURCES AND RESOURCES

The Visitors Information Center at the Chamber of Commerce is best for brochures, maps, general tourist information and personal help; starting point of Scenic Parkway Drive, which takes in most Portland sights, and ends on the summits of Council Crest, Rocky Butte, and Mt. Tabor overlooking the city. 824 SW 5th Ave. (228-9411).

Oregon State Highway Division offers travel information at 12345 N Union Ave. (open May through October only, 285-1631).

The Portland Guidebook by Linda Lampman and Julie Sterling (The Writing Works, Inc., $4.95) is the best and most comprehensive local guide to Portland and its environs.

All telephone numbers are in the 503 area code unless otherwise indicated.

For Local Coverage – *The Oregonian,* morning daily; *The Oregon Journal,* afternoon daily; *Willamette Week* offers a liberally opinionated study of the city.

For Food – Check *The Portland Guidebook* and the weekly newspaper restaurant reviews.

CLIMATE AND CLOTHES: The good news: It doesn't get too cold in Portland (snow pretty rare); it doesn't get too hot here, either (summer temperatures above 90° only last two or three days). However, it certainly does rain. The months from October through May are the worst. June, July,

August, and September are fairly clear, and the average temperature is in the 70s. That's the time when tourists visit the Portland area, so book ahead.

GETTING AROUND: Bus – Portland's Tri-Met system covers three counties; exact-change-only fare is zoned except within the 340-block downtown shopping area (including Old Town, major shopping malls, Art Museum and Historical Society, riverfront) which is free and called "Fareless Square." Complete route and tourist information (and map of Fareless Square) is available from downtown Customer Assistance Office, 522 SW Yamhill (233-3511 for 24-hour route information).

Taxi – Cabs must be called by phone, or picked up at taxi stations in front of the major hotels. They cannot be hailed in the street. Most hotels have direct phone connections to the two largest companies, Broadway Cab (237-1234); Radio Cab (227-1212).

Car Rental – National firms are represented, though the cheapest local service is provided by Budget Rent-A-Car, 834 SW Broadway (222-9123), and at the airport.

MUSEUMS: Exhibitions and displays of the Pacific Northwest — past and present — are given special emphasis in Portland's fine array of cultural institutions, but the rest of the world is well represented too. The Portland Art Museum, the Oregon Historical Society, and the Pittock Museum are all described above in some detail in *Special Places*. Another notable museum:

First National Center – Portland's tallest building, houses two restaurants and a collection of more than 400 paintings, sculptures, and prints by Oregon artists. Many pieces of art are on view on the main floor. To tour the entire building, call 10 days in advance; it's worth it. Between 3rd and 5th and Jefferson and Columbia (225-2361).

LIBRARIES: The open stacks on the third floor of the *Oregon Historical Society* hold an extensive collection of works on Oregon history and early Indian and pioneer life. For contemporary tourist and travel information, visit the *Central Library*, SW 10th Ave. at Taylor (223-7201).

MAJOR COLLEGES AND UNIVERSITIES: The jewel in Portland's academic crown is justly famous Reed College, 2303 SE Woodstock Blvd. (771-1112), a private, liberal arts college of the highest caliber. Other institutions of learning are the University of Portland, 5000 N Willamette Blvd. (283-7911); Lewis and Clark College, 615 SW Palantine Hill Rd. (244-1181); and Portland State University, 724 SW Harrison (229-4433).

PARKS AND GARDENS: Even the freeways into Portland are divided by banks of wild roses and iris; the city is surrounded by green mountains and garlanded with 145 acres of parkland in the city itself. Washington Park, Pittock Acres Park, Mt. Tabor Park, Crystal Springs Gardens, and Tryon Creek State Park are all described above in some detail in *Special Places*. Other notable Portland parks are:

Council Crest Park, above Portland Heights, 82nd Ave.

Rocky Butte, I-80 north to SE 82nd Ave.

Hoyt Arboretum, 400 SW Fairview Blvd.

Westmoreland Park, SE 22nd Ave. at Bybee.

SPECIAL EVENTS: *The Portland Rose Festival,* featuring everything from beauty queens to bicycle races, runs during the second week of June. *Wintering-In Celebration,* on Sauvie Island, is a harvest festival that's held on the last Saturday of September. For other day-by-day listings, see *The Portland Guidebook.*

SPORTS: Basketball – The 1977 NBA champions, the *Trail Blazers,* play their home games at Memorial Coliseum from October through March: tickets at the Coliseum, 1401 N Wheeler (235-8771), or from the Trail Blazer ticket office, 700 NE Multnomah (234-9291).

Soccer – The Portland *Timbers,* with the North American Soccer League, play at Portland Civic Stadium, May–September. Tickets for the stadium, 1844 SW Morrison (248-4245) or Timbers ticket office, 806 SW Broadway (245-6464).

Baseball – The *Beavers,* a farm team for the Pittsburgh *Pirates*, play at Portland Civic Stadium, June–August. Tickets sold at the stadium, 1844 SW Morris (228-7234).

Racing – For racing and parimutuel betting, Portland Meadows Horse Race Track, 1001 N Schmeer Road (285-9144). The season lasts from January to May; and Multnomah Kennel Club Dog Race Track, 22 3rd Ave., Fairview (15 miles from city) (665-2191). Season from May to September.

Bicycling – Rent from Cycle Craft, SW 12th Ave. at Morrison (222-3821). Numerous city and country rides are described in *The Portland Guidebook.*

Fishing – For chinook salmon, try the lower Willamette or Willamette Slough from March through early May. Steelhead are found in the Clackamas River, and its tributary, Eagle Creek, from December through February. But best of all (for fly fishermen) are the Toutle, Washougal and Wind Rivers in southwest Washington state, where you can do battle with the warrior steelhead.

Golf – The metropolitan area has 18 public courses, 9 private clubs. Best public course is Forest Hills Country Club, 20 minutes from downtown in Cornelius (a plus for business golfers — it has showers; 648-4143).

Skiing – The closest is Mt. Hood Meadows; better is Mt. Bachelor, 180 miles from Portland at Bend.

Tennis – The Park Bureau runs four indoor and dozens of outdoor courts. The indoor courts (and a few of those outside) may be reserved by calling 248-4325. Otherwise, first come, first serve. Major tennis center is in Buckman Park, Portland Tennis Center, 324 NE 12th Ave. (233-5959 for reservations).

THEATER: For absolutely up-to-date offerings and performance times, check the daily and weekly publications listed above.

Portland has 13 theaters which offer performances, some locally produced, others traveling shows. Colleges and universities in the area also produce plays and musicals. Best bets for shows: *Portland Civic Auditorium* (226-2876); *Paramount Cabaret* (box office, 226-0034; concert information, 225-0750); *Portland Civic Theatre* (226-3048).

MUSIC: Concerts and opera are held by *Oregon Symphony Orchestra* (228-1353); *Portland Opera Association* (248-4741); free summer concerts in Washington Park between late July and September (information, 248-4287).

NIGHTCLUBS AND NIGHTLIFE: Pop music, jazz, Dixieland, folk, and rock are all offered at Portland's many pubs, taverns, and nightclubs. Current favorites: *Beachcomber,* for jazz, Lake Oswego (636-6677); the *Old Orleans,* for Dixieland, 519 SW 11th Ave. (224-1124); *Earth Tavern,* multimedia shows with music, film, plays, 732 NW 21st Ave. (227-4573); *Red Lion Motor Inn,* 909 N Hayden Island Dr. (283-4466), disco and big band music.

SINS: Though residents claim resolutely that "there is no sin in Portland, we outlawed it years ago," there is; it just isn't very spirited. The mountains, the nearby sea, and the Oregon wildlands are too preoccupying for most residents. Portland is a clean-living city, and so, while the lovelies stripped to bikinis for a swim in the Forecourt Fountain that fronts the Civic Auditorium, 222 SW Clay St., have been known to arouse *lust* in the hearts of men prone to that sort of thing, any one of those males — given a choice between the girl and a season ticket to the Trailblazers' games — would take the tickets and run. *Pride* flourishes among those who know how to pronounce Glisan (the name of a street; rhymes with listen); and *envy* toward the first Portland gardener to produce a red tomato before September. *Gluttony?* It stirs over the Dungeness crab legs sold at $10 a pound at Plancich's Fish Company, 300 NW 13th Ave. — and, since that indulgence can get expensive — over Mrs. Neusihin's pickles, the Portland exclusive that wowed Craig Claiborne when he came to town.

LOCAL SERVICES: Business Services – Contact the Business Service Bureau, 1208 SW 13th Ave. (228-4107); Carlson's Secretarial Services, 117 N State, Lake Oswego (636-7661).

Mechanic – Tune Up Experts, 7510 NE Glisan (253-9548). Ask for John.

Babysitting – Wee-Ba-Bee Attendants (244-8835).

■ **TAKE SOME PORTLAND HOME WITH YOU:** Fresh chinook and silver salmon are two of Portland's best known exports, and airlines are accustomed to seeing passengers board an outbound flight with a cold fin under one arm. Tony's Fish Market, 14th and Washington, Oregon City (656-2870), will supply fresh salmon and crab, specially packed to travel.

BEST IN TOWN

CHECKING IN: Portland is not a city filled with romantic, cozy, historic little hotels tucked away in quaint sections of town. With the notable exception of the Benson, which is older, most Portland hotels are relatively new; but all are convenient and comfortable, and offer a range of facilities in keeping with their price. Expect to pay around $50 (or slightly more) for a double room in one of the hotels we've noted as expensive; $30 to $40 in the moderate range; $15 to $25 at the Mallory, where a modest price does not mean much sacrifice.

The Westin Benson – Built in 1913 by wealthy logger Simon Benson to be Portland's premier hotel. It still is — though the rooms don't really offer the kind of traditional atmosphere you might expect. The hotel, however, now owned by the Westin Corporation, is comfortable and convenient, with a quite good *London Grill* restaurant (open daily) and a respectable *Trader Vic's* as well (closed Sundays). 342 rooms; suites. Pay garage. 309 SW Broadway (228-9611). Expensive.

Portland Marriott – More than a million dollars' worth of millwork went into this Northwest version. It has rooms for 500; two restaurants — both with views of the Willamette River; meeting rooms; banquet facilities; indoor pool; and exercise rooms. 1401 SW Front Ave. (226-7600). Expensive to moderate.

Thunderbird–Red Lion Motor Inns – This giant complex on the Columbia River, just between Portland and Vancouver (Washington), is 10 minutes from the airport. These two inns, together with the *Thunderbird Inn* at the Quay on the

Washington side, provide 810 rooms. Fine restaurants, free parking, live entertainment (there's a grand ballroom at the *Red Lion*), and a large convention center. For either Thunderbird: 1401 N Hayden Island Dr. (283-2111). Red Lion: 909 N Hayden Island Dr. (283-4466). Expensive to moderate.

Red Lion/Lloyd Center – The largest hotel in Oregon and across the street from the largest shopping mall in the Pacific Northwest, the *Red Lion* has 20,000 square feet of meeting space, 526 rooms, 3 restaurants, and 3 lounges. In summer, the best rooms are those cabanas around the pool. Lloyd Center (288-6111). Expensive to moderate.

Mallory Motor Hotel – A step down from the Jacuzzi tubs and poolside cabanas, but a comfortable, quiet hotel that offers a good room and adequate restaurant facilities at a reasonable price. Just across the street from the Civic Theater. 144 rooms; free parking. 729 SW 15th Ave. (223-6311). Inexpensive.

EATING OUT: Portland shines pretty brightly as an eating place. The impact of a certain style of restaurant — small, personal, with creative cuisine (often a mixture of several styles of food, like American and Oriental, macrobiotic and vegetarian) and inviting decor — has had dramatic effects on local eating habits. Residents are out of their own kitchens and around town as never before. Often, the new restaurants are owned by young people who are intensely interested in healthy food in a homey, comfortable atmosphere. Below, our choices of the most interesting dining opportunities, but don't stop there. As you explore any area of the city, you're likely to come across a "find" of your own. Our restaurant selections range in price from $40 or more for a dinner for two in the expensive range, $20 to $35 in the moderate, and $10 or less in the inexpensive range. Prices do not include drinks, wine or tips.

Belinda's – This place is next to a laundromat with an excellent view of a public pay phone, yet it continues to be one of the finest French restaurants in Portland. The wine list is extensive and the entrées — veal, pork, beef, and seafood — are gently coddled in rare French sauces. The owner, who presides over his own stove, thrives on detail. Look for fresh herbs in the salad (he grows them at the rear door) and sample from the scrumptious dessert tray. The house pâté is another must. Open Tuesdays through Saturdays for dinner only; brunch on Sundays. Reservations recommended. Major credit cards. 8324 SE 17th Ave. (232-6606). Expensive.

Rian's Eating Establishment – A favorite downtown lunch and cocktail meeting place. Sandwiches, as well as quiche, chicken Kiev, crab. Closed Sundays. Reservations. All credit cards. In Morgan's Alley (downtown shopping mall), through the wrought-iron gate between SW Park and Broadway (222-9996). Expensive.

Sweet Tibbie Dunbar – A former golf course clubhouse that has achieved genuine charm as a redecorated English pub. House policy is to accept reservations for only one-third of the available tables, so you can go without a reservation and spend a pleasant half-hour in the pub enjoying a drink. Lunches and dinners (Saturday and Sunday dinners only). Credit cards. 718 NE 12th Ave. (232-1801). Moderate.

L'Escargot – At this fine French restaurant, the old oak tables are accented with fresh flowers, flickering candles, and gleaming silver, and the menu features the market's best buy of the day. Try the Pacific salmon delicately sautéed with cantharel mushrooms or the crêpes with one of the chef's savory salads. There are also desserts for every desire. Closed Sundays. Reservations recommended. Major credit cards. 1987 NW Kearney St. (223-6964). Expensive.

Rheinlander – A good spot to feed the kids on grand portions of good German food. Not the place to go for an intime rendezvous for two, since it's filled with families who enjoy being serenaded by a strolling accordian player. Open daily. Reservations. All credit cards. 5035 NE Sandy Blvd. (288-5503). Moderate.

Besides Rian's Eating Establishment, two other Rian's restaurants deserve mention:

Rian's Fish and Ale House – Fine fish and chips, as well as other seafood. Open daily. No reservations. Major credit cards. 600 SW Beaverton-Hillsdale Hwy. (292-0191). Inexpensive.

Rian's Breadbasket – Soup, sandwiches, tamale pie for weekday lunches. For a picnic, they'll prepare an "Emergency Kit" — sandwich, fruit, dessert. Closed Sundays. No reservations. No credit cards. 1100 6th Ave. (in the Standard Plaza, 223-6111). Inexpensive.

Dan and Louis Oyster Bar – A Portland institution. Clams, crab, oysters — quickly, simply, and deliciously prepared. Opened in the days when restaurants didn't worry about decor, and it's still the same today (which means it has a distinct, turn-of-the-century style). Open daily. No reservations. No credit cards. 208 SW Ankeny (227-5906). Inexpensive.

4 and 20 Blackbirds – A greater contrast to Dan and Louis couldn't be imagined. The building is a former mail-order warehouse. The old counter and pillars are intact, but everything else has been swathed in pop-art yellows, blacks, and whites, covered with mirrors and chrome. The pillars have been turned into trees, on which are perched — you guessed it! — the blackbirds. Food is excellent, lovingly prepared quiches, soups, sandwiches. Lunch and dinner. Closed weekends. No reservations. Country Square, Lake Oswego (636-2757). Inexpensive.

Organ Grinder – Not so much a restaurant as a performance at which you can buy pizza and beer. The place has seven — maybe more — pipe organs connected to one keyboard, at which rock tunes are played to accompany silent films. No reservations. Open daily. No credit cards. 5085 SE 82nd Ave. (771-1178). Inexpensive.

Original Pancake House – No kin to the national chain of nearly the same name. From lingonberry to German pancakes, these are Portland's best, and well loved in the city. Closed Mondays and Tuesdays. No reservations. No credit cards. 8600 SW Barbur Blvd. (246-9007). Inexpensive.

Victoria's Nephew – Checkered tablecloths, potted ferns, a huge old "fireside chat" radio on the counter, and tables on the sidewalk; a great place for lunch or English-style high tea. Closed weekends. No reservations. No credit cards. 212 SW Stark (223-7299). Inexpensive.

Rose's Delicatessen – Delicate blintzes, delicious cakes, gigantic sandwiches. The food isn't kosher, but the atmosphere — and the quality of the sandwiches — is vintage New York. Open daily. No reservations (expect a wait during prime meal times). No credit cards. 315 NW 23rd Ave. (227-5181). Inexpensive.

The Skyline – Stuck on an island in the middle of Skyline Boulevard (a major road), this is a drive-in that serves hamburgers and the usual roadside fare. So why do we include it? Because the hamburgers are terrific, and because it's only a five-minute drive from the Portland Zoo complex, where it's easy to work up a good appetite. Has a walk-in, sit-down restaurant inside. Open daily. No reservations. No credit cards. 1313 NW Skyline Blvd. (292-6727, 227-5187). Inexpensive.

Taco Houses No. 1 & 2 – Tacos and beer; the best in the city. Open daily. No reservations. No credit cards. No. 1, 3255 NE 82nd Ave. (252-1695); No. 2, 3550 SE Powell Blvd. (234-6401). Inexpensive.

ST. LOUIS

Ask a St. Louis resident today what he thinks of the city and his answer will drive you crazy with its ambivalence. To live in St. Louis is to be slightly schizophrenic about the place — to love it for what it may be and often to hate it for what it still is.

Only a decade ago, St. Louis had come close to being a forgotten city, a place viewed by most of the country, when mentioned at all, as "first in shoes, first in booze, and last in the National League." But during the late 60s the city started slowly to replenish itself, and now the results of this civic second wind are beginning to show. In old neighborhoods and near suburbs, in the downtown area with its successful new convention center, around Forest Park and along the river, renovation projects are underway. And although committee residents have seen too many false starts in the past to take this spirit of resurgence quite at face value, there *is* a cautious new quality in town: pride.

What accounts for this change of attitude? The past, for one thing, no longer a rote recitation of wagon trains and "Gateway to the West." While the frontier period is not being overlooked, the city is more concerned with exploring the cultural influence, and restoring the physical evidence, of the many diverse ethnic groups which created it: the French, whose elegant mansions still adorn the city's Southside; German burghers, who built solid, but less florid homes in the same area; the Italians and Serbs, whose working-class neighborhoods are still vital communities. Most positive of all are the signs that this interest in heritage and history is directed as much at developing the city's future as investigating its past.

Downtown St. Louis was once a true mercantile center, the profitable middleman in a river of goods that left the city's docks and depots to be sold not only to St. Louisans, but to the residents of small rural communities throughout surrounding states — people for whom the words "the city" could find no grander fulfillment than the buildings, shops, and department stores of downtown St. Louis. Its decline over the years left a vacuum never quite filled by the safe, clean suburban shopping centers that replaced it. Now, businesses are moving downtown once again, drawn by newly constructed office and retail space built and rented at special rates through a city-created tax inducement program. The just-opened convention center and subsequent development of city blocks around it are the first stirrings of a reinvigorated downtown.

Take a walk along the riverfront. There, in the midst of St. Louis revived, is St. Louis eternal — the river and its burden of pleasure craft, barges, and riverboats. Today, St. Louis is the country's busiest inland port, and at the center of it is still Laclede's Landing, where stands the city's largest remaining group of 19th-century buildings, along streets that were part of the original

French fur trading colony laid out by Pierre Laclede Liquest in the 1760s. Nearby is moored the showboat *Goldenrod*, and within walking distance are berths for the riverboats that still journey up and down the Mississippi. And above it all is the gleaming Gateway Arch, a stunning architectural achievement from every perspective.

If there is something essentially ambivalent in the city or its residents, it may be the inevitable result of forging a coherent culture from the two powerful traditions that are the city's heritage: the conservatism of the Old South (but St. Louis is *not* a Southern city) and the unbridled ambition and lack of reserve that fueled early frontier life. There is a large element of truth in the complaint that St. Louis acts like it is an outsized small town. In part, this is because of the pace of life: No one will ever accuse it of being exhausting. But that is not all. In what other American metropolis of two and a half million souls was the sale of *The Happy Hooker* banned?

And yet — during its regular season the St. Louis Symphony's Saturday performances are routinely sold out; the Repertory Theatre of St. Louis is one of the fastest growing companies in the country; the Opera Theater of St. Louis has won raves from coast to coast; Cardinal fans (the baseball Cardinals; St. Louis' football team is also the Cardinals) happily face the rigors of a doubleheader on a typically muggy, enervating summer's day with no more protection from the heat than a "cold one"; and rabid hockey fans risk mayhem and standing-room-only crowds to watch the Blues in NHL playoffs.

The city is a bit paradoxical, then, and many residents maintain an ambivalent attitude toward its present and future. They are heartened that a significant number of people are choosing to live in the city, rather than in distant and antiseptic suburbs; but they worry that the gradual shift of population out of the city and into St. Louis County nonetheless continues. They are encouraged that a whole new generation of St. Louis homeowners are discovering urban neighborhoods and the joys of "do-it-yourself" renovation; but are dismayed by the "ghost town" look of razed blocks and abandoned buildings which still await someone's money and effort. And they are delighted that right now St. Louis has more music to hear, places to go, restaurants to sample, and events to attend for resident and visitor alike than in any time in the past 15 years, much of it in the renovated and restored downtown and riverfront areas; but they remember Gaslight Square, the chic Central West End pub and coffeehouse quarter of the early 60s that was literally killed off by crime and then left to ruin, and they question whether any entertainment area can thrive for long if fundamental economic and social problems aren't solved at the same time.

Ask a St. Louis resident what he likes about the city today, and the answer will probably be a long and enthusiastic list of attractions, but wait a minute, and watch amazement light up his face as he hears what he's saying.

ST. LOUIS AT-A-GLANCE

SEEING THE CITY: A tour of St. Louis must begin along the Mississippi River, where the city began, and the riverfront offers an irresistible focal point: the Gateway Arch, soaring 630 feet above the levee. From its top, all of St. Louis is visible, and miles of countryside beyond, on both sides of the river. Expect a wait for the train to the top (in summer, a long one) and spend the time walking around the base of the Arch, gathering impressions, or visiting the Museum of Westward Expansion in the plaza between the two base columns. 11 N 4th St. (museum phone, 425-4465).

Built in 1966 by architect Eero Saarinen, the Arch is so delicately engineered that its last segment — that arch so far above the ground that spans and connects the two columns — had to wait to be installed until the weather was perfect, so the steel would neither contract nor expand a fraction until in place.

SPECIAL PLACES: Though it's most convenient to get around St. Louis by car, most areas lend themselves to a walking tour. You can park your car for free along the waterfront, for example, and explore on foot the levee, Laclede's Landing, and downtown.

RIVERFRONT AND DOWNTOWN

The Levee – Moored on the river side of the cobblestoned levee are St. Louis' most famous riverboats: the *Goldenrod Showboat,* for dinners and old-fashioned "meller-dramers," and the *Huck Finn* and *Tom Sawyer* for day and night trips up and down the Mississippi.

On the city side of the levee is Jefferson Expansion Memorial Parkway, with the Arch at its center, and in one corner, the Old Cathedral, which is, naturally, the oldest cathedral west (just west) of the Mississippi, 2nd and Walnut Sts. (231-3250). It started its calling as a log cabin in 1764 when the city was founded and took its present form in 1834.

Laclede's Landing – In the 50 years after the Civil War, St. Louis became rich as well as famous, and the entire downtown section boomed and bloomed. What's left of the bloom is Laclede's Landing, a ten-block area just north of the levee on the far side of massive Eads Bridge with some fine examples of cast-iron-fronted buildings (Raeder Place, formerly the Old Missouri Hotel at 806 N 1st, is best of all). It's now the scene of active renovation and home to a new generation of restaurants, galleries, and small shops. Some suggestions while wandering the area: *Kennedy's 2nd Street Company* for a lunch of chili, burgers, and sandwiches, 612 N 2nd St. (421-3655); *The Old Spaghetti Factory* for inexpensive Italian dishes and an old European decor, 727 N 1st St. (621-0276); for a good catfish dinner or oyster appetizer, *2nd Street Diner and Fish Market,* 721 N 2nd St. (436-2222).

Old Courthouse – This courthouse was just two years old in 1847 when an American slave named Dred Scott tested the legality of slavery by suing his owner. The case was heard here; and here, when it was lost, the course of slavery was set. It was the same year Abe Lincoln visited St. Louis. Most interesting today is the building's cast-iron dome, completed in 1859, and the mural which adorns its interior. Two courtrooms have been reconstructed (one from 1870 and one from 1890; the Dred Scott courtroom has been demolished) and the building houses the Museum of Westward Expansion. Also available, of course, is much information on the complete history and full impact of the Dred Scott case. Open daily. Free. 4th St. at Market (425-4465).

St. Louis Sports Hall of Fame – A must for sports fans, with short film clips of various World Series, and memorabilia of different sports and sports figures. Special emphasis, of course, on the Cardinals' own Stan Musial. Open daily. Admission charge. In Busch Memorial Stadium, between Gates 5 and 6, at Walnut St. (421-6790).

Eugene Field House – Primarily an antique toy collection, with some artifacts of the famous St. Louis author Eugene Field, who wrote *Little Boy Blue.* Best to visit at Christmas, when the House prepares a complete Victorian Christmas display. Closed Mondays. Admission charge. 634 S Broadway (421-4689).

SOUTH ST. LOUIS

South St. Louis is primarily German, Italian, and Eastern European. The most determinedly ethnic neighborhood in the area is the Hill (between South Kingshighway and Shaw). From its bocce courts and front yard shrines, to its green, white, and red hydrants, the Hill is 20 blocks of solid Italian consciousness, and great for walking and snacking. Two suggestions: *John Volpi & Co.*, 5256 Daggett (772-8550), closed Mondays, for salami, prosciutto, and Italian sausage; *Amighetti Bakery*, 5141 Wilson (776-2855), closed Sundays and Mondays, for fresh bread and carry-out poorboys.

Anheuser-Busch Brewery – The makers of Michelob and Budweiser offer daily one-hour tours of the brewery and grounds, featuring, naturally, a healthy sampling of the King of Beers. Best on the tour: the stables, a registered landmark building, where the mighty Clydesdale horses reside when they're not on parade. Closed Saturdays, Sundays, and holidays. Free. 610 Pestalozzi St. (577-2626).

Missouri Botanical Garden (Shaw's Garden) – After Henry Shaw got very rich with a hardware store in downtown St. Louis, he decided to repay the city by opening his Southside garden estate to the public. Since 1860 its reputation and its collection have grown apace. Highlights of the 79-acre park: the Climatron, a geodesic-domed tropical greenhouse; Seiwa-En, a beautiful Japanese garden opened in 1977; and the Scented Garden, a special collection of scented plants for the blind which may be touched and handled, with descriptions and explanations in Braille. Open daily. Admission charge. 2101 Tower Grove (577-5100).

Soulard Market – Soulard is the name of both the market and the neighborhood which surrounds it. Since 1847, when the ground was given to the city to be used as a public farmers' market, Soulard Market has been open for business — busiest on Saturday mornings, when everything from live rabbits to homemade apple butter is for sale, but offering something most days. The outside stalls around the main building open whenever fresh goods — meat or poultry, vegetables, fruit, farmers' canned goods or home specialties — come into the city. Closed Sundays, Mondays, and Tuesdays; most active Fridays and Saturdays. 7th St. at Soulard (622-4180).

CENTRAL WEST END

Named for its location along famous Forest Park at the western edge of the St. Louis city limits, Central West End is the city's most sophisticated and elegant section — a warren of small shops, pleasant restaurants, and ornate mansions in the fashionable "places" (private boulevards maintained by the residents; grandest of the grand are Portland Place and Westmoreland Place). All is grist for the walkers' mill, even the private "places," so spend some time just exploring.

Maryland Plaza – A stroller's delight, between Kingshighway and Euclid Avenue, just around the corner from the *Chase Park Plaza Hotel* (see *Best in Town*). With the best people-watching in town, this area is a magnet for politicians, media types, and other glitzy characters. A potpourri of shops and restaurants makes for good food and great buys, too. Some suggestions: 26 Maryland Plaza, an arcade of boutiques featuring everything from seashells and antique clothing to herbs; *Tricia Woo*, 308 N Euclid (367-1869), selling beautiful handmade quilts, unusual toys, and children's and women's clothes. For a bite to eat, if you have money enough left over, try *Europa 390*, 390 N Euclid (367-4562), for lunch of sandwiches and imported beer; *Llywelyn's Welsh Pub*, 4747 McPherson (361-3003), for a plowman's lunch or soup (and of course British beers); or *Balaban's*, 405 N Euclid (381-8085), for a dinner of seafood, French cuisine, or their unusual dinner crêpes. All stores in the area carry the *Maryland Plaza Guide*, which lists shops in the neighborhood. For monthly shows of photography and paintings, try the *Kamp Gallery*, 339 N Euclid (361-6711).

St. Louis Cathedral – It is not just the size of the Cathedral — immense — which is awesome; it is the mosaics which adorn almost the whole interior space — beautiful, ethereal, light bearing; millions of pieces of stone and glass in thousands of shades depicting saints, apostles, and religious scenes. Considered one of the finest examples of mosaic work in this hemisphere, and not to be missed. Tours conducted on Sundays at 12:45 PM. Free. Lindell at Newstead (533-2824).

Powell Hall – Built in 1925 as a movie house, in the days when movie theaters were expected to be miniature replicas of the sumptuous glitter of Hollywood, Powell Hall was renovated in 1965 for the St. Louis Symphony Orchestra, and the best way to see it is by attending a performance. During the intermission you can stroll the aisles and admire the rich velvet seats, marble floors, and 24-karat gold-leaf accents on fluting and floors. On the Grand Tier level is the bar which was given Powell Hall by New York's Metropolitan Opera House. Tours can be arranged during the day. Free. 718 N Grand Blvd. at Delmar (533-2500).

■ **EXTRA SPECIAL:** An hour south from St. Louis just off rt. 55 is *Ste. Genevieve*, one of the oldest permanent settlements west of the Mississippi (established in 1735), and a town which has maintained its bounty of old homes with admirable care. A number of the oldest homes are open daily, as is an excellent old inn, *St. Gemme Beauvais*, 78 N Main St. (314 883-5744). It's a beautifully furnished, eight-room village inn with the best food in town. And not to be missed, if you are in the area during the second weekend of August: Ste. Genevieve's Jour de Fête, when all the old homes are open for a festive two days.

SOURCES AND RESOURCES

The Convention and Visitors Bureau publishes a free guide which lists special events (festivals, street fairs, house tours) and other tourist information; also has maps, brochures and will help with individual problems. 1300 Convention Plaza (421-1023), with a full-time booth on the *Sgt. Floyd*, one of the boats on display along the riverfront beneath the Arch.

The *St. Louis Annual Guide* (published by *St. Louis* magazine, $3.95) is a comprehensive local guide to the city. *St. Louis for Families*, by Paula Knoderer, Carol Hollander, and Bob Broeg (Bethany Press, $3.50), covers every possibility for "doing" the city with kids.

All telephone numbers are in the 314 area code unless otherwise indicated.

For Local Coverage – *St. Louis Globe-Democrat*, morning daily; *St. Louis Post-Dispatch*, evening daily (Thursday's edition carries a calendar of coming events); *The Argus* is the city's famous black community newspaper, published every Friday; *The St. Louis Magazine* is a monthly city magazine with a calendar of events, reviews, and features on the city. The *St. Louis Business Journal* is a weekly update on the business scene.

The St. Louis Symphony Society arranges special tours of any part of the city, with proceeds going to the society's treasury. Information, 712 N Grand Blvd. (533-2500).

The American Institute of Architects has architectural maps of the city, pinpointing interesting buildings (call 621-3484 for information). The Landmarks Association has information on neighborhoods and restoration projects (call 421-6474).

CLIMATE AND CLOTHES: Bad news in St. Louis is summer — from mid-June well into September the heat and humidity are wilting. Dress coolly and be prepared for the worst. Autumn is crisp, cool, and beautiful; winter, cold but with little snow. It rains during all seasons, but spring is likely to be especially stormy, with sudden winds and hard rains blowing up quickly against ink-black skies during tornado season — May and early June.

GETTING AROUND: Bus – The Bi-State bus system serves most of the metropolitan area. Route information, maps, 707 N 1st St. (231-2345).

Taxi – Cabs can be picked up at the major department stores and hotels, hailed in the streets, or ordered by phone. Major companies are Laclede Cab (652-3456); Yellow Cabs (361-2345); and Checker Cab (725-5600).

Car Rental – St. Louis is served by all the major national companies, several have booths at the airport as well as around the city. A reliable local service is Enterprise Leasing, with nine locations around the city (call 863-0055 for information).

MUSEUMS: The story of the movement west is told in murals, graphic displays, and film sequences at the Museum of Westward Expansion under the Arch (*Special Places*). Other museums of interest in St. Louis are:

St. Louis Art Museum, in Forest Park (721-0067). Closed Mondays.

Museum of Science and Natural History, Oak Knoll Park, Clayton (two miles west from Forest Park, 726-2888). Closed Mondays.

Medical Museum and National Museum of Quackery, 3839 Lindell Blvd. (371-5225). Closed Sundays, Labor Day through Easter. Admission charge.

McDonnell Planetarium, Forest Park (535-5810), has special star shows as well as exhibits. Closed Mondays. Admission charge.

MAJOR COLLEGES AND UNIVERSITIES: There are three major universities in the St. Louis area: St. Louis University, founded by the Jesuits in 1818 and the oldest college in the United States west of the Mississippi, Grand at Lindell (658-2222); Washington University, founded by a predecessor of T. S. Eliot, too shy to name the school for himself (at the western end of Forest Park situated in a beautiful campus, 889-5000), and University of Missouri, St. Louis, 8001 Natural Bridge Rd. (553-0111).

PARKS AND GARDENS: Forest Park is America's third largest city park (Central Park and the Portland, Oregon, park system are larger) and it offers far too much to see in even a long day. Highlights are: the zoo, run for years by the much-loved Marlin Perkins. You can visit the exhibits — "Big Cat Country," the famous Monkey House, the walk-through Bird Cage — on foot or by zoo train. The Children's Zoo charges a modest admission price, and you must buy a ticket for the train; all else free (information, 781-0900). Art Museum, on Art Hill, open Wednesdays through Sundays, 2:30–9:30 PM on Tuesdays, maintains a wide-ranging collection and hosts traveling exhibits (721-0067). Jefferson Memorial houses all of Charles Lindbergh's mementos from the famous flight, and has a museum of river history (361-1424). Open daily. Municipal Opera House, in summer especially, is a favorite of residents (361-1900).

SPECIAL EVENTS: *The International Festival* is held during the three-day Memorial Day weekend, across from the zoo in Forest Park. The major attraction is a long line of booths selling ethnic foods, prepared by local groups of different nationalities. *The Historic Pilgrimage,* usually the end of September, is a nine-day program of guided tours to St. Louis' historic homes, museums, and historical sites. Information from the Missouri Historical Association, Jefferson Memorial Building, Forest Park, St. Louis, MO 73112. German food and culture is celebrated during the *Strassenfest,* a weekend celebration usually held in July or August between Market, Olive, and 15th Sts. The Visitors Bureau will have exact dates.

SPORTS: St. Louisans love their professional teams, and sports events are well attended.

Baseball – Busch Memorial Stadium (Broadway at Walnut St., downtown) is home for the National League *Cardinals* (information, 421-3060), who play May–September. Tickets are available at the Stadium and from Famous-Barr and Stix, Baer & Fuller department stores.

Football – The NFL's *Cardinals* (information, 421-1600) are available at Busch Memorial Stadium only.

Hockey – The *Blues* play NHL hockey at the Checkerdome, 5700 Oakland (644-0900).

Horse Racing – Thoroughbred racing at Cahokia Downs, rt. 460, about 20 minutes from St. Louis; harness racing at Fairmount Park, rt. 40 East.

Bicycling – The largest biking event in St. Louis is the Moonlight Ramble, a 17-mile bike ride that starts at 2 AM on the last Sunday of every August and lasts until dawn. American Youth Hostel will have information (644-3560). Biking is always good in Forest Park and bikes can be rented from the Forest Park Boathouse from April to mid-October (information, 367-3423).

Golf – Forest Park has two public courses, 9 and 18 holes respectively. The 18-hole course has a reputation for being tough, but greens and tees are not in the best condition on either. Best public course in the city is the 9-hole course at Ruth Park, 8211 Groby Road (727-4800). It's open all year, modest greens fee.

Tennis – Best for the visitor are the courts at Dwight F. Davis Tennis Center in Forest Park, open during daylight hours; permits for daily play obtained at the Center (information, 367-0220).

THEATER: For absolutely up-to-date offerings and performance times, check the daily and monthly publications listed above. For dinner and a show, especially with children, is the *Goldenrod Showboat,* prototype for Edna Ferber's *Showboat,* where nightly melodramas demand boos and hisses for the villain. Moored at the levee (information, 621-3311). Other choices: the fine *Repertory Theatre of St. Louis,* 136 Edgar Rd. (968-4925); the *American Theater,* 9th St. at St. Charles (231-7000). The *Municipal Opera House* in Forest Park offers its summer stock program of musicals, a St. Louis summer tradition. About 1,400 seats every performance are free; line up outside the Muny about 6:30 PM (361-1900).

MUSIC: Concerts and opera from: *St. Louis Symphony* at Powell Hall (information, 533-2500); *Opera Theater of St. Louis*, Loretto-Hilton Theater (961-0171).

NIGHTCLUBS AND NIGHTLIFE: The tempo of the St. Louis revival is ragtime, and you can hear it at the *National Ragtime Festival,* a five-day ragtime splurge, held in June every year. *Kennedy's 2nd Street Co.,* 612 N 2nd St. (421-3655), features country music Thursdays through Sundays;

Muddy Water Saloon, 724 N 1st St. (421-5335), has consistently good progressive jazz. *Fourth and Pine* (241-2184) has nightly music and a spacious dance floor; *Blarney Stone,* 716 N 1st St. (231-8171), has Irish folk music and good Irish coffee and ale; *Goldenrod,* 400 N Wharf St. (621-3311), has live melodrama. Wednesdays through Sundays.

SINS: The town whose *pride* is a baseball team, the St. Louis Cardinals, also likes to brag that its *sloth* is confined to the zoo (in Forest Park, 781-0900), and that *lust* is equally well penned up, along the 4200 block of Washington and Olive Sts. *Gluttony* provides cheaper thrills yet; the Cleopatra is a sundae dished up at *Cyrano's,* 1059 S Big Bend (721-6500), that turns its tricks with vanilla ice cream topped with a chocolate nut–hot fudge concoction called Elmer's Gold Brick that wraps itself around the ice cream and then hardens.

LOCAL SERVICES: Business Services – Contact Clayton Business Service, 34 N Brentwood (721-3842).

Mechanic – Mike's Service Station, 7500 Big Bend (781-8126), can work on most foreign cars as well as all American automobiles.

Babysitting – A number of agencies are listed in the Yellow Pages, but most will be more expensive than two nonprofessional organizations that provide conscientious babysitters: Missouri Baptist Hospital (432-1212), which provides nursing students with good references and their own transportation; Maryville College (434-4100), which sends trustworthy students. Both institutions are tightly run, relatively strict, and careful.

BEST IN TOWN

CHECKING IN: Whether you want to be within walking distance of the levee, smack-dab downtown, on either end of Forest Park, or conveniently near Lambert Field Airport, quality hotels are available. Prices range from $60 to $70 for a double in our expensive category, $45 to $60 in the moderate, $30 to $45 for an inexpensive hotel.

Marriott Pavilion – In the midst of rebuilt downtown. The "Pavilion" of its title is the Spanish Pavilion, jewel of the 1964 New York World's Fair, dismantled and moved to St. Louis by the then-Mayor Alfonso Cervantes amid great controversy. The pavilion now makes up the two-story lobby of the Marriott, where it is a great success. The hotel offers a coffee shop, two restaurants, and a bar. 341 rooms; free garage, pool, sauna. 1 Broadway (421-1776). Expensive.

Sheraton St. Louis – On the banks of the Mississippi, the hotel has many rooms with river views. All of them have color TV, telephones, and other standard amenities. There are also bars, a dining room and café, and a swimming pool. 910 N 7th St. (231-5100). Expensive.

Chase Park Plaza – The grand old hotel of St. Louis, where limousines routinely line the entrance drive, and celebrities are regular guests. Made an official landmark in 1977, the Chase is beautiful to behold. It isn't an intimate little hotel, with 821 rooms carved from an original 1192, but its prices are surprisingly modest, with all the amenities one would expect of a grand hotel. The new owners are currently modernizing and sprucing up the guest rooms. Barber shop, three restaurants, four bars, shops, garage for guests next door. 212 N Kingshighway (361 2500 or toll-free, 800 325-3391). Moderate.

Cheshire Inn and Lodge – The very image of an English country inn, one block west of Forest Park. Close neighbors are no longer surprised by the English double-decker bus which fetches hotel guests from the airport; the theme is embellished with English antiques in the rooms. Pool, good restaurant, 110 rooms, free parking. Clayton Rd. at Skinker (647-7300). Moderate.

Clayton Inn – This modern hotel in one of St. Louis's wealthy suburbs provides good service, spacious rooms decorated in contemporary style, and fine facilities. There are two restaurants including the Top of the Sevens (closed Sundays) which has a panoramic view of the city, a piano bar, health club with indoor and outdoor pools, sauna, exercise room, and whirlpool; 220 rooms. 7750 Carondelet Ave. (726-5400). Moderate.

Marriott Motor Hotel – At Lambert Field Airport, half an hour from downtown. The hotel features extensive recreational facilities — two pools, tennis courts, putting greens, sauna and exercise rooms — and is good both for business people on short visits and families on the road who'd like to stretch after a day of travel. 433 rooms, free parking. I-70 at the airport (423-9700). Expensive.

Forest Park Hotel – An older hotel undergoing successful renovation, just two blocks from the Chase in the Central West End. Half the hotel is given over to permanent residents, leaving about 100 rooms available for visitors. Hotel has a dining room, coffee shop, barber and beauty shops, cleaners, outdoor pool, and free parking. 4910 W Pine Blvd. (361-3500). Inexpensive.

EATING OUT: Considering St. Louis's large Italian community, it is hardly surprising that the city's premier restaurant serves Italian haute cuisine or that its name is Tony's. But Tony's is more than just good; it is one of the best in the country, a restaurant with a nationwide clientele who swear by it. And like any really fine restaurant, it is expensive. What is more surprising is the host of good restaurants which complement Tony's and the wide variety of cuisines, and very reasonable prices they offer. Our choices below are grouped into broad price categories — expensive, about $50 for a meal for two; moderate, $25 to $35; inexpensive, $10 to $20 — and are guaranteed to get you into the most interesting corners of the city for lunch or dinner. Prices do not include drinks, wine, or tips.

Tony's – According to the *Wall Street Journal,* Tony's owner, Vince Bommarito, is the Vince Lombardi of the restaurant world — a stickler for detail and a perfectionist. The restaurant started out as a spaghetti house, and has grown into a bit of a masterpiece with lavish service, and waiters who study food and drink the way medical students crib for finals. One warning: Tony's takes no reservations, and the wait on Saturday night can take more than three hours. Open Tuesdays through Saturdays for dinner only. Major credit cards. 862 N Broadway (231-7007). Expensive.

Anthony's – Without knowing, you might be justified in assuming that Anthony's owner was trying to steal Vince Bommarito's thunder; you might even suspect bad blood between the two. Blood there is, but not bad, one hopes; Anthony's is owned and run by Tony Bommarito, Vince's brother and partner in that original spaghetti-house-that-became-king. It's dedicated to light, French cuisine, fresh seafood (a rarity in St. Louis), and service that matches brother Vince's place. Anthony's is open for lunch weekdays as well as dinner Mondays–Saturdays. Reservations accepted. Major credit cards. 10 S Broadway (231-2434). Expensive.

Al's Restaurant – Just north of Laclede's Landing, an unlikely but successful combination of riverboat decor and Italian (and American) dishes. Arguably, it has the best steak in town, as well as a very respectable rack of lamb, and an excellent shrimp de jonghe. Open Mondays through Saturdays for dinner only. Reservations accepted every day except Saturday. Most major credit cards. 1st St. at Biddle (421-6399). Expensive.

Cunetto's House of Pasta – Cunetto's is on the Hill, where everything Italian prospers, and where the heart and soul of good food is pasta, hot, fresh, in a variety of styles, augmented by veal, steak, and Italian specialties. Mondays through Fridays, lunch and dinner; Saturdays, dinner only. No reservations (long waits at dinnertime). Major credit cards. 5453 Magnolia (781-1135). Moderate.

Rich & Charlie's Pasta House – Some years ago two young waiters from Tony's decided to start a place of their own. It would be simple fare — sandwiches, pasta, pizza, daily specials of veal and other meat dishes. Now, on Mondays — "All You Can Eat" night — you can barely squeeze in the door. They run a chain, but best, in our opinion, is the Delmar restaurant. Weekdays for lunch, daily for dinners. No reservations. Major credit cards. 8213 Delmar (991-2022). Moderate.

The Empire Café – This chic café features delicious and fancy sandwiches and mouth-watering desserts. No reservations. Most major credit cards. 1923 Park Ave. (231-6003). Moderate.

Lantern House – A real St. Louis surprise, considered one of the country's two best Chinese restaurants by *Esquire*'s Roy de Groot. Best time to go: Sunday lunch for dim sum. Open Tuesdays through Saturdays for lunch; Tuesdays through Sundays for dinner. Reservations advised on weekends. MasterCard only. 6605 Delmar (725-5551). Inexpensive.

Bobby's Creole – Here the specialty is New Orleans–style seafood. Soups, salads, and *beignets* (fritters) are served until 1 AM on weekends. Closed Sundays. Most major credit cards. 6307 Delmar (725-6985). Inexpensive.

Two chains in the St. Louis area to keep in mind for feeding children cheaply but well:

Miss Hulling's Cafeterias – 8th St. at Olive (436-0977) and 11th St. at Locust (436-0840).

Flaming Pit Restaurants – Steak and hamburger stops well above average that offer special children's menus, there are seven *Flaming Pits* throughout the city. Inexpensive.

SALT LAKE CITY

Salt Lake City was born when two great natural forces, history and geology, came together in an accident of fate. To its present-day residents, it was a fortuitous cosmic collision. This kind of epic overview has a particular appeal to the residents of this gleaming oasis in the desert, since Salt Lake City is the headquarters of the Church of Jesus Christ of Latter-Day Saints. Known to most of us as Mormons, disciples of this church believe in divine revelation. And they believe God guided them here. Although the church tries to keep a low profile, evidence of its past work is everywhere, and visitors are immediately aware of the influence of its teachings. All the streets, for example, run at right angles to each other, and are numbered in a grid scale from the center point of Temple Square. This is the plan ordered by Mormon leader Brigham Young in 1847, when he followed the plans envisioned by Mormon prophet Joseph Smith years before. It was Brigham Young who led persecuted and desperately weary Mormons across 1,000 miles of wind-swept prairie and mountains in search of a refuge where no one would bother them. When they arrived, Salt Lake City was a place no one else would covet. The transformation of barren desert into a habitable urban environment was the Mormons' major task, and their history is the legacy of the city.

Geology played its part by placing the Wasatch Mountains to the west of the Great Salt Lake basin. Rising abruptly from the Great Salt Lake Desert, their peaks snatch eastward-bound clouds and wring water from them. This makes the mountains good for skiing, but creates problems for the valley-bound city. The mean precipitation for Salt Lake City itself is 16 inches a year, while the mountains annually reap about 450 inches of precipitation in the form of snow. Even so, Utah is the second driest state in the nation. (First is next-door Nevada.) But the scarcity of water has stimulated irrigation engineers to come up with a number of ingenious, creative solutions. Now there are dams in the mountains to trap the winter snowfall so that upon melting it can be delivered to the farmers in the valleys, who desperately need water to harvest their crops.

Although the lack of water is a problem, scarcity of population is not. In fact, it's quite an advantage, infinitely preferable to the overcrowding which is characteristic of most cities. The heart of the Intermountain area, Salt Lake City absorbs a sizable number of Utah's 1,461,000 residents. The largest city in the state, the city proper houses 167,000 people. More than 660,000 live in the larger Wasatch Front metropolitan district, sandwiched between the mountains to the east, the Great Salt Lake, and its desert to the west.

For a city of its size and relative isolation, the cultural scene is surprisingly active. The Utah Symphony, an important North American orchestra, tours Europe regularly. Ballet West is one of the outstanding ballet groups in the country, and the illustrious Mormon Tabernacle Choir is so well known it needs no description. Several dance companies, a new opera company, and half a dozen theater groups perform throughout the year. A brand-new Bicentennial Center for the Performing Arts has three special buildings designed for concerts, ballet, and art exhibitions. Monday, a slow night in most cities, is a lively time in Salt Lake City, thanks to the Mormon Church. Mormon families are asked to set aside Monday as Family Home Evening, which makes it a good night for family movies and visits to local ice cream parlors. (Mormons have large families, so the emphasis on family togetherness is good for business.)

Brigham Young designed the city so its wide streets and tree-lined boulevards would be its most prominent features. His architectural foresight has stood the test of time, although the home of the Mormon pilgrims, like most other places, has yielded to the tyranny of progress. Ten years of intense building programs have changed the face of Salt Lake City. Main Street has been torn up and completely redesigned, with sparkling fountains, patterned sidewalks, hundreds of new trees, and flower planters. Other streets have received the same treatment, and rundown areas have given way to new buildings like the Salt Palace arena, convention center, and ZCMI and Crossroads malls, enclosed downtown shopping centers. Some delightful, old Victorian mansions remain; portions of others have found a new home at Trolley Square, a shopping center patterned after San Francisco's Ghirardelli Square. The ten beautifully landscaped acres of Temple Square surrounding the Salt Lake Temple and Tabernacle still attract more than four million visitors a year, making it Utah's greatest tourist site.

Although most Salt Lake City residents are Mormons, other ethnic communities exert strong cultural influences. The Guadalupe Center provides a base for the Mexican-Americans' civic activities. The Japanese community's Obon Festival and the annual Greek Festival contribute that eclectic, cosmopolitan flair generally associated with much larger cities. Even in other neighborhoods, many Salt Lake City residents are multilingual. Independent, pragmatic, and idealistic, Salt Lake City people prefer to do things themselves rather than ask for help. However, when other people need help, they will go out of their way. Visitors who get lost find themselves befriended in no time, and often end up as guests in residents' homes. On a larger scale, their altruism is almost legendary. When neighboring Idaho's Teton Dam burst in 1976, thousands of people from Salt Lake City turned out in force to clean up the muck.

An attractive, well-organized city of good-natured people should be enticing enough for just these qualities alone, without the added incentive of the Great Salt Lake, without which, obviously, nothing would be the same. Floating in its briny, warm water is as much a part of the Salt Lake City experience as immersing oneself in its streets and buildings. The heart of the Intermountain region, Salt Lake City is unquestionably a splendid collaboration of nature, civilization, and people who refuse to accept the notion that kindness and what we commonly refer to as progress are mutually exclusive concepts.

SALT LAKE CITY AT-A-GLANCE

SEEING THE CITY: From the top of Capitol Hill, you can look out over the whole city.

SPECIAL PLACES: Salt Lake City's grid pattern is simplicity itself. Everything radiates from Temple Square. Eighteen blocks south is 18th South, five blocks west is 5th West, etc.

CENTRAL CITY

Temple Square – The logical place to start, as it's the heart of the worldwide Mormon Church. Enclosed within a 15-foot wall, the ten acres of Temple Square's grounds draw about four million visitors a year. Within the grounds are the Temple, a granite structure that took 40 years to build; the dome-shaped, acoustically perfect Tabernacle, home of the Mormon Tabernacle Choir; and the Information Center, where you can join any one of many free, daily guided tours. The great Tabernacle organ conducts public recitals every day at noon and 4 PM Thursdays. Tabernacle Choir rehearsals are open to the public Thursdays, 7:30 PM. Tabernacle organ recitals and choir rehearsals are free (531-2534).

Church Office Building – Across the street at Temple Square East is Utah's tallest structure, the Church Office Building, housing the general offices of the Latter-Day Saints Church. Its Genealogical Library is used by thousands of members and non-members daily. It houses the world's largest genealogical collection, and chances are you or your ancestors are listed. Members of the staff will be happy to help you find out. Temple Square (531-2531).

Beehive House – Built by Brigham Young as his official residence in 1854, Beehive House is now a museum operated by the Church. It was the first Governor's mansion and is open to the public daily except Sundays, Thanksgiving, Christmas, and New Year's Day. The patriarch himself is buried half a block northeast in a quiet park. Free. 67 E South Temple and State Sts. (531-2671).

Capitol Hill – Capitol Hill contains the State Capitol, Pioneer Museum, and Council Hall, all within easy reach. A splendid piece of Corinthian architecture, there are free guided tours through the granite and marble Capitol and its many exhibits of Utah products and art (533-5900). Council Hall, across the street to the south, was moved to the hill stone by stone and now houses the Utah Travel Council, where you can pick up brochures and maps (see *Sources and Resources*; 533-5681). Pioneer Museum, to the west of the Capitol, has one of the most complete collections of pioneer relics in the West. Closed Sundays from October to April. Free. 300 N Main St. (533-5759).

Salt Palace and Bicentennial Center for the Performing Arts – Almost anything goes on at the 28,000-seat Salt Palace — conventions, sports events, rock concerts (100 SW Temple, 521-6060). The Bicentennial Arts Center includes a concert hall and art center on the same grounds as the Salt Palace and Capitol Theater (1st South).

ZCMI Center and Crossroads Plaza – Returning to tree-lined Main Street, you'll find two of the largest downtown covered shopping malls in the West. The ZCMI Center, on the east side of the street (15 S Main St.), has over 60 stores inside, some of which serve old-fashioned refreshments like phosphates and iron port. Across the street to the west is the new Crossroads Plaza with 70 stores and numerous theaters and fast-food eateries. 18 S Main St.

MID-CITY

S. E. Temple – Start at the Cathedral of the Madeleine, a Roman Gothic church completed in 1909, which has a beautiful series of German stained glass windows. Further along the street are dozens of exquisite old mansions built by mining magnates at the turn of the century. One of them, the marble and wood former Utah State Historical Society building at 603 E South Temple, is the Governor's mansion.

Trolley Square – Trolley Square has won national acclaim as a restoration project. Ingeniously rebuilt in abandoned trolley barns, this collection of shops, theaters, restaurants, and boutiques attracts a fascinating stream of people. Wandering artists and troubadors entertain in the turn-of-the-century entryways and courtyards. Open 10 AM to 9 PM. 5th South and 7th East Sts. (521-9877).

Liberty Park – Three blocks south on 7th East is 80-acre Liberty Park, with bowers, picnic areas, tennis and horseshoe courts, swimming pool, playground, the Tracy Aviary home for birds, an amusement park, and a boating center. Summer concerts are held in the covered bandstand. 1302 South, 900 East (972-6714).

EMIGRATION CANYON

Pioneer Trail State Park – "This is the place," Brigham Young said when he and his entourage caught their first glimpse of The Valley of the Great Salt Lake. And this is where you'll now find the new Pioneer Trail State Park, with ten renovated buildings from pioneer times, including the Brigham Young Farm Home and the Social Hall (533-5881). This is also the site of the Pioneer Monument and Visitors' Center, with audiovisual exhibits showing the Mormon trek from Illinois to Utah (533-5920). Tours of the buildings are available. Open daily. Donations requested. Emigration Canyon, 2601 Sunnyside Ave.

GREAT SALT LAKE

Great Salt Lake – The most important natural feature of the region, the 73-mile long lake is marshy, salty, sticky, and warm. As you approach it, it may look like nothing more than marshes and weird salt flats, but there are a couple of beaches, and Great Salt Lake State Park where you will undoubtedly find other curious swimmers. The water tastes awful, and stings terribly if it gets in your eyes, so don't splash. You can camp on the south shore year-round, but we warn you, the brine flies are sometimes ferocious. 17 miles west on US 40, I-80.

■ **EXTRA SPECIAL:** The 848,000-acre *Wasatch National Forest* is one of the busiest forests in the country. Located in the High Uintas Primitive Area, the Wasatch National Forest is full of mountain lakes, rugged spruce, dramatic canyons, and mountain peaks as high as 13,400 feet. The Utah State Fish and Game Department operates a winter feeding ground at Hardware Ranch in Logan (245-3131). There are campgrounds at Little Cottonwood, Big Cottonwood, and Mill Creek canyons; call the Salt Lake Ranger Station for information (524-5042). Those closest to the city are the most crowded. Hunting conditions are excellent here. Deer, elk, and moose can be hunted in the fall. A variety of trout swim the streams. In winter, skiers flock to Alta, 25 miles southeast of the city on rt. 210; Brighton, 27 miles southeast on rt. 152; and Snowbird, in Gad Valley, two miles from Alta. To get to the eastern section of Wasatch, take US 40, and rts. 152, 210; to reach the northern part, follow US 89 and 91. For further information, contact the Supervisor's Office, 125 S State St., Salt Lake City 84138 (524-5030, or 942-4059 for campground information; 364-1581 for avalanche information).

SOURCES AND RESOURCES

For brochures and maps, contact the Utah Travel Council, Council Hall, Capitol Hill (533-5681). For information on winter skiing, summer recreations, and fuel availability, call 521-8102. For other events call 533-TIPS.

The best local guide to Salt Lake City is *Great Salt Lake Country,* a free brochure available from the Utah Travel Council.

All telephone numbers are in the 801 area code unless otherwise indicated.

For Local Coverage – *Salt Lake Tribune,* morning daily; *Deseret News,* evening daily; *Utah Holiday*, monthly.

For Food – *Utah Holiday* has a full listing of restaurants in the Salt Lake area, and each issue has a number of articles describing restaurants.

CLIMATE AND CLOTHES: Wintertime is for skiing. Spring is beautiful, but fickle, with apricot blossoms sometimes covered in snow. Summer is hot and dry, with temperatures climbing into the 90s. Fall is gorgeous, especially in the nearby canyons.

GETTING AROUND: Bus – For information on bus schedules in and around Salt Lake, call Utah Transit Authority (263-3737).

Taxi – The best way to get a cab is to call Yellow Cab (521-2100).

Car Rental – All major firms are represented; a cheap local alternative is Payless Car Rental System, 2080 W North Temple (521-9694).

MUSEUMS: *Beehive House,* Brigham Young's former residence, is now a museum; *Hansen Planetarium* features exhibits on astronomy and natural science. On the University of Utah campus, you'll find the Utah *Museum of Natural History,* the Utah *Museum of Fine Arts,* and the Utah Museum of Earth Sciences. Another museum:

Salt Lake Arts Center, at the Bicentennial Center for the Arts, 100 SW Temple.

MAJOR COLLEGES AND UNIVERSITIES: The University of Utah campus has a theater, a special events center, and three museums: Natural History (581-6927), Art (581-7332), and Earth Sciences (581-6927). Between 14th East and 20th East, 1st South and 5th South (581-7200).

SPECIAL EVENTS: On July 24, Salt Lake City celebrates *Pioneer Day,* marking the arrival of the Mormon pioneers. In April and October, thousands of Mormons from all over the world converge on Temple Square for the conferences of the Church of Latter-Day Saints. In July, the *Japanese Obon Festival* is held at the Buddhist Temple, 211 W 1st South. In September, the *Greek Festival* takes place at the Hellenic Memorial Building. For information on special events, call 521-8102 in nonskiing season, or 533-5681.

SPORTS: Hockey – The Salt Lake *Golden Eagles* play at the Salt Palace (363-7681).

Basketball – The NBA *Utah Jazz* plays in the Salt Palace (355-6194).

Baseball – The *Salt Lake Gulls,* affiliated with the *California Angels,* play from mid-April to Labor Day at Derks Field, 65 W 1300 South (363-7676).

Skiing – Utah claims to have the "Greatest Snow on Earth." And certainly, skiers from all over the world enthusiastically attest to its excellence. The season runs from mid-November to May or June. For a recorded ski report, call 521-8102. The major ski resorts within half an hour's drive of Salt Lake City are:

Alta – The granddaddy of them all, Alta, in Little Cottonwood Canyon, has the best and most consistent snow conditions. Alta has six chair lifts, four rope tows, and offers powder and alpine skiing. 25 miles SE of city on rt. 210. (328-8589).

Snowbird – Also in Little Cottonwood Canyon, Snowbird is the newest and most glamorous of the jet-set resorts, with a spectacular tram lift to Hidden Peaks at 11,000 feet. The lift runs in summer, too. In Gad Valley, two miles from Alta.

Brighton – At the top of Big Cottonwood Canyon. The average annual snowfall here is 430 inches. 27 miles SE on rt. 152. (359-3283).

Park City – This is the home of the US Ski Team's National Training Center and has the longest night-skiing run in the nation. Drive 20 miles east on I-80, up Parley's Canyon.

Golf – There are eight public courses in the Salt Lake valley. The best is Mountain Dell, in Parley's Canyon.

Tennis – There are 17 parks in Salt Lake City which have tennis courts. The most popular are the 16 courts (14 lighted) at Liberty Park. Tennis lessons are available (535-7994). The University of Utah has quite a few outdoor public courts.

Swimming – The Great Salt Lake offers an unusual aquatic experience. For fresh-water swimming, try the enormous pool at Lagoon, 15 miles north of the city on I-15.

Fishing, Hunting, Camping, Backpacking, River Running – At Wasatch National Forest (see *Extra Special*), you can fish, hunt, camp, and backpack to your heart's delight. For information, call 524-5030. For information on hunting and fishing regulations, contact Utah Division of Wildlife Resources, 1596 W North Temple (532-2473, 533-9333). For information on backpacking, river running, and primitive wilderness areas in general, call the Bureau of Land Management Office of Public Affairs, 136 E South Temple (524-4227), or the National Park Service, 125 S State (524-4165).

Ice Skating and Sleigh Riding – Sugarhouse Park, 21 S 16th East, for sleigh riding; Bountiful Recreation Center, 150 W 6th North, Bountiful (292-0422), for ice skating.

THEATER: For up-to-the-minute theater listings call 533-8477. *Promised Valley Playhouse* features free performances during the summer of "Promised Valley," a musical about the Mormons. Tickets are available at Temple Square Information Center. Other plays are performed at Promised Valley Playhouse, too, 132 S State (364-5677). The *Pioneer Memorial Theater* and adjacent *Babcock Theater* at the University of Utah stage all kinds of plays, University of Utah campus (581-6961). Theater 138 is at 138 S 2nd East (332-0093).

MUSIC: Salt Lake City has many concerts and dance events. For more information, call 533-8477. The *Mormon Tabernacle Choir* rehearsals are open to the public Thursdays, 7:30 PM. Free. Temple Square. *Utah Symphony Orchestra, Ballet West,* and *Repertory Dance Center* perform at Bicentennial Center for the Performing Arts. Big-name rock and country artists perform at the Salt Palace, 100 SW Temple (363-7681).

NIGHTCLUBS AND NIGHTLIFE: *Between Friends* in the *Salt Lake Hilton,* 150 W 5th South, has fashion shows on Tuesday and Thursday nights plus fine food and music. A 2-week membership for $5 allows you to bring four friends (532-3344). *The Collector* is a fancier disco club that attracts a trendy crowd and also charges membership fees, but out of staters can get a temporary membership card for $10 that admits three people. 32 Exchange Pl. (322-1396).

SINS: To see it from the outside, you would think that the *Magazine Shop,* 228 S Main (359-3295), was a used bookstore. But any dirty old man worth his salt knows that the back room, beyond the off-color comic books near the entrance, is the single small corner into which *lust* has been driven. Outside the city, in the ski resort towns of the surrounding Wasatch Mountain wilderness, women and money abound; Salt Lake City's beggars can be choosers there. But around the great Mormon Tabernacle, the influence of the church is so strong that neither the "thou" or the "jug of wine" are readily bought. And since the Mormon work ethic has banished *sloth* to the ski slopes, *pride* (mainly over the Tabernacle) holds the fort with *gluttony* (with *Snelgrove's* ice cream, and the long, jam-packed menu of frozen concoctions, supplying most of the fuel). "It seems," says one Salt Lake City resident, "that ice cream is the Mormons' biggest vice."

LOCAL SERVICES: Business Services – Aztec Typing Service, 213 E 3rd South (364-6806).

Mechanic – Andy Stevens Automotive, 458 Montague Ave. (328-9222).

BEST IN TOWN

CHECKING IN: Since more than 10 million people a year visit Utah, it's logical to expect a decent selection of hotels in Salt Lake City. And you won't be disappointed. Tourism is Utah's largest single industry, and accommodations are plentiful and varied. Expect to pay between $60 and $106 for a double room in those places we've listed as expensive; between $45 and $60 for those we've designated as moderate; and between $35 and $45 in inexpensive places.

Hotel Utah – Still the grande dame of the state, the Utah is elegant in the traditional sense of the word. Its recent multimillion-dollar facelift hasn't disturbed the old crystal chandelier which still hangs from the mezzanine. More than 200 rooms have been added to the original hotel, for a total of 560, and there is a beautiful new Grand Ballroom. Corner of Main and South Temple Sts. (531-1000). Expensive.

Salt Lake Hilton – The 357-room Salt Lake Hilton exudes an aura of contemporary sophistication. Suites have sunken baths; there is an outdoor swimming pool, therapy pool, sauna, and five dining rooms. A package store on the premises sells liquor. Pets are welcome. 150 W 5th South St. (532-3344). Expensive.

Salt Lake Marriott – The newest hotel in the city, it has two restaurants, two lounges, an indoor-outdoor pool, saunas, a liquor store, and direct access to the Crossroads Mall. Guests have privileges at an adjoining health spa for racquetball, squash, and tennis. The 15-story structure has 518 rooms and is opposite the Salt Palace on the corner of West Temple and 1st South (531-0800). Expensive.

Tri-Arc TraveLodge – This 405-room, 13-story high-rise is built in an unusual arc shape to give every room a view of the valley. The panoramic view from the top is spectacular. When you get tired of looking out the window, you can watch a free in-room movie. With its own heliport. The *13th Floor Supper Club* and the *Golden Spike* restaurants are popular with residents (open daily). Children under 14 free. 161 W 6th South (521-7373). Moderate.

Best Western Little America Hotel – Located on the city's main thoroughfare within walking distance of the downtown shopping area and convention center. This 850-room hotel boasts a recently added tower, two heated pools, a wading pool, and sauna. Children under 12 free. Free bus service to the airport. 500 S Main St. (363-6781). Moderate.

Temple Square Hotel – Another centrally located hotel, this is the city's best modest hostelry. Recently renovated, it offers free parking, and has a coffee shop on the premises. The keynote here is functional rather than fancy. Across the street from Temple Square at 75 W South Temple St. (355-2961). Inexpensive.

EATING OUT: Salt Lake Valley restaurants offer a number of different cuisines, from Continental to seafood, steaks, and chops. Expect to pay between $30 and $50 for two at those places we've listed as expensive; between $15 and $30 at those places designated moderate; under $17, inexpensive. These prices do not include drinks, wine, or tips. *Special note:* The larger restaurants have liquor licenses; otherwise you'll have to bring your own from the nearest state-run liquor store (closed on Sundays). You can expect a small setup fee at many restaurants.

La Caille at Quail Run – One of Utah's finest restaurants. La Caille at Quail Run, set in a château (styled as an 18th-century French maison) a few miles from the city, serves food which is commensurate with its well-appointed surroundings. Dining room overlooks the formal gardens of the restaurant's estate. The menu features veal Marsala, duck Grendier, and on Sundays, Basque cuisine. Trout meunière and eggs Benedict are popular brunch items. Service is prompt, courteous, and efficient. Reservations are a must. Major credit cards accepted. 9565 Wasatch Blvd. (942-1751). Expensive.

The Royal Palace – Located in a converted Jewish synagogue, the Royal Palace assigns each diner a captain, waiter, and busboy. Savory French and Italian specialties if you don't mind the crowd. Dinner only on Sundays. Reservations recommended. Major credit cards. 249 S 4th East (359-5000). Expensive.

Five Alls Restaurant – If you're willing to make the transition from 20th-century Salt Lake to medieval England, drop into the Five Alls for a meal. Waitresses in old-fashioned costumes will rush to serve you anything from prime ribs to sweet English trifle. Closed Sundays. Reservations recommended. Major credit cards. 1450 Foothill Dr. (582-1400). Expensive.

Bratten's Grotto – This restaurant serves only seafood; in fact, it's the only seafood restaurant in town, which is why it's extremely popular with Salt Lake City residents, who willingly stand in line at least 20 minutes to be seated. The complete dinner includes a relish bowl, appetizer, soup, choice of breads, entrée, and dessert. Closed Sundays. Reservations accepted. Major credit cards. 644 E 4th South St. (364-6547). Moderate.

Ryan's Restaurant – Combines privacy with efficient, discreet service. Renowned locally for its steak. Reservations suggested. Major credit cards. 3680 Highland Dr. (467-5511). Moderate.

The Heidelberg – Housed in a converted, thick-walled former flour mill about 15 miles north of the city. In addition to a wide selection of steaks, good choices are sauerbraten, Wiener schnitzel, and rainbow trout American-style. Closed Sundays and Mondays. Reservations necessary. Major credit cards. 600 N Main, Farmington (292-0433). Moderate.

The Cattle Baron – The specialty of the Western states is steak, and here, steak is a many-splendored thing. There are any number of different kinds from which to choose, along with halibut, shrimp, and lobster. A huge, barnlike, 20th-century, pseudo Western dining hall, the Cattle Baron serves excellent food, broiled to your order. Open Wednesdays through Sundays. Reservations advised. Major credit cards. 2110 Emigration Canyon (582-8991). Moderate.

Hare Hollow – Appetizers include fresh vegetables with dip, and plenty of home-baked bread. Breast of chicken and pork chops are very good, too. Reservations suggested. 6121 Highland Dr. (272-5269). Inexpensive.

The Old Spaghetti Factory Restaurant – One of the more popular inexpensive eating places in town, it has lots of friendly ambiance. You may find yourself dining on an old brass bed or in a trolley car, with turn-of-the-century furnishings and memorabilia around. Spaghetti comes in all styles, but try the clam sauce. Open daily. No reservations. 189 Trolley Square (521-0424). Inexpensive.

La Marena Café – Considered a Salt Lake City institution, the café is run by the Catholic Church to fund a variety of projects for the poor. Little atmosphere, but outstanding Mexican food. Guadalupe Center, 346 W 100 South (355-1541). Inexpensive.

SAN ANTONIO

Fed up with politics after failing to win re-election to Congress in 1835, Davy Crockett told his Tennessee constituents, "You kin all go to hell, I'm a goin' to Texas." And so he did. He ended up in San Antonio just in time to join the Texans at the Alamo in their struggle to gain independence from Mexico. He fought alongside Colonels William Travis and James Bowie, who showed Crockett the original bowie knife and said, "You might tickle a fellow's ribs a long time with this instrument before you'd make him laugh." And certainly Santa Anna and his 5,000 soldiers did not go away laughing when the 187 Texas heroes withstood their might, and greatly weakened their ranks, before finally succumbing to the greater force. Though all the fighters for Texas went down in the battle, Crockett (among the last surviving) made his final stand with a lunge at the Mexican general and was promptly dispatched by the swords of the Mexican soldiers.

Today the Alamo still stands and is at the center of a cosmopolitan area which blends the old Texas, with its classic Spanish influence, and the largely Texan-Mexican (Tex-Mex) style of today. Alongside numerous well-preserved reminders of days gone by, the missions and lovely adobe buildings, stand modern steel skyscrapers. Established in 1718 by Spanish missionaries who came to convert the Indians, San Antonio drew thousands of pioneers from around the world. Many ethnic groups remain today, but the largest is the Mexican-Americans, who comprise over half of the city's 800,000 population. The city is largely bilingual, but beyond this mix of cultures is a great disparity in economics; San Antonio is a city of poverty and wealth, with pockets of posh suburbs sharing the same pair of pants with pockets of poverty. Here, where the great post–Civil War cattle boom originated, rich Texas ranchers live in fantastic million-dollar homes, which are as far as you can get from the public housing units occupied by blacks and Mexicans. But over the past few years, the Mexican-Americans have gained political power, and in fact, over half of San Antonio's state legislative delegation and city council is of Mexican descent, including the mayor. There is a lot ahead, however, before the city's poor will see a change in their standard of living.

Military tradition runs deep in the city's blood. Teddy Roosevelt recruited his famous Rough Riders in the bar of the Hotel Menger. Several aviation "firsts" were established at Fort Sam Houston in 1910 by Lt. Benjamin D. Foulouis when he reported, "My first takeoff, my first solo, my first landing, and my first crash on the same day." San Antonio's current military record is somewhat more stable if less flamboyant. Five military installations with more than 60,000 active duty personnel and civilian employees make the federal government the city's major employer. More than 85,000 enlisted men and women a year undergo basic training at Lackland Training Center, the cradle of the Air Force. And at the other end of the military spectrum, 50,000 retirees live here, among them more than 100 retired generals.

Since 1968, San Antonio has moved into the ranks of a tourist attraction. That was the year of HemisFair, a World's Fair celebrating San Antonio's 200th birthday, which left the city with a valuable convention center, Theater for the Performing Arts, and Institute of Texan Cultures. Even more important, the year-long celebration focused attention on the city's forgotten architectural treasures. La Villita, San Antonio's oldest residential neighborhood, was restored with lovely adobe buildings housing authentic Mexican artisan shops. More than 80 homes in the King William section, where the German community lived in grandeur in the 19th century, were restored and feature German stone masonry as well as almost every notable style of American architecture of the past century. And to walk on the Paseo del Rio, the river walk which traces the horseshoe course of the San Antonio River in town, is to step into a primordial tropical paradise of banana palms and bougainvillea only steps away from curio shops, cafés, and San Antonio's business center.

SAN ANTONIO AT-A-GLANCE

SEEING THE CITY: The Tower of the Americas, San Antonio's most visible landmark, at 622 feet, offers the best vantage point from which to view the city and the surrounding countryside. From the observation deck you see flatland stretching to the south and gently rolling hills to the northwest, leading to the Texas hill country. Directly below are the modern buildings of HemisFair Plaza, site of the '68 World's Fair, and a branch of the San Antonio River which cuts a horseshoe path through town. In HemisFair Plaza.

SPECIAL PLACES: The heart of San Antonio is great for walking, with the lovely Paseo del Rio (River Walk) tracing the course of the river, and short distances between many of the attractions. Other interesting sights, including the missions along Mission Trail and the zoo, are best reached by car or bus.

CENTRAL CITY

The Alamo – Where Davy Crockett, Col. James Bowie, Col. Travis, and the 184 other Texas heroes repulsed Mexican dictator Santa Anna and his force of 5,000 in Texas' 1836 struggle for independence. Established in 1718 by Spanish priests as Mission San Antonio de Valero, the original mission has been restored and the site turned into a block-square state park which includes a museum with displays on the Alamo and Texas history, with an excellent weapon collection featuring derringers, swords, and an original bowie knife. Open daily. Free (at Alamo Plaza, 222-1693). At the Remember the Alamo Theater (315 Alamo Plaza, 224-1836) across the street, you can actually be on the scene of the action (the westernmost walls of the original Alamo stood on this site) while watching a multimedia presentation of the battle. Open daily. Admission charge.

La Villita – This little Spanish town in the center of the city looks very much as it did 250 years ago when it was San Antonio's first residential area. Girded by a stone wall, and surrounded by banana palms and bougainvillea, the stone patios and adobe dwellings have been authentically restored and now house artisans' shops where many of the old crafts — glass blowing, weaving, dollmaking, and pottery — are still practiced. Among the other buildings are the restored Cos House built in 1835, where General Cos, commander of the Mexican forces, surrendered to the Texans, and the Old San Antonio Museum, which has displays on Texas history and pleasant outdoor cafés. Open daily. Free. One square city block bounded by the river on the north, Nueva St. on the south, S Alamo St. on the east, and Villita St. on the west. Main office is at 416 Villita St. (299-8610).

HemisFair Plaza – The legacy of the 1968 World's Fair, HemisFair Plaza features the Tower of the Americas with its panoramic view of Texas countryside, a convention center, Theater for the Performing Arts, shops, and several modern buildings which have exhibitions. The Institute of Texan Cultures examines the influence of 26 different ethnic groups, including Mexicans, Germans, Poles, Hungarians, and Irish, who developed the state. Films, slide shows, and exhibitions of artifacts including Mexican stone cooking equipment, and examples of the dress of each of the groups. Closed Mondays. Free (226-7651).

The Museum of Transportation – Shows how people got around in the days of the open country with classic and antique carriages, stagecoaches, hearses, horse-drawn pumpers, until the range gave way to highways and autos. Open daily. Donation requested. Bounded by Commerce, Market, Durango, and Alamo sts. (226-5544).

Paseo del Rio – A branch of the San Antonio River winds like a horseshoe for 2.5 miles through the central business district. Stone stairways lead down to the River Walk which, only 20 feet below street level, is as far from the world of the business district as you can get. Tall trees, tropical foliage, and banana palms line the walks dotted with curio and craft shops, hot nightspots, and outdoor cafés where you can drop tortilla chips to waiting fish. You can get out on the river in a paddleboat or a barge (paddleboat booth at river side under Market St. Bridge), and dine by candlelight aboard some. Make arrangements through barge office, 430 E Commerce St. (222-1701).

El Mercado – The original marketplace has been renovated but still retains its Spanish buildings and old market flavor, with Mexican merchants who do their best to lure you into their shops where you can get beautiful handcrafted objects like onyx chess sets, pottery, silver jewelry. Open daily. 515 W Commerce St. (299-8600).

Spanish Governor's Palace – The only Spanish colonial mansion remaining in Texas. Built in 1749 for the Spanish governors when Texas was a province of Spain, with three-foot-thick walls, a keystone above the door bearing the Hapsburg coat of arms, original Spanish furnishings, and a floor of native flagstone that offers cool refuge even on the hottest Texas days. Open daily. Small admission charge. 105 Military Plaza (224-0601).

Hertzberg Circus Collection – If you're a circus fanatic, you'll go ring crazy here with displays of artifacts tracing the development of the circus from its English origins to P. T. Barnum and the American three-ring extravaganza. Particularly strong in miniatures featuring the original carriage of Tom Thumb and an entire circus in one room. Closed Sundays. Free. 210 W Market St. in Library Annex (299-7810).

SOUTH SIDE

Missions – The Alamo was the first of five missions established under Spanish rule. Except for the Alamo all of the missions are still active parish churches and are located along the well-marked Mission Trail starting at the southern tip of the city. Most notable are:

> **Mission San José** – Called the "Queen of the Missions," the finest and largest example of early mission life. The original parish church, built of limestone and tufa, features "Rosa's Window," an impressive stone carving, and is surrounded by a six-acre compound including a restored mill, Indian quarters, and granary. Open daily. Small admission charge. 6539 San José Dr., six miles south on US 281 (922-2731).

Mission Concepción – The oldest unrestored church in the country is remarkably well preserved with original frescoes made by the padres and Indians from a mixture of vegetable and mineral dyes. Open daily. Small admission charge. 807 Mission Rd. (532-3158).

Buckhorn Hall of Horns – Once an old-time, shoot-em-up saloon, this hall was transported lock, stock, and barrel by the Lone Star Brewing Company to tamer grounds. The collection is as wild as ever — some of the fastest guns in the West, and hunting trophies of everything imaginable from horns and antlers of elk, buffalo, and antelope to whole polar bears and grizzly bears. Open daily. Admission charge. 600 Lone Star Blvd. on the company's grounds (226-8303).

NORTH SIDE

Brackenridge Park – This 343-acre park includes the Southwest's largest zoo. Rock cliffs provide a backdrop for fine displays of animals in their natural settings. Over 3,500 specimens of 800 species are represented and best are the Monkey Island, an outdoor hippo pool, open bear pits, and a children's zoo nursery. Open daily. Admission charge. 3903 N St. Mary's (734-7183).

McNay Art Institute – Small but fine collections include works by Picasso and Chagall among displays of international scope and exhibitions of regional artists. Open daily. Free. 6000 N New Braunfels (824-5368).

■ **EXTRA SPECIAL:** *The Grey Moss Inn*, located in Grey Forest, a wildlife sanctuary only a few minutes from downtown, offers outdoor dining on a tree-shaded patio where you can have charcoal broiled steak, seafood, or chicken prepared on an open grill. You may see a white-tailed deer grazing nearby as you dine. Indoor dining centers around a fireplace. Closed Mondays. Reservations advised. Major credit cards. On Scenic Loop Rd., 12 miles from the Bandera Rd./Loop 410 Interchange (695-8301).

SOURCES AND RESOURCES

General tourist information, brochures, maps, and events calendars are available at the Convention and Visitors Bureau. 321 S Alamo St. (223-9133). *Downtown San Antonio Historic Walking Tours* (free) is a good guide to the area.

All telephone numbers are in the 512 area code unless otherwise indicated.

For Local Coverage – *The San Antonio Express,* morning daily; *The San Antonio Light,* morning and afternoon daily; and *The San Antonio News,* afternoon daily. Available at newsstands. Paseo del Rio Association's *Showboat* lists upcoming events. Available at Visitors Bureau and in hotel lobbies.

CLIMATE AND CLOTHES: Known as the place where "sunshine spends the winter," San Antonio winters are, naturally, sunny and mild with temperatures averaging above 50°. If you like hot weather, summers are pleasant too, with temperatures over 90° and lots of sunshine except for an occasional tropical storm from the Gulf of Mexico.

GETTING AROUND: Bus – San Antonio Metropolitan Transit System serves all sections of the city with the system's El Centro covering a 25-square-block downtown area for 10¢. Complete route and tourist information is available from the Transit Office, 800 W Myrtle St. (227-2020).

Taxi – Cabs may be ordered by phone or picked up at taxi stations in front of major hotels. Some will answer a hail in the street, most will not. Two of the largest companies are Checker (222-2151) and Yellow (226-4242).

Car Rental – All national firms are represented, but one of the best for the budget-minded is *Budget Rent-A-Car,* 338 NE Loop 410 (349-4441).

MUSEUMS: Exhibitions and displays of the Southwest and Texas history are well represented in San Antonio's cultural institutions. The Alamo Museum, the Museum of Transportation, the Hertzberg Collection, the McNay Institute, the Buckhorn Hall of Horns, and the Institute of Texan Cultures are described in *Special Places*. Other interesting museums are:

Witte Memorial Museum, 3801 Broadway (826-0647).

Texas Ranger Museum, 3805 Broadway (824-2537).

San Antonio Museum of Art, 200 W Jones Ave. (226-5444).

ART GALLERIES: Artists and craftsmen from all over the world are finding that San Antonio is an accommodating place to live and work. The art colony is growing rapidly, and galleries are numerous. Try the Raul Gutierrez Gallery of Fine Arts for Western oils, acrylics, and bronzes (8940 Wurzbach; 696-5356), and the Southwest Craft Gallery for handcrafted pieces by well-known Southwest craftsmen (420 Paseo de la Villita; 222-0926).

MAJOR COLLEGES AND UNIVERSITIES: With ten colleges and universities, San Antonio has a large student population. The major educational institutions are the University of Texas at San Antonio, Loop 1604, 17 miles west on I-10 (691-4011), St. Mary's University, One Camino Santa Maria (436-3011), Trinity University, 715 Stadium Dr. (736-7011), the University of Texas Health Science Center, 7703 Floyd Curl (691-6011), Incarnate Word College, 4301 Broadway (828-1261), and Our Lady of the Lake University, 411 SW 24th (434-6711).

SPECIAL EVENTS: A city of fiestas, the most elaborate blowout is the 10-day *Fiesta San Antonio* in mid-April, celebrating Sam Houston's victory over Santa Anna with parades, the Battle of the Flowers, the Fiesta Flambeau in the streets, and the Fiesta River Parade with lighted floats on the river, a king and queen, and lots of food and drink for the subjects. *The Starving Artists Show* in early April has works of art by hungry local artists for nothing much more than $20; everyone is trying to make ends meet so they can eat at the Fiesta.

SPORTS: Basketball – San Antonio's entry in the NBA, the *Spurs,* plays its home games at the Convention Center Arena from October through March; tickets at the Arena in HemisFair Plaza (224-9578).

Baseball – The San Antonio *Dodgers* minor league team plays at V. J. Keefe Field, St. Mary's University, from mid-April to Labor Day (434-9311, tickets).

Swimming – There are 17 municipal pools open May through Labor Day (299-3000 for information.) Best is Alamo Heights Pool, 229 Greeley St.

Golf – There are 17 courses in the city in constant use all year round. Best for visitors is Olmos Basin Municipal Course, 7000 McCullough (826-4041)

Tennis – McFairlin Tennis Center is one of the finest municipal facilities around. Courts are $1.50 for 90 minutes, but call for reservations. 1503 San Pedro Ave. (732-1223).

THEATER: For current performances, check the publications listed above. More than a dozen theaters offer a continuing and varied fare of traveling and locally produced shows. The area's colleges and universities also pro duce plays. For shows: *Fiesta Dinner Playhouse,* Loop 1604 (494-7793); *San Antonio Little Theater,* off the 1500 block of San Pedro (732-8101); *Church Dinner Theater*, 1150 S Alamo St. (224-4085); *Arneson River Theater* on Villita St. and the river (299-8610), where the stage and terraced hillside of the audience are separated by the river, and an occasional passing barge upstages the actors.

MUSIC: The *San Antonio Symphony* performs with guest stars from October through May at 109 Lexington Ave. (225-6161).

NIGHTCLUBS AND NIGHTLIFE: Pop music, jazz, Dixieland, folk, rock, and country-western are all offered at San Antonio's many pubs, taverns, and nightclubs. For a little country, try the *Farmer's Daughter* for the best in local and occasionally big-name stars, 542 N W.W. White Rd. (333-7391). For jazz, try *Jim Cullum's Landing,* 522 River Walk (223-7266) or the *Bwana Dik Club,* 421 E Commerce (223-7276).

SINS: The aristocrats who make up old San Antonio society have fortunes based on land and cattle in a city where oil money is still considered nouveau. Every year cattle baron *pride* reaches the sublime with the Order of the Alamo's election of a Queen of the Fiesta, a celebration held in honor of Texas' victory at the Battle of San Jacinto.

This event attains a level of *gluttony* not in food consumed but in costumes displayed. The cost of gowns for the Queen and her court run into five or six figures; the outfits are so elaborate that their hapless wearers have to be shuttled from function to function standing up in moving vans, like, uh, cattle.

If you want to see some good Texan fury, attend a weekly meeting of the current city council. These take place on Thursdays, and usually run quite long. The various ethnic groups represented have interests divergent enough to keep tempers short, voices high, and manners nonexistent. The *anger* that rages through these meetings only adds to the free-for-all mad melee known here as city government.

LOCAL SERVICES: Business Services – Manpower, 630 Broadway (224-9251).

Mechanic – The Bexar Engine and Transmission Service, 707 S Flores St. (226-9114).

Babysitting – Northside Sitters Club, 7918 Jones-Maltsberger (341-9313).

BEST IN TOWN

CHECKING IN: You can find all of the things you're probably looking for in San Antonio's hotels, like comfortable and convenient accommodations. Expect to pay $50 or more for a double room for a night in the expensive category, $30–40 in the moderate range, and $25 in the inexpensive.

San Antonio Marriott on the River Walk – Directly across the street from the San Antonio Convention Center, the *Marriott* is the city's largest and one of its newest hotels, nestled in a bend of the San Antonio River. The most striking feature is its seven-story atrium with an indoor-outdoor heated swimming pool. *Gambits on the River Walk,* a two-story nightclub, opens up onto the river; *The Cabrillo* features live entertainment; and the *Cactus Flower Café* has riverside dining on its patio. 711 E River Walk (224-4555). Expensive.

Hilton Palacio del Rio – Situated right on the riverside, at the liveliest corner of Paseo del Rio, and making best use of its prime location. The *El Comedor Dining Room* serves al fresco on the River Walk, some of the rooms in this attractive Spanish-style building have river views, and there is an elevator button marked "River" which lets you off at river's edge. Also features a rooftop pool, free coffee in rooms, meeting rooms, shops, and *Durty Nellie's* pub where you can let loose with an Irish lullaby if the spirit moves you. Both the restaurant and the pub are open daily. 500 rooms. 200 S Alamo St. (222-2481). Expensive.

La Mansion del Rio – Opened in 1968, this motor hotel combines a new Spanish-style building with a restored 1852 building that was originally part of St. Mary's University. Nicely designed, with rooms overlooking either the river or an inner courtyard. Features the *Capistrano Room* and *Las Canarias* restaurants and the *El Colegio Bar,* open daily. Also a pool, and free parking. 373 rooms. 112 College St. (225-2581). Expensive.

La Plaza Nacional – This spacious garden hotel is located on nearly 5 acres accented by tropical gardens, tall native Texas trees, and sparkling fountains. Its 250 rooms have balconies overlooking La Villita Historic District. There are four distinctive restaurants and an international menu. Incorporated into the complex are three restored 19th-century bungalows, which are a functional part of the hotel's dining and entertainment facilities. Pool, exercise rooms, sauna, and tennis courts. 555 S Alamo (229-1000). Expensive.

El Tropicano – Six blocks from the heart of downtown, at the north end of the River Walk, and thus a good place from which to tour the river on foot or by water taxi. 110 Lexington Ave. (223-9461). Moderate.

La Quinta – Located two blocks from the river, this two-story Spanish building offers comfortable, convenient accommodations at good prices. Pool, TV, café. 130 rooms. 1001 E Commerce St. (222-9181). Inexpensive.

EATING OUT: Some 26 ethnic groups pioneered Texas, and its current large military population has brought back a taste for exotic dishes from remote areas of the globe, resulting in a wide variety of restaurants. However, it was not for bread alone that the pioneers came or the soldiers went, or they might have done better staying closer to home. San Antonio's best restaurants are Mexican. Non-Texans (outlanders, as they're called down here) are generally surprised (happily) by the prices. Our selections range in price from $30 or more for dinner for two in the expensive range, $15–30 in the moderate range, and under $10, inexpensive. Prices do not include drinks, wine or tips.

La Louisiane – When it opened in 1935, this fine French and Creole restaurant offered full dinners for 75¢ to $1.25. Imminent failure was forecast by residents who said it was too expensive for San Antonio. But they greatly underestimated the size of the hole in some pockets, and its ability to expand with time. Today, a couple can go all out with an elegant $62–$75 production which includes pompano en papillote (poached with oyster and shrimp in white wine sauce), frogs legs sauté meunière, and three vintage wines; or some excellent dishes on a less grand, though by no means $1.25-a-plate-price, scale. La Louisiane has won many national awards for its food and service. The only thing they won't do for you is sew up your pockets. Closed Sundays and Mondays. Reservations advised. Major credit cards. 2632 Broadway (225-7984). Expensive.

The Fig Tree – Long, leisurely dinners with excellent service are the rule at this

19th-century adobe house. In the rare event that you have to wait for a table, have a drink on the balcony overlooking the San Antonio River. Specialty is rack of lamb. In La Villita section, a few blocks from the Alamo site. Open daily for dinner only. Reservations necessary. Major credit cards. 515 Paseo De La Villita (224-1976). Expensive.

Naples – The menu includes all the Italian standards and is particularly good on lasagna and veal, but the specialties are unusual and outstanding — Italian pot roast and Spanish royal red snapper. Generous portions and well-stocked wine cellar. Closed Mondays. Reservations preferred. Major credit cards. 3210 Broadway (826-9554). Moderate.

El Bosque – Excellent Mexican food, located in a country setting 15 minutes from downtown. Try the menu's Extra Special No. 1 which includes the works: enchiladas, refried beans, Spanish rice, tamales, tortillas, chile con queso, guacamole salad. The chiles rellenos are a house specialty. Cocktails and Mexican beer. Closed Mondays and Tuesdays. Reservations recommended. Major credit cards. 12656 West Ave. (494-2577). Inexpensive.

Mi Tierra Café and Bakery – When you tire of souvenir hunting at El Mercado, you can go to the heart of the market square for the real thing — great Mexican food at low prices. The cheese enchiladas are terrific, and the cabrito is good here too. Open daily. No reservations. No credit cards. 218 Produce Row (225-1262). Inexpensive.

Earl Abel's – After feeding hungry families for forty years, Earl has gotten pretty good at it. The place is a godsend for those who have been watching the ravenous animals at the nearby zoo. Offers big servings of standard American fare — broiled filet of trout from the Coast, a chicken liver dinner, a full line of hamburgers, big T-bones, and terrific homemade pecan pie. No reservations. No credit cards. 4200 Broadway (822-3358). Inexpensive.

Church's Fried Chicken – Fast-food chain with a hot twist — chicken and jalapeños. Both spicy and cheap. The headquarters of the national chain, San Antonio has more than 30 Church's so you can't miss them. Open daily. Inexpensive.

Taco Bell – Quick Mexican fare for next to nothing. The burritos and refried beans are tops, and everything else is good and hot. More than a dozen around town. Open daily. Inexpensive.

Mama's – Good food in a family atmosphere with everything from burgers to steaks. Specialty of the house is chicken-fried mushrooms. A volleyball court and basketball hoop are set up in the fenced backyard so kids can work off their energies while mom and pop have a leisurely after-dinner drink. Open daily. 9907 San Pedro (349-2314). Inexpensive.

La Fogata – A newcomer to San Antonio's burgeoning restaurant ranks, *La Fogata* features authentic recipes and foods from Mexico. Cooking is exclusively by charcoal, and though the menu sounds exotic, the prices are down to earth. (No liquor is served.) Closed Mondays. No reservations. No credit cards. 2427 Vance Jackson (341-9930). Inexpensive.

SAN DIEGO

Sparkling and white against a classic aquamarine sea, San Diego looks like what a first-timer to California imagines Los Angeles to be. It's clean, sunny, and radiates glowing self-satisfaction. It is archetypal southern California. San Diego residents call it paradise. (Really.)

Strangers in paradise are usually flabbergasted by the terrific climate. This is one place that really lives up to its outrageous reputation. Residents in this land of eternal spring (71° is the average yearly temperature) tend to gripe when even the merest wisp of cumulus mars the turquoise heaven. Never mind that days without sunshine are few and far between; nothing short of perfect weather will do. You can get spoiled living in paradise.

A lot of people do. About 845,000 live in the city, while the San Diego metro area has 1.8 million people. Although the unemployment rate is higher here than the national average, people would rather be out of work and live in San Diego than work and have to live somewhere else. When the aerospace industry declined toward the end of the Vietnam War, thousands of highly trained engineers, research scientists, and technicians suddenly found themselves out of work. The fact that they did not pick up and leave is generally attributed to the "laid back" San Diego lifestyle. Many of these highly qualified professionals chose to take jobs like washing carpets, or fixing washing machines and cars, rather than forsake those splendid afternoons lounging on the beach. And why not? More than 150,000 visitors come to San Diego every day to do just that.

Tourism is the city's third largest industry. The US government is number one. In fact, 25% of the San Diego labor force works for Uncle Sam. The San Diego Navy complex includes the largest Navy air station on the West Coast. Second most important is the aerospace equipment and missile industry. About 1,000 firms manufacture aviation equipment. (The military-industrial complex thrives in southern California as much as anything else.) San Diego's present size is a direct consequence of the incredible mobilization during WW II. After the Japanese attack on Pearl Harbor, the US moved its Pacific naval headquarters from Honolulu (for obvious reasons) to San Diego. Here were manufactured thousands of B 24 Liberators, which, in turn, pounded thousands of tons of high explosives into the very heart of occupied Europe. Millions of people passed through town during the war years, and many returned to settle when there was peace. This influx swelled the city to the bursting point, necessitating a series of building projects. Then, as America entered the space age, thousands more engineers, rocket specialists, and physicists poured into the area. San Diego gave birth to the Atlas missile, one of the earliest of the sophisticated rockets used to launch man into space.

And originally, it is the place where California began. In 1542, Juan Rodriguez Cabrillo, the Portuguese explorer sailing under a Spanish flag, pulled into the natural shelter formed by San Diego Bay. Cabrillo was later to become known as the "Columbus of California." The first settlement came more than two centuries later, however, when explorer Gaspar de Portolá and a group of Spanish settlers planted San Diego's first European roots. The oldest city in California includes on its list of original settlers the legendary Franciscan, Fray Junipero Serra, founder of the 21-mission trail known as El Camino Real. The first of Fray Serra's missions, San Diego de Alcala, forms the southern end of the chain that lines the coast as far as Sonoma, north of San Francisco. (One wonders what the gentle, pacifist disciple of St. Francis would think of the missiles which are manufactured here now.) Spaced about a day's journey apart, each mission housed about 1,000 Indian converts to Catholicism. The Indians worked as farmers and craftspeople. Food, clothing, and medical care were dispensed by the priests, who also taught the Indians how to irrigate the fields. The missions were the kibbutzim of the 18th century. The missions were also established with military priorities in mind. As the Russians pushed into Alaska, the Spanish government looked toward its string of religious settlements and outposts as strategic bulwarks in the event of an invasion. To the north of San Diego de Alcala, San Luis Rey de Francisco and San Juan Capistrano stood between California's southernmost city and Los Angeles.

In 1810, Mexicans gained control of San Diego, after a successful revolution in the northern Mexican town of Querétaro, led by a revolutionary priest named Hidalgo. The United States seized the land from Mexico in 1846 during its expansionist "manifest destiny" period. Under American rule, San Diego grew slowly, taking a back seat to the mercantile centers of Los Angeles, San Francisco, and Sacramento, the state capital, located on major railroad lines and at the juncture of two of the state's major rivers. San Diego remained an insular village until the center of population moved from "Old Town" to the "New Town" (designed by sugar heir John Spreckels) at the turn of the century. Present-day San Diego follows Spreckels' plan, but it has expanded more than 20 miles to the north, south, and east. San Diego County contains mountains with enough snow for winter skiing and fertile agricultural land. In fact, agriculture is San Diego's fourth largest industry. It is the world's largest producer of avocados. The majority of the more than 500 million avocados grown in California last year came from San Diego. Many eventually found their way into guacamole consumed by visitors and residents. Guacamole is a Mexican hors d'oeuvre, a culinary influence which is just one of the many Mexicanisms permeating the San Diego atmosphere. San Diego's Mexican-Spanish heritage is also reflected in its large Mexican-American population and in its modern architecture as well as in its remarkable old buildings. The Mexican border is only 17 miles to the south, and because of it, San Diego retains a unique character: a blend of American hospitality, traditional border-town sensuality, and the best climate this side of paradise.

SAN DIEGO AT-A-GLANCE

SEEING THE CITY: Cabrillo National Monument, where Juan Rodriguez Cabrillo first saw the West Coast in 1542, still offers the most spectacular view of San Diego. It's the most visited national monument in the US — more popular than the Statue of Liberty. Museum and Visitor Center open daily. Free. Catalina Blvd. on the tip of Point Loma (293-5450).

SPECIAL PLACES: San Diego stretches from the fashionable northern suburb of Del Mar to the Mexican border: all in all, a span of more than 30 miles along the Pacific Coast. It's advisable to concentrate your sightseeing efforts in one particular area at a time. There's no way you can see everything in just a day.

SAN DIEGO

Shelter Island – A manmade resort island in the middle of San Diego Bay lined with boatyards, marinas, and picturesque, neo-Polynesian restaurants. Between July and November, marlin fishermen haul their giant catches into port here to be weighed and photographed. Stop off at Marlin Club Landing, 2445 Shelter Island Drive. If the sight of these monsters makes you yearn for the tug of a giant fish on the line, sign on for a marlin expedition at any of the sportfishing marinas two blocks away on Fenelon Street. You can also fish for albacore, tuna, and yellowtail. To get to Shelter Island, follow Rosecrans Street until you see signs pointing to Shelter Island.

Harbor Island – This is the super deluxe, $50 million resort island. Actually, it started as a landfill project in 1961 when the US Navy offered surplus harbor muck to the Port of San Diego. The Navy was deepening a channel through the Bay. Port officials took them up on their offer and used the 3½ million tons of waste to create Harbor Island. You'd never know, to look at the place. Humble beginnings have yielded fancy beachside promenades, traffic-free malls, restaurants, and hotels. Take Rosecrans to Harbor Drive, then follow signs to Harbor Island.

Mission Bay Park – A 4,600-acre waterfront recreation area. Here you'll find manmade tropical islands, channels, and specific areas where you can water ski, swim, and sail. There are golf courses, hotels, and restaurants here, too. The two-mile stretch of Mission Beach, along the western edge of the park, is one of San Diego's oldest beach communities. A Visitor Information Center is open daily. Take rt. 5 to Mission Bay Drive exit. The Information Center is right off the exit ramp (276-8200).

Sea World – This 80-acre oceanarium is the highlight of the Mission Bay recreation complex. Performing dolphins and Shamu, the three-ton killer whale, entertain regularly. The water show includes the Ding a Ling Brothers' Seal and Otter Circus, too. Backstage you can feed the dolphins and meet the walruses. Yes, there are sharks, too. Open daily. Admission charge. Mission Bay Park (224-3562).

Old Town Plaza – The best way to see Old San Diego is by walking through it. Old Town Plaza (also known as Washington Square) used to be the scene of violent cockfights and bullfights. Duelists chose this as their site for shooting it out. One-hour guided walking tours leave Old Town Plaza daily. Free. San Diego Ave., Mason, Calhoun, and Wallace Sts. (For general park information, call 237-6770.)

Casa de Estudillo – The former commandante of San Diego, José Maria Estudillo, lived here while the city was under Mexican control. It was also the site of Helen Hunt Jackson's book *Ramona,* which describes how the Indians were mistreated. It was built in 1829. Open daily. Free. San Diego Ave. and Mason St. (no phone).

San Diego Union Newspaper Museum – Still going strong, the *San Diego Union* started out in this small, 1860s building. In fact, the newspaper is responsible for restoring it, and for setting up the editorial offices and printing press. Copies of the first *Union* ever printed are still on sale for 25¢. Open daily. Free. 2606 San Diego Ave. (297-2119).

San Diego Historical Museum – Right in back of the Newspaper Museum, this is a good place to get an idea of what Old Town looked like a hundred years ago. A scale-model diorama is on display. Across the alley, you can see Seeley Stable, barns, and a fine collection of horse-drawn wagons and carriages. There's also a slide show of San Diego history. Open daily. Free. 2626 San Diego Ave.

Whaley House – The first brick house in San Diego, built by New Yorker Thomas Whaley. The house is supposed to be haunted by a man who was hung on the grounds in 1852. Haunted or not, the house was the scene of many, lively, high society parties in its day. Ornate 19th-century furnishings still fill the halls. Open Wednesdays to Sundays. Admission charge. San Diego Ave. and Harney St. (298-2482).

Derby-Pendleton House – Behind the Whaley House; this home was built in Portland, Maine, then taken apart, shipped around Cape Horn, and reassembled on this site. Lt. George H. Derby lived here during the Civil War era. On the grounds of this house and Whaley House are a restored trolley car, a pharmacy collection of apothecary paraphernalia, and an herb shop. Open Wednesday to Sundays. Free. 4017 Harney St. (298-2482).

El Campo Santo – At the southern end of San Diego Avenue, you'll find a cemetery containing the graves of many pioneers, soldiers, and bandits. One of the latter, Antonio Garra, was actually executed next to his grave. Unfortunately many of the headstones are missing, but there's enough history here to make a visit compelling. San Diego Ave. and Noell St. (no phone).

Mormon Battalion Memorial Visitors Center – This military museum marks the longest infantry march in US history: 1846 to 1847, when 500 Mormons left their home in Illinois and trekked more than 2,000 miles to San Diego. Only 350 made it. It also has a number of exhibits of the Church of Latter-Day Saints and historical displays. Open daily. Free. In Heritage Park at 2510 Juan St. (298-3317).

Heritage Park – A pocket of preserved Victoriana. The County Parks and Recreation Department is headquartered in the Sherman-Gilbert House. There are several other mansions to explore. Open daily. Free. Juan St. (236-5740).

Serra Museum – Named after Fray Junipero Serra, this lovely mansion houses documents, books, and artifacts on the history of the region during its Spanish colonial, Mexican, and early US periods. The tower gallery is especially fascinating. The museum is on the site of the original European settlement. Open daily. Free. Presidio Park (297-3258).

Balboa Park – A definite must — the cultural heart of the city. Within its 1,200 acres of lawns, groves, lakes, and paths are a complex of fine museums, set in an area of the park known as the Prado, a Shakespearean Theater, and the world-famous San Diego Zoo (each listed below). Open daily. Free. Park Blvd. (239-0512).

San Diego Zoo – Incomparable. One of the finest zoos in the world. For more than 60 years, San Diego has been home to more than 4,000 animals. The zoo covers more than 125 acres, with animals ranging from Australian koala bears to the only New Zealand kiwis in captivity in the country to Indonesian Komodo dragons. Very few of the animals are caged in. The Skyfari Aerial Tramway gives you a great bird's-eye view of everything. Guided bus tours leave frequently from the gate. Open daily. Admission charge. Balboa Park (234-3153, 231-1515).

Timken Art Gallery – Controversial when it was built in 1965 because some people felt it clashed with the prevalent Spanish adobe architecture, the modern Timken houses French, Spanish, Flemish, Russian, and Italian Renaissance art. You'll find

Rembrandt, Bruegel the Elder, and Cézanne on the walls. Open daily. Free. Plaza de Panama, Balboa Park (239-5548).

Fine Arts Gallery – Donated by the Appleton Bridges family in 1926, the original section of the gallery was built to resemble the university at Salamanca, Spain. Two newer wings have since been added. Diego Rivera, the Mexican muralist, Rubens, the painter of big nudes, Rembrandt, and Dali are represented. There are rental and sales galleries, too. Closed Mondays. Admission charge. Plaza de Panama, Balboa Park (232-7931).

Museum of Man – Concerning itself primarily with anthropology and archeology, the Museum of Man bears the distinction of being the only remaining permanent structure from San Diego's 1915 Exposition. Its Spanish colonial tower is remarkable in itself. Exhibits focus on the Southwest Indians. Open daily. Free on Wednesdays; other times, admission charge. El Prado, Balboa Park (239-2001).

Aerospace Museum – San Diego's noted collection of antique planes and gliders was destroyed in an arson fire in 1978, but a public subscription drive and donations of exhibits enabled the museum to open in a new location recently. Ford Bldg., Balboa Park (234-8291).

Reuben H. Fleet Space Theater – The first of its kind. Simulated space travel is the attraction here. Images projected on the 360-degree screen give you the impression you're moving in zero-gravity conditions. As well as the multimedia space blitz, the Science Center has exhibits on astronomy and technology. On Saturday and Sundays there's a free demonstration of lasers. Open daily. Admission charge. Off Park Blvd., Balboa Park (238-1168).

Museum of Natural History – More than a century old, this museum has a collection of birds which nest in the San Diego area, and sharks, whales, and fish who make their home in the surrounding seas. A Sefton seismograph measures tremors and earth movement. There's a giant pendulum to illustrate how the earth rotates. Open daily. Free Tuesdays; other times, admission charge. Across the street from the Fleet Space Theater, Balboa Park (232-3821).

Embarcadero – Another interesting place to walk. From the pier you can see the activities on North Island Naval Air Station across the bay and watch the hundreds of sailboats cruising. Navy ships are open to visitors on weekends, off the Broadway Pier.

Maritime Museum – 113 years ago the *Star of India* sailed forth on her maiden voyage. The oldest square-rigged merchantman afloat, the *Star of India* is berthed here, along with the turn-of-the-century ferryboat *Berkeley* and steam yacht *Medea.* Open daily. Admission charge. Broadway Pier at Harbor Dr. (234-9153).

LA JOLLA

Tidepool – La Jolla, an uncommercial beach 12½ miles north of San Diego, offers opportunities to observe marine life in a natural setting. Visit the tidepools just beyond Alligator Head at La Jolla Cove at low tide to see a veritable profusion of hermit crabs, anemones, and starfish clambering over one another. Make sure you wear tennis shoes — the jagged rocks can cut your feet. From San Diego, take rt. 5 to Ardath Rd. exit. Take Ardath west until it becomes Torrey Pines Rd. Take Torrey Pines west, turn right on Prospect and follow it to Coast Boulevard. Follow signs to La Jolla Cove.

Whale Point – If you visit La Jolla during December, January, or February, visit Whale Point. Every year the giant whales migrate south along this route. Since they've been doing this for the past eight million years or so, we have no reason to believe they'll stop before you read this chapter. To get to Whale Point, follow the shore south from Alligator Head. Opposite the only large building on the beach, there's a small cove known as Seal Rock. From Seal Rock, you'll be able to see another cove, marked by a lifeguard stand and a wall. That's Whale Point.

La Jolla Museum of Contemporary Art – Dramatically situated on the beach, between Seal Rock and Whale Point. The gardens and building are well worth a look. You'll find paintings and sculpture from all over the world. A good place to contemplate art and nature. Closed Mondays. Free. Prospect and Silverado (454-3541).

Sea Caves – A natural formation of seven caves hollowed out by the waves. You get there by walking along the cliffs fronting the ocean. To get to the caves, take Coast Boulevard to the tunnel leading to Coast Walk.

Scripps Institute of Oceanography – One of the most highly esteemed marine study institutes in the world. You can stroll through the grounds, or relax on the Scripps beach. You can't walk on the pier, but the Thomas Wayland Vaughn Aquarium Museum is open to the public. You can watch the fish being fed at 1:30 PM Wednesdays and Saturdays. Open daily. Free. La Jolla Shores Dr. (452-4086).

Torrey Pines State Park – In order to avoid crowding, admission is limited. Get there early. The strange-looking, bent pine trees, which are the outstanding feature, date back to the period when southern California was a pine forest. On the northern side of the park, Los Penasquitos Lagoon offers a spectacular vantage point for watching blue herons and rare egrets. Mule deer come to the southern part of the lagoon to feed. Open daily. Admission charge. Torrey Pines Rd. (755-2063).

■ **EXTRA SPECIAL:** No tour of San Diego would be complete without a visit to *Mexico*. The bustling border city of *Tijuana* is located just 17 miles south of downtown. Many visitors and residents drive here, park their cars on the US side of the border, and walk into Tijuana. (The Tijuana taxis are infamous for overcharging. If you refuse to pay you can end up in jail.) San Diego's new trolley system is a good alternative to driving. The trip to Tijuana takes about 40 minutes and costs $1 each way. You can hop on the trolley at various points along the way, but the route originates at the Amtrak Terminal, C St. and Kettner Blvd., and terminates at San Ysidro (200 feet from the border). Trolleys leave the main stations (in either direction) every 20 minutes from 5:15 AM to 9 PM daily; tickets are purchased at vending machines located at all pick-up points. Tijuana has many crafts shops selling finely wrought ironwork, pottery, and jewelry. Prices are a fraction of what they are at home. You can bring back $100 worth of goods duty-free, once every 30 days. Goods must be declared at retail value at the checkpoint for reentering the US. (If you're driving into Mexico, it's wise to purchase insurance at one of the many insurance offices near the border. It will prevent you from unpleasant detention should you happen to have an accident. Normal US insurance is *not* valid in Mexico.) Tijuana also offers year-round thoroughbred racing, dog racing, jai alai, and bullfighting.

A short drive down a scenic toll road from Tijuana is *Ensenada*, a resort and fishing village. From Ensenada, the road stretches to the south of Baja California. No visas or tourist cards are needed for US citizens in the border areas. You do need a tourist card to travel south of Ensenada.

SOURCES AND RESOURCES

The San Diego Convention and Visitors Bureau distributes brochures and maps. 1200 3rd Ave., Suite 824 (239-9696). There's a Visitor Information Center on East Mission Bay Drive off rt. 5, Mission Bay (276-8200). If you want advance information, write: Mission Bay Lessees Association, 1702 East Mission Bay Drive. For maps and brochures on walking tours of the historic district, stop at the Visitor Information Center at Old Town Plaza (237-6770).

Barry Berndes' The San Diegan (San Diego Guide, $1.95) is the most complete local guide to the San Diego area. You can get a copy by writing *The San Diegan*, PO Box 99127, San Diego 92109, or by calling 275-2213.

All telephone numbers are in the 714 area code unless otherwise indicated.

For Local Coverage – *Evening Tribune,* evening daily; *Union,* morning daily; *Del Mar News-Press*, weekly.

For Food – *Barry Berndes' The San Diegan.*

CLIMATE AND CLOTHES: Rainstorms are few and far between, and almost invariably occur in December, January, and February. During these months, the temperature might drop down into the high 40s at night, so bring a sweater. Daytimes are generally in the 60s. The rest of the year, you can expect bright days and cool evenings with daytime highs in the 70s, lows at night in the 50s. Bathing suits are de rigueur all year round.

GETTING AROUND: Bus – The San Diego Transit System operates frequent buses connecting downtown with the suburbs (233-3004).

Taxi – You can get a cab by calling Yellow Cab (234-6161); Radio Cab (232-6566); Checker Cab (234-4477); Co-Op Cab (280-2667).

Car Rental – The best way to see everything at your convenience is by car. All major national car rental firms are represented. For less expensive rates, try Airways–American Rental Systems (291-9555).

Trolley – The San Diego Trolley is a new, inexpensive way to get around. There are pick-up points throughout the city, but the line originates at the Amtrak Terminal, C St. and Kettner Blvd., and leaves every 20 minutes from 5:15 AM to 9 PM daily. Tickets are dispensed from machines at all trolley stops and cost from 25¢ to $1 depending on your destination, with discounts for senior citizens and the handicapped.

MUSEUMS: Balboa Park contains most of the city museums: the Timken and Fine Arts Galleries, Museum of Man, Aerospace Museum, Reuben H. Fleet Space Center, and Museum of Natural History. The Maritime Museum, Serra Museum, San Diego Union Newspaper Museum, Heritage Park, historic Old Town houses, and La Jolla Museum of Contemporary Art are given fuller descriptions in *Special Places*. Palomar Observatory's giant telescope was, for many years, the most powerful in the world. It's still in use. Photographs of the cosmos are on exhibit. Open daily. County Rd. S6, east of Escondido (742-3476).

MAJOR COLLEGES AND UNIVERSITIES: Scripps Institute of Oceanography (see *Special Places*) is only a part of the University of California at San Diego. The rest of the campus is at University City, La Jolla (452-2230). Other colleges and universities include: US International University, Pomerado Rd. (271-4300); San Diego State University, Alvarado Freeway (265-5200); University of San Diego, Alcala Park (291-6480); Point Loma College, 3900 Lomaland Dr. (222-6474); San Diego Community College District (junior colleges), 3375 Camino del Rio S (230-2000).

SPECIAL EVENTS: San Diego is a summer festival almost all year.

January: *Andy Williams San Diego Open Golf Tournament*, Torrey Pines Golf Course (291-5372; 453-1692); *Rugby Tournament*, Robb Field, 2525 Bacon St. (224-7581).

February: *Indoor Games*, Sports Arena, 3500 Sports Arena Blvd. (224-4171).

March: *Kite Festival*, Ocean Beach (223-1175); *La Costa Tennis Tournament*, La Costa Country Club, Costa del Mar Rd., Carlsbad (438-9111 ext. 431); *Pacific Coast Soaring Championships*, Torrey Pines Glider Port, La Jolla (232-3301).

April: *San Diego Crew Classic*, Bahia Point, Mission Bay Park (488-3642); *Jumping*

Frog Jamboree (preliminaries for Calaveras County annual contest), Del Mar Fairgrounds (755-1161); *PGA Tournament of Champions*, La Costa Country Club, Costa del Mar Rd., Carlsbad (438-9111 ext. 431).

May: *Fiesta de la Primavera*, citywide.

June: *Model Yacht Regatta*, Model Yacht Basin, West Vacation Isle, Mission Bay Park (238-2140); *Annual Camp Pendleton Rodeo*, Camp Pendleton, Area 16 (725-5517); *Shakespeare Festival*, Balboa Park (239-2255).

July: *God Bless America Week* (238-1828); *La Jolla Tennis Championship*, 7632 Draper St. (454-4434); *Southern California Exposition*, Del Mar Fairgrounds (755-1161; 297-0338); *Jazz Festival*, San Diego Stadium (224-4171); *Sun 'n' Sea Festival* parade, aqua games (299-3615); *Festival of the Bells* to celebrate founding of the California missions (281-8449).

August: Annual celebration of *America's Finest City Week.*

September: *Mexican Independence Day* (15 and 16 September); *Cabrillo Festival* (293-5450); *Fiddle and Banjo Contests*, Frank Lane Memorial Park (765-0323).

October: *Oktoberfest*, La Mesa (469-6194); *Borrego Springs Desert Festival*, Borrego Springs (767-6555).

November: *Starlight Yule Parade*, Chula Vista (420-6602); *National Senior Hardcourt Tennis Championships*, La Jolla Beach and Tennis Club (454-7126).

December: *Mission Bay Parade of Lights*, from Quivira Basin to Sea World (276-2800).

SPORTS: There's just about everything for everybody.

Baseball – National League *Padres* play at San Diego's Jack Murphy Stadium, 9449 Friars Rd. (283-4494).

Football – NFL *Chargers* (280-2111) and San Diego State University *Aztecs* (265-6947) play home games at the Stadium, too.

Racing – Thoroughbreds race at Del Mar Race Track, July to September, I-5 to Fairgrounds exit (755-1141 or 299-1340), also at Caliente Race Track, Tijuana (239-8121) (see *Extra Special,* p. 424). Jai alai is played at Fronton Palacio, Tijuana, Fridays through Wednesdays (421-4740).

Bicycling – Hamel's Cyclery and Surf Shop, 704 Ventura Pl., Mission Beach (488-5050); California Bicycle, 633 Pearl St., La Jolla (454-0316); Wheels 'n Things, 2910 Navajo Rd., El Cajon (465-3976).

Fishing – The longest fishing pier on the West Coast is at Point Loma. There are also piers at Mission Bay, San Diego Harbor, and Shelter Island. You don't need a license, and there is no fee for pier fishing. For deep sea fishing, however, you do need a permit. Write to the California Department of Fish and Game Resources Building, 1416 9th St., Sacramento 95814. Marlin, yellowtail tuna, and sailfish run in the spring. Seaforth Sportfishing offers day and overnight excursions, 1717 Quivira Rd. (224-3383).

Golf – For listings of special golf tournaments, see *Special Events*, above. Torrey Pines municipal golf course alongside the ocean is the site of the annual Andy Williams Open. It's also the most famous golf course of all 58 public courses in San Diego County. Golf Central handles arrangements for 10 of these courses, and will help you find partners (299-9009). Mission Bay Golf Course is lit up for night games, Mission Bay Park (273-1221).

Tennis – For special tennis tournaments, see *Special Events*, above. The best public courts are at La Jolla Recreation Center, 615 Prospect St. (454-2071). Others can be found at Cabrillo Playground, 3051 Canon, Point Loma (226-9389); Standley Park, 3585 Governor Dr. (452-8556); and Robb Field, 2525 Bacon St. (224-7581).

Swimming – There are 70 miles of public beaches, not to mention Mission Bay Park's manmade lagoons. La Jolla and Torrey Pines State Park beaches are especially beautiful (see *Special Places*). There are eight municipal swimming pools: Kearney

Mesa Park, Mesa Park, Kerns Memorial Park, Vista Terrace, Swanson, King, Colina del Sol, and Mission Beach Plunge. For information call the Aquatics Department of the City Recreation Office (236-6652).

Surfing and Scuba Diving – La Jolla Cove is the most popular scuba diving spot because the water is particularly clear. Boomer Beach, so named because of the rumbling sound of surf crashing to shore, is the body surfers' first choice. Surfboarders ride the waves at La Jolla Shores.

Sailing and Boating – The City Recreation Department rents motorboats and rowboats for use on lakes (236-5532). They also give sailing courses (488-9895). Seaforth Boat Rentals has sailboats, rowboats, and power boats as well as boats rigged for water skiing. They also rent fishing gear, 1641 Quivira Rd., Mission Bay (223-1681). You can rent sailboats and take sailing lessons at Harbor Island Sailing Academy, 2040 Harbor Island Drive, Harbor Island (291-9568) and Vacation Village Boat Rentals, West Vacation Isle (274-4630).

Whale Watching – You can watch the migrating sea mammals from Cabrillo National Monument, Whale Point in La Jolla, or you can take a whale watching excursion from H & M Landing (224-1144) or Islandia Sport Fishing (222-1164). December, January, and February.

Skiing – The Torrey Pines Ski Club organizes trips to nearby mountains. Write PO Box 82087, San Diego 92138.

Ice Skating – The House of Ice at 5333 Lake Murray Blvd., La Mesa (463-8100), and at 11001 Black Mountain Rd. off Mira Mesa Blvd. W (271-4000) have day and night skating.

Flying – You can rent a Cessna or take flying lessons at Gibbs Flite Center, Montgomery Field (227-0310).

THEATER: *The Old Globe Theater* stages Shakespearean festivals every summer. The Elizabethan theater reproduction housing the festival was destroyed in 1978 by an arson fire, but has been rebuilt with public donations. (239-2255). The rest of the year, the company performs at the next-door Cassius Carter Center Stage in modern musicals and dramas, Balboa Park (239-2255). *Mandeville Center* offers plays, dance concerts, and musical events by members of the University of California San Diego Campus and professional touring groups at Torrey Pines Rd., La Jolla (452-2380). *Marquis Public Theater,* 317 India St. (298-8111) does classics, modern and experimental plays. For intimate cabaret-style musicals, *Coronado Playhouse*, 1775 Grand Way, Coronado (435-4856).

MUSIC: San Diego Convention and Performing Arts Center consists of three separate theaters. The Civic Theater is home of the *San Diego Symphony* and *San Diego Opera Company*, and top-name professional musicians. Golden Hall is the stage for big-name rock artists. Plaza Hall hosts trade expos and exhibits like the annual antiques show. All at 202 C St. (236-6510). *California Ballet* does the Nutcracker Suite at Christmas, other classics the rest of the year, 8276 Ronson Rd. (560-5676). The *San Diego Ballet* performs classics, too, at their home, 526 Market St. (239-4141). *San Diego Youth Symphony* also performs at Civic Theater (233-3232). Free organ concerts are played every Sunday, 2:30 PM, at the Organ Pavillion, Balboa Park. For jazz, visit the *Catamaran,* 3999 Mission Blvd., Mission Beach (488-1081).

NIGHTCLUBS AND NIGHTLIFE: *The Halcyon* is a very popular disco in town at 4258 West Pt. Loma Blvd., Ocean Beach (225-9559). *Bali Hai South Pacific Room* has a Hawaiian nightclub act, 2230 Shelter Island Dr. (222-1181). *Bacchanal* has live music nightly throughout the week and is a popular spot with young singles, 8022 Clairemont Mesa Blvd. (560-8022).

SINS: You really can't blame San Diego residents for puffing up with *pride* over their city's sunshine, its space, its utter cleanliness, and its fantastic zoo (among the best in the country); the city even has good restaurants, and *gluttony* thrives in Old Town State Park, a historic restoration of old San Diego where there are seven Mexican restaurants nearly side by side.

There are thorns in every paradise, however; and lest you overlook *lust,* you should be reminded of Lower Broadway, where virile young men fresh from the frustrations of the nearby naval base let themselves get worked up over a not particularly outstanding assortment of porn palaces. (There is far tonier action at some of the cozy bars in nearby La Jolla.)

LOCAL SERVICES: International Business Investments and Services, 2550 5th Ave. (231-8866).

Mechanics – Tenth Avenue Garage, 843 10th Ave. (232-1428); Jimmy on the Spot Mobile service — he comes to you (560-1140).

Babysitters – Sitter Service Agency, 4138 30th St. (281-7755); Reliable Babysitter Agency, 3439 Adams Ave. (280-2870).

■ **WHEN THE SWALLOWS COME BACK:** Yes, the swallows come back to Capistrano. Every year. Stop in at the Mission of San Juan Capistrano in March for a serenade. It's also open daily the rest of the year. Free. Follow rt. 5 north for 47 miles to Capistrano exit (493-1111).

BEST IN TOWN

CHECKING IN: San Diego has some really fine hotels and resorts, with outdoor athletic facilities and super views. The Hotel Del Coronado, for example, is one of the finest hotels in the world, and hearkens back to Victorian grandeur. Each place has something special to offer, and while we've only listed five of the choicest, there are many others. Expect to pay between $40 and $50 for a double at those places we've noted as expensive; between $30 and $40, moderate, under $30 at places listed as inexpensive.

Little America Westgate – Tops. Located in the heart of the city, the modern, deluxe 225-room hotel is considered one of the finest in the US. Its central location, near the San Diego Convention Center, makes it convenient if you don't have a car. In keeping with the $1 million worth of antiques decorating the premises, the hotel offers fine service. The *Fontainebleau Room* is one of the best restaurants in town (see *Eating Out*). 1055 2nd Ave. (238-1818). Expensive.

Sheraton-Harbor Island – Located within sight of the airport, this 500-room resort and convention hotel has tennis courts, saunas, a swimming pool, and complete convention facilities. Harbor Island has more of the same. 1380 Harbor Island Dr. (291-2900). Expensive.

Half Moon Inn – On Shelter Island, overlooking the bay and the marina with all its sleek and shining boats. This is the newest US member of the august Relais et Chateau hotel group, only the fourth American hotel to be so honored. In addition to 137 luxury rooms, the complex boasts a putting green, shuffleboard courts, and Ping-Pong. Within walking distance are boat yards and sport-fishing operations. 2302 Shelter Island Dr. (phone: toll-free outside California, 800 854-2900; toll-free within California, 800 532-3737; locally 224-3411). Expensive.

Hotel del Coronado – One of the world's great hotels. When it opened in 1888, it was the largest wooden building in the country and the first hotel in the world to have electrical lighting and elevators. Thomas Edison himself supervised the electrical installation. Today, this turreted, rambling 339-room resort is such a landmark that the management offers tours on Saturday afternoons. The nearby *Chart House Restaurant* is very good (see *Eating Out*). On the Coronado Penninsula, 1500 Orange Ave. (435-6611). Expensive to moderate.

Town and Country – One of the best in Mission Valley. Its 1,000 rooms make this the largest hotel in the city. A popular convention hotel; facilities include tennis courts, pools, saunas, barber shop, beauty parlor, and convention rooms. Winter rates are $10 lower than summer rates. 500 Hotel Circle (291-7131). Moderate.

Torrey Pines Inn – A spectacular location overlooking the Pacific and right next door to the famous Torrey Pines Golf Course. You can watch surfers and hang gliders from the hotel windows, and La Jolla's beaches are just out the door. Swimming pool and lounge with entertainment on the premises. 67 rooms. 11480 Torrey Pines Rd., La Jolla (453-4420). Inexpensive.

EATING OUT: San Diego has a wide range of restaurants, the most prevalent being Mexican and seafood. A family of four can eat heartily at a good Mexican restaurant for under $20. There are two local chains which are excellent — Anthony's Fish Grottos and Chart House. Expect to pay $25 to $35 at those places listed as expensive; $15 to $25, moderate; under $15, inexpensive. Prices are for a meal for two, not counting drinks, wine, or tips.

Anthony's Star of the Sea Room – One of the best on the West Coast. Overlooking San Diego Harbor, Anthony's serves fresh-from-the-ocean abalone, and other fish and shellfish. Their clams Genovese is often ordered as an entrée. Open daily except major holidays. Reservations required a day or two in advance. Major credit cards. Harbor Dr. at foot of Ash St. (232-7408). Expensive.

Top o' the Cove – Looking out onto La Jolla Cove, a favorite of show-biz types from LA. If you're in the mood for experimenting, order the langosta con guacamole — it's lobster with avocado and mushrooms in white wine sauce. The restaurant is famous for its hot bread puffs. The soup is good, too. Closed Mondays and holidays. Reservations necessary. Major credit cards. 1216 Prospect St., La Jolla (454-7779). Expensive.

Prince of Wales Grille – Interestingly enough, this is where the one-time Prince of Wales met the woman for whom he abdicated his throne. Grilled dishes are the specialty here. We suggest the crown roast rack of lamb — it's appropriately regal. Closed Sundays and holidays. Reservations required. Major credit cards. Hotel del Coronado, 1500 Orange Ave. (435-6611). Expensive.

Coronado Chart House – One of the chain. This one, in the Hotel del Coronado's boathouse, has Tiffany lamps, antique tables, and a very friendly atmosphere. The view looks out at Glorietta Bay. Steak and lobster are served, and everything is charcoal broiled. Open daily. Reservations are not accepted. Major credit cards. Near Hotel del Coronado, 1701 Strand Way (435-0155). Expensive.

Fontainebleau Dining Room – Waiters wearing white gloves quietly bring you superlative Continental dishes such as veal with bay shrimp. The dessert cart is fabulous. Stunning blue-paneled walls and Louis XIV furniture contribute to that sense of knockout elegance. One of San Diego's very best. Open daily. Reservations necessary. Major credit cards. Little America Westgate Hotel, 1055 2nd Ave. (238-1818). Expensive.

Lubach's – For many years this was considered San Diego's best restaurant. Now, there are other contenders for the title, but Lubach's is still in the ring. Shrimp brochette and calf's sweetbreads financière highlight a menu which includes some fabulous beef and duck dishes. The house salad is great, too, but the wine list is skimpy. Closed Sundays and holidays. Reservations advisable. Major credit cards. 2101 North Harbor Dr. (232-5129). Expensive.

Pisces – The choices here are mainly seafood, although there are some dishes flambéed to lighten things up. The sole with aquavit has a special delicacy. There are some terrific California wines available to complement your meal. Closed holidays. Reservations necessary. Major credit cards. 7640 El Camino Real, Carlsbad (436-9362). Expensive.

Butcher Shop – If, after the theater or other late activity, you crave a good steak, this is the place. The menu is actually a tray filled with the cuts of meat you can order. Meals are served until 1 AM every night. Open daily. Reservations advised. Major credit cards. 1515 Hotel Circle (291-8405). Moderate.

Nino's – Unpretentious surroundings and superior food. Owner Nino Dobrich is in the kitchen all the time to make sure that everything is done just so. The deep-fried zucchini and eggplant are served as an appetizer with every meal. Follow that with spaghetti in butter and garlic and veal Fiorentina and you've got a meal to remember. Closed Mondays and Tuesdays. Reservations advisable. Major credit cards. 4501 Mission Bay Dr. (274-3141). Moderate.

China Camp – The cooking is not Chinese, but it's not quite American, either. Specialties such as drunk steak, begger's hen, and immigrant beef are based on the recipes of the Chinese immigrants who came to California in 1849 to pan for gold. Open daily. Reservations advised. Major credit cards. Pacific Hwy. at Hawthorne (232-1367). Moderate.

Alfonso's – Recipes have been handed down from generation to generation. No, Alfonso won't tell you one of them. You'll probably ask, though, since his Mexican dishes are probably the most popular in town. Try carne asado Alfonso or one of the burrito or taco combination plates. Every dish comes with a marvelous house salad and bread baked in Mexico earlier that day. Ask for Alfonso's Secret — it changes every day, but it's not on the printed menu. Open daily. Reservations advisable. Major credit cards. 1251 Prospect St., La Jolla (454-2232). Inexpensive.

Aztec Dining Rooms – Another hit with aficionados. There are combination plates and five dinner plates, as well as standard à la carte tacos, chiles rellenos, and enchiladas. The guacataco contains shredded beef, guacamole, and hamburger. Mexican beer is available. There are two Aztec dining rooms. Aztec No. 1 is located at the edge of Old Town State Park and offers colorful piñata and pottery decor. Aztec No. 2 offers the same food in a plainer setting. Both are open daily. No reservations necessary. No credit cards. Aztec No. 1, 2811 San Diego Ave., Old Town (295-2965); Aztec No. 2, 2152 San Diego Ave. (295-9514). Inexpensive.

El Chalan – If you've never sampled Peruvian food, this is a good place to start. Actually, the food here is superior to what most Peruvians eat. Start with spicy ceviche, a marinated cold fish salad. You can follow it with papas rellenas — potatoes stuffed with meat, or pescado à la chorrillana, fish sautéed with garlic, onions, peppers and tomatoes. There's real affection between the owner and his clientele. Closed Tuesdays. Reservations suggested. Major credit cards. 5621 La Jolla Blvd. (459-7707). Inexpensive.

Bit of Sweden – All you can eat — and then some — in a help-yourself smorgasbord. There are more salads than you can decently consume, and hot dishes that include roast beef, turkey, baked ham, Swedish meatballs, Swedish pancakes, and stuffed cabbage. Then there's dessert. Closed Mondays. Reservations advisable. No credit cards. 2850 El Cajon Blvd., East San Diego (284-7893). Inexpensive.

Hamburguesa – Stop in for a burger after your tour of Old Town. You can also get great steak and Cobb salad, made with avocado and three different cheeses. Closed Christmas and New Year's Day. Reservations accepted if you call at least an hour in advance. Major credit cards. 4016 Wallace (295-0584). Inexpensive.

SAN FRANCISCO

"San Franciscans are the luckiest people on earth; they not only get a vacation with pay, they have San Francisco to come home to." A Chamber of Commerce press release? No, just the sentiments of one of the lucky ones, *San Francisco Chronicle* columnist Herb Caen, who, like most of its residents, is in love with this city. It is a characteristic of genuine San Franciscans, whether native or transplanted, that they simply can't hear enough praise of the place. And such is the nature of San Francisco that they are very rarely disappointed. A visitor commented on her last day in the city, "I feel sorry for children born here. How sad to grow up and find out the whole world isn't like this." And even Billy Graham has stated publicly that "the Bay Area is so beautiful I hesitate to preach about heaven while I'm here."

Any place that can give pause to Billy Graham must be a remarkably well-endowed piece of geography. And so San Francisco is. The city occupies a hilly peninsula of 47 square miles, shaped something like a slightly crooked thumb pointing northward. On its western border is the Pacific Ocean; to the east is huge, beautiful San Francisco Bay. The waters of the Bay join the Pacific through the narrow northern strait which Golden Gate Bridge spans so spectacularly. When the Bay fills with fog, as it often does, the bridge becomes a single strand of lights riding over clouds. By choosing an inland suburb or an area on the coast, residents can have either the Sun Belt warmth of California's eternal spring or the sharper, foggier weather bred along the shoreline.

Either way, the city's climate is universally desirable for walking, if you can handle the incredibly steep hills. Hidden lanes, small houses circled by picket fences and surrounded by large commercial buildings, stately Victorian façades, stunning murals and other public art, and historical plaques reward even a casual stroll. Grant Avenue provides a tour of Chinatown; Columbus, a glimpse of Italian North Beach and the birthplace of the Beat Generation; and Sutter, a taste of San Francisco's high fashion shops and art galleries.

More demanding is a climb up the city's hills. To live "uphill" in any part of town is more prestigious than downhill, and to live on a famous hill tops all. Nob Hill, original home of the railroad nabobs and now site of several of the city's luxury hotels, is a most elegant address, and Russian Hill has renowned views of the city and the Bay. Along Telegraph Hill's eastern side, Filbert and Greenwich Streets create a series of steps that become wooden sidewalks fronting New England–style cottages, surrounded by gardens and filled with an impressive quiet.

For a city so generously festooned with views, vistas, and vantage points, San Francisco was a long time being discovered. Explorers seeking a northern strait and new lands, among them Sir Francis Drake and Juan Rodriguez Cabrillo, sailed up and down the California coast without spying out the great but hidden inner bay. In 1769, a Spanish land expedition led by Gaspar de Portolá blundered onto San Francisco Bay on a trek north from Mexico. Their goal had been Monterey, and their excitement at discovering one of the world's finest natural harbors was exceeded only by their confusion. The discovery, once made, did not go unheeded. In 1775, another Spaniard, Juan Manuel de Ayala, sailed through the rugged portals which had hidden the bay for so long, and for the first time the full potential of the inlet was realized. Soon after, the area was fully incorporated into Spain's American empire when Father Junipero Serra built Mission Dolores. San Francisco was an early center for the Pacific fur trade, and the 19th century brought New England whalers, Russian trappers, and, when gold was discovered at Sutter's Mill in 1849, nearly everyone else and his brother. By 1850, the population of San Francisco had grown from 900 to 56,000 — prompting Will Rogers to observe a century later that it was "the city that never was a town." (The population is 640,000 today.) Ten years after the gold strike, silver was found in the Comstock Lode, and San Francisco was caught in a second wave of prosperity that carried it to the end of the century. While Levi Strauss made a minor fortune providing Nevada miners with blue jeans, Leland Stanford, Charles Crocker, Collis P. Huntington, and Mark Hopkins financed the transcontinental railroad.

In many ways this uncompromising history influences the city's character today. The Gold Rush brought adventurers from around the world; they were violent, hard men, but they lived together with a certain graceless tolerance. The railroad brought Chinese into the city, and later came Japanese. Russians, Greeks, Mexicans, Filipinos, Scandinavians — all settled in larger and smaller communities around the city over the years. The result is an admirable harmony, and a kind of hodgepodge culture both pleasing and natural: In what other city is the long-time chef of the town's best pizza parlor Chinese? The basis for this culture is respect and tolerance among individual citizens. The city gives birth to new lifestyles, in part, because the civic body politic doesn't get choleric over diversity. It is a natural center of gay life, for example, and gays have been incorporated into the city's mainstream.

San Francisco's tradition of tolerance is responsible for numerous aspects of city life. Bawdy entertainment — much favored by the miners who gave up gold that was like blood for the privilege — is still part of the scene. "Encounter parlors" in North Beach get busted only at election time. Pitchmen outside "topless/bottomless" joints lure passing strollers with cries of "girls" or, if that fails, "eagles, beagles, and a duck." (Remember, curiosity killed the cat.)

What is life like here? Consider this anecdote: In this city of hills, full buses occasionally have trouble negotiating the steepest inclines. A bus driver with a full load may be forced to stop before beginning ascent, to ask a few passengers to get off. Remarkably enough, some always do. This is an absolutely true story, but it is also a parable of sorts, a conundrum to contemplate when standing on Golden Gate Promenade. From there you will see the fine spires of the bridge, with the gold dome of the Palace of Fine Arts shining below, and in the distance, framing the picture, the blue Pacific. If that's not a sight worth getting off the bus for, you're just not resident material.

SAN FRANCISCO AT-A-GLANCE

SEEING THE CITY: Coit Tower on the summit of Telegraph Hill offers a spectacular panorama of San Francisco and the surrounding area — to the north are the waterfront and San Francisco Bay, the Golden Gate Bridge, Alcatraz Island, and on the far shore, Sausalito; downtown San Francisco lies to the south; to the east are Berkeley and the East Bay Hills; and Nob Hill and Russian Hill rise to the west. The tower itself, a 210-foot cylindrical column built in 1934 under the Work Projects Administration, is a striking landmark against the city's skyline. Open daily. Small admission charge. Follow Telegraph Hill Blvd. to the top from Lombard and Kearny Sts. Twin Peaks is another excellent vantage point from which to view the city. Follow Twin Peaks Blvd. to the top. Several cocktail lounges offer fine views, too, and the highest, at 779 feet, is the *Carnelian Room,* the restaurant and bar atop the Bank of America building. 555 California St. (433-7500).

SPECIAL PLACES: San Francisco is a compact city and easy to get around. Most of the attractions are concentrated within a few areas, and the mild weather year-round makes walking pleasant. *San Francisco Discovery Walks* offers visitors a close look at the city's fine architecture, gardens, views, and Victorian interiors for $25, including lunch. Contact Fred Baumeister, 1200 Taylor St., #32 (673-2894).

DOWNTOWN

Civic Center – This seven-square-block area encompasses several attractive buildings and a nicely designed fountain and plaza. Among the buildings are City Hall, a notable example of Renaissance-style grandeur with a 300-foot-high dome; the War Memorial Opera House, site of the signing of the United Nations Charter in 1945 and current home of the San Francisco Opera and Ballet; the Civic Auditorium, scene of cultural and political events since 1915; and the new Louise M. Davies Symphony Hall. The War Memorial Veterans Building houses the San Francisco Museum of Modern Art. Its collection features modern art, and fine permanent collections include works by Matisse, Klee, Calder, and Pollock, while changing exhibits include works by internationally known modern and contemporary artists. Closed Mondays. Admission $2.00, free Thursday nights. McAllister St. and Van Ness Ave. (863-8800). Bounded by Van Ness Ave. and Hyde, McAllister, and Grove Sts., the Civic Center is also a good place to start the 49-Mile Drive, a well-marked trail that takes in many of the city's highlights. Just follow the blue, white, and orange seagull signs.

Union Square – Right in the shopping area, Union Square offers respite from the crowds of people in its throngs of pigeons. You can feed the pigeons, relax on the benches, watch the fashion shows, concerts, and flower displays that are held there in good weather. The elegant *St. Francis Hotel* is on the west side of the square, while the surrounding area contains sidewalk flower stands and the city's finest shops (*Gump's* has a beautiful collection of jade pieces among its many rare imports. 250 Post St.) Bordered by Geary, Post, Powell and Stockton Sts. (982-1616).

Bank of California's Collection of Money – Perhaps you've been wondering what makes those ticker-tape machines tick, and what's really behind all the action. You'll find the answer while looking at the pioneer gold quartz, the silver ingots, and the privately minted gold coins in this fine exhibition of Western currency. Open weekdays during banking hours. Free. 400 California St. (765-0400).

Wells Fargo History Room – The history room features more of Old California, with photographs and relics from Gold Rush days, and the Wells Fargo Overland Stage, the wagon that brought pioneers west, as well as coins from Mother Lode mines. Open weekdays during banking hours. Free. 420 Montgomery St. (396-2619).

Embarcadero Center – This 8½-acre area, housing shopping malls and offices, between the financial district and the waterfront features several notable sculptures, including the Vaillancourt Fountain (100 abstractly arranged concrete boxes with water pouring out of the ends) and a 60-foot sculpture by Louise Nevelson. At noon, street merchants set up stalls and you can pick up a variety of handcrafted goods — leather items, jewelry, macramé, paintings, and sculptures. At the foot of Market St.

Chinatown – The largest Chinese community outside of the Orient, Chinatown is an intriguing 24-block enclave of pagoda-roofed buildings, excellent restaurants, fine import shops featuring ivory carvings and jade jewelry from the Orient, temples, and museums. Grant Avenue is the main thoroughfare — enter through an archway crowned with a dragon (Grant at Bush St.). Best to go on foot or take the California Street cable car, because the area is quite congested and difficult to find parking in. The Old St. Mary's Church, built in 1854 of granite from China, is the city's oldest cathedral. It survived the earthquake, perhaps because of its warning on the façade above the clock dial: "Son Observe the Time and Fly from Evil" (Grant Ave. and California St.). More words of wisdom, as well as regional artifacts, including tiny slippers used for the bound feet of Oriental ladies, pipes from Old Chinatown opium dens, and photographs of early immigrants and some famed telephone operators who memorized the names and numbers of 2,400 Chinatown residents in the old days, can be found at the Chinese Historical Society of America Museum. Closed Sundays and Mondays. Free. (17 Adler Pl. off Columbus Ave., 391-1188). For information on walking tours of Chinatown, contact the Chinese Cultural Foundation, 730 Kearny St. (986-1822).

You haven't really experienced Chinatown fully until you've had dim sum, a breakfast or luncheon feast of a variety of delicate morsels — chopped mushrooms in half-moons of rice dough, deep-fried sweet potato, meat dumplings; try either the original *Yank Sing,* 671 Broadway (781-1111), or the *Hong Kong Tea House,* 835 Pacific Ave. (391-6365). Bordered by Kearny, Mason, Bush Sts. and Broadway.

North Beach – There is no longer a beach here, but this traditionally colorful neighborhood remains intact — mostly Italians, Basques, and artists. The area's great for strolling and eating — there are bakeries and bread shops selling cannolis, rum babas, marzipan, and panettone (a round, sweet bread filled with raisins and candied fruit). There are numerous restaurants and cafés where you can have dinner, espresso, or cappuccino. For lunch or dinner, the *North Beach Restaurant* (1512 Stockton St., phone: 392-1587) has a festive atmosphere and great pastas and veal. Or if you want to make it yourself, you can pick up noodle machines and espresso makers at any of the kitchen specialty shops. At night, the Broadway district offers some of the city's most varied nightlife: from Italian opera and jazz to *Finocchio's* (506 Broadway; 982-9588), for its famous female impersonators. One of the best times of year to visit North Beach is in June, during the street bazaar, when local artists display their wares. Other times, numerous galleries and studios exhibit crafts, paintings, jewelry, and sandals. Washington Square is a nice place to sit in the sun or have lunch with the local paisanos under the statue of Benjamin Franklin (Columbus and Union Sts). Extends north and northwest from Chinatown to San Francisco Bay.

Japan Center – This attractive modern complex is the focal point in culture and trade of San Francisco's substantial Japanese community. The five-acre area contains the *Kabuki Theater*, teahouses, restaurants, sushi and tempura bars, art galleries, a school where you can learn Japanese dollmaking and flower arranging, and the Japanese consulate. The elegantly landscaped Peace Plaza with its five-tiered Peace Pagoda in the center of a reflecting pool is the scene of the April Cherry Blossom Festival and traditional Japanese celebrations, like the Mochi-Pounding Ceremony (in which much preparation and even more pounding result in delicious rice cakes). Speaking of pounding, the Kabuki Hot Springs' shiatsu massage, traditional Japanese baths, whirlpool, saunas, steam bath, and the works will make you feel good as a newly made rice cake (1750 Geary Blvd., 922-6000). Bounded by Laguna, Fillmore, Geary, and Post Sts.

FISHERMAN'S WHARF AND VICINITY

Fisherman's Wharf – This charming waterfront section is at once the center of the commercial fishing industry and California's major tourist attraction, second only to Disneyland. On the wharf at Jefferson Street you walk through an open-air fish market where you can partake in an old San Francisco tradition. Buy a loaf of freshly baked sourdough bread at Boudin's Bread Company and make the ultimate sandwich by adding Dungeness crab purchased at one of the numerous sidewalk stalls. As you munch, stroll around and see some original, off-beat *shtiks* such as a one-man-aviator-band and the "Human Jukebox," who'll play some of his way-out tunes for a small fee. The fishing boats return in the afternoon, and hoist their crates of fish to the pier at the foot of Jones and Leavenworth Sts. If you're up late (about 3 AM), there are few sights at that hour more impressive than the San Francisco fleet leaving the harbor for a day's catch. The wharf restaurants are often crowded and expensive, and you would do better to have a seafood dinner elsewhere (see *Eating Out*). But the wharf vicinity does have many sidewalk stalls selling handcrafted items, and interesting sights have sprung up around this fishing base. Among things to see:

Pier 39 – Reconstructed with wood salvaged from other (demolished) piers, Pier 39 is a new entertainment complex on the northern waterfront. A pleasant day's sojourn can be spent ambling through Pier 39's plethora of shops — crafts, bakery, import, clothing, specialty, toy, jewelry, camera, gourmet delicacies, crystal and silver, and many others. For lunch or dinner, you can choose from among an international roster of cuisines — Mexican, Italian, Japanese, Chinese, Swiss, French, Polynesian; grab a bite at one of the numerous, stand-up, take-out fresh seafood booths; or simply indulge your sweet tooth at *Swensen's,* the famous ice cream parlor. Children can run off excess energy at the Pier's playground and park; weekend sailors and fishermen can charter boats at the marina. Pier 39, on the Embarcadero, just east of Fisherman's Wharf. (Parking garage located across the way on Beach St.)

Balclutha – This British three-masted squarerigger, first launched from Scotland in 1886, had a long and full life as a trading ship, rounding Cape Horn 17 times to San Francisco carrying rice and wine, working as an Alaskan salmon trader, and even doing a stint in Hollywood as a rather oversized prop in sea films. Today *Balclutha,* restored by the San Francisco Maritime Museum Association, is open for public inspection. You can see the wheelhouse, the red-plush upholstered chart house, the captain's cabin, and the hull with its collection of sailing and Barbary Coast memorabilia. Open daily. Admission charge. At Pier 43, Fisherman's Wharf (982-1886).

National Maritime Museum and Historic Park – This huge ship-shaped modernistic building is sure to catch your eye. The museum, now run by the National Park Service, is a treasure trove of photographs tracing shipping development from Gold Rush days to the present: figureheads, massive anchors, shipwreck relics, and beautiful model ships. Just north of the museum, along the Hyde Street Pier, is the Historic Park — five old ships including the steam tug *Hercules* and the steam schooner *Wapama.* Open daily. No admission charge. At the foot of Hyde St. at Jefferson (556-6435).

Bay Cruises – The Blue and Gold Fleet (Pier 39; 781-7877) and the Red and White Fleet (Pier 43½, near Fisherman's Wharf; 546-2805), cruise year-round past Alcatraz Island and the Golden Gate Bridge and then to the shoreline of Marin County rimming the Bay. Departures every day, all day, year-round. Admission charge.

Alcatraz Island – This famed escape-proof federal penitentiary stands out grimly in the Bay 1½ miles from Fisherman's Wharf. Such notorious criminals as Al Capone, "Machine Gun" Kelly, and Doc Barker never returned from their stays here. The prison was closed in 1963 because of exorbitant operating costs and has been open to the public since 1973. The National Park Service runs tours of the prison block, where you see the "dark holes" in which rebellious prisoners were confined in solitude, and the tiny steel-barred cells. Tours leave daily, but make reservations in advance. Charge for the ferry. Departs from Pier 41 (546-2805).

Ghirardelli Square – Originally a chocolate factory, these stately red-brick buildings house import shops where you can find anything from Persian rugs to Chinese kites, outdoor cafés, art galleries, and fine restaurants. *The Mandarin* serves excellent Chinese food; *Maxwell's Plum* has a flashy setting and a stunning bay view; but perhaps sweetest of all is the *Ghirardelli Chocolate Manufactory* (771-4903), where you can watch chocolate being made and then eat the spoils afterward, and if you're truly inspired, the Golden Gate banana split, which tops all — three scoops of ice cream, three flavors of syrup, and a banana bridge rising above mountains of whipped cream. Open daily. Bounded by Beach, Larkin, North Point, and Polk Sts.

The Cannery – Similar to Ghirardelli Square, but canned fruits and vegetables were the products made here. Today this tri-level arcade features chic boutiques and restaurants, and an olive tree–shaded central courtyard where street musicians and mimes strut their stuff. Open daily. Bounded by Beach, Leavenworth, and Jefferson Sts.

Lombard Street – Often referred to as the most crooked street in the world, Lombard St. has 10 hairpin turns in a single block. Drive down slowly, or better yet, stroll, taking time to appreciate the lovely residential facades and flower plantings. Between Hyde and Leavenworth Sts.

GOLDEN GATE — THE PROMENADE AND THE PARK

Golden Gate Promenade – This 3½-mile shoreline trail is among the most spectacular walks (or jogging paths) in America. You meander from Aquatic Park past lush green trees, eroding rocky points, a classy yacht harbor, a grassy park beside an old cobbled seawall, all the while approaching that ultimate of bridges, the Golden Gate. Along the way, you have access to a number of interesting museums. Fort Point, built in 1863 as the West Coast's only Civil War outpost, is now a military museum. Free. (Under the bridge, 556-1693). The Presidio Army Museum, established in 1776 as a Spanish garrison, has artifacts from the Civil War and Spanish-American War. Closed Mondays. Free. Lincoln and Funston Ave. (561-4115). Most unusual is the Palace of Fine Arts, a grand old Beaux-Arts building constructed for the Panama-Pacific Exhibition of 1915. It houses the Exploratorium, a collection of 400 exhibits on perception, which demonstrate just how deceiving the senses can be. Many involve participation, so don't be too perturbed if you reach for something that is not there. Closed Mondays and Tuesdays. Free. 3601 Lyon St. (563-3200).

The Golden Gate Bridge – The loftiest and one of the longest single-span suspension bridges ever constructed. At the bridge, climb to the toll plaza for the view. From here you have several options: You can catch a bus back downtown; turn around, and walk back with the city skyline accompanying you all the way; or follow in the footsteps of great coast trekkers across the Golden Gate Bridge and beyond — north along trails on the ridges and shoreline for 60 miles to Tomales Point. You can walk across the bridge (or under it); if you are driving, take the very first exit north of the bridge, park, and enjoy the terrific view of San Francisco.

California Palace of the Legion of Honor – A memorial for America's WW I dead, modeled after its namesake in Paris, this beautiful classic Greek building houses a fine collection of French art, particularly strong on Impressionist paintings by Monet, Manet, and Degas, and Rodin sculptures. Closed Mondays and Tuesdays. Admission charge includes entry to the de Young Museum (see below). Lincoln Park (558-2881).

Golden Gate Park – Developed from 1,000 acres of rolling sand dunes, Golden Gate Park has all the amenities of a large recreation area. There are bike paths, hiking and equestrian trails, three lakes (where you can sail model boats, or rent real ones, or practice casting), sports fields, and a 25-acre meadow. The park also features a Rose Garden, a lovely Rhododendron Dell, the Strybing Arboretum — over 70 acres rich with 5,000 species of plants and trees from all over the world — and the Conservatory, a greenhouse with lush tropical growth. (Arboretum and Conservatory open daily. Free. Along South Drive and Conservatory Drive respectively.) The *Japanese Tea Garden* is a masterpiece of Oriental landscaping with a half-moon wishing-well bridge, a bronze Buddha, a temple, a teahouse serving jasmine and green tea, and in the spring, magnificent blooms of cherry blossoms. Open daily. (Off South Drive just west of the de Young Museum.) No such lyrical setting could be complete without music, and the Music Concourse offers this with free open-air Municipal Band concerts on Sunday afternoons when weather is good (located between the de Young Museum and the California Academy of Sciences). Two fine museums are part of the park's cultural facilities:

M. H. de Young Memorial Museum – The West Coast's major art museum contains the Western world's finest Oriental collection. Donated by Avery Brundage, the wing contains Chinese jades, bronzes, ceramics, Japanese paintings, delicate lacquered woodwork, and art from India, Korea, and Southeast Asia spanning 6,000 years of Eastern civilization. Also has exhibits of European and Classical works. American Galleries contain the extensive Rockefeller Collection of paintings and furniture. Closed Mondays and Tuesdays. Small admission charge. On the Music Concourse (558-2887).

California Academy of Sciences – The state's oldest scientific institution offers a wide variety of exhibits ranging from the aquarium, with dolphins, piranhas, talking fish, and 14,000 other species, to the farthest reaches of space in the planetarium's changing shows on black holes and UFOs. Open daily. Small admission charge. On the Music Concourse (221-5100).

Cable Car Barn – This lovely brick building is the powerhouse for the current system (you can watch the cable which pulls the cars being threaded through a huge figure eight) and the storehouse for cable car history. The first cable car, invented in 1873 by Andrew Hallidie, and exact scale models of cars servicing all the various lines are on display here at their middle stop. Open daily. Free. At Washington and Mason Sts., near Chinatown (474-1887).

■ **EXTRA SPECIAL:** Within an hour's drive of San Francisco (north along US 101, rt. 37, then rt. 21) is California wine country — the gently rolling hills of *Napa Valley* and *Sonoma County*. This major wine-producing region has numerous wineries which are open for tours and tastings. The beautiful weather is accommodating not only for the vineyards but also for outdoor activity. Among the wineries, the most interesting to visit are Beringer Wines (St. Helena), where you enter the old hillside's aging tunnels and then attend a tasting in the Gothic Rhine House; the Christian Brothers (Mont LaSalle); and the Sterling Vineyard (south of Calistoga), with its striking Aegean-style architecture. You can pick up bread and cheese at any of the valley towns' shops and head to Bothe–Napa Valley State Park (via rt. 29), 1,000 wooded acres of broad-leafed trees, conifers, and redwoods, lovely for picnicking, hiking, and swimming. A few miles farther north is the town of Calistoga, home of the famous health spas and mineral baths, resorts, the interesting Napa County Historical Society Museum, and, best of all, an "Old Faithful" geyser, a 60-foot shower of steam erupting every 50 minutes.

SOURCES AND RESOURCES

The San Francisco Visitor and Convention Bureau, at 1390 Market St., is best for brochures, maps, general tourist information, and personal help. If you write in advance of your trip, the Bureau will send you a valuable package of information, including a three-month calendar of events. You can call 391-2000 anytime for the lowdown on what's going on in town. Their downtown Visitor Information Center provides multilingual service. Powell and Market Sts. (626-5500).

San Francisco at Your Feet by Margot Patterson Doss (Sunset Books, $2.95) is a good walking guide.

All telephone numbers are in the 415 area code unless otherwise indicated.

For Local Coverage – *San Francisco Chronicle,* morning daily; *San Francisco Examiner,* evening daily. Sundays, the two publish a joint edition, including a comprehensive entertainment section, the Datebook.

For Food – Check the *San Francisco Menu Guide* by Dan Whelan and Bella Levin (Danella Publications, $2.95).

CLIMATE AND CLOTHES: Sitting serenely on seven major hills between the Bay and the Pacific, San Francisco is a naturally air-conditioned city, with cool fresh air year-round. Temperatures seldom rise above 75° or drop below 45°, so it's always a good idea to carry a sweater or a light jacket. The sun shines most of the time, although downpours are common between November and March. There are wide contrasts in climate in the San Francisco Bay Area and even within the city itself — most obviously, the frequent fogs along the western or Pacific coastal section. The fog rolls in past the Golden Gate Bridge, bringing a chill to the early evenings along with one of the finest sights imaginable.

GETTING AROUND: Bus – Efficient and inexpensive buses serve the entire metropolitan area. Bus maps appear at the front of the Yellow Pages in the telephone book. For detailed route information contact MUNI (Municipal Transit) of San Francisco, 949 Presidio Ave. (673-MUNI).

Streetcar – Five lines of the MUNI Metro streetcar system run under Market Street, one level above BART, and branch off toward various parts of the city. For route information, call 673-MUNI.

Cable Car – The best way to travel up and over the hills of the city is aboard these famous trademarks; they are pulled along at 9½ miles an hour. There are three lines, and the most scenic is the Hyde Park line, which you can pick up at the turntable at Powell and Market Sts. It will take you over both Nob and Russian Hills to gaslit Victorian Square. For route information call 673-MUNI. The city's cable cars have been on and off their tracks for the past few years to undergo repair.

BART – If you really want to move, this ultra-modern, high-speed rapid transit rail network will whisk you from San Francisco to Oakland, Richmond, Concord, Daly City, and Fremont at up to 80 miles an hour. The system is easy to use, with large maps and boards in each station clarifying routes and fares. For information, contact Bay Area Rapid Transit, 800 Madison Ave., Oakland (788-2278).

Taxi – Cabs can be hailed in the street or called on the phone. Major cab companies are Yellow Cab (626-2345); Veteran's Cab (552-1300); Luxor Cab (552-4040).

Car Rental – There are a few things to remember if you plan to drive in San Francisco: Cable cars and pedestrians always have the right-of-way; curb your wheels when parking on a hill to prevent runaway cars. The national firms all serve San Francisco.

MUSEUMS: The San Francisco Museum of Modern Art, the M. H. de Young Memorial Museum, the California Academy of Sciences, the Wells Fargo Bank History Room, the Chinese Historical Society of America Museum, the National Maritime Museum, the Exploratorium, the California Palace of the Legion of Honor, are all described in *Special Places*. Others are:

Archives for the Performing Arts, 3150 Sacramento St. (922-6750).
California Historical Society, 2090 Jackson St. (567-1898).
The Wine Museum, 633 Beach St. (673-6990).
Mexican Museum, 1855 Folsom St. (621-1224).

MAJOR COLLEGES AND UNIVERSITIES: Two of the country's most prestigious universities are near San Francisco: University of California at Berkeley, Sproul Hall, Berkeley (642-6000), and Stanford University in Palo Alto (497-2300). San Francisco State College, 1600 Holloway Ave. (469-2141), and the University of San Francisco, Golden Gate Ave. and Parker Ave. (666-6886), are in the city.

SPECIAL EVENTS: The *Chinese New Year,* a week-long celebration in January or February (depending on the fullness of the moon) begins with numerous private observances — settling of debts and honoring of ancestors — and then Chinatown goes public with festivals that draw thousands to the streets for the colorful Dragon Parade featuring a block-long dragon, Miss Chinatown USA pageant, marching bands, and elaborate fireworks. To buy reserved bleacher seats, contact the Chinese Chamber of Commerce, 730 Sacramento St. (982-3000).

The *Cherry Blossom Festival* held on two weekends in April at Japan Center (Post and Buchanan Sts.) features traditional tea ceremonies, flower arranging and doll-making demonstrations, bonsai displays, and performances by folk dancers from Japan. The crosstown parade highlights the events with over 50 Japanese performing groups and intricate floats of shrines and temples. For a schedule, call the Japan Center (922-6776).

The *Grand National Livestock Exposition, Horse Show, and Rodeo,* held in late October and early November at the Cow Palace (6 miles south of city on rt. 101), is one of the biggest events in the country with all manner of rodeo events, equestrian competitions, and the best livestock in the West.

SPORTS: The San Francisco Bay Area has everything in professional sports.

Baseball – The San Francisco *Giants* play their home games from April to October in Candlestick Park (for ticket information call 467-8000). On Gilman Avenue, on the southern edge of the city on rt. 101. The *Oakland A's* play at the Oakland Coliseum Stadium (638-4900).

Basketball – The National Basketball Association's *Golden State Warriors* play their home games from October to March at the Oakland Coliseum Arena (635-7800).

Football – The San Francisco *49ers* play at Candlestick Park from August to December (for ticket information call 468-2249). The Oakland *Raiders* play at the Oakland Coliseum Stadium (635-4262).

Racing – For horse racing, Bay Meadows is the place, in San Mateo (574-7223). Seasons are: harness racing — last week of December through mid-February; quarter-horse racing — third week of February through the third week of May; thoroughbred racing — first week of September through the third week of December.

Yacht Racing – The Yacht Racing Association holds several races each year in San Francisco Bay. Good observation points are the Marina and the Vista Point area on the north side of the Golden Gate Bridge (for information call 771-9500).

Bicycling – Rent from Avenue Cyclery, 750 Stanyan, across from Golden Gate Park (387-3155). The park has good bike trails.

Fishing – Fine salmon fishing in the sea beyond the Bay. Season is mid-February to mid-October. Charter boats leave daily early in the morning and return in the afternoon. For information contact Captain Ron's Pacific Charters, 300 Jefferson St. at Fisherman's Wharf (771-2800). You can also cast off San Francisco's municipal pier at Aquatic Park, anytime. No license required.

Swimming – Though much of San Francisco's waters are too rough and cold for swimming, Phelan Beach is good when the weather permits and the current is safe, at Sea Cliff Ave. and El Camino Del Mar (221-5756).

Golf – There are fine courses at Golden Gate Park (751-8987), Lincoln Park (221-9911), and Harding Park (664-4690).

Tennis – Good public tennis courts are in Golden Gate Park on John F. Kennedy Dr. (566-4800).

Horseback Riding – Rent from Golden Gate Stables, Kennedy Dr. at 36th Ave. (668-7360). Seven miles of equestrian trails wind through the park.

Skating – Roller skating is very popular in San Francisco, especially on Sundays in Golden Gate Park when traffic is detoured off the park's roads. You can rent skates at the park entrance on Fulton and 10th sts., or from Skates on Haight, 1818 Haight St. (752-8575).

THEATER: For up-to-date offerings and performance times, check the newspapers listed above. The *American Conservatory Theater* is an excellent resident repertory company and performs classical productions and modern plays from October to May at the *Geary Theater*, 415 Geary St. (673-6440). The *Curran Theater* is best for musicals and often stages traveling Broadway productions, 445 Geary St. (673-4400). The *On-Broadway Theater* presents musical revues, 435 Broadway (398-0800); and the *Golden Gate Theater,* Golden Gate and Taylor Sts. (775-8800) also features Broadway shows. *Club Fugazi,* an old North Beach landmark, has camp productions in a nightclub setting, 678 Green St. (421-4222).

MUSIC: The *San Francisco Opera Company* (in the Civic Center) performs at the War Memorial Opera House featuring celebrated guest artists, from mid-September through November. Since the opera is very popular, it's difficult to get tickets, so the best thing to do is to write in advance: War Memorial Opera House, Box Office, San Francisco, CA 94102 (431-1210). The *San Francisco Symphony* performs in the brand-new Louise M. Davies Symphony Hall from December through May (431-5400). Tickets for the opera, symphony, and ballet can be obtained at Sherman Clay Co., 141 Kearny St. (392-4400), small service charge. During the summer the Symphony gives free open-air concerts on some Sunday afternoons at *Stern Grove*, 19th Ave. and Sloat Blvd. (398-6551). The *San Francisco Ballet* troupe, the country's oldest company and among the finest, performs at the Opera House from December through May and during a summer festival in June (for tickets call 431-1210).

NIGHTCLUBS AND NIGHTLIFE: San Francisco is alive at night and can keep you going whether you're inclined toward jazz or high camp. Much of the nightlife glitters around North Beach, but there's also plenty of activity all around the city. Current favorites: *Earthquake McGoon's,* for traditional Dixieland jazz, 128 The Embarcadero (986-1433), and *Keystone Korner,* 750 Vallejo

St. (781-0697), for jazz; the *Venetian Room* in the Fairmont Hotel (772-5163) for big-name entertainment; *Great American Music Hall,* 859 O'Farrell (885-0750) for major jazz and folk artists; *Old Waldorf,* 444 Battery (397-3884) for rock; *Finocchio's,* 506 Broadway (982-9388), for female impersonators; and *Punch Line,* 444 Battery (397-3884), for comedy. For a view of San Francisco at night try: *Top of the Mark,* 1 Nob Hill in Mark Hopkins Hotel (392-3434), or *Starlite Roof* in the Sir Francis Drake Hotel (392-7755).

SINS: San Francisco is a beautiful city, and an easy one in which to while away a life. From a hillside in the Presidio, overlooking the Golden Gate and Bay, to the rotating bar at the top of the Hyatt Regency, there are an infinite number of ways to laze through a day, *sloth* at its best. Golden Gate Park is full of nooks and crannies, lakes and flowerbeds, a Japanese tea garden and a buffalo range, all of which are easy to enjoy with very little energy expended. And when the fog starts to roll in and it's time to come inside, you can make your way to the lobby of the *Hyatt Regency*, check out the 18-floor-high ceiling, and travel in a glass cage up to the top of the building, into the alcohol and luxury of a bar that slowly rotates 360 degrees, revealing a complete and perfect view to everyone in the place, with no effort on your part.

When it comes to *avarice,* the port of San Francisco has been a delivery point for "stuff" from all over the world for many years. And stuff is what it has. Cost Plus, a multibuilding complex of international supermarkets featuring everything from Danish placemats to African evening clothes to Thai plants to Tibetan prayer bells, is certainly a shopper's must. As is Ghirardelli Square, a slightly more high-tone version of import mania, with an additional dollar or two added to each item to pay for the store owner's supreme good taste in picking merchandise.

As for *lust,* San Francisco rates as one of the prime porno capitals of the world. Here an enormous number of films are made as well as shown, and San Francisco's Broadway was one of the first places in the country to really develop a topless empire of bars and sleaze joints. But now, nude women wrestlers, naked love dancers, and female impersonators share Broadway with little theaters and an interesting mix of restaurants, making the street a bit tamer than it once was.

LOCAL SERVICES: Mechanics – California Garage, for American cars, 1776 Green St. between Gough and Octavia Sts. (474-0279). Foreign Car Repair, for imports, 6027 Geary between 24th and 25th sts. (752-8305).

Babysitting – Bristol Agency, 540 O'Farrell St. (776-9100).

BEST IN TOWN

CHECKING IN: President Taft called San Francisco the town that knows how, and though he probably wasn't talking about hotel accommodations, his statement applies. From the heights of luxury at the "Big Four" hotels on ritzy Nob Hill to downtown accommodations which offer real charm at more moderate prices, San Francisco's hotels are excellent. Where else but in San Francisco will a fresh flower be sent up with breakfast, maybe a grand piano in your suite, or such a good deal as all the food you can eat at a Jewish deli at 10% off if you stay at the adjoining hotel? Our selections range in price from $80 and up for a double room in the expensive bracket; $50 to $75, moderate; and $40 to $50, inexpensive.

Stanford Court – Built on the site of 19th-century Governor Leland Stanford's mansion, in the tradition of Nob Hill elegance and with a touch of original flair, this may be the best hotel in the entire U.S. The drive-in courtyard is covered by a Tiffanyesque glass dome; the rooms have rattan furniture, canopied beds, etchings of old San Francisco, and private baths complete with miniature TVs and heated towel racks. The hotel's restaurant, *Fournou's Oven,* specializes in racks of lamb roasted over an oakwood fire and cream of artichoke soup with hazelnuts. Its well-stocked wine cellar features a tasting room and private wine bins where you can store your personal favorites. You can have coffee or tea in the lobby bar or the fine café. 402 suites and rooms. 905 California St. (989-3500). Expensive.

Mark Hopkins – In the heights of extravagance at Number 1 Nob Hill, with some of the original gables and turrets of railroad magnate Mark Hopkins' 19th-century mansion, and a guest list that has included everyone from Haile Selassie to Frank Sinatra. Rooms feature either classical or contemporary decor, commodious baths and closets, possibly a grand piano (some of the suites have them). The tower rooms have fine views, but the glass-walled *Top of the Mark* lounge is best for a 360-degree panorama of the city. Open daily. 400 suites and rooms. 1 Nob Hill (392-3434). Expensive.

The Fairmont – On the other side of the cable car tracks, but on Nob Hill neither side of the tracks is the wrong one. Adjoining the distinctive old-fashioned main building is a modern tower topped by the *Fairmont Crown* which serves lunch and dinner. Among the other features are the *Tonga Room* for excellent Polynesian fare and dancing, *Canlis'* restaurant, the *Venetian Room* (closed Mondays) for supper and top name entertainment, the *New Orleans Room* for nightly Dixieland jazz, and the *Sweet Corner* for ice cream. 681 suites and rooms. California and Mason Sts. (772-5000). Expensive.

Hyatt Regency – Inside this futuristically designed structure is a 18-story atrium lobby with all the activity of a three-ring circus and a glass-enclosed elevator that whisks you to the top, where there's a revolving bar looking out on San Francisco. The rooms are attractive and modern, and the Hyatt offers all the amenities: convention facilities, shops, color TV, and, for a small fee, in-room movies and privileges at health and racquetball clubs. The Hyatt's lobby is particularly lively, with jazz concerts beginning at 3 PM on Saturdays and 4 PM on Sundays, big-band dancing Fridays from 5:30 to 8:30 PM, and the Regency Strings nightly from 9 PM. 806 rooms. Embarcadero Center (788-1234). Expensive.

Hyatt on Union Square – Quite luxurious, quite elegant. The view from the lavish suites on the 34th floor is simply breathtaking. On the top floor there are two cocktail lounges, one in the restaurant *Hugo's One-Up,* and one called *Reflections,* with a dance floor and piano bar. *Nappertandy's,* off the plaza deck, is popular at lunchtime. There are 700 guest rooms. 345 Stockton St. (398-1234). Expensive.

The Clift – The atmosphere is elegant and subdued. Its one restaurant, the *French Room,* specializes in roast prime ribs and Yorkshire pudding (open daily). Color TV, extension phones in bath, shops, garage. 402 rooms. Geary and Taylor Sts. (775-4700). Expensive.

Holiday Inn – Conveniently near Fisherman's Wharf, with standard accommodations and a pool, which in San Francisco hotels is unusual. Also has meeting rooms, color TV, café, and family plan. 1300 Columbus Ave. (771-9000). Expensive.

Huntington – One of the best values among Nob Hill hotels, with an atmosphere of understated elegance. The rooms are individually decorated and comfortable, and many have a good view of the Bay and the city. *L'Étoile* is a fine French restaurant (closed Sundays). 151 rooms. 1075 California St. (474-5400). Expensive.

St. Francis – This grand old hotel is a San Francisco landmark. Since 1904 it has entertained royalty, presidents, and international celebrities with its old world charm. As a 75th birthday present, the St. Francis recently underwent a massive renovation and added the 32-story Tower, which keeps to the hotel's theme of red velvet, glimmering crystal, and polished rosewood. At the top of the Tower are *Victor's* restaurant, featuring *la nouvelle cuisine,* and the chic *OZ* disco; both have lovely panoramic views of the city. The older sections of the hotel have restaurants, cocktail lounges, and convention facilities. On Union Square (397-7000). Expensive.

Pacific Plaza – One block west of Union Square, this elegant new hotel offers 140 spacious rooms (including nine suites), an atmosphere of serenity, and special touches such as live plants, terrycloth robes, complimentary local telephone calls, parking facilities, conference rooms, and a concierge. On the mezzanine level is *Donatello,* a good Italian restaurant. 501 Post St. (441-7100). Expensive.

Canterbury – This hotel has plenty of charm if you don't mind the downtown noise and the crowds. In the lobby there is a grandfather clock, a terrarium, two aquariums, and lots of human life as well — most on its way to or from *Lehr's Greenhouse,* a tropical garden restaurant with good shrimp creole, a salad bar, and very popular Sunday brunch. The rooms are large and attractive and have color TV and coffeemakers. 250 rooms. 750 Sutter St. (474-6464). Moderate.

Washington Square Inn – New on the scene, within walking distance of Ghirardelli Square and Chinatown. Only 15 rooms, each individually decorated, in a turn-of-the-century house in the North Beach area. Three rooms overlook Washington Square Park and are more expensive. 1660 Stockton St. (981-4220). Moderate.

Cartwright – An efficiently run small hotel with sparkling clean and cheerfully furnished rooms, and very reasonable prices. There are no restaurants, but Continental breakfast is available and the Cartwright adjoins a café. 119 rooms. 524 Sutter St. (421-2865). Moderate.

Drake Wiltshire – Some Eastern touches have enhanced the image of this 55-year-old hotel. Guests can have sauna and shiatsu massage. The rooms are large and comfortable, and the *Fiesta Restaurant* serves solid and reasonably priced meals. 250 rooms. 340 Stockton St. (421-8011). Inexpensive.

Hotel Beresford – For European charm at a reasonable price. Old-fashioned service, a writing parlor off the Victorian lobby, flower boxes in the street windows, and pleasant rooms. The *White Horse* tavern uses fresh vegetables from the hotel's garden, and fish caught by its own boat (open for breakfast and lunch only). 112 rooms. 635 Sutter St. (673-9900). Inexpensive.

EATING OUT: The city has over 2,600 restaurants serving every kind of ethnic fare, seafood, and over 50 kinds of hamburgers. Many of the restaurants are well-known institutions; some, like Trader Vic's, have branched out across the country, often leaving their very best cooks in San Francisco. Our restaurant selections range in price from $40 or more for a dinner for two in the expensive range; $20 to $35, moderate; $15 or less, inexpensive. Prices do not include drinks, wine, or tips.

Trader Vic's – Victor Bergeron is the real Trader Vic, and though he has traveled far and wide, leaving fine restaurants behind him at each stop, the San Francisco restaurant is his real home. The atmosphere is as homey as a South Seas paradise: lush jungle foliage, Polynesian batiks, spears, big-game trophies and skins won by the Trader himself. After one drink (try one of the tropical rum concoctions) you'll feel like you never lived anywhere else. Some prime stops on your gustatory adventure might be bongo bongo soup (cream of puréed oyster), Malay peanut chicken, breast of peach blossom duck, or barbecued double pork loin luau-style.

The service is good, and if you're having trouble deciding, the waiters offer informed suggestions. If you really want to penetrate the heart of things, try to make reservations for the Captain's Cabin, a favored meeting place of the city's social set, where you might see the Trader wandering through. Open daily. Reservations. Major credit cards. 20 Cosmo Pl. (776-2232). Expensive.

Le Club – This intimate French restaurant tucked away in a ritzy Nob Hill apartment house treats all guests elegantly whether they're regulars or first-timers. The atmosphere is that of a fancy private club, with two small dining rooms and a handsome mahogany bar. The French chef renders any classic French dish in addition to house specialties. Open daily. Reservations required. Major credit cards. 1250 Jones St. (771-5400). Expensive.

Ernie's – Dining here is a leisurely affair, so you have plenty of time to enjoy the atmosphere — Victorian yet tasteful. Traditional French dishes have been replaced by *la nouvelle cuisine.* Open daily. Reservations required. Major credit cards. 847 Montgomery St. (397-5969). Expensive.

Maurice et Charles Bistro – A half-hour north of San Francisco in San Rafael is this very popular bistro-style restaurant with scrumptious food. Try the wild boar with chestnut purée or duck breast in green peppercorn sauce. Closed Sundays. Reservations. 901 Lincoln Ave., San Rafael (456-2010). Expensive.

The Mandarin – A Chinese palace with thick beamed ceilings, a delicate cherrywood lotus blossom carving. Mandarin antiques and embroideries — and excellent Chinese food which you watch being barbecued in the Mongolian fire pit. To be set up in style, call owner and hostess Madame Cecilia Chiang a day in advance and order the Mandarin duck (a whole duck prepared with scallions and plum sauce), beggar's chicken, sharkfin soup, or anything she may recommend. Open daily. Reservations. Major credit cards. 900 North Point, in Ghirardelli Square (673-8812). Expensive.

Kansai – A Japanese architect designed this restaurant, which has private dining rooms, a tatami room, and tempura and sushi bars. The specialty here is *kaiseki,* a Japanese formal dinner, which can have as many as 13 courses (this should be ordered a day in advance). Closed Saturdays and Sundays. Reservations necessary. Major credit cards. 325 Sacramento St. (392-2648). Expensive to moderate.

Chez Michel – Here you'll find French cuisine in a chic but casual setting. The brass bar is stunning, the wooden tables are topped with fresh flowers daily, and the ceiling is brightly canopied. *Chez Michel* has nightly specialties that are all wonderfully prepared by their Swiss chef. Dinner hours are 6 PM to 12:30 AM. Closed Mondays. Reservations recommended. Visa and MasterCard. 804 Northpoint (771-6077). Expensive to moderate.

Maxwell's Plum – The San Francisco branch of the New York landmark; perhaps the most elaborately decorated restaurant in the country. Stained glass, ornate crystal chandeliers, elaborate furnishings, a rocking disco complete with a fabulous in-wall fountain, all on a site overlooking San Francisco Bay and the Golden Gate. The menu ranges from hamburgers to haute cuisine, and the desserts are a special treat. Open daily. 900 North Point, Ghirardelli Sq. (441-4140). Expensive to moderate.

Jack's – A local landmark for nearly as long as San Francisco has been on the map. Because of its location in the financial district, many visitors don't know about it and its excellent American and French food. All the grilled entrées are recommended, but the banana fritters with brandy sauce are unbeatable. The decor is unpretentious, as are the prices (particularly the dinner special), and the service is good. Open daily. Reservations. No credit cards. 615 Sacramento St. (986-9854). Moderate.

Tadich's Grill – San Francisco's oldest restaurant (132 years old), and still going strong with what clientele maintain is the freshest seafood in town. Best bets: baked avocado with shrimp diablo, rex sole, salmon, sea bass. Don't pass up the homemade cheesecake for dessert. Closed Sundays. No reservations. No credit cards. 240 California St. (391-2373). Moderate.

Maye's Original Oyster House – The other traditional seafood favorite in San Francisco. After 100 years, owned by the same family using the same secret recipes for broiled calamari, baked creamed crabmeat, and poached salmon in egg sauce. The decor's also original, though there's not much to it (large leather booths). Open daily. Reservations. No credit cards. 1233 Polk St. (474-7674). Moderate.

MacArthur Park – Fresh seafood, barbecued steaks and spare ribs, and a good California wine list. Open daily. Reservations. Major credit cards. 607 Front St. (398-5700). Moderate.

Modesto Lanzone's – Two things are magnificent here — the view of the Bay and the pasta. Modesto, who's around all the time, makes sure that everything's up to par. And so it is — the agnolotti (rounds of dough stuffed with chicken and covered with cream), cannelloni, fettuccine, and gnocchi (pasta made with potato and flour). Closed Mondays. Reservations. Major credit cards. 900 North Point in Ghirardelli Square (771-2880). Moderate.

Schroeder's – Fast, friendly service and large portions of good German food: sauerbraten, potato pancakes, sausages, German beer, and, for dessert, its famous apple strudel. Closed Saturdays and Sundays. Reservations. American Express. 240 Front St. (421-4778). Moderate.

Le Central – For a variation on the Continental theme, a brasserie-style restaurant with bright lights, brick walls hung with French art and the menu written on mirrors and blackboards. Food is in the best brasserie fashion: cassoulet (navy beans simmered with sausages, duck, pork, and lamb), choucroute Alsacienne (sauerkraut cooked in wine with bacon, pork, and sausage), and saucisson chaud (thinly sliced sausage with hot potato salad). Closed Sundays. Reservations advised for lunch and dinner. Major credit cards. 453 Bush St. (391-2233). Moderate.

Original Joe's – Italian family-style meals with a busy counter and bustling table service, and everything from burgers to spaghetti: Joe's Special is a combination of burger, spinach, eggs, and mushrooms. Open daily. No reservations. No credit cards. 144 Taylor St. (775-4877). Inexpensive.

Far East Café – Don't let the neon-lit exterior fool you — inside there are ornate Chinese lanterns and private, curtained booths. The extensive Cantonese menu features all the old classics and, if you call in advance, an excellent family banquet. Open daily. Reservations. Major credit cards. 631 Grant Ave. (982-3245). Inexpensive.

David's – Cheese blintzes with sour cream and jam, stuffed cabbage, gefilte fish with challah, chicken liver with schmaltz, or hot pastrami on Siberian soldiers' bread. And if you really can't get enough, you can move in adjoining the restaurant is David's hotel, where you get a 10% discount on all meals. Open late daily. No reservations. Major credit cards. 474 Geary St. (771-1600). Inexpensive.

Magic Pan Crêperie – For late supper or brunch, featuring hearty soups, avocado or melon salad, and crêpes filled with ratatouille, creamed chicken, beef bourguignonne. Best of all is the Southern praline crêpe, with vanilla ice cream, spiced whipped cream, toasted pecans, and hot praline sauce. There's also a spacious bar up front. Open daily. Reservations. Major credit cards. 341 Sutter St. (788-7397). Inexpensive.

The Hippo – More variations on the good old American hamburger than there are states in the Union. Open daily. Reservations. Major credit cards. Van Ness Ave. at Pacific (771-3939). Inexpensive.

Buena Vista – This saloon has built its reputation on Irish coffee — which some say is the best in the world — and an extensive imported beer selection. The diverse clientele comes to drink, be merry, and *then* eat. Food, although a secondary consideration, is very good here and ranges from steak and veal to hot dogs and enchiladas; breakfasts are a treat and served all day. Community tables are half the fun. Overlooks the bay with views of Alcatraz and Marin County. Open daily. No reservations. No credit cards. 2765 Hyde St. (474-5044). Inexpensive.

SAVANNAH

Savannah is where Georgia began. Here is the quintessential Southern city, possessed of just the right amount of atmosphere and ambience. Nowhere is there total urban dominance by the modern architectural behemoths — skyscrapers etching a skyline while virtually ignoring history and heritage closer to earth. Savannah's roots are too deeply sown in the Georgian soil to permit any such thing. Savannah *is* the South.

The city's beginnings were hardly as auspicious as the present state of restoration would suggest. The site chosen for Savannah had originally been part of a royal grant made in 1663 to the Lord Proprietors of Carolina, but frequent Indian raids (and constant threat of invasion from the Spanish colonists close by) discouraged the Carolina colonists from extending their boundaries to the fullest possible extent. Thus the last of the British colonies in the New World (and likewise last of the 13 original settlements) was ordained by royal proclamation in 1732, when George II turned the rights to these lands over to the "Trustees for Establishing the Colony of Georgia in America."

The leader of these trustees was one General James Oglethorpe, who literally began the new colony as an experiment in regimentation. His intention was to turn English debtors into American citizens by regulating even the most minute segments of their daily lives. The equipment carried to the New World by each would-be settler was meticulously detailed: "To every Man, A Watch-Coat, A Musket, and Bayonet, An Hatchet, An Hammer, An Handsaw, A shod Shovel or Spade . . . And a publick Grindstone to each Ward or Village."

Savannah scarcely survived its colonial period, and the judicious choice of its site was no doubt the reason it ultimately did. Set on Yamacraw Bluff, 15 miles above the mouth of Savannah River, its protected topographical position precluded a substantial number of conventional calamities. But it is the physical layout of the city itself which is Savannah's most enduring heritage. Eschewing the more conventional grid pattern most often used in fledgling colonial urban developments, Oglethorpe chose instead a visionary plan that included separate wards and public squares in regular conformation.

And today, one of the city's many sobriquets is "city of squares." (Others are "the walking city," because everything can be seen on foot; and "forest city," because of the city's treasured Spanish moss-hung trees.) These squares are more than public parks. Landscaped and kept immaculate by a park and tree department nearly as old as the city itself, the squares provide places for shoppers to rest and for bands to play noontime concerts while downtown office people munch brown-bag lunches. Visitors ask, "Why so many squares?" Residents are hard-put to supply an answer. Some say the squares were intended as rallying points in case of Indian attack. Others insist the squares are small versions of English commons. And researchers have substantiated that the pattern of Savannah's squares holds a more than coincidental likeness to those of Old Peking!

Somehow, finding a plausible answer to "Why squares?" is simply not as important as enjoying them. The city has worked hard to beautify them, planting trees and azaleas, and installing benches. In some stand monuments to Georgian heroes: General Oglethorpe (whose name also graces the snobby Oglethorpe Club, which some residents crave to join and others thank the heavens they don't have to), preacher John Wesley, and William Washington Gordon, whose Central of Georgia Railroad first linked seaport Savannah to the midlands and uplands when cotton was king, and the pine tree — source of turpentine and resin products — was crown prince.

Cotton is king no longer. The pine tree is, but because of paper pulp, not resin. Savannah's main industry is papermaking, but the city of 178,000 has a number of strings to its economic bow. With a marvelous deepwater port 18 miles from the Atlantic, the world comes right to Savannah's ocean door.

Most people — as opposed to most industries — come to Savannah not for business but to see the city itself. They come mainly to view the historic preservation and restoration which has been underway with serious intent for about 25 years. In the late 1940s, when the post–WW II trend toward "modernization" threatened to deprive the city of physical evidences of its heritage, a few citizens took countermeasures. Convinced of the economic, historic, and aesthetic value of keeping the city's beautiful architecture intact, they formed the Historic Savannah Foundation as a private undertaking.

With "seed money" provided by individual members, the agency began to purchase homes and offices (Regency, Georgian, and Victorian buildings) otherwise slated for the wrecking ball. The properties were then sold to private buyers who were required to restore and repair them. Proceeds from each sale went toward further purchases by the Foundation.

Instead of parking lots or high-rises, Savannah now enjoys refurbished mansions, town houses, and distinctive offices which not only retain, but *are,* the character of a Southern city that otherwise might have gone with the wind. Most fascinating is the fact that this restoration is a viable, working, and living museum. Functional as well as beautiful, Savannah's buildings are enjoyed by everyone in the community. They are not "look-but-don't-touch, we-close-at-six" museum pieces. Restorers literally live in the houses they have nurtured back to life, and many property owners have been lured from the suburbs back to the city to live and work within the restoration area. Although various of the homes are periodically placed on public view — the owners are understandably proud of what they have done and are quite willing to share their delight with others — the houses in historic Savannah are all mostly just *homes.* As you ramble through the area (hopefully on foot), you may find a home owner blithely washing the car in the front yard of a house more than a century and a half old. Show any real interest, and you will likely be invited in to see what hard work and patience have lovingly wrought.

As a result of this restoration effort, a 2½-mile section of the "old" city has been designated a national landmark district, the largest of its kind in the country. In 1968, Savannah embarked on a multiphased downtown revitalization program to round out the restoration within this district. The city built the $10.4 million Civic and Convention Center, and completely rebuilt the nine-block River Street waterfront. Riverfront Plaza, the cobblestone and brick esplanade which replaced the rotting docks and its eroded shoreline, is an ideal place for romantic strolls, ship watching, or shopping and roaming. The Plaza is lined with more than 65 shops, restaurants, cafés, boutiques, galleries, nightclubs, and the new Hyatt Regency Savannah hotel.

In all, Savannah is an opportunity not to be missed. Which explains, in yet another sobriquet, why it is called "the magnetic city."

SAVANNAH AT-A-GLANCE

SEEING THE CITY: Driving into Savannah across Talmadge Bridge offers a fine introductory view of the city. For the best view from on high, visit the *De Soto Hilton's Harborview Room*, a banquet room on the top floor at Liberty and Bull Sts. (232 0171).

SPECIAL PLACES: Historic Savannah is appealingly negotiable on foot. We recommend at least four walking tours; and count on a minimum of two days to see everything. You can squeeze it all into a morning and afternoon, but by nightfall, exhaustion will be the undisputed victor. Herewith, four walking tours:

Riverfront Plaza – A logical place to start, Riverfront Plaza leads eastward along the Savannah River shoreline. Bordering the thriving seaport's 40-foot-deep channel, the 9-block, brick Plaza is alive with commercial establishments in the 19th-century buildings which were formerly cotton warehouses. Waterfront browsers may be treated to a rock concert or a chamber music recital by an ensemble from the Savannah Symphony. A Riverfront Plaza day tour will undoubtedly whet the appetite for an evening excursion.

Bull Street – If you spend a morning at the Plaza, the afternoon can be spent walking down Bull Street, from City Hall to Forsyth Park, 12 blocks south. Bull is Savannah's principle north-south street, and it contains the city's five most beautiful squares. The six-story City Hall, on River and Bay Streets, stands alongside two brass cannons captured from Cornwallis at Yorktown. The cannons were presented to the Chatham Artillery, a Savannah military unit, by George Washington, in 1791. East of City Hall, Factors Walk, with its iron bridges and narrow street, runs along the city side of the former cotton buildings. After passing City Hall, you will come to the US Customs House, built in 1852 on the same site where Georgia's founder, James Edward Oglethorpe, lived in 1733. It's also where evangelist John Wesley first preached in America. The five squares, not to be missed, are:

Johnson Square – Here, two fountains flow and decks of azaleas are in dazzling flower in spring. Christ Episcopal Church, the first church established in the Colony of Georgia (1773), stands here, too. The present building dates from 1838.

Wright Square – The exquisite Ascension window of the Lutheran Church of the Ascension (1878) is internationally known as a work of art.

Chippewa Square – Here you'll find the First Baptist Church, the oldest of its denomination in Georgia; the Barrow Mansion which now houses an insurance firm; and the Savannah Theater, one of the oldest theaters in continuous use in the country (233-9643).

Madison Square – The carillons and stained glass windows of St. John's Episcopal Church (1840) are well known to church lovers. Here, too, the former Green-Meldrim mansion which served as Sherman's headquarters after Savannah was captured in the Civil War.

Monterey Square – Temple Mickve Israel, consecrated in 1878 for Georgia's oldest Jewish congregation (1773), contains a Torah scroll more than 800 years old. The Gordon and Taylor Street houses fronting Monterey Square are outstanding examples of historic preservations.

From Abercorn to St. Julian Street – Starting at Calhoun Square, at Abercorn and Gordon Streets, walk north toward Massie School (1885), a Greek revival structure which is the public school system's education museum. Alongside stands Wesley Monumental Methodist Church. Four blocks north, at Lafayette Square, is the Colonial Dames House (1849). Two blocks east, beside Troup Square and on parallel Charlton and Macon Streets, are Savannah's two best examples of slum conversion properties, now first-rate town houses. A block and a half north of Troup Square, Colonial Park Cemetery contains the graves of Georgia colonists, with priceless tombstone inscriptions. From the cemetery, it's a two-block walk up Abercorn Street to the Owens-Thomas House (1816) at the corner of State Street, hailed as "America's finest example of English Regency architecture." Now a museum, the house was visited in 1825 by Revolutionary hero Marquis de Lafayette. One block east of Owens-Thomas House, facing Columbia Square, Davenport House, now a museum, is the first architecturally important structure to have been reclaimed by Historic Savannah Foundation. From here, it's a three-block walk north to St. Julian Street, which splits three squares: Reynolds Square at Abercorn Street, Warren Square at Habersham Street, and Washington Square at Houston Street. This section has one of Savannah's largest clusters of restored 18th- and 19th-century homes. Facing Reynolds Square is the *Pink House* (circa 1790), now a fashionable restaurant.

Fort Pulaski – A national monument named for the Revolutionary hero killed in the 1779 Battle of Savannah. Built between 1829 and 1847, Fort Pulaski was captured by Union forces in 1862. Open daily. Admission charge. US 80 near Savannah Beach.

■ **EXTRA SPECIAL:** If you take Skidaway Rd. south to La Roche Ave., then on to the Isle of Hope, you'll find yourself beside the *Intracoastal Waterway* where colonial-style houses stand among moss-hung oaks. Near the Isle of Hope is Bethesda Home for Boys, the oldest orphanage in the country. In March, when the azaleas, redbud, dogwood, and wisteria are at their most radiant, drive south on Abercorn St., turning east at Victory Dr. until you reach Bonaventure Cemetery where the flowers are especially magnificent.

SOURCES AND RESOURCES

Before starting off on a walk, be sure to pick up a map of the city at the Savannah Visitors Center. Their offices are in a converted 1860 railroad station. Take an extra ten minutes to watch their film. It will help give you a feel for the city. Before visiting, you can write 301 W Broad St., Savannah, GA 31402, for information. West Broad and Liberty Sts. (233-3067).

Sojourn in Savannah by Betty Rauers and Franklin Traub (Historic Savannah Foundation, Inc., $2.50) offers detailed information on places of interest around town. It's well illustrated, with etchings, engravings, and reproductions.

All telephone numbers are in the 912 area code unless otherwise indicated.

For Local Coverage – *Savannah Morning News* and *Savannah Evening Press,* dailies, and the *Georgian Gazette,* weekly.

CLIMATE AND CLOTHES: Warm and sunny is the forecast for Savannah most of the year, with temperatures mostly in the 70s. From December through March, you can expect the mercury to drop into the 50s and 40s, and in the height of summer, to climb to the high 80s or low 90s. You can also be pretty sure of afternoon thunderstorms between June and September. Apart from the rains, however, the humidity is hardly ever greater than 60%.

GETTING AROUND: Bus – Savannah Transit Authority operates the municipal bus system, 900 E Gwinnett St. (233-5767).

Taxi – Cabs can be hailed in the streets, downtown. There are taxi stands at the main hotels, but you may prefer to call Abba-Yellow (354-6911).

Car Rental – Avis and Hertz have offices in town. Thrifty Rent-a-Car is a reliable local service (236–6316).

MUSEUMS: Savannah is a treasury of historic and cultural elegance. On your way through the streets of the historic district, the Telfair Academy of Arts and Sciences on Barnard St. (232-1177) recommends itself as one of Savannah's outstanding museums. Other notable museums are:

Savannah Art Association, 119 Jefferson St. (232-7731).

Evans Antique Cars, 313 W River St. (233-3525).

Museum of Antique Dolls, 505 President St. E (233-5296).

Savannah Science Museum, 4405 Paulsen (355-6705). (Zoo and aquarium are on museum grounds.)

Ships of the Sea Maritime Museum, 503 E River St. (232-1511).

MAJOR COLLEGES AND UNIVERSITIES: Armstrong State College, 11935 Abercorn St. Extension (925-4200); Savannah State College, Thunderbolt (356-2186). Both are four-year colleges within the Georgia state university system.

SPECIAL EVENTS: Savannah has three major annual festivals. *Georgia Day,* February 12, celebrates the founding of the colony. Festivities last for a week. *St. Patrick's Day* (March 17) is a one-day event featuring the biggest street parade south of New York. The third weekend in April, "*A Night in Old Savannah,*" is a three-day ethnic fun and food festival in Johnson Square.

SPORTS: Savannah is at the head of one of the country's most popular vacationland areas. Names like Hilton Head, Sea Island, St. Simons, and Jekyll Island are all familiar to lovers of the outdoor life, and all are less than a day's drive from Savannah.

Baseball – The Savannah *Braves,* farm team for the Atlanta Braves, play at Grayson Stadium, Victory Dr. at Bee Rd. (355-8082).

Bicycling – Cycling through the historic district can be an unforgettable experience. The De Soto Hilton hotel rents bikes; so does the Olde Savannah Cycle Shop, 311 W River St. (232-1840).

Swimming and Fishing – Savannah Beach, nostalgically remembered as one end of a rollicking railroad that connected the mainland to the beach, has been a favorite haunt of residents (and visitors) for many years. Here, you can indulge your penchants for swimming, fishing, surfing, crabbing, boating, picnicking, or beachcombing among the dunes.

Golf – The Savannah Inn course, one of the finest in the South, is also open to the public on Wilmington Island (897-1612). The best municipal course is at Bacon Park, Skidaway Rd. and Shorty Cooper Dr. (354-2625). (Shorty Cooper was one of the original golf caddies at Bacon Park.)

Tennis – Best public tennis courts are at Bacon Park, Lake Mayer, and Daffin Park.

THEATER: For complete up-to-date performance schedules, check the daily and weekly publications listed above. *Savannah Civic Center* is the largest auditorium in the city, Orleans Sq. (234-6666). *Little Theater*, Chippewa Sq. downtown (233-7764), is another place for good drama. It occupies the historic Savannah Theater, the oldest theater in continuous use in the US.

MUSIC: The Savannah Civic Center is the home of the *Savannah Symphony Orchestra*, and offers the best concerts, ballets, touring Broadway productions, and dance theater performances, in Orleans Sq. (234-6666).

NIGHTCLUBS AND NIGHTLIFE: Riverfront Plaza is alive with discos and clubs. Two of the most popular are *Night Flight,* a restaurant with live music (234-9565), *Port Royal* (233-2462), and *Bullfrog Springer's Disco and Oyster Bar* (232-7367).

SINS: *Gluttony* has made far deeper inroads than *lust* in Savannah life; for while red lights flicker here and there all over town, with only the most eager lechers seeking out the fancy women and pornographic books stashed away in the odd corners of this fairly conservative city, *gluttony* flourishes in the open, and residents and tourists alike crowd the restaurants to overdose on exotic seafood dishes at the *Pirate's House*, E Broad and Bay Sts. (233-5757). The city's *pride?* A St. Patrick's Day celebration that ranks with those of New York, Boston, and Cleveland.

LOCAL SERVICES: Business Services – Tempo Secretarial Services, 6606 Abercorn St. (355-5512).

Mechanic – Auto Diagnostic Center, 5115 Montgomery St. (352-2285).

Babysitting – Angels and Imps, 614 Jackson Blvd. (355-1068).

■ **SAVANNAH SORTIE:** For a pleasant introduction to Savannah, take a cruise on one of the *Cap'n Sam Cruise Line* sightseeing boats. Cap'n Sam runs regular daily tours of the harbor (a 20-mile, 2-hour trip); twilight cocktail cruises in the evenings; and on summer nights, special dinner/dance cruises. The boats — *Harbor Queen I, Waving Girl,* and *Harbor Queen II* — depart from the foot of Bull Street behind city hall. Call 234-7248 for the cruise schedule and other details.

BEST IN TOWN

CHECKING IN: Savannah has over 3,600 rooms for guests, most of them scattered among the motels within and around the fringe of the city. The city also has four hotels that offer a special elegance. Expect to pay between $45 and $60 for a double at those places we've listed as expensive; between $25 and $45 in the moderate range; under $25 for an inexpensive hostelry.

De Soto Hilton – Occupying the site of the former De Soto Hotel, this retains much of the decor which made its predecessor the queen of the gaslight era's carriage trade. The 264-room De Soto Hilton was built from the ground up after the old De Soto was razed in the mid-60s. Its *Red Lion* cocktail lounge (closed Sundays) is almost an exact replica of the old De Soto's Sapphire Room; its *Pavilion Restaurant* is one of Savannah's finest. The *Harborview Room,* a banquet room on the top floor, offers unquestionably the best panoramic north-south view of Savannah. The De Soto has a bicycle rental desk, arranges golf and tennis games, and offers free garage parking. At the intersection of Liberty and Bull Sts. (232-0171). Expensive.

Hyatt Regency Savannah – This 350-room hotel rises above the Riverfront Plaza, giving guests a view of the oceangoing ships cruising in and out of the harbor. *The Windows* restaurant, overlooking the river, has quickly become a favorite dining spot, along with the more casual *MD's Lounge* and *Patrick's Porch.* Guests can arrange tours and other activities at the concierge's desk in the lobby. Indoor parking. 2 W Bay St. (238-1234). Expensive.

Savannah Inn and Country Club – Ten miles from Savannah on the Wilmington River, this was one of the Roaring Twenties' great resort hotels, and succeeding owners have kept it in first-class condition. Its 210 rooms are distributed between the eight-story hotel, a number of small cottages, and some villas. It has a swimming pool, sauna, restaurant, nightclub, and fishing and boating. Its pride is its 18-hole golf course, one of the South's finest. A modified American plan is available for those who want meals included in the price. Wilmington Island (897-1612). Expensive.

Eliza Thompson House – This quaint 132-year-old, 3-story townhouse in the Historic District has been restored and converted to an inn by Laurie and Jim Widman. The five suites are filled with antiques, as well as with Savannah history books so you can brush up on Georgia's oldest city during your stay. Some suites have fireplaces and all have a hideway kitchen and private entrance. Complimentary sherry makes things even cozier. 7 West Jones St. (236-3620). Expensive.

17 Hundred 90 – One of Savannah's best restaurants recently opened its top two floors as an inn, with 14 rooms, 12 with fireplaces (gas, not wood-burning), all furnished with antiques. A charming resting place in the middle of the city's historic district. 307 E President St. (236-7122). Moderate.

Downtowner – Five blocks west of the De Soto Hilton, built of Savannah gray bricks salvaged from older buildings. Ornamented with wrought-iron balconies, the 204-room, six-story hotel blends in with the architecture of the surrounding historic landmark district. Adjacent to the Civic Center, with a swimming pool. Its *Regency Restaurant and Tavern* is a favorite with Savannah residents. 201 W Oglethorpe (233-3531). Moderate.

Howard Johnson's Downtown – This two-story, 90-room motor hotel has private patios and balconies, which may make it somewhat more appealing than larger, more anonymous hotels. There is a swimming pool, a 24-hour café, a bar which stays open till 2 AM (with entertainment), and ramps for wheelchairs. Pets are welcome. 224 W Boundary St. (232-4371). Moderate.

Holiday Inn Savannah – This two-story building has 209 rooms, two swimming pools, and a laundromat, as well as a café-bar with entertainment. There is a kennel on the premises. Children under 12 are free. 121 W Boundary St. (236-1355). Moderate.

Quality Inn/Heart of Savannah – Its romantic name and size (53 rooms) create a certain intimacy, in contrast to larger hotels. The two great things about it, though, are the free Continental breakfast and the price, about $24 for two. 300 W Bay St. (236-6321). Inexpensive.

EATING OUT: Savannah's restaurants range from elegant to home-style. The seafood here is excellent, and the prices are good, too. Two people can eat very well for $25. Anything which costs more is expensive for Savannah. Anything between $15 and $25 is moderate; under $15, inexpensive. Prices do not include drinks, wine, or tips.

Pirates' House – Located in Savannah's oldest standing building, this made literary history in Robert Louis Stevenson's *Treasure Island.* In any of its 23 dining rooms, a meal is an exquisite experience. Choices include oysters Savannah, several flaming dishes, local seafood, steak, red rice, and exotic desserts. Open daily. Reservations advised. All credit cards. 20 E Broad St. (233-5757). Expensive.

The Olde Pink House – This converted 18th-century mansion specializes in superb Continental and regional dishes. Lunches and dinners are served in the basement Planters' Tavern as well as in the upstairs restaurant. Saturdays, dinners only; closed Sundays. Reservations advised. Major credit cards. 23 Abercorn St. (232-4286). Expensive.

Tassey's Pier – Adjacent to the Thunderbolt Marina, overlooking the Wilmington River on the Intracoastal Waterway. Yachts dock here while crew and passengers come ashore to dine, giving additional credence to Tassey's advertisement: "From the boats to our kitchen." The stuffed flounder and shrimp scampi are highly recommended. So is the Maine lobster even though it's not local. Non-fish-eaters should try the beef champignon. Closed Sundays. Reservations advised. Major credit cards. 3122 River Rd., five miles from Savannah in Thunderbolt (354-2973). Expensive.

The Windows – Savannah's newest exquisite restaurant is in the *Hyatt Regency Savannah,* overlooking the Savannah River. Diners can watch merchant ships come and go while choosing from a Continental menu featuring seafood, duck, and stir-fried Oriental dishes. Open daily; brunch only on Sundays; no lunch on Saturdays. Reservations advised. Major credit cards. 2 W Bay St. (238-1234). Expensive.

Johnny Harris – Specialties here are steaks, prime ribs, barbecues, and chicken. They do their own baking on the premises. In its third generation of continuous ownership, this is where the nationally marketed Johnny Harris Barbecue Sauce originated. Jacket and tie are required on Friday and Saturday nights, but, surprisingly, reservations are not necessary. Closed Sundays. Major credit cards. 1651 E Victory Dr. (354-7810). Moderate.

Regency Restaurant – Well known for beef, seafood, and down-home Southern dishes. Open daily. No reservations needed. Major credit cards. 201 W Oglethorpe Ave. (233-2172). Moderate.

The Pavilion – Another well-known Savannah restaurant, featuring traditional "Old South" recipes from land and sea, with a great buffet. When you're finished eating, go up to the Harborview Room on the top floor for the best view of the city. Open daily. Reservations advised. All credit cards. De Soto Hilton Hotel, Bull and Liberty Sts. (232-0171). Moderate.

17 Hundred 90 – The setting is normal in this 19th-century house, which can accommodate around 100 diners. Savannah residents consider this to be one of their best restaurants: dress appropriately. The seafood casserole is especially good. Closed Sundays. Reservations are advised. Major credit cards. 307 E President St. (236-7122). Moderate.

Anna's Little Napoli – This is the only Italian restaurant in town that offers a complete Italian menu of pasta, veal, and seafood. We recommend the lasagna and veal parmagiana. Open daily. No reservations. Major credit cards. 2308 Skidaway Rd. (234-5083). Inexpensive.

Williams Seafood Restaurant – Family-owned since 1936, this is a good place for generous helpings of fried shrimp, oysters, scallops, chicken, and local seafood. Closed Tuesdays. Reservations advised. Major credit cards. Twelve miles east of Savannah on Savannah Beach Rd. (US 80) (897-2219). Inexpensive.

Mrs. Wilkes' Boarding House – This is one of the "finds" of Savannah — a real, old-time boarding house. Mrs. Wilkes advertises by word of mouth, and while some Savannah people are critical, they admit that is only because when they want home cooking they eat at home. When you walk into Mrs. Wilkes, you'll find everything set out on dining room tables: fried chicken, swordfish steak, potatoes, rice, peas, and other down-home treats. To serve yourself, just spread your arm in that proverbial boarding-house reach. Open 11:30 AM to 3 PM, Mondays through Fridays only. No reservations or credit cards accepted. In the basement of 107 W Jones St. (232-5997). Inexpensive by any standards — about $4 for all you can eat.

Duff's – A family-style restaurant. The food is served from moving turntables which receive continuous replenishment from the kitchen. Open daily. No reservations. Major credit cards. 711 Mall Blvd. (355-5620). Inexpensive.

SEATTLE

Like a promising young boxer, Seattle has suffered some hard blows in recent years and still come out fighting. In spite of high profits and a great psychological boost provided by the ambitious 1962 World's Fair — both more or less unlooked for when the project was initiated — the city was knocked to its knees in the late 1960s with the economic troubles of the aerospace industry, its major employer. Seattle took more than half a decade to recover, but today unemployment in the metropolitan area (population 503,000) is lower than the national average, and the city is in the middle of a splurge of growth. While new skyscrapers get underway, the only reticence in town takes the wholly constructive form of a serious regard for the environmental consequences of growth. The city's guard is up to maintain its status as one of the most livable cities in the country.

Seattle occupies a rich corner of the western frontier, seven hills tucked away by imposing mountain ranges to the east and west. The Olympic Mountains lie on the western horizon line, and the Cascades, with their jagged cliffs crowned by the snow-capped summit of the 14,410-foot Mount Rainier, on the eastern. Immediately to the west is Elliot Bay of the Puget Sound which leads outward to the vast expanse of the Pacific, and on the east is a 24-mile length of fresh water, Lake Washington.

The earliest inhabitants of the region were the Northwest Indians, who were generally more content to trade than to make war with neighbors. Their territory was covered with thick forests, watered by the Puget Sound and Lake Washington, and they lived in comfortable harmony with their surroundings. They had fish and clams for the taking, a moderate climate year-round, and plenty of bark available for the construction of their superb, long canoes.

The European settlers who came in the 1850s couldn't leave well enough alone. They harvested the readily available timber and sent it south to San Francisco. Then they leveled a couple of the more prominent hills to make north-south travel easier. One of those hills, now a concrete canyon in Seattle's downtown, was the lumberjack's principal source of timber. When teams of oxen skidded the new-cut logs down the street to the sawmill, a new American expression was born — Skid Road (now Row). On either side of the Road, you can now hear the strains of rock and jazz from nightclubs where once only the music of box-house bands played. Lumbering, of course, is still one of Seattle's major industries, but the oxen are gone.

Seattle seems to owe its rise to having been in the right place at the right time. There was nothing inevitable about its growth. Olympia, to the south, was an established town when Seattle was little more than a collection of rude huts; Port Townsend was better situated on the Sound; and Tacoma, though it didn't develop as early, was named as the terminus of the Northern Pacific

Railroad. Seattle had a fine deepwater harbor on the Sound, but so did several other 19th-century Washington towns. But in 1887 a "ton of gold" was brought back from Alaska aboard a ship that docked at a Seattle pier and the town was, well . . . golden. Gold fever spread, and the city naturally became a boom town because of its easy access to riches — a protected inland passage to Alaska. Vice flourished in this raw frontier town, if you consider brothels a way of flourishing. The confluence of Seattle lumberjacks and miners on their way to find their fortune in gold in the Klondike brought about a demand for prostitution, which was best satisfied in all the West along Seattle's Skid Road.

After the Gold Rush days, Seattle seemed almost ashamed of itself for its extravagances. It was quick to embrace Prohibition in 1916, three years before the rest of the nation capitulated. Even before WW II, it was a conservative, one-industry town, depending far too heavily on plane production.

Things began to change in 1962. In that year, a group of businessmen put together an audacious undertaking, a World's Fair in Seattle. There had been the Alaska-Yukon Pacific Exposition in 1907 that had created quite a stir, but this was something else. Even the backers were dubious of its success. But the venture turned out profitably and left the city with a different attitude toward itself — a feeling that the city could be first-class in more ways than it thought possible.

The World's Fair gave the city a real boost culturally, leaving it with the valuable legacy of the Seattle Center, a complex which includes an Opera House, Playhouse, Arena Coliseum, the Pacific Science Center with its wide-ranging exhibits, and the futuristically designed Space Needle. The Seattle Repertory Theater is a strong professional group; the Seattle Symphony under the direction of Rainer Meidel is of world class; and the Seattle Opera, culminating its season with a Wagner Ring Festival in the summer, is outstanding.

In sports, too, Seattle hit the big league. The basketball SuperSonics are the most established team and play their games at the Kingdome, Seattle's seat of professional sports. The Kingdome sits on land reclaimed from Elliot Bay that was washed down from a high hill that impeded growth of the city.

With all of its progress toward the future, Seattle still is concerned with its past heritage and has maintained the "old town" alongside the new. Pioneer Square where the city was founded in 1852 has been renovated and designated a historic preservation area. The old brick buildings surrounding the Square are protected from the ruthless movements of progress and the bulldozer. Beyond the stately façades lie galleries, boutiques, and restaurants.

The inner city is unusually healthy; people are moving back into the city to enjoy a new sense of belonging. Off in the distance, the snow-capped peaks of the Cascades and Olympic Mountains, and the expansive stretch of the Puget Sound and Lake Washington, create a magnificent backdrop. But it is the scene of current Seattle — the dynamic activity of a rising city that is attracting residents.

SEATTLE AT-A-GLANCE

SEEING THE CITY: The best view of Seattle and the magnificent Washington landscape is from the top of the *Space Needle*. The observation deck and revolving restaurant offer 360-degree views of the city, the Puget Sound, Lake Washington, and beyond to the snow-covered peaks of the Cascade and Olympic Mountains. Seattle Center (447-3122).

SPECIAL PLACES: Don't be confused by the geographical designations in street addresses, like north or south. Directions which follow avenue names and precede street names (5th Ave. North or North 5th St.) give location in relation to downtown (where only street names and numbers are used).

Seattle Center – The legacy of the 1962 World's Fair, this 74-acre area contains some of the city's finest facilities. Dominating the 50 buildings and the grassy plazas is the Space Needle, a futuristic steel structure that spires 607 feet upward from its tripod base. Among the other highlights are the *Food Circus* (Center House, 305 Harrison St.) where you can sample inexpensive international delicacies, a playhouse, the Opera House, Arena (adjoining buildings on Mercer St.), and Fun Forest Amusement Park (370 Thomas St.) for a variety of entertainment. Information for Seattle Center theater tickets and activities at booth in Center House Building. 5th Ave. N between Denny Way and Mercer St. (625-4234). There are two notable museums in the Center:

Pacific Science Center – Designed by Minoru Yamasaki, these preformed concrete buildings are impressive for their architecture and exhibits. Features astro-space displays, with a large fiberglass moon and a full-scale model of a lunar module, an operating oceanographic model of the Puget Sound which simulates waves, a laserium which uses laser beams to form images, and a reconstruction of a Northwest Indian longhouse. Open daily. Admission charge. 200 2nd Ave. N (625-9333).

Seattle Art Museum Pavilion – Good collection of Northwest painter Mark Tobey, and other regional and contemporary artists including Harry Callahan and Andy Warhol. Closed Mondays. Admission charge. 2nd Ave. N and Thomas St. (447-4795).

Waterfront Park – Overlooks the Puget Sound, but if you really want to know what's swimming around out there you can visit the new aquarium for a close look at native marine life. In the domed viewing room, which is actually a 400,000-gallon tank, you are surrounded by octopus, starfish, dogfish sharks, rock cod, red snapper, scallops, shrimps, anemones, and sea pens. If you're hydrophobic, stick to the standing tanks with their Alaskan sea otters, electric eels, and tropical fish. Open daily. Admission charge. At Pier 59 (625-4357). All along the waterfront there are fish bars where you can pick up a good regional lunch.

Puget Sound Ferry Ride – If looking out at the Sound and up at its marine life isn't enough, you can have the full Sound experience by taking an inexpensive ride along the eastern shore to Bremerton or as far as Victoria, B.C. Ferry Terminal (464-6400).

Pike Place Market – Founded in 1907, this public market is now a historic site with a wide array of stalls offering everything from scrimshaw, leather goods, silver jewelry, prints of the Northwest, to fresh produce and Dungeness crab. Closed Sundays. 1st Ave. between Pike St. and Virginia St.

Seattle Art Museum – The exceptional Oriental collection of Richard E. Fuller features beautiful Chinese jade and bronzes, delicately crafted pottery and snuff bottles, and Indian stone sculptures. Also displays of European painting and modern art. Closed Mondays. Admission charge. In Volunteer Park (447-4710).

Museum of History and Industry – Extensive collection of Pacific Northwest artifacts traces the history of Seattle's first 100 years. A mural depicts the fire that leveled the city in 1889, and the exhibits include almost everything that came afterward — mementos of the Gold Rush, old firefighting equipment, a maritime display, and a Boeing exhibit which follows its development over the past 60 years. Closed Mondays. Free. 2161 E Hamlin St. (324-1125).

Pioneer Square – The site where the city was founded in 1852 has become a historic preservation area, and remains in all its Victorian grandeur today. The classic old brick buildings house some of the city's hottest jazz clubs (like *Parnell's*), best boutiques, and restaurants (for haute cuisine at a moderate price, try lunch at *Brasserie Pittsbourg*, see *Best in Town,* below). When the fire ravaged the district in 1889, the city rebuilt atop the rubble, leaving an underground town, ten feet below. Bill Speidel's Underground Tours guide visitors through the subterranean five-block area, which has some storefronts, interiors, and old waterlines intact. Tours daily. Admission charge. Reservations advised. (610 1st Ave., 682-4646). For gold rush nostalgia, visit the Seattle First National Bank (300 Occidental S, 583-3290), which has murals of scenes from the Rush, and where you can look down (through a glass floor) into the vault where millions in Klondike gold were stored.

International District – Often called the "Gateway to the Orient," Seattle has a large Chinese and Japanese community concentrated in this interesting old section of the city. There are many craft shops, a Buddhist temple, and restaurants serving several varieties of Chinese food. Try the *Bush Garden* for Japanese cuisine in private tatami rooms, 614 Maynard Ave. S (682-6830). The Wing Luke Memorial Museum has a collection tracing the emigration of the Chinese to the Northwest from the 1860s on. Open Tuesdays through Fridays. Free. 414 8th Ave. S (623-5124).

University of Washington Arboretum – Some 200 lakeside acres contain over 5,000 species of plant life from all over the world. Features the largest Japanese Tea Garden outside of Japan. Open all year. Free. Lake Washington Blvd. between E Madison and Montlake (543-2100).

■ **EXTRA SPECIAL:** Just two hours south of Seattle is the spectacular *Mount Rainier National Park* with its 14,410-foot summit of the Cascade range. There are over 300 miles of trails ranging from the super-rough 90-mile Wonderland trail, which circles up to the peak, to short nature walks for mere earthlings. *Paradise Inn* (569-2291) in the park serves hearty mountain meals. Returning to Seattle on rt. 161, you can stop at Northwest Trek, a park zoo, where moose, elk, buffalo, mountain goat, and caribou roam free. The zoo belongs to the animals; visitors tour from a tram and are not allowed off.

SOURCES AND RESOURCES

The Seattle Visitors Bureau offers daily events schedules, maps, and information. 1815 7th Ave. (447-7273).

The Seattle Guidebook by Archie Satterfield (The Writing Works, Inc., $3.95) is the best local guide to Seattle and the surrounding area.

All telephone numbers are in the 206 area code unless otherwise indicated.

For Local Coverage – *Seattle Post-Intelligencer,* morning daily, publishes *What's Happening* on Fridays with coming week's events; *Seattle Times,* afternoon daily, publishes *Tempo* Magazine on Fridays. Both available at newsstands.

For Food – *Best Restaurants Pacific Northwest* by Robert Rubinstein (101 Productions Inc., $2.95).

CLIMATE AND CLOTHES: Seattle's proximity to the Puget Sound keeps the climate mild and moderately moist. Winters are relatively warm with average temperatures around 40° and little or no snow. The wet season is from October to April, so carry an umbrella. Seattle is best in summer and early fall when city and countryside are most accessible.

GETTING AROUND: Bus – Metropolitan Transit provides extensive service in the metropolitan area with an added attraction: Metro's Magic Carpet Service offers free transportation in the downtown-waterfront area. Route information is available at the Metropolitan Transit Office, 821 2nd Ave. (447-4800).

Monorail – The quickest and most exciting way to get from downtown to Seattle Center is via the World's Fair monorail. Leaves every 15 minutes from Westlake Mall, 4th and 5th Aves. at Pine St.

Taxi – Cabs can be hailed in the street or ordered on the phone. Major companies are Far West (622-1717) and Yellow Cab (622-6500).

Car Rental – Seattle is served by the major national firms.

MUSEUMS: Exhibitions on the history, art, industry, and even marine life of the Pacific Northwest and the world are well represented in Seattle's cultural institutions. The Seattle Art Museum, the Pacific Science Center, the Museum of Science and Industry, and the Aquarium are described above under *Special Places*. Other interesting museums are:

Frye Art Museum (contemporary regional works), Terry Ave. and Cherry St. (622-9250).

Foster White Gallery (contemporary regional works), 311½ Occidental S (622-2833).

MAJOR COLLEGES AND UNIVERSITIES: The University of Washington, founded in 1861, is the area's oldest and largest educational institution, at 17th Ave. NE and NE 45th St. (543-2100). Also in the city is Seattle University, 12th Ave. and E Columbia St. (626-6200), and Seattle Pacific University, 3rd Ave. W and W Nickerson St. (281-2000).

SPECIAL EVENTS: *The Seattle Seafair* is a citywide celebration featuring everything from a hydroplane race, a torchlight parade, a beauty contest, a marathon run, to a special appearance by the Pacific Fleet which sends a few ships for open house. Held annually in early August (check papers for exact dates).

SPORTS: Seattle is in the big league nationally — four professional teams play their home games in the Kingdome (201 S King St.). Tickets can be obtained at the Dome but the best bet is to order by phone from the team's ticket office and pick them up at the Dome office.

Basketball – The NBA *SuperSonics* play from October through April (ticket office, 628-8448).

Football – The National Football League *Seahawks*' season is from August through December (ticket office, 827-9766).

Soccer – The *Sounders* play from May through August (tickets, 628-3620).

Baseball – The *Mariners'* baseball season is April through September (ticket office, 628-3300).

Horse Racing – Longacres Racetrack is 11 miles SE via I-5 and I-405 in Renton (226-3131). Season is from mid-May to late September.

Bicycling – Rent from Gregg's Green Lake Cycle, 7007 Woodlawn Ave. NE (523-1822). Green Lake Park and Burke-Gilman Trail are good areas for biking.

Fishing – You can wet a line from the public pier of Waterfront Park or go after the big salmon by renting a boat or taking a charter into the deep sea from Ray's Boathouse, 6049 Seaview Ave. NW (783-9779).

Golf – The city has three good 18-hole municipal courses. Jackson Park, 1000 NE 135th St. (363-4747); Jefferson Park, 4101 Beacon Ave. S (762-4513); West Seattle Course, 4470 35th Ave. SW (932-9792).

Skiing – Close by is Alpental on the Snoqualmie Pass via I-90 (SE). Best is Crystal Mountain 120 miles SE near Mount Rainier.

Tennis – City parks have outdoor courts.

THEATER: For current offerings check the publications listed above. The *Seattle Repertory Theater* performs classical and modern productions from September through April at the Playhouse of the Seattle Center, 225 Mercer St. (447-4730). *Second Stage* and *Intiman* are two small companies that perform at 1419 8th Ave. (447-4651). *American Contemporary Theater* performs contemporary plays at 100 W Rox (285-5110). The *5th Avenue Theater,* 1308 5th Ave. (625-1900), features Broadway plays; and the restored *Paramount Theater,* 901 Pine St. (624-5772), brings in top-name concert artists.

MUSIC: *The Seattle Symphony* (under the direction of Rainer Meidel) and the *Seattle Opera Association* perform at the Opera House from September through April. The Opera's Wagner Ring Festival is in June. The ticket offices for both are in Center House, Seattle Center (Symphony, 447-4736; Opera, 447-4711).

NIGHTCLUBS AND NIGHTLIFE: Some of the area's hottest nightspots are *Northwest Passage,* 1150 114th St. SE, Bellevue (455-9944); *Parnell's,* 313 Occidental S (624-2387); and *Swannie's,* 222 S Main St. (622-9353), for headline comedy acts. Favorite discos are *Sunday's,* 620 1st Ave. N (284-0456), and *Spag's Tavern,* for gays, 924 Pine St. (623-6380).

SINS: To *gluttons,* Seattle offers the Pike Street Market, chockablock with fresh fish, fruits, vegetables, and other goodies; and *Love Season*, for edible underwear, 12001 NE 12th St., Bellevue (455-0533). Love Season, otherwise, is a treasure-trove of erotica styled to fuel the *lust* of all comers. The city's *pride?* An occasional sunny day. If you're so lucky as to encounter one, scurry along to the Bank of California building and take the elevator to the top for a view of Mount Rainier through the glass wall. Or go up the water tower at Volunteer Park off 15th Avenue for a view of Lake Washington, Puget Sound, the Cascades, and the Olympic Mountains.

LOCAL SERVICES: Business Services – Kelly Services, 4th Ave. and Blanchard (382-7171).

Mechanics – Ace and Speed Service, 10215 Greenwood Ave. N (784-2474). Carburetor Specialty Inc., 1134 Broadway (323-7172).

Babysitting – The Student Employment Office at the University of Washington provides reliable and inexpensive student babysitters (543-1840).

BEST IN TOWN

CHECKING IN: Seattle has an abundance and wide variety of accommodations, from grand old hotels and luxury modern high-rises, to an inn on the Puget Sound. There are also convenient, comfortable, and inexpensive accommodations downtown. Expensive accommodations range between $40 and $50 per night for a double room; $30 to $40 in the moderate range; and $20 to $25 at inexpensive hostelries.

Westin Hotel Seattle – Two imposing 40- and 47- story towers in the heart of the shopping district difficult to overlook. Rooms offer spectacular views of the Puget Sound, Mount Rainier, the Cascade and Olympic Mountains. Restaurants include a *Trader Vic's,* the *Market Café* and the *Palm Court* for brunch and live entertainment six nights a week. Open daily. 875 rooms, shops, airport bus. 5th Ave. at Westlake (624-7400). Expensive.

Sorrento Hotel – This small hotel with just 76 rooms has been remodeled and now offers first-class amenities. It is expensive, but provides such luxuries as 24-hour room service, a highly acclaimed restaurant, the *Hunt Club,* and many other extras. Terry Ave. and Madison St. (622-6400). Expensive.

The Park Hilton – One of Seattle's newest hotels, it overlooks the famed downtown Freeway Park, and its *Morilles* dining room has already received high marks on all counts. 6th and Seneca (464-1980). Expensive to moderate.

The Edgewater Inn – Since it's on Pier 67 of the Puget Sound, not only do you get a sea-breeze view of the water, but you can fish from your window (the inn rents fishing gear) and catch your own dinner — the kitchen will cook it to order. Features waterside dining in the *Camelot Room* as well as dancing in the rooftop *Terrace Lounge.* 230 rooms, free parking, and connections to airport terminal. At Pier 67 (624-7000). Moderate.

Mayflower Park Hotel – In the downtown shopping district, the Mayflower offers convenient accommodations in a recently refurnished and renovated setting. Children under 17 with their parents stay free. Free parking, a coffee shop, and a cocktail lounge. 4th Ave. and Olive Way (623-8700). Moderate to inexpensive.

EATING OUT: Seattle's food industry did not really get moving until 1949 when the state passed liquor-by-the-drink regulations, leading to the establishment of good restaurants rather than bottle clubs. There's plenty of nourishment, from wild game, fresh seafood, and steaks, to a wide range of Oriental cuisines in the International District. Our selections range in price from $40 for a dinner for two in the expensive range; $20 to $35 in the moderate; and $15 or less in the inexpensive range. Prices do not include drinks, wine or tips.

The Mirabeau – Its lofty perch — atop the 50-story Seattle–First National Bank Building — is entirely fitting, as it is simply one of the city's best restaurants. The French cuisine — try the veal or wild game — is complemented by a good wine list. Closed Sundays. Reservations. Major credit cards. 1001 4th Ave. (624-4550). Expensive.

Rosellini's Four-10 – Victor Rosellini aims at a big target, not wild game, but the Old World, which he covers admirably with classic Continental and Italian dinners, elegant service and surroundings. The pasta specialties are from old Rosellini family recipes, executed by European-trained chefs. Luncheon specialties include roast duckling and poached salmon stuffed with shrimp sauce. Closed Sundays. Reservations. Major credit cards. 4th and Wall Sts. (624-5464). Expensive.

Canlis' – The first and still the best of the chain. Features excellent dishes, including several cuts of charcoal-broiled steaks, poached fresh salmon in hollandaise sauce, pan-fried Quilcene oysters from nearby Quilcene Bay, and a sweeping view of Lake Union. Closed Sundays. Reservations. Major credit cards. 2576 Aurora Ave. N (283-3313). Expensive.

Daniel's Broiler – A small, intimate, and usually crowded restaurant on the shores of Lake Washington, *Daniel's* has a pretty view and some of the finest stir-fried vegetables and prawns you'll find in the Northwest. Steaks and scampi are also favorites. Open daily for dinner only. Reservations advised. Major credit cards. 200 Lake Washington Blvd. (329-4191). Expensive.

The Broadway – Actually, three places in one: A New York-type bar where wealthy, young Seattleites gather; the Palm Court for casual dining; and the Club Room, with a more intimate and formal atmosphere. The menus are varied, and the wine list extensive. Open daily. 11 AM to 2AM; weekend brunch. Reservations advised. Major credit cards. 314 Broadway E (323-1990). Expensive to moderate.

The Mikado – A by-product of Seattle's large Japanese community. From its sushi bar, with delectable raw fish, through a dinner menu featuring king crab batayaki and shioyaki seafood, the *Mikado* is an experience. Tatami rooms, where you feel a part of the Japanese culture, are available for parties of four or more. Open for dinner only; closed Sundays. Major credit cards. 514 S Jackson St. (622-5206). Moderate.

Duncan's – In the heart of historic Pioneer Square, *Duncan's* is just a short walk from the Kingdome and features a cuisine that can best be described as eclectic Continental. Host Klaus Mager has special menus weekly — dishes from the Middle East one week, the wild game of his native Germany the next. The standing menu offers a wide variety of carefully prepared entrées. Sunday brunch has drawn raves from local critics. Open daily. Reservations advised. Major credit cards. 312 2nd Ave. S (583-0920). Moderate.

Ray's Boathouse – On the waterfront at Shilshole Bay, a great place to have a leisurely dinner while watching the sun go down behind the Olympic Mountains. Seafood offerings are fine and varied. Open daily. Reservations. Major credit cards. 6049 Seaview Ave. NW (789-3770). Moderate.

Jake O'Shaughnessey's – A taste of the old Seattle, with booze bottles lining the mirrored bar walls, the decor of the turn-of-the-century saloon, and six beef and seafood entrées. Specialties are fresh salmon roasted over alder wood, saloon beef, roasted for eight hours in a cast of pure grain roasting salt, and Puget Sound sea stew with ten Sound ingredients. Open daily. No reservations. Major credit cards. 100 Mercer St. in Hansen Baking Company (285-1897). Moderate.

Brasserie Pittsbourg – The decor is informal — white tiled floors, white walls, and paper tablecloths — but the French cuisine is from classical dishes like canard à l'orange and regional specialties with a French twist like the geoduck Pittsbourg — a local king clam sautéed in garlic, butter, and fresh herbs. Closed Sundays. Reservations advised. Major credit cards. 602 1st Ave. (623-4167). Moderate.

Boondock's, Sundecker's, & Greenthumbs – Have a cocktail before starting to peruse the menu — it's a small book. This is one of the Broadway district's first fine restaurants, and it manages to make the meals big — and tasty. You can't go wrong with *Boondock's* Joe's Special, spinach salad, quiches, or wine salami sandwich. There's also a good selection of wines. Open daily. Reservations advised. Major credit cards. 611 Broadway (323-7272). Moderate.

WASHINGTON, DC

In the 1950s, during one of the thaws in the Cold War, President Eisenhower was showing the visiting Nikita Khrushchev around Washington. Every time Eisenhower pointed out a government building, Khrushchev would claim that the Russians had one bigger and better that took only half as long to build. Eisenhower, so the story goes, got pretty weary of this civic one-upmanship, and when they passed the Washington Monument, he said nothing, forcing Khrushchev to ask what the structure was. Eisenhower replied, "It's news to me. It wasn't here yesterday."

Well, the story may be somewhat apocryphal (Eisenhower's reputation as a wit is not luminous) but it does indicate something important about Washington: It is a city filled with imperial architecture — grand, expansive, deliberate — of a kind that simply doesn't happen overnight or by chance. And yet it is a city that did, indeed, happen almost by chance; a city that until WW II seemed to resist almost in its bones being what it has today become: the United States' international showplace.

A walk along the Mall will remove any doubts you have about the quality of Washington's cityscape. The Mall is the grand promenade of the capital, connecting the Capitol to the Lincoln Memorial by two miles of open green and reflecting pools, lined by the excellent Smithsonian museums. Gleaming marble and massively columned buildings on and surrounding this expanse signify that this *is* the seat of the imperial power of the United States of America. These structures, familiar to everyone from picture postcards, take on real dimensions and fulfill the promise of grandeur (particularly at night when they are bathed in floodlights). But this city of wide tree-lined avenues offers enough open space for varied architectural styles to appear highly consistent. Newer government buildings of modern design and neat rows of town houses fit in with federal-style and Greek revival structures. And Washington will retain its impressive mien. A city ordinance limits the height of buildings to 13 stories, so the Capitol remains the city's tallest building. Though others approach it, none surpasses the splendor of this domed edifice.

The fact that Washington is so impressive is especially remarkable if you consider its stormy birth at the turn of the 18th century. Its future then couldn't have looked more bleak. Were it not for a band of disgruntled Continental soldiers who marched into Philadelphia on June 20, 1783, to demand back pay, Congress might well have remained in that most civilized of American cities, and Washington would probably still be a marshy swamp.

For the next seven years, Congress wrangled over the location of the new federal city. In 1790, as a result of a compromise between the North and the South, a site on the Potomac shore was selected, far enough inland to protect against surprise attack, yet accessible to ocean vessels, and at the head of a tidewater. Maryland agreed to give 69.25 square miles of land and Virginia

30.75 square miles to form the square to be known as "The District of Columbia." The city was named for George Washington, who as first president was authorized to oversee its development.

Washington appointed Major Pierre L'Enfant, a French engineer, to lay out the city. L'Enfant arrived on the scene in 1791 and on viewing Jenkins' Hill, the present Capitol Hill, he pronounced it "a pedestal waiting for a monument." He also set about designing avenues 160 feet wide which were to radiate out from circles crowned with sculpture. The city's two focal points were to be the Capitol and the president's house, with Pennsylvania Avenue the principal ceremonial street between.

L'Enfant soon became involved in a controversy over the sale of lots which were to have raised money to finance construction of government buildings, and was fired before the year was out. He spent the rest of his life in relative obscurity, living off the charity of friends. George Washington died in 1799 before the development of the federal city was assured. But President Adams' resolve was firm and Congress was pried from its comfortable surroundings in Philadelphia to the howling wilderness of Washington in November of 1800. Abigail Adams was none too happy with the choice, and wrote to her sister from the new White House: "Not one room or chamber of the whole is finished. . . . We have not the least fence, yard or other convenience without, and the great unfinished audience room I make a drying room of, to hang the clothes in." Abigail was displeased by the White House, and nobody was pleased with the city. The streets were unpaved and mud-rutted, the sewers, nonexistent, and the swampy surroundings infested with mosquitoes (better to stay in the drying room).

During the War of 1812 the city underwent a devastating setback when British troops marched in and succeeded in burning the White House and gutting the Capitol. A torrential thunderstorm saved the city from total destruction, but much was burned beyond repair.

Ironically, for the showplace of democracy, just about the most constructive period of the capital's history took place 50 years later, when Alexander "Boss" Shepherd, governor of the District of Columbia, decided to make Washington worthy of being the capital city in fact as well as in name. Between 1871 and 1874 he succeeded in having the streets paved, gas, sewer mains, and street lights installed, and parks laid out. He thought big, lived high, and used cronyism as his modus operandi. The results were spectacular, as was the debt — $20 million — which left the city bankrupt. The "Boss" was fired; he fled to Mexico, but returned later to a hero's welcome.

Events did not turn out so badly after all for Pierre L'Enfant — or at least for his plans (he, unfortunately, died a pauper in 1825). In 1901 the McMillian Commission was instituted to resurrect L'Enfant's original plans and treat the capital as a work of civic art. Railroad tracks were removed from the Mall, plans were made for the construction of the Lincoln Memorial and Arlington Bridge, and 640 acres of swampland were converted into Potomac parklands. The remains of Pierre L'Enfant were transferred to a grave in Arlington National Cemetery overlooking the city which still bears the stamp of his magnificent design.

First-time visitors to Washington may well wonder if there's a life in

Washington beyond the monuments, buildings, fountains, and statues. Behind the handsome façade lie many Washingtons, but it would take the combined skills of a historian, political analyst, city planner, expert on international, race, and social relations, and a master satirist to explain each one. Writer Ben Bagdikian observes: "In many respects, Washington, DC, is a perfectly normal American city. Its rivers are polluted. The air is periodically toxic from exhaust fumes. It has traffic jams, PTA meetings, and other common hazards of urban life. . . . Beyond its official buildings the natives rise each morning, crowd into buses and car pools, go to work, return at night, to the naked eye no different from the inhabitants of Oklahoma City or Pawtucket, Rhode Island."

All true, but Washington has something which no other city has — the federal government. The District is something of a one-industry town, but the industry is government and that has made all the difference. Nearly half of the 690,000 people living in Washington and its immediate surroundings work for some branch of government (the population of the entire metropolitan area is over three million). As civil servants, they earn relatively high incomes, a factor which provides a solid economic base for the city. Contrary to popular opinion, the population is relatively stable. Even during a change of administration, only about 3,000 officeholders lose their positions. In addition to the permanent government employees, diplomats from more than 137 countries serve in Washington — considered to be the world's top post. The embassies lend a cultural sophistication to the capital, and further diversify the population.

In response to these influences, Washington has developed as a major cosmopolitan center. Restaurants offer nearly as wide a representation of nationalities as do the embassies, and in some cases, even wider — you can eat in a Cuban restaurant, but try to find the Cuban embassy (if you do, it's news to us; it wasn't there yesterday). In the Smithsonian Institution museums you can see anything and everything from the US's only Leonardo da Vinci painting to something even da Vinci, in his wildest dreams, never imagined: the film "To Fly" (at the National Air and Space Museum), projected on a huge screen with dazzling camerawork that scans the countryside and the globe from dizzying heights as if the viewer were in the cockpit of a plane or a spacecraft. (Perhaps this *was* da Vinci's wildest dream.) The cultural picture has never been brighter (remember that it used to be an "event" to have a visiting ballet troupe squeeze onto the stage of a downtown movie theater, or a post-Broadway road show visit Washington's only theater, the National). But today the Kennedy Center draws star artists and provides a home for music, theater, and dance companies. And what better proof of being an established cultural center than having branches of Bloomingdale's, I. Magnin's, and Neiman-Marcus?

Still, there are some shadows across this bright horizon. Washington has a fairly high crime rate, though due to greatly increased police patrols, it's no longer the town of terror it once was said to be. Cold FBI statistics place it 18th on the list of high crime metropolitan areas. Of the District's population, which is largely black, there is a distressingly high rate of unemployment among unskilled workers and teenagers. Following the assassination of Martin Luther King in 1968, extensive parts of downtown Washington were burned, precipitating a white flight to the suburbs. But recently many families have returned to the city and are renovating homes in formerly seedy neighborhoods which are becoming stable integrated communities. Many of the city's worst slums, particularly in the southwest section, have been torn down and in their place stand apartment houses, theaters, restaurants, town houses, and a redeveloped waterfront area.

The forecast ranges from overcast to sunny. With home rule a reality (since 1973), Washington has abandoned its status as "the last colony." Residents may now vote for president, a mayor, a city council, and a nonvoting representative to Congress. Congressional committees which used to have sole discretion on District spending must share the purse strings with elected officials who have the best interests of their Washington constituency in mind, so the future promises further progress.

And so it goes with Pierre L'Enfant's city. It is the Washington he envisioned which you see today. Every visitor to the Capitol should stand on its west terrace and appreciate one of the finest cityscapes in the world. And as you gaze, you might contemplate the words of Henry Adams. Over a century ago, he wrote, "One of these days this will be a very great city if nothing happens to it." Something has and nevertheless, it is.

WASHINGTON AT-A-GLANCE

SEEING THE CITY: The 555-foot Washington Monument commands a panorama of the capital city in all its glory. To the north stands the White House, below stretches the green Mall with the Lincoln Memorial in the west and the Capitol perfectly aligned with it to the east. Beyond to the south and west flows the Potomac, and across the river lies Virginia. Open daily. 15th St. between Independence and Constitution Aves. (426-6839).

SPECIAL PLACES: In Washington, all roads lead to the Capitol. The building marks the center of the District. North/south streets are numbered in relation to it, east/west streets are lettered, and the four quadrants into which Washington is divided (NW, NE, SW, SE designated after addresses) meet here.

CAPITOL HILL AREA

The Capitol – The Senate and House of Representatives are housed in the Capitol which is visible from almost every part of the city. When French architect L'Enfant first began to plan the city he noted that Jenkins' Hill (now called Capitol Hill) was "a pedestal waiting for a monument." And though Washington laid the cornerstone in 1793, the pedestal had to wait through some 150 years of additions, remodelings, and fire (it was burned by the British in 1814) to get the monument we know today. The 258-foot cast-iron dome, topped by Thomas Crawford's statue of Freedom, was erected during the Civil War; beneath it, the massive rotunda is a veritable art gallery of American history featuring Constantino Brumidi's fresco, "The Apotheosis of Washington" in the eye of the dome, John Trumbull's Revolutionary War paintings on the walls, and statues of Washington, Lincoln, Jefferson, and others. The rest of the building also contains many artworks, and though you are free to wander about, the

40-minute guided tours that leave from the Rotunda every quarter hour are excellent and provide access to the Visitors' Galleries of Congress. Congressional sessions start at noon. You can also ride the monorail subway that joins the House and Senate wings with the congressional office buildings, and try the famous bean soup in the Senate Office Building Dining Room. Open daily from 9 to 4:30. Free. 1st St. between Constitution and Independence Aves. (224-3121).

The Supreme Court Building – This neoclassical white marble structure, surrounded by Corinthian columns, and with the inscription on its pediment "Equal Justice Under Law," was designed by Cass Gilbert and completed in 1935. Until then however, the highest judicial body in the nation and one of three equal branches of government met in makeshift quarters in the basement of the Capitol. Now the Court receives equal treatment under the law and meets in an impressive courtroom flanked by Ionic columns when it is in session intermittently from October through June. Sessions are open to the public on a first-come-first-served basis. Open weekdays from 9 AM to 5 PM. Courtroom presentations on the half-hour from 9:30 AM to 3:30 PM, except when court is in session. Free. 1st St. between Maryland Ave. and E Capitol St., NE (252-3211).

The Library of Congress – These magnificent Italian Renaissance-style buildings compose the world's largest and richest library. Originally designed as a research aid to Congress, the Library serves the public as well with 75 million items in 183 languages, including manuscripts, maps, photographs, motion pictures, and music. The exhibition hall displays include Jefferson's first draft of the Declaration of Independence and Lincoln's first two drafts of the Gettysburg Address. Among the Library's other holdings are one of three copies of the Gutenberg Bible, Pierre L'Enfant's original design for Washington, and the oldest known existing film — the three-second "Sneeze" by Thomas Edison. The Coolidge Auditorium has regularly scheduled concerts and literary events. Forty-five-minute guided tours offered Mondays through Fridays. Open daily. Free. 1st St. between E Capitol and B Sts., SE (287-5000).

Folger Shakespeare Library – The nine bas-reliefs on the façade depict scenes from Shakespeare's plays, and inside you can find out anything you want to know about Shakespeare and the English Renaissance. The world's finest collection of rare books, manuscripts, and research materials relating to the foremost English-language playwright, the Library, an oak-paneled, barrel-vaulted Elizabethan palace, also has a model of the Globe Theater and a full-scale replica of an Elizabethan theater complete with a trap door (called the "heavens" and used for special effects). Visitors can see how productions were mounted in Shakespeare's day and how they are done today. Poetry, concerts, and plays by Renaissance and modern authors are presented here. The bookstore features the fine Folger series on the Elizabethan period, as well as editions of Shakespeare's plays. Open daily (closed Sundays from Labor Day to April 15). Free. (544-4600). For information on attending a play see *Theater,* SOURCES AND RESOURCES. 201 E Capitol St., SE (546-4000).

The Museum of African Art – The most extensive collection of African art in this country is on display in the restored town house that was the first home of Frederick Douglass, who worked his way up from slavery to become a noted orator and government official. Exhibits include figures, masks, and sculptures in ivory, wood, bronze, and clay from 20 African nations; also color panels and audiovisual presentations on the people and environment of Africa. One gallery has an intriguing exhibit concerning the influence of Africa's cultural heritage on modern European and American art, and another focuses on the career of Douglass. Delightful gift shop. Open weekdays. Donations suggested. 316–318 A St., NE (357-1300).

Botanic Garden – If you feel like you are overdosing on history, the Botanic Garden provides a pleasant antidote with its azaleas, orchids, and tropical plants, and we're not even going to tell you how big they are or where they're from. Open daily. Free. 1st St. and Maryland Ave. at the foot of Capitol Hill (225-7099).

THE WHITE HOUSE AREA

The White House – Probably the most historic house in America because George Washington never slept here, though every president since him has. It has been the official residence of the head of state since 1800. Designed originally by James Hoban, the White House still appears like an Irish country mansion from the outside; inside there are elegant parlors decorated with portraits of the presidents and first ladies, antique furnishings of many periods, and many interesting innovations added by various presidents like the revolving tray in the Green Room — an invention of Thomas Jefferson's which revolved between pantry and dining room, allowing him to serve such novelties as macaroni and ice cream and waffles without fear of eavesdropping servants. The five state rooms on the first floor are open to the public, and though you won't actually see the business of government going on, you'll be very close to it.

Visitors line up at the East Gate on E Executive Ave. Open Tuesdays through Saturdays 10 AM to noon; until 2 during the summer. VIP tours of seven rooms, instead of the usual five, are available by writing your Congressman in advance. Be sure to specify alternate dates. From 8 AM to 10 AM, Tuesdays through Saturdays. Free. 1600 Pennsylvania Ave. (456-7041).

Lafayette Square – If you do not enter the White House, you can get a fine view of it from this square which was originally proposed by city planner L'Enfant as the mansion's front yard. Statues commemorate Andrew Jackson and the foreign heroes of the American Revolution — Lafayette, de Rochambeau, von Steuben, and Kosciusko. Flanking the square are two early-19th-century buildings designed by Benjamin Latrobe, Washington's first public architect. St. John's Church, constructed along classically simple lines, is better known as the Church of Presidents because every president since Madison has attended services here. Open daily. Free. At 16th and H Sts. NW (347-8766). The Decatur House, built for Commodore Stephen Decatur and occupied after his death by a succession of diplomats, is a federal-style town house featuring handsome woodwork, a spiral staircase, and furniture of the 1820s. Closed Mondays. Small admission charge. 748 Jackson Place, NW (673-4030). Near the southwest corner of the park at 1651-1653 Pennsylvania Ave. NW, is Blair House, the president's official guest house since 1942 and home of the Trumans from 1948 to 1952 when the White House was being renovated (Blair House is not open to the public).

The Ellipse – This grassy 36-acre expanse is the location of the zero milestone from which all distances in Washington are measured, the site of everything from demonstrations and ball games to the national Christmas tree. 1600 Constitution Ave., NW.

Corcoran Gallery of Art – If you think you've seen the Athenaeum portraits of George Washington before, you're probably not experiencing déjà vu. Check your wallet and hopefully you'll see several more reproductions and if you're lucky maybe a few of Jackson, too. This outstanding collection of American art contains some less familiar works as well, including a beardless portrait of Lincoln (your five-dollar bill won't help you here), portraits by John Copley, Gilbert Stuart, Rembrandt Peale, impressionistic works by Mary Cassatt and Childe Hassam, Whistler, Eakins, Bellows, and works by contemporary artists as well. Among the European paintings are a large collection of Corot, and a fine group of Dutch and Flemish 17th-century works. The Corcoran also features exhibitions of fine-art photography and works by artists of the Washington area. Closed Mondays. Free. 17th St. and New York Ave., NW (638-3211).

Renwick Gallery – This beautiful French Second Empire building is worth a visit for its changing exhibits of American crafts and design, the entrance foyer with its impressive staircase, and its 1870 Grand Salon, with overstuffed Louis XV sofas and potted palms. Open daily. Free. Pennsylvania Ave. at 17th St., NW (357-1300).

Daughters of the American Revolution Museum – Though any member of the DAR must prove that she is descended from those who served the cause of American independence with "unfailing loyalty," the museum is open to everyone regardless of the color of their blood. Exhibits feature 28 period rooms including the parlor of a 19th-century Mississippi River steamboat. There's also an extensive genealogical library, where, for a small charge, you can find out who's blue. Closed Saturdays. Free. 1776 D St., NW (628-1776).

Octagon House – This stately red-brick town house is a notable example of the federal style of architecture. The house in which President and Dolley Madison lived for 6 months after the British burned down the White House in 1814 is maintained as a museum to give a picture of the high lifestyle of the early 19th century. American antique furnishings from the federal period include Hepplewhite and Sheraton. Closed Mondays. Donations suggested. 1799 New York Ave., NW (638-3105).

The Organization of American States – Housed in the Pan American Union Building. Its architects, Paul Cret and Albert Kelsey, have blended the styles of North and South America in this building of imposing formality and inviting elegance. The Museum of Modern Latin American Art is just behind the Aztec Garden. Closed Sundays and Mondays. Small fee. 17th St. and Constitution Ave., NW (789-3000).

THE MALL

This two-mile stretch of green from the Lincoln Memorial to the Capitol forms the kind of grand avenue envisioned by Pierre L'Enfant in his original plans for the city.

Lincoln Memorial – From the outside this columned white marble building looks like a Greek temple; inside the spacious chamber with its colossal seated statue of Lincoln, sculpted by Daniel French, it is as inspiring. Carved on the walls are the words of the Gettysburg Address and the Second Inaugural Address. National Park Service guides present brief talks at regular intervals. Always open. Memorial Circle between Constitution and Independence Aves. (426-6841).

Washington Monument – Dominating the Mall is the 555-foot marble and granite obelisk designed by Robert Mills (completed 1884) to commemorate George Washington (as Dwight Eisenhower could have told you). The top (reached by elevator) commands an excellent panoramic view of the city. You can ride down or descend the steps where you see many stones donated by such curious groups as the "Citizens of the US residing in Foo Chow Foo, China" and "Otter's Summit, Virginia's Loftiest Peak." Open daily. Free. 15th St. between Independence and Constitution Aves. (426-6839).

Bureau of Engraving and Printing – If you're interested in money and how it is really made, the self-guided tour which follows the entire process of paper currency production will prove enlightening if not enriching. Everything of a financial character from the one-cent postage stamp to the $500 million Treasury Note is designed, engraved, and printed here. Though it costs only a penny to produce a single note, there are no free samples. Open weekdays. Free. 14th and C Sts., SW (566-2000).

National Archives – The repository for all major American records. The 76 Corinthian columns supporting this handsome building designed by John Russell Pope are nothing compared to the contents. Inside, in special helium-filled glass and bronze cases, reside the very pillars of our democracy — the Declaration of Independence, the Constitution, and the Bill of Rights. Open daily. Free. Constitution Ave. between 7th and 9th Sts., NW (523-3099).

Jefferson Memorial – Dominating the south bank of the Tidal Basin, this domed templelike structure (also designed by John Russell Pope) is a tribute to our third president and the drafter of the Declaration of Independence. The bronze statue of Jefferson was executed by Rudoph Evans and inscribed on the walls are quotations from Jefferson's writings. Open daily. Free. South Basin Dr., SW, at the Tidal Basin (426-6822).

J. Edgar Hoover Building – If you want to find out a little more about an organization which already knows everything about you, take a tour of the FBI. In addition to a film on some past investigative activities, you'll get to see the laboratory and a firearms demonstration. Closed weekends. Free. Pennsylvania Ave. between 9th and 10th Sts. NW (324-3000).

The National Gallery of Art – One of the larger jewels in Washington's rich cultural crown, this gift to the nation by Andrew Mellon, financier and former Secretary of the Treasury, houses one of the world's finest collections of Western art from the 13th century to the present. Among the masterpieces in this huge and opulent white marble gallery are a grand survey of Italian painting including da Vinci's "Ginevra de' Benci," Fra Filippo Lippi's "The Adoration of the Magi," Raphael's "Saint George and the Dragon," works of French Impressionists, a self-portrait by Rembrandt, Renoir's "Girl With a Watering Can," Picasso's "The Lovers," and an extensive American collection. The new seven-story East Building, designed by I. M. Pei, is something of an architectural masterpiece in its own right. An intriguing building of interlocking triangular forms, it houses the Center for Advanced Study in the Visual Arts as well as many exhibition halls. Several visits are necessary to see the whole gallery and there are also tours, films, lectures, and weekly concerts. Open daily. Free. 6th St. and Constitution Ave., NW (737-4215).

Smithsonian Institution – Before James Smithson died in 1829 he willed his entire fortune of half a million dollars "to found in Washington, an establishment for the increase and diffusion of knowledge among men." The wealthy English scientist had never even been to America and probably had no idea how much knowledge would be increased and diffused here in his name. Today the Smithsonian administers numerous museums, galleries, and research organizations; has an operating budget of over $90 million, a staff of over 4,000 and 75 million items in its total collection. The Romanesque red sandstone Smithsonian Institution building, known as "the castle," is the best place to get visitor information on any of the Institution's activities including all of its museums. (All Smithsonian museums are open daily and have free admission; for information on exhibits and special events including lectures, films, and concerts call 357-2020.) 1000 Jefferson Dr., SW (357-1300).

Among the Smithsonian Museums on the Mall are:

National Museum of Natural History – Only 1% of the museum's collection is on display but when you're dealing with a total of some 60 million specimens there's still plenty to see. Features eyefuls of the biggest and the best of most everything from the largest elephant on record — twelve tons from the African bush — to the precious Hope Diamond, at a hefty 44.5 karats, the largest blue diamond known (its only flaw is that it has brought tragedy to all its possessors). The Hall of Dinosaurs has mammoth skeletons. And there's even Martha, who died in the Cincinnati Zoo in 1914 and is now stuffed, the last of the extinct Passenger Pigeons. Open daily. Free. Constitution Ave. at 10th St., NW (357-1300).

National Museum of American History – Everything that has to do with American ingenuity in craftsmanship, design, and industry can be found here along with some things that bear only the most tenuous link. (That's where the real fun begins.) Hall after hall features such items as Eli Whitney's cotton gin, George Washington's false teeth, the flag that inspired "The Star-Spangled Banner," a gargantuan pendulum which was used by French physicist Jean Foucault to demonstrate the rotation of the earth, and a full gallery of first lady mannequins dressed in Inaugural Ball gowns. Open daily. Free. Constitution Ave. Between 12th and 14th Sts., NW (357-1300).

National Air and Space Museum – The largest of the Smithsonian's museums, with displays of aircraft in its vast, lofty interior. Exhibits include the Wright Brothers' plane, Charles Lindbergh's *Spirit of St. Louis,* the Apollo 11 command module, and a walk-through model of a Skylab orbital station. The film "To Fly," shown on a huge screen, is as spectacular as it is dizzying. Planetarium shows are presented in the Albert Einstein Spacearium. Open daily. Free. Independence Ave. between 4th and 7th Sts., SW (357-2700, for show times).

Hirshhorn Museum and Sculpture Garden – Smaller but also superb is this collection donated in 1974 by a Latvian immigrant and self-made millionaire. The Hirshhorn is worth a visit not only for its fine collection but also for a look at the building itself, a circular concrete structure with an open core in which a bronze fountain shoots water 82 feet into the air. Displays include 19th- and 20th-century European and American works, and an attractive sculpture garden which features Rodin's "The Burghers of Calais" and Picasso's "Baby Carriage." Open daily. Free. Independence Ave. at 8th St., SW (357-1300).

Freer Gallery of Art – Prime collection of Far and Near Eastern art amassed by Detroit industrialist Charles L. Freer. Includes Chinese bronze, jade, and porcelain pieces, Greek biblical manuscripts, Japanese ceramics, and Egyptian glassworks. Freer also gathered over 1,000 works of James Whistler. The Peacock Room, Whistler's only known attempt at interior decorating done in peacock and peacock feather motif, should not be missed. Open daily. Free. 12th St. and Jefferson Dr., SW (357-1300).

DOWNTOWN

National Portrait Gallery – Inside this excellent example of Greek revival architecture, many Americans who have gone down in the history of this country have gone up on the walls (in portrait form that is). Among those hanging are all the American presidents, Pocahontas, Horace Greeley, and Harriet Beecher Stowe. In the same building is the National Museum of American Art featuring American painting, sculpture, and graphic arts including Catlin's paintings of the Indians and a choice group of works of the American Impressionists. Both museums (also administered by the Smithsonian) are open daily. Free. 8th St. at F and G Sts., NW (357-1300).

Ford's Theatre – The site of Lincoln's assassination in 1865 by John Wilkes Booth is a national monument. In the past decade, the theater has been restored and reopened and decorated as it was on that fatal night. In the basement there is a museum of Lincoln memorabilia including exhibits capsulizing his life as a lawyer, statesman, husband and father, and president, and the clothes he was wearing when he was shot, the derringer used by Booth to shoot him, and the assassin's personal diary. For theater tickets, call 347-4833. Open daily. Free. 511 10th St., NW (426-6924).

Peterson House – Directly across the street from the theater and museum is the house in which Lincoln died the morning after the assassination. The house is small and sparsely furnished and has been refurnished to appear very much the way it did when Lincoln died. Open daily. Free. 516 10th St., NW (426-6830).

GEORGETOWN

There's not much tobacco left in this area which was once the Union's major tobacco port. It's particularly nice in the spring when you can walk along the Chesapeake and Ohio Canal. The whole area's great for strolling. Besides the Canal (between Jefferson and 31st Sts.) the streets off Wisconsin Avenue house the city's social and political elite in beautiful restored town houses with prim gardens and lovely magnolia trees. The main drags are Wisconsin Avenue and M Street with boutiques, restaurants, and ice cream parlors (try an old-fashioned sundae at *Swensen's*, 1254 Wisconsin Ave.). Most of the action, including the city's hot nightlife, takes place here. In the area at the top of the hill (along R St. east of Wisconsin Ave.), large 18th-century country estates survive and mingle with smaller row houses. For more unusual juxtaposition, the Dumbarton Oaks Garden has beautiful formal gardens and a fine collection of early Christian and Byzantine art. The entrance to the museum is at 1703 32nd St., NW; the entrance to the gardens is at 31st and R sts., NW. Closed Mondays. Small admission charge from April to October (338-8278).

■ **EXTRA SPECIAL:** Just 16 miles south of Washington on Mt. Vernon Memorial Highway is *Mount Vernon*, George Washington's estate from 1754 to 1799, and his final resting place. This lovely 18th-century plantation is interesting not just for its beauty but because it shows a less familiar aspect of the military-political man — George Washington as the rich Southern planter. The mansion which overlooks the Potomac and the outbuildings that housed the shops that made Mount Vernon a self-sufficient economic unit have been authentically restored and refurnished. Some 500 of the original 8,000 acres remain; all are well maintained and the parterre gardens and formal lawns separated from the outlying fields by sunken walls provide a magnificent setting for the mansion. There's also a museum with Washington memorabilia and the tomb of George and Martha lies at the foot of the hill. Plan to spend a few hours touring the buildings and grounds and in the spring or the summer start out early to avoid big crowds. Open daily. Admission charge (703 780-2000).

Also beautifully landscaped and overlooking the Potomac, but with many more tombs and monuments, *Arlington National Cemetery* is a solemn reminder of this country's turbulent history. Here lie the bodies of the many who served in the military forces, among them Admiral Richard Byrd, General George Marshall, Robert Kennedy, Justice Oliver Wendell Holmes, and John Kennedy, whose grave is marked by the Eternal Flame. The Tomb of the Unknown Soldier, a 50-ton block of white marble, commemorates the dead of WW I, WW II, and the Korean War and is always guarded by a solitary soldier. Changing of the guard takes place every hour on the hour. The grounds of the cemetery were once the land of Robert E. Lee's plantation but were confiscated by the Union after Lee joined the Confederacy. *Arlington House* where Lee lived has been restored and is open for public inspection. Cars are not allowed in the cemetery but you can park at the Visitor Center and go on foot or pay and ride the Tourmobile. Open daily. Directly west of Memorial Bridge in Arlington, VA (703 692-0931).

SOURCES AND RESOURCES

The Washington Convention and Visitors Association, 1575 Eye St., NW, Washington, DC 20005 (789-7000), has pamphlets and other information on where to stay, eat, and shop. The Gateway Tour Center, 4th and E sts., NW, has all kinds of tourist information. You can also park your car here in a 1,000-car indoor garage and head for the Mall in a free shuttle bus. *The Walker Washington Guide* by John and Katharine Walker (Guide Press, 7101 Glenbrook Rd., Bethesda, MD 20814; $4.95 plus $1 postage) is the best comprehensive local guide to Washington and its environs.

All telephone numbers are in the 202 area code unless otherwise indicated.

For Local Coverage – The *Washington Post,* morning daily; *Washingtonian* Magazine, monthly. Both are available at newsstands.

For Food – Donald Dresden's *Guide to Eating Out in Washington* (Acropolis Press, $2.95).

CLIMATE AND CLOTHES: Washington has four distinct seasons. Summers are Amazonian, falls New Englandish and lovely, winters cold with some snow and lots of slush (wear boots or suffer), and spring — when the cherry blossoms bloom, and all is beautiful.

GETTING AROUND: Bus – The Metro Bus system serves the entire District and the surrounding area. Transfers within the District are free and the rates increase when you go into Maryland and Virginia. For complete route information call the Metropolitan Area Transit Authority office (637-2437).

Taxi – Cabs in the District charge by the zone and are relatively inexpensive. Sharing cabs is common, but ask the driver whether there is a route conflict if you join another passenger. Cabs may be hailed in the street, picked up outside stations and hotels, or ordered on the phone. Major cab companies are Yellow (544-1212) and Barwood, serving the Maryland suburbs (652-8500).

Car Rental – All the national firms serve Washington.

Subway – The newest way to get around Washington is by Metrorail, the recently opened subway system. The lines that are in operation provide a quick and quiet ride. New lines of the subway to the suburbs and other areas of the city will open up as they are completed, and buses deposit or pick up passengers at these stations. For complete route and travel information and a map of the Metro system, contact the Washington Metropolitan Area Transit Authority office, 600 5th St., NW (637-2437).

Tours – An easy way to get around the principal sightseeing area is by Tourmobile. These 88-passenger shuttle trams allow you to buy your ticket (good for all day) as you board, get on or off at any of the 14 stops, listen to highlights of the sights along the way, and set your own pace. Tourmobiles pass each stop every 20 minutes. For complete tourmobile information contact the office at 1000 Ohio Dr., SW (554-7950).

Gray Line offers narrated bus tours of the District and outlying areas (479-5900). Museum tours as well as special group tours emphasizing historic Washington are run by National Fine Arts Associates, Inc., 5402 Duvall Dr., Bethesda, MD (301 229-1800). From April until mid-October, Washington Boat Lines, Inc. has daily cruises leaving hourly from the foot of Wisconsin Ave. in Georgetown and Lincoln Memorial (554-8000).

MUSEUMS: When it comes to museums, Washington is one of the nation's major showplaces, with the Smithsonian Institution's outstanding museums leading the way. Described in some detail in *Special Places* are the National Gallery of Art, the Smithsonian, Hirshhorn Museum, Freer Gallery of Art, National Air and Space Museum, National Museum of Natural History, National Museum of American History, National Portrait Gallery, National Museum of American Art, and the Renwick Gallery. Also described are the Corcoran Gallery and the Museum of African Art. Other notable museums are:

The Phillips Collection (19th- and 20th-century art), 1612 21st St. (387-0961).

Washington Doll's House and Toy Museum, 5236 44th St., NW (244-0024).

Hillwood, Russian icons, portraits, and Fabergé creations; tours by appointment only. 4155 Linnean Ave., NW (686-5807).

National Geographic Society Exhibition Hall, 17th and M sts., NW (857-7000).

MAJOR COLLEGES AND UNIVERSITIES: Washington has several universities of high national standing — George Washington University, 19th to 24th Sts., NW, F St. to Pennsylvania Ave. (676-6000), American University, Massachusetts and Nebraska Aves., NW (686-2000), Georgetown University, 37th and O Sts., NW (625-0100), Howard University, 2000 6th St., NW (636-6100), and Gallaudet College (for the deaf), 7th St. and Florida Ave., NE (651-5000).

SPECIAL EVENTS: Any town that inaugurates a new president every four years is in good standing when it comes to special events. After the president takes the oath of office every fourth year on January 20, a big parade with all the attendant fanfare makes its way down Pennsylvania Ave.

In between inaugurations there's plenty to keep the District going for four more years. The publications above list exact dates. When you start noticing white single blossoms and a flood of pink double blossoms, it's *Cherry Blossom* time in Washington. In early April, a big festival celebrates the coming of the blossoms and the spring with concerts, parades, balls, and the lighting of the Japanese Lantern at the Tidal Basin.

Around the same time (give or take a few blossoms), is the *Easter Monday Egg Rolling*, when scads of children descend on the White House lawn, and adults are only admitted if accompanied by a child.

House, garden, and embassy tours are given in April and May, allowing entrance to some of Washington's most elegant interiors. For the *Georgetown House Tour* information call 338-1796 and for *Embassy Tour* information call 842-2054.

During the summer, the *American Folklife Festival* sponsored by the Smithsonian Institution sets up its tents on the Mall near the reflecting pool, and groups from all regions of the country do their stuff with jug bands, blues, Indian dance and handicraft demonstrations.

SPORTS: Football – The *Redskins* of the National Football League play their home games at Robert F. Kennedy Stadium from September to December. Tickets are hard to come by for their regular season games and there is a waiting list for season tickets most years, but if you're in town during August or September for pre-season games, chances are much better. Try the Ticketron outlet, 1011 17th St., NW (659-2601), or the stadium box office, E Capitol and 22nd Sts., SE (546-2222).

Basketball – The National Basketball Association's Washington *Bullets* hold court from October to April at the Capital Centre, Capital Beltway and Central Ave. in Landover, MD (301 350-3400). Tickets are available at Ticketron outlets.

Hockey – The *Capitals*, Washington's pro hockey team, play indoors at Capital Centre from January to March and then outdoors at RFK Stadium from April to August. Tickets are available at Ticketron outlets or by calling 301 350-3400.

Boating – The President's Cup Regatta draws the world's fastest speedboats to the Potomac River off Hains Point the first weekend in June.

Bicycling – Rent from Thompson Boat Center, Rock Creek Pky. and Virginia Ave., NW (333-9711). The towpath of the Chesapeake and Ohio Canal, starting at the barge landing in Georgetown, is a good place to ride.

Golf – The best public golf course is the East Potomac-Hains Point Course. In East Potomac Park off Ohio Dr. (554-9813).

Tennis – Washington has some fine public courts and the best bets are the District tennis facilities at 16th and Kennedy Sts., NW (723-2669).

Skating – From November to April you can skate on the rink on the mall between 7th and 9th Sts., NW (347-9041).

Swimming – Year-round facilities are available at the East Capitol Natatorium, 635 North Carolina Ave., SE (724-4495).

THEATER: For current offerings and performance times, check the publications listed above. The opening of the *Kennedy Center* in 1971 gave the District a real cultural boost; it's located off Virginia Ave., NW (254-3600). The center's *Eisenhower Theater* offers musical and dramatic productions, including pre-Broadway shows and Broadway road shows (254-3670). The recently opened *Terrace Theater*, located on the top floor of the center, offers many different productions — modern dance, ballet, dramas, poetry recitals, and so on (254-9895). The *National Theater* presents major productions throughout the year, 1321 E St., NW (628-3393). During the fall, winter, and spring the *Arena Stage* and the *Kreeger Theater* host classical and original plays, 6th and M Sts., SW (488-3300), and the *Ford's Theatre* offers American productions at 511 10th St., NW (347-4833). The *Folger Theatre Group* offers innovative interpretations of Shakespeare's plays as well as more contemporary works at the Folger Library's Elizabethan Theatre, 201 E Capitol St., SE (546-4000). During the summer the *Olney Theater*, about an hour's drive from the District, offers summer stock and well-known casts (rt. 108, Olney, MD, 301 924-3400) and the *Wolf Trap Farm Park for the Performing Arts* presents musicals, ballet, pop concerts, and symphonic music in a lovely outdoor setting (rt. 7 near Vienna, VA — accessible via Dulles Airport access highway, 703 938-3800).

MUSIC: The *National Symphony Orchestra* conducted by Mstislav Rostropovich performs at the Kennedy Center Concert Hall from October through April (254-3776). The *Opera Society of Washington* presents four operas a year at the Kennedy Center Opera house. The *Juilliard String Quartet* performs chamber music concerts on Stradivarius instruments at the Library of Congress Auditorium, 1st St. between E Capitol St. and Independence Ave., SE (287-5502), Friday evenings, from October through April. Tickets are quite inexpensive but should be purchased at Jordan-Kitts Music, Inc., 1330 G St., NW, on Monday mornings beginning at 8:30 AM the week of the concert. During the summer there's music under the stars at *Wolf Trap Farm Park* (703 938-3800) and free concerts by the service bands on the plaza at the West Front of the Capitol, or in front of the Jefferson Memorial. Consult newspapers for where and when.

NIGHTCLUBS AND NIGHTLIFE: For some, Washington is an early-to-bed town but there's plenty of pub crawling, jazz, bluegrass, soul, rock, and folk music going on after dark. You just have to know where to look for it, and best bets are Georgetown, lower Connecticut Ave., and the Capitol Hill areas. Current favorites: *F. Scott's,* one of the classiest bars in town, 1232 36th St., NW (965-1789); *Blues Alley,* for mainstream jazz and Dixieland, 1073 Wisconsin Ave., NW (337-4141); *Charlie's Georgetown,* for dining and listening to Charlie Byrd, a popular jazz guitarist, 3223 K St., NW (298-5985); *Childe Harold,* for blues, country, and bluegrass, 1610 20th St., NW (483-6702); *Desperado's,* another Georgetown favorite with first-rate blues, 3350 M St., NW (338-5220); *Numbers,* a huge modern club with three bars, three dance floors, and a restaurant, 1330 19th St., NW (833-2860); *Jenkins' Hill*, for the District's longest bar where everyone from public servants to students slake their thirst, 223 Pennsylvania Ave., SE (544-6600).

SINS: No matter how you look at it, Washington is a great place for *anger.* Take your pick: There's that very basic statistic about the city that three-quarters of the population, which is black, lives in less than a third of the city's area. Or the fact that *lust* flourishes in the very bosom of the government (between White House offices on one side and Congress on the other). The *Washington Post*'s gossip column "The Ear" prints some of the juiciest tidbits you'll read anywhere; but still, some of the best of it isn't fit to print. Ask any aide.

LOCAL SERVICES: Business Services – WSS Secretarial Service, 2020 K St., NW (457-1848).

Mechanic – Call Carl (24-hour service), 1112 Half St., SW (479-7200).

Babysitting – Child Care Agency, 733 15th St., NW (783-8573).

BEST IN TOWN

CHECKING IN: Washington is a tourist town and there are ample and varied accommodations. You can bed down with history at the old-fashioned Sheraton-Carlton where Calvin Coolidge cut the ribbon and Harry Truman entertained, or at the Watergate, a more recently established landmark. Hotel rooms in the city are at a premium, except during weekends, and reservations should be made in advance. You have a better chance to get bargain rates if you write in advance. Visitors in town for only a few days should stay downtown to make best use of their limited time. Inexpensive taxis, the Metro system, and buses facilitate getting around without having to resort to a car which is difficult and expensive to park. However, if you have a car, major motel chains have facilities at all principal entry points to the district — Silver Spring and Bethesda in Maryland, Arlington, Falls Church, and Alexandria in Virginia. Expect to pay $100 and up for a double room in the expensive range, $75 to $100 in the moderate range, and $40 to $70 in the inexpensive range.

The Madison – Luxurious rooms, excellent service by a well-trained staff, amidst gracious federal-style decor, with extras including interpreters, refrigerators, saunas, and bathroom phones. The *Montpelier Room* is quite a good restaurant. Open for buffet from noon to 3 PM weekdays; Sunday brunch 11 AM–3 PM. There are also two more informal restaurants and a cocktail lounge. 374 rooms. 15th and M Sts., NW (826-1600). Expensive.

The Hay Adams – An incomparable location just off Lafayette Square within a silver dollar's throw of the White House. This older hotel with old-world dignity maintains the standards of the neighborhood with antique furnishings, a paneled lobby, a fine dining room, and good service. Also has cocktail lounge. 170 rooms. 16th and H Sts., NW (638-2260). Expensive.

Fairfax Hotel – Recently restored to an elegance beyond even its original standard. The same management that operates Chicago's distinguished *Tremont* and *Whitehall* hotels has been at work here, and the same taste is evident everywhere. This is as close to an evocation of a classic European hotel as exists in Washington. Facilities include the *Jockey Club* restaurant as well as a cocktail lounge and two meeting rooms. 180 units. 2100 Massachusetts Ave., NW (293-2100 or 800 424-8008). Expensive.

Sheraton-Carlton – Host to many presidents and dignitaries, most making somewhat more of an impression than ribbon-cutter Calvin Coolidge. Truman used to hold his affairs of state here while the White House was being redone, and Jimmy Carter announced his intention to run at the Sheraton-Carlton. The hotel has been recently remodeled and the Italian Renaissance lobby is elegant, the rooms comfortable, the Sunday brunch terrific, and the bar good enough to win approval from Jimmy Breslin. And if you find anything unsatisfactory, the White House is only three blocks away. There are two excellent dining rooms and a cocktail lounge. 235 rooms. 16th and K Sts., NW (638-2626). Expensive.

The Watergate – Though this modern hotel-apartment-office complex doesn't look too historic, appearances can be deceiving, as can small pieces of tape. Large contemporarily furnished rooms, indoor swimming pool and health club, the excellent *Watergate Restaurant* (open daily), cocktail lounge, Les Champs shopping mall with even more dining possibilities, and a location adjacent to Kennedy Center. 238 rooms. 2650 Virginia Ave. (965-2300). Expensive.

Loews L'Enfant Plaza – This imposing modernistic structure is one of Washington's newer luxury hotels. A huge fountain cascades on the plaza; below there is a large shopping mall with chic boutiques and a Metro station, and on the 12th story there's an outdoor swimming pool. The service is high quality, the location conveniently near the Mall, and there are two restaurants and a cocktail lounge. 372 rooms. 480 L'Enfant Plaza, SW (484-1000). Expensive.

Four Seasons – This newest of Washington's luxury hotels is Georgetown's answer to the *Madison.* Its exterior architecture looks a lot like a penitentiary, but the interior is bright and beautiful and the appeal of its rooms has got visitors talking favorably. A traditional concierge offers many personal services including mail delivery. 2800 Pennsylvania Ave., NW (342-0444). Expensive.

Georgetown Inn – Located in the middle of one of Washington's most interesting areas, this handsome brick building is unusually classy for a motor inn. The rooms are well appointed with large beds and bathroom phones and the famous *Rive Gauche* restaurant serves fine Continental cuisine, open daily. Free parking. 95 rooms. 1310 Wisconsin Ave., NW (333-8900). Expensive.

The Canterbury – Located in the downtown business district and not far from the White House, this hotel has 99 suites with a stocked bar in each. Amenities include a complimentary Continental breakfast, underground parking, nightly turn-down service with a Godiva chocolate placed on your pillow, and *Chaucer's* restaurant. Lower weekend package rates are available. 1733 N St., NW (393-3000). Expensive.

Quality Inn–Capitol Hill – This 10-story hotel offers good standard accommodations, an excellent location as well as a restaurant, cocktail lounge, rooftop swimming pool, sauna, gymnasium, and in-room movies. 350 rooms. 415 New Jersey Ave., NW (638-1616). Moderate.

Hotel Washington – One of the city's older hotels, recently refurbished and offering an incomparable view of the White House and various monuments from its rooftop restaurant. Always comfortable, but great during an inaugural parade. Nearby downtown shopping; TV; bathroom phones. 370 rooms. 15th St. and Pennsylvania Ave., NW (638-5900). Moderate.

The Tabard Inn – Located on a charming semi-residential street near the heart of the business district with an ambience rare in an American city. There is a library and small dining room on the first floor. The rooms are furnished with antiques and some of them share baths. 1739 N St., NW (785-1277). Moderate.

The Park Central – Medium size, well located just off Pennsylvania Avenue near the World Bank. *Blackie's Jr.* restaurant; coffee shop, beauty parlor and drugstore. 250 rooms. 705 18th St., NW (393-4700). Moderate.

The Windsor Park South – The rooms are small, clean, and undistinguished but the surroundings are lovely. Close by is Rock Creek Park, and the French Embassy and a beautiful residential neighborhood are just down the street. There are no dining facilities in the hotel. However, there are many restaurants along Connecticut Ave. within a few minutes' walk and the Dupont Circle Metro stop is nearby. 50 rooms. 2116 Kalorama Rd., NW (483-7700). Inexpensive.

The Harrington – This large older hotel situated right in the center of Washington's commercial area has seen better days but provides clean accommodations and is within walking distance of the Mall. High school students flock here on their Big Outing to the nation's capital, and family groups are also drawn because the *Kitcheteria* makes feeding the troops easy and inexpensive. 310 room. 11th and E Sts., NW (628-8140). Inexpensive.

EATING OUT: Considering the international aspects of Washington — 2,000 diplomats attached to 137 embassies and a large number of residents who have lived abroad and brought back a taste for foreign cuisines — it's not too surprising that the District can provide a gastronomic tour de force.

What is surprising is that up until a few years ago this wasn't the case. The great meals even two decades ago were served in private homes and embassies (Jefferson was known to treat his guests to such delicacies as ice cream and imported French wines, but these treats were confined to the White House). But the Kennedys brought a French chef to the White House, and this started a restaurant boom that hasn't stopped yet. There's high quality Continental cuisine and all manner of ethnic food — including Vietnamese. And though it's always helpful to have an ermine-lined wallet or better yet, an expense account, those who have only the yen for good food needn't go hungry. Our restaurant selections range in price from $75 for a dinner for two in the expensive range to $30 to $45 in the moderate range, and $20 and under in the inexpensive bracket. Prices do not include drinks, wine, or tips.

Rive Gauche – This prestigious French restaurant serves haute cuisine at haute prices but the setting is elegant, as is the crowd, and the food is good. The menu and wine list are extensive but the specials of the day are often the best bet, particularly the rockfish Dieppoise prepared in white wine fish stock and cream sauce and garnished with mussels and shrimp. Open daily. Reservations required. Major credit cards. 1310 Wisconsin Ave., NW (333-6440). Very expensive.

Jean-Louis – Named for its chef, this is a small and elegant restaurant with gracious service and fine nouvelle cuisine. Fixed price dinners. Closed Sundays. Reservations necessary. Major credit cards. In the Watergate Hotel, 2650 Virginia Ave., NW (298-4488). Very expensive.

Tiberio – Washington's rising young star, with a repertoire of northern Italian food and pastas including agnolotti in cream, fresh fish and veal specials, and a good wine list (some dishes from southern Italy to boot). Closed Sundays. Reservations. Major credit cards. 1915 K St., NW (452-1915). Very expensive.

Le Pavillon – Though this restaurant may have the highest prices in town, French Chef Yannick Cam offers *nouvelle cuisine* to those who know and appreciate the best. Closed Sundays. Reservations necessary. Major credit cards. 1820 K St., NW (833-3846). Very expensive.

Le Lion d'Or – Reputed to have the finest French food in town, although some say that the service isn't up to par. Try the daily specials, and don't leave without tasting one of the spectacular desserts. Open Saturdays for dinner only; closed Sundays. Reservations advised. Major credit cards. 1150 Connecticut Ave., NW (296-7972). Very expensive.

Jockey Club – Originally (but no longer) operated under the direction of the management of New York's *"21" Club,* this is the newest meeting and eating spot for local movers and shakers. The decor looks more like "21" than the original and the food is almost always of the same high quality. Open daily. Reservations necessary. Major credit cards. 2100 Massachusetts Ave., NW (659-8000). Very expensive.

Le Provençal – As the name suggests, the focus here is on the cuisine of southeastern France and owner/chef Jacques Blanc makes his mark with careful use of aromatics and fine basic ingredients — fresh fish, meat, fowl, and produce. The bouillabaisse is the best in town, the roast duck and sautéed trout dishes are excellent. The surprises come from south of the Mason-Dixon line — such dishes as mussels and crayfish au gratin in sauce Nantua, made from part of the crayfish. Here's the real serendipity — Jacques Blanc instructs others in the arts of haute cuisine. Closed Sundays. Reservations. Major credit cards. 1234 20th St., NW (223-2420). Expensive.

Cantina d'Italia – Still the longest running hit among Italian restaurants (northern Italian cuisine), the changing menu plays well to repeat performances but retains the old showstoppers like fettuccine con salsa di noci (homemade noodles with puréed walnuts, pine nuts, ricotta cheese, and parmesan) and scaloppe di vitello sorrentina (scallops of veal topped with prosciutto, mozzarella, fresh tomato, and parmesan). The only drawback is the basement location which is small and somewhat confining. Closed weekends. Reservations required. Major credit cards. 1214A 18th St., NW (659-1830). Expensive.

La Niçoise – Popular French restaurant with unusual service — waiters maneuvering about on skates. Not only do these versatile waiters skate and serve, but they also perform and at 10:30 there's an amusing, rather bawdy amateur show. Closed Sundays. Reservations required. Major credit cards. 1721 Wisconsin Ave., NW (965-9300). Expensive.

Aux Beaux Champs – The new restaurant in the *Four Seasons* hotel that's the best in Georgetown — and perhaps in all Washington. The service is stylish and the food first rate. 2800 Pennsylvania Ave., NW (342-0444). Expensive.

Le Gaulois – Though small and sometimes overcrowded, it has a top-notch French menu including a full page of daily specials. Closed Sundays. Reservations necessary. Major credit cards. 2133 Pennsylvania Ave., NW (466-3232). Expensive to moderate.

El Tio Pepe – Flamenco dancers and guitar players are the principal elements of atmosphere here. The Spanish food speaks quite nicely for itself — concitas (crabmeat and olives in clam shells), paella à la Valenciana, garlic soup, and homemade chocolate cake that's worth its weight in calories. Closed Sundays. Reservations. Major credit cards. 2809 M St., NW (337-0730). Moderate.

Jour et Nuit – Daily specials, such as lobster royal, are offered in a delightful old Georgetown house-turned-restaurant. The quiet, dignified atmosphere is complemented by very good Continental food. Open daily for dinner; Sunday brunch. Reservations advised. Major credit cards. 3003 M St., NW (333-1033). Moderate.

Gusti's – A downtown standby with consistently good service and traditional Italian specialties such as lasagna and veal scallopine. Open daily. Reservations advised. Major credit cards. 19th and M sts., NW (331-9444). Moderate.

The Broker – A bit off the beaten track in southeast Washington, this stunning restaurant deserves a visit for its unusual and beautifully prepared Swiss dishes. Open daily. Reservations advised. Major credit cards. 713 8th St., SE (546-8300). Moderate.

House of Hunan – New in town, this restaurant already ranks among the finest in the city. Unusual appetizers include shrimp balls and vegetable curls, and special main dishes are crisp whole fish Hunan style, orange beef, and honeyed ham. Open daily. Reservations necessary for dinner. Major credit cards. 1900 K St., NW (293-9111). Moderate.

Old Europe – Features the best German wine list in the District with some French and American labels; standard German dishes as well. Open daily. Reservations. Major credit cards. 2434 Wisconsin Ave., NW (333-7600). Moderate.

L'Escargot – Relaxed atmosphere, good food, for French food fans who shun the tabs of haute cuisine. Specialties like cervelles. Closed Sundays. Reservations. Major credit cards. 3309 Connecticut Ave., NW (966-7510). Moderate.

The Bread Oven – There's nothing like it in downtown Washington — a combined bakery, pastry shop, and restaurant. Stop by for a croissant and coffee in the morning, or enjoy the lunches and dinners — three fixed offerings of a salad platter, a cheese platter, and a rib steak, plus two entrées that change daily. Closed Sundays. Reservations for dinner. Major credit cards. 1220 19th St., NW (466-4264). Moderate.

Germaine's – Fast becoming an "in" place in Washington, Germaine's features a varied Oriental menu — including Japanese, Korean, Vietnamese, and Indonesian foods. Specialties are lemon chicken and squirrel fish. Open daily. Reservations suggested. Major credit cards. 2400 Wisconsin Ave., NW (965-1185). Moderate.

Roma – Solid Italian family-style place, best in warm weather when the large outdoor garden is open and strolling musicians and singers add to the relaxed ambience. All the old favorites are there from pasta to pizza. Open daily. Reservations. Major credit cards. 3419 Connecticut Ave., NW (363-6611). Inexpensive.

Astor – Consistently good Greek food at consistently rock-bottom prices. Known more for its food (try the poililia hors d'oeuvre platter, moussaka, pastitso, or styfado — beef stew) than its atmosphere, the restaurant provides bellydancers upstairs amidst electric blue vinyl and marbelized Formica. There's also an inexpensive wine list with Greek and Mediterranean offerings, many of which are available by the glass. Open daily. Reservations. Major credit cards. 1813 M St., NW (331-7994). Inexpensive.

Iron Gate Inn – A former stable now dedicated to Mideastern food: shish kebab, couscous, and stuffed grape leaves. Speaking of which, there's a charming little grape arbor over the outdoor dining area where you can be served in warm weather. Open daily. Reservations. Major credit cards. 1734 N St., NW (737-1370). Inexpensive.

Vietnam Georgetown – Small and intimate, this simple restaurant serves the best Vietnamese food in town with subtle French overtones. Specialties include deep-fried crispy rolls, shrimp with sugar cane, and beef in grape leaves. Open daily. No credit cards. 2934 M St., NW (337-4536). Inexpensive.

La Ruche – Translation: the beehive, and this small French café buzzes most of the time with Georgetown strollers stopping by for snacks — quiches, pâté and French bread, cappuccino and patisserie, or complete meals. Beer and wine available. Open daily. No reservations. Major credit cards. 1039 31st St., NW (965-2684). Inexpensive.

Sholl's – From businessman to bum, Washingtonians stop off at either location for cafeteria food that actually reflects the seasons: fresh vegetables, creamy puddings, and super homemade pies. Prices anyone can afford. Closed Sundays. No reservations. No credit cards. Open for breakfast, lunch, dinner. 1990 K St. NW and 1433 K St. NW (783-4133). Inexpensive.

Chamberlin's – This cafeteria in the heart of the financial district has been in business for a long time for its above-average cafeteria food served in a no-frills atmosphere. Closed weekends. No reservations. No credit cards. 819 15th St., NW (628-7680). Inexpensive.

The Encore – Kennedy Center's handsome quick-service restaurant offers fairly good food at higher-than-cafeteria prices. Avoid going there before curtain time, because the lines are impossibly long. Open daily. No reservations. No credit cards. 2700 K St., NW (833-8870). Inexpensive.

Patent Pending – The best cafeteria near the Mall. Run by a graduate of the Ecole de Cuisine Française in Dijon, with such dishes as Tomatoes Alice B. Toklas (half a scooped-out tomato stuffed with chick peas vinaigrette, the other half with dill egg salad), Courtyard Salad (fresh mushroom slices, tiny cauliflowers, and tomatoes on a bed of salad greens, under a subtle but spicy yogurt-based dressing), and great soups (lentil, zucchini, or corn chowder). You can dine in a courtyard or in one of two vaulted rooms; there's Dijon mustard on each table. Open daily for lunch. No reservations. No credit cards. At 8th and G Sts., NW, in the National Museum of American Art (638-6503). Inexpensive.

Clyde's – This lively place is frequented by Georgetown students and trendy types. Clyde's serves omelets, pasta, and steaks but is known mostly for its terrific hamburgers and its weekend brunch. There's also Guinness stout on tap that's served at just the right temperature. Open daily. No reservations. Major credit cards. 3236 M St., NW (333-0294). Inexpensive.

You can satisfy your sweet tooth by saving dessert for a visit to either *Häagen-Dazs* or *Swensen's* ice cream parlors. Both have two locations: *Häagen-Dazs,* 1524 Connecticut Ave., NW (667-0350), and 1438 Wisconsin Ave., NW (333-7505); *Swensen's,* 1254 Wisconsin Ave., NW (333-3433), and 5310 Wisconsin Ave., NW (966-8606). Inexpensive.

DIVERSIONS

Introduction

During an editorial meeting to find an appropriate name for this section of the guide, one editor jocularly suggested "Best Sweats." As you can see, it isn't the title we ultimately chose, but it isn't far off the mark either. Twenty years ago it would have been mad to suggest to a woman seeking a week's vacation from her job that she look into a camp where guides would teach her how to live on berries in the wild, identify animal tracks in the snow, and survive alone on a mountain. Today it doesn't seem so crazy, especially to thousands of avid backpackers — men and women — who prepare for their avocation by first attending *formal* survival courses.

That is typical of travelers today. The point is not just to go somewhere, but to do something once you are there — get better at a favorite sport or learn a new one, pursue a hobby, investigate an intriguing idea. Whether you are touring America's utopian communities or climbing Mt. McKinley, the idea is the same: combine an interesting place with a fascinating activity.

So what follows are our suggestions for some of the best places in the country to pursue any of 29 different activities — from downhill skiing (for beginners, intermediates, and experts) to touring America's zaniest local festivals. Within each section you will find all the information you need to organize a theme-oriented trip, including some vital tips on making sure things go the way they should (for instance, the several crucial questions to ask a tennis resort to determine if it has the facilities you need).

Several sections have listings of schools and programs where you can learn more about the subject (like survival schools and sailing programs, mountain climbing courses and scuba diving classes). Where warranted, entries also suggest inns and hotels in the area that are especially attractive.

For the Body

Downhill Skiing

You don't have to be particularly athletically inclined to ski (although learning is faster if you are) or even particularly rich. People all over the US are taking to the hills, with some 1,200 ski areas around the country to practice their art. For no other reason than the sheer number of runs, knowing where to go can be a problem. The selection narrows down considerably if you're only going for a day or a weekend. The primary consideration will be to find a nearby resort that meets your budget and doesn't have long lift lines. For a list of those near you, write to the state travel directors or see magazines like *Ski* and *Skiing; Ski*'s monthly "Where to Ski in Your Region" is full of information on lift rates, kids' programs, tips on avoiding lift lines, and more.

If you have a week to spend, however, the problem of choosing an area becomes more difficult. Vermont, New Hampshire, California, Utah, and Colorado each have several resorts with enough diverse terrain and adequate nightlife, restaurants, and other amenities to prove alluring; there are still others in Idaho, Wyoming, Montana, and New Mexico worth traveling a long way to sample. Some even hold their own alongside — or outshine — their Alpine competitors.

You must first decide in what part of the country to ski — East, Midwest, Rockies, or the Far West. California and the Pacific Northwest get the most snow, with hundreds of inches' accumulation every winter, sometimes at the rate of two feet an hour. But because of the high moisture content of the clouds coming from the sea, and partly because the sun is usually shining and warming the fallen snow, it is often heavy and slushy. The East has its own kind of unfavorable conditions, of which the worst is probably long lift lines. The relatively low altitudes at which most Eastern (and Midwestern as well) skiing is done, combined with weather patterns in the East, result in a lot of freezing and thawing between good snowfalls. Other disadvantages in the East are occasional snow droughts and narrow and heavily traveled trails, which mean that a good snow base can get worn down or glazed over with ice.

For the kind of powder snow that makes for the best skiing, there's no place like the Rockies. These mountains are the only great land barrier for storms moving inland from the West Coast. This means that they get huge quantities of snow, and the overall aridity of the area makes the moisture content low, so that the snow is light, and skis cross it with almost no resistance. Because the water density per cubic centimeter is high (particularly in Utah), the snow has enough body to support a skier through deep powder. The northern Rockies get more snow than the southern Rockies; but snow in the south is drier.

Mountains are smallest in the Midwest, where vertical drops (the perpendicular height from the highest lift-served point to the base of the ski area) may amount to only a few hundred feet, but Midwestern resorts are just the place if you are learning.

The mountains are biggest in the West; the vertical drops are larger and the runs somewhat longer. In the West, too, you will find wide-open bowls. Though their slopes are steep at the top, most intermediates can get down them in good shape by taking long traverses. In the East, trails have been cut narrow to keep snow from blowing off and to provide shelter from the wind. As a result, skiing that is already difficult because of the snow conditions can be even more demanding because the skier must always ski the fall line. Not all the fall lines are horrendously steep, of course, but going straight down takes fortitude even on a gentle slope.

Eastern mountains range in size between the hills of the Midwest and the Western giants. As a rule, if you're just learning to ski, you won't need access to difficult terrain that only a big mountain can provide; what matters will be whether the beginners' area has terrain varied enough to keep you interested. You don't want to spend a week on the slope with the a view of the world's biggest parking lot.

Where you go will also depend on what sort of lodgings you like: not all resorts have condominiums or housekeeping units. Not all have ski dorms (inexpensive) or, for that matter, those friendly rustic old inns where everybody eats in the lodge every night. (They're great for making friends, but wouldn't be much fun for people who like eating every meal in different restaurants.) Most resort towns have modern motels and ski lodges with private baths, saunas, swimming pools, and the like. In New England, in addition, you'll find old country inns — long on charm but not much for plumbing and not always as convenient as some people like.

Some resorts are better for families. Most families are made up of skiers of varying abilities, and if all the hard runs are in one place, and all the easy runs are a five-minute drive away, families are going to have a hard time getting together for lunch or at the end of the day, even if there's some sort of shuttle-bus transportation. If you're taking your family, pick a resort that has a centralized lift layout on one mountain. (Check the trail map in the area's brochures.) Check, too, to see whether nurseries and children's ski schools in which you want to park your kids for the afternoon require that you pick them up for lunch; some resorts provide all-day supervision, some don't.

Nearly every ski resort worth the name has a ski school—and some are quite good. In addition, a number of other resorts sponsor Woman's Way Ski Seminars, which deal with ski problems that seem particularly troublesome to women — stiffness, fear, and motivation; for further information, write Box 1182, Tahoe City, CA 95730 (916 583-2904).

The resorts listed below include a few of the major destinations in the country. At all of them, you'll find a wide variety of lifts, with rates from $15 to $20 a day, lodging places in all price ranges, a variety of packages, and seasons that run generally from mid-November into April (or longer in the Sierra). Note that most resorts are extremely crowded at Christmas and during the Easter holidays. Avoid them then if you like peace and quiet. In any case, reserve well in advance.

EAST

SUGARLOAF USA, Kingfield, Maine: With a 2,637-foot vertical drop, plus 44 trails and slopes and above-timberline skiing in the spring, this is the third biggest ski mountain in the East, and one of the toughest; but there's also a lot of beginner and intermediate terrain, 110 acres of it covered by snowmaking. Best skiing is in March and April. There's a definite Down East feel to the place, and you can lodge right on the mountain in condos or comfortable lodges. Information: Sugarloaf USA, Kingfield, ME 04947 (207 237-2000).

THE MOUNT WASHINGTON VALLEY, near North Conway and Jackson, New Hampshire: With four ski mountains (and interchangeable lift tickets), better than half a dozen ski villages (including Jackson, which one ski writer called the most beautiful in all New England), a bounty of country inns, one of the region's best XC trail networks, and striking scenery at the base of the Northeast's tallest mountain, this is quite a ski area. Black Mountain, with snowmaking and 1,100-foot vertical, offers easy, family-type skiing. At Attitash, the narrow, looping trails draw a fashion-oriented family crowd, and limited lift-ticket sales keep down the weekend crowds. Mt. Cranmore, friendly, easy, and wide open, is great for intermediates; its oddball Skimobile is one of the oldest lifts in New England. Wildcat has narrow, hair-raising trails (built to keep Mt. Washington's winds from denuding the slopes) and a 2,100-foot vertical. Since the area is not well known outside Boston, it's not as crowded as some others, and many good packages are available. Information: Mount Washington Valley Chamber of Commerce, PO Box 385, North Conway, NH 03860 (603 356-3171).

WATERVILLE VALLEY, Waterville Valley, New Hampshire: Known for its snowmaking and careful slopes grooming, this resort also boasts varied terrain on a maximum 2,020-foot vertical; a walking-distance "village" full of spiffy condos; daytime shuttle bus service; membership in the Ski the White Mountains Association, which offers a 5-day Wild Card good for riding lifts of other association members; and a friendly ski week program that brings participants back time and again. Adult racing camps and classes in skiing moguls, powder, and freestyle are also available. Information: Waterville Valley Ski Areas, Waterville Valley, NH 03223 (603 236-8311; toll-free 800 552-0388 from New Hampshire, 800 258-8983 from the rest of the East for snow information; 800 552-4767 from New Hampshire or 800 258-8988 from the rest of the East for reservations).

THE GOLDEN TRIANGLE (BROMLEY, MAGIC MOUNTAIN, AND STRATTON), near Stratton, Vermont: A trio of great ski resorts close together in the south-central part of the state. Bromley, with a 1,334-foot vertical drop, has wide trails and long, well-groomed runs; snowmaking that covers well over three-fourths of the terrain; and one of the best ski schools in the East. The lift setup is such that it's easy to ski off nearly all the chairlifts covering different sections of the mountain from the base. Aptly named Magic Mountain, which has a 1,600-foot vertical, is especially relaxed and friendly. Four lodges, in Swiss style, snuggle right at the base. The lower half of the mountain is for novice or intermediate; the top will challenge the very best skier. Stratton, one of the East's notable destination resorts, has a smooth classic cone of a mountain divided into two separate areas, each with steep sections that are wide, interestingly contoured, so unfailingly well groomed that nobody really has to suffer to get down. There's a 2,000-foot vertical. The crowd tends to be well heeled, mostly families. There are three lodges within walking distance of the base; and lift sales, rentals, the ski shop, ski school meeting place, and children's ski school meeting place and day-care facilities are all easy to get to. It also offers several special body-awareness ski seminars, and a special carousel that tows beginners around in circles until they get the feel of their skis. Shuttle buses link Bromley and Stratton; both can be skied on the same lift ticket. Information: Magic Mountain, Londonderry, VT 05148 (802 824-5566); Stratton and Bromley Vacations, Stratton Mt., VT 05155 (802 824-6915).

KILLINGTON, Killington, Vermont: The home of the longest ski lift in North America, a trail-veined basin big enough to get lost in, has been called a "department store of skiing" for the huge variety of terrain it offers. There are wide long runs, steep and narrow ones (74 trails in all), five interconnected peaks, six lodge facilities, one of the best novice slopes in the East, Vermont's longest vertical drop (3,060 feet), and acres and acres of gladed skiing, which you don't usually find outside the West and Europe. The new Bear Mountain area, where the US Alpine Ski Team trained for the Olympics, offers some of New England's steepest skiing terrain. It also has fantastic snow conditions (which mean skiing from October to May), and the standout snowmaking is expanded every year. It also has some of the East's best learn-to-ski weeks. Information: Killington Ski Resort, Killington, VT 05751 (802 422-3333, 802 422-3711 for reservations).

MOUNT SNOW, near West Dover, Vermont: Walter Schoenecht, the eccentric who founded Mount Snow, left as his legacy a batch of interesting trails and a reputation as a skier's Disneyland that the present owner, the Sherburne Corp., has been hard put to live down, even as the funds that once went into frills were diverted to essentials such as snowmaking and lifts. Nearly half of the 1,700-vertical-foot mountain is now covered by snowmaking (a sixfold increase in the last five years), and the lifts layout is operating more smoothly than ever thanks to a double handful of carefully thought out improvements to serve the 51 trails. Proximity to the East's major metropolitan areas and an abundance of restaurants and nightspots all up and down the valley make Mount Snow one of Vermont's most popular — and busiest — resorts. Information: Mount Snow Ski Resort, Mount Snow, VT 05356 (802 464-8501).

THE MAD RIVER VALLEY (SUGARBUSH, MAD RIVER GLEN, SUGARBUSH NORTH), near Warren and Waitsfield, Vermont: Sugarbush, the most famous in this trio of top-notch resorts in north Central Vermont, is no longer the jet-set favorite it once was, but it still has a certain classy style that makes it less frenetic than, say, Stowe. The runs are as long, steep, narrow, and twisting, and the 2,400-foot vertical as impressive as anything you'll find further north. Eighty percent of the skiing is rated intermediate or advanced; for solid skiers, there are "centered skiing workshops," a sophisticated attempt to combine philosophy and Oriental martial arts with some tough drilling in order to help good skiers improve their skills. With a 1,985-foot vertical, Mad River is, according to some, the toughest mountain in the state. There are lots of moguls and expert trails. But the centralized layout and its uncommercialized family orientation make this a good place to take novice youngsters as well. Sugarbush North (known as Glen Ellen before its 1978 takeover by Sugarbush Management) has the longest vertical of the three (2,645 feet), but is also the easiest. Accommodations in the valley — guest houses and inns, condominiums, motels, hotels, and the posh Sugarbush Inn (802 583-2301) — overlap; each resort has a housing office that can place you. Information: Sugarbush Valley, Warren, VT 05674 (802 583-2381; 800 451-5030 for reservations), and Mad River Glen, Waitsfield, VT 05673 (802 496-3551).

STOWE, Stowe, Vermont: When one ski journalist poked fun at Stowe's lift lines and its variable snow conditions, letters of indignation poured in. This is the East's premier ski resort, and its regulars don't take that position lightly. Nowadays, they have even more to puff up about. A massive snowmaking installation covering half the resort's terrain and a new high-speed, high-capacity double chair lift on Mt. Mansfield have resolved situations that most skiers were willing to tolerate only because the skiing on the 2,150-foot vertical was so good. Meanwhile, a well-coordinated children's ski school–day care set-up has added terrific appeal for young families; and the tough runs that gave Stowe its reputation as an area for experts have yielded the limelight to the 70% of the slopes and trails rated for novices and intermediates. The restaurants, nightlife, and accommodations are as varied and as lively as ever. Information: Stowe Area Association, PO Box 1230, Stowe, VT 05672 (802 253-7321).

WEST

SKI LAKE TAHOE (THE HIGH SIERRA COMPLEX), near Lake Tahoe, California: On the shores of this incredibly deep-blue body of water, Heavenly Valley, Northstar, Alpine Meadows, Squaw Valley (for more about which, see below), and Kirkwood have banded together to offer the greatest concentration of skiing available in America. Alone, each resort offers magnificent terrain; the assemblage is simply mind-boggling. Heavenly Valley, straddling the California-Nevada state line, calls itself America's largest ski resort. The intermediates' haven is on the Nevada side, the beginner/intermediate terrain mainly in California. This is also the resort which is the closest to major-league gambling and low-cost, high-quality lodging in South Lake Tahoe. Alpine Meadows is somewhat smaller, with a smooth lift layout, a respectable 1,800-foot vertical, and 30 acres covered by snowmaking. The upper mountain is full of steep bowls and narrow chutes, but there's usually enough space for traversing; the lower slopes are wide, gentle, beautifully groomed. Kirkwood, whose 2,000-foot vertical has been developed relatively recently, focuses on skiing almost to the exclusion of other activities and après-skiing, so it's a good bet for single-minded types. Olympic and Sentinel Bowls and the snow-filled saddles of the ridges have established Kirkwood's reputation as a place for experts. Northstar, with a 2,300-foot vertical, is more like a private club attached to condominiums; there's a limited-ticket sales policy during crowded times of year. Information: Ski Lake Tahoe, PO Box Z, Incline Village, NV 89450 (702 831-4223).

SQUAW VALLEY, Olympic Valley, California: Five thousand acres of bumps, chutes, gulleys, headwalls, saddles, bowls, and meadows graded for experts, intermediates, and novices. The 1960 Olympic site, and its bustling Olympic Village, are still lively — and lots of fun once you find your way around. Information: PO Box 2007, Olympic Valley, CA 95730 (916 583-6985).

MAMMOTH MOUNTAIN, Mammoth Lakes, California: Mammoth it is. This 11,053-foot blown-out volcano is skiable from late October until early July; the bottom sections are excellent for beginners. Elsewhere, there are rugged runs designed to chill experts. Information: Mammoth Lakes, CA 93546 (714 934-2571).

ASPEN, Aspen, Colorado: The biggest action town in ski-dom, an old mining center, and the granddaddy of American ski resorts, Aspen has a little something for everyone. Aspen Mountain, with its 3,282-foot vertical, is known for its powder, its narrow trails, and celebrated toughies like Ruthie's Run. Aspen Highlands, with its 3,800-foot vertical, has runs of up to 3½ miles. Buttermilk, with its 1,972-foot vertical, is a beginners' and low intermediates' paradise not only for the quality of the snow but also for the width and gentleness of its trails. And there's nightlife and good eating in a quantity and variety that you'll find at few other ski resorts in the world. Information: Aspen Mountain and Buttermilk, PO Box 1248, Aspen, CO 81611 (303 925-1220); Aspen Highlands, PO Box T, Aspen, CO 81612 (303 925-5300).

SNOWMASS RESORT, Snowmass Village, Colorado: Whereas Aspen is best known for its appeal to singles, nearby Snowmass is a family-oriented place that has won a reputation for itself as a Cadillac among family ski areas. One of the largest intermediate mountains in the country, with more than 1,400 acres of skiing, it has over 90 runs ranging down its 3,600-foot vertical. Most accommodations are right on the slope. Information: Snowmass Resort, Box 5566, Snowmass Village, CO 81615 (303 923-2000).

STEAMBOAT, Steamboat Village, Colorado: A relaxed family area on the outskirts of an archetypal Old West town named for its whistling hot springs. The runs (73 of them) are roomy and varied; there are trails, bowls, and powder fields for skiers of all skills; good children's programs; and a 3,600-foot vertical. Steamboat's celebrated, ultra-light "champagne powder" is best experienced in January and February; March and April are good for sunny, warm spring skiing. Information: Steamboat, PO Box 773377, Steamboat Springs, CO 80477 (303 879-0740).

SUMMIT COUNTY (KEYSTONE, COPPER MOUNTAIN, BRECKENRIDGE, AND ARAPAHOE BASIN), Summit County, Colorado: Seventy miles west of Denver via I-70. Breckenridge, among Colorado's first great skiing discoveries, does a brisk business in the family trade. Copper Mountain, which soars above a compact condominium-village complex, is home to a lively Club Med. Three base lift stations lead respectively to beginner, beginner/lower-intermediate, and advanced-intermediate/expert terrain. Keystone has been immaculately designed to take advantage of the natural contours of its mountain; even the easy slopes like the 2,000-foot vertical Schoolmarm are interesting, and the difficult slopes, while hard, are not impossible. The snowmaking system, which covers more than three-fourths of the resort's 460 acres, is the Rockies' most extensive. Arapahoe Basin, the longtime favorite of Denver day-trippers that was recently purchased by Keystone's parent corporation, has added additional expert and late-season (into June) skiing to Summit County's offerings. Its vertical is 1,640 feet. Those at Keystone and Copper are 2,400 feet; 2,390 feet at Breckenridge. Special Ski the Summit lift passes give you access to all four areas. Though shuttle buses are available, a car is helpful. Information: Keystone, PO Box 38, Keystone, CO 80435 (303 468-2316); Copper Mountain, PO Box 3001, Copper Mountain, CO 80443 (303 668-2882); and Breckenridge, PO Box 1058, Breckenridge, CO 80424 (303 453-2368).

VAIL, Vail, Colorado: One of the most magnificent ski complexes in the US, this pioneer of modern American skiing takes up 10 square miles of a mountain up and down a 3,000-foot vertical. There's so much skiing that even experts can spend a week at Vail and never repeat a run. Lodging ranges from small, simple motels to spiffy condo complexes. Information: Vail Resort Association, PO Box 1368, Vail, CO 81657 (303 476-5677).

SUN VALLEY, Sun Valley, Idaho: The ne plus ultra of destination ski resorts, this grande dame offers something for everyone on its 3,400 vertical feet — steilhangs forthe brave and ballroom slopes for the tyro. Baldy, famous for steep-bowl skiing, now boasts an equal variety of intermediate terrain, more like that of Dollar (Sun Valley's other mountain — accessible from Baldy by shuttle bus). Lodging is in Sun Valley proper; at the base of Dollar in a development called Elkhorn; and at Baldy's base in the old mining town of Ketchum. Information: Sun Valley, Sun Valley, ID 83353 (208 622-4111 or toll-free 800 635-8261).

THE BIG MOUNTAIN, Whitefish, Montana: It's often been said that the farther you have to go to get to a resort, the friendlier it's bound to be. And though remarkably *accessible* thanks to decent transportation, the Big Mountain is a good example. Singles can have a great time because of the coziness of the lodges (within walking distance of lifts) and a schedule of parties, and families enjoy it because of the centralized, manageable layout of its 25 miles of runs. Because the mountain is in the northern Rockies, it gets enough snow that you can ski from Thanksgiving until mid-April. Whitefish, 28 miles from the west entrance to Glacier National Park, is an old cowtown turned resort; après-ski can be lively. Information: The Big Mountain, Box 1215, Whitefish, MT 59937 (406 862-3511).

TAOS SKI VALLEY, Taos, New Mexico: The deep powder for which Taos has always been famous is still here, and the lift lines are still notably absent (usually); but the relentlessly steep runs down parts of this 2,613-vertical-footed mountain are no longer the sadistically narrow demons of yore. This, thanks to a recent trail-revamping project that also included smoothing the slopes to take snow cover earlier and keep it longer. Après-ski centers on several cozy American-plan lodges at the mountain's base. The ski school — also famous — is as good as ever; virtually everyone participates. Details: Taos Ski Valley, Taos, NM 87571 (505 776-2291).

ALTA, Alta, Utah: Two things are generally known about this rustic 42-year-old hideaway in Little Cottonwood Canyon, not far from Snowbird and Salt Lake City. First, this is the mother nest for powder skiers; second, the famous Alf's High Rustler run, a ¾-mile chute with a 40° slope, no trees, and frequent avalanches, is possibly the scariest trail in the West. However, not all the runs are steep, and the novice and intermediate bowls offer wonderful views of jagged peaks and forests. Alta is also one of the cozier of American ski resorts, since all après-ski life revolves around the several lodges at base. Lift rates are among the lowest you'll find at any major ski resort. Information: Alta Ski Area, Alta, UT 84092 (801 742-3333; 801 742-2040 for lodging information).

PARK CITY, Park City, Utah: With its many varied trails, night skiing, and snow-making, Park City has always been terrific for intermediates; some of the steep snow-fields will challenge experts as well. The maximum vertical is now 3,100 feet. The town is an erstwhile mining settlement full of shops, health food emporiums, saloons, fancy steak joints — and lots of atmosphere to spare. Information: Park City Ski Area, PO Box 39, Park City, UT 84060 (801 649-8111).

SNOWBIRD, Snowbird, Utah: Like Alta, well known for powder skiing. Where Alta is old-fashioned and home-grown, Snowbird, just a mile to the west, is elegant and ritzy; the fact that it's a multimillion-dollar project shows in the slick condominium towers of unadorned concrete and in the aura of luxury that surrounds the whole scene. As for the skiing, there are superb runs for experts on Snowbird's 3,100 vertical feet, and a respectable quota of runs for novices and intermediates as well. Among the resort's special ski programs are the Mountain Experience (five hours of steep going in the backcountry for experts), free guided skiing tours, and helicopter skiing in the backcountry with the Wasatch Powderbird Guides. For more information, contact Snowbird Ski and Summer Resort, Snowbird, UT 84092 (801 742-2222).

JACKSON HOLE SKI AREA, Teton Village, Wyoming: That the resort has America's biggest vertical drop (4,139 feet) and its longest runs does not explain why it also ranks among the country's least crowded. That is because the first lifts here went up on redoubtable Rendezvous Mountain, and its first reputation was as not only the biggest but also the toughest. Energetic development of the 2,200 vertical feet of Apres Vous, the resort's other, far more forgiving giant, is only beginning to dispel the scare stories. High time: half of Jackson Hole's skiable acreage is rated for experts, its nonexpert terrain is bigger than the entirety of 90% of other US ski resorts. That, plus a compact lift-base arrangement of resorts (so that cars are optional) makes Jackson Hole a good vacation bet for *any* skier. Information: Teton Village Resort Association, Teton Village, WY 83025 (307 733-4005 or toll-free 800 443-6931).

Cross-Country Skiing

You can go striding and gliding across almost any golf course or field when there's even a little snow on the ground. Or you can spend an afternoon tooling down a frozen river or canal, around the edge of a cemetery, or through a city park. You can cross-country in most forests, national and state parks, and even in wildlife management areas (though it's smart not to go off bushwhacking until you're wise in the ways of the wilderness). All you need is a pair of cross-country skis. You don't need elaborate lift facilities. In fact, you don't even need much snow. As long as there is enough to cover the grass, the pavement, or the underbrush, those long, skinny skis will glide along.

Cross-country skiing centers are springing up around the country. They not only offer lessons and provide rentals of cross-country skis (about $7 to $11 a day), but advise on the relative merits of wax vs. nonwax skis (and the kind of wax to use), suggest trails that are marked and tracked by machines to make the going easier, and provide trail maps. In very wild areas, some will also provide guides.

For a complete list of these places, consult the newly enlarged *Ski Touring Guide,* published by the Ski Touring Council, 32 Harmony Rd., Spring Valley, ND 10977 ($5.50), or *Cross Country Ski Magazine,* published three times annually by Times Mirror Magazines, 380 Madison Ave., New York, NY 10017 (212 687-3000; $2.50).

EAST

ACADIA NATIONAL PARK, Bar Harbor, Maine: The 40 miles of carriage roads on Mt. Desert Island, which are not plowed in winter, take you up and down the rugged mountains of the interior and along the coast, and when conditions are right, this is a winter wonderland par excellence. However, because the ocean moderates the temperatures, you can't count on snow; call before traveling. Information: Acadia National Park, rt. 1, PO Box 1, Bar Harbor, ME 04609 (207 288-3338).

SUGARLOAF AREA, Kingfield, Maine: Two miles from Sugarloaf USA, Maine's largest downhill skiing area, the Carrabassett Valley Touring Center has some 60 miles of trails along old logging roads, through forests and over a frozen beaver bog, down an old narrow-gauge railroad track, along a river to a pond, and around some condominiums. Lodgings are in cabins, condominiums, and motels nearby. Information: Carrabassett Valley Touring Center, Carrabassett Valley, ME 04947 (207 237-2205).

THE BERKSHIRES, around Lenox, Massachusetts: Miles and miles of trails through the forests here, some in state parks, some at resorts, and some maintained by special touring centers. Country inns are like hotels with personality or else intimate resorts or house parties at somebody's exceptionally wonderful country home. You'll find a number of major touring centers with ski rental shops, warming huts, and lively programs of special activities — some of them adjoining state forest lands that also have trails. For general information on the area, contact the Berkshire Hills Conference, 20 Elm St., Pittsfield, MA 01201 (413 443-9186).

MOUNT WASHINGTON VALLEY, around North Conway, New Hampshire: Inns, sporting goods stores, the Appalachian Mountain Club (AMC), and the Jackson Ski Touring Foundation maintain over 150 miles of trails at the base of some of the highest peaks in the East. Some curl through the valley, weaving between country inns and art galleries, shops, and quaint restaurants; some plunge into the forests. The most distinctive lodging is at the AMC's Pinkham Notch Camp, off by itself at the northern end of the valley, beloved of rugged outdoor types (although with thick wool blankets and freshly ironed sheets on the narrow bunk beds and shiny tile in the bathroom down the hall, it's not all that spartan). The AMC also maintains two backcountry huts; reservations are required. Information: Appalachian Mountain Club, Gorham, NH 03581 (603 466-2727); Mount Washington Valley Chamber of Commerce, PO Box 385, North Conway, NH 03860 (603 356-3171).

THE ADIRONDACKS, around Lake Placid, New York: This 5½-million-acre wilderness offers some of the most varied touring in the Eastern United States; the area around the site of the 1980 Olympics at Lake Placid is one of its centers. The Bark Eater Lodge (Box 139, Keene, NY 12942; 518 576-2221), offers a variety of guided tours into the wilds and on its own trail system, which is linked to that of the 12-mile-distant Adirondak Loj, a rustic 1880 log structure named by the inventor of phonetic spelling and favored by gung-ho cross-country types (PO Box 867, Lake Placid, NY 12946, 518 523-3441). Both systems connect with the 12 miles of trails at the Mt. Van Hoevenberg Recreation Area, where each trail has been very carefully designed to help skiers of varying ability levels perfect their skills. Various sections of the Northville–Lake Placid Trail, a famous wilderness hiking trail through the valleys between the two towns, are also suitable for cross-country skiing. For a free booklet describing them as well as others in the Adirondacks, write the New York Department of Environmental Conservation, 50 Wolf Rd., Albany, NY 12233 (518 457-7433). Also contact the Lake Placid Chamber of Commerce, Olympic Arena, Lake Placid, NY 12946 (518 523-2445).

NORTHEAST KINGDOM, Vermont: This still quiet, unspoiled section of the Green Mountain State is one of the US's up-and-coming ski-touring areas. You can ski-tour through woods and fields, across lakes, on old logging roads or unplowed secondary roads, or along hiking trails or hunting trails as well as on a number of trails that are prepared and maintained as part of the ski-touring at Burke Mountain Recreation, a downhill ski resort with a 32-mile cross-country trail network (East Burke, VT 05832; 802 626-3305). The Inn on the Common, a fancy, antiquey establishment on the green in one of those picture-postcard towns presided over by a white steepled clapboard church (Craftsbury Common, VT 05827; 802 586-9619), uses the extensive facilities at the 2½-mile-distant Craftsbury Ski Center and at the wonderfully homey Highland Lodge (Greensboro, VT 05841; 802 533-2647).

BLUEBERRY HILL INN, Goshen, Vermont: In the central part of the state, this small inn — a countrified sort of place except for the English silver and china in the antique corner cabinets — has always catered exclusively to cross-country skiers. There are nearly 50 miles of trails — some in loops, some running through the woods to nearby inns — and many special programs. Information: Blueberry Hill, Goshen, VT 05733 (802 247-6535).

STOWE, Vermont: The more-Austrian-than-in-Austria chalet that was always such an attraction of the Trapp Family Lodge (owned by the *Sound of Music* Trapp family) burned in 1980. But the Trapps were never ones to take setbacks lying down, and the cross-country ski center reopened within a week of the fire — much to the satisfaction of Stowe XC-ers: The center was the oldest in the US and one of the finest. (A new lodge opened in the summer of 1982.) Linking up with its especially well-groomed trails are the paths at oh-so-English Edson Hill Manor (Stowe 05672; 802 253-7371); the nearly 100 miles at the Mt. Mansfield Touring Center; and another 20 miles of trails at Topnotch-at-Stowe, a very fancy well-done contemporary resort (Stowe 05672; 802 253-8585). Various other trails connect the Stowe networks to those at Bolton Valley and Smugglers' Notch Ski Areas. Information: Stowe Area Association, PO Box 1230, Stowe, VT 05672 (802 253-7321.)

INN-TO-INN XC, Vermont: Through the woods, fields, and high country; the innkeepers take care of your luggage. Information: Hike-Skitour Vermont, RFD 1, Chester, VT 05143 (802 875-3631); Highland Lodge, Greensboro, VT 05841 (802 533-2647); Churchill House Inn, RD 3, Brandon, VT 05733 (802 247-3300).

MIDWEST

SUPERIOR NATIONAL FOREST, north of Duluth, Minnesota: Minnesota's most concentrated touring opportunities are on the eastern edge of this vast forestland on the Canadian border. There are hundreds of miles of trails in the forest, some under the care of the Forest Service, others maintained by the rustic lodges and inns of the region. For a list of them, and for more information, contact the Superior National Forest, PO Box 338, Duluth, MN 55801 (218 727-6692), and the Minnesota Arrowhead Association, PO Box 204, Duluth, MN 55801 (218 722-0874).

CHEQUAMEGON NATIONAL FOREST, Park Falls, Wisconsin: This northern woodland has about 50 miles of mapped-and-marked loop trails ranging in length from about one mile to about 10, designed primarily for cross-country skiers. But you can also take out over hundreds of miles of snowmobile trails (remarkably peaceful midweek), or along the 60-mile-long section of the North Country Scenic Trail that runs through the forest. It's a straight-line affair, but you can camp en route at Adirondack-style shelters spaced at 8- to 10-mile intervals along the way; the scenery certainly warrants your efforts. Details: Chequamegon National Forest, 157 N 5th Ave., Park Falls, WI 54552 (715 762-2461).

WEST

LASSEN VOLCANIC NATIONAL PARK, Mineral, California: There are only about three miles of marked cross-country trails around the park's small downhill ski area, and just six miles more in the Manzanitas Lake area. But because you can also ski on just about any of the 150 miles of hiking trails (with topography map and compass or guide) or glide along the park roads, which aren't plowed, this is a great place to cross-country ski. The trip through the deep pine woods to the Bumpass Hill thermal area — where mud pots, hot springs, and morning-glory pools roar, bubble, and throw great clouds of warm steam into the cold air — is especially memorable. Notable lodgings: Childs Meadows Resort, Mill Creek, CA 96061 (916 595-4411). More information: California Gift Services, Inc., PO Box 75, Mineral, CA 96063 (916 595-3376).

SEQUOIA AND KINGS CANYON NATIONAL PARKS, near Three Rivers, California: The Sequoia Ski Touring's extensive trail network takes you through groves of the magnificent giant sequoia trees, across white-carpeted meadows, and to cliff-top overlooks that give you wonderful vistas over the Sierra high country. A variety of guided tours is available out of two centers. Lodge at the rustic Giant Forest Lodge (209 565-3381). Information: Sequoia Ski Touring, Sequoia & Kings Canyon Hospitality Service, Sequoia National Park, CA 93262 (209 565-3373).

YOSEMITE NATIONAL PARK, Yosemite, California: The sequoias drown in the snow, the waterfalls freeze into fantastic sculptures, and everything sparkles. Yosemite Mountaineering takes groups on easy overnight trips through just such wonderlands. Special clinics teach you touring, winter camping, touring survival, cross-country racing techniques, ice climbing — and how to handle that XC anathema, a real downhill run. The first weekend in March, the whole place is jammed for the Nordic Holidays — two days of anyone-can-do-it "citizens' races." Lodgings: anything from the primitive cabins at Curry Village to the posh high-ceilinged Ahwahnee. Information: Yosemite Park and Curry Co., Yosemite National Park, CA 95389 (209 373-4171).

STEAMBOAT SPRINGS, Colorado: Some of the best tours in the state can be found around the Scandinavian Lodge outside town; Sven Wiik, the former US Olympic Nordic Team coach who set up the resort and made it one of the first to emphasize cross-country, knew what he was doing when he planned the trips. Especially on Rabbit Ears Pass, you've got the advantages of being up at 10,000 feet — the great views and November-to-May powder — and none of the steep pitches or, for that matter, avalanche danger. The lodge — where you'll eat split pea soup, four kinds of herring, and other Scandinavian favorites, and après-ski in big public rooms decorated with the weavings and the potting of Mrs. Sven Wiik — manages to stay low-key despite the fact that there's a downhill resort practically within schussing distance. Information: Scandinavian Lodge, PO Box 5040, Steamboat Springs, CO 80499 (303 879-0517).

VAIL, Colorado: The Vail/Karhn Ski Touring School, directed by Jean Naumann, is the center of most ski touring in the area. There are easy marked and packed trails on the gentle terrain of a golf course east of town. Guides are available to take beginners through the aspen forests in the valley not far away, and to lead better skiers into the steep country up the valley — the high country around Vail Pass, the rugged and spectacular Gore Range, and the Eagles Nest Wilderness Area. Information: Vail Ski Touring School, 458 Vail Valley Dr., Vail, CO 81657 (303 476-5601, ext. 4380), and the Vail Resort Association, 241 E Meadow Dr., Vail, CO 81657 (303 476-1000).

SUN VALLEY, Idaho: This is one place you don't have to climb to get to the high country: Helicopters take you up to the Douglas fir–covered mountains for trips to Boulder Basin, Corral Creek, and the Pioneer Cabin near Hyndman Peak, where you can picnic in the sun. In addition there are some hundred miles of marked trails which you can do on your own or with guides. Plenty of cozy lodges in the area. More information: Nordic Ski Touring Center, Box 272, Sun Valley, ID 83353 (208 622-4111).

GRAND TETON NATIONAL PARK, near Jackson, Wyoming: Miles and miles of touring in the park along the roads and on the trails — around the edge of Jenny Lake with splendid views of the jagged-tooth mountains, up gentle hills and steeply switch-backed slopes, across frozen flatlands and high-country tundra. From Flagg Ranch, midway between Yellowstone and Grand Teton National Parks along the John D. Rockefeller Jr. Parkway, you can follow a trail back to Huckleberry Hot Springs Campground and, somewhat farther along, a hot springs next to the river where you can strip and soak — and it's not nearly as chilly getting out as you'd expect. Lodgings: motels in Jackson; lodges and condominiums in Teton Village at the base of the big downhill mountain about seven miles from town; dude ranches cum ski touring centers scattered around the valley (including Game Hill Ranch, Bondurant, WY 82922; 307 733-4120); and — really nifty and away from it all — the Togwotee Mountain

Lodge, on a pass about 50 miles from Jackson in the middle of some of the snowiest forests and meadows you'll see anywhere (Box 91, Moran, WY 83013; 307 543-2847). Overnight ski tours are also available. More information: Jackson Hole Chamber of Commerce, Box E, Jackson, WY 83001 (307 733-3316); Grand Teton National Park, PO Box 170, Moose, WY 83012 (307 733-2880).

YELLOWSTONE NATIONAL PARK, Yellowstone, Wyoming: There's an otherworldly look to the place in winter — partly because of the clouds of steam rising from the flats almost everywhere, partly because of the overwhelming emptiness of it all: Geysers roar, fumaroles rumble, and blue pools mild as morning glories explode into showers of scalding water, without a soul to witness the spectacle. There are bison, Canada geese, and elk in such profusion that you stop noticing them after a while. You can make cross-country tours out of the Snow Lodge right next to Old Faithful, or go from West Yellowstone, Montana. In either case, the TWA Services, Yellowstone National Park, WY 82190 (307 344-7311) can provide details. Yellowstone Nordic offers a variety of cross-country adventures (PO Box 488, West Yellowstone, MT 59758, 406 646-7319).

The Best Tennis Vacations

Got some vacation time coming and want to work on your game? You can visit a camp or clinic, or just hole up at a resort with good tennis facilities and play away.

Camps — intensive five-to-eight-hour-a-day programs springing up all over the place nowadays — are usually held at colleges, private schools, or camps that cater to children in other seasons. The accommodations usually aren't much, but there's always plenty of tennis. Clinics, on the other hand, are usually held at hotels or resorts; they're special weekend or week-long programs with instruction provided by the establishment's own pros or by visiting experts. Camps usually cost $50 or $70 a day, clinics about twice that, for room, board, and instruction. Some organizations sponsor several camps and clinics in many different areas around the country.

Whether you tennis-it at a camp or a clinic, you're guaranteed a certain number of hours of court time every day. At the beginning of the program, you're graded, grouped with others of similar ability, and then worked — hard — by instructors who drive you like boot camp drill sergeants. Usually you tackle one stroke at a time. First there will be a demonstration, then simple hitting drills, then more complicated hitting drills in which the stroke is made part of a more complex sequence of moves. You'll end each day with varying degrees of sunburn, blisters, and sore muscles. (One New York jogger arrived at his camp feeling smug and fit; he ended his first day so bushed he could hardly focus on his *Times.*) How successful the course is will depend on where you start. Intermediates who want to add some muscle and bite to their game probably will. But beginners won't leave as Pancho Segura.

Resorts are probably the most relaxing places to spend a tennis vacation. Sign up for a couple of lessons, play tennis when you want, and use the resort's saunas, shops, whirlpool baths, swimming pools, golf courses, and activity programs the rest of the time. In other than clinic situations it's often true that larger resorts catering to groups attract so many beginners that advanced players may be bored; that older, more established resorts attract more advanced players and may not be much fun for beginners; and that a high courts-to-rooms ratio and the presence of a tennis host who arranges games usually means that the tennis program is well enough organized that you won't spend all your time waiting around for a court.

Find out where the resort you're considering fits into this scheme. Also look into the court situation. How many are there, and what kind? How many are lighted? (In some areas, it's just too hot to play during the day.) Can you reserve courts? How far in advance? Can you do it on the phone or must you present yourself in person? Is there any limit to how long you can play? And if you're not taking your own partner, is it easy to scare up a game?

For a complete and up-to-date list of clinics and camps, check the annual January issue of *Tennis* ($1.50 from *Tennis* magazine, 495 Westport Ave., PO Box 5350, Norwalk, CT 06856, 203 847-5811). For tennis resorts, see *Tennis* magazine's November 1981 listing of the US's 50 greatest or its annual February treatment of places to play.

If you travel frequently and like to play when you're away from home, look into *Travelers Tennis and Racketball* (Penthouse Level, New Market Mall, Painesville, OH 44077, 216 352-0791). A $45 fee buys you temporary membership in over 200 private and public tennis clubs and organizations and discounts at many tennis resorts, plus a directory and periodic newsletters and updates.

The number of places to spend tennis vacations is increasing every year. What follows is a list of some good bets.

TENNIS CLINICS

These organizations sponsor clinics at a number of resorts, schools, and college campuses. Each outfit has its own teaching style and methods.

JOHN NEWCOMBE TENNIS CENTERS: Clarence Mabry, former Trinity University tennis coach, is heavily involved in the programs, which are held in Fairfield Bay, Arkansas; New Braunfels, Texas; Fairfield Glade, Tennessee; Sapphire, North Carolina; and Stratton Mountain, Vermont. There's plenty of videotaping. Newcombe himself is only occasionally on hand. Information: PO Box 469, New Braunfels, TX 78130 (512 625-8008).

RAMEY TENNIS SCHOOLS: Headquartered in Owensboro, Kentucky, this organization puts on clinics at college campuses in Galesburg, Illinois; Greencastle and Hanover, Indiana; Faribault, Minnesota; and Springfield, Ohio. Adult weekend programs are held at an indoor club, with deluxe hotel housing, in Owensboro. Information: rt. 6, Owensboro, KY 42301 (502 771-5590).

VAN DER MEER TENNIS UNIVERSITY: Billie Jean King's onetime coach Dennis Van der Meer, one of the most knowledgeable and influential of the nation's teaching pros, personally supervises all clinics held by his organization at Hilton Head, South Carolina, and Sweet Briar, Virginia. Information: Van Der Meer Tennis University, PO Box 4739, Hilton Head, SC 29938 (803 785-9602, or, from outside SC, 800 845-6138).

ALL-AMERICAN SPORTS: Varied camps and clinics emphasize intensive drill sessions rather than mechanical teaching aids, with instruction by noncelebrity pros, in Amelia Island, Florida; Amherst and Mt. Holyoke, Massachusetts; Stowe, Vermont; Southampton, New York; plus Eleuthera, Bahamas; Humacao, Puerto Rico; and Montego Bay, Jamaica. Information: 366 Madison Ave., New York, NY 10017 (212 697-9220 or, toll-free from outside NY, 800 223-2442).

JOHN GARDINER'S TENNIS: The celebrated ranches in Scottsdale, Arizona, and Carmel Valley, California, have spawned a whole new group of tennis clinic programs at resorts in Keystone, Colorado; West Palm Beach, Florida; Sun Valley, Idaho; and Warren, Vermont. The method has you hitting lots of balls under the supervision of well-trained and well-disciplined instructors who hammer the basics into you as you hammer balls. Information: John Gardiner's Tennis, 5700 E McDonald Dr., Scottsdale, AZ 85253 (602 948-2100).

TENNIS RESORTS

EAST

MOUNT WASHINGTON HOTEL, Bretton Woods, New Hampshire: This immense old white Victorian structure gives you spectacular views into the Presidential Range of the White Mountains; miniclinics as well as private and group lessons (some using video) are available. Facilities include 12 clay courts; court reservations are possible. Details: Tennis, Mount Washington Hotel, Bretton Woods, NH 03575 (603 278-1000).

WATERVILLE VALLEY RESORT, Waterville Valley, New Hampshire: A condominium-and-lodge development snuggled into the central New Hampshire forests, popular with families. Facilities: clinics and private instruction; 18 clay courts; court reservations possible. Information: Waterville Valley, NH 03223 (603 236-8311).

THE CONCORD, Kiamesha Lake, New York: With 1,200 rooms scattered through several high-rise hotel structures on 4,000 acres in the Catskills, this place is like a city — but you *can* play all winter long. Facilities: 40 Latexite and Pecton courts, 16 of them indoor and open 24 hours a day; ball machines and video replay and other teaching aids; courts available by reservation only; private and group lessons. Information: The Concord, Kiamesha Lake, NY 12751 (914 794-4000).

TOPNOTCH-AT-STOWE, Stowe, Vermont: An elegant, modern resort. Facilities: All-American Sports clinics; four courts indoors, and ten out (one of them clay); reservations possible. Information: Topnotch, Stowe, VT 05672 (802 253-8585).

STRATTON MOUNTAIN INN, Stratton, Vermont: A 100-room modern ski and summer resort in southern Vermont. Facilities: 16 courts — 4 Plexi-Cushion indoors and 12 outdoors (8 Har-Tru, 2 red clay, and 2 hard-surface); clinics by John Newcombe; reservations possible, but daily limits imposed. Information: Stratton Mountain, VT 05155 (802 297-2500).

SUGARBUSH INN, Warren, Vermont: A jet-set resort in the Green Mountains which manages to be gracious, elegant, and informal all at once. Wonderful food. Facilities: 11 courts — 5 clay, 6 Har-Tru; video replay and ball machines; reservations possible; clinics by John Gardiner. Information: Sugarbush Inn, Warren, VT 05674 (802 583-2301).

THE GREENBRIER, White Sulphur Springs, West Virginia: One of the few turn-of-the-century resorts which hasn't lost even a little of its class. Facilities: 20 courts — 15 Har-Tru outdoors, 5 air-conditioned Dynaturf courts indoors; private lessons and clinics. See also *Resort Hotels.* Information: The Greenbrier, White Sulphur Springs, WV 24896 (304 536-1110).

SOUTH

AMELIA ISLAND PLANTATION, Amelia Island, Florida: This 900-acre condominiums-and-homes development offers terrific beaches, wonderful subtropical forest scenery, plenty of peace and quiet, facilities outstanding enough to have put the place on *Tennis* magazine's list of America's top 50 tennis resorts. You'll find 19 clay composition courts (3 lighted), video replay and ball machines, clinics by All-American Sports, and private and group lessons; Chris Evert Lloyd and John Lloyd are the touring pros, and Chris' brother, Drew Evert, is on the teaching staff. Court reservations are available. See also *Beaches.* Information: Amelia Island Plantation, Amelia Island, FL 32034 (904 261-6161 or 800 874-6878).

GRENELEFE GOLF AND TENNIS RESORT, Cypress Gardens, Florida: A fast-growing resort development which hosts Dennis Van der Meer clinics in winter. Facilities: 12 courts — 8 Har-Tru (all lighted), 4 Laykold (2 lighted); videotape and ball machines; reservations possible; clinics and private lessons. Information: Grenelefe

Golf and Tennis Resort, 3200 State Road 546, Haines City, FL 33844 (813 422-7511).

THE ROYAL BISCAYNE, Key Biscayne, Florida: The courts at this good-sized resort off the Miami shore around the corner from Nixon's old haunt draw locals as well as vacationers; you can almost always find a tennis partner. Facilities: 10 Acryflex courts (4 lighted); video replay and ball machines; court reservations necessary; private and group lessons. Information: 555 Ocean Dr., Key Biscayne, FL 33149 (305 361-5775, 800 325-3535, toll-free).

THE DORAL, Miami, Florida: A veritable city of a resort, this ultra-posh establishment on a 2,400-acre estate offers just about any diversion (including four 18-hole golf courses) that you could ask for, except a beach of its own. There's a swimming pool and plenty of other activities (enough to keep you busy till hell freezes over). Tennis facilities: 19 well-kept courts — 10 of them hard-surface, 9 Har-Tru, 4 lighted; backboard and video replay; court reservations available; tennis hostess; private and group lessons. Arthur Ashe is director of tennis. Information: 4400 NW 87th Ave., Miami, FL 33178 (800 327-6334, toll-free outside Florida, or 305 532-3600).

HARDER HALL GOLF AND TENNIS RESORT, Sebring, Florida: An old-line central Florida resort turned tennis hotspot. Facilities: 12 Plexipave courts — 5 lighted; ball machines and video replay; guaranteed unlimited play; clinics run by Gary Addie; plus private lessons. Information: Harder Hall, Sebring, FL 33870 (813 385-0151 in Florida; 800 237-2491, toll-free elsewhere).

INNISBROOK, Tarpon Springs, Florida: A thousand acres of pine woods, citrus groves, moss-hung cypress trees outside the famous sponge market, and 1000-odd rooms make this quite a big place — but it's well managed and friendly all the same. Facilities: 18 courts — 11 Har-Tru, 7 Laykold, 7 lighted; video replay and ball machines; backboards; court reservations possible; clinics, and private and group lessons. Information: PO Box 1088, Tarpon Springs, FL 33589 (813 937-3124; toll-free, 800 237-0157; in Florida, 800 282-9813 toll-free).

HILTON HEAD ISLAND, South Carolina: Along with its stunning white beaches, quietly elegant new houses, and subtropical forests, this island also has lots of tennis. You'll find most of it at two resorts: the Palmetto Dunes and the Sea Pines Plantation. Palmetto Dunes has 25 courts, 23 of them clay, and 6 of them lighted, and offers Rod Laver Tennis Holidays–sponsored clinics in addition to private and group instruction; the emphasis is on the Australian method, which brought up so many great players of Laver's generation. At Sea Pines — the largest tennis-oriented resort in the world — there are 72 courts (most Har-Tru) clustered in primarily three locations, each a short distance from the beach, shopping, restaurants, and swimming pools. Private lessons are available if you don't want to join one of the resort's own impressive roster of tennis clinics, which include a "Tiny Tots" program for children aged five to eight (life-size cartoon characters are incorporated into the drills), and clinics that focus on singles and doubles strategy, the contact point, preparation, and the like. In addition, there are full-time tennis hostesses and almost daily round-robin tourneys for players of all ages and skill levels. Otherwise, the difference is mainly a matter of style and layout. Sea Pines is big, spread out enough that you need at least a bike to get around, while at the smaller Palmetto Dunes nearly everything is within walking distance. Information: Palmetto Dunes, PO Box 5606, Hilton Head Island, SC 29938 (toll-free 800 845-6130; from South Carolina, 803 785-1161); or Sea Pines Plantation, Hilton Head Island, SC 29928 (800 845-6131).

WORLD OF TENNIS RESORT, Austin, Texas: Townhouses cluster around the groups of courts in the Texas hill country. You feel as if you've got your own courts (almost). Facilities include 26 Laykold and Grasstex courts — 15 lighted, 2 indoors; reservations possible; private lessons and clinics are available. Wimbledon competitor Billy Freer is head teaching pro. Information: World of Tennis Sq., Austin, TX 78734 (toll-free 800 252-9222 from Texas; elsewhere 800 531-5001).

NEWK'S TENNIS RANCH, New Braunfels, Texas: Quiet and unpretentious — but the video replays are in color. At John Newcombe's home base, you lodge in comfortable villas or motel rooms. Facilities: 24 Laykold courts — 4 lighted and covered; ball machines and video replay; practice alleys; many clinics, some with John Newcombe, who is tops. You can reserve the lighted courts, but not the others. (Since there's one court for every two rooms, that's never a problem.) Details: Box 469, New Braunfels, TX 78130 (512 625-9105).

MIDWEST

THE FRENCH LICK SPRINGS HOTEL, French Lick, Indiana: The venerable resort in the hills of the southern part of the state, once *the* spot to sip mineral waters and take a cure, and the first place in America where a chef served tomato juice, is now doing a booming business in conventions — and tennis. Facilities include 21 courts — 8 indoor, 13 outdoors, all lighted; ball machines; court reservations possible, some limits may apply; private lessons. Information: French Lick Springs, French Lick, IN 47432 (812 935-9381).

BOYNE MOUNTAIN LODGE, Boyne Falls, Michigan: A complex of villas, chalets, and lodges in the northern Michigan hills that caters to skiers in winter and to golfers and tennis players in summer. The tennis program was originally designed by the Laver organization. Facilities: 18 courts — 15 Laykold, 2 grass, and 1 clay; video replay, ball machines; reservations possible; clinics and private lessons. Information: Boyne Mountain Lodge, Boyne Falls, MI 49713 (616 549-2441).

WEST

THE ARIZONA BILTMORE, Phoenix, Arizona: An ultra-posh, large-scale, superstar resort. The gold leaf dining room ceiling, the glass mural in the lobby, and the texture of the walls in the lobby were designed by Frank Lloyd Wright; the tile-bottomed Olympic-sized swimming pool compares favorably to the no-holds-barred paradise at San Simeon. Facilities include 18 courts — 17 Plexipave and Supreme, one clay — all but one lighted; plus video replay and ball machines; reservations possible; private lessons and clinics. Information: Arizona Biltmore, Box 2290, Phoenix, AZ 85002 (602 955-6600).

JOHN GARDINER'S TENNIS RANCH, Scottsdale, Arizona: Some people call this Papa Bear of the tennis world the most complete and professional training establishment in the world — and there's good reason for that. Facilities: 24 Plexipave outdoor courts; video replay and ball machines (plus other instructional aids); reservations possible; private lessons and John Gardiner clinics. You can lodge in small casitas, or in four-bedroom casas with their own courts; the one at the Casa Rosewall is on the roof. Champagne on the house when it rains. Information: John Gardiner's Tennis Ranch, 5700 E McDonald Dr., Scottsdale, AZ 85253 (602 948-2100).

JOHN GARDINER'S TENNIS RANCH, Carmel Valley, California: Luxurious. The first Gardiner ranch is still the ultimate tennis resort; and Gardiner himself is on hand with his team of top instructors to take care of the 28 guests who can be accommodated at any given time in the week-long clinic programs (offered April through November). There are 14 Plexipave-surfaced courts. Information: John Gardiner's Tennis Ranch, PO Box 228, Carmel Valley, CA 93924 (408 659-2207).

LA COSTA RESORT HOTEL AND SPA, Carlsbad, California: This super-spa, a favorite among stars of all stripes, has equally well-developed tennis facilities: 25 hard-surface courts — 5 lighted; ball machines; reservations possible but usually not necessary; private lessons by members of a pro staff headed by Pancho Segura. Information: Costa Del Mar Rd., Carlsbad, CA 92008 (714 438-9111).

VIC BRADEN TENNIS COLLEGE, Trabuco Canyon, California: The licensed psychologist and tennis ace whom no less than Jack Kramer called the greatest tennis teacher in the world holds forth here, delivering pre-drill lectures that some standup comics would envy. ("Get to know your navel." "Air your armpits." "Sit down to play.") The facilities are equally impressive: 16 concrete courts — 7 lighted; ball machines; specially designed hitting lanes; a tall teaching tower and video screening rooms; and a huge array of newfangled teaching devices, which are used during Vic Braden clinics. Classroom lectures are also part of the program. Information: 22000 Plano Trabuco Canyon Rd., Trabuco Canyon, CA 92678 (714 581-2990).

SUN VALLEY, Idaho: A great area for tennis. Guests at the Sun Valley Inn, the Sun Valley Lodge, and condominiums at Elkhorn (the well-equipped family-oriented resort community a mile away) have access to around 50 Laykold courts. Reservations are available, as are clinics; videotaping and closed-circuit TV facilities are used. Information: Elkhorn Village Inn, PO Box 1067, Sun Valley, ID 83353 (208 622-4511, or 635-9356), and Sun Valley Resorts, Inc., Sun Valley, ID 83353 (800 635-8261; from Idaho, call 800 632-4104).

Golf: The Greening of America

Golf can be a most frustrating sports interest for travelers in America, especially those who've spent any appreciable time in front of a television set watching the pros cavort (in all their double-knit glory) on some of the world's finest courses. Not only are the courses attractive to the point of distraction, but seeing them so temptingly displayed only heightens their allure.

One would think that the willingness to travel to each course's locale would permit a golfer to satisfy his or her fondest longings. Not so. The fact is that only about half a dozen of the golf courses listed by *Golf Digest* Magazine among the United States' top 50 are open to transient play on any regular basis, and tourists don't do that much better with the second 50. It's enough to make a golfer give up his alligator shirts.

Nonetheless, there are still a host of top courses that are open to traveling players. What follows is a list of a few of those that are truly worth traveling a significant distance to experience.

EAST

TACONIC GOLF CLUB, Williamstown, Massachusetts: One of the least-known top courses in the United States, in the northwest corner of Massachusetts. Though it is the home of the Williams College golf team and the preferred turf of a small local membership, it is open to transient players on weekdays (except from noon to 1:30) and on weekend and holiday afternoons after 1:00 PM. Especially on a fall afternoon, with the leaves just turning on the trees covering the beautiful Berkshire hills, this is a landscape that is right out of America's past, although the very real teeth of this course are apparent in any season. Information: Taconic Golf Club, Water St., Williamstown, MA 01267 (413 458-3997).

THE CONCORD, Kiamesha Lake, New York: It is sometimes hard to take the Catskill Mountains very seriously, especially after several generations of comedians have labored so long to project the image of nonstop gemütlichkeit and sour cream. Yet one of the very best courses in the country is part of the Concord plant on Kiamesha Lake, and it is a track well worth its nickname, "the Monster." It is nearly unconscionably long and almost intolerably difficult, and that's probably why great numbers of masochistic golfers from New York City trudge up to its first tee every weekend. These crowds usually include a number of Japanese players (the most avid, most polite, and sometimes, it seems, most depressingly slow golfers in the world), so you should plan your own assault on the Concord for a weekday. Information: The Concord, Kiamesha Lake, NY 12751 (914 794-4000).

HERSHEY COUNTRY CLUB, Hershey, Pennsylvania: It's difficult to take seriously a course so close to Cocoa and East Chocolate Avenues, but that doesn't change the fact that the two courses at the Hershey Country Club are among the best in the Northeast. The West course is especially challenging, and if the lavish old *Hotel Hershey* is not what it once was, the new clubhouse more than makes up for that for golfers. Chocolate freaks may find the scent in the air a bit distracting, but no one can quarrel with the quality of the golfing challenge. Information: Hershey Country Club, Hershey, PA 17033 (717 533-2360).

THE HOMESTEAD, Hot Springs, Virginia: Three superior courses are the focus of attention at this magnificently kept dowager of a hotel; the golf is among its best features, and the fact that the redoubtable Sam Snead makes his home nearby gives you an idea of just how good it is. The Cascades course, a couple of miles from the Homestead's front door, is the best of the trio of fine tracks; it was the site of the USGA's 1980 Senior Men's Championship. The newer Lower Cascades course is longer. Information: The Homestead, Hot Springs, VA 24445 (703 839-5500).

THE GREENBRIER, White Sulphur Springs, West Virginia: Anyone who regularly attends any sort of meeting, convention, or seminar will inevitably trip over the immense, elegant Greenbrier; but golfers tend to look forward to these conferences with particular relish. The resort's Charles Blair MacDonald–designed courses (the 6,234-yard Lakeside and the 6,659-yard Old White) and the 6,453-yard Greenbrier provide a more than adequate variety of play, and now that Jack Nicklaus has finished his renovation of the Greenbrier layout (the site of the Ryder Cup matches in 1979), its appeal has become even greater. A special attention-getter here is the lavish buffet lunch that's served every day in season in the clubhouse — oh, those peach halves with the freshly whipped cream! Information: The Greenbrier, White Sulphur Springs, WV 24986 (304 536-1110).

SOUTH

DISNEY WORLD, Lake Buena Vista, Florida: Veteran golfers seldom consider this resort complex for their vacations, but this ambitious attempt to be all things to all people has three courses — the 7,222-yard Magnolia and the 6,951-yard Palm at the Golf Resort Hotel, site of the Walt Disney World National Team Championship Golf Classic, and the 6,540-yard Lake Buena Vista. The Magnolia was named for the 1,000 magnolia trees scattered around its lakes and elevated trees; the Palm is rated among the nation's hundred best. Added attractions include South African Phil Ritson's Golf Studio, with lessons and videotaped stroke analysis, and the courses' relative removal from the frenzy of the park proper; it's not unusual for the adults in a Disney World vacation group to hide out on the course while the youngsters try to bring the Magic Kingdom to its knees. Having succeeded, they may then try their luck with the six-hole Wee Links, designed to introduce the game without overwhelming. Information: Disney World Golf Resort, PO Box 78, Lake Buena Vista, FL 32830 (305 824-2200).

DORAL COUNTRY CLUB, Miami, Florida: At the moment, the Doral Country Club stands like a last bastion against the decay that is gripping most of the Miami–Miami Beach tourist axis. But Doral's superb golf facilities (four, plus an executive course) thus far remain unassailed, and the fabled Blue Monster is still the most formidable challenge in the state. It is the site of the annual Doral Open, and the Gold course (where the qualifying rounds for the tournament are often played) offers little diminution in challenge. Information: Doral Country Club, 4400 NW 87th Ave., Miami, FL 33178 (800 327-6334 toll-free).

SAWGRASS GOLF COURSE, Ponte Vedra Beach, Florida: This is no track with which to trifle. For 5 years it was the site of the Tournament Players Championship, and anyone who watched Jack Nicklaus pump a couple of drives into the drink during the 1979 installment knows that this is one of the premier places to play. When the wind blows here, the task can be all but impossible. You also have the opportunity to make the experience as difficult as you choose, for there are four sets of tees from which one can play. It's one of the South's toughest golf tests. Information: Sawgrass Golf Club, PO Box 600, Ponte Vedra Beach, FL 32082 (904 285-2261).

TOURNAMENT PLAYERS CLUB, Ponte Vedra Beach, Florida: This may well be Pete Dye's consummate masterpiece. The 17th hole has become a classic after only one tournament was played here, and this 130-yard island par three drove the pros crazy. It won't treat you any more kindly, so bring enough golf balls. This is by far the most dramatic layout we know, and only the brave of heart should attempt to conquer its sculptured fairways and kindly undulating greens. It's not likely that you'll score very well hereabouts, but it's a comfort to know the pros did no better. Information: Sawgrass Golf Club, PO Box 600, Ponte Vedra Beach, FL 32082 (904 285-2261).

SEA ISLAND GOLF CLUB, St. Simons Island, Georgia: The Sea Island Golf Club is only the most important part of the ten-thousand-acre resort complex known as *The Cloister*. The 36 holes of golf (divided into four distinct nines) all possess ocean views, with the rest of the local landscape dominated by magnolias and pampas grass. The Seaside nine is probably the most challenging of the available quartet, and the four may be played in any order or combination. Information: The Cloister, Sea Island, GA 31561 (912 638-3611).

PINEHURST HOTEL AND COUNTRY CLUB, Pinehurst, North Carolina: There is no golf community in the United States more devoted to the traditional values of the game than Pinehurst. Nongolfers often can't grasp what all the hushed reverence is about, but believers happily play two rounds a day here (on the six courses), visit the World Golf Hall of Fame in between rounds (admission charge), and watch instructional films at the Pinehurst Hotel after dark. Donald Ross–designed Pinehurst #2, home of the annual Hall of Fame Tournament, is the class of the circuits here; the latest and toughest is George and Tom Fazio's panoramic #6. Information: Pinehurst Hotel, PO Box 4000, Pinehurst, NC 28374 (800 334-9560 toll-free; in North Carolina, 800 672-4644).

DORADO BEACH HOTEL, Dorado Beach, Puerto Rico: Though the Rockresort management team no longer minds the tees here, this superb golf center still retains its place as the island's most luxurious escape. There's lively debate about which of the two courses offers the sterner test, but a middle-handicap golfer will be hard pressed to discern the differences as he battles his way through this former grapefruit plantation. Information: Dorado Beach Hotel, Dorado Beach, PR 00646 (800 545-4000, or 809 796-1600).

HARBOUR TOWN GOLF LINKS, Hilton Head Island, South Carolina: The offshore islands along our southeastern coast have received renewed attention since then-President-elect Carter took his first vacation break on St. Simons. But golfers have long known what the general public is just discovering: These islands hold some of the country's best resort terrain. Golfers have their choice of more than a dozen courses; but the magnet is usually the Harbour Town Golf Links, part of the marvelous Sea Pines Plantation development (See *Beaches; Tennis*). With a whopping course rating of 75 — one of the highest in the country — its difficulty needs no elaboration. Only the laid back environment provides some small salve to soaring scores. Pete Dye, who designed Harbour Town, is our personal choice for the game's most creative craftsman, and his talent and handiwork are nowhere better displayed. Information: Harbour Town Golf Links, Sea Pines Plantation, Hilton Head Island, SC 29928 (800 845-6131 toll-free; in South Carolina, 800 922-7042).

WEST

THE WIGWAM, Litchfield Park, Arizona: In a state that is rapidly becoming one of the golfing centers of the nation, none is better than the Gold course, one of a trio of courses at this Phoenix-area resort, operated by the Goodyear tire organization. See also *Resort Hotels.* Information: The Wigwam, Litchfield Park, AZ 85340 (602 935-3811).

LA COSTA HOTEL AND SPA, Carlsbad, California: At this famous Southern California health spa, the late Dick Wilson created a course that bedevils even the pros, so you'll likely welcome the opportunity to repair to the steam room after your first foray. Information: La Costa Hotel, Costa Del Mar Rd., Carlsbad, CA 92008 (714 438-9111).

PEBBLE BEACH GOLF LINKS, Pebble Beach, California: If there is a leading contender for the title of Most Photographed Golf Course, it has to be the ocean-hugging Pebble Beach Golf Links on the windswept Monterey Peninsula. This is one of the relatively rare instances where a first-class US tournament track is actually accessible to the public, and it's an opportunity not to be missed. Information: Pebble Beach Golf Links, Pebble Beach, CA 93953 (408 624-3811).

SPYGLASS HILL, Pebble Beach, California: Barely a short iron away from Pebble Beach and once considered so difficult that the touring pros demanded that several of the tees be moved (and the holes shortened). But even in its edited version you will find Spyglass a handful, and tromping through the ice plants is a botanical education in itself. Information: Spyglass Hill, Pebble Beach, CA 93953 (408 624-3811).

TORREY PINES, La Jolla, California: San Diego is the golfing capital of southern California, with nearly six dozen public courses to satisfy its golf-crazed citizenry. The best of these is the publinx at Torrey Pines (where the Andy Williams tournament is held every year), and both the North and South courses are worth your attention. The rustic, charming Torrey Pines Inn is adjacent. Information: Torrey Pines Inn, 11480 N Torrey Pines Rd., La Jolla, CA 92037 (714 453-4420).

KEYSTONE, Keystone, Colorado: At first glance, Keystone Ranch looks like something out of a John Wayne movie — and it is. The new golf course, opened in June 1980, is laid out on a 9,000-foot mountain plateau framed by snow-capped Rocky Mountain peaks; several holes run around old ranch buildings. Former PGA champion Dave Stockton is the resident pro, and the course is first class from beginning to end. The Keystone Resort is owned by the Ralston Purina Company, and its fine condominium and hotel facilities — used to capacity by skiers in winter — host golfers in summer. Perhaps the greatest attraction of all is the thin air; you'll find your shots going considerably farther than they would at sea level. Information: Keystone Resort, Box 38, Keystone, CO 80435 (303 468-1234).

MAUNA KEA GOLF CLUB, Kamuela, Hawaii, Hawaii: Part of the premier resort of the same name is built on lava flows that have somehow solidified to give the course a linksland character. This is a warm, arid corner of these islands, and much care (and water) is needed to keep the terrain green and true. The spectacular volcanic peak that gives the resort its name is the backdrop for nearly every shot, and the Mauna Kea fairways are among the most scenic in the world. Information: Mauna Kea Beach Hotel, PO Box 218, Kamuela, HI 96743 (808 882-7222).

PRINCEVILLE AT HANALEI, Hanalei, Kauai, Hawaii: The garden spot of the Garden Island, with three spectacular nines (Ocean, Woods, and Lake) in the same terrain you saw in the film *South Pacific.* An additional 18-holer planned by Robert Trent Jones, Jr., will eventually make this one of Hawaii's biggest golf resorts. Weather can be uneven here — the lush forests are the by-product of plentiful rainfall — but the quality of the courses merits the risk. Information: Princeville at Hanalei, PO Box 121, Hanalei, Kauai, HI 96714 (808 826-6561 or 800 367-7090).

GOLF CLINICS

Regular practice under the supervision of a pro on your own home course can't be beat for reducing your handicap. But there's no substitute for an occasional look at your strengths and weaknesses from a new point of view, or for some intensive practice under a new instructor. That's the purpose of the golf clinics that have sprouted up all over the country.

GOLF DIGEST INSTRUCTION SCHOOLS, headquartered in Norwalk, Connecticut: The Harvard of golf schools holds its courses — taught by some of the best teaching pros in the business — at resorts all over the country, year-round. Information: Golf Digest Instruction Schools, 495 Westport Ave., Norwalk, CT 06856 (800 243-6121, or 203 847-5811).

WALT DISNEY WORLD GOLF SCHOOL, Lake Buena Vista, Florida: Developed by South African Phil Ritson, rated among the world's top golf instructors by no less than Gary Player, this program aims to help golfers develop their own styles by building on current skills. In contrast to the other golf programs described here, WDW clinics last only two hours each; signing up for more than one can give the results of a longer program. Videotapes made during lessons can help you chart improvement, and the instructor's tape of his pointers to you, which you can take home, can add punch to your practice time. The unparalleled après-golf activities are just an added bonus. Information: WDW, Box 40, Lake Buena Vista, FL 32830.

THE GOLF SCHOOL AT MOUNT SNOW, Mount Snow, Vermont: These thorough and well-organized programs, offered from May through October, concentrate on making your clinic experience enjoyable as well as instructive — and attract a high repeat business as a result. Unique to this school is a four-to-one student-teacher ratio. Details: Golf School at Mount Snow, Mount Snow, VT 05356 (802 464-3333).

THE GOLF ACADEMY AT STRATTON, Stratton Mountain, Vermont: Director Bob Lendzion and his staff of pros focus on the basics — grip, stance, alignment, and swing — during 2- and 5-day sessions. Information: The Golf Academy at Stratton, Stratton Mountain, VT 05155 (802 297-2200).

Sailing America's Coastal Waters

WINDJAMMER CRUISES

There's no better way to get a feeling for the great age of sailing than on one of the big windjammers (most built before the turn of the century for oystering, fishing, or cargo, and now converted to handle the cruise trade). You can learn knots, help raise anchor and set sail, and fall asleep at night to the creaking of the ship's oak beams.

Most of the boats don't have much in the way of plumbing aboard. On many you'll find simply a supply of wash water on deck, and only on the really luxurious ones will there be wash basins or cold showers in the cabins. However, you don't *have* to do any work; you can spend your days swimming off the side or dozing in the sun. You eat big meals, family-style, and you don't have to help with the cooking unless you feel like it. You cruise a little every day, then stop for a while — to go sightseeing, have a cookout, or take hot showers at a local marina.

Otherwise, what a cruise is like depends a lot on the boat. On smaller vessels, the atmosphere is bound to be chummy (or confining, depending on your attitudes toward spending a week with strangers); they'll also be somewhat more informal and each passenger has more to say about where you go, what you do, and when you do it.

How do you pick a boat? Consider size, plumbing, ports of call, price (usually from $280 to $375 for a week aboard, including meals), means of power, and the policy on children (there may be minimum ages of, say, 14 for girls or 16 for boys).

Here's a sampling of what you'll find:

***MARY DAY*, Camden, Maine:** This 83-foot schooner, the first new windjammer to be built in 30 years, holds 28 passengers (no children under 15) in cabins for one to three; but no running water. Auxiliary power, if you call it that, is supplied by a small boat, good for excursions ashore, but the *Mary Day* herself has no engine. Information: Coastal Cruises, PO Box 798, Camden, ME 04843 (207 236-2750).

SCHOONER *ADVENTURE* AND SCHOONER *ROSEWAY*, Camden, Maine: Largest vessels of the Camden fleet. Built in the Roaring 20s, the 120-foot *Adventure* (fastest on the Coast) is a Gloucester fishing vessel; the 112-foot *Roseway* was built as a yacht and was used for many years as a pilot boat in Boston Harbor. Today both cruise the Maine coast and carry 37 passengers each (no children under 16). Everyone brushes his teeth over the side and sponge-bathes. Information: Yankee Schooner Cruises, PO Box 696, Camden, ME 04843 (207 2364449).

SCHOONER *STEPHEN TABER*, Camden, Maine: A two-masted 68-foot gaff schooner built in 1871 — the oldest continuously active US merchant vessel. This former carrier of bricks and wood pulp has been cruising the Maine coast in the Penobscot Bay region with up to 22 passengers since 1946 (no children under 14). Running water in basins; no auxiliary power. Information: Schooner *Stephen Taber*, 70 Elm St., Camden, ME 04843 (207 236-3520).

THE *HARVEY GAMAGE*, Rockland, Maine: Launched in 1973, and supplied with running water, the 95-foot schooner *Harvey Gamage* is one of the fanciest of the windjammers: the two showers aboard are cold, but they're the only ones you'll find aboard any such ship on the Down East coast. The *Harvey Gamage* is also unusual in welcoming children of any age among its 34 passengers. Cruises take in the Maine coast in summer, the Virgin Islands in the winter. Sailing instruction is provided. Information: Dirigo Cruises, 39 Waterside Land, Clinton, CT 06413 (203 669-7068).

THE *ISAAC H. EVANS*, Rockland, Maine: Built in 1886, this 64½-foot, two-masted schooner spent most of its life oystering and freighting in Delaware Bay; now completely rebuilt, it has cold running water in the cabins, potbellied stoves for heat in the public rooms back aft, and small push boats for going ashore or getting to safe harbor if there's no wind: The ship itself has no engine. Up to 22 passengers at a time (minimum age 16). Information: Captain Doug Lee, PO Box 482, Rockland, ME 04841 (207 594-8007).

***LEWIS R. FRENCH*, Rockland, Maine:** Another two-masted, 64½-foot schooner, this one was built in 1871 as a cargo vessel. Older than the *Issac H. Evans,* but nearly identical in all other ways, it, too, has been completely rebuilt so that it is essentially a new ship on an old design. The small cabins have reading lights and running water; up to 22 guests can be accommodated. Information: Captain John Foss, PO Box 482, Rockland, ME 04841 (207 594-8007).

THE *VICTORY CHIMES*, Rockland, Maine: The largest three-masted passenger-sailing vessel under the American flag, a cargo carrier until 1949, the 132-foot *Victory Chimes* has been ferrying passengers, up to 46 at a time (none under 14), for nearly 30 years. Hot and cold running water in the cabins. A small boat takes passengers ashore once a day. Information: Maine Coast Cruises, Castine, ME 04421 (207 326-8856) in winter; Rockland, ME 04841 (207 596-6060) in summer.

THE *SHENANDOAH*, Vineyard Haven, Massachusetts: This square, topsail engineless schooner launched in 1964 carries up to 29 passengers at a time in cabins for one to four. It puts in at ports throughout southern New England between Nantucket on the east and Mystic on the west. Everybody has a wash basin; you get your hot water from the galley. No children under 10. Information: Coastwise Packet Company, Vineyard Haven, MA 02568 (617 693-1699).

THE SCHOONER *BILL OF RIGHTS*, Newport, Rhode Island: One of the newest of America's windjammers, this 94-foot replica of a topsail schooner that ran contraband during the Civil War carries 32 passengers in 16 staterooms; and puts in at southern New England harbors (Mystic, Nantucket, Point Judith, Block Island, and the Elizabeth Islands). Running water in the cabins. Information: Schooner *Bill of Rights,* PO Box 477, Newport, RI 02840 (401 724-7612).

SAILING SCHOOLS

ANNAPOLIS SAILING SCHOOL, Annapolis, Maryland: Based in Annapolis, this establishment also has schools on the Coronado Peninsula opposite San Diego, California; at Marathon, in the Keys, and at the Sheraton in St. Petersburg, Florida; on the aquamarine waters around St. Croix, the Virgin Islands; outside Charleston, South Carolina; and at the Shore Club in Lake Geneva, Wisconsin. The basic two-day beginners' course includes four hours in the classroom and eight hours in the water; the three- and five-day beginners' courses give you extra time on the water. A variety of programs is available, from five-day cruises (with instructors accompanying you in a power lead boat) to advanced courses (handling auxiliary cruising boats, coastal navigation and piloting, racing, and preparation for bareboat chartering), but are not offered at all of the school's locations. Fees range from about $140 for the two-day course to $195 for the three-day course and $250 for the five-day course (with reductions for couples); on week-long cruises, you pay $590 to $995 per boat, depending on its size. Also available are advanced cruising courses in the Florida Keys, the Virgin Islands, Chesapeake Bay, and the Windwards; and long cruises from Annapolis to St. Croix in spring and fall. Information: Annapolis Sailing School, PO Box 3334, Annapolis, MD 21403 (800 638-9192; from Maryland: 301 267-7205).

THE OFFSHORE SAILING SCHOOL, New York, New York: Run by ex-Olympian Steve Colgate, this school offers 20-hour Learn-to-Sail courses for beginners, with classroom sessions from Sunday (when all courses begin) through Wednesday, and half-day sails alternating morning and afternoon Monday through Saturday. The courses cover all the basics, including navigation and some spinnaker work on 27-foot extra-stable Solings (about $295 to $525, depending on where you go). Learn-to-Cruise courses, designed for graduates and for people with small boat experience, help you handle larger boats and cover all the other things that you have to know to cruise in them — anchoring and docking, heavy-weather sailing, picking up men overboard, and the like. Locations include Atlantic Oakes in Bar Harbor, Maine; South Seas Plantation at low-key and unpretentious Captiva Island, Florida; the super-elegant Tides Inn in Irvington, Virginia, a truly splendid place; and, more informal, Martha's Vineyard, Massachusetts (you stay where you wish); and City Island, outside New York City (basically not so much a vacation school as a place for locals to learn in their spare time). Learn-to-Sail courses are offered at all locations; Learn-to-Cruise courses only at Captiva and Martha's Vineyard. Special racing courses are also offered at Captiva; the advanced racing course is taught by a different internationally known guest expert every week. Information: Offshore Sailing School, 820 2nd Ave., New York, NY 10017 (800 221-4326; from New York: 212 986-4570).

GREAT SAILING AND CRUISING

Some parts of the US coastline are so sail happy that you'd think everybody there owns a boat; if you don't, you can usually charter. Expect to be asked about your sailing experience; most are handled by brokers for private owners. Your experience will determine which boat you get; which you want will depend on how long you plan to cruise, since boats under 26 feet can be a little too cozy for a week on the water.

MARINA DEL REY, California: Ever since this marina, the largest manmade small-boat harbor in the world, was put in nearly 20 years ago, pleasure boaters have been passing through in droves; there are 6,000 slips and plenty of rentals and sailing schools. Information: Department of Small Craft Harbors, 13837 Fiji Way, Marina del Rey, CA 90291 (213 823-4571).

NEWPORT BEACH, California: Joey Bishop and some 10,000 others keep boats in this big, beautiful, busy southern California harbor. There are dozens of marinas; for a list, contact the Newport Harbor Area Chamber of Commerce, 1470 Jamboree Rd., Newport Beach, CA 92660 (714 644-8211).

SAUSALITO, California: Sausalito is the yachting center for San Francisco Bay, with space for over 2,000 boats in its marinas. For a list of yacht brokers, contact the Redwood Empire Association, 360 Post St., San Francisco, CA 94108 (415 421-6554).

SACRAMENTO–SAN JOAQUIN RIVER DELTA, near Stockton, California: Better than a thousand miles of sloughs and cuts, canals and other streams tunnel through the tules (the tall rushes that give this flatland its distinctive appearance), and for some local folk, weekend cruising is a way of life. Most rentals are houseboats, which just about anyone can handle. For a list of liveries and for more information, contact the Stockton Convention and Visitors Bureau, 46 W Fremont, Stockton, CA 95202 (209 943-1987).

LONG ISLAND SOUND, Connecticut and New York: Between the notched shoreline of Connecticut and the rocks-and-sand edge of Long Island, there are literally hundreds of square miles of protected cruising water. The Sunday *New York Times* classified section always contains an extensive listing of boats available for charter. For crewed boats, contact Sparkman & Stephens, 79 Madison Ave., New York, NY 10016 (212 689-9292).

THE MAINE COAST: Straight and bold in the southwest, deeply notched near Boothbay Harbor, and scattered all over with islands like Matinicus (ultra-wild) and Monhegan (crisscrossed with walking paths that take you to bluffs and boulders where you can sun yourself) — the Maine coast offers enough variety to make it among the country's best spots for cruising — provided, that is, you can handle the frequent fogs, the tides, the rocky shores, and the scarcity of marinas. To get details, contact the charter operators: Sparkman & Stephens, 79 Madison Ave., New York, NY (212 689-9292); Robinhood Marina, Robinhood, ME 04530 (207 371-2525), for 32- to 53-foot bareboats; and Seal Cove Boatyard, PO Box 99, Harborside, ME 04642 (207 326-4422), for 19- to -54-foot vessels of various types.

THE CHESAPEAKE BAY, Maryland and Virginia: The sine qua non of cruising in America, 185-mile-long Chesapeake Bay, America's largest estuary, is notched by river mouths, little coves, and harbors where you can tie up and go ashore for a walk through 300-year-old towns; and scattered with quaint islands like Smith and Tangier, where the people started losing their Elizabethan accents only about a decade ago. The cruising season, which begins in April, continues well beyond October, when the Annapolis In-the-Water Boat Show, one of the biggest in US boating, is held. For information and charters, contact Hartge Chesapeake Charters, Galesville, MD 20765 (301 867-7240; bareboats from 26 to 42 feet); or Interyacht, PO Box 49, Annapolis, MD 21404 (301 267-8627; mainly bareboats between 34 and 40 feet).

America's Most Surprising Ocean Beaches

Along America's thousands of miles of lake and ocean shores, you'll find beaches for everyone. Most of the East Coast between the brief busy coast of New Hampshire and Miami Beach is beach-edged; a dotted line of slim barrier beaches, which protect the mainland from the brunt of the ocean's force, extends from Long Island to Florida. There, and along the Gulf Coast of Florida,

Texas, and Mississippi (which has bluer, warmer waters, more gently sloping bottoms, and less surf than East Coast shores), beach grass backs the sand; behind that, further inland, grow scrubby trees and, in the South, tropical vegetation. Often, incredible as it may seem, the deep roots of these fragile plants are all that keep the islands from washing away in storms (as, indeed, they sometimes do anyway).

Beaches up and down the Pacific Coast are, as a rule, better for beachwalking and fishing than for swimming because of riptides and heavy undertow. However, there are exceptions. Water at beaches below Santa Barbara is generally warm enough for dips. Above Santa Barbara it's for the hardy only because of the proximity of the Alaska Current. Around Carmel, the shore is scalloped with coves; north of Fort Ross, it's gravelly and driftwood collecting is terrific. Still farther up the coast, the beaches are edged by forests. The coastlines of Oregon and southern Washington make up one solid strip of beach cut by occasional headlands; but the best concentrations are between Pacific City and Florence, Oregon. Stormwatching in winter is popular there, as is beachwalking afterward to pick up the leavings — driftwood, most commonly, but occasionally brightly colored Japanese fishing floats as well. As for Hawaii, it has some of the best beaches of all; the one on Waikiki is only the most famous.

There are fine beaches, however, at Acadia National Park, in Maine; on Assateague Island, Maryland; at the Cape Cod National Seashore, in Massachusetts; down the New Jersey coast in state parks and in Victorian Cape May; along the Outer Banks of North Carolina; on Padre Island, off the Texas Gulf Coast; in Carmel, California; and along Oregon's great long coast — all of which are described elsewhere in this book (see DIRECTIONS).

Some American beaches allow nude sunbathing; if you're interested, consult the *World Guide to Nude Beaches and Recreation* ($13.95 postpaid from The Naturists, PO Box 132, Oshkosh, WI 54902).

Nancy Bruning's *The Beach Book* ($8.95; Houghton Mifflin) discusses American beaches at length. Below, we list our selection of some of the best.

EAST

OGUNQUIT BEACH, Ogunquit, Maine: This little harbor town, home to about 2,000 souls, is also the site of a three-mile-long strand that is one of the best in New England — partly for its length, partly for the gentleness of the drop-off. The water is "refreshing," as you must expect in Maine. Information: Chamber of Commerce, Box 637, Ogunquit, ME 03907 (207 646-2939).

OLD ORCHARD BEACH, Old Orchard Beach, Maine: This seven-mile strand — 700 feet wide — is the state's longest; the low surf makes it one of the safest on the Atlantic for swimming. Information: Chamber of Commerce, Old Orchard Beach, ME 04064 (207 934-2091).

CRANE BEACH, Ipswich, Massachusetts: This resort town also boasts a wonderful 7-mile-long sweep of dune-backed sand. There's not much surf, so swimming is possible. Most interesting lodgings can be found at Rockport and Gloucester. Information: Chamber of Commerce, PO Box 67, Rockport, MA 01966 (617 546-6575).

FIRE ISLAND, New York: Walk-on ferries from Patchogue, Sayville, and Bay Shore, Long Island (May through October only), take passengers by the thousands to this slip of land, where there are communities for families and gay and heterosexual singles, and the 19,000-acre Fire Island National Seashore, where you can camp (by reservation), swim, hike, surf-cast, or just sit in the sun. Information: Fire Island National Seashore, 120 Laurel St., Patchogue, NY 11772 (516 289-4810).

THE HAMPTONS, Long Island, New York: A great attraction to artists and writers since the 1920s, these towns offer some of the finest beaches in the world, plus restaurants, art galleries, markets, bookstores, gourmet food shops, and parties that keep the area swinging until the wee hours. Rooms are usually difficult to come by on short notice. However, after Labor Day, when the water is at its warmest, the beaches are almost completely deserted. Information: Chamber of Commerce, PO Box 64, Hampton Bays, NY 11946 (516 728-2211).

WATCH HILL BEACH, Watch Hill, Rhode Island: A fine surf beach open to the public in a town so exclusive that little else is. Presiding over the entrance to the beach is the century-old Flying Carousel, one of the oldest in New England. More beaches can be found nearby at Misquamicut and Weekapaug; for information about them and about renting summer houses in the area, contact the Chamber of Commerce, 159 Main St., Westerly, RI 02891 (401 596-7761).

SOUTH

GULF STATE PARK, Gulf Shores, Alabama: These 2½ miles of sugary white sand, lapped gently by the aquamarine Gulf, make up only one short section of the 32-mile stretch between Alabama and Mobile Points — but it's the best section for vacations because of the quality of the facilities at the Gulf State Park Resort (modern, well run, and by now completely recovered from Hurricane Frederick's 1979 attack). Information: Gulf State Park, Box 437, Gulf Shores, AL 36542 (205 968-7531).

AMELIA ISLAND PLANTATION, Amelia Island, Florida: One of the finest beach developments in existence, this one nestled in groves of live oaks and surrounded by salt marshes and dunes has really caught on in the last few years, and from March through May and again from June through August, the 19 tennis courts, 27-hole golf course, 14 swimming pools, bike trails, restaurants, and comfortable condominiums beside the 4-mile-long Atlantic strand are all bustling. Near Jacksonville. Information: Amelia Island Plantation, Amelia Island, FL 32034 (904 261-6161; toll-free 800 342-6841 from Florida, 800 874-6878 from the rest of the US).

THE NORTHWEST COAST, Florida: This may be the whitest sand you'll ever see; it's white like snow, white like sugar. West of Panama City, in the panhandle, US 98 runs next to these beaches (but low dunes protect sunbathers from the sound of the traffic). One US government-owned six-mile stretch, between Fort Walton Beach (pop. 50,000) and Destin (pop. 6,000), is completely undeveloped; there's no parking lot — you just stop your car anyplace along the road. Most of the motels in the area are Mom-and-Pop variety (but nice). Like Destin, whose population has skyrocketed from 1,000 in the last five years, some of the towns east of Panama City are just being discovered as the great tourist destinations they are. St. George Island, near Apalachicola, has 20 miles of beaches, a state park, and a couple of hundred beach houses on stilts, some of which are available for rent through Alice Collins Realty (PO Box 16, St. George Island, FL 32328, 904 670-2758) and Suncoast Realty (St. George Island, FL 32328, 904 670-2247). The loudest noise you'll hear on a busy summer's day is the occasional banging of a screen door. Not far away, the T. H. Stone State Memorial St. Joseph Peninsula State Park has another 20 miles of pure white sand, nice campsites in a grove of trees, and facilities for biking, boating, clamming, fishing. As for temperatures, late March and early April begin the warmweather season, and especially around Fort Walton Beach, the crowds, such as they are, stay on until Labor Day. But even on July 4, you can get off to yourself on the empty strands. The only time that isn't 100% delightful here is in late summer or early fall when the dogflies may be out. Information: Destin Chamber of Commerce, PO Box 8, Destin, FL 32541 (904 837-6241); Greater Fort Walton Beach Chamber of Commerce, PO Box 640, Fort Walton Beach, FL 32549 (904 244-8191); and the Apalachicola Chamber of Commerce, Market St., Apalachicola, FL 32320 (904 653-9419).

SANIBEL-CAPTIVA ISLANDS, Florida: The 20 miles of white sand on this two-island chain off the coast of Fort Myers offers some of the finest, perhaps even *the* finest, seashell collecting in the US. Best pickings are after storms with heavy northwest winds, usually following a cold snap, between January and March, but each tide brings in its share of Florida cones, calico and sponge pectins, yellow, rose, and brown cockles, whelks and pear whelks, paper figs, fighting conchs, and more. Some good areas to search are around the lighthouse at the eastern tip of Sanibel; Bowman's Beach at the island's western end; the southerly tip of Captiva; and the northerly tip of Captiva. The water averages about 72° in winter, 80° in summer. Temperatures range between 65° and 86° in April, between 61° and 77° in November. Motels on the island are hidden away in groves of trees, so the atmosphere is low-key, even during the busy Christmas and spring school holidays. Always reserve in advance, however. Information: Chamber of Commerce, Sanibel, FL 33957 (813 472-1080).

CUMBERLAND ISLAND NATIONAL SEASHORE, Cumberland Island, Georgia: The interior of this 16-mile-long, 3-mile-wide barrier island, the most southerly of Georgia's Sea Islands, is covered with marshes alive with fiddler crabs, oysters, long-legged wading birds like ibis and wood stork, and with groves of weirdly contorted live oaks, willow oaks, magnolia, holly, and pine. The 18 miles of beaches that rim these wildlands are golden and (since the ferry that serves the island from St. Marys, Georgia, makes the 45-minute trip on a fairly limited basis) quite empty as well. All you've got to do is walk a little farther from the ferry dock than anybody else and you'll be alone. Or, if you can plan ahead, write a couple of months in advance to reserve a campsite on the island and spend the night. There are just 16 sites at the developed campground and four primitive sites in the backcountry. Among the couple of pieces of private property that still remain on the island, an inn named Greyfield takes a limited number of guests (912 261-6408; see *America's Special Havens*). Information: Cumberland Island National Seashore, PO Box 806, St. Marys, GA 31558 (912 882-4335).

GULF ISLANDS NATIONAL SEASHORE, near Ocean Springs, Mississippi: In the 70,800 acres of this preserve there are some 52 miles of sugary sand beaches, all of them on three barrier islands off the Mississippi coast — Horn, Petit Bois, and Ship Island. The first two, once national wildlife refuges because of the richness of the wildlife inhabiting the brackish and freshwater ponds and marshes, are accessible only by private or chartered boat; you can go out and camp in your boat or on the shore and have the island to yourself. (Charter boats are widely available in the towns of Gulfport and Biloxi.) Ship Island is accessible by private craft or, from April through September, by a twice-a-day ferry from Gulfport or Biloxi; each boat accommodates 250. That may sound like a lot of people, but once on the island the crowds scatter to the right and left of the boardwalk that leads to the Gulf Coast beach, and you can end up practically alone. Take plenty of sunscreen, a lightweight long-sleeved shirt and trousers: You'll need the protection against the sun since there's scarcely a bit of shade. Information: Gulf Islands National Seashore, 3500 Park Rd., Ocean Springs, MS 39564 (601 875-1864).

HILTON HEAD ISLAND, South Carolina: Not as porcelain-white as the beaches of south Florida, the 12 miles you find here are clean, gently sloping, and almost completely free of crushing waves and strong undertow (except at South Beach, where you've got to be careful). They're also wide — 600 feet at low tide — and hard packed. You can bicycle along them as well as hike, bird-watch, beachcomb (best after fall and winter storms), and swim (April into October). When the weather is too cold for splashing in the surf, you can always take a dip in one of the pools at the several resort hotel/condominium/vacation home developments that made this island famous over two decades ago; among these are Sea Pines Plantation (woodsy, spread out; 803 785-3333), and Palmetto Dunes (everything in walking distance; 803 785-1161). Some of the best golf and tennis facilities in the country are also on the island, along with sailing schools and fishing schools, bike paths, stables, shops, restaurants, and much more. Information: Chamber of Commerce, Box 5647, Hilton Head Island, SC 29938 (803 785-3673).

KIAWAH ISLAND, South Carolina: This 10,000-acre barrier island looks like Hilton Head 15 years ago — that is, almost like a wilderness, as you'll see when you sign up for one of the resort's 2-hour jeep safaris. But when you've had your fill of the tangled jungles, you can stroll down the 10 miles of wide, hard ocean beach (among the best spots on the East Coast for shelling) and pick up elegant disks and stiff pen shells, lettered olives, whelks, and such. Or play tennis or golf; bike along the nearly 8 miles of bicycle paths; or swim in the ocean or any of a half-dozen pools. From May through August, loggerhead turtles lay their eggs on the beach in the dark of the night. As at Hilton Head, the climate is subtropical and balmy, with average highs around 81° in August, 61° in February. Lodgings are provided by the Kiawah Island Inn, plus condominiums, cottages, and private homes. Information: Kiawah Island Company, PO Box 12910, Charleston, SC 29412 (800 845-2471; in South Carolina: 803 768-2121).

THE GRAND STRAND, Myrtle Beach, South Carolina: Stretching for 50 miles from the North Carolina border to Georgetown, this white strand is one of the most popular seaside resorts on the entire Atlantic coast. There are literally dozens of motels crowding the boardwalk — great for people-watching. Fall and winter — still temperate — are more peaceful. Information: Chamber of Commerce, Box 2115, Myrtle Beach, SC 29577 (803 448-5135).

WEST

HUNTINGTON BEACH, California: The "Surfing Capital of the U.S.A.," with its 1,800-foot-long pier (built in 1902 as the Pacific's answer to Atlantic City), is one of the top spots on the Coast to watch surfers catching some of the Pacific's best waves, sometimes right under the barnacle-spiked pilings; a good surfer can stay on top for the distance of two city blocks. Information: Greater Los Angeles Visitors and Convention Bureau, 505 S Flower St., Los Angeles, CA 90071 (213 488-9100).

PISMO BEACH, California: The giant Pismo clams once found in such numbers that farmers plowed them up for hog and cattle feed are still plentiful enough on this wide, 21-mile-long strand that it's not so difficult to get your limit — 10 per day of at least 4½ inches in width. Best shelling is at extreme low tides, year-round. Otherwise, you can swim (best from August through November) and go surfing or fishing or just drive down the beach. (This is the last oceanfront community where the latter activity is permitted.) Dune buggies are available to rent nearby. Motels are mainly at the north end of the strand, atop rocky cliffs; some have their own short narrow beaches, accessible by twisty wooden staircases. Information: Pismo Beach Chamber of Commerce, 581 Dolliver St., Pismo Beach, CA 93449 (805 773-4382).

POINT REYES NATIONAL SEASHORE, Point Reyes, California: Just north of San Francisco, this triangle of land holds the US Weather Bureau's record for the foggiest, windiest station between Mexico and Canada. So, though three-mile-long Limantour and four-mile-long Drake's Beaches are safe for swimming, Point Reyes is not the place you come for fun in the sun. Rather, you come for the solitude and great walks — especially along Pacific-pounded Point Reyes and McClure's beaches. People stop for picnics on the former, then move on; McClure's is nearly deserted most of the time because of the difficult access (a steep narrow trail). Inland, where weather is less changeable, 100 miles of hiking trails show off wildflowers, marshes, and wildlife. Also visit the historic Point Reyes Lighthouse, the re-created Miwok Indian Village, and the Morgan horse-breeding farm. Motels are in Inverness. Information: Point Reyes National Seashore, Point Reyes, CA 94956 (415 663-1092).

KAANAPALI, Maui, Hawaii: The longest of all Hawaii's great beaches, this one takes in about three miles of golden sand near Lahaina, the old whaling station; flat water makes it good for swimming. Edging the beach: an area full of hotels and golf courses on land owned by the Amfac Corporation, whose careful master plan has kept the architecture handsome and harmonious. Information: Hawaii Visitors Bureau, 2270 Kalakaua Ave., Honolulu, HI 96815 (808 923-1811).

Scuba: The Wild Blue Under

Just about anyone can use a snorkel, mask, and flippers (invented, incidentally, by Benjamin Franklin) wherever the water is clear enough — in Hawaii, along the coast of Block Island, Rhode Island, or at Florida's John Pennekamp Reef State Park (see DIRECTIONS). The Virgin Islands offer some fine snorkeling as well.

Scuba diving is something else. Handling everyday procedures and emergencies with equal aplomb takes training and practice. And so, while you can buy the gear you need at any diving shop, most diving shops will only refill tanks for — and rent equipment only to — divers who have passed special certification courses that require one or two nights a week for about six weeks, partly in a swimming pool and partly in open water. For details, contact the sponsoring organizations: the National Association of Underwater Instructors (NAUI), PO Box 14650, Montclair, CA 91763 (714 621-5801); the Professional Association of Diving Instructors (PADI), 1243 E Warner Ave., Santa Ana, CA 92705 (714 540-7234); or your local YMCA.

SHORT COURSES

You can get your certification (or C card) on your vacation if you work at it every day. Several establishments in Hawaii offer short courses, with a good deal of work in the clear warm waters around the coral reefs. They include the Sea Sage Diving Centers, 4-1378 Kuhio Hwy., Kapaa, Kauai, HI 96746 (808 822-3841); and Gold Coast Divers, PO Box 2064, Kailua Kona, HI 96740 (808 329-1328).

SOME GREAT DIVING SPOTS

Check local diving shops for up-to-the-minute information about conditions.

LA JOLLA COVE, La Jolla, California: Starting in this 50-yard-deep, 100-yard-wide notch in the southern California coastline, the San Diego–La Jolla Underwater Park takes in about 7 miles of underwater scenery up the coast as far as Torrey Pines; within that area there's a look-but-don't-touch area where you can see vast quantities of kelp, abalone, lobster. One of the best sights is the edge of the 17-mile-long submarine canyon — an 11,000-foot drop-off. Information: Parks and Recreation Department, Coastal Division (714 236-6652), and, for details about La Jolla hostelries, the San Diego Convention and Visitors Bureau, 1200 Third Ave., Ste. 824, San Diego, CA 92102 (714 232-3101).

JULIA PFEIFFER BURNS STATE PARK, Big Sur, California: Forty-two miles south of Monterey, where the mountains shoulder down to the sea, divers in wet suits watch sea lions, some 50 varieties of fish, and occasional whales coming by to scrape barnacles from their backs on rocky chimneys in the sea floor. All this and kelp beds, too. Nepenthe, a redwood pavilion designed by a Frank Lloyd Wright disciple, on a cliff 800 feet above the sea, is the place to eat and see what's going on in the area (408 667-2345). Information: Julia Pfeiffer Burns State Park, rt. 1, Big Sur, CA 93920 (408 667 2315).

HAWAII'S KONA COAST, Hawaii, Hawaii: On the leeward side of Hawaii Island there's good diving in the Pine Trees area (lava-tube caves big enough to drive a Volkswagen through, lionfish, lobsters, and a spectacular canyon) and the Red Hills area (good caves, including one in which you'll almost always see a shark, shrimp, and banded coral). Everywhere there are arches, coral, clear warm water, and fish. This island is good for diving because it's new in geologic terms and there's not a lot of sand to cover up food for the fish. Information: Gold Coast Divers, PO Box 2064, Kailua Kona, HI 96740 (808 329-1328).

BUCK ISLAND REEF NATIONAL MONUMENT, St. Croix, Virgin Islands: A mile and a half off the coast, this island has one of the finest marine gardens in the Caribbean, accessible via an underwater snorkel trail. Scuba divers can visit the underwater grottoes. Half- and whole-day trips are widely available in Christiansted. Information: PO Box 160, Christiansted, St. Croix, VI 00820 (809 773-1460).

VIRGIN ISLANDS NATIONAL PARK, St. John, Virgin Islands: National Park Service Rangers lead underwater snorkel tours for beginners; scuba divers can marvel at the coral reefs (flowerlike, vivid, full of tiny organisms). Information: the Superintendent, Virgin Islands National Park, PO Box 7789, St. Thomas, VI 00801 (809 775-2050).

TRIPS

The establishments that sponsor scuba courses for beginners usually also run extensive dive trip schedules to dive sites accessible only by boat, for experienced and/or certified divers; for lists of these operators in the area you want to visit, write PADI or NAUI (two of the national scuba-instruction certification organizations listed on p. 513). The following outfits also sponsor trips on a more or less regular basis.

CALIFORNIA: *The Diving Locker,* 1020 Grand Ave., San Diego, CA 92109 (714 272-1120), to Clemente Island and Coronado Island.

FLORIDA: Diving trips to the Keys are sponsored by the *Reef Shop Dive Center,* Rt. 1, Box 7, Islamorada, FL 33036 (305 664-4385); *The Diving Site,* 12399 Overseas Hwy., Marathon Shores, FL 33050 (305 289-1021); *Pennekamp Diving Headquarters,* 105920 Overseas Hwy., Key Largo, FL 33037 (305 451-1151); *Hall's Diving Center,* 1688 Overseas Hwy., Marathon, FL 33050 (305 743-5929); and *Key West Pro Dive Shop,* 1605 N Roosevelt Blvd., Key West, FL 33040 (305 296-3823). In the Palm Beach area, contact *Norine Rouse Scuba Club of the Palm Beaches,* 4708 N Dixie, W Palm Beach, FL 33407 (305 844-2466), for trips to see sunken ships full of porkfish, grunts, coneys, and other exotic fish. Around Pompano Beach, where the waters have reefs and drop-offs: *Professional Diving Schools of Florida,* 1540 N Federal Hwy., Pompano Beach, FL 33062 (305 785-0780).

ILLINOIS: In the Chicago area you can dive to some thirty Lake Michigan wrecks off charters operated by *Aquaventure,* 1655 Oakton St., Des Plaines, IL 60018 (312 297-7414). May through October are the best months, with visibility ranging up to 15 feet; full dive suits are always required.

NEW YORK: Dives to the wrecks of the *Coimbra Lightburne,* the *San Diego,* and the *Oregon* are sponsored by the *Coastal Diving Academy,* 108 W Main, Bay Shore, NY 11706 (516 666-3127). Dives in Lake George, Lake Erie, Seneca Lake, and the St. Lawrence River are the specialty of the *Nypenn Divers,* 400 Prospect St., Binghamton, NY 13905 (607 729-4988).

TEXAS: Along the coast of Padre Island not far from Corpus Christi, you can dive off oil platforms or three sunken Liberty ships; the water is warm and very clear. Information from *Padre Island Dive Shop,* 4455 S Padre Island Dr., Corpus Christi, TX 78411 (512 855-2821).

Touring America's Waterways

In the days before cities were strung together by highways, people traveled from one settlement to another along rivers and chains of lakes — and there were hundreds of them. Quite a few have been dammed up, polluted, or defaced by highways and factories. But there are still enough open and visible water courses to suit the needs of most recreationists, and you don't have to be an expert paddler to enjoy them. Some are easy enough for beginning canoeists in open-deck canoes. Others — whitewater torrents as wild now as they were 200 years ago — are serviced by experienced boatmen who will take you down in big rubber rafts.

FLATWATER CANOEING

The following waterways offer extensive opportunities for paddling trips easy enough for almost anyone — though you should check on conditions before you put in, since recent rainfalls or strong winds can turn normally navigable lakes and streams into trouble spots. Canoes are usually available for rent at about $7 to $15 a day, with packages and reductions available for multiday tours. The liveries are usually your best source of information about campsites en route. Most provide shuttle services from point of entry to final landing. Fees are based on the total road mileage involved.

EAST

THE ALLAGASH, Maine: As much a region as a 90-mile-long river and chain of lakes, the Allagash sweeps and swirls through one of the greatest wilderness areas in the East as it heads northward from near Churchill Lake along the US-Canadian border to its confluence with the St. John River. Countless other lakes and streams, in equally wild country, are accessible by portages — so you can canoe and fish to your heart's content. April through June are high-water months; fall foliage, which flames bright in early October, changes the scene once again. For more information on routes and liveries, contact: Maine Bureau of Parks and Recreation, Augusta, ME 04333 (207 289-3821).

THE ADIRONDACK CANOE ROUTES, New York: You feel like a 19th-century woodsman when you paddle through this hundred-mile-long chain of river-and-portage-connected lakes in New York's North Country. The waters are on the cold side, but clean enough to drink, and lovely for swimming and fishing. You can camp in three-sided log lean-tos on the shores of the lakes and on islands in the middle. The terrain along the route is mountainous, rocky, forested, and, except for the shelters, completely undeveloped. Information: New York State Department of Environmental Conservation, 50 Wolf Rd., Albany, NY 12233 (518 457-3522).

THE DELAWARE RIVER, Pennsylvania, New York, New Jersey: From the foothills of the Catskill Mountains in southern New York state to the Delaware Water Gap on the border of Pennsylvania and New Jersey, the Delaware ripples through some 120 miles of dense woodlands — the sort you wouldn't expect to find so close to the East's big cities. Liveries include Bob Lander's Ten Mile River Enterprises, Inc. (RD 2, Narrowsburg, NY 12764, 914 252-3925); Jerry's Three River Canoe Rentals and Campgrounds (PO Box 7, Pond Eddy, NY 12770, 914 557-6078); Kittatinny Canoes (Dingmans Ferry, PA 18328, 717 828-2700).

THE SHENANDOAH RIVER, Virginia: Snaking between the Massanutten Mountains and the Blue Ridge on this majestic stream, you will almost always have a panorama of forested hills in view — though occasionally the banks are given over to farmlands or summer homes. This goes on for nearly 100 miles, but the most popular trip is the 45-mile stretch between Luray and Front Royal, which can be paddled in a weekend. Foliage peaks in late September, while the fish (and, alas, the blackflies) are most active in early June. Shenandoah River Outfitters (RFD 3, Luray, VA 22835, 703 743-4159) provides canoes and shuttle service for this trip at standard rates.

SOUTH

THE BUFFALO RIVER, Arkansas: This 148-mile-long stream in northern Arkansas is speckled by gravel bars and edged by forests and cliffs full of waterfalls, caves, fern falls. The seasons — from the pink and white springs to the lush summers and through the stunning orange and red autumns — make each trip down the Buffalo a delight. Current is no problem; long pools alternate with rapids and riffles. Information: Buffalo National River, PO Box 1173, Harrison, AR 72601 (501 741-5443).

THE WHITE RIVER, Arkansas: What with the ghostlike early morning fogs, the mountains, and the cave-pocked bluffs along the shore, the plentiful wildlife and the good trout fishing, this 100-mile Arkansas stream provides a beautiful trip. Information: Batesville Chamber of Commerce, 409 Vine St., Batesville, AR 72501 (501 793-2378).

THE EVERGLADES NATIONAL PARK, Florida: In still water, the paddling is more strenuous, but the scenery — mangroves, big buttonwood trees, bays, and tunnels — is worth the effort. There are several short trails and one 100-miler that will keep you paddling for days. Winter months are best; you see more birds and the weather is more invigorating. Information: Everglades National Park, PO Box 279, Everglades, FL 33030 (305 247-6211).

OKEFENOKEE NATIONAL WILDLIFE REFUGE, Georgia: Leachings of decaying vegetation stain these still south Georgian waters black as a moonless night; and, smooth as glass, they reflect every leaf and twig of the moss-veiled cypress forests through which many of the canoe trails will take you. (Others cut through "prairies" — water-rooted versions of the ones you find in Kansas.) A limited-permit system ensures that when you canoe through the swamp, you'll have the campsite all to yourself. Route and rental information and permits: US Fish and Wildlife Service, PO Box 117, Waycross, GA 31501 (912 283-2580).

BLACK CREEK, Mississippi: Canoeing this Mississippi stream through forests of cypress, pines, and oaks, you camp on snow-white sandbars; and since the current is gentle, you can simply float if you want. Longest trip is about 45 miles, three days of canoeing, starting at Big Creek. Half the trip runs through National Forest land. For information on the trip and canoe rentals: De Soto National Forest, Black Creek Ranger District, PO Box 248, Wiggins, MS 39577 (601 928-4422).

MIDWEST

BLUE RIVER, Indiana: From Fredericksburg to this southern Indiana stream's confluence with the Ohio, there are 58-plus miles of clear deep green water edged by forests of redbud, dogwood, oak, maple. Good fishing for rock bass, especially in early summer. Details: Blue River Marina, PO Box 235, Milltown, IN 47145 (812 633-4806), and the Old Mill Canoe Rental, PO Box 60, Fredericksburg, IN 47120 (812 472-3140).

AU SABLE RIVER, Michigan: Along the 240 canoeable miles of this twisting Midwestern waterway you'll find quiet wooded shores, some in the Huron National Forest, and plenty of good fishing. Information: Oscoda–Au Sable Chamber of Commerce, 100 W Michigan Ave., Oscoda, MI 48750 (517 739-7322).

BOUNDARY WATERS CANOE AREA, Minnesota: Wild and vast, this system of streams, narrows, and island-dotted lakes created by glaciers eons ago offers — with surrounding Superior National Forest, nearby Voyageurs National Park, and Ontario's Quetico Provincial Park — some of the most extensive canoeing on the continent. Guides, liveries, and complete outfitting services are widely available in Grand Marais, Ely, and Crane Lake, Minnesota. Information: Superior National Forest, PO Box 338, Duluth, MN 55801 (218 727-6692).

OZARK NATIONAL SCENIC RIVERWAYS, Missouri: The Current River and its tributary the Jacks Fork, which make up the Riverway, together offer some 140 miles of woods, caves, springs, sinkholes, and pleasant, easy-to-negotiate pools and riffles. Route and rental information: Ozark National Scenic Riverways, PO Box 490, Van Buren, MO 63965 (314 323-4236).

WEST

RUSSIAN RIVER, California: Fast enough to be fun, but not too fast, the 60 miles of this California stream from the Lake Mendocino Dam to the Pacific are safe almost year-round and understandably popular. The waters — deep pools, small riffles, and moderate rapids — swirl you between steep forested banks, past shores full of vineyards, orchards, and stands of redwood that hide summer cottages, to open spaces where you can smell the salt air. Rentals and information: Burke's Russian River Canoe Rentals, PO Box 602, Forestville, CA 95436 (707 887-1222).

MISSOURI RIVER, Montana: Central Montana's wonderfully stark sagebrush-and-sandstone-cliff wilderness is nearly treeless except for occasional cottonwoods; and as it's a great place for sun, it's also among the best in the West (where most streams are wildwater torrents) for easy canoeing. May, June, and July are best for wildlife watching; the cottonwoods turn to gold in late September and October. Information: Missouri River Outfitters, PO Box 1212, Fort Benton, MT 59442 (406 622-3295).

WHITEWATER RAFTING

When you're knifing through the 20-foot-high waves of a river racing downstream at the rate of 50,000 or 60,000 cubic feet per second, and your clothes are drenched with the spray, and you can hardly hear the screams of your fellows for the noise of the river (something like the roar of a dozen freight trains), and when the same scenario repeats itself day after day — even the wildest roller coaster seems tame.

But even when the same river is flowing at its normal 5,000 cubic feet per second, and even in the East, where the torrential stretches of wilderness rivers are so short that whitewater trips usually last only a day, it's not hard to understand why river-running can get into your blood. Few other means of wilderness travel put you so close to the forces of nature. And if you're not the rugged, hardy type, another way to get deep into the wilderness without some kind of noisy motor simply doesn't exist. All of the country's mightiest rivers are accessible on trips run by commercial operators — both small outfits who take their craft down one or two streams in a given region, and larger organizations that have developed programs nationwide. Among the latter are the Sierra Club, 530 Bush St., San Francisco, CA 94108 (415 981-8634); the American River Touring Association, 445 High St., Oakland, CA 94601 (415 465-9355); and OARS, PO Box 67, Angels Camp, CA 95222 (209 736-4677).

Depending on where you go and when and who takes you, you may wield a paddle (with the guide in the rear shouting out instructions) or you may go along as just a passenger. In the very wildest waters, you'll probably go in big catamaran rafts. On other trips down other rivers, the outfitter will pack along inflatable canoes or kayaks, and you can get out and do some paddling on your own, even closer to the water level, when you tire of watching the cliffs, rocky banks, and forests go by — that is, if you're not tired out from the swimming, picnicking, hiking, fishing, and other diversions that the outfitters normally program into excursions. Between the river, the sourdough pancake breakfasts, the steaks and spuds dinners, the companionable evenings around the campfires, and the lullaby the river sings to you through the quiet canyon nights — a trip down a great waterway is one of those memorable vacation adventures that brings out the poet in you.

THE COLORADO RIVER (GRAND CANYON SECTION), Arizona: The most challenging of all river trips, and one of the most popular, is also, some people will tell you, one of the great moments of human experience. You shoot some 100 rapids — Badger Creek, Soap Creek, 25 Mile, House Rock, Unkar, Nevills, Sockdolager, Grapevine, and dozens of others that don't even have names — as you run the 280 miles between the most common put-in area near Lee's Ferry and the headwaters of Lake Mead. The soaring sculptured walls and the glowing colors of their rock layers are as grand when seen from below as they are when you stand on the Canyon rim. And, though the flow is controlled by the Glen Canyon Dam upstream, so that no single season is more tumultuous than any other, the river itself changes all the time. Summers are busy and hot; in spring you'll find temperatures in the comfortable 70s and 80s, blooming desert plants, and smaller crowds. For a complete list of outfitters (who go downstream in everything from dories to motor-powered rafts), write the Superintendent, Grand Canyon National Park, PO Box 129, Grand Canyon, AZ 86023 (602 638-2411).

THE MAIN SALMON, Idaho: A good trip for beginning your river-running career, Lewis and Clark's "River of No Return" offers enough deep-rolling rapids to keep you interested, but not so many that you'll spend your river hours in terror. On the 100-mile stretch between Cork Creek and Spring Bar, not far from Riggins — the stretch most commonly floated by commercial outfitters — there are warm springs and quiet pools where you can get out and splash, sandy beaches, spectacular canyons, desert hills, and, on the north-facing slopes, stands of Douglas fir. In one 10-mile stretch, the banks rise so steeply from the water's edge that there's not even a trail along the shore. Runs during high-water in May or June are wildest; the following months through Labor Day are quieter on the water. Actually, the river is floatable for 237 miles between North Fork and the confluence of the Salmon and the Snake. For a list of outfitters, including some who will take you the whole route, write the Idaho Outfitters and Guides Association, PO Box 95, Boise, ID 83701 (208 345-2648), or the Salmon National Forest, Box 780, North Fork, ID 83466 (208 865-2383).

THE MIDDLE FORK OF THE SALMON, Idaho: Along the 106-mile stretch floated by most outfitters — between Boundary Creek and the confluence with the Main Salmon — this river takes you through the River of No Return Wilderness, over 80 or more wild rapids, and into the second deepest gorge on the continent (Hell's Canyon on the Snake is the deepest). During rest stops and overnights, you can explore creeks and waterfalls, side canyons, and hot springs. Information: Challis National Forest, Challis, Idaho 83226 (208 879-4321). The American River Touring Association operates here. For details, contact ARTA, 445 High St., Oakland, CA 94601 (415 465-9355).

THE SELWAY RIVER, Idaho: Too rocky for floating most of the time, this is among the most challenging whitewater courses in the country during peak spring runoff in the last two weeks in June and the first two in July. (Trips book up well in advance.) You wouldn't want to pit yourself against the Selway on a first river trip, but it's a good bet for veteran floaters. The river's course takes you through the 1,239,840-acre Selway-Bitterroot Wilderness, among the US's largest, most of which is passable only on foot or by boat. Information on outfitters: Bitterroot National Forest, West Fork Ranger Station, Darby, MT 59829 (406 821-3269), or the Nezperce National Forest, Moose Creek Ranger Station, Grangeville, ID 83530 (208 983-2712).

THE ROGUE RIVER, Oregon: A National Scenic River, the 40 miles between Grave Creek and Foster Bar, about 25 miles from the Pacific, offer Class IV rapids, high canyons, rock gorges, wildlife, good fishing (for steelhead, chinook, and silver salmon), and historic sites — Zane Grey had a cabin at Winkle Bar. There's whitewater on rapids like Mule Creek Canyon and Devil's Staircase, but since there are long stretches of smooth water between them, commercial trips on the Rogue are good for families. Most operators run trips run between Grave Creek and Foster Bar. Private parties must have permits to run that stretch between late May and Labor Day. More information: Siskiyou National Forest, Galice Ranger District, PO Box 1131, Grants Pass, OR 97526 (503 479-3735).

YOUGHIOGHENY RIVER, Pennsylvania: The trip down the 6½-mile wild section of this famous Eastern whitewater stream lasts only a little over half a day — but you get quite a run for your money. The scenery, at any rate, is beautiful: laurel and rhododendron in the spring, wraithlike mists and lush forests in summer, and bright leaves in autumn. Four concessioners provide guided trips. Information: Ohiopyle State Park, PO Box 105, Ohiopyle, PA 15470 (412 329-4707 or 4704).

THE CHATTOOGA, South Carolina: After seeing "Deliverance," which was filmed here, a lot of people who didn't know any better tackled the whitewater in metal canoes, and the canoes usually ended up on the river's bottom, torn to pieces, or wrapped around rocks. In other words, this is no canoe trip for beginners. But in a raft, and with a guide, almost anyone can shoot the rapids. Wildwater, Ltd. (Long Creek, SC 29658, 803 647-5336) will show you how to scout them — great for helping you understand swift water. Other outfitters include Nantahala Outdoor Center, US-19 West, Box 41, Bryson City, NC 28713 (704 488-2175) and Southeastern Expeditions, 1955 Cliff Valley Way, Ste. 220, Atlanta, GA 30029 (404 329-0433).

THE RIO GRANDE, Texas: A stretch of the Rio Grande within Big Bend National Park takes you through some of the most isolated country in America. You won't find much whitewater, but the floating is spectacular. Most trips run through either Santa Elena Canyon, Boquillas Canyon, or Mariscal Canyon. Santa Elena is deepest, and, because of Rockslide Rapids, wildest; Mariscal, most remote; Boquillas, 22 miles from end to end, the longest and great for sunsets. Go in April to see a spectacular wildflower display, in May to see the bird migrations, or in October, which is locals' favorite time because of the great weather and the ordinarily reliable water flows. One portion of the river was recently designated a Wild and Scenic River. Information: Big Bend National Park, TX 79834 (915 477-2251).

THE GREEN RIVER (GRAY AND DESOLATION CANYONS), Utah: Were you to put in on the Green below Flaming Gorge and float all the way to Lake Powell, several hundred miles later, you wouldn't find more interesting river country than this stretch between Sand Wash (about 35 miles southwest of Myton) and Green River City (some 96 miles later). Gray Canyon has the biggest rapids by far, but there are some in Desolation which, in the words of one river rat, will "eat you up if you don't know what you're doing." Views from the boat take in stands of Douglas fir, cottonwood groves, and petroglyphs from the Fremont culture of 1,500 years ago. Floating season is May through late September; spring is wildest, July and August hottest. Information: Bureau of Land Management, PO Box AB, Price, UT 84501 (801 637-4584).

THE COLORADO RIVER (CATARACT CANYON SECTION), Utah: In all the 300-mile-long Colorado River system, this stretch of water in Canyonlands National Park offers some of the most technically demanding whitewater and some of the most exciting rafting in the country — even if you don't go in the spring, when the flow is ten times normal. Cataract Canyon lies just downstream of the Green's confluence with the Colorado; trips through the canyon begin either on the Green or the Colorado, and can continue downstream to the headwaters of Lake Powell. For information and a list of outfitters: Canyonlands National Park, Moab, UT 84532 (801 259-7167).

THE CHEAT RIVER, West Virginia: The great granddaddy of all Eastern whitewater runs, this one, through the Appalachian foothills, has more bumps, holes, waves, and hydraulics than any other 12-mile watercourse in the East. In all, there are some 38 major rapids laid practically end to end. The trip, which lasts a day, is most exciting in spring, but wild enough for almost anybody through October. Information: Travel Development Division, Office of Economic and Community Development, State Capitol, Charleston, WV 25305 (304 348-2286).

THE NEW RIVER, West Virginia: Actually one of the oldest rivers in the world, this Appalachian Mountain stream is edged by forests whose vegetation hides all sorts of tumbledown buildings, relics of long-gone railroad-shipping boom days. That gives you something to look at during the flatwater stretches, but unless you go during a very low-water period, there won't be very many of them. When the waves are 8 to 15 feet high in the rapids, as they are during spring runoffs, it's all you can do to hang on to your paddle. Wildwater Expeditions, Unlimited, Inc. (PO Box 55, Thurmond, WV 25936, 304 469-2551), runs a first-rate operation; for a list of other outfitters who run this superscenic river, write the Travel Development Division, Office of Economic and Community Development, State Capitol, Charleston, WV 25305 (304 348-2286).

Goin' Fishing: The Best Spots in America

America's number one participation sport has hooked 25% of the US population, so it's no wonder that huge amounts of money, not to mention bureaucratic time and effort, go into massive stocking programs. Just where you'll find all these fish at any given time can vary from year to year, depending on water conditions, weather, chemicals, and from season to season, as fish seek out the water temperatures they need to exist.

A long familiarity with the habits of fish in a single lake is almost a guarantee of hefty stringers, but, as the professional bass fishermen who fish many different lakes can tell you, it's enough to have reliable knowledge of the species' habits, and of the water temperatures, bottom conformations, shoreline, and so on, of the area you're fishing — information that is easily obtained from local fish and game authorities and from area marinas and bait and tackle shops.

EAST

Ocean fishing is big in all the coastal states — mainly for bluefish and stripers that migrate up and down the coast as they seek out congenial water temperatures. Inland, fishermen work the lakes and stalk the wily trout in streams and rivers.

MOOSEHEAD LAKE, near Greenville, Maine: The largest body of water in Maine, a sportfishing resort for over a century, provides landlocked salmon and brook and lake trout; deep waters (246 feet) and good oxygenation make the fishing good throughout the season — despite heavy fishing pressure from a variety of fishing camps around the shores. Information: Chamber of Commerce, Greenville, ME 04441 (207 695-2702).

OCEAN CITY, Maryland: The white marlin capital of the world sends fishermen out to the Baltimore and Washington Canyons, about 50 miles off shore, for dolphin, bonita, tuna, and wahoo. Surf casting and jetty fishing can also produce good fishing. Information: Chamber of Commerce, Rt. 1, PO Box 310A, Ocean City, MD 21842 (301 289-8559).

LAKE WINNIPESAUKEE, near Laconia, New Hampshire: The largest body of water in New Hampshire (72 square miles) offers some of the best stringers of lake trout and landlocked salmon in New England. Some 240 miles of shoreline on the mainland, and still more on 278 scattered islands, provide good habitat for bass and pickerel. Salmon are most active in April, May, and June (at the surface); later you've got to fish deeper. Lake trout are liveliest in April and May. Information: Lakes Region Association, PO Box 300, Wolfeboro, NH 03894 (603 569-1117), and the New Hampshire Fish and Game Department, 34 Bridge St., Concord, NH 03301 (603 271-3421).

BATTENKILL RIVER, near Manchester, Vermont: This famous Vermont fishing stream, a forest-edged, sun-dappled angler's idyll, is heavily fished, but its long, slow, waist-deep pools give the brookies and browns who inhabit it "a two-day look at every visitor" (according to one local veteran), and since the fish are not hatchery-bred, they don't regard man as a friend. The upshot is that the average fisherman doesn't get much: The stream is what you'd call a challenge. A nationally known tackle company headquartered nearby can answer your questions about when and where. Contact: Orvis, 10 River Rd., Manchester, VT 05254 (802 362-3434).

NEW RIVER, near Hinton, West Virginia: This fascinating fishing stream produces good creels of trophy white bass, smallmouth bass, muskellunge, walleye, rock bass, channel catfish, and carp. Best spots are downstream of the Bluestone Dam and at the New/Gauley confluence. Details: Department of Natural Resources/Wildlife, 1800 Washington St., E. Charleston, WV 25305 (304 348-2771).

SOUTH

The Southern fisherman heads for the Gulf or the Atlantic, where offshore oil rigs and artificial reefs draw huge populations of big fish, or for big impoundments managed with fishing in mind (in Arkansas, Kentucky, and Tennessee); crappie and largemouth bass are usually available, but depending on the area, you'll also get smallmouth, trout, stripers. Try western North Carolina and northern Georgia for trout.

LAKE EUFAULA, near Eufaula, Alabama: One of the finest largemouth fisheries in the country, not just for the quantity of fish available for the taking but also for their size. This impoundment of the Chattahoochee River along the Georgia-Alabama line is the site of many annual tournaments. Spring and fall are best. Information: Chamber of Commerce, Eufaula, AL 36027 (205 687-3879).

THE WHITE RIVER, Lakeview, Arkansas: Local fishermen call this wilderness Ozarks stream the trout capital of the world; the lake water released through turbines in the Bull Shoals Dam and Reservoir at the mouth of the White produce the 54° tailwaters that are ideal for trout propagation. For a list of outfitters, request the *Ozark Mountain Region Guide* from the Arkansas Department of Parks and Tourism, One Capitol Mall, Little Rock, AR 72201 (501 371-1511; or toll-free 800 482-8999 from Arkansas, or 800 643-8383 from the rest of the US).

BOCA GRANDE PASS, Boca Grande, Florida: One of the world's most famous fishing grounds, for the silvery legions of fighting tarpon that invade the Gulf every summer, will give you the liveliest action in June; the season extends from March through October. Information: Charlotte County Chamber of Commerce, 98 Tamiami Trail, Punta Gorda, FL 33950 (813 639-2222).

TEN THOUSAND ISLANDS, near Marco Island, Florida: This trackless mangrove wilderness of creeks, oyster-bottomed coves, and rivers, stretching 60-odd miles along the Gulf Coast, is one of the best US spots for snook, a battling tropical fish found only in southern Florida; May through July is the season. Information: Chamber of Commerce, 1700 N Tamiami Tr., Naples, FL 33940 (813 262-6141).

DESTIN, Florida: City officials call Destin "the world's luckiest fishing village," and with over 100 party boats and charters (the state's largest fishing fleet) charging into the Gulf every day, they just may be right. The quarry: pompano, grouper, king mackerel, sailfish. Information: Chamber of Commerce, PO Box 8, Destin, FL 32541 (904 837-6241).

THE KEYS, Florida: Islamorada, Marathon, and Key West are the three main centers in the area for bonefish, permit, and tarpon; Islamorada's sportfishing fleet is one of the US's largest. Information: Chamber of Commerce, 3330 Overseas Hwy., Marathon, FL 33050 (305 743-5417); Greater Key West Chamber of Commerce, 402

Wall St., Key West, FL 33040 (305 294-2587); and the Chamber of Commerce, PO Box 915, Islamorada, FL 33036 (305 664-4503).

ALLIGATOR ALLEY, between Naples and Fort Lauderdale, Florida: Along the canal that parallels rt. 84, bass and bluegills feed and reproduce in nearly ideal conditions (it's said that more tolls have been paid by fisherman than cross-state drivers). Fishing is best at low water. Information: Naples Chamber of Commerce, 1700 N 9th St., Naples, FL 33940 (813 262-6141).

LAKE OKEECHOBEE, Okeechobee, Florida: Some of the world's finest black crappie fishing can be found at this inland sea, the second largest body of fresh water located entirely within the US; you can also take bluegill and bass, plus catfish that sometimes take two hands to display. Season: November to April. Information: Okeechobee County Chamber of Commerce, 55 S Parrott Ave., Okeechobee, FL 33472 (813 763-6464).

BILLFISH ALLEY (DE SOTO CANYON), near Pensacola, Florida: Paralleling the coast for a hundred miles, this offshore depression offers an abundance of white and blue marlin, sailfish, tuna, dolphin, wahoo, and swordfish. (Best fishing is May through October.) Details: Visitor Information, 803 N Palafox, Pensacola, FL 32501 (904 433-3065); Chamber of Commerce, PO Box 640, Ft. Walton Beach, FL 32549 (904 244-8191); Panama City Beach Resort Council, PO Box 9473, Panama City Beach, FL 32407 (904 234-6575 in Florida; or toll-free from out of state, 800 874-7107).

LAKE JACKSON, near Tallahassee, Florida: Legendary catches of big largemouth bass are still par for the course at this angling hot-spot. Information: Chamber of Commerce, PO Box 1639, Tallahassee, FL 32302 (904 224-8116).

LAKE BARKLEY and KENTUCKY LAKE, near Cadiz, Kentucky: The 220,000 acres of water (with 3,500 miles of shoreline) shared by these two impoundments offer some of the state's most consistently fine bass fishing. Information: Land Between The Lakes, Tennessee Valley Authority, Golden Pond, KY 42231 (502 924-5602).

GRAND ISLE, Louisiana: Internationally known for the deep sea fishing it offers, especially around offshore oil rigs, this angling center offers quantities of party and charter boats. Details: Nez Coupe Souvenir & Tackle Shop, PO Box 171, Grand Isle, LA 70358 (504 787-3352).

OUTER BANKS, North Carolina: The proximity of the Gulf Stream to this slender finger of sand has brought good fishing close to shore. There are blue and white marlin, bonito, tuna, dolphin, barracuda, wahoo, sailfish, Spanish and king mackerel, and bluefish aplenty. Best fishing from April through November. Information: Outer Banks Chamber of Commerce, PO Box 90, Kitty Hawk, NC 27949 (919 261-2626).

CURRITUCK SOUND, Knotts Island, North Carolina: This huge shallow expanse of water between Kitty Hawk and the Virginia line offers some of the best freshwater fishing in the country — largemouth (no lunkers, but plenty of fish), plus rock bass, speckled trout, and white perch. The size and the hundreds of islands inside its bounds make a guide an essential. Good catches are the rule April through November, especially during southerly winds. Information: Elizabeth City Chamber of Commerce, 502 Ehringhaus St., Elizabeth City, NC 27909 (919 335-4365).

LAKES MARION and MOULTRIE, near Santee, South Carolina: This 171,000-acre impoundment of the Santee and Cooper Rivers, the first in the country with a landlocked striped bass program, offers some of the best fishing for these fighters, and has produced world's-record channel catfish, black crappie, and bowfin. Crappie and largemouth are especially plentiful. Information: Santee-Cooper Country, Drawer 40, Santee, SC 29142 (803 854-2131).

MIDWEST

Michigan, Minnesota, and Wisconsin together boast nearly five million fishing licenses, so it's not surprising that the angling is lively. Best is fishing for trout on Michigan's

Au Sable, Manistee, Pine, Rifle, and upper Muskegon Rivers; for steelhead in April; and for smallmouth bass in lakes in the northwest part of the lower peninsula.

In Minnesota, on the other hand, walleye is the fish — but you can also get smallmouth on the waters along the Canadian border; pike in the north, muskie in the Boy River chain, the Mantrap chain, and Big Lake and Leech Lake; and kamloops and native steelhead in the streams that empty into Lake Superior.

Missouri's fishing is mainly in the big southwestern reservoirs, but there's also float fishing for bass and panfish on the Jack's Fork, the Meramec, the Eleven Point, Niangua, James, Big Piney, and Current Rivers.

Ohio's western basin produces some of the US's best walleye fishing in spring and summer — off reefs, island shorelines, and submerged shoals.

Wisconsin produces salmon beginning in August around Kenosha, Milwaukee, and Racine. Fishermen troll for lake trout in summer and go for cohos and brown trout between Bayfield and Washburn. There are smallmouth in all the northern lakes, especially on the Door County peninsula in July and August.

LAKE MILLE LACS, near Brainerd, Minnesota: The fact that between opening day and late July the harvest of walleyes allegedly ran to 2½ tons of fish a day (or about 400,000 over the whole period one year) gives you an idea of the scope of the fishing here. Information: Chamber of Commerce, Brainerd, MN 56401 (218 829-2838).

WEST

Salmon fishing in Alaska is the standard by which all other salmon fishing is matched; you can get kings in May and June and silver salmon in autumn. But California is the bigger fishing state, with over two million holders of fishing licenses and 500 charter boats leaving from ports up and down the coast — for salmon in the north, and for yellowtail, albacore, and bonito in the south.

Trout reigns as king in Colorado. Ditto for Idaho; the Black Hills of South Dakota; western Montana; and the mountain lakes of California and Washington. Idaho's Snake, Clearwater, and Salmon Rivers are visited every year by huge quantities of steelhead and chinook in October, November, March, and April.

Hawaiian catches hold nearly half of the International Game Fish Association records for blue marlin — but there's also adventure to be had in going for bonefish (not in the flats as in Florida but in deep water) and surf-casting.

In Oregon and Washington, charters go for salmon and tuna from June through September. Chinook and silver run in summer and early fall, and steelhead in winter.

Meanwhile, there are walleye in Missouri River impoundments in South Dakota, and in North Dakota, smallmouths around islands and flooded butte tops of the various impoundments. In Utah, 200-mile-long Lake Powell has crappie, striped bass, and walleye; bass are active March through May and late September and early November.

THE SACRAMENTO RIVER, near Redding, California: Especially from Redding to Hamilton City (October through March), this river offers some of the best of the country's king salmon fishing. Hefty 25- to 30-pounders are common, and 40-pounders are occasionally pulled out. The Balls Ferry area south of Redding and the mouths of the American and Feather Rivers are also good, as is the steelhead fishing in the Klamath River: This is outdoor country par excellence. Information: Chamber of Commerce, PO Box 850, Red Bluff, CA 96080 (916 527-6220), and the Shasta-Cascade Wonderland Association, PO Box 1989, Redding, CA 96099 (916 243-2643).

THE KONA COAST, Hawaii, Hawaii: Most of those record fish caught in Hawaii were pulled in off the Kona coast. Charters are plentiful around the port of Kailua. Information: Hawaii Visitors Bureau, 2270 Kalakaua Ave., Honolulu, HI 96815 (808 923-1811); in Kailua, stop in at the HVB at World Square (808 329-1782).

COLUMBIA RIVER, below the Bonneville Dam, Oregon: May and June shad runs are so huge that nearly everyone catches one of these strong-running, high-leaping fish; stringers of 25 (the limit) are not uncommon. Information: Chamber of Commerce, Port Marina Park, Hood River, OR 97031 (503 386-2000); Smith's War Surplus, 1737 Cascade, Hood River, OR 97031 (503 386-3040).

ILWACO, Washington: Mid-April to October a fleet of charter boats goes out into the Pacific for kings and cohos and silvers at the Salmon Capital of the World; 300,000 salmon are caught offshore every year. Some fishermen, in fact, complain that they get their three-salmon limit almost as soon as they leave shore, and don't know what to do with the rest of the day. Information: Peninsula Visitors Bureau, PO Box 850, Long Beach, WA 98631 (206 642-2400).

FIREHOLE RIVER, Yellowstone National Park, Wyoming: With headwaters near Old Faithful, this river is small by Western standards; the rainbows and browns that inhabit it are most commonly just 10 to 16 inches long; and the fish big enough to keep (those over 16 inches) are hard to catch, even in late May and June and again from late August until season's close in late October, when the Mayfly and caddis-fly hatches bring the trout into action. But the Firehole is one of the nation's great "total experience" rivers: Rarely will you fish here without seeing wildlife, and the scenery — forests, mountains, and clouds of steam rising from the great meadows that flank the stream — is superb. Information: Bud Lilly's Trout Shop, Box 698, West Yellowstone, MT 59758 (406 646-7801 or, in winter, 406 586-5140).

FISHING SCHOOLS

In the last few years, a number of fishing pros and tackle manufacturers have taken it upon themselves to teach the bumbling angler the fine art of filling up a stringer — so even if you didn't grow up in a fishing family, you can quickly begin acquiring the skills necessary to keep you hauling them in with the best. Some provide instruction in fly-fishing and concentrate on trout; others teach you bait- and spin-casting techniques.

FENWICK FLY FISHING SCHOOLS, based in Westminster, California: The company that took the lead in mass-producing first-rate fly rods some 20 years ago now turns out top-notch fishermen at the two- to five-day courses it offers at locations all over the US and Mexico. The emphasis differs with the school locale; you can learn fly-fishing, bass and muskie tactics, steelhead techniques, and more. Information: Fenwick/Woodstream Company, PO Box 729, Westminster, CA 92683 (714 897-1066).

AMERICAN SPORTSMAN'S CLUB FLY FISHING SCHOOL, Steamboat Springs, Colorado: When you attend this organization's seminars, you live, with your 12 fellow students, at the ASC's rustic lodge — and you think trout from morning till night. This may not be to your taste, but you can't dispute the results. A 6-mile-stretch of the Elk River, a top Colorado fly-fishing stream which flows through lush meadows near the lodge, is leased for the school's exclusive use. Details: ASC, 8000 E Girard, Ste. 219, Denver, CO 80231 (303 755-7096).

BUD LILLY'S FLY-FISHING SCHOOL, West Yellowstone, Montana: More informal programs are run daily in this scenic area by well-known Montana fisherman Bud Lilly. Special courses are offered for ladies. Information: Bud Lilly's Trout Shop, Box 698, West Yellowstone, MT 59758 (406 646-7801).

H. L. LEONARD ROD COMPANY FLY-FISHING SCHOOLS, Central Valley, New York: The nation's oldest cane fly-rod maker, which started out in the instruction business with one-night-a-week courses for locals, now dazzles anglers from all over with three-day programs (May through September) in the Catskills; you practice on the Delaware and put up at the comfortable-rustic Buckhorn Lodge. Details: H. L. Leonard Rod Company, PO Box 393, Central Valley, NY 10917 (914 928-2301).

JOAN AND LEE WULFF FISHING SCHOOLS, Lew Beach, New York: Two of the nation's most famous fishermen share their expertise with anglers of all skill levels at their school in the Catskills. The Beaverkill (above) is one of several productive waters where you can practice. Mid-April through mid-July. Information: Joan and Lee Wulff Fishing School, Lew Beach, NY 12753 (914 439-4060).

ORVIS FLY-FISHING SCHOOL, Manchester, Vermont: This manufacturer of fine fishing gear, in business since 1856, has taught the intricacies of the sport to such luminaries as Supreme Court Justice Potter Stewart, and in the opinion of some who know the field, its program — which includes practice in the company's stocked ponds, dry runs on the famous Battenkill (see p. 521), and classroom sessions — is one of the best of its kind. In fall, Orvis sponsors a shooting school. Information: Orvis, 10 River Rd., Manchester, VT 05254 (802 362-3434).

Mountain Climbing and Mountains

Like all great sports, mountaineering allows the participant to choose the severity of the test — to match skills to challenge. Climbs can range from simple but rugged hikes requiring some technical work (that is, the use of chocks, nuts, ropes, ice axes, and crampons to get over vertical rock faces and icy surfaces) to high-altitude expeditions lasting weeks and requiring specialized skills, great reserves of strength and endurance, and sophisticated equipment. But one rule applies to all climbing: You are only as safe as your judgment and training are good. And it is always exhilarating.

Climbing is not a forbidding sport for a beginner, but the only way to start is with training. Best is a beginner's one-day course; in the West, at either the School of American Mountaineering in Grand Teton National Park, Moose, WY 83012 (307 733-2297); or Yosemite Mountaineering in Yosemite National Park, Yosemite, CA 95389 (209 372-1000). In the East there is one school, Eastern Mountain Sports, North Conway, NH 03860 (603 356-5433). A one-day course will give a not too strenuous introduction to belaying, anchoring, rappelling, and moderate-angle climbing; and even with these modest skills you will be able to take rocks which in your pre-course life you'd have judged unclimbable.

Better than a one-day course (which is really more orientation and encouragement than adequate training for more rigorous climbs) is a week or multiweek course, which provides an active, exciting vacation. The one you pick will depend on where you want to be and what you want to learn — rock work, snow and ice techniques, or expedition planning. Some courses concentrate on one subject; others combine the three.

CLIMBING SCHOOLS

PALISADE SCHOOL OF MOUNTAINEERING, Bishop, California: Week-long courses operating out of a base camp in the Palisades, a 10-mile-long crest of jagged peaks and glaciers. You can learn ice and snow climbing, rock climbing, expedition planning. Information: PO Box 694, Bishop, CA 93514 (714 935-4330).

BOB CULP CLIMBING SCHOOL, Boulder, Colorado: Classes in the basics as well as for advanced climbers, semi-private and private lessons in rock and ice work. Information: 1335 Broadway, Boulder, CO 80302 (303 442-8355).

FANTASY RIDGE SCHOOL OF ALPINISM, Estes Park, Colorado: Half-day to ten-day ice-, snow-, rock-climbing, and mountaineering seminars all year. Information: PO Box 2106, Estes Park, CO 80517 (303 586-5758).

LUTE JERSTAD ADVENTURES, Portland, Oregon: Lute Jerstad sponsors various courses at a number of locations around the region. You can learn rock skills or snow and ice travel. Information: PO Box 19527, Portland, OR 97219 (503 244-4364).

RAINIER MOUNTAINEERING, Tacoma, Washington: Seminars in snow and ice climbing. Information: 201 St. Helens St., Tacoma, WA 98402 (206 627-6242).

AMERICA'S MOUNTAINS — FOR THE CLIMBING

LONGS PEAK, near Estes Park, Colorado: The easiest way to this 14,255-foot summit in Rocky Mountain National Park involves nothing more than a long, albeit challenging walk from the Longs Peak Ranger Station and up boulder fields through the Keyhole (about eight miles). The north face route is less crowded, but climbing skills are required. For technical climbs, you must register with park rangers. Information: Rocky Mountain National Park, Estes Park, CO 80517 (303 586-2371).

MT. KATAHDIN, near Millinocket, Maine: The 5,267-foot peak in Baxter State Park, the northern terminus of the Appalachian Trail, rises sharply as you get close to the 4,000-foot timberline. Most routes don't require ropes, and the climb takes a day — but slopes full of loose rock can make the going tough. Information: Baxter State Park, 64 Balsam Dr., Millinocket, ME 04462 (207 723-5140).

MT. WASHINGTON, near North Conway, New Hampshire: The view from the 6,288-foot summit — the "second greatest show on earth," according to no less than P. T. Barnum — attracts hikers by the thousands. The trails up are steep, but not *that* steep. The danger, instead, lies in the weather, reputedly the worst in the world. It is treacherous, and ferocious snowstorms *do* blow up on a regular basis with practically no warning—even in summer. Information: The Appalachian Mountain Club, Pinkham Notch Camp, Gorham, NH 03581 (603 466-2727).

MT. MARCY, near Lake Placid, New York: This 5,344-foot Adirondack peak can be reached in a day over a variety of routes — most of them steep trails that make you wish you were in better shape. The forests at the bottom — full of ferns and trees whose foliage seems almost electric green — may remind you of the Pacific Northwest rain forests. Information: New York State Department of Environmental Conservation, Bureau of Publications, 50 Wolf Rd., Albany, NY 12233 (518 457-3521).

MT. HOOD, near Government Camp, Oregon: The 11,235-foot summit of this inactive volcano has been conquered by a blind man, a man with no legs, several adventurers with artificial limbs, a five-year-old, a 79-year-old woman, and travelers on skis, bikes, and in tennis shoes; only Mt. Fuji is more popular as a summit destination. Nonetheless, this climb takes technical know-how and preparation; it is the inexperienced, poorly equipped climber who is most apt to be injured (and well over a hundred people have lost their lives on the mountain). Most people follow the southside route, which departs from the new Wy'East Day Lodge, where you can register and get current conditions at a 24-hour climbing station. Then you're off for the beautiful trip — beginning at midnight, past scenic glaciers and fumaroles. For details on routes, contact the Mt. Hood National Forest, 19559 SE Division St., Gresham, OR 97030 (503 667-0511).Guided trips are available through the Mazamas Hiking and Climbing Club, 909 NW 19th Ave., Portland, OR 97204.

MT. RAINIER, near Ashford, Washington: Visible on a clear day for over a hundred miles in all directions, this 14,410-foot mountain, the fifth highest in the lower 48 states, is lush with wildflowers and giant forests below the 6,500-foot timberline, heavily glaciated above it. The two-day trip to the top, which takes you through fields of crevasses and crumbling lava, is long, strenuous, and demanding — but anyone in good condition can do it with a guide. Information: Mt. Rainier National Park, Tahoma Woods Star Route, Ashford, WA 98304 (206 569-2211).

THE GRAND TETON, near Jackson, Wyoming: Looking at it from below, you'd never think that relatively inexperienced climbers could safely attack the awe-inspiring 13,770-foot summit. However, the granite rock (solid enough that you can trust it) offers plenty of handholds and footholds — everything you need to climb a mountain, one step at a time, with some training and the proper equipment. Exum Mountain Guides, which operates the School of American Mountaineering (Moose, WY 83012, 307 733-2297) will take you up on the two-day climb to the top after you've spent two days in the climbing school. Information: Grand Teton National Park, PO Box 170, Moose, WY 83012 (307 733-2880).

Wilderness Trips on Foot

Building your backpacking skills to the point that you can go deep into a trackless wilderness for a few weeks and come out none the worse for wear takes some time. But it's not impossible. Day hikes, for example, are a good introduction. All the national parks and forests, state parks and forests, and various other public lands have trails of various lengths that are perfect for simple walks. You'll be breaking in your boots so that over extended treks blisters will be less likely to develop, and you'll be building up your stamina.

From there, short trips close to home are your best bet. Or you can sign up for one of the various outdoor programs that school tenderfeet in wilderness and hiking skills. Guided trips build confidence and provide companionship. A few areas of the United States have the counterparts of the hikers' huts scattered all over the Alps; you don't have to carry a tent or even food.

Then there are thousands of square miles of hikable terrain all over the country, with easy trails for novices, more rugged ones (steeper, less well maintained) for better hikers, and huge wildernesses where you can hike cross-country with just a topographic map and compass.

OUTDOOR TRAINING SCHOOLS

Some adults are lucky enough to have learned how to handle themselves in the wilderness when they were young — in the company of backpacking-loving relatives. Others must acquire camping skills on their own, and learn about everything from tree identification to back country first aid from books. For the very timid, however, there's no better introduction to woodcraft than one of the handful of outdoor training schools offered by a number of organizations around the country. The National Outdoor Leadership School (NOLS) and Outward Bound, listed below, are among the most important. You can find out about others in magazines like *Backpacker* (1 Park Ave., New York, NY 10016) and *Outside* (1165 N Clark, Chicago, IL 60610), where most advertise their services.

OUTWARD BOUND, based in Greenwich, Connecticut: With schools on Hurricane Island in Maine, and in Colorado, Minnesota, North Carolina, New Mexico, and Oregon; at each, the aim is to help you grow by challenging you. Information: Outward Bound, 384 Field Point Rd., Greenwich, CT 06830 (203 661-0797 or 800 243-8520).

NATIONAL AUDUBON SOCIETY ECOLOGY CAMPS, based in New York, New York: These July and August programs held in Connecticut, Maine, Wisconsin, and Wyoming, focus on area ecosystems; you lodge in cabins, bungalows, and lodges in each area and do your learning on field trips. Great for families. Information: National Audubon Society, 4150 Dartley, Ste. 5, Boulder, CO 80303 (303 499-0219).

AMERICAN FORESTRY ASSOCIATION CONSERVATION RETREATS, Cashiers, North Carolina: Young and old, singles, couples, and families lodge in the comfortable High Hampton Inn while attending classes in subjects as varied as backcountry first aid, fly casting, mountain folklore, orienteering, small woodlot management, passive solar design, wood for home heating, growing Christmas trees, wildflower identification, and gemology. Information: AFA, 1319 19th St., NW, Washington, DC 20036 (202 467-5810).

BOULDER OUTDOOR SURVIVAL SCHOOL, Provo, Utah: The mountains, deserts, and canyonlands of Utah are the setting for this small but venerable institution's 14- and 30-day programs. You learn primitive fire-building techniques, trap-and-snare construction, plant identification, primitive direction finding, shelter construction, and more. But increased self-confidence and spiritual awareness, and enhanced interpersonal relationships, are equally important benefits. Information: BOSS, PO Box 7215, University Station, Provo, UT 84602 (801 224-5183).

AMERICAN HIKING SOCIETY, based in Washington, DC: This hikers' lobbying organization sponsors occasional trail cleanup trips. Information: 1701 18th St., NW, Washington, DC 20009 (202 234-4609).

NATIONAL WILDLIFE FEDERATION CONSERVATION SUMMITS, based in Washington, DC: Classes and informative field trips in Colorado, New York State, North Carolina, and Wisconsin, held from June through August, focus on natural history and ecology; the seminars are short and the programs are wonderful for families. Information: National Wildlife Federation, 1412 16th St., NW, Washington, DC 20036 (703 790-4363).

NATIONAL OUTDOOR LEADERSHIP SCHOOL (NOLS), based in Lander, Wyoming: This organization, originally established to school wilderness-trip leaders in certain outdoor skills, offers courses in backpacking, minimum-impact camping, cross-country skiing, kayaking, and climbing, in Alaska, Washington, and Wyoming all year. Information: Box AA, Lander, WY 82520 (307 332-6973).

EASY LONG TRIPS

On these trips, you don't have to pack anything more than the clothes you'll need for the time you're away from home. Hikers' huts and inns provide your shelter.

YOSEMITE NATIONAL PARK, Yosemite, California: The High Sierra camps in this park are among the few places in the US where you can stay in the mountains overnight without having to camp out. The five villages of sex-segregated tent-dormitories are roughly nine miles apart; hot showers, linen, blankets, soap, and towels, and breakfast and dinner are provided for about $50 per person per night. Reservations (available in writing beginning December 1, and usually gone within two weeks) are essential. Information: Yosemite Park & Curry Co., Yosemite National Park, CA 95389 (209 373-4171).

GLACIER NATIONAL PARK, West Glacier, Montana: You can't exactly backpack from Sperry to Granite Park — the two rugged stone chalets in this park — but you can do overnight backpacks first to one and then to the other, returning to your car between times. Only the restrooms, in separate buildings, and the kitchens at both chalets have been modernized, so they're much as they were when built around World War I. Both are lit after dark by candlelight, both are in the National Register of Historic Places, and both are open only in July and August; rates are around $35 a night including three meals. Reserve well in advance. Information: Belton Chalets, Inc., PO Box 188, West Glacier, MT 59936 (406 888-5511).

WHITE MOUNTAINS NATIONAL FOREST, around North Conway, New Hampshire: In the heart of the Presidential range, a system of hikers' huts maintained by the Appalachian Mountain Club gives you almost unlimited hiking variety — both above and below tree line. No two are quite alike: Lakes of the Clouds, situated at the edge of two icy blue lakes above tree line, seems relatively new; the Madison Hut, just above tree line, is built of stone and seems almost ancient. Blankets (but not linen), dinner, and breakfasts are provided for the nightly charge, about $25 a person. Reservations are essential. Information: the AMC, Pinkham Notch Camp, Gorham, NH 03581 (603 466-2727).

INN-TO-INN HIKING, around Vermont: A group of country inns in the area have teamed up to offer special trips during which you sleep in big brass beds under antique quilts, soak off your sore muscles in claw-footed bathtubs, and either carry your own gear in a pack between inns — or go with a group and have everything ferried from one overnight stop to the next by car. Two organizations offer similar trips: Hike-Skitour Vermont, RFD #1, Chester, VT 05143 (802 875-3631), and the Churchill House Inn, Brandon, VT 05733 (802 247-3300).

GUIDED TRIPS

Not all organizations that sponsor trips for groups furnish the gear you'll need; some provide everything, while some will set you up with everything but a sleeping bag. Make sure to confirm this in advance, and find out whether the rates — usually from about $25 to $55 per day — include food, sleeping gear, lodging the night before the trip begins (if necessary), guides, equipment, and the like. For extensive lists of organizations offering group backpacking trips, consult Pat Dickerman's *Adventure Travel,* the best source of information about North American trips ($9.45 postpaid from Adventure Guides, Inc., 36 E 57th St., New York, NY 10022, 212 355-6334).

AMERICAN FORESTRY ASSOCIATION, headquartered in Washington, DC: Trips lasting five to ten days are offered in Montana, Idaho, Colorado, Wyoming, Arizona, California, West Virginia, and Washington state — most with pack stock carrying the gear. Fees include food and all the gear you need except your clothes and sleeping bag. Information: American Forestry Association, 1319 18th St., NW, Washington, DC 20036 (202 467-5810).

APPALACHIAN MOUNTAIN CLUB, Gorham, New Hampshire: This group's guided overnight hikes give you insight into the White Mountains' natural and social history. Information: AMC, Pinkham Notch Camp, Gorham, NH 03581 (603 466-2727).

CAMP DENALI, McKinley Park, Alaska: Expeditions and seminar-type wilderness workshops give you a chance to explore subarctic tundra, rocky ridges, cross glacial streams with groups of up to 24. The first two weeks in June offer superb birding and wildflower viewing (under 24 hours of daylight); in late August and early September, sandhill cranes can be seen in migration, one of nature's great spectacles. Information: Camp Denali, McKinley Park, AK 99755 (907 683-2302 September through May, 907 683-2290 the rest of the year).

KENAI GUIDE SERVICE, Kasilof, Alaska: Backpacking above timberline, June through August, at the base of dark, rocky pinnacles, alpine meadows and gorges, glaciers and cliffs, snowfields. Information: Kenai Guide Service, PO Box 40, Kasilof, AK 99610 (907 262-5496).

THE SIERRA CLUB, headquartered in San Francisco, California: The conservation organization offers a variety of backpacking, rafting, and skiing trips, including some, the so-called service trips, on which you clean up the trails in a specific area. Information: Sierra Club, Outing Department, 530 Bush St., San Francisco, CA 94108 (415 981-8634).

UNIVERSITY OF THE WILDERNESS, headquartered in Evergreen, Colorado: Five- to ten-day trips take you through the mountains, deserts, river canyons, and swamps of the southern and western US; seminars and workshops in writing about and photographing the wilderness also available. Information: University of the Wilderness, PO Box 1687, Evergreen, CO 80439 (303 674-9724).

BEST BACKPACKING SPOTS

There's good backpacking all over the country — even in the Midwest, where most of the forests have given way to farms and pastures. Best hiking and backpacking, however, lie in one of 11 general regions — Alaska, the Northwest Coast ranges, the Cascade range (slightly inland in Washington, Oregon, and northern California), the Columbia Plateau (just slightly inland from the Cascades), the Rockies (swooping through Idaho, western Montana, most of Wyoming and Colorado, and northern New Mexico), the Great Desert (covering most of Nevada), the Sierra (in California), the Colorado Plateau (northern Arizona, northwestern New Mexico, the southern two-thirds of Utah), the Ozarks of northern Arkansas and southern Missouri, the Appalachians (extending from northern Maine through Tennessee and Virginia), and the north woods of northern Michigan and Wisconsin and Minnesota. Each area has its particular characteristics.

Alaska's mountains, valleys, forests, and oceans are all wilderness; the climate is wet and temperate in the southern part of the state, drier and much colder (with winters that fall to 50° below) north of the Alaskan range, and drier and colder yet north of the Brooks range, where large trees simply do not exist and the vegetation has to hug the ground to survive the winds. Trails and cross-country travel are both possible, but mosquitoes, bad in June, sometimes make the wilds unpleasant.

The Northwest Coast ranges, with peaks less than 8,000 feet, are primarily distinguished by their weather — wet, with about 200 inches of rain each year — and the resultant lush growth of cedars, firs, hemlocks, spruces, redwoods, ferns, mosses, shrubs. Summer is the driest season; trail use is usually moderate. The Cascade range, paralleling the Northwest Coast range, has peaks up to 10,000 feet, somewhat lighter precipitation, dense forests except in areas covered by relatively recent lava flows, good trails — and all-around fine wilderness. The Sierra, made famous by John Muir, are known for their good hiking — and with reason. Not only are there awesome glaciated granite peaks (which are characteristic), but the climate is somewhat drier than along the coast, with low-altitude forests of ponderosa, yellow, and lodgepole pine, and white and red fir giving way to alpine lakes and lichen-covered granite boulders as you follow uphill trails (which are plentiful); in addition, mosquitoes and other pests are usually absent. It's not hard to understand why the area is heavily trafficked.

The Columbia Plateau, on the other hand, gets relatively little use. Home of some of the largest populations of cougar in the country, of eagles, hawks, salmon, and sturgeon (and relatively insect-free because of the overall aridity), it has areas of recent volcanic activity, like moonscapes; ponderosa pineland; alpine terrain; and canyons like the celebrated Hell's Canyon and Snake River Canyon. A good many people float the streams, but scarcely anyone ventures uphill. The Great Desert area, cut by mountain ranges of sculptured rock, is the wildest and least used. People think of it as hot and boring. Actually, it boasts a wide variety of terrain: handsome stands of the weird Joshua tree (in the Mojave Desert), the cactus of the Sonora Desert (archetypical desert), and sagebrush and cottonwood country in its Great Basin section. There aren't many designated backpacking trails, but if you've got the experience to go cross-country, this is a place to do it.

The Colorado Plateau is characterized by its weirdly shaped buttes, canyons, mesas, and a range of environments from desert to alpine. It's hikable so long as you're prepared.

The Rockies, on the other hand, require less experience. More than 40 monuments, forests, and parks make this Valhalla for foot travelers; there are snow-capped peaks, fields of wildflowers, alpine lakes, icy streams, slopes full of conifers and deciduous trees. With the Sierra, this is the US's prime backpacking territory.

The Ozarks offer some backpacking through dense forests in low mountains and shallow valleys, scattered with caves and underground rivers; this is especially good if you want to travel cross-country, though long trails have recently become more abundant. The northwoods, on the contrary, are full of trails. Flat and rolling countryside makes the going fairly easy as well, and huge numbers of lakes offer fine campsites.

In the East, the Appalachians make for the best backpacking. The peaks are lower and more rounded than those in the West, but many of the grades are just as steep as those in the rest of the country. The Appalachian Trail runs the length of the chain from Maine to Georgia; the Long Trail runs for 265 miles along the spine of the Green Mountains in Vermont. (For details about these long trails, contact the Appalachian Trail Conference, PO Box 236, Harpers Ferry, WV 25425, 304 535-6331; or the Green Mountain Club, PO Box 889, Montpelier, VT 05602, 802 223-3463).

In addition to these long trails, there is yet a third — the recently designated North Country Trail, the country's longest, which runs for 3,246 miles from Crown Point, New York, across seven states to Four Bears Memorial Park, North Dakota. Information: North Country Trail Association, PO Box 311, White Cloud, MI 49349 (207 794-6062).

OUACHITA NATIONAL FOREST, Hot Springs, Arkansas: Some of the state's best hiking is to be found along the ridge-climbing, viewful, 175-mile-long Ouachita National Recreation Trail and its 40-odd miles of spurs. Details: Ouachita National Forest, PO Box 1270, Hot Springs, AR 71901 (501 321-5202).

OZARK NATIONAL FOREST, Russellville, Arkansas: More than 80 miles of the Ozark Highlands Trail have been completed. The woods are most beautiful in spring, when dogwoods bloom by the thousand, and during fall foliage season. Details: Ozark National Forest, PO Box 1008, Russellville, AR 72801 (501 968-2354).

TONTO NATIONAL FOREST, Phoenix, Arizona: The largest national forest in the state, with more than 2.8 million acres, a good trail system, and four wilderness areas that take in everything from desert at an altitude of 1,500 feet to fir and pine forest at 7,000 feet. You'll find desert, mountains, and canyons, grassland, piñon, and ponderosa pine in the Mazatzal Wilderness; a maze of box canyons and arid mountains covered with chaparral in the Sierra Ancha Wilderness; and forbidding, barren mountains soaring from the desert floor in the Superstition Wilderness. Experience in desert travel is important (and you must carry water). Information: Tonto National Forest, PO Box 29070, Phoenix, AZ 85038 (602 261-3205).

KLAMATH NATIONAL FOREST, Yreka, California: Here are outstanding backpacking possibilities in a state that is full of them, because of the size (almost 1.7 million acres) and the fine forests of pine, cedar, fir, and hemlock that cover mountains ranging up to 8,000 feet. You can hike hundreds of miles of trails, most just moderately steep, and cross-country in the roadless areas of the Salmon-Trinity Alps Primitive Area and the Marble Mountain Wilderness (pine and fir forests, meadows, icy streams, alpine lakes). In the spring and fall, you'll see a spectacular wildfowl show, as birds from Canada and Alaska, moving along the Pacific flyway, converge on the eastern part of the forest. The Pacific Crest Trail also runs through the Klamath. Information: Klamath National Forest, 1312 Fairlane Rd., Yreka, CA 96097 (916 842-6131).

NEZPERCE NATIONAL FOREST, Grangeville, Idaho: An incredible trail system — 2,700 miles — makes this 2.2-million-acre forest one of the best for backpacking in the Rockies. An elevation range from 1,000 feet to 10,000 feet makes for plenty of variety — lowland meadows and cool mountain forests. A portion of the River of No Return Wilderness Area, the largest classified wilderness in the US, lies within the Nezperce. Details: Nezperce National Forest, 319 E Main, Grangeville, ID 83530 (208 983-1950).

SUPERIOR NATIONAL FOREST, Duluth, Minnesota: One of the finest forest areas in the country, these 3 million acres take in a million acres of virgin forest scattered with lichen-covered granite outcrops and lakes — about two thousand of them, with rocky shorelines, on some, and islands and sand beaches. The fishing — for walleye, musky, northern pike, trout, and bass — is superb; some people come for that alone. Information: Superior National Forest, PO Box 338, Duluth, MN 55801 (218 727-6692).

TOIYABE NATIONAL FOREST, Reno, Nevada: The largest national forest in the lower 48 states, the Toiyabe is scattered across central, southern, and western Nevada, and the east slopes of the Sierra Nevada Range in eastern California. The Toiyabe has High Sierra environments with alpine lakes, icy streams, and coniferous forests; and desert country with cactus, creosote bush, yucca, and above that juniper and piñon pine. Hundreds of miles of trails poke into every corner of its 3.4 million acres; those in California's Hoover Wilderness near Yosemite are heavily used, while those in the high desert ranges of central Nevada are quiet. Temperatures are not as forbidding as you might expect. For a few brief weeks, generally in October, you can gather the tasty piñon pine nuts, long an important food staple for the native Americans of Nevada and California, and a great delicacy nowadays. Information: Toiyabe National Forest, 111 N Virginia St., Reno, NV 89501 (702 784-5331).

WILLAMETTE NATIONAL FOREST, Eugene, Oregon: You can do outstanding backpacking on good trails through 1.7 million acres, 300,000 of which have been designated as wilderness: the 16,200-acre Diamond Peak Wilderness, a cluster of volcanic peaks covered with fir, hemlock, pine, and meadows, scattered with lakes; the 100,208-acre Mount Jefferson Wilderness, which surrounds an extinct, glacier-covered volcano; the 285,302-acre Three Sisters Wilderness, whose 330 miles of trails take you through cedar, fir, pine, and spruce forests, alpine tundra, meadows, and expanses of basalt and obsidian left from recent volcanic activity; and the 46,655-acre Mount Washington Wilderness, most of which is lava flow, lakes, ponds, and flatland. Information: Willamette National Forest, PO Box 10607, Eugene, OR 97440 (503 687-6521).

SISKIYOU NATIONAL FOREST, Grants Pass, Oregon: The low mountains in the southwestern corner of the state are covered by wonderful flowering bushes — wild lilac, azaleas, and rhododendrons among them — and crossed by fine fishing streams, including the celebrated Rogue. You can hike along the Rogue River Trail, a part of the new 36,038-acre Wild Rogue Wilderness, through the rugged Coast Range; but the prime backpacking area is the Kalmiopsis Wilderness, 179,650 acres of rocky hills and low canyons where you'll see interesting hardwoods and shrubs, some quite rare. Hornets, yellow jackets, and rattlesnakes are common. Superb fishing in fall during the massive salmon and steelhead migration. Information: Siskiyou National Forest, PO Box 440, Grants Pass, OR 97526 (503 479-5301).

ASHLEY NATIONAL FOREST, Vernal, Utah: The 236,509-acre High Uintas Primitive Area — a wonderful expanse of lakes, forests, meadows, and rocky mountains, which the Ashley National Forest shares with the Wasatch National Forest — is what most people come to hike, but similar environments can be found throughout the forest, particularly on the east, and they're far less crowded. Lakes, streams full of trout, and exposed sandstone formations are also here. Information: Ashley National Forest, 437 E Main, Vernal, UT 84078 (801 789-1181).

For the Mind

Regional American Theaters

A note in the program tells you to keep the aisles free of obstructions, and when the lights go down (there's no curtain) and the actors come whooping down the aisles around you, you know why.

Regional theater isn't always so exuberant, but it's not provincial either. The old situation, in which all you had in the hinterlands was dinner theater and summer stock of varying quality, no longer exists. Regional theater — theater out of New York City — has entered its prime, and some of the most exciting and innovative productions, the kind that "lower the drawbridge between actor and audience," in the words of one critic, go onto stages outside Manhattan. Regional theaters provide actors an opportunity to get back to the basics, and give talented local authors and first-timers a chance to get their works produced. Meanwhile, whether the play ends up on Broadway or never gets more than a reading, audiences get some lively dramatic experiences.

EAST

THE HARTFORD STAGE COMPANY, Hartford, Connecticut: Housed in a $2.5 million structure designed by Robert Venturi, this innovative organization presents an eclectic assortment of about six plays during its season; the focus is on American playwrights. Information: the Hartford Stage Co., 50 Church St., Hartford, CT 06103 (203 525-5601).

LONG WHARF THEATRE, New Haven, Connecticut: In two separate theaters, you'll see Shakespeare and Shaw, revivals and premieres, plus many new works — some fully staged, some given as readings. Many, many Long Wharf productions go on to Broadway. Among past hits: *The Gin Game, Sizwe Banzi Is Dead, The Shadow Box.* Information: Long Wharf Theatre, 222 Sargent Dr., New Haven, CT 06511 (203 787-4282).

TRINITY SQUARE REPERTORY COMPANY, Providence, Rhode Island: A dozen major productions of modern and original works and classical dramas are staged annually in two theaters. Trinity Rep makes headlines for itself as much for its characteristic style — verging on the flamboyant — as for the plays themselves. Information: Trinity Square Repertory Company, 201 Washington, Providence, RI 02903 (401 351-4242).

ARENA STAGE, Washington, DC: One of the oldest, most consistently admired American theater companies, this one, founded in 1950, is noted for developing American drama and for introducing foreign (particularly Eastern European) plays to the US. Three stages seat 827, 514, and 180; the last is used for small musical revues and experimental works. Jon Voight and James Earl Jones have performed here; past productions include *After the Fall* by Arthur Miller; *Teibele and Her Demon,* an adaption of an Isaac Bashevis Singer short story; *A Lesson from Aloes* by Athol Fugard; *Tomfoolery* by Tom Lehrer; George Bernard Shaw's *Major Barbara*; and *Design for*

Living by Noel Coward. Reservations essential. Information: Arena Stage, 6th and Maine Ave., SW, Washington, DC 20024 (202 488-3300).

SOUTH

ACTORS THEATRE OF LOUISVILLE, Louisville, Kentucky: In recent years, the two stages here have become bright spots on the American theater scene. The annual Festival of New American Plays, initiated in 1977, has gained international critical attention and has sent graduates on to successful runs on both coasts. The four dozen or so productions each season, both classics and innovative new works, are presented in a main auditorium and a smaller upstairs theater — both located in a grand old columned building that has been designated a National Historic Landmark. Information: Actors Theatre of Louisville, 316–320 W Main St., Louisville, KY 40202 (502 584-1205).

DALLAS THEATER CENTER, Dallas, Texas: You'll see conventional dramas on the main stage, plays by contemporary authors — six a season, many of them premières — in a downstairs theater. Preston Jones' *A Texas Trilogy* got its start here. Information: Dallas Theater Center, 3636 Turtle Creek Blvd., Dallas, TX 75219 (214 526-8210).

ALLEY THEATRE, Houston, Texas: Classical drama and new works chosen for ideas and language (usually nine a season) are presented on a multispace stage in one theater, two or three plays in another. Members of the theater's own company alternate between the two stages, both of which are located in a stunning concrete-and-glass structure in the Houston Civic Center. The Alley is one of the country's oldest regional theaters. Information: Alley Theatre, 615 Texas Ave., Houston, TX 77002 (713 228-9341).

MIDWEST

CINCINNATI PLAYHOUSE IN THE PARK, Cincinnati, Ohio: World premières of plays by new American playwrights, classics, rarely presented works, musicals, and comedies, in two theaters (with 219 and 629 seats respectively) are the staples of this much-praised regional professional company. Information: Cincinnati Playhouse in the Park, PO Box 6537, Cincinnati, OH 45206 (513 421-3888).

GOODMAN THEATRE, Chicago, Illinois: Again, two stages — the first for classical dramas and modern plays (including frequent world premières), the second for intimate or avant-garde productions. The second oldest regional theater in the country, the Goodman also mounts an annual production of the holiday favorite, *A Christmas Carol.* Information: Goodman Theater, 200 S Columbus Dr., Chicago, IL 60603 (312 443-3800).

ORGANIC THEATER, Chicago, Illinois: Producing three new plays a season, this creative repertory company has been described as "visceral," "imaginative," "loud," "funny," and "original." Sometimes the actors and directors (an "extended family," in the words of one long time member, because the troupe has been together for so long) pick the play, then improvise at will; sometimes the group itself writes the material from scratch or from an as-yet-unscripted novel (*Bleacher Bums* and Mary Renault's *The King Must Die* in recent years). Sometimes who will play what role isn't decided until the first preview. It sounds chaotic — but it works. David Mamet's *Sexual Perversity in Chicago* started out here. Information: Organic Theater, 3319 N Clark St., Chicago, IL 60657 (312 327-5588).

GUTHRIE THEATER, Minneapolis, Minnesota: With 1,441 seats, the Guthrie is the largest of the country's regional theaters. It also has the longest season (nine months) and the largest resident company (30 actors), and its house, which shares a handsome contemporary building with the Walker Art Center, is one of the most unusually designed, with a unique thrust stage that gives audiences access to three sides of the stage; no member is more than about 50 feet from the actors. Classical drama, Middle European revivals, and American plays rotate in repertory Mondays through Saturdays. Michael Moriarty and Tovah Feldshuh are among scores of actors who got their start, or polished their skills, on the Guthrie stage. Information: Guthrie Theater, 725 Vineland Pl., Minneapolis, MN 55403 (612 377-2224).

MILWAUKEE REPERTORY THEATER, Milwaukee, Wisconsin: In a six-play season, classics alternate with premières of new works by talented contemporary playwrights, at the Todd Wehr Theater in the Performing Arts Center and the intimate Court Street Theater. The MRT's annual production of Charles Dickens' *A Christmas Carol* is a Milwaukee holiday favorite. Information: Repertory Theater, 929 N Water St., Milwaukee, WI 53202 (414 273-7121).

WEST

MARK TAPER FORUM, Los Angeles, California: One of the nation's best-respected regional theaters, the Mark Taper won a Tony Award for theatrical excellence in 1977; Michael Cristofer's *The Shadow Box,* which was produced here, won a Pulitzer in the same year. On the main stage, you'll see many premières and an occasional revival; the subject matter tends towards the timely, the currently problematical. Also under the Forum wing, however, are the Improvisational Theater Project, the Forum Lab (where new works are developed), and Hollywood's Aquarius Theatre, where touring companies of Broadway hit productions and other big-box-office numbers are presented. Information: Mark Taper Forum, 135 N Grand Ave., Los Angeles, CA 90012 (213 972-7654).

AMERICAN CONSERVATORY THEATER (ACT), San Francisco, California: A bit of Shakespeare, some Coward, some Chekhov and a Lillian Hellman have played to capacity audiences at this San Francisco theater, which started out in Pittsburgh and moved to the coast only in the mid-sixties. There's also a new playwrights series, and the annual year-end production of *A Christmas Carol* is a Bay Area tradition. Information: ACT, 450 Geary St., San Francisco, CA 94102 (415 673-6440).

SEATTLE REPERTORY THEATRE, Seattle, Washington: Modern and contemporary comedies and dramas, both classics and premières, are performed on the open-thrust stage of the Seattle Center Playhouse. Information: Seattle Repertory Theatre, Seattle Center, PO Box B, Queen Anne Station, Seattle, WA 98109 (206 447-4764).

Outdoor Dramas

Paul Green, who in his long career as a dramatist wrote some of the best of these native American epic plays, called this dramatic form "a people's theater," and anticipated the day when it would ripen into something like outdoor drama of the Greeks. Whether we ever see that day, 1¾ million travelers every year are pilgrimaging to woodland amphitheaters across the country to watch these spectacles of war and peace, statesmen and villains, heroes and plain folk, prejudice, feuds, murder, night riders, love and suffering — the very stuff of American history acted out a lot larger than most of it was lived.

Outdoor drama is not a subtle art form, but pageants are not meant to be. These summer spectacles have two compelling virtues that would win audiences in any case: They are natively American, based on legends, stories, tall tales, and real history told in the very places where the legends occurred, the history was lived; and they are exciting — colorful, enthusiastically acted, compulsively produced with horses charging, guns and cannon exploding, flames leaping, and extravagant costuming and good music. And they are also generally inexpensive; reserved seats (which you should consider) usually cost less than $7 a head; unreserved even less. For a complete list of American outdoor dramas (there are more than 50), send a self-addressed and stamped envelope to Institute for Outdoor Drama, 202 Graham Memorial 052A, University of North Carolina, Chapel Hill, NC 27514 (919 933-1328).

EAST

TRAIL OF THE LONESOME PINE, Big Stone Gap, Virginia: The love story of a mountain girl and a mining engineer from the East, set in the days when coal and iron discoveries were changing the lives of the mountain people. It's a true story, presented not far from where the couple wooed, in this part of the state so deeply affected by mining. July and August. Ticket information: June Tolliver Playhouse, PO Box 700, Big Stone Gap, VA 24219 (703 523-1235).

THE HATFIELDS AND THE McCOYS and HONEY IN THE ROCK, Beckley, West Virginia: The saga of the most famous feuding families in America (complete with a runaway daughter, a stillborn baby, killings, bounties, and betrayal) alternates in repertory with the story of the formation of West Virginia during the Civil War. Indians coined the phrase "honey in the rock" to refer to natural gas which escaped from cracks in rocks and which they worshiped (as you'll see in a scene in which gas jets under the stage are ignited). Late June through early September. Tickets: PO Box 1205, Beckley, WV 25801 (800 642-2766 toll-free from West Virginia in summer; or 304 253-8313).

SOUTH

THE GREAT PASSION PLAY, Eureka Springs, Arkansas: The quaint hillside town where Carry Nation made her last temperance speech also puts on a May-through-October pageant about Christ's last days. Tickets: Elna M. Smith Foundation, Box 471, Eureka Springs, AR 72632 (501 253-8781).

THE ARKANSAW TRAVELLER FOLK THEATRE, Hardy, Arkansas: An evening of good food, good country music, and comedy based on the legend of the Arkansaw Traveller. (When visiting a fellow mountain man, the Traveller asks about a leaky roof; the man explains that when it's raining he can't fix it, and when it's not, he doesn't need to.) Late May through early September. Ticket details and information about dinner beforehand: Arkansaw Traveller, PO Box 536, Hardy, AR 72542 (501 856-2256 or 501 793-2291).

CROSS AND SWORD, St. Augustine, Florida: Paul Green's production of Pedro Menéndez de Avilés' founding of St. Augustine, the first settlement in the US, was first seen in 1965, the year the city celebrated its 400th birthday; it now plays mid-June through late August. William Gibson's *The Body and the Wheel* annually plays five nights around Easter. Information: PO Box 1965, St. Augustine, FL 32084 (904 471-1965).

THE STEPHEN FOSTER STORY, Bardstown, Kentucky: A musical about how the composer wooed and won his Jeannie with the light brown hair (whose real name, it turns out, was Jane). At the town's Talbott Tavern, you can sleep in the room Louis Philippe of France occupied during visits in the early 1800s, and stuff yourself on fried chicken, biscuits, and some of the richest pies in the South (107 W Stephen Foster Ave., Bardstown, KY 40004, 502 348-3494). Early June through early September. Tickets: Stephen Foster Story, PO Box D, Bardstown, KY 40004 (502 348-5971).

THE LEGEND OF DANIEL BOONE, Harrodsburg, Kentucky: This popular drama focuses on the history of the great pioneer, at Old Fort Harrod State Park — a 28-acre preserve set up to honor the first permanent white settlement in Kentucky. Mid-June through late August. The Trustees' House — the Shaker-inspired restaurant and inn at nearby Shakertown at Pleasant Hill (606 734-5411; see *America's Special Havens*); and the lovely Beaumont Inn (Harrodsburg, KY 40330, 606 734-3381) are area musts. Tickets: PO Box 365, Harrodsburg, KY 40330 (606 734-3346).

HORN IN THE WEST, Boone, North Carolina: This story of how the earliest American pioneers rebelled against the royal governor and went west was written by Kermit Hunter, a celebrated creator of outdoor dramas. Late June through mid-August. Information: PO Box 295, Boone, NC 28607 (704 264-2120).

UNTO THESE HILLS, Cherokee, North Carolina: Kermit Hunter also wrote this piece about the Cherokee Indians from 1540 until 1838, when they were herded westward over the Trail of Tears; it's presented mid-June through late August at the Mountainside Amphitheater, on the edge of the Oconaluftee Indian Village, a replica of a Cherokee settlement of 200 years ago (see *Indian America*). Information: PO Box 398, Cherokee, NC 28719 (704 497-2111).

THE LOST COLONY, Manteo, North Carolina: A fixture of the summer season on the Outer Banks since 1937, America's first outdoor drama tells the story of the mysterious disappearance of Sir Walter Raleigh's first English colony in 1587 with Indian dances, fireworks, and grand court scenes. Mid-June through late August. Information: The Lost Colony, PO Box 40, Manteo, NC 27954 (919 473-2127; 919 473-3414 for reservations).

TEXAS, Canyon, Texas: The struggle between farmers and cattlemen in the not-always-so-gay 1880s, and how it affected a batch of young lovers, is presented at Palo Duro State Park, near Amarillo, mid-June through late August, in a 1,000-foot-deep, 100-mile-long canyon so impressive that in many ways it turns out to be the star of the show. Information: PO Box 268, Canyon, TX 79015 (806 655-2181).

THE LONE STAR, Galveston, Texas: The story of the founding of the Texas Republic features a cast of over 80 (including six horses), cannon and gunfire, a burning house, and a couple of really spectacular battle scenes. Alamo heroes Davy Crockett and David Bowie are on hand, along with Sam Houston and the Mexican general Santa Anna. Early June through late August. Details: The Lone Star, PO Box 5253, Galveston, TX 77551 (713 737-3440).

BEYOND THE SUNDOWN, Livingston, Texas: Driven across the Southeast from Alabama to Louisiana, the Alabama-Coushatta Indians finally took refuge in East Texas — and promptly got caught up in the hostilities between the armies of Mexico, led by General Santa Anna, and those fighting for Texas under Sam Houston. Both factions tried to draw the tribe into the war, but the chiefs opted to move once again rather than fight, and it was only the coming of peace, and the grant of a parcel of land — the kernel of today's reservation, where the drama is held — that spared the tribes yet another journey. While you're in the area, you can watch demonstrations of bead-work and pine-needle–basketmaking at a tourist complex on the reservation, and tour the unspoiled Big Thicket National Preserve nearby. Details: Beyond the Sundown, RR3, Box 640, Livingston, TX 77351 (713 563-4391).

MIDWEST

TECUMSEH!, Chillicothe, Ohio: The Shawnee war chief's struggle with William Henry Harrison over the Northwest Territory involves a cast and crew of 140, a dozen horses, and thirteen stages, in performance late June through early September. Tickets: PO Box 73, Chillicothe, OH 45601 (614 775-0700).

TRUMPET IN THE LAND, New Philadelphia, Ohio: Moravian missionaries, Indian converts, and the Revolutionary War on America's first frontier, complete with horses, a massacre, dances, and humor. This Paul Green work is presented from late June to early September about a mile from Schoenbrunn Village, a restoration of the settlement where many of the events took place. Tickets: PO Box 275, Dover, OH 44622 (216 339-1132).

SHEPHERD OF THE HILLS, Branson, Missouri: Harold Bell Wright's novel of this name is reenacted on the farm where the 1902 Ozarks drought it depicts actually took place. Branson is near Table Rock Lake, a 43,100-acre impoundment where you can swim, water ski, fish, go boating; and Silver Dollar City, an amusement park themed around crafts. The drama is staged late April through October. Tickets: Shepherd of the Hills Farm, Rt. 1, PO Box 770, Branson, MO 65616 (417 334-4191).

THE BLACK HILLS PASSION PLAY, Spearfish, South Dakota: The same man, one Josef Meier, has been playing Christ since 1939. He also produces, directs, and owns the show, which runs June through August in Spearfish and mid-February through mid-April in Lake Wales, Florida. Details on the Spearfish production: PO Box 489, Spearfish, SD 57783 (605 642-2646). Information about the winter show: PO Box 71, Lake Wales, FL 33853 (813 676-1495).

WEST

TRAIL OF TEARS, Tahlequah, Oklahoma: The story of the Cherokees from the end of the tragic march over the Trail of Tears until the beginning of this century. The story is presented at Tsa-La-Gi, the Cherokee Heritage Center, where, among other attractions, you can tour a re-creation of an early 18th-century Cherokee village, where Cherokees in costume dance, play at stickball, and work at crafting baskets, weapons, pots, and tools. Mid-June through late August. You can lodge nearby at the pleasant Tsa-La-Gi Inn (918 456-0511). Pageant tickets: PO Box 515, Tahlequah, OK 74464 (918 456-6007).

THE RAMONA STORY, Hemet, California: Townspeople turn out in droves for the barbecues and assorted goings-on held to honor this dramatization of the Helen Hunt Jackson novel, a sort of Indian *Romeo and Juliet.* Raquel Welch played Ramona a few years back. Six performances are presented in late April and early May; to get tickets, you've got to reserve by the preceding January, through the Ramona Pageant Association, PO Box 755, Hemet, CA 92343 (714 658-3111).

America's Music Festivals: Summers of Sound

All over the country, throughout the summer, musicians get together to regale audiences with the glorious sounds of music — not just symphonies, string trios, chorales and cantatas, but also breakdowns, rags, gospel choruses, and a lot of country fiddling and picking. They're playing in mansions and amphitheaters, rustic gardens and antique opera halls, huge band shells, and even the California vineyards. Some festivals are one-day happenings. Some mean round-the-clock music for a weekend or more. Some fill seats (or lawns, as the case may be) nightly for a whole summer.

State tourist organizations can tell you about the ones in the area you want to visit. Or, for a list of bluegrass events, you can contact *Bluegrass Unlimited* magazine for its annual festival edition ($1.50; PO Box 111, Broad Run, VA 22014, 703 361-8992).

Expect to pay from $5 to $25 each for tickets, depending upon where, what, when, and whom. Should you order in advance? By all means, most especially if the object of your trip is to hear a specific performance. Usually, you will be able to get seats at the last minute (and at the big festivals you can always sit on the lawn), but advance planning will ensure that you get to sit where you want. A good rule is to make ticket arrangements as soon as you have decided when and where you are going.

EAST

THE BERKSHIRE MUSIC FESTIVAL AT TANGLEWOOD, Lenox, Massachusetts: The Boston Symphony Orchestra, summering at this old Massachusetts mountain estate, performs Friday and Saturday nights and Sunday afternoons, July through August, in an enormous band shell surrounded by lawns; professional chamber music concerts and chamber symphony programs presented by music students — the Barenboims and Horowitzes of the future — at the Berkshire Music Center. You'll find a bounty of great country inns in the area — most notably the Red Lion Inn in Stockbridge (described in *America's Special Havens*). Festival details: Berkshire Music Festival, Lenox, MA 01240 (413 637-1600).

THE CHAUTAUQUA INSTITUTION, Chautauqua, New York: Founded in 1874 as a training camp for Sunday school teachers, this lakeside community of quaint Victorian guesthouses and hotels is a learning festival where music keeps company with plays, lectures, and courses in the other arts, psychology, politics, philosophy, crafts, and just about any other subject you can name. July and August. Details: PO Box 1095, Chautauqua, NY 14722 (716 357-5635).

THE LAKE GEORGE OPERA FESTIVAL, Glens Falls, New York: Favorite operas are sung in English by professional performers from all over the US during July and August in this most delightful of American vacation areas; Sunday evenings, there are Opera-on-the-Lake cruises. Tickets: Lake George Opera Festival, PO Box 425, Glens Falls, NY 12801 (518 793-3858).

CARAMOOR FESTIVAL, Katonah, New York: On weekends, late June through late August, chamber and orchestral concerts are presented on an Italian Renaissance-style estate — the large works in an outdoor theater surrounded by 15th-century Venetian columns, the chamber concerts in a Spanish-style courtyard. You can make the hour-long trip in special buses from New York City's Lincoln Center. Tickets: Caramoor, Box R, Katonah, NY 10536 (914 232-4206).

KOOL JAZZ FESTIVAL, New York, New York: America's first and oldest jazz festival, born in 1953 as the Newport Jazz Festival and held in New York City since 1972, offers mostly big-name performers, with a few up-and-comers along the way, the last week in June and the first week in July at various locations around the city. Information: Kool Jazz Festival, PO Box 1169, New York, NY 10023 (212 787-2020).

THE SARATOGA PERFORMING ARTS CENTER, Saratoga Springs, New York: The watering hole of the horsey set, this genteel old town is also home to the giant amphitheater where the Philadelphia Orchestra and George Balanchine's New York City Ballet perform early July through late August, while programs of theater and dance are presented in a smaller theater nearby. Throughout the summer, big-name pop entertainers also appear. Tickets: SPAC Box Office, Saratoga Springs, NY 12866 (518 587-3330). The Gideon Putnam Hotel, on the grounds of the Saratoga Spa State Park (where you can still take the waters orally or in a variety of mineral baths), is posh and comfortable in that particular way that spells affluence (518 584-3000).

NEWPORT MUSIC FESTIVAL, Newport, Rhode Island: Three times daily, for two weeks every July, first-rate young artists perform classical music otherwise relegated to obscurity by short-sighted critics in the gilt and marble ballrooms of the town's glorious mansions. Lodgings by the sea: the Inn at Castle Hill (401 849-3800, see *America's Special Havens),* and the Sheraton–Islander Inn (401 849-2600). Good food: the Black Pearl (401 846-5264). Tickets: 50 Washington Sq., Newport, RI 02840 (401 846-1133).

MARLBORO MUSIC FESTIVAL, Marlboro, Vermont: Fine musicians playing earnestly together under the direction of Rudolf Serkin make such music every weekend from early July through mid-August that most tickets sell out within a couple of weeks of an early April mailing. You may latch onto one of the hundred available for seating under a canopy outdoors by presenting yourself at the box office about an hour before curtain time (8:30 PM on Saturday, 2:30 PM on Sunday). To get on the mailing list, write the Marlboro Music Festival at 135 S 18th Street, Philadelphia, PA 19103 (215 569-4690) before early June and after mid-August, or at Marlboro, VT 05344 (802 254-

8163) in the summer. Pleasant lodgings, about 15 miles from Marlboro: the Inn at Sawmill Farm in West Dover (802 464-8131). For more information about the inn, see *America's Special Havens.*

OLD FIDDLERS' CONVENTION, Galax, Virginia: One of the largest and best-known festivals devoted to traditional music, this institution of half a century's duration is held annually during the second full weekend in August. Information: Box 655, Galax, VA 24333 (703 236-6355).

THE ANNUAL HAMPTON JAZZ FESTIVAL, Hampton, Virginia: The Hampton Coliseum, where it's held, sells out well in advance for performances by top names in soul and jazz, annually the last weekend in June; generally Friday through Sunday. Box office: PO Box 7309, Hampton, VA 23666 (804 838-4203).

WOLF TRAP FARM PARK, Vienna, Virginia: At this national park for the performing arts, you'll get a cross section of what's going on in the American and international music scene: Big-name performers in the world of classical and popular music, ballet, opera, and modern dance may fill up the lawns and the big open-air pavilion, while next the air reverberates with the music of folk singers or bluegrass musicians like Bill Monroe or Doc Watson, or even tap-dance groups or country-and-western performers like Tammy Wynette — all of whom have been on stage in the last few years. Early June into September. Tickets: 1624 Trap Rd., Vienna, VA 22180 (703 938-3810).

NATIONAL FOLK FESTIVAL, Vienna, Virginia: An annual event since 1934, this noncommercial festival now held at Wolf Trap Farm Park in late July is the oldest and largest multicultural folk festival in the United States. Crafts demonstrations and storytelling are part of the goings-on, and a few other traditional arts are represented as well; but the real emphasis is on the music — bluegrass, blues, gospel and ballad singing, old-time fiddling, Tex-Mex, ethnic, and country music — and the nation's best performers in each genre appear. Joint sponsors are the National Park Service and the National Council for the Traditional Arts. Information: NCTA, 1346 Connecticut Ave., NW, #1118, Washington, DC 20036 (202 296-0068).

SOUTH

MOUNTAIN DANCE AND FOLK FESTIVAL, Asheville, North Carolina: Square dancers and cloggers keep time to the music of mountain pickers, fiddlers, ballad singers, dulcimer players every August for this half-century-old event. Information: Chamber of Commerce, PO Box 1011, Asheville, NC 28802 (704 258-5200).

SPOLETO USA, Charleston, South Carolina: Gian Carlo Menotti's important Italian arts festival made its stateside debut in 1977 with concerts in public parks and gardens, and other interesting Charleston sites, including the restored Dock Street Theater, and has been going strong ever since, every year for seventeen days beginning in late May. Tickets: PO Box 704, Charleston, SC 29402 (803 722-2764).

MIDWEST

THE RAVINIA FESTIVAL, Highland Park, Illinois: The Chicago Symphony Orchestra holds forth in the open-air pavilion of a 36-acre woodland park from late June to mid-August, when a month of dance programming featuring at least one well-known company, begins. Chamber music, concert opera, one-composer celebrations, recitals, and educational programs have given the festival a reputation for adventurous programming. Information: Ravinia Festival, PO Box 896, Highland Park, IL 60035 (tickets: 312 432-1236; schedules: 312 782-9696).

BEANBLOSSOM BLUEGRASS MUSIC FESTIVAL, Beanblossom, Indiana: This blink-and-you-miss-it settlement in the hilly southern part of the state really hops just once every year in June, when country music star and festival organizer Bill Monroe brings his musicians to town for a big bluegrass marathon. Of the thousands who come to watch the scheduled concerts in the wooded amphitheater, many set up tents and park their campers in a nearby field, and the air rings with the fiddling and picking of their jam sessions into the wee hours. Information: Bill Monroe, 3819 Dickerson Pike, Nashville, TN 37207 (615 868-3333).

THE BLOSSOM MUSIC CENTER, Cuyahoga Falls, Ohio: When the Cleveland Orchestra isn't playing at this woods-rimmed, cedar-shingled shell halfway between Akron and Cleveland, you'll find pop concerts — everything from the Beach Boys and Barry Manilow to jazz and ballet. Mid-June into September. Tickets are available from Ticketron nationwide. Information: Blossom Music Center, 1145 W Steels Corners Rd., Cuyahoga Falls, OH 44223 (216 929-3048).

CINCINNATI MAY FESTIVAL, Cincinnati, Ohio: Massed choruses and opera superstars perform cantatas and other ambitious choral works annually during the last two weekends in May. James Conlon is music director. Information: Cincinnati Music Festival Association, Music Hall, 1241 Elm St., Cincinnati, OH 45210 (513 621-1919).

WEST

CARMEL BACH FESTIVAL, Carmel, California: Works by Bach and others are performed in recitals (sometimes two a day), daily evening concerts, and matinees at the halls and churches of this lovely sophisticated village on the northern California coast, for two weeks in late July every year. Tickets: Carmel Bach Festival, PO Box 575, Carmel, CA 93921 (408 624-1521). Information about the many inns and interesting hotels and restaurants — a specialty in these parts — is available from the Carmel Business Association, PO Box 4444, Carmel, CA 93921 (408 624-2522). Two Carmel favorites: the Victorian-era Pine Inn (408 624-3851) and Sea View Inn (408 624-8778).

MONTEREY JAZZ FESTIVAL, Monterey, California: The sellout concerts that make up this event held annually the third weekend in September feature some of the biggest names in the business. Some concerts are themed around an instrument or a type of music. Tickets: Monterey Jazz Festival, PO Box JAZZ, Monterey, CA 93940 (408 373-3366).

THE ASPEN MUSIC FESTIVAL, Aspen, Colorado: Constant musical activity of one sort or another — jazz, choral, orchestral, and operatic pieces, chamber works, and about anything else you can name — makes this festival, which is held annually from late June through late August, one of the nation's liveliest. Sometimes the performers are name soloists on the order of Pinchas Zukerman and Maureen Forrester; sometimes you'll be hearing students. No matter. The repertoire of medieval through contemporary works is always interesting, and the performances are thoughtful and well executed. There's plenty of backpacking, hiking, swimming, fishing, horseback riding, and other outdoor activity going on during the off-hours. Tickets: PO Box AA, Aspen, CO 81612 (303 925-3254).

CENTRAL CITY OPERA, Central City, Colorado: American talent shows its stuff in imaginative productions sung in English in a tiny, acoustically perfect, turn-of-the-century opera house. During its July and August run, the festival also has embraced dance, jazz, theater. Tickets: Central City Opera Festival, 1615 California St., Ste. 510, Denver, CO 80202 (303 623-7167 for information; 303 571-4435 for tickets).

NATIONAL OLD TIME FIDDLERS' CONTEST, Weiser, Idaho: Parades, BBQ dinners, tractor-pulling contests — and near-nonstop fiddling at daytime and nighttime competitions, and jam sessions in between times — keep this town of 4,000 hopping every year the third full week in June. Weiser is the self-styled "fiddling capital of America" and the home of the Fiddlers' Hall of Fame, and the contest attracts some 300-plus contestants and nearly 5,000 spectators from all over the US and Canada. Information: Chamber of Commerce, Weiser, ID 83672 (208 549-0452).

SANTA FE OPERA, Santa Fe, New Mexico: Familiar and unfamiliar works, plus American premières and a lot of unusual compositions, alternate in repertory during

July and August. Tickets in advance are a must: Santa Fe is presenting some of the nation's best opera. Information: PO Box 2408, Santa Fe, NM 87501 (505 982-3851).

PETER BRITT GARDENS MUSIC AND ARTS FESTIVAL, Jacksonville, Oregon: For two weeks every August, some 30 orchestral concerts and chamber recitals are presented outdoors in the spectacular Britt Music Pavilion and the tiny ballroom of a restored turn-of-the-century hotel, as part of the Northwest's oldest music festival, founded to honor pioneer vintner, horticulturist, and daguerreotypist Peter Britt. Reserve your lodgings well in advance because of the concurrent Oregon Shakespearean Festival, some 15 miles away in Ashland. Tickets: Peter Britt Gardens Music and Arts Festival, PO Box 1124, Medford, OR 97501 (503 779-0847).

GRAND TETON MUSIC FESTIVAL, Teton Village, Wyoming: From mid-July until late August, for six weeks, you'll find great music in these oft-climbed mountains — sometimes it's contemporary, sometimes not; sometimes the artist or composer talks about the pieces beforehand. Tickets: Grand Teton Music Festival, PO Box 310, Teton Village, WY 83025 (307 733-3155).

Restored Towns and Reconstructed Villages

Williamsburg, Virginia, is only the most famous of America's restored towns: All over the country historical villages have been reconstructed — some simply repaired and restored, others pieced together from brand-new buildings or from original structures collected from numerous sites — to graphically recreate the day-by-day life of earlier periods in American history. At the best of these, curators hire craftspeople to demonstrate everyday tasks of the era, and provide lectures, walking tours, and an array of special events. In general, the larger the restoration, the wider the variety of crafts and the longer the roster of special activities you'll find.

And, though not all museum villages are as authentic as Williamsburg, where the quest for historical accuracy extends to making male craftspeople's shoes from the same kind of leather that would have been used in the 18th century, curators at most museum villages take considerable pains to make sure that at least the most obvious things are correct. There's no better place to enjoy yourself learning history.

EAST

MYSTIC SEAPORT, Mystic, Connecticut: Gulls wheel and cry overhead while you're walking around the 17 acres of this reconstructed New England sea village, where, along with the usual crafts, there's a ship's chandlery, sail loft, ship model shop, and hoop-maker's place. You can watch shipwrights at work restoring the *Charles W. Morgan,* America's last surviving wooden whaleship; and browse through the US's largest collection of small boats. And there's more: More ships; formal exhibits of scrimshaw, marine art, and figureheads; steamboat cruises; schooner races; demonstrations of sail-setting and furling and other marine skills; and, at Christmas, a lively program of period merriment (lantern-light tours, lots of old-fashioned decorations, and the like). Information: Mystic Seaport, Mystic, CT 06355 (203 536-2631). (See *Mystic,* DIRECTIONS)

PLIMOTH PLANTATION, Plymouth, Massachusetts: This reconstruction of the Pilgrims' village now includes a dozen-plus houses, fort, Wampanoag campsite (summers), and the famous replica of the *Mayflower.* Its sails are made of flax and sewn by hand, its beams pegged together with "tree nails" made from 120-year-old cider vats. Both aboard ship and in the Village, men and women in period dress portray actual residents of the 1627 Plymouth through speech, manner, and attitude, while pursuing the daily routine of the farming community. The Pilgrims, it turns out, did not wear tightly fitting, somber clothes, but instead, like other 17th-century farmers and working folk, loose and colorful garments. Closed December through March. Information: Plimoth Plantation, Box 1620, Plymouth, MA 02360 (617 746-1622). As for actual colonial landmarks, nearby Duxbury and Kingston have street upon street of old homes. In Plymouth itself you can visit the houses of the Pilgrims, their burial sites, and a grist mill. Good time to go: Thanksgiving, when there's a public feast and religious service at the town's Memorial Hall, and a reenactment of the Pilgrim's Progress to church. More information: Plymouth Area Chamber of Commerce, 85 Samoset St., Plymouth, MA 02360 (617 746-3377).

OLD STURBRIDGE VILLAGE, Sturbridge, Massachusetts: Things are so authentic at this re-created village that sheep help to trim the grass on the village green, and the general store is stocked with just those items a 19th-century shopper would have expected. Hard-working ladies cook up savory goodies on open hearths, using 19th-century "receipts," and blacksmiths, broom-makers, coopers, printers, and artisans go about their work the traditional way. The purpose is to show rural America turning into industrial America, and so in addition to the farm and the grist mill, there are exhibits like the carding mill. Sturbridge is one of the most respected establishments of its type, the largest living history center in the Northeast, and even without its huge assortment of period theatricals, speechmakings, church services, concerts, and other special events, you could go back many times and never see it all. At Thanksgiving, the Village fathers put on a magnificent period feast; reservations are usually gone by April. Information: Old Sturbridge Village, Sturbridge, MA 01566 (617 347-3362). At the Publick House, a quaint old inn outside the restoration area, Christmas brings a wonderful Edwardian Yule feast-cum-pageant complete with scarlet-coated beefeaters and a boar's head (617 347-3313; see *America's Special Havens*).

STRAWBERY BANKE, Portsmouth, New Hampshire: Rescued from demolition, the settlement that flourished here on the New Hampshire coast for over 150 years beginning in 1695 is now being restored. Five houses are furnished and open for tours, and about 14 others are in various stages of completion. Some of the antique structures are being scraped and painted, others exhibit collections of textiles and tools, early photographs, architectural details, and archeology. In all, there are 85 exhibit rooms in 6 different buildings, plus 5 houses furnished to illustrate a given era in local history, plus craft shops and a coffee shop in yet other restorations. Information: Strawberry Banke, PO Box 300, Portsmouth, NH 03801 (603 436-8010).

THE FARMERS' MUSEUM AND VILLAGE CROSSROADS, Cooperstown, New York: The message here is how, in the 75 years between the end of the Revolution and the beginning of the Civil War, the plain people of America built a nation where only forests had stood. The museum's Main Barn section has displays about men's jobs (sugaring off to planting, hop-picking to hunting), women's tasks (spinning and weaving, laundering and, because a woman's work was never done, much more), and the activities of tanners and tinsmiths, barrel makers, felt-hat makers, and many other craftsmen. Alongside exhibits of the tools these jobs required, craftspeople are hard at work. Outside, there's a dirt-laned village where you'll see more of the same in period buildings set up to look like shops and houses, while cows, chickens (bred to authentic scrawniness) and guinea hens wander around on the lawns. Special programs include a Harvest Festival in the fall; seminars dealing with American culture during the first two weeks of July; and scattered throughout the year, craft workshops for the interested amateur as well as the professional. Also in the area: a fine Georgian-style resort hotel, the Otesaga (607 547-9931; see *America's Best Resort Hotels),* and the cozy Cooper Inn

(607 547-2567). Information: New York State Historical Association, Cooperstown, NY 13326 (607 547-2533).

GENESEE COUNTRY MUSEUM, Mumford, New York: A collection of about 50 early American buildings gathered from upstate New York and restored on this rolling 125-acre site reflects American life of about 150 years ago. New additions include an elegant Italianate home and its two-story carriage house. You'll also see a pottery, bandstand, farm, parsonage, pioneer settlement, a variety of homes, an inn, a Methodist church, and a score of shops and offices, all peopled by costumed "villagers." The unusual Gallery of Sporting Art explores man and his animals. Open from May through Columbus Day weekend. Information: Genesee Country Museum, Box 1819, Rochester, NY 14603 (716 538-6822).

HOPEWELL VILLAGE NATIONAL HISTORIC SITE, near Elverson, Pennsylvania: This settlement is the most far-ranging restoration of the kind of iron-producing center that flourished in this corner of southeastern Pennsylvania starting about 1770. The ironmaster's home, charcoal house, waterwheel, blast machinery, casting house, cold-blast furnace, tenant houses, and barns are all open year-round. In summer many of the processes are demonstrated. Information: Hopewell Village, RD 1, PO Box 345, Elverson, PA 19520 (215 582-8773).

SHELBURNE MUSEUM, Shelburne, Vermont: A collection of collections of Americana housed in 35 historic buildings moved to the 45-acre site from all over the state. You'll see hundreds of carousel figures, cigar store Indians, cradles, dolls, dresses, horse-drawn vehicles, quilts, rugs, ship figureheads and shop figures, tin bathtubs, tools for woodworking and toys. The collection of decoys is the largest in the US. To see all the exhibits, go between mid-May and mid-October; only a few buildings are open in winter (and only on Sundays). Best lodgings in the area are at the classy Basin Harbor Club, on Lake Champlain (802 475-2311; see *America's Best Resort Hotels).* Eat at the Dog Team (great for home cooking and sticky buns, 802 388-7651). Information: Shelburne Museum, Shelburne, VT 05482 (802 985-3344).

JAMESTOWN, Jamestown, Virginia: The first colonial capital eventually simply died away. Fences, foundations, hedgerows, property ditches, and even streets that you see now as you walk through parts of the Colonial National Historical Park are all that remain except for the Glasshouse, restored and fitted out so that craftsmen can make glass as they did here three centuries ago. Three- and five-mile drives through the park are punctuated by signs explaining Virginia's early life and industries. Nearby, at the 25-acre state-sponsored Jamestown Festival Park, you'll see museum buildings, a reconstructed fort, Indian exhibits, a working 17th-century pottery, and reproductions of the three famous ships which, though hardly bigger than yachts, got the settlers across the ocean. Information: Jamestown Festival Park, PO Drawer JF, Williamsburg, VA 23185 (804 253-4838); Colonial National Historical Park, Yorktown, VA 23690 (804 898-3400); Williamsburg–James City/County Chamber of Commerce, PO Box HQ, Williamsburg, VA 23185 (804 229-6511). (See *Tidewater Virginia,* DIRECTIONS.)

COLONIAL WILLIAMSBURG, Williamsburg, Virginia: All the superlatives apply to this restoration of Virginia's 18th-century cultural, social, and legislative center — not just for the sheer size of the collection (150,000 items, 88 colonial and early-19th-century buildings, and several hundred reconstructions), but also for the variety of crafts demonstrated (36 in all), the historical authenticity, and the craftworkers' knowledgeability. Winter months are least busy; the entire summer, and spring and autumn on weekends can be hectic. Shops can accommodate only a few people at a time, and you can imagine what it's like when thousands descend on the place. Information: Colonial Williamsburg Foundation, Williamsburg, VA 23187 (800 582-8976 from Virginia; 800 446-8956 from the rest of the US). (See *Tidewater Virginia,* DIRECTIONS.)

SOUTH

HISTORIC ST. AUGUSTINE, St. Augustine, Florida: The Spanish in the New World were cruel, but their settlement was quite civilized in other ways, or so it will seem when you tour this restored section of the US's oldest permanent settlement. The plain stucco houses line a narrow street across from the Castillo de San Marcos (the fort which protected the town) and fill a couple of side streets as well. At work in some buildings are a silversmith, a wizened old Spanish cigarmaker with lightning-fast hands and an even quicker tongue, and a weaver who does her thing with spinnings from the backs of dogs and cats, ponies and pigs. The settlement's story is told at a Chamber of Commerce Visitor Center — a good place to begin any visit — and at the outdoor drama *The Cross and the Sword* (see *Outdoor Dramas*). Special events include an annual Blessing of the Fleet on Palm Sunday weekend and, on Easter Sunday, a "Parada de los Caballos y Coches," an Easter parade of horse-drawn carriages. Information: St. Augustine and St. Johns County Chamber of Commerce, 10 Castillo Dr., St. Augustine, FL 32084 (904 829-5681).

WESTVILLE 1850, Lumpkin, Georgia: Life in the South wasn't all barbecues and 16-inch waistlines. Some people lived in modest homes, gathered eggs and made the baskets to put them in, milked cows and made the jugs to store the milk, shod the horses, repaired buggies, dried fruits, stored vegetables, made syrup from sugar cane, ginned cotton and baled it, and made furniture — all things you'll see at this nifty recreated village. Extra craftsmen are on hand for the Fair of 1850, held the first week in November, and there are Maypole dances on May Day, a barbecue on July 4, and a Yule Log ceremony in early December. Information: Westville, PO Box 1850, Lumpkin, GA 31815 (912 838-6310).

MIDWEST

LINCOLN'S NEW SALEM STATE PARK, Petersburg, Illinois: Edgar Lee Masters' home, the setting for his *Spoon River Anthology*, is a mere two miles from the town where Abraham Lincoln courted Ann Rutledge, tended store, worked as a postmaster, studied law, learned surveying, and, in 1837, got himself elected to the legislature. A variety of buildings have been reconstructed next to the Onstott Cooper Shop (an original structure which has been restored) on a site presented to the state by William Randolph Hearst. Extra craftworkers are brought in for Christmas in New Salem, held usually the first Saturday and Sunday in December. Nearby, Ann Rutledge and Edgar Lee Masters are buried in Petersburg's Oakland Cemetery. Information: Lincoln's New Salem State Park, RR 1, Petersburg, IL 62675 (217 632-7611).

GREENFIELD VILLAGE, Dearborn, Michigan: The Henry Ford Museum's phenomenal collection of American decorative arts, tools, and implements of agriculture, communications, lighting, transportation, and power covers 14 acres — but that's only what you'll see in Dearborn. Set up on an adjacent 240 acres are, for starters, the courthouse where Abe Lincoln practiced law as a circuit rider; Edison's laboratories; homes or birthplaces of the Wright Brothers, H. J. Heinz, Robert Frost, Noah Webster, William Holmes McGuffey (of *McGuffey's Reader* fame), and nearly 100 other structures that figure strongly in US history, all moved from their original sites. Lodgings: the Georgian-style Dearborn Inn, or in reconstructed homes of Walt Whitman, Edgar Allan Poe, Patrick Henry, Oliver Wolcott, and Barbara Fritchie (313 271-2700; see *America's Special Havens*). For more information, contact the Henry Ford Museum and Greenfield Village, Dearborn, MI 48121 (313 271-1620)

LUMBERTOWN USA, Brainerd, Minnesota: The town that calls itself Paul Bunyan's home is also the site of a recreated 1870 logging center with bunkhouse, mess hall, saloon, and nearly 30 other buildings. Closed mid-September through mid-May. Details: Chamber of Commerce, Brainerd, MN 56401 (218 829-2838).

STUHR MUSEUM OF THE PRAIRIE PIONEER, Grand Island, Nebraska: The cottage in which native son Henry Fonda was born is on display here along with some 57 other structures that give a vivid impression of what life was like for the ordinary pioneers here on the south-central Nebraska prairie. The village is open from May through September only; you can visit two museums also on the property year-round. Nearby: Harold Warp's Pioneer Village and the 1864 Fort Kearny State Historical Park, once an important stop on the Oregon Trail. Information: Stuhr Museum, 3133 W Hwy. 34, Grand Island, NE 68801 (308 384-1380).

HAROLD WARP'S PIONEER VILLAGE, Minden, Nebraska: This antique collection installed in a collection of 24 buildings compactly arranged on a 20-acre site shows you "man's progress since 1830." That means, in part, that you'll see not one old-time kitchen setup, but several (from 1830, 1860, 1890, 1910, 1930, 1950, and 1980). Stoves, refrigerators, autos and trucks, farm machinery, farm tractors, bikes, boats, planes, fire engines, streetcars, steam engines, locomotives, and many other familiar objects get the same thorough treatment. Information: Harold Warp's Pioneer Village, Minden, NE 68959 (308 832-1181).

WEST

BODIE STATE HISTORIC PARK, near Bridgeport, California: Within 20 years of the discovery of gold in 1859, Bodie was, in the words of its pastor Reverend F. M. Warrington, "a sea of sin lashed by the tempests of passion." It had 30 mines, breweries, 65 saloons, ale stoops, pothouses, restaurants, gin mills, and opium dens; and, on Maiden Lane and Virgin Alley, plenty of ladies — Eleanor Dumont (alias Madame Mustache), Nellie Monroe, French Joe, and Rosa May. Very little of Bodie has withstood the years of fire and heavy snowstorms since its heyday; the buildings that have survived are maintained by the California State Park system in a state of "arrested decay" — that is, minor repairs are made and walls are shored up, but no attempt is made to make Bodie look any different than it did when it was at last abandoned. Peering through windows as you take the mapped-out walking tour, you'll spot old-fashioned condiments and canned goods on a general store shelf; caskets inside the morgue; a pipe organ in the Methodist church. It's all so eerie that you'll understand why the park rangers who take care of Bodie like company. Open all year but inaccessible (because of snow) except in summer. Information: Bodie State Historic Park, PO Box 515, Bridgeport, CA 93517 (no phone).

COLUMBIA STATE HISTORIC PARK, Columbia, California: The "gem of the southern mines" never quite died out like Bodie but only decayed, so restoration was relatively simple. Walking tours mapped out by the state take you past all the important structures. After your tour, you can pan for color in Matelot Gulch, ride a stagecoach, sip sarsaparilla, get a haircut at California's oldest barbershop, or eat the '49-er delicacy known as Hangtown Fry. Plenty of camping and hiking is available in the surrounding Stanislaus National Forest. Lodgings: at the restored 1851 Gunn House in Sonora (209 532-3421) and at the very-Victorian City Hotel (209 532-1479; see *America's Special Havens,* City Hotel, Columbia). More information: Columbia State Historic Park, PO Box 151, Columbia, CA 95310 (209 532-4301); the Tuolumne County Chamber of Commerce, PO Box 277, Sonora, CA 95370 (209 532-4212); the Stanislaus National Forest, 19777 Greenley Rd., Sonora, CA 95370 (209 532-3671).

POLYNESIAN CULTURAL CENTER, Laie, Oahu, Hawaii: Studying at the Mormon-operated Brigham Young University Hawaii Campus, students from all over the South Pacific put themselves through school by working at this 42-acre reconstruction of traditional villages of Fiji, Hawaii, New Zealand's Maori culture, Samoa, Tahiti, the Marquesas, and Tonga. The crafts, singing, dancing, and food preparation are all things the students have grown up with, so it couldn't be more authentic. Closed Sundays. Nearby lodgings: Laniloa Lodge (808 293-9282). More information: Polynesian Cultural Center, 2301 Kalakaua Ave., Ste. C304, Honolulu, HI 96815 (808 923-1861 or 808 293-3333).

Utopias and Religious Settlements

Ever since the Pilgrims fled England for the New World, Americans have been leaving settled areas for wildernesses where they could set up their own civilizations, far from the corrupting influences. Sometimes the new settlements survived. For instance, the Amana Colonies — founded over a century ago — still thrive, even though the communal ownership of property was dissolved in the 1930s. In parts of Ohio, Pennsylvania, and Maryland, the Amish still live by the old ways, though buggies are not quite so common as they once were.

A good many others were not so successful. All through American history, religious settlements and attempted Utopias have come and gone like Christmas shoppers through a revolving door. Often, however, the communities that they built have withstood the ravages of time, and the last few years have seen a number of these settlements restored as museum villages. Some are open year-round, some only in summer; it's wise to call before you go. Admission fees are low — a few dollars for passes that will allow you to tour all the buildings, or 50¢ to $1 or so for each restored structure. Some are free.

BISHOP HILL, near Galesburg, Illinois: The first major Swedish settlement in the US, this community near the Mississippi River was not a big success. Eric Jansson, the dissident Swedish Lutheran who came here in the early 1840s and persuaded some 800 of his fellows to follow him in 1846, was assassinated in 1850 — and it was all downhill after that. In 1861, communal ownership of property was dissolved. Dissidents among the dissidents withdrew. Mismanagement of remaining property ensued. The community went into debt, and Bishop Hill crumbled. However, a good many of the descendants of the original settlers stayed on, so the buildings did not all decay. By the 1960s, when people got interested in the colony, 13 of the 16 original structures were still standing, among them the Bjorkland Hotel, the blacksmith shop, the Greek Revival Steeple Building (full of replicas of 19th-century rooms and topped by a one-handed clock) and the colony church, which could seat 1,000 worshipers. An 11-mile-long path leads you past other landmarks. In November every year, a Julemarknad — Swedish Christmas market — is held. Nearest motels are in Galesburg, where you can visit Carl Sandburg's birthplace, see the granite boulder under which his ashes were placed, and, on the campus of Knox College, stroll around the school's original building, the site of the Lincoln-Douglas debates. Information: Bishop Hill State Historic Site, Box D, Bishop Hill, IL 61419 (309 927-3345).

NAUVOO, Nauvoo, Illinois: Chicago was little more than a one-horse town when the followers of Mormon leader Joseph Smith arrived here and started building simple frame houses with wood brought down from their forests in Wisconsin; by 1846, the town was 20,000 strong, full of gardens, and topped by an immense white marble temple. Schisms developed, as schisms will, partly because of disagreements within the Mormon band itself over the polygamy issue; Joseph Smith ended up lynched at the jail in Carthage; and Brigham Young, another Mormon, led the group westward just as in the famous old grade B movie on the subject. Over the years, while Salt Lake City was abuilding, the houses in Nauvoo were burning, one by one. But the neat grid of streets is still clear as ever, and scattered here and there are enough buildings that you can get a pretty good idea of how it was back then. Most of them are open for tours and manned by Mormon missionaries, who, it seems, are aiming to convert you just by presenting facts (almost always interesting). Jonathan Browning, maker of the famous rifles, was a Mormon, as you'll learn; you'll tour his studio and home and see an interesting device he worked out that would churn butter and rock a baby in a cradle at the same time. The Mormons were replaced in Nauvoo by a group of French Utopian thinkers called Icarians. They did not flourish or even leave a mark on the city. Following them came a very traditional group of Germans, who found that the land would grow grapes and that the cellars of the Mormon houses were perfect for ripening blue cheese. These businesses flourish in Nauvoo today, and when you eat a meal at the Hotel Nauvoo you can sample them both. The hotel (open mid-March through October) also has very plain, but air-conditioned and quite comfortable, bathroom-down-the-hall rooms (217 453-2211). A good time to visit, if you can plan for lodgings well in advance, is the weekend before Labor Day, when people from all over the area stream into town for the Grape Festival. Among the parades for grown-ups and kids and other small-town doings, there's a ceremony called the Wedding of the Wine and Cheese. For more information, contact the Nauvoo Chamber of Commerce, Nauvoo, IL 62354.

NEW HARMONY, Indiana: This quiet little town in southwestern Indiana near the confluence of the Wabash and Ohio Rivers has been home to two Utopian settlements. The first was led by Harmonist George Rapp, who, with his 700-plus followers, turned the forests and swamplands they found here in 1814 into 30,000 acres of farms, factories, and homes in a bare ten years. The later venture was led by Robert Owen, a Scottish intellectual who drew distinguished scholars, writers, and educators to New Harmony, established free kindergartens, education for women, a library, and many other firsts. That settlement declined, but many sturdy Harmonist buildings survived and are open year-round. Particularly fascinating are the Workingmen's Institute, a former trade school now filled up with Indian artifacts, lacy antique underwear, a stuffed eight-legged calf, and the oddest lot of other knickknacks you'll see in a long time; and the re-created Labyrinth, a maze made out of hedges that you can actually try to walk through. The original, built by George Rapp's Harmonists, was supposed to represent the choices taken during a lifetime. A variety of special programs take place in the striking new Atheneum, designed by architect Richard Meier and opened to the public in 1979. The carefully designed New Harmony Inn, modern but Shaker-simple, a real symphony of polished woods, itself is worth the trip (812 682-4491; see *America's Special Havens),* there's good food at the Red Geranium (812 682-4431) and the Greenroom (812 682-4704). Information: Historic New Harmony, New Harmony, IN 47631 (812 682-4474).

AMANA COLONIES, Iowa: The Community of True Inspiration, a Lutheran splinter group under the leadership of Christian Metz, founded this group of seven equidistant towns — now a National Historic Landmark — about 1855 as a communal society in which everybody shared all goods, all gains, and even ate together. Reorganized some three-quarters of a century later in 1932, the Amana Colonies today have a good deal more community feeling than you find in other parts of the US. You can tour the Amana refrigeration plant, in which descendants of the original settlers own stock, and watch the production of microwave ovens, refrigerators, freezers, air-conditioners, and such. The story of life in the good *old* days is told at the Horse Barn Farm Museum in South Amana (a scale-model village and antique tools); at the Amana Heim Museum in the town of Homestead (full of original pioneer items); and at the Heritage House in Amana (exhibits of potting, ice-cutting, bookbinding, woodworking, wine making, soap making, along with an Amana doctor's washhouse and woodshed, and a schoolhouse). Amana, Middle Amana, High Amana, West Amana, East Amana, South Amana, and Homestead all have interesting little shops where you can buy local produce — woolens, furniture, baked goods, sausages, and other foods and crafts. And they all have a number of atmospheric restaurants like Bill Zuber's Dugout, which like the others is great for German food (319 622-3911). More information: Amana Colonies Travel Council, Amana, IA 52203 (319 622-3051, 319 622-3441).

SHAKER VILLAGE OF PLEASANT HILL, near Harrodsburg, Kentucky: A belief in celibacy effectively guaranteed the demise of this outgrowth of the Quaker religion founded by Mother Ann Lee, but the legacy has been enormous. The Shaker conviction that religion should not be separated from the secular concerns of human life meant that much effort and ingenuity were expended on the tiniest details of life; every physical object was considered a prayer, and engineered for perfection. The tools and furniture that resulted fetch high prices at auctions today; they're bound to make an impression on you when you see them in this restoration's 27 original buildings. There are many special events. Information: Shaker Village of Pleasant Hill, Harrodsburg, KY 40330 (606 734-5411).

HANCOCK SHAKER VILLAGE, near Pittsfield, Massachusetts: The best place in the East to see Shaker architecture. The standout is the Round Stone Barn, three-storied and designed for efficiency, but beautiful enough to bring Le Corbusier and other great architects to mind. In all, 18 buildings on the property are filled with Shaker furniture and Shaker "spirit drawings." The four-story Church Family Building housed a hundred men and women; and there's a laundry and machine shop, wash house, and icehouse. Once a year, for a week in August, the museum stages Worlds' People's Dinners, which are open to the public (by reservation only), along with cooking and craft demonstrations. Country inns are plentiful: the big, rambling Red Lion Inn in Stockbridge (413 298-5545; see *America's Special Havens*), the cozy Village Inn in Lenox (413 637-0020), and the Williamsville Inn in West Stockbridge, good for imaginative food (413 274-6580). Information: PO Box 898, Pittsfield, MA 01202 (413 443-0188).

THE CANTERBURY SHAKER VILLAGE, Canterbury, New Hampshire: One of two remaining active Shaker communities. The 24 white frame structures that stand here now were once home to 400 Shakers; the gardens were laid out a century ago to feed them. The mall is lined with enormous sugar maples planted by the Shakers for orphans they had adopted to care for. Tours of the village take you to or through the museum, ministry, sisters' shop, laundry, school, Meetinghouse (with separate entrances for men and women), and various residential buildings. Information: Shaker Village, Canterbury, NH 03224 (603 783-9977).

OLD SALEM, Winston-Salem, North Carolina: Founded in 1766 by a group of Moravians from Pennsylvania, Salem's church directed not just spiritual life but also secular doings — and business prospered. At the restoration, you can see fire engines, decorative arts, and household items, plus craft shops, the oldest tobacco shop still standing in America, and the immense Single Brothers House, where 14-year-old boys came to live while they learned a craft. Special events are planned for Easter, July 4th, and Christmastime. Information: Greater Winston-Salem Chamber of Commerce, PO Box 1408, Winston-Salem, NC 27102 (919 725-2361).

SCHOENBRUNN VILLAGE STATE MEMORIAL, near New Philadelphia, Ohio: Concerned about the education of the Indians, the Moravian church sent missionaries into the wilderness, and six separate settlements were established in this area. David Zeisberger and his force of Christian Indians, converts, and missionaries cleared the wilderness and within a couple of years had put up some 60 log structures. But by that time, England and the colonies were at war, and Schoenbrunn was caught between the firing lines. The missionaries and their congregations departed, leaving the settlement to crumble. What you see now — a church, school, and a baker's dozen other structures — is a recreated area built since the 1920s. Sometimes craftspeople are on hand to demonstrate spinning and weaving or tending the gardens, planted with red and calico corn, sweet corn, herbs, turnips, and pumpkins. *Trumpet in the Land,* an outdoor drama presented in an amphitheater nearby, tells the story (see *Outdoor Dramas*). Information: Schoenbrunn Village State Memorial, PO Box 129, New Philadelphia, OH 44663 (216 339-3636).

ZOAR STATE MEMORIAL, Zoar, Ohio: Another group of German Separatists who, like George Rapp, refusing to accept the Lutheran doctrine, found themselves alternately ignored and persecuted until it seemed easier to leave the Old World than to stay; and on Rapp's example, they bought a tract of land on the Tuscarawas River and crossed the ocean. The system of communal ownership under which the community eventually flourished in Zoar was not inspired by the Bible so much as by necessity imposed during the very lean times of the settlement's first years. When you visit today, you see it as it was during the lifetime of leader Joseph Baumeler: the red brick houses with their tile roofs and bright trim are spic and span; the bakery, tin shop, and garden house look for all the world as if they were still open for business; and the fantastic community garden, geometric in design, which is still so neat you'd say it had been laid out by some Prussian drill sergeant. A good time to see it all is during the Zoar Harvest Festival, held annually on the first weekend in August, when there are art and music festivals and tours of private homes in the area. Zoar State Memorial is closed from November through March. Nearby: Atwood Lake Lodge in Atwood Lake Park is modern, comfortable, beautifully situated, and quite reasonable besides (216 735-2211). Information: Zoar State Memorial, Zoar, OH 44697 (216 874-3211).

OLD ECONOMY, Ambridge, Pennsylvania: When Father George Rapp left New Harmony, Indiana, he came here — and proceeded to create something even grander than the settlement he had left. There was, first of all, his own Great House, which had 25 rooms ranged around two wings, and a vault for spare cash. Then there was the Feast Hall, a single room which could seat 1,000 diners. Both structures, plus the wine cellars, storehouse, hat shop, shoe shop, cabinetmakers' shops, community kitchens, and a number of dwellings have been restored and are open to the public. Why did the Rapp settlement finally die out? The loss of Rapp's leadership upon his death in 1847, coupled with competition from other industries, dwindling numbers, and some poor investments, rang the death knell. The society was dissolved in 1905. Christmas festivities, German style, are staged annually. Information: Old Economy Village, Great House Square, Ambridge, PA 15003 (412 266-4500).

EPHRATA CLOISTER, Ephrata, Pennsylvania: This religious experiment, begun in 1732 by a German Seventh-Day Baptist named Conrad Beissel, lasted until 1813 — despite celibacy and despite the rigorous lifestyle demanded of its practitioners: They slept on beds which were more like narrow benches, laid their heads on wooden pillows, walked down straight and narrow hallways and through doorways so low they had to stoop. There was, of course, plenty of symbolism behind all of it — and that, among other things, is what you learn about when you tour the handsome buildings. You'll also learn why singing was permitted, and, at the *Vorspiel* historical pageant, presented in summer, you'll hear some of the original music of Ephrata. For information about visiting Ephrata, in the heart of Pennsylvania Dutch country, contact: Ephrata Cloister, 632 W Main St., Ephrata, PA 17522 (717 733-6600).

America's Great Museums

Some of the best in the world can be found in the US — not just art museums, but natural history museums and science museums where the visitor is invited to touch, climb, experiment, try out, push buttons, and learn. Most have fascinating shops where you can buy reproductions of objects in the collections — postcards, statuary, textiles, jewelry, knickknacks.

For a complete listing of both major and minor museums of the urban areas you plan to visit, see the individual city reports in THE AMERICAN CITIES. Herein, a distillation of the best: art museums, museums of science and industry, natural history museums — the country's very best.

Those listed here are worth some time — a half-day is usually adequate — and return visits. They're popular, especially on weekends. To get the most from your time, try to visit midweek. Most have special exhibits for the holidays, changing exhibitions that supplement the permanent collections, and a schedule of concerts, lectures, and short courses that are well worth investigating, even on a short visit. Hours usually vary with the season; most are closed one day a week. Admission prices are low; in Washington, DC, many of the museums are free; in New York City, there's often a "pay-what-you-wish-but-you-must-pay-something" donation "requested."

EAST

BALTIMORE MUSEUM OF ART, Baltimore, Maryland: Strong on modern art, thanks to the Cone Collection — paintings, prints, and sculptures of Matisse, Picasso, and other French post-Impressionists donated by the two wealthy Cone sisters — the museum also has period rooms that highlight the architectural, artistic, and historic growth of Maryland, through furniture and artifacts, some dating to the 1600s; the Wurtzburger collection of African, pre-Columbian, and Polynesian art; a vast print collection; and a spectacular new outdoor sculpture garden. Information: Baltimore Museum of Art, Art Museum Dr. (Charles and 31st), Baltimore, MD 21218 (301 396-7101).

MUSEUM OF FINE ARTS, Boston, Massachusetts: This great, vast old museum in the heart of Boston, not far from Fenway Park, sits alongside a lovely 12-acre park near the bank of the Charles River; on sunny days, you can spot artists with sketch pads in hand on the green. Inside, you'll find an extensive permanent collection of Impressionists (including many Monets), works by American portrait and landscape painters, and American decorative arts (Duncan Phyfe chairs, Paul Revere silver, and other such blue-blooded items). The collection of Egyptian architectural casts and artifacts is the largest outside Cairo; the Asiatic collection is the earth's largest under one roof. And the I. M. Pei addition is the talk of the architectural world. Information: Museum of Fine Arts, 465 Huntington Ave., Boston, MA 02115 (617 267-9300 or, for weekly events, A-N-S-W-E-R-S).

ISABELLA STEWART GARDNER MUSEUM, Boston, Massachusetts: One of the world's magnificent private galleries. The collections are housed in a 15th-century-style Italianate mansion built between about 1899 and 1903, with capitals, columns, fireplaces, fountains, staircases, and other architectural elements imported from Europe by the museum's founder, Mrs. Jack Gardner, a not-so-proper Bostonian who drank beer as well as tea, and further disgraced herself in the eyes of Boston society by being born in New York City. Mrs. Jack — as she was called — lived on the top floor of her four-story mansion during her lifetime, maintaining the rest of the house as a museum, which by the terms of her will is open to the public, with the proviso that the arrangement of paintings, furniture, and other objects remain as it was during her lifetime. As a result, objects that seem to have as much sentimental as aesthetic value are exhibited alongside Rembrandts, Titian's "The Rape of Europa," and other pieces collected with the advice of Bernard Berenson, the art scholar who coined the term "squillionaire." (The Museum *Guide* is a good thing to have.) The sounds of the lovely fountain in the marble and plaster courtyard in the center of the house, and the smell of the flowers growing around it, are almost always with you as you inspect the results of Mrs. Gardner's acquisitiveness — Tintorettos, Manets, Botticellis, Whistlers, one Corot, and one of the 36 surviving works of Vermeer. When your feet are tired, you can take lunch or tea at a café on the premises; also find out about the concerts held from September through June. Information: Isabella Stewart Gardner Museum, 2 Palace Rd., Boston, MA 02115 (617 566-1401).

THE AMERICAN MUSEUM OF NATURAL HISTORY and THE HAYDEN PLANETARIUM, New York, New York: In the 40 halls and galleries of this behemoth, you'll find rooms and rooms of dinosaur bones; one of the largest collections of rocks and gems in the US; fabulous life-size dioramas of animals, prehistoric people, and vegetation; a fine exhibit about reptiles from the prehistoric days to the present, and much more. Especially interesting is the new Hall of Asian Peoples, which traces Eastern culture through the 19th century. Don't miss the great whale — a huge replica of a blue whale hanging from the ceiling of the Great Hall. The adjacent Hayden Planetarium has shows daily; and on weekend evenings, there's a multimedia sound-and-light show using laser beams (fine for families and a must for young adults — but you'll need reservations). Phone the Planetarium for times (212 724-8700). For Museum hours and programs: American Museum of Natural History, Central Park West at 79th St., New York, NY 10024 (212 873-4225).

THE FRICK COLLECTION, New York, New York: Henry Clay Frick, a coke and steel magnate who died in 1919, commissioned the architect Thomas Hastings to design a house that could function equally well, later on, as a museum, and so it's not surprising that the surroundings, sumptuous with their elegant furnishings and thick carpets, are so perfectly suited to the elegant collection of paintings and objets d'art, including Renoir's "Mother and Children," Vermeer's "Officer and Laughing Girl" and "Girl Interrupted at Her Music," Fragonard's "The Progress of Love," Holbein's portraits of Sir Thomas More and Thomas Crowell, and works by Gainsborough, Turner, Reynolds, Lawrence, and nearly everyone else (or so it sometimes seems) who ever inspired an art lover to rapture. All in all, the Frick is relaxing, hospitable, and among the most accessible museums anywhere. Information: Frick Collection, 1 E 70th, New York, NY 10021 (212 288-0700).

METROPOLITAN MUSEUM OF ART, New York, New York: Home of America's most extensive art collection. There are works of great masters from the Middle Ages to the present day, a vast assemblage of Greek and Roman sculptures, Oriental art, costumes throughout the ages, jewelry, musical instruments, decorative arts from all ages, and special exhibitions of stunning quality. The fine Egyptian collection includes mummies, funerary objects, and even linen sheets taken from tombs; the new Sackler Wing contains a whole temple. A variety of tape-recorded audio tours that hit the high spots of the collections will help you handle the mind-boggling presentation. At Christmas, a tree is hung with 18th-century Neapolitan ornaments — each one a sculpture in its own right. Closed Mondays. Information: Metropolitan Museum of Art, 5th Ave. at 82nd St., New York, NY 10028 (212 535-7710).

MUSEUM OF MODERN ART, New York, New York: Possibly the most complete museum of modern art in the world. The permanent collections — concerned with 20th-century art — include works of abstractionists, expressionists, conceptualists, film-makers (there are daily film programs), industrial designers, photographers, and others. It is not a showplace of works of the very avant-garde; but then neither will you encounter Botticellis or Titians. Look for the completion of a major expansion program in the spring of 1983. Information: Museum of Modern Art, 11 W 53rd St., New York NY 10019 (212 956-6100).

THE GUGGENHEIM MUSEUM, New York, New York: The first visual encounter you'll have when you come to this museum will be with the Frank Lloyd Wright–designed structure that houses the collection. Perfectly round, with a domed roof, the building is constructed so that the exhibits are ranged along the walls of a quarter-mile-long ramp that spirals upward for six floors. Standing at the bottom, looking toward the skylight at the top, you can't help but wonder if Wright had read William Butler Yeats' "Turning and turning in the widening gyre . . ." It's also hard to understand the criticism that greeted the new building in October 1959; it was dubbed "a marshmallow" and even "a clothes washer." More charitable commentators said only that the building overpowered the art on display. Whether you agree will depend on how you feel about Wright *vis à vis* Kandinsky (one of the largest assemblages of his work in the world is here), Chagall, Delaunay, Picasso, and other Impressionist, modern, contemporary, and avant-garde artists represented in the permanent collections and in the ever-changing exhibitions that make the Guggenheim so lively. Information: The Guggenheim, 5th Ave. and 88th St., New York, NY 10028 (212 860-1313).

WHITNEY MUSEUM OF AMERICAN ART, New York, New York: Devoted to American art, primarily that of the 20th century, and the work of living artists, the Whitney presents some 15 exhibitions annually in its Marcel Breuer–designed building. The permanent collection includes works by Calder, de Kooning, Hopper, Johns, O'Keeffe, Nevelson, Prendergast, Segal, Sheeler, and Warhol. Information: Whitney Museum of American Art, Madison Ave. at 75th St., New York, NY 10021 (212 570-3676).

FRANKLIN INSTITUTE, Philadelphia, Pennsylvania: A huge, vital, hands-on science museum with four floors of displays about energy, aviation, math, communications, weather, time. You can board a 707 jet, ride a locomotive, wind through a 15,000-times-lifesize heart, watch manmade lightning, and, in the adjoining Fels Planetarium, take in daily star shows. Information: Franklin Institute, 20th St. and The Parkway, Philadelphia, PA 19103 (215 564-3375).

PHILADELPHIA MUSEUM OF ART, Philadelphia, Pennsylvania: Housed in an imposing edifice of Minnesota dolomite, which Lord Dunsany called the most beautiful building in America, are Van Gogh's "Sunflowers," Cézanne's "Bathers," Marcel Duchamp's "Nude Descending a Staircase," Picasso's "Three Musicians," and the famous statue of Diana that topped New York City's first Madison Square Garden. Along with the excellent Impressionist collection, there's a Japanese Tea House, designed to convey the atmosphere as well as the art of Japan, a Chinese scholar's study, a large collection of arms and armor, and distinguished collections of china, porcelain, glass, jade, graphics, sculpture, and decorative arts. Information: Philadelphia Museum of Art, 26th St. and The Parkway, Philadelphia, PA 19103 (215 763-8100).

THE CORCORAN GALLERY OF ART, Washington, DC: In its gracious, skylit halls full of American art — among the finest collections of American art anywhere, in fact — are prestigious assortments of works by Sargent and Copley. You'll also find European paintings, however (some by Corot, some by the animal sculptor Antoine Barye, as well as Renaissance drawings), and a variety of changing exhibitions of contemporary art and photography. One block beyond the White House. Information: Corcoran Gallery of Art, 17th and New York Ave., NW, Washington, DC 20006 (202 638-3211).

THE SMITHSONIAN INSTITUTION, Washington, DC: Completed in 1855, the red Gothic castle on the Mall now functions mainly as office space for the staff that oversees the Smithsonian's scattered museums and galleries — seven on the Mall, six (including the National Zoo) in other parts of DC, one in New York City, and a dozen scientific research facilities around the country. The total collection contains over 75 million items and gains almost a million more every year; only about 1% are displayed at any given time, so there's always something new to see. The museums of American History, Natural History, and Air & Space are among the most popular in Washington. Information: Smithsonian Institution, 1000 Jefferson Dr., SW, Washington, DC 20560 (202 357-1300).

THE HIRSHHORN MUSEUM AND SCULPTURE GARDEN, Washington, DC: One of the newest museums under the Smithsonian's wing and the most modern of the city's museums of modern art, the Hirshhorn houses, in part, the ever-astonishing collections amassed by Joseph Hirshhorn, who grew up in such poverty that he never even owned a toy. He spent much of the fortune he made in stocks and uranium buying art (the way some people buy clothes). The painting collection focuses on American art, and includes works by Eakins, Davis, Estes, Gorky, Henri, Hopper, de Kooning, and Noland; European masters like Bacon, Grosz, and Magritte are also represented. The extraordinary vitality of the sculpture collection reflects the greatness of Calder, Daumier, Degas, Matisse, Picasso, and David Smith — whose works are displayed. For this variety alone the Hirshhorn would be fascinating; the building itself — circular and fortresslike — is intriguing as well. Information: Hirshhorn Museum, Independence Ave. at 8th St., Washington, DC 20560 (202 357-2700).

NATIONAL GALLERY OF ART, Washington, DC: Housed in a John Russell Pope–designed building whose 500,000 square feet make it one of the world's largest marble structures, this museum built to introduce Americans to the cream of European art is what one local critic called "the sort of place paintings would aspire to if masterpieces went to heaven." Columns of Tuscan marble, floors of green marble from Vermont and gray marble from Tennessee, and walls of Indiana limestone and Italian travertine produce an effect that is unadulteratedly sumptuous; the museum's contents are, if possible, even more awe-inspiring. Leonardo da Vinci's "Ginevra de Benci" (America's only Leonardo), Jan Vermeer's "Woman Holding a Balance," a Rembrandt "Self-Portrait," Jean-Honoré Fragonard's "A Young Girl Reading," Auguste Renoir's "A Girl With a Watering Can," and Claude Monet's "Rouen Cathedral, West Façade" are among literally thousands of breathtaking canvases and sculptures — gifts of hundreds of donors — housed in the original building and the striking new East Building, designed as a grouping of interlocking triangles by I.M. Pei & Partners. It can all be a bit bewildering, so, as an introduction, you might want to join one of the regular tours; rent a tape tour; or pick up the excellent "Brief Guide." A monthly calendar lists special events, which include free films, lectures, and concerts. Information: National Gallery of Art, 4th St. and Constitution Ave., NW, Washington, DC 20565 (202 737-4215).

MIDWEST

THE ART INSTITUTE OF CHICAGO, Chicago, Illinois: El Greco's "Assumption of the Virgin," Seurat's "Sunday Afternoon on the Island of Grand Jatte," and Grant Wood's "American Gothic" are among the works in the Art Institute's outstanding collections, which also include excellent post-Impressionist and Impressionist works, Japanese prints, Chinese sculpture and bronzes, and European and American prints and drawings. The new American Galleries are wonderfully conceived to show off the development of US culture; the Chagall stained glass windows and the Trading Room, reconstructed from the old Chicago Stock Exchange, as well as the Thorne Miniature Rooms (which tell the history of decorative arts in miniaturizations of real furniture), are not to be missed. Information: Art Institute of Chicago, Michigan Ave. at Adams, Chicago, IL 60603 (312 443-3600).

FIELD MUSEUM OF NATURAL HISTORY, Chicago, Illinois: The more than 13 million artifacts and specimens displayed in 42 exhibit halls and 6 galleries are organized around anthropology, botany, ecology, geology, and zoology. The most famous are the pair of fighting elephants in the main hall, the butterflies, Bushman (the gorilla from the Lincoln Park Zoo, now stuffed but looking otherwise remarkably alive), and an exciting reproduction of a Pawnee earth lodge. At a "Place for Wonder," you can touch less precious specimens of the types of things you see in the museum. The new "Maritime Peoples of the Arctic and the Northwest Coasts" exhibit documents the life and culture of these peoples with some 2,500 objects. Information: Field Museum, Roosevelt Rd. at Lake Shore Dr., Chicago, IL 60605 (312 922-9410).

MUSEUM OF SCIENCE AND INDUSTRY, Chicago, Illinois: Chicago's most popular attraction has computers to question, buttons to push, rides to ride, and so on, as part of some 2,000 displays examining the principles of science (as well as other subjects). High points: Colleen Moore's fairy castle of a doll house; the computerized nutrition exhibit "Food for Life"; and the Sears circus exhibit, full of dioramas of circus scenes, piped-in circus music, and a dynamic short film (the kind you want to sit through twice in a row). The working coal mine, the walk-through human heart, and the German submarine are every bit as much fun as they always have been. And there are new exhibits on newspapers, Nobel prizewinners, and computers. Information: Museum of Science and Industry, 57th and Lake Shore Dr., Chicago, IL 60637 (312 684-1414).

MILWAUKEE PUBLIC MUSEUM, Milwaukee, Wisconsin: The basic theme here is how man and other living creatures adapt to the environment, but there are a lot of variations, and exhibits relate not only to Indians, history, geology, and world cultures of the distant past, but also to aspects of American society. This sprawling institution really shines, however, when it comes to the making of dioramas. At a North Coast Indian exhibit, for instance, smells and sounds come at you from all sides. A rattlesnake hisses. When the buffalo charge, you can hear the thundering of their hooves on the earth — getting louder and louder. The geese honk at a wildlife exhibit. At a portrayal of an East African bamboo forest, you hear the sounds of an elephant come crashing through the trees. Particularly interesting is the Streets of Old Milwaukee section, where the 19th-century city has been recreated, right down to flickering gaslights, telephone poles wrapped with wire to keep horses from chewing them, and a kite tangled up in the treetops. The same ingenuity is at work in the European village of shops and homes, a new exhibit which portrays 33 cultures of the Old Countries. Information: Milwaukee Public Museum, 800 W Wells, Milwaukee, WI 53233 (414 278-2700).

THE MINNEAPOLIS INSTITUTE OF ARTS, Minneapolis, Minnesota: The exterior is architecturally classic, and it houses an equally classic variety of Old Masters, Chinese and ancient art, and decorative arts. In addition, the museum presents films, recitals, and lectures. Information: Minneapolis Institute of Arts, 2400 3rd Ave. S, Minneapolis, MN 55404 (612 870-3046).

WALKER ART CENTER, Minneapolis, Minnesota: Offering a vivid overview of major 20th-century art styles, this art center housed in a striking contemporary building complements the Institute's classic collections; originates many touring exhibitions; and conducts a lively program of music, dance, film, theater, and educational activities. Information: Walker Art Center, Vineland Pl., Minneapolis, MN 55403 (612 375-7600).

DETROIT INSTITUTE OF ARTS, Detroit, Michigan: One of the US's most unusual collections of Old Masters and modern artists lines the walls and hallways of the Institute, which is the fifth largest fine arts museum in the country. Italian art is only one of the areas in which the museum has large holdings; French painting and decorative arts and the Dutch and Flemish painters are also well represented here. There are several Egyptian mummies and suits of medieval armor on display, as well as a large collection of African and native American art. A bust of Lincoln by Gutzon Borglum (who carved Mt. Rushmore) shares the lawn with Tony Smith's contemporary *Gracehoper*. Sundays the Institute presents Brunch with Bach, and there are frequent special exhibitions, lectures, and films. Details: Detroit Institute of Arts, 5200 Woodward Ave. (corner of Kirby Ave.), Detroit, MI 48202 (313 833-7900).

CLEVELAND MUSEUM OF ART, Cleveland, Ohio: One of the major American museums and one of the few of its kind that is still free to the public, this privately owned institution boasts an enviable collection that takes in all periods and cultures. Under the long directorship of the renowned Oriental art scholar Sherman E. Lee, galleries were organized chronologically, with the decorative arts pieces displayed alongside paintings and sculpture of the same era and area. The constantly growing collection currently numbers over 45,000 objects; the arts of the Near and Far East, India, pre-Columbian America, Europe, America, Africa, and ancient Egypt, Greece, and Rome are represented. The Oriental collection is one of the finest in the Western world, and the museum has particularly strong medieval, European painting, and decorative arts collections; of late, the collection of contemporary paintings has been growing rapidly. Throughout the year there are frequent concerts and films, with gallery talks and lectures every Sunday afternoon. The original 1916 building overlooks a garden and lagoon; a decade-old wing designed by Marcel Breuer houses the special exhibitions galleries, the musical arts department, and the education department (one of the largest professionally staffed education departments in the country). A number of Cleveland's other cultural institutions face the museum across a grassy oval. Information: Cleveland Museum of Art, 11150 East Blvd. at University Circle, Cleveland, OH 44106 (216 421-7340).

WEST

THE LOS ANGELES COUNTY MUSEUM OF ART, Los Angeles, California: The best museum in the state, and the largest built in the US in over 30 years, the LA County Museum has three separate pavilions — one devoted to changing exhibitions, one given over to the Leo S. Bing Theater (where there are weekly film presentations and frequent lectures and concerts), and the third — the Ahmanson Gallery — mainly to an eclectic permanent collection that encompasses exhibits of ancient times, the present, and years in between. Though the collections are relatively recent, they're excellent, particularly the Indian and Islamic holdings. A sculpture garden contains works by Moore, Calder, and others. Information: Los Angeles County Museum of Art, 5905 Wilshire Blvd., Los Angeles, CA 90036 (213 857-6111).

ASIAN ART MUSEUM OF SAN FRANCISCO, San Francisco, California: The Avery Brundage Collection — one of the world's finest of Oriental objects — represents most of the museum's holdings, which include some 10,000 sculptures, architectural elements, paintings, bronzes, ceramics, and decorative objects illustrating stylistic developments of Asian art. The museum shares an entrance with the M. H. de Young (below), but the two are distinct institutions. Information: Asian Art Museum of San Francisco, Golden Gate Park, San Francisco, CA 94118 (415 558-2993).

CALIFORNIA PALACE OF THE LEGION OF HONOR, San Francisco, California: The collections housed in this graceful building in the French neoclassical style (based on the Legion of Honor in Paris) are predominantly French, but you'll also find the largest graphics collection in the western US. With the M. H. de Young Memorial Museum (below), it comprises the Fine Arts Museums of San Francisco. Information: Lincoln Park, San Francisco, CA 94121 (415 558-2881).

M. H. DE YOUNG MEMORIAL MUSEUM, San Francisco, California: One of the western US's largest municipal art museums. Collections include paintings, sculpture, and decorative arts from ancient Egypt through the 20th century. There are galleries devoted to American painting and decorative arts; to the traditional arts of Africa, Oceania, and the Americas; and to period rooms from Europe and America. Fra Angelico, Rembrandt, Rubens, Titian, El Greco, Goya, Hals, Van Dyck, Gainsborough, and Reynolds are represented. Information: M. H. de Young Memorial Museum, Golden Gate Park, San Francisco, CA 94118 (415 558-2887).

DENVER ART MUSEUM, Denver, Colorado: Besides having an excellent collection that takes in the period from AD 1100 to the present, the Denver Art Museum has top collections of pre-Columbian art and artifacts, native American art, Oriental art, and textiles, plus holdings in American, European, and contemporary art. The seven-story $6.5 million structure, which looks something like a medieval castle with its slitlike windows, was designed around the exhibits; some display halls completely recreate another time and place. Information: Denver Art Museum, 100 W 14th Ave. Pkwy., Denver, CO 80204 (303 575-2793).

AMON CARTER MUSEUM OF WESTERN ART, Fort Worth, Texas: This museum started out chronicling America's westward expansion, with a huge collection of paintings, castings, and sculpture by Frederic Remington and Charles Russell. But gradually, the museum has adopted American art as a whole as its theme, and, in addition to western pieces, you'll also see 19th century landscapes and genre paintings by such artists as Winslow Homer, Albert Bierstadt, and Thomas Moran; a selection of the 500,000-item American photography collection is also always on view. A new theater provides a home for films, lectures, and symposiums. Information: Amon Carter Museum, 3501 Camp Bowie Blvd., Fort Worth, TX 76107 (817 738-1933).

FORT WORTH ART MUSEUM, Fort Worth, Texas: This museum contains only works from the 20th century; Ben Shahn, Andy Warhol, Chagall, Calder, Matisse, Rauschenberg, and Picasso are represented. Along with the Amon Carter and Kimbell museums, this institution is located on Will Rogers Square. Information: Fort Worth Art Museum, 1309 Montgomery St., Fort Worth, TX 76107 (817 738-9215).

KIMBELL ART MUSEUM, Fort Worth, Texas: This result of a bequest by Kay Kimbell contains an incredible array of works by Cézanne, Goya, Gainsborough, Rembrandt, Van Gogh, and others. Information: Kimbell Art Museum, Will Rogers Rd. W, Fort Worth, TX 76107 (817 332-8451).

Space Centers: The Future Now

The Saturn V Rocket on display at the Alabama Space and Rocket Center — one of three such space centers in the US — is as long as a football field and as wide as a two-lane highway; the sheer size of it is adequate testimony to the scope of the space program. There are plenty of reasons to visit. At each center you will be given facts and figures that may give you pause the next time you start to agree with someone who calls the space exploration program a waste of money. You'll be offered the opportunity to take over the controls of a rocket; experience weightlessness in a zero-gravity machine; and in a dozen other ways retrace the small steps that were such great leaps for mankind. Outside there are "rocket parks" — greenswards where mammoth spacecraft grow like so many monster asparagus stalks.

EARTH'S LARGEST SPACE MUSEUM, Huntsville, Alabama: Formerly the Alabama Space and Rocket Center, this institution tells you what's happening on the space scene — and looks into the future as well. The current emphasis is the Space Shuttle program, and not long ago, a new "ride" that simulates a trip in the much-talked-about craft was introduced; you're tilted, rattled, shaken, assailed by roars and flashing lights, and given a you-are-there feeling that makes you wish you were. In comparison to such exhibits, some of the older space-related displays look like Tin Lizzies: some of the youngsters who come here, born long after Sputnik and Yuri Gagarin, look on things like the Mercury Sigma Rocket, piloted by Walter Schirra in 1961, as ancient history. But this is by and large a very lively place, and you can fire a rocket engine, land a mooncraft by computer, rendezvous with the Russian Soyuz, man the controls of a spaceship flying through an asteroid belt, see the Apollo 16 moonship. Aboard the Spaceship *Lunar Odyssey*, you can even experience space travel, from the deafening roar of the lift-off to star-spangled wild-blue-yonder views and weightlessness in a simulated outer-space trip. Miss Baker, the tiny squirrel monkey who (with another monkey named Able) made a 10,000 mph flight aboard a Huntsville-built Jupiter rocket in 1959, lives in the museum's elaborate monkeynaut exhibit with Norman, her new spouse. Outside: rockets, rockets, and more rockets, including the 363-foot-long Saturn V. Also in Huntsville, you can take bus tours of the NASA Marshall Space Flight Center, home of the Space Shuttle, where you'll see testing towers, firing grounds, Skylab, a model of the space shuttle, and a buoyancy-simulator underwater training tank used by astronauts. Information: Alabama Space and Rocket Center, Tranquillity Base, Huntsville, AL 35807 (toll-free 800 633-7280 or, from Alabama, 800 572-7234).

THE JOHN F. KENNEDY SPACE CENTER, Kennedy Space Center, Florida: The Kennedy Space Center is on Merritt Island, and is home of all NASA launchings; Cape Canaveral, across the Banana River, is the site for launchings of Department of Defense flights. This 25-square-mile spaceport is a hotbed of space-related activity — everything from data-gathering and tracking to fuel storage and manned-flight launches. The best way to see it is on the 2-hour-long bus tour, which takes in the launching and landing sites of the Space Shuttle, Mission Control, and more. As the pace of the Space Shuttle program is stepped up, the amount of activity that you are apt to see will increase dramatically — as will the number of launchings. Very little is closed to visitors at this time; even the Space Shuttle areas were toured up until 3 hours before blast-off. In any event, the new (and still expanding) Visitor Center where you meet the tours itself offers abundant attractions, including a lunar roving vehicle, a replica of an Apollo Lunar Module, and a baker's dozen theaters, minitheaters, and tape programs that tell you about flights past and future. If you opt for a tour around Christmas or in summer, be sure to arrive as close as possible to the Center's 8 AM opening to avoid lines.

Afterward, you can swim off unspoiled beaches along the 25-mile Cape Canaveral National Seashore, go deep-sea fishing, and, at the Merritt Island National Wildlife Refuge, see alligators, panthers, and some 200 species of birds. Cocoa Beach, where most motels are just a shell's throw from the Atlantic, is the place to lodge.For more information: Kennedy Space Center Tours, Visitor Center TWA 810, Kennedy Space Center, FL 32899 (305 452-2121).

THE LYNDON B. JOHNSON SPACE CENTER, Houston, Texas: An important research and development center for the US's Space Shuttle flight program. You can learn about the subject at the Visitor Center, where you see moon rocks, space suits, rocket engines, and spacecraft from the Mercury, Gemini, Apollo, Skylab, and Apollo-Soyuz test missions, and other impedimenta of the space age. NASA films shown all day long show you what each mission was like. Self-guided walking tours of the JSC take you to the Mission Simulation and Training Facility (Building 5), where astronauts practiced their complex Skylab tasks as well as Building 9A (devoted to Space Shuttle paraphernalia), Building 31A (where lunar samples are studied), and two others. Guided tours of Mission Control are also available daily. For information: Lyndon B. Johnson Space Center, Houston, TX 77058 (713 483-4321).

TO SEE A LIFT-OFF

"It's like being inside of a flame — no heat, but your entire body shakes, your bones and organs shake, the earth shakes." That is one writer's description of watching a launch: They're definitely worth seeing. There are approximately 10 a year from Cape Canaveral and Kennedy Space Center, and you can watch lift-offs from either site along rt. A1A, which passes between Cape Canaveral and Patrick Air Force Base. (For launch information, call toll-free within Florida, 800 432-2153.) It is hard to plan a vacation around a launching, because variable weather conditions make a strict schedule impossible. There is a special viewing area, three miles from the launching pads, for which you can make reservations through the Kennedy Space Center.

Factory Tours: Watching the Work

Every year, literally hundreds of companies welcome thousands of visitors to their plants. Newspapers show off their printing presses, breweries their mash tubs, distilleries their warehouses and their quality-control systems, soft-drink companies their bottling plants, wineries their vineyards and aging rooms. Each region has a specialty. There are maple sugar houses and marble quarries in Vermont, tobacco warehouses and cigarette factories in Kentucky and North Carolina, petrochemical works in Louisiana, oil fields and coal mines in Wyoming, lumber mills and wood products plants in the Pacific Northwest. Most big companies have plants in several parts of the country. If you're interested in seeing how a specific product is made, write the corporate headquarters and ask about tours.

Below, you'll find a very brief sampler of some industrial tours available to the general public. There are hundreds more, however. To find out about them, contact the state tourist offices and chambers of commerce in the areas you plan to visit.

And always phone ahead. Companies may need to line up someone to take you around, and that takes time. Even when the operation does have a regularly scheduled tour program, you've got to be sure that it will not be temporarily closed down because of vacations or model changeovers. If you have children, you need to make sure they are old enough to go on the tour. (There's usually an age limit of anywhere from 7 to 16.) This may seem a lot of trouble, but the excitement of the factories — the speed of the machines, the clanks and the screeches, the roars and the buzzes — will make all the planning worthwhile.

EAST

PROCTER & GAMBLE MANUFACTURING COMPANY (BALTIMORE PLANT), Baltimore, Maryland: Ivory, Camay, Tide, Cheer, Bold, Downy, Joy, and other P&G products are bottled, boxed, or wrapped here, then packed into cartons for shipping. You watch the process, then get refreshments and gift packs to take home. Tour season is October through May; no children under 14. Information: P&G Manufacturing, PO Box 2077, Baltimore, MD 21203 (301 752-2440, ext. 329).

SCOTT PAPER COMPANY, Winslow, Maine: Wood pulp (made 12 miles away by the same company at the most modern pulp mill in the world, which you can also tour) is slushed up in blenders, beaten with chemicals, and turned into rolls of Scottowels, Scottissue, and Cut-Rite Waxed Paper stock that measures 5 feet in width, 6 feet in diameter. Information: Scott Paper, Skowhegan, ME 04976 (207 453-9301).

MILTON BRADLEY COMPANY, East Longmeadow, Massachusetts: Games and toys, from cutting and drawing and the counting of the pieces to the final packaging. Information: Milton Bradley Company, 443 Shaker Rd., East Longmeadow, MA 01028 (413 525-6411).

ANHEUSER-BUSCH, Merrimack, New Hampshire: One of the few Anheuser-Busch breweries where the tour is guided (rather than self-guided), this brewery is also notable for being the home of the famous Clydesdales. Information: Anheuser-Busch, 1000 Daniel Webster Hwy., Merrimack, NH 03054 (603 889-6631).

CORNING GLASS CENTER, Corning, New York: An area has been set aside for visitors where fine Steuben glass is hand-formed and engraved. Adjacent is a museum that houses one of the US's best glass collections, and a science center in which the properties and new uses of glass are tested. Information: Corning Glass Center, Corning, NY 14830 (607 974-8814).

EASTMAN KODAK, Rochester, New York: In one of the buildings you visit on ninety-minute tours here, you'll see injection molding of spools, reels, and film canisters; in another, you'll see how the film is actually inserted. The plant, which is so big that you see most of it from a bus, is among three Kodak Rochester installations open to visitors; for details about the others, which manufacture cameras and projectors and optical items such as lenses, contact Eastman Kodak, 200 Ridge Rd. W, Rochester, NY 14650 (716 722-2465).

FAIRLESS WORKS, US STEEL CORPORATION, Fairless Hills, Pennsylvania: The US Steel Corporation's only basic steel plant on the East Coast produces some 4 million ingot tons of steel annually. The most impressive part of your visit (partly by bus) may be your stop at the open hearth shop, where molten iron is charged into open hearths and to the rolling division, where ingots are rolled into slabs and then into 1/3-mile-long ribbons. No children under 16. Information: Fairless Works, US Steel Corporation, Fairless Hills, PA 19030 (215 736-4440).

BUREAU OF ENGRAVING AND PRINTING, Washington, DC: At the world's largest securities manufacturing establishment, you can watch the making of currency on 25-minute self-guided tours. Information: Bureau of Engraving and Printing, Washington, DC 20228 (202 447-9709).

SOUTH

GERBER PRODUCTS, Fort Smith, Arkansas: Everything from baby cereal to strained peas and applesauce, at every stage, through canning, packaging, and shipping. Winter is least active. Information: Personnel, PO Box 1547, Fort Smith, AR 72901 (501 782-8671).

VILLAZON AND COMPANY, Tampa, Florida: Cigars, hand- and machine-made, from leaf to banding. Mornings are most active, and production peaks during September, October, and November. Information: 3104 N Armenia, Tampa, FL 33607 (813 879-2291).

McILHENNY COMPANY, New Iberia, Louisiana: An aged mash made of pickled peppers is mixed with 100-grain vinegar in barrels, then put through three progressively finer strainers to make Tabasco sauce, and, finally, bottled, labeled, and packed into cartons. All in the middle of a mysterious bayou. Information: McIlhenny Company, Avery Island, LA 70513 (318 365-8173).

CANNON MILLS COMPANY, Kannapolis, North Carolina: From the cotton bale to the terrycloth on your towel rack. The loops are made by a special weaving process. Information: Cannon Mills, 230 West Ave., Kannapolis, NC 28081 (704 933-1221, ext. 2776).

MIDWEST

CATERPILLAR TRACTOR, Peoria, Illinois: When the immense yellow tractors roar off the assembly line like so many mechanized elephants, everything shakes, even the concrete floor. By appointment only. Information: Tour Coordinator, Caterpillar, 100 NE Adams St., Peoria, IL 61629 (309 675-4578).

KITCHENS OF SARA LEE, Deerfield, Illinois: On what is one of the best plant tours in the country, you'll see the production of the cheese cakes, coffee cakes, dessert cakes, pound cakes, crumb cakes, and Danish pastries named after the daughter of one Charles Lubin, who, back in 1950 — when most people claimed that consumers would not buy expensive bakery goods in supermarkets — proved that just the opposite was true and made himself a multimillionaire as a result. Your visit begins with an orientation session that tells you about the procedures you'll be seeing; then ventures into the 576,000-square-foot baking area, where you'll see the making of Danish pastries, and watch the lapping of the over 100 layers of dough and butter that gives them their flakiness, as well as the production of cheese cakes from the mixing and the baking to the freezing, packing, and shipping. You'll get a peek at the computer room where the baking operations are controlled, and — at the end, you'll be served refreshments (Danish in the morning, cake in the afternoon) designed to make you a Sara Lee convert. The tours are so popular that reservations are always necessary. Note, however, that even on the best of days, you won't see all of Sara Lee's goodies in production. For details, contact the Sara Lee Kitchens, 500 Waukegan Rd., Deerfield, IL 60015 (312 945-2525).

PROCTER & GAMBLE MANUFACTURING COMPANY, Iowa City, Iowa: Crest, Gleem, Prell, Scope, Head & Shoulders, and Lilt. Free samples at the end of the tour. Information: Procter & Gamble, 2200 Lower Muscatine Rd., Iowa City, IA 52240 (319 351-2310).

DE KLOMP WOODEN SHOE AND DELFT FACTORY, Holland, Michigan: America's only Delft factory, situated in a resort colony with a Dutch heritage, also makes wooden shoes. Information: De Klomp Wooden Shoes, 257 E 32nd St., Holland, MI 49423 (616 396-2292).

THE HOMESTAKE MINE, Lead, South Dakota: Here, you can see the aboveground operations of the largest gold producer in the Western Hemisphere. No tours on Saturdays and from November through April. Information: Lead Civic Association, Lead, SD 57754 (605 584-1020).

PARKER PEN COMPANY, Janesville, Wisconsin: Pens come out of this plant at 1400 N Parker Dr. at the rate of 50,000 to 100,000 a day. The manufacture of each one requires some 130 separate operations; the final inspector signs the certificate with the pen he's approved. Information: Parker Pen Company, PO Box 5100, Janesville, WI 53547 (608 754-7105).

KOHLER COMPANY, Kohler, Wisconsin: Bald clay is piped through miles of tubing into plaster of Paris molds. After two days of drying, this "greenware" is smoothed by hand, then sprayed with red, brown, black, avocado, gold, gray, parchment, and even white glazes. You'll see bathtubs, lavatories, toilets, faucets, showerheads, and kitchen sinks being produced; this is the world's largest pottery of plumbing fixtures under one roof. The tempting showroom at the end of the tour shows off all the latest in the plumber's world, including a few nifty devices that are priced for rich folks' houses. No tours in late July and early August. Information: Kohler Company, Kohler, WI 53044 (414 457-4441).

OSHKOSH B'GOSH, INC., Oshkosh, Wisconsin: Bib overalls, from the laying out and the cutting to the finished products, from size 1 to size 60. Information: Oshkosh B'Gosh, PO Box 300, Oshkosh, WI 54902 (414 231-8800).

WEST

PENDLETON WOOLEN MILLS, Pendleton, Oregon: From fleece to finished virgin wool garments. Information: PO Box 969, Pendleton, OR 97801 (503 276-6911), or PO Box 1691, Portland, OR 97207 (503 226-4801).

THE BOEING COMPANY (747/767 PLANT), Everett, Washington: By virtue of being big enough to hold 50 planes in various stages of completion, the final assembly building which you tour is the largest building in the world by cubic volume —62 acres under one roof! Information: Boeing Company, PO Box 3707 (OA-65), Seattle, WA 98124 (206 342-4801).

THE WEYERHAEUSER COMPANY, Longview, Washington: The world's largest forest products plant. Sawmill tours are available from mid-June through Labor Day only. Information: Weyerhaeuser, PO Box 188, Longview, WA 98632 (206 425-2150).

For the Spirit

National Parks: A Checklist

Set aside by Congress for their exceptional array of one-of-a-kind scenic, geological, and historic features, the national parks are the Metropolitan Museums of America's natural history. You won't find *all* of the country's most marvelous natural features in the system — but almost.

Nevertheless, park boundaries are drawn arbitrarily, and usually take in only the areas where the marvels are found in greatest concentration. National forests, national wildlife refuges, state parks, and other government-protected preserves often surround the parks or take in similar countryside — and they're far less crowded.

Here is a list of the parks and adjacent recreation areas and attractions. Unless otherwise indicated, all of them offer camping and ranger programs; permits are usually required for overnight hiking trips into the backcountry.

Almost all parks will be crowded during a mid-July to mid-August summer "rush hour," and it may be necessary to reserve your campsite in advance. But you will also find naturalist programs scheduled with a frequency that you wouldn't encounter at other times of year — say, in other summer months, or during spring, fall, and winter. Then, on the other hand, you may have the country's most marvelous natural features almost all to yourself.

For folders on the individual areas, you can write the superintendents of the parks you're interested in, or address your query for information about more than one park to the National Park Service, Public Inquiries, Room 1013, Interior Building, Washington, DC 20240 (202 343-4747). For a small fee, The Superintendent of Documents, US Government Printing Office, Washington, DC 20402, can send you booklets on archeology, fishing, backcountry travel, and camping in the national park system, as well as an interesting publication describing the dozens of lesser-used parks and a comprehensive listing of parks. Michael Frome's excellent *National Park Guide* (Rand McNally, $7.95) describes all of the natural areas in considerable detail.

EAST

ACADIA NATIONAL PARK, Bar Harbor, Maine: With its fjords, towering shoreline cliffs, rocky coves, and trail-crossed inland forests, this 38,524-acre national park, the only one in New England, offers some of the most spectacular scenery in a beautiful state. Ocean Drive, the sea-hugging section of the 20-mile-long Park Loop Road, takes you to Great Head, high over the surf; to tide pools full of brightly colored marine life; to Otter Point, where you can watch the lobster boats and pleasure craft out at sea; and to brief but golden Sand Beach. Somes Sound, the East Coast's only fjord, is also in the park. Acadia National Park, Bar Harbor, ME 04609 (207 288-3338). See also *Acadia National Park,* DIRECTIONS.

SHENANDOAH NATIONAL PARK, Front Royal, Virginia: Crisscrossed by some 465 miles of trails — 94 of them along the Appalachian Trail — Shenandoah National Park's 194,078 acres are about as close to paradise as a hiker can get. The 105-mile-long Skyline Drive, which crosses and recrosses the top of the ridge along which the park sprawls, makes the place wonderful for Sunday drivers as well — particularly in May, when the pink azalea is in bloom; in June, when the mountain laurel is blossoming; and from mid- to late October during the fall color display. You can go riding, cycling, or fishing, or join the rangers for nature walks and campfire talks — and even today, when you look up into the night sky, you won't have any trouble figuring out why the Indians named the area "Daughter of the Stars." The Skyline Drive continues for nearly 500 miles more, as the Blue Ridge Parkway. You can follow it or find other diversions closer at hand in the George Washington National Forest, which flanks the park. Information: Shenandoah National Park, Luray, VA 22835 (703 999-2243). See also *Shenandoah National Park,* DIRECTIONS.

SOUTH

HOT SPRINGS NATIONAL PARK, Hot Springs, Arkansas: Five thousand acres in the Ouachita Mountains, 47 mineral hot springs, and 4 spas at "Bath House Row" (where baths go for about $5 each), make this one of the nation's most unusual national parks. Nearby: DeGray and Ouachita lakes, immense impoundments where you can swim, fish, go boating; and the Ouachita National Forest, great for backpacking and hiking. From mid- to late May, the magnolias bloom; mid-October brings the equally spectacular fall foliage show. Information: Hot Springs National Park, PO Box 1860, Hot Springs, AR 71901 (501 624-3383). See also *Hot Springs National Park,* DIRECTIONS.

EVERGLADES NATIONAL PARK, Homestead, Florida: The park's 1½ million acres of mangrove swamps and watery plains provide a wonderful feeding ground for waterbirds, ducks, and all manner of tropical bird life: egrets, brown pelicans, yellow-crowned and black-crowned night herons, roseate spoonbills, great white herons, wood ibis. Go in summer to see giant loggerhead turtles laying their eggs on the beaches at Cape Sable, or in winter and early spring for the best bird-watching. Nearby: A Seminole Indian reservation, good for arts and crafts; the Audubon Society's 6,000-acre Corkscrew Swamp Sanctuary, home of the largest remaining stand of virgin bald cypress in the US. Information: Everglades National Park, PO Box 279, Homestead, FL 33030 (305 247-6211). See also *Everglades National Park,* DIRECTIONS.

MAMMOTH CAVE NATIONAL PARK, Mammoth Cave, Kentucky: The 52,000-plus acres of woodlands take in what used to be known as "the greatest cave that ever was." That was back in the days ladies had to don bloomers to visit, but a trip along the cave's 230 miles of mapped corridors will convince you that it isn't far from true, even today. Information: Mammoth Cave National Park, Mammoth Cave, KY 42259 (502 758-2251). See also *Mammoth Cave National Park,* DIRECTIONS.

GREAT SMOKY MOUNTAINS NATIONAL PARK, near Gatlinburg, Tennessee: The committee who picked the area for a park site called it "Exceptional, for the height of the mountains, depths of the valleys, ruggedness of the area, and unexampled variety of trees, shrubs, and plants." That this statement remains true is particularly amazing when you consider that the park lies within a day's drive of almost all the major cities in the East and the Midwest; the Smokies get the heaviest use of any park in the system. Yet, with about 5,000 acres, 800 miles of hiking trails, and scenic parkways which never seem to end, you can usually get off by yourself, even in summer, the busiest season. Spring, fall, and winter are also lovely — spring for the wildflowers (April) and rhododendrons and azaleas (late June); fall for the crisp air and flaming colors; winter for the solitude. Information: Great Smoky Mountains National Park, Gatlinburg, TN 37738 (615 436-5615). See also *Great Smoky Mountains National Park,* DIRECTIONS.

BIG BEND NATIONAL PARK, on the US-Mexican border near Terlingua, Texas: Formed as the Rio Grande wore away at the hardened sediments of an inland sea that covered the area millions of years ago, Big Bend is one of the best places in the park system to study desert life, which is far livelier than you'd expect. The rocky, pine- and juniper-covered Chisos Mountains — which change colors as the sun moves through the sky — shelter coyotes, ringtails, pronghorns, mule deer, lizards, snakes, and some 400 species of birds. You can take it all in from hiking trails and primitive roads, or from the river, on commercial rafting trips. Information: Big Bend National Park, TX 79834 (915 477-2251). See also *Big Bend National Park,* DIRECTIONS.

GUADALUPE MOUNTAINS NATIONAL PARK, near Salt Flat, Texas: Just south of the New Mexico line, this 77,500-acre 1966 addition to the park system preserves a spectacular exposure of what some geologists consider the world's most significant and extensive fossil reef, a reminder that many years ago the entire area was covered by a shallow sea. Especially noteworthy: Texas' highest peak, Guadalupe (8,751 feet, accessible by trail); the whitish, thousand-foot cliffs known as El Capitan; and the rugged countryside which takes in desert vegetation, ponderosa pine, southwestern white pine, and Douglas fir. The first two weeks of November, when the canyon foliage takes on its autumn colorations, are particularly beautiful. Information: Carlsbad Caverns National Park, 3225 National Parks Hwy., Carlsbad, NM 88220 (915 828-3385).

VIRGIN ISLANDS NATIONAL PARK, St. John, Virgin Islands: Nearly two-thirds of tiny St. John Island is taken up by the tropical forests, sparkling beaches, and Danish ruins of this 15,150-acre national park. Offshore there are wonderful coral reefs, vividly colored and full of neon-bright fish. You can swim, snorkel, go for bonefish (spooky and tough to catch) or marlin, tuna, sailfish, and wahoo, hike through the forests to former plantations and pre-Columbian Indian petroglyphs, and camp just a stone's throw from the beach. Information: Virgin Islands National Park, PO Box 7789, St. Thomas, Virgin Islands 00801 (809 775-2050).

MIDWEST

ISLE ROYALE NATIONAL PARK, near Houghton, Michigan, in Lake Superior: With some 160 miles of trails, this 539,280-acre park on the largest island in Lake Superior is one of the best places for hiking in the US — and certainly in the Midwest. You can also go boating, or fish in inland streams, bays, and in Lake Superior for trout, northern pike, or perch. Information: Isle Royale National Park, 87 N Ripley St., Houghton, MI 49931 (906 482-3310). See also *Isle Royale National Park,* DIRECTIONS.

VOYAGEURS NATIONAL PARK, International Falls, Minnesota: While it is possible to drive to the edge of this 205,000-acre park, access to most of the forests, bogs, and lakes (four big ones and some two dozen smaller ones) is almost entirely by houseboat, runabout, cruiser, and canoe: Backpacking will never be as popular here as it is, say, at Isle Royale, though exploring an island on foot can be fun. For the moment, powerboating on the big lakes is the main activity, along with fishing for northern pike, trout, smallmouth bass, and walleye and, in winter, cross-country skiing, snowmobiling, and ice fishing. Outfitters renting everything from boats to camping gear are widely available. Information: Voyageurs National Park, PO Box 50, International Falls, MN 56649 (218 283-9821). See also *Voyageurs National Park,* DIRECTIONS.

WEST

GLACIER BAY NATIONAL PARK, Gustavus, Alaska: With over three million acres, this meeting place of water, ice, and land is one of the widest expanses of terrain in the national park system; inland peaks that rise to 15,300 feet are home to bear, coyote, wolf, and wolverine, while the shoreline is inhabited by whales and seals. You can hike on 4 miles of trail near park headquarters or head cross-country. The monument is accessible only by airplane or boat. Information: the Superintendent, Glacier Bay National Park, Gustavus, AK 99826 (907 697-3341).

DENALI NATIONAL PARK, McKinley Park, Alaska: North America's tallest mountain, 20,320-foot Mount McKinley, towers over the spectacular Alaska Range, which dominates the scenery in this recently renamed 3,029-square-mile subarctic wilderness — but if you come specifically to see Denali, the "high one," you may be disappointed: the mountain is cloud-covered for more than half of every summer season. However, the park does offer you an excellent opportunity to hike in both tundra and taiga and to look for Alaskan grizzly, moose, caribou, Dall sheep, and wolf, as well as many other species of mammals, birds, and flora — and the landscape will quite simply take your breath away. Information: Denali National Park, Box 9, McKinley Park, AK 99755 (907 683-2294). See also *Denali National Park,* DIRECTIONS.

GRAND CANYON NATIONAL PARK, Grand Canyon, Arizona: "The world's most wonderful spectacle," according to naturalist John Burroughs. True or not, no other natural formation in the US comes close to equaling the Canyon's size, color, or geological significance. Information: Grand Canyon National Park, PO Box 129, Grand Canyon, AZ 86023 (602 638-2411). See also *Grand Canyon National Park,* DIRECTIONS.

PETRIFIED FOREST NATIONAL PARK, near Holbrook, Arizona: Part of the Painted Desert — a vast area of bright-colored sandstone, shale, and clay formations — 93,493-acre Petrified Forest National Park is made up of six areas where the fallen trees of a 200-million-year-old forest have gradually filled with minerals, turned to stone, and been stained by traces of carbon, iron, and manganese in brilliant reds, purples, and blues. The logs of jasper, agate, and other quartzes that resulted — some 100 feet long — lie helter-skelter on the ground. (Concessionaires sell bits of the stuff collected on private properties outside the park.) The 50,000 park acres designated as wilderness make for great hiking and camping; best seasons are spring (particularly from late April through early June, when desert wildflowers are in bloom) and fall. Information: Petrified Forest National Park, AZ 86028 (602 524-6228). See also *Petrified Forest National Park,* DIRECTIONS.

LASSEN VOLCANIC NATIONAL PARK, near Mineral, California: This park has mud pots, fumaroles, hot springs, and such, just like Yellowstone; but Lassen is far less crowded. The park's center, 10,457-foot Lassen Peak, is one of the most recently active volcanoes in the lower 48 states. Information: Lassen National Park, Mineral, CA 96063 (916 595-4444). See also *Lassen Volcanic National Park,* DIRECTIONS.

REDWOOD NATIONAL PARK, near Crescent City, California: Northern California's 106,000-acre park, 7 miles wide, stretches for 46 Pacific-pounded miles adjoining Six Rivers National Forest, and takes in sand and pebble beaches, creeks, cliffs, and huge stands of virgin redwoods, including the earth's tallest tree, measured in 1963 at 367.8 feet. In 1980, UNESCO added the park to its prestigious World Heritage List of places worthy of preservation for the good of mankind. Most of the other redwoods reach 200 feet. Information: Redwood National Park, 1111 Second St., Crescent City, CA 95531 (707 464-6101). See also *Redwood National Park,* DIRECTIONS.

SEQUOIA AND KINGS CANYON NATIONAL PARKS, near Three Rivers, California: The two parks, administered as one, take in a 65-mile-long, 1,300-square mile expanse of rugged canyons, peaks, and gorges. But the purpose of the park is to preserve groves of giant sequoia, which, with the coastal redwoods, are among the last surviving members of a large group which was widespread eons ago. Information: Sequoia and Kings Canyon National Parks, Three Rivers, CA 93271 (209 565-3341). See also *Sequoia and Kings Canyon National Parks,* DIRECTIONS.

YOSEMITE NATIONAL PARK, Yosemite, California: A 1,189-square-mile parkland, with groves of sequoias, brushy chaparral, alpine vegetation, immense waterfalls (at their most thunderous in May and June), and huge monoliths. One of them, El Capitan, is the world's largest mass of visible granite. You can take backpacking, mule, horseback, or naturalist trips led by rangers; go to mountain climbing school (see Climbing Schools, *Mountain Climbing*); or take a summer photography workshop with

Ansel Adams. Information: Yosemite National Park, PO Box 577, Yosemite, CA 95389 (209 372-4461). See also *Yosemite National Park,* DIRECTIONS.

MESA VERDE NATIONAL PARK, near Durango, Colorado: Fourteen hundred years ago, Indians came to this land, lived on the mesa tops, built elaborate new homes in the sides of the cliffs — and then disappeared. Just why that happened, nobody knows, but it's hard not to speculate when you visit this 52,035-acre park. With park rangers, you can tour the 200-room Cliff Palace, 200 feet up; Spruce Tree House, amazingly well preserved; and Balcony House. Even history-haters will get hooked on matters archeological. Other area attractions: The old Denver and Rio Grande narrow-gauge railroad, which runs from Durango, through deep forested canyons, to the quaint old mining town of Silverton (call 303 247-2733 for train information); the San Juan National Forest, great for hiking and fishing; and a variety of other national monuments: the Aztec Ruins and Chaco Canyon, near towers, pueblos, and cliff dwellings scattered around the Four Corners area; Navajo, near Kayenta and Tuba City, Arizona; and Canyon de Chelly, near Chinle, Arizona, in the Navajo reservation. Lodgings are available in Mesa Verde at Far View Lodge, modern, beautifully situated, and aptly named (303 529-4421). In Durango, you'll find the refurbished Victorian-era Strater Hotel (303 247-4431) along with some 50 other hostelries. For park information, contact the park superintendent in Mesa Verde National Park, CO 81330 (303 529-4461); for details about the surrounding area, write the Cortez Chamber of Commerce, Box 968, Cortez, CO 81321 (303 565-3414).

ROCKY MOUNTAIN NATIONAL PARK, Estes Park, Colorado: The 265,679 acres — 415 square miles — of high peaks and luxuriant forests that were set aside as a park in 1915 are today virtually unspoiled, and make excellent hiking. You can go to the top of 14,255-foot Longs Peak, one of the park's 59 peaks over 12,000 feet, or stroll to lovely Emerald Lake, its shores formed by towering peaks. Information: Estes Park Chamber of Commerce, PO Box 3050, Estes Park, CO 80517 (303 586-4431) and Rocky Mountain National Park, Estes Park, CO 80517 (303 586-2371). See also *Rocky Mountain National Park,* DIRECTIONS.

HALEAKALA NATIONAL PARK, on the island of Maui, Hawaii: Whether, after your trip to this 28,660-acre preserve, you'll remember the spectacular drive to the headquarters over the highest paved road in the mid-Pacific, or the stunning emptiness of the 19-square-mile crater of this now-dormant volcano, is a toss-up. The highway clings precariously to the mountainside, and offers views of mists, cloud banks, pastureland, ocean. The vast, silent caldera — ribboned with hiking trails where you can stay overnight in primitive cabins — is dotted by cinder cones, lava flows, and spatter vents. In the Kipahulu District of the park, on the Pacific, you can splash in waterfall pools that tumble into each other on the way to the sea. Information: Haleakala National Park, PO Box 369, Makawao, Maui, HI 96768 (808 572-7749). See also *Haleakala National Park,* DIRECTIONS.

HAWAII VOLCANOES NATIONAL PARK, near Volcano, Hawaii: 4,077-foot Kilauea, dubbed the drive-in volcano because of its accessibility, is just one of two that are still active in this 229,177-acre park; and between it and 13,680-foot Mauna Loa, something is usually acting up. You may see Kilauea letting out fountains of lava (once, a fountain sprayed 1,900 feet into the air). You may see rivers of lava. You may feel Mauna Loa's tremors. You will probably see steam — along Steaming Bluff it will swirl around you like a fog. You'll see brand-new land, created in 1979, when lava from the volcano's east rift zone erupted. And at the Hawaiian Volcano Observatory, you can watch seismographs at work. The Volcano House is a good place to lunch, dine, lodge; there's also an around-the-clock sauna heated by natural volcanic steam vents (808 967-7321). Nearby: Puuhonua-o-Honaunau National Historic Park, on the Kona Coast at Honaunau, the site of an ancient Hawaiian temple. Information: Hawaii Volcanoes National Park, HI 96718 (808 967-7311).

GLACIER NATIONAL PARK, West Glacier, Montana: Properly called Waterton-Glacier International Peace Park, because it adjoins Canada's Waterton National Park, this Montana area's million-plus acres — a phenomenal 1,600 square miles — take in precipitous peaks, knife-edged ridges, 40 glaciers, and approximately 700 miles of hiking trails. Grizzlies live here in abundance, along with bighorn sheep, mountain goats, mule deer, and hawks. Fifty-mile-long Going-to-the-Sun Road provides magnificent vistas. There are marvelous places to stay in the park as well: Sperry and Granite Park Chalets, built around the time of the First World War and hardly modernized since, are accessible only by footpath — but if you can get there, you can see what it feels like to live in a house without electricity. Far fancier are the bigger local establishments — Lake McDonald Lodge and Many Glacier Hotel inside the park, and Glacier Park Lodge, just outside — which are like sets for a Nelson Eddy musical. Nearby: a chairlift ride at Big Mountain, near Whitefish; Flathead Lake, south of Kalispell, the largest natural freshwater lake west of the Mississippi; Flathead National Forest; and Bigfork, a tiny artsy town. Good lodgings are available at Big Mountain and at the Flathead Lake Lodge (406 837-4391) in Bigfork. Time your visit for early summer and you'll catch the resort full of rodeo cowboys, who come to improve their skills at a special rodeo school. Park information: Glacier National Park, West Glacier, MT 59936 (406 888-5441). See also *Glacier National Park,* DIRECTIONS.

CARLSBAD CAVERNS NATIONAL PARK, near Carlsbad, New Mexico: Lying underneath the rugged foothills of the Guadalupe Mountains, Carlsbad Cavern is only the best known of the dozens of caves in this national park; the grotto is as noteworthy for its immensity as for its variety of formations. From May through September, you can watch hundreds of thousands of bats leaving the caverns each evening. In another part of the park, lantern tours through an undeveloped cave are available. Information: Carlsbad Caverns National Park, 3225 National Parks Hwy., Carlsbad, NM 88220 (505 785-2233). See also *Carlsbad Caverns National Park,* DIRECTIONS.

THEODORE ROOSEVELT NATIONAL PARK, Medora, North Dakota: Some 70,374 acres of the badlands that so enchanted the former president when he first came to the area as a big game hunter in 1883 are preserved in this park, and when you visit, you'll easily comprehend the attraction that led Roosevelt to purchase two ranches in the area: The buttes and canyons, carved by wind and water into fantastic shapes, make the scenery extraordinarily beautiful, and the countryside is full of wildlife — buffalo, prairie dogs, eagles, and more. For more information: Superintendent, Theodore Roosevelt National Park, Medora, ND 58645 (701 623-4466).

CRATER LAKE NATIONAL PARK, near Crater Lake, Oregon: Formed by the collapse of a volcano some 6,840 years ago, 21-square-mile, 1,932-foot-deep Crater Lake is the deepest in the United States (and second deepest, next to Canada's Great Slave Lake, in the Western Hemisphere), and boasts some of the most brilliantly blue waters you'll see anywhere. Within 100 miles: Umpqua, Winema, Rogue River National Forests; the Oregon Shakespearean Festival in Ashland; Jacksonville, home of Peter Britt Gardens Music and Arts Festival; and the whitewater raft trips down the Rogue. Information: Crater Lake National Park, PO Box 7, Crater Lake, OR 97604 (503 594-2211). See also *Crater Lake National Park,* DIRECTIONS.

WIND CAVE NATIONAL PARK, near Hot Springs, South Dakota: Set in the Black Hills, this 28,059-acre park is home to bison, prairie dogs, pronghorn antelope, and an unusual cave full of exotic crystal formations — frostwork crystals made of calcite, aragonite, and boxwork, a honeycomb affair made of crystalline fins. You can see these on traditional walks through the cave, on special candlelight tours through unelectrified sections, and on spelunking tours where you do your locomoting on all fours. Nearby: many hot springs; Mount Rushmore National Memorial (where the heads of Washington, Teddy Roosevelt, Lincoln, and Jefferson are carved in granite cliffs); aptly named Jewel Cave National Monument; Custer State Park, home of one of the world's largest herds of bison; and Black Hills National Forest (good camping). You shouldn't miss the State Game Lodge in Custer State Park, where you can eat buffalo steaks (605 255-4541). According to one commercial buffalo rancher, buffalo tastes like beef wished it did — flavorful, but tender as a filet mignon. Information: Wind Cave National Park, Hot Springs, SD 57747 (605 745-4600).

BADLANDS NATIONAL PARK, Interior, South Dakota: Erosion has left the landscape of this 244,300-acre preserve sculpted into canyons and cliffs, spires and gullies, all banded with the bright colors of the many layers of clay and sandstone deposited here over millennia. Information: Superintendent, Badlands National Park, Interior, SD 57750 (605 433-5361).

ARCHES NATIONAL PARK, near Moab, Utah: Through some of the numerous arches already discovered in Arches National Park's 73,389 acres, you can see the park's vast expanse of canyons and, off in the distance, the snow-capped peaks of the LaSal. Eight arches are located at the Windows. Trim, tapered Delicate Arch, the park's most celebrated landmark, is higher than a seven-story building. Landscape Arch is the world's longest known natural stone bridge. Though only a few miles north of Canyonlands, the formations here are geologically quite different, and a visit to both will teach you a lot about how the earth came to be what it is. Going with one of the several local jeep and river trip outfitters will give you a good grasp of the land's story. Information: Canyonlands National Park, Moab, UT 84532 (801 259-7165) and the Grand County Travel Council, 805 N Main, Moab, UT 84532 (801 259-7531).

BRYCE CANYON NATIONAL PARK, Bryce Canyon, Utah: The Paiutes called the stunning giant rock formations along the edge of the Paunsaugunt Plateau here "red rocks standing like men in bowl-shaped canyons." But when you drive along the 34-mile-long parkway on the plateau's edge, you may think the results of 60 million years of silt and clay deposits and water action resemble castles and cathedrals, Hindu temples and skyscrapers, chessmen and such. The colors — pink, orange, and scarlet, striped with lavender and blue, or cream, white, and yellow — are even more vivid at sunset. It's just as phenomenal when you see them close up; be sure to stop for at least a short hike. Information: Bryce Canyon National Park, Bryce Canyon, UT 84717 (801 834-5322). See also *Bryce Canyon National Park,* DIRECTIONS.

CANYONLANDS NATIONAL PARK, near Moab, Utah: The Green and Colorado Rivers, which meet in this area, have carved deep and winding gorges in the reddish-orange sandstone. The buttes, cliffs, mesas, spires, columns, and pillars — like mad Ludwig's castles in Bavaria — are truly fantastic. Some of the 337,559 acres of juniper and pinyon are still unexplored; those which are charted can be seen on jeep tours out of Moab or float trips down the Green and Colorado Rivers (see *Touring America's Waterways*). Nearby: Arches National Park; Manti-LaSal National Forest (cool woodlands); Glen Canyon National Recreation Area, surrounding Lake Powell (good for water sports); Natural Bridges National Monument; and Hovenweep National Monument, a chain of prehistoric Indian dwellings. Lodgings are available in Moab and Monticello. Information: Grand County Travel Council, 805 N Main, Moab, UT 84532 (801 259-7531), and Canyonlands National Park, Moab, UT 84532 (801 259-7165).

CAPITOL REEF NATIONAL PARK, near Torrey, Utah: According to local legend, Butch Cassidy once used this isolated area as a hiding place, but it was only recently that the rest of America woke up to its beauties: sandstone monoliths, colored in deep rich reds that in some light seem almost luminous, and soaring 400 to 700 feet above the valley floor; petroglyphs and pictographs of prehistoric Indians that keep company with names that the early pioneers carved on the cliffs; and subtle, lovely desert vegetation. You can see it all either from your own car, on jeep tours conducted by a local outfitter, or on foot — along short hiking trails or by going cross-country along dry river beds. Backpacking is also possible. Nearby: Anasazi State Park (more prehistoric Indian history); the Bureau of Land Management's Calf Creek Recreation Area (good for camping, mainly). Information: Capitol Reef National Park, Torrey, UT 84775 (801 425-3871).

ZION NATIONAL PARK, near Springdale, Utah: It was the Mormons, settling here in the 19th century, who called the central feature of this 146,570-acre park "Zion," or "heavenly city of God," and who gave many of its features their strange-sounding names — Kolob Canyons and Mt. Moroni. Backcountry trails are rugged, but full of marvels, like the amphitheater of sculptured cliffs or the "Hanging Gardens" — rock walls draped with columbine, monkey flower, maiden-hair ferns, and scarlet lobelia — which you see along the Narrows Trail. Park roads give you terrific views of the canyon walls, colored crimson, purple, pink, orange, and yellow. Horseback trips are also available. Within a 125-mile radius, you can visit the North Rim of the Grand Canyon; Bryce Canyon National Park; Cedar Breaks National Monument; and the Dixie National Forest. Cedar City, about 25 miles from the park's northern boundary, is home to the Utah Shakespeare Festival every summer. Information: Zion National Park, Springdale, UT 84767 (801 772-3256). See also *Zion National Park,* DIRECTIONS.

MT. RAINIER NATIONAL PARK, near Longmire, Washington: The dormant ice-clad volcano which is the raison d'être of this park is only its most striking feature. The 241,920 acres also have cathedral-like forests of Douglas and Pacific silver fir, western red cedar, Sitka spruce, western hemlock. The park is a wonderland of glaciers, and boasts the lower 48's most extensive single-peak glacier system, as well as its longest glacier (Carbon), and its largest (Emmons). Nearby are the Snoqualmie National Forest and the Crystal Mountain Resort, a ski development that does a brisk business in summer. Most accommodations — motels, inns, and lodges — are along rt. 7 from Tacoma. Information: Mt. Rainier National Park, Tahoma Woods Star Route, Ashford, WA 98304 (206 569-2211). See also *Mt. Rainier National Park,* DIRECTIONS.

NORTH CASCADES NATIONAL PARK, near Sedro Woolley, Washington: Ice falls and waterfalls, hanging valleys and ice caps, and some 300 glaciers, plus canyons, granite peaks, and mountain lakes and streams make this a rugged 789 square miles. It's not for that reason only, however, that you'll find some of the most extensive opportunities for outdoor recreation in the area. In addition to the park, you'll find the 167-square-mile Ross Lake National Recreation Area (which lies between the park's north and south units); the 97-square-mile Lake Chelan National Recreation Area (adjoining the south units on its southern border); and surrounding the four units, the Mount Baker–Snoqualmie, Wenatchee, and Okanogan National Forests. You'll find especially interesting lodgings at the rustic North Cascades Lodge (509 682-4711) in Stehekin, at the north end of Lake Chelan and accessible only by boat or float plane from the town of Chelan. Information: North Cascades National Park, 800 State St., Sedro Woolley, WA 98284 (206 855-1331).

OLYMPIC NATIONAL PARK, near Port Angeles, Washington: These 1,400 square miles lay claim to some of the wettest weather in America; sixty living glaciers; alpine meadows; deep lush valleys; everything is green rain forests full of fungi, lichens, and some 70 species of moss, draped over branches and growing on tree trunks. There are stands of Sitka spruce and Douglas fir, sometimes 300 feet tall and 1,000 years old. Huge Roosevelt elk inhabit the park, their numbers making the herd the largest in the country. Seals, sea lions, and whales can be seen when you hike along the beaches in the Pacific coast section. Nearby: the Olympic Highway, circling the peninsula; Olympic National Forest; the San Juan Islands, a still fairly unspoiled resort area in Puget Sound, accessible by ferry from Anacortes, Washington, and Sidney, British Columbia. Information: Olympic National Park, 600 E Park Ave., Port Angeles, WA 98362 (206 452-4501). See also *Olympic National Park,* DIRECTIONS.

GRAND TETON NATIONAL PARK, near Jackson, Wyoming: This 40-mile-long string of snow-capped and glacier-covered mountains dominates the skyline as do few other mountains in the nation. The 13,770-foot Grand simply towers over big skinny Jackson Hole, the valley on the south end of the park. Surrounding are Teton, Shoshone, and Targhee National Forests, all heavily forested and trail-crossed. Information: Grand Teton National Park, PO Drawer 170, Moose, WY 83102 (307 733-2880). See also *Grand Teton National Park,* DIRECTIONS.

YELLOWSTONE NATIONAL PARK, in the northwest corner of Wyoming, just east of West Yellowstone, Montana: Old Faithful is the most famous thermal feature in this park full of thermal features. There are countless geyser basins, mud pots, bubbling springs, hot pools that are blue, red, orange, and yellow, depending on the temperature of the water and the plants that can survive there. Yellowstone has a reputation for being crowded — and it is, at its major points of interest. Go into the backcountry, however, and you can have trails almost to yourself. Information: Yellowstone National Park, WY 82190 (307 344-7381). See also *Yellowstone National Park,* DIRECTIONS.

America's Most Exciting Amusement Parks and Theme Parks

Sixty or seventy years ago, the American Sunday changed forever. Until then, America's amusement parks were run as sedate adjuncts to picnic groves, usually owned by the companies that ran trolleys and interurban train lines. At some unrecorded moment, a trolley line executive realized that people loved the rides a lot more than the picnics, and before long picnicking as a Sunday afternoon pastime went the way of oil lamps. Huge entertainment complexes sprang up beside piers and boardwalks across the country. Roller coasters didn't go very fast (one attendant was chided for eating his lunch on board), but they stirred the masses. "It was something dreadful," scrawled a shaken Agatha Wales on the back of a postcard after her ride on the Venice, California, roller coaster. "I was never so frightened in my life. And if the Dear Lord will forgive me this time, I will never ride it again." Most folks were simply thrilled.

Today, more time, money, and talent is going into the business than ever before — and the results are spectacular. Not only are the parks clean, green, and flowering, but you can take in zippy, chills-down-the-spine shows and even top-name entertainers after you've whirled over some of the scariest roller coaster tracks in history.

Admission fees — usually under $14, with reductions for children — generally buy all the rides and shows you want, though occasionally you'll have to pay extra to play games at the penny arcade. A couple of parks — Disneyland (in California), Walt Disney World (in Florida), and Knott's Berry Farm — charge on a per-ride, per-attraction basis.

EAST

SIX FLAGS GREAT ADVENTURE, Jackson, New Jersey: The company that brought America Six Flags Over Texas (and with it, the concept of rides-and-live-shows entertainment complexes behind all those listed below) has completely changed the face of the park (the largest in the Northeast) since it took over; but the great rides — the coasters, the 15-story-high Ferris wheel, the giant log flume — are still there, along with a dual wooden coaster, the Lightning Loops (a loop coaster that shuttles forward and backward), performing dolphins and a high dive act. A 450-acre drive-through safari park adjoins the rides area, bringing the total acreage to 1,100. Special rock concerts are held here all year. Information: Six Flags Great Adventure, PO Box 120, Jackson, NJ 08527 (201 928-2000).

HERSHEYPARK, Hershey, Pennsylvania: Though Krackle Bars and Hershey Kisses stroll the grounds, the park's theme is Pennsylvania's German, Dutch, and English cultural heritage — carried out through an artfully reconstructed Tudor castle; food shops offering local specialties like Belgian waffles and funnel cakes; and a Crafts Barn where artisans work at tole painting and caricatures and the like. The fast, old wooden roller coaster known as The Comet is among the best in the US; the sooper-dooperLooper, a steel-tube coaster that shoots you around steeply banked turns and upside down through one enormous vertical loop was the first of its kind on the East Coast. And there are 35 other rides. Also included in your admission is a trip through ZOOAMERICA, a small but high-quality zoo that showcases the plants and animals of five different North American environments; its peregrine falcons, prairie dogs, and other home-grown mammals look as exotic to most visitors as the African creatures displayed at other parks. Information: Hersheypark, Hershey, PA 17033 (717 534-3916). See also *Pennsylvania Dutch Country,* DIRECTIONS.

THE OLD COUNTRY, Williamsburg, Virginia: Run by the people who operate Busch Gardens/Tampa and the Anheuser-Busch Breweries, this is one of the most beautiful US parks. The site — 500 acres of ravine-cut woodlands — is one large reason. Not much of it has been manicured or tamed, and the rides (Rhine cruises, steam train trips, skyrides, and the like) have been chosen and installed to make the most of the scenery. The Loch Ness Monster — an absolutely terrifying double-looped, upside-down roller coaster that drops riders 114 feet in 5 seconds — is one of the best rides in the country. The food stands out, too; you'll find not only hamburgers, but also European specialties — sausages, cheeses, pastas, schnitzels. And, as befits a park with a European theme, there are musical revues, oompah bands, import shops, and a giant Festhaus — a party hall like those in Munich, except that this one is twice the size of a football field. Visiting the Old Country makes a fine complement to sightseeing around Colonial Williamsburg, the unique citywide museum of 18th-century America. (See *Tidewater Virginia,* DIRECTIONS.) For information: PO Drawer FC, Williamsburg, VA 23185 (804 253-3350).

KINGS DOMINION, Richmond, Virginia: Great roller coasters — not just the double, wooden racing roller coaster (one of three similar chillers in the US), but also a loop-the-loop which catapults you through a vertical loop, and then reverses the whole procedure and drops you into a 168-foot-long slide. The big new attractions are the fifth coaster and the 17-story-high Lost World, a man-made mountain that conceals three different adventures. Fred Flintstone and other Hanna-Barbera characters entertain. Information: Kings Dominion, Doswell, VA 23047 (804 876-5331).

CAROWINDS, Charlotte, North Carolina: The theme is Carolina's history, with a good assortment of rides and shows and five coasters, including one that turns riders upside down four times and a wild new whitewater rapids ride. Information: Carowinds, PO Box 240516, Charlotte, NC 28224 (704 588 2600).

SOUTH

OPRYLAND USA, Nashville, Tennessee: The wooded site on the banks of the Cumberland River on the edge of this Southern city was pretty to begin with, and the architects made the most of the landscape by leaving all but a handful of the original trees while adding dozens of their own, and hundreds of flowers. The park is a treat to behold. But Opryland really shines when it comes to music — not just country and western and bluegrass, as you might expect from the park's name, but also rock 'n' roll, gospel, Broadway show tunes, and more. There are thrill rides, too: a twisting corkscrew roller coaster that hurtles you upside down; a tight-turning coaster that has you flying through the treetops; a flume; the new-and-wild Grizzly River Rampage (a.k.a.

G-R-R), a huge and satisfyingly long whitewater rafting adventure; and more. Every Memorial Day weekend, there's a big Opryland Gospel Jubilee, for which some of the country's top-name gospel groups perform in the park's Theater-by-the-Lake; and now and then throughout the year, television specials are taped in the Grand Ole Opry House (and tickets are free to Opryland visitors). For more information, contact Opryland, 2802 Opryland Dr., Nashville, TN 37214 (615 889-6611).

SIX FLAGS OVER GEORGIA, Atlanta, Georgia: Loosely themed around the six countries whose flags have flown over Georgia, Six Flags climbs a forested hillside on the western edge of the city. There are graded paths for strolling, gazebos for sitting and inhaling the sweet Southern air, and plenty of Coca-Cola and watermelon. The roller coaster, the Great American Scream Machine, ripples around a reflecting lake that makes it seem even higher than it really is; one of the scariest around. In addition to that, a *triple* loop coaster, a new whitewater raft trip, and 39-odd other rides, there are live shows, magicians and musicians that stroll the grounds, jugglers, puppeteers, and, in summer, fireworks. By the way, the six flags belong to Britain, France, Spain, the US, the Confederacy, and of course, the state of Georgia. Information: Six Flags over Georgia, PO Box 43187, Atlanta, GA 30378 (404 948-9290).

WALT DISNEY WORLD, Lake Buena Vista, Florida: Phenomenally successful in its first decade, this 43-square-mile resort complex holds even more promise for its second since the October 1, 1982, opening of the $800 million Epcot Center. More than twice the size of the Magic Kingdom — WDW's Disneyland-like rides and attractions area — this new "thinking man's theme park" examines technology and global cultures in a number of pavilions that feature some of Disney's most advanced special effects to date. Yet the 45 attractions of the Magic Kingdom, presided over by that fairytale castle, and River Country, the ultimate in old-fashioned swimming holes, look as terrific as ever. So do the three golf courses, the tennis courts, the one-of-a-kind campground, the dinner shows, the shopping villages, and the spiffy resorts. Information: Walt Disney World, PO Box 40, Lake Buena Vista, FL 32830 (305 824-4538; for reservations, 305 824-8000).

SIX FLAGS OVER TEXAS, Arlington, Texas: Developed (like the Atlanta park under the same management) around the theme of six countries which have, over the years, called Texas their colony (Mexico, Spain, France, the Republic of Texas, the Confederacy, the US), Six Flags over Texas, halfway between Dallas and Fort Worth, was the first of the successful theme parks. When it was founded in 1961, it would have been called "Texas under Six Flags" but for the protest of a Texas director that "Texas ain't never been under nuthin'." Summers are hot — but nearly everything that can be air-conditioned, including the grape arbors, is. The assortment of rides and good-clean-fun entertainment is similar to that at its sister park in Atlanta. Information: Six Flags over Texas, PO Box 191, Arlington, TX 76010 (817 461–1200).

ASTROWORLD, Houston, Texas: Also owned by the Six Flags organization, this park is big, clean, as glossy as the Space City itself, and full of rides and wholesome family shows. As of 1977, it was also the home of the first reconstruction of the famous Coney Island Cyclone — one of the most exciting roller coasters ever built. A new shuttle loop coaster went in in 1978 and in the spring of 1980, the park acquired a wild river rapids ride. Astroworld, 9001 Kirby Dr., Houston, TX 77054 (713 748-1234).

MIDWEST

CEDAR POINT, Sandusky, Ohio: While many other old-fashioned amusement parks went into decline about twenty years ago, this fixture of the Great Lakes summer scene was just getting renovated, and today it's quite a place. There's a midway that really looks like a midway instead of some make-believe European country, and a host of nifty one-of-a-kind rides: Gemini (a traditional racing wooden coaster whose 125-foot-high first hill drops 118 feet at a 55° angle); one of the tallest Ferris wheels in the world (with views out over Lake Erie, which laps at the boundaries of the park); a movie theater with a 67-by-88-foot screen that makes you feel you're part of the action; 13 live shows; four carousels; an enormous arcade; and a marine complex where you can watch performing dolphins and sea lions. Cedar Point has nearly 60 rides (more than any other park), and a ride capacity of 75,000, which means less queuing for all. Stay at the big, rambling Hotel Breakers, built in 1905 and fitted out with Tiffany stained glass windows and chandeliers. Knute Rockne, who perfected the forward pass on the Cedar Point beach, married an employee of the hotel. For details about the hotel and the park, write Cedar Point, CN 5006, Sandusky, OH 44870 (419 626-0830).

KINGS ISLAND, near Cincinnati, Ohio: The prototype for Richmond's Kings Dominion. The rides — even the layout — are similar. Especially notable here is the world's longest, highest, and fastest roller coaster, The Beast, and the world's first suspended coaster, The Bat. On the 1,600-acre grounds, there's also a good golf course, the College Football Hall of Fame, and a campground. Information: Kings Island, Kings Island, OH 45034 (513 241-5600).

SIX FLAGS OVER MID-AMERICA, Eureka, Missouri: Like the other parks in the chain, this one near St. Louis will show you a something-for-everyone good time. The park also lays claim to the world's highest parachute drop ride and the Screamin' Eagle roller coaster — no longer the highest and fastest of them all, but still plenty exciting. Information: Six Flags over Mid-America, PO Box 60, Eureka, MO 63025 (314 938-4800).

MARRIOTT'S GREAT AMERICA, Gurnee, Illinois: The Marriott Corporation masterminds two great parks — one in this town near Chicago, the other in northern California. So far, both have the same theme areas — New Orleans, historic America, and so on; plus a Farmers' Market (an assemblage of food boutiques where you can get Mexican, Chinese, and Spanish specialties, Belgian waffles, deli sandwiches, made-from-scratch french fries, and more, in a compact area); bands playing march music and Dixieland; giant loop roller coasters; brand-new designed-to-look-antique 100-foot-high double-decker carousels; and the Pictoriums, movie theaters where the image projected measures 70 by 96 feet. Both also boast a variety of Broadway-style original show productions. The Gurnee park's latest highlight is the world's largest double-racing wooden roller coaster. Information: Marriott's Great America, PO Box 1776, Gurnee, IL 60031 (312 249-1776).

WEST

DISNEYLAND, Anaheim, California: This dream of Walt Disney's is as fantastic as you've probably heard, as magical as Tinkerbell's fairy dust, and perfect to the last detail. Thrill rides aren't the big deal. Instead, you have "adventures" — you get bombarded by cannonballs fired by pirates in the Caribbean, visit a haunted mansion, explore the frontier, or fly through outer space. The special effects are truly astounding. During the summer Main Street Electrical Parade, you see floats and creatures outlined in thousands of tiny white lights. For a list of local motels, write the Greater Los Angeles Visitors and Convention Bureau, 505 S Flower St., Los Angeles, CA 90071 (213 488-9100). For Disneyland information: Guest Relations Office, 1313 Harbor Blvd., Anaheim, CA 92803 (714 999-4565).

KNOTT'S BERRY FARM, Buena Park, California: This park just down the road from Disneyland started out as, yes, a berry farm, then grew like Topsy when Mrs. Walter Knott began serving chicken dinners and Mr. Walter Knott took to concocting entertainments to amuse people who queued up for Mrs. Knott's chicken. It isn't another Disneyland. Nor is it an Opryland. Here, old things — antiques — are scattered throughout the three sections (an early California village, a Roaring 20s area, a frontier village). Here you'll spot an old wagon wheel, there some airplane parts, narrow-gauge locomotives, cable cars, antique carousels (one is mule-powered). In addition to the rides (about 75 in all, including some real white-knucklers), you can watch can-can dancers, marionettes, a summer ice show, a singing-and-dancing extravaganza; and play games in the largest penny arcade west of the Mississippi. And there's plenty of good eating right on the grounds: Sicilian pizza, extra-juicy hot dogs, among other things — if you don't want Mrs. Knott's fried chicken, that is. Information: Greater Los Angeles Visitors and Convention Bureau (address above) for area information; Knott's Berry Farm, 8039 Beach Blvd., Buena Park, CA 90620 (714 827-1776).

SIX FLAGS MAGIC MOUNTAIN, Valencia, California: The third in a trio of Southern California diversions, Magic Mountain is the place to go to get spun around, shaken like a rag doll, and flipped head over heels till you almost wished you'd stayed home. There are, in fact, so many coasters and spinning wheel rides that for years the place looked more like a test ground for scaffolding than a place to have a good time. No longer, though: It's green and clean as a whistle. And a new area, Spillikin Handcrafter's Junction, is almost funky: You can watch craftsmen turning pots, blowing glass, working with leather and wood — and then buy the products. And since the Six Flags organization took over a few years ago, the place has really blossomed, with new live shows, puppet performances, and music and dance revues, so that the offerings are more balanced than ever before; you can have a good time even if you don't ride the rides. For lodging information, contact the Greater Los Angeles Visitors and Convention Bureau (address above). Park details: Magic Mountain, Valencia, CA 91355 (805 255-4100).

MARRIOTT'S GREAT AMERICA, Santa Clara, California: But for the lack of an American Eagle wooden roller coaster and a slightly lusher look (the result of the northern California climate), this park is a twin to the Great America in Gurnee, Illinois, described above. Information: Great America, PO Box 1776, Santa Clara, CA 95052 (408 988-1776).

America's Best Resort Hotels

American resorts are playgrounds for adults — full of golf courses, tennis courts, horseback riding trails and horse stables, bike paths, hiking paths, swimming pools, lake beaches, and other facilities too costly for the average homeowner's backyard.

Any decent resort should offer these kinds of activities. The list below is a selection of American resorts that give just a bit more — more activities, better service, greater style — or simply have just a bit more panache than their competitors. For any resort you will pay more than for a hotel or motel. At our choices, prices are likely to be even higher. But remember: Rates are usually reduced — sometimes cut in half — during off-season (the timing of which will vary depending upon where the resort is, and when it experiences its heaviest crowds). When you are budgeting, be sure to ask whether greens fees, tennis court fees, and the costs of other activities are included in the price of your room. If not, they can add as much as $15 or $20 a day to your budget.

EAST

THE BALSAMS GRAND RESORT HOTEL, Dixville Notch, New Hampshire: This fairy-tale castle — immense and white, with red tile roofs — sits at the base of 800-foot cliffs alongside a manmade lake, surrounded by 15,000 acres of the forests and stony peaks of northernmost New Hampshire. The 6,525-yard Donald Ross–designed 18-hole golf course, built against the side of a mountain and full of sloping fairways, is a challenge; even the 9-hole executive course, a mere 2,020 yards long, will require every club in your bag. There's also tennis, swimming, hiking, and trout fishing. Information: The Balsams, Dixville Notch, NH 03576 (603 255-3400).

MOUNTAIN VIEW HOUSE, Whitefield, New Hampshire: In continuous operation since 1865, this hostelry set on a plateau overlooking the Presidential Range reflects every bit of the care that has been bestowed on it. Witness the magnificent flower arrangements on all the tables in the comfortable but well-put-together public rooms, and the immaculate grooming of the golf course, a 9-holer that can be played off two sets of tees as 18 holes. There's also tennis, hiking, an Olympic-sized swimming pool. Information: Mountain View House, Whitefield, NH 03598 (603 837-2511).

SPALDING INN CLUB, Whitefield, New Hampshire: Not far from Mountain View House, this snug resort shares with that establishment a certain feeling of gracious but unpretentious elegance encountered at few other hotels in the country. The maintenance is superb, from the lawns and gardens and white-trimmed clubhouse and cottages to the four clay tennis courts, the nine holes of par-three golf, and the heated swimming pool. But the Spalding Inn Club is perhaps best known for its bowling green, and several national competitions have been held here. The resort runs on the full American plan, and the food is good and interesting enough to quell any desire you may have to eat around. Information: Spalding Inn Club, Whitefield, NH 03598 (603 837-2572).

THE OTESAGA, Cooperstown, New York: The building's fine turn-of-the-century Georgian exterior with its large columns and its stately colonnaded lobby is a good deal more formal than the resort itself, which is mannerly but not straight-laced. You can swim in Lake Otsego, at the foot of the resort's lawns, or go sailing, fishing, golfing, or tennis playing. There's a wonderful noontime buffet, a heated pool, nightly dancing. Cooperstown, of course, is a village of museums: the Farmer's Museum, the Baseball Hall of Fame, the Fenimore House. Information: The Otesaga, Box 311, Cooperstown, NY 13326 (607 547-9931).

GROSSINGER'S, Grossinger, New York: This Catskills establishment is a Jewish mother among resorts. There's more food on your plate at breakfast, lunch, and dinner than you can possibly eat, and it's so good that you consume every bite anyway, and when the waitresses (who won't take no for an answer) scurry to the kitchen and bring you more, you clean your plate again. There are too many activities, too many lectures and demonstrations, too much after-dark entertainment, and so many facilities that you can't possibly take advantage of everything. At Grossinger's, for instance, you won't find just one Olympic-sized swimming pool, but two; not one golf course but two; and there are two health clubs; sixteen tennis courts — and some 600 old-fashioned or *House Beautiful*–spiffy rooms. A lively day camp program for youngsters through age 17 offers the same variety of activities. There's skating, skiing, and tobogganing in winter. The kitchen is kosher (meat and dairy products are prepared separately and never served together). Information: Grossinger's Hotel, Grossinger, NY 12734 (914 292-5000).

THE BASIN HARBOR CLUB, Vergennes, Vermont: In its tenth decade of summer resort operation, and in the third generation of the Beach Family proprietorship, the Basin Harbor Club sits right on the banks of Lake Champlain a few miles away from the Shelburne Museum in Shelburne. It's clearly an operation designed for a well-heeled clientele, but appears far more informal than most, more like an assemblage of summer homes at an exclusive lake resort. Which makes sense, since lodging is in 70 cottages (some beautifully appointed, some as modest as most people's lake resort places). There's a golf course (fairly level), tennis courts, swimming pool, boats for rent, and a children's program. Rocks along the shore of Lake Champlain are great for sunning. On July 4, the resort celebrates with a buffet breakfast, brass band performances and other special goings-on, and a big fireworks display. Open mid-June to mid-October. Information: Basin Harbor Club, Vergennes, VT 05491 (802 475-2311).

WOODSTOCK INN, Woodstock, Vermont: The town, a picture-postcard affair whose village green is rimmed by colonial homes and presided over by a quaint old church whose steeple boasts four sets of Paul Revere bells, deserved an inn like this; but when the old Woodstock Inn burned not long ago, nobody really expected a new hostelry quite so fine as this Rockresort. You can swim, play tennis on any of 10 courts or golf on a superb Robert Trent Jones course, go biking — or, in the area, shop for antiques or take off on hikes in the forests. In winter, you can downhill ski at Suicide Six, cross-country ski on any number of trails, go for sleigh rides, and more (there are special holiday celebrations for Thanksgiving, Christmas, Washington's Birthday). Information: Woodstock Inn, Woodstock, VT 05091 (802 457-1100).

SOUTH

MARRIOTT'S GRAND HOTEL, Point Clear, Alabama: A rambling structure of weathered cypress occupies a corner of a 500-acre expanse of live oaks and spreading pines that grow right down to the soft white sand that edges Mobile Bay. The extensive facilities include 27 holes of golf, card rooms, a swimming beach and a freshwater pool, sailboats for sailing, speedboats for waterskiing, courts for tennis, bikes for cycling, greens for lawn bowls, and a big air-conditioned yacht for Gulf of Mexico fishing trips. But the atmosphere is low-key and nobody feels obliged to scurry around to take advantage of it all. Information: Grand Hotel, Point Clear, AL 36564 (205 928-9201).

BOCA BEACH CLUB, Boca Raton, Florida: You know you're entering a special hotel from the moment you arrive: Cozy armchairs and a goblet of champagne or a flagon of fresh orange juice are offered even before you check in; and registration is accomplished at lovely antique desks attended by a smiling, attentive staff. The guest rooms are large and tastefully furnished, and the hotel's site on a spit of land between the Intracoastal Waterway and the Atlantic guarantees a watery vista no matter where a room is situated. The best rooms in the house, however, are those on the ground floor; these offer lanais for lounging and direct access to the beach on the Atlantic side. There are also a large terraced pool, numerous tennis courts, and a golf course right on the grounds. Information: Boca Raton Hotel and Club, East Camino Real, Boca Raton, FL 33432 (305 395-3000); toll-free 800 432-0150 from Florida, 800 327-0101 from the rest of the US).

THE BREAKERS, Palm Beach, Florida: American millionaires built this great marble palace of a hotel — the third on the property — in 1925–26 to show Europeans that they had taste, and so it is filled with Flemish tapestries, watercolors and oils, crystal chandeliers, hand-painted and vaulted ceilings, and other works by some 1,200 craftsmen. On the 140-acre property are some large cottages, two 18-hole golf courses including the Breaker's Ocean (one of the best courses on Florida's east coast), 14 tennis courts, and an Olympic-size saltwater swimming pool. Information: The Breakers, Palm Beach, FL 33480 (305 655-6611).

THE KING AND PRINCE, St. Simons Island, Georgia: The centerpiece of this unpretentious 30-year-old Spanish-style palacio-by-the-sea is the splendid dining room, a former ballroom hung with a quartet of vast brass chandeliers and lined on both sides with arched windows that look out over the gardens on one side and the surf-pounded Atlantic (illuminated after dark) on the other. In addition to its lovely gardens planted with oleanders and azaleas, the resort boasts beautiful rooms with lazy ceiling fans, suites with sunken living rooms and entrances directly on the long beach, and lounges full of Chinese Chippendale and Queen Anne furniture. The bridal suite, a circular room atop a spiral staircase, has a king-sized bed and a panoramic view of the ocean. It's all very quietly elegant, but not so stuffy that you feel embarrassed to walk barefoot outside. Activities: golf, tennis, swimming, riding, biking, surf-fishing. Information: King and Prince Hotel, PO Box 798, St. Simons Island, GA 31522 (912 638-3631).

THE CLOISTER, Sea Island, Georgia: This famous old Georgia shore resort — one of the East Coast's most noteworthy — is the kind of almost clubby place to which young people who came here originally on vacation with their parents return on their honeymoon, then come back time and time again, bringing their own youngsters; where, even when guests don't know each other at the start, conversations come easily, simply because everyone shares (if nothing else) a dedication to the resort's old-fashioned good manners. That means dressy evenings of dinner and dancing, and afternoons on the tennis courts or the links (absolutely superb; see *Golf*), or riding, shooting, fishing, boating, cycling, or swimming (either at the beach or in two lovely pools). The facilities are first-class all the way, the grounds are immaculately kept, and the 260-plus rooms all look so fresh that even regulars marvel. Details: The Cloister, Sea Island, GA 31561 (912 638-3611).

THE HOMESTEAD, Hot Springs, Virginia: One of the very finest American resorts, this complex of impressive red brick buildings has immense colonnaded salons where string orchestras play classical music at high tea every day and health clubs where you can soak in mineral baths or take saunas or get massaged within an inch of your life. You can go swimming, play tennis or golf on any of three wooded courses, go riding through the 16,000 acres of Alleghany Mountain forests that belong to the resort, or pass an evening dining and dancing in dressed-up style. This is a big hotel (615 rooms), but it's so well ordered that you can hardly tell when the house is full. Information: The Homestead, Hot Springs, VA 24445 (703 839-5500).

THE TIDES INN, Irvington, Virginia: A gracious establishment founded in 1947 on a peninsula on the western shore of Chesapeake Bay about an hour's drive from Williamsburg, this resort follows the best tradition of family-owned resorts, with fine service and elegant facilities — billiard and Ping-Pong, seven tennis courts, an Olympic-sized swimming pool overlooking the Rappahannock River, a 9-hole putting green, a 9-hole par-3 golf course, Sir Guy Campbell's 6,500-yard championship 18, George Cobb's 7,000-yard 18-hole course, and dining salons where the place settings are crystal and real silver. The feeling at the Tides Golf Lodge, across the inlet, is rustic-modern, casual — completely different. Information about the pair: Tides Inn, Irvington, VA 22480 (804 438-5000); toll-free 800 552-3461 from Virginia, 800 446-9981 from the rest of the US).

THE GREENBRIER, White Sulphur Springs, West Virginia: Staying here will take you back to the Ginger Rogers–Fred Astaire era: You can't help but feel like dressing for dinner, and going dancing in the Old White Club afterward — that, despite the fact that it's also difficult not to wear yourself out on the riding trails, hiking paths, tennis courts, and golf courses that fill up the hotel's 6,500 acres. Everything about this place is elegant, from the endless string of parlors ornamented with Chinese vases and priceless screens, centuries-old oil paintings, real English antique furniture and such, to the long menu full of every conceivable fish, fowl, meat, salad, appetizer, dessert, to the accommodations in comfortable bedrooms and "cottages," a short walk away from the hotel, like Fifth Avenue apartments. Information: The Greenbrier, White Sulphur Springs, WV 24986 (304 536-1110).

MIDWEST

THE GRAND HOTEL, Mackinac Island, Michigan: The fact that there are no cars on this island except fire trucks gives it a turn-of-the-century feel you'll seldom find elsewhere in the US today; the hotel simply completes the picture. A rambling white structure with about 260 rooms, set on 500 acres of lawns and trees adjoining a 2,000-acre state park and overlooking the Straits of Mackinac, the recently renovated Grand Hotel is old-fashioned from the pillared veranda (so long you could barely recognize a friend standing at the opposite end) to the horse drawn surreys that meet guests at the ferry, the afternoon teas, the ornate staircase, and the 19th-century furnishings. By some accounts, this is the world's largest summer resort. Cycling, horseback riding, golfing, and tennis are the activities. Closed November through mid-May. Information: Grand Hotel, Mackinac Island, MI 49757 (906 847-3331).

WEST

THE WIGWAM, Litchfield Park, Arizona: One of the top resorts in the country, founded around WW I as an R & R spot for Goodyear Tire and Rubber Company executives, numbers about 200 rooms in one- and two-story adobe casitas surrounded by palm- and eucalyptus-shaded gardens. Golf is the main activity because of the two excellent Robert Trent Jones–designed courses — the 7,220-yard Gold Course, cleverly filled with sand traps, and the much easier 6,100-yard Blue Course, par 70, which offers well-bunkered fairways and many water holes. A third course was designed by Robert Lawrence (par 72). There are also eight tennis courts (six of them lighted), plus ball machines, practice alleys, and a good program of clinics and private instruction. Other activities: horseback riding, steak broils, shuffleboard and lawn sports, swimming in a big pool. Information: The Wigwam, Litchfield Park, AZ 85340 (602 935-3811).

THE ARIZONA BILTMORE, Phoenix, Arizona: Frank Lloyd Wright's ideas for what a great resort ought to be were part of the inspiration for this grand duchess of desert resorts. In the light of the rest of Wright's work, the gold-leaf ceiling in the dining room, the glass sculpture in the lobby, and some of the other very Gatsbyesque features of the place may seem strange — but that won't diminish your enjoyment. The kitchen is good enough to bring diners from all over the valley, and there are afternoon teas and an endless assortment of facilities — 18 tennis courts, two 18-hole golf courses, two swimming pools (one of them lined with Catalina tile, comparable to the one at William Randolph Hearst's San Simeon). Information: Arizona Biltmore, Box 2290, Phoenix, AZ 85002 (602 955-6600; for reservations, 800 228-3000).

MARRIOTT'S CAMELBACK INN, Scottsdale, Arizona: This resort at the foot of Mummy Mountain, facing its namesake across the valley, was built in 1935 of adobe mud dug up for the foundation; recently added condominiums and hotel units bring the total number of rooms on the 120 acres to about 400. To accommodate all the guests there are two swimming pools, 10 tennis courts, plus two of the fancier of the area's 18-holers, as well as a staff big enough to make room service and overall maintenance head and shoulders above that of most far smaller establishments. You can also go biking, hiking, riding on an Indian reservation a few miles away; play Ping-Pong, billiards, shuffleboard — or get massaged in the whirlpool. Information: Marriott's Camelback Inn, PO Box 70, Scottsdale, AZ 85252 (602 948-1700).

THE LODGE AT PEBBLE BEACH, Pebble Beach, California: The California coast — "The finest meeting place of land and water in existence," according to one admirer — deserves no less than this magnificent old hotel. The interior is only a part of the charm. The Pebble Beach Golf Links, a leading contender for the title of Most Photographed Golf Course, and the Robert Trent Jones–designed Spyglass Hill course are among the most famous golf courses in existence, for good reason; they're also among the few tournament-class courses open to the public. And there are still other courses in Pebble Beach. If you don't like golf, you can go shopping in nearby Carmel; sightseeing along the celebrated Seventeen Mile Drive, with magnificent views of the rocky shore; horseback riding through the private 5,328-acre Del Monte Forest, which surrounds the lodge; swimming; or play tennis at the nearby Beach Club. Information: The Lodge at Pebble Beach, Seventeen Mile Dr., Pebble Beach, CA 93953 (408 624-3811).

MARRIOTT'S SANTA BARBARA BILTMORE, Santa Barbara, California: The sections of the hotel's 21 Montecito acres not taken up with the Spanish mission–style buildings where the guest rooms are located are filled up with gardens of eucalyptus, junipers, monkey trees, and oaks. The rooms are luxurious — with extra long, extra wide beds, good mattresses, oversized showerheads, and Royal Velvet bath towels.

There's an Olympic-sized swimming pool across from the hotel, plus an additional one on the property, and a quarter-mile-long beach. In the area, there's golf, fishing, and tennis. Summer, when daytime temperatures in the eighties are moderated by a constant ocean breeze, is the prime season. Information: Santa Barbara Biltmore, 1260 Channel Dr., Santa Barbara, CA 93108 (805 969-2261).

THE BROADMOOR, Colorado Springs, Colorado: When this magnificent hostelry was built by mining magnate Spencer Penrose and Charles Tutt in 1918, it was with the idea that this would be one of the world's most fashionable hotels, that it would be "permanent and perfect." It is. One of the interesting things about the Broadmoor is that in late winter and early spring you can sometimes enjoy winter and summer sports in the same day — skiing in the morning, for instance, golf or tennis in the afternoon. As for the building itself, it's everything you'd expect of a structure put up at the time with the assistance of hundreds of European craftsmen: Not only are there art objects from around the world in all the public rooms, but incredible ornamentation embellishes walls, ceilings, and floors alike. Information: The Broadmoor, Colorado Springs, CO 80901 (303 634-7711).

THE MAUNA KEA BEACH HOTEL, Kamuela, Hawaii, Hawaii: Some say this is the most fantastic work yet of Laurance Rockefeller, the major domo of the Rockresorts group that originally developed this property along with a handful of other fantastic, one-of-a-kind, built-from-scratch luxury resort hotels. Now managed by Westin Hotels, the Mauna Kea seems to have grown up out of the landscape; it's an asset to the surroundings rather than an eyesore. There are many diversions: an infuriating Robert Trent Jones golf course with stupendous Pacific views from every green; a swimming pool; charter boats; riding; snorkeling; scuba diving. All over the hotel there are artifacts from Asia and the Pacific — food implements and ancient ceremonial bowls, tapas, masks, tikis. Information: Mauna Kea Beach Hotel, Kamuela, HI 96743 (808 882-7222).

Inn Sites: America's Special Havens

When standardization finally overtook the hotel industry, at least one great anxiety — where to stay — was removed from travel. Travelers could be assured of finding acceptable accommodations in even the most remote corner of the country. But a new worry arose: What happened to those *special* places, the inns and hotels with special charm, with atmosphere, with a personal spirit and style and history all their own?

They still exist. The trend toward cookie-cutter construction simply increased the number of total hotel and motel rooms; it didn't destroy those unique hostelries that still grace this country from Maine to Oregon. They tend to become the "finds" of lucky patrons who would publish their credit card numbers before they would broadcast the name and location of their favorite country hideaway.

But, being made of sterner stuff, we offer a listing of *our* favorite places all across this country. Some are traditional New England inns, perfect for a ski weekend or a trip through the forests when the foliage is at its most brilliant; some are luxurious hideaways; some are rugged western lodges where the horses are spirited and the campfire stories tall.

EAST

GRISWOLD INN, Essex, Connecticut: The "Gris" is a favorite port of call for Connecticut River sailors, who may tie up just a few steps from the inn's front door.

Landlubbers arriving by car are just as welcome, and all are quickly infused with the friendly spirit radiating with the warmth from the potbellied stove. There's much to catch the eye — an outstanding collection of historic lithographs, steamboat relics, a large collection of historic firearms, many ships' name plaques, and a fine group of marine oils by Antonio Jacobsen. The beds, mostly brass, are in rooms that long ago developed port or starboard lists. But the hospitality and fine New England food more than make up for the absence of plumb joints. Sunday is a special eating day, featuring a buffet-style Hunt Breakfast. The all-you-can-eat groaning board seems about to buckle under everything from eggs and bacon to creamed beef and lamb kidneys. The *Tap Room* is immodestly acclaimed as "the most handsome barroom in America," and the description is not far from wrong. But it has a rival for the title in the adjacent Covered Bridge Room, which is hung from floor to ceiling with the prints and the paintings in the inn's standout collection. Information: Griswold Inn, Essex, CT 06426 (203 767-0991). William G. Winterer, innkeeper. 21 rooms.

COPPER BEECH INN, Ivoryton, Connecticut: The decor of this elegant, charming, and immaculate inn installed in a turn-of-the-century Victorian mansion and now run by Paul and Louise Ebeltoft, looks more like your rich old aunt's country estate than a commercial enterprise. The bedrooms have huge, old-fashioned, claw-footed bathtubs. There's an old greenhouse that's been converted into a lounge (with a piano), and the three dining rooms are full of fresh flowers, crystal, gleaming silver, and the incredible smells of baby pheasant, rack of lamb, pâté, lobster bisque, veal *chasseur,* and other delights that have put the inn on Connecticut's culinary map. Big breakfasts are not part of the picture, which is just as well because lunch and dinner are so good. Information: Copper Beech Inn, Main St., Ivoryton, CT 06442 (203 767-0330).

CURTIS HOUSE, Woodbury, Connecticut: The inn, reputedly Connecticut's oldest, is located in a town with more than 30 antique shops, 20 on Main Street alone. Original beams and fireplaces set the atmosphere in the spacious dining rooms. The bedrooms have colonial furniture, a number of them with pretty canopied beds. Bright, oval rag rugs cover the wide-board floors. The kitchen's specialties include French onion soup, turkey pot pie, and roast turkey. Information: Curtis House, Woodbury, CT 06798 (203 263-2101). Garwin Hardisty, innkeeper. 18 rooms.

BLUE HILL INN, Blue Hill, Maine: In operation on Blue Hill Bay since 1840, this inn is, according to the innkeepers, "the only inn in Maine which has never been operated as anything but an inn." Wingback armchairs, fireplaces, traditional wallpapers, ruffled curtains, and extra wool blankets make the bedrooms as cozy as they can be. But the real attraction here is the Maine coastline, best seen on foot, but accessible by bicycle, Moped, or car. The sea reaches into the meadowland all along this crabbed and twisting shoreline, so you keep seeing bits of the Atlantic wherever you go. Craft shops in Blue Hill carry famous Rowantrees pottery as well as other ceramic goods. Chamber music is performed several times a week in the summer by the students of Kneisel School of Music. The inn serves country-style breakfasts every morning, after which you are free to explore the coast or visit beautiful Deer Isle and Mt. Desert Island not far away. The inn's first-rate dinners are rich in chowders and fresh seafood; you'll also dine well on veal marsala, roast beef, and mandarin chicken breasts. Information: Blue Hill Inn, Blue Hill, ME 04614 (207 374-2844). Fred and Jean Wakelin, innkeepers. 9 rooms.

THISTLE INN, Boothbay Harbor, Maine: It's not the rooms (which are plain and old-fashioned) that make up the recently renovated Thistle Inn's attraction, so much as the warm and friendly atmosphere (especially in winter, when it's the only place in town that's open). In the tavern, a hangout for natives as well as a drawing card for weekenders, an upturned dory supports the bar and a piano player seldom has trouble getting together a chorus. The drinks are so hearty that most people are surprised by their size. In the restaurant, specialties include flambée scallops, haddie in a cheese sauce, Downeast steak (doused with a Newburg sauce filled with big chunks of lobster). Lobster pie is also a favorite. Information: Thistle Inn, Boothbay Harbor, ME 04538 (207 633-3541). Jerry Sheehan, innkeeper. 8 rooms.

CENTER LOVELL INN, Center Lovell, Maine: This old house had been around since 1805 when William Mosca, a graduate student in sociology and children's literature in New Haven, came up from Connecticut and decided to turn the place into the kind of friendly bed-and-breakfast he had encountered in England. But Mosca's family is Italian, and so what he ended up with turned out to be, in his words, "a typical New England home — except Italian," a place of "bed-and-breakfast friendliness with Italian food but without Italian tackiness." The food, all of it cooked as his grandmothers would have done it, is a point of pride with Mosca. He drives all the way to New York just to get the right cheeses and the right salami for his antipasto platters. Other specialties include Nicolo Firenze, a boneless half of chicken with an unusual stuffing, and gamberi al forno Roma, baked shrimp stuffed with crab. Three or four times a year — for New Year's Eve, Memorial Day, July 4, and one evening during the week of the big, locally famous Fryeburg Fair every autumn — Mosca lays out an eight-course banquet. Even if your visit is not timed so that you can enjoy the feasting, however, there's plenty to keep you busy when you visit: hiking and antiquing in summer; craft-shopping at the Fryeburg Fair and leaf-peeping in the fall; alpine skiing (within 10 to 30 minutes); and cross-country skiing on an extensive network of old logging roads that begins right at the back door. (One Boston writer called the trails here New England's best.) Information: Center Lovell Inn, Center Lovell, ME 04016 (207 925-1575). William and Susan Mosca, innkeepers. 4 rooms.

THE GREENVILLE INN, Greenville, Maine: Dominating this town on the edge of the wilderness surrounding giant Moosehead Lake, this rambling old mansion built by lumber barons in 1895 seems a lonely outpost of civilization, with its elegant paneling, leaded-glass windows, and fine detailing (ceramic-tiled fireplaces, for instance, and a shower arranged so that the spray comes at you from all sides). But the turn-of-the-century life that the structure was built to serve no longer exists. The furniture that replaced the lumber barons' is more comfortable than spiffy; and the style is informal and low-key: The Greenville Inn, whose rooms are set up to handle families as well as couples, is a very friendly, very family-oriented sort of place. There are two dining rooms (one with a wonderful cherry mahogany ceiling, the other with views of Moosehead Lake), and the lounge is very popular with locals. Nowadays, the food is a bit fancier: the gourmet menu changes every 4 to 6 weeks. Information: Greenville Inn, Box 1194, Greenville, ME 04441 (207 695-2206). Bob and Alice Stein, innkeepers. 6 rooms.

THE ISLAND INN, Monhegan Island, Maine: The century-old frame structure sitting on a picturesque bluff overlooking the tiny harbor between Monhegan and its satellite island of Manana is open summers only. Operated by a Monhegan native and his wife, the inn has a large, bright dining room where boiled lobster is the specialty, and fresh, simply prepared fish — striped bass, haddock, bluefish — fills the menu. An all-you-can-eat buffet on Sunday nights draws scores of Monhegan visitors who have spent the day exploring the awesome, 150-foot cliffs that face the pounding surf to the east. Although the inn has its own generator, most of the island goes without electricity. The yellow gleam of the kerosene lamps through the windows of the surrounding wood-shingled houses makes a pretty sight as you walk along the village's single dirt road. More than 600 varieties of flowering plants — including the trailing yew, unique to the island — and up to 200 species of birds may be seen along the many woodland trails. Information: The Island Inn, Monhegan Island, ME 04852 (207 372-9681). Robert Burton, innkeeper. 45 rooms.

ROBERT MORRIS INN, Oxford, Maryland: The most famous Robert Morris — used his wide connections to raise money for the American Revolution, and when other backers failed to appear, he did not hesitate to pay the troops out of his own pocket. Alas, what the war couldn't do bad speculations accomplished a few years later, when he went bankrupt from a series of frontier land deals. His father's home, carefully preserved over the years, today is Tidewater Maryland's finest inn. Many of the rooms are decorated in vintage Americana, and you may climb into a high four-poster with the aid of a small stepladder or snuggle into a trundle bed. The slate on the tavern floor was quarried in Vermont, and public rooms and guest rooms alike are decorated with early braided or rag rugs. Best known to sailors, who tie up at the inn's anchorage on the Tred Avon River; to fishermen, who use the inn as a headquarters for excursions up and down the Chesapeake Bay shore; and to local gourmands, who swear its restaurant does the best things possible to bay crabs and the local oysters, the inn is a must for anyone touring the area. Information: Robert Morris Inn, Oxford, MD 21654 (301 226-5111). Ken and Wendy Gibson, innkeepers. 35 rooms.

WHEATLEIGH, Lenox, Massachusetts: This 33-room Italianate palazzo was built by an American railroad man and banker in the gay nineties, and ranks as the most elegant inn in all New England, if not in North America. Surrounded by gardens and lawns, the structure is all blond bricks and terra cotta and limestone detailing. There are loggias and arcades, stained-glass windows, a magnificent swooping staircase, lovely fireplaces, a proper library with glass-fronted bookcases and rich dark paneling, and, everywhere, ornately carved ceilings, moldings, mantelpieces, and walls. Travelers with a weakness for such things have reason to rejoice at the arrival of a pair of new innkeepers who seem genuinely glad to welcome guests to their palace of a home-sweet-home. Nowadays, Wheatleigh can get you hooked — all too easily. Information: Wheatleigh Inn, Lenox, MA 01240 (413 637-0610). Susan and Linfield Simon, innkeepers. 15 rooms.

JARED COFFIN HOUSE, Nantucket, Massachusetts: The gas lamps ornamenting the façade of this inn have been converted to electricity, but they still cast a flattering glow on the 1845 brickwork — and give you an inkling of the marvels you will find inside: high ceilings; wonderfully ornate moldings; elegant chests and desks in Chippendale, Sheraton, and American federal style; many canopied beds, several draped with crewel-embroidered fabric; oriental rugs; scrumptious seafood; and, most important of all, the extraordinary warmth and friendliness evinced by every staff member from the chambermaid to the desk clerk to the waitresses and the innkeepers themselves. Spring, summer, and fall are busy; winter — except during the year-end holidays, when the innkeeper stages a special celebration — is delightfully peaceful. This is the island's best-known and most popular inn, and you'll need reservations well in advance. But the planning always pays off when you return from a day of soaring along some cliff's-edge road on your bike, or tennis, golf, or soaking up the sun at the beach. Information: Jared Coffin House, Nantucket, MA 02554 (617 228-2400). Philip Whitney Read, innkeeper. 46 rooms.

HANCOCK INN, Hancock, Massachusetts: The accommodations here are modest, but the fact that they exist at all is a marvel when you consider the state of the structure when manager Chester Gorski arrived a few years ago. Some of the wood was rotted, some of the pipes had burst, and the chimneys, the septic system, and the wiring were in bad shape. Chester took care of all that, then addressed himself to the more cosmetic matters of painting and wallpapering while his wife Ellen haunted the tag sales and auctions in search of antiques to give the smallish rooms a bit more personality than they might otherwise have had. The result — a building that is, if not yet quite like new, then at least sturdy and snug against the cold Berkshire winters — is comfortable enough to keep the place full of skiers from the first snow fall until the end of the season at nearby Jiminy Peak. But the great attraction is the food served in the romantic, Franklin-stove–warmed dining room. Chester, it seems, can wield the tools of the chef as well as those of the handyman, and turns out a veritable parade of first-class dishes, from *billi bi* (a cream of mussel soup) and chicken Kiev to lobster bouillabaisse, sautéed scallops flambée in gin and cream, and a filet mignon in a cream and mushroom sauce spiked with cognac. Ellen has a way with salads, and the white wine vinaigrette in which she tosses some unusual mixtures of vegetables (perhaps watercress and endive with a bit of romaine and raw shredded beets) is a standout; her cheesecake, sometimes blended with ground pistachios or hazelnuts, ranks among guests' favorites. Exactly what you'll find on the menu when you visit depends on the season and the availability of ingredients — but it will always be Continental and traditional and so good that you'll pity the poor soul who comes here on a diet. More information: Hancock Inn, rt. 43, Hancock Village, Hancock, MA 01237 (413 738-5873). Chester and Ellen Gorski, innkeepers. 9 rooms.

RED LION INN, Stockbridge, Massachusetts: This fine rambling three-story clapboard structure built in 1773 as a stagecoach stop occupies a prominent place on Main Street, which, except for the traffic that clogs the intersection during the busy summer season, looks just as if Norman Rockwell ought to have painted it. He did. His home was just across the road, and the country's largest and finest collection of his paintings can be seen not far away, in the Old Corner House. Still, there's more to Stockbridge than Rockwelliana — Lenox's Berkshire Music Festival and Berkshire Theater Festival, and the Jacob's Pillow Dance Festival at Lee, among other things — and the inn hums throughout the hot-weather months with overnight guests, diners, and a good many other folk who have simply stopped in to ogle the high-ceilinged Victorian parlors and their gleaming silver and mahogany embellishments; or to sit on the long front porch, where two rows of rocking chairs bob back and forth from early morning until well after dusk. The inn is well worth seeing, even if you can't get a bed for the night. Certainly, the inn's restaurants — the outdoor patio restaurant, all cool and green; the cozy, dark Widow Bingham's Tavern, with its candles and checkered tablecloths; and the main dining room, full of sparkling silver and white napery — are among the most charming spots for meals in an area that is full of appealing eateries. Hearty soups begin many dinners here; they conclude with one of New England's spiciest Indian puddings. Information: Red Lion Inn, Stockbridge, MA 01262 (413 298-5545). Betsy Holtzinger, innkeeper. 100 rooms.

PUBLICK HOUSE, Sturbridge, Massachusetts: This is not one of those cozy country inns where it's you and the innkeeper against the rest of the world. Instead, this hostelry — which opened as one of our not-quite-yet-a-nation's finest restaurants in 1771 — is most popular for its food; and the hungry pour by the bus load and car load through its doors, and then chow down on fresh fish and lobster pie and wonderful sticky buns. A lucky and foresighted few have reserved in advance, and, when they've sated themselves on the innkeeper's savory offerings, waddle up the creaky, crooked stairs and throw themselves down on a bed in one of the cozy rooms. About a decade ago, the innkeeper initiated a splendid pageant-cum-feast, a revival of the Yuletide celebration known in merrie Olde England, with a Boar's Head Feast, a Yule Log Procession, and the telling of moving tales of the season; held thrice daily on two Saturdays and Sundays preceding Christmas, it now sells out well in advance. A newer event, Yankee Winter Weekends, keep the inn filled from January through March. You're welcomed with a syllabub (Chablis with cream) and Joe Froggers, giant ginger cookies; and then fed goodies nearly around the clock: breakfasts of fried mush and deep-dish apple pie and hickory-smoked bacon; snacks of curried meatballs, aged cheddar, roasted chestnuts, codfish cakes and chowder and hot buttered rum; and dinners of roasted venison and other exotic concoctions. Then, as in summer, you can leave the inn for a visit to Old Sturbridge Village, a reconstruction of a New England village that might have existed at about the time of the Industrial Revolution (see *Restored Towns and Reconstructed Villages*). If the Publick House is full, look into the nearby *Colonel Ebenezer Crafts Inn,* also run by the Publick House; it's smaller and somewhat more personal. Information: Publick House, Sturbridge, MA 01566 (617 347-3313). Buddy Adler, innkeeper. 25 rooms.

LONGFELLOW'S WAYSIDE INN, Sudbury, Massachusetts: Originally known as the *Red Horse Tavern,* the inn changed its name in 1863, the better to bask in the fame Longfellow created for it when he wrote of local lore in *Tales of a Wayside Inn,* a series of poems whose most celebrated section begins, "Listen, my children, and you shall hear . . ." The building in which Longfellow set his work, which had been purchased by Henry Ford along with the surrounding 3,000 acres in the 1920s, was partially destroyed by fire, after some two-and-a-half-centuries of existence, in the mid-50s; but with Ford Foundation help, it was soon restored. The former plans were somewhat modified: Many of the original guest rooms were turned into museumlike room settings showing how the inn probably looked in the early 18th century; and eight new rooms were added. As inn rooms go, they're not spectacularly charming, but with their reproduction furnishings, early American color schemes, and well-constructed bathrooms, they're comfortable enough. They are, moreover, wonderfully quiet. The surrounding acreage insulates you from highway hubbub, and, because the inn's principal trade is in meals, when the diners have departed, you have the establishment practically to yourself; you feel you've got your own private estate. Meals consist of sturdy New England fare, including tasty breads, cakes, and pies out of the inn's own ovens, made from flour ground by the mill on the premises. Also on the grounds is the schoolhouse that inspired "Mary Had a Little Lamb," and a classic New England chapel, complete with blinding white clapboards and soaring steeple, where countless New England sweethearts have tied the knot. Information: Wayside Inn, Sudbury, MA 01776 (617 443-8846). Francis J. Koppeis, innkeeper. 10 rooms.

BRADFORD INN, Bradford, New Hampshire: Tired of careers in Philadelphia, Tom Best and his wife Woody itched for a new challenge, and restoring this inn — a solid but unimposing high-ceilinged, turn-of-the-century roominghouse in one of those quiet New England towns where big trees and 200-year-old houses keep company on Main Street with a clapboard church and the town's small businesses — promised to be just the thing. And so they began. They tore up floors and replaced them, laid carpet, repaired roofs, built a handsome bar, and scattered their own collections of knickknacks, and some inherited from parents and grandparents, around the inn; and, after what seemed like eons, the new hostelry was ready for business.

"You might still discover a crack in the plaster or a tear in the wallpaper," says Woody, "but you'll always find everything absolutely clean; I see to that myself; plenty of blankets and towels and hot water — and good food." Tom, in a newly equipped kitchen, cooks the house specialties — beef in wine, a lobster Newburg that some people travel a hundred miles to enjoy, and the unique Mack Pie. Details: Bradford Inn, Bradford, NH 03221 (603 938-5309). Tom and Woody Best, innkeepers. 12 rooms.

HILLSIDE INN, East Hebron, New Hampshire: The Hillside has grown like Topsy over the years — an addition here, a few cottages there. But ten of the rooms are in the original building, and they are charming with their early American decor, their antique furnishings, and their views over lovely Newfound Lake or a country road outside. The modern rooms, which have two double beds and sliding glass doors that open into the water, are wonderfully spacious. The cottages are great for families of all sizes. And then, too, the lakeside location is as peaceful as it can be. One of the most charming things about the inn, however, is its dining room — big and old-fashioned with its broad-plank floors, and full of antique chairs and tables and hutches crammed with antique silver and dishes. Broad windows give you delightful views over the water, and fresh flowers, cut from the decorative gardens that take up some of the inn's 70 acres, embellish all the tables. In summer, you can play croquet or badminton, hit tennis balls on two clay tournament-class courts, go sailing or rowing, or venture into the nearby White Mountains for a hike; during the winters that the inn is open, there's skiing and tobogganing. For information: Hillside Inn, East Hebron, NH 03232 (603 744-2413). David Weigel, innkeeper. 17 rooms.

FITZWILLIAM INN, Fitzwilliam, New Hampshire: The "Rules of the House" provide an accurate insight into what you're likely to find: "This is a New England country inn, in the heart of a New England country village, and we have some customs that may seem strange to you. Please try to understand our ways and abide by our requests." If you find this off-putting, you'll be encouraged by rule number one: "We have no room keys to give you — everyone trusts everyone else in the country. However, we do lock the outside doors early. If you're going to be out, please pick up a house key at the desk. The innkeeper is shy about answering the door in his PJs." Modern intrusions are unwelcome in this wooden hostelry dating from 1796. The innkeeper has been quoted as saying that when a prospective guest asks if the rooms have phones and television sets, he politely refers them to "the nice motel just down the road." Information: Fitzwilliam Inn, Fitzwilliam, NH 03447 (603 585-9000). Charles and Barbara Wallace, innkeepers. 22 rooms.

THE JOHN HANCOCK INN, Hancock, New Hampshire: John Hancock never slept here or even stopped for a short mug of ale while inspecting the nearby landholdings left to him by a rich uncle. But the inn does boast that its 1789 opening makes it the oldest operating inn in New Hampshire. Located in the Monadnock region, the "Currier and Ives corner of the Granite State," in one of those quintessentially New England towns with a white-steepled church, a bandstand on the green, and a half dozen bright clapboard houses stuck away in a fuzz of leaves, the inn is full of small neat rooms with twin canopy beds or white ruffled curtains and tiny-print wallpapers. Nothing out of the ordinary, really. But there's one exception, and that room, number 16, happens to be more beautiful than nearly any other room in any other inn in the region. The murals that are its most striking feature, creations of an itinerant artist named Rufus Porter, depict the scenes of the area in heavenly blues. The furniture is mahogany, the bedspread and curtains are white. Somehow, sleeping here seems almost like spending the night in the great outdoors; the work is so lively that you get an odd, you-are-there feeling. The only other remnant of Porter's work, curiously, is found inside the closet of one of the rooms down the hall. The restaurant serves food that is New England-plain; offerings include the roast duckling, the seafood casserole, and the prime rib — served daily and not just once or twice a week as in many other restaurants of similarly small size. The bar, however, with sleigh seats for benches and giant bellows for tables, is exceptionally homey. Information: The John Hancock Inn, Hancock, NH 03449 (603 525-3318). Glynn and Pat Wells, innkeepers. 10 rooms.

LYME INN, Lyme, New Hampshire: Lyme is as delightful a New England village as you'd ever want to find, with its big green common, its fine clapboard church, its well-stocked country store — not to mention its handsome inn, a gathering place for the town citizenry, a favorite lodging place for visiting parents of students at nearby Dartmouth College, and a Lyme tourist attraction in its own right. All the rooms are furnished with delightful antiques. The structure itself, put up in 1809, is full of walls that slant, hallways that narrow then inexplicably widen, and stairways that twist and climb every which way, apparently without rhyme or reason. But such quirks only add to its charm. A fascinating collection of framed samplers, hanging on the walls of the dining rooms, is worth close scrutiny, not only for the workmanship but perhaps for the messages as well, from "God Bless Our Home" to more religious aphorisms. Information: Lyme Inn, Lyme, NH 03768 (603 795-2222). Fred and Judy Siemons, innkeepers. 15 rooms.

NEW LONDON INN, New London, New Hampshire: You may travel through New England for the length of a normal lifetime and assume you've seen most of what is good and fair when, suddenly, you discover a delight like New London. Here is a perfection of New England towns, not so much restored, one senses, as preserved. And in the middle of all this beauty, across from the town green, sits the three-story, clapboard-sided, antique-furnished New London Inn. Built in 1792, it is famous for a deal made in 1941 with a retired town tax collector named Calvin Sargent. Sargent, grandson of the original builder of the hostelry, had a hankering for security. Moreover, he liked the old place. So he offered the innkeepers $5,000 to room-and-board him for life (he was 73 at the time); the offer was accepted — and Sargent outlived the owners, enjoying the fruits of his contract well into his hundredth year. You may not stay so long, but there's plenty to keep you busy while you're there: in summer, water sports on three lakes so clean you can drink out of them; and, in winter, downhill and cross-country skiing. Information: New London Inn, New London, NH 03257 (603 526-2791). George Adame, innkeeper. 26 rooms.

THE MAINSTAY INN, Cape May, New Jersey: Cape May, one of our nation's oldest seaside resorts, is a treasure of Victorian architecture, and the Mainstay Inn — just a few blocks from the Atlantic — is one of its gems. From the inn's white picket fence to the green wicker chairs that sit on its veranda, to the imposing 12-foot mirror in the entrance hall and beyond, this late-19th-century former gambling house has been lovingly restored and exquisitely furnished in pure Victorian style by a dedicated young couple. Breakfast and tea only. Information: The Mainstay Inn, 635 Columbia Ave., Cape May, NJ 08204 (609 884-8690). Tom and Sue Carroll, innkeepers. 12 rooms.

THE INN AT THE SHAKER MILL FARM, Canaan, New York: When Ingram Paperny uncovered this abandoned early-19th-century mill, it had neither bedrooms nor public rooms and was sorely in need of an expert carpenter. But the structure, set beside a hillside waterfall, so tempted its discoverer that he set up his own wood shop and began its careful conversion to inn. The rooms — no frills, but comfortable enough — reflect the heritage of austerity left by the Shakers who lived in the area — in Old Chatham, New York, where there's now an extraordinary collection of material on display, and just across the state line in Hancock, Massachusetts, now home to the popular Shaker Village. The setting in the foothills of the Berkshires is one of great beauty, and so the inn attracts an interesting crowd, everyone from magazine editors to mycologists to multilingual United Nations employees. Information: The Inn at the Shaker Mill Farm, Canaan, NY 12029 (518 794-9345). Ingram Paperny, innkeeper. 12 rooms.

THE 1770 HOUSE, East Hampton, Long Island, New York: Like so many other American inns, the 1770 House has had several lives (in this case, first as a home, later as a store, then as a boarding house, and finally as the dining hall of a boys' school), and over the years hardly anybody bothered to give it the care it required. And so, when Sid and Miriam Perle bought the place several years ago, the building was a wreck. Thanks to their efforts, however, the structure has never looked better. The exterior, clapboards painted white with coal-black shutters at the windows, makes the inn a creditable addition to a venerable neighborhood. Inside, the old and the new work together to delightful effect. (Especially striking: the large colonial fireplace in the taproom, especially popular for cocktails and snacks after the local summer theater lets out; the Perles' wonderful clock collection; and the stained glass that is used as a decorative accent throughout the inn.) The 1770 House is open year-round, but the dining room serves meals only on weekends in winter. Information: The 1770 House, 143 Main St., East Hampton, NY 11937 (516 324-1770). Sidney and Miriam Perle, innkeepers. 7 rooms.

GURNEY'S INN, Montauk, Long Island, New York: If you define an inn as a colonial hostelry on an elm-shaded New England street, this may not be the place for you: You won't find the antique lamp or the ancient patchwork quilt, the spinning wheel or the stenciled wall. You lodge in cottages or motel-type rooms; dress up for dinner and go dancing to live music in the lounge after you've supped; or just hole up in your room and take in a television show when you've had your fill of the spa facilities (excellent enough to attract the likes of Cheryl Tiegs and Alvin Ailey). But Gurney's Inn is a personable place, and when you go out on the beach, one of those endless, surf-pounded Atlantic strands, you put civilization thousands of miles behind you. The shore is delightful for jogging or sunbathing in summer, and even better for walks in the fall — if you don't mind the whip of the wind, the tingle of the cold, and spray in the face as the price of a beach to call your own. Information: Gurney's Inn, Montauk, NY 19154 (516 668-2345). Nick and Joyce Monte, innkeepers. 128 rooms.

THE 1740 HOUSE, Lumberville, Pennsylvania: Built around an early-18th-century stable by two other refugees from urban America, the 1740 House is one of the best inns in Bucks County, which is full of inns — not so much because it's particularly quaint (because it isn't: the rooms are heated and air-conditioned, the floors are carpeted wall to wall, the baths are tiled, and the furnishings are W. & J. Sloane's finest). Rather, the 1740 House prospers year after year because it is one of those unfailingly well-managed places where everything works, and because it is located in the kind of countryside where everyone dreams, at least once, of making a second home: a woodsy region that shelters antique houses, run through by a mighty river and a placid canal where you can canoe or ice skate; where the towns have grown (always tastefully) just enough so that there are interesting shops, movie theaters or playhouses, and restaurants and snack bars where you're as apt to find quiche on the menu as hamburger. In Bucks County, as at the 1740 House, you can have your comforts and get away from it all, too. Hearty breakfasts (served in a sunny room overlooking the canal) and full dinners are available at the inn; you'll have to go elsewhere for lunches and bring your own drinks. Information: The 1740 House, River Rd., Lumberville, PA 18933 (215 297-5661).

CLIFF PARK INN, Milford, Pennsylvania: This early-19th-century farmhouse-turned-inn, a typical Pocono Mountains resort hotel set on a 900-foot cliff that towers over the Delaware River, has been run by five generations, since 1900, of the same family — and so if you come here expecting someplace homey, you won't be disappointed. There are cushy chintz sofas in the parlors, lace spreads on the beds, and polished floors throughout. But the Cliff Park Inn also has something of the elegance of a country club, in part because, ever since the golf course was added in 1913, back in the days that golf was just catching hold in America, golf has been one of the guests' favorite pastimes. (In fact, the resort is open only when the weather is apt to be temperate enough for a round, just between Memorial Day weekend and the end of November in these parts.) Most rooms are upstairs in the main building; a half dozen cottages are also available not far away. Information: Cliff Park Inn, Milford, PA 18337 (717 296-6491). Harry W. Buchanan, innkeeper. 18 rooms.

THE 1661 INN, Block Island, Rhode Island: The uniqueness of this pretty, simple structure perched above the village that clusters about the harbor, comes mostly from the beauty of its site on a meadow rising up 12 miles off Point Judith, an hour's ferry ride away. But the atmosphere — informal enough that before-dinner wine-and-cheese hours seem to make perfect sense — figures strongly as well; the special house drinks — the Monhegan Moro, a wild combination of sweet and dry vermouth, and the Island of the Little Gods Mind Boggler, white wine with cranberry juice — are something else again. Lunches and dinners are served at the owners' other property, the mansard-roofed, Victorian Manisses Hotel, recently opened after an extensive restoration-cum-labor-of-love. Block Island is one of the best places in the East for biking; there's also good snorkeling, picnicking, salt- and freshwater fishing, bird-watching, and beach-combing — below the steep Monhegan cliffs for shells, driftwood, and other flotsam. Information: The 1661 Inn, Block Island, RI 02807 (401 466-2421). Joan and Justin Abrams, innkeepers. 26 rooms.

THE INN AT CASTLE HILL, Newport, Rhode Island: This three-story Victorian mansion, built on a 32-acre water's-edge site in 1874 by the son of the Swiss American naturalist Louis Agassiz, is one of those mansions which Newporters call, inexplicably, "cottages." However, though it's a plain sort of place by the standards of William

Wetmore's Stanford White–designed Château-sur-Mer, and Cornelius Vanderbilt's Richard Morris Hunt–designed The Breakers, you may have a tough time stretching your imagination to call it a cottage. In the first place, it's huge; and in the second place, it's more elegant than most Fifth Avenue apartments. The chestnut paneling gleams. Tiffany lamps shed their soft glow on fantastically carved Victorian furniture, much of it original to the house. Oriental rugs protect the polished floors. In the dining room, you'll sit on velvet-covered chairs, drink coffee poured from silver urns, and eat your food with silver cutlery. Innkeeper Paul McEnroe, who has kept an inn since the beginning of the American innkeeping renaissance, is a thoroughgoing professional and a gracious human being, and knows how to make every guest feel at home; the wonderful New Year's Eve dinner dance sells out well in advance as a result. The menu offers a Neptune's bounty of clams and lobsters and other seafood prepared, more often than not, with a Continental flair. Rooms are located in the main house and in a newer area out back; for charm, the former are best. Information: The Inn at Castle Hill, Newport, RI 02840 (401 849-3800). Paul McEnroe, innkeeper. 10 rooms.

THE OLD TAVERN, Grafton, Vermont: Restored, along with some 25 other Grafton buildings, by the Windham Foundation, as a part of one of the country's most extensive restoration projects, the Old Tavern is one of America's most beautiful inns. Everything gleams: the wooden floor boards throughout the main building and the annex across the street, the furniture, the tops of the tables in the dining room, the silver tableware, the glasses, and the china. All of the sleeping rooms are furnished with the loveliest sort of antiques — lace tester beds, wing chairs covered with chintz, Chippendale-style highboys, and such. When you consider all that, and the delightful setting in picture-postcard-perfect Grafton, you may call the Old Tavern one of your favorite inns, despite the fact that it's more elegant than warm, more institutional than intimate; so many people love the place so well, in fact, that you'll be hard put to get a room at the last minute — especially on a weekend. It's important to reserve well in advance, and to query the desk clerk carefully about the available rooms: No two are alike, and some are more wonderful than others. The surrounding area is gorgeous, too: In Grafton alone, there's the general store, the cheese company, and a lovely covered bridge. Information: The Old Tavern, Grafton, VT 05146 (802 843-2231). Lois Copping, innkeeper. 35 rooms.

NORWICH INN, Norwich, Vermont: Just across the Connecticut River from Dartmouth College, the Norwich Inn has been in operation since 1797, and the people of the town take a proprietary interest in the establishment; it's a sort of a landmark in the area. And so, when new innkeepers arrived in June 1979 and started turning wonderful things out in the kitchen, Norwichians beamed. Now, when you visit the handsome Terrace Dining Room, glassed-in porch, carpeted and filled with plants so that it seems almost like a greenhouse, you can order rack of lamb, veal piccata, Norwich scallops (cooked in sherry with a hint of garlic), or a special filet of sole, wrapped around an almond-and-spinach stuffing. And you can order from one of the most extensive wine lists in the area — fine Champagne, first-growth French wines, and reasonably priced bottles both imported and domestic, some of which you usually can't get anymore. Norwich, one of those immaculately kept towns whose clapboard and brick homes and tall trees defined most people's idea of how a New England town should look, is as charming as ever; and Dan & Whitt, a big old general store where you can buy hardware and grain for yourself and your animals, rifles and flannel and soaps and just about anything else you can name, is still doing its booming business. In summer, you can go hiking and biking, and in winter you'll want to go for a ski. Information: Norwich Inn, Norwich, VT 05055 (802 649-1143). Al and Doreen Twachtman, innkeepers. 27 rooms.

KEDRON VALLEY INN, South Woodstock, Vermont: Horseback riders love this inn because of its collection of 30 riding horses and its network of 250 miles of trails;

but it is a pleasant, unpretentious sort of place to go and stay for a night, a weekend, or longer, even if you don't ride. You can go swimming or hiking in summer; in winter and early spring, sleigh rides, skiing, snowshoeing, and maple sugaring are the order of the day. Rooms are located in both of the inn's two handsome early-19th-century brick buildings, and in a more modern, motel-type log building in the back. The food is good enough that you'll be glad there's plenty of it. On weekends, a buffet dinner gives you the chance to fill your stomach with as much crab Newburgh and rare roast beef as it can handle; and at Sunday brunch, you can sample red flannel hash. All breads and pies are baked in the kitchen, and there's always a maple-sugar–cured ham at dinner. Information: Kedron Valley Inn, South Woodstock, VT 05071 (802 457-1473). Paul and Barbara Kendall, innkeepers. 32 rooms.

HARTNESS HOUSE, Springfield, Vermont: A cockamamie jumble of dormers, arched windows, fieldstones, bay windows, and other fancies of the typical Victorian architect, this mansion was originally the home of an inventor and "machine tool genius" who at one time held the post of governor of Vermont, one James Hartness. Some of the rooms, including a wonderfully handsome turret room, are located here; other more modern quarters can be found in an addition in the back. The inn also has three stately dining rooms, and the attractive Crown Point Pub. Outside, under a spreading maple, there's a swimming pool, and, just beyond, a weird object that looks like a tank turret tipped partly over — James Hartness's telescope. The area around Springfield, along the Black River, was for many years a center for the manufacture of precision machine tools, and Springfield came to be known as "the cradle of invention." The American Precision Museum, which is nearby in Windsor, is well worth visiting to learn the story. Also in the area is the St. Gaudens National Historic Site, across the river in Cornish, New Hampshire. Information: Hartness House, Springfield, VT 05156 (802 885-2115). George and Cherrill Staudter, innkeepers. 42 rooms.

THE INN AT WEATHERSFIELD, Weathersfield, Vermont: Mary Louise Thorburn had spent years entertaining a house full of people (and loving it), and after the nest emptied out, running an inn seemed the natural thing to do. She and husband Ron looked all over for the perfect place, and in 1978 they came to Weathersfield, a perfect gem of a New England town some 19 miles from Woodstock. They saw this inn with its six white pillars and wavy-paned glass; fell in love with the design, the layout, and the setting on 12 acres of lawns and trees, back from the road; bought the place practically on the spot, and in 1980, opened for business as one of those very special places where visitors feel not so much like paying customers as welcome guests in someone's home. And what a home: The floors are wide-planked throughout, the rooms are all furnished in antiques — some with four-posters, one with a magnificent old bedstead canopied with a single piece of hand-crocheted lace. There are enough antique quilts in the house to dazzle a museum textiles curator, and the bedsheets are flowered, ruffled, or edged with lace. (Atop every mattress, Mrs. Thorburn has laid an electric pad: just the thing to warm your toes on a cold Vermont night after the fire on your hearth — there's one in every room — has died down.) Afternoons are given over to bountiful English teas — the heady liquid brewed in sterling pots and accompanied by salmon mousse on bread rounds, fresh vegetables with a dip, and some wonderful sweet — perhaps an English trifle or a tipsy pudding. Breakfasts — made up of sausage or ham, and Belgian waffles, well-sauced *fines herbes* omelettes, eggs Benedict, Scotch eggs, or red velvet hash with poached eggs — are so generous that you may be able to make tea do for lunch, especially if you know you have one of the Thorburns' delightful dinners, confected of imaginative appetizers, soups, entrees, and desserts, to look forward to. For more information, contact the Inn at Weathersfield, PO Box 165, Weathersfield, VT 05151 (802 263-9217). Ron and Mary Louise Thorburn, innkeepers. 7 rooms.

INN AT SAWMILL FARM, West Dover, Vermont: Abandoned barns, uniquely adaptable because of their huge open spaces, seem to make a special sort of inn — or so you would conclude upon seeing this fine establishment, the creation of Rodney Williams, an architect, and Ione, his wife, a professional decorator. The spaces are good, to begin with: The living room is high-ceilinged, just big enough for two sitting areas, but not so big that you can't sit and see the fire burning in the huge hearth; the dining rooms are small enough that you can almost feel you're at someone's very elegant dinner party; and there are all manner of comfortable nooks and crannies where you can go to read a book or just lie down and snooze. Ione has furnished the whole place with bright-colored fabrics, and, because the Williamses' daughter is married to a Fieldcrest executive, everything from the towels and the sheets to the blanket covers, the carpets, and the bedspreads is color-coordinated. Meanwhile, the Williamses' son Brill has become quite a chef, and the ingredients he uses are always just a little fresher and a little more perfect than the garden variety. The food reflects that fact. The Marlboro Music Festival is nearby, and keeps the inn full in summer; and in fall, the flaming foliage draws crowds. In winter, people come to ski on Mount Snow, just down the road, or to cross-country over the river and through the woods. So, no matter when you want to visit, you're best advised to reserve well in advance. Information: Inn at Sawmill Farm, PO Box 8, West Dover, VT 05356 (802 464-8131). Rodney, Ione, and Brill Williams, innkeepers. 20 rooms.

SOUTH

ROD AND GUN CLUB, Everglades City, Florida: Times have changed since the 1920s, when industrialist Barron Collier converted an old gulfside house, popular with hunters and fishermen for years, into a private club, and made it a hideaway for very important persons (including a scattering of US presidents). So the club is now open to the public. But much of the flavor of the early days remains, and there are mounted sport fish and hunting specimens on the walls; the emphasis here is still on the water and its creatures. A marina serves private boats. Charters and guides are available for hire, as are skiffs and canoes for some fine fishing — for grouper, tarpon, or the battling snook (a special treat because it's not commercially available); the chef will prepare your catch for a small fee. The inn is just about a mile from the entrance to Everglades National Park, and in February the place hops with a special seafood festival. Other diversions: the heated pool (which is screened because of the mosquitoes), or just sitting around on the pleasant veranda. Tennis courts are nearby. Information: Rod and Gun Club, Everglades City, FL 33929 (813 695-2101). Martin Bowen, innkeeper. 18 rooms in separate cottages.

CHALET SUZANNE, Lake Wales, Florida: The style of many places can be suggested in a word or phrase — Victorian, early American, motel modern. Chalet Suzanne is what you'd call eclectic. Left to her own devices in the depths of the Depression, with two children to care for, a tiny young widow named Bertha Hinshaw decided to start a restaurant. Talent and energy made this central Florida endeavor a huge success over the years, and by the time Bertha Hinshaw died not long ago, in her 90s, the inn had its own orange groves, a private airstrip, one of the finest and most original kitchens in the state, and a reputation for being one of the oddest-looking inns this side of paradise, for the Chalet Suzanne, as the establishment came to be called, after Mrs. Hinshaw's daughter, eventually came to reflect her passion for collecting anything and everything, but particularly tiles, and her penchant for putting together elements of architectural styles from all around the globe, everything from turrets to bare-wood decks. What could have been bizarre or garish is here simply exquisite. Fortunately, thanks to the dedicated care of Carl Hinshaw, Bertha's son, and his wife and children, the spirit of Bertha Hinshaw lives on. Not only worth visiting for itself, Chalet Suzanne makes a fine home base for sightseeing expeditions. Information: Chalet Suzanne, PO Drawer AC, Lake Wales, FL 33853 (813 676-1477). Carl and Vita Hinshaw, innkeepers, 30 rooms.

GREYFIELD INN, Cumberland Island, Georgia: A one-of-a-kind inn on a one-of-a-kind island in the Atlantic, just northeast of the Georgia-Florida state line, this establishment was built by the Thomas Carnegies around the turn of the century for their daughter and her husband, and, substantially unaltered, was opened as an inn several years ago by a Carnegie granddaughter, Mrs. Lucy Ferguson. If something this far off the beaten track, accessible only by boat or chartered plane, appeals to you, then you may not mind that there are no tennis courts or swimming pool, and that the only recreation on the island, really, is reading, conversation, shelling, walking, and looking for wildlife — hundreds of different kinds of birds, armadillo, alligators. And when you've had enough of that, you can just sit around in the house and savor the lifestyle of the turn-of-the-century rich. Meals are served buffet style. Information: Greyfield Inn, Drawer B, Fernandina Beach, FL 32034 (904 261-6408). Karen Chaplin, innkeeper. 9 rooms.

THE INN AT PLEASANT HILL, Shakertown, Kentucky: The Shakers — an ascetic, communal sect that originated in England in the middle of the 18th century — are usually associated with upstate New York and bordering Massachusetts, where more than 200 years ago Mother Ann Lee established the country's first major Shaker settlements. However, the Shakers went west in the 19th century, and eventually settled in Kentucky — at Auburn and near Harrodsburg at Pleasant Hill (see *Utopias*). As part of the nationwide revival of interest in the Shakers, particularly in their architecture and design, all 27 of the original buildings at Pleasant Hill have been restored, and twelve of them are fitted out with guest rooms and appropriate reproductions of Shaker furniture — chairs and trundle beds, sconces, mirrors, and, everywhere, pegs to hang things up as the Shakers did. The nonprofit organization that administers Pleasant Hill has provided every room with its spiffy tiled bath, air-conditioning, and a television set; but otherwise the feeling is one of authenticity. A dining room in the Trustees' House offers big Kentucky-style breakfasts featuring grits, eggs, sausage, biscuits, and all the rest; lunches and dinners are also belt-looseners. Information: Inn at Pleasant Hill, Rt. 4, Harrodsburg, KY 40330 (606 734-5411). Ann Voris, innkeeper. 70 rooms.

LaMOTHE HOUSE, New Orleans, Louisiana: Built in the early 1800s by a successful planter named Jean LaMothe, this exquisite example of an early New Orleans townhouse is a delightful place to call home while you visit this exciting city. From the courtyard and its lush plantings to the foyer, hung with a Waterford crystal chandelier, and throughout the elegantly antique-furnished establishment, you can't help but find yourself transported to the city's earlier, gentler days. But you won't find the discomforts: All of the rooms are air-conditioned, and each has a private bath, a color TV, and a phone. Continental breakfast, the only meal served, is always an event: Everyone sits at a long banquet table, and lingers long afterward over chicory coffee drawn from a Sheffield urn at least two centuries old. The inn is just a few blocks from the heart of the French Quarter and its jazz, good food, and intriguing shops. Information: LaMothe House, 621 Esplanade Ave., New Orleans, LA 70116 (504 947-1161). Mrs. Mimi Munson Langguth, innkeeper. 15 rooms.

MAISON DE VILLE, New Orleans, Louisiana: This gem of a hotel in the heart of the French Quarter offers you a choice of accommodations: There's the *maison,* where magnificent antique-furnished rooms-with-balconies give you views over the street or a lush courtyard. Or, out back, there are the remodeled circa-1743 slave quarters, where Tennessee Williams is supposed to have worked on his *Streetcar.* And then, a stroll away on Dauphine Street, there are the delightful Audubon Cottages, where John James Audubon lived and worked from 1821 to 1826. Built in the Creole brick-and-post style (something like the old European half-timbered buildings), they have perhaps the most elegant rooms of all, with luxuriously furnished bedrooms, kitchens with stocked refrigerators, and private gardens. The whole Maison de Ville complex stands out even more, however, for the services: Tables in restaurants and space on sightseeing tours are booked by an omniscient concierge; shoes left outside your door are shined; a classic

French breakfast is served on a tray, along with a copy of the *Times-Picayune* and a rose. And when you return after a night on this fun-loving town, you'll find a piece of chocolate on your pillow. The bed, of course, has been turned down. Information: Maison de Ville, 727 Toulouse St., New Orleans, LA 70130 (504 561-5858). William Prentiss, innkeeper. 14 rooms, 7 suites.

HOUND EARS LODGE AND CLUB, Blowing Rock, North Carolina: Skiing down south? Yep, up here in the Blue Ridge Mountains. It can be pretty good, too, both here at the lodge and nearby. Open all year, this friendly resort has a fine 18-hole golf course as well as swimming, tennis, and other outdoor activities. On foot and by car, there's a lot to do and see — for children as well as adults. The lodge operates on the modified American plan, and meals are served to overnight guests only. Information: Hound Ears Lodge and Club, Blowing Rock, NC 28605 (704 963-4321). Bill Jeffcoat, innkeeper. 25 rooms.

NU-WRAY INN, Burnsville, North Carolina: If you like to get high on mountains, and you're east of the Rockies, this is the place. Nearby are the Pisgah National Forest, one of the wildest woodlands in the East (don't miss Linville Gorge), and Mt. Mitchell, at 6,684 feet, the highest east of the Mississippi. The inn, at about half that altitude, will keep your feelings on the up side with its good food and friendly atmosphere — despite the fact that you're awakened every morning without fail at 8 by the ringing of a bell and summoned to breakfast a half hour later by that same bell. The meal is worth it. The call to dinner (served by reservation) is less jarring; a Reginaphone, an old-fashioned music box, that is just one of the many Wray family antiques scattered around the inn, is your summons. Information: Nu-Wray Inn, Box 156, Burnsville, NC 28714 (704 682-2329). Rush T. Wray, innkeeper. 35 rooms.

SNOWBIRD MOUNTAIN LODGE, Robbinsville, North Carolina: As the name implies, this is a place for the birds — and those who love to watch them. From the inn's 3,000-foot setting bordering the Nantahala National Forest, the views above and below you are breathtaking. Birders and hikers have their choice of trails, from the gentle to the rugged. The forest covers 450,000 acres, including a 50,000-acre Cherokee reservation with a restored village and many exhibits and demonstrations for visitors. If you're still addicted to your car, there are some spectacular tours in the area, particularly to 30-mile-distant Fontana Dam and its 30-mile-long TVA lake. The inn serves all meals but has no bar. Information: Snowbird Mountain Lodge, Joyce Kilmer Forest Rd., Robbinsville, NC 28771 (704 479-3433). Bob and Connie Rhudy, innkeepers. 22 rooms.

SWORD GATE INN, Charleston, South Carolina: Charleston is known for its glorious old homes, and the carefully restored Sword Gate Inn, housed in an 18th-century mansion in the heart of the city's historic section, is ideal for getting you into the spirit of the city while you visit. The furnishings were selected with sensitivity and acute care for detail, and everything, from the gingham comforter to the freshly cut flowers, is directed toward a guest's comfort and delight. Breakfast — delicious and informal — is the only meal offered. Bikes and tours of the city are arranged at your request. Information: Sword Gate Inn, 111 Tradd St., Charleston, SC 29401 (803 723-8518). David and Suzanne Redd, innkeepers. 5 rooms.

THE RED FOX TAVERN, Middleburg, Virginia: Jefferson slept here; Washington surveyed the land hereabouts; and Civil War rebels used this building, constructed in 1728, as headquarters. (The bar is made from the table used by J. E. B. Stuart's surgeon.) Later, because Middleburg lies in the heart of the Virginia hunt country (and some 800 horse owners live in the immediate area), the inn prospered as a social center for the horsey set. And then, gradually, the inn went into a decline, and might well have gone the way of countless other old American buildings had it not been for the energetic ministrations of a local lady who wanted to do some good for the community and have a little fun at the same time. And so it was that the Red Fox

Tavern was filled up with Williamsburg wallpapers and wonderful antique furniture and paintings, which, like so many of the people who come here once again for their hunt breakfast, speak of horses as if there were no other subject in the world. In the dining room (wide-board, pegged floods; a stone wall; fireplaces; Windsor chairs), wonderful meals are served: classic Southern breakfasts, and lunches and dinners that mix local specialties like crab cakes and peanut soup with steaks, chops, and Continental offerings such as veal with mushrooms and cream. Music and lighter fare are available in the pub out back. Horses are available for rent, and there's plenty to watch — if not the National Beagle Trials, then at least plenty of races and shows. Details: The Red Fox Tavern, Washington and Madison Sts., PO Box 385, Middleburg, VA 22117 (703 687-6301). Turner Reuter, Jr., innkeeper. 6 rooms.

WAYSIDE INN, Middletown, Virginia: This establishment has been important in the area ever since it opened in 1797 — at first, as a stopping place for planters traveling down the old Shenandoah Turnpike; later, during the Civil War, as the site of the crucial battle of Cedar Creek; then, as this history-rich valley attracted the new automobile traveler, as "America's First Motor Inn." The Wayside's present vitality, however, is largely attributable to a Washington banker and antique fancier who restored and refurbished the inn with great zest, then filled up the rooms with a wealth of Oriental, Victorian, Empire, and early American antiques. One of the more popular of the several dining rooms is the 1742 slave kitchen; the setting, with the huge fireplace and a fire crackling on the hearth, is as inviting as the home-grown vegetables, home-baked breads and pastries, and various other specialties you'll find on your table. (The peanut soup and baked ham are not to be missed.) In summer, there are professionally mounted plays at the 260-seat Wayside Theater not far away. Information: Wayside Inn, 7783 Main St., Middletown, VA 22645 (703 869-1797). Marjorie Alcarese, innkeeper. 21 rooms.

THE COUNTRY INN, Berkeley Springs, West Virginia: The six imposing white pillars on the front of this building suggest formality. But don't be deceived: This country inn is about as friendly a place as an inn can be. (There's nothing formal about a place that keeps a stack of board games in its rec room.) And so the inn is a great place to stay when you come into the area — to visit 6,000-acre Cacapon State Park (where there's hiking, riding, cross-country skiing, swimming, and tennis); to tour hour-distant Harpers Ferry National Historical Park, where John Brown staged his notorious raid, or Charles Town, with its old-fashioned opera; or simply to take the waters in Berkeley Springs, where, at one of the oldest spas in the country, the administering state parks department offers Turkish and Roman baths, massages, and mineral baths at rates that are almost unbelievably low. Moreover, the eating at the inn could hardly be better: Concoctions like chicken-cucumber-onion soup keep company on the menu with country dishes made from local hams, chickens, and vegetables. Information: The Country Inn, Rt. 522, Berkeley Springs, WV 25411 (304 258-2210). Jack and Adele Barker, innkeepers. 40 rooms.

THE GENERAL LEWIS INN, Lewisburg, West Virginia: What started out as a private home on a hilltop back in 1798 and grew over the years into a magnificently situated mansion, with columns in the front and a sweep of beautiful lawns all about, has been an inn since 1929 — much to the delight of traveling Americans enamored of antique-furnished rooms and hearty country meals of ham, fried chicken, and steak. It's a classic inn in a lovely old-fashioned town. Information: The General Lewis Inn, Lewisburg, WV 24901 (304 645-2600). Col. Charles May, innkeeper. 34 rooms.

MIDWEST

ABE MARTIN LODGE, Nashville, Indiana: Like many other Indiana state park lodging places, the rustic stone-and-log Abe Martin Lodge at Brown County State Park is not long on antique-filled sleeping accommodations and fancy cuisine. Guest quarters both in the lodge and in the nearly two dozen surrounding cabins tend toward the plain but comfortable, and food toward the homestyle; fried chicken and biscuits are the order of almost every day. But few far more sumptuously furnished hostelries can boast such a setting — in the midst of 15,000 acres of wooded hills (a landscape that gives the lie to stories about Indiana being pancake-flat and consecrated to cornfields); the scenery is gorgeous during the pink and white springs, when the dogwoods and redbuds deluge the hills with a rosy blizzard, and in the blazing autumns, when the hardwoods turn scarlet, yellow, and all the colors in between. The result is similar to the Great Smokies, if on a slightly smaller scale. Nearby Nashville, a small town gone touristy, is nonetheless quaint and distinctively Hoosier, with its galleries and simple antique stores. Information: Abe Martin Lodge, PO Box 25, Nashville, IN 47448 (812 988-4418).

NEW HARMONY INN, New Harmony, Indiana: Associated with a restoration of two 19th-century communes that flourished here (see *Utopias*), the New Harmony Inn may be the most beautiful new hostelry in America: The lines are spare and clean as those of a Shaker building, and the variety of woods used as furniture, floors, stairways, and moldings provides a visual treat. The spreads on the high beds are in natural colors as well; only the bathroom tiles are colored — and they are vivid indeed, as bright blue, in some cases, as the unusual glass-roofed swimming pool out back. (Tennis, golf, riding, and other outdoor activities are available nearby.) Apart from Continental breakfasts available at the Entry House, no meals are served. But you can get a terrific lunch or dinner at the *Red Geranium,* a couple of minutes' walk from the inn. Information: New Harmony Inn, New Harmony, IN 47361 (812 682-4491). Gary Gerard, innkeeper. 45 rooms.

DEARBORN INN COLONIAL HOMES AND MOTOR HOUSES, Dearborn, Michigan: Begun by Henry Ford in 1931 for very important visitors and Ford corporate officials, this cluster of motor houses and colonial homes (faithful reproductions of the finest examples of American Georgian architecture) is now an interesting inn open to the public. All the rooms are fine, but the homes, with their reproductions of early American furniture, are particularly charming. The inn serves all meals, offers room service, has a heated pool and courts for tennis and shuffleboard, and livens up Friday and Saturday nights with dancing. Across the way is Mr. Ford's grand display of Americana, Greenfield Village and the Henry Ford Museum. A public golf course is nearby. Information: Dearborn Inn Colonial Homes and Motor Houses, 20301 Oakwood Blvd., Dearborn, MI 48123 (313 271-2700). Adrian A. de Vogel, innkeeper. 180 rooms.

NATIONAL HOUSE INN, Marshall, Michigan: The one-man preservation drive launched by a former Marshall mayor, one Harold Brooks, over a half century ago is finally bearing fruit, and hundreds of people are now actively involved in breathing new life into the town's beauty spots. Brooks bought several choice homes — the finest examples of 19th-century architecture in the area — and held them until he found buyers willing to restore and preserve the structures in their original style. Later, thanks to an enlightened zoning code and community cooperation, more and more homes were saved, so that by now 6 of them are in the National Register and 15 more are listed by the state as historic landmarks; all are examples of fine Victorian workmanship. The National House (1835) is the oldest operating inn in Michigan. It started as a hotel, went through several transformations — once into a windmill factory and another time into an apartment house — and has in recent years been restored in the Victorian style of its distinguished neighbors. From the doorknobs to the bed linens, everything has been done with a reverence for the original. The highlight of the year is the town's annual Historic Home Tour, the first weekend after Labor Day, when thousands come here to tour the restored houses. Information: National House Inn, 102 S Parkview, Marshall, MI 49068 (616 781-7374). Steve Poole, innkeeper. 15 rooms.

LOWELL INN, Stillwater, Minnesota: Built more than half a century ago, this gracious, colonial-style inn, with its 13 columns and high portico, has been run by the Palmer family since 1930 with a greater-than-usual degree of sensitivity to the proper care and feeding of guests. The bedrooms have been recently redone (but no televisions were added to disturb the peace), and each of the three popular dining rooms has a different motif: The Garden Room, stone-floored, with wrought-iron tables and chairs, has a pretty trout pool from which you can pick your supper; the George Washington Room, full of bright napery and gleaming silver, reflects the colonial period; and the Matterhorn Room, whose specialty is fondue, is full of Swiss woodcarvings that seldom fail to evoke *oohs* and *ahs* from about everyone who sees them. Lowell, which is just about 18 miles from St. Paul, is chockablock with antique shops; and after the bustle of the Twin Cities seems about the most heavenly place on earth. Information: Lowell Inn, 102 N 2nd St., Stillwater, MN 55082 (612 439-1100). Arthur and Maureen Palmer, innkeepers. 21 rooms.

ST. GEMME BEAUVAIS, Ste. Genevieve, Missouri: A number of the late-18th- and early-19th-century buildings in this surprise of a town, whose founding in 1732 makes it Missouri's first permanent settlement, have been restored — among them the Amoureaux House, part of which dates from 1770; the Beauvais House, about the same age; the 1790 Green Tree Tavern, the town's first inn; and St. Gemme Beauvais, its only operating inn. As befits the town's French heritage, the hostelry's breakfasts and lunches (the only meals served) feature Continental concoctions like quiche, crêpes, and omelettes; in keeping with the age of the structure, the parlors and guest accommodations are almost entirely done up in Victorian antiques — immense carved bedsteads that make you feel small no matter how much you ate for lunch, ornately framed mirrors, dressing tables with marble tops, a handsome old dining table and chairs. Lace curtains, flowered wallpapers, and draperies in the Victorian manner complete the effect, which is every bit as charming as the town itself. No wonder the citizens of St. Louis, less than two hours away, are so fond of the place. Open all year. Information: St. Gemme Beauvais, 78 N Main, Box 231, Ste. Genevieve, MO 63670 (314 883-5744). Frankye and Boats Donze, innkeepers. 8 rooms.

BUXTON INN, Granville, Ohio: Granville — in the middle of the state, near Denison University, the Heisey Glass Museum, and the Indian Mound Museum — is anybody's idea of how a Middle American town should look: spotlessly clean, with tree-lined streets, graceful buildings, inviting homes, and pleasant shops. It's a perfect setting for the tiny Buxton Inn (not to be confused with its larger, busier, neighbor, the Granville Inn). The rooms have been furnished with a keen eye for the right antiques; several of the chandeliers are especially worth noting. And so, too, is the food. There's a fireplace in the front dining room, which has low ceilings to enhance its cozy atmosphere. Lunch and dinner, served every day, include French-American specialties like seafood coquille cardinale, Louisiana chicken (rolled in seasoned flour, sautéed, and served with a cream sauce, toasted almonds, and artichoke hearts), and tournedos chasseur. Also don't miss the bean soup. Information: Buxton Inn, 313 E Broadway, Granville, OH 43023 (614 587-0001). Orville and Audrey Orr, innkeepers. 3 rooms.

GOLDEN LAMB INN, Lebanon, Ohio: Midway between Cincinnati and Dayton and in a town of 9,000, Ohio's oldest inn has, since its founding in 1803, provided lodging to ten presidents, DeWitt Clinton, Henry Clay, Mark Twain, and a very cross Charles Dickens (who complained that he couldn't get a drink; for a short while the inn was a temperance hotel). The location, smack in the middle of town, is its single unappealing characteristic nowadays — but the antique-furnished rooms, all done in period style and some fitted out with four-posters, are among the most pleasant in the area, and the Inn makes a fine base for a couple of days while you go canoeing or fishing on the Little Miami River, take the youngsters to a nearby amusement park, or visit the state museum or the Warren County Museum, where a collection of Shaker artifacts shows off the culture of this religious group, which came to the area nearly two centuries ago.

The food at the inn is good, and overnight guests get preferred seating. Try some of the Shaker items on the menu. Information: Golden Lamb Inn, 27 S Broadway, Lebanon, OH 45036 (513 932-5065). Jackson B. Reynolds, innkeeper. 18 rooms.

WHITE GULL INN, Fish Creek, Wisconsin: Fish Creek is just what it sounds like, Door County's gift to those who just want a small, far-out-of-the-way place near water where things are fairly quiet and the eating's good, something like Montauk or Cape Cod. As for the food you can't beat the Fish Boil dinner, the best of the day's catch from Lake Michigan with boiled potatoes, a tasty coleslaw, and homemade cherry pie. And then there's the Early American Buffet, with delights like turkey dumpling soup, maple-glazed carrots, baked ham, and corn and clam pie. Wash it down with a beer and amble down to the harbor and then back to bed for a good night's sleep to prepare for another day of the same. Some call it escape, others simply see it as a recharge. Either way, the pleasure's all yours. Information: White Gull Inn, PO Box 175, Fish Creek, WI 54212 (414 868-3517). Andrew and Jan Coulson, innkeepers. 12 rooms and a 2-bedroom housekeeping cottage.

WEST

ARIZONA INN, Tucson, Arizona: When Isabella Greenway (the state's first woman congressional delegate) opened this as an inn in 1930, it was primarily a desert oasis for the mighty, the mighty rich, and the well-heeled well-knowns — Rockefellers, Churchills, movie stars, and such. But the inn, no longer off in the desert by itself and no longer beyond the reach of lesser souls, has found itself surrounded by Tucson. No matter, it goes its own luxurious way in the manner and spirit in which it was conceived.

The gardens will astonish you first — 12 acres of lawns and flowers scattered with bushes and trees and criss-crossed by lovely footpaths; to take care of them, the inn employs more gardeners than some inns can welcome as guests. Inside, the color scheme is more subdued — a Mexican-American symphony of corals, beiges, grays, and reds that harmonizes with the desert surroundings. A full-time decorator on the staff keeps things looking their best. A heated pool, a vivid blue, is shaded on one side (to the delight of those for whom the glaring desert sun can sometimes be too much), and lunch is served poolside. You can play tennis (at night, as well as during the day, since the courts are floodlit), practice your putting on a green, play croquet and badminton, or, not far away, go riding or enjoy a round of golf. A good portion of the staff has worked at the inn for a couple of decades or more, and the unfailing professionalism of the staff's service reflects the fact. The food is good, too, and the Continental menu attracts diners from all over the state. Information: Arizona Inn, 2200 E Elm St., Tucson, AZ 85719 (602 325-1541). Robert Minerich, innkeeper. 85 rooms, 8 suites, 4 private homes.

TANQUE VERDE RANCH, Tucson, Arizona: When is a dude ranch a country inn? When the dude ranch is, like this one, 12 miles outside Tucson on the edge of the 1.4-million-acre Coronado National Forest and the lovely 63,000-acre Saguaro National Monument, the last word in luxury and personable charm. The Tanque Verde, part of which used to be a stagecoach stop, is no run-of-the-mill dude ranch. It has four tennis courts, indoor and outdoor swimming pools and a therapy pool, saunas, exercise rooms, and other luxuries. Some of the rooms have fireplaces, some have patios, and all have phones (but there are no TVs). Antiques are scattered here and there throughout the inn. Some 200 species of birds, from the bridled titmouse to the bald eagle, have been identified in the area, and the inn is so popular with bird-watchers that bird-banding (under the supervision of Chuck Cochran, who is engaged in a national project) is a regular activity. Riding, however, is still the big deal, and you can do it to your heart's content (or your bottom's protest) on your choice of some 80 horses, on supervised trail rides that take place several times daily. And when all is said and done, there's the Dog House Bar, a bunkhouse converted to a bottle club. Information:

Tanque Verde Ranch, Rt. 8, PO Box 66, Tucson, AZ 85710 (602 296-6275). Bob Cote, innkeeper. 47 rooms, 13 suites.

VAGABOND HOUSE INN, Carmel, California: It's one thing to restore a neglected but fundamentally magnificent old building. It's a trick of quite another sort to take a group of efficiency "units" from the early 1940s and transform them into a charming inn worthy of its unique natural surroundings. But that's what the present and former innkeepers have done here on the loveliest part of the northern California coast. Antiques collected over the years crowd the inn's rooms; the needlepoint wrought by one diligent lady, sewn into covers for the cushions that are scattered on several plump sofas, or framed and hung on the walls in the company of a fascinating lot of prints and watercolors, is still omnipresent; the ticking of the old clocks collected by Chuck Watts is still one of the characteristic sounds of the inn, along with the chattering of the squirrels who inhabit a wonderful main garden patio centered on an immense old live oak, dotted with rhododendron and camellia bushes, and hung here and there with baskets of ferns, begonias, and fuchsias. Each room faces that patio, and each has a character all its own, depending on the particular mix of maple and wicker, bentwood and books, brass and quilts; all of the rooms have a fireplace. The combination of such details makes the inn one of the loveliest places to stay when you come to visit this area; to see the much-photographed Point Lobos and the redwoods at Big Sur; and browse through the shops of Carmel. The inn serves only breakfast, but there's no dearth of good restaurants in the area. Information: Vagabond House Inn, 4th and Dolores Sts., PO Box 2747, Carmel, CA 93921 (408 624-7738). Dennis Levitt and Jewell Brown, innkeepers. 12 rooms.

CITY HOTEL, Columbia, California: Thanks to a State Parks Department historic preservation project, this once fabulously prosperous Gold Rush town three hours from San Francisco is a living museum of the area's mid-19th-century boom days, and from spring through fall the town is jammed with sightseers. A highlight of nearly everyone's visit is a stop at this two-story brick hotel, restored in the 70s to the tune of over half a million dollars. The gold diggers of those long-gone days liked their comforts every bit as much as the tourists do, and when they struck it rich, they would usually go all out to treat themselves. And so a hotel in a town like this was apt to be just as grand as you find the City Hotel, the passion for the good life reflected in the furnishings — tufted settees, marble-topped washstands and bureaus, Victorian bedsteads in burled wood or brass, Oriental rugs, a rosewood piano, brass hat racks and chandeliers gleaming at every turn. What you don't expect is a wine list as excellent and extensive as the one you find in the gorgeously furnished restaurant, or a kitchen that is not only so competent but so talented; some people come to Columbia just for the food. Information: City Hotel, PO Box 1870, Main St., Columbia, CA 95310 (209 532-1479). Ron Erickson, innkeeper. 9 rooms.

ST. ORRES, Gualala, California: The shoddiness of most contemporary building notwithstanding, a renaissance of interest in fine workmanship has quietly been taking place in America. As just one example, consider this inn on the northern California coast, a Russian palace of a structure built of redwood and salvaged materials around a tumbledown old guest house by a couple of carpenters-with-a-dream, and then named for the family that homesteaded the land. The interior is an exercise in woodworking virtuosity. Redwood paneling on the bedroom walls is meticulously tongue-in-grooved and laid in intriguing patterns that are as distinguished as those of an ancient fresco, or, for that matter, the ones you find in the velvet quilts that were hand-stitched by a talented local craftswoman for the beds. And the dining room — a three-storied space walled partially in redwood-framed stained glass and topped by another onion dome — may be more arresting than any other restaurant in the country. In such a setting, you expect original meals, and you get them — wonderful variations on Continental classics for which some people drive all the way from San Francisco; a concoction known as chocolate decadence may make a chocoholic of you even if you don't have a sweet tooth. The totality is so marvelous that the peaceful setting amongst the beaches, coves, and redwoods is just icing on the cake. Information: St. Orres, PO Box 523, Gualala, CA 95445 (707 884-3303). Eric Black, Richard Wasserman, Ted Black, Rosemary Campiformio, innkeepers. 8 rooms, 3 cottages.

HERITAGE HOUSE, Little River, California: Because so many early California settlers were homesick when they first arrived here from New England, they built their houses in styles that would remind them of the East Coast, and left this part of the West liberally sprinkled with New Hampshire cottages and Down East farmhouses like the one at the core of the main building of this inn on California's northern coast (which, incidentally, Baby Face Nelson once used as a hideout). But even though the original structure has been added to many times over the three decades since the present innkeeper came here in 1949, most of the rooms are not in the farmhouse but in small, medium, large, and extra-large guest cottages surrounding it. Each set of quarters is different. Some of the old ones, originally sited elsewhere in the Coast region, were knocked down, transported to Little River, reassembled with varying degrees of fidelity to the original, and then luxuriously furnished; others were built from salvaged lumber. All the rooms have private baths; many have fireplaces or pot-bellied stoves and — most important of all — views of the ocean, which is what you come here for in the first place. As for the kitchen, it eschews the Continental in favor of the best of American cuisine — everything from the tiny pancakes to the cream soups and meat and fish entrées. Information: Heritage House, 5200 Highway I, Little River, CA 95456 (707 937-5885). L. D. Dennen, innkeeper. 60 rooms.

UNION HOTEL, Los Alamos, California: This old hotel, originally built in 1880 and rebuilt, after a fire, in 1915, had gone through more than 25 owners and nearly as many incarnations — as pool hall, dance hall, rooming house, and candidate for the wrecker's ball — when, in 1972, a meat wholesaler from not-far-distant Los Angeles, casting about for a new career, discovered the place and decided that running an inn was just what he had always wanted to do. He hired a carpenter, Jim Radhe, and bought a couple of old barns, a trio of old sheds, and a garage to use as lumber to re-create the façade of the first Union Hotel as portrayed in an old print. And then he went out antique hunting. When he came home from his travels, he had enough furniture and knickknacks to give the empty building the cluttered look that a structure of its vintage deserved. Look around you, and marvel: Here are century-old gaslights from Mississippi and chairs hand-carved in Alabama, a mantelpiece from a Pasadena mansion and a vintage Singer sewing machine; there you see the chandeliers that once graced the home of Lee J. Cobb, a lamp used in the filming of *Gone With the Wind,* a grandfather clock, a 150-year-old bar made of African mahogany and an ivory-inlaid Brunswick pool table. Scattered around the guest rooms, you'll find a mahogany armoire that conceals a Murphy bed, a brass-and-iron bedstead inset with cloisonné work, and countless antique four-posters, quilts, crocheted bedspreads, and vintage Bibles. After all this Victorian clutter, the spacious dining room (where unpretentious home cooking is the order of the day) and the rough-paneled Western bar (which you enter through swinging doors that once admitted customers to a Southern bordello) are a welcome change. The inn is open only Friday through Sunday nights (year-round), and the meals vary according to the innkeeper's whim. Kids are charged for their food according to how much they weigh on a big butcher scale. Information: Union Hotel, 362 Bell St., Los Alamos, CA 93440 (ask the operator for Los Alamos 2744). Richard and Teri Langdon, innkeepers. 14 rooms.

THE MacCALLUM HOUSE, Mendocino, California: East is East and West is West and they meet here, four hours north of San Francisco. Mendocino, Nantucket West to many, is another example of how the early California settlers brought New England to the coast. The MacCallum House happens to be one of the prettier expressions of the Easterners' homesickness. Built in 1882 by lumber magnate William H. Kelley as a wedding present for his daughter Daisy and her husband Alexander MacCallum, this three-story Victorian mansion, trimmed with jigsaw-cut woodwork and fronted by a wonderful expanse of windows, was bought by two San Franciscans, Bill and Sue Norris, in 1974, about 20 years after Daisy's death. With the house, they purchased almost all of the furnishings, and so, when you visit, you can browse through Daisy's library (which includes some handsome leather-bound books, some volumes in French and German, some books on travel and religion, and a good many romantic novels) and admire the Tiffany lamps, Persian carpets, and carved footstools that belonged to the MacCallums themselves until not long ago. Some of the guest rooms are in the main building, but the Norrises have also rebuilt the old carriage house, the barn, and the greenhouse, and most guests are accommodated there. Continental dinners are served in the library from April through December. A short walk from town are the headlands at Russian Gulch State Park that can be described by only one word — spectacular. Information: The MacCallum House, PO Box 206, Mendocino, CA 95460 (707 937-0289). Sue Norris, innkeeper. 20 rooms.

HOTEL LEGER, Mokelumne Hill, California: Restored and refurbished in 1960, the pleasant Victorian interior of this century-old former beer hall, and its two-storied veranda (pillars below and railing above), seem to recreate, for a moment, the Gold Rush days of the mid-19th century here, and sometimes you can almost imagine how it was in Mok' Hill that famous weekend of legend when no less than 17 hangings took place in one night. The rooms are old-fashioned, with flowered wallpaper, high Victorian beds, and plenty of rocking chairs. The surrounding Mother Lode Country is less gussied-up than some other sections of California's former mining regions, and it's a welcome change. But if you don't want to go out exploring, you can just laze around the swimming pool out back among the orange trees. Prime rib is served in the dining room on weekends. Information: Hotel Leger, PO Box 50, Mokelumne Hill, CA 95245 (209 286-1401). Sue Clark, innkeeper. 13 rooms.

SAN YSIDRO RANCH, Montecito, California: Originally owned by the Franciscan Missions, this 540-acre resort near Santa Barbara, which opened in 1893, enjoyed a long season as the choice vacation spot of the rich and the famous: Laurence Olivier and Vivien Leigh were married here; Jack Kennedy honeymooned with Jackie here; John Galsworthy, Aldous Huxley, Sinclair Lewis, Winston Churchill, Somerset Maugham, Bing Crosby, Jack Benny, and many others stayed here; and Ronald Colman owned the place from the mid-30s until his death in 1958. But in the 60s, the legend began to fade, and the inn started to fall apart and was well down the road to total ruin when James Lavenson, former president of New York's great *Plaza Hotel,* put up the money to clean up, fix up, and paint up. And so, when you visit today, the tennis courts, stables, restaurant, and swimming pool are all as spiffy as they were when Galsworthy revised his *Forsyte Saga* there (if not more so: Some of the cottages that house guests now have their own Jacuzzis). You can hole up in your bungalow and never see the light of day, or mix with fellow guests at the bar and in the dining room, the kitchen, whose specialties include a smattering of the French and a smattering of the American, is good enough that among those who drop in to say "Hi!" to the chef is none other than Julia Child. Special meals grace the tables on Easter, Thanksgiving, Christmas, and New Year's Eve. Information: San Ysidro Ranch, 900 San Ysidro La., Montecito, CA 93108 (805 969-5046). James and Susie Lavenson, innkeepers. 38 cottages.

THE INN AT RANCHO SANTA FE, Rancho Santa Fe, California: It was one of those classic corporate bloopers: The Atcheson, Topeka and Santa Fe Railroad bought up some 9,000 acres of cheap land to plant three million eucalyptus trees to provide — company officials hoped — an endless supply of railroad ties. Nobody had bothered to think, however, that eucalyptus trees grow crooked, not straight — and though the trees took off, there wasn't a tie to be had in the bunch. The railroad then went into the citrus business, and, later, started up a residential development, one of the first planned communities in the country. The inn was first built to house prospective purchasers and it just kept on growing until it became what you find here today — a sedate and very restful complex of unpretentious but comfortably furnished cottages nestling in the luxuriant shrubbery on the grounds surrounding the original building. There are three tennis courts, and, nearby, two fine golf courses and a beach. The inn will pack you off with a box lunch. There's a wonderful large library and a high-ceilinged lounge; and the whole thing is just 27 miles from San Diego. Information: The Inn at Rancho Santa Fe, PO Box 869, Rancho Santa Fe, CA 92067 (714 756-1131). Dan D. Royce, innkeeper. 75 rooms.

WINE COUNTRY INN, St. Helena, California: Here, in the Napa Valley, some 70 miles from San Francisco, is a rarity: a brand-new, built-from-scratch, old-fashioned country inn. Ned and Marge Smith spent years dreaming, talking, sketching, and planning inns; they traveled to classic inn country, lived there as guests, and picked the brains of innkeepers. And when they were ready a few years ago, they built their own, a marriage of the old and new made in inn Heaven. Each room is different; most have fireplaces and all have character. Thanks to the Smiths' big dream and careful attention to detail, it all works as it should. Breakfast is the only meal, and it's served in a large, attractive common room. There are many fine restaurants in the area, and the menus for most of them are all available at the inn for your perusal. Information: Wine Country Inn, 1152 Lodi La., St. Helena, CA 94574 (707 963-7077). Jim Smith, innkeeper. 25 rooms.

MANSION HOTEL, San Francisco, California: California versions of the Old World bed-and-breakfast place have started sprouting all over the West Coast in the last few years. Some are installed in rambling old Victorian homes, some in sleek, contemporary town houses done up so that they look like something straight out of *Architectural Digest.* All are centrally located or in good residential neighborhoods, near public transportation, and, while not inexpensive, do give you good value for your money, providing not only complete breakfasts (and sometimes the use of the refrigerator and laundry facilities as well), but also the chance to meet new people and get some personal guidance about what to see and do. *Bed and Breakfast International* (151 Ardmore Rd., Kensington, CA 94707; phone 415 525-4569) can make your arrangements for such lodgings in a number of cities; most are in the area around San Francisco. This city, unlike many others of its size, is also blessed with an inn — a completely separate operation, but nonetheless worth looking into. The Mansion Hotel, created by a one-time ad man, boasts 18 rooms with bath — some almost *House & Garden* charming — particularly the John Muir Room and the elegant Empress Josephine Room with its Louis XIV canopy bed and matching mirrored armoire, private sundeck, and bar; Barbara Streisand and Robin Williams have been among recent guests. Room rates include fresh flowers in your room; complimentary wine, coffee, tea, and sherry; mansion Magic Concerts — and, of course, breakfast in bed. Other facilities include an elegant restaurant, a music parlor, game room and library, billiard room, and even a sauna. The mansion is San Francisco's only designated Landmark Hotel. Information: Mansion Hotel, 2220 Sacramento St., San Francisco, CA 94115 (415 929-9444). Robert Pritikin, innkeeper. 18 rooms.

SONOMA HOTEL, Sonoma, California: This old wood-and-adobe structure, which started out in the 1870s as a dry goods store and meeting hall, was carefully restored in 1976 by the present owners, so that it now has a delightful Gay Nineties ambience. All the rooms have dresser-armoire-and-bedstead suites made in Europe around the turn of the century; Room 3, named after the Mexican General Vallejo, who laid out the town, and furnished with his own exquisite carved rosewood bedroom suite, currently on loan from the Sonoma League for Historic Preservation, is particularly lovely. In the morning, when you go downstairs for Continental breakfast in the inn's charming lobby, the management will help you plan a good tour of the surrounding wine country and nearby points of interest like the Jack London State Historic Park at Glen Ellen, where you can see the ruins of London's own Wolf House as well as the home of his widow, filled with London memorabilia. Information: Sonoma Hotel, 110 W Spain St., Sonoma, CA 95476 (707 996-2996). Dorene and John Musilli, innkeepers. 17 rooms.

SUTTER CREEK INN, Sutter Creek, California: One of the oldest country inns in the West, this green-shuttered bit of New England-in-California, built in 1859 by a wealthy merchant for his eastern bride, came into the possession of Jane Way, a somewhat psychic palm reader, graphologist, and former housewife, in 1966. Jane turned the place into an inn. She installed canopy beds, double beds, and beds that swing, ever so gently, by chains from the ceiling. (If you can't get used to the motion, you can stabilize your mattress.) Some of the bathtubs were sunken into the floors. Fireplaces and Franklin stoves were installed. Outbuildings were converted to guest rooms. Chintz by the yard was swathed around squashy sofas, draped over beds, and hung at the windows. There are plenty of antiques, but they're the kind that look as if they don't mind being used. The place feels comfortable, reflecting (with a greater degree of fidelity than is usual) the personality of the innkeeper herself. Jane doesn't serve lunch or dinner — she leaves that to other innkeepers in the area; but instead she offers her guests the chance to congregate first thing in the morning over a big eggs-and sausage breakfast in the brick-walled kitchen, a room as warm as the flash of the copper utensils hung from beams and walls alike. When the conversation lags, Jane may add brandy to your coffee (if you haven't already done so), or swirl it with a cinnamon stick, just because it's more festive that way. Or she might be persuaded to tell you how she came to terms with the ghost she encountered when she first arrived at the inn, or about her father, who is known locally for having brought France's Colombard grape to California. Or, because she is well versed in local history, she might tell you the sad tale of John Sutter, who had built up one of the state's biggest ranches when a carpenter working in the area discovered gold on one of his streams in 1848 and set off a gold rush that had prospectors killing his cattle, destroying his land, and ruining his hopes for a comfortable old age. Only the memory remains: Sutter Creek today is beautifully kept, an antiquer's delight. For more information: Sutter Creek Inn, 73 Main St., Sutter Creek, CA 95685 (209 267-5606). Jane Way, innkeeper. 16 rooms.

AHWAHNEE HOTEL, Yosemite National Park, California: Built in 1927 in a deep wide valley guarded by granite mountains, ostensibly to accommodate the growing number of visitors arriving in the park by automobile, this marvelous establishment is rustic but luxurious, with slate floors, beamed ceilings, a cavernous lobby, and immense windows in even the smallest sitting rooms to give you views into the park. The Ahwahnee is the kind of place where dressing up for dinner is the order of the day. Yet the old stone structure manages at the same time to so harmonize with the surroundings that even Frank Lloyd Wright admired it. Meals in the imposing, playing-field-sized dining room, especially notable for its towering picture windows and heavily beamed ceiling, are highlighted by salmon (sometimes broiled, sometimes poached in white wine) and prime rib. Like the park, the hotel is open all year. But you'd be hard-pressed to say which season is best for a visit. In summer, there's hiking all through the Sierra, and you can sign up for rock climbing schools or special programs dealing with high-altitude ecology. In winter, the favored pastimes include downhill and cross-country skiing, snowshoeing to some of the frozen waterfalls, or races and winter games sponsored by the park concessionaire. At Christmas, during what usually turns out to be the high point of the Ahwahnee's season, the hotel hosts the annual Bracebridge Dinner, wherein a section from Washington Irving's *Sketch Book* is reenacted in song and drama: The good Squire Bracebridge, an English country gentleman who is seated at the head of the dining room on a table set up on a dais, entertains his guests (you, a few hundred others, and assorted satin-, velvet-, and fur-clad actors and singers) over a fabulous six-course dinner that includes a flaming plum pudding and a peacock pie. The pageantry is gorgeous, and so the limited number of tickets that will reserve your place at the table sell out almost as soon as they're made available to the public. Ticket ordering procedure changes occasionally, so write well in advance for details. Ahwahnee Hotel, Yosemite Park and Curry Co., Yosemite National Park, CA 95389 (209 373-4171). 121 rooms.

BURGUNDY HOUSE, Yountville, California: The rolling hills, bucolic landscapes, and usually sunny skies of California's three great wine-producing areas — the Mendocino, Napa, and Sonoma valleys — seem a world apart from usually congested, often-foggy or rainy San Francisco, even though they're just 90 minutes away. And so, when you come to the Napa Valley town of Yountville, which celebrated its sesquicentennial last year, you have scenery, delightful weather, and the Burgundy House besides. This relatively new inn — installed in a circa-1872 former antique shop, brandy distillery, and speakeasy with two-foot-thick fieldstone walls — has been decorated in eclectic style by innkeeper Mary Keenan, with all manner of antique pieces, many of them French. One room has its own patio, a few have private baths, and all have fine views over treetops or vineyards. No matter which you get, you'll be welcomed with a decanter of wine. And there's more of the same in a big common room, where many guests gather in the late afternoons or evenings and for breakfast; this is the kind of place where strangers become fast friends fast. (Nearby Bordeaux House, under the same management, is every bit as companionable, despite its sleek, contemporary look; this establishment is your best bet if you want your own bath.) Between meals at any number of fine local restaurants, you can go out for some antique-shopping, ballooning, or soaring; visit one of the several local spas for massages, or steam or mud baths; or go out and taste some wine. A tip on touring the vineyards: To stay sober, take only a couple of swallows of each variety, and, for clarity's sake, concentrate on just one or two varieties as you go from vineyard to vineyard. (Each vineyard has its specialty — Blanc de Blanc and Cuvée de Pinot Noir, for instance, at Domaine Chandon, one of the most interesting in the Yountville area.) Information: Burgundy House, 6711 Washington St., Yountville, CA 94599 (707 944-2855). Mary and Bob Keenan, innkeepers. 12 rooms.

C LAZY U RANCH, Granby, Colorado: This establishment, situated at about 8,000 feet on the Continental Divide, is the real thing, a working ranch as well as the western version of a country inn. The emphasis, of course, is on horseback riding, and you're given your own personal mount to ride as little or as much and whenever you want for the duration of your stay. But other horsing around also figures: country fairs and rodeos, and, in June, roundups. The C Lazy U is also a guest ranch, though, and so you'll find a heated pool, a whirlpool and sauna, tennis and racquetball court, skeet-shooting ranges, Ping-Pong tables, miles of trails for hiking, and horseshoe court. And if that won't keep you busy, you can always go fishing — or just take a drive through the mountains. The large lodge, which faces a lake where you can ice-skate in winter, is surrounded by guest cottages. All the rooms are cozy and comfortable; the food is solid and plentiful; and evenings are convivial. Information: C Lazy U Ranch, PO Box 378, Granby, CO 80446 (303 887-3344). George and Virginia Mullin, innkeepers. 12 rooms, 24 suites.

RANCHO ENCANTADO, Tesuque, New Mexico: Surrounded on three sides by the Tesuque Indian Reservation and on the fourth by the Sante Fe National Forest, this top-notch Old Southwest resort hotel came into being in the 1920s as a very ordinary sort of desert lodge. But in the late 60s, Betty Egan, a Cleveland widow with four children, came here to start life over again. She took the place in hand and turned it into the exciting complex it is today, a luxurious Western guest ranch — more than a hotel, more than an inn; the sort of establishment where you expect to find cowbells and dried peppers and Indian weavings hanging here and there, the occasional rawhide chair, and lots of red tile. The guest rooms, all furnished with antiques and Southwestern Indian art and artifacts, all have their own patios; most have either stoves or fireplaces. The tri-level dining room, walled in white adobe, looks out across the desert, some 170 acres of which make up the Rancho Encantado spread. For fun, you can swim in a heated outdoor pool, play tennis, go riding (on horses you hire by the hour), or join in many other indoor or outdoor activities. Food is Mexican or Continental. (Be sure to try the sour cream chicken enchiladas and the carne asado, steak marinated with chili strips.) There are big feasts for Thanksgiving and Christmas. The European Plan (no meals included in rates) prevails except in November and December. Information: Rancho Encantado, Rt. 4, PO Box 57C, Santa Fe, NM 87501 (505 982-3537). Betty Egan, innkeeper. 22 rooms.

SALISHAN LODGE, Gleneden Beach, Oregon: A dedicated environmentalist who was also a thoroughgoing sybarite couldn't find a better spot for a vacation than this unusual modern resort on the Oregon coast about 90 miles west of Portland. Here, everything harmonizes with the spectacular landscape of lagoons, woods, beach, and ocean. Every bedroom, lounge, and dining room is further testimony to the good taste of the resort's designers and the architectural integrity of the complex. The creation of Oregon manufacturer John D. Gray, Salishan stands as one proof that good design and reverence for the environment can also be good business.

Rooms — all with fireplaces, big bathrooms, and oversized windows that frame forest views — are located in 15 villas that are connected by bridges and covered walkways. The dining room is also exceptionally handsome, and the kitchen is noted for its way with seafood, particularly salmon, which comes barbecued, baked in puff pastry, and fixed just about any other way you can imagine. The wine list is so extensive that it has an index; it lists everything from an unpretentious Beaujolais to a Lafite Rothschild that costs more than a whole weekend's stay at some very nice places. The resort even has its own art gallery and publishes a botanical guide to the flora on the grounds and in the area. And every guest is assigned his own parking space (a feature much appreciated by the Cadillac-Mercedes-BMW crowd that gravitates here). To round things out, there is an indoor swimming pool, therapy pool, and a variety of health club facilities (exercise rooms, saunas, and such); tennis courts are located both indoors and outdoors; and golf is available on the property. Bird-watching, collecting driftwood, and studying the trees and the wildflowers can keep you plenty busy, however. Information: Salishan Lodge, PO Box 118, Gleneden Beach, OR 97388 (503 764-2371). Russ Cleveland, innkeeper. 150 rooms, 3 suites.

TIMBERLINE LODGE, Timberline, Oregon: Those who lived through the Great Depression remember that the WPA (Works Progress Administration) was the whipping boy of everyone who condemned the New Deal as a waste, and that the men who worked for the organization were widely considered no better than a bunch of lazy bums. Timberline Lodge, built by the WPA with youths from the CCC (Civilian Conservation Corps) more than halfway up snow-capped, 11,200-foot Mt. Hood, puts the lie to that notion. Hundreds of Oregonians — trained to chisel stones, blacksmith, carve, and carpenter by locals and by craftsmen imported from Europe — created a structure that is truly monumental, from its 400-ton chimney (a hundred feet high) and its 750-pound bronze-and-brass weather vane, to the cathedral of a lobby, the massive staircases, and the giant-sized doorway. Even the details are dazzling: the chairs made of hardwood, wrought iron, and rawhide; the newel posts carved with animals and birds from sawed-off telephone poles; stained glass murals portraying local scenes and creatures; hand-wrought chandeliers and lamps; rugs hooked from the blankets and uniforms used by the workers; and on and on. The ensemble is a structure in harmony with the mountain it calls home, a work of unusual architectural design and impressive craftsmanship — and a monument to American determination. When you visit, you'll lodge in rooms filled up with sturdy blond furniture, hand-woven rugs, and appliquéd spreads and curtains. Every room has a private bath and a good view (either of valley or peak). There's a heated pool and a sauna; you can ski the year around, and in summer you can hike or climb as well. At Christmastime, Richard Kohnstamm, who has been here for over two decades, celebrates the season with such verve that even stay-at-homes don't miss the hearth fires. Information: Timberline Lodge, Government Camp, OR 97028 (503 272-3311). Richard Kohnstamm, area operator. 60 rooms.

EXCELSIOR HOUSE, Jefferson, Texas: In the 19th century, this community 200 miles east of Dallas on the Louisiana border was a booming cotton-shipping center. But then the world, in the person of the railroads, passed it by. Business suffered, "progress" ceased, and Jefferson came into the 50s and our own era of high interest in things historic virtually unscarred by the wrecker's ball. The brick-and-timber, grillwork-embellished Excelsior House, a New Orleans–style construction that was one of the town's most prominent buildings, was bought in 1961 by the Jesse Allen Wise Garden Club, and its members set about sanding and painting, polishing and papering, to return the hotel to the grandeur it knew back in the days when it was welcoming the wealthy and the famous (among them, even a few presidents). The rooms are now furnished with warm cherry, mahogany, and maple dressers and sleigh beds, canopy beds, and Jenny Lind–style spool beds. In the public rooms, there are oriental rugs underfoot and chandeliers of crystal and porcelain overhead. Some of the ceilings are pressed tin, some are plaster. The windows are draped in the Victorian style. Breakfast, for which you convene on the sun porch, is the only meal served — but what a meal it is: ham and eggs, grits, and heaps of the fluffy, bite-sized Orange Blossom Muffins for which the hotel is famous. Also memorable are a visit to Jay Gould's luxurious private railway car, which was restored by the garden club after it was found rotting away in a field, and a leisurely tour of the town's several other historical sights. Information: Excelsior House, 211 W Austin St., Jefferson, TX 75657 (214 665-2513). 14 rooms.

CAPTAIN WHIDBEY INN, Coupeville, Washington: The chief claim to fame of the peaceful, wooded island 50 miles north of Seattle where Coupeville is located is this resort, built some three-quarters of a century ago, high above the sea, of the reddish logs of the locally plentiful madrona tree. A fixture of the Pacific Northwest vacation scene almost since the beginning, it is popular, however, not so much because of any superabundance of activities (it's as quiet as the island itself) but because it is a personality kid, a one-of-a-kind, through and through. Dominating the lobby is a huge fireplace built of stone and surrounded by easy chairs. The shelves of the library are jammed with books. The window-walled dining room, where you can order from a wine list as distinguished as any in the area and a menu that features all kinds of fish and crustaceans fresh from the cold local waters, gives you views of the ocean and beyond it in the east, the snowy summit of Mt. Baker. And the ceiling of the bar, a favorite watering hole in this part of the world, is hung with hundreds of empty bottles whose labels bear inscriptions testifying to the good times had during the consumption of their contents. Rooms in the main building, all of them simply furnished, are like miniature log cabins; they share the baths at the end of the hall. For privacy and space, you want the rooms facing the lagoon. Information: Captain Whidbey Inn, 2072 W Whidbey Island Inn Rd., Coupeville, WA 98239 (206 678-4097). John Stone and Geoff Stone, innkeepers. 25 rooms.

JAMES HOUSE, Port Townsend, Washington: Dreaming of a future as the West's greatest port, this community boomed as rich men working on getting richer poured into town. Of the great houses they built along the city's streets to show off their substance, Francis Wilcox James's was the most impressive. Built in 1889, at a cost of around $10,000 — back in the days when $2,000 or $3,000 would pay for more than adequate living quarters, and $4,000 was all that was required to construct something really splendid — this porticoed, dormered, many-chimneyed, peak-roofed, shingle-sided Queen Anne–style mansion fell on hard times in the years after the railroads passed Port Townsend by, and left the early dreams unrealizable. The ceilings were lowered, the large rooms were partitioned into cubicles. Then, in the 60s, Bill and Frances Eaton saw the house, loved it, bought it, and over the course of a decade, restored it. The present owners, Rod and Deborah LaMontagne, have also given it heavy doses of TLC, as you can see when you visit: From the banisters and the parquet floors to the carved settees and the high-standing bedsteads, the James House gleams. Every room is handsome in its way, and every room looks toward the mountains, but for style and view, the Bridal Suite (which has its own fireplace, a private bath, and a balcony) takes the prize. It has an especially handsome massive bedstead inset with burled walnut panels. Breakfast is the only meal served; everyone gathers around a big oak table for home-baked breads and all manner of other goodies. Information: James House, 1238 Washington St., Port Townsend, WA 98368 (206 385-1238). Rod and Deborah LaMontagne, innkeepers. 12 rooms.

Vacations on Farms and Ranches

In the country, city people rediscover the sound of songbirds and the smell of grass. Suburbanites get the chance to poke around an area where the nearest neighbors live miles away. Parents can say to their children, "No, milk does not start out in cartons" — and then prove it. Youngsters can see people who live differently, think differently, and have different values, so that "when it comes time to think about their future," in the words of one father, who has taken his eight kids to farms in Virginia, Wisconsin, North Dakota, Idaho, and Colorado over the course of a decade, "their decisions will be based on knowledge and actual experience rather than guesswork and fiction." Even if there were no lessons to be learned, however, a stay at a farm or ranch would be a decidedly pleasant way to pass a couple of weeks, so it's no wonder that all over the country there are hundreds of farms and ranches welcoming guests.

No two are quite alike. On the one hand, there are the guest farms and dude ranches with tennis courts, fancy swimming pools, square dances, hayrides, jam-packed recreation programs, and the like; guests are the main business and facilities and amenities focus on accommodating them. On the other hand, there are family farms and working ranches where raising cows, chickens, chinchillas, horses, beefalo, pigs, wheat, or pinto beans is the central activity, and the owners take guests only to bring in a little extra money, or to make friends and exchange views on the very different ways in which they establish their homes, bring up their children, make a living. In these places, there won't be many other guests, and you'll fill up your days with trips to town, berry-picking expeditions, swims in nearby rivers or ponds, fishing in the streams, going out for hayrides, milking cows, going to night markets or county fairs, driving the Holsteins in from the pasture, digging potatoes, hunting for fossils or arrowheads, gathering eggs, etc. You'll stay in the farmer's own house (and usually, share a bath) or in an adjacent cottage with housekeeping facilities; you may also share some or all of his meals (eggs fresh from the henhouse and vegetables from the garden, apple strudel, cinnamon buns, maple-syrup baked beans, homemade donuts, and such). Nobody will drag you out of bed at 5 AM, but you can rise with the sun (and the farmer) if you wish, and since there's been no cocktail lounge to keep you up into the wee hours, you may even feel that is no burden. The slower pace of life in the country (you'll learn that it's no myth) almost guarantees that you'll end the vacation rested instead of exhausted — and the warmth of the hosts assures that you'll feel as if you're staying in the home of a friend right up until the time comes to pay the bill.

How much will that be? At a family farm or ranch the weekly rates, including meals, begin at $135 per person (with reduced rates for children under 12); and from about $200 or up at the guest-oriented guest farms, lodges, inns, dude ranches. (The more extensive the facilities, the higher the rates.) When cabins, cottages, bunkhouses, and extra farmhouses with housekeeping facilities are available, you can pay as little as $150 a week for the entire family, and fresh eggs, vegetables, and milk are sometimes thrown in for next to nothing.

In the listing below — which ought to give you an idea of what's available — inexpensive means you'll pay about $135 to $175 per person per week, moderate about $200 to $325, and expensive about $350 and up. However, sometimes the rates include unlimited use of facilities and all the riding you want — and sometimes one or more of the activities cost extra. Be sure to find out what's included when you price the ranches. Also look at how the ranch management defines a week: Will your money buy you six nights' lodging or seven, seven days' stay or eight?

For a comprehensive list of farms and ranches of all kinds, plus addresses, phone numbers, rates, size, activities, and previous guests' comments, see Pat Dickerman's *Farm, Ranch & Country Vacations* ($9.45 postpaid from Farm & Ranch Vacations, Inc., 36 E 57th St., New York, NY 10022, 212 355-6334). Herewith, a short list of some of the most typical:

FAMILY FARMS

THE RODGERS DAIRY FARM, West Glover, Vermont: About 35 miles from the Canadian border in Vermont's unspoiled Northeast Kingdom, three generations of the Rodgers family run a 350-acre dairy farm on the same property which their Scottish ancestors settled in the early 1800s — and provide lodgings to city folk in a century-old, 17-room, white clapboard farmhouse surrounded by maple-shaded lawns ringed with an old-fashioned split-rail fence. Daytimes, you can watch the cows being milked by machine and learn to ride the pony and to reach under the clucking hens to gather eggs — scary but fun. You can make friends with the dogs and the kittens, pull weeds in the gardens, and gather vegetables which will appear on the big dinner table within the hour. If it's haying time you can help pick up bales of hay, stack them on the haywagons, and unload them in the barn. Or, if you want, you can drive a few miles to Shadow Lake for a swim, or to Barton, 12 miles away, to see what it's like to be in a town with 1,051 inhabitants (many more than in the villages of Glover and West Glover, pop. 650, combined), take in an auction or two, or just sit in lawn chairs under the maple trees. In winter, there's snowmobiling and cross-country skiing. Information: James and Nancy Rodgers, Rodgers Dairy Farm, West Glover, VT 05875 (802 525-6677). Inexpensive.

ETHILTON FARMS, Hartford, Wisconsin: Milt and Ethel Bliss have been giving guests such a warm welcome to their 160-acre farm for the last quarter-century that when holidays and birthdays come around, the couple is showered with cards and notes of good wishes. When you come to visit, you stay (usually with one or two other families, five or six other guests in all) right in the Blisses' farmhouse. You share their bathrooms and eat at their big tables, and by the time you leave, if you don't feel like a member of the family, you're bound to conclude that the Blisses are the most personable people you've met in your life. Mrs. Bliss, who has written three books — about her experiences with her guests, about the couple's year in India, and about organic gardening — is something of a human dynamo. It is mainly because of her diligence, for instance, that she can comment, "We could get along for weeks without a trip to the supermarket." She tends an immense garden all summer long, then cans, freezes, and stores the harvest so that it shows up on the table (as soups, hot dishes, juices, and the like) all through the year. The 120 tillable acres of the property are partly planted with wheat that is ground or processed right on the farm for breads and cereals — and the cereals are topped with cream from the Ethilton Farms cows. (What else?) As for Mr. Bliss, he goes to bed with the chickens and has done half a day's work before sunrise; and then usually has energy left over to fill you in on the plight of the modern farmer, or to tell you about his days working with various government agencies in this country and four others. Children love Ethilton Farms: There are eggs to gather, hay bales to climb over, cows to milk, woods to explore, and on and on. Tennis, golf, and quite a lot of sightseeing are also available, even though this is quite a rural area. And it's all just 125 miles from Chicago. Information: Milt and Ethel Bliss, N1234 County Highway O, Hartford, WI 53027 (414 474-7258). Inexpensive.

WILSON'S PINTO BEAN FARM, Yellow Jacket, Colorado: Everything at this southwestern Colorado establishment is comfortable and homey — but don't expect luxury: The trailer which guests occupy is not a late model, and the three guest rooms in the farmhouse are not large. Yet to visit Esther, Art, and the Wilson children (in their teens and twenties) is to experience real, honest-to-goodness farm life — 1,100 acres of pinto beans, wheat, and alfalfa; an assortment of farm animals; and a shed where you'll see the huge modern farm machinery used for planting and harvesting crops. The Wilsons grow much of their own food, and Esther's home-churned butter, home-baked bread, kosher dills, sweet pickle chips, apricot jam, and chokecherry jelly turn up on the big family table with the regularity of clockwork, along with apple, cherry, and plum pies. Biking and horseshoe pitching are favorite activities, as is hiking to Canyon Pasture, where you can see the remains of a settlement, now overgrown with sagebrush, which once housed more people than similar, better-preserved structures at nearby Mesa Verde National Park (described in *National Parks*). Also nearby in the red earth country of the Four Corners region where the farm is located are the Hovenweep and Canyon de Chelly National Monument. Open March through November. Information: Arthur and Esther Wilson, PO Box 252W, Yellow Jacket, CO 81335 (303 562-4476). Inexpensive.

DUDE RANCHES

WHITE STALLION RANCH, Tucson, Arizona: Yot get the feeling of wide-open spaces on this 4,000-acre spread northwest of Tucson, at the foot of the rugged Tucson Mountains, within a 100,000-acre game preserve. The White Stallion is the only guest ranch in the area that can also claim a longhorn cattle operation — but riding is the point here — owners Allen and Cynthia True raise quarter horses and Belgians, and once a week the local cowboys stage a rodeo in the ranch arena. Wranglers will take you into the saguaro-dotted desert around the ranch house just about any time you please. And when you are not on horseback, the time is filled with hayrides, movies, barbecues and cookouts, lawn games, and hikes. Or you can stake out a spot at poolside or in the cozy library, or visit the hot tub therapy room, or have a round of golf nearby, or a game of tennis on the ranch's Laykold courts. Everyone is on a first name basis, the place is friendly and very informal, despite the size (about 65 guests in all). Open October through the first Sunday in May. Information: Allen and Cynthia True, White Stallion Ranch, Rt. 28, PO Box F-567, Tucson, AZ 85704 (602 297 0252). Expensive.

THE COLORADO TRAILS RANCH, Durango, Colorado: See the Old West, hear its tales, and get the flavor of cowboy life — and at the same time lodge in a tidy little cabin with your own bath, carpeting, and electric heat, at this 525-acre mountain ranch just outside Durango, in the southwestern corner of Colorado. With up to 80 other vacationers, you can take riding lessons, go on trail rides and hayrides and overnight pack trips, swim in a heated pool, play tennis, fish for trout, square dance. The staff puts on steak fries, variety shows, melodramas, and powwows around the campfire. But there's never any pressure to do anything, and though sing-alongs may at first seem corny, somehow everyone ends up enjoying them. Counselors take kids (with groups of their peers) on special activities each day; the arrangement seems to give each generation just the right amount of time together and apart. Open June to early September; plan to reserve six months in advance. Information: Ginny and Dick Elder, Colorado Trails Ranch, PO Box 848, Durango, CO 81301 (303 247-5055). Expensive.

WORKING RANCHES

DEER FORKS RANCH, Douglas, Wyoming: It takes about an hour to drive through the rangelands of eastern Wyoming from the town of Douglas to the 5,900-acre spread where the Middleton family grazes cows, grows hay, raises horses, and welcomes guests. The two rustic housekeeping cabins with private baths where guests stay are quite comfortable; both have fully equipped kitchens and the new cabin even has a small washing machine. If you can ride, you may be rounding up cows from the far corners of this vast ranch, and if you can't, you'll soon learn how. Hiking, arrowhead-hunting, trout fishing, and eating (three times a day) will also keep you busy. Too, depending on the season, you may find yourself stacking bales of hay, separating steers from heifers, or helping the vet do pregnancy tests. One day you may drive in to see the rodeo, or state fair, or a cattle auction; another, you may join the Middletons and their friends and relatives for a branding. Open year-round. Information: Ben and Pauli Middleton, Deer Forks Ranch, Rt. 6, Douglas, WY 82633 (307 358-2033). Inexpensive.

THE G BAR M RANCH, Clyde Park, Montana: Like many other ranches in the West, this one in the Bridger Mountain foothills, just east of Bozeman, is both a vacation spot for dudes and a working spread, with most of its 3,300 acres given over to cattle, and four rooms in the ranch house (and two outlying log cabins) fitted out for visitors. Riding, of course, is the main feature; you'll go out to check fence and water holes, help doctor calves that got too curious about porcupines, carry salt to the cattle on summer range in the high country, and so on; and George Leffingwell, one of the owners, puts even the most inexperienced rider at ease. Because the ranch is a private game sanctuary, you'll often see mule deer, golden eagles, and coyotes, along with moose, elk, and bear on occasion. You can also go fishing or hiking, hunt fossils, and photograph wildflowers. Once every week there's an all-day ride and a supper ride, and on Saturday nights, there's music. Otherwise, you won't find much of an activities program — and most people like it that way: "It's like coming home after being away for a long time," one visitor explains. Everyone — ranch family, vacationers, and ranch hands — has meals (including breakfasts of sourdough pancakes and chokecherry syrup) together, and in the course of mealtime talk, you'll learn about the area's history and ecology, the economics of operating a cattle ranch, and the independent spirit of the Western rancher. Open from May into September. Information: the Leffingwells, the G Bar M Ranch, PO Box AE, Clyde Park, MT 59018 (406 686-4423). Moderate.

THE HALTER RANCH, Big Sandy, Montana: In the center of the Missouri River Wilderness Waterway, 80 miles east of Great Falls, Montana, the Halter family raises cattle, horses, hay, and barley on 3,000 acres of meadows and rugged breaks along the White Cliffs of the Missouri River, described in Lewis and Clark's journal. Gay Halter Pearson and husband Ron will show you how to ride or milk a cow, or take you on overnight trail rides or trips in inner tubes down the Judith River. Gay's father, Jerry Halter, who is active in efforts to make the area a wild river waterway, can regale you with tales of the homesteads, forts, and Indian ruins in the area, some of which you'll see when (ranch work permitting) he takes you on float trips down the Missouri. All the guests — usually one family at a time, never more than two — seem to fit easily into the Halter's life, and they're exceptional people. Open from April into November. Information: Gay Halter Pearson, Box 408, Big Sandy, MT 59520 (406 378-2549). Moderate.

A Short Tour of Indian America

When people discuss early American history, their starting point is usually the 17th or 18th century, and the founding of Jamestown, the colonial settlements, or George Washington and the heroics of the American Revolution. But long before any of this took place, long before the white man ever arrived, the real history of this country was the story of the American Indian. During the period of the last glaciation, some 25,000 to 50,000 years ago, the area which is now the Bering Strait was a broad plain about 1,000 miles wide. Nomadic peoples wandered across this land bridge from Siberia into what is now Alaska. Before them stretched a vast uninhabited land, as diverse as it was silent, from the frozen ice caps of the north to the primordial swamp of the Southeastern tropics. These people roamed freely over the land and truly discovered what we have come to call North America. They lived in direct and respectful relationship to the soil. In the Far North, they became ice-hunters. In the rich forests of the North, hunting bands tracked the caribou, deer, beaver, and small fur-bearing animals. In the Eastern woodlands and warm Southeastern region, agriculture reached a high stage of development and was the center of ceremonial life. The Great Plains was inhabited by both farmers and hunters, people who would become great warriors after the introduction of the horse in 1750. Along the Pacific coast settled tribes who were primarily fishermen. The culture of native North America reached its most sophisticated point among the Pueblos, who lived in communal villages in the Southwest, and developed a hardy strain of maize capable of surviving in this arid region.

All of these people came to be known as Indians, for no better reason than that Christopher Columbus, landing one day in Santo Domingo, thought he was in the Indies, off the coast of Asia. As the Indians settled in different parts of North America, they adopted diverse lifestyles; but they remained fundamentally similar in many ways. They were a most remarkably resourceful people. Isolated from the rest of the world, they not only survived on their own, but they created rich cultures around the mysteries and miracles of nature. In addition to the wide variety of maize grown by different tribes, Indians developed pumpkins, beans, squash, tobacco, potatoes, sweet potatoes, chocolate, tomatoes, vanilla, and peanuts — all native and unique to this continent. The different tribes spoke their own languages, and though these may have derived from several parent tongues, at one time at least 200 mutually unintelligible languages were spoken by the American people. In these languages, the Indians told stories of the wonders of creation. The Navajo mythology involves a series of ascents through different worlds inhabited by spirits and beings of both good and evil. The story of emergence from the Black World that was "darker than the darkness of all the moonless nights of many winters" is as beautiful and rich as the story of Adam and Eve. Other tribes created their own legends, songs, dances, and ceremonies. Some lived in fear of nature, others praised its benevolence, but all reacted to it directly, channeling tremendous amounts of physical and emotional energy into their rituals. In New Mexico the Indians painted a series of murals with iron oxide to glorify nature. Elsewhere in the Southwest, they built subterranean chambers of worship, called kivas. In the Southeast, immense ceremonial mounds of earth were filled with sculpture, and many stand today, still protecting the secrets of the rituals for which they were created.

The European explorers who came to the Americas in the 16th, 17th, and 18th centuries came for conquest, and with their arrival, the story of the American Indian takes a tragic turn; it becomes, to a great extent, a tale of exploitation. In 1492,

Columbus sailed to the New World and encountered the Indians; he remarked on the "artless and generous quality" they had "to such a degree as no one would believe but he who had seen it." In return for their good will, Columbus sent 600 Indians back to Spain to work as slaves. During the following centuries the Spanish, British, and, in their turn, Americans waged nearly constant war against the Indians. There was outright massacre, exemplified by the 1890 incident at Wounded Knee, when 300 unarmed Sioux men, women, and children, gathered to celebrate a Ghost Dance (itself a frenetic ritual which Indians believed would save them from decimation by the white invaders), were surrounded and gunned down by the Seventh Cavalry of the United States Army. Less horrific, but just as pernicious, was systematic subjugation by the government of the United States. In 1835, the Five Civilized Tribes of the East (Cherokee, Seminole, Creek, Choctaw, and Chickasaw) were forcibly relocated to Indian Territory in Oklahoma, only to have most of the land taken away from them by the government for white homesteading after the Civil War. From 1887 to 1934 the General Allotment Act divided communal Indian lands, and reduced the total number of Indian-owned acres in America from 138,000,000 to 48,000,000. Even in pathetic reservation enclaves, civil rights were denied the Indians. (Not until 1968, with the Civil Rights Act, were the provisions of the Bill of Rights extended to reservation Indians.)

Though many tribes have become extinct, the American Indian still survives (with a population of 830,000), a testament to human dignity and endurance. Except in the Southwest, the Indian tribes no longer occupy their original lands, and their members are beset with problems — discrimination, as well as extremely high unemployment and high alcoholism and suicide rates. But the story of the real discoverers of America is not finished. In recent years, many young Native Americans have become radicalized by the plight of their people: In 1969 Indians occupied Alcatraz Island; in 1972 many marched on Washington, presenting the federal government with a list of demands (called the Trail of Broken Treaties paper); and in 1973, Indians occupied the Pine Ridge Reservation on the site of the Wounded Knee Massacre, bringing broad international recognition to their plight.

But improvement in Indian affairs demands more than recognition; the gap is one of understanding that can only be bridged by direct contact. In recent years, this has become possible with the growth of tourism in Indian communities. Even some militant members of Indian society believe that this is a positive trend, one which will allow their tribes to practice their own unique lifestyles while sustaining themselves economically. And so, from the commercialized Seminole reservations in Florida to the settlements in the Southwest, where tribes still inhabit the lands of their ancestors — some of the most beautiful country in America — you can glimpse the complex dances, ceremonies; and examine the magnificent handcrafted baskets, jewelry, patchwork, and painting of these ancient civilizations. The cultures that you'll encounter in this Indian America — though at the root of our nation's heritage — are as foreign as those of remotest Egypt and the Orient.

When you enter Indian America, it is best to meet the people on their own terms. Do not take photographs of ceremonies, rituals, or individuals without express permission. Similarly, do not use recording devices, sketch pads, and notebooks. It is advisable to behave as unobtrusively as possible, refraining from applause, loud talking, or even questions about the significance of rituals. In some cases, explanations may be offered. Otherwise it is best to watch what is going on around you and do research before or afterward. Keeping these few things in mind, you will undoubtedly find an adventure in Indian America truly rewarding.

Described below are several highlights of Indian America — reservations and other Indian lands, ceremonies, beautiful natural settings, and excellent museums.

For information about arts and crafts businesses owned and operated by Native Americans, get a copy of the free *Source Directory* published by the Indian Arts &

Crafts Board (Room 4004, US Department of the Interior, Washington, DC 20240, 202 343-2773).

And for an overview of American Indian heritage, consult the following:

Indians of North America, by Harold E. Driver (University of Chicago Press, $7.95), a reconstruction of the native American culture with an emphasis on the 20th century and the post-60s era.

I Have Spoken: American History Through the Voice of the Indians, edited by Virginia L. Armstrong (Chicago: Swallow Press, $7.95).

EAST

MICCOSUKEE TRIBAL ENTERPRISE, near Miami, Florida: Some 550 members of the Miccosukee tribe (which was not officially recognized until 1962) live on this reservation on the northern border of the Everglades National Park. A Cultural Center has exhibits tracing the history of the tribe, which shares a language and hunting and fishing techniques with the Seminoles, who also live in Florida. The lifestyle on the reservation is still fairly traditional. In the school system, English takes second place to Mikasuki, the tribal language. Many Miccosukees live in chickees, which are palmetto thatched-roof dwellings, and some work as artists, making baskets, cypress wood carvings, and clothing of patchwork cloth (available at the Cultural Center). A quarter-mile east of the Cultural Center is the Miccosukee restaurant which serves traditional Indian fare: frybread, catfish, and Everglades' frogs' legs. One of the best times to visit is at the end of December during the Music and Arts Festival, when musicians and artists and craftsmen from many tribes converge on the reservation to play everything from traditional music to Indian rock. On US 41, 26 miles west of Miami. Information: PO Box 440021, Miami, FL 33144 (305 223-8380).

CHEROKEE, North Carolina: Adjacent to the Great Smoky Mountains National Park, this beautiful area is the country where the Cherokees lived before they were forcibly relocated to Oklahoma in 1835 along a route now called the Trail of Tears. But some Cherokees remained, hiding in the mountains, and others returned later. Today, this is the center of the Cherokee people, and many work here in the tribal government, in factories that produce moccasins and quilts, and in tourist businesses. One of the best times to visit is in the fall during the Fall Festival when Cherokees from all over return home and participate in traditional dances, games, and arts and crafts demonstrations. The event customarily begins the Tuesday of the first full week in October. For exact dates, check with the Cherokee Chamber of Commerce, Cherokee, NC 28719 (704 497-9195). Of interest at Cherokee are:

Oconaluftee Indian Village: A replica of a Cherokee village which depicts life of the 18th century, with guided tours. Included are a seven-sided council house, ceremonial chambers, and lectures at various sites where members of the tribe, dressed in authentic costumes, demonstrate crafts, cooking, and weapon-making. Open May through October. Off rt. 441 on Drama Rd. For a little more history come to life, see the drama *Unto These Hills,* which recounts the story of the Cherokee people in an amphitheater during the summer (see *Outdoor Dramas*). Mountainside Theater on Drama Rd. Information: Oconaluftee Indian Village, Cherokee, NC 28719 (704 497-2315 or 704 497-2111).

Museum of the Cherokee Indian: Owned by the Eastern Band of Cherokee Indians, this museum has multimedia theaters and innovative exhibits that focus on the history of the tribe with examples of clothing and implements used for farming, hunting, and fishing. Open daily year-round. Admission charge. On Drama Rd. Information: Museum of the Cherokee Indian, PO Box 770A, Cherokee, NC 28719 (704 497-3481).

Qualla Arts and Crafts Mutual: Best of the area's many craft shops, this is the official cooperative marketing center of the Cherokees. The work is authentic, and many items here are rarely available elsewhere, such as white oak, river cane, and honeysuckle vine baskets, animal sculptures made of buckeye, walnut, and wild cherry, pottery, and beadwork. On rt. 441 near the Museum. Information: Qualla Arts and Crafts Mutual, PO Box 277, Cherokee, NC 28719 (704 497-3103).

WEST

Some 16.5 million acres in northern Arizona and neighboring New Mexico and Utah form the Navajo territory, the largest Indian reservation in America. The Navajos are the most populous of the Indian tribes, with over 100,000 members, many of whom live in villages of traditional dwellings called hogans, six-sided pit houses built of logs, cemented with clay, and covered with earth. The Navajos were influenced by the Spaniards, becoming primarily a pastoral rather than agricultural people, but they did pick up farming, weaving, and sand-painting from the Pueblos. They are also more open about their ceremonies than the Pueblos, providing visitors with an opportunity to observe sacred rituals.

WINDOW ROCK, Arizona: The town is the seat of Navajo tribal government and is a good place to begin a trip into Navajo territory. You can view displays about the tribe's history and culture at the newly renovated Tribal Museum; learn a bit about how the Navajos see their environment and live in harmony with it at the recently revamped Navajo Zoological and Botanical Park; shop for crafts at the Navajo Arts and Crafts Enterprise; and take any number of excursions into the surrounding countryside. The Recreational Resources Department can suggest destinations and can give you dates for various Navajo dances. Among the biggest of the local festivities is the Intertribal Indian Ceremonial, held annually in nearby Gallup from the second Thursday in August through the following Sunday. The Window Rock Motor Inn's café offers Navajo dishes like frybread sandwiches (602 871-4108). Information: Navajo Tribe, Recreational Resources Department, PO Box 308, Window Rock, AZ 86515 (602 871-4941, ext. 1645), or Gallup Chamber of Commerce, PO Box 1395, Gallup, NM 87301 (505 722-2228).

MONUMENT VALLEY NAVAJO TRIBAL PARK, Arizona and Utah: The valley is a classic Western scenic wonder with high mesas, sculptured buttes, natural bridges, earth arches, chiseled canyons and gorges, huge sandstone monoliths, and has been used in filming innumerable Westerns, including a few early John Wayne films. A 16-mile road (a 1 ½-hour drive) winds its way through the valley and can be negotiated by most cars, except during the winter, when four-wheel-drive vehicles are advisable. Visitors should not photograph Navajos or their possessions without permission. Camping is available at the park headquarters, where there is also a Navajo arts and crafts shop. 25 miles north of Kayenta off rt. 163. Information: Box 93, Monument Valley Tribal Park, UT 84536 (801 727-3287).

NAVAJO NATIONAL MONUMENT, Kayenta, Arizona: The largest and most intricate of Arizona's cliff dwellings are preserved in this rugged country. There are two areas, each of which contains a remarkable 13th-century pueblo ruin. Betatakin Area is the site of the monument headquarters, and the Visitors' Center offers exhibits, slide shows, a Navajo arts and crafts shop, and a campground. Betatakin is the most accessible of the areas, and the ruin across the canyon may be viewed from a foot trail, or visited on a three-hour guided tour (daily in summer; no tours in winter). Other areas may be reached via horseback (reserve from headquarters in advance) or by a strenuous hike. 32 miles southwest of Kayenta off rt. 160. Information: Navajo National Monument, Tonalea, AZ 86044 (602 672-2366).

HUBBELL TRADING POST NATIONAL HISTORIC SITE, Ganado, Arizona: Dating back to the 1870s, this is the oldest continuously active trading post on the Navajo reservation. The post and Hubbell home depict the life of an unusual trader and his family, and have displays on the history of the area, and beautiful Navajo sand paintings, handwoven rugs, silver work, and other jewelry. The National Park Service runs guided tours of the home, which is 1 mile west of Ganado off rt. 264, and there are usually Navajo weaving and silversmithing demonstrations at the Visitors Center. Information: Hubbell Trading Post, Ganado, AZ 86505 (602 755-3475).

FIRST, SECOND, AND THIRD MESA, Arizona: The Hopis are exceptional jewelry makers and farmers and live in a close communal relationship in apartment villages on three isolated ridges of land which stand high above the Arizona desert. The best place to stay is on the Second Mesa, at the Hopi Cultural Center which has a motel, café, campground, museum, and restaurant where you can get hominy stew, frybread, piki, and other native foods. At the Hopi Arts and Crafts Guild, you can purchase the finest of Hopi crafts — silver jewelry, pottery, Kachina dolls, and baskets. The studio of Charles Loloma, the most important of contemporary Indian jewelers, and Old Oraibi, the oldest continuously occupied town in the United States, are on the Third Mesa. A variety of ceremonies, including the Snake Dance (in August) are open to visitors, but the exact dates are usually not announced till very close to the event, so check at the Cultural Center. On rt. 264 at Pinon Rd., four miles northwest of rt. 87. Information: Hopi Tribe, Box 123, Oraibi, AZ 86039 (602 734-2441).

Nowhere in the United States do you get a better sense of the Indian past than among the Pueblos, the desert peoples of New Mexico. The aridity of the climate has left many ancient ruins intact, and the tribes live among them on the land of their ancestors in pueblos, communal villages of adobe or sandstone dwellings that blend unobtrusively into their surroundings. The pueblos described below are within driving distance of Santa Fe or Albuquerque.

ACOMA, New Mexico: Perhaps the most spectacular of the pueblos, this village sits on a 368-foot-high mesa, commanding a panoramic view of the New Mexico plain. The pueblo has been inhabited for some 1,000 years, and though many of the families have homes in nearby farming villages, Acoma is open to visitors year-round. Among the buildings are the mission of San Esteban, established in 1629 and constructed of adobe walls ten feet thick; a subterranean ceremonial chamber known as a kiva on the main plaza (off-limits to visitors); and several small craft shops where delicate Acoma pottery with geometric and bird pattern motifs can be purchased for prices lower than at trading posts elsewhere. Tribal members lead tours daily. Small admission charge and photographic fee. On rt. 23, 60 miles west of Albuquerque. Information: PO Box 309, Pueblo of Acoma, NM 87034 (505 552-6606).

TAOS, New Mexico: Sitting at the base of the Sangre de Cristo range, which culminates in New Mexico's highest point, the Taos pueblo is a stronghold of tribal tradition. The people are devout in their religious observances, and subsist as farmers. Near the multistoried adobe dwelling, craftsmen display fine leatherwork, moccasins, and drums, as well as golden-hued pottery. The San Geronimo Fiesta in late September is open to the public and features extraordinary dancing, a greased-pole climbing contest, and other festivities. The town of Taos, 2½ miles south, is primarily an artists' colony, and the work of residents and of other artists is displayed at some 80 galleries all over town. Area information: Chamber of Commerce, Drawer I, Taos, NM 87571 (505 758-3873).

Once dominant on the northern plains, the Sioux — nomadic buffalo hunters who lived in conical tents of animal hide called teepees — were the prototype for the American Indian image. Today, the buffalo no longer roam, and the tribe is beset with economic problems, but the Sioux still maintain their dignity. The area is not highly developed commercially, but if you do visit, the rewards will be great.

OGLALA SIOUX PINE RIDGE RESERVATION, South Dakota: This 2.3-million acre reservation — where, at Wounded Knee, some 300 unarmed Sioux were slaughtered in 1890 in a massacre commemorated by a simple gravesite — is now the home of nearly 15,000 Sioux. You can visit the Holy Rosary Mission, where there are exhibits on Sioux culture and displays of fine Sioux crafts: bead work, quill work (an intricate type of weaving employing porcupine quills), and magnificent paintings on buffalo hide that display a visionary quality — despite the fact that life in the past was beset by tragedy, they depict a happy life that might have been. The Tribal Office can give you information about ceremonies to which the public is welcome — among them the Sun Dance, a late August religious observance of both atonement and thanksgiving that involves much elaborate drumming and dancing. There are also powwows and rodeos throughout the summer. The reservation is located 120 miles south of Rapid City on rt. 18. Information: PO Box 468, Pine Ridge, SD 57770 (605 867-5821).

MUSEUMS

HEARD MUSEUM OF ANTHROPOLOGY AND PRIMITIVE ARTS, Phoenix, Arizona: One of the world's best, this museum founded in the late 1920s focuses on the Indian cultures of the Southwest. The collection of Kachina dolls, assembled and donated in small part by Barry Goldwater, is perhaps the museum's best known; even though some 97% of the collection may be in storage at any given time, there are still rooms full of these painted and feathered likenesses of supernatural beings on display. But there are also exhibits of jewelry, baskets, textiles, ceramics, and artifacts of the area's ancient inhabitants. Of a pair of additional galleries devoted to changing exhibitions, one focuses on contemporary Southwestern Indian arts and crafts while the other compares this native culture to others around the world. Information: Heard Museum, 22 E Monte Vista Rd., Phoenix, AZ 85004 (602 252-8840).

MUSEUM OF THE AMERICAN INDIAN, New York, New York: One of the world's largest anthropological museums, this institution houses an immense, uniquely representative collection of the artifacts of the cultures of the American Indian; it ranks among the world's biggest such collections and represents everything from precious ornaments to commonplace tools, from paleo-Indian projectile points to abstract paintings by contemporary Indian artists, covering the hemisphere from Atlantic to Pacific, from the Arctic to the Antarctic. In the gift shop, you can buy original Indian handcrafted *objets,* as well as books on native American culture. Information: Museum of the American Indian, Broadway at 155th, New York, NY 10032 (212 283-2420).

GILCREASE INSTITUTE OF AMERICAN HISTORY AND ART, Tulsa, Oklahoma: A gift to the city of Tulsa from oil millionaire Thomas Gilcrease, whose mother was a Creek Indian. The extensive collection on the American Indian focuses on anthropology, with exhibits of archaeological artifacts, on art, with paintings of Indians by Remington, Russell, Catlin, Bodmer, Miller, Bierstadt, and such prominent contemporary Indian artists as Blackbear Bosin (Comanche), Allan Houser (Apache), and Fred Kabotie (Hopi); there's also a large collection of authentic Indian crafts dating from the 15th century to the present. Information: Gilcrease Museum, 1400 N 25 West Ave., Tulsa, OK 74127 (918 581-5311).

WHEELWRIGHT MUSEUM, Santa Fe, New Mexico: Changing exhibits focus on the history, culture, and problems faced by contemporary tribes. The museum recreates a 19th-century trading post and displays baskets, beadwork, and art by early artists. Closed Mondays from November through April. Details: Wheelwright Museum, 704 Camino Lejo, Santa Fe, NM 87501 (505 982-4636).

SIOUX INDIAN MUSEUM, Rapid City, South Dakota: This fine facility, operated by the Indian Arts and Crafts Board of the Department of the Interior, transmits a feeling for the Sioux past with its collection of 19th-century Sioux artifacts — clothing, games, moccasins, pipe bags, and baby carriers. Another gallery broadens the scope with changing exhibits, usually shows of contemporary artists from many different tribes. Information: Sioux Indian Museum, PO Box 1504, West Blvd. between Main and St. Joe sts., Rapid City, SD 57709 (605 348-0557).

Dam Nation

The politics of water and the ecology of America's "big dams" are just beginning to be understood, but the bane of environmentalists can, for all that, make quite a pleasant vacation experience. First of all, dams are clean-lined and beautiful to look at; they're impressively huge. All the bigger ones — including those listed here — offer tours of the powerhouses of pumping stations, or at least have visitors' centers with exhibits that explain what the dams do. In the West, you can also watch boats being locked through navigation systems, or fish fighting their way up fish ladders to their upstream spawning grounds. And when you've seen the dam, you can enjoy yourself on the huge reservoirs they impound.

GLEN CANYON DAM, near Page, Arizona: Five million cubic yards of concrete, 1,560 feet across, rise 710 feet above the bedrock across the Colorado River between sheer walls of red Navajo sandstone. Behind: Lake Powell, 186 miles long and with 1,800 miles of shoreline. You can fish for crappie or striped and largemouth bass; the largest stripers are nearing 20 pounds. Around the lake is the million-acre Glen Canyon National Recreation Area. For details, contact its Superintendent at PO Box 1507, Page, AZ 86040 (602 645-2471).

OROVILLE DAM, Oroville, California: Rising 770 feet above Oroville's business district, this is the highest dam in the US and the highest earth-fill dam in the US. Lake Oroville, with 162 miles of shoreline, backs up behind the dam, and there's good boating and fishing — for silver and king salmon, rainbow and brown trout, largemouth and smallmouth bass, crappie, bluegill, and catfish. Information: Lake Oroville State Recreation Area, 400 Glen Dr., Oroville, CA 95965 (916 534-2409); Plumas National Forest, 159 Lawrence St., Quincy, CA 95971 (916 283-2050); and Tahoe National Forest, Nevada City, CA 95959 (916 265-4531).

KENTUCKY DAM, near Gilbertsville, Kentucky: The 206-foot height and 8,422-foot length make this structure across the Cumberland River the largest in the TVA system; together with the Barkley Dam on the Tennessee River, near Cadiz, not far away, it impounds some 220,000 acres of water with 3,500 miles of forested, cove-notched shoreline. Both Kentucky Lake and Lake Barkley are great for crappie and largemouth fishing; and a multitude of activities are available at Kenlake, Kentucky Dam Village, and Lake Barkley State Resort Parks, and at the TVA's own 170,000-acre Land Between the Lakes, all on the shores of the two impoundments. Recreation information: Office of Tourism Development, Capitol Plaza Tower, Frankfort, KY 40601 (502 564-4930).

FORT PECK DAM, near Glasgow, Montana: The largest earth-fill dam in the US, the second largest in the world, this $75 million, 21,026-foot-long structure rises 250½ feet above the Missouri River. Fort Peck Lake, with 1,600 miles of lakeshore, is the fourth largest reservoir in the world. And the Glasgow mayor said it could be built for $1 million! Recreation information: Glasgow Chamber of Commerce, Box 832 Glasgow, MT 59230 (406 228-2222).

HOOVER DAM, Boulder City, Nevada: This 726-foot-high structure, the highest concrete dam in the western hemisphere, was selected by the American Society of Civil Engineers as one of the country's Seven Modern Wonders of Civil Engineering — and when you take the 528 foot elevator ride down 52 stories to the power plant, you will probably agree. Some 115 miles long, with 550 miles of shoreline, Lake Mead (behind the dam) is by volume one of the world's largest manmade reservoirs. Recreation information: Lake Mead National Recreation Area, 601 Nevada Hwy., Boulder City, NV 89005 (702 293-4041).

JOHN DAY DAM, near Biggs, Oregon: For this $487 million project, the US Army

Corps of Engineers rerouted highways and moved one entire town and parts of two others (Boardman, Arlington, and Umatilla, respectively). The most impressive part of a visit — providing construction work is completed by the time you visit — may be the navigation locks which lift ships 113 feet in 15 minutes — but all sorts of superlatives apply to the whole operation. Lake Umatilla stretches for about 75 miles behind the dam. Recreation information: The Dalles–John Day Project, Resources Section, PO Box 564, The Dalles, OR 97058 (503 298-8732).

FLAMING GORGE DAM, near Vernal, Utah: In the Green River's Red Canyon, this $66 million, 502-foot-high dam impounds a 91-mile-long reservoir in the Flaming Gorge National Recreation Area — 195,054 acres of bright red and orange rock chimneys and spires, rust-colored canyons, pine-clad mountains. Recreation information: Ashley National Forest, Dutch John, UT 84023 (801 885-3315).

GRAND COULEE DAM, Coulee Dam, Washington: The world's largest concrete dam, this one completed in 1942 is higher than a 46-story building and nearly a mile long, used up 11,975,521 cubic yards of concrete, and has a spillway twice as high as Niagara Falls. Yet it's dwarfed by the immense granite cliffs on either side. The spillway is floodlit on summer nights. Recreational opportunities are available in the 100,059-acre Coulee Dam National Recreation Area, Box 37, Coulee Dam, WA 99116 (509 633-1360).

Historic Canals

When Charles Dickens traveled through Ohio in the 1840s, he did it on a canal boat — and hated every minute of it, from the cramped quarters to the odoriferous companionship of the mules brought aboard between stints of pulling. No doubt thousands of other passengers agreed.

Nevertheless, the canals that linked inland cities to lakes and rivers from Maine to Chicago provided the fastest transportation until the railroads flourished. Then canal boomtowns died out, and canals (like much of the Erie Canal, which linked Lake Erie and the Atlantic Ocean) were filled in and paved over, or left to crumble.

Still, canals have not been forgotten. Cruising on these wave-free waterways is relaxing, and several short trips are available for only a few dollars a person. Also, Midlakes Navigation Company, Ltd., PO Box 61, Skaneateles, NY 13152 (315 685-8500), has cruises on parts of the New York State Barge Canal System which parallels the old waterway. The American Canal Society, 809 Rathton Rd., York, PA 17403, keeps its members posted on what they can see where with a newsletter (membership is about $8). Here are a few canal sites you can visit:

EAST

THE C & D CANAL MUSEUM, Chesapeake City, Maryland: An old stone pump house on the Chesapeake and Delaware Canal still houses the steam engines used until 1927 to power a wooden waterwheel, a mechanical marvel fitted out with buckets that transferred water from Back Creek into the canal at the rate of 1.2 million gallons an hour. Information: US Army Corps of Engineers, Chesapeake City, MD 21915 (301 885-5622).

OLD ERIE CANAL STATE PARK, DeWitt to Rome, New York: Some 35 miles of the celebrated Erie Canal are maintained by the State for recreational use, and in summer you can go hiking and biking, and in winter, snowmobiling. Picnic areas and connecting paths to nearby recreation areas are strategically located. Information: Central New York State Parks Department, Recreation and Historic Preservation Commission, Jamesville, NY 13078 (315 492-1756).

CANAL TOWN USA, Canastota, New York: Located in a yellow clapboard building directly across the street from the canal, this small, decade-old museum is filled with artifacts related to canal days, models of canal boats, and displays on Canastota history. Information: Canal Town USA, Canastota, NY 13032 (315 697-3451).

OLD ERIE CANAL VILLAGE, Rome, New York: At an 1840s canal village on a restored section of waterway, you can take steam train rides and cruises on the horse-drawn packet boat *Independence.* Twelve old buildings — among them one set up as a farm vehicle museum with over 25 contraptions on view — plus a canal museum can be visited. Open May through October. Information: City of Rome Tourism Department, City Hall, Liberty Plaza, Rome, NY 13440 (315 336-6000).

THE CANAL MUSEUM, Syracuse, New York: Changing exhibits dealing with life on the canals are set up in the building where canal boats were weighed to determine the tolls they'd pay. Information: Canal Museum, Weighlock Building, 301 E Water St., Syracuse, NY 13202 (315 471-0593).

ALLEGHENY PORTAGE RAILROAD NATIONAL HISTORIC SITE, Cresson, Pennsylvania: The eastern and western divisions of the state-run Pennsylvania Canal were linked by this railroad. Visitors see some of the stone railroad ties, a quarry where they were made, and a couple of the engine houses; and demonstrations of stone cutting, spinning, weaving are presented in summer. Slide programs at the Visitors' Center set up in the old Lemon House Tavern tell the story. Information: PO Box 247, Cresson, PA 16630 (814 886-8176).

CHESAPEAKE AND OHIO CANAL NATIONAL HISTORICAL PARK, near Washington, D.C.: A 1924 flood put an end to the uneven career of this 184-mile-long waterway between Georgetown and Cumberland, Maryland. The woodsy towpath is ideal for hiking and biking; the sections of the canal that aren't dry are great for canoeing. A Visitors' Center near Great Falls, Maryland, in an old tavern, has exhibits that tell the story. Information: C&O Canal National Historical Park, PO Box 4, Sharpsburg, MD 21782 (301 739-4200).

MIDWEST

ILLINOIS AND MICHIGAN CANAL HEADQUARTERS BUILDING, Lockport, Illinois: What some people call the best preserved canal town in America has a number of old canal locks (as well as a modern one), a fine 19th-century block of storefronts, some stone sidewalks — and the only canal museum in the US that illustrates the construction, operation, and demise of a single waterway. Information: Will County Historical Society, 803 S State St., Lockport, IL 60441 (815 838-5080).

CANAL FULTON PARK, Canal Fulton, Ohio: A full-sized replica of the mule-drawn canal barges that once plied the Ohio-Erie Canal is the focus. A festival held every July recreates the era. Information: Canal Fulton Heritage Society, Canal Fulton, OH 44614 (216 854-3808).

ROSCOE VILLAGE, Coshocton, Ohio: This once-busy community on the Ohio-Erie Canal, now restored, is a fine place to see a Disney version of what rough-and-ready canal life was like. You can ride a horse-drawn trolley and canal boat replica, and visit a blacksmith shop, general store, post office, drugstore, tavern, and several homes — plus a wonderful peppermint-pink ice cream parlor with one of those tinkling Vox Regina music boxes. Many lively special events. Information: Roscoe Village, Coshocton, OH 43812 (614 622-9310).

America's Military Academies

From the establishment of West Point in 1802 to the opening of the Air Force Academy in April 1954, the academies have always provided a variety of spectacles from pomp-and-circumstance full-dress parades to museums of military equipment, cannon, and guns. The grounds are manicured, delightful for walking; the settings usually breathtaking. Be sure to time your visit to catch a parade; and ask about athletic events and guided tours which are often available.

US AIR FORCE ACADEMY, Colorado Springs, Colorado: After you've seen the Visitor Center and its displays about cadet life, a self-guided tour (takes about two hours) of the 18,000-acre grounds will include the school's chapel — a "chapel of the future" when it was built in 1963 in the shape of a 17-spired tetrahedron pyramid 150 feet high, with separate chapels inside for various faiths. Schedule your visit for 10:30. Every weekday (except during summer vacations and some other breaks), the cadets — in uniform — assemble, then march in formation to the dining hall to the accompaniment of martial music. A real goose-bump raiser. You can lodge in Colorado Springs — the state's second biggest town — at any number of motels; most prestigious is the Broadmoor, a very posh, very old, and very famous resort (The Broadmoor, Colorado Springs, CO 80901, 303 634-7711). For information on the Academy: US Air Force Academy, Colorado Springs, CO 80840 (303 472-4040).

US COAST GUARD ACADEMY, New London, Connecticut: Your visit to this pretty campus begins at the modern Visitor Pavilion, where you can browse through exhibits and watch a multimedia show depicting cadet life, then pick up a map for a self-guided tour that takes in the chapel; the Academy's museum, notable for its intriguing collection of vessel models; and when it's in port, the sailing bark *Eagle,* now used for cadet training cruises. Once weekly in spring and fall, usually on Fridays or Saturdays, cadets parade in review. An added attraction of this nautically minded corner of Connecticut is the interesting selection of inns, the best of which includes the venerable Griswold Inn — a bustling place on Main Street in Essex that has been putting up travelers for centuries (203 767-0991) — and the Copper Beech, in Ivoryton, the former home of a Connecticut ivory trader, full of high-ceilinged, four-postered sleeping chambers (203 767-0330). See *America's Special Havens.* For Academy information, contact the US Coast Guard Academy, New London, CT 06320 (203 442-1092).

US MERCHANT MARINE ACADEMY, Kings Point, New York: On Long Island's picturesque North Shore, and overlooking Connecticut, Long Island Sound, and New York City and its bridges, this Academy occupies what used to be the Chrysler estate (as well as parts of others on Long Island's "Gold Coast"). At the Main Gate, you can get maps and information about what to see — displays about the history of the Merchant Marine and their ships at the American Merchant Marine Museum, and regimental reviews, held on some Saturdays in fall and spring at 10 AM. For information: US Merchant Marine Academy, Kings Point, NY 11024 (516 482-8200).

US MILITARY ACADEMY, West Point, New York: Opened on July 4, 1802, with a class of ten, this Academy is probably the most famous and most visited of the service schools, and for good reason. It fairly reeks of military tradition. The campus is beautiful, as manicured as any parkland, full of Gothic buildings, and magnificent views like the one from Trophy Point, above the Hudson River. ("The fairest of the fair and lovely Highlands of the North River, shut in by deep green heights and ruined forts, and looking down upon the distant town of Newburgh," according to Charles Dickens, who visited in 1842.) The chapel, a lofty granite Gothic structure which seems even more majestic because of the several flights of stairs you've got to trek up to get into it, holds the largest church pipe organ in the country. The museum — stuffed with military artifacts from the Stone Age to the bombs and tanks of the present — is the largest of all military museums in the world. At Trophy Point, you can see a few links of the heavy iron chains the American Revolutionaries stretched across the river to block British ships during that war. Cadet reviews are held during spring and fall; for times and dates, call ahead. Country inns come and go in the area. Among the nicest are the Bird and Bottle in Garrison (914 424-3000); and the Beekman Arms in Rhinebeck (914 876-7077). You can eat or lodge in any of these. Also interesting, for food:

the Culinary Institute of America's Escoffier Room in Hyde Park, where top chefs of the future are in rigorous training (914 471-6608). For Academy information: The US Military Academy, West Point, NY 10996 (914 938-2638).

US NAVAL ACADEMY, Annapolis, Maryland: On certain Wednesday afternoons during fall and spring, and during commissioning week, the 4,500 spit-and-polished midshipmen have a 3:45 PM dress parade on Worden Field. During the academic year when the temperature is above 55°, the Brigade of Midshipmen assembles in Tecumseh Court for reports, a drum and bugle performance, and a march to lunch. There's more to see: the crypt of John Paul Jones, somewhat like Napoleon's in Paris; the chapel, really a large cathedral, complete with stained glass windows; trophies in the fieldhouse (and an explanation of how the goat came to be the Navy's mascot); a museum full of naval history exhibits (closed Mondays). Pamphlets outlining a self-guided walking tour are available, as are guided tours (except in winter; call 301 263-6933). For times and more information: US Naval Academy, Annapolis, MD 21401, 301 267-2291). For meals and interesting lodgings, don't miss Annapolis' 18th-century Maryland Inn, (Church Circle, Annapolis, MD 21401, 301 263-2641), also a good base for walks through the narrow streets of this historic city and for visits to the various federal mansions (including the Chase-Lloyd House, where Francis Scott Key was married). Earl "Fatha" Hines and Charlie Byrd are frequent performers in the Maryland Inn's King of France Tavern.

Great Horse Races

Ever since President Washington closed Congress on October 24, 1780, so that he and the senators could attend the races at this country's first racetrack, Baltimore's Pimlico, Americans have been competing against each other on horseback.

Every breed has its set of competitive events. Standardbreds, bred to trot (with diagonal legs moving in synchronization) or, more commonly, to pace (with lateral legs moving together), pull sulkies around dirt ovals. Thoroughbreds ridden by tiny jockeys in bright-colored silks charge down flat tracks or leap their way over steeplechase courses. Quarter horses run for million-dollar purses, while Western horses work out at rodeos.

ALL ABOUT HORSES

KENTUCKY HORSE PARK, Lexington, Kentucky: Possibly the best place in the country to get a feeling for American horse life, this $35 million facility which opened in September 1978 on 1,032 acres in the heart of the Kentucky bluegrass country represents not just the thoroughbreds which are born and bred in the area, but also Morgans, Arabians, Appaloosas, and just about any other breed you can name. With a stirring 25-minute film on the history of man and horse, and a 40,000-square-foot museum full of dioramas, computers, and various displays about horses the size of dogs, horses and Roman chariots, horses in the wild West, and more. At the Model Farm, you can see a farrier, a harnessmaker, and over 25 different breeds of horses, and learn about the day-by-day care of the horses in residence. You can go horseback riding, take pony rides, cruise the grounds in horse-drawn omnibuses, watch appropriately costumed drivers hitch up landaus — and take in dozens of special events: polo games, thoroughbred and standardbred exhibition races, steeplechase meetings, dressage exhibitions, horse pulling contests, quarter horse sprints, cross-country races (the kind in which Britain's horsey Princess Anne competed in the Olympics). Also available are 265 sites for camping, tennis courts, recreation areas, a fine lively activities program, and a good-size swimming pool. Information: Kentucky Horse Park, 4089 Iron Works Pike, Lexington, KY 40511 (606 233-4303).

GREAT RACES

Of the hundreds of races that give horse racing the largest paid attendance of any US sport, these are among the biggest.

THE BLUE GRASS STAKES, Lexington, Kentucky: With a $150,000-added purse, this is the biggest event of the 15-day spring meeting at Keeneland Race Course — old, famous, and very beautiful at this time of year with the dogwoods and flowering crabs in full bloom. Because the race is run nine days before the Kentucky Derby, over a course just an eighth of a mile shorter than the Derby's mile and a quarter, it is a steppingstone to the Triple Crown. The $150,000-added Spinster, for fillies and mares three years old and up, highlights a 16-day October season and determines, at least in part, which horse will be named champion in her respective division. Four times a year, there are thoroughbred sales — yearlings in July and September, breeding stock in November, all ages in January. The highest price ever paid for a horse at public auction — $1.6 million — was paid here at Keeneland in 1979 for a colt by Hoist the Fling. There's a small area where spectators can come and watch this money change hands. Tickets and information: Keeneland Association, PO Box 1690, Lexington, KY 40592 (606 254-3412).

THE KENTUCKY FUTURITY, Lexington, Kentucky: The Red Mile, named for the color of the clay on the track, has two seasons every year — the first from late April through June at night; the second for nine days in late September and early October in the afternoons. The Kentucky Futurity — a mile-long $100,000 race for three-year-old trotters, the third leg of the Triple Crown for trotters — comes at the end of September/October: The fact that the fillies and colts who enter have raced against each other for months by the time they get here makes for exciting races. The Red Mile is known as the fastest standardbred track in the world. Right in the middle of the October meeting is the Tattersall Sale (the equivalent of Keeneland's big yearling sale). On Show Day, the Sunday halfway through the October meeting, all the horse farms in the area hold open houses, complete with burgoo (a kind of oatmeal gruel) and music — and anyone can come. Information: Tom White, The Red Mile, PO Box 420, Lexington, KY 40585 (606 255-0752).

THE KENTUCKY DERBY, Louisville, Kentucky: Always the highlight of the spring meet, this race, modeled after England's English Derby, was established in 1875 and has been run over the same course ever since (though the original mile-and-a-half distance was trimmed to 1¼ miles in 1896). It's a big deal for the horse owners because of the big purse (more than $300,000); for the horses because of the competition and the distance (which is considerable for a three-year-old so early in the season); and for all of Louisville, for which this is a social as well as a sporting event. Reserved seat tickets are sold on a renewal basis — which means that those who have them get first chance at them in succeeding years — and 99% of ticket holders renew. However, general admission tickets are sold on the day of the race. Information: Churchill Downs, Louisville, KY 40208 (502 636-3541).

THE PREAKNESS, Baltimore, Maryland: The middle jewel of the Triple Crown is raced the third Saturday in May for more than $250,000 on the 1 3/16-mile, dirt flat track at the Pimlico Race Track. The Preakness, one of the oldest races in America, started in 1873 and attracts three-year-old thoroughbreds from all over the country. The regular racing season at Pimlico runs mid-March through May on both the flat track and the ⅞-mile turf course. Information: Maryland Jockey Club, Pimlico Race Course, Baltimore, MD 21215 (301 542-9400).

THE HAMBLETONIAN, East Rutherford, New Jersey: Named for the greatest sire of them all (every trotter and pacer are said to be related to this famous horse), this jewel in the Triple Crown for trotters — recently moved to the Meadowlands from its home of 25 years at the Illinois Du Quoin State Fair — is one of the fastest races of them all. Information: Hambletonian Stakes, Meadowlands Racetrack, East Rutherford, NJ 07073 (201 935-8500).

ALL-AMERICAN FUTURITY, Ruidoso Downs, New Mexico: The richest race since the dawn of civilization, with a $2.5 million gross purse ($1 million of which goes to the winner), is not a race of thoroughbreds but of quarter horses — originally bred primarily for ranch work with powerful hind quarters that make them superb sprinters, and now infused with thoroughbred blood. Between 14,000 and 18,000 people make their way every summer to southern New Mexico to watch over 200 horses go through eliminations that leave 10 fast ones to compete on a quarter-mile dash down a straight track. Held on Labor Day. Information: Ruidoso Downs Race Track, Ruidoso Downs, NM 88346 (505 378-4431).

THE BELMONT STAKES, Elmont, New York: The third and final leg of the races for the Triple Crown by the best of the country's three-year-old thoroughbreds. Held every year the first week in June, with the highest purse and the longest track (1½ miles) in the Crown. Secretariat holds the record at 2:24. The regular racing season at Belmont Park, where the race is held, is mid May through July, and late August to mid-October. Information: Belmont Park, PO Box 90, Jamaica, NY 11417 (212 641-4700).

THE TRAVERS, Saratoga Springs, New York: The oldest active stakes race in the country — a mile-and-a-quarter run for three-year-old thoroughbred colts — is held at the oldest active racetrack in the country, the Saratoga Race Course, where they've been racing almost every year since 1864. Many US tracks have been designed after Saratoga. In the Travers, the colts are so closely matched that it's usually a pretty exciting race. The Saratoga season runs for four weeks, from about the end of July until about the end of August and there are stakes races of one sort or another almost every day, with big races on Saturdays: the Alabama, $100,000 for 3-year-old fillies; the Whitney, for three-year-olds and up; and the Hopeful, a $75,000 race for two-year-olds whose winner, historically, has often gone on to win the Triple Crown races the following year. Information: Saratoga Race Course, c/o New York Racing Association, PO Box 90, Jamaica, NY 11417 (212 641-4700).

THE INTERNATIONAL TROT, Westbury, New York: In Europe, trotting trainers are more concerned with gait and style, and a European trotting race is a pretty race. You can see the difference between European trotters and American at the $250,000 International Trot, the world championship of trotting, held at Roosevelt Raceway every July or August during the summer meet (other meets are held late February through April and mid-October to early December). Information: Roosevelt Raceway, Westbury, NY 11590 (516 222-2000).

THE MESSENGER STAKES, Westbury, New York: The second most important race of the Roosevelt Raceway year, this one held at the end of October or beginning of November is the third leg of the Triple Crown for three-year-old pacers and helps decide who gets divisional honors and who gets named the horse of the year. The purse is $150,000. Information: Roosevelt Raceway, Westbury, NY 11590 (516 222-2000).

THE CANE PACE, Yonkers, New York: This $500,000 race, usually held in mid-summer, with the Little Brown Jug (Delaware County Fair, Delaware, Ohio) and the Messenger Stakes (see above), make up the Triple Crown of pacing; the race is similar to the Messenger in many ways, right down to the half-mile track (somewhat slower, because of the turns required, than the mile-long track at the Meadowlands, in East Rutherford, New Jersey). As for all other staked races, competitors have been entered (and payments made to keep their entrance status current) almost from birth. Information: Yonkers Raceway, Yonkers, NY 10704 (914 968-4200).

THE YONKERS TROT, Yonkers, New York: Worth an estimated $325,000, this is one of the three glamour events of trotting (with the Kentucky Futurity and the Hambletonian described above) held in summer. Information: Yonkers Raceway, Yonkers, NY 10704 (914 968-4200).

ROLLING ROCK RACES, Ligonier, Pennsylvania: Steeplechase racing is not common in the US, and that's surprising, because it's fast, dangerous, and exciting, as you can imagine when you think of a pack of horses charging over a course full of high jumps made of brush (hedges) or timber (like split-rail fences). The Rolling Rock races, held on a 12,000-plus-acre country estate, are among the best-run and the best-paying of the year's calendar of steeplechase races. Held annually in the fall (formerly in October, now always in September), with six races a day for two days, the whole town — and people from hundreds of miles around — turns out. Kids get out of school. The high school band comes to entertain. People picnic on the tailgates of station wagons and recreational vehicles — and just sit and enjoy the colorful woods and the rolling hills. You watch from reserved box seats or from grandstands, and park either near the box seats or in one of three hay fields a few blocks away. Reserved seat tickets start going by June. Information: Rolling Rock Racing Association, The Bigelow, Suite 1115, Bigelow Sq., Pittsburgh, PA 15219 (412 471-3344).

THE COLONIAL CUP INTERNATIONAL STEEPLECHASE, Camden, South Carolina: The $50,000 cup makes this late fall event, first held in 1970, the very biggest in steeplechase racing; with the Rolling Rock races and the Temple Gwathmey at Belmont Park, it is one of the jewels of the Triple Crown of steeplechase racing. But unlike its fellows, the Colonial Cup is an international race, and participants come from around the world. There are no timber races as at Rolling Rock, but instead special "national fences" made of plastic brush — 17 obstacles in all. The Carolina Cup, held in the spring, is older and draws bigger crowds (though the purse is not so large). Information: Colonial Cup, PO Box 280, Camden, SC 29020 (803 432-6513).

RODEOS

Beyond the fact that the rodeo cowboy's skills are rooted in the life of the Wild West, the rodeo system today has very little to do with that romantic era. In the first place, there's big money involved — hundreds of thousands of dollars in prizes for all the different events. Then, too, the cowboys are more like Olympic athletes: They train hard and work hard to get where they are. All rodeos sanctioned by the Professional Rodeo Cowboys' Association (PRCA) — the larger of the two cowboy "leagues" — include bareback, saddle bronc, and bull riding; calf roping and team roping; and steer wrestling. Often there's also barrel racing (for women), sanctioned by the Girls' Rodeo Association; plus chuckwagon races and the like. All of these rodeos — the US's biggest and most important — are associated with livestock shows or big state or county fairs.

THE NATIONAL WESTERN STOCK SHOW AND RODEO, Denver, Colorado: At the largest indoor rodeo in the country, some 1,000 entrants vie for over $300,000 in prize money every January. The venerable annual (the biggest of the US's livestock exhibitions) also has plenty of exhibits that tell you everything you didn't know about livestock matters from saddles to beef production. All over the place there are kids grooming animals in preparation for judging and onlookers numbering in the thousands. Information: 1325 E 46th Ave., Denver, CO 80216 (303 623-1166).

THE NATIONAL FINALS RODEO, Oklahoma City, Oklahoma: At the end of the year, the top 15 money-winners qualify for the National Finals — and from there they all have equal chances for the championships in the various divisions. There are 10 performances, all held the first week in December; most tickets sell out by May. Information: Fullerton Ticket Agency, Civic Center Music Hall, Oklahoma City, OK 73102 (405 235-1306), and the Chamber of Commerce, 1 Santa Fe Plaza, Oklahoma City, OK 73102 (405 232-6381).

SOUTHWESTERN EXPOSITION AND FAT STOCK SHOW RODEO, Fort Worth, Texas: The world's oldest indoor rodeo, held in the heart of cowboy country at the end of January every year, pays nearly $225,000. Information: Southwestern Exposition, PO Box 150, Fort Worth, TX 76101 (817 335-9346).

HOUSTON LIVESTOCK SHOW AND RODEO, Houston, Texas: This event, which runs for two weeks beginning the last week in February, features a Texas-size rodeo, held in the Astrodome; and the world's largest livestock show, which fills up the Astro Arena with horses, chickens, pigs, and cattle, for display and for sale at auction. In 1979, five chickens went for $22,000 and the grand champion steer for $70,000. Tickets and information: Houston Livestock Show, PO Box 20070, Houston, TX 77225 (713 791-9000).

CHEYENNE FRONTIER DAYS RODEO, Cheyenne, Wyoming: The oldest US rodeo and the granddaddy of them all is a long-standing tradition in Wyoming. In addition to the usual competitive events, there are night shows (generally featuring country and western performers like Charley Pride or Dolly Parton) and chuckwagon races. Last full week in July. Information: Frontier Days, PO Box 2385, Cheyenne, WY 82001 (307 634-7794).

FOR MORE INFORMATION

There are complicated systems for the way the thoroughbreds and standardbreds race; an understanding will help you enjoy the races more and make wiser bets. The Thoroughbred Racing Associations, 3000 Marcus Ave., Lake Success, NY 11042 (516 328-2660), publishes lists of major races and a booklet describing the sport. The US Trotting Association, 750 Michigan Ave., Columbus, OH 43215 (614 224-2291), publishes a history of the sport and free booklets that tell you how to read the tote board and what's going on during the races. Similar information about steeplechasing is available from the National Steeplechase and Hunt Association, PO Box 308, Elmont, NY 11003 (516 437-6666). For information about rodeos, write the PRCA, 101 Prorodeo Dr., Colorado Springs, CO 80919 (303 593-8840).

Oddities and Insanities

America is full of offbeat attractions — museums given over to one subject (cartoons, buttons, soup tureens), whole festivals entirely devoted to matters that you'd consider entirely inconsequential, big blowouts or festivals that completely take over a town, and "world's best," "world's only," "world's first," etc. Around every corner there's something unexpected. A sampling:

EAST

BARNUM FESTIVAL, Bridgeport, Connecticut: A ten-day flurry of Jenny Lind contests, fireworks, circus parades, flea markets in the great showman's home town. Mid-June to early July. Information: Barnum Festival, 804 Main St., Bridgeport, CT 06604 (203 367-8495).

NATIONAL CRAB PICKING CONTEST, Cambridge, Maryland: Faster than you can imagine. Part of the Jaycees' Bay Country Festival, held every year in August. Information: Roger Webster, 2 Shady Dr., Cambridge, MD 21613 (301 228-8644).

NATIONAL MUSKRAT SKINNING CONTEST, Cambridge, Maryland: As part of the Outdoor Show held here annually each winter since 1938, contestants aim to skin five animals faster than any other competitor. Information: Roger Webster, 2 Shady Dr., Cambridge, MD 21613 (301 228-8644).

THE NEWSPAPER HOUSE, Rockport, Massachusetts: A cabin made entirely of chemically treated rolled newspapers at 52 Pigeon Hill in this shop-crammed resort town north of Boston. Information: Chamber of Commerce, Rockport, MA 01966 (617 546-6575).

LAKE CHARGOGGAGOGGMANCHAUGGAGOGGCHAUBUNAGUNGAMAUGG, Webster, Massachusetts: The name, in the language of the Nipmuc Indians, means "I fish on my side, you fish on your side, and no one fishes in the middle." Local fishermen call it Lake Webster. Largemouth and smallmouth bass, pickerel, and rainbow and brown trout have an almost ideal environment. Information: Webster-Dudley-Oxford Chamber of Commerce, Box 100, Webster, MA 01570 (617 943-0558).

LUCY THE MARGATE ELEPHANT, Margate, New Jersey: Constructed around 1881 along with similar curiosities by one James Lafferty, Lucy is a 75-foot-long and 65-foot-tall elephant building, a former hotel. Now she stands as a national historic landmark. There's a small museum inside, and you can climb onto her howdah, an observatory. Information: Save Lucy Committee, PO Box 3000, Margate, NJ 08402 (609 822-6519).

NATIONAL POLKA FESTIVAL, Hunter, New York: Top bands, a dance floor that holds 1,000 in the largest tent in the US, ethnic foods, and daily dance contests. August. Information: PO Box 297, Hunter, NY 12442 (518 263-3800).

MUSEUM OF CARTOON ART, Port Chester, New York: Exhibits of cartoon making, cartoon history, and the work of a thousand different cartoonists. The collection, the largest of its kind in the world, is newly housed in the first house in the world to be constructed entirely of reinforced concrete. Information: Comly Ave., Port Chester, NY 10573 (914 939-0234).

WORLD CHAMPIONSHIP SNOW SHOVEL RIDING CONTEST, Ambridge, Pennsylvania: You sit on coal shovels or spades, then slide down a 153-foot snow-covered slope; the idea is to get down before your opponents — still sitting on the shovel. Held every winter in January. Information: Beaver County Tourist Promotion Agency, 699 Fifth St., Court House, Beaver, PA 15009 (412 728-5700).

BEAN SOUP FESTIVAL, McClure, Pennsylvania: Thousands of gallons of bean soup are stirred up in 35-gallon iron kettles to accompany 25 roast hogs and the usual small-town festival doings every year in September. It's a great feast. Information: Bean Soup Festival, Box 8, McClure, PA 17841 (717 658-8425).

UNITED CHURCH OF CHRIST GAME SUPPER, Bradford, Vermont: A church supper where the goodies on the table are beaver, boar, bear, coon, pheasant, rabbit, venison, Moufflon ram, and whatever else the locals have hunted that year; the sittings sell out within days of tickets going on sale. November. Information: United Church of Christ, Bradford, VT 05033 (802 222-4418).

CONVENTION OF THE AMERICAN SOCIETY OF DOWSERS, Danville, Vermont: A gathering of novice and experienced dowsers with reports, workshops, meetings, and a Sunday morning public Dowsing on the Green. One four-day weekend in September preceded by a two-day dowsing school. Information: American Society of Dowsers, Danville, VT 05828 (802 684-3417).

WORLD'S FAIR, Tunbridge, Vermont: A country fair with pony pulling contests, oxen judging, and fiddlers' and band concerts (among other things) with a reputation for no-holds-barred wildness. Mid-September. Information: Vermont Department of Agriculture, 116 State St., Montpelier, VT 05602 (802 828-2428).

FEAST OF THE RAMSON, Richwood, West Virginia: The publisher of this town's newspaper once threatened to put the juice of the ramp — a wild onionlike vegetable peculiar to the shady coves of Appalachia — in the printing ink, and the townspeople panicked. Once you've eaten ramps, the smell hangs around you for days, but the annual feast devoted to the green is much loved nonetheless. April. Information: Chamber of Commerce, 50 Oakland Ave., Box 587, Richwood, WV 26261 (304 846-6790).

SOUTH

NATIONAL PEANUT FESTIVAL, Dothan, Alabama: Peanut recipe contests, parades, arts and crafts shows, hog herding contests, sheep dog trials, and greased pig scrambles are the staples at this small-town-bash-grown-to-state-fair-size. Boiled peanuts are for sale everywhere. Mid-October. Information: National Peanut Festival Association, PO Box 976, Dothan, AL 36302 (205 793-4323).

WORLD'S CHAMPIONSHIP DUCK-CALLING CONTEST, Stuttgart, Arkansas: The competition for the title of Queen Mallard is followed by various duck-calling competitions, some for kids, some for women, some for men in hale, mating, feed, and comeback calls. The event takes place annually the weekend of Thanksgiving. Information: Chamber of Commerce, Box 932, Stuttgart, AR 72160 (501 673-1602).

INTERNATIONAL WORM FIDDLING CONTEST, Caryville, Florida: Worm fiddlers drive wooden stakes into the ground and drag metal bars across the stakes to create a vibration that brings the worms to the surface, where they are bagged for fish bait. Saturday before Labor Day. Information: Joanne Palmer, PO Box 21, Caryville, FL 32427 (904 548-5116).

WORLD CHAMPIONSHIP SWAMP BUGGY RACES, Naples, Florida: With their high wheels, these homemade conveyances that can get through mud and water under nearly any conditions are a way of life in this part of the country; a flooded 40-acre marshland on the edge of the Everglades provides the racecourse twice a year, usually the last Sundays in October and February. Information: Swamp Buggy Days, PO Box 3105, Naples, FL 33939 (813 774-2701).

INTERNATIONAL KITE FLYOFF, Sarasota, Florida: Awards go to the highest flier, the most original kite, the biggest kite, and the smallest kite. The Kite Flying Champion of the World is usually on hand. The event is always held in January on the Saturday closest to Ben Franklin's birthday. Information: Sheraton-Sandcastle, 1540 Ben Franklin Dr., Sarasota, FL 33577 (813 388-2181).

INTERNATIONAL SANDCASTLE CONTEST, Sarasota, Florida: Not just mounds of sand, but crocodiles 50 feet long, octopuses, pyramids, whales, poodles, and mermaids are sculpted in an attempt to win the first prize — a week's free stay at the Sheraton-Sandcastle Resort on Lido Beach, where the event is held annually on the first Saturday in May. Information: Sheraton-Sandcastle, 1540 Ben Franklin Dr., Sarasota, FL 33577 (813 388-2181).

WORLD'S CHICKEN PLUCKIN' CHAMPIONSHIP, Spring Hill, Florida: Teams compete at this small community northwest of Tampa to establish new world records (to be listed in *Guinness).* Also part of the goings-on is a Miss Drumstick Contest, in which competitors' torsos are enveloped in flour sacks; and there's plenty of music, singing, dancing, and food. October. Information: Spring Hill VFW–Post 10209, 7504 Spring Hill Dr., Spring Hill, FL 33526 (904 796-0398).

GREAT EASTER EGG HUNT, Stone Mountain, Georgia: One of the biggest Easter egg hunts in the US, with 20,000 brightly colored hard-boiled eggs hidden in a meadow. The park where it is held, on the outskirts of Atlanta, also has two Easter sunrise services, one at the mountain's base, the other at its peak. Information: Stone Mountain Park, PO Box 778, Stone Mountain, GA 30086 (404 469-9831).

INTERNATIONAL BANANA FESTIVAL, Fulton, Kentucky: The twin cities of Fulton, Kentucky, and South Fulton, Tennessee, celebrate the area's role as "Banana Crossroads of the United States" and "Banana Capital of the World" with banana-eating contests, a banana bake-off, and a one-ton banana pudding that serves 10,000 — half to a third of the people who put in an appearance in these communities about 50 miles from Paducah and 127 miles from Memphis. And it's free — and so are the bananas handed out to all comers. August. Information: International Banana Festival, PO Box 428, Fulton, KY 42041 (502 472-2975).

THE CRAWFISH FESTIVAL, Breaux Bridge, Louisiana: Such a major event is involved in serving up these little crustaceans in all imaginable forms that the townspeople can put on the festival only every other year. In May in even-numbered years. Information: Breaux Bridge City Hall, Breaux Bridge, LA 70517 (318 332-2171).

LOUISIANA FUR AND WILDLIFE FESTIVAL, Cameron, Louisiana: Trapshooting, retriever dog trials, duck- and goose-calling contests, nutria- and muskrat-skinning contests, fur judging, and more. Second weekend in January. Information: Braxton Blake, Cameron, LA 70631 (318 775-5335).

NATIONAL HOLLERIN' CONTEST, Spivey's Corner, North Carolina: Left over from the days before telephones, when each mountain man had his own holler. In 1976, a three-legged dog barked along with the hollerers. June. Information: Ermon Godwin, PO Box 332, Dunn, NC 28334 (919 892-4133).

EASTER EGG FIGHTS, Sugar Hill, North Carolina: Descendants of this Piedmont town's early German settlers, following a 160-year-old custom, test the durability of their hard-boiled brightly colored eggs by banging the small ends together. The contestant that ends up with the least damage wins. Early on Easter Sunday. Area information: Chamber of Commerce, Cherryville, NC 28021 (704 435-3451).

CHITLIN' STRUT, Salley, South Carolina: The chitlin' capital of the world serves up over five tons of these boiled, deep-fried hog intestines every year in November. Information: Town of Salley, Box 484, Salley, SC 29137 (803 258-3485).

EASTER FIRES PAGEANT, Fredericksburg, Texas: Costumed Easter bunnies and bonfires in a pageant which got its start back in the days when parents told their youngsters that what were actually the bonfires of ready-to-attack Indians were the cookfires of Easter bunnies boiling eggs. Easter Eve. Information: Chamber of Commerce, PO Box 506, Fredericksburg, TX 78624 (512 997-3444).

THE WURSTFEST, New Braunfels, Texas: Crowds of nearly 140,000 come around to gobble mettwurst, blutwurst, bratwurst, leberwurst, wurstkabobs, pork hocks, sauerkraut, dumplings and all the rest at an extravaganza that nods to the heritage of the people who settled here. November. Information: Wurstfest Association, PO Box 180, New Braunfels, TX 78130 (512 625-2385).

MIDWEST

POPE COUNTY DEER FESTIVAL, Golconda, Illinois: All day and part of the night for one weekend in November, the hunters come in their orange hats and Day-Glo vests to consume tons of BBQ, pie, and coffee. Information: Milton Baker, Pope County Deer Festival, Golconda, IL 62938 (618 683-4466).

NATIONAL HOBO CONVENTION, Britt, Iowa: Thousands of vacationers and even some hobos converge on this little town every year in August — and have been since 1900. Information: Chamber of Commerce, Britt, IA 50423 (515 843-3867).

INTERNATIONAL PANCAKE DAY, Liberal, Kansas: The main event is a foot race in which women in house dresses, aprons, and head scarves run an S-shaped course through town while flipping flapjacks in skillets — a strange activity which got its start some 500 years ago in England. Shrove Tuesday. Information: International Pancake Day, PO Box 665, Liberal, KS 67901 (316 624-1106).

WORLD'S LONGEST BREAKFAST TABLE, Battle Creek, Michigan: Where else but in the Breakfast Capital of the World would you find four blocks of end to end picnic tables laden with products of the Big Three (Kellogg's, Post, and Ralston-Purina)? June. Information: Chamber of Commerce, PO Box 16, Battle Creek, MI 49016 (616 962-4076).

THE MAGIC GET-TOGETHER, Colon, Michigan: After the great illusionist Harry Blackstone moved here in the 20s, the town became a magicians' colony of sorts; Abbott's Magic Company, founded by one of the pilgrims, puts on this extravaganza of "illusions," as magic tricks are known in the business. August. Information: Abbott's, Colon, MI 49040 (616 432-3235).

NATIONAL CHERRY FESTIVAL, Traverse City, Michigan: A half million journey here annually for one of the nation's biggest festivals — where they can enjoy cherry sundaes at an ice cream social, cherries in pancakes for breakfast, cherry desserts made by area cherry growers' wives, cherry pie eating (and baking) contests, and three parades. One week in July. Information: National Cherry Festival, PO Box 141, Traverse City, MI 49684 (616 947-4230).

NATIONAL FENCE PAINTING CONTEST, Hannibal, Missouri: Kids dressed up like Tom Sawyer compete as part of the Tom Sawyer Days, held every year the first week in July. There's also frog jumping, a baby beauty contest, a mud volleyball game (played in a pit full of pure Mississippi mud), and raft race. Information: Chamber of Commerce, PO Box 230, Hannibal, MO 63041 (314 221-1101).

THE PUMPKIN SHOW, Circleville, Ohio: Crowds up to half a million come for what Ohioans call "the greatest free show on earth" — and down piles of pumpkin ice cream, pumpkin pie, pumpkin fudge, pumpkin candy, pumpkin milk shakes, pumpkin cookies, and even pumpkin hamburgers. October. Information: Chamber of Commerce, Circleville, OH 43113 (614 474-4923).

BUZZARD DAY, Hinckley, Ohio: Buzzard Town USA got its name because of a flock of 50 or so of the big birds that spend most of the warmer months here; the day they return from their wintering grounds (or a day close to it) every March there are bazaars where you can buy chocolate buzzards, buzzard cookies, T-shirts, and bumper stickers, and a big pancake breakfast. Information: Chamber of Commerce, Box 354, Hinckley, OH 44233 (216 278-2554).

INTERNATIONAL CHICKEN FLYING MEET, Rio Grande, Ohio: An organized version of what farm boys have been doing from hay lofts, trees, cliffs, and other high places for years, on Bob Evans' farm. May. Information: ICFM Secretary, 3776 S High St., Columbus, OH 43207 (614 491-2225).

LUMBERJACK WORLD CHAMPIONSHIPS, Hayward, Wisconsin: Events in sawing (single-man bucking, two-man bucking, power sawing), log rolling, speed climbing, tree topping, ax throwing, canoe jousting, lumberjack relays, and chopping contests at a museum village, Historyland, that traces the history of the area. July. Information: Historyland, Hayward, WI 54843 (715 634-4811).

WEST

THE FUR RENDEZVOUS, Anchorage, Alaska: This action-packed event features the World Championship Sled Dog Race, an Eskimo blanket toss exhibition, fur auction, fur style show, pancake feed, and about 130 other events, including baseball games on snowshoes, curling bonspiels, a cross-country snowmobile race, and more. One of the nation's ten largest festivals. Ten days in February. Information: Fur Rendezvous, PO Box 773, Anchorage, AK 99510 (907 277-8615).

CALAVERAS COUNTY FAIR & JUMPING FROG JUBILEE, Angels Camp, California: This ordinary county fair features the International Frog Jump Finals, which climax a season of frog-jumping events across the country. The 2,800 contestants jump bullfrogs in an attempt to beat Davy Crockett's 1976 20-foot-3-inch record. Frogs are for rent. May. Information: Frogtown, PO Box 96, Angels Camp, CA 95222 (209 736-2561).

MULE DAYS, Bishop, California: The Mule Capital of the World puts on a Mule Days Parade with an assemblage of 200 entries — mule teams, riding teams, pack strings and comedy entries (in which mules carry outhouses or beds); plus mule shoeing contests, a One-Mile Mule Run, a Mule Sale, a braying contest (for people), and a variety of other events. Memorial Day weekend. Information: Chamber of Commerce, 690 N Main St., Bishop, CA 93514 (714 873-8405).

INDIO DATE FESTIVAL, Indio, California: A ten-day county fair with some unusual entertainment: races of camels and ostrich (who behave so unpredictably that everybody else is upstaged). February. Information: Chamber of Commerce, Indio, CA 92201 (714 347-0676).

INTERNATIONAL SURF FESTIVAL, Manhattan Beach, California: Also at Hermosa, Torrance, and Redondo Beaches, this event is the big deal of a surfer's year. Late July or August. Information: Chamber of Commerce, 425 15th St., Manhattan Beach, CA 90266 (213 545-5313).

WORLD'S CHAMPIONSHIP PACK BURRO RACE, Fairplay, Colorado: Contestants drag, push and pull their stubborn animals over the rugged mountains. Last full weekend in July. Information: Burro Race Committee, Box 412, Fairplay, CO 80440.

WORLD'S LARGEST OPEN-AIR HOT SPRINGS SWIMMING POOL, Glenwood Springs, Colorado: In winter, clouds of steam make you feel you're totally alone in a fog. Information: Chamber of Commerce, 1102 Grand Ave., Glenwood Springs, CO 81601 (303 945-6589).

NATIONAL BASQUE FESTIVAL, Elko, Nevada: The population of this little town skyrockets as merrymakers from all over come to chorus the Basque National Anthem, watch Basque games and contests (walking weight carries, tugs of war, handball, woodchopping and sheephooking contests, and 250-pound and granite-ball lifts), and enjoy Basque meals and Basque dancing and singing. July. Information: Chamber of Commerce, PO Box 470, Elko, NV 89801 (702 738-7135).

WORLD CHAMPIONSHIP COW CHIP THROWING CONTEST, Beaver, Oklahoma: Pasture discus fans from around the world compete in this highly specialized athletic event; there's a special division for politicians. Also on the schedule: an amateur talent show, and an egg-throwing contest. April. Information: Chamber of Commerce, PO Box 878, Beaver, OK 73932 (405 625-4726).

WORLD POSTHOLE DIGGING CHAMPIONSHIP, Boise City, Oklahoma: Men, women, and children compete. The event is part of the annual Santa Fe Trail Daze festival in late May or early June. Information: Chamber of Commerce, PO Box 1027, Boise City, OK 73933 (405 544-3344).

INTERNATIONAL BRICK AND ROLLING PIN THROWING CONTEST, Stroud, Oklahoma: Hurlers from this small town compete against teams from Stroud, England, Stroud, Canada, and Stroud, Australia, for the best throws with bricks (for men) and rolling pins (for women). July. Information: Chamber of Commerce, 219 W 3rd, Stroud, OK 74079 (918 968-3321).

NATIONAL ROOSTER CROWING CONTEST, Rogue River, Oregon: Roosters from across the nation attempt to best the 1979 record set by White Lightning—112 crows in 30 minutes. Last Saturday in June. Information: Chamber of Commerce, PO Box 353, Rogue River, OR 97537 (503 582-0242).

OREGON STRAWBERRY FESTIVAL, Lebanon, Oregon: Bigger than the National Strawberry Festival (Manistee, Michigan, in early July), this Oregon festival stars the world's largest strawberry shortcake (a 5,700-pounder that is 16 feet long, 12 feet wide, 8 feet high and served with 300 gallons of ice cream and 3,000 pounds of strawberries). June. Information: Chamber of Commerce, 1040 Park St., Lebanon, OR 97355 (503 258-7164).

WORLD'S CHAMPIONSHIP SNOWSHOE SOFTBALL TOURNAMENT, Winthrop, Washington: Teams from all over the Pacific Northwest battle it out on snowshoes one day every February in this tiny, old-fashioned western town. Besides the softball, there's jousting, a relay tourney, and a chariot race — all on snowshoes. Details: Chamber of Commerce, Box 402, Winthrop, WA 98862 (509 996-2125).

DIRECTIONS

Introduction

Herein are America's 66 most spectacular itineraries, from Maine's coastal road to the least visited of the major Hawaiian islands. Our most splendid national parks are listed below, with information on what to see and do while visiting them, as well as the best driving routes across the country. Each entry has been organized to cover about a three-day touring period — whether spent driving a particular route or visiting a park. Most entries include a *Best en Route* section which identifies interesting and special accommodations or restaurants in the area. Entries are not exhaustive or comprehensive; they discuss the highlights of the areas, and in *Best en Route,* offer suggestions for especially fine accommodations. They are, in one sense, starting points for a longer visit. If, however, you are pressed for time, you will find that by following the itineraries, you will see the most notable spots (and attractive accommodations) in the area.

We have organized these itineraries by general geographical areas — East, South, Midwest, and West — and you can locate a particular place by looking first for its state under the appropriate area heading. By connecting several itineraries together, it is possible to construct a driving route of an entire state or group of states. For example, by combining the individual itineraries covering the Great Smoky Mountain National Park, Okefenokee Swamp, the Everglades, and the Florida Keys, you can put together a reasonable touring schedule for a whole section of the southeastern United States.

East

Mystic Seaport, Connecticut, to Providence, Rhode Island

Mystic Seaport, a restored whaling village and nautical museum, is located about 150 miles northeast of New York City, off I-95 in Mystic, Connecticut. A driving tour will take you through several grimy, industrial New England towns, but you can escape the Interstate at exit 71, South Lyme. Bear left at the end of the ramp, then left again at the junction of rt. 156, going in the direction of East Lyme (the sign is very confusing). This is a charming back road that winds through forgotten little towns of country stores, antique shops, and boatyards fronting Long Island Sound.

NIANTIC, Connecticut – A village of New England Gothic wood-frame homes. Cross a drawbridge flanked by marinas and restaurants. As you reach the opposite side of the bridge, you'll pass the entrance to the Millstone Nuclear Power Plant. One wooded interlude beyond, and you'll find yourself in a long strip of curio shops, gas stations, and shopping centers. This is antique country, too, and there are innumerable places to stop and browse. In the distance, that inviting cluster of soft spruce hills punctuated by a church spire is your next destination: New London.

NEW LONDON, Connecticut – An 18th- and 19th-century whaling port, now housing the US Coast Guard Academy. You'll see a lot of military jeeps and rugged seamen; in all, New London has a rather faded air, similar to some of the waterfront industrial districts in London, England, for which the town was named. As you enter, follow signs to the business district and pull into a parking space on Bank Street near the Fishers Point Ferry Landing, with its polished wood waiting room. In winter, a wet, fierce wind blows in from Long Island Sound, but in warmer months, the cool breeze is ideal. You might want to stroll along the Captain's Walk, a cobblestone promenade offering a view of the water. On the corner of Bank St. and Captain's Walk, there's a lovely shop selling an intriguing combination of stained glass Tiffany lamps, mobiles, plaques, and live plants. Across the street, Caruso's Music Shop sells drums decorated with garishly colored windmills. The main sites in New London include: The Lyman Allyn Museum, a hodgepodge collection of Egyptian, Greek, Roman, medieval, Renaissance, and antique furniture (100 Mohegan Ave., 443-2545); Tale of the Whale Museum, with whaling implements (3 Whale Oil Row, 442-8191); Olde Town Mill, the oldest industrial power plant in the country, in use in 1650, with a museum of colonial manufacturing (Mill and Main, 442-7924).

MYSTIC, Connecticut – Take I-95 12 miles north to exit 90. As you exit the Interstate, you'll pass the Mystic Aquarium, with sea lions, seals, and more than 2,000 species of marine life (536-3323). About a half mile south of I-95 on rt. 27 is Mystic Seaport Museum (536-2631). Even in the middle of winter, the parking lot is crowded, but then it is possible to wander through the seaport without encountering hordes of people. In summer, the place is jammed. It takes at least three hours to see everything. Mystic Seaport consists of neat rows of sparkling white buildings along the banks of the Mystic River, which feeds into Long Island Sound. There are four major historic ships, a working shipyard, a recreated 19th-century community area with craftspeople, and a formal exhibit area. Visitors may board the 1882 training ship *Joseph Conrad;* the fishing schooner *L. A. Dunton;* and the 1841 whaling ship, *Charles W. Morgan.* The *Morgan,* a National Historic Landmark, is undergoing an extensive restoration that visitors are permitted to watch. In summer, there are daily demonstrations of sail setting and furling, chantey singing, and other maritime skills. You'll probably gasp in astonishment as you enter the exhibit building with an assortment of giant ships' figureheads. Exhibits of scrimshaw (engraved whale tusks) depicting old clipper and whaling ships bear testimony to years of patient craftsmanship. The guides are senior citizens who volunteer their time, warmth, and experience. But there's more than enough to see: the chandlery, the ropemaking factory, rigging and sailmaking lofts, and model ship exhibits. Be sure to stop at the Mystic Scale Model, to see the town as it was in the 19th century. Stepping outside again, you'll realize how much love and care has gone into preserving the peaceful beauty and dignity of the village. There is something truly timeless about it.

WESTERLY, Rhode Island – About 12 miles east of Mystic on rt.1, Westerly, a Rhode Island town of dignified, white colonial mansions, stretches to the coast of Block Island Sound. Westerly includes Watch Hill, an exclusive residential community, and Misquamicut State Beach. Florence Nightingale's cap is on exhibit at Westerly Hospital, Wells St. (596-4961). Be careful driving around town. Westerly has only five principal streets, but it's a tricky place and you can easily get lost and end up back in Pawcatuck, Connecticut. Keep bearing right around the circle to avoid this.

PROVIDENCE, Rhode Island – The capital of Rhode Island, about 50 miles from Westerly on I-95 or rt. 1, another delightfully empty road that hugs the coast, is a city with a low-level skyline. Take the Broadway exit off I-95 and bear right. Drive straight along that street and then bear left until you get to Kennedy Plaza and the US Courthouse on Exchange St., a building with several interesting classical sculptures depicting Justice. Circle the plaza, take a left on Dorrance, and when you pass the Westminster Mall, a pedestrian shopping plaza, turn left on Friendship St. Cross the intersecting street and head up the hill, past the Rhode Island School of Design Art Museum (224 Benefit St., 331-6363). This area, known as College Hill, includes Brown University, whose main gate is on George St. (863-1000), and Rhode Island School of Design, known as RISD, on Benefit St. (331-3511). Both campuses have concerts, films, plays, lectures, and cultural exhibits throughout the year. Brown is in the Ivy League varsity league. Interspersed with the college buildings are a number of historical houses. These splendid colonial estates, columned mansions, and gardens are like entering another world. Some of the houses are open daily. By the way, George Washington really did sleep in the Stephen Hopkins House (Benefit and Hopkins Sts., 861-2935). The easiest way to return to I-95 is by following Thayer St. to I-195, which feeds into I-95. I-95 will take you back to New York or on to Boston, about 45 miles northeast.

BEST EN ROUTE

Larchwood Inn, Wakefield, Rhode Island – Built in 1831, this country inn is known for its delicious, fresh seafood, elegant yet comfortable furnishings, and cozy atmosphere. Close to swimming, boating, fishing, and surfing, as well as bicycling and cross-country ski routes. 176 Main St., Wakefield, RI 02879 (401 783-5454).

The Biltmore Plaza, Providence, Rhode Island – A major renovation has brought this lovely old hotel back to life. Its rooftop restaurant, *L'Apogée,* has notable French food. Kennedy Plaza, Providence (401 421-0700; toll-free 800 225-7654).

The Ancient Mariner, Mystic, Connecticut – After wandering around the seaport, a seafood meal is a must. Chowder here is hearty, homemade, authentic New England clam. Seafood Thermidor is well stocked with scallops, shrimp, and other shellfish. 34 W Main St. (203 536-2581).

The Maine Coast and Acadia National Park, Maine

To drive along Maine's coastline is to spend some honest time with nature. Not the kind of ski-lodge nature that seems to be little more than an entertainment, letting you come and go as you will and ending conveniently at the doors of a warm lodge. Nature in Maine comes mostly on its own terms, and those are terms of force — the fundamental force of the open Atlantic, the obdurate resistance of the rocky coastline against which it washes.

What makes this an honest trip, if you are observant, is a single revelation: that the forces at work here are totally oblivious to human beings. Watch eddies of the sea suck and slap against some stark slab of stone, perhaps at Acadia National Park, where the process is particularly well defined; the edge of the continent is being constantly, imperceptibly worn away, altered, but it is not an action within the scope of our time scale. It is not something that happens for any motive. It is natural force; it is nature. We don't even have language to describe such a process and its relation to us. Words like indifferent or oblivious imply knowledge, intention, will. They don't nearly represent the implacable force of water and stone, the inhuman beauty of it. Only by seeing it does this become comprehensible.

Perhaps the best road in the country to see this sea and stone contest — east of the California/Oregon coastal road — is Maine's rt. 1. It stretches from Kittery to the Canadian border, but the section most interesting in a short two- or three-day drive is from Portland to Acadia National Park.

This route allows you to stop along the way at any number of villages and towns of unique Maine flavor. All along this craggy coast, America's history is evident. No so much the history of great battles or the sites of events which altered destiny; but history with a small *h,* a sense of one's own past. We are all, in some part, Yankees. There's more than a little twinge of recognition while viewing something studied but never before seen, like the widow's walks that border the roofs of so many of the houses along the coast. It's this kind of familiar history that nudges your consciousness all along this coastal route.

Anyone in search of a few days' respite from the current century will hardly be disappointed by the state of Maine.

PORTLAND – Is a good place to begin your drive along the coast. It's a city, like countless others, with the requisite number of hotels and places to eat. The true flavor of Maine, however, lies beyond the city limits. Head out along rt. 95 due north, which in Maine is known as "Down East."

BATH – Is now — and has always been — a shipbuilding center. There's a Marine Museum (963 Washington St.) that portrays local history in a unique way — you are ferried down the Kennebec River, stopping at four separate museum sites en route. Each deals with a different phase of Maine's maritime past.

WISCASSET – Is an ideal place to sample life as it was in the late 1800s. Many of the homes of that era are still occupied today. Originally built by wealthy merchants and shippers, they are lovingly maintained by their present owners. Of the several homes open to the public, the Nickels-Sortwell Mansion (Main and Federal Sts.) offers a clear-cut example of 19th-century federalist elegance — at least as it existed in Maine.

BOOTHBAY HARBOR – Has been discovered by tourists, but that should not detract from its interest as a place to visit. It is, rather, a tribute to the Yankee ingenuity that early recognized the salability of picture-postcard scenes, incomparable lobster suppers, and singular charm. Enjoy the appealing (albeit commercial) displays that have been concocted for your amusement: the Railway Village (just north of town) with its narrow-gauge train that carries passengers; the Schooner Museum (100 Commercial St.) complete with an antique fishing boat, the *Sherman Zwicker,* that you can board and explore. There's also the public aquarium (admission free) at McKown Point. And be sure to eat your fill of the local delicacy — lobster. You'll find it served in a variety of styles, delicious and relatively inexpensive.

While there are several fine places to stay right in Boothbay Harbor, there's something quite special just across the bay on Monhegan Island. You'll enjoy a stay overnight at the Island Inn. It's family-owned and over a century old, and there's a sort of time-stood-still feeling about the entire island. Most of the island has no electricity; peace and seclusion are the main elements of island entertainment, and you can explore the island in solitude, discovering the wildflowers and birds on your own. It's only a short ferry ride from the mainland to this gentler time.

ROCKLAND – A modern port city, the world's largest lobster distribution point, and the takeoff place for the ferry to two very special Maine islands — North Haven and Vinalhaven. North Haven is an island with a number of summer estates. Vinalhaven is a fishing village of about 1,100 Down East residents. There are no tennis courts, swimming pools, or movies; but there are church suppers (with baked beans, brown bread, and homemade pies), walks along the often foggy shores, and the constant coming and going of island fishermen. Both islands are accessible via the Maine State Ferry Service from Rockland (207 594-5543). North Haven has no commercial accommodations; Vinalhaven has two: Bridgeside Inn (207 863-4854) and Tidewater Motel (207 863-4618); but local families also take in travelers.

CAMDEN – Should be a stop between Rockland and Mt. Desert Island (described below) simply because it is such a beautiful harbor town. Surrounded by high hills (there is good skiing here in the winter, and winter sports at Camden Snow Bowl) and a number of beautiful old homes, it is a town for walking around in, for a long lunch, or for shopping — especially if you are shopping for one of Maine's 3,344 islands. The town is something of a center for real estate agents dealing in islands, and the place to start is with the real estate ads in *Down East* magazine, published in neighboring Rockport, and available throughout the state.

MT. DESERT ISLAND – An exceptional place, one of the most wildly beautiful spots in the country, with 35,000 acres devoted to spectacular Acadia National Park; the peak for which it was named (by the French explorer Champlain in 1605) is Mt. Cadillac, the highest spot on the Atlantic coast (which, at 1,530 feet, is hardly gargantuan, but offers a marvelous view of Frenchman's Bay from its height); its major town, Bar Harbor, has been synonymous with wealth and society for five decades.

In its heyday — from the 1890s through the 1940s — Bar Harbor was simply too posh for the likes of most folks; the old wealth, certainly, is still on the island (as you will see when you peek at the mammoth estates in the hills as you drive the park's loop road). But today Bar Harbor is far too open, too raucous, too egalitarian to appeal to its original crowd. It opens and closes with the summer season, and for people on the way to the splendors of Acadia, it offers fun shops (wander Main Street with an eye out for the Rock Shop and Bar Harbor Pottery especially), many hotels, and a host of good seafood restaurants.

But the real attraction of Mt. Desert is Acadia. It is the only national park to have been purchased with private funds, an effort organized by Dr. Charles Eliot of Harvard and George Bucknam Dorr when lumber interests threatened the island. The nation accepted the gift in 1916. Parts of the park are off the island, on Isle au Haut and Schoodic Point on the mainland, but the main attractions are accessible from the six-mile loop road which circles Mt. Desert's portion of Acadia.

Start a tour at the Visitors' Center (at the entrance near Bar Harbor) with exhibits on the ecology and history of the island. There you pick up information on camping and sports (golf, cycling, horseback riding, hiking, swimming, and an array of winter activities), and maps of the driving routes as well as the hundreds of trails that score the island's "mountains." The Ocean Drive loop culminates in the crown of Mt. Cadillac, and along the way gives ample opportunities to stop for a descent straight to rocky shore, where sea and stone meet.

Special treats, available at the harbors of the island's towns (Bar Harbor, Northeast Harbor, Bass Harbor), are sea cruises of nearby islands directed by naturalists. You search for eagles' nests or signs of porpoises and seals; or learn about the lobster trade; or make forays to historical museums on out-islands. Information at the Visitors' Center or from the companies which offer the cruises, located on the harbors mentioned above. Acadia is New England's only national park and it is a major treasury of authentic wilderness. For information: the Superintendent, Acadia National Park, RFD #1, PO Box H1, Bar Harbor, ME 04609 (207 288-3338).

BEST EN ROUTE

There is a delicate art to planning a trip to New England, and Maine is no exception. Summer and winter are high seasons; book well in advance. The three weeks from late September to mid-October are leaf-peeping season, a magic time to be here, but crowded, especially in the delightful New England inns which are themselves incentive enough for a trip. An optimum time to visit is after leaf peeping and before winter, when life has returned to nontourist normal, and with luck, the weather is fine. But that is just the period (mid-October to mid-November) when the Maine inns begin closing for the season, and you must plan in advance to get the ones you want. (An incentive: Rates during this period can be cut in half.) Our favorite Maine inns:

Homewood Inn, Yarmouth – Beyond Portland on beautiful, foggy Casco Bay, this traditional New England inn has hearty food, a popular Monday night clambake, tennis, pool, boating, and gameroom. Closed from mid-October to early June. Drinkwater Point, Yarmouth, ME 04096 (207 846-3351).

Island Inn, Monhegan Island – This century-old frame structure sitting on a picturesque bluff over the tiny harbor between Monhegan and its satellite island of Manana is open summers only. Fresh fish — striped bass, haddock, bluefish — are regulars on the menu; the cooking is not fancy, but the service is cheerful and quick. An all-you-can-eat buffet on Sunday nights brings in hikers returning from the awesome 150-foot cliffs that face the pounding surf to the east. Although the inn has its own generator, most of the island goes without electricity, and the yellow gleam of kerosene lamps through the windows of the wood-shingled houses makes a pretty sight as you walk along the village's solitary dirt road. Among the many woodland trails are no less than 600 varieties of flowering plants — including the trailing yew, unique to this island — and birders may espy up to 200 species during the year here. Monhegan Island, ME 04852 (207 372-9681).

Whitehall Inn, Camden – A classic Maine house, wrapped around with a deep, cool porch decorated with lots of green, potted plants. It was here that Edna St. Vincent Millay (a resident of the town from the time she was 18) gave the first public recitation of *Renascence.* Camden, ME 04843 (207 236-3391).

Asticou Inn, Northeast Harbor, Mt. Desert Island – An elegant, but comfortable, resort that maintains its style in simple ways. It encourages repeat visits, and likes to get to know its visitors. Open from mid-June to mid-September. In the very backyard of Acadia National Park. Northeast Harbor, Mt. Desert Island, ME 04662 (207 276-3344).

Maryland's Eastern Shore

On the eastern coast of Maryland, the Eastern Shore is among the most charming and unspoiled historic sections of the country. Dating from pre-Revolutionary times, the Eastern Shore has retained the simple elegance that characterized the region when Lord Baltimore and his followers established their first settlements. Although part of the Eastern Seaboard, the environment is surprisingly remote from urban and suburban 20th-century America. Loyalties in this part of the world tend to run deep. Local residents are known to assert, "I don't give a damn about the whole state of Maryland 'cause I'm from the Eastern Shore . . ."

The Eastern Shore is more than just a few scattered plantations separated by open green. It retains a neat harmony of spreading rivers and streams, large and small farms, fine homes, with grounds that stretch to the water's edge. Mention the bay in this part of the country and you'll find it means only one thing: the Chesapeake, 200 miles long, from 4 to 30 miles wide, fed by 150 rivers, and containing more than 7,000 miles of tidewater shoreline. Here, you can taste some of the best oysters, crabs, and clams in the country, within sight of fishermen on the bay to remind you this is the region's most important occupation. Take I-40 northeast from Baltimore about 35 miles, then head 5 miles south on rt. 213 to Chesapeake City.

CHESAPEAKE CITY – The Maryland port of the Chesapeake and Delaware Canal. Built in 1829 for $2 million, the canal shortens the water route between Baltimore and Philadelphia by more than 275 miles, and has been a constant source of jobs for people in the surrounding community. The canal was purchased by the US government in 1919 and lowered to sea level in 1927 for $10 million. Since then, it has served as an important commercial line in the inland waterway connecting Maine to Florida, and has been used for leisure vessels as well. The largest waterwheel in the world can be found in the stone pumphouse, along with a scale model of the original canal, on the government property. The wheel was used to control water levels until the early 1900s. (For information, contact the Old Lock Pump House; 301 885-5621.)

WARWICK – About 12 miles south of rt. 213 on rt. 282. Overlooking the Bohemia River, Warwick is the site of the Bohemia Manor, a symmetrical brick building designed in the Georgian style by Thomas F. Bayard, US senator from Delaware between 1922 and 1929. The land is part of a larger plot purchased by Bayard's ancestor

Augustine Herman, who made a deal for the land with George Calvert, the first Lord Baltimore, in 1659. Calvert gave Herman 15,000 acres in exchange for Herman's skillful maps of the region. With the successful completion of his map project, Herman became the first to propose a canal connecting the Chesapeake and Delaware Bays. He is now buried close to Bohemia Manor (for information, contact Warwick City Hall; 301 398-0200).

CHESTERTOWN – About 22 miles south of Warwick on rt. 213. This tranquil, pretty, pre-Revolutionary town facing the Chester River contains several historic two-story brick houses. Across town, away from the river, Washington College spreads across 20 acres. Founded in 1780 by Reverend William Smith, this small liberal arts college, named after George Washington (who served on the Board of Visitors and Governors), now has an enrollment of about 800 students (Washington Ave.). Pre-Revolutionary buildings include: the Wickes House (100 E High St.), Palmer House (532 W High St.), Geddes-Piper House (Church Alley), and Widehall and the Customs House (both at High and Front Sts). On the third Saturday in September, there's a candlelight walking tour that takes you past the wide, sweeping lawns of the town's homes, into the public and colonial homes decorated with ornate, carved mantelpieces and unusual Americana. For information, call Peggy Johnstone at 301 778-3645. For general information on historic homes and tours, call Chestertown Town Hall (301 778-0500).

WYE MILLS – About 25 miles south of Chestertown on rt. 213, this tiny colonial town grew up around an early-18th-century gristmill which has now been restored and is operated by college students. The Wye Church, built in 1721, is also in use. Nearby stands the Wye Oak, the official state tree. It has provided shade for 450 years and is one of the tallest white oaks in the country.

EASTON – About 12 miles south of Wye Mills on rt. 50 is the self-proclaimed "Colonial Capital of the Eastern Shore." Easton is often swamped with envious Northerners, some of whom become so enchanted that they return to purchase old estates upon retirement. Easton has some fine local antiques, artwork, and artifacts. During the second week in November, Easton celebrates the Waterfowl Festival. Wildfowl artists and carvers from all over the East Coast participate in this major festival. Historic attractions in town include the Third Haven Meeting House, built in 1682, and the Talbot County Historical Society and Museum. (For information, contact Easton Chamber of Commerce, 301 822-4606; or the Tourism Council of the Upper Chesapeake, 301 758-2300.)

OXFORD – Take rt. 333 southwest from Easton, until you reach the end of land. Here, you can ride on the oldest "free running" ferry in the nation. The Oxford-Bellevue ferry shuttles back and forth across the Tred Avon River, offering a fine view of the enclosed port and this small boating community.

ST. MICHAELS – When you leave the ferry, take rt. 329 to rt. 33 northeast about 8 miles. St. Michaels is the home of an authentic 19th-century lighthouse and the Chesapeake Bay Maritime Museum, which contains maritime paraphernalia and old sailing vessels docked just outside the building. Narrated cruises of the Miles River can be taken from the museum aboard *The Patriot.* (For information, contact the Chesapeake Bay Maritime Museum; 301 745-2916.)

TILGHMAN ISLAND – Continue southwest on rt. 33 to its southern tip. Tilghman Island isn't an island, it's a point of land and home port for a portion of the Chesapeake Bay skipjack fleet, the last commercial sailing fleet in North America. The island is a haven for fishermen and boaters, and fishing boats and a skipjack are available for charter.

BLACKWATER NATIONAL WILDLIFE REFUGE – Returning to Easton, pick up rt. 50 south through Cambridge to rt. 16, and past Church Creek to rt 335, about 20 miles. The refuge contains the greatest variety and quantity of waterfowl in the US. There are driving tours, walking tours, and a visitors information center. (For information, call the Refuge at 301 228-2677).

CRISFIELD – About 55 miles southeast of Easton, the place to catch ferries to two excellent retreats, Smith and Tangier Islands. Three ships ferry passengers, mail, and freight to the islands where colonies of the Chesapeake Bay watermen live and work. Both Smith and Tangier Islands are flat, sandy, and surrounded by marshland. Smith Island, a miniature version of the mainland, has tiny frame houses with small gardens, wharves, crab shanties, and very little commercialism. You won't ever find a town hall here because there's no local government. Nearly everything is part of the United Methodist Church. Tangier Island is more developed, with a new anchorage for visiting sailors, a high school, and a local government headed by a mayor. (For more information, contact the Somerset County Tourism Commission at 301 651-2968).

BEST EN ROUTE

Tidewater Inn, Easton – Almost a legend, certainly a landmark. Activities in town center around this colonial inn, especially during Waterfowl Festival. The restaurant is famous for fish and other local produce; 120 rooms. Dover and Harrison Sts., Easton, MD 21601 (301 822-1300).

The Robert Morris Inn, Oxford – Located in the former home of a financier, the inn has been redecorated recently. Adjacent to Tred Avon River ferry. Close to tennis, golf, sailing, swimming, and bicycling. Dining room open to the public. PO Box 70, Oxford, MD 21654 (301 226-5111).

Mrs. Crockett's Chesapeake House, Tangier Island – Another secluded guest house close to nautical activities. Tangier Island is in Virginia waters. Tangier Island, VA 23440 (804 891-2331).

Mrs. Kitching's, Smith Island – A five-room guest house on remote Smith Island, near all water sports. Ewell, Smith Island, MD 21824 (301 425-3321).

The Berkshires, Massachusetts

Up and down the East Coast, the Berkshires are famous for art and music in the summer, foliage in the fall, and downhill and cross-country skiing in the winter. Nobody seems to be quite sure how it all began — whether vacationers began going to the Berkshires because of the excellence of the music and art; or whether artists and musicians began going because that's where the summer people went; or whether it's simply that everybody loves a vacation in the Berkshire Mountains — musicians, artists, and just plain folks included.

More correctly referred to as the Berkshire Hills (although you'll swear they look just like mountains when you see them), the area of Berkshire County fills the western quarter of the state, stretching from Connecticut to Vermont along the 50-mile border Massachusetts shares with New York. However, the Berkshires begin in earnest west of I-91, from Great Barrington in the south to the Mohawk Trail and Vermont in the north. Running straight through this area is rt. 7, connecting the major Berkshire towns (major in influence, not in size; only Pittsfield is a city of any size): Great Barrington, Stockbridge, Lenox, Pittsfield, Williamstown, and slightly to the east, North

Adams. Rt. 7 is a good road on which to start your trip, but remember the unique advantage of Berkshire geography: The outside boundaries of the Berkshires form an almost-perfect square, which in turn makes an almost-perfect driving route. Follow the square and you'll be able to take in all the significant cultural, educational, and historical activities that give the Berkshires its special cachet.

Summer is, of course, prime time for artistic offerings. From the world-famous Tanglewood Concerts and the Jacob's Pillow dance performances to the less well known theatrical offerings and the galleries presenting works of art and crafts, the Berkshire area is synonymous with both excellence and innovation in the arts.

A formidable rival to summer is the fall season, when the Berkshire Hills explode into color. The season starts in mid- or late September, but finding foliage at its colorful peak is about as chancy as finding perfect snow on a ski trip: You never know if nature will cooperate. Still, there are some general rules about when foliage will peak in a particular area. In late August, the harbingers stand out as solitary spots of gold or scarlet against the green hillsides. By mid-September, swamp maples are ablaze at the higher elevations and the northern part of the region. Most of the area, however, doesn't peak until October.

Snow always changes the face and appeal of a northern area — and the Berkshires are no exception. Mt. Greylock, highest peak in the state, provides a glorious setting for skiing and snowmobiling. For information on ski conditions, call toll-free 800 628-5030; 800 292-6633, in Massachusetts.

During the summer months there's so much going on that even old-timers have to consult newspaper listings to plan their cultural days. You'll find an exhaustive listing of them in local papers throughout the Berkshires, divided into areas, each providing a complete rundown on what's happening in any location. For advance information on the whole area, any season: Berkshire Hills Conference, 20 Elm St., Pittsfield, MA 01201 (413 443-9186). Request the booklet *Circle Tours,* which describes six trips through the Berkshires. The conference also has lists of golf and tennis courts. Information on the Mohawk Trail area: Northern Berkshire Chamber of Commerce, 69½ Main St., North Adams, MA 01247 (413 663-3735); and Mohawk Trail Association, Main St., Charlemont, MA 01339 (413 339-4962).

STOCKBRIDGE – This beautiful town is something of the archetypical Berkshire village, in part because it has appeared so often in that role in so many famous paintings by resident Norman Rockwell. Reproductions of its buildings and its people have graced the covers of *Saturday Evening Post* and *McCall's* dozens of times. You can see the originals of many famous covers ("The Four Freedoms," for example) at the Norman Rockwell Museum (Main St. and Elm St.; 413 298-3822), a lovingly preserved collection of Rockwell work. Just down the street is the marvelous Red Lion Inn, justly one of New England's most famous hostelries.

Two interesting stops: Chesterwood, the home of sculptor Daniel Chester French, and the Mission House. Chesterwood (two miles northwest of town; 413 298-3579) is maintained by the National Trust for Historic Preservation. You can visit the home, its gallery, and the gardens. Mission House (in town, Main and Sergeant Sts.; 413 298-3383) was built in 1739 by the Rev. John Sergeant, who preached to the Berkshire

Indians. (Relations were warm between Indians and white settlers. Today, about a mile out of town, stands a marker reading: "The Ancient Burial Place of the Stockbridge Indians, Friends of Our Fathers.") Today the house is a museum of early colonial life.

BECKET – Is the host-town for the oldest dance festival in America, Jacob's Pillow. For eight weeks in summer this occasion draws dance groups from all over the world; its own resident company performs as well. PO Box 227, Lee, MA 01283 (413 243-0745), for schedule and reservations.

LENOX – Is generally acknowledged as the star town of the Berkshires, probably because it is the summer home of the Boston Symphony Orchestra. Culture fairly hangs in the air. Every summer, the Tanglewood Concerts draw crowds of thousands each weekend. And there's more than one way to enjoy your music at Tanglewood: at the Music Shed you can join the throngs who lie about on blankets, picnicking, drinking, dreaming, and enjoying the symphony concerts; Chamber Music Hall offers more intimate programs to smaller audiences; Theater also presents chamber music programs. All these things — and more — take place on the 210-acre estate, Tanglewood, near where Nathaniel Hawthorne lived and wrote. The grounds are manicured to perfection. You can tour them and the Hemlock Gardens as well. For information on Tanglewood's schedule: Symphony Hall, 251 Huntington Ave., Boston, MA 02115 (617 266-1492), or from June, Festival Ticket Office, Lenox, MA 01240 (413 637-1940).

Nearby is the Pleasant Valley Wildlife Sanctuary (W Mount Rd.), maintained by the Massachusetts Audubon Society. Guided trails show you much of western Massachusetts nature, and a beaver colony as well. There are small jewel-like lakes at almost every turn in this part of the Berkshires. One of the nicest is Stockbridge Bowl (south off rt. 183).

PITTSFIELD – Offers as its main summer event the South Mountain Concerts, which feature opera, chamber music, and young people's concerts (call 443-6517 for schedules and information). Other attractions are not seasonal, and open all year. Hancock Shaker Village is an original Shaker community built around 1790. There's a round barn, restored homes and buildings, and many exhibits of Shaker life. It's located five miles west of town. The Berkshire Museum (39 South St.) houses an impressive collection of Old Masters, early American works, and some very modern works, as well as some natural history exhibits. If you loved *Moby Dick,* you'll want to visit Arrowhead (780 Holmes Rd.), Herman Melville's home from 1850 to 1863. The Berkshire Historical Society maintains this home with its Melville memorabilia, furniture, and period costumes.

WILLIAMSTOWN – Is the home of Williams College. There's also the Williamstown Theater Festival (Park and Main Sts.) and the Clark Art Institute (South St.), a jewel box of a museum presenting outstanding examples of French Impressionists, old silver, porcelains, and sculpture.

It is at Williamstown that you turn the "corner" of the Berkshire route and join the Mohawk Trail toward North Adams and Greenfield beyond. Before reaching North Adams, to the south nature provides some spectacular attractions here with the proximity of Mt. Greylock and its lookout tower; the Natural Bridge formation (scientists estimate that it's been around for about 55 million years!); and the Savoy Mountain State Forest and Mohawk Trail intersection, with a host of camping, picnicking, swimming, hunting, fishing, cabins for rent.

NORTH ADAMS – The Fall Foliage Festival is held in the last weeks of September to celebrate the coming of color with a no-holds-barred Oktoberfest blowout. A perfect time to visit. Contact the Northern Berkshire Chamber of Commerce (address above) for details.

BEST EN ROUTE

Below are our choices from a wide variety of eating and sleeping places. The Berkshires are home to some of the best inns in the country — truly an embarrassment of riches. We suggest you examine a couple of the inn books listed in the bibliography, GETTING READY TO GO. In the meantime, our choices:

The Red Lion Inn, Stockbridge – The atmosphere here is homey, friendly, and full of small-town charm. Inn dates back to 1773; some rooms are furnished in original antiques. Your bed may be a four-poster or a canopy. Rates are higher during summer weekends; winter, there are fewer rooms open. Restaurant serves three meals a day, noted for good, dependable, Yankee cuisine. Rt. 7, Stockbridge, MA 01262 (413 298-5545).

The Springs, New Ashford – Your hosts, the Grossos, have been feeding visitors for 50 years in informal, hearty style. Rt. 7, New Ashford, MA 01237 (413 458-3465).

Mill on the Floss, New Ashford – An 18th-century house is the setting. The food is Continental and good. Dinner only; closed Sundays. Rt. 7, New Ashford, MA 01237 (413 458-9123).

Le Jardin, Williamstown – Country inn combines gracious surroundings with fine French cuisine. Closed during November. 777 Cold Springs Rd., Williamstown, MA 01267 (413 458-8032).

The Restaurant, Lenox – Informal setting with very eclectic cuisine including vegetarian dishes, seafoods, duckling. Interesting wine list. Dinners from $4.50. 15 Franklin St., Lenox, MA 01240 (413 637-9894).

The Stockpot – Though the service is on the leisurely side, the food here is worth waiting for, particularly the breakfast casserole (ham, cheese, and eggs), the quiches, and the homemade desserts. Try the chess pie (pecans and raisins topped with whipped cream) or the sour cream coffee cake. You can buy some of Stockpot's comestibles in *The Back Burner,* a little shop behind the restaurant. On Pine St., Stockbridge, MA 01262 (413 298-3592).

Cape Cod, Martha's Vineyard, and Nantucket, Massachusetts

If you look imaginatively at a map of Massachusetts, Cape Cod takes on the shape of a squat foot — wrapped in an elfish slipper that rises and curls at the toes — taking a step into the Atlantic. The cape is 70 miles long, from Buzzards Bay where it leaves the mainland of southern Massachusetts to the tip of its toe at Provincetown. It juts at least 30 miles into the Atlantic, far enough to be washed by the warmer waters of the Gulf Stream; consequently, the cape has cooler summers and milder winters than the mainland.

Below it, accessible by ferry, are the two most famous islands in America: Martha's Vineyard and Nantucket, where the homes and villages of America's 19th-century seafaring community are still intact and still inhabited.

What is special about the cape and the islands has everything to do with the sea. It is the sea that provides the sailing, swimming, and beaches so attractive in summer. (Cape Cod has 300 miles of beaches — almost all clean and beautiful — and two kinds of water: on its northern, protected shore, waters are calm and warmer; southern and eastern beaches, facing the open Atlantic, are cold, with high, exciting waves.) It is the sea that is responsible for its history. The Pilgrims landed at Provincetown about a month before they went ashore the mainland at Plymouth; and its beautiful, perfectly preserved 19th-century homes and villages are products of the area's successful ventures into worldwide shipping 150 years ago. (There was a time when Nantucket captains were as likely to meet one another in the Banda Islands as on the streets they shared as neighbors at home.) And it is the sea — and the sand it torments — that makes Cape Cod one of the most interesting ecological studies a layman is likely to stumble across.

That's the good news. The bad news is, of course, that nasty commercialism has corrupted much of this tranquillity — filling up the open spaces with fast-food chains, assaulting the eyes and ears of the beholder with a concrete barrage. But only in some places! Yankee foresight blew the whistle on galloping commercialism some years ago. Two specific areas of the cape are protected by law from 20th-century excesses: the 28,000-acre Cape Cod National Seashore, with its 35-mile stretch of untamed shoreline; and old rt. 6A leading along the north coast of the cape to the seashore. Here you'll be able to discover villages with their heritage intact. Village elders must give their okay for so much as a shingle to be changed. And consequently, very few changes take place.

For a look at what might have happened without these protective laws, take a drive along rt. 28 (along the south shore), which is up to its neon in the 20th century. Nothing has escaped modernization here. Rt. 28 is bordered on both sides with drive-ins, stores, and restaurants with "klever" names like "Leaning Tower of Pizza."

And so the formula for sightseeing on Cape Cod can be shaped according to your personal preference: If you're looking for up-to-the-minute action, follow rt. 28; if you seek peace and a sense of history, take rt. 6A; and if you're in a rush to get to Provincetown, take I-6, which bisects the cape.

In order to see both Cape Cod *and* the neighboring Martha's Vineyard and Nantucket Island, it makes sense to sweep the northern shore up to Provincetown (rt. 6A), and return via the outer shore along the southern coast as far as Hyannis Port (rt. 28). Here pick up the ferry for the two offshore islands and later return to the cape at Woods Hole. (You could fly, but the ferry is preferable if you've got the time.)

One further caveat: Everybody loves Cape Cod. In peak season the whole area fairly groans under the weight of all its adoring visitors (Provincetown leaps from a population of 5,000 to 55,000 in summer). Places are crowded, and the natives can be cranky and out-of-sorts. If you can time your vacation for either spring or late fall, you'll be able to see much more nature. And you'll be able to find some local folks with time to sit and chat. However, if you want crowds, excitement, and big names, July and August are your time.

SANDWICH – Is the first town along rt. 6A, and it is rewardingly historic. The Sandwich Glass Museum (rt. 130) exhibits remarkable examples of this town's famous glass. The First Church of Christ (1848) features a spire that was copied from a design by

England's Christopher Wren. Everything Americana from antique cars to a Civil War gristmill can be seen at the Heritage Barn Plantation (rt. 6A, Grove and Pine Sts.). And children will be delighted with the Yesteryears Doll Museum (River and Main Sts.).

YARMOUTH PORT – Is notable for three restored original houses: Capt. Bangs Hallet House (18th century) on Strawberry La.; Col. John Thatcher House (1680) on rt. 6A; and Winslow Crocker House (1780), also on 6A.

"THE DENNISES" – Consist of four towns: Port, South, East, and West Dennis. Together they offer a combination of old and new: historical houses to tour, and June through Labor Day, current theater offerings at the Cape Playhouse (on rt. 6A, 385-3911 for schedule and reservations). The Dennis Pines Golf Course, in East Dennis, features an 18-hole course (385-3166 for information).

BREWSTER – Has two interesting museums: Drummer Boy (two miles west), a 35-acre site with American Revolution scenes; and the Cape Cod Museum of Natural History (Main St.) with live animals and marine exhibits. Sealand of Cape Cod (three miles on 6A in West Brewster) offers marineland shows and a penguin rookery.

EASTHAM – Is the gateway town to the Cape Cod National Seashore. In addition, the town's Historical Society maintains several restored homes for touring. It is just off rt. 6 in an 1869 schoolhouse, with exhibits.

CAPE COD NATIONAL SEASHORE – Cape Cod is a peninsula without bedrock — it is all sand. Before white men came here in any numbers, the cape had stands of hardwood and topsoil, which protected the Atlantic shoreline from the sea's fury. When the hardwood went, the sea and the wind played havoc with the sand — shores around Truro and Wellfleet were eaten away, the same sand was deposited along the moors surrounding Provincetown. The Cape Cod National Seashore came into being in 1961 after years of appalling disregard almost put an end to this 28,000-acre chunk of the cape. It now runs from Eastham to Provincetown, and includes six towns, much private property, and four public areas. No camping is allowed, except in privately owned campgrounds. There are four picnic areas. From June through Labor Day the National Park Service conducts guided tours and evening lectures. There are many self-guided trails and interpretive shelters. For more information: the Superintendent, Cape Cod National Seashore, South Wellfleet, MA 02663 (617 349-3785). Visitor's Center at Race Rd., Provincetown, MA 02657 (487-1256).

WELLFLEET – Has numerous beaches for swimming, and a wealth of inland freshwater ponds. Fishing and sailing are also well provided for here — the town marina can accommodate 150 boats. Wellfleet Bay Wildlife Sanctuary runs a summer day camp for kids with the emphasis on natural history appreciation. The Audubon Society of Massachusetts sponsors the sanctuary and maintains its many self-guided nature trails.

PROVINCETOWN – Is the name most familiar to first-timers on the cape. It attracts artists and celebrities, has a large homosexual summer community, and is exceedingly liberal and easy-going — in rather startling contrast to the town's early history as the first landing site of the Pilgrims.

In 1899 Charles Hawthorne established the Cape Cod School of Art in Provincetown, and its reputation as an art center was established. Several leading artists summer here (including Robert Motherwell), and the town's long Commercial Street has at least a dozen good galleries, side by side with museums (Provincetown Museum adjoining the Pilgrim Monument overlooking the city, the Heritage Museum, and the city's oldest house at 27 Commercial St.). The Provincetown Playhouse on the Wharf gained national recognition for its excellence and innovation in theater. Unfortunately, a tragic fire in 1976 destroyed the theater as well as the Eugene O'Neill Theater Museum.

To return via the south shore (rt. 28) you must backtrack for a period of time. An interesting stop, which you would have passed on your way to Provincetown, is Truro.

TRURO – May be a welcome change from Provincetown's hustle and commotion. Sparsely settled, Truro is known for the excellence of its fishing and swimming, and for the Highland Light, which dates back to 1795 and can be seen 20 miles out to sea.

Less publicized is the locally known fact that a large part of Truro's summer population is comprised of New York City psychiatrists on vacation.

CHATHAM – Is one of the many towns on the cape with a working gristmill that offers for sale the corn you can see being ground into meal. This one dates back to 1797 (Shattuck Pl. off Cross St.).

HYANNIS – Has become synonymous with the Kennedy family, but long before the clan and its "compound," Hyannis drew its share of visitors because of its marvelous swimming beaches. There's an annual Antiques Fair held in July (National Guard armory) and musical theater-in-the-round is held in the Melody Tent (W Main St., 775-9100 for schedule and prices). Hyannis is also port city for the ferry services to the islands. There are day trips for sightseeing, as well as auto ferry service. You must reserve well in advance for space on the ferries, by calling 540-2022 locally, or the toll-free numbers, 1-800-352-7104 within Massachusetts or 800-225-3122 from anywhere in the Northeast. In summer you should make ferry reservations by mail: Woods Hole, Martha's Vineyard and Nantucket Steamship Authority, PO Box 284, Woods Hole, MA 02543.

NANTUCKET – Lies 30 miles south of Cape Cod. It is not by chance that both Captain Ahab and First Mate Starbuck of the ill-fated *Pequod* were Nantucket men. Nothing could have seemed more likely to Melville's readers, and besides, one Captain George Pollard of Nantucket did lose a ship to an enraged sperm whale. Nantucket was once the whaling capital of the world, and you know it the instant the ferry gets within sight of Nantucket town. Main Street is lined with elegant 19th-century homes (many open for viewing); the Whaling Museum offers a whaling boat among other exhibits.

The island is only 49 square miles and can boast 50 miles of sand-dune-protected beaches. The Gulf Stream hovers offshore, warming the waters to an amazing 70° much of the summer. There are eight beaches, most with lifeguards, bathhouses, and food facilities. Sailing enthusiasts can rent all sizes of boats. Bicycle lanes coexist peacefully with roads for cars.

MARTHA'S VINEYARD – Is connected by the ferry system. It's five miles by sea from Cape Cod. If you've ever heard that New Englanders are feisty and independent, consider the latest goings-on on Martha's Vineyard. In 1977, the state legislature decided to take away the island's individual representation, incorporating it into a single district with Cape Cod. Natives of the island didn't take too kindly to this, and they formed a group to push for secession. They received offers from states in the US for annexation — including Hawaii. A compromise has been worked out so you won't have to say you've been to Martha's Vineyard, Hawaii!

A sprawling 10 miles wide and 20 miles long, this island requires that you have some wheels to see all there is. You can rent cars, bikes, or mopeds. Shuttle buses scurry between the main resort towns, and taxis and tour buses are available.

The primary resort towns are: Vineyard Haven, shopping center for the entire island; Gay Head, famous for its multicolored clay cliffs looming above the ocean; Oak Bluff; Menemsha; and Edgartown.

Edgartown is the oldest settlement on the island, a fact well documented by the Dukes Historical Society Museum (School and Cooke Sts.). Built in 1765, there are some marvelous examples of colonial architecture here, a Jacobean fireplace, and seven open fireplaces. The return to the mainland is done by ferry (remember to reserve!), this time arriving at Woods Hole on Cape Cod.

MASHPEE Route 28A leads northward and back to mainland Massachusetts. But before leaving Cape Cod, detour inland to Mashpee, which is in the heart of the cape and in the heart of cranberry country. Descendants of the Mashpee Indians still gather cranberries from the many bogs. There's also the Wampanoag Indian Museum (rt. 130), with a diorama and exhibits of Indian lore; the Old Indian Meeting House (1648); and the Mashpee burial grounds (rt. 28, south of town).

BEST EN ROUTE

Old Yarmouth Inn, Yarmouth Port – Open all year. The oldest place (1676) on the cape, you won't find the inn advertised anywhere. They don't need to — their delighted clientele does it for them. It's good for rooms and meals — 14 rooms in all, each with private bath. Food is, happily, mainly seafood caught locally, vegetables are similarly fresh. The restaurant is closed on Mondays, Tuesdays, and Wednesdays off-season. Old King's Highway, Yarmouth Port, MA 02675 (617 362-3191).

Jared Coffin House, Nantucket Island – Open all year. Numerous celebrities have stayed here, beginning in 1821 when it was built. Now historically restored, the hotel offers old-hotel elegance to its guests — 49 rooms; formal dining room complete with piano during evening meals. During December (21st through New Year's Day) a gala "Twelve Days of Christmas" celebration keeps things running in high gear on this now year-round island. 29 Broad St., Nantucket, MA 02554 (617 228-2400).

White Mountains, New Hampshire

There's a pleasant, comfortable feeling about the White Mountains, similar to the pleasing quality of a George Gershwin tune. As you drive along roads that wind through deep, tree-lined gorges and sparkling clear mountain brooks, breathing the clean, fresh smell of pine everywhere, you get an inescapable sense that "all's right with the world."

Smack in the center of the state, the White Mountains offer New Hampshire countryside at its best. Some 140 miles north of Boston on I-93 (which is the only interstate through the area), our route starts at Plymouth and wanders through some of the best sightseeing and skiing land in the state.

PLYMOUTH – As you approach the White Mountain National Forest, 1,600 square miles of one of the oldest mountain ranges in the Appalachian chain, you might want to take a brief detour onto rt. 25 at Plymouth, about 60 miles north of Manchester, for a quick look at the Polar Caves. As the name implies, Polar Caves are reminders of the great glaciers that passed this way around 50,000 years ago, then retreated to the north. The Hanging Boulder, an 80-ton rock that seems to hang in midair, has been suspended that way for countless thousands of years; it isn't likely to fall on your head. You can also catch a glimpse of some of the glacial ice left behind during the great retreat. It's still sticking to the cavern floor.

WHITE MOUNTAIN NATIONAL FOREST – As you return the eight miles to I-93, you'll pass the southern boundary of the national forest. There are 18 campgrounds here; Pinkham Notch is the headquarters of the Appalachian Mountain Club Huts System (for information and reservations, call 466-2727). If you're passing through during the fall, you'll be overwhelmed by the foliage, reds and oranges fanning out in all directions like spectacular flames, and you might wonder why they're called the White Mountains. If you stop to look, you'll be able to see the slender, white birch trunks for which these mountains are named. In summer, the subtle green leaves of the white birch ripple with those of the brown sugar maple, giving the mountains an unforgettable depth and richness. Since the White Mountains are older than the Rockies, geological forces have had more time to smooth them into rounded formations.

Information: White Mountain National Forest, PO Box 638, Laconia, NH 03246 (603 524-6450).

THE FLUME – The road narrows to become rt. 3 just before you reach the Flume. The Flume is a narrow natural gorge flanked on both sides by 70- to 90-foot-high granite walls, and set in the fir, spruce, and birch forest of Franconia Notch State Park. Intertwined along the cliffs is an intricate set of catwalks that allows you to get several unusual perspectives of the Flume Brook and its waterfall.

THE OLD MAN OF THE MOUNTAINS – As you leave the Flume, driving slowly, take in the view of Mt. Liberty. Just three miles to the north, you'll see the Old Man of the Mountains, a magnificent, craggy, Lincolnesque profile carved naturally into the side of a mountain. This is New Hampshire's most famous landmark, and is often used as a symbol of the state. Skiers are no doubt more familiar with this part of the world as the site of the Cannon Mountain Aerial Tramway and Mittersill Ski Area.

FRANCONIA NOTCH – Known as "the Switzerland of America," Franconia Notch is located between the Kinsman and Franconia ranges of mountains and is traversed by rt. 3. The Old Man of the Mountains is on the east side of the notch. The southern flank of the Presidential Range stretches across the horizon, sedate as those grand men of history for whom they are named. Mount Lincoln and Mount Lafayette are the closest to Franconia, but as you proceed northeast on rt. 3, you'll pass Mount Cleveland; then, the approach to Mount Washington, the tallest of the Presidentials. Jefferson, Adams, and Madison stand to the north; Monroe, Franklin, Eisenhower, Clinton, Jackson, and Webster to the south.

MOUNT WASHINGTON – Ascending this mountain is an adventure whether you climb, take the cog railway, a chauffeured car, or drive yourself. All of these dramatic, rugged paths lead to the rocky summit at 6,288 feet. That might not sound high to you, and certainly it's not by Rocky Mountain standards, but Mount Washington is the tallest peak in the Northeast. Unless you're an expert climber, we recommend going up in a vehicle. Mount Washington is known as "Misery Mountain" because of its foul weather. There's the chance of snow no matter when you go, and the average temperature for the year never climbs above 30°. Even if you drive in mid-August, when the neighboring valleys are in the humid 80s, you'll need a heavy sweater before you get to the top of Mount Washington. If you're climbing, be sure to check weather conditions before setting out. It has taken the lives of 43 people in the past 80 years, and although there are lodges on the mountain slopes to accommodate expeditions, there are some very slippery, dangerous spots along the way. If driving your own car, make sure you stop frequently while descending to let your brakes cool off. The road is so steep that it is possible to burn the lining from brake drums before reaching the bottom. If you don't want to risk it, take the Cog Railway. It's been going since 1869, and it's a safe way to reach the stark, windswept mountain peak.

CRAWFORD NOTCH – Another good vantage point for gazing at the Presidentials. Crawford Notch State Park has camping, fishing, hiking, and picnicking facilities (in Bartlett on rt. 302, 374-2272). Traveling southeast on rt. 302, you'll pass Attitash Ski Area, Alpine Slide (a 4,000-foot-long ride down a mountain), and Mount Cranmore Ski Area.

NORTH CONWAY – About 20 miles south of Crawford Notch you can ride up a mountain on a skimobile (call 356-5544 for information). There's also a restored Victorian railway in town.

KANCAMAGUS HIGHWAY – North Conway and Conway have grown into resort towns of pinewood shopping centers and motels. If it seems overdeveloped for your taste, we suggest heading west on rt. 112, known as the Kancamagus Highway. This is one of the most glorious drives anywhere in the United States, and goes into the deep recess between the Presidential Mountains, to give a closer look at what you've already seen from a distance, returning you to I-93 45 miles later.

BEST EN ROUTE

Dana Place Inn, Jackson – A 12-room hotel, with swimming pool and river swimming, tennis courts, fishing, close to cross-country and downhill skiing and golf. Pinkham Notch Rd., Jackson, NH 03846 (603 383-6822).

Lovett's by Lafayette Brook, Franconia – Guest house and cabins, some with fireplaces in living rooms, a swimming pool, pond, and cross-country skiing. Close to golf, tennis, and fishing. Personal service and excellent cooking. 32 rooms. Profile Rd., Franconia, NH 03580 (603 823-7761).

The Jersey Shore: Atlantic City to Cape May, New Jersey

There are good beaches all along the intercoastal waterway of New Jersey's Atlantic Ocean shoreline, but the most famous section of all is the 50-mile stretch of wide, beautiful seashore and gentle surf that begins just south of Atlantic City and ends at Cape May Point. It has some of the best beaches on the Eastern Seaboard and an unusual geographic conformation that makes for fabulous fishing: The oceanfront land is actually a series of narrow islands that run parallel to the mainland, with a tidal bay in between. Fishermen can choose deep-sea fishing or the calmer waters of the protected bays.

This section of the Jersey shore was *the* place to summer in the late 1800s. Anyone who was anyone went to the seashore somewhere along the Jersey Shore (locally it's never referred to as "the New Jersey shore"). This popularity — exemplified by Atlantic City, made famous in the Depression game of Monopoly — ultimately led to overexposure and a recession; since WW II, as successive waves of "beautiful people" flocked first to Florida and then to European and Caribbean beaches rather than prosaic New Jersey, the major resorts suffered severe setbacks.

In desperate attempts to lure tourists back, many of these towns began casting about for other means of creating excitement — amusement parks, convention facilities, special activities. This is good news and bad news for the contemporary visitor. Good news because it makes the shore — with its quiet surf and wide beaches — a great place to take small children (when the beach scene gets tiring, you can head for boardwalk and pier entertainments); bad news because amidst the hurly-burly you might just overlook the very best aspect of some shore towns — the lovely Victorian and Edwardian houses which hide in streets behind the gaudy boardwalks.

These islands and mainland communities form what is called the Jersey Cape. The islands themselves are connected by Ocean Drive — actually a series of bridges designed as a scenic, efficient beltway for traffic up and down the Cape. The towns along Ocean Drive stir the memory of anyone raised on the East Coast — Atlantic City, Ventnor City, Margate City, Strathmore, Sea Island City, Avalon, Stone Harbor, Wildwood, Cape May. A stop at any one of them will prove entertaining, but the high points are certainly Atlantic City, America's newest gambling center; Wildwood; and beautiful Victorian

Cape May. Information: Atlantic City Visitors' Bureau, Convention Hall, Atlantic City, NJ 08401 (609 348-7044); Wildwood Public Relations Department, PO Box 609, Wildwood, NJ 08260 (609 522-1407); Cape May County Chamber of Commerce, PO Box 74, Cape May Courthouse, Cape May, NJ 08280 (609 465-7181).

ATLANTIC CITY – On November 2, 1976, New Jersey legalized casino gambling, and Atlantic City slammed into high gear to become Las Vegas' East Coast competition. Bets are still out on just how the current wheeling and dealing for real estate will change Atlantic City, but the effect is bound to be dramatic, and, backers hope, lucrative. Nonetheless, Atlantic City is the only spot in the eastern two-thirds of the country in which Americans can legally gamble in a casino. The first casino to open was the lavish Resorts International at North Carolina and Boardwalk, followed in 1979 by the new Caesar's Boardwalk Regency at Arkansas and Boardwalk, and Bally's Park Palace Hotel and Casino. More are sure to follow. For a while yet, it will be possible to enjoy remnants of the old Atlantic City — the world-famous boardwalk, all eight miles of it; the piers, teeming with amusement centers; the famous wicker rolling chairs, once the height of luxury for anyone wishing to take in the sights and the salt air; the tram, which snakes along between the hotels and Convention Hall; the Miss America pageant and of course, the saltwater taffy.

WILDWOOD – Strikes something of a balance between the quieter pleasures of a visit to Cape May, and the ritz, swank, and swizzle of Atlantic City. Wildwood has a fine, wide beach, an appropriately lively boardwalk, with six amusement piers, and a reputation for good after-dark entertainment, offered by a varied array of nightclubs with comedians and singers, jazz bands and Dixieland groups, etc.

CAPE MAY – Where the clocks all stopped somewhere toward the end of the 19th century — and that suits the townfolk just fine. That particular time warp has proved to be a gold mine in tourist trade. The determined and dogged theme of this town is Victoriana. There are so many original and preserved Victorian wood-frame buildings still in mint condition that Cape May has been declared a national landmark. Attempts at modernization are squashed as quickly as possible. (A recent one involved the city's 139 gaslights, which conservationists claim are a waste of energy, urging conversion to electricity. But the locals know well that authenticity is essential to tourism. And, since tourism is the major source of income for Cape May, the outcome was inevitable.)

Indeed authenticity is lovingly protected in this town. Its 600 Victorian buildings stand busily side by side, each resplendent in its gingerbread excesses, scalloped widow's walks traced along scalloped rooftops, columned verandas bedecked with latticework trims; even the gardens seem just right for a nosegay framed with a lace doily.

Visitors can choose from a number of ways of enjoying this old-fashioned community. There's a historic walking tour four days a week. It lasts about an hour and a quarter, leaving from the information booth at Washington and Ocean Streets. A horse-drawn tourist trolley covers a similar route, offering sightseers a 25¢ Victorian tour for the slightly inflated 20th-century price of $1.50. There's a Victorian pedestrian mall which offers a delightful alternative to the shopping malls we have come to love and hate out in suburbia; and even a Victorian bandstand where concerts are presented weekly, a free offering by the community. At Convention Hall visitors are treated to an almost continuous flow of entertainment ranging from free ballroom dancing, teen discos (a $1.75 charge for this), and concerts, to antique shows, kiddie cartoon shows, and so on. Consult the calendar of events posted at the information office just outside the hall on Beach Drive at the boardwalk.

But for pure self-indulgence and excess you just can't beat the experience of living in one of these authentic Victorian mansions-turned-guest house during your stay in town. A Victorian guest house might well feature afternoon tea served on the veranda, or an antique fourposter bed in your room, or a tour of the house, but it most definitely will not include any 20th-century trappings.

Probably the most famous of these guest houses is the Mainstay Inn, known locally as the Victorian Mansion. Authenticity is fiercely maintained by the present owners, a young couple who delight in sharing their wealth of Victoriana with interested visitors. This house-with-a-past was built in 1856 as an Italian villa and has gone through some fascinating changes. Your room might be one of the "front rooms" which means you'll luxuriate in 12-foot ceilings and a splendid view. Or you might choose one in the "new wing" that was built in 1896 to accommodate the six house maids.

For those who prefer the out-of-doors to Victorian parlors, there's nearby Cold Springs Campground. Here on 25 acres there are 100 campsites which include the usual facilities, plus general activities centers.

At the very tip of the cape is the Cape May Point State Park. Although there is no swimming allowed here due to the insidious currents, called "Cape May rips," visitors love to search the beach for "diamonds" — bits of wave-polished quartz that shine brilliantly in the sand. There's also a nearby bird sanctuary and lighthouse.

Also at the tip of the cape is the Cape May–Lewes, Delaware, ferry. Passengers may embark here for the 70-mile ride to Delaware. Make advance reservations by writing PO Box 827, N Cape May, NJ 08204 (609 886-2718).

BEST EN ROUTE

The Mainstay Inn, Cape May – Built in 1872, with original furnishings, a grand dining room, and veranda. A few blocks from the ocean. Rates include a Continental breakfast on the porch in summer; and full breakfast in the house during winter months. Closed December through March. 635 Columbia Ave., Cape May, NJ 08204 (609 884-8690).

Seventh Sister Guest House, Cape May – A seven-room inn built in the late 1800s. Most rooms have an ocean view, and the house has a comfortable porch facing the sea. Baths are shared. 10 Jackson St., Cape May, NJ 08204 (609 884-2280).

Windward House, Cape May – A shingled cottage in the heart of the historic district with seven rooms. 24 Jackson St., Cape May, NJ 08204 (609 884-3368).

Resorts International Hotel Casino, Atlantic City – This hotel has a wide variety of restaurants and bars, and of course, they all surround a gambling casino. The Superstar Theater features top-name entertainment. There are seven fine restaurants, including a 24-hour buffet. Some of the 756 rooms and suites have ocean views. Expensive, but packages available. N Carolina and Boardwalk, Atlantic City, NJ 08404 (609 344-6006).

Adirondack Park and Mountains, New York

For some people the ideal vacation is a complete return to nature. They seek out rugged wilderness locations, and gently ease their "civilized" bodies into the comforting rhythms of nature. The Adirondack Parkland offers almost unlimited challenges and opportunities for this sort of communion with the elements. There are over five million acres in this area, nearly all protected by law from the "modern improvements" of man. There are mountains; more lakes than you can count, several of them very famous (Saranac Lake, Lake George, Lake Placid); many campsites tucked away in the miles of forests; and the old Indian Canoe Route.

The Adirondack Park and Mountains encompass just under 9,000 square miles, just about filling the entire northeastern section of New York state, from Lake Champlain and the Vermont border to as far south as Glens Falls. The area is popular year-round; in winter, for skiing and snow sports (Lake Placid was the site of the 1980 Winter Olympics); in summer for its lakes, forests, and fishing; in autumn for the spectacular foliage of its wooded mountains. It's an especially attractive vacation area because among the isolated fields, lakes, and mountains of the interlaced parklands are cities of reasonable size, which can be visited — or avoided — as you choose.

The deliberate underdevelopment of the Adirondack Parkland is the very foundation of its charm and appeal. However, roads are few and they don't always lend themselves to a straight route, especially if you really want to get a sense of the scope of the area. However, with some backtracking and patience you can circle the entire parkland in a few days, allowing plenty of flexibility for stopping, looking, enjoying, and relaxing.

The Adirondack Mountains are about 4 hours from New York. Our route starts at Lake George and goes in a counterclockwise loop through the area; along the way you will have ample opportunities for exploring on your own. For information: Division of Tourism, Department of Commerce, 99 Washington Ave., Albany, NY 12245 (518 474-4116).

LAKE GEORGE VILLAGE – Is the most populous (30,000 accommodations for tourists) and most commercial town in the area. The lake itself is a 32-mile jewel set comfortably at the base of some very impressive mountains. There are dozens and dozens of state-owned islands in the lake. Lake George Village is an active, exciting place, with some of the drawbacks of a tourist center. The natural pleasures of swimming, boating, and fishing have almost been superseded by more profitable ventures like Storytown USA (five miles south on rt. 9), a theme park with six fairy-tale areas.

The entire Adirondack area is a mine of early American history, especially for the French and Indian War period. Lake George is no exception. Fort William Henry (Canada St.) is a reconstructed fort, with interesting displays. You will be shown a 45-minute edited version of "The Last of the Mohicans" as part of the tour of this 200-year-old fort. An impressive number of relics from the French and Indian War are on display.

Explore the scenic beauty of Lake George on one of the cruise vessels operated by the Lake George Steamboat Co. (Steel Pier and Beach Rd.). There are twilight cruises, long and short versions as well, aboard powerboats or the paddlewheel *Minne-Ha-Ha* (668-5777 for specific times and departures). An eagle's-eye view of the area is yours for the driving. Take rt. 9 a half mile south to Prospect Mountain State Parkway. At the end of the spectacular five-mile climb, you transfer to the free view-mobile for the final ascent to Prospect's peak.

BLUE MOUNTAIN LAKE – Is west on rt. 28 from Lake George. In addition to the glorious scenery you'll also find the Adirondack Lake Center for the Arts (located in the village) with an art gallery, concerts, films, and exhibits. The Adirondack Museum (one mile north on rt. 30) offers a 20-building display of a wealth of historical treasures (mostly on the history of the area). Nearby Blue Mountain has nature trails and some overlooks at its peak.

Rt. 30 north will take you past Long Lake. Tupper Lake lies just north. The attraction is Big Tupper Mountain with its excellent skiing facilities including a chair lift (which operates in summer for sightseeing), T-bar, beginners' lift, and various snack bars. There is golfing, boating, swimming, and camping all around the lake.

SARANAC LAKE – World famous as a health resort, Saranac spas have been visited by a host of celebrities (including Robert Louis Stevenson, whose cottage is open to the public) and a lot more just plain folks. This area, too, is versatile as a winter and summer sports resort. There are boat races, art exhibits, and concerts. The Dickert Memorial Wildlife Collection (housed in the Saranac Lake Free Library, 100 Main St.) has some marvelous mounted specimens of local wildlife. In winter, Mt. Pisgah ski center — at the end of the village — has a ski lift.

LAKE PLACID – Is the largest town in the Adirondacks. Synonymous with the 1932 and 1980 Winter Olympics, the sports facilities are superior here. At the Olympic Arena and Convention Hall (Main St.) you can enjoy winter and summer skating as well as ice shows, concerts, and other performances. On the famous Mt. Van Hoevenberg Bobsled Run (seven miles southeast on rt. 73) you can skim down the run in an Olympic-type bobsled for $5. During winter months there are afternoon races (December to March). It's also a good cross-country ski area.

Not to overlook the fine arts, the Center for Music, Drama, and Art (Saranac Ave. at Fawn Ridge) offers concerts, performances by the repertory company, and art exhibits (523-2512 for specific information).

John Brown's Farm Historical Site (John Brown Rd. off rt. 73) gives you a glimpse into the famous abolitionist's life — his furnishings, his home, and his gravesite.

Lake Placid, too, has a variety of cruises around the lake. Trips leave from Holiday Harbor (north on rt. 86 to Mirror Lake Drive; 523-3301 for complete information).

AUSABLE CHASM – A scenic wonder on rt. 9 north not to be missed. There are any number of ways to view this incredible gorge which slashes from 100 to 200 feet deep along its route. Footbridges cross its 20-to-50-foot width. You can take a self-guided walking tour and see the quaintly named rock formations: "pulpit rock," "elephant's head," "cathedral rock." May to September, you can also take a guided boat ride down a natural flume through the rapids. (Just to settle any arguments, it's pronounced: "Oh-SAY-bl.")

FORT TICONDEROGA – Played a strategic part in our nation's history. Originally built in 1675 by the French, it changed hands in its active life about a dozen times, was burned, and almost destroyed. Now restored according to the original French plans, it houses a museum with many original weapons, uniforms, and other war trappings. Live fife-and-drum performances and cannon firings add realistic touches.

Although there is much to do in Adirondack towns, there is much more to do in the Adirondack countryside, and chances are you're here to camp, fish, swim, and hike. Below, a list of some of the campgrounds in the area with telephone numbers for more information and reservations. For complete information: Division of Tourism, Department of Commerce, 99 Washington Ave., Albany, NY 12245 (518 474-4116).

Lewey Lake at Indian Lake (209 sites). Climb Snowy and Blue Ridge Mts., fish, swim, canoe, hike (518 648-5266).

Moffit Beach at Speculator (257 sites). Camp on Sacandaga Lake. Swim, fish, hike, canoe (518 548-7102).

Luzerne at Lake Luzerne (165 sites). Nearby dude ranch provides mounts, trails, Friday night rodeos. Swim, hike (518 696-2031).

Lake George Islands at Glen Island (398 sites). Register at Glen, boat to any of 55 islands. Sites all have fireplace, tent platform, semiprivate dock. Four different boat launching sites. Swim, hike, fish, canoe (518 644-9684).

Rogers Rock at Hague (304 sites). Supervised hikes up the 1,000-foot Rogers Rock. View over Lake George. Swim, fish, hike, canoe (518 585-6746).

Putnam Pond at Ticonderoga (56 sites). Miles of trails branch out from here to forest ponds and lakes (518 585-7280).

Cranberry Lake at Cranberry Lake (173 sites). Over 50 miles of wilderness trails, some with rustic lean-tos. 20 miles of Oswegatchie Inlet for boaters. Swim, fish, hike, canoe (315 848-3614).

Ausable Point at Peru (121 sites). Remote area, near rapids. Swim, fish, canoe (518 561-7080).

Higley Flow at Colton (143 sites). Administered by the state Parks and Recreation Department. Excellent fishing, swim in Raquette River (315 265-2010).

BEST EN ROUTE

The Lodge, Lake Clear – German food in rustic and woodsy surroundings. The lodge itself is pure old-Adirondack in style with mounted moose heads hung on the walls. The menu is fixed and served family style — and everyone gets to know everyone else over a hearty meal. Reservations are a must for dinner and for the few available rooms. The Lodge on Lake Clear, Lake Clear, NY 12945 (518 891-1489).

The Saranac, Saranac – A learning laboratory for students of hotel administration at nearby Paul Smith College. Here, if you have a complaint, you have a vast army of folks to hear you out. 101 Main St., Saranac Lake, NY 12983 (518 891-2200).

Hudson River Valley, New York

Rip Van Winkle slept here. So did George Washington. And you can, too, in any number of charming inns and hotels as you explore the magnificent Hudson River and the valley which surrounds it. There is so much scenic beauty, so many historical reference points, and so many downright fascinating bits of folklore that you will find yourself totally caught up in the charm and mystery of this area.

Our route follows the east and west banks of the Hudson from New York City to Rip Van Winkle Bridge about 20 miles south of Albany. This is the entry point to the Catskill Mountain area to the west, and the Adirondacks to the north. At the bridge, our itinerary crosses from the east to the west bank, and returns toward New York City. For a comprehensive, mile-by-mile guide to this route, see *The Hudson River Tourway* by Gilbert Tauber (Doubleday Dolphin Books, $4.95).

If for no other reason, this is a compelling route for the sheer beauty of the Hudson. In its 315 mile course from the Adirondacks to the sea, the Hudson changes style from a shimmering, three-mile-wide expanse (called Tappan Zee by the early Dutch — zee being Dutch for sea) to a sinuous serpent squeezed by the towering Palisades downriver nearer New York City. To see the river reflect the setting sun is one of the enchantments of New York life.

Throughout local history men have compared the Hudson to Germany's Rhine. And men of great wealth, seeking to exploit the similarities, have built palatial estates along its banks. Lacking any definable style, these pseudo-villas and châteaux have been lumped together into the tongue-in-cheek category of "Hudson Valley Gothic." Many of these mansions are open to the public and are well worth a look.

British and American forces fought for this area inch by inch during the Revolutionary War. The Hudson was the key to holding the great northern territories beyond, and the towns up and down the valley hosted in turn patriots and King's men.

And finally, less tangible, but very real, is the air of folklore and mystery — the delicious shiver of the supernatural — that cloaks the high mountains and heavily forested valleys. There's the goblin who sits atop Dunderberg whose churlish moods control the winds whipping up the river below. And, of course, there's the Headless Horseman; this is his turf.

TARRYTOWN – Just 25 miles north of New York City, deep in Washington Irving's "Sleepy Hollow" country. Sunnyside, Irving's home for 24 years, is open to the public. You can see his books, manuscripts, household furnishings, and some statues of his characters (W Sunnyside La., off Broadway). Nearby is one of those incredible Hudson Gothic mansions, Lyndhurst (635 S Broadway), built in 1838 by Alexander Jackson Davis and home of railroad tycoon Jay Gould from 1880 to 1893. The 67-acre estate offers stunning interiors and vistas as well as outdoor concerts and festivals in warm months (for concert information, 914 631-0046).

GARRISON – Two mansions here must not be missed. Boscobel, built by S. M. Dyckman for his wife in 1806, remains a glorious villa housing a collection of rare and beautiful antiques. The grounds are manicured in English formal style; and the view of the Hudson is spectacular. Nearby is Dick's Hilltop Castle, intended as a near-replica of the Alhambra by its owner, dreamer Evans Dick. The poor soul lost all his money in the stock market disaster of 1911 and his dream house was never finished. Four years and $3 million had gone into it. What's there, however, is quite enough to behold.

POUGHKEEPSIE – Two families have immortalized their names as well as their town: the Vassars for their prestigious women's college; and the brothers Smith for their cough drops. Besides Vassar, visit the Glebe House (635 Main St.), built about 1767 as a rectory for the Episcopal church, and the Clinton House (Main St. at White St.), home of the governor during the brief period in 1777 when Poughkeepsie was state capital. There are some beautiful old houses in town.

HYDE PARK – A name familiar to most Americans as the home town of Franklin Delano Roosevelt. He spent most of his life here; and, with his wife Eleanor, is buried here in the rose gardens on the Roosevelt estate. Visitors may browse through FDR's books, collections, and other personal treasures in the estate museum and library. As a mini-bargain, the admission price here also entitles you to visit the Vanderbilt Mansion down the road. Designed by Stanford White and built in 1895, this "Gothic" is a study in lavish excesses.

RHINEBECK – For a bit of history-come-alive don't miss the Old Rhinebeck Aerodrome (off rt. 9 on Stone Church Rd.). In addition to a spiffy collection of World War I aircraft still in working order, there's a Waldo Pepper–type simulated dogfight overhead staged Sunday afternoons, May through September and Saturday afternoons as well from early July to the end of the season. It's very real. And what with the aviators in goggles and flowing white scarves you'll find yourself searching the cast for a glimpse of Robert Redford — or at least the Red Baron. Rhinebeck is a lovely old town, with the oldest inn in the country, the Beekman Arms.

KINDERHOOK – Just east of Kinderhook (rt. 13) is the Old Chatham Shaker Village, a restoration of the 18th-century community. Visitors can go into the homes and see the marvelously simple items created by these people. There is also an herb garden, bookstore, and gift shop. From this point one either continues northward into the Adirondacks, or crosses the river (via the Rip Van Winkle Bridge in Hudson) and returns south along the west bank of the Hudson.

CATSKILL – Is the gateway to the famous mountain resort area. It is also the site of Mr. Van Winkle's famous nap. The Catskill Game Farm (12 miles west off rt. 32) delights kids with its touch-and-feed areas for tame deer and other animals. Catskill Park is a forest preserve that contains six campgrounds, hundreds of miles of marked nature trails, a ski run with chair lift, and all the glories of nature. Hunter Mountain is a popular ski area here.

WOODSTOCK – Now forever to be associated with the flower children of the 60s, but established in 1895 by a wealthy Englishman as a colony for intellectuals and artists. The Art Students League of New York set up a summer program here a few years later. Still healthy and active today, Woodstock continues to be synonymous with the arts. Each summer there are cultural events presented to the public: Woodstock Artists Association Gallery (28 Tinker St. at Village Green) features traveling exhibits by local and nationally known artists; Woodstock Playhouse (rt. 212 at rt. 375, 679-2436); and the Maverick Concerts (Maverick St., 679-6936). Call ahead for schedules and information.

KINGSTON – Is one of New York's oldest towns, a place that has survived every curve ball thrown by history — and there have been a number. First a Dutch trading post, then an English colony, and finally American (the state constitution was signed here in 1777), the city suffered attacks by various parties at every juncture — Indians, Dutch, British, Americans. A century ago its major industry was cement; that played out, but today it still prospers with a diverse economy, including a large IBM complex. This town has more than 15 original early American homes in the old stockade area (the stockade was built in 1658) that can be toured. Some of the houses on the tour made up a segment of the Underground Railroad for escaped slaves headed for Canada. After the tour, you will still have time to peek into the New York State Senate House and Museum (312 Fair St.).

NEW PALTZ – Was founded by French Huguenots in 1768. Today restored homes and a church from this original settlement are open to the public. Equally an attraction is the marvelous Mohonk Mountain House, a delightful New Paltz inn.

NEWBURGH – For more than a year (between April 1782 and August 1783) George Washington and the Continental Army had headquarters here. It was from here that the successful conclusion of the war was announced, and needless to say, the headquarters are a fascinating place to visit — the Jonathan Hasbrouck House (Liberty St.), where Washington stayed, and the New Windsor Cantonment (off rt. 32), which is a reconstruction of the army's winter camp. Ironically, it's not open in the winter.

MOUNTAINVILLE – Not far away is the Storm King Mountain Art Center, a cut-stone French château housing some important pieces of sculpture, including some by David Smith. The view from here is quite Alpine in feeling — the river narrows between towering mountains, and one is impressed with the distant vistas.

Weary from your historical exploration? Take a rest pause at the Brotherhood Winery (North St. in Washingtonville, off rt. 94). Established by monks many years ago, it remains America's oldest functioning winery. Tour the caverns where the aging casks lie in state, learn a bit about wine making, and then sample some of the finished products (914 496-9109 for hours).

WEST POINT – The United States Military Academy, training grounds for some of our nation's top military leaders. This famous institution was founded in 1802. There are some places you'll want to see, spots remembered from all those movies: the chapel with its stained glass windows; the kissing rock; and Trophy Point, with its crow's-eye view of the Hudson.

BEST EN ROUTE

Beekman Arms, Rhinebeck – This just might be the oldest continuously operating inn in the US. It is built over an original stone tavern (circa 1700); the main portion of the existing hotel was built in 1760. During the Revolution it was known as Bogardus Tavern to the regulars who used it — among them Washington and Lafayette. Rhinebeck, NY 12572 (914 876-7077).

Bear Mountain Inn, Bear Mountain – Open all year. Recently renovated at a cost of millions, this charming old inn was built in the style of a Swiss chalet. Besides the main inn, accommodations are available in the Overlook Lodge and in small rustic cabins. Bear Mountain, NY 10911 (914 786-2731).

Mohonk Mountain House, New Paltz – Open all year, this world-famous resort offers a variety of all-season sports, a relaxing atmosphere in the 1869 Victorian mansion, and overwhelming panoramic scenery. Rooms include three meals a day; the dining room is open to the public as well as guests. Miles of nature trails lead guests on self-guided tours. Cross-country skiing and horseback riding are two favorite sports. Lake Mohonk, New Paltz, NY 12561 (914 255-1000).

For food:

La Crémaillère, Banksville – Owned and operated by one of New York City's finest French restaurateurs, this inn captures the best of a French country inn. The rustic walls are hung with original oils depicting various French provinces, open fireplaces warm body and soul, lovely china pieces decorate the small wood bar. The food is outstanding, worthy of the multi-star ratings the restaurant has received. Closed every Monday, and the month of February. Call ahead for directions and reservations. Banksville, NY (914 234-3306).

Escoffier Restaurant of the Culinary Institute of America – Combining the best of creative cooking with a new experience in dining out. The institute offers a two-year cooking course to serious chefs. The final phase includes cooking for the public (that's us) in one of two dining rooms on the premises: the Escoffier Room, formal and extremely serious in its approach to haute cuisine; and the Rabelais Grill, with windows overlooking the kitchen where the student chefs are hard at work. Lunches and dinners are served Tuesdays through Saturdays. (Dinners, it should be noted, are serious, three-hour affairs.) Rt. 9, Hyde Park, NY 12538 (914 471-6608).

Niagara Falls and Buffalo, New York

If you're searching for an unspoiled vacation paradise far away from crowds and confusion, Niagara Falls is definitely not your destination. It is, in fact, a major tourist attraction, second only to New York City in the entire eastern United States. Big and bawdy, Niagara Falls generally makes things seem larger than life — its commercialism is tackier and somehow more annoying than in other areas, its industrial pollution more offensive. Yet despite all these excesses, Niagara Falls manages, quite literally, to rise above it all.

It is ironic that the single most devastating threat to the future of the falls comes not from the abuses of man, but rather from a weakness in nature. The shale and limestone foundations of the riverbed are slowly being washed away by the sheer force of the water plunging over the falls. As this erosion continues, the falls will be forced backward until they flatten out altogether and become little more than a series of rapids in the river.

But there's still time to pack the car and leave a note for the newspaper boy to say you're leaving. Scientists estimate that all this will take another few tens of thousands of years. In the meantime you can visit the falls. And while you find yourself marveling over their massive beauty, you might even have a kind thought or two for the commercial-minded folks whose various enterprises make it so ridiculously easy for you to see the attractions.

You can also shuttle over the several bridges across the Niagara River and see the whole thing from the Canadian vantage points.

And once you've had enough of the wonders of nature and are craving some intellectual stimulation, you can drive to nearby Buffalo, an upstate cultural oasis complete with major art galleries, museums, and a symphony orchestra — not to mention three major-league professional sports teams.

NIAGARA FALLS – The falls are formed as the waters of Lake Erie race downhill to join Lake Ontario, becoming en route the Niagara River. The river gathers strength and power in the narrows, and then plunges almost 200 feet, forming the world-famous falls. A small island in the river splits this whitewater juggernaut at the point of its mighty dive, dividing it into two falls instead of one: the American Falls — 182 feet high and 1,076 feet wide; and the Horseshoe (Canadian) Falls — 176 feet high and 2,100 feet wide. There is a minor falls, much smaller, called Bridal Veil.

The indomitable little island responsible for this twofold masterpiece is Goat Island, named for its former residents. Its 70 acres are prime viewing locations, making it a popular attraction. In addition to scenic walks almost at the brink of the falls, the island features a heliport for sightseeing choppers, and an elevator which takes visitors to the falls' base. From here the fearless may don the heavy-weather gear provided by the tour leader and walk along the path just behind the incredible wall of water — as drenching as it is deafening.

If you can dream up an offbeat angle from which you'd like to view the falls, chances are someone has already thought of it and has turned it into a prosperous business. Would you like an aerial view of the falls? The selection includes: Spanish Aerocars, cable cars that cross over the whirlpool and rapids; helicopter rides; or any of several observation towers. The two best viewing towers are on the Canadian side, on a 250-foot escarpment across from the falls. They are the 524-foot Skylon Tower (viewing height about 770 feet above the falls) and the 416-foot Panasonic Tower (viewing height about 665 feet).

At ground level there are any number of ways to view. The View-mobile offers miniature trams which run a 30-minute course between Prospect Point and Goat Island, allowing passengers to get on and off at any of several stops along the route. Of the various boat trips, the *Maid of the Mist* is the most famous. (Actually there are three sightseeing boats named *Maid of the Mist,* so you won't have too long to wait.) For the very daring there are giant rafts which depart from below the falls and make a whitewater tour of the downriver rapids.

And don't forget night viewing. The Horseshoe Falls is lighted by four billion candlepower in rainbow colors every night. The energy for this Technicolor extravaganza is provided by the falls itself.

Residents of the American side will grudgingly, but honestly, admit that the Canadian side is more pleasant (meaning less commercial). There are several bridges which span the river, and crossovers are made as hassle-free as both countries' customs can manage. The Canadian side offers a wide range of falls-oriented attractions in addition to the towers already mentioned. The Niagara Power Project (four miles north of town, rt. 104) uses exhibits and demonstrations to help the layman understand how all this raw natural power is harnessed and put to work for us. Another learning experience is at the Geological Museum (Prospect Park) where audiovisual presentations illustrate the various rock formations in the area, and specifically how they affect the future of the falls. The museum also offers a lovely rock garden, and a nature trail.

Many festivals and special events are scheduled during the peak summer months. At the huge Artpark (seven miles north of town, Robert Moses Parkway) there are 200 acres on which dance performances, concerts, and other artistic presentations are held (716 745-3377 for schedules).

The Tuscarora Indian Reservation is nearby (five miles northeast of town) and invites the public to two annual events each summer: Maid of the Mist Festival, with authentic dances, parades, and folklore; and the Picnic which is a sharing of Indian foods and a celebration of the lifestyles of this offshoot tribe of the mighty Iroquois nation. For information: the Niagara Falls Convention and Visitors Bureau, 300 4th St., PO Box 786, Falls Street Station, Niagara Falls, NY 14303 (716 278-8112).

BUFFALO – Is the second largest city in New York (population 463,000) and has all the cultural, industrial, and other urban trappings you would expect in a large city. What's surprising is the breadth of scope of its fine arts centers and its physical beauty. Virtually surrounded by parks, Buffalo's pride is Delaware Park, which was designed by world-famous landscape architect Frederick Law Olmsted. (He also designed New York City's Central Park.) Delaware boasts not only spectacular grounds and landscaping, but also a golf course, a zoo (with some buffalo, of course), and two museums: The Albright-Knox Art Gallery (1285 Elmwood Ave.), with its impressive collection of contemporary American and European works, as well as 18th-century English and 19th-century French and American artists; and the Buffalo and Erie County Historical Society (25 Nottingham Court at Elmwood Ave.), which plunges you into the rich history of the area.

There's boating and fishing on nearby waters including Lake Erie, and skiing within an hour of the city. For sports spectators, there are Buffalo's three professional teams: the *Bills* (football), who play in Rich Stadium (Abbott Rd. and US 20); the *Braves* (basketball) and the *Sabres* (hockey), who play in Memorial Auditorium (Main and S Park Sts.).

Famous in its own right, the Buffalo Philharmonic Orchestra now boasts guest appearances by its former conductor, the illustrious young Michael Tilson Thomas. Home base is the Kleinhans Music Hall, known for its superior acoustics (26 Richmond Ave., 885-4632 for performance schedules).

BEST EN ROUTE

Red Jacket Inn, Niagara Falls, NY – Some rooms have private patios overlooking the Niagara River (which at this point is actually an island strait). Has a pool, babysitters, and on weekends, entertainment. 7001 Buffalo Ave., Niagara Falls, NY 14304 (US side) (716 283-7612).

Ameri-Cana, Niagara Falls, Ontario, Canada – About 4 miles outside the hustle and bustle of downtown, amid spacious grounds with a play area, this motor inn has rooms as well as several efficiencies and kitchen units. It makes a great home base if you've got a small mob with you. 8444 Lundy's La., Niagara Falls, Ontario, Canada L2H 1H4 (356-8444). Moderate.

Old Red Mill, Williamsville, NY – Eleven miles northeast of Buffalo, this restaurant has several interesting dining areas: a lovely old house with fireplaces and a few converted railroad cars. 8326 Main St., Williamsville, NY 14221 (716 633-7878).

Old Orchard Inn, East Aurora, NY – Converted into a fine restaurant, this old home serves family style in a warm, rural atmosphere. Blakely Rd., East Aurora, NY 14052 (716 652-4664).

Pennsylvania Dutch Country, Pennsylvania

Actually the Pennsylvania Dutch aren't Dutch at all. They came here in the 18th century from Germany seeking the freedom to worship as they wished, and in William Penn's country they found it. They also found natives who couldn't pronounce the word Deutsch — and so Dutch it has been ever since. The center of this large area — which officially encompasses the counties of Lancaster, York, Dauphin, Lebanon, Berks, and Lehigh — is Lancaster, the middling-size city in southern Pennsylvania that sits just short of halfway between Philadelphia and Harrisburg.

The freedom these devout people sought was the right to observe and practice Jesus' teachings as they interpreted them — their interpretation being as literal as literal could be. With typical brevity, they summed up their beliefs: "God said it/ Jesus did it/ I believe it/ And that settles it!"

In reality, what we mean by "Pennsylvania Dutch" actually incorporates three bodies of faith: the Amish, most rigid in their literal interpretation of the Bible, shunning all things modern, and living physically austere lives based on the style of their forefathers; the Mennonites, more accepting of the outside world, but still what is called in the area "plain"; and the Moravians, also called the "fancy Dutch," mainly German Lutherans and Reformed Church members whose farms are made noticeable by the "hex signs" which adorn barns.

Some Amish will not speak to strangers; their homes may not be toured; they may not be photographed. Despite their refusal to use any modern technology (they travel by horse and buggy), they are superior farmers. Each year droves of tourists sample their distinctive and now famous foods — shoofly pie, scrapple, and chicken-corn soup.

Luckily all is not buttoned up in Pennsylvania Dutch country. There are many Mennonites whose source of income is the tourist trade, and it is possible to rent rooms in a Mennonite family farmhouse during a visit, rather than stay in a local hotel. You can hire a Mennonite guide for a personalized tour of the countryside, thereby gaining an edge on commercial tour groups. These unusual and interesting additions to your visit can be arranged at the Mennonite Tourist Information Center (2209 Mill Stream Rd., Lancaster, PA 17602, 717 299-0954). Because the area is so large, to get a true feeling for the plain and fancy peoples you should have an advance plan — an organized idea of what you want to see, or buy, or eat. Information: Pennsylvania Dutch Visitors Bureau, 1799 Hempstead Rd., Lancaster, PA 17601 (717 299-8901).

LANCASTER – The largest concentration of authentic Pennsylvania Dutch sights are clustered here and just outside town along rts. 30 and 340. Farmers' markets are perhaps the biggest draw in town, and with good reason. Here the prize of the crops are offered for sale — along with flowers, plants, homemade baked goods, canned relishes, and old-country-style sausages and bolognas. There are seven such markets, but the most popular is the Central Market (Penn Sq.), open from 6 AM to 5 PM on Tuesdays and Fridays. Almost as lavish in its abundance is the Southern Market (102 S Queen St.), open Saturdays from 5 AM to 5 PM.

For a better understanding of Amish life, you can visit several simulated Amish communities. The Amish Homestead (three miles east on rt. 462) shows farming techniques as practiced by the first Amish settlers, and a tour of an 18th-century house; the Amish Farm and House (six miles east on rt. 30) offers a tour and a lecture, "The Plain People"; and a Disneyesque version of what's happening, called Dutch Wonderland, located on rt. 30, is a theme park complete with gardens, shows, and shops. There are several ways to get an overall view of Lancaster. There are many commercial sightseeing tours offering preplanned itineraries. Or you might be interested in a self-guiding auto tape tour. The tape and player can be rented for about $6 from many commercial establishments. (Ask at the Information Center for one nearby.)

BIRD-IN-HAND – Is where you can learn about those traditional folk-art hex signs. At the Hex Barn and Wagonland (off rt. 340) you can watch them being made, and then buy some of the finished products. Here, too, is a splendid collection of horse-drawn vehicles, including the typical Amish wagons, and even a surrey with fringe on top. At the Country Crafts Museum and Gallery (west on rt. 340, north on Mt. Sidney Rd.) there's a charming exhibit of antique toys, dower chests, and other folk furnishings. And on many roads in this area, you'll cross antique covered bridges, many in their original state. Outside Bird-in-Hand is the excellent Plain 'n Fancy Farm restaurant (on rt. 340) with a representative menu of Pennsylvania Dutch favorites. Amost anywhere you stop to eat in Pennsylvania Dutch country is an experience in overabundance as well as plain good cooking, in a culture that traditionally equates well stuffed with good health. Be prepared to be as dazzled by the sheer size of the spread as by the flavor of the food.

HERSHEY – Milton Hershey was a Mennonite whose lifestyle appears to have been pretty worldly, and if not his lifestyle, at least his sweet tooth, which has also affected just about every American child since the Hershey Chocolate Factory was built in 1903. The townsfolk and descendants of Milton Hershey don't appear to be overly modest either. Much of this town bears his name, from the Hershey Gardens to Hersheypark (a theme park with rides and amusements), to Hershey Stadium (sporting events), to just about everything else. One thing you'll not want to miss is the tour of Chocolate World, where you'll watch a simulated step-by-step version of how chocolate is made, from cacao bean to Hershey Kiss.

Hershey's major nonchocolate event is Original Pennsylvania Dutch Days, an annual event held for one week the end of July. Quilting bees, arts and crafts demonstrations, and a plentitude of good foods are all part of the fun.

KUTZTOWN – Is famous for its Pennsylvania Dutch Folk Festival held every year in early July. Serious shoppers throng to this event to buy the many handicrafts, sample the culture and food, and enjoy historic exhibits of the plain and the fancy Dutch. While here, be sure to visit the Crystal Cave, a natural phenomenon discovered back in 1871 and now improved with indirect lighting and safe walkways. You'll see crystal formations, natural bridges, and caverns.

While the annual events and farmers' markets are warm-weather major attractions of the area, you should realize that the crowds they draw create a distraction and a disadvantage. For this reason you might want to time your visit during the off-season (spring, fall, or winter), when the tourist traffic is lighter and you stand a better chance of fading into the background and gaining truer insights.

Whatever your choice of season remember that you'll enjoy your stay much more if you do your homework in advance. Tourist brochures and detailed maps are easily obtained from the tourist bureaus, and they are absolutely essential. There are 220 noteworthy sights to see and visit in Lancaster County alone!

BEST EN ROUTE

Visiting a Mennonite Farm – If you wish to do this, you must call or write ahead to the Mennonite Information Center. They will send you an up-to-date listing of the farms that welcome overnight visitors. Some serve breakfast, others do not. A double room (no private bath) costs about $14 and up. The Mennonites are afraid of publicity and are fearful to say in print that they will serve meals because of the avalanche of tourists to the area. Individual tourists are often lucky enough to form their own personal relationships with their Mennonite hosts. Information: 2209 Millstream Rd., Lancaster, PA 17602 (717 299-0954).

Host Farm Resort, Lancaster – If a total family vacation is the goal. Guests choose from a barrage of activities — sports, amusements, even cabaret shows — with emphasis on "something for everyone." 2300 Lincoln Hwy. E, Lancaster, PA 17602 (717 299-5500).

General Sutter Inn, Lititz – For food and accommodations. The inn has been around since 1764 and is comfortable, clean, unfancy; the food is marvelous. 14 E Main St., Lititz, PA 17543 (717 626-2115).

Groff's Farm, Mt. Joy – For food only. Housed in a 230-year-old home, the food is all made from the freshest ingredients. The wine is made here and housed in the cellar (you'll be invited down for a tour and tasting after dinner by Abe or Betty Groff). There are two seatings, 5 PM and 7:30 PM, and if it happens to be your birthday, Betty Groff will grab her huge trumpet and march through the house's many dining rooms serenading your good health. If her music doesn't turn you on, but her cooking does, you can take home a copy of one of her cookbooks. Reservations are a must. RD 3, PO Box 912, Mt. Joy, PA 17552 (717 653-2048).

Newport and Block Island, Rhode Island

Newport, America's first resort town, is so crammed with history that you can take a leisurely stroll past a row of 19th-century millionaire's mansions, stop in for a drink at a tavern that has been doing business since 1673, and visit a house where George Washington conferred with French strategists during the Revolutionary War — all in the course of an afternoon. Like old sedimentary rock, the town is composed of different time layers. There is colonial Newport — refuge from religious intolerance; 18th-century Newport — bustling and prosperous seaport; and late-19th-century Newport — summer playground of the super-rich. And thanks to the work of the Preservation Society and Restoration Foundation of Newport, all of these towns remain intact in 20th-century Newport, an architectural museum of glittering mansions, impressive 17th- and 18th-century homes, and some of the oldest houses of worship in America. Add to these attractions a pleasant shoreline and snug harbor in Narragansett Bay and you have a place where history and recreation are in fine balance.

Founded in 1639 by victims of the Massachusetts elders' religious intolerance, Newport attracted settlers of all religious convictions, including Quakers and Jews. In the 18th century the town prospered as a seaport and merchants built fine homes with the profits they made from transporting rum to the West Indies and slaves from Africa. It was during this period, in the 1730s, that wealthy planters and merchants from the Carolinas and West Indies began to spend their summers here, making Newport America's first resort. The British occupation during the Revolution put an end to Newport's first golden age; the second did not begin until after the Civil War, when people like the Astors, the Belmonts, and the Vanderbilts began to build their summer "cottages" in Newport — "cottages" modeled after the grand palaces and châteaux of Europe.

A center for yachting and all kinds of sea sports, Newport is on the tip of the large island for which the state is named, in Rhode Island Sound. It has several excellent beaches, but even better are on Block Island, about 12 miles south of the mainland, and accessible by ferry from Newport (as are Providence and New London, Connecticut). Newport and Block Island are a morning's drive from Boston and New York.

NEWPORT – To get oriented at once, stop at the Chamber of Commerce (10 America's Cup Ave.) for a free visitor's guide, maps, and information on current happenings in town. There are frequent musical programs, especially in summer. Newport's bookstores carry many guidebooks to the town; one excellent one is *Newport: A Tour Guide,* by Anne Randall, which offers well-planned walking routes. Newport is so compact that you can walk or bicycle just about everywhere, but if you like your sightseeing sitting down and exertionless, Viking Tours (847-6921) offers a two-hour city bus tour and a one-hour harbor/bay boat ride as well as walking tours.

If you have come to Newport, you have come at least in part to see its mansions. The Preservation Society of Newport (118 Mill St.) offers a very good tour of some of Newport's most stunning "summer cottages." Hunter House (54 Washington St.), built in 1748, is the only colonial mansion on the tour. This stately home once served as the headquarters of the commander of French forces in the American Revolution. The Breakers (Ochre Point Ave.), a 70-room mansion overlooking the Atlantic, is the most splendid of all of Newport's great houses. Built in 1895 for Cornelius Vanderbilt, the building was designed to resemble a northern Italian Renaissance palace. The finest examples of Newport "cottages" from the Gilded Age stand garden-by-grounds along Bellevue Avenue. In the course of a stroll down this impressive street you will pass the city's most famous homes. The Elms, built in 1901 for a Philadelphia coal magnate, was modeled after the Château d'Asnières near Paris. After touring the house, which is completely furnished with museum pieces, you can walk around the grounds and admire the formal French gardens and collection of rare trees and shrubs from all over the world. Marble of all kinds and colors was used to build Marble House, completed in 1892 for William K. Vanderbilt. This palatial home contains all of its original furnishings. Château-sur-Mer, built in 1852, is one of the finest examples of ornate Victorian architecture in America. Rosecliff, where scenes from Paramount's "Great Gatsby" were filmed, was designed by Stanford White after the Grand Trianon at Versailles and built in 1902. Also on Bellevue Avenue are the International Tennis Hall of Fame and Tennis Museum, an 1881 casino where the first tennis matches were played, and Belcourt Castle, which houses the largest stained glass collection in the world.

Another way to see Newport's mansions is to take the Cliff Walk, a three-mile trail between the mansions and the sea.

Away from mansion row, you leave the Gilded Age to step back in time to the federal and colonial eras. At the Old Colony House (Washington Sq.), Washington conferred with Rochambeau. The Wanton-Lyman-Hazard House (17 Broadway), built in 1675, is the oldest residence in Newport. The Newport Historical Society (82 Touro St.) houses a fine collection of old Newport silver, porcelain, furniture, toys, and dolls, as well as a marine museum. Nearby is Touro Synagogue (85 Touro St.), considered an architectural gem as well as a symbol of religious liberty. Built in 1763, the synagogue is the oldest in the US. (Open daily except on Saturdays and religious holidays.)

At the corner of Church and Spring Streets, Trinity Church, built in 1726, is the most perfectly preserved colonial wooden structure in the country. The church was modeled after the London churches of Christopher Wren, and contains many artifacts of early American life. A few blocks away from the church is the Redwood Library, built in 1748 and a National Historic Site. Legend has it that the Old Stone Mill adjacent to the library was built by Norsemen, but excavation dates this building at about 1673.

At the Samuel Whitehorne House (416 Thames St.), you can see some of the exquisitely crafted furniture, silver, and pewter that once graced the homes of wealthy Newport merchants.

If, after seeing Newport's colonial treasures, you crave a few for yourself, you can shop for fine reproductions of colonial furniture, silver, and brassware at the Brick Market (Thames St.). Antique shops line Franklin and Spring Streets, and the boutiques on cobblestoned Bowen's Wharf at the waterfront (off Thames St.) carry everything from sweaters to scrimshaw. (Be sure to try some of the seafood restaurants here too.)

BLOCK ISLAND – Offers an antidote to too much shopping and sightseeing. This pear-shaped bit of rolling meadowland is 12 miles at sea in Block Island Sound and just an hour's ferry ride from Newport. There are a few historical things to see on Block Island: Settler's Rock, where the first settlers landed in 1661; the Palatine Graves, where an ill-fated ship met a watery fate (commemorated in a poem by Whittier); the Block Island Historical Society, with exhibits on the island's history. (The island has a bad reputation with sailors. The site of over 200 shipwrecks, it was for a good part of the 18th century a haven for pirates, smugglers, and sea thieves.) But mostly, this is a place to loll on the beach, take long walks by the sea, or do some serious fishing. The waters off Block Island support tuna, bluefish, cod, striped bass and flounder, and there are over 300 inland ponds. Block Island is an excellent vantage point for bird-watching: It is filled in fall and spring with migrations of birds on the Atlantic flyway. At the northern end of the island, Mohegan Bluffs, rising 200 feet above sea level, offer long ocean vistas. A suggestion: Leave your car on the mainland, and rent a bike to get around; the whole island covers only 11 square miles. It has a fine harbor, and sailors up and down the coast put up here for a day, biking around the island's beaches for a day, picnicking, and shopping.

BEST EN ROUTE

The Inn at Castle Hill, Newport – Formerly the home of Alexander Agassiz, the son of the famous 19th-century naturalist. Rooms have excellent views of Narragansett Bay. The inn itself has been declared a historical monument. The restaurant here is quite good; there's a varied menu, but the specialty is, of course, seafood. Ocean Dr., Newport, RI 02840 (401 849-3800).

1661 Inn, Block Island – The 1661 is a Block Island tradition. As is fitting in a place so married to the sea, the restaurant serves excellent seafood. Both the restaurant and the inn are closed from late fall until the end of May, but the building's annex, with 9 rooms, is open year round. A Continental breakfast is included. PO Box 367, Block Island, RI 02807 (401 466-2421).

Vermont: A Short Tour

"Winter or summer," one Vermonter says, "being here is the name of the game." It's true. You can't go wrong in Vermont, no matter when you go. From the beautiful southern villages that inspired artist Norman Rockwell to the elaborate ski resorts flanking the Green Mountains, it's all stunning. There are several routes to the Green Mountain State. If you're coming from Boston, take I-93 to I-89 directly to Burlington, Vermont's largest city, on Lake Champlain. With Burlington as your base, you can explore the northern part of the state, wander along the Canadian border, then journey through the southern section on your way back to Boston.

BURLINGTON – Is a town that dates back to the Revolution. Revolutionary War hero Ethan Allen is buried here in Greenmount Cemetery. Burlington's location on Lake Champlain makes this a major navigational center for ship traffic between the United States and Canada. It was the site of a major naval battle during the War of 1812. From Battery Park, you can get a marvelous view of the tranquil lake and spruce-lined shores. It's hard to believe that any place this peaceful could have been a battlefield. Lake Champlain and Vermont's inland lakes provide a variety of catch, plentiful and safe for consumption. Ferries cross Lake Champlain every 50 minutes. Destination: Port Kent, New York. The crossing takes 2½ hours round-trip (for information, contact Lake Champlain Transportation Company, King Street Dock, 864-9804). There is a swimming area at North Beach. Apart from the lake itself, the highlight of Battery Park is Beansie the hot dog man. Beansie sells hot dogs, chili, and french fries from his van during the warmer months. In winter, he takes his van and his hot dogs to Florida. In town, the University of Vermont (656-3480), Trinity College (658-0337), and St. Michael's College (655-2000) campuses present films, concerts, plays and sports activities throughout the academic year.

SOUTH HERO – Just north of Burlington on one of Lake Champlain's islands. Allenholm Farms sell fresh apple cider, and hot apple and pumpkin pies in late September–early October, when Vermont's foliage is at its height. The apples come from the Allenholm orchards. Pick up some milk at a country store and feast while gazing at the lake. To get to South Hero, take rt. 7 to rt. 2 northeast. You'll pass through Sand Bar Wildlife Area and State Park, another good spot for picnicking.

STOWE – If you ski, you've undoubtedly heard of Stowe. Even if you don't, it's worth a trip. Take rt. 7 north to rt. 104A east. (When you pass Cambridge, keep your eye out for a genuine Vermont covered bridge. No longer in use, it's now standing off to the side of the highway.) Head south on rt. 108 at Cambridge Junction–Jeffersonville, the prettiest part of the state, according to many residents. A few miles south of the turnoff, you'll pass through Smugglers Notch, an important hideout for contraband goods passing between the United States and Canada during the War of 1812. The rugged, hairpin road through the notch is impassable during winter, but you can cross-country ski. There are downhill ski areas at Smugglers Notch, Mount Mansfield — the tallest peak in the state — and nearby Underhill and Bolton Valley. Mount Mansfield explodes into view as you round a hill. When the sun is shining behind its snow-covered peak in winter, Mount Mansfield is, in the words of one Vermonter, "most amazing." (High praise from a Vermonter.) Marking the end of the Green Mountains, Mount Mansfield's 4,393 feet are laced with trails and caves. In August, you can pick blueberries as you hike. Stowe, one of the most famous ski areas in New England, is just down the road on rt. 108.

HUNTINGTON GORGE – From Stowe, continue south to rt. 89 east, toward Burlington, taking the Richmond exit. Follow rt. 2 toward Jonesville, take a right on the steel bridge crossing the Winooski River (Winooski is an Indian word for onion), and follow the road to Huntington Gorge, a secluded picnic and swimming spot. Here, the Huntington River narrows to a waterfall. But be careful — there are no lifeguards.

JAY PEAK – Alternately, from Stowe, you can head north on rt. 100 all the way to Canada. Just before you reach the border, take the turnoff for rt. 101 north to Jay Peak ski area. To return to Burlington, head west on rt. 105 to St. Albans, formerly an important railroad stop along the route to Canada. Here you can pick up I-89 south to Burlington.

SHELBURNE – Just south of Burlington, home of the Shelburne Museum, with restored Americana from the 1880s (985-3344). You can see what an old Vermont village used to look like. There are farm buildings, a grocery store, a pharmacy, feed shops, a dentist's office, and even the steamboat *Ticonderoga,* which used to ply its way across Lake Champlain. If you're fortunate enough to be passing through Shelburne at sunset, go to Shelburne Point, the tip of a little finger of land pointing northwest on the shores of Lake Champlain. The sunsets are no less than magnificent from this vantage point, and there's a beach and a restaurant at the marina.

LINCOLN GAP – Wandering south along rt. 7, through Vergennes, you'll encounter a number of good restaurants and inns. South of Vergennes, you might want to detour east on rt. 17, through Bristol, to Lincoln Gap, a winding passageway which has challenged Vermonters for years. Many drivers return again and again, but the legendary gap has claimed a number of them over the years. One Vermonter cautions that the road "is really a horror, and if you persist, sooner or later it'll get you."

MIDDLEBURY – On the western boundary of the Green Mountain National Forest, site of Middlebury College and the Bread Loaf Writers' School, where Robert Frost taught. There's a Robert Frost Mountain here, a Robert Frost Wayside Recreation Area, and Middlebury College Snow Bowl, a family ski area popular with Middlebury residents, but not yet familiar to out-of-staters. There's a good climbing trail at neighboring Ripton. Continue southeast on rt. 125, which runs into rt. 100 south, to get to Killington and Pico Peak ski areas.

PLYMOUTH – Birthplace of President Calvin Coolidge. His former home is now a museum. His son, John Coolidge, runs Plymouth Cheese, a small factory where everything is made by hand. Coolidge and his team of hardy Vermonters keep the place open even when the world is covered with snow. The cheddar is delicious. (Speaking of Vermont specialties, if you're in the state in late winter, take a special trip to St. Johnsbury, home of the Maple Grove Maple Factory, the world's largest maple candy factory. For Vermonters, maple sugaring time is a celebration of spring. To get to St. Johnsbury, take rt. 2 east from Burlington.)

ROUTE 100A – This scenic road takes you past Calvin Coolidge State Forest to Plymouth Union and Round Top ski area, which is usually not overrun with tourists. At Ludlow, the Okemo Mountain ski area has good ski conditions. From Ludlow, take rt. 100 south to its end at South Londonderry, site of Ball Mountain Dam Recreation Area, and pick up rt. 30 southeast to Brattleboro.

You've probably noticed by now that Vermont has no billboards on its highways and very few bottles littering the roadsides. Vermonters are very proud of their state and have passed a number of strict conservation laws designed to protect the countryside from abuse. Visitors are welcome, but must share this respect for the land.

BRATTLEBORO and STRATTON – In the winter, these are, of course, two of

Vermont's more popular ski resorts. If you're driving through during the summer months, though, you might look into one of the area's special summer events, such as Brattleboro's Annual Arts and Crafts Show or Stratton's lovely Annual Art Festival. In the fall, the foliage displays in this region are quite spectacular; pack a picnic lunch and set off through the trees. (For a map and booklet tracing scenic autumn foliage tours, write to the Agency of Development and Community Affairs, Travel Division, 61 Elm St., Montpelier, Vermont 05602.)

BEST EN ROUTE

North Hero House, Champlain Islands – A 23-room inn with tennis and water sports facilities, with an ideal lakefront location. Bicycles provided. Champlain Islands, North Hero, VT 05474 (802 372-8237).

Middlebury Inn, Middlebury – Close to Middlebury College and the Shelburne Museum. This 75-room inn is near golf, tennis, bicycling, skiing, and swimming. Dining room is open to the public. Court Sq., Middlebury, VT 05753 (802 388-4961).

Waybury Inn, East Middlebury – Built in 1810 as a stagecoach stop, it has 11 rooms. This is a popular spot for hearty meals, even if you don't plan to spend the night. Rt. 125, East Middlebury, VT 05740 (802 388-4015).

Okemo Inn, Ludlow – Built in 1810, this has a homey feel, with a grand New England fireplace. Ludlow, VT 05149 (802 228-2031).

Walloomsac Inn, Bennington – A fine old-timer dating from 1764. Large rooms, some with four-poster beds, old-fashioned bathtubs on legs, and a sprawling porch. Open mid-May to Nov. 1. 67 Monument Ave., Old Bennington, VT 05201 (802 442-4865).

Shenandoah National Park, Virginia

For 80 miles along the spine of the Blue Ridge Mountains in northwestern Virginia, overlooking the beautiful valley of the Shenandoah River, lies Shenandoah National Park. More than 95% of the park's 190,000 acres are wooded — stands of deciduous hardwood (oak, hickory, hemlock) that explode into color during the first short, cold days of autumn. Through the park runs the 105-mile Skyline Drive, as well as a 95-mile section of the Appalachian Trail, the entire length of which winds from Georgia to Maine.

Bounded by the Blue Ridge Mountains on the east and the Alleghenies to the west, the Shenandoah Valley is the heart of the mighty Appalachian Mountain chain, an area loved and revered by Indians and white men for centuries (Shenandoah is Indian for "Daughter of the Stars"). George Washington surveyed land here, and was so awed by its special splendor that he became a large landowner. Eventually he required all of his tenants to plant at least four acres of apple trees — a legacy Americans can still enjoy while gazing from the park's overlooks and trails to the glorious apple orchards that blanket the valleys below. The park was established in 1935 to make inviolate a goodly portion of the Shenandoah area. It extends from the town of Front Royal in the north to just east of Waynesboro in the south, and is only a couple of hours' drive from the Washington, DC, area. Waynesboro is connected by I-64 to Richmond and the "colonial triangle" towns of Williamsburg-Yorktown-Jamestown.

FRONT ROYAL – Take in some of the attractions at the northern edge of the park before entering. Most interesting is the Thunderbird Museum and Archeological Park (five miles south of town on rt. 340). Amphibious vehicles transport you across the Shenandoah River to a major archeological dig. You will have the opportunity to watch archeologists at work, and see displays on the local geology. The Blue Ridge Mountains here form the most southeasterly wave of the Appalachians, formed of lava a billion years old. The area has nature walks, picnic facilities, and craft shops. Warren Rifles Confederate Museum (Chester St., Front Royal) houses many relics of the Civil War including furniture, rare photographs, weapons, and other typical war memorabilia.

If you're visiting the Shenandoah Valley in the fall, plan to attend the annual Festival of Leaves held in Front Royal the third week in October (when the foliage is at its peak). The festival, one of the largest in all Virginia, offers a wide variety of attractions: craftsmen, tours of historic homes and churches, and an art show with over 50 artists exhibiting. (For information: Chamber of Commerce, PO Box 568, Front Royal, VA 22630, 703 626-3185.)

And if you find yourself seduced by the beauty of the Shenandoah River, and want to get to know it better before entering the park, a short drive north into West Virginia's eastern panhandle will bring you to Harpers Ferry, where you can join a Shenandoah River whitewater rapids expedition. Each trip takes about five hours, including a Southern hospitality–style picnic, and is organized by Blue Ridge Outfitters (304 725-3444 in Harpers Ferry) between May and November.

SHENANDOAH NATIONAL PARK – Every autumn the park produces just about the most spectacular show of fall foliage to appear anywhere in the United States. The Skyline Drive charges straight along the crest of the Blue Ridge for the entire length of the park, surrounded by successive waves of Appalachian hills — the Blue Ridge nearest, Alleghenies to the west — rising and falling into the distance. It is an unparalleled leaf-peeping experience, marred only by the inconvenience of having to share it with so many other people. Park vistas are as beautiful in the spring and summer as they are in autumn. Flowers and blossoming trees carpet the valleys in infinite varieties of color and depth. If you want to see the foliage, by all means brave the park in September and October; if you want to see the park, however, avoid the autumn crowds.

The park has two Visitors' Centers: Dickey Ridge, just within the northern entrance at Front Royal, and Big Meadows, where rangers have deliberately checked the growth of the forest to allow a huge, green meadow to flourish in the sunshine. There, myriad varieties of park plants — orchids, violets, wildflowers — grow in profusion. A visit to the park should include a stop at one of the centers — preferably first — to pick up literature and check out daily activities. Rangers lead nature walks through different parts of the park, advise on trails, and of course, provide information on camping. Shenandoah has two lodges, campgrounds (about 20), and a policy allowing off-trail camping. However, campers must have permits, available from rangers.

There are two distinct ways of seeing the park. Skyline Drive has numerous stops and overlooks, many with short trails leading from them, which allow visitors to drive the park's length, stopping where they wish. Certainly you can enjoy the many beautiful vistas along the route doing this, and with some luck even see some of the park's wildlife — deer, or perhaps a bear. However, the only way to get more than a passing acquaintanceship with Shenandoah is simply to plunge into it, and with more than 300 miles of hiking trails and paths — some quite arduous, others little more than strolls — as well as the Appalachian Trail, Shenandoah is a park made for hiking.

Swamp Trail, near Big Meadows, is an easy two-mile walk which encompasses the three major environments typical of the entire mountain area: forest, meadow, and mountain swamp. Available at the Visitors' Center is a short brochure which describes what you see along the trail. Because it is level along most of its length (a mile out and a mile back), Swamp Trail is a pleasant walk for families with children of different ages and different levels of endurance. The trail up Hawksbill Mountain is a good deal more rigorous (three miles long), but very rewarding: Along its route are numerous stopping points that offer spectacular views of the valley. The trail is often used in the summer by rangers leading groups of visitors.

A walk around Stone Man Mountain reveals something about the underpinnings of the entire mountain chain in this area. Formed of ancient lava galvanized by eons of slow heat, along Stone Man (and elsewhere in the park) high cliffs of lava break into great columns of stone, called columnar jointings, which developed as the lava which made them cooled and separated. Here and wherever stone is exposed, you will see strange, circular bubbles of color in the rock. These were caused by gas which percolated through the lava as it cooled, nearly a billion years ago.

Though 95% forest, the park has very little virgin woodland left. When it was established in 1935, and the last of the local residents were moved to nearby locations, generations of farmers had practiced the time-honored method of quick-burning to clear forests and prepare fields for planting and almost nothing was left of the original Blue Ridge forests. Today's woodlands represent a masterwork of reforestation. Even more tragic was the loss of the area's native chestnut trees. These were once the most common tree in the mountains, and certainly the most useful. Their wood was excellent for furniture, their foliage provided tannic acid required for tanning, and their nuts were a cash crop. But 70 or 80 years ago a fungus deadly to the trees entered the US from the Far East, and devastated the native forests. Today scientists are trying to develop resistant breeds, but nothing has appeared to replace the thousands of acres of chestnuts.

At Limberlost, in Whiteoak Canyon, you can see some of the very few virgin trees left in the park. Here there is a stand of original hemlock trees, and some 500-year-old white oaks. Information: the Superintendent, Shenandoah National Park, Luray, VA 22835 (703 999-2266).

BEST EN ROUTE

Shenandoah has four major campgrounds (and many camps) and numerous off-trail, limited-facility camping sites. It also has a unique off-trail "camp where you like" system, but as noted before, all campers must have permits, and these specify how many people are allowed in the party, and for how long the party may be out. The park also has two excellent lodges, Skyland and Big Meadows. For reservations at either, write ARA Virginia Skyland Co., PO Box 727, Luray, VA 22835 (703 743-5108). Skyland is a Shenandoah tradition, begun in 1894 by George Pollock. It has 158 rooms, a full dining room, a stable, and craft shops. Big Meadows offers the same features, with only 96 rooms. Both are open April through October, with reservations required about 2 months in advance for any time except foliage season (then 8 months, minimum).

Tidewater Virginia

One of the richest historical areas in the country is Virginia's coast — traditionally called Tidewater Virginia — on the Chesapeake Bay. Here, almost within call of one another, are Williamsburg, Jamestown, and Yorktown; the beautiful 18th-century plantation homes along the James, York, Rappahannock, and Potomac Rivers; and to the west and north, Richmond and Fredericksburg, with a wealth of surrounding Civil War sites. There is hardly a period of early American history, from initial exploration to the War Between the States, not represented by some vital detail here.

Begin a tour of Tidewater Virginia at the beginning. The "colonial triangle" between the James and the York Rivers is the most highly concentrated area of historical sites in the whole country. The three points of the triangle are: Jamestown, where America began; Williamsburg, where patriots plotted the future of the nation-to-be; and Yorktown, where the war ended and the nation was born. And all three are conveniently linked by the Colonial Parkway so you can travel with ease between the three.

WILLIAMSBURG – Is the first reconstruction of a historical area ever undertaken in the US, and it is still the best. Work was begun on restoring the 18th-century town in 1926; no detail was too insignificant, no project too large in this staggering project. Visitors to Williamsburg can actually experience life as it was lived in colonial days. Craftsmen ply their trades exactly as they did then, sheep graze on the green, a horse-drawn cart takes you down Duke of Gloucester Street with its array of taverns and shops all busy at their 18th-century businesses. Take a stroll over to Market Square and watch the militia train and drill. A good introduction to colonial Williamsburg can be found at the Visitors' Information Center (Colonial Pkwy. and rt. 132 Y). Of the 400 buildings that have been restored there are some you won't want to overlook: the Governor's "Palace," as it was called by the disgruntled colonists whose taxes paid the bills for this luxurious mansion; the College of William and Mary, built in 1693 and the second-oldest college in America; and two jovial and famous meeting places, Raleigh and Wetherburn's Taverns.

Make reservations well in advance. Williamsburg is a very popular destination for families with children. There are a great many motels and hotels near town. Within the town itself is the Williamsburg Inn (Frances St.), a joy to see or visit for its painstaking authenticity. One perfect touch is the costumed colonial dame who plays a harp during the evening meal. (See *Restored Towns and Reconstructed Villages,* DIVERSIONS, p. 544, for more information about Williamsburg.)

JAMESTOWN – Williamsburg became the seat of the royal government in 1699. Before that, Jamestown had been the center of the royal colony, and the site of the first successful English settlement in America. John Smith and his group of 103 settlers arrived in Jamestown in May 1607. Today it is an island; at the time, it was connected to the mainland by a narrow isthmus that the James River eventually ate away. The first years of the colony were extremely hard, with little help from the London Company, which sponsored the journey, and in general fate dealt the town a rather hard hand. By 1699, when the government was moved, it had been burnt down once, set afire another time, and finally abandoned.

Today the area is the Colonial National Historical Park. For the most part one sees diggings indicating where buildings were and how extensive the settlement was. The one remaining building of the period is the Glasshouse, restored and fitted out as it was originally, with craftspeople blowing glass. But history comes most vividly alive at Jamestown Festival Park, which is located in the harbor of the James River (not part of Jamestown itself). Here are full-scale replicas of the three tiny ships on which the first settlers made their journey: the *Susan Constant,* the *Godspeed,* and the *Discovery.* You can actually board the *Susan Constant* and see the cramped quarters that housed those courageous families. There is also a recreation of John Smith's fort, which you can tour, as well as several special exhibit houses. (For more information, see *Restored Towns and Reconstructed Villages,* DIVERSIONS, p. 544.)

YORKTOWN – Is the third city of colonial significance linked by the Parkway. Yorktown had been an important tobacco shipping port until the Revolutionary War began. In the autumn of 1781 British Commander Cornwallis got boxed in here by a combination of the French fleet along the coast and French and American ground troops, led by George Washington. On October 9 a siege began, and ten days later Cornwallis surrendered. The Revolutionary War was over. Unlike Jamestown, however, Yorktown is a functioning city today, surrounded on all sides by the Yorktown Battlefield. After a stop at the Yorktown Victory Center (on rt. 238) for information and brochures, you can take a walk through the battlefield, which is carefully designed to explain the battle and its significance. Of special interest is the Moore House (on rt. 238), where the capitulation papers were drawn up (they were signed on a British ship), and the Swan Tavern (Main St. and Ballard), a reconstruction of an early-18th-century tavern, now a shop. Before leaving the Williamsburg-Jamestown-Yorktown area, consider a visit to the Old Country, a splendid amusement park outside Williamsburg (five miles on rt. 60) which is fully described in *Amusement Parks and Theme Parks,* DIVERSIONS, p. 571.

TIDEWATER PLANTATIONS – Along any and all of the rivers, inlets, bays, and peninsulas of Tidewater Virginia and the Chesapeake Bay you are likely to find lovely Georgian homes fully restored and inhabited, which date from the tobacco trade days of the mid-1800s. However, from Williamsburg west along the north shore of the James River are a number of the most famous plantations and plantation homes in America. Most are open to visitors, and in any case even if one house is closed on the particular day you visit, grounds are always open. About eight miles outside Williamsburg is Carter's Grove, built in the 1750s and restored as part of the Colonial Williamsburg project. Across the river from Jamestown is the Rolfe-Warren House, built almost 100 years earlier, on land given by Indian Chief Powhatan to his daughter Pocahontas and her groom John Rolfe. Along the James River north shore route are: Sherwood Forest, home of President John Tyler; Westover, Byrd's own home, built in the 1730s as the focal point of his 179,000-acre fiefdom; Berkeley, birthplace of President William Henry Harrison; and Shirley, home of the immensely powerful Hill-Carter family.

PORT OF HAMPTON ROADS – The quest for history is only one of the attractions of the Tidewater area. The business — and pleasure — of the sea itself plays a large role in the life of the peninsula. The Port of Hampton Roads incorporates four cities — Newport News, Hampton, Portsmouth, and Norfolk — and is a center for shipping, shipbuilding, and seafood. It is also the entry point to Virginia's beaches, either around Cape Henry to Virginia Beach, or through the toll bridge and tunnel to the peninsula of Virginia that hangs below Maryland.

From Yorktown, rt. 17 and I-64 lead into the center of these seafaring towns. A fitting stop is the Mariner's Museum (Clyde Morris Blvd., in Newport News). It offers a wealth of ships' fittings, models, cannon, maps, and instruments. While in Newport News consider the harbor cruise (from the Boat Harbor at the end of Jefferson St.) which takes you around Hampton Roads and historic Fort Monroe, in the very waters where the *Monitor* met the *Merrimac.*

BEST EN ROUTE

Williamsburg Inn, Williamsburg – Genteel luxury, in a perfectly restored, perfectly maintained 18th-century atmosphere. Located in the center of Williamsburg, the inn offers history outside the front door and a golf course outside the back. Reservations Office, Colonial Williamsburg Foundation, PO Box B, Williamsburg, VA 23185 (804 229-1500).

Tides Lodge, Irvington – Primarily a golf establishment that offers numerous entertainments of the outside, athletic variety (yachting, tennis, canoeing, jogging, swimming, fishing) for the family. Associated with the elegant Tides Inn nearby. Irvington, VA 22480 (804 438-6000).

Smithfield Inn, Smithfield – Just south of Newport News, but well beyond the built-up port area of Hampton Roads. Very few rooms (six), very reasonable rates, and excellent food. The town of Smithfield is replete with 18th-century houses. 112 Main St., Smithfield, VA 23430 (804 357-4358).

Harpers Ferry and Monongahela National Forest, West Virginia

West Virginia really is the stuff that country music is made of — country roads, rocky cliffs, Blue Ridge Mountains, almost heaven. But it's much more than mountaintops and John Denver lyrics. The small towns built into these old hills are strongholds of America's history. This is where John Brown's ill-fated raid on Harpers Ferry took place, where one of the bloodiest and most crucial battles of the Civil War was fought, and where hundreds of mule-drawn barges navigated the Chesapeake and Ohio Canal, carrying coal to fuel the young nation. The towns are within a few hours' drive of each other through beautiful backcountry, including Monongahela National Forest, a thickly wooded preserve of forest with tranquillity and wild and woolly whitewater canoeing.

HARPERS FERRY, West Virginia – Though this lovely hillside town overlooking the confluence of the Potomac and Shenandoah Rivers appears tranquil today, it was the site of John Brown's raid on the federal arsenal in 1859 as part of his plan to arm a slave rebellion and to establish a free state in the Blue Ridge Mountains. The abolitionist force succeeded in capturing the arsenal, but they were surrounded by the local militia, and Brown was captured by Colonel Robert E. Lee and hung for treason and murder a month and a half later. A half-mile walking tour through the Harpers Ferry National Historical Park (Shenandoah St.) links several restored homes, a gun-making museum, the engine house where Brown was caught, blacksmith shop, confectionary, tavern, and Jefferson Rock, which commands a fine view of the area's rivers and hills.

SHARPSBURG, Maryland – The headquarters of the Chesapeake and Ohio Canal National Historical Park (the park itself is ten miles south of US 70 along rt. 65). This 185-mile canal was begun in 1828 to link Washington, DC, and Pittsburgh. It never reached its final destination, but it is still among the longest and best preserved canals built during the early 1800s. Construction of the canal was halted at Cumberland, Maryland, in 1850 because railroads became a more efficient means of transportation. The canal was used until 1924 to carry coal, crops, and lumber from the West Virginia mountains to Georgetown. At its peak, some 500 mule-drawn barges navigated the waterway, with 75 locks through which they were raised and lowered. Many of the locks and aqueducts have been restored, and interesting old buildings line the banks of the canal, which is now operated by the National Park Service. Trails and campsites along the entire length of the canal are available for hikers and bicyclists.

The Antietam National Battlefield and Cemetery Site lies one mile north of Sharpsburg on rt. 65. On this site, the Union forces stopped the first Confederate invasion of the North in what was one of the bloodiest battles of the war. Iron tablets and battlefield maps describe the events. The Visitors' Center houses a museum; musket and cannon demonstrations, historical talks, and bicycle tours are scheduled throughout the year.

CHARLES TOWN, West Virginia – Charles Washington, brother of George, founded and designed this town in 1786. Of interest here are numerous historic homes as well as the Jefferson County Courthouse (N George and E Washington Sts.), which was the site of the 1859 trial of John Brown, and the site of his gallows (S Samuel and Hunter Sts.). The Jefferson County Museum (N Samuel and E Washington Sts.) has everything of John Brown's that's not amoldering in the grave. Just outside town is Harewood, an estate built by another Washington brother, Samuel, and the site of the wedding of James and Dolley Madison. Nearby are Claymount Court (Summit Point Rd.), built by George's grandnephew, Bushrod; and Happy Retreat (Blakely Pl.), an earlier home of Charles.

BERKELEY SPRINGS, West Virginia – For many years, this resort city was called Bath, after the famous spa in England. George Washington noted the mineral springs while surveying the region for Lord Fairfax. Fairfax donated the springs to Virginia in 1756 and they have been public property ever since. Not one to mingle with the commoners, Fairfax bathed in a private hollow that's known as the Fairfax Bathtub. Today, however, the hoi polloi bathe right at the center of town in the Berkeley Springs Park, a state-run facility with health baths, warm springs, a swimming pool, and even a Roman bathhouse.

Cacapon Park, ten miles south of town (off rt. 522), is a 6,155-acre park at the base of Cacapon Mountain with excellent facilities for golf, tennis, horseback riding, fishing, swimming, and boating.

LOST RIVER STATE PARK, near Moorefield, West Virginia – The parklands were once a vacation spot of the Lee family of Virginia and now have facilities for swimming, tennis, picnicking, and riding. One of the original cabins has been restored and turned into a museum. Nearby stands unusual Ice Mountain (it has ice at its base even on the hottest summer days). The mountain is honeycombed with cold underground passages that keep the ice frozen.

MONONGAHELA NATIONAL FOREST, West Virginia – The forest covers over 833,000 acres in the heart of the Alleghenies, stretching southwest from the Maryland border for 100 miles through West Virginia backcountry, a region of rounded mountains and twisting valleys. Monongahela is a "reconstructed" forest. Fifty years ago, it was a wasteland that had been stripped of its huge stands of timber and scarred by mining and fires. The replanting program began in 1920 and the region is blanketed once again with deep forests inhabited by whitetail deer, black bear, and wild turkey.

The best route through Monongahela starts at Petersburg, at the northeast corner of the forest, and heads south via rt. 28 through the Alleghenies to Minnehaha Springs at the Virginia border. The road runs along the south branch of the Potomac. Seneca Rocks, towering 1,000 feet above the river, are the area's major landmark. Mountain climbers from all over come here to claw their way up the rugged stone face of this immense stone cliff. Nearby is Spruce Knob, at 4,862 feet, the highest peak in West Virginia. (West Virginia's average altitude is the highest of any state east of the Mississippi.) This area of the forest is being developed as a national recreation area. The 100,000 acres have excellent facilities for hiking and camping. Starting at the Seneca Rocks, there's some whitewater canoeing for a distance of 15 miles along the headwaters of the Potomac.

Near Greenbank is the National Radio Astronomy Observatory, a huge radio telescope with which astronomers are recharting the heavens. Tours of the complex are given during the summer months and a film explains the work done at the observatory. The facility is open daily from mid-June through Labor Day; weekends only from Memorial Day to mid-June, and in September and October.

At Cass (just south of Greenbank, off rt. 7) is the depot of a state-owned railroad with a steam locomotive that runs through the rugged mountains along the route of an old logging railroad up to the summit of Bald Knob, the second-highest mountain in the state. The eight-mile trip takes two hours with a stop for exploring and picnicking. The trip to the top of the mountain takes 4 ½ hours.

Further south is Mill Point, to the west of which lies Cranberry Glades, a large outdoor botanical laboratory centered around a big cranberry bog. The area is particularly beautiful during the fall, but worth a visit at any time. Nearby, the Cranberry Mountain Visitors' Center has instructive displays. While you're there, take a short hike up Hill Creek where within half a mile there are three lovely waterfalls.

Monongahela National Forest now has over 30 campgrounds and more are being built. There are almost 2,000 miles of streams with excellent trout and bass fishing. In season, there is hunting for bear, deer, and wild turkey. For more information contact Monongahela National Forest Headquarters, USDA Building, Sycamore St., PO Box 1231, Elkins, WV 26241 (304 636-1800).

BEST EN ROUTE

The Greenbrier, White Sulphur Springs, West Virginia – Just south of Monongahela, this magnificent resort has been favored by celebrities ranging from Robert E. Lee to the Duke of Windsor and 20 American presidents since the springs were first used in 1778. Originally a mineral spa, the Greenbrier has been a resort for 202 years and is famous for having as many employees as guests — a standard few modern resorts can match. There are three 18-hole golf courses, one of which was recently redesigned by Jack Nicklaus, 20 tennis courts, 2 Olympic-sized pools, miles of riding trails, skeet and trap shooting, an art colony, theaters, nightclubs, restaurants, and a spa. There's also a notable diagnostic clinic on the premises. After roughing it in the Monongahela National Forest, nothing could be better than being pampered here for a day or two. Station A, White Sulphur Springs, WV 24986, just west of town on rt. 60 (304 536-1110; toll-free, 800 624-6070).

Cacapon Lodge, near Berkeley Springs, West Virginia – This state-run facility in the park provides good standard accommodations and easy access to all the facilities in the park. Berkeley Springs, WV 25411 (304 258-1022).

South

Hot Springs National Park, Arkansas

Does the name Hot Springs conjure up images of steam rising from the ground? Does its reputation as a health resort make you think it's a place only good for a rest cure? A place where you might, conceivably, be bored?

If you've only thought of Hot Springs, Arkansas, as a place to bring your aching joints on those unfortunate occasions when they seem to creak, you're in for a huge surprise. Hot Springs is the hottest tourist attraction in Arkansas. And it's only 50 miles from Little Rock, the state capital.

A city of some 35,000, Hot Springs is the center of Hot Springs National Park. This, in itself, is unusual, since most national parks are miles from large, populated centers. The place has certainly come a long way from the day in 1541 when explorer Hernando de Soto christened it "the valley of vapors." At that time, it was a secluded section of Indian territory. It was, in fact, the Indians themselves who led de Soto and his exhausted team of explorers to the bubbling pools of water, where they were rejuvenated after a bath. The legendary curative properties of these 47 thermal springs became known all the world over. In 1832, the 4,000 acres of Hot Springs were declared a federal reservation. In 1921, they became a national park.

The fabled Bathhouse Row has been offering regimens of baths and massages long enough to be listed on the National Register of Historic Places. There are 9 bathhouses, 4 of which are on Bathhouse Row. Before stepping into the mineral baths, you should be examined by a physician. (It's not required, just recommended.) You do need a referral from a licensed physician for physiotherapy sessions at any of the hydrotherapy facilities. The springs themselves are located on the western slope of Hot Springs Mountain. A huge reservoir collects the more than one million gallons flowing through 45 of the thermal springs every day, and channels them to the bathhouses. (You can see two of the bubbling springs behind the Maurice Bathhouse on Central Avenue. The rest are not visible to the public.) You might be surprised at the blue-green algae floating on the surface of the springs, since algae traditionally make their home in colder waters. The springs puzzle geologists, too, but for other reasons. They theorize that rain seeps through a fault in the earth under Hot Springs Mountain, then rises along layers of rock to bubble out through the fault. But how is it heated? Perhaps by molten rock deep inside the earth, or by radioactive minerals. It could be the result of inner seismic friction, or unexplained chemical reactions.

The spa is merely one aspect of this multifaceted vacation area. From February to April, thoroughbred horses race at Oaklawn Park, a handsome track. The season reaches its climax during the week-long Racing Festival of the South in the second week of April. The Racing Festival culminates in the running of the Arkansas Derby on the final day. The races kick off a lively, diversified summer and fall season. In June, Hot Springs is the scene of the Arkansas Fun Festival; in July, the Miss Arkansas Pageant; in October, the Arkansas Oktoberfest. Special performances of an outdoor drama are staged at the 1,600-seat Mid-America amphitheater.

Other places of interest include: Arkansas Alligator Farm (847 Whittington Ave.); IQ Zoo (380 Whittington Ave.); Wildwood 1884 (Victorian Mansion, 808 Park Ave.); Josephine Tussaud Wax Museum (250 Central Ave.); the Magic Springs Family Fun Park (rt. 70 east); Animal Wonderland (two miles west of city on rt. 270); the Fine Arts Center (815 Whittington Ave.); and the Mid-America Center Museum.

For a touch of tranquillity follow rt. 270 west to the gently rolling Ouachita Mountains, one of the oldest mountain ranges on the continent. Here, you'll find three manmade lakes on the Ouachita River: Lakes Ouachita, Hamilton, and the smallest, Lake Catherine. These lakes are the pride of Hot Springs, each offering fishing, swimming, water skiing, sailing, and scuba diving. You can camp at Lake Catherine, 12 miles west of Malvern. There are also campsites along the southern shores of Lake Ouachita, and an unbeatable 18 miles of hiking trails through the forests. You can join guided nature walks during the summer. Lake Ouachita offers a unique camping opportunity. If you rent a Camp-a-Float motorized barge, you can take your car or camper onto the water and travel around the 48,000-acre lake without having to land.

For complete information on accommodations and resort facilities in Hot Springs, and a free travel kit, write Hot Springs Chamber of Commerce, PO Box 1500, Hot Springs AR 71901 (800 643-1570 outside of state; 1 800 272-2081 within Arkansas). For a free travel kit, write Hot Springs Advertising Commission, PO Box 1500, Hot Springs National Park, Hot Springs, AR 71901, or contact the Arkansas Department of Parks and Tourism, #1 Capitol Mall, Little Rock, AR 72201 (501 371-1511; or toll-free, 800 643-8383 out of state, and 800 482-8999 in Arkansas). Since it attracts people from all over the world, Hot Springs isn't one of those national parks where you can look forward to hot dogs on stale rolls and rubbery hamburgers. There's an abundance of restaurants: American, German, Italian, Czechoslovakian, Mexican, and kosher. Information: the Superintendent, Hot Springs National Park, PO Box 1219, Hot Springs, AR 71901 (501 321-5202).

BEST EN ROUTE

Arlington Hotel, Hot Springs – In the middle of the city, with its own hot mineral water bathhouse, the hotel has 2 swimming pools, 3 restaurants, and 500 rooms. Central and Fountain Sts., Hot Springs, AR 71901 (501 623-7771; or toll-free 800 643-1502).

The Ozarks, Arkansas

They call it "the Natural State." Down home, pickin' and strummin', come-as-you-are Arkansas. Unpretentious part of the world, when you get right down to it. Home of the Ozarks, one of the great capitals of American folk myth and heritage. This is the home of country roads, leading through gentle, blue-green mountains, twisting along the edges of gorges that catapult into white, frothy rivers. If you can imagine a banjo or fiddle in the background, you've got the whole picture. To get to the Ozarks from Little Rock, the capital, take I-30 and rt. 67 north about 110 miles.

NEWPORT-JACKSONPORT – On the banks of the White River, famous for its fine trout. You might want to stop at Jacksonport State Park just north of Newport, to picnic. If you have enough confidence in your casting abilities, you can fish in the river for your meal. Jacksonport was once a rough-and-ready frontier river town, and its old courthouse is now a museum. The *Mary Woods II,* a White River paddle-wheel tugboat, is also on display. According to local history, Jacksonport citizens liked the river city so much, they refused to let the railroad come in; the station was built three miles south, in Newport. As a result, Jacksonport declined.

BATESVILLE – Follow the river northwest along rt. 14, about 35 miles up the road, and you'll be able to step back into the 19th century, since this town is very much as it was during the days when paddle-wheelers steamed into dock, full of passengers and cargo. For two weeks during the summer, Arkansas College in Batesville holds Folklore Workshops in conjunction with the Ozark Folk Center, 40 miles away in Mountain View.

MOUNTAIN VIEW – Home of the Ozark Folk Center, and a good place for first-timers to get acquainted with the crafts, customs, and music of the Ozarks. Since it opened in 1973, Ozark Folk Center has been a country music and folk history lover's dream. In addition to mountain craft exhibits and workshops, the 80-acre center is alive with music. If you happen to be passing through in April, you'll probably be swept up in a crowd of about 100,000 people, all flocking to town for the Arkansas Folk Festival, two weekends of jug band, fiddle, jew's harp, mountain dulcimer, and banjo strummin' sessions. If you don't like crowds, but hanker after that foot-stompin' music, stop by between late spring and October. The Ozark Folk Center's 1,043-seat auditorium has concerts almost every night. There are also free concerts at the county courthouse every Saturday night, and in October, a two-week Family Harvest Festival at the center. Traditional pottery, quilting, shucking, spinning and weaving — you can see it all at the folk center. And you can take some home — from the center's shop. For information call the Ozark Folk Center, 501 269-3851.

BLANCHARD SPRINGS CAVERN – In the Sylamore District of the Ozark National Forest, about 15 miles north of Mountain View on rt. 5. Considered to be one of the most spectacular underground natural environments in the state, Blanchard has only been open to the public since 1973. You can walk along Dripstone Trail, an intricate labyrinth that crisscrosses the palatial subterranean caverns, taking you past stalactites, a Christmas-tree-shaped stalagmite, a frozen waterfall, and a cavern called the Ghost Room. More difficult is the Discovery Trail, open during summer months only. There are outdoor nature trails and camping areas here, too. Be sure to call for reservations (501 757-2213) at least three days in advance during the summer months, even if you only want to tour.

MOUNTAIN HOME – Some fabulous river and lake country lies just to the north of Blanchard Springs. If you stay on rt. 5, you'll pass the junction of the rushing waters of the White and Buffalo Rivers. About 50 miles north of Mountain View, you'll come to Mountain Home, sitting between Norfork Lake and Bull Shoals, two of the Ozarks' most famous lakes. Both lakes are great for canoeing, swimming, and water skiing. Bass, bream, crappie, catfish, stripers, and rainbow trout swim around in the clear water just waiting to be caught, and there are Ozark guides who'll take you to where the fish are biting. You can even join a night fishing expedition on a pontoon boat. On the shores of Bull Shoals Lake, Bull Shoals State Park has campsites and a dock (on rt. 178). Near Buffalo Point National Recreation Area on the shores of the Buffalo River, you can rent a canoe for an unforgettable trip along one of America's wild rivers. The 132-mile Buffalo River flows through spectacular blue mountains, and there are no artificial dams to obstruct the water's flow. The National Park Service maintains cabins and campsites along the riverbanks.

HARRISON – "The hub of the Ozarks," Li'l Abner country. Here you'll find Dogpatch, USA, a theme park filled with cartoonist Al Capp's notable characters (on rt. 65).

EUREKA SPRINGS – A delightful Victorian town just east of 28,000-acre Beaver Lake. A fashionable health spa in the 1880s, Eureka Springs has 63 natural springs within the city limits, more than Hot Springs, Arkansas' most popular thermal spa resort. The kids will love the shuttle bus, designed to look like a trolley car. Here, too, you can hear country music concerts during the summer in Basin Spring Park bandshell, weekday nights. From May through October, the Great Passion Play is performed near the seven-story-tall Christ of the Ozarks statue, in a 4,200-seat amphitheater (daily except Mondays and Thursdays). For information, contact Eureka Springs Chamber of Commerce, Eureka Springs, AR 72632 (501 253-8737).

BEAVER LAKE – Rt. 62 loops around the north shore of Beaver Lake. Here you can visit Pea Ridge National Battlefield Park, site of a decisive 1862 Civil War battle, after which Missouri stuck firmly to the Union.

OZARK NATIONAL FOREST – On your way back to Little Rock, take rt. 62 south to Fayetteville, home of the University of Arkansas' main campus (575-2000). Then follow rt. 71 south, past Devil's Den and Lake Fort Smith State Parks, to I-40 east. (There's a Travel Information Center to the west of the intersection of rt. 71 and I-40.) On your way back to Little Rock, you might want to stop at Clarksville, the heart of the 1.1-million-acre Ozark National Forest. You can get off the Interstate and wander north along rt. 21, through dense, uninhabited forest. As you breathe in the scent of spruce and pine, you might find yourself humming to the tune of some banjo song you heard a few nights ago. This is the time to enjoy the cool, rushing sounds of the forest. Information: the Superintendent, Ozark National Forest, PO Box 1008, Russellville, AR 72801 (501 968-2354).

BEST EN ROUTE

Ozark Folk Center Lodge, Mountain View – A 60-room lodge in woodsy surroundings. Right next to the Folk Center. A good place to choose if you want rustic environment and a chance to be where it's all happening. Mountain View, AR 72560 (501 269-3871).

Crescent Hotel, Eureka Springs – A landmark, built in 1886. Most of the 76 rooms have different Victorian furniture. The limestone hotel has a restaurant, swimming pool, tennis court, coffee shop, and rooftop garden lounge. Close to 12 springs. Closed January and February. 75 Prospect St., Eureka Springs, AR 72632 (501 253-9766).

Everglades National Park, Florida

In most of America's national parks you have little more to do than arrive and open your eyes to be impressed. The Everglades is far more demanding. Here you must know something about ecology, and something about what you're looking at, to appreciate the full splendor of this magnificent swamp wilderness.

The Everglades is America's only subtropical wetlands. Fed by the waters of southern Florida's huge Lake Okeechobee, the entire southern tip of the state was once more or less like the Everglades today — a huge tract of mangrove swamps, seas of saw grass, hammocks of hardwood trees, and millions of birds, fish, snakes and alligators, and insects (especially mosquitoes). As southern Florida developed, the slow draining waters of Okeechobee were channeled for irrigation, and swamps drained. Bit by bit southern Florida dried out.

In 1947, alarmed by the destruction of these unique wetlands, the federal government set aside 1,400,533 acres 30 miles west of Miami as Everglades National Park. Despite various (and continuing) threats to the park, it remains today: the third largest of America's national parks, 2,188 square miles of the world's most delicate ecological system, stretching to Florida's southern and western Gulf coasts.

You must understand the delicacy of the Everglades if you are to enjoy its understated pleasures. It is actually a freshwater river (its Indian name is Pa-Hay-Okee — "River of Grass") 100 miles long, 50 miles wide, just inches deep. This strange stream travels along an incline of only three inches a mile, and moves so slowly that a single drop of water takes years to reach the Gulf from Lake Okeechobee. This slow river provides nourishment for a vast and complex system of life, and is a perfect laboratory in which to see the interdependence and sensitivity of an ecosystem. Where the earth rises so much as three inches, the plant life in the 'glades changes from saw grass to hardwood forest. Where ripples appear in a pond, a small fish is eating mosquito larvae; a large fish, a bream perhaps, will dine on the larvae-eater; bass hunt the bream; gar will feed on the bass; and the gar is menu-fodder for the alligator who originally made (or deepened) this pond with his tail in the winter.

About 200 miles north of the Tropic of Cancer, the Everglades is the meeting point of subtropical and temperate life forms. In this it is unique in the US: Here you see mangrove, West Indian mahogany, and the poisonous manchineel tree, and in a nearby hammock rising from the saw grass, pine and hardwood trees. Alligators and whitetail deer share the same stomping ground.

The entrance to the Everglades is on rt. 27 about 12 miles beyond Homestead. Rt. 27 ends at the park entrance; from here you follow the main park road for the 38-mile journey through the park to Flamingo, Florida, on the

Florida Bay. There are several ways to see the 'glades: by car, you can drive to various stopping places along the road; on foot, where trails follow into the heart of things (with ranger guides); by small outboard or canoe, following the water routes. In any case, first stop is at the Visitors' Center outside the park, where you can see exhibits on park wildlife and ecology, and pick up information on guided tours, "swamp tromps" (more about these later), and park activities and rules.

If you are driving, the next stop is Royal Palm Station (about two miles beyond the center), where you can follow boardwalks over the saw grass and watch for animal life. (That saw grass, by the way, has mean, serrated edges on three sides. It chews clothes or flesh with equal ease, so be careful.)

Beyond Royal Palm the road runs through pine forests to Long Pine Key Area, a good picnicking spot. Note the pines. They manage to survive only because they are sturdily fire resistant. You may see a number of them with fire-blackened trunks. Almost every summer fires sweep through parts of the 'glades. Most trees are killed, but pines burn only on the outside; their corky bark protects them. In summer, the saltwort marshes which flank many of the forests dry out, and are torched by summer lightning. True to the beautifully balanced nature of the 'glades system, these fires are actually restorative, and clear the way for new growths of plants and trees.

Pa-Hay-Okee is the next stop on the car route. From here you have access to a high platform and boardwalks that overlook Shark River Basin, where alligators and fowl gather. The alligators form an important link in the chain of life in the Everglades. During the dry season — autumn through spring — they settle into sloughs and dig deep holes with their tails. In late winter as the marshes dry out, fish get caught in these " 'gator-holes," which become teeming pools of fish life. This is crucial for the wading birds, which nest near these ample sources of food and are assured a food supply.

Seven miles beyond Pa-Hay-Okee is Mahogany Hammock, the largest stand of mahoganies in the US. Boardwalks allow you to wander into it. A bit further on you drive to Paurotis Pond, where you encounter the first mangrove trees. Here salt and fresh water begin to mix, and the mangrove is the only tree which thrives in salt water. They are great colonizers, and live in a constant drama of creation and destruction all along the Gulf shore. They settle into the swampy salt water of the coast, and as they drop seeds and throw out breathing roots they capture material and actually begin "building" earth bulwarks against the sea. As seagulls and other sea birds collect around them, dropping guano, this earth becomes rich and fertile. Then hurricanes sweep the coast, and everything is ripped out of the swampy ground and thrown inland.

The main park road ends at Flamingo, where you'll find a hotel, campgrounds, and boats for hire (including houseboats) for excursions into portions of the 'glades only accessible by waterway.

Serious visitors should plan to spend most of their time out of their cars, on ranger marked foot trails or on a "swamp tromp" into the very slime of the marshes. (There is also a tram ride available from late December through August at Shark Valley off rt. 41, which skims the northern border of the park.) For the less hardy, foot trails are a comfortable way to have an intimate experience of the 'glades.

Gumbo Limbo Trail begins at Royal Palm and explores the interior of Paradise Key, where exotic air plants and hardwood trees grow; also at Royal Palm, Anhinga Trail is a likely route to spot a number of alligators and a variety of birds from an elevated walkway. You might just be lucky enough to sight some of the delicate Virginia whitetail deer along the Pineland Trail (beginning about two miles from Long Pine Key area). (These little deer are the prey of the Florida panther, which, sadly, lives in dwindling numbers here in the Everglades.) At the Pa-Hay-Okee Overlook you'll get a perspective of the expanse of saw grass that makes up the Shark River basin.

For the more intrepid who would like to meet nature's challenge, from December through March there are the frequent "slough slogs" or "swamp tromps" — walking expeditions led by park naturalists which get you into things. Quite literally. You'll need old clothes and shoes that you don't mind getting muddy and wet. And be sure to have plenty of mosquito repellent handy. There are several different destinations you can select from: out to a 'gator hole; a tree island; or a major mangrove stand. Ask for up-to-date schedules at the Visitors' Center.

The Wilderness Waterway is just about the most challenging test the Everglades can cook up for the outdoors person. It is a 99-mile water trail which corkscrews through the Ten Thousand Islands area. Although the water lanes are well marked, there is sufficient room for error that travelers are requested to take all precautions when undertaking this journey. By powerboat it is quite possible to complete the course in about six hours. However, any serious nature observer will opt for the canoe and the serenity it offers en route. There are minimally outfitted campsites, each wryly nicknamed, along the water lanes: "Hell's Bay" ("hell to get into and hell to get out of"); "Onion Key," the bare-bones remains of a 20s land developer's dream; and a crude pit outhouse and fireplace campsite known as "The Coming Miami of the Gulf." The waterways begin at Everglades City and extend to Flamingo.

The somewhat less athletic and daring boater might prefer to take a guided-boat cruise. One such cruise departs every evening from Flamingo to tour Florida Bay; this is a good opportunity to view Florida's blazing sunsets and watch the indigenous birds returning to roost for the evening. From November through May, there are daily cruises from Everglades City to explore Upper Chokoloskee Bay.

The not-so-visible members of the Everglades family run the gamut from the lowly and much-hated mosquito all the way to the signature 'gator who is most often spotted when his eyes break water while the rest of him hides beneath the swampy water's surface. Fish are tropical and abundant, each with a role in the food cycle that maintains the Everglades. Schools of dolphin can usually be spotted from the coastal shorelines. Recreational fishing is permitted, but many creatures are protected by law from any molestation or harm by man. Information: the Superintendent, PO Box 279, Homestead, FL 33030 (305 247-6211).

BEST EN ROUTE

Rent a Houseboat in Everglades National Park – Accommodations are hard to come by in the immediate Everglades area. A houseboat might just be the answer. There's a wide range of prices depending on the duration of your rental. All rentals include everything from fuel and other boating essentials such as lifelines and jackets, to inside essentials such as bedding and linens and cooking utensils. Before you go, look into the park rules, for example: no pets are allowed on board any boat; float plans must be filed with wilderness boating office; and in some areas, the larger outboard motors are banned or restricted (check with Park rangers). Make peak season reservations 4 months in advance. Flamingo Houseboat Corp., c/o Everglades National Park, Flamingo, FL 33030 (813 695-3101).

Omni International, Miami – Newest hotel complex in this golden land of hotel complexes. This one boasts a 556-room hotel located in a large shopping mall. The Treasure Island Amusement Park is also in the mall, promising to lure and amuse the kiddies with a variety of rides, bumper cars, and the like. 16th St. and Biscayne Blvd., Miami, FL 33132 (305 374-0000).

Florida Keys and John Pennekamp Coral Reef State Park, Florida

Curving 150 miles out into the Gulf of Mexico from the southern tip of mainland Florida, the Florida Keys dot the waters like periods following a phrase. And in many ways, this archipelago is an afterthought to that great landmass above, centered around Miami, with its glittering nightlife and crowded swimming beaches. The 42 islands that make up the Keys are generally tucked soundly away by 11 at night, have very few swimming beaches despite the availability of water (the shallow waters coupled with fierce coral discourage swimming), and few glamorous resorts. The local hotel with five stories — a midget by Miami resort standards — is a skyscraper hereabouts.

What the Keys do have, however, are some of the finest seascapes around — the blue waters of the Atlantic to the east and south, and the green seas of the Gulf of Mexico on the northern side. As you drive along the Overseas Highway (US 1), a toll-free road composed of highway spanning the islands with 42 bridges (some only 100 feet long, others stretching as much as seven miles) you'll be surrounded on all sides by sea and sky. Even on the Keys themselves, many of which are only a few hundred yards wide, you can see through the mangroves, Caribbean pine, and silver palmetto to the sea, which is the overwhelming presence here. And though you can't see it from the car, below the surface the view is even more dramatic. The Keys are surrounded by an offshore coral reef, a section of which can be seen close up at the John Pennekamp State Park in Key Largo. It is a slightly hallucinogenic underwater scene as bright blue and green tropical fish move in and out of the sculptured reefs of white, pink, and orange coral.

The story of the Overseas Highway is interesting. In the late 1880s, Henry Flagler, an associate of John D. Rockefeller, aimed to establish a "land" route to Cuba by extending the Florida East Coast Railroad line to Key West. From there, he planned a ferry shuttle for the final 90 miles to Havana. He invested some $20 million in the construction of tracks but the 1929 crash destroyed his project. Six years later, the Labor Day Hurricane of 1935 wiped out most of what remained of the tracks. At that point, the government stepped in and began building the Overseas Highway along the same route.

Of the 42 keys linked by the highway, there are several major islands with accommodations, restaurants, shops, and their own unique characteristics. Much of this local flavor has to do with the natives of the area. They're Floridians, but they call themselves Conchs. Descended from the London Cockneys who settled in the Bahamas, the Conchs also incorporate Cuban, Yankee sailor, and Virginia merchant blood. Conchs have always been people of the sea — fishermen, boatsmen, underwater salvagers. They could hardly be otherwise, living as they do, surrounded by water. And when you are in their territory, you can easily share their pleasures. Fishing is king in these parts, with over 600 varieties of fish in the surrounding waters. Besides the challenges to anglers, the availability of fresh fish has stimulated Key chefs to dream up such creations as Conch chowder, turtle steak, and in their land-bound flights of fancy, Key lime pie, which must be yellow, not green, to be the genuine article.

JOHN PENNEKAMP CORAL REEF STATE PARK, Key Largo – Key Largo is the first of the keys and the longest, but what is actually most interesting here is under water. Running parallel to the Key for 21 miles is the country's only underwater state park and the location of the sole living coral reef in the continental United States. The park is a snorkeler's and scuba diver's heaven, encompassing 150 square miles of the Atlantic Ocean, hundreds of species of tropical fish, and 40 different varieties of coral. Laws forbid taking anything from the water, so the area will be preserved for others to see.

To get an overview of the reef and surrounding sea, take a tour on the glass-bottom boat. Though somewhat commercialized, it provides valuable information on the ecological balance of the reef and journeys several miles out onto the high seas to the reef's most spectacular section, where you'll see beautifully colored coral formations and other marine life, including barracuda, giant sea turtles, and sharks, from a dry vantage point. But as the water gets bluer and bluer, the ride gets rougher and rougher, so take the antiseasickness tablets they offer at the beginning of the trip.

You can also venture into the water under better circumstances for scuba diving tours of the reef. You can rent everything you'll need at the park headquarters — wet suits, tanks, skin diving gear, and boats to get out to the reef.

Closer to shore, water trails for canoeing in the mangrove swamp offer alternatives for those who want to stay above water. And for those who want to go in, the swimming beach has a roped-off area which is good for a dip or some casual skin diving.

There are 60 campsites, all with tables and charcoal grills, and some with electrical hookups and water. Reservations for the sites should be made at least two months in advance — the park is a very popular destination. Reservations and information: John Pennekamp State Park, PO Box 487, Key Largo, FL 33037 (305 451-1202).

ISLAMORADA, Upper Matecumbe Key – A sportfishing center in an area that's famous for fishing. The many coral reefs in the surrounding shallow waters attract scuba and skin divers as well. The Coral Reef Resort sponsors diving trips here (PO Box 575, Islamorada, FL 33036, 664-4955). The Underwater Coral Gardens, two colorful coral deposits and the wreck of a Spanish galleon, offer the possibility of underwater exploration and photography, and can be reached by charter boat.

LONG KEY – Stop here for some underwater hunting of crawfish — lobsterlike crustaceans without the pincers. There are dive shops all along the route, indicated by the red-and-white-striped divers' flags, which arrange private or group snorkeling expeditions to nearby reefs where you stalk (swim after) your prey.

MARATHON – This large key, midway down the archipelago, has recently been developed as a tourist center and already has an airport, an 18-hole golf course, and a convention center. Despite these efforts, Marathon retains much of the original character of a fishing village. There are over 80 species in the Gulf and ocean waters which can be taken with rod and reel or nets from charter boats or the key's bridges. (For information on the many fishing contests held throughout the year, write to the Chamber of Commerce, 3330 Overseas Hwy., Marathon, FL 33050.) The competition is rough and the fish smart. Long Key has the distinction of being home to the world's only school for fish — Flipper's Sea School, where you can watch dolphins, porpoises, and sea lions as they are taught the tricks that will wow audiences all over the country. Hall's Diving Center is a good place to rent gear (1688 Overseas Hwy., 743-9474).

BIG PINE KEY – The largest of the Lower Keys contains 7,700 acres thick with silver palmetto, Caribbean pine, and cacti. Tiny Key deer were thought to be extinct until they reappeared here, and it is possible to spot rare white heron. The Bahia Honda State Recreational Area (five miles east on US 1) has camping, boating, scuba and skin diving rentals, picnicking, and coral-free swimming.

KEY WEST – The southernmost community in the United States and the point closest to Cuba (a 90-mile swim). This famous key combines Southern, Bahamian, Cuban, and Yankee influences in a unique culture that can be seen in its architecture, tasted in its cuisine, and felt in its relaxed, individualistic atmosphere. Traditionally, fishermen, artists, and writers are drawn to this tranquil slip of sand and sea. Ernest Hemingway was among its early devotees, and lived here during his most productive period, during the writing of *To Have and Have Not, For Whom the Bell Tolls, Green Hills of Africa,* and one of the greatest of his short stories, "The Snows of Kilimanjaro." His Spanish colonial–style house of native stone, surrounded by a lush garden of plantings from the Caribbean, is now a museum with many original furnishings and Hemingway memorabilia on display (907 Whitehead St.). Among the others who have been attracted to Key West are Harry Truman (who established a "Little White House" here), John James Audubon, Tennessee Williams, John Dos Passos, and Robert Frost.

To get your bearings, take the Conch Tour Train, a 90-minute narrated tram ride that covers 14 miles, passing all the highlights of town. The train leaves several times a day from one of two depots: Duval and Front Streets, and Old Mallory Square. Since Key West is best for strolling, after the train ride you can visit the places that sounded most interesting, or walk to the key's galleries, craft, and shell shops.

The Lighthouse Museum (Truman Ave. and Whitehead St.) has many military exhibits including a Japanese submarine captured at Pearl Harbor. The Audubon House (205 Whitehead St.), where the artist worked on paintings of Florida Keys wildlife in 1831 and 1832, has a complete set of *Birds of America* engravings on display.

Fishing dominates sports here as elsewhere in the Keys. In addition to fishing in the ocean and Gulf from boats and bridges, there are two fine collections of local marine life. The Municipal Auditorium (Whitehead St. on Mallory Sq.) features live fish. But if you want to see these fish in their natural environment, probably the best way is to scuba dive around the coral reefs. The Key West Pro Dive Shop sponsors trips and rents gear (1605 N Roosevelt Blvd., PO Box 580, Key West, FL 33040, 305 296-3823).

BEST EN ROUTE

Indies Resort and Marina – This 159-room hotel has two dining rooms (one of which is five stories high — a veritable skyscraper in the Keys), a new cocktail lounge, golf course, tennis courts, marina, and fresh- and saltwater pools. Marker 61, Duck Key, FL 33050 (305 289-1000).

Pier House, Key West – Located in the heart of the restored Old Town Key West area, this 101-room hotel has 3 dining areas and a pool. 1 Duval St., Key West, FL 33040 (305 294-9541; toll-free, 800 432-3414; toll-free in Florida, 800 327-8340).

Eden House, Key West – An old guesthouse, built back in the early 20s, now stands as the best of traditional designs, and the price is right. 1015 S Fleming St., Key West, FL 33040 (305 296-6868).

Okefenokee Swamp, Georgia

If you've ever hummed *Way Down Upon the Suwannee River* while you were taking a shower, or waiting for a bus, you already have a connection to the Okefenokee Swamp. In fact, you're even ahead of Stephen Foster, who'd never seen the Suwannee River when he wrote the song. He originally called it *Way Down Upon the Pedee River,* but luckily for Okefenokee lovers, he switched names, thereby immortalizing a curious wandering waterway that begins in this southeast Georgia marshland and flows 230 miles through northeast Florida into the Gulf of Mexico. If you've ever hummed *Way Down Upon St. Marys River,* you are already no doubt familiar with the aquatic interrelationships within the 660 square miles of the Okefenokee Swamp. St. Marys is the other Okefenokee river.

The powerful, mysterious marshland of watery caverns lined with elegant, luxurious cypress trees dripping with moss used to be known as the "land of the trembling earth," a name bestowed upon it by its original inhabitants, the Creek Indians. Many thousands of years earlier, the swamp had been a vast expanse of salt water. Trail Ridge, now Okefenokee's eastern border, was at that time an ocean reef. But shifting land formations locked the water in, and it became a breeding ground for swamp vegetation. The first white settlers arrived in 1853, making their living by fishing, hunting 'gators, and picking wild herbs to sell. Swampers still lead a fairly rugged life, plying their boats up and down the Suwannee in search of cooters, the giant turtles they sell in local markets. Youngsters earn pocket money by catching snakes for people to keep as pets and crayfish for fishermen to use for bait. The worn, wooden porches of swampdwellers' cabins are very often covered with the drying leaves of a plant called deer's tongue, which is used as a medicine and to flavor pipe tobacco.

There are several ways to get to the Okefenokee Swamp from Savannah, Georgia. If you take I-95 south along the coast, you'll find any number of interesting places to stop. At Brunswick, 60 miles south of Savannah, pick up rt. 84 east about 50 miles, to the Okefenokee Swamp.

SAPELO ISLAND – About fifty miles south of Savannah is the Sapelo Island National Estuarine Sanctuary, as the island is officially named. The number of visitors allowed here is restricted because it has been set aside by the Georgia Department of Natural Resources to study and protect the salt marshes—and their marine life—surrounding the island. This island is so unspoiled that ecologists use it as a base for measuring the pollution levels of other areas. Along with lots of deer and wild turkey and the University of Georgia Marine Institute laboratories, the lovely South End mansion is here. Originally built as a plantation house in the 1800s and once owned by tobacco tycoon R. J. Reynolds, South End is sometimes used by former President Carter and his family for vacations. Tours of the island are given on Wednesdays and Saturdays only (reservations required; phone 912 264-7330); you get to the island by ferry from Darien (it's a half-hour boat ride).

MARSHES OF GLYNN – About 30 miles further south, the Marshes of Glynn stretch west from the highway. Georgia-born poet Sidney Lanier composed an epic poem to the marsh in 1878. "The Marshes of Glynn" is not exactly something you would hum at a bus stop, but "Glooms of the live oaks, beautiful-braided and woven/With intricate shades of the vines that myriad-cloven/Clamber the forks of the multi-form boughs" gives you a pretty good idea of life in the sea-marsh. When you see the intricate, misty Marshes of Glynn rising on the horizon alongside I-95, you can well imagine the problems poet Lanier must have had wrestling to create some meaning out of the tropical morass.

SEA ISLANDS – Barely ten miles further south, these legendary islands hug the Georgia coast. Fabled for their exquisite resorts and superior outdoor sports facilities, St. Simons, Jekyll, and Sea Islands have a unique charm. Jekyll, the most southerly island, was a private club for millionaires until 1946, when it became a state park, with nine miles of beach, a wildlife refuge, and restored millionaires' cottages.

OKEFENOKEE NATIONAL WILDLIFE REFUGE – You'll come to the turnoff for Okefenokee, rt. 40, about 30 miles south of St. Simons. From here, it's about 18 miles west on rt. 40 to Folkston, site of the Suwannee Canal Recreation Area. From Folkston, the eastern entrance to the National Wildlife Refuge, you can take guided boat trips, or rent one yourself. There are also hiking trails and a nature drive. In 1937, the government declared Okefenokee a National Wildlife Refuge. Since then, rare species of woodpecker, nuthatch, and flying squirrel nest in the trees, protected by federal law. Mud turtle, snapping turtle, and Florida cooter swim among the water lilies, along with an inordinate variety of frogs, toads, and snakes. Although some, like the king and blue racer snake, are not dangerous, others, such as the diamondback rattler and cottonmouth, have claimed the lives of many. If you're taking a guided excursion in a flat-bottomed boat, the swamp guide will explain how to watch out for these reptiles. If the wind is blowing in one direction, and the grass is leaning a different way, you can be pretty sure there's a snake in there somewhere. But don't be afraid — most snakes are scared of people and won't go out of their way to attack. Your guide might also bend down and touch a lit match to the surface of the swamp, where methane gas bubbles up from the dying vegetation below. It's this churning, seething, subsurface activity which evoked the fascinating Creek Indian image, "trembling earth." Within the boundaries of the refuge are several state parks, including the Stephen C. Foster State Park in Fargo and the Laura S. Walker State Park in Waycross. The park boasts camping, picnicking, fishing, and swimming facilities; and Okefenokee Swamp Park, also in Waycross, site of the Swamp Ecological Center and takeoff point for boat journeys through the swamp. Information: Okefenokee National Wildlife Refuge, PO Box 117, Waycross, GA 31501 (912 496-7156).

BEST EN ROUTE

King and Prince Beach Hotel, St. Simons Island – A resort inn alongside the sea with a good beach, swimming pool, tennis courts, and bike rental. Close to golf, horseback riding, fishing, sailing, and skeet shooting. Dining room open to visitors as well as guests. 94 rooms. PO Box 798, St. Simons Island, GA 31522 (912 638-3631).

Sheraton by the Sea, Jekyll Island – As you'd expect from a former millionaires' paradise, Jekyll Island resorts are still deluxe. This 160-apartment beachfront resort complex set among landscaped grounds has a swimming pool, restaurant, and lounge. 1175 N Beachview Dr., Jekyll Island, GA 31520 (912 635-2521; toll-free, 1 800 841-6262; toll-free in Georgia, 1 800 342-6872).

Mammoth Cave National Park, Kentucky

An ancient Chinese sage, believing that it is better to be soft and yielding than hard and inflexible, was fond of pointing out that stone, the most rigid of substances, always gives way to water. If Lao-tse were around today, he would find the perfect example of his teachings in Mammoth Cave, a huge system of underground chambers and passageways in central Kentucky that has been hollowed out of stone entirely by the seepage of rainwater and the flowing action of underground streams.

Mammoth Cave National Park is off I-65, about 100 miles from Louisville and the same distance from Nashville. The entrance to the main cave is about seven miles west of Cave City, Kentucky. One of the largest known caves in the world, Mammoth contains chambers that are two-thirds the length of a football field. Its tallest dome is 192 feet high; its deepest pit is 106 feet deep. Although the entire cave complex lies beneath an area only ten miles in diameter, its known passageways and chambers (hundreds of miles of passageways have yet to be explored) wind and twist through five separate levels for a distance of 180 miles.

If its size alone isn't enough to impress you, there are the cave's fantastic formations: Disney-like shapes in stone that twist and turn, ripple and flow, in infinite variation. Most of these natural sculptures, like strange yet familiar objects in a dream, remind you of a hundred different things at once, but some — usually the larger ones — are so strongly suggestive of particular objects that they have been named: King Solomon's Temple, the Pillars of Hercules, Frozen Niagara, the Giant's Coffin, the Bridal Altar Room (which has actually been used for weddings). Adding to the dreamlike effect, clusters of gypsum crystals, like rare flowers, hug many of the cave's walls, turning them into exotic hanging gardens.

National Park Service guides conduct daily tours of the most spectacular formations and chambers in the cave. (No solo exploring is allowed.) And if you weary of the park's subterranean wonders, above ground there are 51,000 acres of beautiful Kentucky woodlands to roam.

The origins of Mammoth Cave go back about 240 million years to a time when a succession of seas covered this part of the country. The seas left layers of mud, shells, and sand that hardened into limestone and sandstone. After the last sea drained away, rainwater, containing small amounts of carbonic acid, seeped into fissures in the limestone layers, dissolving some of the stone as it percolated down. Over time, the cracks widened and a system of underground streams developed which hollowed out the cave. As the streams cut deeper and deeper into their beds, they continuously lowered the floor of the cave, allowing more and more of the upper regions to dry.

Water not only carved out this mammoth house of stone, it furnished and decorated it as well. As it seeped through the limestone in the dry parts of the cave, it evaporated, leaving a mineral deposit called travertine (also known as cave onyx). Water dripping from the ceiling of the cave over centuries formed icicles of travertine, or stalactites. Water flowing over rock formed waterfalls of travertine, or flowstone. In a similar way, water shaped the cave's pillars, temples, and altars. Even as you marvel at these formations and gasp at the vastness of this underground palace, water, seeping through the limestone and flowing in underground streams, continues the process begun eons ago.

Human beings knew about Mammoth Cave 3,000 years ago. The remains of a mummified man who was apparently killed by a falling boulder while he was chipping minerals from the cave walls indicate that the woodland Indians used to mine gypsum here.

Kentucky pioneers discovered the cave in 1798; since then it has had a varied history. During the War of 1812, saltpeter, an ingredient in gunpowder, was extracted from bat guano found on the floor of Mammoth Cave. As almost the only source of saltpeter in the entire country, the cave played an important role in winning the war.

In the 1840s, when the cave was privately owned, a doctor attempted to cure tubercular patients by having them live in the constant temperature (54°) and humidity (87%) of the cave for several weeks. A few patients died and the rest emerged sicker than when they'd entered.

Throughout the 19th century, the curious came from far and near to see the cave's wonders by the flickering light of whale-oil lamps. Occasionally, the famous were drawn as well. Edwin Booth, the celebrated Shakespearean actor, recited Hamlet's soliloquy in a chamber of the cave now called Booth's Amphitheater. And in 1851, Jenny Lind sang sweetly in these subterranean halls.

There are three main entrances to the cave: the natural or Historic Entrance, and two manmade entrances known as Frozen Niagara and Carmichael. You can purchase tickets for a variety of different cave tours at the Visitors' Center near the Historic Entrance. (Beware of official-looking solicitors who offer to sell you tickets on the way to the Visitors' Center; these people are usually employed by owners of small private caves nearby.)

There are five main tours to choose from — one to suit just about every age and level of endurance. (All tours require sturdy shoes and a warm sweater.) The easiest trip is Frozen Niagara (½ mile, one hour), which takes you to a variety of formations, the largest of which is Frozen Niagara itself. On the Historic Trip (two miles, two hours), you will see the Rotunda Room, where bat guano was processed into saltpeter during the War of 1812; Lost John, the mummified Indian gypsum miner; and Mammoth Dome, the highest dome in the cave. You will also see the famous blindfish of Mammoth Cave in the underground streams along this route. Through long evolutionary adaptation to the perpetual darkness of the cave, these colorless fish have lost the use of their eyes.

To see the most beautiful gypsum formations in the cave, take the Scenic Trip (four miles, four hours), on which you will stop for lunch in the Snowball Room, 267 feet underground. The Scenic Trip ends at Frozen Niagara.

You will see the cave in an entirely different light when you take the Lantern Trip (three miles, three hours). While electricity makes it easy to see everything, only lantern light creates the proper shadowy atmosphere for cave viewing.

If all of these tours seem a bit tame, there is the Wild Cave Trip (five miles, six hours), a rugged route that leads through crawlways and gives you a taste of what spelunking is all about — hard hats, headlamps, and all. Persons in wheelchairs need not miss out on Mammoth Cave. A special tour (½ mile, 1½ hours) is available for the physically handicapped.

When you finally emerge from your tour, blinking in the sunlight and dazzled by all the wonders underground, you can restore your senses with a short (one mile) walk on the Cave Island Nature Trail, which begins and ends near the Historic Entrance. Giant sycamores and beech trees line this trail, which leads to the bottomlands of the Green River. There, underground streams emerge from the caverns below ground. Several other trails wind through the woods on this side of the park.

The least developed and, in many ways, the most beautiful part of the park is its north side. Here, you can walk along the stream beds past waterfalls and natural bridges, or meander along the steep bluffs that afford lovely views of the Kentucky hills. To get to this little-known side of the park, take the car ferry run by paddle wheel and guided by cables across the Green River.

If you have just returned from the Wild Cave Trip and have had enough hiking for the day, thank you, you can board the *Miss Green River* for a leisurely cruise. The twilight cruise is the best for seeing wildlife: As you sit in comfort, you glide past beaver, turtles, deer, and snakes on the riverbank. Not as exciting as the *African Queen* maybe, but a very pleasant way to pass an hour. You can buy tickets for the cruise at the Visitors' Center.

If your fishing gear is just languishing in the trunk of the car, you can put it to good use in the Green River or in the scenic Nolin River, which runs along the park's eastern boundary. Permits are required and are available from the Kentucky Department of Fish and Wildlife Resources, 1 Game Farm Rd., Frankfort, KY 40601 (502 564-3046).

Before you head north to Louisville for the Kentucky Derby (held on the first Saturday of May at Churchill Downs), northeast to the beautiful Bluegrass Country around Lexington, or west to the lake country that borders Tennessee, don't forget to stop at the craft shop at Mammoth Cave National Park. Here you can buy woven items, pottery, metal crafts, baskets, brooms, wood carvings, and dulcimers handmade in the Kentucky hills. Information: the Superintendent, Mammoth Cave National Park, Mammoth Cave, KY 42259 (502 758-2328).

BEST EN ROUTE

There are numerous hotels and motels in the area, at Cave City and Bowling Green. Farther afield in central Kentucky, in the general direction of Louisville and Lexington, are a couple of inns of interest which could be comfortably incorporated into a Mammoth Cave visit.

Doe Run Inn, Brandenburg – Close to the Indiana-Kentucky border near the Ohio River, 40 miles southwest of Louisville. The inn incorporates the remains of an early Kentucky mill, and is simple, unadorned, and comfortable. One reason for visiting is to eat — chicken, ham, biscuits, traditional Kentucky fare done with great attention. Rt. 2, Brandenburg, KY 40108 (502 422-2042).

Boone Tavern Hotel, Berea – Run by Berea College and staffed by students; guests are welcome at all college activities. About 40 miles south of Lexington. Main St., Berea, KY 40403 (606 986-9358).

Bayou Country, Louisiana

Technically, a bayou is a bit of waterway that has wandered away from — or been left by — a main river. A huge, slow river will create bayous as it flows across any flat plain, cutting new waterways as rising sediment changes its course, then abandoning them when it changes direction yet again. Thus are bayous — independent slow-moving streams — born.

That's the dictionary definition of a bayou, but it doesn't begin to describe the bayou country of southern Louisiana, where the Mississippi River flows so slowly, and over such a wide and meandering course, that it has bred bayous like bastard children, a whole world of them, filled with swampgrass patrolled by alligators and cypress forests festooned with Spanish moss. Bayou country — called Acadiana — starts west of New Orleans, and covers 22 parishes (counties) from Auoyelles Parish down to the Gulf Coast.

Bayou is actually the French mispronunciation of the Choctaw word "bayuk," meaning creek or stream. The Choctaw Indians were the first inhabitants of this region. In the mid-1700s they were joined by the Acadians, French inhabitants of Nova Scotia whom the British exiled from Canada. (You may remember *Evangeline,* Longfellow's tragic poem on their trek.) These Acadians — "Cajuns" as they came to be known down here — adapted to the temperate climate, settled in, and gradually turned the bayou country into a French-American enclave unlike anything in the world.

The marriage of bayou and French was felicitous; today the culture remains, though not untouched, still unique. Whimsical "franglais" crops up everywhere: horse races at Evangeline Downs begin with the cry *"Ils sont partie"* instead of "They're off." The unofficial motto of this part of the country is *Laissez le bon temps rouler,* which, if not authentic French, nonetheless translates into an accurate summary of Cajun attitudes —"Let the good times roll."

On a map, Acadiana is located in south central Louisiana, west of Baton Rouge. Its eight parishes include a few largish cities, some spectacular gardens, some local oddities like salt islands that you're not likely to see anywhere else, and a lot of history kept alive by the Cajuns.

Due to its sprawling size, Acadiana is not a region that lends itself to an organized driving route. Part of the charm of a visit here is in meandering along like the bayous themselves, traveling wherever highways lead you. A detailed map of Acadiana is absolutely essential, as some of the roads here will not even show up on large maps of the state. Request a driving map from the Lafayette Convention and Visitors' Commission, POB 52066 OCS, Lafayette, LA 70505 (318 232-3737).

There are dozens of little towns, each with its own festival or its unique claim to fame. Remember that you are in the South where the pace is much less hectic than in other regions of the United States. The people are very outgoing — friendlier and more willing to sit for a spell and chat. Add to this Southern hospitality and French charm — and you have the basic ingredients for a most memorable vacation. Allow enough time to let yourself get into the slow swing. Certainly try some of the regional cuisine — like crawfish — that has never made it north of Lafayette. Join in the local festivals. In short . . . *Laissez le bon temps rouler!*

ATCHAFALAYA BASIN – Running down the eastern third of Acadiana, the Basin is a good place to begin getting familiar with the country — and incredible country it is. The Basin is a swamp 1,300 square miles in area, stretching from near Lafayette south to the Gulf. Three times larger than Okefenokee Swamp in Georgia (see p. 686), it receives little notice outside the state because it is totally undeveloped for tourists, with one exception. For an adventure through Atchafalaya Basin, you can take the boat tour that leaves from McGee's Landing near Henderson (exit 115 off rt. I-10). For advance reservations, call 318 228-8523.

LAFAYETTE (intersection of US 167 and I-10) – The undisputed center of Acadiana. A city with a population of some 100,000, it boasts the usual variety of municipal auditoriums, centers, and museums. But these are not the things that have drawn you down to bayou country. There are uniquely Cajun places and events here you'll not want to miss. The Acadian Village (1½ miles off Hwy. 167, north on Ridge Rd.) is a bayou town that has been relocated and restored to reflect life in 1755, the year the first wave of French exiles arrived here from Acadia in Nova Scotia. Visitors can walk through town, stopping at the general store, several open houses, the trading post, and a blacksmith shop. The heart of the village is the Chapel of New Hope (the chapel remains a symbolic heart today because this village exists not only as a historic restoration, but also as a fund-raising center for the Alleman Center for Louisiana's handicapped citizens).

Adjacent to the village, and also part of the Alleman Center, are the Around-the-World Tropical Gardens — a horticulturist's walking tour of the hot-weather areas of the world: semitropical US, Latin America, Asia, Africa, and the Pacific Islands. (Both village and gardens are open daily, 10 AM to 5 PM.)

In March and April, Lafayette hosts the Azalea Trail festivities, when antebellum homes throughout the area open to the public, and millions of azaleas grown in the area burst into bloom; it is the perfect time to visit the town.

BREAUX BRIDGE (nine miles northeast of Lafayette, rt. 94 and I-10) – Here the Crawfish Festival is held in April or May in even-numbered years. This "crawfish capital of the world" is actually a picturesque Acadian town located on the banks of the Bayou Teche — from whose waters come the crawfish that tempt up to 50,000 hungry visitors. Local restaurants serve this delicacy in dozens of different ways, all Cajun and all delicious.

ST. MARTINVILLE – This is the area where a great many Acadians first settled, and the town is filled with references to that epic story and Longfellow's poem about it. (In fact, you might well want to reread the poem before you visit. It will heighten your appreciation of the town.) In town you can visit Evangeline's grave. The city has a life-size bronze statue of Evangeline, a gift from actress Dolores del Rio after filming the movie here. The town courthouse has a small, intriguing display of early French aristocratic coats of arms, but even more interesting is the Acadian Museum, on the grounds of Longfellow-Evangeline Commemorative Area just outside town, with live demonstrations of early crafts. The museum is said to be in the house of the man who was "Gabriel" in Longfellow's poem. The grounds of the area are extensive, 157 acres, with camping facilities, a pool, and a restaurant.

NEW IBERIA (Hwy. 90 and Hwy. 14) – The center of the sugar cane industry as well as the home of the romantic Bayou Teche. Here, too, is a stately old mansion very much in the manner of stately old mansions you've always associated with the Old South, called Shadows-on-the-Teche. It's vintage 1830 and is now one of 12 historic properties in the area owned and maintained by the National Trust for Historic Preservation.

Just outside of town are two of those geographical oddities mentioned earlier — islands formed by salt domes which pushed up from the sea-level marshlands millions of years ago. These dome-islands are, as you might imagine, rich in salt. In fact it is mined right there. (Salt from here served the entire Confederate army for the duration of the war.) But there is also an astonishing amount of other natural resources, including oil reserves, and some of America's most fertile earth.

AVERY ISLAND – Though small, it is packed with things to see and marvel over. Jungle Gardens and Bird Sanctuary were both developed by the late Edward Avery McIlhenny. The Gardens are a 200-acre landscaped paradise, featuring exotic growing things from all over the world. The Bird Sanctuary is famous for its huge rookery for egrets. Enormous flocks of herons and egrets and other birds protected here can be seen in warm months. Ducks and other migrating fowl can be seen in winter. Here on Avery Island grow all those tiny-but-fiery little peppers that go into the supersecret recipe for Tabasco sauce. You can tour the Tabasco plant if you like, but they guard their secret formula very jealously.

A final note about Avery Island: It is one of the primary US producers of fur-bearing nutria. Nutria, lest you ask, are fur-bearing mammals also known as coypus, originally from South America. A number of years ago a hurricane allowed some domestic nutria to escape from their cage. They discovered the bayou agreed with them, and proceeded to overpopulate. They are caught today for their fur.

JEFFERSON ISLAND – Another nearby salt dome, this island has a history richly laced with intrigue, glamour, and adventure. Originally a hide-out of Jean Lafitte (pots of foreign gold and silver were unearthed here in 1923), it was much later bought by Joseph Jefferson, who designed and built the "Big House." (Jefferson was a famous actor during the late 1800s who toured the world with his Rip Van Winkle for 40 years.) In 1917 Jefferson Island was bought by Lyle Bayless, whose son is responsible for the present beauty of the island.

BEST EN ROUTE

Lafayette is a very ordinary city when it comes to lodgings; there are many, many hotels and motels which are comfortable, reasonable, and handy, but which offer little else than convenience. While you are in the bayou country you certainly won't have trouble finding accommodations, but neither are you likely to have the trip "made" by some surprise inn. One exception may be:

Asphodel, near Jackson – A plantation village in the heart of plantation country. Asphodel is the plantation, open for tours only; the village has smaller buildings:

an inn/restaurant, gift shop, and breakfast room. Cuisine is excellent, mixing Creole cooking with the best of others. Rooms come with "Southern breakfast" (grits, eggs, bacon, and much more). Write Asphodel Plantation, Rt. 2, Box 89, Jackson, LA 70748 (504 654-6868).

It's hard to get a bad meal in Acadiana, but you must be prepared to eat native: jambalaya, gumbo, crawfish (or crawdaddies or crayfish).

Natchez Trace Parkway, Natchez, Mississippi, to Nashville, Tennessee

For several hundred years before white men settled in the Mississippi and Ohio Valleys, the Natchez, Choctaw, and Chickasaw Indians used one major trail to pass north and south. Worn down to a permanent roadbed, the trail — or Trace — wandered for 450 miles from the lower Mississippi River into what was to become central Tennessee. When Kentucky and Tennessee filled up with hunters and trappers, and then settlers, the Trace entered the history of commerce. Settlers traded with Southern port cities, especially Natchez where the trail began, and the Trace — then called the Natchez Trace —was the portage route back home. "Kaintuck" boatmen floated downriver on the Mississippi's currents, but were obliged to return home on foot, carrying their boats and canoes on their backs. Between the late 1700s and about 1820, the Natchez Trace was a constant thoroughfare.

The coming of steamboats changed the history of the Trace. By 1819 there were 20 steam-driven ships plying the Mississippi — up- and downstream — eliminating the need for overland portage.

Parts of the Natchez Trace still exist, and today the entire route is commemorated by the Natchez Trace Parkway, a modern highway being built under the auspices of the National Park Service and still under construction, that runs from Natchez, Mississippi, northward through a slip of Alabama, to Nashville, Tennessee. The parkway does not replace the Trace, but it does follow the original route as closely as possible, and there are numerous spots along the way where travelers can park and actually walk (or ride horseback) along the Trace. The parkway is far from completed. Its longest continuous section stretches from Jackson, Mississippi, to Kirkville, 180 miles of quiet two-lane highway with numerous points of interest — Indian mounds, sites of Civil War battles, areas of natural interest, and above all, portions of the Trace which cross the parkway's route — marked by signs. You can follow the Natchez Trace Parkway from Nashville south to Natchez (realizing that the entire route is not yet completed) or from Natchez to Nashville. We start our itinerary, as did the boatmen who used the Trace, at Natchez, traveling north to Tennessee. Information: the Superintendent, Natchez Trace Parkway, NT 143, Tupelo, MS 38801 (601 842-1572).

NATCHEZ – Before beginning the journey north, spend some time in Natchez itself. When the boatmen ended their downriver journeys here in the first decades of the 19th century, they found a city on its way to getting rich, obsessed with elegance and style, supported by the profitable cotton trade. The rivermen saw little of this elegance or opulence, however. With their wages stuffed in their pockets, they spent most of their time in Natchez-Under-the-Hill, everything a shantytown river city should be. Gamblers, killers, adventurers, and traders gathered there on their respective businesses.

There is little of Natchez-Under-the-Hill to see today, but there is a great deal to see and do in Natchez itself. It is known as the city "where the Old South still lives," and in town are two antebellum homes of note: Stanton Hall (401 High St.) and Rosalie (100 Orleans St.). Rosalie is the earlier of the two homes, built about 1820. There are a number of antebellum homes in the area open to the public, and a list is available from the Pilgrimage Headquarters (PO Box 347). For a month every spring — early March to April (and/or two weeks in early October) — the Pilgrimage and Natchez garden clubs sponsor a daily tour that includes some 30 of the finest antebellum homes in the country. Everything possible is done to create the aura of the Old South; ladies in hoop skirts greet visitors in their spacious parlors, formal gardens are pruned, preened, and open to the public, and the evenings are given over to an annual Confederate Pageant.

Within city limits is the Grand Village of the Natchez Indians (US 61, on Jefferson Davis Blvd.), a National Historic Landmark that has yielded archeological proof that Natchez is the site of the Natchez Indians' largest village (the "Grand Village"). The Natchez culture peaked in the mid-1500s, and came to a disastrous end in 1730 when the French wiped out the entire tribe.

NATCHEZ TRACE PARKWAY – When completed, the parkway will run the full 450 miles between Natchez and Nashville, crossing and recrossing the Trace many times in its course. Today only three segments are open (a total of almost 330 miles): between Lorman and Jackson, Mississippi (about 63 miles); between Jackson and Tupelo, Mississippi (about 180 miles); and between Cherokee, Alabama, and Duck River, Tennessee (about 85 miles). Other shorter segments are located north of Natchez, east of the Mississippi-Alabama state line and east of Tupelo. However, roads leading to these sections are clearly marked, so it is possible to leave from either terminus city and follow the route of the Trace.

The parkway is completely free of all commercialism. You will find no hotels or restaurants along the road. Park rangers patrol the parkway carefully to protect it from spoilage. (Food and accommodations are available in towns off the parkway.) There are picnicking facilities along the parkway, and campsites at three campgrounds. Campsites can't be reserved in advance, and there is a 15-day limit on maximum stays at any campsite. The parkway headquarters is just north of Tupelo, where the parkway intersects rt. 45. There you can get maps and information, and see a film on the Trace and its history. The parkway features self-guiding tours along the Trace, and rangers at headquarters can provide information on them.

Today the significance of the Natchez Trace is the history that is buried on it or near it. The parkway offers a way of following the Trace while having the most significant aspects of it pointed out as you go. Indian mounds, remains of inns or "stands," as they were called, and living history demonstrations presented by rangers give a sense of what the Trace was like when it was a footpath that cut through steaming swamps and flatlands, plagued by insects, disease, roving bands of cutthroats (the boatmen who used the Trace were returning home from profitable trading ventures on the Mississippi; as they walked along the dark lane of the Trace, often with hedges six feet above their heads, they would be set upon by thieves), and unfriendly Indians. At frequent intervals along the parkway there are rest stops with picnic tables and facilities, usually located at especially scenic spots.

Just 12 miles outside of Natchez on the parkway is Emerald Mound, one of the largest Indian ceremonial mounds ever found in the United States. Built sometime in the 300 years before 1600, Emerald Mound covers nearly eight acres, and is representative of the Mississippian Indians who predated the Natchez and Choctaws, who still lived in the area when white explorers discovered it.

Outside Tupelo is Chickasaw Village, the remains of a fortified Chickasaw camp and starting point of a self-guided tour through the area. Much of the country around the Trace saw action during the Civil War, and there are numerous markers along the route noting points of historical interest. Though it is off the parkway, anyone interested in the war will certainly want to visit the Tupelo National Battlefield, where some 10,000 Confederate horsemen met 14,000 Union troops. The cavalry engaged the Union forces three times on July 14, 1864, and were defeated each time, at a ghastly price in men and horses. Finally the Union troops retreated north, after buying enough time for General Sherman to move his force by rail to begin the attack on Atlanta.

The segment of parkway beyond Tupelo has one special feature, a short section of the actual Trace which can be driven, called the Old Trace Loop Drive. About 2½ miles of the Trace have been paved (though very narrow) and turned into a one-way loop drive for automobiles, featuring several scenic overlooks. Trailers are not recommended to try the loop.

BEST EN ROUTE

Texada, Natchez – Pronounced "te-hada." A fully restored 1792 mansion, part of the yearly Pilgrimage Tour, that offers accommodations for overnight guests. Rooms are in the main house, and one has twin sleigh beds. There is also a three-bedroom guest cottage. 222 S Wall St., Natchez, MS 39120 (601 445-4283).

The Burn, Natchez – Antebellum elegance; six rooms for guests. 712 N Union St., Natchez, MS 39120 (601 445-8566).

For food:

Carriage House Restaurant, Natchez – In the courtyard of Stanton Hall, the restoration project of the Pilgrimage Garden Club. The menu emphasizes early Southern food, and is excellent. 401 High St., Natchez, MS 39120 (601 445-5151).

Cock of the Walk, Natchez-Under-the-Hill – Atmosphere of the flatboat days, when boatmen fought one another to earn the right to wear the red feather, signifying they were "cock of the walk." The tavern features red-shirted waiters, serving only one dish — the Mississippi specialty of catfish, with all the trimmings. Natchez-Under-the-Hill, Natchez, MS 39120 (601 446-8920).

Outer Banks and Cape Hatteras National Seashore, North Carolina

The elements reign supreme on the Outer Banks, a 175-mile ribbon of sandy islands — linked together by a single highway — running faintly parallel to the North Carolina coast. The ocean and the wind lash at the shoreline, changing its shape, washing away and replacing sand, building dune after dune. A large wave falling across the sand at a particularly narrow point can make two islands where once there was one, and there are spots where only a few hundred feet separate a crashing Atlantic from the calm Pamlico Sound. The visitor will gaze in awe at what the ocean and the wind can do, because a trip to these five islands (north to south: Bodie, Pea, Hatteras, Ocracoke, and Cape Lookout), and especially to the Cape Hatteras National Seashore, is a trip not of doing, but of simply being there and witnessing the ever-writing hand of nature.

Except for one stretch of superhighway — the "motel row" from Kitty Hawk to Nags Head, an area tolerated for the tourists it brings — the Outer Banks are America's seaside wilderness, where man has been defeated by nature and has admitted it. And a good thing, too. With almost all the motels in one area, the rest of the land is under the auspices of the National Park Service and protected from development.

Ghosts haunt the Outer Banks. More than 500 ships sank within just a few miles of its shores, earning it the title "Graveyard of the Atlantic." It began with Sir Richard Grenville's *Tiger* in 1585 and continues today; most recent victim was the seagoing tug *Marjorie McAllister* in 1969. Most famous was the Federal gunboat *Monitor;* it survived a mismatch with the Confederacy's *Merrimac* in March of 1862, but on December 31 of that same year it went under in a Hatteras storm.

The irregular coastline and manic weather made these shores the perfect lair for pirates. In the early 1700s, Edward Teach (Blackbeard) and his band holed up in Ocracoke. It was here, in 1718, that Blackbeard was killed, most of his treasure going down with him. It still waits on the ocean floor.

This section of ocean offers excellent sport, with scores of fish to be pulled in by surf casters: tuna, mackerel, marlin, and unfortunately, even the occasional dolphin, that cagey sea creature known for antics like swimming near shore and laughing at the hook-and-line hunters.

There's no telling what nature will do next: Birds roost here by the thousands on their way north and south in warm and cold seasons, making the Outer Banks one of the country's prime bird-watching spots. The trees that held the sands in place centuries ago are gone, having been felled for shipbuilding by the fishermen who lived here. Today, the fishermen and their villages have all disappeared, and only wildflowers — thousands of them — whip in the breezes.

Three approaches link the banks with the mainland: from the north, two toll bridges, one at Point Harbor at the end of rt. 158; the other, the extension of rt. 64, running across Roanoke Island and through Manteo before coming out near Nags Head. From the south, a ferry connects Cedar Island and Ocracoke Village. Free ferry service runs from Cedar Island to the city of Hatteras. (For more information and to make reservations on the ferry to Ocracoke, call 919 928-3841 or 919 225-3551; reservations are accepted by phone or in person within 30 days prior to the crossing. For details on free ferry service to Hatteras, call 919 986-2353.)

KITTY HAWK A visit can start from either end of the Outer Banks islands, but we'll begin in the north, at Kitty Hawk, because there isn't a schoolchild alive who doesn't associate this little town and stretch of beach with Wilbur and Orville Wright, and that day in 1903 when a new era began. Commemorating the two bicycle makers from Dayton stands a majestic monument, the Wright Brothers National Memorial, two miles south of town on the rt. 158 bypass. A Visitors' Center (open year round, free admission) displays original plans for the "flying machine," scale models of the craft, and reconstructions of hangars, workshops, and living quarters.

The drive south on rt. 158 through Kill Devil Hills and Nags Head is disappointing; simply ignore the motels that line the road, and contemplate the scenery to come. Nags Head is the last town before the Cape Hatteras National Seashore officially begins, and the beach just south of town boasts spectacular sand dunes, some rising as high as 135 feet. Climb to the top of one or two for an unobstructed view miles in all directions.

CAPE HATTERAS NATIONAL SEASHORE – A Visitors' Center near the southern end of Bodie Island (signs point the way) is open daily, except Christmas. Also stop in at the Bodie Lighthouse, which has an observation platform for viewing the bird life that roosts in the neighborhood.

Before continuing south, cross the bridge to Manteo on Roanoke Island. Just north of town is the Fort Raleigh National Historical Site, commemorating the English colony settled in 1585 by Walter Raleigh and found empty and mysteriously abandoned in 1586. Historians are still puzzled by the disappearance of the colony, and the single word, "croatoan," found carved on a fencepost. Today, visitors can tour a reconstruction of the earthwork fort, excavations marking the original site, and a nature trail that traces Roanoke Sound. The site is open daily. Next to the site is Elizabeth Garden, a memorial to the colonists, featuring herb gardens, sculpted lawns, and a nightly presentation (in summer) of the historical drama *The Lost Colony.* (See *Outdoor Dramas*, p. 537.) The gardens are closed mid-December to early January.

Pea Island is the next bit of land south of Bodie, home of the Pea Island National Wildlife Refuge, 5,880 acres maintained by the US Fish and Wildlife Service. All year long this is one of the East Coast's most populated avian roosting places, but especially exciting in fall or spring when birds head south or north. Expect to see great snow geese, gadwalls, Canada geese, loons, grebes, herons, brant, whistling swans, and countless other species of aquatic and migratory birds.

The drive south on rt. 12 on Hatteras Island deserves unhurried attention because each spot is worth a stop: Markings along the road indicate places for swimming, fishing, viewing hulls of wrecked vessels, climbing dunes, and spying on wildlife. At the "elbow" of Hatteras Island is the village of Buxton, and just south, toward the sea, is the Cape Hatteras Lighthouse, America's tallest at 208 feet. A marvelous view is afforded from the lighthouse observatory (open daily except Christmas). The balcony is closed for safety reasons. If you spend enough time watching the waves and the shifting sands, you'll feel that you're watching the shape of the island change, sand washing away and returning in different configurations. Perhaps nowhere in the country can one better witness the ocean's power, for right off Cape Hatteras the cold Atlantic waters first mingle with the warm Gulf Stream. The effect is swirling, crashing waves, an awesome show of nature's force. Nearby is the Museum of the Sea with exhibits on the island's centuries of maritime activity and industry (open daily, except Christmas).

The town of Hatteras, south of Buxton on rt. 12, is known only as a place to stop for a bite to eat or a quick look around. Stop and talk to some natives, and listen for their cockneylike accent. The story goes that Hatteras Village was settled by survivors of a ship that left Devon, England, and capsized off the coast. To this day, villagers have a "Devon" twang to their speech.

The final island in the national seashore chain is Ocracoke, physically the most beautiful. The only city is Ocracoke Village at the island's southern tip, where the ferry from Cedar Island docks and picks up passengers for the return trip. Stop in the Visitors' Center there (open daily except Christmas) to pick up brochures on the island's many walks and sights. Before boarding the ferry back to the mainland, arrange with a local boat captain for a ride to Cape Lookout National Seashore, the next set of islands to the south. There are no cars — and no roads — on this newly cited national monument to nature, but you can walk around and catch glimpses of the wild horses, unfettered vegetation, and the remains of abandoned fishing villages. Of all the areas in the Outer Banks, this is one of the most fascinating, and well saved for last. There is little to do, but so very much to see and experience.

For more information on campgrounds and anything else in the Outer Banks: the

Superintendent, Cape Hatteras National Seashore, Manteo, NC 17954 (919 473-2117). National Park rangers are more than willing to help with all your questions by mail, on the phone, or in person. They'll even teach the novice how to surf cast (in summer only); just bring your own tackle.

BEST EN ROUTE

Make reservations to stay in either Kill Devil Hills or Nags Head at the northern end of the island chain outside of the seashore park; there is a wide choice of motels and restaurants. (Most establishments close from mid-October to early April; be sure to call or write for exact dates.)

Sea Ranch, Kill Devil Hills – Has an indoor-outdoor pool, indoor tennis, golf privileges, and a night club with entertainment. It is north of town, on rt. 158 at milepost 7, PO Box 325, Kill Devil Hills, NC 27948 (919 441-7126).

Chart House, Kill Devil Hills – In the same area, with comfortable accommodations and a selection of recreational activities — private beach, pool, golf, picnic facilities. Also on rt. 158 at milepost 7.5. PO Box 432, Kill Devil Hills, NC 27948 (919 441-7418).

While in the area be sure to try *Port O' Call* restaurant, an especially good seafood place with daily specials. On rt. 158 at milepost 9 (919 441-7484). Another good seafood restaurant is Evans' Crab House at the rt. 158 by-pass at milepost 10 (919 441-5994).

Sea Oatel, Nags Head – Sits on its own beach, with most of its rooms overlooking the sea, on rt. 158 at milepost 16.5. PO Box 489, Nags Head, NC 27959 (919 441-7191).

Blue Heron, Nags Head – Has its own beach as well, and bargain rates, very near the Sea Oatel on rt. 158. R.R. 1, PO Box 741, Nags Head, NC 27959 (919 441-7447).

Hatteras Island, Rodanthe – On the north end of Hatteras Island on rt. 12. It offers one- and two-bedroom apartments, and has a pool and a playground. Write to the motel at PO BOX 8, Rodanthe, NC 27968 (919 987-2345).

Island Inn, Ocracoke – A surprise in the town of Ocracoke on Ocracoke Island, with very comfortable rooms overlooking the harbor, and best of all, perhaps the best food in the area. PO Box 7, Ocracoke, NC 27960 (919 928-4351).

There is a choice of clean and well-managed campsites on the Outer Banks: Oregon Inlet (on Bodie Island), Cape Point (Buxton, on Hatteras Island), in Ocracoke, in Salvo (south of Nags Head), and in Frisco (northeast of Hatteras). The first three are open year-round; the other two, summers only. Information from the Cape Hatteras National Seashore (address above).

Great Smoky Mountains National Park, Tennessee and North Carolina

When most people consider US national parks, their thoughts turn to nature's spectacles — shooting geysers, roaring rivers carving out vast canyons, forests turned to stone. The most popular of the national parks has no such superstars, but still attracts nearly nine million visitors annually (more than twice the draw of any other park) with its almost perfect serenity. Spread across the northwest corner of North Carolina and the southeastern tip of

Tennessee, the Great Smoky Mountains National Park offers 800 square miles of quiet beauty — virgin forest blanketing a third of the land; 16 rounded ancient mountains reaching 6,000 feet or higher; drives with inspiring views; more than 700 miles of marked trails for hiking and horseback riding; over 600 miles of streams for fishing; lush and varied vegetation; and a romantic, bluish mist from which the Great Smokies derive their name. They are the oldest mountains in America and among the oldest on earth, formed during the Appalachian Revolution, a period that began about 230 million years ago and which lasted many millions of years. The Great Smokies rose as the earth's crust gradually buckled and thrust upward. Whipped, worn, and shaped by eons of storms, winds, and rains, the Smokies survived the weather's onslaught, and today their altitude is better than 5,000 feet for 36 miles along the main crest. Clingman's Dome, the highest peak, arches 6,643 feet upward, and like its neighbors, almost always wears a veil of blue "smoke." Therein lies one of the Smokies' mysteries. What the Indians once called "smoke" we now know is a mist formed by a mixture of water vapor and oils secreted by plants.

The Smokies support an incredible variety of plants. Nurtured by 80 inches of rain a year, more than 150 species of trees flourish in the park. Some trees here were seedlings when the Europeans came to America, including giants with trunks measuring 25 feet in circumference. Hemlocks, pines, oaks, yellow poplars, mountain laurel, and rhododendrons can be seen as you drive along US 441, which bisects the park. As you drive or climb upward, you encounter diverse flora — Southern, New England, and Canadian plant life all on one mountain.

Mt. Le Conte (6,593 feet) is one of the Smokies to explore thoroughly. You can enjoy the view from a distance, but a mountain is more than a big thing to be seen from a car window. To fully appreciate its beauty, ascend Mt. Le Conte by foot or on horseback. There is no road leading up. At its base, southern plants (like dogwood) abound. Higher up, New England sugar maples and yellow birches appear. And thriving near the top are spruce, fir, and balsam trees, all native to southern Canada. During the Ice Age, the glacier advance stopped north of the Smokies. As a result, northern plants migrated southward, in order to survive, and mingled with local species.

On the way up Mt. Le Conte, the visitor can follow the Alum Cave Trail. Crossing Alum Cave Creek, the hiker confronts another of the park's mysteries: the laurel hells. Laurels and rhododendrons tangle together so inextricably as to be almost impenetrable. Actually, "hellish" is hyperbolic — this vegetation is interesting and beautiful. No one knows why no trees grow on this ground. Perhaps fires swept the area and the rhododendron–mountain laurel brush established itself before trees could. But getting out of a hell can be tricky off the paths. Even bears have difficulty breaking through any other way.

Did someone say bears? Yes, there are many black bears in the Smokies. The black bear is the smallest species of bear in North America, weighing 200 to 300 pounds. Chances are you won't come across any, but if you meet a bear while hiking, yell or bang pans. If these noises don't scare him away, run. On no account approach a bear.

However, there is no need to practice 100-yard dashes in preparation for a visit to the Great Smokies. Bears tend to shy away from humans, and hikers on trails rarely encounter them. Occasionally, backcountry bears will raid hikers' packs and food supplies, so when camping at night, hang your packs on tree limbs over eight feet high, which will support them but not the bears. In warm weather some bears will rummage through litter baskets in search of food. Bolder bears will even beg for food from tourists. Avoid feeding or approaching them. Bears that rely on handouts forget how to forage for food when the tourist season ends. Certainly do not imitate the man who tried to push a bear into his car so that he could take the bear's picture next to his wife. As gentle as bears may seem, they can suddenly turn mean.

Back on the main track, the Alum Cave Trail leads not to Alum Cave (there is no Alum Cave), but to a bluff with a good view. Legend has it that Confederate soldiers came up here to mine alum for gunpowder. What is here is an overhang of black slate 150 feet high and about 300 feet long.

For the hiker who finds the climb long, there are overnight shelters. To use the shelters you need a permit, which you should obtain from a ranger before you set out. On the summit there is a glorious view and a resting spot — Le Conte Lodge — well worth the trek up.

Clingman's Dome, the highest peak in the Smokies, is another worthwhile climb. (Its 6,643-foot peak can be reached by car.) The winding road up leads to a parking lot. From there a paved half-mile trail leads to the summit, continues spiraling up the ramp of an observation tower, and ends in a serene and beautiful view from the Smokies' highest point. The smooth asphalt trail provides access to the view for those in wheelchairs.

Another tranquil spot is Cades Cove, a green Tennessee valley in the park's western reaches. A few farmers still tend fields there. A one-way road circles past their cabins, barns, and a gristmill from the days of the pioneers. Many of the 19th-century pioneers who settled this area now rest in the Methodist churchyard.

Gregory Bald is a good example of the kind of wide, green, open meadowlands typical of the Smokies' mountaintops, but which are something of a mystery. There is no obvious reason for mountaintop meadowlands, and none of the explanations put forward by park naturalists — wind, fire, or prolonged dry spells killing tree life, making way for meadows — is entirely satisfactory. It has even been proposed that the meadows are sites of early Indian ceremonies.

Gregory Bald and Clingman's Dome are among the park sites on the famous Appalachian Trail. Stretching from Maine to Georgia, the Appalachian Trail zigzags for 68 miles along the park's crest. Altogether, there are about 700 miles of trails in the Great Smoky Mountains National Park, and many of them can be hiked easily in a day or less. Horseback riding is permitted on about half of them.

For motorists, there are 226 miles of paved roads in the park. The two main roads are US 441 and Newfound Gap Road. US 441 cuts across the park between Knoxville, Tennessee, and Asheville, North Carolina. Newfound Gap Road, filled with hairpin turns, affords the motorist splendid views of the mountains as it winds across the park between Gatlinburg, Tennessee, and Cherokee, North Carolina.

Gatlinburg, the western entrance to the park, sees a large share of the park's visitors. Having just 3,000 permanent residents, Gatlinburg is wall-to-wall motels and tourist shops and can accommodate 23,000 people nightly.

On the park's southern side is Cherokee, the capital of the Cherokee Indian reservation, with the Oconaluftee Indian Village, a replica of an 18th-century Cherokee village, and the Qualla Arts and Crafts Mutual, which has high-quality crafts. (For more information see *A Short Tour of Indian America,* p. 608.)

The Great Smoky Mountains National Park is open year-round. The blue mist is thickest in the fall as the leaves start to decay, but the mountains are smoky and majestic during any season. Even on the busiest summer day, you can find peace and seclusion here. There is no mystery about why the Great Smoky Mountains National Park is so popular. Information: the Superintendent, Great Smoky Mountains National Park, Rt. 2, Gatlinburg, TN 37738 (615 436-5615).

BEST EN ROUTE

Visitors have several lodging options. The park runs six developed campgrounds available on a first come-first served basis. Those at Cades Cove, Elkmont, and Smokemont are open year-round. There are 98 primitive backcountry campsites which can be reserved in advance (at least 30 days), most of which are simply clearings with water, and 17 shelters (with chain link fencing fortified against bears) along the Appalachian Trail and other trails for which you must obtain a permit 24 hours before setting out on your hike. Listed below are other lodgings inside the park and in nearby towns such as Gatlinburg. For further information on park facilities and reservations contact Park Headquarters, Great Smoky Mountains National Park, Rt. 2, Gatlinburg, TN 37738 (615 436-5615).

Le Conte Lodge, Great Smoky Mountains National Park – This secluded retreat atop Mt. Le Conte is accessible only by foot or horse trail. The lodge is on park grounds but privately run, and can accommodate 40 people with plenty of fresh mountain air and hearty mountain fare. Open from late March through October, space must be reserved. Contact Le Conte Lodge, PO Box 350, Gatlinburg, TN 37738 (615 436-4473).

Wonderland Club Hotel, Great Smoky Mountains National Park – Old-fashioned atmosphere with good service and food in a quiet setting. Similar to Le Conte, but this hotel can be reached by car. Open early May through October; reservations recommended. Rt. 2, Gatlinburg, TN 37738 (615 436-5490).

Mountain View Hotel, Gatlinburg, Tennessee – The town's first hotel retains something of the old flavor in atmosphere and decor. Dining room, swimming pools, balconies, playground, color TV, free parking; 116 rooms. Rt. 73 E and Parkway, Gatlinburg, TN 37738 (615 436-4132).

Big Bend National Park, Texas

If the call of the wild has got your number, strike out for Big Bend National Park. It's as remote as you can get in the Southwest without actually setting foot into one of the more obscure sections of northern Mexico. Big Bend is literally just that — a big bend in the Rio Grande in southern Texas. If you look at the map, you can see that it's set in that little pocket of Texas that sags slightly to the left of the main body of the state. Although it's not as far south or as far west as you can go by any means, it hugs an interesting corner of the state. It's also nowhere near anyplace you're likely to call civilized. The closest town is Marathon, Texas, about 40 miles north. And the only thing really noteworthy about Marathon, Texas, is that you have to go through there to get to Big Bend. If you're coming from Dallas/Fort Worth, 545 miles northeast, take I-20 to rt. 18 south at Monahans. Rt. 18 runs into rt. 385 south at Fort Stockton, which takes you through Marathon, all the way to Persimmon Gap Ranger Station. Continue on to the administration building and Visitors' Center at Panther Junction in Big Bend National Park.

Because it's in such an out-of-the-way part of the world, lots of people don't make it out here. Not that the folks and wildlife in Big Bend really mind — they adore having these isolated, 706,558 acres of canyons and desert all to themselves. You might not understand why anyone would want to live here at all if you go down to the park's lower elevations in summer, when the scorching heat makes it almost too hot to breathe. Dust fills the air, whirling in conical clouds with only an occasional thunderstorm to break the dry agony. Legends about the intolerable July temperatures include the one about a Big Bend coyote chasing a Big Bend jackrabbit. Even though both are swift animals, the story goes, it was so hot, "they was both walkin'." But since the park's altitude ranges from 1,850 to 7,835 feet, there are places to cool off.

However, if you visit in spring, there's a good likelihood you'll experience a jubilant awe in the presence of rocky cliffs overflowing with white and crimson blossoms. The land, barren and parched in summer, is reborn after the heavy winter rains. Although the scenery is a knockout, we can't promise you a sunny garden. We'd love to tell you that the weather is glorious in the spring but, to be perfectly honest, Big Bend is notoriously unpredictable when it comes to climate. In February, it can hit the 90s on a Monday and snow six inches or more later in the week. And very often, the temperature climbs 40° during the day, only to drop faster than a stone falls off a cliff after dark.

How did Big Bend get such an ornery climate? Millions of years ago the entire area was covered with water. Layers and layers of sand filtered down to the bottom, forming sedimentary rock — in some places, more than 1,000 feet thick. When the ocean dried, the Rio Grande poked its wet nose into the neighborhood and began winding its way through the rocky plains, wearing a groove in the earth along its path. This is the same process of water eroding rock that was a part of the making of the Grand Canyon.

Any trip to Big Bend should begin at the Visitors' Center at Panther Junction. From there, continue along the road to the Basin Ranger Station, where you can rent horses, pack animals, and guides for day or overnight expeditions. You can also camp here, at the Chisos Basin campground. (Since the Chisos Basin is more than 5,000 feet high, be sure to bring a sleeping bag even in the summer.) You can see spectacular sunsets from here, as the sky cascades into a medley of pink, orange, and purple. Because the desert atmosphere is especially clear, the shimmering changes of color are intense and powerfully moving. Whitetail deer occasionally wander past; skunk and wild pig also make this their home. You can hear the coyote wail as it gets dark, an eerie, echoing prelude to a harmonious serenade of night birds. Lizards come out in the morning, which is really the best time for human exploration, too. Big Bend National Park takes in an entire mountain range — the Chisos Mountains. The shallow Rio Grande cuts its way through the gorges of Boquillas Canyon and the 1,500-foot-high Santa Elena Canyon. It's a great place for fishing for catfish.

You don't have to rough it to see these canyons, although many people prefer the greater intimacy of traveling on foot or horseback. A good driving road leads to Santa Elena and Boquillas Canyons. In fact, you can drive for 187 miles through Big Bend. If you want to hike, the rangers will tell you about the trails. There's one to Lost Mine Ridge that takes about three hours, round trip, and another good one to South Rim, on the Mexican border. Inquire at Panther Junction Visitors' Center. Information: the Superintendent, Big Bend National Park, Big Bend, TX 79834 (915 477-2251).

About 450,000 visitors come to Big Bend National Park every year — not a huge crowd as parks go, but still a considerable increase over the intrepid handfuls who braved it in 1944, when this area came under federal jurisdiction. But the national park is only part of a mammoth, exquisite stretch of land, known as the last surviving huge wilderness of Texas. It's still as raw here today as it was when the frontiersmen and women arrived to conquer the Wild West. If you ever wondered how it must have felt to set out for untamed territory, there are three areas northwest of Big Bend that will fill your yearning for challenge. Follow the road at the northwestern boundary of Big Bend National Park that leads along the Rio Grande.

SOLITARIO – About 12 miles north of Lajitas, Texas. Solitario is an arid, isolated, craterlike bowl in the middle of nowhere. Geologically remarkable because it contains traces of four distinct eras, Solitario contains ancient Paleozoic rocks; limestone dating from the Cretaceous sea era; hardened lava flows; and most recent, contemporary erosion. The terrain is so harsh that on a good day, you can expect to cover about 15 miles with a sturdy four-wheel-drive vehicle. Solitario is aptly named — there's nothing here but the elements, although there have been stories of ghosts appearing around campfires.

FRESNO AND CHORRO CANYONS – Just to the west of Solitario, in the uplands, these canyons appear magically in the wilderness like Shangri-la in a burst of rushing waterfalls and green, shady trees. This is truly an oasis. Upper Madrid Falls in Chorro Canyon is the Garden of Eden to this part of the world, but after its discovery by settlers in 1870, it was lost to memory for 100 years. Next door the one-mile-wide Fresno Canyon separates Solitario from the Bofecillos Mountains and escapes the annual floods which are endemic to the region. The sheltered canyon provides refuge to wild birds, butterflies, and water-loving animals. Fresno Canyon came to public attention in 1916 when the US Cavalry stationed itself there to head off Pancho Villa and his men, who were hiding in a nearby creek.

COLORADO CANYON – A few miles north of Redford, before you reach the town of Presidio. This was one of the few areas in this part of the world that was never settled by the Indians. No shards have ever been found in the hollows of these canyon walls. Colorado Canyon is great for canoes or kayaks, with a few whitewater rapids to heighten the adventure. During a normal half-day trip, you'll go through an unforgettable passage lined with cliffs towering more than 800 feet high. Don't be frightened if you come across bear feeding along the riverbank — they'll be more startled than you.

BEST EN ROUTE

Chisos Mountains Lodge, Big Bend National Park – A small lodge with motel-type units, restaurant, and a supply store, dramatically situated at 5,400 feet. Reservations required year-round. Big Bend National Park, TX 79834 (915 477-2291).

Antelope Lodge, Alpine – Well-appointed cottages in a country setting. 27 units. PO Box 338, Alpine, TX 79830 (915 837-2641).

Padre Island National Seashore, Texas

Like the coasts of New Jersey and the Carolinas, Texas' Gulf of Mexico shoreline is blessed with a series of long, lean islands that lie just offshore, and that follow the great arc of the Gulf Coast with almost perfect fidelity. The last and longest of these islands is Padre Island, 140 miles of sand and grass that stretches along the south Texas coast from Port Aransas just above Corpus Christi to Port Isabel, where Mexico and Texas meet like two lips puckering to kiss the Gulf.

Padre Island is really two islands, separated by a tiny channel of sea: Padre, the longer, more northerly island; and South Padre, which ends at Port Isabel. North Padre is 115 miles long, 80 miles of which is sand, grass, and sea, where you stand a good chance of witnessing nothing but the work of nature — waves beating against the shore, acres of grasslands, and if you're lucky, not another human being, just the thousands of birds and shore animals that live here or visit during migrations. This is Padre Island National Seashore.

Development is contained almost entirely on the 25 miles of South Padre, in settlements predominantly confined to the northern and southern extremities, where you will find the motels, hotels, restaurants, resort communities, condominiums, and highways that have made the south Texas coast famous. And if it weren't enough to have these civilizations coexisting, Padre Island is an anomaly because the two ways of life get on together very well.

Two "port" cities — Port Aransas in the north and Port Isabel in the south — are the main points of development as well as being two of the three gateways to Padre; the third gateway is rt. 22, which runs east out of Corpus Christi, becomes the Laguna Madre Causeway, and arrives on the isle just north of where Padre Island National Seashore begins. If you've come to visit the seashore, you'll almost have to stay in or near one of the "port" cities; that's not so bad. If you've come to visit the cities and enjoy their very relaxed, sun-filled, pleasure-dome existence, that's not so bad, either, so long as you make some time to visit what nature has wrought.

PORT ARANSAS – Actually on Mustang Island, an "adopted" part of the Padres. The University of Texas Marine Science Institute is here, a reminder of the area's primary — if not only — industry, the sea. Charter trawlers crowd the town's small harbor waiting to plow the bountiful Gulf waters in search of tarpon, sailfish, snapper, tuna, and countless other breeds of fighters. A hefty catch is almost guaranteed every time you set out with rod and reel. (Many of the deep-sea party boats come equipped with motorized reels: Get a nibble, flick the switch, and land your catch. If, like many people, you feel this method eliminates the "sport" in fishing, be sure to check out the equipment when you rent.) May through July, the town is filled with anglers in for the Deep-Sea Roundup, a contest to see who can land the biggest and who can land the most. Other attractions center around the 18 miles of sparkling white beach, focal point for surfers, surf casters, swimmers, and surfside drives. Mustang Island is almost entirely undeveloped except for Port Aransas.

There is direct access to the National Seashore from Port Aransas, but before going over, there is a mainland diversion well worth your time, the Aransas National Wildlife Refuge. To get there take rt. 35 through the mainland city of Aransas Pass, and just beyond the tiny hamlet of Lamar. The 54,000 acres of the Aransas National Wildlife Refuge have been set aside for the nearly extinct whooping crane, visible in the colder months when the cranes come down from Canada. (The refuge is open daily, admission is free.) There is an observation tower and an information station, as well as trails for spying on the natives by foot or car. An alternative to a park visit is a cruise up Aransas Bay past the water side of the refuge for less obstructed views of the cranes. Cruises leave from Lamar, and must be arranged at that town's harbor.

PADRE ISLAND NATIONAL SEASHORE – Return to Port Aransas and take rt. 53 south, the single highway which links Mustang Island with North Padre. After making the crossing, one of the first sights is Malaquite Beach and an excellent campground for trailers and the hearty few who tent on the beach. (Up and down Padre the beaches are open for overnight guests, usually for a token fee of about $2 a night. For more information, contact the Superintendent, address below.)

There are no cities, villages, towns, or any other recognizable examples of man's existence in the national seashore park. Once upon a time, the grasslands that cover the inland portions of the island — from the beaches of Laguna Madre in the west to the beaches of the Gulf of Mexico in the east — were grazing land for cattle. Padre Nicholas Balli, the Spanish monk after whom the island chain is named, started raising livestock here in 1800, but the cattle, cowboys, and monks are gone, and the grasses are returning to the sandy soil.

Other men have been here in the last 500 years, mostly Spaniards in the 16th, 17th, and 18th centuries, chasing or being chased by pirates. And the shallow waters of the Gulf side took their toll of vessels, including many a royal treasure ship. It's acknowledged by the residents and seashore personnel that millions of dollars in gold are probably buried in the Padre sand, or lost just off the coast. For this reason, the seashore is off-limits to metal detectors and modern-day treasure hunters. The natural splendor will not be violated by fortune seekers.

To travel around the national seashore other than on foot assumes that you own or have rented a four-wheel-drive vehicle. The paved road runs out just a few miles south of Malaquite Beach, and only jeeps have a chance of reaching the island's heartland. Park rangers patrol in helicopter and jeep, spending much of their time dragging half-buried cars out of the sand.

However you go, watch for the diverse and utterly fascinating collection of animal life. On the ground, the island is crawling with creatures like coyote, ground squirrels, gophers, and kangaroo rats. At least 12 different types of snake are known to reside in the tall grasses, including two species of rattlers. Watch out for these unfriendly fellows. (Campgrounds and other areas designated for two-legged guests can be assumed safe from potentially dangerous visitors.) In the air and alighting everywhere are hundreds of birds of different species: herons, willets, black skimmers, marsh hawks, pelicans, avocets, horned owls, peregrine falcons, and swarms of sanderlings. They come from Mexico and Central America in the spring, or pass through on their way south in fall and early winter. Year-round, Padre is an avian amusement park.

Of course, wherever you go, there is fishing. The beaches of Padre are regarded as among America's best for variety and sheer volume. Standing on the beach throwing your tackle to the surf, you may be the only person visible for miles. There may not be another soul to hear your victory shout after a half-hour fight with a shark — a fairly common catch in this part of the Gulf.

Just south of Malaquite Beach is the Grasslands Trail, a well-marked trek through the tall grasses and on to the dunes. The walk offers a look at many types of the island's native growth, including sea oats, railroad vines, croton, wild indigo, and a last vestige of Virginia live oak. The dune walk is also impressive for its museumlike representation of how dunes are formed. You may think that the dunes — in every stage of formation from small sand drifts to hills — have been prepared as some kind of exhibit. But no, these are real drifts, in the normal and natural process of being shaped by wind, weather, and sand shifts. Especially if you aren't going to get to the wilder, uninhabited southern reaches of the seashore, the Grasslands Trail is well worth taking. Information: the Superintendent, Padre Island National Seashore, 10235 S Padre Island Dr, Corpus Christi, TX 78418 (512 937-2621).

SOUTH PADRE ISLAND – Because no road runs the full length of either North or South Padre, you'll have to get back on mainland roads to reach South Padre. The southern tip of the island is being carefully developed as a vacation paradise, so hotels and motels and miles of sporting pleasures line the white-yellow beach and turquoise water. The causeway through Port Isabel comes out near Isla Blanca Park. There you'll find a bathhouse and cabanas, plus overnight accommodations for sleeping under the stars. There are also food concessions, water-skiing facilities, a trailer park, and a children's recreation area.

PORT ISABEL – Just across the Laguna Madre and connected to South Padre by the Queen Isabella Causeway is Port Isabel, a growing, but still peaceful, resort town — one of the South's first vacation centers, the favorite of Texas society dating back to the mid-1800s. Port Isabel is primarily a fishing town, with the world's largest shrimping fleet tying up here and a little further into the bay at the port of Brownsville, and the harbor is home port for many deep-sea charter fishing boats.

Just west of town on rt. 100 is the smallest state park in this state famous for big things, the Port Isabel Lighthouse Historic Site. The lighthouse dates from the 1850s when "gold rush fever" made Port Isabel a popular stop for folks on the way west. The lighthouse also overlooks the site of Fort Polk, a Mexican War camp and depot that was commanded by General Zachary Taylor. The last land battle of the Civil War was also fought in the neighborhood, at Palmito Hill. The lighthouse is open daily, 9 AM to 5 PM, with an admission charge.

If you're in Port Isabel, take a quick drive across the Mexican border to Matamoros, a shopping and visiting town featuring markets for jewelry, leather, and clothing, plus some authentic Spanish restaurants and nightclubs. They accept American currency, and only proof of citizenship is necessary to cross the border.

At the end of any visit through the untamed nature and sand expanses of North Padre Island, you'll find South Padre, and especially Port Isabel, quiet, relaxed enclaves perfect for enjoying a warm sun, sparkling water, and deluxe accommodations. For more information on accommodations and activities on South Padre: The South Padre Island Tourist Bureau, PO Box 2095, South Padre Island, TX 78597 (512 943-6434.)

BEST EN ROUTE

There is no shortage of top-flight accommodations in either Port Aransas or Port Isabel.

The Beachhead, Port Aransas – Just a boardwalk away from the beach. One- and two-bedroom apartments available with kitchens; parking, a coin laundry, and a heated pool. Balcony views look over the Gulf. PO Box 293, Port Aransas, TX 78373 (512 749-6261).

Executive Keys, Port Aransas – Sits on the Gulf, with balcony views from almost every room. Recreation facilities include lawn games, golf privileges, volleyball. All of the two- and three-bedroom kitchen-equipped suites have dishwashers and such amenities. PO Box 1087, Port Aransas, TX 78373 (512 749-6272).

Island Retreat, Port Aransas – A fisherman's delight, offering fish cleaning and freezing facilities for guests. Most apartments have balconies on the Gulf and convenience appliances. Also has two pools, access to the ocean, and a raft of recreational activities. PO Box 637, Port Aransas, TX 78373 (512 749-6222).

Hilton Sea Island Hotel, South Padre Island – The cream of South Padre Island's hotel-apartment offerings, with a large new condominium tower, a private beach, a club for dining and dancing, an Olympic-sized pool, and tennis. PO Box 2081, South Padre Island, TX 78597 (512 943-2685).

Bahia Mar, South Padre Island – The Hilton's competition, with two pools and saunas, tennis courts, a putting green, and entertainment nightly. Choice of accommodations from rooms to apartments and town houses. PO Box 2280, South Padre Island, TX 78597 (512 943-1343).

Most people on the island cook for themselves, and there is a shortage of good restaurants besides the cafés and roadhouses that line the highways. For first-class meals, locals and long-time summer residents drive into Corpus Christi or Brownsville. When on South Padre Island, you might try the *Jetties* (Rt. 100, 943-6461) for a wide choice in seafood, and known especially for fresh jumbo Gulf shrimp.

For more information, contact these local service organizations: Corpus Christi Area Convention and Tourist Bureau, PO Box 2664, Corpus Christi, TX 78403; Cameron County Park Board, PO Box 666, Port Isabel, TX 78578.

Midwest

The Lincoln Heritage Trail

The Lincoln Heritage Trail blazes 2,200 miles along the folkloric roads of Illinois, Indiana, and Kentucky, Abraham Lincoln's home states. Here, his voice still echoes around every bend: eloquently in government chambers, softly in great Victorian mansions, and jokingly in the backwood cabins of his close friends. Along the trail, memories of Mr. Lincoln are vividly recollected through re-enactments of scenes from America's past and reconstructions of stately buildings, quaint homesteads, and entire 19th-century towns. The route that follows is a living history book, tracing Lincoln's footsteps through colonial America.

SPRINGFIELD, Illinois – Here you will see and hear more about Abraham Lincoln than anywhere else in the US. Start with Lincoln's private residence (the only home he ever owned) on 8th and Jackson Sts. One of a row of handsome period homes, it has been repainted in its original colors of Quaker brown and apple green and furnished with some actual Lincoln family possessions. Informative tour guides minutely detail Lincoln's home life. Open daily 8 AM to 5 PM.

The Old State Capitol on Public Square, where Lincoln gave his famous "House Divided" speech, has undergone complete reconstruction, and the stunning second-floor legislative chamber looks as if a session had just adjourned. The Illinois State Historical Library is located on the bottom floor. Open 8:30 AM to 5 PM daily. On summer evenings the "Sound and Light Show" colorfully spotlights Mr. Lincoln's accomplishments in Springfield. Presented on the mall facing the building at 9 PM except Monday.

A 117-foot granite obelisk marks the Lincoln Tomb site in Oak Ridge Cemetery. The tomb's rotunda contains a single statue of Lincoln and a few bronze plaques creating a solemn and dignified tribute, at the rear of the memorial a monument to Lincoln is enclosed in a semicircular chamber, flanked by flags and remnants of the longest funeral procession in history. On the opposite wall are the crypts of Mary Todd Lincoln and three of the couple's four sons.

A few miles from Springfield off rt. 66, in the city of Lincoln, are the Lincoln College Museum, which houses an impressive array of memorabilia, and the Postville Courthouse, where almost-7-feet-tall Charlie Ott impersonates Lincoln and relates anecdotes of his travels as a circuit court lawyer. Maps outlining the route Lincoln rode and documents stating the bylaws of this early court system cover the walls.

NEW SALEM, Illinois – The next site on the trail is the village of New Salem, reconstructed to look exactly as it did when Lincoln visited in the 19th century. Here you'll see mammoth oxen pulling covered wagons along dirt roads lined with tiny log cabins. A visit to the cabins finds period-costumed women kneading dough, cooking over flaming hearths, and spinning wool. During summer months, beginning at sunset, you can watch the delightful outdoor drama, "Your Obedient Servant, A. Lincoln," staged under the stars. All dialogue in this lively account, which ranges from Lincoln's birth in Kentucky to his death in Ford's Theater, is taken verbatim from historical records.

VINCENNES, Indiana – The trail through Lincoln country cuts into Indiana at the border town of Vincennes, the original capital. Called the "Birthplace of the West," it's a tribute to early American growth. Visit the George Rogers Clark Memorial and Visitors Center, an awesome structure in which are hung several massive murals by Ezra Winter. Headsets, distributed at the entrance, explain each mural and its relevance to the American past.

The Log Cabin Visitors' Center provides tickets for the "Trailblazer" tour on a trolley-like bus that winds its way through the "Mile of History" in the Old State Capital.

HISTORIC NEW HARMONY, Indiana – Take a break from Lincolniana and visit New Harmony, another landmark in American history. Originally a tract of wilderness on the banks of the Wabash, the village grew from settlements of religious and utopian communal sects. First came the Rappites (or Harmonites), led by Father George Rapp, who preached that the second coming of Christ would occur in their lifetime. Later came the Owenites, a group of experimenting intellectuals looking to improve the quality of life.

The placid walkways of New Harmony are lined with restored, sparsely furnished houses and Rappite dormitories. Ticket books purchased at the Visitor Reception Building provide access to many buildings: the Atheneum — an architectural award winner; the Roofless Church; the Opera House; and the Theater Museum and Workshop. Be sure to wander through the labyrinth — a reconstruction of the Rappite maze symbolizing the twisting road of life to perfect harmony.

LINCOLN CITY, Indiana – Now pick up the Heritage Trail in Lincoln City (off US 231 south) at the Lincoln State Park and the Lincoln Boyhood National Memorial. Here, the cabin Abe's father, Thomas, built after journeying from Kentucky has been reconstructed. You can try your hand at rail-splitting, watch farmers plow fields with horse rigs, or hike the various nature trails. The grounds are open daily from dawn to dusk; the visitors center is open daily from 8 AM. to 5 PM. Closed January 1 and December 25.

JEFFERSONVILLE, Indiana – Off rt. I-65, you'll enter the town of Jeffersonville. Perched on the banks of the Ohio River, The Howard Steamboat Museum (housed in James Howard's former home) displays intricately carved models of his 19th-century masterpieces. Outside the window, the *Belle of Louisville* steamboat still chuffs by.

Cross the Ohio River into Louisville. For a complete report on the city and its attractions, see *Louisville,* THE AMERICAN CITIES.

HODGENVILLE, Kentucky – Abe Lincoln's life in Kentucky began in a tiny cabin nestled among the bluish-green, "Knob" hills of north central Kentucky. Take I-65 to Hwy. 61 and the Abraham Lincoln Birthplace and National Historic Site in Hodgenville. A section of this national park is actually Sinking Springs Farm, where Lincoln was born in 1809. An elaborate memorial building has been erected around the original family cabin. A faulty land deed uprooted the family when Lincoln was only two, and provoked their move to Knob Creek, where the family lived for 7 years. The primitive Lincoln log cabin stands reconstructed among the lushest of bluegrass hills.

BARDSTOWN, Kentucky – Continue northeast on Hwy. 31E for a pleasant stop at Bardstown, where you'll find the Federal Hill estate, better known as "My Old Kentucky Home." Tour the grand estate and its mansion where Stephen Foster supposedly wrote the famous song. Have lunch in Bardstown under the cozy brick arches of *La Taberna Restaurant,* at 5th St. and Xavier Dr.

LEXINGTON, Kentucky – Next, it's north to Lexington via rt. 68, the scenic palisades road. In Lexington, off rt. 68 (which becomes Broadway), on W Main Street is Mary Todd Lincoln's childhood home. This grand house personifies her life in the aristocracy and contradicts Lincoln's background completely: Meticulously crafted antiques and exquisitely detailed carpets crown the polished wooden floors. 578 W Main St. Open 10 AM to 4 PM, Tuesdays through Saturdays. Admission charge.

BEST EN ROUTE

New Harmony Inn, Historic New Harmony, Indiana – This inn's 45 rooms all have simple wood furnishings and some have working fireplaces, kitchenettes, and small balconies. The atmosphere of the inn reflects the quiet, easy pace of the community. No television or radio. Complimentary Continental breakfast served in the adjoining building. The New Harmony Inn, Historic New Harmony, IN 47631 (812-682-4491).

Overlook Restaurant, Leavenworth, Indiana – This restaurant has a wonderful view of the Ohio River and the best in home-style cooking: Heaping portions of mashed potatoes, vegetables, and biscuits accompany southern-fried chicken and other entrées. On Hwy. 62 in Leavenworth, IN (812-739-4264).

Isle Royale National Park, Michigan

Imagine yourself on a remote island where there are no cars, no roads, and where the only sound you are likely to hear at night is the call of a loon, the cry of a wolf, or wind in the pines. If the thought appeals, your destination should be Isle Royale, largest of the 200 islands and islets that make up Isle Royale National Park in Lake Superior. Isle Royale — dominant island for which the park was named — lies parallel to the northwest shore of Lake Superior, like a long candle flame pointing north. The island is 44 miles long and between five and eight miles wide. Open in summer only, this isolated bit of wilderness in Lake Superior has changed little since French trappers took possession of the island and named it in honor of Louis XIV.

Though closer to the Minnesota-Canada border, the park officially is part of Michigan. You can reach Isle Royale from both the Michigan and the Minnesota shores of Lake Superior. Access from Michigan is through the town of Houghton, by seaplane or ferry. (It is about a six-hour ferry ride to Isle Royale; a splendid grace period in which to leave civilization behind and contemplate the real isolation of the island.) The route to Houghton from St. Ignace (the town at the northern end of the Mackinac Straits bridge, which links Michigan's upper and lower peninsulas) takes you through the land of Hiawatha, the Ojibwa Indian immortalized in Longfellow's poem.

The shorter route to Isle Royale is from Minnesota. The ferry leaves Grand Portage, just below the Canadian border, 150 miles north of Duluth. The Duluth-to-Grand Portage section of I-65 offers one of the most scenic shore drives in the United States. And in Grand Portage, you can visit the national monument which marks the site of the "great depot" of early fur trading days.

Another ferry runs from Copper Harbor, about 50 miles north of Houghton. The trip takes about 4½ hours. Ferries accommodate passengers only; cars are not allowed on the island. There are ample parking facilities at both points of departure. For information on ferry schedules and reservations, write the Superintendent of the park.

Hundreds of millions of years ago, lava flows formed the earliest rock of which Isle Royale is made. During the glacial period, a layer of ice a mile high covered the island, but when the ice melted and the resulting lake receded a bit, Isle Royale emerged — "an island of rock rising abruptly from the lowest depths of the lake in irregular hills to a height varying from 100 to 450 feet above the level of the lake," as Michigan's first state geologist put it in 1841. A thin layer of soil, in some places no more than a few inches deep, covers the rock of Isle Royale like icing on a cake, but it is enough for spruce, balsam, pine, poplar, and birch to thrive.

As you make your way across the water to Isle Royale, leaving the mainland shore farther and farther behind, you will begin to get a sense of the isolation which has deeply affected the island's ecology. Only birds and animals that have been able to fly, swim, or drift across from the mainland are found on Isle Royale, with two exceptions. When moose suddenly appeared for the first time on the island in 1912, it was assumed that they had walked across from the Canadian shore on the thick ice that had formed on the lake that winter. The moose multiplied so fast that the plant moose browse became scarce on the island and overpopulation threatened to reduce the herds. Fortunately, in the winter of 1948–49, wolves crossed the ice from Canada, restoring the old relationship of hunter and hunted and ecological balance.

Rock Harbor Lodge at the island's eastern end, Windigo Inn at its western (closed since 1974), and a couple of lighthouses on the shore are just about the only buildings on Isle Royale. (Park headquarters are just offshore on Mott Island, in Isle Royale's Rock Harbor.) Although in prehistoric times, and again in the 19th century, men came to the island to mine its copper, there have never been any permanent settlements.

Over 160 miles of hiking trails, springy with moss and spruce needles, take the place of roads on Isle Royale. The trails lead to lookout towers with sweeping views, sheltered inlets along the pebbled shore, abandoned copper mines now buried deep in blueberry thickets, and silent inland lakes (over 20 of these), where at sunrise or sunset, you are likely to glimpse a moose. More than 30 campsites are scattered across the island.

Hiking offers an opportunity to observe some of the island's abundant wildlife, which includes beaver, muskrat, mink, weasel, squirrels, the snowshoe hare, and red fox as well as moose. There are also wolves, but they are extremely shy of human beings. Herring gulls and warblers are plentiful, but you will also see pileated woodpeckers, osprey, and the bald eagle among the 200 species of birds that inhabit the island. There are hundreds of common wildflowers as well as such rarities as yellow lady's slipper, bog kalmia, swamp candle loosestrife, and some 30 different species of orchids.

Such unspoiled wilderness has its price. You won't, for example, find flush toilets at the campsites. Noncampers can stay in the comparative luxury of the Rock Harbor Lodge, but in general, if you turn pale at the thought of roughing it, Isle Royale is probably not for you.

One of the best ways to explore the island's interior is to walk its length. To do this, take the Greenstone Ridge Trail, which connects Rock Harbor Lodge at the eastern end of the island with Washington Harbor at the western end 40 miles away. This hike will take you several days. A much shorter but very rewarding walk is the trail to Mount Franklin, where you can continue on to Ojibway Lookout, offering a fine view of the Canadian mainland from the tower. If you take the trail that leads to Monument Rock, a 70-foot-high natural tower that has been sculpted by waves and ice, you can continue past the Rock to one of the copper pits mined by prehistoric Indians with fire and stone hammers 4,000 years ago. Beyond this ancient mine is Lookout Louise, which offers the best views in the entire park.

A fine trail leads to the old Rock Harbor Lighthouse, built in 1885 to guide the boats sent by mining companies to take out the island's copper. The lighthouse guards what one member of the team on the US Linear Survey of 1847 called "the most beautiful harbor in Lake Superior." This same gentleman reported seeing mirages of islands and mountains off Isle Royale's coast.

On the west end of the island, a trail leads from Washington Creek, to an abandoned copper pit that was mined until the turn of the century when it was no longer considered profitable. A privately owned boat makes a full circuit around the island several times each week. (For information, write Sivertson Brothers Fisheries, 366 Lake Ave. S, Duluth, MN 55802, 218 722-0945). There are also shorter excursions to nearby islands, boat rentals at Rock Harbor Lodge, and a marina for small private craft at Rock Harbor. If you want to canoe, bring your own boat. The best canoeing is between Siskiwit Lake and the northeast end of the island.

Anglers will find pike, walleye, perch, and even some whitefish in the island's inland lakes, brook trout in its streams, and lake trout in Lake Superior. You don't need a license for the inland waters of the park. If you plan to do backcountry camping rather than use campsites, you must obtain a permit from the headquarters in Rock Harbor.

In the evening, if you would like to learn more about the flora and fauna you have seen during the day, you can attend one of the illustrated lectures that are given nightly at Rock Harbor Lodge and Daisy Family Campground. Information: the Superintendent, Isle Royale National Park, PO Box 271, Houghton, MI 49931 (906 482-3310).

BEST EN ROUTE

Rock Harbor Lodge, Isle Royale – At the eastern end of the island, this offers 20 housekeeping lodges, 60 lodge rooms, a dining room and snack bar. You can buy camping supplies and food here as well. Reservations between mid-June and Labor Day: National Park Concessions, PO Box 405, Houghton, MI 49931 (906 482-2890); for information the rest of the year: National Park Concessions, Mammoth Cave, KY 42259 (502 773-2191).

Isle Royale Campsites – There are over 30 campsites along the shores and inland lakes. Every campsite offers screened Isle Royale shelters and minimal facilities. There are usually enough shelters for all, but it's best to bring your own tent just in case. A park ranger will tell you which sites are free and how long you will be able to stay at each site.

St. Croix River, Minnesota and Wisconsin

Many people say the territory around the St. Croix River is haunted. They say that spirits of the Indians who lived here for many generations are still a strong presence in the birch and pine forests lining the riverbanks. There are even some who say the Indians' shadowy birchbark canoes still make their way through the tributaries and creeks feeding into the St. Croix, and that you can hear the rustle of paddles breaking water if you listen in the silence.

More prosaic travelers, less inclined to give credence to tales of ghostly wanderers, are nonetheless enchanted by the magic of the St. Croix — a 164-mile stretch of water separating Minnesota and Wisconsin that was one of the first to be granted federal protection under the Wild and Scenic River Act of 1968. It's surprising to find such a relatively unspoiled section of country close to a big city, but you don't have to travel very far from the cosmopolitan Twin Cities, Minneapolis–St. Paul, to get to the lower St. Croix. It's just 25 miles northeast of St. Paul on rt. 36.

Although the lower St. Croix valley is dotted with attractive villages, the untamed upper St. Croix hasn't changed much from Indian times. In fact, the Ojibwa (or Chippewa), descendants of the Algonquin, still harvest wild rice from the fertile crannies hidden among the small inlets lacing the surrounding marshes. But the placid waters bear a history of conflict.

The Dakota Indians lived here first, treasuring the river for its fish, the land for its wild rice, and the forest for its many kinds of game. (Otter, beaver, black bear, and deer still make their home in these woods, although animals like the buffalo and big wolf are now extinct.) After more than 350 years of wars, the Dakota were driven out by the Chippewa, who had moved in from the East after unsuccessfully trying to defend their land from Iroquois attack. While the Chippewa and Dakota battled, the French explorers and traders arrived, calling the Dakota by their French name, the Sioux. After the Chippewa victory, the Sioux fled north and west, eventually to be vanquished by the whites.

The French used the St. Croix as a fur connection, establishing many trading posts along its banks and developing the waterway into a flourishing commercial route. Beaver pelts were sold and shipped to Canada, and from there to Europe, where they found their way to the haberdashers of the fashionable. The intense struggle to control this resource-rich territory was not confined to the Indians and the French. The British were avid for supremacy, too, and in 1763, when the French and Indian wars were finally over, the Union Jack flew from the masts and flagpoles along the St. Croix. The Hudson Bay Company and other trading enterprises of the period conducted a brisk business until the War of 1812, when the United States imposed a ban on foreign trading activity in the area. Then the loggers arrived. Thousands of men felled hundreds of thousands, perhaps even millions, of trees, mostly white pine, and the river was used to float logs. Innumerable lumberjacks perished while dynamiting logjams which clogged the river's flow. The lumbering era is a strong part of the historic legacy of the valley, and St. Croix residents still compete in logrolling contests. The logging came to an end when there were no longer enough trees for the industry to operate profitably. Since then, the region has been marked for conservation and many people are working through a number of organizations to prevent further exploitation and destruction of the forest.

STILLWATER – The birthplace of Minnesota. A riverfront town 25 miles from St. Paul, Stillwater's the kind of place where they consider you a newcomer unless at least one generation of your family is in the cemetery. But don't let that throw you — it's a great place to visit, full of charming old buildings, fine antique shops, emporiums, and cafés. If you're in the mood for chartering an old twinstack steamwheel boat, go to Jubilee Charter Boat (Stillwater Landing), where you can rent the 300-passenger *Jubilee* for business conferences, parties, and weddings. If you're traveling with fewer than 299 people, we suggest you phone to inquire about alternative arrangements. If you can't get on the boat for that day, poke around town. There's been a lot of talk lately about developing Stillwater into the Sausalito of Minnesota, but a number of concerned planners refuse to okay any drawing-board schemes that would threaten to turn the town into a tourist trap. For information on logrolling contests, fireworks, and the pageantry of Stillwater's annual Lumberjack Days (midsummer), contact St. Croix Valley Area Chamber of Commerce, Stillwater, MN 55082 (612 439-7700).

MARINE-ON-ST. CROIX – You can bike from Stillwater on carefully marked trails. At one time a dynamic lumberjack town, Marine-on-St. Croix has lost much of that rip-roaring, freewheeling atmosphere that characterized its formative years during the tree-tumbling era, but you can muse about what the old days must have been like in O'Brien State Park overlooking the river.

TAYLORS FALLS AND ST. CROIX FALLS – Canoe enthusiasts will probably head straight for these two towns sitting across the river from each other about 28 miles north of Stillwater. This is the dividing line between the upper and lower St. Croix. Here, the picturesque, tranquil southern stretch becomes rugged whitewater. (Actually, it's the other way around, since the St. Croix flows from north to south, but as you're most probably driving from the south, it will seem as if the peaceful part of the river ends and the wild section begins.) The land is relatively unsettled from this point north, which makes it ideal for back-to-the-woods people. The dramatic disparity between upper and lower St. Croix has its roots in the glacial and postglacial era, which formed two great lakes out of melting ice about 10,000 years ago. The water melting from glacial Lake Grantsburg, which covered much of Minnesota, flowed south, forming the St. Croix. When the entire mass of ice covering the hemisphere began to recede, glacial Lake Duluth, the predecessor of Lake Superior, was unable to drain east because of a huge section of ice that refused to melt. The excess water began cutting its way through sand, gravel, and boulders of what is now the St. Croix valley, in the process forming the great gorge known as the Dalles. The path of the new glacial river also bored giant kettle holes which are responsible for the tricky currents that challenge today's canoeists. (You can rent canoes from Taylors Falls Canoe Company, Taylors Falls, MN 55084, 612 465-6315; the company organizes canoe trips, too. Across the river in Wisconsin, you can rent canoes from Wild River Cabins, St. Croix Falls, WI 54024, 715 483-9343. It also rents rowboats, pontoons, and fishing gear.) If you are unwilling to tackle the frothy, churning waters of the Upper St. Croix in a canoe, you might consider a day trip on the St. Croix Dalles as a safer alternative. Excursions take you past geological formations in the river, while guides explain what each is and how it was formed. Daily June through October. Muller Boat Company (Taylors Falls, MN

55084, 612 465-6315). Muller Boat Company also operates the *Katy M,* a paddlewheeler. For maps showing canoe routes throughout Minnesota, contact the W. A. Fisher Company (123–125 Chestnut St., Virginia, MN 55792, 218 741-9544). If you enjoy looking at the great outdoors, but don't care to spend the night, you can head back to Minneapolis–St. Paul on rt. 8 west to I-35 south.

BEST EN ROUTE

Lowell Inn, Stillwater – A 50-year-old hotel and restaurant built in red brick colonial style, known as the "Mount Vernon of the West." It's run by the 11 members of the Palmer family. 102 N Second St., Stillwater, MN 55082 (612 439-1100).

Honeysuckle Farm, Rush City – Only 35 miles northwest of St. Croix Falls and 60 miles north of Minneapolis–St. Paul, this 134-acre farm grows corn, hay, and oats. There are cows, chickens, and pigs. Close to St. Croix River, it can accommodate eight guests. Carl and Beverley Heinrich, Rt. 2, Rush City, MN 55069 (612 358-4525).

Voyageurs National Park and Boundary Waters Canoe Area, Minnesota

Centuries before there were roads in North America, the Indians in their birchbark canoes traveled a network of lakes, streams, and connecting portage trails that stretched from the Rocky Mountains to the St. Lawrence River. In the heyday of the great fur trade, French-Canadian voyageurs plied this natural highway, paddling and portaging huge quantities of furs east to Montreal, and great numbers of soldiers, explorers, and missionaries west to the frontier. The last of the voyageurs disappeared in the 1830s, but in Voyageurs National Park and the Boundary Waters Canoe Area in northern Minnesota, you can still get a taste of what it was like on the old voyageur highway in the days when the splash of a paddle was the only manmade sound on these waters and the wilderness stretched as far as the eye could see.

Voyageurs National Park and the Boundary Waters Canoe Area are part of the oldest land mass in the world. Glaciers shaped this land, scooping out its lake basins, scoring its surface with an intricate maze of waterways, polishing its ancient boulders smooth. Except for an occasional sandy beach or rocky cliff, a canopy of trees — spruce, pine, fir, balsam, aspen, and birch — covers the land to the water's edge.

Voyageurs National Park, one of the country's newest national parks (it was established in 1975), extends almost 40 miles along Minnesota's northeast border. Numerous streams and over 50 lakes — ranging in size from Rainy Lake, 35 miles wide, to Rat Lake, barely 300 yards across — make up a third of the park's 205,000 acres. At the heart of the park lies the wild and scenic 75,000-acre Kabetogama Peninsula. You can hike, fish, and of course canoe here, and stay in accommodations that range from tentsites accessible only by water to fine lakeside resorts. As in the days of the voyageurs, wild rice grows in the shallow waters of the park, and deer, moose, wolves, beaver, and bear inhabit its deep woods.

Just east of Voyageurs National Park lies the vast Boundary Waters Canoe Area (BWCA), one million acres of Minnesota's Superior National Forest, most of which have been reserved exclusively for the use of canoeists. The BWCA stretches nearly 100 miles along the border between Minnesota and Ontario's million-acre Quetico Provincial Park, another protected canoeing area. With its myriad lakes interconnected by innumerable streams and portage trails, and its access to Quetico's waters, the BWCA offers the canoeist an almost infinite number of route possibilities. Motorboats and cars are allowed only in certain parts of this canoeist's paradise, and even the air space is restricted. Travel permits are required.

VOYAGEURS NATIONAL PARK – Access to the park's perimeter is from International Falls, Minnesota, which is linked to Virginia and Duluth, Minnesota, by rt. 53. To enter the park, a boat or floatplane is needed. These can be hired at the many resorts surrounding the park. In the winter, ice roads, snowmobiles, and skis provide access. Chief among the sights to see at Voyageurs is the spectacular Crane Lake Gorge near the park's eastern edge, where the Vermilion River churns through a narrow chasm between vertical walls of rock before tumbling into the lake. Trails line both sides of the mossy canyon.

At the east end of Rainy Lake, the well-preserved Kettle Falls Hotel, built in 1913, recalls the days when only trappers, traders, fishermen, and lumberjacks passed through these parts. Because of a quirk in the boundary line here, you can stand at Kettle Falls on the Minnesota side and look south to Canada.

Canoeing is not especially difficult or dangerous in the park as long as you pay attention to the weather. A storm or even a stiff wind on some of the bigger lakes can whip up waves that will easily swamp a canoe. To avoid this problem, it is best either to wait out the wind or plan a trip through the smaller lakes. You can obtain maps and the services of a guide at local resorts, and canoes and supplies from outfitters at a number of places, including International Falls and Crane Lake. (In International Falls, contact Johnson Canoe Outfitters, PO Box 529, International Falls, MN 56649, 218 377-4411.)

Another major Voyageurs recreation is fishing. The waters of Lakes Rainy, Namakan, and Kabetogama are known for their walleye, northern pike, and smallmouth bass. In the smaller lakes and streams are lake trout. For bigger game, try Shoe Pack Lake on Kabetogama Peninsula for the famed muskellunge, which can weigh up to 60 pounds or more.

The most developed part of the park is Crane Lake, a cluster of resorts, summer homes, and marinas on the south shore of Crane Lake. Here you can arrange for anything from water skiing to backcountry fishing via floatplane. More resorts and swimming beaches ring Lake Kabetogama.

Camping is free throughout the park. For information on camping and recreational facilities: the Superintendent, Voyageurs National Park, Box 50, International Falls, MN 56649 (218 283-9821).

BOUNDARY WATERS CANOE AREA – Main gateway to BWCA is through Ely, Minnesota (other routes are through Grand Marais or, by canoe, through Voyageurs lake system). If you go by paddle and portage, it is possible to follow the Canada-US border all the way from Rainy Lake at the western end of Voyageurs to the eastern end of BWCA, and beyond to Grand Portage, on the shores of Lake Superior.

This 275-mile route retraces the final leg of the 2,000-mile journey made annually by the Northwestern voyageurs, who transported furs from the northwest trading posts in the Rockies to the central depot of the fur trade in Grand Portage. Here, the "Montrealers," who had paddled across the Great Lakes to meet them, collected the furs to take east. The voyageurs used to paddle 18 hours a day, but assuming you will be traveling at a more leisurely pace, this trip should take about three weeks.

Within the Boundary Waters Canoe Area, any number of canoe routes are possible, ranging from a day-long excursion to a summer-long voyage. Almost all the possible routes are listed in *Suggested Canoe Routes,* available from Boundary Waters Canoe Area, Forest Service, US Department of Agriculture, PO Box 339, Duluth, MN 55801. Maps of all major canoeing trails in Minnesota and Quetico Provincial Park in Ontario are sold at W. A. Fisher Co., 123–125 Chestnut St., Virginia, MN 55792 (218 741-9544).

If you are entering the BWCA from Ely, stop in at the Voyageurs Visitors' Center just east of town on rt. 169 to have a look at the full-sized replica of a voyageur's birchbark canoe. There are other exhibits as well. Maps, travel permits (required for all canoeing), camping permits, and advice are dispensed here free of charge. (Travel permits are also available from district rangers and some canoe outfitters anywhere in the Superior National Forest.)

Like Voyageurs National Park, the BWCA doesn't offer many whitewater thrills. (Where there are rapids, they are generally too rough to navigate and you have to take a portage trail around them.) What it does offer, however, is the chance to canoe in solitude. If you choose one of the less traveled routes that require longer portages, you may be lucky enough to have almost the whole route to yourself.

The time of year can also make a difference: Peak months at BWCA are July and August, but the prime season for canoeing runs from May through October. Unfortunately, May and June are also the prime months for mosquitoes and black flies.

Canoe outfitters in Ely and Grand Marais can supply you with everything you might need for your trip, including guides, food, and the canoe itself.

If you plan to cross over into Canadian waters, you must check in at a US customs post at Ely, Crane Lake, or Grand Marais, as well as at a Canadian customs post. The Canadians charge a small daily fee for camping and canoeing permits.

After your canoeing adventure, you can rest your newly developed paddling muscles by taking a scenic drive on Honeymoon Trail or the Gunflint or Sawbill Trails in the magnificent Superior National Forest. Wherever you travel in this huge wilderness preserve, you won't be far from one of its 2,000 lakes.

Not far from the eastern edge of the Boundary Waters Canoe Area in the Superior National Forest is Grand Portage and the Grand Portage National Monument, which marks the site of the central trading depot of the voyageurs. From Grand Portage, in the summers, you can take a ferry to Michigan's remote Isle Royale National Park, an island wilderness in Lake Superior. Information: Boundary Waters Canoe Area, Forest Supervisor, PO Box 338, Duluth, MN 55801 (218 727-6692, ext. 321).

BEST EN ROUTE

The Voyageurs National Park area abounds with fishing camps, lodges, and resorts. The Park Service will provide lists of these. Voyageurs is a new national park, and facilities are by no means complete, with many resorts and hotels still under construction or in the planning stages.

Kettle Falls Hotel, Rainy Lake – A long-time favorite of fishermen. Accessible only by boat and plane, on the east end of the 40-mile lake that stretches along the US-Canada border. Open mid-May to October. Kettle Falls Hotel, 622 12th Ave., International Falls, MN 56649 (218 374-3511).

Whispering Pines – On the shore of Lake Kabetogama. Accessible by car via a primitive road. Open mid-May to October. Whispering Pines, Orr, MN 55771 (218 374-3321).

West

Denali National Park and Preserve, Alaska

With the passage of the Alaska Lands Bill on December 2, 1980, the park's name was changed from Mt. McKinley National Park to Denali National Park and Preserve. Denali, an Athabascan Indian word meaning "The Great One," refers, of course, to the commanding peak, Mt. McKinley.

Mt. McKinley is our giant. Nothing in our part of the world is higher, and at more than 20,000 feet, Mt. McKinley approaches — admittedly just barely — Himalayan altitudes. (The Greater Himalayas tower above it at 25,000 to 29,000 feet [Mt. Everest]; but McKinley competes handily with the Lesser Himalayas, whose peaks rise 7,000 to 15,000 feet above the Vale of Kashmir.) Just a couple of hundred miles from the Arctic Circle, Mt. McKinley is the heart and soul of surrounding Denali National Park and Preserve, about 5 million acres of the austere, wild tundra country that is one of the greatest natural wonders in the US.

McKinley is actually two peaks, its double summits separated by two miles of glacial ridge. First viewed, it is an imposing sight: North Peak rises 19,470 feet, South Peak, 20,320. No matter how many pictures you see, how many articles you have read, nothing quite prepares you for it: the startled recognition, an audible gasp or sigh, unrestrained exclamations of wonder.

Climbers have been on the South Peak since the early 1900s when "sourdoughs," gold prospectors with some free time, decided to get to the top to see what the country looked like from up there. In a show of Bicentennial enthusiasm a few years back, nearly 80 climbers made it to the summit of South Peak in July 1976. The fatality rate for McKinley climbers is low, but the last 7,000 feet are covered in sheer ice and snow, and make very difficult climbing. (Parties interested in scaling McKinley or Mt. Foraker *must* apply to the National Park Service first. Because of the difficulty of the slope, only experienced, healthy climbers with tested skill and proper equipment should consider the challenge.)

Mt. McKinley is just one of the attractions of this huge, isolated tundra world — a world, alas, few get the opportunity to visit. The park is designed to protect its year-round, native inhabitants; man is an afterthought. There are few roads through the park navigable by car, and those that exist are closed to private traffic for much of their distance (shuttle buses roam between campgrounds, taking visitors to park offices, sighting stations, other camps, etc.). The park is open year-round, but its access road is closed from October until late May. Spring arrives late in the year, not until June or early July, when the wildflowers, nesting birds, and mosquitoes come out in full force.

An added treat, as if calculated to give extra pleasure to the three or four months allowed to visitors, sunlight lasts 18 to 20 hours each day in the warm season; consequently, many activities are scheduled for 6 AM to take advantage of the early morning light, when the mountain shimmers cold-blue and ice-white, before clouds can obscure Mt. McKinley's uppermost 5,000 feet.

Perhaps the greatest attraction of the park is its vital animal life: caribou, grizzly bear, surefooted Dall sheep, wolf, and a huge variety of smaller, furred, warm-blooded beasts. One of the surprises of the park is its array of flora, including a variety of miniature trees — one-foot willows, knee-high birch — which have adapted to the incredible cold of winter and limited water by developing root systems reaching yards into the earth, where the temperature may be 50° warmer than on the surface. They literally grow down instead of up. Mosses and lichen grow like tufts of beard on the tundra's rough face, providing vital food supplies to caribou and other nonhibernating winter creatures. In summer, visitors habitually learn to identify hundreds of plant species by their shapes and color when sighted across a broad meadow or hanging from a sheer canyon wall.

Denali National Park and Preserve is not a place to visit casually. The only road into its interior begins in the town of McKinley Park, 123 miles south of Fairbanks, 240 miles north of Anchorage. For years after the park was established in 1917 it remained without direct road access to these main cities — railroad and private aircraft linked it to the outside world (and still do, along with commercial air service from the two towns). Today, rt. 3 passes the entrance to the park on its run from Anchorage to Fairbanks. The road into the park is almost 90 miles long, running due west past many scenic canyons, passes, and riverbanks. Only the first 15 miles are paved. The first sight of Mt. McKinley occurs a few miles in, but it isn't until mile 60, at Highway Pass, that you can get a full view of its magnificent peaks.

Private vehicles are not allowed on the park road after Savage River Bridge, at mile 14.5 (except for visitors with confirmed reservations for campsites further along the park road). Campsites are spread intermittently along the road, and a free shuttle bus links guests along the road and the many trails, sights, and camps. The bus is also something of a mobile social center, a place for picking up the latest on where caribou herds have been sighted. The shuttle bus runs from Riley Creek Campground to Wonder Lake (at the northern edge of the park), making stops along the way wherever passengers request. Shuttle service runs regularly from 6 AM to 5 PM (check for exact times at the Visitors' Center). There is a bus stop next to the McKinley Park Station Hotel.

The Eielson Visitors' Center sits just off the park road some 65 miles in from the entrance. At an elevation of 3,730 feet, it offers good views of the mountain's twin peaks and the awesome spectacle of the Muldrow Glacier, stretching from McKinley to within a mile of the park road. Exhibits at the center detail glacial geology and mountain-climbing expeditions of the past. Make a point of stopping at the center, especially if you plan to hike or stay overnight. Information on weather conditions, animal activity, and other potentially lifesaving data are available from the rangers stationed there.

Along the park road you're sure to pass a number of places worthy of a stop. The Teklanika River is a classic example of the glacial rivers that flow on their curled courses north from the Alaska Range. Dall sheep, those surefooted mountain climbers, can be spotted as mere dots on the sides of Igloo Canyon. Grizzly bear activity centers around Sable Pass, though no one knows exactly why. (No matter where you spot grizzlies and other animals throughout the park, don't frighten them, or attempt to pet or feed them. They only *look* friendly.) Wildflowers spreading across the vast fields of Stony Hill Overlook are a summer contribution to the scene. And at Wonder Lake, the last stop on the restricted-use park road at the northern end of the park, magnificent reflections of the mountains are cast on the mirrorlike surface.

Hikers and backpackers should obtain a backcountry-use permit before setting out on their treks. Fishing licenses are not required, but a limit of ten fish a day per fisherman is imposed. (Fishing in the park is far from Alaska's best due to silty lakebeds and streams, and shallow ponds.) Tours can be arranged at the McKinley Park Station Hotel for a full day's excursion into the park. For information on all aspects of park life and visiting, write: the Superintendent, Denali National Park and Preserve, Box 9, McKinley Park, AK 99755 (907 683-2294).

BEST EN ROUTE

McKinley Park Station Hotel, McKinley Park – Just inside the entrance to the park. Filling meals are offered day and night — an especially desirable amenity for the early riser who wants to make that 6 AM appointment with nature. Information: Box 87, McKinley Park, AK 99755 (907 683-2215).

In Denali National Park and Preserve – A choice of several campgrounds along the park road offers the best opportunity to see, and *feel,* tundra life. The camps are: Sanctuary River, Teklanika, Igloo Creek, Wonder Lake, Savage, and Riley Creek. Motorists can drive to Savage and Riley Creek without camping permits, but other sites are on the controlled-access portion of the road. Bring warm clothing, a waterproof shelter, mosquito netting and/or repellent, camp stoves (no wood is available in the park). For campsite information: Superintendent, Denali National Park and Preserve, McKinley Park, AK 99755 (907 683-2294).

Camp Denali – A wilderness camp north of Wonder Lake, in the park. Camp Denali features log cabins and a communal dining room. Guided tours are conducted daily from the site, as are four-, five-, and nine-day "Sourdough Vacations" into the wilderness. Write Camp Denali, PO Box 67, Denali National Park and Preserve, AK 99755 (907 683-2302 in winter; 907 683-2290 in summer).

Tongass National Forest, Alaska

John Muir, the Scottish naturalist who wrote thousands of words about Yosemite and this country's Western wilderness, was rendered almost speechless by the beauty of the southeastern panhandle of Alaska. "Never before this had I been embosomed in scenery so hopelessly beyond description," he wrote in *Travels in Alaska.* His words capture the nature of this area, much of which is still preserved as a wilderness in Tongass National Forest. The Tongass is the largest of the national forests, encompassing 16 million acres, reaching nearly the entire length of the rugged 400-mile coastline of southern Alaska from north of Juneau to south of Ketchikan, east from the outermost islands of the Alexander Archipelago to the border of British Columbia in the west. The panhandle is also bordered by two parallel mountain ranges. To the west, the peaks of the submerged Fairweather Range form the islands of the archipelago; to the east looms the Coast Range, with many peaks between 5,000 and 10,000 feet and numerous glaciers. In between is enough land to leave even the hardest to impress breathless: America's only remaining frontier — more than 11,000 evergreen-covered islands, fjords whose flanks rise precipitously from the water's edge, huge walls of moving ice, glaciers carving and molding the coastline, and lush, moss-blanketed rain forests rising toward the Coast Range.

The Inside Passage runs the entire length of the Tongass. This waterway which once provided gold seekers with access to the Klondike is well protected from the bitter northwesterly winds by the outlying islands, and makes for pleasant passage by ferry along the foot of the Coast Range. Fjords and rivers flow into the Passage and the surrounding lowlands are blanketed by thick stands of hemlock, cedar, and spruce. In the summer, wildflowers abound: Fireweed, shooting stars, iris, and anemone color the marshes and meadows of the Tongass.

This region does not conform to stereotyped notions of Arctic harshness. If you're looking for huskies pulling sleds and boundless snow, the weather will not fulfill your expectations. Sitka, a city with a climate typical of the region, has an average temperature of 56° in August and 32° in January. This moderation is caused by the Japan Current, which brings warm temperatures and plenty of rain. Sitka collects an average of 85 inches of rain annually, with June the driest month and October the wettest. During the summer months it gets dark around midnight, so there is plenty of light for exploration of the Tongass.

The national forest is a rich wildlife area. Brown and black bear, trumpeter swans, deer, coyote, moose, and mountain goats all roam the islands and coastal region. Those with keen eyes will spot the bald eagle, a bird that has been hunted close to extinction in the lower 48 states but still thrives in Alaska. Fishing is outstanding, with salmon up to 50 pounds not uncommon. In addition, many varieties of trout inhabit the freshwater lakes and streams of the Tongass.

Even bigger and better than a 50-pound salmon is another natural phenomenon of the Tongass — the glacier. Alaska possesses the largest expanse of glacial ice in the world outside of Greenland and Antarctica. The panhandle's active glacier system offers a view of a broad succession of glacial stages. The glaciers that carved, shaped, and plowed much of this region are of fairly recent origin. Geologists estimate that about one million years ago, during the Pleistocene period, the sea level was hundreds of feet lower than it is today; glaciers moved from the heights of the Coast Range toward the sea, gouging the deep fjords and river valleys visible in Tongass today.

Glaciers originate in snowfields located in the higher regions of mountains. The only prerequisite for glacier formation is a snow cover that deepens over the years as more snow accumulates than melts. As successive layers build up, the accumulated weight exerts increased pressure on the underlying layers. When pressure is sufficient, snow crystallizes into ice. Movement of the glacier begins when the weight of the accumulation exceeds the strength of the ice. The immense pressure exerted by the sheer mass of the ice makes the ice "flow," something like cold molasses; glacial ice is not brittle.

The glaciers that exist in Alaska today are remnants of a "Little Ice Age," which began in the 14th century and lasted for some 300 years. Due to a warming trend in the climate during the latter half of the 19th and first half of the 20th century, the Alaskan glaciers are receding.

The only glacier accessible by highway, Mendenhall Glacier, is reached by rt. 7 and Mendenhall Loop Rd., just 13 miles from Juneau. Mendenhall is over 12 miles long and is 1½ miles wide at its face. The National Forest Service maintains trails alongside the glacier so that you can view the river of ice from excellent vantage points. If you're lucky, you'll see an example of calving, when a large slab of cobalt blue ice plummets from the glacier's face into Mendenhall Lake.

In Glacier Bay National Park and Preserve, the retreat of Muir Glacier, which bares the rocky deposits (glacial moraines) left in its wake, illustrates how virgin forest grows on seemingly barren soil. Only lichens and moss can survive in the most recently exposed regions. However, in the areas exposed during earlier years (those farther from the glacier's face), small willows take hold and are followed by spruce and hemlock that mature into a forest. When the glacier moves inexorably forward during the next ice age, the forest will be swept aside.

The few major cities in the panhandle serve as excellent departure points for fishing, camping or hiking forays into the Tongass, and also provide comfortable modern accommodations. Inaccessible by highway, the cities are reached by air, cruise ship, or the Alaska Marine Highway System, a state-run ferry service linking Seattle, Washington, with the panhandle. Reservations and information can be obtained by contacting the Division of Marine Transportation, Pouch R-DOT, Juneau, AK 99811 (907 465-3941).

Southernmost Ketchikan is renowned for its salmon fishing, and the many sportfishing lodges in the area offer anglers a chance to go after king salmon. The Tongass Historical Society Museum (629 Dock St.) has a collection of Indian artifacts and items used by Southeastern Alaska pioneers. Petersburg and Wrangell are the next stops on the Marine Highway. The Clausen Memorial Museum (Second and F Sts.) in Petersburg has a good collection of historical fishing gear. The Bear Tribal House (on Chief Shakes Island) of the Tlingit Indians has a fine totem pole collection.

To the northwest lies Sitka, which was known as the Paris of the Pacific during the 19th century when it was the major trading outpost of the Russian Empire. St. Michael's Russian Orthodox Cathedral (on Lincoln St.) is one of the best surviving examples of Russian peasant cathedral architecture in the free world, and contains a treasure of ecclesiastical art and splendid gifts from the Czar. The Sheldon Jackson Museum (on Jackson College campus) has an outstanding collection of Aleut, Eskimo, and Indian artifacts. In early July, the city hosts the All-Alaska Logging Championships.

Juneau, the state capital, located at the northern end of the Inside Passage, has the widest range of accommodations. A walking tour links 15 points of historic interest. The Alaska State Museum (in the Subport area) has extensive collections of pioneer memorabilia from the Russian American period and Gold Rush era as well as Aleut, Eskimo, and Indian crafts and artifacts. Bus tours of the Mendenhall Glacier region are available from the city.

Only a boat or short plane ride away from these cities lies the wilderness of the Tongass. The Forest Service maintains campgrounds in these areas and close to the cities too. In addition, 146 cabins in the outlying areas, on the seacoast, or near rivers or lakes, offer excellent opportunities to get back to nature. They have no bedding, plumbing, or electricity, but some of the lakeside cabins include a skiff. When you go this way, you see the Tongass for what it is — a gift from the earth. For further information and reservations contact the Tongass Forest Regional Supervisor, PO Box 1628, Juneau, AK 99802 (907 586-7484). For further information on the cities and the rest of the panhandle, contact Alaska Division of Tourism, Pouch E, Juneau, AK 99811 (907 465-2010).

BEST EN ROUTE

Hilltop Motel, Ketchikan – Some 46 rooms with restaurant and lounge, located directly across from the airport and ferry terminal. 3434 Tongass Ave., Ketchikan, AK 99901 (907 225-5166).

Bell Island Hot Springs, Bell Island – King and coho salmon sportfishing lodge, 20 minutes by air from Ketchikan. Restaurant, Olympic-sized pool, cabins, boat rentals. Contact: Reservations Office, Bell Island Hot Springs Resort, 1113 Fifth Ave. S, No. 108, Edmonds, WA 98020 (206 776-7100).

Shee Atika Lodge, Sitka – Situated on the waterfront, the facilities of this hotel include a restaurant and marina. Box 78, Sitka, AK 99835 (907 747-6241 or toll-free: 800 426-0670).

Baranof Hotel, Juneau – Located in the center of the city, this 201-room hotel has a restaurant, coffee shop, airport limousine service, meeting rooms, and nightly entertainment. 127 N Franklin St., Juneau, AK 99801 (907 586-2660).

Sheffield House, Juneau – This 104-room hotel has a restaurant, lounge, and live entertainment. 51 W Egan Dr., Juneau, AK 99801 (907 586-6900).

Grand Canyon National Park, Arizona

On first looking at the Grand Canyon, even the firmest atheist may feel intimations of some higher power. An awesome force created this vast expanse of beautiful sculptures of the earth. Level upon level of rock of intricate and seemingly infinite formations rise out of this huge chasm in the earth and seem to be patterns of some master design. As your eye traces the layers and reaches the far rim of the Canyon, your gaze keeps rising as if expecting to see a sign, perhaps the artist's signature emblazoned across the sky. And you may find confirmation for your beliefs. On the other hand, you may, at this point, begin searching for some scientific explanation. Whether the force was natural or supernatural, the instrument of the sculpting is right in front of you, at the bottom of the canyon. You've only to look at the Colorado River.

The reason you might have overlooked the river in the first place is simple. The Colorado follows a winding course through the canyon and is not even visible at certain points along the rim, and where it is, it appears to be a narrow gentle stream. Looks have never been more deceiving. At the floor of the canyon, you see this gentle stream for what it really is — the wide and mighty Colorado. And only then do you begin to understand this tremendous force which has cut an awesome course through vast stretches of rock and time. The canyon is 277 miles long, between 4 and 18 miles wide, and more than a mile deep. While the area around it has been "under construction" for two billion years, the canyon itself is a relative newcomer — geologically speaking. The Colorado River began eroding layers of sediment about a million years ago. This downward cutting of the river, coupled with a general rise in the earth's surface, created a natural amphitheater in which the epic story of the preceding ages has been exposed — literally — to the naked eye.

The story told by the multiple layers of the Grand Canyon is extraordinary. Initially the area surrounding the canyon (long before the canyon existed) was flat. Over millions of years wind, heat, and pressure buckled the land into mountains, which were then flattened over millions of years by erosion. Mountains formed again, eroded to deserts, and were covered by a shallow sea. All of this is recorded in the canyon, a great book written in by the hands of time and force. The rock layers exposed to view are like steps in a staircase of natural history. At the bottom of the gorge is the first step, Vishnu, the hard shiny black rocks of the Precambrian age, which are among the oldest exposed rocks on earth. As we move up the staircase, the changes in hue, texture, and fossil remains between layers is truly incredible; there is the Redwall limestone, a 500-foot-thick deposit of gray-blue limestone, outstanding because of its sheer cliffs and traces of amphibian and fern fossils; above that is the Coconino sandstone, the solidified remains of sand dunes in which fossilized footprints indicate lizard life. And at the top is the pale gray Kaibab limestone (at 180 million years, the toddler of the Grand Canyon family), a rich exhibition case for fossils from the shallow sea that once covered the area — sponges, sharks' teeth, corals, and bivalves.

Though geologists could spend lifetimes exploring the area, the canyon has attractions beyond. Hikers, bikers, river adventurers, naturalists, and just plain lookers-on have equal claim on the wonder. Between the South Rim and North Rim (an average distance of 9 miles as the crow flies, but 21 miles by the rugged Kaibab hiking trail, and more than 200 miles by automobile) there is a vast expanse with something to see at every point, from the magnificent views, to four distinct climatic zones, to many species of plants and animals.

The South Rim is the more heavily visited of the two and the best place for an introduction to the Grand Canyon. Crowded in the summer, but open year-round, the South Rim features extensive facilities for visitors amidst a lovely background of juniper and piñon forest, and open fields of Arizona blue lupine, yellow wild buckwheat, and purple asters. The South Rim Visitors' Center, Yavapai Museum, and Tusayan Ruin and Museum offer orientation exhibits on the geological history of the area and the peoples who lived in the canyon. At the center you can pick up information on all the daily and weekly activities, from nature hikes along the rim led by rangers to more strenuous excursions into the canyon. South Rim drives cover 35 miles and have excellent overlooks. The eight-mile West Rim drive, closed to automobile traffic from May 1 to Labor Day, has a free shuttle bus service linking key points. Ranger-naturalists are stationed at Hopi Point, Mohave Point, and Pima Point for interpretive talks on the geology, botany, animal life, and peoples of the Grand Canyon. The West Rim drive provides the best overview of the canyon, and the frequent buses that run from early morning till evening allow visitors to enjoy the sights at their own pace. Bicycles may be rented during the summer; scenic airplane and helicopter flights are available year-round.

Trails for hiking down into the canyon start at the South Rim and, if you know your limits, can provide more intimate acquaintance with the wonders therein. The Bright Angel Trail, with rest stations at 1½ and 3 miles, and the steep South Kaibab Trail are best for hiking. You can take supervised nature walks or do it on your own, but remember that the canyon gets hotter as you descend and is hottest at midday. Take your hike in the early morning or late afternoon, bring plenty of water and food along, and a hat for protection from the sun, and don't forget that going down is the easy part. Leave twice as much time for hiking back up. If you're an experienced hiker, there are a number of more rigorous and extended hikes to the river and up to the North Rim.

One of the most interesting and certainly less strenuous ways to see the canyon is by muleback. There are one-day rides and overnight trips into the inner gorge; riders stay overnight at the small guest ranch alongside Bright Angel Creek, where comfortable cabins can soothe even the most saddle-sore.

There are a wide range of lodgings at the South Rim from the private concessions in the park — the rustic Bright Angel Lodge, the modern Yavapai and Thunderbird Lodges — to several park-run or privately operated campgrounds. Since the canyon is such a popular attraction, reservations should be made in advance, particularly during the summer months.

Less accessible from major highways and cities, the North Rim is also less crowded and offers different views of the Canyon from a magnificent setting. Tall blue-green firs, scarlet gilias, and roaming deer can be seen on the North Rim, which is closed in the winter because of heavy snows (open from mid-May to mid-October). The 26-mile Cape Royal Drive has magnificent overlooks including Point Imperial, which at 8,801 feet is the highest point on the canyon rim and features spectacular views of the subtle hues of the Painted Desert, Marble Canyon, and the Colorado River. The North Rim has some organized activities (Transept Trail Walk, led by a ranger-naturalist, geology talks at Cape Royal, evening campfire programs at the campground near the Grand Canyon Lodge, muleback trips) but is more a place for solitary communion with nature. The most outstanding vista is Toroweap Point, which, far off the beaten track (reached only by dirt road), offers an amazing view, 3,000 feet down a sheer vertical wall to the snake-shaped Colorado.

The Grand Canyon Lodge provides modest accommodations on the North Rim. A campground near the inn allows stays of up to one week.

Of all the ways to see the canyon, none is more exciting than rubber rafting the roaring Colorado. Various commercial enterprises offer trips on relatively stable rubber rafts powered by outboard motors. On these, you get to see the canyon from the bottom up — cat's claw, yucca, blackbrush, the pink Grand Canyon rattlesnake — and above rise the sheer cliffs of rock almost older than time itself. Shooting along the rapids, you get a sense of the power that has revealed it all. Information: the Superintendent, Grand Canyon National Park, Grand Canyon, AZ 86023 (602 638-2411).

BEST EN ROUTE

There is a variety of accommodations in the Grand Canyon National Park. The National Park Service runs several campgrounds which are available on a first come-first served basis. For overnight hikes you need to have a permit and should reserve in advance by contacting the Backcountry Office at the address given above. Several concessions operate motels and hotels in the park. Listed below are two of several places in the park run by the Grand Canyon National Park Lodges Company. You should reserve rooms three to four months in advance by contacting the company at South Rim, Grand Canyon, AZ 86023 (602 638-2401).

El Tovar – This recently renovated hotel is the oldest and most luxurious of the Grand Canyon accommodations. Some suites have balconies overlooking the Canyon and there is a good dining room serving prime ribs and filet mignon. South Rim.

Yavapai Lodges – This complex has 196 modern units and 150 standard motel rooms in the older section; cafeteria. Grand Canyon Village.

Petrified Forest National Forest, Arizona

In one of those great moments of motion pictures, Humphrey Bogart, playing a desperate criminal in "The Petrified Forest," allows his sensitive side to rule and frees his captive, Bette Davis, at the ultimate cost of his own life. But in this case, it was more than the dame that compelled him. Certainly the desert landscape of the Petrified Forest, at once desolate and inhospitable, yet strangely beautiful in all its harshness, can turn a person's head and heart. And such a change in conscience is not a special effect of the movie but is part of the real life here as well. The Petrified Forest Visitors' Center has a display of apologetic letters, in some cases long confessionals written as much as 20 years later, from visitors who have broken the park rules and taken samples of petrified wood, only to find that the wood weighs more heavily on their minds than on their bookshelves. The Petrified Forest has a powerful impact on the minds and imaginations of those who see it.

You have simply to go there to feel its power; you will undoubtedly be surprised by what you find. The Petrified Forest is really nothing like a forest at all but rather a high arid desert region in northeastern Arizona. No living trees stand, and the predominant forms of vegetation are cactus and yucca growing sparsely around mesas and buttes that bake in the unrelenting sun.

But there are trees, or at least the remains of trees, and thousands of them, lying supine and glowing in the desert heat. In fact, the 147-mile area encompassed by the park contains the richest collection of petrified wood in the world, ranging from huge prone logs to small brilliantly colored chips — burning oranges, deep reds, rusts, and yellows, mixed with the dark shades of black, blue, and purple, and lighter shades of white, gray, and tan. The only color you won't see much of is green, for this is a forest turned to stone. And the colors of the logs are part of the landscape as well. The northern portion of the park adjoins the Painted Desert, which really is just that, except that the colors are natural in this series of plateaus, buttes, and low mesas, remarkable for the bright reds, oranges, and browns in layers of sandstones, shales, and clays. The area is something of an outdoor gallery — the Painted Desert and the Petrified Forest, which might more aptly be called the sculpted desert, exhibiting nature's work in various media as the colors and forms change from minute to minute with the intensity of sun and the formidable shadows of late afternoon or early morning.

In the dawn of its history, the Petrified Forest was actually a forest. About 200 million years ago, what is now a high desert plateau was a low-lying swamp basin with dense beds of ferns, mosses, and trees growing in marshlands and along streams. Groves of conifers flourished on hills and ridges above this basin. Over long periods of time, natural forces felled the trees, and flooding streams transported them to the floor of the floodplain where they were gradually buried under thousands of feet of mud, sand, and silica-rich volcanic ash (left from earlier volcanic activity). Water carrying the silica and other minerals seeped through the sediment and filled in each wood cell, retaining the details of the wooden mold. The silica left glasslike deposits of white, gray, and tan shades, while traces of iron in the water colored the logs yellow, orange, red, and rust, and manganese created the blacks, blues, and purples. During a period of mountain-building activity 70 million years ago, an upheaval lifted the layer high above sea level, and gradual erosion left the rainbow logs exposed. Geologists believe that many other logs are buried below the surface to a depth of 300 feet.

Though more logs will be exposed in the continuing evolutionary process, what is on the surface is truly remarkable and can be seen in several hours. The park's major features, six separate forests with concentrations of chips and huge chunks of onyx, agate, and jasper, are linked by a 28-mile road. The Visitors' Center, open year-round, is a good place to stop first to see specimens of polished petrified wood, exhibits explaining the petrification process, and of course, the letters from petty and grand petrified-wood thieves whose consciences got the better of them. Rainbow Forest is a magnificent highlight, for its beautiful colors, and the evidence of the petrification process; many trunks exceed 100 feet in length, and brilliant chips of onyx, agate, carnelian, and jasper tint the desert sand. At Long Logs, logs are piled one on top of the other, and a partially restored Indian pueblo built of petrified wood chunks overlooks the area. A parking lookout located on a ridgetop above Jasper Forest looks out on masses of logs, opaque in color, strewn on the valley floor. One of the park's most unusual sights is Agate Bridge, a huge single log with over 100 feet exposed and both ends encased in sandstone.

Newspaper Rock is a mammoth chunk of sandstone with intriguing uninterpreted picture writings of prehistoric Indians. Nearby is Blue Mesa, where a one-mile loop of paved trail leads along a blue-gray ridge carved by the winds into intricate sculptures. Exploration of the vast unmarked surroundings must be arranged with park rangers; without natural water sources or trails, the Petrified Forest is not for casual hiking.

The Painted Desert is at the northern end of the park. After stopping at the Administration Building for displays on how traces of iron have stained the layers of clay and sandstone many shades from bright red to pale blue, take the six-mile loop drive, stopping at several overlooks, and see it for yourself. The colors seem ever-changing and appear most vivid in early morning or late afternoon, or after rain, a most uncommon event.

There are no lodging facilities inside the park and camping is not permitted. Removing petrified wood from the park is also strictly forbidden. However, if you want a sample of petrified wood, you can purchase some taken from private lands outside the park at the Painted Desert Oasis and Rainbow Forest lounges located near the park entrances. But leave the park intact as federal law, nature's law, and, as many have found, the law of their consciences dictate. The beauty of the Petrified Forest is there for all to behold. You really can't take it with you — at least not in your pocket, but only in the image of your mind's eye. Information: the Petrified Forest National Park Headquarters, AZ 86028 (602 524-6228).

BEST EN ROUTE

The park has no overnight facilities but there are many motels in Holbrook, 25 miles to the west, and one in Chambers, 21 miles east.

Tonto, Holbrook – This 38-room motel has an outdoor pool, TV and telephone in every room, and will accommodate pets. Within walking distance of two restaurants. 602 Navajo Blvd., Holbrook, AZ 86025 (602 524-6263).

Romney, Holbrook – This 32-room motel has color TV in every room, a full-service restaurant, and accepts pets. 310 W Hopi Dr., Holbrook, AZ 86025 (602 524-6231).

Best Western Chieftain, Chambers – This 51-room motel is located near the Navajo Reservation. Facilities include a pool, a service station, and a restaurant serving Spanish, American, and Indian food such as Navajo tacos — frybread sandwiches with beans and other vegetables. Reservations are advisable: PO Box 697, Chambers, AZ 86502, on I-40 (602 688-2754).

Big Sur and the Monterey Peninsula, California

Big Sur is a 50-mile stretch of Pacific coast south of the Monterey Peninsula and Carmel-by-the-Sea. Its name, Big Sur, is a corruption of a Spanish phrase meaning "Big South." California rt. 1 hugs the rugged coastline from Monterey, through Big Sur, to Morro Bay, 125 miles to the south. Convict chain gangs spent almost two decades carving the twisting highway out of solid cliffs, a highway that is unquestionably the most dramatic on the entire Pacific Coast.

The Monterey Peninsula and Carmel lie 125 miles south of San Francisco, 350 miles north of Los Angeles. Carmel is 4 miles south of the town of Monterey.

MONTEREY – California's first capital, with more than 40 buildings built before 1850. The Old Custom House is the oldest government building in California, dating back to 1827. It has historic material on display (Custom House Sq.). Monterey Presidio, now a US Army language training center, dates from 1770, when it was built by Franciscan Father Junipero Serra, founder of California's Mission Trail (Pacific St.). California's first Constitution was drafted in Colton Hall, in 1849; the building dates from 1848 (Pacific St. and Colton Hall Park). Enamored with what he sensed as "the haunting presence of the ocean," author Robert Louis Stevenson in 1789 lived and worked at what is now called the Robert Louis Stevenson House when the building was French Hotel (530 Houston St.). Cannery Row, site of 20th-century author John Steinbeck's famous novel, has long since given way to chic shops and elegant eateries.

SEVENTEEN-MILE DRIVE – Despite its name it's only 12 miles long, but it takes you from the beaches and cypress trees of Pacific Grove to Carmel. Stop off at Seal Rock, Cypress Point, Pebble Beach Golf Links (site of the annual Crosby Pro-Am Tournament), and Pebble Beach, enclave of the super-rich.

CARMEL-BY-THE-SEA – A picturesque seaside artists' colony. Almost 25% of the permanent population of 4,500 people are working artists. Carmel's quaint, untouched quality is attributable to some of the most stringent zoning laws in the country, passed in 1929. Since then, neon signs, traffic signals, and dozens of other garish accoutrements have been prohibited. Carmel's narrow streets are lined with intriguing little boutiques, shops, 65 art galleries, and some of California's finest restaurants. The Carmel Mission, the most perfectly restored of all the California missions, was founded in 1770 by Father Junipero Serra, who loved it so much he arranged to be buried there. In 1960, Pope John raised the Mission to the status of a Minor Basilica, the second religious landmark so designated in the American West (Lasuen Dr.). South of Carmel, Point Lobos Recreation Area, a 1,255-acre park, has some of the most beautiful scenery along the California coast. Be sure to visit China Cove, Bird Island, and the wonderful stands of cypress. Colonies of seals and sea lions live on the rocks. Despite the fact that there are no wolves in the area, the Spanish called it "Lobos" (Spanish for "wolf") because the barking of the seals reminded them of the sound of wolves. The park has a Visitors' Center, hiking trails, campsites, and fishing spots (four miles south of Carmel on rt. 1). The Bach Music Festival takes place every July. For information on events in Carmel-by-the-Sea, contact the Carmel Business Association, Carmel, CA 93921 (408 624-2522).

CARMEL VALLEY – Follow the Carmel Valley Road east into the land of strawberry fields, orchards, grazing pasture, and artichoke farms. Because of its sunny, warm climate, the valley is an ideal choice for vacationers. You can play golf, ride horses, swim, play tennis, hunt wild boar and deer in season, or fish for trout in the Carmel River. Carmel Valley Begonia Gardens is ablaze with the colors of 15,000 flowers. The Korean Buddhist Temple is a good place to experience a contemplative foreign religion (Robinson Canyon Rd.). Most hotels and motels in Carmel Valley are resorts. For information on accommodations and events, contact the Carmel Valley Chamber of Commerce, PO Box 288, Carmel Valley, CA 93924 (408 659-4000).

THIRTY-MILE DRIVE – The 30 miles between the Monterey-Carmel area and Big Sur are some of the most dramatic in the country. It takes about an hour to drive along the coast-hugging, twisting road. Here, the Santa Lucia Mountains encounter the sea.

Bixby Creek Bridge, just south of Carmel, is a 260-foot-high observation point where you can park you car, watch the ocean pound the beach, and gaze hypnotically at the Point Sur Lighthouse, which flashes every 15 seconds.

BIG SUR – The most famous piece of shoreline on the continent. In fact, it's so familiar to TV and movie audiences, it is almost unnecessary to talk about it. The rolling grassy hills of Big Sur end abruptly at cliffs towering high above the sea. There are many places to stop and watch sea otters, seals, and sea lions near the shore. You might even see whales spouting, farther out to sea. Below the cliffs, waves crash over the boulders. You won't need to be told which specific spots on the road are especially scenic — when you round a hairpin curve and find yourself gasping and grabbing for your camera, you'll know you've found one.

In the town of Big Sur, you can stroll along the beach, have a picnic overlooking the water, shop or browse in the town's art galleries, or visit the redwood trees, inland. Be sure you stop in at Nepenthe, a restaurant on an 800-foot cliff that was originally built by a student of Frank Lloyd Wright. Nepenthe has evolved over the years into Big Sur's main hangout and social center (408 667-2345). Pfeiffer–Big Sur State Park, a deep forest of redwood and other trees, provides a change of scenery from the bare, grassy hills of Big Sur. It has horseback riding, hiking trails, fishing spots, picnic areas, campgrounds, food service, and a lodge. At Jade Cove, you can hunt for jade at low tide. For information contact Big Sur Information Center, Big Sur, CA 93920 (408 667-2353).

SAN SIMEON – About 40 miles to the south of Big Sur, William Randolph Hearst's fabled castle, San Simeon, contains sections of castles from other parts of the world which the late newspaper tycoon shipped to his Pacific estate. Amazingly reconstructed, the majestic rooms, halls, courtyards, and swimming pools are no less than stunningly elegant. Tours will take you through this regal $50 million treasurehouse, now a state historical monument of 123 acres overlooking the ocean. Tickets may be purchased in advance by writing Hearst Reservation Office, Department of Parks and Recreation, PO Box 2390, Sacramento, CA 95811 (805 927-4621).

MORRO BAY – Named for the massive volcanic spire jutting out almost 600 feet above the sea. Morro Bay State Park, a 1,483-acre tract with horseback riding, hiking trails, picnic areas, and campsites, also has a natural history museum on local marine biology and ecology.

BEST EN ROUTE

Ventana Inn, Big Sur – Dramatic, contemporary elegance with exposed beams, high ceilings, balconies, patios, and windows looking over mountains and ocean. All rooms have patchwork quilts and hand-painted furniture. Swimming pool, sauna, Jacuzzi whirlpool, and hiking trails. Rt. 1, Big Sur, CA 93920 (408 667-2331).

Pine Inn, Carmel – A Victorian establishment with stained glass, electrified gas lamps, marble-topped tables, wooden chests, and brass beds. A penthouse that sleeps eight has a fireplace. Each of the 49 bedrooms is furnished differently. PO Box 250, Carmel, CA 93921 (408 624-3851).

Sea View Inn, Carmel – Although the sea view is partially blocked by tall pines, this inn was built around 1906 and has retained much of its original atmosphere, if not its $3-a-night original prices. There are eight bedrooms, six with private bath, and some have window seats and rocking chairs. A delicious breakfast is included. PO Box 4138, Carmel, CA 93921 (408 624-8778).

Death Valley National Monument, California

One of the largest of our national monuments, Death Valley National Monument covers 3,000 square miles, 550 of which are below sea level. It is located 140 miles west of Las Vegas on rts. 190 and 95, and 300 miles northeast of Los Angeles on I-14 and rt. 90, on the California side of the California-Nevada border, in the Mojave Desert. Originally, the 140-mile valley was called Tomesha ("red-hot earth") by the Indians, but was given its present name by a party of prospectors who got lost in the valley during the Gold Rush.

To the 49ers and the early settlers, Death Valley was a deadly obstacle to be overcome in order to reach the riches of California. Modern travelers find it an exciting, dramatic place that can be explored in relative safety. Death Valley can be a unique side trip on journeys from southern California to Las Vegas, Yosemite, or Sequoia–Kings Canyon National Parks.

Death Valley and environs form a region of extremes. At 282 feet below sea level, it is the lowest point in the entire Western Hemisphere. Only 70 air miles away stands the highest point in the continental US — Mt. Whitney, 14,494 feet above sea level. Death Valley is also one of the hottest places on earth, with temperatures recorded as high as 134° in the shade (the all-time world record is 136°, recorded in Libya, in 1922). Summertime is a good time to stay away.

If a scientist were to tell you he or she was going to Death Valley to study fish, you might justifiably raise a skeptical eyebrow. However, there are several species of fish in the streams of Death Valley that do not exist anywhere else in the world. There are, in fact, more than 40 species of life indigenous only to Death Valley. Despite its great heat and minuscule rainfall (less than two inches a year), Death Valley has springs and several streams that flow all year. There's even a small swamp. During migration periods, Death Valley is visited by such unlikely guests as Canada and snow geese, herons, and ducks.

In addition to Death Valley's valid claims on things that are the highest, the lowest, the oldest, and the biggest, it might also be the richest. There are many legends about the fabulous lost mines of Death Valley. These may or may not be true, but at one time it certainly had some of the nation's most lucrative mines. There were boom towns with colorful names like Bullfrog and Skidoo, towns that died when the mines played out, although today you'll pass what remains of these once-vibrant mining centers on your way to monument headquarters, north of Furnace Creek. At the Furnace Creek Visitors' Center, you can pick up brochures and maps explaining how to take a self-guiding auto tour. There are slide shows, nature exhibits, and lectures.

Death Valley is actually the floor of what was once a large inland lake.

When the Sierra Nevadas were thrust up from the earth, they cut off the lake's supply of rainwater. (Today, the western slopes of the Sierras are green with vegetation, while just a few miles away the eastern slopes are parched and dry.) The Devil's Golf Course is the name for a bed of salt pinnacles, some of which are as high as four feet and still growing.

If there's one mineral that Death Valley is famous for, it's borax. The borax mines were established in the 1880s, when roads in Death Valley were built for the legendary 20-mule teams that hauled the borax out of the valley. Three of the modern roads in Death Valley follow the route of the old 20-mule teams. Near Mustard Canyon, there's a display of artifacts from the Harmony Borax Works.

However, the most famous landmark in Death Valley is Scottys Castle. Walter Scott (or "Death Valley Scotty," as he was known) had once been a performer in Buffalo Bill's Wild West Show. He built an elaborate, lavishly furnished castle in Grapevine Canyon at the north end of Death Valley, claiming he had paid for it with gold from a secret mine. The castle, standing like a mirage on the edge of the desert, has been famous ever since it was built. The romantic tale of a secret gold mine is, unfortunately, untrue. The castle was actually built by Albert M. Johnson, a wealthy Chicago businessman who came to Death Valley and quickly became close friends with the flamboyant ex-cowboy. Other well-known Death Valley landmarks are Zabriskie Point, Titus Canyon, Telescope Peak — 11,049 feet high — and directly below it, Badwater, the lowest point in the valley. There are nine campgrounds scattered throughout the valley, among them: Furnace Creek, Mahogany Flat, Mesquite Spring, Sunset Campground, and Texas Springs. Reservations for campsites are not accepted. There's almost always plenty of room for everyone. The tourist season runs from mid-fall to mid-spring, and the weather is pleasant during the winter. If you're planning to do any hiking during your visit, keep in mind at all times that Death Valley got its name for a reason. You should *always* carry plenty of extra water.

Death Valley's stark visual appeal evokes a strong emotional response. While other western national parks and monuments allow visitors to view the beauty of the West, Death Valley invites you to experience something of the spirit of the Old West — the determination, drive, and sense of hope that made this part of America what it is today. The men, women, and children who were the original pioneers knew that they faced the very real possibility of death as they started out across this valley. Most of them made it and went on to start new lives in California; some lie buried beneath its sands. You can't visit Death Valley without instinctively finding yourself thinking about the soul and spirit of the people who crossed it in covered wagons over a century ago. It's a monument to the American spirit and to the spirit of the pioneers who traveled the American West.

Each of the canyons and mountains surrounding Death Valley seems to have its own special colors. Golden Canyon has bright golds and rich purples; Mustard Canyon is various shades of ocher. The Black Mountains have reds, greens, and tans. One particularly interesting canyon is Mosaic Canyon, whose gray rock surfaces are embedded with colorful pebbles that have been worn down by erosion, making the canyon look as if someone decorated it with brilliant mosaics.

Within a few hours' drive of Death Valley, there are a number of ski resorts, among them: June Mountain, Mammoth Mountain, and Wolverton. Just 120 miles from Death Valley lies the southernmost glacier field in the Northern Hemisphere, located near the town of Big Pine on rts. 190 and 395.

Information on Death Valley: the Superintendent, Death Valley National Monument, Death Valley, CA 92328 (714 786-2331).

BEST EN ROUTE

Reservations at both the inn and the ranch listed below can be made through Furnace Creek Inn, Death Valley, CA 92328.

Furnace Creek Inn, Death Valley – Luxurious, well-known hotel with swimming pool, tennis, lounge with entertainment, and palm-lined gardens. 69 rooms, open mid-October through April. One mile south of Visitors' Center on rt. 190 (714 786-2345).

Furnace Creek Ranch, Death Valley – More casual accommodations in cottages and motel units, swimming pool, golf, tennis, horseback riding, restaurant, cocktail lounge, and service station. Adjacent to trailer park and landing strip for light planes. 225 rooms. Open all year. Next to Visitors' Center on rt. 190 (714 786-2345).

Lake Tahoe, California

Lake Tahoe is so much more than a lake resort that its name is almost misleading. It is equally famous for its incomparable outdoor sports facilities, especially skiing; sophisticated gambling casinos offering the best nationally known entertainers; and, of course, the lake itself. The largest mountain lake in North America, Tahoe is 22 miles long, 12 miles wide, and has 71 miles of shoreline. At an altitude of 6,229 feet, it is 1,664 feet deep, and contains enough water to cover the entire state of California to a depth of more than one foot. Despite its size and the heavily populated sections of its shoreline, the water is pure enough to drink. In fact, there's enough of it to supply every person in the United States with five gallons of water every day for five years.

If you look at a map of California and Nevada, you'll find Lake Tahoe nestled at the notch where California's eastern boundary starts to slant southeast. Actually, two-thirds of the lake belongs to California, one-third to Nevada. South Lake Tahoe is 209 miles from San Francisco, on I-80 to Sacramento, then rt. 50. At South Lake Tahoe, you have a choice: rt. 50 to rt. 28, north, along the developed eastern shore in Nevada, or rt. 89, which runs into rt. 28, around the northern edge of the lake in California.

There are two theories about Lake Tahoe's origins. One argues that the lake was a huge crater gouged out of the crown of the Sierra Nevadas during the Ice Age. Another puts the lake's beginnings at three million years ago, when volcanic lava hardened, trapping the Tahoe waters in a deep, geological cup. However it began, present-day Tahoe offers something for nearly everyone.

Luxury-seekers will find ultramodern hotels and casinos at the southern end of the lake. Outdoor sports enthusiasts will find skiing, boating, swimming, fishing, hiking, golf, and tennis in abundance everywhere. Campers seeking solitude and untrammeled nature have access to any of the three national forests around the lake — Tahoe, 696,000 acres to the north of the lake; Toiyabe, 3.1 million acres on the eastern edge in Nevada; and Eldorado, 886,000 acres to the southwest.

Starting at the US Forest Service Visitor Information Center, at the southern tip of the lake on rt. 89, one mile north of Camp Richardson (916 541-0209), you can trace the shoreline by car north and west through California, or through Nevada. The corkscrew road winding through the ponderosa pine and spruce along the western edge of the lake is considerably more rugged than the strip fronting the eastern shoreline. California offers much better sightseeing, since rt. 89's intricate twists and turns reveal dramatic, panoramic views. You'll have to take it slowly — the road is peppered with 10-mile-an-hour zones, and, on a weekend, clogged with people. And take it *very* slow if the weather is foggy, rainy, or snowy — rt. 89 can be treacherous.

EMERALD BAY – Greets you almost as soon as you begin to make your way north. You might well experience déjà vu — the feeling you've been here before. This is one of the most photographed sites in the state. Eagle Falls, a canyon above the bay, has crystal-clear pools for swimming.

DESOLATION VALLEY WILDERNESS – In startling contrast to Emerald Bay's fairyland splendor, these 41,000 forbidding acres of lake-dotted granite form a barren landscape laced with dozens of hiking trails. Experienced hikers have been known to gripe that the trails are as mannerly as a city park's.

TAHOE CITY – Ski country. You can pick up interchangeable lift tickets for slopes at Northstar, Alpine Meadows, Heavenly Valley, Squaw Valley, and Kirkwood. For information, contact Ski Lake Tahoe, Incline Village, NV 89450 (800 648-5494, toll-free; in Nevada and Hawaii, 702 831-4222). North Lake Tahoe Chamber of Commerce is located at 850 North Lake Blvd., Tahoe City, CA 95730 (916 583-2371).

SQUAW VALLEY – Five miles north of Tahoe City, the site of the 1960 Olympics. One of the most famous ski areas in the world, with 26 chairlifts, cable cars, and complete accouterments. The aerial tram operates all year (916 593-6985).

INCLINE VILLAGE – At the northern end of the lake, in Nevada. Lakeshore Boulevard is lined with expensive houses, showy hotels, casinos, and other attractions which make this "The Entertainment Capital of Lake Tahoe." Robert Trent Jones designed the two championship 18-hole golf courses, notorious for their water hazards. Golf Incline, as it's called, becomes Ski Incline from December through April (702 831-1821). The Lake Tahoe Racquet Club has 26 courts (702 831-0360).

PONDEROSA RANCH – As familiar to you now as your own living room, you can catch a glimpse of the set of the TV series *Bonanza* from the Incline golf courses. More than 350,000 people visit the ranch every year. A pre-breakfast horseback ride leaves the Ponderosa Stables at 8 AM (702 831-0691).

MT. ROSE – Detour north on rt. 27 for a bird's-eye perspective of the lake and environs. In winter, Mt. Rose has three ski slopes. In summer, there are 40 campsites in the Mt. Rose Campground (702 882-2766).

TOIYABE NATIONAL FOREST – Slightly to the east of the shoreline, known for its challenging hiking trails — so "uncontrolled" that inexperienced hikers are cautioned to stay away. Reservations must be made in advance for the 54 campsites, operated by the US Forest Service. Contact Ticketron in San Francisco (415 788-2828).

CAVE ROCK – Used as a natural barrier against enemy attack by the Paiute Indians. Today, the natural cave is a tunnel for cars, with a lookout point.

ZEPHYR COVE – Cruise to Emerald Bay on the MS *Dixie,* a triple-deck ship offering dinner, cocktail, and midnight disco cruises as well as daylight passenger excursions. The ship can be hired for special charter cruises off-season, October through April. During the spring and summer months, reserve well in advance (702 588-3508).

STATELINE – Gambling country. This is what Tahoe is most famous for. Take your pick — you'll find slot machines, craps and keno tables, roulette wheels, and giant names in nightclub entertainment all over town. Harrah's, Sahara Tahoe, Harvey's, and Caesar's Tahoe are the most famous casinos. Barney's, next to Harrah's, has a smaller casino and gives discount coupons to guests at other hotels. South Tahoe Nugget also distributes coupons. It's about three-quarters of a mile east of Barney's on rt. 50. For information and reservations, contact the South Lake Tahoe Visitors Bureau, PO Box 17727, South Lake Tahoe, CA 95706 (916 544-5050).

BEST EN ROUTE

River Ranch Lodge, Tahoe City, California – A 21-room inn. Write PO Box 197, Tahoe City, CA 95730 (916 583-4264).

Hyatt Lake Tahoe, Incline Village, Nevada – Big casino and nightclub activity, plus water sports, tennis, and golf nearby. 460 rooms. PO Box 3239, Incline Village, NV 89450 (702 831-1111).

Coeur du Lac Condominiums, Incline Village, Nevada – For information on rentals, write PO Box 7107, Incline Village, NV 89450 (702 831-3318).

Harrah's, Stateline, Nevada – World-famous super-resort with a 150-yard-long casino, famous entertainers in the showroom, 4 lounges, and a full range of activities. Also, 540 rooms and 24-hour action. The hotel's Summit Restaurant has lake views from the window, and serves Continental specialties like pheasant with choucroute and champagne sauce. PO Box 10, Reno, NV 89504 (800 648-3773, toll-free from Arizona, California, Idaho, Oregon, and Utah; everywhere else, 702 329-4422).

Del Webb's Sahara Tahoe, Stateline, Nevada – A casino with 1,200 slot machines, superstar nightclub/lounge, and luxury facilities. 540 rooms, and here, too, nonstop action. The hotel's House of Lords Restaurant serves filet mignon Béarnaise and flambé desserts. PO Box C, Stateline, NV 89449 (800 648-3322, toll-free from Arizona, California, Idaho, Oregon, and Utah; everywhere else, 702 588-6211).

Harvey's, Stateline, Nevada – More than 1,600 slot machines, all gambling facilities, and several restaurants. Top of the Wheel serves Polynesian and American specialties. The Sage Room serves steak and seafood, and the El Dorado Room serves a buffet. 200 rooms. PO Box 128, Stateline, NV 89449 (702 588-2411).

Christiana Inn, South Lake Tahoe, California – If you're looking for quieter accommodations close to the scene, this small, European-style chalet a mere 100 yards from the ski lifts at Heavenly Valley might suit your purpose. Dining room offers an extensive Continental menu and wine list. Two rooms and three suites. PO Box 6870, S Lake Tahoe, CA 95729 (916 544-7337). While you're in Heavenly Valley, try the Top of the Tram Restaurant (steak, chicken, trout entrées). The price of Sunday brunch includes the tram. Keller Rd. (916 544-6263).

Palm Springs and Joshua Tree National Monument, California

Palm Springs is in Coachella Valley, 100 miles southeast of Los Angeles. It was at one time an important stop on the stagecoach route from Prescott, Arizona, to Los Angeles. Today, the drive from LA to Palm Springs takes about two hours on I-10, which, in LA, is the San Bernardino Freeway.

The sun shines an average of 350 days a year in Palm Springs and the air is pure. The average daytime temperature is 88°; nighttime average, a comfortable 55°. Since the humidity is always low, you can enjoy the heat without suffering from that muggy, clammy feeling that accompanies high humidities.

Palm Springs was discovered hundreds of years ago by the Agua Caliente Indians. Agua Caliente means "hot water" in Spanish, and it was, in fact, the discovery of hot springs in the earth which led to the area's development into a spa and, later, a resort. The Agua Caliente Indians considered these springs to have miraculous healing powers. The springs were opened to the public around the turn of the century, and whether or not they healed anyone, they have provided a miracle for the Agua Caliente tribe, which is still the largest single landowner in Palm Springs. The 180 members of this tiny tribe own over ten square miles of tremendously valuable land within the city limits.

People are more attracted to Palm Springs' warm, dry climate, its desert scenery, and superb resort facilities than to the springs themselves. For the rich, Palm Springs offers all the luxurious goods and services money can buy. For anyone, rich or poor, it offers what money cannot buy — a sparkling environment and delightful climate. Despite the fact that Palm Springs has over 200 hotels and hosts about two million visitors annually, it is nevertheless a very small town, with a permanent population of 36,000. The town probably has the world's highest number of swimming pools per capita — over 7,000, one for every five people. Not everyone in Palm Springs is rich, although sometimes it seems that way. In winter, the wealthy, the famous, and the powerful come to play, and prices for everything soar as high as Mt. San Jacinto, the peak overlooking the city. During the summer, temperatures rise and prices drop.

No matter when you come, you'll find active nightclubs, dozens of fascinating (and expensive) boutiques, and sports activities that range from horseback riding through the nearby canyons to balloon trips through the desert. Known as "Golf Capital of the World," Palm Springs has 40 golf courses, and is the site of more than 100 major golf tournaments each year, including the Bob Hope Celebrity Classic and the Standard Brands–Dinah Shore Championship. There are hundreds of tennis courts and an increasing number of important annual tennis championships. The round of constant events and festivals includes rodeos, horse shows, the Desert Circus, art festivals, major league exhibition baseball games, charity balls, and designer fashion shows.

Clothing designers often launch new styles in Palm Springs, so you can find next year's fashions this year. Check out the elegant specialty shops on Palm Canyon Drive, the main thoroughfare.

The main places of interest include the Palm Springs Desert Museum, a lavish new cultural center with an excellent art museum, a history museum with unusual Indian artifacts, and outstanding facilities for the performing arts (135 E Tahquitz-McCallum Way). The Living Desert Reserve has plants in natural settings with landscaped paths; Moorten Botanical Gardens offers more than 2,000 kinds of desert plants from all over the world (1701 S Palm Canyon Dr.). San Jacinto Wilderness State Park, atop the 10,780-foot mountain, has more than 50 miles of hiking trails, picnic areas, and six campgrounds. Its 13,000 acres can be reached only by an aerial tram ride. The park is the site of numerous activities — some serious and some purely fanciful — throughout the year. It is part of the larger San Bernardino National Forest. Information on Palm Springs: the Palm Springs Convention and Visitors' Bureau, Municipal Airport Terminal, Palm Springs, CA 92262 (714 327-8411).

THE INDIAN CANYONS – Filled with plants, bubbling hot springs, magnificent waterfalls, ancient Indian cliff dwellings, and pictographs on the canyon walls. Don't be surprised if it reminds you of Shangri-la — these canyons were used as the film location for the original movie version of *Lost Horizon,* James Hilton's novel about the fabled hidden paradise. The canyons are closed to visitors during the summer. Tahquitz Canyon is now closed year-round due to the constant danger of fire. The canyons are part of the Agua Caliente Indian Reservation.

INDIO – "Date Capital of the World" (the kind that grows on trees, rather than the kind you go out with), and site of the National Date Festival in February. Decor is neo–Arabian Nights, with camel and ostrich races. A movie called "The Sex Life of a Date" has been playing at Shield's Date Gardens for the past few years.

JOSHUA TREE NATIONAL MONUMENT – Created in 1936 over howls of protest from mining companies that wanted to exploit the region. The monument is a haven for the strange Joshua tree and other desert wildlife and plants. The Joshua tree was given its name by early pioneers who felt that it resembled the prophet Joshua raising his arms in supplication to God or perhaps pointing the way for them to go.

Start your tour at the Twentynine Palms Oasis, site of the monument's headquarters, Visitors' Center, and museum. A hike along the short nature trail will acquaint you with the plants and animals that live here. The park spreads 870 square miles south of the oasis, with good major roads. Split Rock, one of the monument's best-known landmarks, is a giant split boulder more than three stories high with a natural cave underneath.

Ten miles south of Pinto Wye, Cholla Cactus Gardens and nature trail cover several acres. The gardens are filled with a species of cactus known as jumping cholla, so called because it seems to jump out at you to give you a painful sting. It's probably a good place to skip if you have young children with you. Wonderland of the Rocks in Hidden Valley is the most popular site on monument grounds. Thousands of years of desert winds have carved the rocks into bizarre shapes resembling sailing ships, monsters, cabbages, kings, and assorted other oddities. The best examples of Joshua trees stand at Keys View, which offers impressive views of the San Bernardino Mountains, San Jacinto, and the distant waters of the Salton Sea. Information: the Superintendent, Joshua Tree National Monument, 74485 National Monument Dr., Twentynine Palms, CA 92277 (714 367-7511).

BEST EN ROUTE

Canyon Hotel Racquet and Golf Resort, Palm Springs – Luxury resort with three heated pools, golf, tennis, restaurants, coffee shop, and nightclub with entertainment. Children under 15 not admitted mid-December through Easter except for Christmas and Easter. Closed mid-June to mid-September. 470 rooms. 2850 S Palm Canyon Dr., Palm Springs, CA 92262 (714 323-5656).

Gene Autry Hotel, Palm Springs – Not as expensive as Canyon, with three heated pools, tennis, restaurant, nightclub with entertainment. 186 rooms, 12 cottages. Closed mid-June to mid-September. 4200 E Palm Canyon Dr., Palm Springs, CA 92264 (714 328-1171).

La Siesta Villa, Palm Springs – Nineteen rooms in self-contained villas, all with fireplaces and kitchen units. Heated pool. Children under 14 not accepted. 247 W Stevens Rd., Palm Springs, CA 92262 (714 325-2269).

Sun Spot Hotel, Palm Springs – Heated pool, laundromat, putting green, and airport transportation. Tennis and golf privileges; 20 rooms, 10 with kitchens. Southeast of downtown Palm Springs. 1035 E Ramon Rd., Palm Springs, CA 92262 (714 327-1288).

Sheraton Plaza, Palm Springs – Opened in January 1981, this new luxury resort is set on 13 acres with 250 rooms (74 are suites), a lavish garden courtyard, swimming pool, tennis courts, and exercise room. Other amenities include a fine restaurant, poolside dining, and live entertainment nightly at *Harvey's Bar. The Wine Bar* features award-winning California wines by the glass or by the bottle. Within walking distance of the town's shops, restaurants, and attractions. At Tahquitz-McCallum Way and Calle Encilla (714 320-6868 or toll-free, 800 325-3535).

Redwood National Park and Lassen Volcanic National Park, California

Millions of years ago, redwoods grew throughout vast areas of North America. Now they're found only in a narrow band of land along the coast of northern California and southern Oregon, and rarely grow more than 50 miles inland since the conifer needs the coastal fog's moisture, which it absorbs through its needles.

REDWOOD NATIONAL PARK – Established in 1968, Redwood National Park consists of several fragments of land in California near the Oregon border. About a quarter of the park's 106,000 acres is divided into three state parks — Jedediah Smith State Park, nine miles northeast of Crescent City, where Redwood National Park maintains its headquarters and Visitors' Center; Del Norte Coast Redwoods State Park, 7 miles southwest of Crescent City; and Prairie Creek Redwoods State Park, near the southern boundary of Redwood National Park at Orick. When the national park was created, the existing parklands were augmented with other redwood groves purchased from lumber companies and private owners. It now has about 40 miles of rugged shoreline with spectacular bluffs. Altogether, Redwood National Park is 55 miles long, but only ten miles wide at its widest point. If you're coming from San Francisco (330 miles to the south), you'll enter the park at Orick.

Just to the north of Orick is the site where the park was dedicated. Nearby stands Lady Bird Grove, a group of immense trees named in honor of Mrs. Lyndon B. Johnson, the former First Lady. Along Redwood Creek, you'll find the tallest trees on earth. A redwood grove gives the feeling of a cathedral. The huge trees grow close together, shutting out the sunlight from above. The branchless trunks soar 80 to 100 feet straight up before the bows spread out to form the roof of the grove. Few smaller trees can grow in their shadow. Although redwoods are related to the giant sequoias which grow in the High Sierras, it's quite simple to distinguish the two — the tall, slender trunk and dark brown bark of a redwood differs from the sequoia's bright reddish-brown color and comparatively massive trunk. The scientific name for the coast redwood is *Sequoia sempervirens.*

Tragically, *sempervirens* (Latin for "living forever") has become a misnomer for the tree. In the 100 years that commercial logging has been active in this region, more than 85% of the original redwood forest has been cut down. In 1978, vast new tracts of land were acquired by the park, almost doubling its size. Unfortunately, however, all but a few thousand acres had already been cut over by the lumber companies. A National Park Service study done in the 1960s estimates that virtually all of the original forest outside the parks will be gone by the 1990s. Presently, there are over 250,000 acres of redwood parks in the state.

Nature designed the redwood for durability. It can grow either from seeds or sprout from roots and stumps of old trees. Its bark is often more than a foot thick and is remarkably fire-resistant. There are natural chemicals in the fiber of the tree that make it incredibly resistant to decay, disease, or fire. The durable, everlasting quality of the redwood is the main reason for the demise of the original groves. The wood's durability and resistance to decay make it superb for items like picnic benches and siding of houses, and it has incredible insulation properties.

The Howard Libby Tree is the tallest known tree on earth — 367.8 feet high, and 44 feet in circumference. Sadly, the forest's tranquillity is occasionally disrupted by the sound of chain saws in the adjacent groves that are owned by lumber companies. To the north of Redwood Creek, Prairie Creek State Park gets as much rain as an Amazon rain forest (about 100 inches a year, most of which falls in winter). The park is filled with redwood, big-leaf maple, Douglas fir, and luxuriant foliage and flowers. Fern Canyon's 50-foot-high walls are swathed with mosses and lichens, and 40 miles of trails stretch through the area's 12,000-acre forest. In the broad meadows of the state park, a herd of about 200 Roosevelt elk roams free. Gold Bluffs, at the western edge of Prairie Creek State Park, fronts directly on the sea. Rugged promontories jut into the Pacific and huge waves break over the jagged rocks. South of Eureka is the Avenue of Giants, 33 miles of majestic groves. There are more than 100 campsites at Gold Bluffs and Prairie Creek.

Del Norte Coast Redwoods State Park, 7 miles southwest of Crescent City, is unusual because its virgin redwood forest extends right to the steep bluffs overlooking the rocky shore. The best views are from the coast-winding Damnation Trail. In late spring, this section is ablaze with azaleas. There are campgrounds at Mill Creek. The northernmost section of Redwood National Park, Jedediah Smith State Park, stands at the northeastern edge of the coastal redwood belt. It contains redwoods as well as inland species like ponderosa pine. The largest trees are in the Frank Stout Memorial Grove, where the star attraction is the 340-foot Stout Tree. There are campsites and good swimming at a sandy beach along the Smith River (nine miles northeast of Crescent City). Despite efforts of the Save-the-Redwood League, vast areas of the forest surrounding the park continue to be leveled by lumber companies. Conservationists are attempting to raise enough money to purchase and preserve virgin forests that are now in private hands. Until they succeed in buying the remaining forest, your visit to Redwood National Park is likely to include the depressing sight of huge redwood logs being carried out of the forest on lumber trucks. Information: Redwood National Park, Crescent City, CA 95531 (707 464-6101).

LASSEN VOLCANIC NATIONAL PARK – About 160 miles southeast of Redwood National Park. Lassen Peak last erupted in 1914, making it one of the most recent active volcanoes in the continental United States. After centuries of peace, Lassen's 20th-century eruptions lasted for seven years, culminating in massive explosions in May 1915 that catapulted five-ton rocks into the air, mowing down all life on the northeast side of the mountain for several miles. Volcanic dust fell as far away as Nevada. In 1916, the volcano and the surrounding area were set aside as a national park. (You could say it opened with a bang.) The smallest of the national parks in California, 106,000-acre Lassen is a mini-Yellowstone, with bubbling mud pots, boiling hot springs, and hissing steam vents known as fumaroles. Like Yellowstone, most of Lassen's major sites are easily accessible by car. Lassen Volcanic National Park headquarters are in Mineral, on rt. 36, nine miles from the park entrance, where you can stop for information. Or you can take rt. 44 east from Redding about 40 miles to the Visitors' Center at Manzanita Lake. The 30-mile Lassen Park Road winds through the western section of the park which contains the major attractions, including 10,457-foot Lassen Peak. More than 150 miles of hiking trails lead to thermal areas and lakes. Lassen Peak Trail will take you on a 2½-mile climb to the summit of Lassen Peak; a shorter, easier trail leads to Bumpass Hell, a section of hot springs, mud pots, and fumaroles in the southwestern corner of the park. (Bumpass is named for an early guide who plunged a leg into a steaming mud pot.) Nearby you'll find Little Hot Springs and the Sulphur Works. In winter you can ski in the southwestern corner of the park.

Summit Lake, in the park's center, is the embarkation point for pack trips to the eastern areas. Cinder Cone, in the northeast corner, was set aside as a national monument several years before Lassen became a park. The stark, black cylindrical cone is surrounded by colorful formations of volcanic ash called the Painted Dunes. To the east of Cinder Cone lie the aptly named Fantastic Lava Beds, a mass of black volcanic stone deposited when Cinder Cone erupted in 1857. If you are somewhat intimidated by the thought of visiting volcanoes, keep in mind that Cinder Cone is considered "dormant." That doesn't mean, however, that new eruptions are impossible. Information: the Superintendent, Lassen Volcanic National Park, Mineral, CA 96063 (916 595-4444).

BEST EN ROUTE

Dehaven Valley Farm, Westport – A refurbished 19th-century farmhouse with porcelain washstands and pitchers, antique towel racks, and fresh flowers in eight bedrooms. Sheep graze outside the house, which is within walking distance of the beach and an old logging road. PO Box 128, Westport, CA 95488 (707 964-2931).

The Benbow Inn, Garberville – Built in the 1920s to resemble an English Tudor mansion, with dark wood paneling, stone fireplace, and shaded terrace. Facilities include a nine-hole golf course, hiking trails, fishing, hunting, swimming, canoeing. Closed January through March. 445 Benbow Dr., Garberville, CA 95440 (707 923-2124).

Mineral Lodge, Mineral – Set in a valley with a mountain view, the lodge consists of several buildings, a swimming pool, restaurant, tennis, and gift shop. In Mineral. For information write PO Box 168, Mineral, CA 96063 (916 595-4422)

Sequoia and Kings Canyon National Parks, California

Sequoia and Kings Canyon National Parks are the backpackers' highway into the majestic Sierra Nevada of Southern California. By car you can see a bit — the giant sequoias, for which Sequoia is named, the forests which surround them, the lower-elevation sights. But only two major roads enter the 1,300 square miles of the parks: One is closed most of the winter by mammoth snowfalls; the other meanders into and out of the western corner of Sequoia so quickly that one feels it is intimidated by the mountains to the east. What you don't see by car is almost everything but the trees: the largest mountain peaks, especially Mt. Whitney, tallest peak in the continental US (at 14,495 feet); the animals; the streams; and the thousands of miles of backcountry, mountain trails for hiking, camping, horse and mule packing, fishing. These *are* the High Sierra experience.

Geographically and administratively, Sequoia and Kings Canyon are one park, covering end to end about 850,000 acres. But the two boast radically different physical features. Sequoia, the southwestern corner of which is accessible by car, is home of the world-renowned giant sequoia trees, the largest living things known on earth (not to be confused with coastal redwoods — *Sequoia sempervirens* — which are taller than *Sequoradendron* but not nearly so broad). Forests of the giant sequoia used to cover the hemisphere; now they are found only on the western faces of the Sierra Nevada, at middle elevations (still thousands of feet above sea level, however). East of the stands of sequoia, the park begins to rise with the Sierra Nevada, culminating at the park's eastern edge in Mt. Whitney, Mt. Muir (14,045 feet), and Mt. Langley (14,042 feet). Then, as quickly as they sprouted, the great peaks fall away to lower elevations, and outside the parks the country breaks into deep, long valleys.

Kings Canyon stretches north of Sequoia, sharing with it one entire border. Made a national park in 1940 (50 years after Sequoia), Kings Canyon has the same wild, rugged mountain beauty of eastern Sequoia, and has the additional attraction of sheer canyon ledges for which it gained fame. Mountains of 13,000 feet are not at all uncommon in the eastern region of Kings Canyon, and running through them, from the northern reaches of Kings Canyon to Mt. Whitney in Sequoia, is John Muir Trail, the 220-mile mountain walking path that threads through the most spectacular, isolated, and peaceful vistas of both parks. Immediately to the east and north of the parks is John Muir Wilderness Area, with Inyo National Forest just beyond.

There is no more fitting tribute to naturalist John Muir than these trails and protected areas. It seems that most of America's beautiful parks and natural wonderlands have at some time in their histories required the guardianship of a farseeing and usually heroic protector; for many that person was one man — John Muir. Sequoia and the High Sierra are perhaps his most remarkable testaments. In the late 1880s, Muir fought the government, and the lumber companies, to protect the sanctity of these natural treasures, long before most people recognized their beauty and spiritual importance. In 1890, thanks to Muir's devotion, Sequoia National Park was officially created, the country's second such refuge. (Yellowstone Park had been established 18 years earlier. Yosemite Park followed Sequoia by a mere five days.)

Automobiles are given limited access in Sequoia and Kings Canyon; there is, however, a beautiful drive along the 50 or so miles of Generals Highway, the stretch of rt. 198 which begins southwest of Sequoia near the town of Three Rivers and winds through the mighty stands of sequoia in the park's southwestern corner, joining rt. 180 outside Sequoia to meander into Kings Canyon. (The road into Kings Canyon is closed in winter due to snow — as much as 20 feet at a time in some places.)

If you start the driving tour at the western corner of Sequoia, you will drive past some of the most magnificent examples of sequoia in the world — several of the mightiest named for American generals. General Sherman Tree is one of the world's tallest trees. It rises 272 feet on a 101.6-foot circumference. It is the subject of thousands of photographs; not one expresses the sheer awe you'll feel when standing next to its thick, reddish-brown trunk, wondering if it ever stops. Estimates of the age of General Sherman put it at a little over 2,500 years. Estimates of the tree's weight place it at 2,000 tons, with enough wood to build 40 five-room houses. It is as high as the Capitol in Washington, and no less a national treasure. The General Sherman Tree is part of Giant Forest, of special interest because it offers a view of sequoia in every stage of development, from sapling (they grow from seeds about the size of a pinhead) to high in the sky (if not quite so high as the few reigning monarchs of the forests).

As you drive the full length of the Generals Highway you will pass several other magnificent trees, especially in Grant Grove (actually part of Kings Canyon), where the road joins rt. 180 and turns north on the way to the heart of Kings Canyon. There stands the General Grant Tree, a full five feet shorter than Sherman, but six feet larger in circumference, and considered by many to be the more awe-inspiring spectacle. Robert E. Lee Tree is nearby, and a few minutes' walk from the grove is Big Stump Basin, where you can see what remains of these colossi after loggers get to them, as they did in the late 19th century despite Muir's efforts. The fourth largest tree in the range is Hart Tree, standing in the Redwood Mountain Grove, west of Generals Highway in Sequoia National Forest.

Halfway along Generals Highway you will come to Lodgepole Visitors' Center, with exhibits on the trees and other aspects of park life. By all means plan to stop for a while. The Visitors' Center (there is also a Visitors' Center in Grant Grove and a visitor contact station at Cedar Grove in Kings Canyon) has information on a huge array of available activities in the park, and is a starting point for guided hiking tours. There is no question that the best way to see the parks is with backpack, tent, and time to hike around. Ranger-guided trips to the mountains and through the sequoia forests give a feeling for the land that is impossible to have from the road, even with frequent stops. The place to organize these journeys is at the Visitors' Center.

But making plans and seeing exhibits is not the only incentive for stopping at Lodgepole. Rising some 6,725 feet above sea level (4,000 feet above the Kaweah River), it offers a magnificent view of the parks and all their treasures. The eastward view is most impressive, looking toward the spiny backbone of the Sierras. A short walk from the rock is Crescent Meadow and Tharp's Log, the log cabin headquarters of 19th-century explorer Hale Tharp. A climb up Beetle Rock is best saved for late afternoon and the experience of a sunset closing out the day over the park. And the strong-winded should hike down to Crystal Cave, a marble cavern highlighted by guided tours given by park rangers.

For an exciting overnight trip, get in a tour to Bearpaw Meadow. The walk on the High Sierra Trail is 11 miles of scenery that rivals the best of Muir Trail. Make reservations in advance with the park concession for facilities there. If you are roughing it, you must get a backcountry permit from the visitors' center. If you feel like continuing on past Bearpaw, the High Sierra Trail continues eastward until it meets Muir Trail at Wallace Creek. From there, you can make side trips to Mt. Whitney, Big Arroyo, or Kern Canyon. Be sure to tell park personnel where you plan to be, and when you plan to come back.

The center of activity in Kings Canyon is Cedar Grove, reached by rt. 180. The ranger station at Cedar Grove has the most current information on hikes, as well as a campsite. From Cedar Grove, hikes can go in almost any direction on miles of trails. The least explored areas are to the north, into the heart of Kings Canyon Park. You will find lakes of all sizes and mountain after mountain. It must be done on foot or horse or muleback. There is little stopping you from tackling the miles of trails and countless opportunities for individual exploration. After all, that's why John Muir fought for it. Information: the Superintendent, Sequoia and Kings Canyon National Parks, Three Rivers, CA 93271 (209 565-3341).

BEST EN ROUTE

Although nothing in the Sequoia and Kings Canyon area really earns a *Best en Route* rating, there are ample alternatives for accommodations — in nearby hotels and motels, in park lodges, and in campsites throughout the national parks and forests.

There are more than a dozen in the two parks. The Lodgepole Campground is run on a reservation-only basis and they can be made through Ticketron outlets. Sequoia and Kings Canyon Hospitality Service, Sequoia National Park, CA 93262 (209 565-3373), has information about the two park-run lodges, Giant Forest Lodge in Sequoia Park (209 565-3373) and Grant Grove Lodge in Kings Canyon (209 335-2314).

While in the parks, there are a number of stores and supply stations to help outfit you for a hike or overnight. They are located near the campsites, and also sell the fishing licenses that are a necessity if you plan to tackle the lakes and streams for the many varieties of native catch, especially the magnificent golden trout. Mules, burros, and horses can be rented at Giant Forest, Grant Grove, Cedar Grove, and Mineral King for pack trips throughout the parks.

Other campsites are available in the Sequoia National Forest, on Hume Lake (where boating, swimming, fishing, and other accommodations are the featured attractions), in Inyo National Forest, and at Stony Creek Campground (on Generals Hwy., south of Grant Grove in Kings Canyon).

Hotel and motel accommodations outside the park are limited to four nearby towns: Three Rivers, just south of Sequoia; Visalia to the west; and Porterville and Fresno.

Yosemite National Park, California

A good many of California's finest physical resources are the product of the Sierra Nevada, the mountain range that runs for 250 miles parallel to the Nevada border. The gem in this mountainous necklace is Yosemite National Park, 1,189 square miles of mountains, valleys, granite spires and monoliths, waterfalls and forests in central eastern California.

Yosemite was established as a national park in 1890, but the natural history of Yosemite spans many millions of years, starting during an ancient age when a shallow arm of the Pacific covered what is now the Sierra Nevada chain and the great Yosemite Valley of California. The sea dried up and subsequent volcanic activity caused molten rock to infiltrate the underlying sedimentary layers. In time, these layers were eroded and the igneous rock, granite, was exposed. Later upheavals of the earth tilted these layers to the west, creating the steep eastern flank and long western slope of the mountains we know today. As a consequence of the angle of the mountains, the flow of streams became more rapid, cutting deep V-shaped valleys into the granite. Then, during Ice Ages two or three million years ago, glaciers gouged the valley into a U-shaped trough with a round bottom and sheer sides. Finally, the melting glaciers formed a lake whose bed is the present valley floor.

Today the valley is Yosemite's main attraction, though by no means all that the park has to offer. Carpeted with meadows and forests, and watered by the Merced River, the valley is seven miles long and one mile wide. Its walls rise 2,000 to 4,000 feet from the valley floor, featuring some of the geological wonders of the world. First and foremost is El Capitan, at 3,604 feet the largest known single block of granite in the world, a huge sheer outcropping which does not have a single fracture on its entire perpendicular wall, a challenge to even veteran rock climbers. Towering above the lower end of the valley, directly across from El Capitan, are the 2,900-foot Cathedral Spires. On the north side of the valley stand the Three Brothers, a trio of leaning peaks piled on top of each other to a height of 3,800 feet. Beyond, the upper valley broadens with a semicircle of granite domes — Sentinel Basket, North Dome, and the massive Half Dome. These huge granite deposits were formed by exfoliation, a process in which the surface layers of rock released from subterranean pressures peel, chip, and crumble into rounded contours on their way toward ultimate dissolution. Though this shaping force is completely imperceptible, the valley's magnificent waterfalls demonstrate the process of gradual dissolution still at work. The most spectacular of the valley's falls is Yosemite, noted for its height; the Upper Fall plunges 1,430 feet over the north wall (a height equal to nine Niagara Falls), and the Lower Fall immediately below is a drop of more than 300 feet. Combined with the cascades in between, the fall's double leap measures 2,565 feet, making Yosemite the highest waterfall on this continent. With the valley's other waterfalls — Ribbon, the misty Bridalveil, Nevada, Vernal, and Illilouette — Yosemite offers one of the most amazing water spectacles anywhere.

In January 1981, the Yosemite General Management Plan began to serve as the approved, long-term guideline for the park. It is likely that this plan will limit the number of visitors entering the park to avoid its overuse. There is also a provision for the employee housing and its supporting maintenance and storage facilities to be relocated outside the park's boundaries.

Yosemite Village, the center of activities in the park with campgrounds, lodging, shops, and restaurants, is a good place to begin a visit. The Yosemite Valley Visitors' Center, open year-round, offers exhibits on the geological development of the area, and information on the wide range of activities — ranger-guided walks, lectures, and demonstrations (the Yosemite *Guide* provides a schedule of the week's activities). After a stop at the Visitors' Center and a tour of the valley via free shuttle bus has oriented you, over 700 miles of trails outside the valley can be covered by horse, mule, or foot.

No matter how you choose to go, there are several highlights of the park that you should not miss. Glacier Point offers a sweeping 180° panorama of the High Sierra. Half Dome rises in front of you, Nevada and Vernal Falls are prominent, and in the background are the snowy peaks of Yosemite's backcountry. The road to Glacier Point (closed in winter) winds through red fir and pine forest and meadow. You can hike to the valley floor along one of several trails. Four-Mile Trail, which is really 4.6 miles, zigzags down steeply, while Pohono Trail rounds the south rim, and arrives on the valley floor near Bridalveil Fall, a total of 13 miles.

Tuolumne Meadows is a gateway to the high country and, at 8,600 feet, the largest alpine meadow in the High Sierra. Though it is closed in the winter, during the summer the park operates a campground here and a full-scale naturalist program exploring high-altitude ecological systems.

The Mariposa Grove is the largest of the park's three groves of mammoth sequoias. Over 200 of the beautiful old redwoods here measure more than 10 feet in diameter. Among them is the tunnel tree (now supine), which was so large that people used to drive through the hollow area at the base. The Grizzly Giant is not hollow; but if it were, a Mack truck carrying the tunnel tree could drive straight through it.

In addition to its scenic attractions, Yosemite offers a wide variety of summer and winter recreational activities. The miles of trails offer hiking for everyone from tenderfoot to trailblazer. Wilderness permits are required for backcountry travel and are issued at the ranger station on a first-come, first-served basis or by reservation. Stables at Curry and Wawona rent horses and mules and offer a variety of guided trips from one-day excursions to six-day saddle trips through the High Sierra. If you're afraid of mules and horses, bike rentals at Yosemite Lodge and Curry Village provide wheels. For those who like to live dangerously the vertical granite walls of the valley beckon with some of the finest climbing areas in the world. Actually, the Yosemite Mountaineering School (209 372-4611) gives lessons, eliminating most of the danger but none of the challenge of scaling a sheer cliff.

In wintertime, Yosemite becomes a snow-covered paradise, with Badger Pass for downhill skiing, over 90 miles of trails for cross-country skiing, an outdoor ice-skating rink at Curry Village, and magnificent mountainous vistas blanketed in white.

At every time of year Yosemite has something to offer and while you are there at any season (most people come in the summer) you imagine how those cliffs would appear during another — perhaps covered with snow — or how the falls thunder as the snow melts. But no matter what you imagine about Yosemite, a visit will more than fulfill its promise. Information: the Superintendent, PO Box 577, Yosemite National Park, CA 95389 (209 372-4461).

BEST EN ROUTE

The National Park Service runs some 20 developed campgrounds in the park. Group campsites must be reserved in advance. Individual campsites are assigned on a first-come, first-served basis, except between April and October 31, when the Yosemite Valley campgrounds are on an advance campsite reservation system. Reservations are required and can be made in person at over 150 Ticketron outlets in California or by mail from throughout the United States to: Ticketron Reservation Office, PO Box 2715, San Francisco, CA 94126. *Campsites cannot be reserved by phone.*

Ahwahnee Hotel – This classy structure of stone and native timber dates back to 1927. Good dining room, two bars, entertainment, and lots of well-designed public areas. In Yosemite Valley (209 373-4171).

Yosemite Lodge – A combination of cabins and modern hotel rooms built around a central area with two restaurants, cafeteria, swimming pool, bike rental, shops, and, in the summer, an ice cream cone stand. In Yosemite Valley (209 373-4171).

Camp Curry – Rustic tents, cabins, and hotel rooms with access to a cafeteria, public lounge, fast food service, pool, and bike rental facility. The Mountaineering School has its headquarters here, and in the winter, there's an ice skating rink. In Yosemite Valley (209 373-4171).

Rocky Mountain National Park, Colorado

The North American Rocky Mountains stretch from northern New Mexico and southern Colorado to the Columbia Range and the Rocky Mountain Trench in Canada, 300 miles north of the US-Canada border. And this massive range is part of an even larger series of mountains, the North American Cordillera, that includes the Brooks Range in Alaska and Mexico's Sierra Madres, the mountains that follow Mexico's eastern and western coasts.

In the US, the highest peaks in the Rockies are those of the Front range, so named because it is the first range of the chain to rise from the Great Plains in north central Colorado. Some 410 miles of the Front range have been set aside as the Rocky Mountain National Park, and within its 263,793 acres are more than 80 peaks above 10,000 feet, more than 50 above 12,000 feet, innumerable mountain valleys (averaging 8,000 feet above sea level), and Longs Peak at 14,255 feet. It is a spectacular area of glacial moraines (great piles of rocks where the advance of glaciers finally stopped), mountain lakes, alpine valleys, and tundras. The area has five small glaciers, and a myriad of hiking and horse trails, peaks, canyons, and roads.

The Colorado Rockies began formation about 70 million years ago; they rose and were worn down by wind and water erosion over the next 30 million years. A 15-million-year period of volcanic activity and faulting threw them up once again. The mountains that appeared were at the mercy of wind and water for eons, but its present form was stamped on the chain only a million years ago, when the first of three distinct glacial periods began. Portions of mountains were leveled by the incredible force of the glaciers; chasms appeared as mountain walls were cut through; valleys dug where the glaciers' heads buttressed against unyielding mountain faces. Many of the beautiful mountain lakes that dot the park today are the remnants —called cirques — of deep pits dug by the inexorable force of glaciers grinding against bedrock.

The first settlers in the area were Indian tribes more than a thousand years ago. In recent centuries the land was controlled by the Utes and the Arapahoes. Arrowheads, pottery, tools, and hand hammers are just some Indian artifacts that have been found in the park region. Some trails still in use today bear the marks of the earlier Indians who crossed this mountainous terrain.

However, the Louisiana Purchase, in 1803, brought ownership of this land to the United States government. The first American pioneers, Colonel Stephen Long (1820), William Ashley (1825), and John C. Frémont (1843), paved the way for other adventurers to follow. The mountains became the goal of many Easterners seeking gold in the late 1850s and early 1860s. In 1859, Joel Estes saw the Front Range, and within a year had settled his family there, in Estes Park, the area now named for him (just three miles from the main entrance to the park). Estes loved the beauty and isolation of the area, and when neighbors moved within a few miles of him several years after he settled, he got disgusted and moved farther west. Within a year he was back again, unable to live without the rugged spectacle of the mountains surrounding him. He was not alone in his appreciation. An Irish earl built a huge estate in the Front Range and publicized the beauty of the area. In 1914, the region became a national park, largely due to the hard work and constant writing of Enos Mills, a great naturalist and author. He believed that this wonderful wilderness should be maintained, as a park, in order to preserve the clean air and lofty peaks. He once wrote: "He who feels the spell of the wild, the rhythmic melody of falling water, the echoes among the crags, the bird songs, the wind in the pines . . . is in tune with the universe."

Rocky Mountain National Park is open all year, though many facilities — and roads — within the park close during the snows, between October and May. The park is approached through the beautiful alpine valley, Estes Park. In the town of Estes Park you can take an aerial tramway to the top of Prospect Mountain (8,900 feet) for your first, overwhelming view of the Rockies to the west. From the town, there are two possible entrances into the park — through the Fall River entrance directly onto the Trail Ridge Road, the main driving route through the park, or through the more southerly entrance at Beaver Meadows. If it is your first visit, by all means take the slightly more roundabout route through the Beaver Meadows entrance, where you will be able to stop at the Visitors' Center for orientation. Rangers will provide maps of the entire park. There are more than 300 miles of trails in the park, designed for amateurs as well as experienced hikers. There is a ½-mile trail at Bear Lake (at the end of the short drive south from Beaver Meadows) which circles the lake. If you are a serious hiker you may want to try the 16-mile route to the top of Longs Peak, highest peak in the range. Though long, it is by no means an impossible feat — about 200 hikers a day reach the pinnacle during the summer. The view from the top is unsurpassed. Rangers at the Beavers Meadows Visitors' Center have information on hikes, camping and campgrounds, activities, and facilities in the park.

There are two driving routes across the park: Trail Ridge Road, which starts at the Fall River entrance and meanders west and then south to Grand Lake (the park's western entrance point); and the shorter Fall River Road, an offshoot of the Trail Ridge that runs slightly north of the longer road. Fall River is a narrow, one-way dirt road with a 15 mph speed limit that is strictly enforced, but it offers marvelous opportunities for photographs, both of the peaks in the park, and of park wildlife. The entire park is a wildlife refuge, natural habitat of elk, deer, black bear, coyote, and the increasingly scarce mountain lion and bobcat. You will certainly see bighorn sheep — called Rocky Mountain sheep — which are the park's emblem, and if you do any hiking, especially in spring (which comes late here), you will see the alpine wildflowers that flourish in the meadows below timberline. Summer is brief in the mountains — a few weeks in late July and August — and the winters are long and harsh, and above timberline flora is that of the tundra — lichen, tiny flowers, scrub trees with deep roots that can survive the freezing winters, deep snows, and rocky, barren terrain above 12,000 feet.

Trail Ridge Road, the park's main road, offers an exquisite view of Longs Peak and leads you through the Mummy Range, where you rise above the 11,500-foot timberline and lose sight of the stands of spruce, pine, and fir. At Fall River Pass, where the road turns gradually southward, you can stop at the Alpine Visitors' Center, where exhibits explain the alpine tundra through which you are driving. The Center also has a snack bar for light meals. If you follow Trail Ridge Road to its end at Grand Lake you will cross the Continental Divide at Milner Pass (10,760 feet). The Divide is the mountain ridge that weaves in and out of the Rocky peaks from Mexico all the way through Canada — the point at which all waters on the continent break, those falling on the western slopes joining water systems that lead to the Pacific Ocean, those falling on the eastern slopes joining water systems that lead to the Gulf of Mexico or the Atlantic. Farther north the Divide often appears as no more than a gentle rise in the road, but at Milner Pass, where the north fork of the Colorado River begins, you get a real sense of its significance. From here, Trail Ridge Road follows the Colorado to the western entrance and egress point of the park at Grand Lake and Lake Granby, which border the park on its southwest edge. Grand Lake has a good boat harbor and, at an altitude of 8,380 feet, is one of the highest boating facilities in the world. Every August, Grand Lake hosts a buffalo barbecue. Information: the Superintendent, Rocky Mountain National Park, Estes Park, CO 80517 (303 586-2371).

BEST EN ROUTE

Hobby Horse Motor Lodge, Estes Park – Adjacent to a stable and golf course, with riding trails in the surrounding area. It has its own trout pool for children, as well as a heated swimming pool. PO Box 40, Estes Park, CO 80517 (303 586-3336).

McGregor Mountain Lodge, Estes Park – At the entrance of Rocky Mountain National Park, overlooking Fall River Canyon. PO Box 1969, Estes Park, CO 80517 (303 586-3457).

Machin's Cottages in the Pines, Rocky Mountain National Park – Comfortable, well-appointed cottages that accommodate groups of up to 12 people. Cottages have completely equipped kitchens, fireplaces, and cozy living rooms. PO Box 88, Estes Park, CO 80517 (303 586-4276).

Hawaiian Islands: A Survey

Hawaii attracts just under 4 million visitors a year, and it is a tragedy that at least half of these people never get beyond the traditional tourist centers of Honolulu and Waikiki, Maui, or the Kona Coast of Hawaii island. None of the major Hawaiian Islands are untouched by tourism, but several — Molokai, Kauai, and the lesser-developed sections of Maui and Hawaii — genuinely reflect the original Polynesian and plantation cultures that are unique to the islands. This doesn't mean developed areas are to be avoided. There is an allure and excitement in Honolulu and Waikiki which grab you the minute you step off the plane, and Maui's beautiful western coast has some of the finest resort hotels in the world, with unmatched facilities and activities. But it does mean there is another Hawaii, far closer than the historic islands, just beyond the resorts. By careful planning you can have both, and that makes Hawaii one of the most exciting vacation spots in the United States.

The state of Hawaii consists of 132 islands, some no more than bare rocks hardly above waterline, that stretch across 1,600 miles of the north Pacific Ocean from Hawaii island in the southeast to Kure and the Midway Islands in the northwest. The largest islands are clustered together in the southeastern end of the chain, about 2,500 miles southwest of Los Angeles, and these make up what most of us think of as "Hawaii": Hawaii, Kahoolawe, Maui, Lanai, Molokai, Oahu, Kauai, and Niihau. There are international airports on Oahu (Honolulu) and Hawaii (Hilo). Interisland travel is extremely easy, by jet, "commuter" plane, or by helicopter.

Of the eight major islands, only six are open to tourism. Kahoolawe, a 45-square-mile dot in the ocean between Hawaii and Maui, has been a US Navy bombing range since WW II, and is uninhabited. Niihau, off Kauai's western coast, is privately owned (73 square miles) and devoted to a colony of pure Hawaiians living as did their ancestors. No tourists or journalists are allowed, although colony members can leave the island for the Kauai sugar cane plantation of the island owners. Herewith a brief survey of the six inhabited and accessible major islands:

HAWAII – Called the "Big Island," with just about twice as much land area as the rest of the chain combined (just over 4,000 square miles), with a year-round population of under 100,000. Hawaii has two active volcanoes, Kilauea and Mauna Loa.

MAUI – A fascinating combination of sophisticated resorts (along the western coast) and rural, mountainous inlands. The 729-square-mile island is dominated by Haleakala, a 10,023-foot dormant volcano surrounded by a large national park.

LANAI – The smallest island open to tourists (140 square miles), and in the first stages of developing tourist facilities. Most of the land is devoted to growing pineapples, and much of the island is owned by Dole Company.

MOLOKAI – Most famous for the leper colony on the isolated peninsula of Makanalua. This early colony was taken over by Father Damien, a Belgian priest, in 1873, from which time he strove to make it a home for the people who were persecuted elsewhere. Molokai has some of the most spectacular cliffs in the islands, and today is very much the plantation island that it was 75 and 100 years ago, although Sheraton and other organizations have built (and are building) low-profile, luxurious resorts along one coast.

OAHU – The capital island, with Honolulu and Waikiki Beach and an infinite variety of activities, restaurants, sights, and nightlife. The 608-square-mile island supports four-fifths of the population of the entire state (see *Honolulu,* THE AMERICAN CITIES).

KAUAI – A splendid combination of plantation Hawaii and resorts, restaurants, and activities. The island has 533 square miles, and some of the most beautiful country in the world, including the spectacular, inaccessible mountain coast of Na Pali.

Hawaii, Hawaii

Slightly smaller than Connecticut, Hawaii is the largest island in the Hawaiian chain. It is also the youngest, and that makes it a living text of how, and of what, the entire chain was formed. It is the island of active volcanoes, where periodic eruptions of Kilauea and Mauna Loa (the two living volcanoes that form Hawaii Volcanoes National Park) pour tons of lava across the countryside and into the sea. The forces at work on this island have wrought a variety of landscape which typifies the natural processes gradually shaping and reshaping the entire chain; but here, because the island is large enough to feel like a small subcontinent, you can travel from the rich earth of the sugar cane fields (and on the famous southwestern Kona Coast, America's only coffee fields) to the strange, sparse moonlike rockbeds of lava in the park and along the eastern coast. Green tropical jungle and gray, twisted rock — those are the muscle and bone which form the face of Hawaii.

The most recent volcanic action on Hawaii is recent indeed. Kilauea erupted in the fall of 1977, and as usual the event was anticipated by the scientists living in the park, who constantly monitor the moods of the volcanoes. Hundreds of people — sightseers, photographers, journalists, and the idly curious — flew or cruised over to the island to watch the eruption. Villages — all but one — in the path of the lava flow were evacuated, and no one was injured. In the village that was not evacuated, the villagers waited calmly for the noise and fury to pass, secure in the knowledge that their prayers to Pele, the goddess of fire who lives in these volcanoes (whichever of the two is hotter at the moment), would not be unanswered. The eruption came as scheduled, the lava flowed as expected, and as anticipated by the villagers, the lava stopped short of the protected village, diverted into a handy ditch which no one remembered digging.

The attractions of Hawaii are manifold: It has a glittering resort area, the Kona Coast, which offers accommodations and activities of every sort; it has many, many small communities that are untouched by commercialism and that represent agricultural Hawaii as well as any in the islands; and it has the volcanoes, and thus the lava-torn landscape, which is unique in all the world. It is a very large island, with capacity to accommodate many more visitors than it currently gets. With an international airport at Hilo, on the northeastern coast, it can be the Hawaiian entrance or exit point for travelers.

Allow at least four days to see Hawaii (appropriately nicknamed "the Big Island"). There are really three major areas to explore: Hilo and the northern Hamakua Coast; the Kona Coast; and the national park. The route described below starts at Hilo and circles counterclockwise past the Hamakua area, to the Kona Coast, and ends at the park.

HILO – Offers an unparalleled opportunity to see Hawaii's thriving orchid industry nose-to-blossom. Two nurseries in town give tours, and both are fascinating for anyone with even the vaguest interest in the whys and wherefores of plants — especially the exquisite orchids grown here. Orchids of Hawaii (575 Hinano St.) shows people around its nursery for the asking; Kamaaina Crafts (1477 Kalanianaole Ave.) charges a small fee for its tour.

The Lyman Mission House and Museum (276 Haili St.), built in 1839 as the home of an early missionary, has exhibits on the ethnic makeup of the islands, as well as artifacts of early Hawaiian culture. Nearby is a very genuine, and very large, artifact: the Naha Stone, which adorns the front yard of the Hilo Library (300 Waianuenue Ave.). The stone weighs in excess of two tons, and according to an ancient legend the man who could lift the stone would become king of all the islands. The man who did so was King Kamehameha I — known to history as Kamehameha the Great because he did indeed conquer all the islands (more with the help of cannon than brute strength). For shopping, a pleasant diversion is the bazaar at Waiakea Village Market Place (400 Hualani St.).

HAMAKUA COAST – Northward along rt. 19 the views are staggering. Atop high pali (cliffs), the road looks over the windward coast and the not-very-peaceful Pacific Ocean. This road was constructed to accommodate nature, not man, and you will soon develop a rhythm in your driving as you curve, plunge, curve, and climb around waterfalls and valleys. All along the route you will see the state "Hawaiian Warrior" signs that indicate scenic overviews. Don't fail to stop. When Hawaiians think a view is good enough to warrant special note, mainlanders had better take them at their word. Off the highway at the small village of Honomu is Akaka State Park, with two of the most beautiful waterfalls on the island. Highest is Akaka Falls itself — a 442-foot ribbon of water that plunges daintily down a jungle cliff. Nearby are jungle walks among lush, if eerie, plants. Laupahoehoe Point — a small leaf of lava that pushes into the brutal, angry Pacific — is an excellent spot for picnicking. The point is marked by a Warrior sign, and you must drive from the road down a rough, mile-long spur road to the point itself. There the picnic area is bathed in a fine sea spray, and you can watch the sometimes terrifying fury of the sea smashing against the rocks. In 1947 a small community here was lost to the sea when a giant tidal wave washed over the point. A plaque commemorates the spot.

The end point of the northward rt. 19 road is Waipio Valley, where rt. 19 joins rt. 25, the only navigable point through the Kohala Mountains. Here there is a lookout tower with fine views of the northeastern end of the island, and drivers with four-wheel vehicles who offer tours through the rough roads of the valley.

PUUKOHOLA HEIAU NATIONAL HISTORIC SITE – Where rt. 19 crosses the base of the Kohala Mountains and turns south to follow Hawaii's eastern coast stands this historic site, an ancient temple (approximately 15th century) and altar which young King Kamehameha I rebuilt in 1791, dedicated to a god of war. Behind this act of piety was cold and cunning ambition. He invited his chief island rival to the dedication cermony, and there killed him. With that act Kamehameha initiated his drive to conquer not just the island of Hawaii, but all the major islands in the chain. Just down the road from the heiau is one of the island's most elegant resorts, the Mauna Kea Beach Hotel, and beyond it Puako, a small village that has some of the best examples in the islands of Hawaiian petroglyphs. At Puako, rt. 19 becomes the Queen Kaahumanu Highway, cutting across a lava desert and skirting a number of beautiful, and as yet relatively undeveloped, beaches.

KAILUA-KONA – Major town on the Kona Coast and starting point of a series of resorts that stretches to Keauhou. Most of the town's contemporary attractions — hotels, shops, restaurants, and bars — are on Alii Drive. There, also, is Hulihee Palace, a summer resort built in 1838 for the Hawaiian royal family that today houses a museum of furnishings and memorabilia of the period. Kailua-Kona is a major center for deep-sea fishing along the Kona Coast (one of the best fishing grounds for big game fish in the world), and there are numerous charter operations along Kailua wharf. This is also a fine place for a late afternoon stroll, to watch the charters return to port, and the weighing of the catches.

KEALAKEKUA BAY – Where British Captain James Cook was killed in 1779. Cook was the first Western explorer to discover the Hawaiian Islands (named by him the Sandwich Islands), when he sailed into Kauai's Waimea Bay in 1778 in search of fresh water. He was greeted joyfully by the Hawaiians, who regarded him as something of a god, and who recognized his courage and mastery of the sea. Cook's expedition stayed for only a few weeks, but returned in November 1778 to Kealakekua Bay on Hawaii island. Here too he was accorded great respect, but relations between islanders and sailors gradually soured. An open break came on February 14, 1779, when a brief battle erupted between the two groups; it ended with the death of Captain Cook. It has become legend that the islanders dismembered and ate Cook, but this is not true. They gave him a hero's burial, which involved dismemberment and special burial in the earth; Cook's men — who were upset at having only certain portions of their captain returned to them — misinterpreted the proceedings as cannibalism. The spot where Cook fell is marked by a monument, and today the bay is a marine preserve.

CITY OF REFUGE NATIONAL HISTORICAL PARK – An ancient and sacred area that was once a sanctuary for Hawaiian criminals. Fugitives had to swim the perilous Honaunau Bay to reach the City of Refuge. Once there, they were entitled to pardons from the resident priest and could then return home, free from stigma and the threat of death. Today visitors can explore this bit of antiquity, watch craftsmen carve canoes with the same tools and methods used by early Hawaiians, marvel at the perfect remains of the Great Wall, the formidable carved images used to scare off invaders. There are taped tours and information brochures available at the Visitors' Center.

HAWAII VOLCANOES NATIONAL PARK – When either of Hawaii's two active volcanoes — Kilauea, 4,077 feet, and Mauna Loa, 13,680 feet — rumbles, bubbles, or actually erupts, people flock from around the world to watch. Both volcanoes are within the park, which is dedicated to collecting and disseminating information on volcanic phenomena. The Visitors' Center (about two miles within the park's boundaries) has volumes of material on the effects of these two volcanoes, as well as information on activities within the park — camping and hiking within Kilauea's crater, ranger-led hikes, special events. While you visit, anything could happen. You might see Kilauea releasing fountains of steam or rivers of lava (the Chain of Craters road, once fully passable, is nearly closed today because lava flows have blocked it at so many points); you might feel tremors from Mauna Loa; you certainly can watch the seismograph at the observatory. At Volcano House (the park's inn and restaurant, just across from the Visitors' Center) you can spend the night on the edge of Kilauea crater, and have a box lunch packed for a day's hike the next morning. Information: the Superintendent, Hawaii Volcanoes National Park, Hawaii, HI 96718 (808 967-7311).

BEST EN ROUTE

Mauna Kea Beach Hotel, Kamuela – As close to paradise as most of us will ever get. A valuable art collection is exhibited throughout the main rooms and halls for all to touch and appreciate; gardens delight the eye at every turn. It has three fine dining rooms, spacious and lavishly decorated rooms, and a Robert Trent Jones–designed golf course with a world-famous water hole over the crashing Pacific. Tennis, beach, horseback riding, and pool. PO Box 218, Kamuela, Hawaii, HI 96743 (808 882-7222).

Kona Village Resort, Kona Coast – Some 95 bungalows dot the 65-acre expanse of this village, each designed and decorated in the style of one of the islands of the South Pacific. Facilities include tennis courts, water sports, sailing. There is a Polynesian luau every Friday night and a paniolo (cowboy) steak fry on Wednesdays. PO Box 1299, Kailua-Kona, Hawaii, HI 96740 (808 325-5555).

Volcano House, Hawaii Volcanoes National Park – This is the first place to fill up when scientists at the observatory predict a major eruption. This gracious, comfortable inn and restaurant will require advance reservations even during periods of quiet. Surely it must be one of the few hotels in Hawaii that routinely lights a cozy fire in the evenings. Hawaii Volcanoes National Park, HI 96718 (808 967-7321 or toll-free 800 325-3535).

Kauai, Hawaii

Kauai is a spectacular island by any standards: oldest in the archipelago — first formed, and, therefore, first to cool — most lush, verdant, and rich with soil, a land where anything will grow. Papaya, mango, coconut, hundreds of varieties of exotic plants and orchids, bougainvillea and cactus, litchi, banana trees, mimosa —an endless list. And every growing edible — as well as almost every other species — was brought by someone: the first Hawaiians, the missionaries, Western explorers, the Japanese, mainland visitors. Without human help, the islands get only one new species of plant every 10,000 years.

On the windward side, everything is green. The razor-sharp pinnacles of the volcanic fissures along Na Pali coast, the spectacular rock chasms that spill down the windward side of the island into dense jungle valleys, pouring forth myriad waterfalls, are covered with a light down of lichen. And that which is not green is red — the ferrous red of iron-permeated soil, further evidence (if any were needed) of the now utterly extinct volcanoes which heaved this island thousands of feet from the sea bed.

Even the misconceptions that visitors carry to the island are dominated by geography. Kauai is known as one of the wettest spots on earth. As a consequence, nervous vacationers, hungry for sunburn and body surfing, shun it for the more developed but secure havens of Maui or Oahu. But it rains only 60 to 80 inches a year on the northern, wetter, and windward side of the island; only 15 to 20 inches a year leeward. Way up on Mt. Waialeale (Why-ali-ali), it rains some 480 inches a year, easily one of the wettest places in the world, and source of the constant waterfalls that appear and disappear like silver whiskers on the faces of distant valley walls; source also of Kauai's rotten weather reputation. But Waialeale is in the middle of the island, 5,000 feet up, and it actually acts as a rain barrier for the southern half of Kauai. Windward is wet, especially in winter, but spring and summer bring good holidaying weather to the entire island.

LIHUE – By necessity most vacationers begin their visit to Kauai here, the island's commercial center, and site of its only public airport (a 20-minute flight from Oahu). Whether coming for a week (advised) or a day (popular but a pity), Lihue is the point of arrival, and offers the first glimpse of the marriage of sugar cane and tourism that characterizes Kauai right now. Best about Lihue is its location on Kauai's eastern coast, midway on the road which circles the island (Kauai is a slightly dented and bashed circle, 32 miles across; the road would make a complete circle around the island except for the interruption of the impassable Na Pali cliffs). But there are good reasons for staying outside the city, up or down the coast.

Best reason: Once beyond Lihue — which sports a Pizza Hut, McDonald's, and other American inevitables — you plunge almost instantly into old Hawaii. The towns and villages still live in the grip of the two monoliths of island life, the missionary church (most Kauaians are Catholic) and the plantation. Little towns like Hanapepe (which means "working babies") are part of a genuine frontier plantation culture. Another good reason: Scattered along the coast are numerous fine resorts, and most of the historic and geological sights that make a driving tour enchanting.

South and west from Lihue the road leads to Waimea Canyon, a "must see," and eventually ends at Kokee State Park — quite literally perched over a 1,000-foot drop into the westernmost valley of Na Pali. That is the final destination of the drive south (perhaps a whole 19 miles from Lihue), but along the way is much to see.

POIPU BEACH – With waters, like those along most of the beaches of the island, that are shallow a long way out, and subject to fits of rock along the sea floor where sand ought to be; but nonetheless a decent beach for swimming and sunning. Serious body surfers will want to walk a quarter of a mile north, around a promontory, to Brennecke Beach, best on the island for that sport. (All island beaches, even those fronted by posh resorts, are public, open, and free.) Poipu Beach has two of the best posh resorts on the island, the Waiohai and the Kiahuna.

SPOUTING HORN – An outjutting of volcanic rock, so eaten by the sea that when a strong roller comes in, the sea water spurts through a hole 10 to 15 feet into the air; a sad sigh whispers through this natural pneumatic tube with each spout. It provides a good illustration of the power the sugar cane companies have traditionally held on Kauai. Years ago, the spout shot as high as 80 feet into the air; high enough that salt spray was flung across the cane fields — perhaps 200 yards away — killing patches of cane. The plantation managers dynamited the horn, widening the hole so that the spout stayed within a reasonable height. Now the horn is protected by the state, but at the time no one thought it strange that a private company would summarily destroy a unique natural formation to protect a few rows of cane.

WAIMEA CANYON – Nowhere on the island are you so close to the staggering power of the earth itself as when peering into the depths of this 3,600-foot canyon, ten miles long. The original Hawaiians believed this was the work of Pele, goddess of fire. It hardly makes more sense to try to imagine the force necessary to have left these huge wedges of mountain hanging just so; to have honed these cliffs to such sharp precision; to have etched such regular and undeviating patterns across miles and miles of rock. When a helicopter swings across the canyon, hanging 1,000 feet or so above the Waimea River at the bottom of the ravine and whizzing along the length of the valley, you can suffer vertigo just watching.

KOKEE STATE PARK – Has a lovely, tiny museum, a large picnic area, a restaurant (hamburgers and other sandwiches), and some comfortable cabins for about $10 a day (make reservations at least three months in advance, Kokee Lodge, PO Box 518, Kekaha, Kauai, HI 96752, 808 335-6061). It's a good place to stop after Waimea Canyon, and before going the few miles more to road's end at Na Pali lookout. It is also the starting point of miles of hiking trails which botanists and backpackers will find irresistible.

NA PALI COAST – Is the highlight of any trip to Kauai. Here the windward side of the island breaks into a series of splendid, jagged, jungle valleys thousands of feet deep, like patterns cut into fine crystal. They stretch from the mountains to the sea, and are accessible only by foot (and some not even by foot), air, or sea. There are numerous legends and superstitions surrounding Na Pali. It was here that an entire tribe of Hawaiians disappeared forever several centuries ago. And here that the legendary Menehune — a race of dwarfs, credited with constructing much of the stonework on the island — are said to have hidden when they mysteriously disappeared. Some islanders believe they still live in Na Pali. (Lest you don't quite believe in the existence of the Menehune, Captain James Cook, who landed here in 1778, mentions in his report to the British Admiralty seeing a group of very light-skinned, diminutive women.) Late last century, a leper named Koolau fought off the entire state militia by guerrilla warfare waged from the jungles of Na Pali. He refused to go to the leper colony on Molokai, and took his family into the depths of the jungle, where presumably they lived and died.

From the lookout 4,000 feet above the ocean, is a magnificent view down Kalalau Valley to the water. There are some hiking trails into Na Pali from the eastern side of the island, but most frequent access is from the other side, where Kauai's main, circular road ends at Hanalei and Haena. From there you can hike to beaches two, six, or ten miles along the coast, following wave upon wave of valley. Or take the easy way out, and hire a helicopter from Lihue (three companies make the journey, charging about $90 for an hour's ride) to spin you through the valleys. You can be dropped for as long as you want on any of the perfectly isolated black or white sand beaches at the foot of each valley.

HANALEI – "South Pacific" was filmed here, and a marvelous old plantation town it is. The town has a thrown-together, informal museum, Hanalei Museum, but of more interest is Waioli Mission House, built in 1841, and filled with period furnishings. It's a piece of genuine New England Hawaii. There's also good scuba and snorkeling in the area.

BEST EN ROUTE

Waiohai, Poipu Beach – This newcomer to the Poipu Beach scene has 460 spacious bedrooms done in fresh, cool colors and outfitted with well-stocked wet bars and luxurious dressing rooms. An early morning dip in one of its three swimming pools or a stroll along its lovely curve of sandy beach should be followed by breakfast on your lanai overlooking the sea; ask for the house specialty—macademia nut muffins. Poipu Beach (phone: 742-9511 or 800-227-0848).

Kiahuna Plantation, Poipu Beach – Privacy, comfort, and quiet are the keynotes at this condominium resort of one- and two-bedroom apartments. Spacious rooms, full kitchens, daily maid service, 10 tennis courts, and an 18-hole golf course are some of the amenities provided. Its white-verandahed and ceiling-fanned dining room, the Plantation Gardens, is part of the original plantation house and offers a seafood menu as well as a view of the surrounding extensive gardens. RR 1, PO Box 73, Poipu Beach, Koloa, Kauai, HI 96756 (808 742-6411).

Princeville at Hanalei, Hanalei – The finest golf course on the island, a 27-hole course designed by Robert Trent Jones, using the spectacular coastline and sea to best advantage. All accommodations are in condominiums, and there are tennis courts and four restaurants on 10,000 acres on the former Princeville Ranch. PO Box 121, Hanalei, Kauai, HI 96714 (808 826-6561; 800 367-7090, toll-free).

Maui, Hawaii

The second largest island in the Hawaiian chain has a very strange shape, an even more interesting history, and topography that accounts for some of the most beautiful country in the islands. Given only a day or two, you will undoubtedly end up on the beaches of West Maui, where beautiful hotels and condominiums stretch from Kaanapali to Kapalua, or on the resort strip of East Maui, from Kihei to Wailea. You could do worse. But with just a couple more days, and a car to help negotiate the long — for the islands — distances between stops, you can add to that the lush valleys around Wailuku and Kahului, and the heights of Haleakala National Park. The result would be almost a mini-survey of Hawaii's geologic and cultural history — a dormant volcano; verdant, fertile valleys devoted to cane and pineapples; and a west coast village that was a standard stop on the whaling route 150 years ago, a town where missionaries and New England whalers literally fought for the hearts and the minds of the Hawaiian people.

Maui is formed of three distinct geographic areas. With enough imagination, you can imagine the island in the form of a steer's head facing east. West Maui, with the gold coast strip of hotels and beach, and the well-preserved whaling town of Lahaina, forms the ear of this steer. Inland, West Maui is mountainous, wild, and, in part at least, unexplored. Where the ear joins the head, at Wailuku and Kahului, the mountains break and there is much flat and fertile farmland. To the east the island rises steadily along the slopes of dormant Mt. Haleakala, its summit 10,023 feet above the sea. At the snout of the hypothetical steer is the village of Hana.

Most tourists begin their visit to Maui at Kahului airport (a 27-minute flight from Oahu), and from there head west for Lahaina and the resorts beyond, south for Kihei and Wailea, or east on rt. 37 to Haleakala.

LAHAINA – The capital of the Hawaiian islands from 1795 until 1843, when King Kamehameha III moved the court to Honolulu. Of far greater impact on the town and its people were the whaling ships, which made Lahaina a regular stop from the early

1800s until petroleum replaced whale oil as a source of light at the end of the century. During the 80 or 90 years during which whalers tied up at the town's docks, life was constant turmoil. Missionaries saved souls and sailors seduced and drank, and in general the Hawaiians were harassed and harangued on all sides. A great deal of the original whaling town still exists, in part due to the hard work of Lahaina's contemporary citizens, who have spent a good part of recent years in restoration work. An interesting and historic place to visit is Baldwin House, the home of medical missionary Dr. Dwight Baldwin in the mid-nineteenth century. In the vicinity, you will undoubtedly see a huge, spreading banyan tree (in the town square near Front St.). It was planted in 1873 to commemorate 50 years of missionary work on the island, and it stands still strong and hale today. Across the street from the tree is the town's most famous manmade landmark, the Pioneer Inn, an old rake of a hotel that opened at the turn of the century; in the harbor in front of that is the *Carthaginian II,* a ship of recent vintage true-rigged like a brig of the whaling era. Just why all the whalers were interested in Maui will be made graphically clear if you visit anytime during the winter months, when the annual migration of humpback whales is underway. The whales breed in Hawaiian waters in the winter (in summer they live much farther north in Arctic seas), and standing on the dock you can see them cavorting between Maui and Lanai from December through April.

KAANAPALI TO NAPILI – This four-mile stretch of beach has been called "a sort of rarefied Waikiki." Even the qualifying "rarefied" tends to do it a disservice. If the beach is not quite so spectacular as Waikiki, the resorts which line it have been far more sensitively and sensibly developed than those that pile up like a freeway crash along Honolulu's pride. The beach is neatly divided by a huge outcropping of black volcanic rock, called Black Rock in English and Kekaa in Hawaiian. At the base of this beauty is the Sheraton-Maui Hotel. Five other hotels and an equal number of condominium complexes make up the Kaanapali Beach Resort, which also includes the famous Royal Kaanapali Golf Courses (two of eight 18-hole courses on the island) and Whaler's Village. The full impact of the whaling industry on Maui is described in detail in the many exhibits of this combination shopping bazaar and museum that allows adults to shop while kids entertain themselves with a huge whale skeleton and other such delicacies.

KAPALUA – Beyond Kaanapali, the coast of West Maui is almost one uninterrupted stretch of holiday condominiums to the northwest tip of the island. Two particularly beautiful beaches can be found here, the beach at Napili Bay and Kapalua Beach, perhaps the most perfect crescent beach on the island. Kapalua Beach is surrounded by the exquisite scenery of another of Maui's planned resort developments, Kapalua, set on panoramic acreage formerly used to grow pineapples. Kapalua Bay Hotel, condominium communities, two Arnold Palmer–designed golf courses, 10 tennis courts, and a small shopping center are the central features of the resort.

WAILUKU – Another early Maui city that has survived — and thrived — in the 20th century. On Maui's northern coast, close to (almost part of) Kahului and its airport, Wailuku has its own remnants of early Hawaii. A staunch emblem of Maui's missionary past is Kaahumanu Congregational Church (rt. 30), built in 1832. It is a simple building that reflects much of the spirit and the form of early church work here and throughout the islands. Wailuku is also a good place to make forays to Iao Valley, in the mountains of inland West Maui. Along the way on rt. 32 you pass the Maui Historical Museum, Hale Hoikeike, with exhibits on all aspects of Maui history. It is a good place to stop before continuing to road's end a few miles farther west, at Iao Valley's Kepaniwai Park. The park is the approximate point where King Kamehameha the Great (grandfather of the King Kamehameha who moved the royal court from Maui to Oahu) finally trapped his Mauian enemies in the basin of Iao Valley and decimated them, assuring the loyalty of all the major islands in the chain. This happened in the 1790s, and the carnage was so great that the stream which runs through the valley was named Wailuku — "Bloody River."

KIHEI AND WAILEA – The western coast of East Maui is on the dry leeward side of Haleakala. Six miles of the coast are known as Kihei, and better known as "sunny" Kihei because of the sparse average annual rainfall. Kihei is almost one long strip of golden beach from beginning to end, and not too many years ago the land fronting the beach—the same land that is now chockablock with low- and high-rise condominiums —was virtually virgin territory. So while Kihei has its beach to recommend it, it is often pointed to as a worst-case example of unchecked development, while the planned resort of Wailea, just south, is considered a model of the way to go. Wailea, too, has glorious beaches, but they are backed by resort property irrigated to the ultimate in verdure, and the two 18-hole golf courses, 14-court tennis center, shopping center, three condominium villages, and two first-class hotels complement rather than violate the landscape.

HALEAKALA NATIONAL PARK – "The House of the Sun" — Mt. Haleakala — dominates the entire eastern half of Maui. The approaches from the west are a peaceful contrast to the tourist frenzy of the coastal resort areas. Here is countryside virtually untouched by commercialism, a series of pastoral scenes that could represent almost any mountainous region in the world. Because of the mountain, Maui enjoys a unique climate system, hot on the coasts, fertile and moist on the flat plains between West Maui and the mountain, and progressively cooler weather as the altitudes increase. Some 10,000 feet high, Haleakala is the largest dormant volcano in the world. Its crater is an immense 19-square-mile hole 3,000 feet deep, honeycombed with trails and devoted to a national park. On the way to the park's entrance you will pass (on rt. 377) the Kula Botanical Gardens, where experts will explain the way in which Maui's unique climate is used to grow simple garden vegetables (the best in the islands) beside exotic tropical orchids.

Park headquarters, at about 7,000 feet, is a necessary stop to collect information on campgrounds, the mountain, and activities like horseback riding, hiking, and renting simple cabins maintained by the National Park Service in the crater. These must be reserved at least three months in advance (address below), and camping is strictly controlled; only 25 overnight campers are allowed in the park at one time. No matter how warm it may be at the base of Haleakala, you will need some light wrap at the summit.

The view from the top is spectacular. From there you see West Maui, and the neighboring islands of Hawaii, Lanai, Molokai, and Oahu. It was from the summit of Haleakala that Maui the god lassoed the sun to force him to make his daily trip across the sky more slowly. And dawn atop the mountain is one of the finest experiences a traveler can behold.

The park extends to Maui's eastern coast in a single eight-mile strip. The area encompasses a stretch of ecologically delicate jungle, where the rangers are struggling to maintain an environment that protects and encourages the tropic growths. The area also includes the Seven Pools, a series of pools and streams that spill into one another like a pyramid of champagne glasses filled to overflowing. This eastern area of the park, which encompasses the Kipahulu Valley, can be reached by circling East Maui on the Hana Highway, a scenic route that is in itself one of the island's sightseeing attractions. The road is rough, winding, and very narrow, which makes it difficult to stop to enjoy the views, but there are three lookout points along the way before it ends in Hana, a tiny village populated mainly by part Hawaiians who work on the Hana Ranch and by wealthy out-of-town celebrities seeking seclusion. Beyond Hana, another 10 miles of rutted road leads around to the park again, to the point where the lowest of the Seven Pools spills into the sea. Information: the Superintendent, Haleakala National Park, PO Box 369, Makawao, Maui, HI 96768 (808 572-7749).

BEST EN ROUTE

Sheraton-Maui Hotel, Kaanapali – Certainly one of the most dramatic locations on the island, with lobbies at the base and top of stark Black Rock. Facilities include the beach, which is virtually outside the door, swimming pools, tennis courts. Kaanapali Beach, Lahaina, Maui, HI 96761 (808 661-0031, and toll-free 800 325-3535).

Royal Lahaina Resort, Kaanapali – Overlooking Kaanapali's beautiful beach (along with neighbor Sheraton-Maui), with a 12-story tower and a number of cottages around its grounds. Facilities include tennis courts and golf next door. Kaanapali Beach Resort, Lahaina, Maui, HI 96761 (808 661-3611).

Hotel Hana-Maui, Hana – Sixty-one rooms on the island's far east coast; though intimate, the hotel spreads across 20 acres and the only real distraction from the perfectly blue Pacific is tennis and a pitch and putt golf course. Hana, Maui, HI 96713 (808 248-8211).

Molokai, Hawaii

There is a distinct hierarchy of development among the Hawaiian islands, and once you understand the forces at work it is a pretty accurate measure of the state of the local agricultural economy. Most of the major islands — Maui, Hawaii, Kauai, Molokai — have been dependent on agriculture at one time or another during this century. And time and again that industry has failed, forcing the islands, one after another, to develop adequate tourist facilities to replace the lost farming income. It has happened most recently on Kauai, which for years had a thriving sugar cane industry, with plantations of thousands and thousands of acres. In the last decade, however, the island has repeatedly lost business to the Far East, where cane is produced at perhaps one-tenth the cost (primarily because of inhumanly low labor costs). And so Kauai began developing tourist facilities — very cautiously and with great consideration — to replace the vacuum left by sugar cane.

All this is happening right now on Molokai. Throughout the 19th century Molokai was known as "the Forgotten Island." Its population decreased year by year as islanders went elsewhere for work. Then, early in the 20th century, pineapples were introduced and the island began a gradual renaissance; Dole and Del Monte bought large chunks of the island, and people returned to Molokai for pineapple jobs. But as in the case of sugar cane on Kauai, impossibly cheap labor in the Far East has meant that island pineapples are simply too expensive, and production is threatened.

Right now Molokai has only one full-fledged resort, the new Sheraton-Molokai. More are on the drawing boards, but for the time being the island seems almost in a state of suspension, awaiting the future. The sense of quiet and solitude which has always characterized it was never more marked than it is right now. In some places — the closed Dole Pineapple plantation town — there is an eerie sense of history just passed, of an era having closed so recently that it still vibrates in the air; and yet elsewhere on the island this solitude is splendid and serene — for example, along the jagged, wild, inaccessible cliffs east of Makanalua Peninsula, or at the many coves and beaches which swimmers have entirely to themselves for hours on end. It is certainly an island that can be visited on a day trip from Oahu; the visitor flies either to Molokai airport (well outside the town of Kaunakakai) to see the whole island, or to Kalaupapa to visit the historical site and colony on Makanalua peninsula. But Molokai has wild roads and beautiful vistas as yet unmapped on any standard tourist itinerary, and a two- or three-day visit will offer a feeling of Hawaii unavailable on any of the more developed islands.

KAUNAKAKAI – Eight miles east of the airport which bears its name; through here most tourists enter Molokai. The town may surprise you. With its main street and the wooden façade of its stores, it looks remarkably like a Western frontier town. There is a distinct "cowboy" atmosphere about it which is typical of many towns throughout the islands. In the case of Kaunakakai, this atmosphere is more a reflection of the general character of Molokai towns than proximity to the island's huge Puu O Huko Ranch. With a population slightly over 500, the town has little to offer in the way of tourist facilities, but much about it speaks of the island's recent history. You will note, for example, the fine, long wharf — extending a half mile into the sea — which is almost empty today. It was built to accommodate the huge barges on which pineapples were shipped for processing. Today there is little work done on it.

PAPOHAKU BEACH – The west coast site of Molokai's new Sheraton Hotel, as well as a number of often-empty and as yet undeveloped beaches. The coast tends to be rocky, with occasional underwater coral reefs that can be an unpleasant surprise as you swim. Even the Sheraton's beach is better for sunning than swimming. On the way to Papohaku, along rt. 46, you will pass the deserted Dole Pineapple plantation town of Maunaloa. It is well worth a look as a kind of living museum exhibition of contemporary company towns in Hawaii.

PALAAU STATE PARK – Along Molokai's northern coast, overlooking Makanalua Peninsula and the Kalaupapa settlement. The peninsula is 1,600 feet below the park, at the base of a series of jagged, wild cliffs that become inaccessible farther along the eastern coastline. The present view is not the original overlook. This can be found at the beginning of the Jack London Trail (also in the park), the tortuous switchback trail that leads from the overlook to the peninsula below. It is navigable by foot or mule only, and takes several hours.

HALAWA VALLEY – Fills Molokai's northeastern end. Accessible only by rt. 45, which begins in Kaunakakai and follows the island's coast east and north. The valley is at least a half-day's excursion from the airport, but offers a real sense of Molokai today, and the best views of the magnificent cliffs at road's end. (The road, by the way, becomes increasingly narrower as it turns northward, twisting and turning along the mountains that rise like a ship's prow along the island's northern coast.) Immediately outside of Kaunakakai on rt. 45 are a number of ancient fish ponds. Dating as far back as the 15th century, these ponds were built as fattening-up farms for the fish trapped inside, assuring the availability of a fresh fish meal whenever the royal whim desired one. All the major islands have ruins of these royal fish ponds, but the ones on Molokai are in the best state of preservation and are therefore worth a stop.

At the end of rt. 45 is deserted Halawa Valley. Once a thriving community valley patchworked with taro farms, in 1946 the warnings of the giant tidal wave (tsunami) forced the evacuation of all the families from the valley. They never returned. Most of this valley is now the privately owned Puu O Huko Ranch. It is a junglelike wilderness with two spectacular waterfalls, a lagoon, and some swimming beaches. The interior hides a wealth of wild birds and deer which attract knowledgeable hunters.

KALAUPAPA – The community on Makanalua Peninsula. In 1866 the entire peninsula was declared a leper colony by royal decree, and sufferers throughout the islands were forced to go there. Its isolation acted as a perfect buffer, protecting the healthy islanders from the disease they feared and shunned. The suffering inflicted on victims of the disease was intense: No provisions were made for food, shelter, clothing, or the basic necessities of life. Lepers were peremptorily dumped on the island, and left there to die (often with whatever family members consented to join them and care for them in exile). In 1873 a Belgian priest, Father Damien de Veuster, chose to join the lepers, and for the next 16 years he labored to provide shelter and food for them, and to build a living community where only disease and despair had ruled human relations. In 1889 he died of leprosy, but he left behind a real community. Today the peninsula is under the auspices of the Hawaii State Department of Health, and about 100 persons live there. It is destined to be closed sometime in the future. It is their peninsula, but visitors are welcome. Hansen's disease is completely under control today by virtue of various sulfa drugs, and adults are completely safe. Children under 12 are not allowed on the peninsula. Several organizations offer tours of the peninsula, which can be approached by air, by sea, or by foot or mule from the overlook at Palaau State Park. One touring company is Damien Tours, PO Box 1, Kalaupapa, Molokai, HI 96742 (808 567–6171).

BEST EN ROUTE

Hotel Sheraton-Molokai, Kepuhi Beach – Sheraton is the first in the sweepstakes to develop Molokai into a recognized tourist stop, and their entry is topnotch. With 290 rooms spread over some 33 buildings on the ground, the hotel has tennis courts, an 18-hole golf course, and of course, a beach. Its main dining room is beautifully designed, using some traditional Hawaiian building materials. PO Box 1977, Mauna Loa, Kepuhi Beach, Molokai, HI 96770 (808 552–2555 or 800 325–3535, toll-free).

Hotel Molokai, Kaunakakai – In a palm grove about two miles from town. Rooms are distributed among buildings throughout the grounds, and though it hasn't the recreational facilities of the new Sheraton, the Molokai is much more conveniently placed, in the center of the island rather than on the isolated western coast. At press time, the hotel was slowly being converted into condominiums. PO Box 546, Kaunakakai, Molokai, HI 96748 (808 553–5347; toll-free, 800 367–7040).

Oahu, Hawaii

Oahu, home of four-fifths of Hawaii's population, is quite appropriately nicknamed "the Gathering Place." Since Kamehameha III moved the royal court to Honolulu from Maui in 1843, Oahu has been the social, political, and industrial center of the entire archipelago. Since WW II it has also been the center of tourism, and several Oahu sites and cities have become synonymous with Hawaii itself: Honolulu, Diamond Head, Waikiki, and Pearl Harbor. (For a detailed report on these Honolulu sites, see *Honolulu,* THE AMERICAN CITIES.) Just as you must get off Oahu to the Neighbor Islands to see all of Hawaii, you must get out of Honolulu to see all of Oahu. On the other hand, simply because of Honolulu, Oahu offers an immense variety of activities.

WAIKIKI BEACH – Not unlike Miami Beach, a miracle of shoulder-to-shoulder tall hotels with the expected complement of souvenir shops, restaurants, discos, bars, and other tourist attractions. The beach itself is the most extravagant stretch of sand in all the islands. It was the exclusive spot of the ancient Alii (royalty), who came here for their royal sunning and surfing. The beach today remains as physically beautiful as any you will see in the world — when you can see it, that is. It is usually well hidden beneath a layer of supine bodies out for a day's sun. Even sunrise joggers must jockey for a bare stretch of sand. Waikiki is not a deserted island paradise. There are some splendid hotels and restaurants along this strip. There are also honky-tonk traps and tacky stores.

From Honolulu and Waikiki the route we describe below roughly follows the southern, eastern, and northern coasts of the island in a large 110-mile loop. The first part of this loop, rt. 72, covers the entire eastern tip of Oahu, from Diamond Head to Kailua. Ask at your hotel or at the desk of any car rental agency for a booklet of Oahu itineraries called the *Drive Guide.* It contains helpful maps and interesting descriptions of the routes.

OAHU'S SOUTHERN TIP – The road really starts at Diamond Head, the spectacular volcanic crater that has become the symbol of Hawaii. The volcano which formed this perfect crater has been extinct for at least 150,000 years, and early Hawaiians, for whom it was just as much a landmark as it is for Hawaiians today, thought it resembled nothing so much as a fish head. There are a number of relatively tough hiking paths in the crater that can be entered from Makalei Place, off Diamond Head Road.

Rt. 72 passes through two affluent neighborhoods beyond Diamond Head, the Kahala district and Hawaii Kai, a development initiated by Henry Kaiser, the man who during WW II turned the making of Liberty ships into a five-week project. Hanauma Bay at Koko Head Park is where the Elvis Presley film "Blue Hawaii" was filmed years ago, and it has one of the most beautiful underwater parks in the country. It's an excellent place for snorkeling or scuba diving because the waters are so perfectly clear. Nearby is Halona Blow Hole, a submerged lava tube that turns sea water into a saltwater geyser as waves roll in.

Here, too, is Sea Life Park (259-7933), with a number of standard aquatic exhibits (dolphins, seals, whales) as well as a fascinating see-through tank filled with coral and various forms of sea life which would normally live in a coral reef. At feeding times you can watch scuba divers plunge into the water to lead a happy parade of turtles, multicolored fish, manta rays, eels, and small and larger sharks happily intent on the food being distributed. For confirmed landlubbers it is a fascinating performance. The easternmost point on the island is Makapuu Point, marked by a lighthouse. This is the point at which the trade winds divide, some continuing north, some south, across the island. At Kailua, to the north, it is possible to cut inland and return to Honolulu via the Pali Highway (rt. 61). En route are the Nuuanu Pali Tunnels and the scenic masterpiece, Pali Lookout. This is where Kamehameha I drove the defenders of Oahu over the steep cliffs to their deaths. Today the view from these heights is as grand as it is fear-inspiring. The Pali Highway is mountainous, leading through lush tropical rain forests, numerous curves, and arriving abruptly in the teeming urban Honolulu.

EASTERN OAHU – The coastal loop continues beyond Kailua as rt. 83, the Kamehameha Highway. This road takes you along the eastern and northern coasts of the island. Each of the islands has at least one — and usually several — mountains or ridges that form some familiar shape. On Maui there is the John F. Kennedy profile in Iao Valley; on Kauai, Queen Victoria's profile. All the islands are of volcanic origin, and in the fury of an eruption lava turns, twists, and tears into a fantastic variety of shapes. Oahu's major profile is the Crouching Lion, visible from rt. 83. Like all of these figures, the exact resemblance is iffy, and depends as much on the viewer's perspective and good will as the actual shape of the formation. But what is interesting is that myths always collect around these profiles. A bit beyond the Crouching Lion is the lovely

Sacred Falls, an 87-foot waterfall that plunges into a pool. Visitors are welcome to swim in the pool and cavort in the falling water, but the waterfall is a hard mile's hike beyond the parking spot, and you should be prepared for about an hour's tramp.

The culmination of the drive along the eastern shore is the Polynesian Cultural Center in Laie (293–9291). Though it is a commercial enterprise, the center has excellent reconstructions of villages of all the major cultures of the Pacific — Marquesas, Samoan, Tongan, Hawaiian, Tahitian, Fijian, Maori. Contemporary members of these cultures practice early island crafts, and a number of genuine rituals are offered in evening programs. There are also luaus and stage shows with audience participation several times a day. A mixture of museum and Disneyland, the center is informative and a great deal of fun as well.

NORTHERN OAHU – Where rt. 83 rounds the top of the island and turns southwest, it runs smack dab into a spot that is guaranteed to raise goose pimples on any surfer's surface — Sunset Beach, home of the Big Waves, including the notorious Banzai Pipeline. Here, every winter, international competitions are held. More cerebral, but thrilling in its own right, is nearby COMSAT — earth station for international commercial satellite communications. Ahead on the north shore is Waimea Falls Park (638–8511), another natural-wonder-gone-professional. The famous and incredibly beautiful waterfall is now made easy to see via the park's round-trip tram ride. The 1,800-acre park offers a variety of botanical gardens, forests, and restaurants.

From here the highway turns south and heads toward Honolulu.

BEST EN ROUTE

Kahala Hilton, Honolulu – This deluxe hotel has a magnificent setting on a tropical lagoon inhabited by dolphins and turtles. Many of the 308 rooms have separate dressing rooms and lanais overlooking the lagoon, mountains, or beach. All have large baths and are decorated with interesting handmade wall hangings. Its Maile Restaurant is one of the best in the Honolulu area. 5000 Kahala Ave., Honolulu, Oahu, HI 96816 (808 734-2211).

Royal Hawaiian, Honolulu – Fondly known as "the Pink Palace" or "Pink Lady," this 525-room hotel was *the* place to stay in the 1930s, when luxury liners steamed into Honolulu with elegant passengers who stayed for months. The pink stucco Mediterranean-style building retains its glittering chandeliers and long corridors, although it has changed hands since then and is now managed by Sheraton. Avoid the new tower; it's the gracious, older rooms that really give this place its charm. 2255 Kalakaua Ave. (922-4422).

Hyatt Regency, Honolulu – The two octagonal towers of this hotel atop the ritzy Hemmeter Center are a visual landmark in Waikiki, and its Great Hall with a tropical garden, three-story waterfall, and massive hanging sculpture is a sightseeing spot in its own right. Each of the 1,234 rooms is handsomely furnished and decorated with some fine Hawaiian prints. 2424 Kalakaua Ave. (922-9292).

Craters of the Moon National Monument, Idaho

Everyone wants to know what the moon really looks like. For centuries we lived with intense speculation, some of it informed by science, much indebted to imagination. For a decade now we have lived with reality: Those incredible pictures of a flat, gray, pockmarked surface scarred by all the flying debris of space for eons, flanked by strange, craggy rocks rising from Swiss cheese holes in the ground; and in front, standing with a flag unfurled in a vacuum, the astronaut, looking as awkward and out of place as a snowman learning to walk. These pictures have become part of our consciousness, our definition of what space travel is about. And while all the rigmarole of space is familiar — the liftoff, the orbit, the lunar module — the moon remains a mystery. What did the first astronauts feel? What would it be like to visit the moon?

It's not impossible. And no further away than Idaho. When scientists wanted to familiarize prospective astronauts with the lunar surface, they brought them here: to Craters of the Moon National Monument, in the valley of the Snake River, in the middle of Idaho.

It's not unfamiliar territory to many people, especially skiers. Some 70 miles to the west is Idaho's Sun Valley, one of the state's finest skiing centers. For travelers coming from (or going to) Sun Valley, Craters of the Moon makes a delightful day diversion from the main route I-84 or the road to Sun Valley, rts. 93 and 75.

Craters of the Moon National Monument is as close to being on the moon as you can get without leaving earth. The next best thing to actually being there, touring Craters of the Moon will give you an understanding of that extraterrestrial splendor which we spend billions of dollars trying to reach. (In fact, that's another good reason to stop by. You can find out whether or not you like the moon, at a price you can afford. If it's not exactly your slice of cheese, you can turn toward Sun Valley happy that you have not signed on for one of those excursions to the moon scheduled to start in the 1980s. If it's your cup of tea, you can put your name on the list.) Kids are likely to be irrevocably affected, and you might have to live with a junior astronaut until you can convince your son or daughter to apply to medical school.

Coming south from Sun Valley, or north from I-84, you must drive at least a section of rts. 93 and 75 before getting to the turnoff for Craters of the Moon. Along the road are two diversions worth considering.

SHOSHONE INDIAN ICE CAVES – Idaho has a number of caves — some discovered, some not — related to its volcanic origins. The Shoshone Indian Caves are a constantly cool (about 32°) series of caves (or one long cavern really) that simply won't change temperature no matter how hot the weather is outside. There are tours every half hour between May and October. (Be sure to bring a sweater.) On the grounds is an Indian museum and the statue of Chief Washakie of the Shoshone tribe. Admission charge. About 43 miles south of Sun Valley, 15 miles north of Shoshone on rt. 75.

SHOSHONE FALLS – Although quite a detour from the route — 30 miles south of the town of Shoshone — the falls are well worth the drive. Larger than Niagara, these waterfalls drop 212 dramatic, turbulent feet into the Snake River. (Evel Knievel fans will remember Snake River because of his world-famous, daredevil jump across Snake River Canyon, which is further along the meandering Snake.) Like all parts of the Snake, the drama of the falls is affected by the flow of water, which is, in its turn, affected by rainfall, and more important, the amount of irrigation along its course through Idaho. During the heat of the summer irrigation is at its height, the falls are at their nadir.

CRATERS OF THE MOON NATIONAL MONUMENT – Craters of the Moon is 60 miles northeast of Shoshone, along rt. 93. You'll know you're in the right part of the country a few miles before you reach Carey, Idaho, when you pass a series of lava beds; if you miss them, don't worry. There'll be plenty more when you get to where you're going.

Craters of the Moon is a land of lava on lava — stark, black, and cinder-blown. Its visual impact is stunning: miles of black lava rising and falling over the otherwise broad, flat valley, with abrupt, jagged peaks and huge cinder and lava cones — some 800 feet high — dotting the landscape. The entire area was the product of a series of volcanic explosions which over eons added successive layers of lava to rock and lava already laid down. So startling is the effect of seeing the monument that its equally startling geographic history takes some time to appreciate.

Beneath the entire monument area are ice caves; running through them (or below them) is the great fissure in the earth known as the Great Rift. In three great epochs of upheaval, the Great Rift exploded in waves upon waves of white-hot magma — spewing molten rock at 2,000° out of the fissure itself — throwing tons of debris and rock into the air to form the volcanic cones which appear across the area. The cones belong to one of the earlier series of eruptions; the ubiquitous black lava actually belongs to a much more recent cataclysm — between 1,600 and 2,000 years ago. That is well within recorded history, a thought to keep in mind as you survey the broken, jagged, black landscape of the monument.

The human history of the monument is nowhere near as intriguing as its natural history. Indians certainly knew — and passed through — the area (you will see trail markers and cairns piled in various spots; they are Indian artifacts, though it is not known today exactly to what use they were put). But it does not seem to have been an important part of the world for them. The area was discovered by white men in 1833, and proclaimed a national monument in 1924.

The place to start any tour of the monument is at the Visitors' Center, where there are exhibits and displays on the area's amazing formations and natural history which describe the process in detail. From the Visitors' Center there is a seven-mile loop drive which will take you by car past most of the monument's best-known landmarks. Among things not to miss are Indian Tunnel, an 830-foot lava tube used as a cave by the Indians on treks through the lava fields, and Devils Orchard, one of the oldest lava formations in the area. A warning: Take along water, even when you are driving. In summer, the sun bakes the lava, burns the foot, and parches the throat. (In winter, the entire area is covered in deep snow, and turns into marvelous cross-country ski terrain.)

For the more adventurous, there are numerous trails and walks to bring you face to face with lava, and let you explore the monument on foot. (To do any hiking or camping, you must obtain a permit at the Visitors' Center.) There is much to recommend the on-foot approach. Since much of the monument is unreachable by car, it is the only way to really see the vast area of lava fields which are virtually unexplored. And by venturing into the (relative) unknown on foot, you will discover the monument's great secret: Far from being a sterile, hostile, bleak landscape, it is alive with plants, birds, and animals. Hundreds of species of flora have adapted to the area; there are mountain bluebirds, nighthawks, and sparrows galore; and in the back reaches of country you will see mule deer, hear coyote, and if you're very lucky, spot a distant bobcat. Camping and any other information on the monument: the Superintendent, Craters of the Moon National Monument, PO Box 29, Arco, ID 83213 (208 527-3257 or 527-3207).

BEST EN ROUTE

You will certainly have no trouble finding hotels and motels within striking distance of Craters of the Moon. However, most recommendable are several lodges in the Sun Valley/Ketchum, Idaho, area.

Sun Valley Lodge and Inn – The lodge and inn are separate physical entities, but part of the Sun Valley Resort. The lodge is a classic, rustic redwood ski lodge (of recent vintage) with 141 rooms, some with fireplaces; also, two good restaurants. The Inn is a more family-oriented operation, with 115 rooms in a rambling, neo-Tyrolean building. Some shops and restaurants are in a mall separating the two buildings. Sun Valley Rd., Sun Valley, ID 83353 (208 622-4111 or toll-free 800 635-8261, outside Idaho).

Heidelberg Inn – More in the Alp tradition of Idaho resorts, the Heidelberg is a kind of Austrian Alp motel, pleasanter to stay at than to try to describe. Some of its 30 rooms have fireplaces and kitchenettes. Warm Spring Rd., Sun Valley, ID 83353 (208 726-5361).

Tamarack Lodge – A very comfortable resort lodge with 27 rooms. PO Box 495, Sun Valley Rd., Ketchum, ID 83340 (208 726-3344).

Flint Hills, Kansas

If you look at a map, you will find that the Flint Hills run from the Kansas-Oklahoma border into the northern third of the Sunflower State. The north-south axis of the hills lies about 45 miles east of Wichita, or about a quarter of the distance between the Missouri state line in the east and the Colorado foothills of the Rockies that form Kansas' western edge.

Flint Hills, so named because of the chunks of flint found in the soil, are among the last surviving plains of prairie grassland. Although at one time the plains formed a belt that ran from Chicago to the edge of the Rockies, and from Canada to Texas, now scarcely 1% of the original 400,000 square miles of tallgrass remain. Most of the land has been razed to provide homes on the range, or has been reduced to stubble by machines and grazing herds.

Once the plains were subject to long droughts and brush fires—the stereotypical picture of this area of Kansas. But modern technology is changing that image of the plains, with the planting of fire lines, the building of large reservoirs, and the construction of superhighways. Also, the Flint Hills are probably not as dry and devoid of plant life as you might have thought. Trees line the area's streams, which in turn nourish wild plums; wild flowers seem to thrive on the streams' grassy slopes with blooms for every warm season; larkspur, cornflower, indigo, wild red rose, and clover mingle on the hillsides.

For the most part, this section of Kansas looks much as it did when pioneers passed through on their way west, and settlers stayed to farm the rich soil in other parts of the state. The farms are vastly larger now, the fields tended by giant clanking machines, but the prairie that served as a home for herds of buffalo and pronghorn antelope is still prime grazing territory. The area is also known for its sprawling cattle ranches and rich oil deposits.

Cattle fed on the grasses of Kansas grow exceptionally large and healthy, although it was not until the turn of the century that agricultural scientists understood why. Under the prairie lies limestone chock-full of protein and minerals. The prairie roots, going down into the earth as deep as six yards, tap this remnant of an ancient seabed and bring its nourishment to the stems and leaves, making extraordinarily rich fodder. Cowboys still ride the hills on horseback and in four-wheel drives, searching for the stragglers of their grazing herds. You can join these lone sailors in a sea of golden grass by driving through Flint Hills. If you have a jeep, you can get away from the paved highways that crisscross the plains here, but even if you stick to the civilized paths, you cannot help being transported, for a moment, to the simpler life of the past.

Although Kansas is known for its sudden, severe thundershowers and storms that often bring tornadoes, there are only a few twisters during the spring.

The route we suggest will lead you through Flint Hills en route from Kansas City to Oklahoma City.

TOPEKA – State capital since 1861, this was the site of bitter conflict between abolitionists and proslavery factions during the Civil War. After years of being known as Bleeding Kansas, the state joined the Union. Sites in town include: State House, housing artwork depicting pioneer and Civil War years (Capitol Square, 296–0111). The zoo has exhibits of exotic tropical flowers and trees as well as animals (Gage Park, 272–5821). Nearby, the Reinish Memorial Rose and Rock Gardens provide an oasis of fragrant tranquillity in spring, summer, and autumn (Gage Park). The Kansas State Historical Society Museum has exhibits on state history, an old airplane, and models of pioneer establishments (10th and Jackson Sts., 296–3251).

EMPORIA, FLINT HILLS – Take I-35 about 50 miles southwest from Topeka. This is the heart of the Flint Hills region and its major cattle market. Tens of thousands of cattle are sent to the slaughterhouse from this town of 25,000 every year. Emporia is the home of William Allen White, the late publisher of the *Emporia Gazette,* one of America's most respected editors. His bust stands in Peter Pan Park. For information on park activities, call the City Manager (342–5127). Emporia State University presents concerts, plays, and films throughout the year (1200 Commercial). The Way College emphasizes Biblical studies (1300 W 12th). Lyons County Lake and Park, a 528-acre recreation area, has swimming, boat launching, fishing, and camping. Campsites do not have hookups (11 miles north of town on rt. 170). For information, call the State Forestry, Fish and Game Commission office in Emporia, 342–0658.

FLINT HILLS NATIONAL WILDLIFE REFUGE – About 5,000 acres, primarily devoted to waterfowl. In winter, as many as 20 bald eagles nest on the grounds, as well as many other species. Among them: snow geese, blue geese, greater and lesser Canadian geese, mallard ducks, great horned and snowy owls. Whitetail deer, coyote, red fox, and rabbit live here too. The best time to visit is fall, either before or after the hunting season, when the refuge is closed to human visitors. Open the rest of the year. Free. From Emporia, take rt. 99 south about three miles. After you cross the river bridge, you'll see an unnumbered county road running east to Hartford. Follow it for about 20 miles to the refuge (392–5553).

FALL RIVER AND TORONTO DAM AND LAKE STATE PARKS – Known as the twin reservoirs of the "Kansas Ozarks," the combined recreation area consists of 2,000 acres, with 40 miles of shoreline. Fishing, boating, swimming, hiking, and camping. The parks are 55 miles south of Emporia on rt. 99, then east for 20 miles on rt. 96 (658–2455).

WICHITA – Kansas' largest city (population 261,800) and leading manufacturing center, and headquarters of four aircraft companies. Places of interest include: Wichita

Art Museum, containing American and European canvases and sculpture (619 Stackman Dr., Sim Park); Wichita Art Association, containing two modern galleries and a children's theater (9112 E Central); Wichita Historical Museum, containing pioneer paraphernalia (3751 E Douglas Ave.); Wichita State University, with Frank Lloyd Wright buildings and a contemporary art museum (N Hillside and 17th Sts.). Kids will enjoy Cow Town Historic Wichita, a restored frontier village with Wyatt Earp's jail. Open daily, March through October (1717 Sim Park Dr.).

Glacier National Park, Montana

Montana's Glacier National Park is measured in millions: one million acres carved by the movement of massive glaciers millions of years ago, visited by more than a million people every year. These 1,600 square miles shared by the US and Canada are known variously as Waterton Park, Glacier International Peace Park, and simply Glacier, although the giant ice sheets to which the park owes its name and its geography have long since disappeared. There are still some 50 small glaciers throughout the park — snow masses deep enough to compact the lower levels into ice and heavy enough to creep downhill. The largest of these, Grinnell, covers 300 acres and contains ice 400 feet thick. In the summertime, streams of water from Grinnell and the other glaciers cascade down the mountainside, gathering volume as they merge and tumbling into the deep cold lakes. This spectacular descent and many other features of this Alpine wilderness in the northwest region of Montana (just west of St. Mary) merit at least a one-week visit.

Glacier's six large lakes (all five miles or more in length) stretch from the park's edges into its interior; it has some 200 smaller lakes and glacial ponds, 1,000 waterfalls, over 50 streams full of rushing, grinding ice, and 700 miles of trails and paths for hiking and horseback riding as well. The Blackfoot Indians considered the area sacred because of its awesome beauty.

The snow does not melt in Glacier until June (usually mid-June), and although the park is open from June until October 15, September may bring the snow once again, requiring the closing of certain park roads and campgrounds. Nevertheless, having a snowball fight in summer, fishing in a mountain stream, or watching a mountain goat seemingly defy gravity in search of vegetation along a mountain slope are experiences worth waiting for, and worth returning for, in the event that you are turned away at the park entrance in July because of a sudden summer snowstorm.

Enter the park from Browning, along US 2 (access from the south via US 89). Within park boundaries, you will be urged to follow park regulations, not only because of the geography of the park, which can be treacherous, but to protect the park's rich and abundant animal life. The 57 species of animals, including the mountain goat, mule, deer, moose, beaver, muskrat, mink, bighorn sheep, coyote, and wolf, are somewhat overshadowed by the presence of one particular inhabitant — the grizzly bear. Glacier is one of the few US parks which is home to grizzlies, and although these 500-plus-pound carnivores are extremely shy, hikers are encouraged to make noises along the trail, indicating their presence. (You really don't want to surprise a sleeping grizzly.) A tin can containing a few pebbles or a bell tied to a knapsack or belt will do the trick.

In addition to the variety of animal life, there are at least 200 types of birds, running the gamut from hawks and eagles that swoop overhead to grouse and dippers that inhabit the woods and streams. As in any wildlife preserve, these creatures are not easy to spot, and it is likely that you will leave having spied only an occasional mountain goat or sleepy marmot. But if you have a few days to spare, the best assurance of getting a taste of the park's resources is to hike and camp in any of the 15 campgrounds. What you discover on your own can be augmented by participating in one of the daily walks or campfire programs conducted by ranger naturalists at the visitors' centers or campgrounds. The rangers will point out the myriad variety of plants and explain how the knife-edged ridges and glacial peaks were formed eons ago, an invaluable part of your visit.

By far the best way to see the park is on foot, on short walks from the Visitors' Center at Logan Pass, St. Mary's, or Apgar, or longer treks (some guided) lasting several days. At Glacier Valley you can rent horses for horseback journeys through the park.

If you cannot manage more than a drive through Glacier, you will still have the experience of one of the best routes in America. The park's Going-to-the-Sun Road, starting in St. Mary on rt. 89, is an unforgettable 50 miles of twisting, cliff-hanging mountain roadway linking the east and west sides of the park. (Vehicles over 30 feet long or over 8 feet wide are banned from the road, and even a slight snow necessitates strict regulations.)

Along the way, you skirt the edge of St. Mary Lake, with its backdrop of snow-capped peaks and Douglas firs, reaching the first of 17 parking turnouts about five miles beyond the lake. Here you have access to a view of Triple Divide Peak, where — as the name implies — mountain waters divide and enter three larger water systems: the Arctic via Hudson Bay, the Gulf of Mexico via the Mississippi system, and the Pacific Ocean via the Columbia River.

After many other magnificent vistas and views of the park's towering peaks (including 10,080-foot Mount Jackson), you reach the highlight of the drive, the crossing of the Continental Divide at Logan Pass. From this 6,664-foot elevation, you have a 100-mile view of the countryside — a spectacular panorama that justifies Glacier's reputation as the Alps of America.

There is a Visitors' Center here, where you can get directions to Hidden Lake. The 1½-mile hike along a self-guided nature trail, which is part boardwalk, part trail, and part wildflower garden, offers a fine view of the calm, deep blue lake 800 feet below — a perfect finale to a lovely walk.

Your drive along the Going-to-the-Sun Highway eventually leads into McDonald Valley. Lake McDonald — complete with a roadside exhibit of fossil algae and McDonald Lodge — is a good place to picnic and rest before going on your way. If you are ready for more hiking, you should head over to Avalanche Campground, and pick up an easy two-mile trail that leads to Avalanche Basin. Technically called a "glacial cirque," this is a natural amphitheater with 2,000-foot walls and six waterfalls — a spectacular sight that gives you a sense of what the park's interior is like without the strain of a longer trek.

The park's largest lake, McDonald is a center of activity. You can swim, take a boat tour from the dock at Lake McDonald Lodge, or hike to Sperry Glacier, where Sperry Chalets offer overnight stays complete with prepared meals and box lunches. Reservations are required. The chalets are also a good spot from which to plan a fishing expedition, an activity that requires no license at Glacier, and spans a season from mid-June to mid-October.

There is also fishing at Two Medicine Lake in Two Medicine Valley, southwest of McDonald. Rainbow and brook trout, mackinaw, and pygmy whitefish are caught commonly, while cutthroat, Dolly Varden trout, and kokanee are available during seasonal migrations. Two Medicine Lake is a good place for camping, hiking, and boating, as well.

If you enjoy horseback riding, you should stay in Many Glacier Valley long enough to join the popular all-day trip through Alpine meadows filled with wildflowers to Iceberg Lake — another clear mountain lake filled with huge chunks of ice that break off from the banks of the iceberg. You can also arrange a hiking trip with cook, packer, and packhorse, or a shorter guided pack trip with a highly recommended, park-approved outfitter — Rocky Mountain Outfitters (Columbia Falls, MT 59912; after June 1, address letters to East Glacier Park, MT 59434).

There are many other sights in the park — Red Eagle Lake, located in a glacial cirque with some spectacular falls and an impressive gorge; Flattop Mountain, near Lewis Range, where the juxtaposition of forest and meadow makes it a favorite for hiking and picnicking; and Grinnell Lake, where a trail leads to the largest glacier in the park.

If you have driven through the park, but still not had your fill of wildlife adventure and/or isolation of the mountain pines, you should take Chief Mountain International Highway (rt. 17) to Waterton Lakes National Park in Canada. Actually an extension of Glacier, it offers more of the same, with fewer crowds. Information: the Superintendent, Glacier National Park, West Glacier, MT 59936 (406 888–5441).

BEST EN ROUTE

If you prefer sheets and blankets to the stars above and mud below, there are several good hotels, motels, and lodges at the park. If you wish to stay at one of the chalets at Sperry or Granite Park, write to Belton Chalets, Inc., B. Ross Luding, PO Box 188, West Glacier, MT 59936; otherwise information on accommodations in and around the park is available through Glacier Park, Inc., headquartered during the park season in the Glacier Park Lodge at the southeast corner of the park on rt. 49, East Glacier, MT 59434 (406 226–4841), from October through May at 1735 E Fort Lowell Rd., Suite 7, Tucson, AZ 85719 (602 795–0377). In the park are:

Lake McDonald Lodge – This lodge was originally built in 1914. In a setting of giant cedars, its hunting lodge atmosphere and lakeside locale make this a good choice if you want to go fishing, boating, or riding. Make early reservations. The lodge is often booked months in advance. Open mid-June to mid-September. Twelve miles northeast of Going-to-the-Sun Hwy. (406 888–5431).

Glacier Park Lodge – Offers a pool, playground, attractive setting, and good restaurant serving prime ribs, mountain trout. Open mid-June through mid-September. In the southeast corner of the park on rt. 49 (406 226–9311).

Many Glacier Hotel – Rustic accommodations overlooking Swiftcurrent Lake with easy access to boating, fishing, hiking, and riding. Dancing and entertainment nightly supplement good, hearty fare at the restaurant. Open mid-June to mid-September. Twelve miles west of Babb off rt. 89 (406 732–4311).

Carlsbad Caverns National Park, New Mexico

If you're driving across the Chihuahuan Desert in New Mexico and those vast undulating horizontal stretches of sand are beginning to appear endless rather than beautiful, there's something nearby that can satisfy the direction of your fancy — Bat Flight at Carlsbad Caverns. Here, every night at sunset from May through October, 5,000 bats per minute spiral out of the open-mouthed darkness of the cave, as many as a million in one viewing. For an hour or more, the bats, on their way out to feed for the night, create a blackening vortex against the sky which widens into a gray streak as they set off into the stillness of nightfall.

Carlsbad Caverns National Park is in New Mexico's southeastern corner, just 15 miles from the Texas border to the south and 27 miles from Carlsbad, New Mexico, to the northeast. As you approach Carlsbad Caverns, you begin to sense that there is something unique about the place; the monotony of the terrain is broken by the rise of the foothills of the Guadalupe Mountains which stand a few miles across the Texas border. But it is underground in this hilly, desert region that everything spectacular is happening. Underneath the surrounding terrain (the national park encompasses 73 square miles) is an intricate network of caves, with the main cavern the largest known underground cavity in the world. For a long time, no one knew about any of this. In the 1800s, New Mexico residents noticed the nightly bat flights from a nearby cave and named it Bat Cave. But they left the bats and the cave alone until 1901 when the deposits of bat guano near the cave's entrance attracted commercial interest. A mining operation was set up, and between then and 1923, 200 million pounds of guano were extracted from the cave for fertilizer. During that time, James Larkin White, a local boy, explored the inside of the cave and discovered its marvelous limestone formations. Armed with just a kerosene lamp, however, White was only on the tip of an iceberg; inside the cave lie 14 acres of caverns, caves, and formations, culminating in the Big Room, the largest underground chamber found anywhere in the world. Moreover, some of the caves in the surrounding network have still not been completely explored. But the main cavern, with its stalagmite and stalactite formations of magnificent design and infinite variety — some joining and creating monumental pillars, others densely clustered in fragile and delicate patterns — is a testament to nature's artistry.

The beginnings of this subterranean gallery go back more than 200 million years when a vast inland sea covered the entire area. At the edge of this sea, limestone-secreting organisms built the massive Capitan Reef. In the course of millennia, the sea dried up and the reef was buried under several thousand feet of sediment. Then, approximately 20 million years ago, during a period of mountain building activity, a huge fault split the reef and thrust mountains upward. The thick layers of sediment above the reef began to erode and ground water containing carbon dioxide began to seep through and down into the tiny fractures of the limestone mass, changing the limestone into calcium bicarbonate, a substance easily dissolved, creating open spaces. The water table gradually lowered, carving great cavities within the rock. The erosion was accelerated as massive blocks of porous rock, no longer supported by water, collapsed, increasing the size of chambers. The seepage of surface rain and melted snow from above continued, carrying dissolved limestone to the walls of the cavern, where it solidified as the water evaporated. Drop by drop, eon by eon, the water deposited more limestone, creating many formations — stalactites that hang like icicles from the ceiling, and stalagmites that reach up from the ground. Where the two have fused stand massive pillars.

To get a good feeling for nature's work at Carlsbad Caverns, you will need about half a day. (The park is open all year.) After stopping off at the Visitors' Center to consult background displays on the history of the cavern, follow a short trail to the entrance of the cavern, where a self-guided tour begins (visitors are given portable tape recorders with tapes). Remember to wear a sweater because the cave stays a pleasantly cool 56° year-round. The natural entrance to the cave is imposing — an arch 90 feet wide and 40 feet high. The walk is a total of three miles, beginning with a relatively steep descent down switchback trails to a depth of 829 feet. As you progress, the main points of interest are described on the tape, but look all about and take your time to appreciate the immensity and beauty of what lies around you. You walk along the main corridor through a succession of amazing chambers — the circular King's Palace, with its ornate limestone decorations and curtains of glittering cave onyx, the Queen's Chamber, noted for its delicate "elephant ear" formations, and the Papoose Room, a low-ceilinged chamber with numerous stalactites. Larger than both the King's and Queen's chambers is the Big Room, which fulfills its title with a 255-foot ceiling in an area the size of 14 football fields. The room's magnificent and huge totem poles, pillars, and domes are most striking.

If you are pressed for time or cannot make the descent by foot, there is an elevator and a shorter tour of 1½ miles, mainly of the Big Room.

Incongruous as it may seem after walking through the cavern's natural chambers, there is a lunchroom at the bottom where you can stop off for a meal. Except for the lunchrooms and the elevator which brings you to the surface after you complete the tour (unless you actually want to follow three miles of trails back up), little has been done to alter the natural state of the caverns. The lighting is well hidden in underground cables and brings out the subtle hues in the limestone formations.

If electric lights and lunchrooms do not fit into your idea of how to explore a cavern, the park has preserved New Cave for the ultimate in underground adventures. You reach this totally undeveloped cave via unpaved roads and then trek up a steep and primitive 1¼-mile trail. The tour is a strenuous three-hour walk. You discover the spectacular formations only with the help of the lights you are carrying. Tours are given daily during the summer and weekends by reservation the rest of the year. Reservations are required (505 785-2233). You needn't be an experienced spelunker, but you have to be ready for a rough excursion.

Above ground, visitors can stroll along a self-guided nature trail or take the daily guided tour and view the arid desert vegetation and large variety of cacti, and hopefully some of the area's wildlife — fawns, mule, deer, and lizards. For the more adventurous, there is backcountry camping with plenty of contact with the wilderness — the trails are poorly defined, and the desert, rugged and dry.

But neither trailblazer nor tenderfoot should miss the bat flight any evening from May to October (the bats hibernate in winter). While everyone sits in the amphitheater at the cave's mouth, waiting for the bats to come whirling out of the mouth of the cave, a park naturalist explains the flight, but is usually upstaged in mid-sentence when thousands of bats pour out of the cave and into the darkening horizon. Information: the Superintendent, Carlsbad Caverns National Park, 3225 National Park Hwy., Carlsbad, NM 88220 (505 785–2233).

BEST EN ROUTE

Although you can get a permit at the Visitors' Center for rugged backcountry camping, there are no developed overnight facilities in the park. The town of Carlsbad, 27 miles northeast of the park along US 62, offers a wide range of motels and hotels. White City, a privately owned town seven miles northeast of the Visitors' Center, has a motel and a few shops as well.

Rodeway Inn, Carlsbad – This 107-room motel has a café, color TV, heated indoor pool, exercise room, playground, dancing, and entertainment on Saturday nights. PO Box 640, 3804 National Parks Hwy., Carlsbad, NM 88220 (505 887–5535; toll-free, 800 228–2000).

Stevens, Carlsbad – Pool, attractive restaurant, free coffee in rooms, dancing and entertainment; 181 rooms. PO Box 580, 1829 S Canal St., Carlsbad, NM 88220 (505 887–2851).

Motel 6, Carlsbad – Pool, 80 rooms and low rates. 3824 National Parks Hwy., Carlsbad, NM 88220 (505 885–8807).

Cavern Inn, White City – This motel has 132 rooms, a restaurant, pool, and accepts pets. PO Box 128, White's City, NM 88268 (505 785–2291).

Crater Lake National Park, Oregon

The Klamath Indians have their own explanation for the creation of this spectacular, brilliant blue, deep lake in the Cascade Mountains of southern Oregon. Llao, god of the underworld, was chased back into his secret passage to the netherworld. The good gods on the earth's surface plucked a mountain from its base and threw it after the fleeing Llao. It landed, point down, sealing Llao's escape route forever, and creating the crater that now is the focal point for more than 600,000 visitors each year.

Geologists offer an equally splendid version of the story. Ten thousand years ago the great peaks of the Northwest Cascades rose from the earth — Rainier, Hood, Shasta, Adams, and further south, Mt. Mazama. Several of them existed over pockets of natural gas, and 6,600 years ago one of these pockets exploded — literally tearing the insides out of Mt. Mazama and covering an area of 35 square miles with pumice and molten earth. Having vomited everything from within, the sides of Mt. Mazama collapsed, forming a caldera of 21 square miles nearly 2,000 feet deep. This great volcanic bowl gradually filled with rainwater and melted snows and became — as it was named millenniums later — a Crater Lake. So stable is the lake that the water level barely changes season to season, year by year; and the water itself is very cold — 55° in the warmest summers (not for swimming), and pure: Rangers advise visitors to drink from the lake water when they get to its shore; the water, they claim, is 20 times cleaner than the country's cleanest tap water.

Whichever version makes a believer of you, Crater Lake is a sight not to be missed. Oregon's only national park (established in 1902 after long years of fighting), it is famous for animal and plant life, miles of hiking trails, a drivable road running 33 miles around the rim of the crater, and the lake, 1,932 feet deep, second deepest on the continent after Canada's Great Slave Lake. The park's vistas are unparalleled both for their natural beauty and for the many natural viewing places created as if expressedly for the visitors who flock here.

Although far off the beaten path from southern Oregon's few big cities (Medford is about 60 miles south, Roseburg a bit further west), Crater Lake's Rim Road is as ideal a method for viewing this wonder as any man could have devised. Almost 100 miles of trails, most starting from the Rim Road, snake through the park, up adjacent mountains for panoramic views of the lake or down to the lake's shores. There you can find boat trips around the lake, and to its two islands — Phantom Ship and Wizard.

Until 1853, Crater Lake was unknown to white men. Then a gold prospector, John Wesley Hillman, stumbled upon it while searching with a party of gold diggers for the famous Lost Cabin Mine. It was called "Deep Blue Lake" by the few who knew of its existence, and the discovery wasn't made public for 31 years. Official expeditions were made during that time, and in 1873, a government geologist sounded its depths at 2,008 feet, a respectable finding for the limited equipment of the day.

The man most crucial to the lake's fate first saw it in 1885. William Gladstone Steel was a Kansan transplanted to the great new West. Once he laid eyes on this spectacle, he committed his life to its preservation. He personally led a crusade to save it from homesteaders, lumber interests, and prospectors. Teddy Roosevelt, perhaps the greatest conservationist to inhabit the White House, made Crater Lake a national park on May 22, 1902. In 1913, Steel was rewarded for his long crusade with an appointment as the park's superintendent.

Crater Lake National Park is a 250-square-mile tract surrounded on almost every side by national forests. Except for a small panhandle of land at the southern entrance (included within the park's boundaries to protect stands of ponderosa pines), the park is a near-perfect rectangle. There are three entrances. From the south (driving north from Klamath Falls, about 50 miles) take rt. 62 to the southern entrance and soon enter the Rim Road. The western entrance, at Union Creek, is where rt. 62 crosses the western border of the park. From the north, you enter from rt. 138, passing through the park's Pumice Desert before reaching the Rim Road.

It is probably most convenient to begin in the south, for the Visitors' Center at Rim Village, the only settlement along the rim, is nearest to the southern road, and in summertime, the Rim Road is one way, going clockwise. (Take this into consideration if you plan to enter from the north; it will take 30 miles to reach the Visitors' Center.) If you enter from the south, you will see the Pinnacles about six miles south of the Rim Road from Kerr Notch (along the crater's southeast edge), fluted columns and spires of pumice and earth, pieces of earth thrown into the wind by Mt. Mazama's explosion 6,000 years ago. At this spot, the particles hit vents of gas and steam from within the earth, and turned solid.

Begin a visit at the Visitors' Center and the nearby Sinnott Memorial, an excellent orientation point. Talks on the origin of the lake are given at the Sinnott Memorial daily, and exhibits are open. (Visitors' Center is open daily mid-June to Labor Day, 8:30 AM to 7 PM). Cross-country skiing is popular here during winter months. Information is available at the Visitors' Center. During winter months, only the park's south entrance is open.

There are two reasons to go to Crater Lake: one is to sail *on* it, and the other is to get *above* it, to look down on it, as did the men — Indian and white — who discovered it. Two walking tours worth investigating start at the Visitors' Center. A 1½-mile trail runs to the top of Garfield Peak, 1,900 feet above the lake's surface. The other trail is Discovery Point Trail, taking the modern-day explorer to the spot where John Hillman first laid eyes on this unexpected vision.

Fishing is allowed without a license, but there is a daily limit of ten fish per person; the lake has trout and a species of small salmon. Nightly campfire programs are held at Mazama Campground and the Crater Lake Lodge.

From the Visitors' Center you enter the Rim Road (strictly one way — going clockwise — in the summer) and you'll have to struggle to keep your eyes on the road and off the scenery. Fortunately, nature anticipated your needs, and numerous natural stopping places mark the circular route. There are numerous trails and tracks which lead from stopping places up nearby summits (for even larger views), or down to the lakefront.

The first stop at the mountain is called "the Watchman," with a 1½-mile trail to its summit, overlooking the lake from 1,800 feet. Further along, on the northeast side, you'll run across Cleetwood Trail, and its one-and-a-bit-mile path down to the lake's shores. It is a steep path down, steeper coming back up, and don't take more than you can comfortably carry. But do go down, for at the end of the trail the boat trips on Crater Lake begin, 2½-hour circles around the lake and to the islands in the middle. Boat trips have guides on board explaining what you pass and what to look for. Inquire at the Visitors' Center before heading down Cleetwood Trail as to times and availability of boat trips.

Other stops along the route include the 2½-mile trail up Mount Scott, the highest point in the park. A little further on is the turnoff for the drive up to the top of Cloudcap, 1,600 feet above the lake. All these paths and roads give different perspectives on the vastness of the lake below, views of the Cascade Range to the north, and the full scope of Oregon scenery all around.

The major drawback to Crater is winter, for when it comes, the park closes up almost totally. There are accumulations of snow of 50 feet by the time winter has had its say, and the north entrance is closed almost the entire season. While park accommodations close completely, there is a choice of ski facilities open within the park's grounds. The Rim Road opens in early June if the snow is cleared. Certain roads and trails may be closed during peak season due to conservation considerations.

And a last note: Although you'll undoubtedly have the experience of sneaking up on "tame" wild animals like deer, squirrels, chipmunks, marmots, and foxes, don't feed or try to pet them. This is especially true of the bears that scavenge among the garbage cans at night and early in the morning. For more information on facilities, park accommodations, travel suggestions: the Superintendent, Crater Lake National Park, Crater Lake, OR 97604 (503 594-2211).

BEST EN ROUTE

Crater Lake Lodge, Rim Village – Just what you'd expect of a well-managed, comfortable but rustic national park lodge. There are 76 rooms, and a number of cabins available; plus some stores in Rim Village. There is nightly entertainment — campfire programs — and easy access to information on ranger tours, boat rides, lectures, and other park activities. Open June 15 to mid-September. Reservations required. Crater Lake National Park, Crater Lake, OR 97604 (503 594-2511).

Also in Crater Lake National Park – Two campgrounds within the park offer a variety of camping facilities: Mazama, in the southcentral, and the primitive Lost Creek. All are run on a first come-first served basis; there is a nominal charge for Mazama, Lost Creek is free. Information from the Superintendent, Crater Lake National Park, Crater Lake, OR 97604 (503 594-2211).

Diamond Lake Resort, Diamond Lake, Oregon – Just seven miles north of the park's northern entrance, in Diamond Lake, this lodge has 92 rooms, on the lakefront (of . . . Diamond Lake). Diamond Lake, OR 97731 (503 793-3333).

The Oregon Coast

One of the most awesome drives in the country is along Oregon's northwest Pacific Coast, from Astoria at the mouth of the Columbia River all the way to the Oregon-California border at Pelican Beach. Here you can see how land has been — and is still being — sculpted by the enormous, slow force of the sea. Very little of the land along the coast is privately owned, and as a result you can stop at hundreds of points along the road that are part of state and federal forests. Most of the coast is lined with steep cliffs; 20 million years ago, when the coastline was formed, the land was level with the Pacific. The route can be driven north to south or south to north; we start at the northernmost point, Astoria, and work south. To get from Portland to Astoria take rt. 30, a 75-mile drive. The coast road is rt. 101.

ASTORIA – At the mouth of the Columbia River, known for its salmon. It's both a river fishing and a commercial deep-sea fishing center. From the top of the Astoria Column on Coxcomb Hill, you can see the harbor, ocean, and inland, the wooded mountains. Astoria Column commemorates the first American settlement in Oregon country during the pioneer era. Four miles south of Astoria on rt. 101, Ft. Clatsop National Memorial marks the site where Lewis and Clark spent the winter of 1805–1806. Ten miles south of Ft. Clatsop, the small town of Gearheart has an excellent 18-hole golf course.

SEASIDE – Two miles south of Gearheart. Formerly the premier resort on the coast, it has now lost some of its grandeur, although it is still one of Oregon's busiest shore resorts. A seawall along the coast forms a two-mile boardwalk above the beach. Tillamook Head, five miles from Seaside on an old logging road that juts west to the ocean, stands more than 1,200 feet above sea level and provides a sweeping view of the northern territories and the offshore Tillamook Lighthouse. South of Seaside, rt. 101 turns east along the Necanicum River, through green lowlands where commercial farms grow lettuce and peas. At Cannon Beach Junction, a road lined with towering hemlocks leads to Cannon Beach, named for the cannon that washed ashore from a wrecked American ship in 1846.

ARCH CAPE – Carved into a bluff at Neah-kah-nie Mountain. Barely five miles down the road, Manzanita is both a beach and mountain resort, located in a cove protected by rugged headlands to the north. From here the road turns inland, crosses the Nehalem River, and passes through Wheeler. Next door to Wheeler, Hoevet was at one time a prosperous mill town. Seven miles south of Wheeler, Rockaway has broad beaches, the arched Twin Rocks, an offshore formation, and attractive resort facilities.

TILLAMOOK BAY – The bay's main town is Tillamook, center for Oregon's inland dairy region. Cape Meares, just west of town, offers a broad view of the ocean from a 700-foot-high overlook. Cape Meares is the first stop on the Three Capes Scenic Drive, which also leads to Cape Lookout and Cape Kiwanda, near Pacific City.

NESKOWIN – About 30 miles south. The beaches attract beachcombers who hunt for Japanese floats, colored glass balls used as net supports by Oriental fishermen. The floats cross the Pacific on the Japan Current. Cascade Head, southwest of Neskowin, stands 1,400 feet high and juts out to sea.

DEVIL'S LAKE – Fourteen miles south of Neskowin, the lake offers good fishing and claims to be the source of the shortest river in the world, "D" River, which flows only 400 yards from Devil's Lake to the Pacific. Just west of Devil's Lake, Lincoln City is the center of the largest concentration of resort facilities on the coast.

DEPOE BAY – Fifteen miles south of Devil's Lake. Five miles north of town, Boiler Bay State Park runs along the coast. South of the park, huge heaps of shells, some more than an acre in size, mark the remains of Indian feasts. Depoe Bay's harbor is nearly always filled with trawlers, and charter boat fishing is available. Offshore, water spouts from an aperture in the rocks known as Spouting Horn. Look for the geyser of spray shooting skyward from the ocean. The Depoe Bay Aquarium has exhibits on local marine life (rt. 101 in the middle of town). About 4 miles south, Cape Foulweather viewpoint overlooks an impressive stretch of ocean, and just south of there, Devil's Punch Bowl State Park looks out to Otter Rock, a seabird rookery that was once the home of thousands of sea otters. At the base of a sandstone bluff, waves rush through two openings and boil up inside the rocky caldron, receding in a wash of foam. This formation is called Devil's Punch Bowl. For information on Depoe Bay parks, contact

City Hall Recreation Department (Depoe Bay, OR 97341, 765-2361). About ten miles south of the Devil's Punch Bowl, Newport spreads across a steep, ridged peninsula between the ocean and Yaquina Bay. The resultant sheltered harbor offers year-round surfing, scuba diving, fishing, clamming, and crabbing. While in Newport, be sure to sample the delicious Dungeness crab and Yaquina Bay oyster.

FLORENCE – Here, the coastline alters in character. The steep, craggy headlands give way to a 50-mile stretch of sand dunes extending to the Coos Bay area. Behind the low foredunes along the shore stretches a chain of freshwater lakes. Beyond the lakes are huge dunes, some reaching as high as 250 feet, and extending as far as three miles inland. Half-buried pine and spruce mark the dunes' eastward march. Jessie M. Honeyman State Park contains Cleawox Lake, locked in by the dunes, and a dense, evergreen forest laced with trails. South of Honeyman is Oregon Sand Dunes Recreational Area, part of Siuslaw National Forest. You can take a dune buggy ride or hike over the dunes, but be careful: It's easy to get lost. Winds can whip up and become blinding in a short time, covering your footprints. Dune hiking is also more taxing than hiking on hard-packed ground.

COOS BAY – South of the dunes area, mile-long McCullough Bridge crosses Coos Bay, site of the lumber town of North Bend. The Coos Bay region is the West's main lumber port. Shore Acres, Sunset Bay, and Cape Arago state parks, west of Coos Bay, overlook protected coves and Simpson's Reef offshore. From the headland, sea otters and sea lions can be seen playing on offshore reefs.

CAPE BLANCO – Forty miles south of Coos Bay, a road leads to Cape Blanco, the most westerly point in Oregon. The flat, grassy cape juts two miles into the Pacific, overlooking Blanco and Orford Reefs to the south. The Cape Blanco Lighthouse on the headland was built in the 1870s. Port Oxford, six miles south of the Cape Blanco turnoff, is a small harbor town protected by a cape to the north called the Heads. Many trails lead through underbrush to secluded beaches and tidal pools. Humbug Mountain, six miles south of Port Oxford, rises 1,750 feet; Humbug Mountain State Park has fishing, swimming, and camping facilities (it is part of Siskiyou National Forest).

GOLD BEACH – At the mouth of the Rogue River, 22 miles south of Humbug Mountain. During the 1850s a good deal of gold was dredged from the Rogue, but in 1861, floods swept the deposits into the ocean. (Small amounts of gold can still be found along the beaches.) The stretch of coastline from here to the California line is probably the most rugged in Oregon. Innumerable coves and tidal pools remain, virtually untouched. Cape Sebastian, 7 miles south of Gold Beach, and 35 miles from the California border, is a 700-foot promontory reaching out to the sea, with many trails branching inland from the coast. Harris State Park, six miles from California, has miles of beach and a view of offshore bird rookeries.

BEST EN ROUTE

Crest Motel, Astoria – Perched on a hilltop overlooking the Columbia River, with mountains on the far shore. Accommodations are in three buildings, one of which houses two large suites. 26 rooms in all. 5366 Lief Ericson Dr., Astoria, OR 97103 (503 325-3141)

Tu Tu Tun Lodge, Gold Beach – Set in the woods on the banks of the Rogue River. All rooms overlook the water. A riverboat stops to pick up passengers at the lodge dock daily. Swimming pool, fishing, and hiking trips. 96550 N Bank Rogue, Gold Beach, OR 97444 (503 247-6664).

Jacksonville Inn, Jacksonville – Located 100 miles inland from Gold Beach, in the heart of what was once gold rush country. Built in 1863, the Inn has been through several incarnations, as a bank, hardware store, professional offices, and a repair shop. Each of the eight bedrooms is lovingly furnished with antiques. The dining room serves substantial meals of steak, seafood, and Continental dishes. An interesting 19th-century town, Jacksonville has a number of frontier era buildings to explore. 175 E California St., Jacksonville, OR 97530 (503 899-1900).

Badlands National Park, South Dakota

About 60 miles southeast of Rapid City, South Dakota, on I-90, Badlands National Park covers more than 170 square miles, haunting southwestern South Dakota with a presence of irregular, awesome hills carved in pastel colors brilliant enough to make even Dorothy's magical rainbow seem commonplace. It was raised in status from a national monument to a national park in 1978.

The Indians called this region "Maco Sica," or badlands, because of its barren terrain and weird shapes. In their travels across the land, they left numerous arrowheads, knives, and other weapons and accessories which are still being found. Later, the French-Canadian explorers and trappers who passed through on their way south labeled the stark prairie "les mauvaises terres," which also means badlands. General Alfred Sully took one look at the place and called it "a part of hell with the fires burned out."

The journey starts in Rapid City.

RAPID CITY – Settled in the late 1870s after gold was discovered in the Black Hills, Rapid City now has a population of 44,000, and spreads across a section of Black Hills plateau. Main sites in town include: South Dakota School of Mines and Technology, with exhibits of fossils and geological artifacts, including specimens of local minerals (St. Joseph St.); Dahl Fine Arts Center, with giant murals showing scenes of US history and assorted Americana (713 7th St.); Bear Country animal park, home of roaming buffalo, wolves, bison, deer, mountain lion, antelope, and various smaller furry native creatures (eight miles south on rt. 16). At Black Hills Reptile Gardens you can see rattlesnakes being milked, alligators being wrestled, and snakes from all over the world (six miles south on rt. 16). Chapel in the Hills is a replica of an 800-year-old Norwegian church set among rolling hills in a tranquil valley (Chapel Rd.). The Horseless Carriage Museum offers exhibits of old-fashioned cars, clothes, musical instruments, machinery, and other nostalgia. It is located ten miles south on rt. 16. Before heading for Badlands National Park, take a look at the surrounding countryside from Skyline Drive, a scenic route in the southwest part of town. Then, having surveyed the turf, pick up I-90 southeast to the monument. You can enter at Wall, 55 miles from Rapid City, but it's advisable to choose the Cactus Flat entrance about 15 miles further down the road, as it takes you to Cedar Pass headquarters and the Visitors' Center.

BADLANDS NATIONAL PARK – Over 80 million years ago this entire area was submerged, the underwater surface of a shallow sea. Sediment of rock, clay, and sand slowly swept across the plains from the west. Forty to fifty million years later, the water disappeared, leaving marshy plains surrounding the powerful White River to the north. Slow-moving streams brought water through the more arid southern regions. This period was known as the Oligocene Epoch, an important segment of the period known as the Age of Mammals. A great variety and number of animals roamed the prairies and plains. Many, like their dinosaur predecessors, became extinct. Others, such as giant sea turtles, three-toed horses, and large, rhinoceros-like animals, evolved into species we know today. After these animals died, their remains sank into the soft marshes or settled on the bottom of a nearby riverbed. Gradually, winds and rivers from the west brought even greater quantities of sediment, most of which came from volcanic disturbances. Winds and infrequent rains continued, drying out the badlands even further. Grasslands replaced marshes. Strange, statuesque shapes produced by sediment took form. Today, the land is a sweeping sculpture garden with buttes rising above weaving gullies of dry sand. Different colored layers created by volcanic ash, clay, and stone stand in the open, clearly visible. Fossils lie imbedded in and underneath these geological structures. Nor has the process stopped. These strange formations are constantly changing shape, molded by easterly winds and sudden downpours.

No matter how desolate the landscape appears, there is plenty of wildlife. Occasionally, you can spot a juniper or red cedar among the stark surroundings. Likewise, yucca, green skunk, and rabbit brush thrive on the recently fallen slopes and valleys which hold greater moisture. Most animals inhabiting the area seek refuge in those moist prairies on the park's circumference, but in the badlands you can see buffalo, along with herds of deer and antelope. The jackrabbit, cottontail, and chipmunk keep close to the shrubs in an attempt to avoid their predatory neighbor, the coyote. Occasionally, you can catch sight of the golden eagle, cliff swallow, rock wren, and snowy owl.

In the late 1800s, the badlands were overrun with tourists and geologists seeking souvenirs and fossils. In an attempt to preserve the area, Congress passed legislation creating Badlands National Monument in 1929. In 1939, a presidential proclamation, in cooperation with the state of South Dakota, set aside 110,000 acres to be administered by the National Park Service and the Department of the Interior.

Though there are entrances at both sides of the Badlands National Park (40 miles apart), the entrance at the northeast corner, just south of Cactus Flat, takes you to headquarters and the Visitors' Center, which is located further down the road on the left, near Cedar Pass. Inside, there are displays, exhibits, and recorded slide programs. In the summer, guides conduct nature hikes and evening nature programs in the amphitheater. If you're interested in horseback riding through the monument grounds, you should inquire at the Visitors' Center.

You can drive for 22 miles along a paved road lined with parking areas and lookouts with explanation markers describing geological and botanical phenomena. There are two main hiking trails: the ¾-mile Door Trail, and the longer Cliff Shell nature trail. Both take you into the middle of the multicolored plateaus and soft clay surroundings so you can see them at close range. If you are a photographer, be sure to set out in the early morning or late afternoon, when the rainbows and stripes carved into the jagged hills are clearest. There are campsites at Sage Creek.

If you enter at Cedar Pass, you can drive through the monument and exit at the western Pinnacles entrance, picking up I-90 at Wall for the return trip to Rapid City. Or, you might want to stop in Kadoka, about 30 miles east of Cedar Pass, on the far eastern boundary of Badlands National Park. Information: the Superintendent, Badlands National Park, PO Box 72, Interior, SD 57750 (605 433–5460).

KADOKA – Only 815 people live in this town, but if you're interested in looking at some of the biggest petrified logs in the neighborhood as well as fossilized fish from the period when South Dakota was partially underwater, stop in at Badlands Petrified Gardens, off E Kadoka exit of I-90.

BEST EN ROUTE

Cedar Pass Lodge, Badlands National Monument – In the heart of the rugged badlands, not far from the monument Visitors' Center. Accommodations consist of 19 cabins and a main building with a restaurant and a gift shop. Badlands National Park, PO Box 5, Interior, SD 57750 (605 433–5460).

Black Hills, South Dakota

The fabled Black Hills cover about 6,075 square miles of southwestern South Dakota along the Wyoming border. Famous for mineral deposits and pure grazing land, the Black Hills are actually green: a blend of oak, elm, ash, pine, and aspen. They are, in reality, a far cry from the ominous-sounding name bestowed upon the hills by the Indians, who found them sacred and mysterious.

According to folklore, Paul Bunyan and his blue ox, Babe, created the Black Hills. Hungry, the huge Babe swallowed a stove in the hope of finding nourishment. Unfortunately, his stomach couldn't adapt to this hefty substance and he died. Unable to find a suitable burial ground, Paul Bunyan poured soil over his faithful companion. With time, the rain carved brooks and streams into the mound and brisk winds and birds brought seeds to the undeveloped hills. Thus the Black Hills. To tour the Black Hills from Rapid City, South Dakota, take rt. 16 southwest for 13 miles to Rockerville.

ROCKERVILLE – A veritable ghost town. In its glory during the late 1870s, when $1 million worth of gold was mined out of the surrounding hills, but the town's supply of the valuable mineral ran dry as suddenly as it was found. By 1882, most residents moved further west, leaving empty saloons and cabins to the animals that roamed the hills. But nowadays, the town comes alive in summer, as visitors come to see the old-time saloon, general store, and soda parlor. Mock gunfights are held during the day. In the evenings, there's vaudeville at the Rockerville Meller Drammer Theater, a gaslight theater. All attractions are part of Rockerville Gold Town, rt. 16.

KEYSTONE – One of the first pioneer towns in the area. This is the official address of Mt. Rushmore, three miles from the center of town (see *Mt. Rushmore,* p. 783). You can see Mt. Rushmore from the Rushmore Aerial Tramway, a half mile south of Keystone, on rt. 16A. Also on rt. 16A, you can mine for gold ore and keep anything you find at Big Thunder Gold Mine.

HILL CITY – About ten miles west of Keystone on rt. 16. Here, an 1880s steam train takes you through the Black Hills, past the settings used in the TV series *Gunsmoke.* You can go by train and connecting car to Keystone and back. To make reservations, write 1880s Train, PO Box 1880, Hill City, SD 57445 (605 574-2222). About five miles south of Hill City stands 7,242-foot Harney Peak, the highest point in South Dakota. Look for the detour leading from rt. 385. It will take you to the base of the mountain. From here you must hike to the summit. Harney Peak provides an elegant view of "the Needles," a section of granite pinnacles.

CUSTER – About 25 miles southwest of Keystone on rt. 16 west and rt. 385 south. Nestled along French Creek, this is one of the oldest towns in the Black Hills. Though quartz, mica, beryl, and gypsum are mined in the immediate area, it was gold that brought the town its prosperity. In fact, the first gold strike in the state occurred in 1874 in Custer State Park, where you can swim, fish, and hike. Within the park's 72,000 acres roams one of the largest bison herds in the world. (The park is five miles east on rt. 16A, seven miles north on rt. 89.) Crazy Horse Memorial, now under construction, will be the world's largest sculpture when it's finished. Sculptor Korzak Ziolkowski, formerly an assistant to Gutzon Borglum, the artist who carved Mt. Rushmore, is working on the memorial dedicated to the life of Crazy Horse, the Indian leader who defeated Lt. Col. George Custer and the 7th Cavalry. It is also dedicated to the enduring spirit of man. You can visit Ziolkowski's home and studio, where there's a completed model of the work in progress (five miles north of Custer on rt. 16).

JEWEL CAVE NATIONAL MONUMENT – About 14 miles west of Custer on rt. 16. A myriad of crystal formations create beautiful images and designs. Walking tours and more rigorous spelunking tours are conducted during the summer months, but you should be in good physical condition before considering one. Visitors' Center and exhibit room provide background on local geology (about 14 miles west of Custer on rt. 16). The last weekend in July, the Gold Discovery Days Pageant at Custer attempts to recreate the time of the great gold discovery of 1874. Celebrations include a carnival, a rodeo, and a re-enactment of Gold Rush events.

WIND CAVE NATIONAL PARK – Designated a national park by President Theodore Roosevelt in 1903, the cave got its name from the strong wind currents which blow through its entrance. The winds are believed to be caused by external atmospheric pressures. Most of the 28,000-acre park is above ground, and consists of woodlands and open prairies. Elk, bison, and prairie dogs wander freely among the wildflowers and trees, making this area a favorite of photographers. It's about 15 miles south of Custer on rt. 385.

BLACK HILLS NATIONAL FOREST – The forest covers more than one million acres of dense pine forest seemingly wedged into the crevices of the rugged, jagged hills. Established in 1897, Black Hills National Forest is home to elk, deer, antelope, and mountain goats. Camping, hiking, fishing, and horseback riding facilities are available. Information: the Superintendent, Black Hills National Forest, PO Box 792, Custer, SD 57730 (605 673-2251).

LEAD – Pronounced "leed." Unlike neighboring towns, Lead never ran dry of gold. Homestake Mine has been in operation since 1877. The largest working gold mine in the Western Hemisphere, Homestake offers tours from May through October (on rt. 14A and rt. 85). In winter, Lead is an active ski resort as people arrive to challenge the slopes of Terry Peak, at 7,076 feet the highest ski mountain east of the Rockies. The chair lift to the summit gives you an unparalleled view of Montana, North Dakota, Nebraska, and Wyoming (1½ miles southwest on rt. 14A).

DEADWOOD – Less than five miles east of Lead on rt. 85, Deadwood is primarily a tourist town. Once, however, it was the "get rich quick" spot after Custer ran dry. Wild Bill Hickok, Calamity Jane, and Preacher Smith roamed the streets and caroused at the very well attended saloons. It was here that Wild Bill Hickok lost not only a game of poker but his life. He and other Wild West characters are buried at Mt. Moriah Cemetery. Every summer, Wild Bill Hickok's death is re-enacted at the Old Town Hall. The play is called *The Trial of Jack McCall* (Lee St.). The first weekend of August, Deadwood holds a rodeo and a parade down Main St. to celebrate the "Days of '76." For information call the Chamber of Commerce (605 578–1876).

BEST EN ROUTE

Sylvan Lake Resort, Custer State Park – Located near Sylvan Lake, a popular resort area, this hotel offers fishing and riding. You can stay in cabins or in a standard hotel room. There is a restaurant on the premises. Open May until October. Sylvan Lake Resort, PO Box 752, Custer State Park, Custer, SD 57730 (605 574–2561).

State Game Lodge, Custer State Park – Motel units and cabins, stocked fishing streams, and fine horseback riding trails. Restaurant and cocktail lounge. Pets are welcome. State Game Lodge, Custer State Park, Custer, SD 57730 (605 255–4541).

Rushmore View Motor Lodge, Keystone – Provides a terrific view of Mt. Rushmore without crowds and traffic. Open May until October. PO Box 197, Keystone, SD 57751 (605 666–4466).

Mt. Rushmore National Memorial, South Dakota

Located in Keystone, off rt. 16A, Mt. Rushmore National Memorial rests in the eastern portion of South Dakota's Black Hills, surrounded by trees, streams, and rolling green meadows. The portraits of Presidents Washington, Jefferson, Lincoln, and Theodore Roosevelt, which are carved into the granite cliffs, rise above all else in the area. Mt. Rushmore has become a symbol of America, fittingly known as "the Shrine of Democracy."

Looking at the site from nearby Harney Peak, a 7,242-foot mountain, Mt. Rushmore's designer, Gutzon Borglum, spotted the rectangular block that was later to serve as the base for his presidential masterpiece, and became excited with the possibilities. "There's the place to carve a great national memorial," Borglum exclaimed. "American history shall march along the skyline."

Upon closer inspection, Borglum found Mt. Rushmore was, indeed, ideal for his intended project. Despite a few minor flaws, the surface was smooth, rising 6,000 feet above sea level. The rock face which rested on the southeast corner of the slab was 1,000 feet long and 400 feet wide, and provided maximum daylight and optimum illumination.

Curiously enough, Mt. Rushmore got its name by accident. In fact, there is no connection between the name and the shrine to the four presidents. In the late 19th century, the Black Hills became a haven for gold seekers. Inevitable land disputes followed. One miner, involved in a interminable conflict, hired the services of an Eastern lawyer to settle his claim. The lawyer's name was Rushmore. One day, as he was riding past the rocky plateau with his client, the lawyer inquired as to its name. Kidding, the miner responded that its name was Mt. Rushmore. And 45 years later, in 1930, Mt. Rushmore became the official name.

But the idea to construct a shrine was not as easily accepted. In 1923, Doane Robinson, South Dakota state historian and poet, proposed building a monument dedicated to famous Western heroes such as Lewis and Clark, Kit Carson, and the famous Sioux Indian Red Cloud. But local citizens were reticent to support the idea, failing to grasp the potential significance of such a romantic memorial. Robinson refused to give up, and finally managed to win the support of two influential and wealthy South Dakota residents, Representative William Williamson and Senator Peter Norbeck. Both agreed that the giant sculpture would bring fame and fortune to the quiet Midwestern state, a state primarily known for its mineral-rich Black Hills and never-ending prairies. Robinson and his colleagues found the needed support and in 1924, Gutzon Borglum was called to survey the terrain and discuss the project. Foreseeing the possibilities and intrigued by the challenge, Borglum left Confederate Memorial, which he was carving at Stone Mountain outside Atlanta, Georgia, and headed for the Black Hills.

It was Borglum's idea to create a national memorial that would embrace the merits and symbolize the ideals of our most celebrated presidents. But many people were critical. Wanting no manmade sculpture to destroy the beauty of the rich Black Hills, they made fund raising difficult. Traveling extensively to raise funds, Borglum finally found enough money to begin his greatest work. Aware that people might only react to its size, he declared, "I did not and don't intend that this shall be just a damn big thing, a three-day tourist wonder."

On August 10, 1927, President Calvin Coolidge rode a horse three miles from nearby Keystone to dedicate the beginning of Mt. Rushmore's construction. Sporadic funding forced the project to continue for 14 years, with actual construction taking 6½ years. Borglum, with the help of his son, Lincoln, supervised throughout, overseeing 36 crew members, some of whom came from Borglum's Stone Mountain sculpture in Georgia. Between 1927 and 1941, when the project was completed, nearly $1 million was spent, all but $153,992 from the federal government. Borglum died in March 1941, just prior to Mt. Rushmore's completion. Nevertheless, his lifelong dream became reality only a few months later, under his son's supervision. Since that time, no addition or refinement has been made, despite numerous proposals.

When looking at Mt. Rushmore, you can see the painstaking detail that Borglum inscribed into the tough granite surface; George Washington's jacket collar and Teddy Roosevelt's spectacles are two examples. The faces weren't sculpted by traditional methods. More than 450,000 tons of rock were removed; the outer surface was disassembled with dynamite. Drillers, lowered from above the sculpture, rested on "swing seats" as they chipped away stone just a few inches from the desired depth. Then a smaller drill was used to form a crude outline of the individual faces. The final smooth surface was created by a technique called "bumping" — using an air hammer.

However, even with all the fine detail, it is still the dimensions of the monument which create its impressive aura. The faces measure 60 feet from top of head to chin; the mouths stretch over 18 feet across, and the average nose is 20 feet long. The finished project is a perfect example of that love of size that swept 20th-century America. Mt. Rushmore ranks as one of the largest sculptures in the world, comparable to the ancient Egyptian pyramids and sphinxes.

The symbolism in this "Shrine of Democracy" is as grand and potent as its physical dimensions. Addressing congressional peers in 1928, William Williamson stressed the symbolic, allegorical significance of the memorial. "Washington symbolizes the founding of our country and the stability of our institutions," he said. "Jefferson, our idealism, expansion, and love of liberty; Lincoln, our altruism and sense of inseparable unity. Roosevelt typifies the soul of America — its restless energy, rugged morality, and progressive spirit."

More than two million visitors a year come to Mt. Rushmore, which was carved from 1927 to 1941. The memorial's visitor center is open daily, from

8 AM to sundown. In summer it remains open through early evening. No camping or picnicking permitted. Information: Mt. Rushmore National Memorial, Rt. 16A, Keystone, SD 57751 (605 574–2523).

BEST EN ROUTE

Palmer Gulch Lodge, Hill City – Down-home ranch accommodations with horseback riding, fishing, hiking, and swimming. Cabins can accommodate between 3 and 8 guests. PO Box 295, Hill City, SD 57745 (605 574–2525).

Powder House Lodge, Keystone – Only four miles from Mt. Rushmore, in a mountain setting. Accommodations consist of cabins and motel units. Restaurant has a salad bar and specializes in roast beef. Open May through September. Keystone, SD 57751 (605 666–4646).

Great Salt Lake, Utah

There's a stretch out west, familiar to anyone who has crossed the country on I-80 — that ultimate of American superhighways — where all life seems to stop. On both sides of the shimmering blacktop spread vast reaches of sand, blinding white in the unrelenting sun. The air is hot, dry, and stagnant, and the monotonous flatness inspires mirages. But sometimes, the harsher a place seems, the more interesting it turns out to be, and this is the case with the Great Salt Lake Desert region in Utah.

As you continue driving you will encounter what looks like a gray-blue inland sea which is either the Great Salt Lake or the largest mirage you're ever likely to see. If you're still on I-80, west of Salt Lake City, the lake is no illusion. And as you get closer to the lake, you will find that it is no anomaly in relation to the surrounding landscape, but only to our general concept of lakes and seas. This 30-by-70-mile body of water does not teem with life as one would expect. It is North America's dead sea by virtue of its high salt concentration — 18% to 24% in the southern and eastern waters and as much as 28% in the lake's northern reaches (almost eight times saltier than seawater). The only life that the lake supports is some primitive algae, bacteria, a kind of brine shrimp (¼ inch long and feathery, a semitransparent crustacean used for tropical fish food), and swarms of stingless brine flies that blacken the shores from May to September. Naturally, the water is unfit for drinking, hardly ideal for swimming, and not exactly a fisherman's dream. But what it does offer is eight billion tons of salt, deposits of magnesium, lithium, gypsum, potash, boron, sulfur, and chloride compounds that have lured chemical firms to this liquid mine; and for everyone else, some of the most fantasy-fulfilling floating, wading, and bobbing imaginable.

With a little knowledge of natural history, everything begins to fall into place. The arid and desolate area that surrounds the lake appears as inhospitable as it does because it was once covered by the lake's salty waters. Today's Great Salt Lake is merely a drop in the bucket compared to this earlier sea. Only 23,000 years ago freshwater Lake Bonneville (formed from the melting snows of successive ice ages) stretched from Salt Lake City east into Nevada and north into Idaho, covering an area comparable to Lake Michigan. The lake reached depths exceeding 1,000 feet and encompassed 20,000 square miles. (The terraced striations marking its former shorelines are still visible today on the flanks of the Wasatch Mountains of the Rockies.) When the last of the glaciers waned and the ice retreated northward, weather in this region became hotter and drier. Lake Bonneville shrank below the level of its outlet, and its feeder streams continued to bring in salt which could not escape. Though some water flowed in, the amount was not sufficient to offset evaporation, and the lake grew saltier and saltier. Today, the remnant of this once vast inland sea is so salty that no swimmer can sink in it. The Southern Pacific's rail causeway, built in 1903, divides the lake into two sections of differing salinities. To the south of the dike-supported track, the lake appears bluer because the freshwater inflow dilutes the salinity; the north side approaches saturation. But either side of the tracks provides ample testing grounds for experiments in human buoyancy.

Great Salt Lake State Park Saltair Beach at the southern end of the lake (15 miles west of Salt Lake City on I-80) is one of the two places the public has access to the lake. (For a full report on Salt Lake City, see *Salt Lake City,* THE AMERICAN CITIES.) There is a small entrance fee and the park provides all required equipment — parking lot, concessions, changing rooms, and open-air showers. After you park and change, it's only you and scientific method, so get in there. In the summertime the water will be quite warm, around 80°. The lake is shallow and you will undoubtedly have to wade out a few hundred yards before you can draw any conclusions. But once you are in chest- or neck-deep water you can experiment as you wish. (Floating is easy. You can float sitting up or with arms or legs out of the water. Two can float in tandem, etc.) But there are positions you shouldn't try — any which involve putting your face in or under the water. You won't sink, but that burning sensation in your eyes and nasal and oral passages will make you wish you never set eyes on the Great Salt Lake. After your swim, you will want to rinse off at the open showers to remove the white salty residue left on your body. The park is open year-round and has facilities for camping and boating; you can sunbathe anywhere along the beach (but keep your suit on because Utah law does not look kindly on nudity). There are boat ramps but no rentals. Motorboats are not used because the high salt concentration has a corrosive effect on the motor and metal. Those with boats can get information from the rangers on how to reach some of the lake's islands.

Antelope Island, the other point for public access, is less crowded and can be reached via a 16-mile boat ride or by car (63 miles north along the east shore, reached via Layton, and then a paved road from the mainland). Antelope Island also provides camping and picnic facilities all year. The island is a good jumping-off point for boat trips because it provides access to several other lake islands — Egg and Fremont, where you can see birds and other animals including horses and sheep that are brought here for summer grazing. Gunnison Island in the northwest quadrant of the lake can only be reached via boat and is a nesting site for the great white pelican. Amidst these scrubby bushes and rock heaps, you can spot this magnificent bird, as well as terns and gulls.

Though you'd hardly suspect it as you lie in the warm waters of the Great Salt Lake or watch the seagulls soar, there are a dozen well-developed ski resorts within an hour's drive in the Wasatch Mountain Range east of Salt Lake City. The base elevation is 8,000 feet and the season stretches from November through April, so when it gets too cold to float (although folks of polar-bear habits do immerse themselves year-round), there are plenty of places to ski in what Utahns claim is the greatest skiing spot on earth. There's a good cover of snow, and unlike on the lake, on the slopes the law of gravity prevails — if you fall, you're down. For further information on the Great Salt Lake, contact the Superintendent of the Great Salt Lake State Park, Saltair Beach, PO Box 323, Magna, UT 84044 (801 533-4081).

BEST EN ROUTE

Though there are no developed campsites, you are allowed to drive your car or recreational vehicle onto the beach and spend the night at the Great Salt Lake State Park Saltair Beach. A wide range of accommodations are available in Salt Lake City.

Hotel Utah, Salt Lake City – Still the grande dame of the state; elegant from the crystal chandelier which hangs above the mezzanine to the beautiful new Grand Ballroom. Main and S Temple Sts., Salt Lake City, UT 84111 (801 531-1000).

Salt Lake Hilton, Salt Lake City – This hotel in the city exudes an aura of contemporary sophistication. Suites have sunken baths; there is an outdoor swimming pool, therapy pool, sauna, and five dining rooms. 150 W 5th St. South, Salt Lake City, UT 84101 (801 532-3344).

Zion and Bryce Canyon National Parks, Utah

According to official Utah sources, one-seventh of all the national parks in the United States lie within a 200-mile circle in southern Utah. Two of the most spectacular, Zion and Bryce Canyons, are only 90 miles apart. From Salt Lake City, I-15 proceeds on to Zion National Park. From there, rt. 15 east to rt. 89 north takes you to Bryce Canyon. Continue on rt. 89 north when you leave Bryce Canyon. This will take you into rt. 28, which feeds into I-15 for the trip back to Utah's capital.

ZION NATIONAL PARK – A series of dramatic gorges and canyons, Zion is geologically part of the area which includes the Grand Canyon, 125 miles to the south, and Bryce Canyon, 89 miles northeast. From the air, the three canyons look like a series of steps, with Grand Canyon the first, Zion in the middle, and Bryce Canyon, the top. The middle sibling of this vast natural canyon-scape is younger than the Grand Canyon, and older than Bryce. It dates back to the Mesozoic era, a period no doubt more familiar to you as the time when dinosaurs stalked the earth. (It is possible to see dinosaur footprints in the rocks at Zion if you look diligently enough.) At first a sea, then a desert, Zion's layered buttes and canyons are actually the scars of incredibly harsh climatic changes. These shifts created psychedelic purple, lilac, yellow, and pink rock walls and gorges which shimmer in the clear light. When you see it, you'll know why they call this "the land of rainbow canyons." Most geologists believe Zion Canyon was formed by the Virgin River, which carved a gorge out of deep layers of sediment left from the shallow seas which covered the area. Others attribute its birth to a fissure opening along a fault line, or glacial activity. The erosion theory seems to hold the most weight, since the fast-flowing Virgin River moves over soft, easily eroded rock. We're not sure whether the river was named after explorer Thomas Virgin or the Virgin Mary. There seems to be a running debate among historians, just as there is among geologists. Undebated is the comment of one of the first settlers to explore Zion: Ebenezer Bryce said, "It's one helluva place to lose a cow." (Pets are not permitted on the trails anyway. You'll just have to take Elsie someplace else.) The 229 square miles of Zion National Park (established 1919) were apparently named by a 19th-century Mormon, though who the name-giver was and when it was named are lost to history. We do know that Zion means "heavenly resting place."

Zion is most impressive for the intense and rugged beauty of its canyons, some of which are impassable even today just as they were when white explorers began visiting the area last century, and for the splendid incandescence of the color of its rock formations. There is a breathtaking drive on the Zion–Mt. Carmel Highway, which runs along the canyon valley, zigzagging up Pine Creek Canyon and through the 5,607-foot-long tunnel. This road connecting I-15 and rt. 89 is all the more remarkable when you consider that it was completed in 1930, the year Zion and Bryce Canyons were first photographed from the air.

Any visit should begin at the Zion Visitors' Center near the southern entrance, where there's a museum of geological exhibits and an information center. From the lobby, you'll have an excellent view of multicolored Zion Canyon. If you want to hike along any of the 65 miles of trails, you'll have to pick up a permit at the Visitors' Center before setting out. And be sure to check weather conditions — the trails around the canyon rim are sometimes closed due to snow. From the Visitors' Center, you can also embark on horseback trips to the west rim of Zion Canyon and Sandbench Trail. For a combined driving-hiking expedition, drive to the Temple of Sinawava, eight miles from the south entrance of the park. Inside the amphitheater-shaped temple are the two giant pillars for which the temple got its name: the altar and the pulpit. Once you reach the temple, the road stops, so you'll have to get out and walk. From here, it's a mile along the most popular footpath in the park to the beginning of the Narrows Gorges, where the Virgin River, sometimes no more than 20 feet wide, races through the giant walls of rock where columbine, shooting star, and cardinal flowers grow in spring. You can join a guided nature hike during the summer and camp along the fir-, pine-, and moonflower-lined banks of the river. It's five strenuous miles to Angel's Landing at the top of the canyon, but the view is worth it. There is a two-day backpacking trip along the 12-mile West Rim Trail. The southeastern section of Zion National Park is desert. Parunweap Canyon is the home of lizards, cacti, and Indian cliff dwellers' ruins dating back 500 years. Information: the Superintendent, Zion National Park, Springdale, UT 84767 (801 772-3256).

KANAB – En route to Bryce Canyon, this town of about 13 motels and a handful of restaurants has the distinction of being 20 miles east of a set of coral pink sand dunes used as a location for many a Hollywood movie.

BRYCE CANYON NATIONAL PARK – The Paiute Indians called the stone formations at Bryce Canyon "red rocks standing like men in a bowl" and thought the twisted shapes were evil creatures that had been cast into stone by a vengeful god. The configurations at Bryce Canyon National Park do look disturbingly human and many have been named after the things they resemble. Technically, Bryce's canyons are not canyons at all, but breaks in the earth, tremendous pink and white limestone amphitheaters as deep as 1,000 feet. Standing at the edge of the Paunsaugunt Fault (Paunsaugunt means home of the beaver), Bryce Canyon National Park is laced by an intricate network of tributaries of the Paria River. You can get a great view of the splintered rock plateau stretching away toward the river from the 9,105-foot-high Rainbow Point. (We recommend taking it easy at Bryce Canyon. The 8,900-

foot altitude will tire you quickly. There are plenty of places to rest along the park's trails.)

As at Zion, the best place to start your explorations of Bryce Canyon's 36,000 acres is the Visitors' Center. Here you'll find some interesting geological and archeological exhibits. If you want to take a guided tour on foot or horseback, this is the place to arrange it. There is also a minibus tour, which leaves from Bryce Canyon Lodge. There are 20 miles of driving roads around the rims of the canyons. (Some are closed between November and April due to snow.) Of the several fascinating hiking trails, the most popular is the Navajo Loop Trail, a two-hour excursion which takes you more than 500 feet into a canyon, past the curiously named Wall Street, Temple of Osiris, and Thor's Hammer rock formations. The five-mile Peekaboo Loop passes the so-called Hindu Temples, Wall of Windows, and Three Wise Men. Thousands of other formations stretch, seemingly endlessly, beyond the Fairyland Tower Bridge. Although the Paunsaugunt Fault was given its name because of a preponderance of beaver, hunting for pelts has pretty much wiped them out. You should, however, be able to spot skunk, gray fox, marmot, chipmunk, and squirrel without too much difficulty. Hawk, dove, and owl are among the more prevalent species of winged creatures hovering over Bryce Canyon. This is also one of the best places in the country for photography. Light sparkles here, illuminating the canyons so that they seem to glow from an inner fire. Dawn and dusk are the best times to take pictures. There are two campgrounds, each with a 14-day restriction. Information: the Superintendent, Bryce Canyon National Park, Bryce Canyon, UT 84717 (801 834-5322).

BEST EN ROUTE

Zion Canyon Lodge, Zion National Park – A group of cabins with a total of 120 rooms. There are horseback riding facilities and a snack bar/restaurant. Zion Canyon Lodge is managed by TWA Services, Inc. PO Box TWA, Cedar City, UT 84720 (801-586-7686).

Bryce Canyon Lodge, Bryce Canyon National Park – A collection of cabins with a total of 120 rooms, some with ornamental fireplaces. Bryce Canyon Lodge is managed by TWA Services, Inc., PO Box TWA, Cedar City, UT 84720 (801 586-7686).

Bryce Canyon Pines Motel and Restaurant, Bryce Canyon – About six miles from the park. Facilities include a restaurant and coffee shop, heated swimming pool, and horseback riding. Some of the 34 rooms have fireplaces. Bryce Canyon Pines, Hwy. 12, Panguitch, UT 84759 (801 834-5336).

Mt. Rainier National Park, Washington

Swathed in glaciers, Mt. Rainier reaches 14,410 splendid, icy feet into the sky. A formidable, awesome presence, it is the tallest peak in Washington state (fifth tallest in the lower 48), situated 60 miles southeast of Seattle. Exploring Mt. Rainier's perilous slopes might not be your idea of a holiday. (Not everyone likes to hang upside down from a precipice, fastened to firmament by the mere grace of rope and pick.) Whether or not you would enjoy the challenge of climbing the mountain, your first encounter with Mt. Rainier is sure to be unforgettable.

Even those who are not enamored of mountains, insisting that "when you've seen one, you've seen 'em all," almost invariably return from a visit to Mt. Rainier converted. A solitary giant laced with frosty crevices, this mountain dominates the surrounding area. In fact, the 235,404 acres of Mt. Rainier National Park seem to have been selected specifically to provide natural settings of pine, wildflowers, and lakes against which the craggy Rainier can be seen to best advantage.

A curious combination of glacial and volcanic activity, Mt. Rainier is the product of relatively recent geological phenomena. One would be hard put to establish its precise age, since the mountain itself is the product of those momentous eruptions occurring within the last million years which are also responsible for Mt. Baker, near the Canadian border, Lassen Peak in northern California, and the other peaks in the Cascade Range, to which Rainier belongs.

Climbers approaching Columbia Crest, Mt. Rainier's summit, have reported mini-geysers of steam spurting through the ice, a sign of volcanic activity below. The steam has carved intricate mazes in the mountain's ice, forming a labyrinthine network of ice tunnels and caves which provide mountaineers with protection against the brutally chilling winds that sweep across the craters near the mountaintop. In 1870, the first team to climb Mt. Rainier spent the night before their ascent to the pinnacle safely nestled in one of these burrows. Without these natural caves and tunnels to provide shelter, they would probably have died from exposure. Mt. Rainier's glacial system, the most extensive "single peak" network in the country (apart from Alaska), consists of 41 glaciers. Their age is estimated to be a mere 10,000 years, a legacy of the last, massive Ice Age Retreat. Carbon Glacier is Mt. Rainier's longest — six miles; Emmons Glacier, almost 4½ miles long by 1 mile wide, the largest. If you're curious about geological activity, this is the best place for observing icy and subterranean thermal forces in action. The Nisqually Glacier moves between 50 feet and 400 feet a year. Whereas most glaciers seem to be shrinking, Mt. Rainier's expand, flowing down toward the valleys.

Declared a national park in 1899, Mt. Rainier National Park is surrounded by national forests. Snoqualmie National Forest forms the eastern, northern, and western boundaries. Gifford Pinchot National Forest is to the south.

To get to Mt. Rainier National Park from Seattle, take I-5 south about 32 miles to Tacoma, then pick up rt. 410, which will take you directly to Mt. Rainier; or, you can drive inland on rt. 169, picking up rt. 410 in Enumclaw.

MT. BAKER–SNOQUALMIE NATIONAL FOREST – Stretches 160 miles from the Canadian border to Yakima. Spruce and fir trees cover 2,513,000 acres which include Mt. Baker, a 10,778-foot dormant volcano, 390 glaciers, and 2,500 miles of trails, including sections of the Pacific Crest Trail. Ski centers at Snoqualmie Pass, White Pass, Stevens Pass, Mt. Baker, and Mt. Pilchuck. Campsites open in summer. On rt. 410, just north of Mt. Rainier National Park. Park headquarters located at 1601 2nd Ave., Seattle, WA 98101 (206 442-5440).

CRYSTAL MOUNTAIN – A year-round resort with excellent ski facilities in winter. Year-round chair lift offers a breathtaking view, sweeping from Mt. Rainier to Mt.

Hood in Oregon. The Washington Cascade Crest Trail leads to nearby mountains. In Snoqualmie National Forest on rt. 410 (206 663-2265).

GIFFORD PINCHOT NATIONAL FOREST – More than 1.2 million acres of fir and spruce, dominated by Mt. Adams and Mt. St. Helens. Mt. St. Helens, dormant since 1842, stirred to life in March 1980. A series of earthquakes and minor eruptions culminated in a massive explosion that blasted nearly 1,300 feet off the top of the 9,677-foot mountain on May 18, 1980. The story of the eruptions is presented in two Forest Service interpretive centers: One is located on rt. I-5, 15 miles north of Vancouver, Washington, and the other is at Lewis and Clark State Park on Jackson Highway, about 12 miles south of Chehalis. Mt. Adams, a 12,326-foot monster with glaciers, forests, and lava flows, is the Pacific Northwest's second largest peak. At its base, the Pacific Crest Trail leads from the western side of the mountain through Goat Rocks Wilderness. There are 57 campgrounds in different parts of the forest. Open in summers. Borders Mt. Rainier National Park to the south. Headquarters located at 500 E 12th St., Vancouver, WA 98660 (206 696-4041).

MT. RAINIER NATIONAL PARK – Enter the park via Mather Memorial Parkway, a 50-mile paved road that takes you to the White River entrance where the road forks. You can continue south to Stevens Canyon and the Ohanapecosh Visitors' Center and campground, or east, to the Sunrise Visitors' Center and campgrounds, near Frozen Lake and Mt. Fremont, a respectable 7,230 feet. The campground is about a mile from the road. Stevens Canyon Road, a section of the 117-mile network of paved roads, takes you along the southern boundary, past the Tatoosh Range, and 5,995-foot Eagle Peak. The road passes Longmire, Paradise Visitors' Center, and the Nisqually entrance and ranger station, in the southwest corner of the park. The visitors' center distributes free information on hiking and climbing. Be sure to pick up the booklet entitled *Fragile, Handle with Care* before setting out. Guides conduct expeditions from Paradise Visitors' Center in summer. In winter, Paradise is headquarters for snowshoe walks and cross-country skiing. At Paradise, Longmire, or Sunrise Visitors' Centers, you can pick up the Wonderland Hiking Trail, a 90-mile route that encircles the base of Mt. Rainier. Wonderland takes you past Box Canyon, waterfalls, fields with wildflowers in season, Golden Lakes, Carbon River, Carbon Glacier, and the Mowich Glaciers. Campsites are spaced every 12 miles along the trail. Northern Loop Trail extends 17½ miles from Wonderland Trail through backcountry meadows, to Chenuis Mountain, at an elevation of 6,400 feet. Pick up a permit at a visitors' center if you intend to camp overnight at any of the sites along the 300-mile network of interlacing trails.

The 1963 US Mt. Everest Expedition trained on Mt. Rainier, but you don't have to be preparing to tackle the world's largest mountain to get to Rainier's peak. You can take a one-day or a five-day course in mountain climbing techniques at the national park's Paradise Guide House, Rainier Mountaineering Inc. (201 St. Helens, Tacoma, WA 98402, 206 627-1105). All climbers are required to register at one of the visitors' centers before setting out, and there are restrictions on the number of people allowed in each party. Park officials have also set requirements for health, equipment, and leadership qualifications. All expeditions are monitored. Every year, about 2,500 people brave the slopes between the end of May and Labor Day. Even in good weather, sudden storms can envelop the mountain in gales of Himalayan ferocity, and, on quiet days, the glacial movements sometimes form new crevasses. At any moment, sudden rockfalls can tear out hunks of trail. The best time to climb is mid-July, after the summer storms have passed, but before the constant summer heat wears down the ice, causing unstable mountain conditions. Generally, the climb takes two days, with an overnight stop at Camp Muir, a shelter at 10,000 feet. You can rent or buy camping gear at Paradise Guide House. Information: write the Superintendent, Mt. Rainier National Park, Ashford, WA 98304 (206 569-2211).

BEST EN ROUTE

Crystal Mountain, Crystal Mountain – A self-contained Alpine village with Silver Skis Chalet and Crystal Chalets condominiums, with heated pool, night skiing, and grocery stores. Crystal House, Crystal Inn, and Alpine Inn, the three hotels on the premises, have 120 rooms. 100 condo units available all year. Off rt. 410. Write Crystal Mountain, Inc., Crystal Mountain, WA 98022 (206 663-2265).

Alta Silva, Crystal Mountain, Washington – A small, rustic, chalet-style apartment complex. Horses are available for summertime excursions. Fishing and hunting trips organized. Each unit has a full kitchen, fireplace, and sleeps four to nine; economical for larger groups, moderate to expensive for couples. On rt. 410. Write Alta Silva, PO Box 198, Star Route, Enumclaw, WA 98022 (206 663-2238).

Mt. Rainier National Park, Washington – Near Paradise Visitors' Center, elevation 5,400 feet, Paradise Inn has lodge-type lobby with two open fireplaces, cocktail lounge, snack bar. Dining room. 117 rooms. Open from mid-June to Labor Day. Near Longmire Visitors' Center, elevation 2,700 feet, National Park Inn offers meal service and a gas station. Open daily mid-April through December; weekends and holidays the rest of the year. 16 rooms. For reservations, write Manager, Paradise Inn or National Park Inn, Mt. Rainier Hospitality Service, 4820 S Washington, Tacoma, WA 98409 (206 475-6260).

Olympic National Park, Washington

The heart of the Olympic peninsula in western Washington state, Olympic National Park covers 1,400 square miles of diverse terrain. On the western edge of the peninsula lies a 50-mile stretch of wild Pacific beachfront. Hundreds of offshore islands nestle among the inlets and coves which are home to many communities of seals and other marine and amphibious creatures. Inland, numerous small lakes dot the landscape, filling glacial pits which scarred the earth when giant masses of ice withdrew to the north at the end of the Ice Age about 10,000 years ago. The lakes are part of a thriving water system, and the Olympic peninsula is the wettest spot in the continental US, with an average annual precipitation of 50.7 inches. It is cloudy more than 220 days each year, and wet 160 days. Temperatures are in the 70s in summer, in the 30s in winter. Here, too, are junglelike, complex, and primeval rain forests, with ancient ferns nearly as tall as the trees. Not far from the rain forests, glacier-capped mountains tower into the sky. The biggest is Mt. Olympus, a 7,965-foot peak in the center of the park. All told, about 60 glaciers cover some 25 square miles of mountainous terrain, in frosty juxtaposition to the lush vegetation nearby.

Discovered in 1592 by the Spanish explorer Juan de Fuca, for whom the strait connecting the Pacific with Puget Sound was later named, the Olympic Peninsula was home to the Coast Salish Indians, an artistic civilization with an intense economic and spiritual kinship to the sea. In 1804, explorers Lewis and Clark found their way to the peninsula. They were followed by a stream of trappers and traders, whose presence brought germs to which the Indians were not immune. A series of appalling epidemics and conflicts with the white settlers wiped out many of the original inhabitants. Today, the descendants of the Salish survivors live in reservations. The Quileute and Hoh Indian reservations are actually part of Olympic National Park's coastal area. The Ozette and Makah Indian reservations can be found in the northwestern corner of the peninsula; the Skokomish and Nisqually Indian reservations, in the southeast. Olympic National Park itself was established in 1938, and the coastal area came under federal protection in 1953.

Located 75 miles west of Seattle, Olympic National Park is accessible from US Highway 101, which loops around the peninsula. From Seattle, you can take a Washington State Ferry across Puget Sound to the Kitsap Peninsula, then take another ferry across the Hood Canal near the site of a floating bridge that was destroyed by a windstorm in February 1979. Or, if you prefer, take I-5 south from Seattle to Olympia and pick up US Highway 101 north. This road loops around the eastern, northern, and western coasts of the peninsula. You have to pick up US 12 at Aberdeen to complete the circular route to Olympia, a distance of 50 miles.

The major entrance to Olympic National Park is Port Angeles, site of the largest of three Visitor Information Centers and the Pioneer Memorial Museum with exhibits on local fauna, flora, and minerals. Heart o' the Hills Road, a path 18 miles long that ascends to an elevation of nearly a mile, begins here. Halfway up, at Lookout Point, you can see across the Strait of Juan de Fuca to British Columbia, and to Mt. Baker, when visibility is good. Perched at the top of the road, Hurricane Ridge Lodge is a good place to catch your breath and pick up more information. If you plan to explore the wilderness or camp, you must get a permit here. You can embark on Big Meadow Nature Trail on foot, or you can continue by car along an unpaved mountain road to Obstruction Point, at 6,450 feet. Unless it's shrouded in fog, Mt. Olympus should be staring you smack in the face. A number of the park's hiking trails commence from Obstruction Point. One leads to Deer Park Campground. You can't reserve space in advance at any of the campsites, so it's advisable to carry rain gear if you plan to sleep outdoors. The maximum stay permitted at any site is 14 days.

Lake Crescent is about 15 miles west of Port Angeles on rt. 101, still in mountain country. Stop in at the Visitor Information Center at Storm King for brochures and camping permits. On the western shore of the lake, you can pick up the road to Soleduck Hot Springs, Soleduck Campground, and the Seven Lakes Basin.

Named after the mythological home of the Greek gods, and covered by six glaciers, some as thick as 900 feet, 7,965-foot Mt. Olympus gets about 200 inches of snow and rain a year, making it the wettest spot of the lower 48.

On the western edge of the park stands the Hoh rain forest; the Visitor Information Center will provide you with information on the numerous species of shrubs, fungi, mosses, and trees. This is the home of the giant Sitka spruce, which often grows as high as 40 feet. Roosevelt elk, deer, bear, raccoon, and dozens of different species of birds live in this neck of the woods.

One of the park's finest attributes is its Pacific Coast area, 50 miles of rugged beachfront studded with giant rocks. Home of seagulls, eagles, seals, and sea lions. Campsites open in summer. Fishing boats can be chartered at La Push. Unlike the Makah Indians (below), the Quinault Indians at the reservation five miles to the south do not welcome tourists. Information: the Superintendent, Olympic National Park, 600 E Park Ave., Port Angeles, WA 98362 (206 452-4501).

MAKAH INDIAN RESERVATION – About 10 miles west of Lake Crescent, pick up a small road running north from Sappho, bearing left onto rt. 112 northwest to Clallam Bay. Continue to the northwesternmost tip of the peninsula at Neah Bay, a fishing village where the Makah Indians operate several charter fishing companies, motels, and crafts shops. There's a museum at Neah Bay containing the archeological material excavated by teams from Washington State University. There are campsites at Makah Bay, one mile south of Neah Bay. For information contact the travel secretary at the Makah Tribal Office, PO Box 115, Neah Bay, WA 98357 (206 645-2205).

OLYMPIC NATIONAL FOREST – Forms the eastern and northern borders of the national park with 651,000 acres of rain forest vegetation. Campsites in the Quinault Lake and Hood Canal area open in summer. For information, contact Olympic National Forest Headquarters, Federal Building, Olympia, WA 98501 (206 753-9534).

BEST EN ROUTE

Olympic National Park – Lodges run by the same concession that handles accommodations in Big Bend, Mammoth Caves, Isle Royal, and Blue Ridge National Parks. Lake Crescent Lodge has 33 one- and two-room cabins and 20 motel units and is near hiking trails, boating, and fishing areas. There are 16 campgrounds in the park. For information or reservations, write National Park Concessions, Inc., Star Route 1, Box 11, Port Angeles, WA 98362 (206 928-3211).

Makah Motel, Makah Reservation – Leased from the Makah Indian tribe, there are 11 rooms, some with kitchens. Open all year. PO Box 251, Neah Bay, WA 98357. On Main St. (206 645-2366).

Makah Restaurant, Makah Reservation – Across the street from the motel, serving seafood, hamburgers, steaks, and french fries. Open daily. On Main St., Neah Bay (206 645-2476).

Devils Tower National Monument, Wyoming

In the film *Close Encounters of the Third Kind,* François Truffaut holds up a picture of Devils Tower, asking, "Have you ever seen anything like this?" "Sure," says Richard Dreyfuss. "I've got one just like it in my living room."

If you've seen the movie, you undoubtedly know that Devils Tower is the site selected for encounters of the third kind (physical contact) with beings from another planet. And, if you've seen the movie, you're also aware that one aspect of the initial contacts is the implantation of a psychic image of Devils Tower in the minds of American men and women, who then become obsessed with visions of the tower, which they are driven to reproduce by sketching, painting, or even sculpting a giant replica.

Whether or not you've seen the film, your first encounter with Devils Tower

National Monument will most probably be overwhelming. A gargantuan landmark rising suddenly in the middle of a vast Wyoming plain, Devils Tower is the only outstanding physical feature in the northeastern sector of the state. On a clear day you can see it from as far as a hundred miles away.

Devils Tower is close to the western edge of the Black Hills National Forest in South Dakota. If you're coming from Rapid City, South Dakota, or the Black Hills, take I-90 or rt. 34 west (rt. 34 becomes rt. 24 when you cross the Wyoming state line). It's about 90 miles. You can also get there on rt. 14. Devils Tower National Monument covers 1,346 acres of land between the towns of Sundance and Hulett.

Pioneers traversing the Great Plains by horse and wagon used it as a guidepost, as had the first white explorers and, before them, the Indians. Some of those Indians called it Mateo Tepee, meaning Grizzly Bear Lodge. Others referred to it as Bad God's Tower, and it was by this name the first US Geological Survey party became acquainted with it in 1875, later Americanizing its name to Devils Tower. According to one legend, the Bad God (Satan) beats on the top of the tower as on a drum to frighten the land during thunderstorms. Kiowa Indians, however, mythologically ascribe the tower's origin to an incident in which several bears tried to attack seven young Indian maidens. The Great Spirit saved them by lifting the rock on which they were standing to a great height; thus, the tower. In this version, those deep, vertical ridges on the sides of the tower were formed by the bears' frustrated scratching in an attempt to reach their prey. When the animals died from exhaustion, the Great Spirit lifted the little girls to the sky and transformed them into the constellation Pleiades. We don't know whether or not President Theodore Roosevelt was aware of these myths, but in 1906, he decided Devils Tower was important enough to become the country's first national monument.

Since then, it has intrigued visitors from all over the world. Geologists, curious about the huge rock, have come to its base at the foot of the Belle Fourche River, fascinated by the layers of sedimentary rock and vegetation. According to scientific estimates, the tower dates back about 50 million years, the end product of a geological process involving molten rock bubbling up from the center of the earth and cooling. The fluted, strangely symmetrical sides of the monolith also provide a visible lesson in how plants are formed. Although the formidable, barren-looking tower hardly seems a hospitable environment for botanical life, the rock attracts lichens which slowly erode the solid mineral surface into tiny fragments. As dust blows in from the prairie, little pockets of soil nestle in the cracks, attracting moss and liverwort. As the soil deepens, grass and wildflowers grow. Sagebrush and other shrubs cluster closer to the base, while, lining the very bottom, aspen and pine trees take root. About a half mile from the base, a prairie dog community burrows intricate underground mazes. Once considered the enemy of farmers because of the holes they dig, these little ground squirrels are now an endangered species. (The colony at Devils Tower is one of the few protected communities of prairie dogs in the US.)

If you want to climb to the top of the tower, make sure you get special permission from the supervisor at the Visitors' Center. (We're pretty sure you won't see any UFOs when you get up there. Devils Tower officials insist no one has reported any. But there has been an influx of visitors hopeful of a sighting in the wake of the movie.) Scaling the sides has become a lot more feasible since 1893, when William Rogers reached the summit. Instead of climbing, he actually wedged a wooden ladder device between the vertical ridges of the rock. In 1937, the first team of three climbers reached the top by traditional methods. If you're contemplating the climb, remember there are now 38 ways to reach the acre-and-a-half top of the giant, tree-stump-shaped tower. And when you get there, you'll probably encounter falcons' and hawks' nests. The park supervisor will give you a book of regulations when you apply for special permission to ascend. If you're not up for an assault on the tower itself, you might just want to wander along the Tower Trail, and watch the prairie dogs burrow. You'll also catch glimpses of rabbit, chipmunk, and, if you're lucky, whitetail and mule deer. (Deer come out to feed at sunset.) The Visitors' Center will provide you with a guide to the nature trail and a list of 89 birds known to inhabit the monument grounds.

Although inclement weather tends to keep people away in winter, Devils Tower National Monument is open year-round. Because of its isolated location, you'll find yourself alone with the four staff members if you head out there any time between October and March. There are cross-country ski trails lacing the grounds, and plenty of room to stretch, but the 51 campsites might well be closed due to snow since the rangers don't maintain the road in rough weather. "It's mostly a summer park," Devils Tower superintendent Homer Robinson explained. "That's when we run the campfire programs, nature walks, and climbing expeditions."

Whether you come to climb, to explore the geology and nature, to photograph the mysterious, dramatic rock, or to muse about the spectacular possibility of creatures from outer space landing on the top, you'll be fascinated by Devils Tower's mystique, as have thousands of others. And who knows? After seeing the real thing, you might decide that you, too, want one just like it in your living room. Information: the Superintendent, Devils Tower National Monument, Devils Tower, WY 82714 (307 467-5370) or the Wyoming Travel Commission, I-25 at Etchepare Circle, Cheyenne, WY 82002 (307 777-7777 or toll-free, 800 443-2789).

BEST EN ROUTE

Dampier's Paradise Valley, Four Corners – About 45 miles southeast of Devils Tower, with ranch house, trailer hookup, and cabins. Near hiking, rodeos, and trout fishing. Accommodations for 30 guests. James and Marilyn Dampier, General Delivery, Four Corners, WY 82715 (307 746-4797).

Grand Teton National Park and Jackson Hole, Wyoming

Grand Teton National Park is located just south of Yellowstone National Park in northwestern Wyoming near the Idaho border. The park encompasses

310,000 acres of the most spectacular part of the Teton Range, the "youngest" stretch of peaks in the Rockies — a mere 10 million years old.

Early French-Canadian fur trappers gave the Tetons their name, French for "big breasts." Perhaps they had been a long time on the trail, or their naming of the mountains represented wishful thinking, for there is nothing smooth, soft, or voluptuous about the jagged, irregular spires of the Teton Range. The name is doubly ironic since there are three mountains named Teton: Grand, Middle, and South Teton. In 1806, when John Colter left the Lewis and Clark expedition to explore Yellowstone, directly north of Jackson Hole, he brought back fantastic tales of boiling springs, powerful geysers, and sulfurous fumes spouting from the earth. People back East didn't believe his wild stories and nicknamed the place "Colter's Hell." If Yellowstone is Colter's Hell, then by rights the Grand Tetons, with their tranquil, majestic beauty, should be called "Colter's Heaven." Although there are higher mountains in North America, the Tetons have a special visual impact because their sheer volcanic mass rises abruptly without foothills from the peaceful flat valley of Jackson Hole, Wyoming.

Jackson Hole ("hole" is an old fur trappers' term for an enclosed mountain valley) is about 50 miles long and 6 to 12 miles wide, with several highways leading to different parts of the valley. The town of Jackson is south of Grand Teton National Park. Coming from Yellowstone National Park, take the Jackson Hole Highway, which runs alongside the Snake River from Yellowstone. Most of the valley is accessible by automobile year-round.

GRAND TETON NATIONAL PARK – As you head for park headquarters at Moose Visitors' Center, be sure to stop at the spectacular Signal Mountain overlook. (Moose, Colter Bay, and Jenny Lake Visitors' Centers distribute information on hiking, fishing, camping, and the history of the Grand Tetons.) There are hundreds of miles of hiking trails crisscrossing the park, many of them following ancient Indian trails past hidden streams and icy mountain lakes. One three-hour excursion includes a boat ride across Jenny Lake and a vigorous hike of two miles to Hidden Falls and Inspiration Point. The tour leaves the East Shore Dock at Jenny Lake about every half-hour from 7 AM to 6 PM. A bit more difficult is the Skyline Trail which climbs to an elevation of two miles above sea level. There's another, less strenuous hike, along the Indian Paintbrush Trail, known for its resplendent wildflowers and wonderful views of the lakes and mountains. Both Skyline and Indian Paintbrush Trails are suitable for people in reasonably good physical condition. (Be forewarned, however, that the park rangers' idea of "reasonably good physical condition" might well be considerably more rigorous than your own.) You can rent canoes and boats on Jackson and Jenny Lakes, launch your own (you must have a permit, available from Moose Visitors' Center). There are scheduled boat rides on Jackson Lake, the longest in the valley. Guided rubber raft trips down the Snake River leave from Jackson Lake Lodge. The trips range from tame to wild-and-woolly, but they all give you a chance to see elk, antelope, bighorn sheep, moose, buffalo, and black bears roaming freely along the shores. There are over a dozen routes to the summit of Grand Teton Mountain, 13,770 feet high. Some are relatively easy, but one is considered to be among the most difficult in the nation. Exum Mountain Guides of Jenny Lake offers a two-day mountain climbing course, and has guides to take you up Mt. Owen, Mt. Moran, or Grand Teton in summer (PO Box 570, Wilson, WY 83014, 733-2276). You can rent horses at Colter Bay, Jenny Lake, or Jackson Lake Lodge. There are five campgrounds, and permits are required for wilderness camping.

For information, write the Superintendent, Grand Teton National Park, PO Box 170, Moose, WY 83012 (307 733-2880).

BRIDGER-TETON NATIONAL FOREST – Adjoins the national park to the east, and extends north to flank Yellowstone National Park. Combined with Bridger National Forest, the land takes in more than three million acres of forest, river, mountain, and wilderness. Trout fishing in streams, mountain lake fishing, 3,000 miles of hiking trails, and the National Elk Refuge are the major attractions. There are 12 campgrounds and an aerial tramway which rises to 10,500 feet — great for sightseeing in summer, skiing in winter. Information: the Superintendent, Bridger-Teton National Forest, FS Building, Jackson, WY 83001 (307 733-2752).

TARGHEE NATIONAL FOREST – Stretches from the western boundary of Grand Teton National Park to Idaho, covering more than 1.6 million acres. Fishing, rafting, swimming, and camping in summer; skiing in winter at Grand Targhee Winter Sports Area in Alta, Wyoming. Information on Targhee National Forest: the Superintendent, Targhee National Forest, 420 N Bridge St., St. Anthony, ID 83445 (208 624-3151).

JACKSON HOLE – One of the nation's foremost ski resorts, with the biggest vertical drops and longest runs to be found anywhere in the US. There are three world-famous ski resorts in the Jackson Hole area: Teton Village, with Rendezvous Peak; Snow King; and Grand Targhee, all of which are located in the national forest. Teton Village, 12 miles west of Jackson, has more extensive beginning and intermediate slopes than those found at 90% of the major ski resorts in the country, as well as some of the toughest slopes around. An excellent place for a family whose members have different levels of skiing ability. Snow King Mountain, at Jackson, is renowned for its challenging, steep slopes. Grand Targhee is an hour's drive from Jackson over Teton Pass, on rts. 22 and 33, but it offers excellent skiing from the very early fall to very late spring. Jackson Hole has more than just impressive ski facilities, excellent food, and après-ski entertainment. In fact, its most important feature is something other ski areas often lack — snow. In one recent year, the US Forest Service had already recorded 161 inches of new snow by the opening day of the ski season — more than most ski resorts get in an entire year. In summer, more than 130,000 people come to Jackson Hole to sign on for quiet, leisurely Snake River floating excursions, or more exciting whitewater trips. There are more than a dozen float trip operators in the area. Two of the best are Barker-Ewing (PO Box 1243, Jackson, WY 83001, 307 733-3410) and Jack Dennis Float Trips (PO Box 286, Jackson, WY 83001, 307 733-3270). The Jackson Hole area has the best fishing in the Rockies; local cutthroat trout are legendary. Information: Jackson Hole Ski Area, Teton Village, WY 83025 (307 733-4005, or toll-free 800 445-6931).

BEST EN ROUTE

Jackson Lake Lodge, Grand Teton National Park – Boating and fishing expeditions, swimming, horseback riding, and restaurant. 385 rooms. Grand Teton Lodge Company, PO Box 240, Moran, WY 83013 (307 543-2855).

Jenny Lake Lodge, Grand Teton National Park – Log cabins in rustic setting. Boating and fishing expeditions, hiking trips, horseback riding, and restaurant. 30 rooms. Grand Teton Lodge Company, PO Box 240, Moran, WY 83013 (307 733-4647).

Colter Bay Village, Grand Teton National Park – Log cabins with full water sports and horseback riding facilities. Restaurant. 209 rooms. Grand Teton Lodge Company, PO Box 240, Moran, WY 83013 (307 543-2855).

Alpenhof, Teton Village – Chalet-style mountain lodge with pool, sauna, close to skiing. Fireplaces in lounge, good American and Continental restaurant. 40 rooms. PO Box 288, Teton Village, WY 83025 (307 733-3242).

Hitching Post Lodge, Jackson – Specializes in cookouts and chuck wagon breakfasts. Heated pool. 17 rooms. Open May through September. PO Box 521, Jackson, WY 83001 (307 733-2606).

Yellowstone National Park, Wyoming

Nowhere on earth is the raw power of nature more apparent than at Yellowstone National Park. We learn as schoolchildren that the face of the earth is constantly changing — mountain ranges are formed and then eroded; lakes are born and then slowly degenerate into swamps; ice ages come and go, forever changing the contour of the land. But all these things take thousands, even millions of years, and the inner forces that shape the earth we live on are rarely perceptible to us.

At Yellowstone, however, the awesome grandeur of the earth's primal forces can be seen, felt, smelled, and heard. The ground rumbles as a geyser shoots thousands of gallons of scalding water into the air, steam hisses and roars from crevasses in the earth, hellish sulfurous odors fill the air, mud flats boil and bubble. Yellowstone combines the grandeur of creation with the mightiness of destruction.

Yellowstone was the first national park to be established anywhere in the world (1872). Yellowstone is the largest of our national parks, covering 3,474 square miles — about two-thirds the size of Connecticut. Although most of the park lies in northwestern Wyoming, it also stretches into Montana and Idaho. There are entrances at Gardiner, Montana (north), West Yellowstone, Montana (west), Jackson, Wyoming/Grand Teton National Park (south), Cody, Wyoming (east), and Cooke City, Montana (northeast). The entrance at Gardiner is open all year. The other entrances are closed to cars from mid-December through March. The John D. Rockefeller Memorial Parkway leads from Grand Teton National Park to the south entrance of Yellowstone. Western, Northwest Orient, and Frontier Airlines serve nearby cities and provide bus transportation to the park. All Yellowstone entrances are open in winter to snowmobiles and heated snow coaches and are also accessible on foot—skis or snowshoes. Yellowstone's winter season runs from mid-December through March.

The superstar of Yellowstone is Old Faithful. It has been erupting on an average of once every 64½ minutes ever since it was discovered over 100 years ago. The average period between eruptions is deceptive; the period between performances has varied from a record low of 33 minutes to a record high of 2 hours and 28 minutes. Though not the largest geyser in Yellowstone, Old Faithful is among the most dependable, shooting thousands of gallons of steaming water from 120 to 170 feet into the air for periods of two to five minutes.

Over 200 other geysers in the park make Yellowstone the greatest geyser region in the world. (Only three other areas in the world have concentrations of geysers — Iceland, New Zealand, and Siberia.) Yellowstone also has an estimated 10,000 hot springs, mud pots, and fumaroles (natural vents in the earth that shoot out superheated steam). The fuel for this thermal activity lies 15,000 feet below the surface of the earth where a chamber of magma (molten rock) heats the overlying layers of stone. A geyser occurs where groundwater seeps into underground crevasses in the red-hot rocks. The water is superheated to over twice its boiling point. At first, the pressure of the thousands of gallons of overlying water prevents the superheated liquid from turning to steam. Finally the pressure becomes so great that some of the water is pushed out through the cone of the geyser. As the pressure drops, the superheated water instantly distills into steam and blasts out of the geyser's cone.

Geyser basins cover less than 2% of Yellowstone. Even without the geysers, Yellowstone would still be an important national park. The Grand Canyon of the Yellowstone, with a waterfall twice as high as Niagara and canyon walls splashed with multicolored rock, deserves that status by itself. There's also a unique petrified forest, with trees that remained upright just as they were when they were covered with volcanic dust and turned to stone thousands of years ago. Yellowstone Lake is the largest mountain lake in North America and one of the highest lakes of its size in the world; only Lake Titicaca in Peru has a higher elevation.

All Yellowstone's major attractions are accessible by car. The famous Grand Loop is a 142-mile-long road that traces a circular route around the park. Counting the trip into and out of the park, your visit to Yellowstone will be about 200 miles long. You should plan on a minimum of two or three days to see the major attractions.

The park's headquarters and museum and the Mammoth Hot Springs are near the Gardiner entrance. At the springs you will see bizarre-looking terraced pools formed on the side of Terrace Mountain by mineral-rich water from the hot springs. Some of the terraces are growing at the rate of a foot a year as the hot springs dissolve the subterranean limestone beds under the mountain and redeposit the minerals on the surface. Terrace Mountain is quite literally turning itself inside out. Over the course of a few years, you could watch a mountain growing before your eyes.

The Norris Geyser Basin is 21 miles south of Mammoth Hot Springs. A Visitors' Center has explanatory exhibits and guided walks through the main basin. There's also a two-mile-long trail through the lower basin.

The west entrance (via rts. 20 and 191) joins the Grand Loop at Madison Junction. Heading south, the Grand Loop goes along the banks of the Firehole River, a stream that's fed by dozens of hot springs in its bed.

Old Faithful is just 16 miles south of Madison Junction, where there is a Visitors' Center with fine exhibits and dioramas. The surrounding geyser basins — Upper, Midway, and Lower — have some of the best geysers, hot springs, and mud pots in the park.

The John D. Rockefeller Memorial Parkway joins the Grand Loop 17 miles east of Old Faithful. The road hugs the shore of Yellowstone Lake all the way up to its northern end. Yellowstone Lake has great fishing for cutthroat trout (although there are strict catch limitations). Boats and tackle are available at Grant Village along the Rockefeller Highway and at Fishing Bridge on the north shore.

North of Fishing Bridge, the Grand Loop leads to the 24-mile-long Grand

Canyon of the Yellowstone. The river has carved a twisting canyon 1,200 feet deep. The predominant color of the stone face of the canyon walls is, of course, yellow, but the canyon is also tinted with colors ranging from pale saffron to bright orange.

The Upper Falls of the Yellowstone mark the beginning of the canyon. The water moves with such force that it appears to arch through the air rather than fall. Farther along is the magnificent Lower Falls, which are twice as high as Niagara. The Upper Falls are easy to see; the best view of the Lower Falls is from a trail leading to them. Inspiration Point, which juts far out into the canyon, offers incredible views of the river raging below.

At Tower Junction, the northeast entrance road joins the Grand Loop. Nearby, the spectacular Tower Falls drop 132 feet. From Tower Junction, the Loop leads past Yellowstone's petrified forest to the park headquarters at Mammoth Hot Springs.

There are four hotels/motels along the Grand Loop (see *Best en Route*) and some of the major campgrounds are at Bridge Bay, Grant Village, Lewis Lake, Madison Junction, Pebble Creek, and Tower Fall. Keep in mind, however, that Yellowstone is packed to the treetops with tourists during mid-summer, especially in July and August. If you are planning to visit during that period, try to make reservations well in advance of your trip. The park service has a radio station that gives visitors recorded messages about lodging, campsites, and other information.

One message that is constantly repeated is a warning that it is illegal to feed the animals, especially the bears. Bears can turn from cute, cuddly creatures to vicious wild animals in a split second.

Yellowstone presents the park service with a dilemma. It is one of the most popular national parks and millions of people visit each year, causing traffic jams and leaving behind tons of litter. Visitors are constantly demanding that the park service expand the facilities. In doing that, however, some of the unique character of Yellowstone would be destroyed. The last major expansion program took place in the late 1950s. In 1959, Yellowstone was shaken by a series of huge earthquakes that knocked down half a mountain — almost as if the earth were reasserting its sovereignty over Yellowstone and cautioning those who wanted to exploit and commercialize this region that they should regard Yellowstone with awe and treat it with proper respect.

For more information on facilities and campgrounds in Yellowstone contact: National Park Service, PO Box 168, Yellowstone National Park, WY 82190, five miles south of the north entrance at Mammoth Hot Springs (307 344-7381).

BEST EN ROUTE

TWA Services, Inc., is a concessionaire that offers lodging, meals, and tours around the park. For further information, contact TWA Services, Yellowstone Division, Yellowstone National Park, WY 82190 (307 344-7311).

Old Faithful Snow Lodge – The only accommodations open during the winter season (mid-December to mid-March) as well as the summer. 185 rooms. On Loop Rd. next to Old Faithful.

Lake Yellowstone Hotel and Cabins – Overlooks lake and provides easy access to boating and fishing. Open in summer. Two miles south of Lake Jct. Loop Rd.

Canyon Village – Centrally located near the Grand Canyon of the Yellowstone. 598 cabins, open in the summer. Loop Rd. at Canyon Jct.

Mammoth Hot Springs Hotel and Cabins – 106 rooms, 109 cabins, some with view of the springs. Open in summer. Five miles south of north entrance on Loop Rd.

INDEX

Index